HAMMOND
DISCOVERY
WORLD ATLAS

HAMMOND INCORPORATED
MAPLEWOOD, NEW JERSEY 07040

Hammond Publications Advisory Board

ENTIRE CONTENTS © COPYRIGHT MCMLXXXIX BY HAMMOND INCORPORATED
All rights reserved. No part of this book may be reproduced or utilized in any form or by any means, electronic or mechanical, including photocopying, recording or by any information storage and retrieval system, without permission in writing from the Publisher.
                    PRINTED IN THE UNITED STATES OF AMERICA

BOMC offers recordings and compact discs, cassettes and records.
For information and catalog write to BOMR, Camp Hill, PA 17012.

Library of Congress Cataloging-in-Publication Data
Hammond Incorporated.
    Hammond discovery world atlas.
    "Terrain maps of land forms and ocean floors": p.
    Includes indexes.
    1. Atlases. 2. Zip code – United States. I Title.
II. Title: Discovery world atlas.
G1021.H2683 1988   912   88-675304
ISBN 0-8437-1224-4
ISBN 0-8437-1223-6 (pbk.)

CONTENTS

Introduction to the World Atlas
Introduction to the Maps and Indexes
Gazetteer-Index

Terrain Maps of Land Forms and Ocean Floors I-XVI

Contents/Legend I
World II
North America IV
Canada V
United States VI
Middle America VIII
South America IX
Europe X
Western Europe XI
Africa XII
Asia XIII
Pacific Ocean XIV
Australia and New Zealand XVI

World and Polar Regions

World 1, 2
Arctic Ocean 4
Antarctica 5

Europe

Europe 6
United Kingdom and Ireland 8
Norway, Sweden, Finland, Denmark and
   Iceland 16
Germany 20
Netherlands, Belgium
   and Luxembourg 23
France 26
Spain and Portugal 29
Italy 32
Switzerland and Liechtenstein 35
Austria, Czechoslovakia
   and Hungary 38
Balkan States 41
Poland 44
Union of Soviet Socialist Republics 46

Africa

Africa 52
Northern Part 54
Southern Part 57

Asia

Asia 58
Near and Middle East 60
Turkey, Syria, Lebanon and Cyprus 63
Israel and Jordan 66
Iran and Iraq 68

Indian Subcontinent
   and Afghanistan 70
Japan and Korea 73
China and Mongolia 76
Burma, Thailand, Indochina and
   Malaya 79
Southeast Asia 82

Australia and Pacific Ocean

Australia and New Zealand 85
Pacific Ocean 88

South America

Northern Part 90
Southern Part 93

North America

North America 94
Canada 96
Newfoundland 99
Nova Scotia and Prince Edward
   Island 100
New Brunswick 102
Quebec 104
Ontario 107
Manitoba 110
Saskatchewan 112
Alberta 114
British Columbia 116
Mexico 118
Central America 121
West Indies 124

United States

United States 126
Alabama 129
Alaska 130
Arizona 131
Arkansas 132
California 133
Colorado 134
Connecticut 135
Delaware 146
Florida 136
Georgia 137
Hawaii 130
Idaho 138
Illinois 139
Indiana 140
Iowa 141
Kansas 142

Kentucky 143
Louisiana 144
Maine 145
Maryland 146
Massachusetts 147
Michigan 148
Minnesota 149
Mississippi 150
Missouri 151
Montana 152
Nebraska 153
Nevada 154
New Hampshire 155
New Jersey 156
New Mexico 157
New York 158
North Carolina 159
North Dakota 160
Ohio 161
Oklahoma 162
Oregon 163
Pennsylvania 164
Rhode Island 147
South Carolina 165
South Dakota 166
Tennessee 167
Texas 168
Utah 169
Vermont 155
Virginia 170
Washington 171
West Virginia 172
Wisconsin 173
Wyoming 174

The Fifty States 175
World Index 177
Map Projections 193
World Air Distances 196
World Statistical Tables 198
Geographical Comparisons 200
World Distribution Maps 202
Development of Continents and
   Oceans 218
The Ice Ages 219
The Geologic Record 220
Life Support Cycles 222
Man's Impact Upon Nature 224

The current edition of the Hammond World Atlas features an outstanding new section devoted to THE PHYSICAL WORLD — a series of terrain maps of land forms and ocean floors. These physical maps were originally produced as sculptured terrain models, thus simulating the earth's surface in a highly realistic manner. The three-dimensional effect is both instructive and pleasing to the eye.

As in previous editions, the atlas is organized to make the retrieval of information as simple and quick as possible. The guiding principle in organizing the atlas material has been to present separate subjects on *separate* maps. In this way, each individual map topic is shown with the greatest degree of clarity, unencumbered with extraneous information that is best revealed on separate maps. Of equal importance from the standpoint of good atlas design is the treatment of all current information on a given country as a single atlas unit. Thus, the basic reference map of an area is accompanied on adjacent pages by all supplementary information pertaining to that area. For example, except for individual United States maps, the detailed index for a given map always appears on the same page as, or on the pages immediately following, the reference map. This same map index provides population data for the many cities, towns and villages shown on the map. Highlight information on the area, i.e., the total population and area, the capital, the highest point, is listed in the summary fact listings accompanying each unit. An adjacent locator map relates the subject area to the larger world beyond. A three-dimensional picture of the area is exhibited by means of the accompanying full-color topographic map. A separate economic map defines the vital agricultural, industrial and mineral resources of the area. In the case of the foreign maps, the flag of each independent nation appears on the appropriate page. Finally, certain country units contain special subject maps dealing with the history, climate, demography and vegetation of the area.

The back of the book contains a second type of index. This is a multi-paged "A-to-Z" index of places that appear on the maps. The use of this map index is essential when the name of a place is known but its country, state, or province is unknown.

Of course, the maps have been thoroughly updated. These revisions echo the new nations, shifting boundaries and the fluid internal divisions of many countries. New communities generated by the opening up of resources in the developing nations are also noted. Up-to-date geographical information, both foreign and domestic, is received daily by the atlas editors. A worldwide correspondence and thorough research brings to the atlas user the latest geographical and demographic information obtainable.

In closing it may be said that the atlas has truly been designed for contemporary use. Just as the information presented on the following pages is as current and up to date as the editors and cartographers could issue it, so the design and organization has been as well planned as possible to create a work useful to present generations.

President
HAMMOND INCORPORATED

Introduction to the Maps and Indexes

The following notes have been added to aid the reader in making the best use of this atlas. Though he may be familiar with maps and map indexes, the publisher believes that a quick review of the material below will add to his enjoyment of this reference work.

Arrangement — The Plan of the Atlas. The atlas has been designed with maximum convenience for the user as its objective. The first part of the atlas is devoted to the physical world — terrain maps of land forms and the sea floor. The rest of the atlas contains the general political reference maps, area by area. All geographically related information pertaining to a country or region appears on adjacent pages, eliminating the task of searching throughout the entire volume for data on a given area. Thus, the reader will find, conveniently assembled, political, topographic, economic and special maps of a political area or region, accompanied by detailed map indexes, statistical data, and illustrations of the national flags of the area.

The sequence of country units in this American-designed atlas in international in arrangement. Units on the world as a whole are followed by a section on the polar regions which, in turn, is followed by pages devoted to Europe and its countries. Following the maps of the European continent and its countries, the geographic sequence plan proceeds as follows: Africa, Asia, the Pacific and Australia, South America, North America, and ends with detailed coverage on the United States.

Political Maps — The Primary Reference Tool. The most detailed maps in each country unit are the *political maps.* It is our feeling that the reader is likely to refer to these maps more often than to any other in the book when confronted by such questions as — Where? How big? What is it near? Answering these common queries is the function of the political maps. Each political map stresses *political* phenomena — countries, internal political divisions, boundaries, cities and towns. The major political unit or units, shown on the map, are banded in distinctive colors for easy identification and delineation. First-order political subdivisions (states, provinces, counties on the state maps) are shown, scale permitting.

The reader is advised to make use of the *legend* appearing under the title on each political map. Map *symbols*, the special "language" of maps, are explained in the legend. Each variety of dot, circle, star or interrupted line has a special meaning which should be clearly understood by the user so that he may interpret the map data correctly.

Each country has been portrayed at a *scale* commensurate with its political, areal, economic or tourist importance. In certain cases, a whole map unit may be devoted to a single nation if that nation is considered to be of prime interest to most atlas users. In other cases, several nations will be shown on a single map if, as separate entities, they are of lesser relative importance. Areas of dense settlement and important significance within a country have been enlarged and portrayed in inset maps inserted on the margins of the main map. The reader is advised to refer to the linear or "bar" scale appearing on each map or map inset in order to determine the distance between points.

The *projection* system used for each map is noted near the title of the map. Map projections are the special graphic systems used by cartographers to render the curved three-dimensional surface of the globe on a flat surface. Optimum map projections determined by the attributes of the area have been used by the the publishers for each map in the atlas.

A word here as to the choice of place names on the maps. Throughout the atlas names appear, with a few exceptions, in their local official spellings. However, conventional Anglicized spellings are used for major geographical divisions and for towns and topographic features for which English forms exist;

i.e., "Spain" instead of "España" or "Munich" instead of "München." Names of this type are normally followed by the local official spelling in parentheses. As an aid to the user the indexes are cross-referenced for all current and most former spellings of such names.

Names of cities and towns in the United States follow the forms listed in the *Post Office Directory* of the United States Postal Service. Domestic physical names follow the decisions of the Board on Geographic Names, U.S. Department of the Interior, and of various state geographic name boards.

It is the belief of the publishers that the boundaries shown in a general reference atlas should reflect current geographic and political realities. This policy has been followed consistently in the atlas. The presentation of *de facto* boundaries in cases of territorial dispute between various nations does not imply the political endorsement of such boundaries by the publisher, but simply the honest representation of boundaries as they exist at the time of the printing of the atlas maps.

Indexes — Pinpointing a Location. Each political map (except for individual United States maps) is accompanied by a comprehensive index of the place names appearing on the map. If you are unfamiliar with the location of a particular geographical place and wish to find its position within the confines of the subject area of the map, consult the map index as your first step. The name of the feature sought will be found in its proper alphabetical sequence with a key reference letter-number combination corresponding to its location on the map. After noting the key reference letter-number combination for the place name, turn to the map. The place name will be found within the square formed by the two lines of latitude and the two lines of longitude which enclose the co-ordinates — i.e., the marginal letters and numbers, the diagram below illustrates the system of indexing.

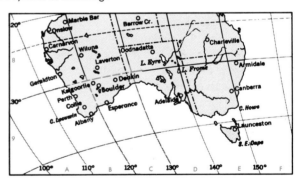

Where space on the map has not permitted giving the complete form of the place name, the complete form is shown in the index. Where a place is known by more than one name or by various spellings of the same name, the different forms have been included in the index. Physical features are listed under their proper names and not according to their generic terms; that is to say, Rio Negro will be found under Negro and not under Rio Negro. On the other hand, Rio Grande will be found under Rio Grande. Accompanying most index entries for cities and towns, and for other political units, are *population figures* for the particular entries. The large number of population figures in the atlas makes this work one of the most comprehensive statistical sources available to the public today. The population figures have been taken from the latest official censuses and estimates of the various nations.

Population and area figures for countries and major political units are listed in bold type *fact lists* on the margins of the indexes. In addition, the capital, largest city, highest point, monetary unit, principal languages and the prevailing religions of the country concerned are also listed. The Gazetteer-Index of the World on the following pages provides a quick reference index for countries and other important areas. Though population and area figures for each major unit are also found in the map section, the Gazetteer-Index provides a conveniently arranged statistical comparison contained in two pages.

Relief Maps. Accompanying each political map is a relief map of the area. These are in addition to the terrain maps of land forms in the front of the atlas. The purpose of the relief map is to illustrate the surface configuration (TOPOGRAPHY) of the region. A shading technique in color simulates the relative ruggedness of the terrain — plains, plateaus, valleys, hills and mountains. Graded colors, ranging from greens for lowlands, yellows for intermediate elevations to browns in the highlands, indicate the height above sea level of each part of the land. A vertical scale at the margin of the map shows the approximate height in meters and feet represented by each color.

Economic Maps — Agriculture, Industry and Resources. One of the most interesting features that will be found in each country unit is the economic map. From this map one can determine the basic activities of a nation as expressed through its economy. A perusal of the map yields a full understanding of the area's economic geography and natural resources.

The agricultural economy is manifested in two ways: color bands and commodity names. The color bands express broad categories of *dominant land use*, such as cereal belts, forest lands, livestock range lands, nonagricultural wastes. The red commodity names, on the other hand, pinpoint the areas of production of *specific* crops; i.e., wheat, cotton, sugar beets, etc.

Major mineral occurrences are denoted by standard letter symbols appearing in blue. The relative size of the letter symbols signifies the relative importance of the deposit.

The manufacturing sector of the economy is presented by means of diagonal line patterns expressing the various *industrial* areas of consequence within a country.

The fishing industry is represented by names of commercial fish species appearing offshore in blue letters. Major waterpower sites are designated by blue symbols.

The publishers have tried to make this work the most comprehensive and useful atlas available, and it is hoped that it will prove a valuable reference work. Any constructive suggestions from the reader will be welcomed.

Sources and Acknowledgments

A multitude of sources goes into the making of a large-scale reference work such as this. To list them all would take many pages and would consume space better devoted to the maps and reference materials themselves. However, certain general sources were very useful in preparing this work and are listed below.

STATISTICAL OFFICE OF THE UNITED NATIONS.
Demographic Yearbook. New York. Issued annually.

STATISTICAL OFFICE OF THE UNITED NATIONS.
Statisical Yearbook. Nw York. Issued annually.

THE GEOGRAPHER, U.S. DEPARTMENT OF STATE
International Boundary Study papers. Washington. Various dates.

THE GEOGRAPHER, U.S. DEPARTMENT OF STATE.
Geographic Notes. Washington. Various dates.

UNITED STATES BOARD ON GEOGRAPHIC NAMES.
Decisions on Geographic Names in the United States.
Washington. Various dates.

UNITED STATES BOARD ON GEOGRAPHIC NAMES.
Official Standard Names Gazetteers. Washington. Various dates.

CANADIAN PERMANENT COMMITTEE ON
GEOGRAPHICAL NAMES.
Gazetteer of Canada series. Ottawa. Various dates.

UNITED STATES POSTAL SERVICE.
National Five Digit ZIP Code and Post Office Directory.
Washington. Issued annually.

UNITED STATES POSTAL SERVICE.
Postal Bulletin. Washington. Issued weekly.

UNITED STATES DEPARTMENT OF THE INTERIOR.
BUREAU OF MINES.
Minerals Yearbook. 4 vols. Washington. Various dates.

UNITED STATES GEOLOGICAL SURVEY.
Elevations and distances in the United States. Reston, Va. 1980.

CARTACTUAL.
Cartactual — Topical Map Service. Budapest. Issued bi-monthly.

AMERICAN GEOGRAPHICAL SOCIETY.
Focus. New York. Issued ten times a year.

THE AMERICAN UNIVERSITY.
Foreign Area Studies. Washington. Various dates.

CENTRAL INTELLIGENCE AGENCY.
General reference maps. Washington. Various dates.

A sample list of sources used for specific countries follows:

Afghanistan
CENTRAL STATISTICS OFFICE.
Preliminary Results of the First Afghan Population Census 1979. Kabul.

Albania
DREJTORIA E STATISTIKES.
1979 Census. Tiranë.

Argentina
INSTITUTO NACIONAL DE ESTADISTICA Y CENSOS.
Censo Nacional de Población y Vivienda 1980. Buenos Aires.

Australia
AUSTRALIAN BUREAU OF STATISTICS.
Census of Population and Housing 1981. Canberra.

Brazil
FUNDACAO INSTITUTO BRASILEIRO DE GEOGRAFIA
E ESTATISTICA.
IX Recenseamento Geral do Brasil 1980. Rio de Janeiro.

Canada
STATISTICS CANADA.
1981 Census of Canada. Ottawa.

Cuba
COMITE ESTATAL DE ESTADISTICAS.
Censo de Población y Viviendas 1981. Havana.

Hungary
HUNGARIAN CENTRAL STATISTICAL OFFICE.
1980 Census. Budapest.

Indonesia
BIRO PUSAT STATISTIK.
Sensus Penduduk 1980. Jakarta.

Kuwait
CENTRAL OFFICE OF STATISTICS.
1980 Census. Al Kuwait.

New Zealand
DEPARTMENT OF STATISTICS.
New Zealand Census of Population and Dwellings 1981.
Wellington.

Panama
DIRECCIÓN DE ESTADISTICA Y CENSO.
Censos Nacionales de 1980. Panamá.

Papua New Guinea
BUREAU OF STATISTICS.
National Population Census 1980. Port Moresby.

Philippines
NATIONAL CENSUS AND STATISTICS OFFICE.
1980 Census of Population. Manila.

Saint Lucia
CENSUS OFFICE.
1980 Population Census. Castries.

Singapore
DEPARTMENT OF STATISTICS.
Census of Population 1980. Singapore.

U.S.S.R.
CENTRAL STATISTICAL ADMINISTRATION.
1979 Census. Moscow.

United States
BUREAU OF THE CENSUS.
1980 Census of Population. Washington.

Vanuatu
CENSUS OFFICE.
1979 Population Census. Port Vila.

Zambia
CENTRAL STATISTICAL OFFICE.
1980 Census of Population and Housing. Lusaka.

This alphabetical list of grand divisions, countries, states, colonial possessions, etc., gives page numbers and index references on which they are shown on the largest scale as well as area and population of each unit. The index reference shows the square on the respective map in which the name of the entry may be located.

Country	Page No.	Index Ref.	Area Square Miles	Area Square Kilometers	Population
*Afghanistan	70	A 2	250,775	649,507	15,540,000
Africa	54, 57	......	11,707,000	30,321,130	469,000,000
Alabama, U.S.A.	129	......	51,705	133,916	3,893,888
Alaska, U.S.A.	130	......	591,004	1,530,700	401,851
*Albania	43	E 5	11,100	28,749	2,590,600
Alberta, Canada	114	......	255,285	661,185	2,237,724
*Algeria	54	F 6	919,591	2,381,740	17,422,000
American Samoa	89	J 7	77	199	32,297
Andorra	31	G 1	188	487	31,000
*Angola	57	K14	481,351	1,246,700	7,078,000
Anguilla	124	F 3	35	91	6,519
Antarctica	5	......	5,500,000	14,245,000	....
*Antigua and Barbuda	124	G 3	171	443	72,000
*Argentina	93	H10	1,072,070	2,776,661	28,438,000
Arizona, U.S.A.	131	......	114,000	295,260	2,718,425
Arkansas, U.S.A.	132	......	53,187	137,754	2,286,435
Aruba	124	E 3	75	193	55,148
Ascension Island, St. Helena	1	......	34	88	719
Asia	58	......	17,128,500	44,362,815	2,633,000,000
*Australia	86	......	2,966,136	7,682,300	14,576,330
*Austria	38	B 3	32,375	83,851	7,507,000
*Bahamas	124	C 1	5,382	13,939	209,505
*Bahrain	60	F 4	240	622	358,857
*Bangladesh	70	F 3	55,126	142,776	87,052,024
*Barbados	125	G 4	166	430	248,983
*Belgium	25	E 7	11,781	30,513	9,855,110
*Belize	122	C 2	8,867	22,966	144,857
*Benin	54	G10	43,483	112,620	3,338,240
Bermuda	125	H 3	21	54	67,761
*Bhutan	70	G 3	18,147	47,000	1,298,000
*Bolivia	90	G 7	424,163	1,098,582	5,600,000
*Botswana	57	L16	224,764	582,139	819,000
*Brazil	90	K 6	3,284,426	8,506,663	119,098,992
British Columbia, Canada	117	......	366,253	948,596	2,744,467
British Indian Ocean Terr.	58	L10	29	75	2,000
Brunei	83	E 4	2,226	5,765	192,832
*Bulgaria	43	F 4	42,823	110,912	8,862,000
*Burkina Faso	54	F 9	105,869	274,200	6,908,000
*Burma	81	B 2	261,789	678,034	32,913,000
*Burundi	57	M12	10,747	27,835	4,021,910
California, U.S.A.	133	......	158,706	411,049	23,667,565
*Cambodia (Kampuchea)	81	E 4	69,898	181,036	5,200,000
*Cameroon	54	J10	183,568	475,441	8,503,000
*Canada	96-97	......	3,851,787	9,976,139	24,343,181
*Cape Verde	1	......	1,557	4,033	324,000
Cayman Islands	124	B 3	100	259	16,677
*Central African Republic	54	K10	242,000	626,780	2,284,000
Central America	122-123	......	197,480	511,475	21,000,000
Ceylon, see Sri Lanka					
*Chad	54	K 8	495,752	1,283,998	4,309,000
Channel Islands	11	E 8	75	194	133,000
*Chile	93	F10	292,257	756,946	11,275,440
*China, People's Rep. of	77	......	3,691,000	9,559,690	958,090,000
China, Republic of (Taiwan)	77	K 7	13,971	36,185	16,609,961
*Colombia	90	F 3	439,513	1,138,339	27,520,000
Colorado, U.S.A.	134	......	104,091	269,596	2,889,735
*Comoros	57	P14	719	1,862	290,000
*Congo, Rep. of	57	J12	132,046	342,000	1,537,000
Connecticut, U.S.A.	135	......	5,018	12,997	3,107,576
Cook Islands	89	K 7	91	236	17,695
*Costa Rica	122	E 5	19,575	50,700	2,245,000
*Cuba	124	B 2	44,206	114,494	9,706,369
*Cyprus	64	E 5	3,473	8,995	629,000
*Czechoslovakia	39	C 2	49,373	127,876	15,276,799
Delaware, U.S.A.	146	R 3	2,044	5,294	594,317
*Denmark	19	......	16,629	43,069	5,124,000
District of Columbia, U.S.A.	146	......	69	179	638,432
*Djibouti	55	P 9	8,880	23,000	386,000
*Dominica	125	G 4	290	751	74,089
*Dominican Republic	124	D 3	18,704	48,443	5,647,977
*Ecuador	90	E 4	109,483	283,561	8,354,000
*Egypt	54	M 6	386,659	1,001,447	41,572,000
*El Salvador	122	C 4	8,260	21,393	4,813,000
England, U.K.	11	......	50,516	130,836	46,220,955
*Equatorial Guinea	57	H11	10,831	28,052	244,000
*Ethiopia	54-55	O 9	471,776	1,221,900	31,065,000
Europe	6	......	4,057,000	10,507,630	676,000,000
Faerøe Islands, Denmark	19	B 2	540	1,399	41,969
Falkland Islands & Dependencies	93	H14	6,198	16,053	1,812
*Fiji	89	H 8	7,055	18,272	588,068
*Finland	16	O 6	130,128	337,032	4,788,000
Florida, U.S.A.	136	......	58,664	151,940	9,746,342
*France	26	......	210,038	543,998	53,788,000
French Guiana	90	K 3	35,135	91,000	73,022
French Polynesia	89	L 8	1,544	4,000	137,382
*Gabon	57	J12	103,346	267,666	551,000
*Gambia	54	C 9	4,127	10,689	601,000
Georgia, U.S.A.	137	......	58,910	152,577	5,463,105
*Germany, East (German Democratic Republic)	20	......	41,768	108,179	16,737,000
*Germany, West (Federal Republic)	20	......	95,985	248,601	61,658,000
*Ghana	54	F10	92,099	238,536	11,450,000
Gibraltar	31	D 4	2.28	5.91	29,760
*Great Britain & Northern Ireland (United Kingdom)	8	......	94,399	244,493	55,672,000
*Greece	43	F 6	50,944	131,945	9,599,000
Greenland	4	B12	840,000	2,175,600	49,773
*Grenada	125	G 4	133	344	103,103
Guadeloupe & Dependencies	124	F 3	687	1,779	328,400
Guam	89	E 4	209	541	105,979
*Guatemala	122	B 3	42,042	108,889	7,262,419
*Guinea	54	D 9	94,925	245,856	5,143,284
*Guinea-Bissau	54	C 9	13,948	36,125	777,214
*Guyana	90	J 2	83,000	214,970	820,000
*Haiti	124	D 3	10,694	27,697	5,009,000
Hawaii, U.S.A.	130	......	6,471	16,760	964,691
Holland, see Netherlands					
*Honduras	122	D 3	43,277	112,087	3,691,000
Hong Kong	77	H 7	403	1,044	5,022,000
*Hungary	39	E 3	35,919	93,030	10,709,536
*Iceland	19	B 1	39,768	103,000	228,785
Idaho, U.S.A.	138	......	83,564	216,431	944,038
Illinois, U.S.A.	139	......	56,345	145,934	11,426,596
*India	70	D 4	1,269,339	3,287,588	683,810,051
*Indiana, U.S.A.	140	......	36,185	93,719	5,490,260
*Indonesia	83	D 7	788,430	2,042,034	147,490,298
*Iowa, U.S.A.	141	......	56,275	145,752	2,913,808
*Iran	68	F 4	636,293	1,648,000	37,447,000
*Iraq	68	C 4	172,476	446,713	12,767,000
*Ireland	15	......	27,136	70,282	3,440,427
Ireland, Northern, U.K.	15	F 2	5,452	14,121	1,543,000
Isle of Man	11	C 3	227	588	64,000
*Israel	67	B 4	7,847	20,324	3,878,000
*Italy	32	......	116,303	301,225	57,140,000
*Ivory Coast	54	E10	124,504	322,465	7,920,000
*Jamaica	124	C 3	4,411	11,424	2,161,000
*Japan	75	......	145,730	377,441	117,057,485
*Jordan	67	D 3	35,000	90,650	2,152,273
*Kampuchea (Cambodia)	81	E 4	69,898	181,036	5,200,000
Kansas, U.S.A.	142	......	82,277	213,097	2,364,236
Kentucky, U.S.A.	143	......	40,409	104,659	3,660,257
*Kenya	57	O11	224,960	582,646	15,327,061
Kiribati	89	J 6	291	754	57,500
Korea, North	74	D 3	46,540	120,539	17,914,000
Korea, South	74	D 5	38,175	98,873	37,448,836
*Kuwait	60	E 4	6,532	16,918	1,355,827
*Laos	81	D 3	91,428	236,800	3,721,000
*Lebanon	64	F 6	4,015	10,399	3,161,000
*Lesotho	57	M17	11,720	30,355	1,339,000
*Liberia	54	E10	43,000	111,370	1,873,000
*Libya	54	J 6	679,358	1,759,537	2,856,000
Liechtenstein	37	J 2	61	158	25,220
Louisiana, U.S.A.	144	......	47,752	123,678	4,206,312
*Luxembourg	25	J 9	999	2,587	364,000
Macau	77	H 7	6	16	271,000
*Madagascar	57	R16	226,657	587,041	8,742,000
Maine, U.S.A.	145	......	33,265	86,156	1,125,027
*Malawi	57	N14	45,747	118,485	5,968,000
Malaya, Malaysia	81	D 6	50,806	131,588	11,138,227

*Member of the United Nations

Country	Page No.	Index Ref.	Area Square Miles	Area Square Kilometers	Population
*Malaysia	81	D 6	128,308	332,318	13,435,588
	83	E 4			
*Maldives	58	L 9	115	298	143,046
*Mali	54	F 8	464,873	1,204,021	6,906,000
*Malta	32	E 7	122	316	343,970
Manitoba, Canada	110		250,999	650,087	1,026,241
Martinique	125	G 4	425	1,101	328,566
Maryland, U.S.A.	146		10,460	27,091	4,216,975
Massachusetts, U.S.A.	147		8,284	21,456	5,737,037
*Mauritania	54	D 8	419,229	1,085,803	1,634,000
*Mauritius	57	S19	790	2,046	959,000
Mayotte	119	P14	144	373	47,300
*Mexico	119		761,601	1,972,546	67,395,826
Michigan, U.S.A.	148		58,527	151,585	9,262,078
Midway Islands	154	A 5	1.9	4.9	453
Minnesota, U.S.A.	149		84,402	218,601	4,075,970
Mississippi, U.S.A.	150		47,689	123,515	2,520,638
Missouri, U.S.A.	151		69,697	180,515	4,916,759
Monaco	26	G 6	368 acres	149 hectares	25,029
*Mongolia	77	E 2	606,163	1,569,962	1,594,800
Montana, U.S.A.	152		147,046	380,849	786,690
Montserrat	125	G 3	40	104	12,073
*Morroco	54	E 5	172,414	446,550	20,242,000
*Mozambique	57	N16	303,769	786,762	12,130,000
Namibia (South-West Africa)	57	K16	317,827	823,172	1,200,000
Nauru	89	G 6	7.7	20	7,254
Nebraska, U.S.A.	153		77,355	200,349	1,569,825
*Nepal	70	E 3	54,663	141,577	14,179,301
*Netherlands	25	F 5	15,892	41,160	14,227,000
Netherlands Antilles	124	F 3	390	1,010	246,000
Nevada, U.S.A.	154		110,561	286,353	800,493
New Brunswick, Canada	102		28,354	73,437	696,403
New Caledonia & Dependencies	89	G 8	7,335	18,998	133,233
Newfoundland, Canada	99		156,184	404,517	567,681
New Hampshire, U.S.A.	155		9,279	24,033	920,610
New Herbrides, see Vanuatu					
New Jersey, U.S.A.	156		7,787	20,168	7,364,823
New Mexico, U.S.A.	157		121,593	314,926	1,302,981
New York, U.S.A.	158		49,108	127,190	17,558,072
*New Zealand	87		103,736	268,676	3,175,737
*Nicaragua	122	D 4	45,698	118,358	2,703,000
*Niger	54	H 8	489,189	1,267,000	5,098,427
*Nigeria	54	H10	357,000	924,630	82,643,000
Niue	89	K 7	100	259	3,578
North America	94		9,363,000	24,250,170	370,000,000
North Carolina, U.S.A.	159		52,669	136,413	5,881,813
North Dakota, U.S.A.	160		70,702	183,118	652,717
Northern Ireland, U.K.	15	F 2	5,452	14,121	1,543,000
Northwest Territories, Canada	96	G 3	1,304,896	3,379,683	45,741
*Norway	16	F 7	125,053	323,887	4,092,000
Nova Scotia, Canada	100		21,425	55,491	847,442
Ohio, U.S.A.	161		41,330	107,045	10,797,624
Oklahoma, U.S.A.	162		69,956	181,186	3,025,290
*Oman	60	G 6	120,000	310,800	891,000
Ontario, Canada	107,108		412,580	1,068,582	8,625,107
Oregon, U.S.A.	163		97,073	251,419	2,633,149
*Pakistan	70	B 3	310,402	803,944	83,782,000
*Panama	122	G 6	29,761	77,082	1,830,175
*Papua New Guinea	82	B 7	183,540	475,369	3,010,727
	89	E 6			
*Paraguay	93		157,047	406,752	2,973,000
Pennsylvania, U.S.A.	164		45,308	117,348	11,863,895
Persia, see Iran					
*Peru	90		496,222	1,285,215	17,031,221
*Philippines	83		115,707	299,681	48,098,460
Pitcairn Islands	89	O 8	18	47	54
*Poland	45		120,725	312,678	35,815,000
*Portugal	30		35,549	92,072	9,933,000
Prince Edward Island, Canada	100	E 2	2,184	5,657	122,506
Puerto Rico	124-125		3,515	9,104	3,186,076
*Qatar	60	F 4	4,247	11,000	220,000
Québec, Canada	105, 106		594,857	1,540,680	6,438,403
Réunion	57	R20	969	2,510	491,000
Rhode Island, U.S.A.	147	H 5	1,212	3,139	947,154
Rhodesia, see Zimbabwe					
*Romania	45	F 3	91,699	237,500	22,048,305
*Rwanda	57	N12	10,169	26,337	4,819,317
Sabah, Malaysia	83	F 4	29,300	75,887	1,002,608
Saint Helena & Dependencies	1		162	420	5,147
Saint Kitts and Nevis	124	F 3	104	269	44,404

Country	Page No.	Index Ref.	Area Square Miles	Area Square Kilometers	Population
*Saint Lucia	125	G 4	238	616	115,783
Saint Pierre & Miquelon	99	B 4	93.5	242	6,041
*Saint Vincent & the Grenadines	125	G 4	150	388	124,000
San Marino	32	D 3	234	60.6	19,149
*São Tomé and Principe	57	G11	372	963	85,000
Sarawak, Malaysia	83	E 5	48,202	124,843	1,294,753
Saskatchewan, Canada	113		251,699	651,900	968,313
*Saudi Arabia	60	D 4	829,995	2,149,687	8,367,000
Scotland, U.K.	13		30,414	78,772	5,117,146
*Senegal	54	D 9	75,954	196,720	5,508,000
*Seychelles	58	J10	145	375	63,000
Siam, see Thailand					
*Sierra Leone	54	C10	27,925	72,325	3,470,000
*Singapore	81	F 6	226	585	2,413,945
*Solomon Islands	89	G 6	11,500	29,785	221,000
*Somalia	55	R10	246,200	637,658	3,645,000
*South Africa	57	L18	455,318	1,179,274	23,771,970
South America	90		6,875,000	17,806,250	245,000,000
South Carolina, U.S.A.	165		31,113	80,583	3,121,833
South Dakota, U.S.A.	166		77,116	199,730	690,768
South-West Africa (Namibia)	57	K16	317,827	823,172	1,200,000
*Spain	31		194,881	504,742	37,430,000
*Sri Lanka	70	E 7	25,332	65,610	14,850,001
*Sudan	54	M 9	967,494	2,505,809	18,691,000
*Suriname	90	J 3	55,144	142,823	354,860
*Swaziland	57	N17	6,705	17,366	547,000
*Sweden	16	J 8	173,665	449,792	8,320,000
Switzerland	37		15,943	41,292	6,365,960
*Syria	64	G 5	71,498	185,180	8,979,000
Taiwan	77	K 7	13,971	36,185	16,609,961
*Tanzania	54	N13	363,708	942,003	17,527,560
Tennessee, U.S.A.	167		42,144	109,153	4,591,120
Texas, U.S.A.	168		266,807	691,030	14,229,288
*Thailand	81	D 3	198,455	513,998	46,455,000
*Togo	54	G10	21,622	56,000	2,472,000
Tokelau	89	J 6	3.9	10	1,575
Tonga	89	J 8	270	699	90,128
*Trinidad and Tobago	125	G 5	1,980	5,128	1,067,108
Tristan da Cunha, St. Helena	5		38	98	251
*Tunisia	54	H 5	63,378	164,149	6,637,000
*Turkey	64	D 3	300,946	779,450	45,217,556
Turks and Caicos Islands	124	D 2	166	430	7,436
Tuvalu	89	H 6	9.78	25.33	7,349
*Uganda	57	N11	91,076	235,887	12,630,076
*Ukrainian S.S.R., U.S.S.R.	50	D 5	233,089	603,700	49,755,000
*Union of Soviet Socialist Republics	46, 50		8,649,490	22,402,179	262,436,227
*United Arab Emirates	60	F 5	32,278	83,600	1,040,275
*United Kingdom	8		94,399	244,493	55,672,000
*United States of America	126-127		3,623,420	9,384,658	226,504,825
*Upper Volta (Burkina Faso)	54	F 9	105,869	274,200	6,908,000
*Uruguay	93	J10	72,172	186,925	2,899,000
Utah, U.S.A.	169		84,899	219,888	1,461,037
*Vanuatu	89	G 7	5,700	14,763	112,596
Vatican City	32	B 6	108.7 acres	44 hectares	728
*Venezuela	92		352,143	912,050	14,313,000
Vermont, U.S.A.	155		9,614	24,900	511,456
*Vietnam	81	E 3	128,405	332,569	52,741,765
Virginia, U.S.A.	170		40,767	105,587	5,346,818
Virgin Islands, British	125	H 1	59	153	11,006
Virgin Islands, U.S.A.	125	H 1	132	342	96,569
Wake Island	89	G 4	2.5	6.5	302
Wales, U.K.	11	D 5	8,017	20,764	2,790,462
Wallis and Futuna	89	J 7	106	275	9,192
Washington, U.S.A.	171		68,139	176,480	4,132,180
Western Sahara	54	D 6	102,703	266,000	76,425
*Western Samoa	89	J 7	1,133	2,934	158,130
West Virginia, U.S.A.	172		24,231	62,758	1,950,279
*White Russian S.S.R. (Byelo-russian S.S.R.), U.S.S.R.	50	C 4	80,154	207,600	9,560,000
Wisconsin, U.S.A.	173		56,153	145,436	4,705,521
World	5		57,970,000 (land)	150,142,300	4,415,00,000
Wyoming, U.S.A.	174		97,809	253,325	469,557
*Yemen, People's Democratic Republic of	60	E 7	111,101	287,752	1,969,000
*Yemen Arab Republic	60	D 6	77,220	200,000	6,456,189
*Yugoslavia	43	C 3	98,766	255,804	22,471,000
Yukon Territory, Canada	96	C 3	207,075	536,324	23.153
*Zaire	57	L12	905,063	2,344,133	28,291,000
*Zambia	57	M14	290,586	752,618	5,679,808
*Zimbabwe	57	M15	150,803	390,580	7,360,000

HAMMOND
THE PHYSICAL WORLD
Terrain Maps of Land Forms and Ocean Floors

CONTENTS

THE WORLD II-III

NORTH AMERICA IV

CANADA V

UNITED STATES VI-VII

MIDDLE AMERICA VIII

SOUTH AMERICA IX

EUROPE X

WESTERN EUROPE XI

AFRICA XII

ASIA XIII

PACIFIC OCEAN XIV-XV

AUSTRALIA/NEW ZEALAND XVI

RELIEF MODELS BY ERNST G. HOFMANN, ASSISTED BY RAFAEL MARTINEZ

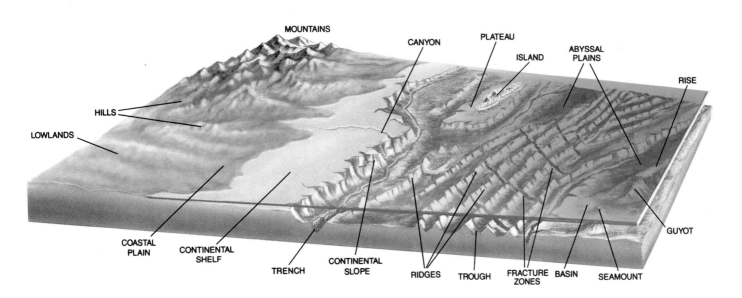

The oblique view diagram above is designed to provide a detailed view of the ocean floor as if seen through the depth of the sea. Graduating blue tones are used to contrast ocean floor depths: from light blue to represent shallow continental shelves to dark blues in the greater depths. Land relief is shown in conventional hypsometric tints.

In this dramatic collection of topographic maps of continents, oceans and major regions of the world, Hammond introduces a revolutionary new technique in cartography.

While most maps depicting terrain are created from painted artwork that is then photographed, Hammond now premiers the use of a remarkable sculptured model mapping technique created by one of our master cartographers.

The process begins with the sculpting of large scale three-dimensional models. Once physical details have been etched on the models and refinements completed, relief work is checked for accurate elevation based on a vertical scale exaggerated for visual effect.

Finished models are airbrushed and painted, then photographed using a single northwesterly light source to achieve a striking three-dimensional effect. The result is the dynamic presentation of mountain ranges and peaks on land, and canyons, trenches and seamounts on the ocean floor. Never before have maps conveyed such rich beauty while providing a realistic representation of the world as we know it.

LEGEND FOR TERRAIN MAPS

International Boundaries — · · —	Mountain Peaks ▲
State and Provincial Boundaries — · —	National Capitals ⊛
Other Boundaries — — — —	Other Capitals ⊚
Boundaries Along Rivers	Canals

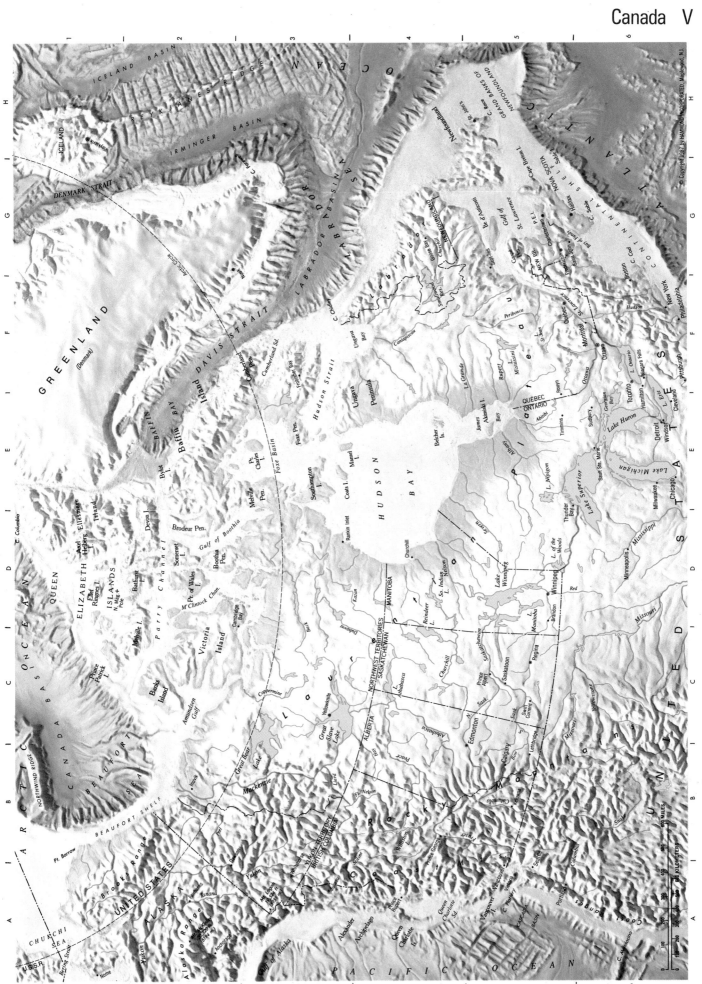

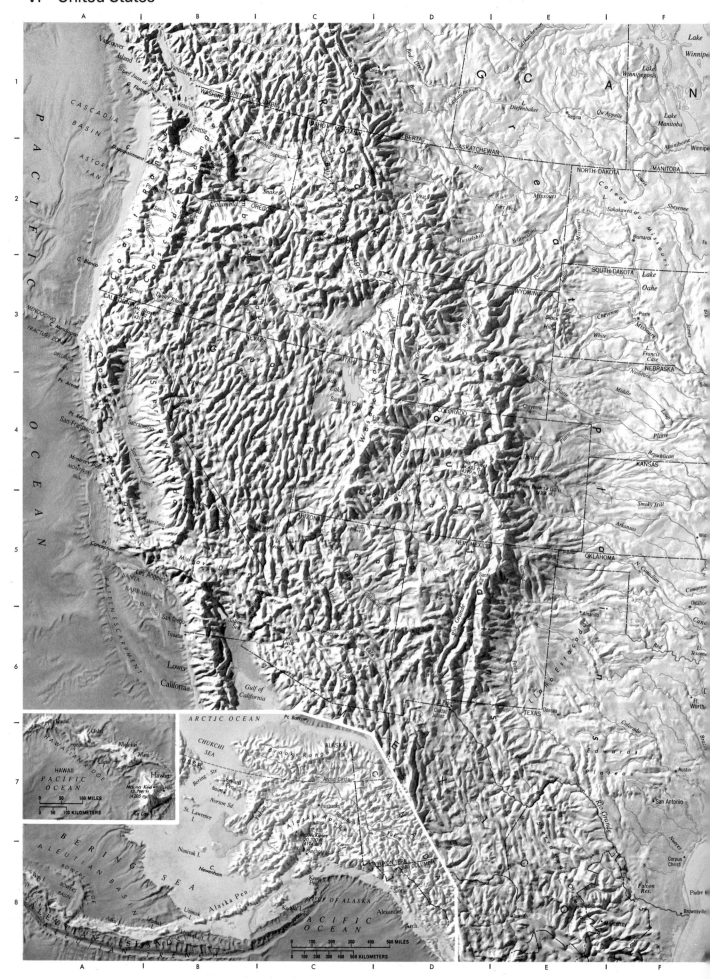

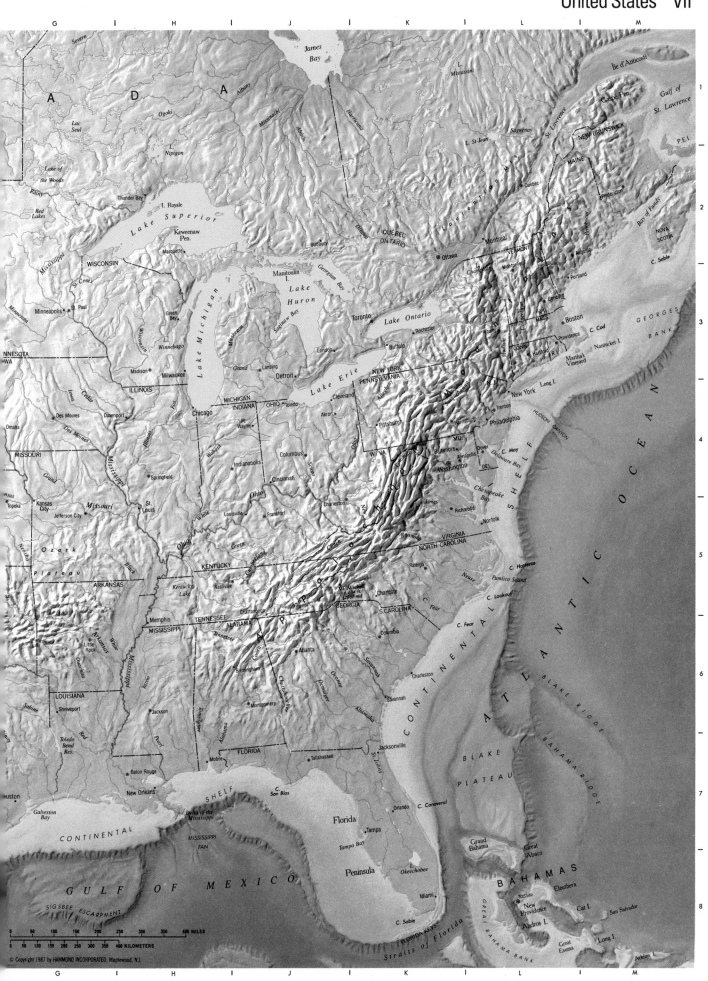

G H I J K L M

CANADA

James Bay

Île d'Anticosti

Gulf of St. Lawrence

P.E.I.

Gaspé Pen.

NEW BRUNSWICK

MAINE

Fredericton

NOVA SCOTIA

C. Sable

Bay of Fundy

QUEBEC ONTARIO

Ottawa

Montréal

VERMONT

Montpelier

N.H.

Concord

Augusta

Portland

Boston

MASS.

C. Cod

GEORGES BANK

Martha's Vineyard

Nantucket I.

R.I.

Hartford

CONN.

Providence

Lake Superior

I. Royale

Keweenaw Pen.

Marquette

WISCONSIN

Lac Seul

Ogoki

L. Nipigon

Lake of the Woods

Rainy

Red Lakes

Thunder Bay

Toronto

Lake Ontario

Rochester

Buffalo

NEW YORK

Albany

Hudson

New York

Long I.

Trenton

N.J.

HUDSON CANYON

Lake Huron

Manitoulin I.

Georgian Bay

Saginaw Bay

Mackinac

Green Bay

L. Winnebago

Madison

Milwaukee

Lansing

Detroit

Lake Erie

Cleveland

Akron

PENNSYLVANIA

Pittsburgh

Harrisburg

Allegheny

Philadelphia

SHELF

Minneapolis

St. Paul

MINNESOTA

IOWA

Des Moines

Davenport

ILLINOIS

Chicago

Ft. Wayne

INDIANA

MICHIGAN

OHIO

Toledo

Columbus

Cincinnati

W. VA

MD.

Baltimore

Annapolis

Dover

DEL.

Delaware Bay

C. May

Washington

Omaha

MISSOURI

Springfield

St. Louis

Indianapolis

Ohio

Louisville

Frankfort

Charleston

Chesapeake Bay

Richmond

Norfolk

Kansas City

Jefferson City

Topeka

KENTUCKY

Nashville

Kentucky Lake

VIRGINIA

NORTH CAROLINA

Roanoke

Raleigh

Neuse

Pamlico Sound

C. Hatteras

Ozark Plateau

ARKANSAS

Black

Memphis

Chattanooga

TENNESSEE

GEORGIA

S. CAROLINA

Charlotte

Columbia

C. Fear

C. Lookout

ATLANTIC OCEAN

Little Rock

Ouachita

MISSISSIPPI

ALABAMA

Birmingham

Atlanta

Savannah

C. Fear

Charleston

CONTINENTAL

BLAKE RIDGE

BAHAMA RIDGE

LOUISIANA

Jackson

Montgomery

Mobile

FLORIDA

Tallahassee

Jacksonville

BLAKE PLATEAU

Grand Bahama

Great Abaco

Shreveport

Baton Rouge

New Orleans

CONTINENTAL SHELF

C. San Blas

Delta of the Mississippi

Florida

Orlando

C. Canaveral

Galveston Bay

GULF OF MEXICO

MISSISSIPPI FAN

Tampa

Tampa Bay

Peninsula

L. Okeechobee

Miami

BAHAMAS

Nassau

New Providence

Eleuthera

Cat I.

SIGSBEE ESCARPMENT

C. Sable

Straits of Florida

Andros I.

Great Exuma

GREAT BAHAMA BANK

Long I.

San Salvador

Acklins I.

0 50 100 150 200 250 300 350 400 MILES
0 50 100 150 200 250 300 400 KILOMETERS

© Copyright 1987 by HAMMOND INCORPORATED, Maplewood, N.J.

G H I J K L M

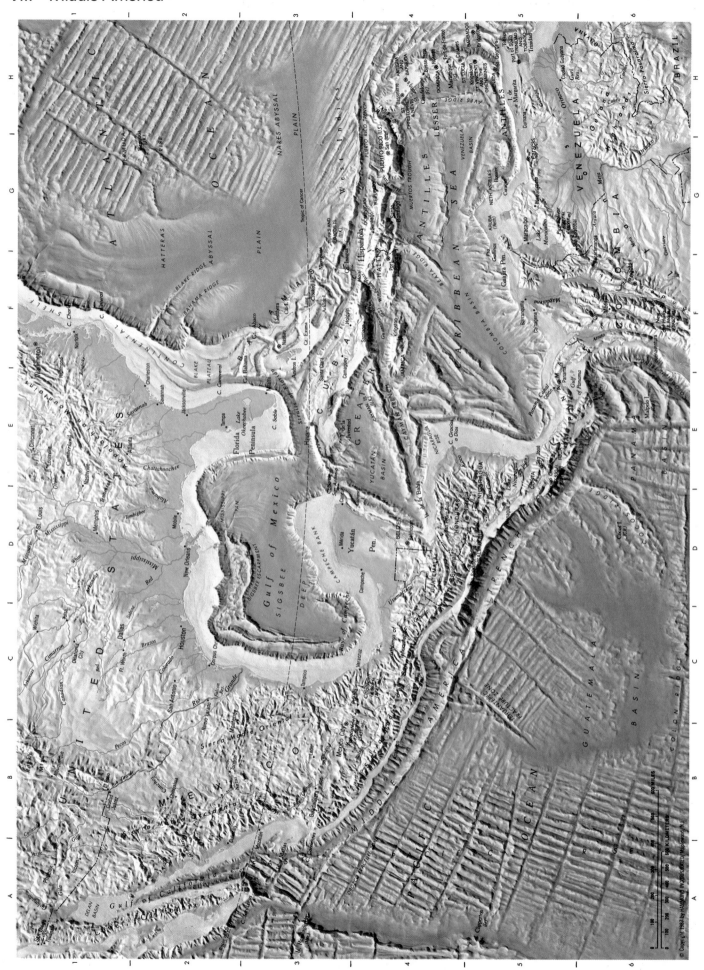

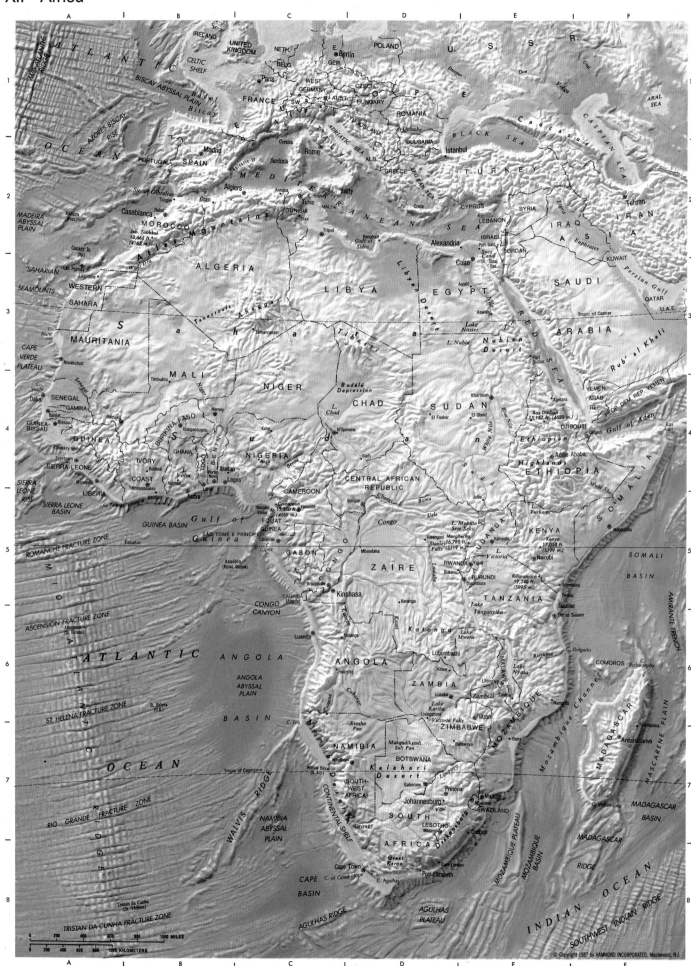

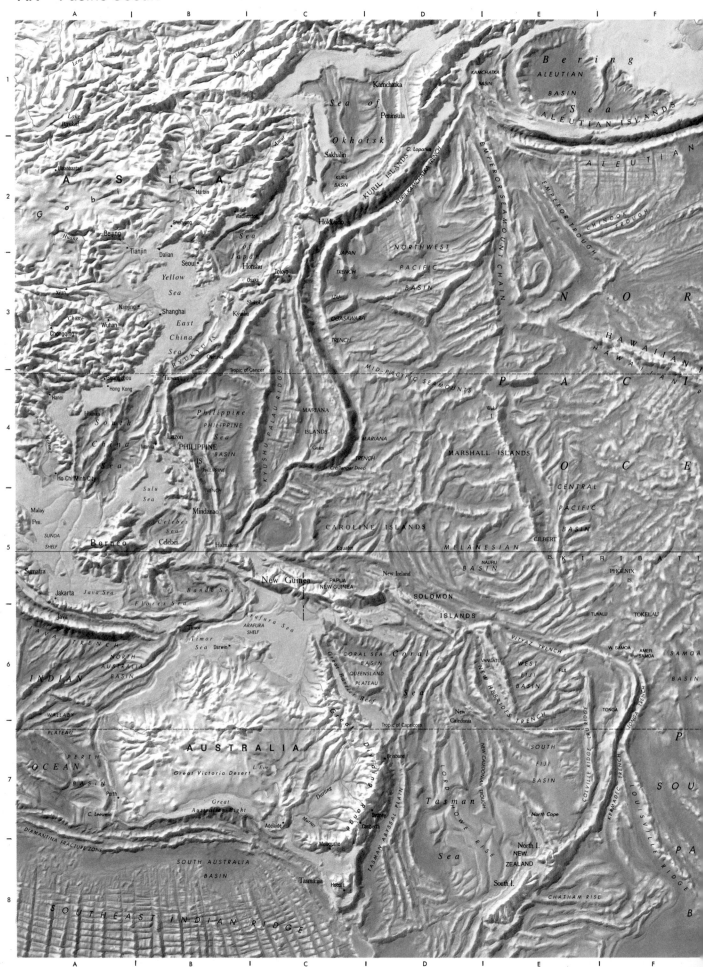

Lena

Aldan

Lake
Baykal

Kamchatka

Sea of

Okhotsk

KAMCHATKA
BASIN

Bering

ALEUTIAN

BASIN

Kamchatka

Peninsula

ALEUTIAN ISLANDS

Sea

Ulaanbaatar

A S I A

G   o   b   i

Harbin

Amur

Sakhalin

C. Lopatka

KURIL
BASIN

KURIL ISLANDS

KURIL KAMCHATKA TRENCH

EMPEROR SEAMOUNT CHAIN

A L E U T I A N

EMPEROR TROUGH

CHINOOK   TROUGH

Beijing

Shenyang

Vladivostok

Hokkaido

Huang

Tianjin

Dalian

Seoul

Sea

of

Japan

Honshu

Tokyo

JAPAN

TRENCH

IZU

NORTHWEST

PACIFIC

BASIN

N   O   R   R

Xian

Yellow

Sea

Nanjing

Osaka

Shikoku

Kyushu

OGASAWARA

Chang

Wuhan

Shanghai

East

China

Sea

TRENCH

MID-PACIFIC SEAMOUNTS

HAWAIIAN

Chongqing

RYUKYU IS.

Okinawa

Tropic of Cancer

P   A   C   I   I   R

HAWAIIAN

Guangzhou

Taiwan

Hanoi

Hong Kong

Philippine

KYUSHU-PALAU RIDGE

MARIANA

Wake
I.

Hainan

South

China

Sea

PHILIPPINE

Philippine

Sea

BASIN

ISLANDS

MARIANA

MARSHALL ISLANDS

O   C   E

Luzon

PHILIPPINE
IS.

Manila

PHILIPPINE

Guam

TRENCH

Ho Chi Minh City

TRENCH

Sulu
Sea

Mindanao

CENTRAL

PACIFIC

BASIN

Malay
Pen.

SUNDA
SHELF

Celebes
Sea

Borneo

Celebes

Halmahera

CAROLINE ISLANDS

Equator

MELANESIAN

GILBERT

Sumatra

Jakarta

Java Sea

Banda Sea

New Guinea

PAPUA
NEW GUINEA

New Ireland

NAURU
BASIN

PHOENIX
IS.

K   I   R   I   B   A   T   I

Java

Flores Sea

SOLOMON

ISLANDS

IS.

TUVALU

TOKELAU

JAVA   TRENCH

Timor

ARAFURA
SHELF

Arafura Sea

VITYAZ TRENCH

W. SAMOA

AMER.
SAMOA

SAMOA

BASIN

Timor
Sea

Darwin

VANUATU

WEST

FIJI

BASIN

FIJI

INDIAN

NORTH
AUSTRALIA
BASIN

Coral Sea
BASIN

Coral

Sea

NEW HEBRIDES TRENCH

TONGA

WALLABY

Great Barrier Reef

QUEENSLAND
PLATEAU

New
Caledonia

Tropic of Capricorn

P

PLATEAU

OCEAN

PERTH

BASIN

AUSTRALIA

Great Victoria Desert

L. Eyre

Brisbane

Dividing

Gulf

NEW CALEDONIAN TROUGH

COLVILLE RIDGE

LAU RIDGE

SOUTH

FIJI

BASIN

LORD

HOWE

RISE

SOU.

KERMADEC TRENCH

TONGA TRENCH

LOUISVILLE RIDGE

PA

Perth

C. Leeuwin

Great

Australian Bight

Darling

Adelaide

Murray

Sydney

Canberra

Melbourne

Tasman

TASMAN ABYSSAL PLAIN

Sea

North Cape

North I.

NEW

ZEALAND

DIAMANTINA FRACTURE ZONE

SOUTH AUSTRALIA

BASIN

Tasmania

Hobart

South I.

CHATHAM RISE

S O U T H E A S T   I N D I A N   R I D G E

B

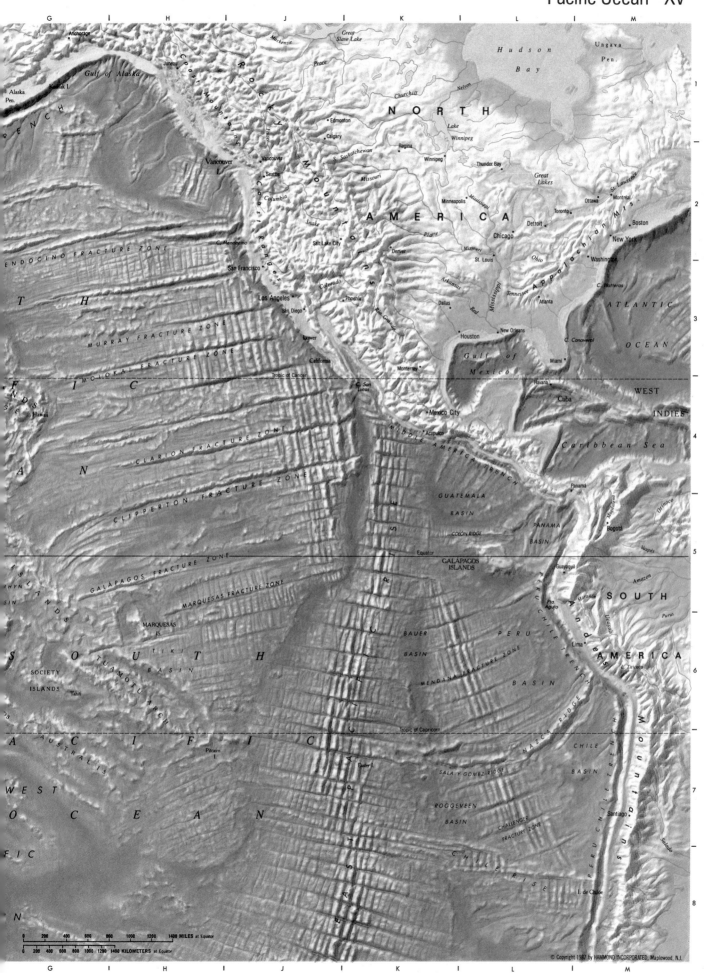

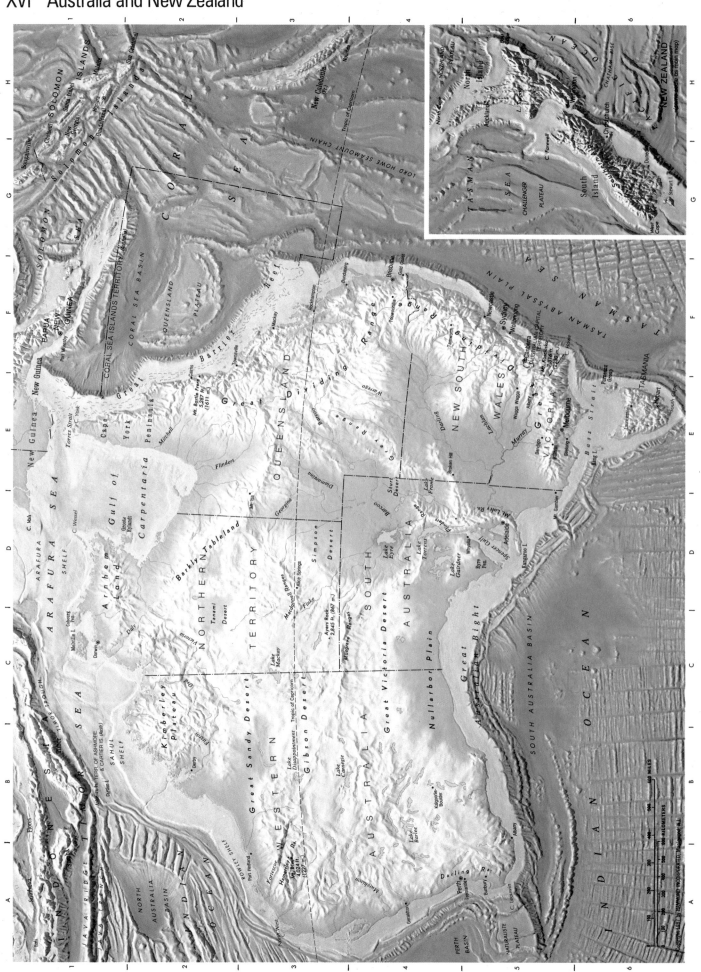

This map has been prepared with the North Pole as the mathematical center. From it, distances to any part of the world may be measured. On Mercator's map of the world, the polar regions are so scattered that their relatively small area and availability for flight routes are disregarded. Today, with airplanes following great circle courses, often within the Arctic Circle, polar projection maps are indispensable to the people of this air-minded age.

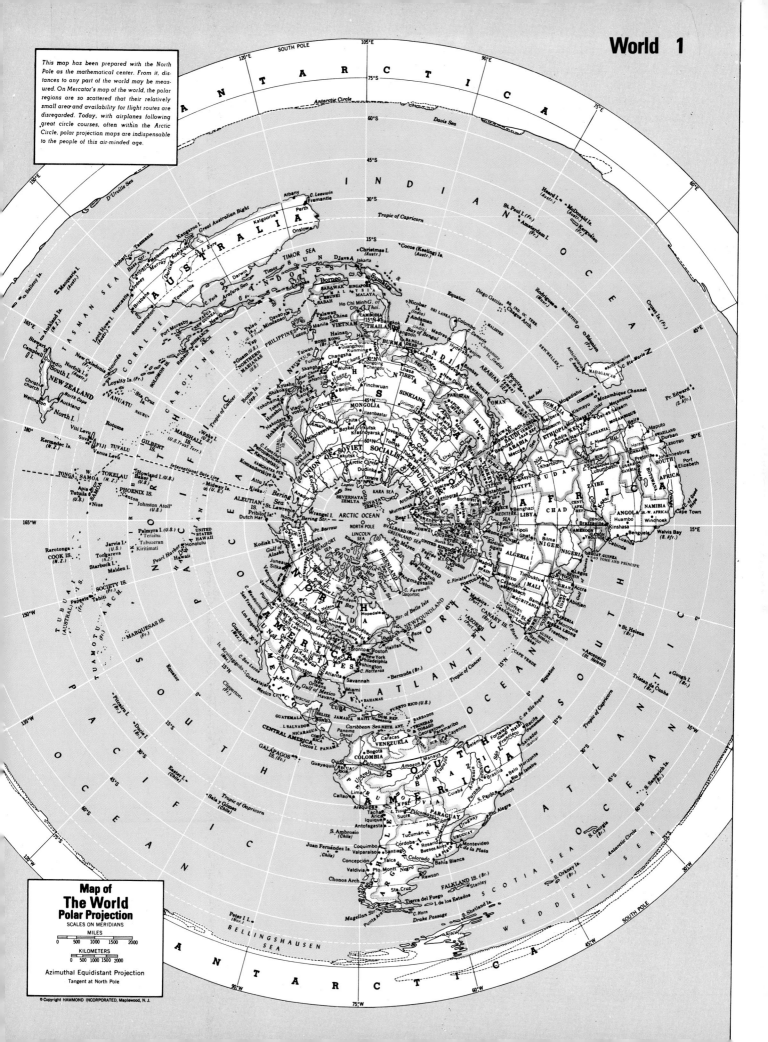

Map of The World Polar Projection

SCALES ON MERIDIANS

MILES
0   500   1000   1500   2000

KILOMETERS
0   500 1000 1500 2000

Azimuthal Equidistant Projection
Tangent at North Pole

The World

BRIESEMEISTER ELLIPTICAL
EQUAL-AREA PROJECTION

Capitals of Countries ....⊗
Other Capitals.........................⊛
International Boundaries..... − − −

Scale 1:80,000,000

Time Zones

STANDARD	Areas using half hour deviations.
TIME	
ZONES	Areas not using zone system.

NOTE: Standard time zones in the U.S.S.R. are always advanced one hour.

LAND AREA 57,970,000 sq. mi.
(150,142,300 sq. km.)
WATER AREA 139,781,000 sq. mi.
(362,032,790 sq. km.)
TOTAL SURFACE AREA 197,751,000 sq.mi.
(512,175,090 sq. km.)
POPULATION 4,415,000,000

Antarctica
AZIMUTHAL EQUIDISTANT PROJECTION
Scale 1:62,000,000

ANTARCTICA
+ SOUTH POLE

Alaska (gulf), U.S.	D17	Borden (isl.), Canada	B15	Farewell (cape), Greenl.	D12
Alaska (pen.), U.S.	D18	Bristol (bay), U.S.	D18	Finland	C8
Alaska (range), U.S.	C17	Brodeur (pen.), Canada	B14	Foxe (basin), Canada	C13
Alaska (reg.), U.S.	C17	Brooks (range), U.S.	C17	Franz Josef Land (isls.),	
Aleutian (isls.), U.S.	D18	Chelyuskin (cape), U.S.S.R.	B4	U.S.S.R.	A7
Alexander (arch.), U.S.	D16	Cherskiy, U.S.S.R.	C1	Frederikshåb, Greenl.	C12
Alexandra Land (isl.),		Chukchi (pen.), U.S.S.R.	C18	Garry (lake), Canada	C14
U.S.S.R.	A8	Chukchi (sea)	C18	George Land (isl.), U.S.S.R.	B7
Amundsen (gulf), Canada	B16	Columbia (cape), Canada	A13	Godhavn, Greenl.	C12
Anadyr (gulf), U.S.S.R.	C18	Cook (inlet), U.S.	D17	Godthåb (Nûk) (cap.),	
Anadyr' (riv.), U.S.S.R.	C1	Cumberland (sound), Canada	C13	Greenl.	C12
Arctic Ocean	A15	Davis (str.),	C12	Graham Bell (isl.), U.S.S.R.	A6
Atlantic Ocean	D11	Denmark (strait)	C11	Great Bear (lake), Canada	C16
Attu (isl.), U.S.	D1	Devon (isl.), Canada	B14	Great Slave (lake), Canada	C16
Axel Heiberg (isl.), Canada	A14	Dezhnev (cape), U.S.S.R.	C18	Greenland	B12
Baffin (bay), Canada	B13	Disko (isl.), Greenl.	C12	Greenland (sea)	B10
Baffin (isl.), Canada	C13	Dmitriya Lapteva (str.),		Grise Fiord, Canada	B13
Banks (isl.), Canada	B16	U.S.S.R.	B2	Grønnedal, Greenl.	C12
Barents (sea)	B8	Dnepr (riv.)		Gunnbjørn (mt.), Greenl.	C11
Barrow (pt.), U.S.	B16	Dvina, Northern (riv.),		Gyda (pen.), U.S.S.R.	C6
Bathurst (isl.), Canada	B14	U.S.S.R.	C7	Hammerfest, Norway	B9
Bear (isl.), Norway	B9	East (Dezhnev) (cape),		Hayes (pen.), Greenl.	B13
Bear (isls.), U.S.S.R.	B1	U.S.S.R.	C18	Hekla (mt.), Ice.	C11
Beaufort (sea)	B16	East Siberian (sea),		Holman Island, Canada	B15
Belyy, U.S.S.R.	B6	U.S.S.R.	B1	Holsteinsborg, Greenl.	C12
Bering (sea)	C18	Edge (isl.), Norway	B8	Hope (inlet), Norway	B8
Bilibino, U.S.S.R.	C1	Ellef Ringnes (isl.), Canada	B15	Iceland	C10
Bol'shevik, U.S.S.R.	A4	Ellesmere (isl.), Canada	B14	Igarka, U.S.S.R.	C5
Boothia (gulf), Canada	B15	Faddeyevskiy (isl.),		Igloolik, Canada	B14
Boothia (pen.), Canada	B14	U.S.S.R.	B2	Indigirka (riv.), U.S.S.R.	C1

Inuvik, Canada	C16	October Revolution (isl.),	
Ivigtut, Greenl.	D12	U.S.S.R.	B5
Isachsen, Canada	B15	Olenek, U.S.S.R.	C4
Jan Mayen (isl.), Norway	B10	Omolon (riv.), U.S.S.R.	C1
Julianehåb, Greenl.	D12	Oymyakon, U.S.S.R.	C2
Juneau, U.S.	D16	Pangnirtung, Canada	C13
Kalâtdlit-Nunat		Peary Land (reg.), Greenl.	A11
(Greenland)	B12	Pechenga, U.S.S.R.	C8
Kane (basin)	B13	Pechora (riv.), U.S.S.R.	C6
Kanin (pen.), U.S.S.R.	C7	Pond Inlet, Canada	B13
Kara (sea), U.S.S.R.	B6	Port Radium, Canada	C15
Karasovey (cape), U.S.S.R.	B6	Pribilof (isls.), U.S.	D18
Karskiye Vorota (str.),		Prince Charles (isl.),	
U.S.S.R.	B7	Canada	C13
Kem', U.S.S.R.	C8	Prince of Wales (cape), U.S.	C18
Khatanga, U.S.S.R.	B4	Prince of Wales (isl.),	
King Christian IX Land (reg.),		Canada	B14
Greenl.	C11	Prince Patrick (isl.),	
King Christian X Land (reg.),		Canada	B16
Greenl.	B11	Providenya, U.S.S.R.	C18
King Frederik VIII Land (reg.),		Queen Elizabeth (isls.),	
Greenl.	B11	Canada	B15
Kiruna, Sweden	C8	Repulse Bay, Canada	C14
Knud Rasmussen Land (reg.),		Resolute, Canada	B14
Greenl.	B12	Reykjavik (cap.), Ice.	C11
Kodiak, U.S.	D17	Rocky (mts.), Canada	D16
Kola (pen.), U.S.S.R.	C8	Rudolf (isl.), U.S.S.R.	A6
Kolguyev (isl.), U.S.S.R.	B7	Sachs Harbour, Canada	B16
Kolyma (range), U.S.S.R.	C1	Saint Lawrence (isl.), U.S.	C18
Kolyma (riv.), U.S.S.R.	C2	Saint Matthew (isl.), U.S.	C18
Komsomolets (isl.), U.S.S.R.	A5	Salekhard, U.S.S.R.	C6
Kort, U.S.S.R.	C8	Scoresby (sound), Greenl.	B10
Kotel'nyy (isl.), U.S.S.R.	B2	Scoresbysund, Greenl.	B10
Kotuy (riv.), U.S.S.R.	B4	Severnaya Zemlya (isls.),	
Kotzebue, U.S.	C18	U.S.S.R.	A4
Kraulshavn, Greenl.	B13	Seward, U.S.	D17
Kuskokwim (riv.), U.S.	C17	Seward (pen.), U.S.	C18
Lancaster (sound), Canada	B14	Shannon (isl.), Greenl.	B10
Laptev (sea), U.S.S.R.	B3	Siberia (reg.), U.S.S.R.	C3
Lena (riv.), U.S.S.R.	C3	Sitka, U.S.	D16
Lincoln (sea)	A12	Somerset (isl.), Canada	B14
Logan (mt.), Canada	C17	Søndre Strømfjord	
Longyearbyen, Norway	B8		C12
Lyakhov (isls.), U.S.S.R.	B3	Spitsbergen (isl.), Norway	B9
Mackenzie (bay), Canada	B16	Srednekolymsk, U.S.S.R.	C2
Mackenzie (mts.), Canada	C16	Sukkertoppen, Greenl.	C12
Mackenzie (riv.), Canada	C16	Susuman, U.S.S.R.	C2
Mackenzie King (isl.),		Svalbard (isls.), Norway	B9
Canada	B15	Sweden	C9
Markovo, U.S.S.R.	C1	Taymyr (pen.), U.S.S.R.	B4
Mayo, Canada	C16	Taymyr (riv.), U.S.S.R.	B4
M'Clure (str.), Canada	B15	Taz (river), U.S.S.R.	C5
McKinley (mt.), U.S.	C17	Thule, Greenl.	B13
Melville (bay), Greenl.	B13	Thule A.F.B. (Dundas),	
Melville (isl.), Canada	B15	Greenl.	B13
Melville (pen.), Canada	C14	Tiksi, U.S.S.R.	B3
Mezen', U.S.S.R.	C7	Tingmiarmiut, Greenl.	C12
Morris Jesup (cape), Greenl.	A11	Trail (isl.), Greenl.	B10
Mould Bay, Canada	B16	Tromsø, Norway	B9
Murmansk, U.S.S.R.	C8	Tuktoyaktuk, Canada	C16
Mys Shmidta, U.S.S.R.	C1	Uelen, U.S.S.R.	C18
Nanortalik, Greenl.	D12	Umnak (isl.), U.S.	D18
Narssaq, Greenl.	D12	Unalaska (isl.), U.S.	D18
Narvik, Norway	C9	Unimak (isl.), U.S.	D18
Nar'yan-Mar, U.S.S.R.	C7	Union of Soviet Socialist	
Navarin (cape), U.S.S.R.	C18	Republics	C2
Nettilling (lake), Canada	C13	United States	C2
New Siberian (isls.),		Upernavik, Greenl.	B12
U.S.S.R.	B2	Ural (mts.), U.S.S.R.	C6
Nikolayevsk, U.S.S.R.	D2	Ushakov (isl.), U.S.S.R.	B5
Nome, U.S.	C18	Ust'-Kuyga, U.S.S.R.	C3
Nord, Greenl.	A10	Vaygach (isl.), U.S.S.R.	C6
Nordvik-Ugol'naya, U.S.S.R.	B4	Verkhoyansk, U.S.S.R.	C3
Noril'sk, U.S.S.R.	B5	Verkhoyansk (range),	
Norman Wells, Canada	C16	U.S.S.R.	C3
North (cape), Ice.	C11	Victoria (isl.), Canada	B15
North (cape), Norway	B8	Vil'kitskogo (str.),	
Northeast Foreland (pen.),		U.S.S.R.	B4
Greenl.	A10	Viscount Melville (sound),	
Northeast Land (isl.),		Canada	B15
Norway	B8	Vorkuta, U.S.S.R.	C6
North Magnetic Pole, Canada	B15	Wainwright, U.S.	B18
North Pole		Wandel (sea), Greenl.	A10
Norton (sound), U.S.	C18	White (sea), U.S.S.R.	C8
Norway	C9	Whitehorse, Canada	C16
Norwegian (sea)	C10	Wiese (isl.), U.S.S.R.	B6
Novaya Sibir' Isl.		Wilczek Land (isl.)	
U.S.S.R.	B2		B6
Novaya Zemlya (isls.),		Yamal (pen.), U.S.S.R.	C6
U.S.S.R.	B6	Yana (riv.), U.S.S.R.	C3
Novyy Port, U.S.S.R.	C6	Yellowknife, Canada	C15
Nûk, Greenl.	C12	Yenisey (riv.), U.S.S.R.	C5
Nunivak (isl.), U.S.	D18	York (cape), Greenl.	C17
Ob' (gulf), U.S.S.R.	B6	Yukon (riv.), U.S.	C17
Ob' (riv.), U.S.S.R.	C6	Zhigansk, U.S.S.R.	C3
		Zyryanka, U.S.S.R.	C2

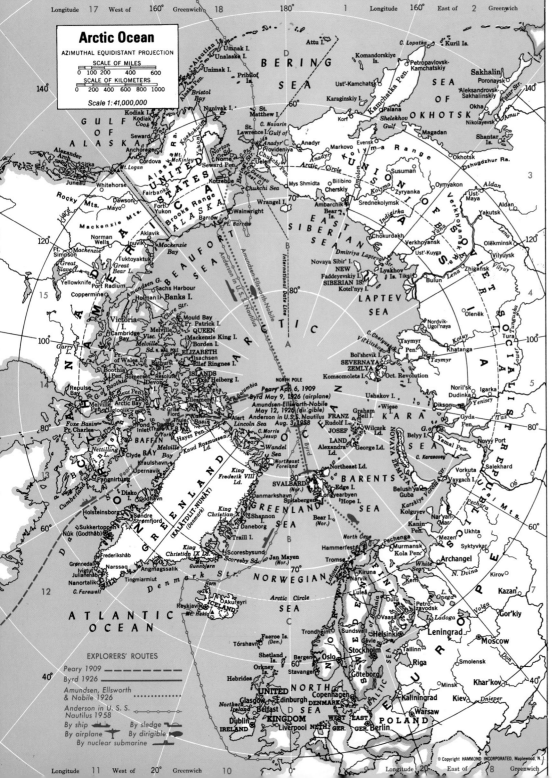

Antarctica
AZIMUTHAL EQUIDISTANT PROJECTION

SCALE OF MILES

0 200 400 600 800

KILOMETERS

0 200 400 600 800 1000

© Copyright HAMMOND INCORPORATED, Maplewood, N.J.

EXPLORERS' ROUTES

Palmer 1820 ++++++++++
Amundsen 1910-12 ············
Scott 1910-13 ···············
Byrd 1928-30 — — — — —
Fuchs 1957-58 ooooooooooo
By ship 🚢   By sledge   By airplane ✈
By snow tractor 🚜

Adare (cape)	B9	Larsen Ice Shelf	C16
Adelaide (isl.)	C15	Lazarev Station	C1
Adélie Coast (reg.)	C7	Levick (mt.)	B8
Alexander (isl.)	B15	Lister (mt.)	B8
American Highland	B4	Little America	B10
Amery Ice Shelf	C4	Luitpold Coast (reg.)	B17
Amundsen (bay)	C3	Lützow-Holm (bay)	C3
Amundsen (sea)	B13	Mackenzie (bay)	C4
Amundsen-Scott Station	A14	Mac-Robertson Land (reg.)	B4
Antarctic (pen.)	C15	Marguerite (bay)	C15
Balleny (isls.)	C9	Marie Byrd Land (reg.)	B13
Banzare Coast (reg.)	C7	Markham (mt.)	A8
Barr Smith (mt.)	A8	Mawson	C4
Batterbee (cape)	C3	McMurdo (sound)	B9
Beardmore (glac.)	A8	Mertz Glacier Tongue	C8
Bellingshausen (sea)	C14	Mirnny	C5
Berkner (isl.)	B16	New Schwabenland (reg.)	B1
Biscoe (isls.)	C15	Ninnis Glacier Tongue	C8
Bouvet (isl.)	D1	Norvegia (cape)	B18
Bouvetøya (Bouvet) (isl.)	D1	Oates Coast (reg.)	B8
Bransfield (str.)	B15	Palmer (arch.)	C15
Budd Coast (reg.)	C6	Palmer Land (reg.)	B15
Byrd Station	A12	Palmer Station	C15
Caird Coast (reg.)	B17	Peter I (isl.)	B14
Charcot (isl.)	C15	Prince Edward (isls.)	E2
Clarie Coast (reg.)	C7	Prince Olav Coast (reg.)	C3
Coats Land (reg.)	B17	Princess Astrid Coast (reg.)	B1
Colbeck (cape)	B10	Princess Martha Coast (reg.)	B18
Coronation (isl.)	C16	Princess Ragnhild Coast (reg.)	B2
Daly (cape)	C4	Prydz (bay)	C4
Darnley (cape)	C4	Queen Mary Coast (reg.)	C5
Dart (cape)	B12	Queen Maud (mts.)	A12
Davis (sea)	C5	Queen Maud Land (reg.)	B1
Davis Station	C4	Riiser-Larsen (pen.)	C2
Drake (passage)	C15	Ronne Entrance (inlet)	B15
Dumont d'Urville Station	C7	Ronne Ice Shelf	B15
Edward VII (pen.)	B11	Roosevelt (isl.)	A10
Edward VIII (bay)	C4	Ross (sea)	B9
Eights Coast (reg.)	B14	Ross Ice Shelf	A10
Elephant (isl.)	D16	Sabine (mt.)	B9
Ellsworth Land (reg.)	B14	Sabrina Coast (reg.)	C6
Enderby Land (reg.)	B3	Sanae Station	B18
English Coast (reg.)	B15	Scotia (sea)	D16
Executive Committee (range)	B12	Scott (mt.)	C10
Farr (bay)	C5	Scott Station	B9
Filchner Ice Shelf	B16	Shackleton Ice Shelf	C5
Ford Ranges (mts.)	B11	Sidley (mt.)	B12
Gaussberg (mt.)	C5	Siple (mt.)	B12
George V Coast (reg.)	C8	South Georgia (isl.)	D17
Getz Ice Shelf	B12	South Magnetic Pole	C7
Goodenough (cape)	C7	South Orkney (isls.)	C16
Graham Land (reg.)	C15	South Polar (plat.)	A1
Grytviken	D17	South Pole	A4
Hearst (isl.)	B16	South Sandwich (isls.)	D17
Hilton (inlet)	B16	South Shetland (isls.)	C16
Hobbs Coast (reg.)	B12	Sulzberger (bay)	B11
Hollick-Kenyon (plat.)	B13	Thurston (isl.)	C14
Hope (bay)	C16	Transantarctic (mts.)	B17
Indian Ocean	C3	Victoria Land (reg.)	B8
James Ross (isl.)	C16	Vincennes (bay)	C6
Joinville (isl.)	C16	Vinson Massif (mt.)	B14
Kainan (bay)	B10	Walgreen Coast (reg.)	B13
Keltie (cape)	C7	Weddell (sea)	C16
Kemp Coast (reg.)	C3	West Ice Shelf	C5
King George (isl.)	C16	Wilhelm II Coast (reg.)	C5
Kirkpatrick (mt.)	A8	Wilkes Land (reg.)	B7
Knox Coast (reg.)	C6		

Weddell Sea

Traverse of Cross Section Shown Below

+ SOUTH POLE

ANTARCTICA

Ross Sea

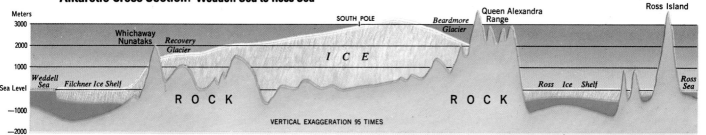

Antarctic Cross Section: Weddell Sea to Ross Sea

Meters
3000
2000
1000
Sea Level
-1000
-2000

Whichaway Nunataks — Recovery Glacier — SOUTH POLE — Beardmore Glacier — Queen Alexandra Range — Ross Island

Weddell Sea — Filchner Ice Shelf — ICE — ROCK — ROCK — Ross Ice Shelf — Ross Sea

VERTICAL EXAGGERATION 95 TIMES

Information Based on American Geographical Society's "Antarctic Map Folio Series"

Aberdeen, Scotland D3
Adriatic (sea) F4
Aegean (sea), Greece G5
Albania G4
Ålborg, Denmark F3
Alps (mts.) E4
Amsterdam (cap.),
　Netherlands E3
Andorra E4
Antwerp, Belgium E3
Arad, Romania G4
Araks (riv.), U.S.S.R. J5
Archangel, U.S.S.R. J2
Armenian S.S.R., U.S.S.R. ..J4
Astrakhan, U.S.S.R. J4
Århus, Denmark E3
Atlantic Ocean C4
Austria F4
Azerbaidzhan S.S.R.,
　U.S.S.R. J4
Azov (sea), U.S.S.R. H4
Baku, U.S.S.R. J4
Balaton (lake), Hungary F4
Balearic (isls.), Spain E5
Balkan (mts.) G4
Baltic (sea) F3
Barcelona, Spain E4
Barents (sea) J1
Basel, Switzerland E4
Belfast (cap.), N. Ireland ...D3
Belgium E3
Belgrade (cap.), Yugoslavia ..G4
Bergen, Norway E2
Berlin (cap.), E. Germany ...F3
Bern (cap.), Switzerland E4

Bilbao, Spain D4
Birmingham, England D3
Biscay (bay) D4
Black (sea) H4
Bologna, Italy F4
Bonn (cap.), W. Germany ...E3
Bordeaux, France D4
Bornholm (isl.), Denmark ..F3
Bosporus (str.), Turkey G4
Bothnia (gulf) F2
Braşov, Romania G4
Bratislava, Czech. F4
Bremen, W. Germany E3
Brest, France D4
Bristol, England D3
Brno, Czech. F4
Brussels (cap.), Belgium ...E3
Bucharest (cap.), Romania ..G4
Budapest (cap.), Hungary ...F4
Bug (riv.) G3
Bulgaria G4
Burgas, Bulgaria G4
Burgos, Spain D4
Calais, France E3
Cardiff, Wales D3
Carpathian (mts.) G4
Caspian (sea), U.S.S.R. J4
Cartagena, Spain D5
Caucasus (mts.), U.S.S.R. ..J4
Channel (isls.) D4
Cologne, W. Germany E3
Como, Italy E4
Constanţa, Romania G4
Copenhagen (cap.), Denmark ..F3
Córdoba, Spain D5
Cork, Ireland D3

Corsica (isl.), France E4
Cracow, Poland F3
Crete (isl.), Greece G5
Crimea (pen.), U.S.S.R. H4
Czechoslovakia F4
Danube (riv.) G4
Dardanelles (str.), Turkey ...G5
Debrecen, Hungary G4
Denmark E3
Denmark (str.) B2
Dnepropetrovsk, U.S.S.R. ..H4
Dnieper (riv.), U.S.S.R. H3
Dniester (riv.), U.S.S.R. G4
Don (riv.), U.S.S.R. J4
Donets (riv.), U.S.S.R. H4
Douro (riv.), Portugal D4
Dover, England E3
Drava (riv.) F4
Dresden, E. Germany F3
Dublin (cap.), Ireland D3
Dvina, Northern (riv.),
　U.S.S.R. J2
Ebro (riv.), Spain D4
Edinburgh (cap.), Scotland ..D3
Elba (isl.), Italy E4
Elbe (riv.) F3
El'brus (mt.), U.S.S.R. J4
England, U.K. D3
English (chan.) D3
Erfurt, E. Germany F3
Estonian S.S.R., U.S.S.R. ...G3
Etna (mt.), Italy F5
Faeroe (isls.), Denmark D2
Finisterre (cape), Spain C4

Finland G2
Finland (gulf) G3
Florence, Italy F4
France E4
Frankfurt, W. Germany E3
Frisian (isls.) E3
Garonne (riv.), France D4
Gdańsk, Poland F3
Geneva, Switzerland E4
Geneva (lake) E4
Genoa, Italy E4
Georgian S.S.R., U.S.S.R. ..J4
Gibraltar D5
Gibraltar (str.) D5
Glasgow, Scotland D3
Göteborg, Sweden F3
Granada, Spain D5
Graz, Austria F4
Greece G5
Guadalquivir (riv.), Spain ...D5
Guadiana (riv.) D5
Hague, The (cap.),
　Netherlands E3
Hamburg, W. Germany F3
Hammerfest, Norway G1
Helsinki (cap.), Finland G2
Hungary F4
Iceland C2
Ionian (sea) F5
Ireland D3
Irish (sea) D3
Istanbul, Turkey G4
Italy E4
Jan Mayen (isl.), Norway ...D1
Jönköping, Sweden F3
Kalinin, U.S.S.R. H3

Kaliningrad, U.S.S.R. G3
Kaluga, U.S.S.R. H3
Kama (riv.), U.S.S.R. K3
Karl-Marx-Stadt, E. Germany ..F3
Karlsruhe, W. Germany E4
Karlstad, Sweden F3
Kassel, W. Germany E3
Katowice, Poland F3
Kattegat (str.) F3
Kaunas, U.S.S.R. G3
Kavalla, Greece G4
Kazan, U.S.S.R. J3
Kecskemét, Hungary F4
Kharkov, U.S.S.R. H4
Kherson, U.S.S.R. H4
Kiel, W. Germany F3
Kielce, Poland G3
Kiev, U.S.S.R. H3
Kirov, U.S.S.R. J3
Kirovograd, U.S.S.R. H4
Kishinev, U.S.S.R. G4
Kjölen (mts.) F2
Kola (pen.), U.S.S.R. H2
Krasnodar, U.S.S.R. H4
Kristiansand, Norway E3
Kristiansund, Norway E2
Krivoy Rog, U.S.S.R. H4
Kuopio, Finland G2
Kursk, U.S.S.R. H3
Kuybyshev, U.S.S.R. K3
Ladoga (lake), U.S.S.R. H2
Lapland (reg.) G2
Latvian S.S.R., U.S.S.R. G3
Leeds, England E3
Leghorn, Italy E4

Le Havre, France E4
Leipzig, E. Germany F3
Leningrad, U.S.S.R. H3
León, Spain D4
Liechtenstein E4
Liège, Belgium E3
Lille, France E3
Limerick, Ireland D3
Limoges, France E4
Linköping, Sweden F3
Linz, Austria F4
Lions (gulf) E4
Lisbon (cap.), Portugal D5
Liverpool, England D3
Ljubljana, Yugoslavia F4
Łódź, Poland F3
Lofoten (isls.), Norway F2
Loire (riv.), France E4
London (cap.), England E3
Luxembourg E4
Lyon, France E4
Madrid (cap.), Spain D4
Majorca (isl.), Spain E4
Málaga, Spain D5
Malta F5
Manchester, England D3
Marmara (sea), Turkey G4
Marseille, France E4
Mediterranean (sea) E5
Minsk, U.S.S.R. G3
Moldavian S.S.R., U.S.S.R. ..G4
Monaco E4
Moscow (cap.), U.S.S.R. H3
Munich, W. Germany F4
Murcia, Spain D5

Murmansk, U.S.S.R. H2
Nantes, France D4
Naples, Italy F4
Netherlands E3
Nice, France E4
North (Nordkapp) (cape) ...G1
Norway G1
North (sea) D3
Northern Ireland, U.K. D3
Norway F2
Norwegian (sea) D2
Nuremberg, W. Germany ...F4
Odense, Denmark F3
Oder (riv.) F3
Odessa, U.S.S.R. H4
Onega (lake), U.S.S.R. H2
Orenburg, U.S.S.R. K3
Orkney (isls.), Scotland D3
Orléans, France E4
Oslo (cap.), Norway F2
Palermo, Italy F5
Palma, Spain E5
Paris (cap.), France E4
Perm', U.S.S.R. K3
Ploieşti, Romania G4
Plovdiv, Bulgaria G4
Plymouth, England D3
Po (riv.), Italy E4
Poland F3
Portugal D4
Poznań, Poland F3
Prague (cap.), Czech. F3
Pyrenees (mts.) D4
Reykjavík (cap.), Iceland ...B2
Rhine (riv.) E3
Rhône (riv.), France E4

AREA 4,057,000 sq. mi.
(10,507,630 sq. km.)
POPULATION 676,000,000
LARGEST CITY Paris
HIGHEST POINT El'brus 18,510 ft.
(5,642 m.)
LOWEST POINT Caspian Sea -92 ft.
(-28 m.)

Population Distribution

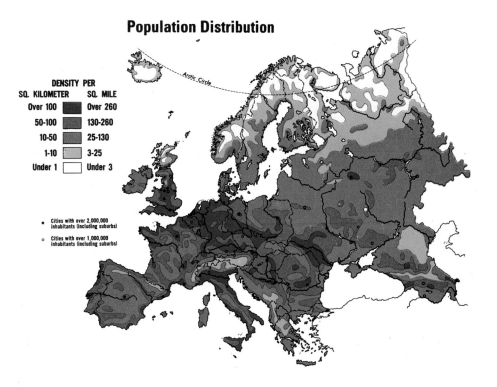

DENSITY PER

SQ. KILOMETER	SQ. MILE
Over 100	Over 260
50-100	130-260
10-50	25-130
1-10	3-25
Under 1	Under 3

• Cities with over 2,000,000 inhabitants (including suburbs)

○ Cities with over 1,000,000 inhabitants (including suburbs)

Vegetation

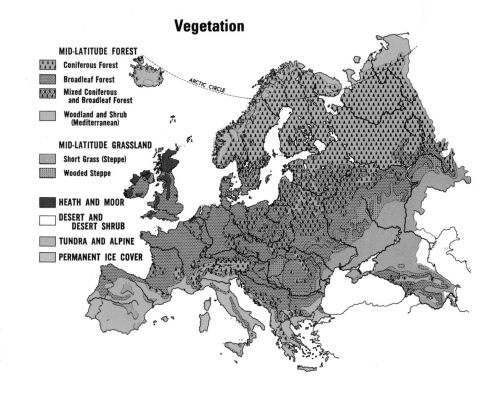

MID-LATITUDE FOREST

Coniferous Forest

Broadleaf Forest

Mixed Coniferous and Broadleaf Forest

Woodland and Shrub (Mediterranean)

MID-LATITUDE GRASSLAND

Short Grass (Steppe)

Wooded Steppe

HEATH AND MOOR

DESERT AND DESERT SHRUB

TUNDRA AND ALPINE

PERMANENT ICE COVER

© Copyright HAMMOND INCORPORATED, Maplewood, N. J.

Rhône (riv.), France	E4
Riga, U.S.S.R.	G3
Romania	G4
Rome (cap.), Italy	F4
Rostov, U.S.S.R.	J4
Rotterdam, Netherlands	E3
Russian S.F.S.R., U.S.S.R.	H3
Saarbrücken, W. Germany	E4
Saint George's (chan.)	D3
Salzburg, Austria	F4
San Marino	F4
Saragossa, Spain	D4
Sarajevo, Yugoslavia	F4
Saratov, U.S.S.R.	J3
Sardinia (isl.), Italy	E4
Sava (riv.)	F4
Scotland, U.K.	D3
Seine (riv.), France	E4
Sevastopol', U.S.S.R.	H4
Seville, Spain	D5
Shetland (isls.), Scotland	D2
Sicily (isl.), Italy	F5
Skagerrak (str.)	E3
Sofia (cap.), Bulgaria	G4
Sognefjorden (fjord), Norway	E2
Southampton, England	D3
Spain	D4
Stockholm (cap.), Sweden	F3
Strasbourg, France	E4
Stuttgart, W. Germany	E4
Sweden	F2
Switzerland	E4
Szeged, Hungary	F4
Tagus (riv.)	D5
Tampere, Finland	G2
Taranto (gulf), Italy	F5
Tbilisi, U.S.S.R.	J4

Tiber (riv.), Italy	F4
Tiranë (cap.), Albania	F4
Trieste, Italy	F4
Trondheim, Norway	F2
Turin, Italy	E4
Turkey	H5
Turku, Finland	G2
Tyrrhenian (sea)	F4
Ufa, U.S.S.R.	K3
Ukrainian S.S.R., U.S.S.R.	G4
Union of Soviet Socialist Republics	H2
United Kingdom	D3
Ural (mts.), U.S.S.R.	L2
Valencia, Spain	D5
Valletta (cap.), Malta	F5
Vatican City	F4
Venice, Italy	F4
Vienna (cap.), Austria	F4
Vistula (riv.), Poland	F3
Volga (riv.), U.S.S.R.	J4
Volgograd, U.S.S.R.	J4
Wales, U.K.	D3
Warsaw (cap.), Poland	G3
Weser (riv.), Germany	E3
West Germany	E3
White (sea), U.S.S.R.	H2
White Russian S.S.R., U.S.S.R.	G3
Wrocław, Poland	F3
Yugoslavia	F4
Zagorsk, U.S.S.R.	H3
Zagreb, Yugoslavia	F4
Zaporozh'ye, U.S.S.R.	H4
Zhitomir, U.S.S.R.	G3
Zürich, Switzerland	E4

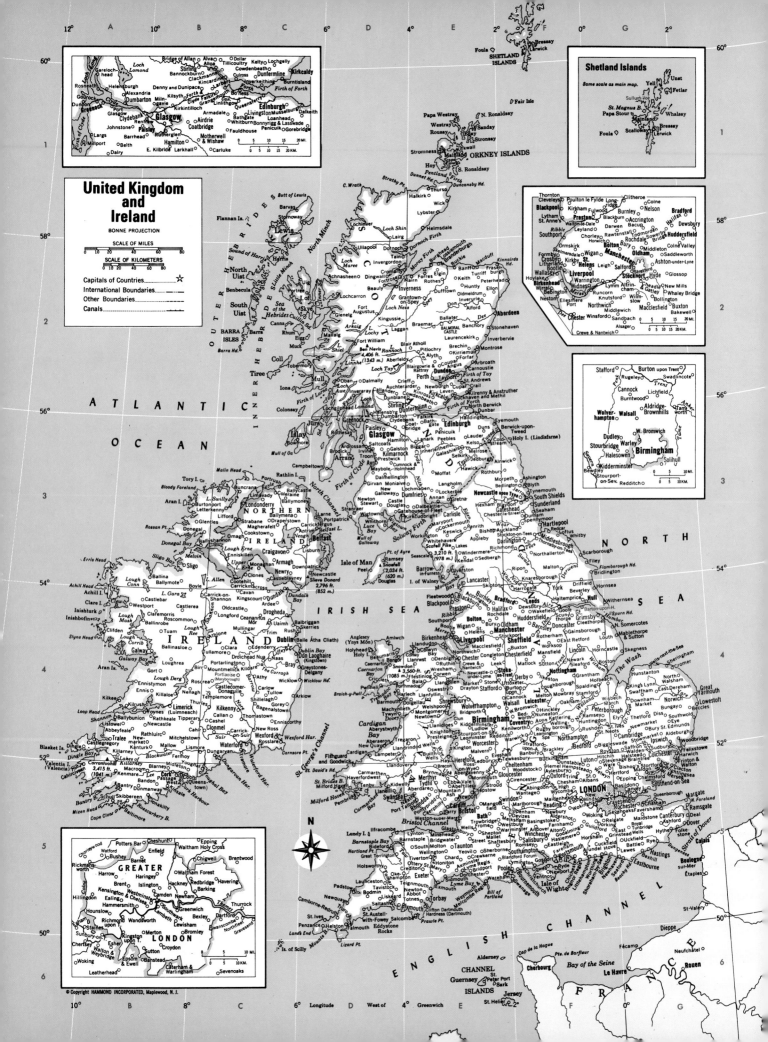

UNITED KINGDOM

AREA 94,399 sq. mi. (244,493 sq. km.)
POPULATION 55,672,000
CAPITAL London
LARGEST CITY London
HIGHEST POINT Ben Nevis 4,406 ft. (1,343 m.)
MONETARY UNIT pound sterling
MAJOR LANGUAGES English, Gaelic, Welsh
MAJOR RELIGIONS Protestantism, Roman Catholicism

IRELAND

AREA 27,136 sq. mi. (70,282 sq. km.)
POPULATION 3,440,427
CAPITAL Dublin
LARGEST CITY Dublin
HIGHEST POINT Carrantuohill 3,415 ft. (1,041 m.)
MONETARY UNIT Irish pound
MAJOR LANGUAGES English, Gaelic (Irish)
MAJOR RELIGION Roman Catholicism

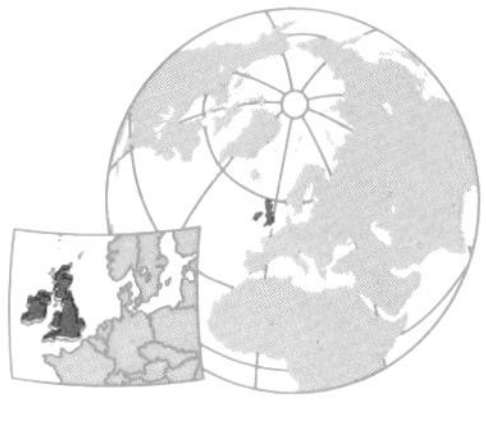

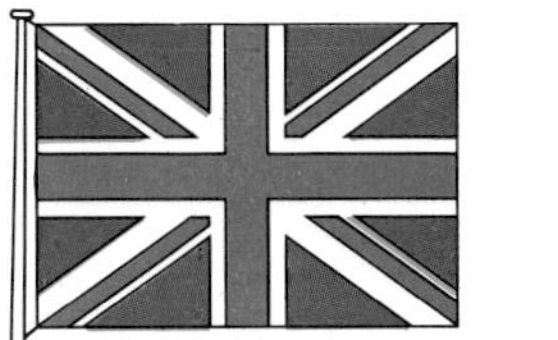

UNITED KINGDOM

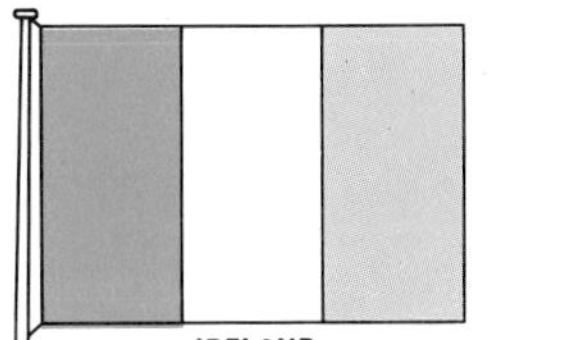

IRELAND

ENGLAND

AREA 50,516 sq. mi. (130,836 sq. km.)
POPULATION 46,220,955
CAPITAL London
LARGEST CITY London
HIGHEST POINT Scafell Pike 3,210 ft. (978 m.)

WALES

AREA 8,017 sq. mi. (20,764 sq. km.)
POPULATION 2,790,462
CAPITAL Cardiff
LARGEST CITY Cardiff
HIGHEST POINT Snowdon 3,560 ft. (1,085 m.)

SCOTLAND

AREA 30,414 sq. mi. (78,772 sq. km.)
POPULATION 5,117,146
CAPITAL Edinburgh
LARGEST CITY Glasgow
HIGHEST POINT Ben Nevis 4,406 ft. (1,343 m.)

NORTHERN IRELAND

AREA 5,452 sq. mi. (14,121 sq. km.)
POPULATION 1,543,000
CAPITAL Belfast
LARGEST CITY Belfast
HIGHEST POINT Slieve Donard 2,796 ft. (852 m.)

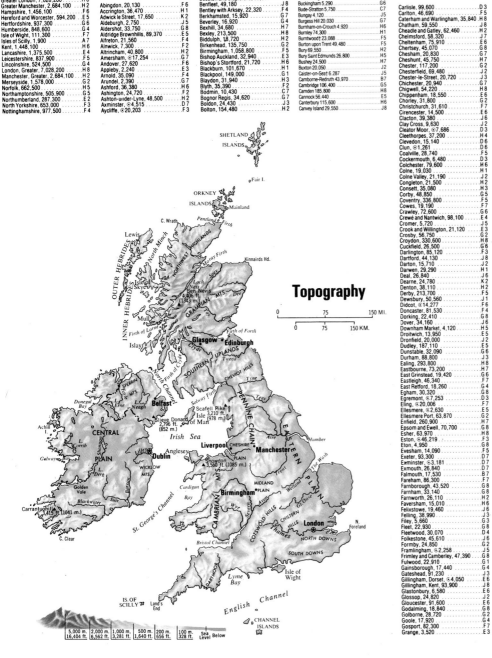

Topography

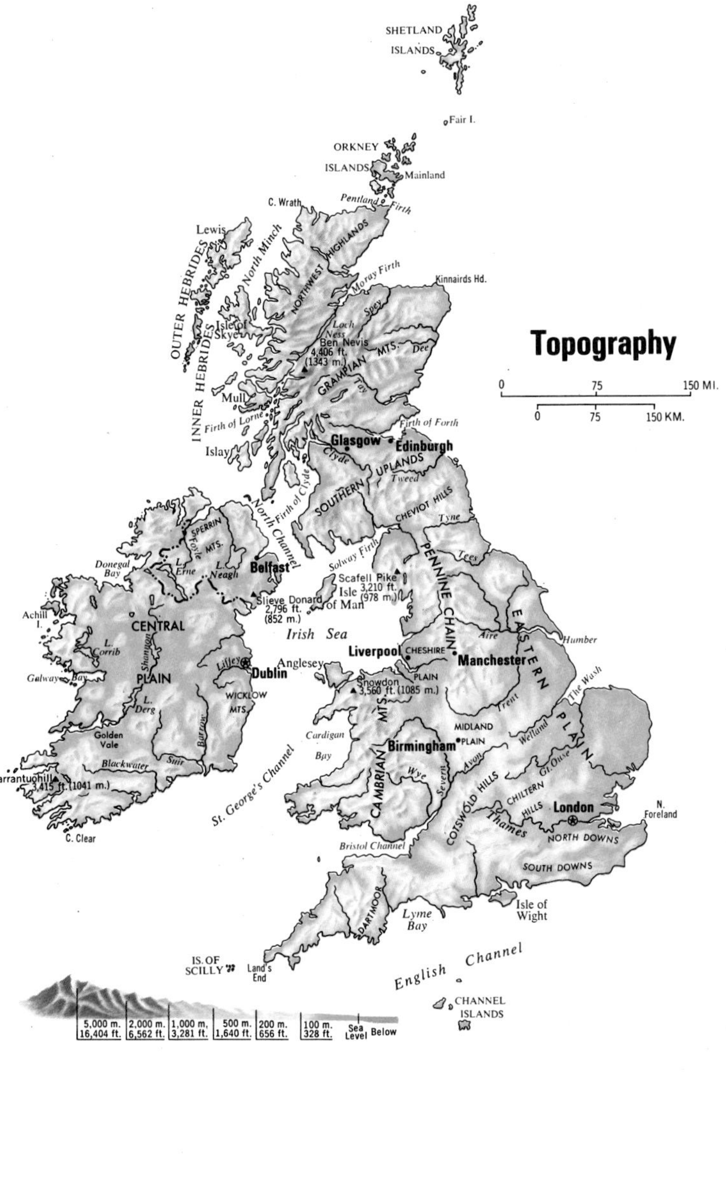
SHETLAND ISLANDS
Fair I.
ORKNEY ISLANDS
Mainland
C. Wrath
Pentland Firth
Lewis
OUTER HEBRIDES
North Minch
NORTHWEST HIGHLANDS
Moray Firth
Kinnairds Hd.
Isle of Skye
INNER HEBRIDES
Loch Ness
Ben Nevis 4,406 ft. (1343 m.)
GRAMPIAN MTS.
Dee
Mull
Firth of Lorne
Firth of Forth
Islay
Glasgow
Edinburgh
Clyde
SOUTHERN UPLANDS
Tweed
CHEVIOT HILLS
Tyne
Firth of Clyde
North Channel
SPERRIN MTS.
Donegal Bay
L. Erne
L. Neagh
Belfast
Solway Firth
Scafell Pike 3,210 ft. (978 m.)
Isle of Man
PENNINE CHAIN
Tees
Slieve Donard 2,796 ft. (852 m.)
Achill I.
CENTRAL PLAIN
L. Corrib
Shannon
Irish Sea
Liverpool
CHESHIRE PLAIN
Manchester
Aire
Humber
EASTERN PLAIN
Galway Bay
Liffey
Dublin
Anglesey
Snowdon 3,560 ft. (1085 m.)
WICKLOW MTS.
Trent
The Wash
L. Derg
Barrow
CAMBRIAN MTS.
MIDLAND PLAIN
Birmingham
Welland
Golden Vale
Blackwater
Suir
Cardigan Bay
Severn
Avon
Gt. Ouse
Wye
COTSWOLD HILLS
CHILTERN HILLS
Carrantuohill 3,415 ft. (1041 m.)
St. George's Channel
London
Thames
N. Foreland
NORTH DOWNS
C. Clear
Bristol Channel
SOUTH DOWNS
DARTMOOR
Lyme Bay
Isle of Wight
IS. OF SCILLY
Land's End
English Channel
CHANNEL ISLANDS
0 75 150 MI.
0 75 150 KM.
5,000 m. 16,404 ft.
2,000 m. 6,562 ft.
1,000 m. 3,281 ft.
500 m. 1,640 ft.
200 m. 656 ft.
100 m. 328 ft.
Sea Level
Below

ENGLAND

COUNTIES

Avon, 920,200 . . . E 6
Bedfordshire, 491,700 . . . G 5
Berkshire, 659,000 . . . F 6
Buckinghamshire, 512,000 . . . G 6
Cambridgeshire, 563,000 . . . G 5
Cheshire, 916,400 . . . E 4
Cleveland, 567,900 . . . F 3
Cornwall, 405,200 . . . C 7
Cumbria, 473,600 . . . D 3
Derbyshire, 887,600 . . . F 5
Devon, 942,100 . . . D 7
Dorset, 575,800 . . . E 7
Durham, 610,400 . . . F 3
East Sussex, 655,600 . . . H 7
Essex, 1,426,200 . . . H 6
Gloucestershire, 491,500 . . . E 6
Greater London, 7,028,200 . . . H 8
Greater Manchester, 2,684,100 . . . H 2
Hampshire, 1,456,100 . . . F 6
Hereford and Worcester, 594,200 . . . E 5
Hertfordshire, 937,300 . . . G 6
Humberside, 848,600 . . . G 4
Isle of Wight, 111,300 . . . F 7
Isles of Scilly, 1,900 . . . A 7
Kent, 1,448,100 . . . H 6
Lancashire, 1,375,500 . . . E 4
Leicestershire, 837,900 . . . F 5
Lincolnshire, 524,500 . . . G 4
London, Greater, 7,028,200 . . . H 8
Manchester, Greater, 2,684,100 . . . H 2
Merseyside, 1,578,000 . . . G 2
Norfolk, 662,500 . . . H 5
Northamptonshire, 505,900 . . . G 5
Northumberland, 287,300 . . . E 2
North Yorkshire, 653,000 . . . F 3
Nottinghamshire, 977,500 . . . F 4
Oxfordshire 541,800 . . . F6
Shropshire (Salop) 359,000 . . . E5
Somerset 404,400 . . . E6
South Yorkshire 1,318,300 . . . F4
Staffordshire 997,600 . . . E5
Suffolk 577,600 . . . H5
Surrey 1,002,900 . . . G6
Sussex, East 655,600 . . . H7
Sussex, West 623,400 . . . G7
Tyne and Wear 1,182,900 . . . H3
Warwickshire 471,000 . . . F5
West Midlands 2,743,300 . . . F5
West Sussex 623,400 . . . G7
West Yorkshire 2,072,500 . . . J1
Wiltshire 512,800 . . . E6
Yorkshire, North 653,000 . . . F3
Yorkshire, South 1,318,300 . . . F4
Yorkshire, West 2,072,500 . . . J1

CITIES and TOWNS

Abingdon, 20,130 . . . F 6
Accrington, 36,470 . . . H 1
Adwick le Street, 17,650 . . . K 2
Aldeburgh, 2,750 . . . J 5
Aldershot, 33,750 . . . G 8
Aldridge Brownhills, 89,370 . . . E 5
Alfreton, 21,560 . . . F 4
Alnwick, 7,300 . . . F 2
Altrincham, 40,800 . . . H 2
Amersham, ⊙17,254 . . . G 7
Andover, 27,620 . . . F 6
Appleby, 2,240 . . . E 3
Arnold, 35,090 . . . F 4
Arundel, 2,390 . . . G 7
Ashford, 36,380 . . . H 6
Ashington, 24,720 . . . F 2
Ashton-under-Lyne, 48,500 . . . H 2
Axminster, ⊙4,515 . . . D 7
Aycliffe, ⊙20,203 . . . F 3
Aylesbury, 41,420 . . . G 7
Bacup, 14,990 . . . H 1
Bakewell, 4,100 . . . J 2
Banbury, 31,060 . . . F 5
Banstead, 44,100 . . . H 8
Barking, 153,800 . . . H 8
Barnet, 305,200 . . . H 7
Barnsley, 74,730 . . . J 2
Barnstaple, 17,820 . . . D 6
Barrow-in-Furness, 73,400 . . . D 3
Barton-upon-Humber, 7,750 . . . G 4
Basildon, 135,720 . . . J 8
Basingstoke, 60,910 . . . F 6
Bath, 83,100 . . . E 6
Batley, 41,630 . . . J 1
Battle, ⊙4,987 . . . H 7
Bebington, 62,500 . . . G 2
Bedford, 74,390 . . . G 5
Bedlington, 27,200 . . . F 2
Bedworth, 41,600 . . . F 5
Beeston and Stapleford, 65,360 . . . F 5
Benfleet, 49,180 . . . J 8
Bentley with Arksey, 22,320 . . . F 4
Berkhamsted, 15,920 . . . G 7
Beverley, 16,920 . . . G 4
Bexhill, 34,680 . . . H 7
Bexley, 213,500 . . . H 8
Biddulph, 18,720 . . . H 2
Birkenhead, 135,750 . . . G 2
Birmingham, 1,058,800 . . . F 5
Bishop Auckland, 32,940 . . . E 3
Bishop's Stortford, 21,720 . . . H 6
Blackburn, 101,670 . . . H 1
Blackpool, 149,000 . . . G 1
Blaydon, 31,940 . . . H 3
Blyth, 35,390 . . . F 2
Bodmin, 10,430 . . . C 7
Bognor Regis, 34,620 . . . G 7
Boldon, 24,430 . . . J 3
Bolton, 154,480 . . . H 2
Bootle 71,160 . . . G2
Boston 26,700 . . . G5
Bournemouth 144,100 . . . F7
Bracknell† 34,067 . . . G8
Bradford 458,900 . . . J1
Braintree and Bocking 26,300 . . . H6
Brent 256,500 . . . H8
Brentwood 58,690 . . . J8
Bridgwater 26,700 . . . E6
Bridlington 26,920 . . . G3
Bridport 6,660 . . . E7
Brigg 4,870 . . . G4
Brighouse 35,320 . . . J1
Brightlingsea 7,170 . . . J6
Brighton 156,500 . . . G7
Bristol 416,300 . . . E6
Broadstairs and Saint Peter's 21,670 . . . J6
Bromley 299,100 . . . H8
Bromsgrove 41,430 . . . E5
Buckfastleigh 2,870 . . . C7
Buckingham 5,290 . . . G6
Bude-Stratton 5,750 . . . C7
Bungay 4,120 . . . J5
Burgess Hill 20,030 . . . G7
Burnham-on-Crouch 4,920 . . . H6
Burnley 74,300 . . . H1
Burntwood† 23,088 . . . F5
Burton upon Trent 49,480 . . . F5
Bury 69,550 . . . H2
Bury Saint Edmunds 26,800 . . . H5
Bushey 24,500 . . . H7
Buxton 20,050 . . . J2
Caister-on-Sea† 6,287 . . . J5
Camborne-Redruth 43,970 . . . B7
Cambridge 106,400 . . . G5
Camden 185,800 . . . H8
Cannock 56,440 . . . E5
Canterbury 115,600 . . . H6
Canvey Island 29,550 . . . J8
Carlisle, 99,600 . . . D 3
Carlton, 46,690 . . . F 5
Caterham and Warlingham, 35,840 . H 8
Chatham, 59,550 . . . J 8
Cheadle and Gatley, 62,460 . . . H 2
Chelmsford, 58,320 . . . J 7
Cheltenham, 75,910 . . . E 6
Chertsey, 45,070 . . . G 8
Chesham, 20,830 . . . G 7
Cheshunt, 45,750 . . . H 7
Chester, 117,200 . . . G 2
Chesterfield, 69,480 . . . J 2
Chester-le-Street, 20,720 . . . J 3
Chichester, 20,940 . . . G 7
Chigwell, 54,220 . . . H 8
Chippenham, 18,550 . . . E 6
Chorley, 31,800 . . . G 2
Christchurch, 31,610 . . . F 7
Cirencester, 14,500 . . . E 6
Clacton, 39,380 . . . J 6
Clay Cross, 9,630 . . . J 2
Cleator Moor, ⊙7,686 . . . D 3
Cleethorpes, 37,200 . . . H 4
Clevedon, 15,140 . . . D 6
Clun, ⊙1,261 . . . D 6
Coalville, 28,740 . . . F 5
Cockermouth, 6,480 . . . D 3
Colchester, 79,600 . . . H 6
Colne, 19,030 . . . H 1
Colne Valley, 21,190 . . . J 2
Congleton, 21,500 . . . H 2
Consett, 35,080 . . . H 3
Corby, 48,850 . . . G 5
Coventry, 336,800 . . . F 5
Cowes, 19,190 . . . F 7
Crawley, 72,600 . . . G 6
Crewe and Nantwich, 98,100 . . . E 4
Cromer, 5,720 . . . J 5
Crook and Willington, 21,120 . . . E 3
Crosby, 56,750 . . . G 2
Croydon, 330,600 . . . H 8
Cuckfield, 26,500 . . . G 6
Darlington, 85,120 . . . F 3
Dartford, 44,130 . . . J 8
Darton, 15,710 . . . J 2
Darwen, 29,290 . . . H 1
Deal, 26,840 . . . J 6
Dearne, 24,780 . . . K 2
Denton, 38,110 . . . H 2
Derby, 213,700 . . . F 5
Dewsbury, 50,560 . . . J 1
Didcot, ⊙14,277 . . . F 6
Doncaster, 81,530 . . . F 4
Dorking, 22,410 . . . G 8
Dover, 34,160 . . . J 6
Downham Market, 4,120 . . . H 5
Droitwich, 13,950 . . . E 5
Dronfield, 20,000 . . . J 2
Dudley, 187,110 . . . E 5
Dunstable, 32,090 . . . G 6
Durham, 88,800 . . . J 3
Ealing, 293,800 . . . H 8
Eastbourne, 73,200 . . . H 7
East Grinstead, 19,420 . . . G 6
Eastleigh, 46,340 . . . F 7
East Retford, 18,260 . . . G 4
Egham, 30,320 . . . G 8
Egremont, ⊙7,253 . . . D 3
Eling, ⊙20,006 . . . F 7
Ellesmere, ⊙2,630 . . . E 5
Ellesmere Port, 63,870 . . . G 2
Enfield, 260,900 . . . H 7
Epsom and Ewell, 70,700 . . . G 8
Esher, 63,970 . . . H 8
Eston, ⊙46,219 . . . F 3
Eton, 4,950 . . . G 8
Evesham, 14,090 . . . F 5
Exeter, 93,300 . . . D 7
Exminster, ⊙3,181 . . . D 7
Exmouth, 26,840 . . . D 7
Falmouth, 17,530 . . . B 7
Fareham, 86,300 . . . F 7
Farnborough, 43,520 . . . G 8
Farnham, 33,140 . . . G 8
Farnworth, 26,110 . . . H 2
Faversham, 15,010 . . . H 6
Felixstowe, 19,460 . . . J 6
Felling, 38,990 . . . J 3
Filey, 5,660 . . . G 3
Fleet, 22,930 . . . G 8
Fleetwood, 30,070 . . . D 4
Folkestone, 45,610 . . . J 6
Formby, 24,850 . . . G 2
Framlingham, ⊙2,258 . . . J 5
Frimley and Camberley, 47,390 . . . G 8
Fulwood, 22,910 . . . G 1
Gainsborough, 17,440 . . . G 4
Gateshead, 91,230 . . . J 3
Gillingham, Dorset, ⊙4,050 . . . E 6
Gillingham, Kent, 93,900 . . . J 8
Glastonbury, 6,580 . . . E 6
Glossop, 24,820 . . . J 2
Gloucester, 91,600 . . . E 6
Godalming, 18,840 . . . G 8
Golborne, 28,720 . . . G 2
Goole, 17,920 . . . G 4
Gosport, 82,300 . . . F 7
Grange, 3,520 . . . E 3
Grantham 27,830 . . . G5
Gravesend 53,500 . . . J8
Great Grimsby 93,800 . . . G4
Great Torrington 3,430 . . . C7
Great Yarmouth 49,410 . . . J5
Greenwich 207,200 . . . H8
Guildford 58,470 . . . G8
Guisborough 14,860 . . . F3
Hackney 192,500 . . . H8
Hale 17,080 . . . H2
Halesowen 54,120 . . . E5
Halifax 88,580 . . . J1
Haltemprice 54,850 . . . G4
Haltwhistle† 3,511 . . . E2
Hammersmith 170,000 . . . H8
Haringey 228,200 . . . H8
Harlow 79,160 . . . H7
Harrogate 64,620 . . . F4
Harrow 200,200 . . . B5
Hartlepool 97,100 . . . F3
Harwich 15,280 . . . J6
Haslingden 15,140 . . . H1
Hastings 74,600 . . . H7
Hatfield† 25,359 . . . H7
Havant and Waterloo 112,430 . . . G7
Haverhill 14,550 . . . H5
Havering 239,200 . . . J8
Hayle† 5,378 . . . B7
Hazel Grove and Bramhall 40,400 . . . H2
Heanor 24,590 . . . F4
Hebburn 23,150 . . . J3
Hedon 3,010 . . . G4
Hemel Hempstead 71,150 . . . G7
Hereford 47,800 . . . E5
Hertford 20,760 . . . H7
Hetton 16,810 . . . J3
Hexham 9,820 . . . E3
Heywood 31,720 . . . H2
High Wycombe 61,190 . . . G8
Hillingdon 230,800 . . . G8
Hinckley 49,310 . . . F5
Hinderwell† 2,551 . . . G3
Hitchin 29,190 . . . G6
Hoddesdon 27,510 . . . H7
Holmfirth 19,790 . . . J2
Horley† 18,593 . . . H8
Hornsea 7,280 . . . G4
Horsham 26,770 . . . G6
Horwich 16,670 . . . G2
Houghton-le-Spring 33,150 . . . J3
Hounslow, 199,100 . . . G 8
Hove, 72,000 . . . G 7
Hoylake, 32,000 . . . G 2
Hoyland Nether, 15,500 . . . J 2
Hucknall, 27,110 . . . F 4
Huddersfield, 130,060 . . . J 2
Hugh Town, ⊙1,958 . . . A 8
Hull, 276,600 . . . G 4
Hunstanton, 4,140 . . . H 5
Huntingdon and Godmanchester, 17,200 . . . G 5
Huyton-with-Roby, 65,950 . . . G 2
Hyde, 37,040 . . . H 2
Ilfracombe, 9,350 . . . C 6
Ilkeston, 33,690 . . . F 5
Immingham, ⊙10,259 . . . G 4
Ipswich, 121,500 . . . J 5
Islington, 171,600 . . . H 8
Jarrow, 28,510 . . . J 3
Kendal, 22,440 . . . E 3
Kenilworth, 19,730 . . . F 5
Kensington and Chelsea, 161,400 . . G 8
Keswick, 4,790 . . . D 3
Kettering, 44,480 . . . G 5
Keynsham, 18,970 . . . E 6
Kidderminster, 49,960 . . . E 5
Kidsgrove, 22,690 . . . E 4
King's Lynn, 29,990 . . . H 5
Kingston upon Thames, 135,600 . . H 8
Kingswood, 30,450 . . . E 6
Kirkburton, 20,320 . . . J 2
Kirkby, 59,100 . . . G 2
Kirkby Lonsdale, ⊙1,506 . . . E 3
Kirkby Stephen, ⊙1,539 . . . E 3
Knutsford, 14,840 . . . H 2
Lambeth, 290,300 . . . H 8
Lancaster, 126,300 . . . E 3
Leatherhead, 40,830 . . . G 8
Leeds, 744,500 . . . J 1
Leek, 19,460 . . . H 2
Leicester, 289,400 . . . F 5
Leigh, 46,390 . . . H 2
Leighton-Linslade, 22,590 . . . F 7
Letchworth, 31,520 . . . G 6
Lewes, 14,170 . . . H 7
Lewisham, 237,300 . . . H 8
Leyland, 23,690 . . . G 1
Lichfield, 23,690 . . . F 5
Lincoln, 73,700 . . . G 4
Liskeard, 5,360 . . . C 7
Litherland, 23,530 . . . G 2
Littlehampton, 20,320 . . . G 7

(continued on following page)

Liverpool, 539,700 G 2
Loftus, 7,850 G 3
London (cap.), 7,028,200 H 8
London, ★12,332,900 H 8
Long Eaton, 33,560 F 5
Longbenton, 50,120 J 3
Looe, 4,060 C 7
Loughborough, 49,010 F 5
Lowestoft, 53,260 J 5
Ludlow, ⊙7,466 E 5
Luton, 164,500 G 6
Lydd, 4,670 H 7
Lyme Regis, 3,460 E 7
Lymington, 36,780 F 7
Lynton, 1,770 D 6
Lytham Saint Anne's, 42,120 G 1
Mablethorpe and Sutton, 6,750 H 4
Macclesfield, 45,420 H 2
Maidenhead, 48,210 G 8
Maidstone, 72,110 J 8
Maldon, 14,350 H 6
Malmesbury, 2,550 E 6
Malton, 4,010 G 3
Malvern, 30,420 E 5
Manchester, 490,000 H 2
Mangotsfield, 23,000 E 6
Mansfield, 58,450 K 2
Mansfield Woodhouse, 25,400 F 4
March, 14,560 H 5
Margate, 50,290 J 6
Market Harborough, 15,230 G 5
Marlborough, 6,370 F 6
Matlock, 20,300 J 2
Melton Mowbray, 20,680 G 5
Merton, 169,400 H 8
Middlesbrough, 153,900 F 3
Middleton, 53,340 H 2
Middlewich, 7,600 H 2
Mildenhall, ⊙9,269 H 5
Millom, ⊙7,101 D 3
Milton Keynes, 89,900 F 5
Minehead, 8,230 D 6
Moretonhampstead, ⊙1,440 C 7
Morpeth, 14,450 F 2
Mundesley, ⊙1,536 J 5
Nelson, 31,220 H 1
Neston, 18,210 G 2
Newark, 24,760 G 4
Newbury, 24,850 F 6
Newcastle upon Tyne, 295,800 H 3
Newcastle-under-Lyme, 75,940 E 4
Newham, 228,900 H 8
Newhaven, 9,970 H 7
Newport, 22,430 F 7
New Romney, 3,830 J 7
Newton Abbot, 19,940 D 7
Newton-le-Willows, 21,780 H 2
New Windsor, 29,660 G 8
Northallerton F 3
Northam, 8,310 C 6
Northampton, 128,290 F 5
Northfleet, 27,150 J 8
North Sunderland, ⊙1,725 F 2
Northwich, 17,710 H 2
Norton, 5,580 G 3
Norton-Radstock, 15,900 E 6
Norwich, 119,200 J 5
Nottingham, 280,300 F 5
Nuneaton, 69,210 F 5
Oadby, 20,700 F 5
Oakham, 7,280 G 5
Okehampton, 4,000 D 7
Oldham, 103,690 H 2
Ormskirk, 28,860 G 2
Oswaldtwistle, 14,270 H 1
Oxford, 117,400 F 6
Padstow, ⊙2,802 B 7
Penryn, 5,660 B 7
Penzance, 19,360 B 7
Peterborough, 118,900 G 5
Peterlee, ⊙21,846 J 3
Plymouth, 259,100 C 7
Polperro, ⊙1,491 C 7
Poole, 110,600 E 7
Porlock, ⊙1,290 D 6
Portishead, 9,680 E 6
Portland, 14,860 E 7
Portslade-by-Sea, 18,040 G 7
Portsmouth, 198,500 F 7
Potters Bar, 24,670 H 7
Poulton-le-Fylde, 16,340 G 1
Preston, 94,760 G 1
Prestwich, 32,850 H 2
Queenborough, 31,550 H 6
Radcliffe, 29,630 H 2
Ramsbottom, 16,710 H 2
Ramsgate, 40,090 J 6
Rawtenstall, 20,950 H 1
Rayleigh, 26,740 J 8
Reading, 131,200 G 8
Redbridge, 231,600 H 8
Redcar, ⊙46,325 F 3
Redditch, 44,750 E 5
Reigate, 55,600 H 8
Richmond upon Thames, 166,800 H 8
Rickmansworth, 29,030 G 8
Ripley, 18,060 F 4
Rochdale, 93,780 H 2
Rochester, 56,030 J 8
Rothbury, ⊙1,818 E 2
Rotherham, 84,770 K 2
Royal Leamington Spa, 44,950 F 5
Royal Tunbridge Wells, 44,800 H 6
Rugby, 60,380 F 5
Rugeley, 24,440 E 5
Runcorn, 42,730 G 2
Rushden, 21,840 G 5
Ryde, 23,170 F 7
Rye, 4,530 H 7
Ryton, 15,170 H 3
Saddleworth, 21,340 J 2
Saint Agnes, ⊙4,747 B 7
Saint Albans, 123,800 H 7
Saint Austell-with-Fowey, 32,710 C 7
Saint Columb Major, ⊙3,953 B 7
Saint Helens, 104,890 G 2
Saint Ives, Cornwall, 9,760 B 7
Saint Neots, 17,940 G 5
Salcombe, 2,370 D 7
Sale, 59,060 H 2
Salford, 261,100 H 2
Salisbury, 35,460 F 6
Saltburn and Marske-by-the-Sea, 21,170 G 3
Sandbach, 14,280 H 2
Sandown-Shanklin, 14,800 F 7
Sandwich, 4,420 J 6
Saxmundham, 1,820 J 5
Scarborough, 43,300 G 3
Scunthorpe, 68,100 G 4
Seaford, 18,020 H 7
Seaham, 22,470 J 3
Seascale, ⊙2,106 D 3
Seaton, 4,500 D 7
Seaton Valley, 35,880 J 3
Sedbergh, ⊙2,741 E 3
Selsey, ⊙6,491 G 7
Sevenoaks, 18,160 J 8
Shaftesbury, 4,180 E 7
Sheffield, 558,000 J 2
Sherborne, 9,230 E 7
Sheringham, 4,940 J 5
Shildon, 15,360 F 3
Shoreham-by-Sea, 19,620 G 7
Shrewsbury, 56,120 E 5
Silloth, ⊙2,662 D 3
Sittingbourne and Milton, 32,830 H 6
Skelmersdale, 35,850 G 2
Skelton and Brotton, 15,930 G 3
Sleaford, 8,050 G 5
Slough, 89,060 G 8
Solihull, 108,230 F 5
Southampton, 213,700 F 7
Southend-on-Sea, 159,300 H 6
Southport, 86,030 G 1
South Shields, 96,900 J 3
Southwark, 224,900 H 8
Southwold, 1,960 J 5
Sowerby Bridge, 15,700 H 1
Spalding, 17,040 G 5
Spenborough, 41,460 J 1
Spennymoor, 19,050 F 3
Stafford, 54,860 E 5
Staines, 56,380 G 8
Stamford, 14,980 G 5
Stanley, 42,280 H 3
Staveley, 17,620 K 2
Stevenage, 72,600 G 6
Stockport, 138,350 H 2
Stockton-on-Tees, 165,400 F 3
Stoke-on-Trent, 256,200 E 4
Stourbridge, 56,530 E 5
Stourport-on-Severn, 19,430 E 5
Stowmarket, 9,020 J 5
Stratford-upon-Avon, 20,080 F 5
Stretford, 52,450 H 2
Stroud, 19,600 E 6
Sudbury, 8,860 H 5
Sunbury-on-Thames, 40,070 G 8
Sunderland, 214,820 J 3
Sutton, 166,700 H 8
Sutton Bridge, ⊙3,113 H 5
Sutton in Ashfield, 40,330 K 2
Swadlincote, 21,060 F 5
Swanage, 8,000 E 7
Swindon, 90,680 F 6
Tamworth, 46,960 F 5
Taunton, 37,570 D 6
Tavistock, ⊙7,620 C 7
Telford, ⊙79,451 E 5
Tenbury, ⊙2,151 E 5
Tewkesbury, 9,210 E 6
Thetford, 15,690 H 5
Thirsk, ⊙2,884 F 3
Thornaby-on-Tees, ⊙42,385 F 3
Thorne, ⊙16,694 F 4
Thornton Cleveleys, 27,090 G 1
Thurrock, 127,700 J 8
Tiverton, 16,190 D 7
Todmorden, 14,540 H 1
Tonbridge, 31,410 H 8
Torbay, 109,900 D 7
Torpoint, 6,840 C 7
Tower Hamlets, 146,100 H 8
Tow Law, 2,460 H 4
Trowbridge, 20,120 E 6
Truro, 15,690 B 7
Turton, 22,800 H 2
Tynemouth, 67,090 J 3
Upton upon Severn, ⊙2,048 E 5
Urmston, 44,130 H 2
Uttoxeter, 9,100 E 5
Ventnor, 6,980 F 7
Wainfleet All Saints, ⊙1,116 H 4
Wakefield, 306,500 J 2
Wallasey, 94,520 G 2
Wallsend, 45,490 J 3
Walsall, 182,430 E 5
Waltham Forest, 223,700 H 8
Waltham Holy Cross, 14,810 H 7
Walton and Weybridge, 51,270 G 8
Walton-le-Dale, 27,660 G 1
Wandsworth, 284,600 H 8
Wantage, 8,490 F 6
Ware, 14,900 H 7
Wareham, 4,630 E 7
Warley, 161,260 E 5
Warminster, 14,440 E 6
Warrington, 65,320 G 2
Warwick, 17,870 F 5
Washington, 27,720 J 3
Watchet, 2,980 D 6
Watford, 77,000 H 7
Wellingborough, 39,570 G 5
Wells, 8,960 E 6
Wells-next-the-Sea, 2,450 H 5
Welwyn, 39,900 H 7
Wem, ⊙3,411 E 5
West Bridgford, 28,340 F 5
West Bromwich, 162,740 F 5
West Mersea, 4,730 H 6
Westminster, 216,100 H 8
Weston-super-Mare, 51,960 D 6
Weymouth and Melcombe Regis, 41,080 E 7
Whickham, 29,710 J 3
Whitchurch, ⊙7,142 E 5
Whitehaven, 26,260 D 3
Whitley Bay, 37,010 J 3
Widnes, 58,330 G 2
Wigan, 80,920 G 2
Wigston, 31,650 F 5
Wilmslow, 31,250 H 2
Wilton, 4,090 F 6
Winchester, 88,900 F 6
Windermere, 7,860 E 3
Winsford, 26,920 G 2
Wirral, 27,510 G 2
Wisbech, 16,990 H 5
Witham, 19,730 H 6
Withernsea, 6,300 H 4
Wivenhoe, 5,630 J 6
Woking, 79,300 G 8
Wokingham, 22,390 G 8
Wolverhampton, 266,400 E 5
Wombwell, 17,850 K 2
Woodhall Spa, 2,420 G 4
Woodley and Sandford, ⊙24,581 G 8
Woodstock, 2,070 F 6
Wooler, ⊙1,833 F 2
Worcester, 73,900 E 5
Workington, 28,260 D 3
Worksop, 36,590 F 4
Worsbrough, 15,180 J 2
Worsley, 49,530 H 2
Worthing, 89,100 G 7
Wymondham, 9,390 J 5
Yateley, ⊙16,505 G 8
Yeovil, 26,180 E 7
York, 101,900 F 4

OTHER FEATURES

Aire (riv.) F 4
Atlantic Ocean A 7
Avon (riv.) F 5
Avon (riv.) F 7
Axe Edge (mt.) H 2
Barnstaple (bay) C 6
Beachy (head) H 7
Bigbury (bay) C 7
Blackwater (riv.) H 6
Bristol (chan.) C 6
Brown Willy (mt.) C 7
Cheviot (hills) E 2
Cheviot, The (mt.) E 2
Chiltern (hills) G 6
Cleveland (hills) F 3
Colne (riv.) G 8
Cornwall (cape) B 7
Cotswold (hills) E 6
Cross Fell (mt.) E 3
Cumbrian (mts.) D 3
Dart (riv.) D 7
Dartmoor National Park C 7
Dee (riv.) D 4
Derwent (riv.) G 3
Derwent (riv.) H 3
Don (riv.) F 4
Dorset Heights (hills) E 7
Dove (riv.) J 2
Dover (str.) J 7
Dungeness (prom.) J 7
Dunkery (hill) D 6
Eddystone (rocks) C 7
Eden (riv.) E 3
English (chan.) D 8
Esk (riv.) D 2
Exe (riv.) D 7
Exmoor National Park D 6
Fens, The (reg.) G 5
Flamborough (head) G 3
Formby (head) G 2
Foulness Island (pen.) J 6
Gibraltar (pt.) H 4
Great Ouse (riv.) H 5
Hartland (pt.) C 6
High Willhays (mt.) C 7
Hodder (riv.) H 1
Holderness (pen.), 43,900 G 4
Holy (isl.), 189 F 2
Humber (riv.) G 4
Irish (sea) B 4
Kennet (riv.) F 6
Lake District National Park D 3
Land's End (prom.) B 7
Lea (riv.) G 6
Lincoln Wolds (hills) G 4
Lindisfarne (Holy) (isl.), 189 F 2
Liverpool (bay) D 4
Lizard, The (pen.), 7,371 B 8
Lundy (isl.), 49 C 6
Lune (riv.) E 3
Lyme (bay) D 7
Manacle (pt.) C 7
Medway (riv.) H 6
Mendip (hills) E 6
Mersea (isl.), 4,423 J 6
Mersey (riv.) G 2
Morecambe (bay) D 3
Mounts (bay) B 7
Naze, The (prom.) J 6
Nene (riv.) H 5
New (for.) F 6
North (sea) J 4
North Downs (hills) G 6
North Foreland (prom.) J 6
Northumberland National Park E 2
North York Moors National Park G 3
Orford Ness (prom.) J 5
Ouse (riv.) G 4
Ouse (riv.) G 6
Parrett (riv.) E 6
Peak District National Park F 4
Peak, The (mt.) J 2
Peel Fell (mt.) E 2
Pennine Chain (range) E 3
Plymouth (sound) C 7
Portland, Bill of (pt.) E 7
Prawle (pt.) D 7
Purbeck, Isle of (pen.), 39,500 F 7
Ribble (riv.) E 4
Saint Alban's (head) F 7
Saint Bees (head) D 3
Saint Martin's (isl.), 106 A 8
Saint Mary's (isl.), 1,958 A 8
Scafell Pike (mt.) D 3
Scilly (isls.), 1,900 A 7
Selsey Bill (prom.) G 7
Severn (riv.) E 6
Sheppey (isl.), 31,550 J 6
Sherwood (for.) F 4
Skiddaw (mt.) D 3
Solent (chan.) F 7
Solway (firth) D 3
South Downs (hills) G 7
Spithead (chan.) F 7
Spurn (head) H 4
Stonehenge (ruins) F 6
Stour (riv.) E 7
Stour (riv.) H 6
Stour (riv.) J 6
Swale (riv.) F 3
Tamar (riv.) C 7
Taw (riv.) D 7
Tees (riv.) F 3
Test (riv.) F 6
Thames (riv.) H 6
Tintagel (head) C 7
Torridge (riv.) C 7
Trent (riv.) G 4
Tresco (isl.), 246 A 8
Tweed (riv.) E 2
Tyne (riv.) F 3
Ure (riv.) F 3
Ver (riv.) H 7
Walney, Isle of (isl.), 11,241 D 3
Wash, The (bay) H 5
Weald, The (reg.) H 6
Wear (riv.) F 3
Weaver (riv.) G 2
Welland (riv.) G 5
Wey (riv.) G 6
Wharfe (riv.) E 3
Wirral (pen.), 432,900 G 2
Witham (riv.) G 4
Wolds, The (hills) G 4
Wye (riv.) D 5
Wyre (riv.) G 1
Yare (riv.) J 5
Yorkshire Dales National Park E 3

CHANNEL ISLANDS

CITIES and TOWNS

Saint Anne E 8
Saint Helier (cap.), Jersey, ⊙28,135 E 8
Saint Peter Port (cap.), Guernsey, ⊙16,303 E 8
Saint Sampson's, ⊙6,534 E 8

OTHER FEATURES

Alderney (isl.), 1,686 E 8
Guernsey (isl.), 51,351 E 8
Herm (isl.), 96 E 8
Jersey (isl.), 72,629 E 8
Sark (isl.), 590 E 8

ISLE of MAN

CITIES and TOWNS

Castletown, 2,820 C 3
Douglas (cap.), 20,389 C 3
Laxey, 1,170 C 3
Michael, 408 C 3
Onchan, 4,807 C 3
Peel, 3,081 C 3
Port Erin, 1,714 C 3
Port Saint Mary, 1,508 C 3
Ramsey, 5,048 C 3

OTHER FEATURES

Ayre (pt.) C 3
Calf of Man (isl.) C 3
Langness (prom.) C 3
Snaefell (mt.) C 3
Spanish (head) C 3

WALES

COUNTIES

Clwyd, 376,000 D 4
Dyfed, 323,100 C 6
Gwent, 439,600 D 6
Gwynedd, 225,100 C 4
Mid Glamorgan, 540,400 D 6
Powys, 101,500 D 5
South Glamorgan, 389,200 A 7
West Glamorgan, 371,900 D 6

CITIES and TOWNS

Aberaeron, 1,340 C 5
Abercarn, 18,370 B 6
Aberdare, 38,030 A 6
Abertillery, 20,550 B 6
Amlwch, 3,630 C 4
Bala, 1,650 D 5
Bangor, 16,030 C 4
Barmouth, 2,070 C 5
Barry, 42,780 B 7
Beaumaris, 2,090 C 4
Bedwellty, 25,460 B 6
Bethesda, 4,180 D 4
Betws-y-Coed, 720 D 4
Brecknock (Brecon), 6,460 D 6
Brecon, 6,460 D 6
Bridgend, 14,690 A 7
Brynmawr, 5,970 B 6
Builth Wells, 1,480 D 5
Burry Port, 5,990 C 6
Caernarfon, 8,840 C 4
Caerphilly, 42,190 B 6
Cardiff, 281,500 B 7
Cardigan, 3,830 C 5
Chepstow, 8,260 E 6
Chirk, ⊙3,564 D 5
Colwyn Bay, 25,370 D 4
Criccieth, 1,590 C 5
Cwmamman, 3,950 D 6
Cwmbran, 32,980 B 6
Denbigh, 8,420 D 4
Dolgellau, 2,430 D 5
Ebbw Vale, 25,670 B 6
Ffestiniog, 5,510 D 5
Fishguard and Goodwick, 5,020 B 5
Flint, 15,070 G 2
Gelligaer, 33,820 A 6
Harlech, ⊙332 C 5
Haverfordwest, 8,930 B 6
Hawarden, ⊙20,389 G 2
Hay, 1,200 D 5
Holywell, 8,570 G 2
Kidwelly, 3,090 C 6
Knighton, 2,190 D 5
Llandeilo, 1,780 C 6
Llandovery, 2,040 D 5
Llandrindod Wells, 3,460 D 5
Llandudno, 17,700 D 4
Llanelli, 25,870 C 6
Llanfairfechan, 3,800 D 4
Llangefni, 4,070 C 4
Llangollen, 3,050 D 5
Llanguicke, ⊙15,029 D 6
Llanidloes, 2,390 D 5
Llantrisant, ⊙27,490 A 7
Llanwrtyd Wells, 460 D 5
Llwchwr, 27,530 D 6
Machynlleth, 1,830 D 5
Maesteg, 21,100 D 6
Menai Bridge, 2,730 C 4
Merthyr Tydfil, 61,500 A 6
Milford Haven, 13,960 B 6
Mold, 8,700 G 2
Montgomery, 1,000 D 5
Mountain Ash, 27,710 A 6
Mynyddislwyn, 15,590 B 6
Narberth, 970 C 6
Neath, 27,280 D 6
Nefyn, ⊙2,086 C 5
Newcastle Emlyn, 690 C 5
Newport, Dyfed, ⊙1,062 C 5
Newport, Gwent, 110,090 B 6
New Quay, 760 C 5
Newtown, 6,400 D 5
Neyland, 2,690 B 6
Ogmore and Garw, 19,680 A 6
Pembroke, 14,570 C 6
Penarth, 24,180 B 7
Penmaenmawr, 4,050 C 4
Pontypool, 36,710 B 6
Pontypridd, 34,180 A 6
Porthcawl, 14,980 D 6
Porthmadog, 3,900 C 5
Port Talbot, 58,200 D 6
Prestatyn, 15,480 D 4
Presteigne, 1,330 D 5
Pwllheli, 4,020 C 5
Rhondda, 85,400 A 6
Rhyl, 22,150 D 4
Risca, 15,780 B 6
Ruthin, 4,780 D 4
Saint David's, ⊙1,638 B 6
Swansea, 190,800 C 6
Tenby, 4,930 C 6
Tredegar, 17,450 B 6
Tywyn, 3,850 C 5
Welshpool, 7,370 D 5
Wrexham, 39,530 E 4

OTHER FEATURES

Anglesey (isl.), 64,500 C 4
Aran Fawddwy (mt.) C 5
Bardsey (isl.), 9 C 5
Berwyn (mts.) D 5
Black (mts.) D 6
Braich-y-Pwll (prom.) C 5
Brecon Beacons (mt.) D 6
Brecon Beacons National Park D 6
Caldy (isl.), 70 C 6
Cambrian (mts.) D 5
Cardigan (bay) C 5
Carmarthen (bay) C 6
Cemmaes (head) C 5
Dee (riv.) D 4
Dovey (riv.) D 5
Ely (riv.) B 7
Gower (pen.), 17,220 C 6
Great Ormes (head) C 4
Holy (isl.), 13,715 C 4
Lleyn (pen.), 25,800 C 5
Menai (str.) C 4
Milford Haven (inlet) B 6
Pembrokeshire Coast National Park C 6
Plynlimon (mt.) D 5
Preseli (mts.) C 6
Radnor (for.) D 5
Rhymney (riv.) B 6
Saint Brides (bay) B 6
Saint David's (head) B 6
Saint George's (chan.) B 5
Saint Gowans (head) C 6
Severn (riv.) E 5
Snowdon (mt.) D 4
Snowdonia National Park D 4
Taff (riv.) B 7
Teifi (riv.) C 5
Towy (riv.) D 6
Tremadoc (bay) C 5
Usk (riv.) B 6
Wye (riv.) D 5
Ynys Môn (Anglesey) (isl.), 64,500 C 4

★Population of met. area.
⊙Population of parish.

SCOTLAND
(map on page 13)

REGIONS

Borders, 99,409 E 5
Central, 269,281 D 4
Dumfries and Galloway, 143,667 E 5
Fife, 336,339 E 4
Grampian, 448,772 F 3
Highland, 182,044 D 3
Lothian, 754,008 E 5
Orkney (islands area), 17,675 E 1
Shetland (islands area), 18,494 F 2
Strathclyde, 2,504,909 C 4
Tayside, 401,987 E 4
Western Isles (islands area) 29,615 A 3

CITIES and TOWNS

Aberchirder, 877 F 3
Aberdeen, 210,362 F 3
Aberdour, 1,576 D 1
Aberfeldy, 1,552 E 4
Aberfoyle, 793 D 4
Aberlady, 737 F 4
Aberlour, 842 E 3
Abernethy, 776 E 4
Aboyne, 1,040 F 3
Acharacle, ⊙764 C 4
Achiltibuie, ⊙1,564 C 3
Achnasheen, ⊙1,078 C 3
Ae, 239 E 5
Airdrie, 38,491 C 2
Alexandria, 9,758 A 1
Alford, 764 F 3
Alloa, 13,558 C 1
Alness, 2,560 D 3
Altnaharra, ⊙1,227 D 2
Alva, 4,593 C 1
Alyth, 1,738 E 4
Ancrum, 266 F 5
Annan, 6,250 E 6
Annat, ⊙550 C 3
Annbank Station, 2,530 D 5
Applecross, ⊙550 C 3
Arbroath, 22,706 F 4
Ardavasar, ⊙449 B 3
Ardersier, 942 E 3
Ardgay, 193 D 3
Ardrishaig, 946 C 4
Ardrossan, 11,072 D 5
Armadale, 7,200 C 2
Arrochar, 543 D 4
Ascog, 230 A 2
Auchenblae, 339 F 4
Auchencairn, 215 E 6
Auchinleck, 4,883 D 5
Auchterarder, 1,738 E 4
Auchtermuchty, 1,426 E 4
Auldearn, 405 E 3
Aviemore, 1,224 E 3
Avoch, 776 D 3
Ayr, 47,990 D 5
Ayton, 410 F 5
Bailivanish, 347 A 3
Baillieston, 7,671 B 2
Balallan, 283 B 2
Balerno, 3,576 D 2
Balfron, 1,149 B 1
Ballantrae, 262 C 5
Ballater, 981 F 3
Ballingry, 4,332 D 1
Ballinluig, 188 E 4
Balloch, Highland, 572 D 3
Balloch, Strathclyde, 1,484 B 1
Baltasound, 246 G 2
Banchory, 2,435 F 3
Banff, 3,832 F 3
Bankfoot, 868 E 4
Bankhead, 1,492 F 3
Bannockburn, 5,889 C 1
Barrhead, 18,736 B 2
Barrhill, 236 D 5
Barvas, 279 B 2
Bathgate, 14,038 C 2
Bayble, 543 B 2
Bearsden, 25,128 B 2
Beattock, 309 E 5
Beauly, 1,141 D 3
Beith, 5,859 D 5
Bellsbank, 3,066 D 5
Bellshill, 18,166 C 2
Berriedale, ⊙1,927 E 2
Bieldside, 1,137 F 3
Biggar, 1,718 E 5
Birnam, 659 E 4
Bishopbriggs, 21,570 B 2
Bishopton, 2,931 B 2
Blackburn, 7,636 C 2
Blackford, 529 E 4
Blair Atholl, 437 E 4
Blairgowrie and Rattray, 5,681 E 4
Blanefield, 835 B 1
Blantyre, 13,992 B 2
Blyth Bridge, ⊙441 E 5
Bo'ness, 12,959 C 1
Boat of Garten, 406 E 3
Boddam, 1,429 G 3
Bonar Bridge, 519 D 3
Bonhill, 4,385 B 1
Bonnybridge, 5,701 C 1
Bonnyrigg and Lasswade, 7,429 D 2
Bowmore, 947 B 5
Braemar, 394 E 3
Breasclete, 234 B 2
Brechin, 6,759 F 4
Bridge of Allan, 4,638 C 1
Bridge of Don, 4,086 F 3
Bridge of Weir, 4,724 A 2
Brightons, 3,106 C 1
Broadford, 310 B 3
Brodick, 630 C 5
Brora, 1,436 E 2
Broxburn, 7,776 D 1
Buchlyvie, 412 B 1
Buckhaven and Methil, 17,930 F 4
Buckie, 8,145 E 3
Bucksburn, 6,567 F 3
Bunessan, ⊙585 B 4
Burghead, 1,321 E 3
Burnmouth, 300 F 5
Burntisland, 5,626 D 1
Cairndow, ⊙874 D 4
Cairnryan, 199 D 6
Callander, 1,805 D 4
Cambuslang, 14,607 B 2
Campbeltown, 6,428 C 5
Cannich, 203 D 3
Canonbie, 234 F 5
Caol, 3,719 C 4
Carbost, ⊙772 B 3
Cardenden, 6,802 D 1
Carloway, 178 B 2
Carluke, 8,864 E 5
Carnoustie, 6,838 F 4
Carnwath, 1,246 E 5
Carradale, 262 C 5
Carrbridge, 416 E 3
Carron, 2,626 C 1
Carsphairn, 186 D 5
Castlebay, 284 A 4
Castle Douglas, 3,384 E 6
Castle Kennedy, 307 D 6
Castletown, 902 E 2
Catrine, 2,681 D 5
Cawdor, 111 E 3
Chirnside, 888 F 5
Chryston, 8,322 C 2
Clackmannan, 3,248 C 1
Clarkston, 8,404 B 2
Closeburn, 225 E 5
Clovulin, ⊙315 C 4
Clydebank, 47,538 B 2
Coalburn, 1,460 E 5
Coatbridge, 50,806 C 2
Cockburnspath, 233 F 5
Cockenzie and Port Seton, 3,539 D 1
Coldingham, 423 F 5
Coldstream, 1,393 F 5
Coll, 305 B 2
Colmonell, 218 D 5
Comrie, 1,119 E 4
Connel, 300 C 4
Cononbridge, 914 D 3
Corpach, 1,296 C 4
Coupar Angus, 2,010 E 4
Cove and Kilcreggan, 1,402 A 1
Cove Bay, 765 F 3
Cowdenbeath, 10,215 D 1
Cowie, 2,751 C 1
Craigellachie, 382 E 3
Craignure, ⊙544 C 4
Crail, 1,033 F 4
Crawford, 384 E 5
Creetown, 769 D 6
Crieff, 5,718 E 4
Crimond, 313 G 3
Crinan, ⊙462 C 4
Cromarty, 492 E 3
Crosshill, 535 D 5
Crossmichael, 317 D 6
Cruden Bay, 528 G 3
Cullen, 1,199 F 3
Culross, 504 C 1
Cults, 3,336 F 3
Cumbernauld, 41,200 C 1
Cumnock and Holmhead, 6,298 D 5
Cupar, 6,607 E 4
Currie, 6,764 D 2
Dailly, 1,258 D 5
Dalbeattie, 3,659 E 6
Daliburgh, 261 A 3
Dalkeith, 9,713 D 2
Dalmally, 283 D 4
Dalmellington, 1,949 D 5
Dalry, 5,833 D 5
Dalrymple, 1,336 D 5
Darvel, 3,177 D 5
Daviot, ⊙513 D 3
Denholm, 581 F 5
Denny and Dunipace, 10,424 C 1
Dervaig, ⊙1,081 B 4
Dingwall, 4,275 D 3
Dollar, 2,573 E 4
Dornoch, 880 D 3
Douglas, 1,843 E 5
Doune, 859 D 4
Drongan, 3,609 D 5
Drumbeg, ⊙833 C 2
Drummore, 336 D 6
Drumnadrochit, 359 D 3
Drymen, 659 B 1
Dufftown, 1,481 E 3
Dumbarton, 25,469 B 1
Dumfries, 29,259 E 5
Dunbar, 4,609 F 4
Dunbeath, 161 E 2
Dunbeg, 939 C 4
Dunblane, 5,222 E 4
Dundee, 194,732 F 4
Dundonald, 2,256 D 5
Dunfermline, 52,098 D 1
Dunkeld, 273 E 4
Dunning, 564 E 4
Dunoon, 8,759 A 2
Dunragit, 323 D 6
Duns, 1,812 F 5
Duntochter, 3,532 B 2
Dunure, 452 D 5
Dunvegan, 301 B 3
Dyce, 2,733 F 3
Eaglesfield, 581 E 5
Eaglesham, 2,788 D 5
Earlston, 1,415 F 5
East Calder, 2,690 D 2
East Kilbride, 71,200 B 2
East Linton, 882 F 5
Eastriggs, 1,455 E 5
Ecclefechan, 844 E 5
Edinburgh (cap.), 470,085 D 1
Edzell, 658 F 4
Elderslie, 5,204 B 2
Elgin, 17,042 E 3
Elie and Earlsferry, 807 F 4
Ellon, 2,855 F 3
Embo, 260 E 3
Errol, 762 E 4
Evanton, 562 D 3
Eyemouth, 2,704 F 5
Fairlie, 1,029 D 5
Falkirk, 36,901 C 1
Falkland, 998 E 4
Fallin, 3,159 C 1
Fauldhouse, 5,247 C 2
Ferness, ⊙287 E 3
Ferryden, 740 F 4
Findhorn, 664 E 3
Findochty, 1,229 E 3
Fintry, 296 B 1
Fochabers, 1,238 E 3
Forfar, 11,179 F 4
Forres, 5,317 E 3
Fort Augustus, 670 D 3
Forth, 2,929 C 2
Fortrose, 1,150 D 3
Fort William, 4,370 C 4
Foyers, 276 D 3
Fraserburgh, 10,930 G 3
Friockheim, 807 F 4
Furnace, 220 C 4
Fyvie, 405 F 3
Gairloch, 125 C 3
Galashiels, 12,808 F 5
Galston, 4,256 D 5
Gardenstown, 892 F 3
Garelochhead, 1,552 A 1
Gargunnock, 457 B 1
Garlieston, 385 D 6
Garmouth, 352 E 3
Garrabost, 307 B 2
Gartmore, 253 B 1
Gatehouse-of-Fleet, 835 D 6
Giffnock, 10,987 B 2
Gifford, 575 F 5
Girvan, 7,597 D 5
Glamis, 190 F 4
Glasgow, 880,617 B 2
Glasgow, ★1,674,789 B 2
Glenbarr, ⊙691 C 5
Glencaple, 275 E 5
Glencoe, 195 C 4
Glenelg, ⊙1,468 C 3
Glenluce, 725 D 6
Glenrothes, 31,400 E 4
Golspie, 1,374 E 3
Gordon, 320 F 5
Gorebridge, 3,426 D 2
Gourock, 11,192 A 1
Grangemouth, 24,430 C 1
Grantown-on-Spey, 1,578 E 3
Greenlaw, 574 F 5
Greenock, 67,275 A 2
Gretna, 1,907 E 5
Gullane, 1,701 F 4
Haddington, 6,767 F 5
Halkirk, 679 E 2
Hamilton, 45,495 C 2
Hamnavoe, 307 G 2
Harthill, 4,712 C 2
Hatton, 315 G 3
Hawick, 16,484 F 5
Heathhall, 1,365 E 5
Helensburgh, 13,327 A 1
Helmsdale, 727 E 2
Hill of Fearn, 233 D 3
Hillside, 692 F 4
Hillswick, ⊙696 G 2
Hopeman, 1,248 E 3
Huntly, 4,078 F 3
Hurlford, 4,294 D 5
Inchnadamph, ⊙833 D 2
Innellan, 922 A 2
Innerleithen, 2,293 E 5
Insch, 881 F 3
Inveraray, 473 C 4
Inverbervie, 853 F 4
Invercassley, ⊙1,067 D 3
Invergordon, 2,385 D 3
Invergowrie, 1,389 E 4
Inverie, ⊙1,468 C 3
Inverkeithing, 6,102 D 1
Inverness, 35,801 D 3
Inverurie, 5,534 F 3
Irvine, 48,500 D 5
Isle of Whithorn, 222 D 6
Jedburgh, 3,953 F 5
John O'Groats, 195 E 2
Johnshaven, 544 F 4
Johnstone, 23,251 B 2
Kames, 230 C 5
Keiss, 344 E 2
Keith, 4,192 F 3
Kelso, 4,934 F 5
Kelty, 6,573 D 1
Kemnay, 1,042 F 3
Kenmore, 211 E 4
Kilbarchan, 2,669 A 2
Kilbirnie, 8,259 A 2
Kilchoan, ⊙764 B 4
Kildonan, ⊙1,105 E 2
Killearn, 1,086 B 1
Killin, 600 D 4
Kilmacolm, 3,348 A 2
Kilmarnock, 50,175 D 5
Kilmaurs, 2,518 D 5
Kilninver, ⊙247 C 4
Kilrenny and Anstruther, 2,951 F 4
Kilsyth, 10,210 B 1
Kilwinning, 8,460 D 5
Kinbrace, ⊙1,105 E 2
Kincardine, 3,278 C 1
Kinghorn, 2,163 D 1
Kingussie, 1,036 D 3
Kinlochewe, ⊙1,794 C 3
Kinlochleven, 1,243 D 4
Kinloch Rannoch, 241 D 4
Kinloss, 2,378 E 3
Kinross, 2,829 E 4
Kintore, 970 F 3
Kippen, 529 B 1
Kirkcaldy, 50,207 D 1
Kirkcolm, 346 C 6
Kirkconnel, 3,318 E 5
Kirkcowan, 354 D 6
Kirkcudbright, 2,690 E 6
Kirkhill, 210 D 3
Kirkintilloch, 26,664 B 2
Kirkmuirhill, 2,575 E 5
Kirkton of Glenisla, ⊙331 E 4
Kirkwall, 4,777 E 2
Kirriemuir, 4,295 E 4
Kyleakin, 268 C 3
Kyle of Lochalsh, 687 C 3
Kylestrome, ⊙745 D 2
Ladybank, 1,216 E 4
Laggan, 393 D 3
Lairg, 572 D 2
Lamlash, 613 C 5
Lanark, 8,842 E 5
Langholm, 2,509 E 5
Larbert, 4,922 C 1
Largs, 9,461 A 2
Larkhall, 15,926 E 5
Lauder, 639 F 5
Laurencekirk, 1,416 F 4

(continued)

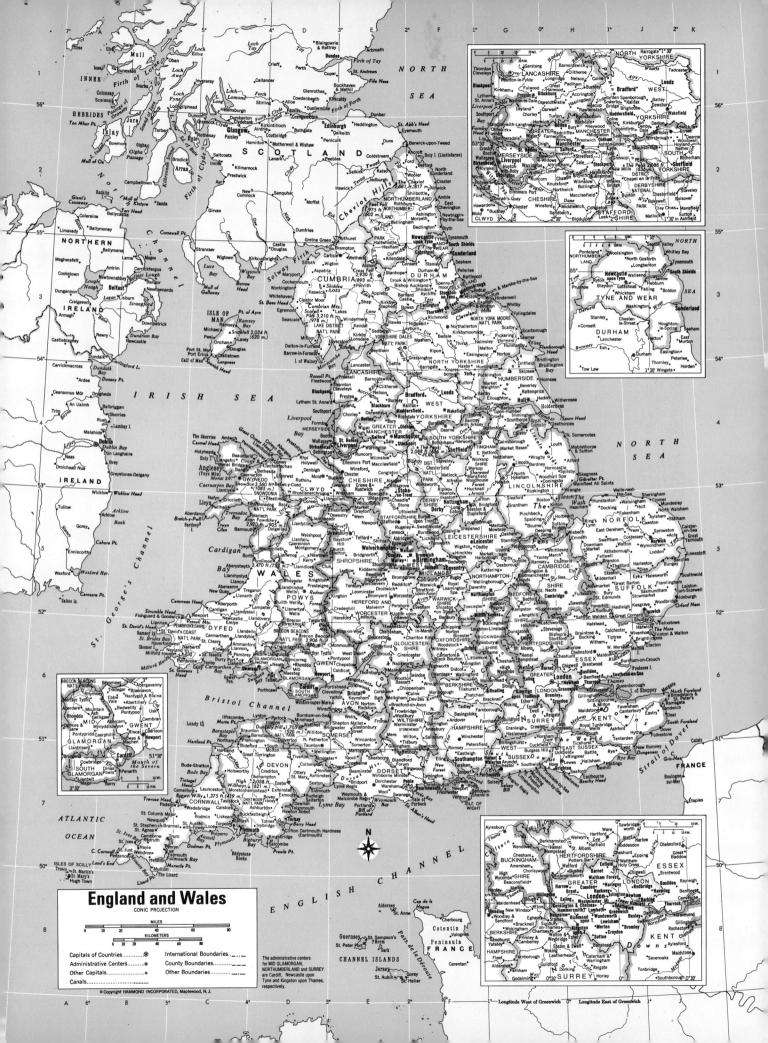

England and Wales

CONIC PROJECTION

MILES
KILOMETERS

Capitals of Countries............⊛
Administrative Centers............◉
Other Capitals............●
Canals............

International Boundaries............
County Boundaries............
Other Boundaries............

The administrative centers for MID GLAMORGAN, NORTHUMBERLAND and SURREY are Cardiff, Newcastle upon Tyne and Kingston upon Thames, respectively.

© Copyright HAMMOND INCORPORATED, Maplewood, N.J.

Lennoxtown, 3,070 .... B 1
Lerwick, 6,195 .... G 2
Leslie, 3,303 .... E 4
Lesmahagow, 3,906 .... E 5
Leswalt, 237 .... C 6
Letham, 804 .... F 4
Leuchars, 2,482 .... F 4
Leurbost, 461 .... B 2
Leven, 9,507 .... F 4
Leverburgh, 223 .... B 3
Lhanbryde, 1,184 .... E 3
Lilliesleaf, 212 .... F 5
Limekilns, 812 .... D 1
Linlithgow, 6,098 .... C 1
Linwood, 10,510 .... B 2
Lionel, 187 .... B 2
Livingston, 21,900 .... C 2
Loanhead, 5,971 .... D 2
Lochailort, ⊙673 .... C 4
Lochaline, 213 .... C 4
Lochans, 355 .... D 6
Locharbriggs, 2,561 .... E 5
Lochawe, 200 .... C 4
Lochboisdale, 382 .... A 3
Lochcarron, 204 .... C 3
Lochgelly, 7,754 .... D 1
Lochgilphead, 1,217 .... C 4
Lochgoilhead, 216 .... D 4
Lochinver, 283 .... C 2
Lochmaben, 1,304 .... E 5
Lochmaddy, 307 .... A 3
Lochore, 2,994 .... D 1
Lochwinnoch, 2,064 .... A 2
Lockerbie, 3,135 .... E 5
Lossiemouth and Branderburgh, 5,817 .... E 3
Lumsden, 248 .... F 3
Luncarty, 584 .... E 4
Lybster, 554 .... E 2
Lyness, ⊙454 .... E 2
Macduff, 3,682 .... F 3
Machrihanish, 212 .... C 5
Maidens, 536 .... D 5
Mallaig, 903 .... C 4
Markinch, 2,366 .... E 4
Mauchline, 3,612 .... D 5
Maud, 634 .... F 3
Maybole, 4,703 .... D 5
Mayfield, 8,232 .... D 2
Meigle, 357 .... E 4
Melrose, 2,197 .... F 5
Melvaig, ⊙1,794 .... C 3
Methlick, 315 .... F 3
Methven, 806 .... E 4
Mid Yell, 220 .... G 2
Millport, 1,161 .... A 2
Milnathort, 1,099 .... E 4
Milngavie, 10,846 .... B 1
Minnigaff, 658 .... D 6
Mintlaw, 657 .... F 3
Moffat, 2,041 .... E 5
Moniaive, 342 .... E 5
Monifieth, 7,100 .... F 4
Montrose, 4,704 .... F 4
Morar, 184 .... C 4
Motherwell and Wishaw, 72,991 .... C 2
Muirkirk, 2,607 .... E 5
Muir of Ord, 1,339 .... D 3
Musselburgh, 17,045 .... D 2
Muthill, 672 .... E 4
Nairn, 5,821 .... E 3
Neilston, 4,358 .... B 2
Nethy Bridge, 431 .... E 3
New Abbey, 339 .... E 6
Newarthill, 7,003 .... C 2
Newburgh, Fife, 2,124 .... E 4
Newburgh, Grampian, 447 .... G 3
Newcastleton, 903 .... F 5
New Cumnock, 5,077 .... D 5
New Deer, 601 .... F 3
New Galloway, 337 .... D 5
Newmains, 6,847 .... C 2
Newmarket, 613 .... B 2
Newmill, 449 .... E 3
Newmilns and Greenholm, 3,509 .... D 5
New Pitsligo, 1,125 .... F 3
Newport-on-Tay, 3,762 .... F 4
New Scone, 3,830 .... E 4
Newtongrange, 4,555 .... D 2
Newton Mearns, 6,901 .... B 2
Newtonmore, 894 .... D 3
Newton Stewart, 1,983 .... D 6
Newtown Saint Boswells, 1,101 .... F 5
Newtyle, 664 .... E 4
North Berwick, 4,317 .... F 4
North Tolsta, 527 .... B 2
Oakley, 3,499 .... C 1
Oban, 6,515 .... C 4
Old Kilpatrick, 3,256 .... B 2
Oldmeldrum, 1,103 .... F 3
Oykel Bridge, ⊙742 .... D 3
Paisley, 94,833 .... B 2
Palnackie, 225 .... E 6
Patna, 2,867 .... D 5
Peebles, 6,049 .... E 5
Penicuik, 10,476 .... D 2
Penpont, 364 .... E 5
Perth, 43,098 .... E 4
Peterculter, 3,226 .... F 3
Peterhead, 14,846 .... G 3
Pierowall, ⊙735 .... E 1
Pitlochry, 2,468 .... E 4
Pitmedden, 313 .... F 3
Pittenweem, 1,548 .... F 4
Plockton, 288 .... C 3
Poolewe, ⊙1,794 .... C 3
Port Appin, ⊙2,172 .... C 4
Port Askaig, ⊙1,795 .... B 5
Port Bannatyne, 730 .... A 2
Port Charlotte, 240 .... B 5
Port Ellen, 932 .... B 5
Port Glasgow, 22,189 .... A 2
Portgordon, 814 .... F 3
Portknockie, 1,217 .... F 3
Portmahomack, 226 .... E 3
Portpatrick, 643 .... C 6
Portree, 1,374 .... B 3
Portsoy, 1,717 .... F 3
Port William, 517 .... D 6
Prestonpans, 3,272 .... D 1
Prestwick, 13,218 .... D 5
Queensferry, 5,339 .... D 1
Reay, 283 .... E 2
Renfrew, 18,880 .... B 2
Renton, 3,443 .... A 1
Rhu, 1,540 .... A 1
Rhynie, 333 .... F 3
Rigside, 1,195 .... E 5
Rosehearty, 1,220 .... F 3
Rosneath, 946 .... A 1
Rothes, 1,240 .... E 3
Rothesay, 6,285 .... A 2
Rutherglen, 24,091 .... B 2
Saint Abbs, 203 .... F 5
Saint Andrews, 12,837 .... F 4
Saint Combs, 738 .... G 3
Saint Cyrus, 340 .... F 4
Saint Margaret's Hope, 210 .... F 2
Saint Monance, 1,205 .... F 4
Saline, 831 .... C 1
Saltcoats, 14,861 .... D 5
Sandbank, 850 .... A 1
Sandhead, 248 .... D 6
Sandwick, 603 .... B 2
Sanquhar, 2,030 .... D 5
Sauchie, 6,082 .... C 1
Scalasaig, ⊙137 .... B 4
Scalloway, 896 .... G 2
Scarinish, ⊙875 .... B 4
Scourie, ⊙745 .... C 2
Scrabster, 273 .... E 2
Selkirk, 5,635 .... F 5
Shader, 258 .... B 2
Shawbost, 458 .... B 2
Shieldaig, ⊙550 .... C 3
Shotts, 9,512 .... C 2
Skateraw, 674 .... F 3
Skelmorlie, 1,535 .... A 2
Skipness, ⊙765 .... C 5
Slamannan, 1,584 .... C 2
Spean Bridge, 235 .... D 4
Springholm, 340 .... E 5
Stanley, 1,385 .... E 4
Stenhousemuir, 8,203 .... C 1
Stevenston, 11,786 .... D 5
Stewarton, 5,165 .... D 5
Stirling, 29,799 .... C 1
Stonehaven, 4,837 .... F 4
Stonehouse, 7,900 .... D 5
Stornoway, 5,371 .... B 2
Stow, 485 .... F 5
Strachan, ⊙390 .... F 3
Strachur Bay, ⊙678 .... C 4
Stranraer, 10,174 .... C 6
Strathaven, 5,464 .... D 5
Strathpeffer, 874 .... D 3
Strichen, 962 .... F 3
Stromeferry, ⊙1,724 .... C 3
Stromness, 1,680 .... E 2
Strontian, ⊙764 .... C 4
Struan, ⊙772 .... B 3
Swinton, 235 .... F 5
Tain, 2,057 .... D 3
Tarbert, Strathclyde, 1,391 .... C 5
Tarbert, W. Isles, 479 .... B 3
Tarbolton, 2,224 .... D 5
Tarland, 452 .... F 3
Tayport, 2,848 .... F 4
Thornhill, Central, 443 .... D 4
Thornhill, Dumf. & Gall., 1,510 .... E 5
Thurso, 9,113 .... E 2
Tillicoultry, 4,320 .... C 1
Tobermory, 652 .... B 4
Tolob, ⊙2,033 .... G 2
Tomatin, 214 .... D 3
Tomintoul, 306 .... E 3
Torphins, 499 .... F 3
Tradespark, 425 .... E 3
Tranent, 7,212 .... F 5
Troon, 11,656 .... D 5
Tullibody, 6,082 .... C 1
Turriff, 3,051 .... F 3
Tweedsmuir, ⊙105 .... E 5
Twynholm, 274 .... D 6
Tyndrum, ⊙1,153 .... D 4
Uddingston, 5,278 .... B 2
Uig, Highland, 103 .... B 3
Uig, W. Isles, ⊙1,948 .... A 2
Ullapool, 807 .... C 3
Uphall, 3,035 .... C 1
Viewpark, 9,812 .... C 2
Walkerburn, 842 .... F 5
Watten, 347 .... E 2
Wemyss Bay, 323 .... A 2
West Barns, 659 .... F 5
West Calder, 2,005 .... C 2
West Kilbride, 3,883 .... D 5
West Linton, 705 .... D 2
Whitburn, 11,647 .... C 2
Whitehills, 875 .... F 3
Whithorn, 990 .... D 6
Whiting Bay, 352 .... C 5
Wick, 7,804 .... E 2
Wigtown, 1,118 .... D 6
Winchburgh, 2,409 .... D 1
Yetholm, 435 .... F 5

OTHER FEATURES

A'Chralaig (mt.) .... C 3
Ailsa Craig (isl.), 3 .... C 5
Almond (riv.) .... E 4
Annan (riv.) .... E 5
Appin (dist.), 2,006 .... C 4
Ardgour (dist.), 315 .... C 4
Ardle (riv.) .... E 4
Ardnamurchan (pen.), 764 .... B 4
Argyll (dist.), 4,940 .... C 4
Arkaig, Loch (lake) .... C 4
Arran (isl.), 3,564 .... C 5
Askival (mt.) .... B 4
Assynt (dist.), 833 .... C 2
Athol (dist.), 1,082 .... D 4
Atlantic Ocean .... B 2
Avon (riv.) .... C 1
Avon (riv.) .... E 3
Awe, Loch (lake) .... C 4
Ayr (riv.) .... D 5
Ayr, Heads of (cape) .... D 5
Badenoch (dist.), 2,717 .... D 4
Baleshare (isl.), 64 .... A 3
Balmoral Castle .... E 3
Barra (sound) .... A 3
Barra (isl.), 1,005 .... A 4
Barra (head) .... A 4
Barra Isles (isls.), 1,092 .... A 4
Battock (mt.) .... F 4
Beauly (riv.) .... D 3
Beinn Dearg (mt.) .... D 3
Beinn a Ghlo (mt.) .... E 4
Bell Rock (isl.), 3 .... F 4
Ben Alder (mt.) .... D 4
Ben Avon (mt.) .... E 3
Benbecula (isl.), 1,355 .... A 3
Ben Cruachan (mt.) .... C 4
Ben Lawers (mt.) .... D 4
Ben Lui (mt.) .... D 4
Ben Macdhui (mt.) .... E 3
Ben Mhor (mt.) .... A 3
Ben More (mt.) .... B 4
Ben More (mt.) .... D 4
Ben More Assynt (mt.) .... D 2
Ben Nevis (mt.) .... D 4
Bernera (isl.), 276 .... B 2
Berneray (isl.), 131 .... A 3
Berneray (isl.), 6 .... A 4
Bidean nam Bian (mt.) .... D 4
Black Isle (pen.), 7,209 .... D 3
Blackwater (res.) .... D 4
Boisdale, Loch (inlet) .... A 3
Bracadale, Loch (inlet) .... B 3
Braemar (dist.), 7,624 .... E 3
Breadalbane (dist.), 3,649 .... D 4
Bressay (isl.), 248 .... G 2
Broad (bay) .... B 2
Broad Law (mt.) .... E 5
Broom, Loch (inlet) .... C 3
Brough Ness (prom.) .... F 2
Buchan (dist.), 40,089 .... F 3
Buddon Ness (prom.) .... F 4
Burray (isl.), 209 .... F 2
Burrow (head) .... D 6
Bute (isl.), 8,423 .... C 5
Bute (sound) .... C 5
Butt of Lewis (prom.) .... B 2
Cairn Gorm (mt.) .... E 3
Cairngorm (mts.) .... E 3
Cairn Toul (mt.) .... E 3
Caledonian (canal) .... D 3
Canna (isl.), 22 .... B 3
Carn Ban (mt.) .... D 3
Carn Eige (mt.) .... C 3
Carrick (dist.), 21,425 .... D 5
Carron (riv.) .... C 1
Carron (riv.) .... C 3
Cheviot (hills) .... F 5
Cheviot, The (mt.) .... F 5
Clisham (mt.) .... B 3
Clyde (riv.) .... D 5
Clyde (firth) .... D 5
Coll (isl.), 144 .... B 4
Colonsay (isl.), 137 .... B 4
Copinsay (isl.), 3 .... F 2
Cowal (dist.), 15,548 .... C 4
Creag Meagaidh (mt.) .... D 4
Cromarty (firth) .... D 3
Cuillin (hills) .... B 3
Cuillin (sound) .... B 3
Dee (riv.) .... D 5
Dee (riv.) .... F 3
Dennis (head) .... F 1
Deveron (riv.) .... F 3
Don (riv.) .... F 3
Doon (riv.) .... D 5
Dornoch (firth) .... E 3
Duirinish (dist.), 1,085 .... B 3
Duncansby (head) .... F 2
Dunnet (head) .... E 2
Earn (riv.) .... E 4
Earn, Loch (lake) .... D 4
Eday (isl.), 179 .... F 1
Eddrachillis (bay) .... C 2
Eden (riv.) .... F 4
Egilsay (isl.), 39 .... F 1
Eigg (isl.), 69 .... B 4
Eil, Loch (lake) .... C 4
Eishort, Loch (inlet) .... B 3
Enard (bay) .... C 2
Eriboll, Loch (inlet) .... D 2
Ericht, Loch (lake) .... D 4
Eriskay (isl.), 219 .... A 3
Erisort, Loch (inlet) .... B 2
Esk (riv.) .... F 5
Etive, Loch (inlet) .... C 4
Ewe, Loch (inlet) .... C 3
Eye (pen.), 850 .... B 2
Fair Isle (isl.), 65 .... F 3
Fetlar (isl.), 88 .... G 2
Fife Ness (prom.) .... F 4
Findhorn (riv.) .... E 3
Flannan (isls.), 3 .... A 2
Formartine (dist.), 10,768 .... F 3
Forth (riv.) .... B 1
Forth (firth) .... F 4
Forth and Clyde (canal) .... B 2
Foula (isl.), 33 .... F 2
Fyne, Loch (inlet) .... C 5
Galloway (dist.), 54,972 .... D 5
Galloway, Mull of (prom.) .... D 6
Gare Loch (inlet) .... A 1
Garioch (dist.), 6,863 .... F 3
Garry, Loch (lake) .... D 3
Gigha (isl.), 174 .... C 5
Girdle Ness (prom.) .... G 3
Glass (riv.) .... D 3
Glen More (dist.), 55,035 .... D 3
Goat Fell (mt.) .... C 5
Gometra (isl.), 10 .... B 4
Grampian (mts.) .... D 4
Great Cumbrae (isl.), 1,296 .... A 2
Gruinard (bay) .... C 3
Hallandale (riv.) .... E 2
Harris (sound) .... A 3
Harris (dist.), 2,175 .... B 3
Hebrides (sea) .... B 3
Hebrides, Inner (isls.), 14,881 .... B 4
Hebrides, Outer (isls.), 29,615 .... A 3
Helmsdale (riv.) .... E 2
Herma Ness (prom.) .... G 2
Holy (isl.), 10 .... C 5
Holy Loch (inlet) .... A 1
Hoy (isl.), 419 .... E 2
Inchcape (Bell Rock) (isl.), 3 .... F 4
Inchkeith (isl.), 3 .... D 1
Indaal, Loch (inlet) .... B 5
Inner (sound) .... C 3
Inner Hebrides (isls.), 14,881 .... B 4
Iona (isl.), 145 .... B 4
Isla (riv.) .... E 4
Islay (isl.), 3,816 .... B 5
Jura (isl.), 210 .... C 5
Jura (sound) .... C 5
Katrine, Loch (lake) .... D 4
Kerrera (isl.), 27 .... C 4
Kilbrannan (sound) .... C 5
Kinnairds (head) .... G 3
Kintyre (pen.), 10,077 .... C 5
Kintyre, Mull of (prom.) .... C 5
Knapdale (dist.), 4,082 .... C 5
Kyle of Tongue (inlet) .... D 2
Laggan (bay) .... B 5
Lammermuir (hills) .... F 5
Lennox (hills) .... B 1
Leven (lake) .... E 4
Leven, Loch (inlet) .... D 4
Lewis (dist.), 20,047 .... B 2
Liddel Water (riv.) .... F 5
Linnhe, Loch (inlet) .... C 4
Lismore (isl.), 166 .... C 4
Little Minch (sound) .... B 3
Lochaber (dist.), 13,813 .... D 4
Lochnagar (mt.) .... E 4
Lochy, Loch (lake) .... D 3
Lomond, Loch (lake) .... D 4
Long, Loch (inlet) .... D 4
Lorne (dist.), 12,162 .... C 4
Lorne (firth) .... C 4
Loyal, Loch (lake) .... D 2
Luce (bay) .... D 6
Luing (isl.), 151 .... C 4
Lyon (riv.) .... D 4
Machers, The (pen.), 6,192 .... D 6
Mainland (isl.), 12,747 .... E 1
Mainland (isl.), 12,944 .... G 2
Mar (dist.), 23,931 .... F 3
Maree, Loch (lake) .... C 3
May, Isle of (isl.), 10 .... F 4
Merrick (mt.) .... D 5
Minginish (dist.), 772 .... B 3
Moidart (dist.), 155 .... C 4
Monach (sound) .... A 3
Monadhliath (mts.) .... D 3
Moorfoot (hills) .... E 5
Moray (firth) .... E 3
Moriston (riv.) .... D 3
Morven (dist.), 398 .... C 4
Morven (mt.) .... E 2
Muck (isl.), 24 .... B 4
Muckle Flugga (isl.), 3 .... G 2
Mull (isl.), 2,024 .... C 4
Mull (head) .... F 1
Mull (sound) .... C 4
Nairn (riv.) .... D 3
na Keal, Loch (inlet) .... B 4
Naver (riv.) .... D 2
Ness, Loch (lake) .... D 3
Nevis, Loch (inlet) .... C 3
Nith (riv.) .... E 5
North (chan.) .... C 5
North (sound) .... F 1
North (sound) .... G 4
North Esk (riv.) .... F 4
North Minch (sound) .... B 3
North Ronaldsay (isl.), 134 .... F 1
North Uist (isl.), 1,469 .... A 3
Oa, Mull of (prom.) .... B 5
Ochil (hills) .... E 4
Oich (riv.) .... D 3
Orchy (riv.) .... D 4
Orkney (isls.), 17,675 .... F 1
Oronsay (isl.), 2 .... B 4
Outer Hebrides (isls.), 29,615 .... A 3
Oykel (riv.) .... D 3
Pabbay (isl.), 4 .... A 3
Papa Stour (isl.), 24 .... F 2
Papa Westray (isl.), 106 .... F 1
Paps of Jura (mt.) .... C 5
Park (dist.), 210 .... B 2
Peel Fell (mt.) .... F 5
Pentland (hills) .... D 2
Pentland (firth) .... E 2
Pladda (isl.), 2 .... C 5
Quoich, Loch (lake) .... C 3
Raasay (isl.), 163 .... C 3
Rannoch (dist.), 1,177 .... D 4
Rannoch, Loch (lake) .... D 4
Rhinns, The (pen.), 8,295 .... C 6
Roag, Loch (inlet) .... B 2
Rona (isl.), 3 .... B 3
Ross of Mull (pen.), 585 .... B 4
Rousay (isl.), 181 .... E 1
Rudha Hunish (cape) .... B 3
Rudh Re (cape) .... C 3
Rum (isl.), 40 .... B 3
Ryan, Loch (inlet) .... C 5
Saint Kilda (isl.), 65 .... A 2
Saint Magnus (bay) .... F 2
Sanda (isl.), 9 .... C 5
Sanday (isl.), 11 .... B 3
Sanday (isl.), 592 .... F 1
Scalpay (isl.), 483 .... B 3
Scalpay (isl.), 5 .... C 3
Scapa Flow (chan.) .... E 2
Scarp (isl.), 12 .... A 2
Scridain, Loch (inlet) .... B 4
Scurdie Ness (prom.) .... F 4
Seaforth, Loch (inlet) .... B 3
Seil (isl.), 326 .... C 4
Sgurr a Choire Ghlais (mt.) .... D 3
Sgurr Alasdair (mt.) .... B 3
Sgurr Mor (mt.) .... C 3
Sgurr na Lapaich (mt.) .... C 3
Shapinsay (isl.), 346 .... F 1
Shetland (isls.), 18,494 .... G 2
Shiant (sound) .... B 3
Shiel, Loch (lake) .... C 4
Shin (falls) .... D 3
Shin, Loch (lake) .... D 2
Shona (isl.), 17 .... C 4
Sidlaw (hills) .... E 4
Sinclair's (bay) .... E 2
Skye, Isle of (isl.), 7,183 .... B 3
Sleat (pt.) .... B 4
Sleat (dist.), 449 .... C 3
Small Isles (isls.), 171 .... B 4
Snizort, Loch (inlet) .... B 3
Soay (isl.), 5 .... B 3
Solway (firth) .... E 6
South Esk (riv.) .... F 4
South Ronaldsay (isl.), 776 .... F 2
South Uist (isl.), 2,281 .... A 3
Spean (riv.) .... D 4
Spey (riv.) .... E 3
Start (pt.) .... F 1
Stinchar (riv.) .... D 5
Strathbogie (dist.), 7,959 .... F 3
Strathmore (valley) .... E 4
Strathspey (dist.), 6,668 .... E 3
Strathy (pt.) .... E 2
Stroma (isl.), 8 .... E 2
Stronsay (isl.), 436 .... F 1
Sumburgh (head) .... G 2
Sunart, Loch (inlet) .... C 4
Swona (isl.), 3 .... E 2
Taransay (isl.), 5 .... A 3
Tarbat Ness (prom.) .... E 3
Tarbert, East Loch (inlet) .... B 3
Tarbert, Loch (inlet) .... B 5
Tarbert, West Loch (inlet) .... A 3
Tay (riv.) .... E 4
Tay (firth) .... F 4
Tay, Loch (lake) .... D 4
Teith (riv.) .... D 4
Teviot (riv.) .... F 5
Thurso (riv.) .... E 2
Tiree (isl.), 875 .... B 4
Tolsta (head) .... B 2
Tor Ness (prom.) .... E 2
Torridon, Loch (inlet) .... C 3
Trossachs, The (valley) .... D 4
Trotternish (dist.), 1,948 .... B 3
Tweed (riv.) .... F 5
Tyne (riv.) .... F 5
Ulva (isl.), 23 .... B 4
Unst (isl.), 1,124 .... G 2
Vaternish (dist.), 162 .... B 3
Vatersay (isl.), 77 .... A 4
West Burra (isl.), 501 .... G 2
Westray (firth) .... E 1
Westray (isl.), 735 .... E 1
Whalsay (isl.), 870 .... G 2
White Coomb (mt.) .... E 5
Wigtown (bay) .... D 6
Wrath (cape) .... C 2
Wyre (isl.), 36 .... F 1
Yarrow (riv.) .... E 5
Yell (isl.), 1,143 .... G 2
Ythan (riv.) .... F 3

★Population of met. area
⊙Population of parish.

Agriculture, Industry and Resources

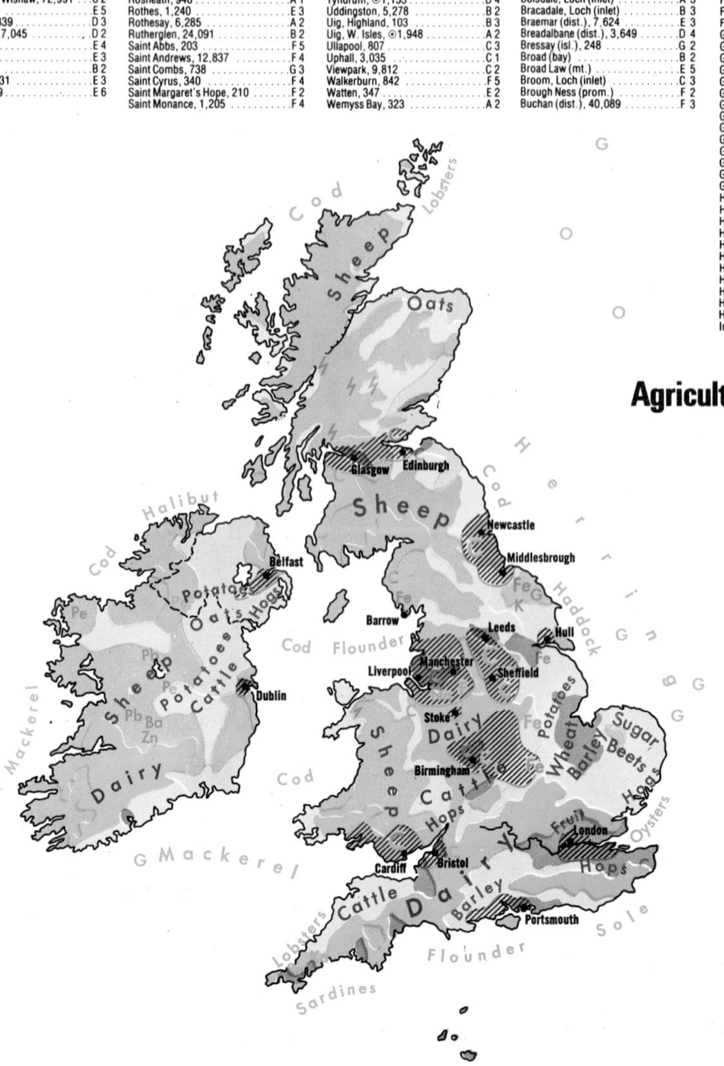

DOMINANT LAND USE

- Cereals (chiefly oats, barley)
- Truck Farming, Horticulture
- Dairy, Mixed Farming
- Livestock, Mixed Farming
- Pasture Livestock

MAJOR MINERAL OCCURRENCES

Ba	Barite	Na	Salt
C	Coal	O	Petroleum
F	Fluorspar	Pb	Lead
Fe	Iron Ore	Pe	Peat
G	Natural Gas	Sn	Tin
K	Potash	Zn	Zinc
Ka	Kaolin (china clay)		

Water Power
Major Industrial Areas

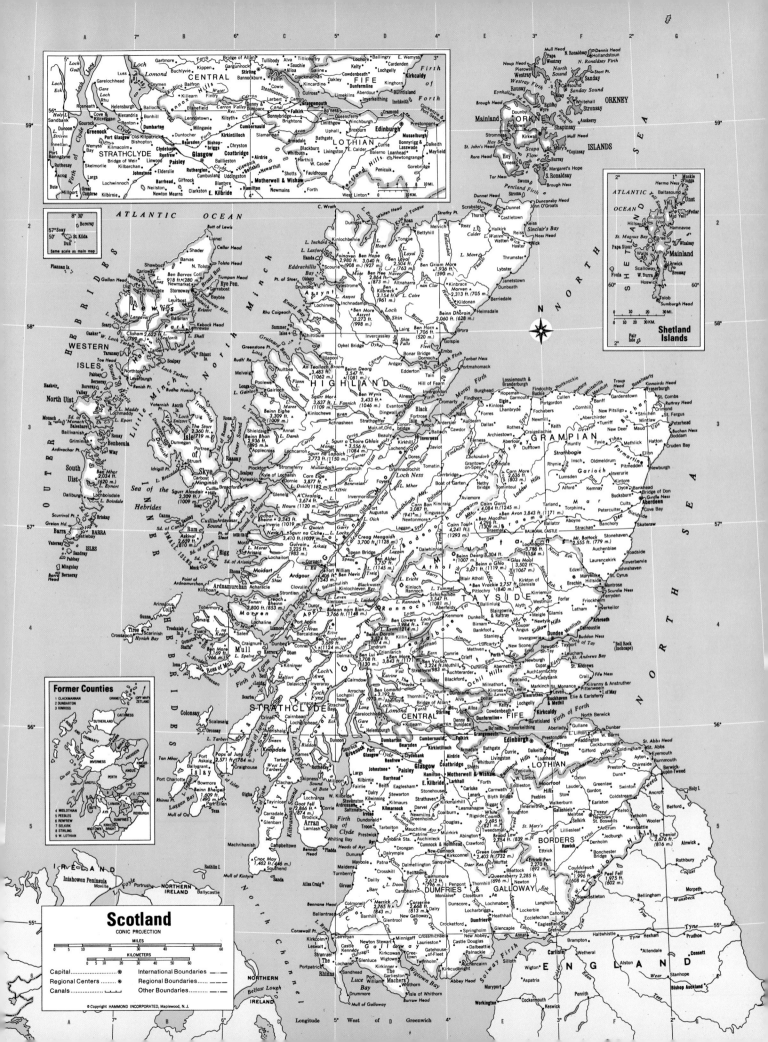

Scotland

CONIC PROJECTION

14 United Kingdom and Ireland
(continued)

IRELAND

Carlow 34,237 H6
Cavan 52,618 G4
Clare 75,008 D6
Cork 352,883 D7
Donegal 108,344 K2
Dublin 852,219 J5
Galway 149,223 D5
Kerry 112,772 B7
Kildare 71,977 H5
Kilkenny 61,473 G6
Laois 45,259 G6
Leitrim 28,360 E3
Leix (Laois) 45,259 G6
Limerick 140,459 D7
Longford 28,250 F4
Louth 74,951 J4
Mayo 109,525 C4
Meath 71,729 H4
Monaghan 46,242 H3
Offaly 51,829 F5
Roscommon 53,519 E4
Sligo 50,275 D3
Tipperary 123,565 F6
Waterford 77,315 F7
Westmeath 53,570 G5
Wexford 86,351 H7
Wicklow 66,295 J5

CITIES and TOWNS

Abbeydorney, 188 B 7
Abbeyfeale, 1,337 C 7
Abbeylara, ‡290 F 4
Abbeyleix, 1,033 G 6
Achill Sound, ‡1,163 B 4
Aclare, ‡336 D 3
Adare, 545 D 6
Aghada-Farsid-Rostellan, 461 E 8
Aghadoe, ‡497 B 7
Aghagower, ‡693 C 4
Ahascragh, 221 E 5
Annagry, 201 E 1
Annascaul, 236 B 7
An Uaimh, 4,605 H 4
An Uaimh, *6,665 H 4
Ardagh, Limerick, 213 C 7
Ardagh, Longford, ‡974 F 4
Ardara, 683 E 2
Ardee, *3,183 H 4
Ardee, 3,096 H 4
Ardfert, 286 B 7
Ardfinnan, 510 F 7
Ardmore, 233 F 8
Ardrahan, ‡239 D 5
Arklow, 6,948 J 6
Arthurstown, 1,188 H 7
Arva, 370 F 4
Ashford, 341 J 5
Askeaton, 844 D 6
Athboy, 705 H 4
Athea, 328 C 7
Athenry, 1,240 D 5
Athleague, ‡955 E 4
Athlone, 9,825 F 5
Athlone, *11,611 F 5
Athy, 4,270 H 6
Athy, *4,654 H 6
Aughrim, 451 J 6
Avoca, ‡620 J 6
Bagenalstown (Muinebeag), 2,321 H 6
Baile Átha Cliath (Dublin) (cap.), 567,866 K 5
Bailieborough, 1,293 G 4
Balbriggan, 3,741 J 4
Balla, 293 C 4
Ballaghaderreen, 1,121 E 4
Ballina, Mayo, 6,063 C 3
Ballina, *6,369 C 3
Ballina, Tipperary, 336 E 6
Ballinagh, 459 G 4
Ballinakill, 300 G 6
Ballineen D 8
Ballinamore, 808 F 3
Ballinasloe, 5,969 E 5
Ballincollig-Carrigrohane, 2,110 D 8
Ballindine, 232 C 4
Ballingarry, Limerick, 422 D 7
Ballingarry, Tipperary, ‡574 F 6
Ballinlough, 242 D 4
Ballinrobe, 1,272 C 4
Ballintober, ‡867 E 4
Ballintra, 197 E 2
Ballisodare, 486 E 3
Ballivor, 287 H 4
Ballybay, 754 G 3
Ballybay, *1,159 G 3
Ballybofey-Stranorlar, 2,214 F 2
Ballybunion, 1,287 B 7
Ballycanew, ‡460 J 6
Ballycarney, ‡294 J 6
Ballycastle, ‡724 C 3
Ballyconnell, 421 F 3
Ballycotton, 389 F 8
Ballydehob, 253 C 8
Ballyduff, 406 B 7
Ballygar, 359 E 4
Ballygeary, 725 J 7
Ballyhaise, 274 G 3
Ballyhaunis, 1,093 D 4
Ballyheigue, 450 B 7
Ballyjamesduff, 673 G 4
Ballylanders, 266 E 7
Ballylongford, 504 B 6
Ballymahon, 707 F 4
Ballymakeery, 272 C 8
Ballymore, ‡447 F 5
Ballymore Eustace, 433 J 5
Ballymote, 952 D 3
Ballyporeen, ‡810 E 7
Ballyragget, 519 G 6
Ballyroan, ‡478 G 6
Ballyshannon, 2,325 E 3
Ballytore, ‡580 H 5
Baltimore, 200 C 9
Baltinglass, 909 H 6
Baltray, 236 J 4
Banagher, 1,052 F 5
Bandon, 2,257 D 8
Bandon, *4,071 D 8
Bannow, ‡798 H 7
Bansha, 184 E 7
Bantry, 2,579 C 8
Barna, ‡1,734 C 5
Belmullet, 744 B 3
Belturbet, 1,092 G 3
Bennettsbridge, 367 G 6
Birr, 3,319 F 5
Birr, *3,881 F 5
Blanchardstown, 3,279 H 5
Blarney, 1,128 D 8
Blessington, 637 J 5
Boherbue, 372 C 7
Borris, 430 H 6
Borris-in-Ossory, 276 F 6
Borrisokane, 769 E 6
Borrisoleigh, 471 E 6
Boyle, 1,727 E 4
Boyle, *1,939 E 4
Bray, 14,467 K 5
Bray, *15,841 K 5
Brí Chualann (Bray), 14,467 K 5
Broadford, 226 C 7
Brosna, 250 C 7
Bruff, 547 D 7
Bruree, 243 D 7
Bunbeg-Derrybeg, 878 E 1
Bunclody-Carrickduff, 929 H 6
Buncrana, 2,955 G 1
Buncrana, *3,334 G 1
Bundoran, 1,337 E 3
Burtonport, ‡1,288 E 2
Buttevant, 1,045 D 7
Cahir, 1,747 F 7
Cahirciveen, 1,547 A 8
Callan, 1,283 G 7
Camolin, 306 J 6
Campile, 231 H 7
Cappamore, 567 E 6
Cappawhite, 305 E 6
Cappoquin, 872 F 7
Carbury, ‡894 H 5
Carlingford, 559 J 3
Carlow, 9,588 H 6
Carlow, *10,399 H 6
Carndonagh, 1,146 G 1
Carnew, 570 H 6
Carrickmacross, 2,100 H 4
Carrickmacross, *2,475 H 4
Carrick-on-Shannon, 1,854 F 4
Carrick-on-Suir, 5,006 F 7
Carrigaholt, ‡493 B 6
Carrigaline, 951 E 8
Carrigallen, 230 F 4
Carrigart, ‡753 F 1
Carrigtwohill, 622 E 8
Carrowkeel, ‡326 G 1
Cashel, 2,692 F 7
Castlebar, 5,979 C 4
Castlebar, *6,476 C 4
Castlebellingham, 407 J 4
Castleblayney, 2,118 H 3
Castleblayney, *2,395 H 3
Castlecomer-Donaguile, 1,244 G 6
Castledermot, 583 H 6
Castlefin, 610 F 2
Castlegregory, 216 A 7
Castleisland, 1,929 B 7
Castlemartyr, 491 E 8
Castlepollard, 693 G 4
Castlerea, 1,752 D 4
Castletown, ‡504 F 6
Castletownbere, 812 B 8
Castletownroche, 399 D 7
Castletownshend, 170 C 9
Causeway, 215 B 7
Cavan, 3,273 G 3
Cavan, *4,312 G 3
Ceanannus Mór, 2,391 G 4
Ceanannus Mór, *2,653 G 4
Celbridge, 1,568 H 5
Charlestown-Bellahy, 677 D 4
Charleville (Rathluirc), 2,232 D 7
Clara, 2,156 F 5
Claregalway, ‡594 D 5
Claremorris, 1,718 C 4
Clashmore, ‡379 F 8
Clifden, 790 B 5
Cloghan, 404 F 5
Clogh-Chatsworth, 324 G 6
Clogheen, 530 F 7
Clogherhead, 649 J 4
Clonakilty, 2,430 D 8
Clonaslee, 285 F 5
Clondalkin, 7,009 J 5
Clonegal, 202 H 6
Clones, 2,164 G 3
Clonfert, ‡430 E 5
Clonmany, ‡936 G 1
Clonmel, 11,622 F 7
Clonmel, *12,291 F 7
Clonmellon, 328 H 4
Clonroche, 222 H 7
Clontuskert, 351 E 4
Cloone, ‡460 F 4
Cloughjordan, 480 E 6
Cloyne, 654 E 8
Coachford, 290 D 8
Cóbh, 6,076 E 8
Cóbh, *7,141 E 8
Coill Dubh, 920 H 5
Collon, 262 J 4
Collooney, 546 E 3
Cong, 233 C 4
Convoy, 654 F 2
Coolaney, ‡352 D 3
Coolgreany, ‡603 J 6
Cootehill, 1,415 G 3
Cootehill, *1,542 G 3
Cork, 128,645 E 8
Cork, *134,430 E 8
Corofin, 342 C 6
Courtmacsherry, 210 D 8
Courtown Harbour, 291 J 6
Creeslough, 269 F 1
Crookhaven, ‡400 B 9
Croom, 756 D 6
Crosshaven, 1,222 E 8
Crossmolina, 1,077 C 3
Crusheen, ‡405 D 6
Culdaff, ‡621 G 1
Daingean, 492 G 5
Delvin, 223 G 4
Dingle, 1,401 A 7
Doaghbeg, ‡701 F 1
Donabate, 426 J 5
Donegal, 1,725 F 2
Doneraile, 799 D 7
Dooagh-Keel, 649 A 4
Doon, 387 E 6
Douglas, ‡4,448 D 8
Drimoleague, 415 C 8
Drishane, ‡1,548 C 7
Drogheda, 19,762 J 4
Drogheda, *20,095 J 4
Droichead Nua, 5,053 H 5
Droichead Nua, *6,444 H 5
Dromahair, 177 E 3
Drumcar, ‡1,215 J 4
Drumconrath, ‡1,044 H 4
Drumkeerin, ‡467 E 3
Drumlish, 205 F 4
Drumshanbo, 576 E 3
Dublin (cap.), 567,866 K 5
Dublin, *679,748 K 5
Duleek, 658 J 4
Duncannon, 228 H 7
Dundalk, 21,672 H 3
Dundalk, *23,816 H 3
Dunfanaghy, 303 F 1
Dungarvan, 5,583 F 7
Dungloe, 940 E 2
Dunkineely, 288 E 2
Dún Laoghaire, 53,171 K 5
Dún Laoghaire, *98,379 K 5
Dunlavin, 423 H 5
Dunleer 855 J4
Dunmanway 1,392 C8
Dunmore 522 D4
Dunmore East 656 G7
Dunshaughlin⊙ 283 H5
Durrow, Laois 596 G6
Durrow, Offaly⊙ 441 F5
Easky 184 D3
Edenderry 2,953 G5
Edenderry* 3,116 G5
Elphin 489 E4
Emyvale 281 G3
Ennis 5,972 D6
Ennis* 10,840 D6
Enniscorthy 5,704 J7
Enniscorthy* 6,642 J7
Enniskerry 772 J5
Ennistymon 1,013 C6
Eyrecourt 314 E5
Fahan⊙ 1,023 G1
Falcarragh 506 E1
Feakle⊙ 398 D6
Fenit 360 B7
Ferbane 1,064 F5
Fermoy 3,237 E7
Fermoy* 4,033 E7
Ferns 712 J6
Fethard, Tipperary 1,064 F7
Fethard, Wexford⊙ 637 H7
Foxford 868 C4
Foynes 624 C6
Frankford (Kilcormac) 1,089 F5
Frenchpark⊙ 693 E4
Freshford 585 G6
Galbally 258 E7
Galway 27,726 C5
Galway* 29,375 C5
Geashill⊙ 751 G5
Glandore⊙ 695 C8
Glanmire-Riverstown 1,113 E8
Glanworth 335 E7
Glenamaddy 315 D4
Glenbeigh 266 B7
Glencolumbkille⊙ 787 D2
Glengarriff 244 C8
Glenties 734 E2
Glenville⊙ 264 D7
Glin 623 C6
Golden⊙ 640 F7
Gorey 2,946 J6
Gorey* 3,024 J6
Gormanston⊙ 1,384 J4
Gort 975 D5
Gowran 402 G6
Graiguenamanagh-Tinnahinch 1,303 H6
Granard 1,054 F4
Greencastle 322 H1
Greenore 882 J4
Greystones-Delgany 4,517 K5
Gurteen 165 D3
Hacketstown 574 H6
Headford 673 C5
Holycross⊙ 902 F6
Hospital 525 E7
Inchigeelagh⊙ 516 C8
Inishannon 190 D8
Inistioge 179 G7
Inniscrone 582 C3
Johnstown 303 G6
Kanturk 2,063 D7
Keel-Dooagh 649 A4
Kells⊙ 423 G6
Kells (Ceanannus Mór) 2,391 G4
Kenmare 903 B8
Kilbaha⊙ 471 B6
Kilbeggan 635 G5
Kilcar 273 D2
Kilcock 827 H5
Kilconnell⊙ 629 E5
Kilcoole 679 K5
Kilcormac 1,089 F5
Kilcullen 880 H5
Kildare 3,137 H5
Kildysart 239 C6
Kilfenora⊙ 441 C6
Kilfinane 561 D7
Kilgarvan 228 B8
Kilkee 1,287 B6
Kilkelly 225 D4
Kilkenny 9,838 G6
Kilkenny* 13,306 G6
Killala 368 C3
Killaloe 871 D6
Killarney 7,184 C7
Killarney* 7,541 C7
Killavullen 221 D7
Killenaule 592 F6
Killeshandra 432 F3
Killimor 221 E5
Killinaboy⊙ 297 C6
Killorglin 1,150 B7
Killucan-Rathwire 290 G4
Killybegs 1,094 E2
Kilmacrennan 274 F1
Kilmacthomas 396 G7
Kilmallock 1,170 D7
Kilmeadan⊙ 262 G7
Kilmihill 284 C6
Kilmoganny 181 G7
Kilmore Quay 273 H7
Kilmurry⊙ 387 C6
Kilnaleck 273 G4
Kilronan 243 B5
Kilrush 2,671 C6
Kilsheelan⊙ 665 F7
Kiltimagh 978 C4
Kilworth 360 E7
Kingscourt 1,016 H4
Kingstown (Dún Laoghaire) 53,171 K5
Kinlough 160 E3
Kinnegad 362 G5
Kinnitty⊙ 420 F5
Kinsale 1,622 D8
Kinsale* 1,989 D8
Kinvara 293 D5
Knightstown 236 A8
Knock⊙ 1,202 D4
Knocklong 248 D7
Knocknagashel 168 C7
Labasheeda⊙ 468 C6
Laghy⊙ 625 E2
Lahinch 455 C6
Lanesborough-Ballyleague 906 E4
Laracor⊙ 404 H4
Laytown-Bettystown-Mornington 1,882 J4
Leenane⊙ 271 B4
Leighlindridge 379 H6
Leitrim⊙ 544 F3
Leixlip 2,402 H5
Letterkenny 4,930 F2
Letterkenny* 5,207 F2
Lifford 1,121 F2
Limerick 57,161 D6
Limerick* 63,002 D6
Liscarroll 231 D7
Lisdoonvarna 459 C5
Lismore 884 F7
Lismore⊙ 1,041 F7
Listowel 3,021 C7
Littleton 322 F6
Longford 3,876 F4
Longford* 4,791 F4
Lorrha⊙ 685 E5
Loughrea 3,075 E5
Louisburgh 310 B4
Louth 208 J4
Lucan-Doddsborough 4,245 J5
Luimneach (Limerick) 57,161 D6
Lusk 553 J4
Macroom 2,256 C8
Malahide 3,834 J5
Malin⊙ 552 G1
Mallow 5,901 D7
Mallow* 6,506 D7
Manorhamilton 858 E3
Manulla⊙ 660 C4
Maryborough (Portlaoise) 3,902 G5
Maynooth 1,296 H5
Meathas Truim 546 G4
Midleton 3,075 E8
Midleton* 4,666 E8
Milford 763 F1
Millstreet 1,319 D7
Milltown 260 A7
Miltown-Malbay 677 C6
Minard⊙ 397 A7
Mitchelstown 2,783 E7
Moate 1,378 F5
Mohill 868 F4
Monaghan 5,256 G3
Monasterevan 1,619 H5
Moneygall 282 F6
Monivea⊙ 405 D5
Mooncoin 413 G7
Mount Bellew 275 D5
Mountcharles 445 E2
Mountmellick 2,595 G5
Mountmellick* 2,864 G5
Mountrath 1,098 F5
Moville 1,089 G1
Moycullen⊙ 498 C5
Moynalty⊙ 583 H4
Muff 240 G1
Muinebeag 2,321 H6
Mullagh 293 H4
Mullaghmore⊙ 629 D3
Mullinahone 262 F7
Mullinavat 343 G7
Mullingar 6,790 G4
Mullingar* 9,245 G4
Naas 5,078 H5
Navan (An Uaimh) 4,605 H4
Nenagh 5,085 E6
Nenagh* 5,174 E6
Newbliss⊙ 547 G3
Newbridge (Droichead Nua) 5,053 H5
Newcastle 2,549 D7
Newcastle* 2,680 D7
Newmarket 886 C7
Newmarket-on-Fergus 1,052 D6
New Pallas⊙ 1,271 E6
Newport, Mayo 420 C4
Newport, Tipperary 582 E6
New Ross 4,775 H7
New Ross* 5,153 H7
Newtown Forbes⊙ 495 F4
Newtownmountkennedy 882 J5
Newtownsandes 268 C6
O'Briensbridge-Montpelier 237 D6
Oldcastle 759 G4
Old Leighlin⊙ 309 G6
Oola 348 E6
Oranmore 440 D5
Oughterard 628 C5
Passage East 408 G7
Passage West 2,709 E8
Patrickswell 415 D6
Pettigo 332 F2
Piltown 456 G7
Portarlington 3,117 G5
Portlaoise 3,902 G5
Portlaoise* 6,470 G5
Portlaw 1,166 G7
Portmarnock 1,726 J5
Portumna 913 E5
Queenstown (Cóbh) 6,076 E8
Rahan⊙ 531 F5
Ramelton 807 F1
Raphoe 945 F2
Rathangan 868 G5
Rathcoole 1,740 J5
Rathcormac 191 E7
Rathdowney 892 F6
Rathdrum 1,141 J6
Rathgormuck⊙ 231 F7
Rathkeale 1,543 D7
Rathluirc 2,232 D7
Rathmore 437 J5
Rathmullen 486 F1
Rathnew-Merrymeeting 954 J6
Rathowen⊙ 294 F4
Rathvilly 230 H6
Ratoath 300 J5
Riverstown 236 E3
Rockcorry 233 H3
Rosapenna⊙ 822 F1
Roscommon 1,556 E4
Roscommon* 2,821 E4
Roscrea 3,855 F6
Rosscarbery 309 C8
Rosses Point 464 D3
Rosslare 588 J7
Rosslare Harbour (Ballygeary) 725 J7
Roundstone 204 A5
Roundwood 260 J5
Rush 2,633 J4
Saint Johnston 463 F2
Scarriff 619 E6
Schull 457 B8
Scotstown 264 H3
Shanagolden 231 C6
Shannon Airport 3,657 D6
Shannon Bridge 188 F5
Shercock 313 G4
Shillelagh 246 J6
Shinrone 365 F5
Shrule 288 C4
Sixmilebridge 567 D6
Skerries 3,044 J4
Skibbereen 2,104 C8
Slane 483 H4
Sligo 14,080 E3
Sligo* 14,456 E3
Sneem 285 B8
Spiddal⊙ 819 C5
Stepaside 748 J5
Stradbally, Laois 891 G5
Stradbally, Waterford 158 F7
Strokestown 563 E4
Swanlinbar 257 F3
Swinford 1,105 C4
Swords 4,133 J5
Taghmon 369 H7
Tallaght 6,174 J5
Tallow, 883 F 7
Tarbert, 485 C 6
Teltown, ‡739 H 4
Templemore, 2,174 F 6
Templetuohy, 197 F 6
Termonfeckin, 328 J 4
Thomastown, 1,270 G 7
Thurles, 6,840 F 6
Thurles, *7,087 F 6
Timoleague, 257 D 8
Tinahely, 450 H 6
Tipperary, 4,631 E 7
Tipperary, *4,717 E 7
Toomevara, 272 E 6
Tralee, 12,287 B 7
Tralee, *13,263 B 7
Tramore, 3,792 G 7
Trim, 1,700 H 4
Trim, *2,255 H 4
Tuam, 3,808 D 4
Tuam, *4,952 D 4
Tubbercurry, 959 D 3
Tulla, 415 D 6
Tullamore, 6,809 G 5
Tullamore, *7,474 G 5
Tullaroan, ‡301 G 6
Tullow, 1,838 H 6
Tullow, *1,945 H 6
Tynagh, ‡452 E 5
Tyrrellspass, 289 G 5
Urlingford, 652 F 6
Virginia, 583 G 4
Waterford, 31,968 G 7
Waterford, *33,676 G 7
Waterville, 547 A 8
Westport, 3,023 C 4
Wexford, 11,849 H 7
Wexford, *13,293 H 7
Whitegate, 370 E 8
Wicklow, 3,786 K 6
Wicklow, *3,915 K 6
Woodenbridge, ‡620 J 6
Woodford, 198 E 5
Youghal, 5,445 F 8
Youghal, *5,626 F 8

OTHER FEATURES

Achill (isl.), 3,129 A 4
Allen (lake) E 3
Allen, Bog of (marsh) H 5
Aran (isl.), 773 D 2
Aran (isls.), 1,499 B 5
Arklow (bank) K 6
Arrow (lake) E 3
Awbeg (riv.) D 7
Ballinskelligs (bay) A 8
Ballycotton (bay) F 8
Ballyheige (bay) B 7
Ballyhoura (hills) E 7
Ballyteige (bay) H 7
Bandon (riv.) D 8
Bann (riv.) J 6
Bantry (bay) B 8
Barrow (riv.) H 7
Baurtregaum (mt.) A 7
Bear (isl.), 288 B 8
Blacksod (bay) A 3
Blackstairs (mt.) H 6
Blackwater (riv.) D 7
Blackwater (riv.) H 4
Blasket (isls.) A 7
Bloody Foreland (prom.) E 1
Blue Stack (mts.) E 2
Boderg (lake) E 4
Boggeragh (mts.) D 7
Boyne (riv.) J 4
Brandon (head) A 7
Bride (riv.) E 7
Broad Haven (harb.) B 3
Brosna (riv.) F 5
Bull, The (isl.), 5 A 8
Caha (mts.) B 8
Carlingford (inlet) J 3
Carnsore (pt.) J 7
Carrantuohill (mt.) B 7
Clare (riv.) D 5
Clare (isls.), 168 A 4
Clear (cape) B 9
Clear (isl.), 192 C 9
Clew (bay) B 4
Comeragh (mts.) F 7
Conn (lake) C 3
Connacht (prov.), 390,902 C 4
Connemara (dist.), 7,599 B 5
Cork (harb.) E 8
Corrib (lake) C 5
Courtmacsherry (bay) D 8
Curragh, The H 5
Dee (riv.) H 4
Deel (riv.) D 7
Deele (riv.) F 2
Derg (lake) E 6
Derravaragh (lake) G 4
Derryveagh (mts.) E 2
Dingle (bay) A 7
Donegal (bay) D 3
Drum (hills) F 7
Dublin (bay) J 5
Dundalk (bay) J 4
Dunmanus (bay) B 8
Dursey (isl.), 38 A 8
Ennell (lake) G 5
Erne (riv.) E 3
Errigal (mt.) E 1
Erris (head) A 3
Fanad (head) F 1
Fastnet Rock (isl.), 3 B 9
Feale (riv.) C 7
Fergus (riv.) D 6
Finn (riv.) F 2
Finn (riv.) G 3
Flesk (riv.) C 7
Foyle (inlet) G 1
Foyle (riv.) G 2
Galley (head) D 9
Galtee (mts.) E 7
Galtymore (mt.) E 7
Galway (bay) C 5
Gara (lake) D 4
Garadice (lake) F 3
Gill (lake) E 3
Glyde (riv.) H 4
Golden Vale (plain) E 7
Gorumna (isl.), 1,108 B 5
Gowna (lake) G 4
Grand (canal) G 5
Greenore (pt.) J 7
Gweebarra (bay) D 2
Hags (head) B 6
Helvick (head) G 7
Hook (head) H 7
Horn (head) E 1
Iar Connacht (dist.), 10,774 C 5
Inishbofin (isl.), 236 A 4
Inishbofin (isl.), 103 E 1
Inisheer (isl.), 313 B 5
Inishmaan (isl.), 319 C 5
Inishmore (isl.), 864 B 5
Inishowen (head) H 1
Inishowen (pen.), 24,109 G 1
Inishtrahull (isl.), 3 G 1
Inishturk (isls.), 83 A 4
Inny (riv.) A 8
Inny (riv.) F 4
Inver (bay) E 2
Ireland's Eye (isl.) K 5
Irish (sea) K 4
Joyce's Country (dist.), 2,021 B 4
Kenmare (riv.) A 8
Kerry (head) A 7
Key (lake) E 3
Kilkieran (bay) B 5
Killala (bay) C 3
Killary (harb.) A 4
Kinsale (harb.) E 8
Kippure (mt.) J 5
Knockboy (mt.) B 8
Knockmealdown (mts.) F 7
Lady's Island Lake (inlet) J 7
Lambay (isl.), 24 K 4
Laune (riv.) B 7
Leane (lake) B 7
Leane (lake) G 4
Lee (riv.) D 8
Leinster (mt.) H 6
Leinster (prov.), 1,498,140 G 5
Lettermullan (isl.), 221 B 5
Liffey (riv.) H 5
Liscannor (bay) B 6
Long Island (bay) B 9
Loop (head) A 6
Lugnaquillia (mt.) J 5
Macgillicuddy's Reeks (mts.) B 7
Macnean (lake) F 3
Maigue (riv.) D 6
Maine (riv.) C 7
Malin (head) F 1
Mask (lake) C 4
Maumturk (mts.) B 5
Melvin (lake) E 3
Mizen (head) B 9
Moher (cliffs) B 6
Monavullagh (mts.) F 7
Moy (riv.) C 3
Mulkear (riv.) E 6
Mullaghareirk (mts.) C 7
Mulroy (bay) F 1
Munster (prov.), 882,002 D 7
Mweelrea (mt.) B 4
Mweenish (isl.), 198 B 5
Nagles (mts.) E 7
Nenagh (riv.) E 6
Nephin (mt.) C 3
Nore (riv.) G 7
North (sound) B 5
Omey (isl.), 34 A 5
Oughter (lake) G 3
Ovoca (riv.) J 6
Owenmore (riv.) D 3
Owey (isl.), 51 D 1
Paps, The (mt.) C 7
Partry (mts.) C 4
Pollaphuca (res.) J 5
Punchestown H 5
Rathlin O'Birne (isl.), 3 C 2
Ree (lake) F 5
Roaringwater (bay) B 9
Rosses (bay) D 1
Rosskeeragh (pt.) D 3
Royal (canal) G 4
Saint Finan's (bay) A 8
Saint George's (chan.) K 7
Saint John's (pt.) D 2
Saltee (isls.) H 7
Seven (heads) D 8
Seven Hogs, The (isls.) A 7
Shannon (riv.) E 6
Sheeffry (hills) B 4
Sheelin (lake) G 4
Sheep Haven (harb.) F 1
Sheeps (head) B 8
Sherkin (isl.), 82 C 9
Silvermine (mts.) E 6
Slaney (riv.) H 7
Slieve Aughty (mts.) D 5
Slieve Bloom (mts.) F 5
Slieve Gamph (mts.) D 3
Slievenaman (mt.) F 7
Sligo (bay) D 3
Slyne (head) A 5
South (sound) C 5
Stacks (mts.) B 7
Suck (riv.) E 5
Suir (riv.) G 7
Swilly (inlet) F 1
Tara (hill) H 4
Tory (isl.), 273 E 1
Tory (sound) E 1
Tralee (bay) B 7
Trawbreaga (bay) F 1
Ulster (part) (prov.), 207,204 G 2
Valencia (Valentia) (isl.), 770 A 8
Valentia (isl.), 770 A 8
Waterford (harb.) G 7
Wexford (bay) J 7
Wicklow (head) K 6
Wicklow (mts.) J 6
Youghal (bay) F 8

NORTHERN IRELAND

DISTRICTS

Antrim, 37,600 J 2
Ards, 52,100 K 2
Armagh, 47,500 H 3
Ballymena, 52,200 J 2
Ballymoney, 22,700 J 1
Bainbridge, 28,800 J 3
Belfast, 368,200 J 2
Carrickfergus, 27,500 K 2
Castlereagh, 63,600 K 2
Coleraine, 44,900 H 1
Cookstown, 27,500 H 2
Craigavon, 71,200 J 3
Down, 48,800 K 3
Dungannon, 43,000 H 3
Fermanagh, 50,900 F 3
Larne, 29,000 K 2
Limavady, 25,000 H 1
Lisburn, 80,800 J 2
Londonderry, 86,600 G 2
Magherafelt, 32,200 H 2
Mourne (Newry and Mourne), 75,300 J 3
Moyle, 13,400 J 1
Newtownabbey, 71,500 J 2
North Down, 59,600 K 2
Omagh, 41,800 G 2
Strabane, 35,500 G 2

CITIES and TOWNS

Ahoghill, ‡1,929 J 2
Annalong, 1,001 K 3
Antrim, 8,351 J 2
Ardglass, 1,052 K 3
Armagh, 13,606 H 3
Armoy, ‡1,051 J 1
Augher, ‡1,986 G 3
Aughnacloy, ‡1,885 H 3
Ballycastle, 2,899 J 1
Ballyclare, 5,155 J 2
Ballygawley, ‡2,165 G 3
Ballykelly, 1,116 G 1
Ballymena, 23,386 J 2
Ballymoney, 5,697 J 1
Ballynahinch, 3,485 J 3
Banbridge, 7,968 J 3
Bangor, 35,260 K 2
Belfast (cap.), 353,700 J 2
Belfast, *551,940 J 2
Bellaghy, ‡2,265 H 2
Belleek, ‡2,487 E 3
Beragh, ‡2,137 G 2
Bessbrook, 2,619 J 3
Brookeborough, ‡2,534 G 3
Broughshane, 1,288 J 2
Bushmills, 1,288 J 1
Caledon, ‡1,828 H 3
Carnlough, 1,416 J 2
Carrickfergus, 16,603 K 2
Carrowdore, 2,548 K 2
Castledawson, 1,162 H 2
Castlederg, 1,766 F 2
Castlewellan, 1,488 K 3
Claudy, ‡2,507 G 2
Clogher, ‡1,888 G 3
Coalisland, 3,614 H 2
Coleraine, 16,354 H 1
Comber, 5,575 K 2
Cookstown, 6,965 H 2
Craigavon, 12,740 J 3
Crossgar, 1,098 K 3
Crossmaglen, 1,085 H 3
Crumlin, 1,450 J 2
Cullybackey, 1,649 J 2
Derrygonnelly, ‡2,539 F 3
Dervock, ‡1,191 J 1
Donaghadee, 4,008 K 2
Downpatrick, 7,918 K 3
Draperstown, ‡2,247 H 2
Dromore, Bainbridge, 2,848 J 3
Dromore, Omagh, ‡2,224 G 3
Drumquin, ‡1,982 F 2
Dundrum, ‡2,245 K 3
Dungannon, 8,190 H 3
Dungiven, 1,536 H 2
Dunnamanagh, ‡2,242 G 2
Ederny and Kesh, ‡2,497 F 2
Enniskillen, 9,679 F 3
Feeny, ‡1,459 H 2
Fintona, 1,190 G 3
Fivemiletown, ‡1,649 G 3
Garvagh, ‡2,363 H 2
Gilford, 1,592 J 3
Glenarm, ‡1,728 J 2
Glenavy, ‡2,360 J 2
Glynn, ‡1,872 K 2
Gortin, ‡2,033 G 2
Greyabbey, ‡2,646 K 2
Hillsborough, 1,021 J 3
Holywood, 9,892 K 2
Irvinestown, 1,457 F 3
Keady, 2,145 H 3
Kells, ‡2,560 J 2
Kesh, ‡2,497 F 3
Kilkeel, 4,090 K 3
Killough, ‡3,295 K 3
Killyleagh, 2,359 K 3
Kilrea, 1,196 H 2
Kircubbin, 1,075 K 3
Larne, 18,482 K 2
Limavady, 6,004 H 1
Lisburn, 31,836 J 2
Lisnaskea, 1,443 G 3
Londonderry, 51,200 G 2
Loughbrickland, ‡2,056 J 3
Maghera, 2,085 H 2
Magherafelt, 4,704 H 2
Markethill, ‡2,352 H 3
Millisle, 1,172 K 2
Moneymore, 1,178 H 2
Moy, ‡2,349 H 3
Moygashel, 1,086 H 3
Newcastle, 4,647 J 3
Newry, 20,279 J 3
Newtownabbey, 58,114 K 2
Newtownards, 15,484 K 2
Newtownbutler, ‡2,663 G 3
Newtownhamilton, ‡1,936 H 3
Newtownstewart, 1,433 G 2
Omagh, 14,594 G 2
Pomeroy, ‡1,786 H 2
Portaferry, 1,730 K 3
Portavogie, 1,310 K 3
Portglenone, ‡2,061 H 2
Portrush, 5,376 H 1
Portstewart, 5,085 H 1
Randalstown, 2,799 J 2
Rathfriland, 1,886 J 3
Rostrevor, 1,617 J 3
Saintfield, ‡2,198 K 3
Sion Mills, 1,588 G 2
Sixmilecross, ‡1,980 G 2
Stewartstown, ‡1,759 H 2
Strabane, 9,413 G 2
Strangford, ‡1,987 K 3
Tandragee, 1,725 J 3
Tempo, ‡2,282 G 3
Trillick, ‡2,167 G 3
Warrenpoint, 4,291 J 3
Whitehead, 2,642 K 2

OTHER FEATURES

Bann (riv.) H 2
Belfast (inlet) K 2
Blackwater (riv.) H 3
Bush (riv.) H 1
Derg (riv.) F 2
Divis (mt.) J 2
Dundrum (bay) K 3
Erne (lake) F 3
Foyle (inlet) G 1
Foyle (riv.) G 2
Giant's Causeway H 1
Lagan (riv.) K 2
Larne (inlet) K 2
Magee, Island (pen.), 1,581 K 2
Magilligan (pt.) H 1
Main (riv.) J 2
Mourne (mts.) J 3
Mourne (riv.) G 2
Neagh (lake) J 2
North (chan.) K 1
Rathlin (isl.), 109 J 1
Red (bay) K 1
Roe (riv.) H 1
Saint John's (pt.) K 3
Slieve Donard (mt.) K 3
Sperrin (mts.) G 2
Strangford (inlet) K 3
Torr (head) K 1
Ulster (part) (prov.), 1,537,200 G 2
Upper Lough Erne (lake) F 3

*City and suburbs.
‡Population of district.

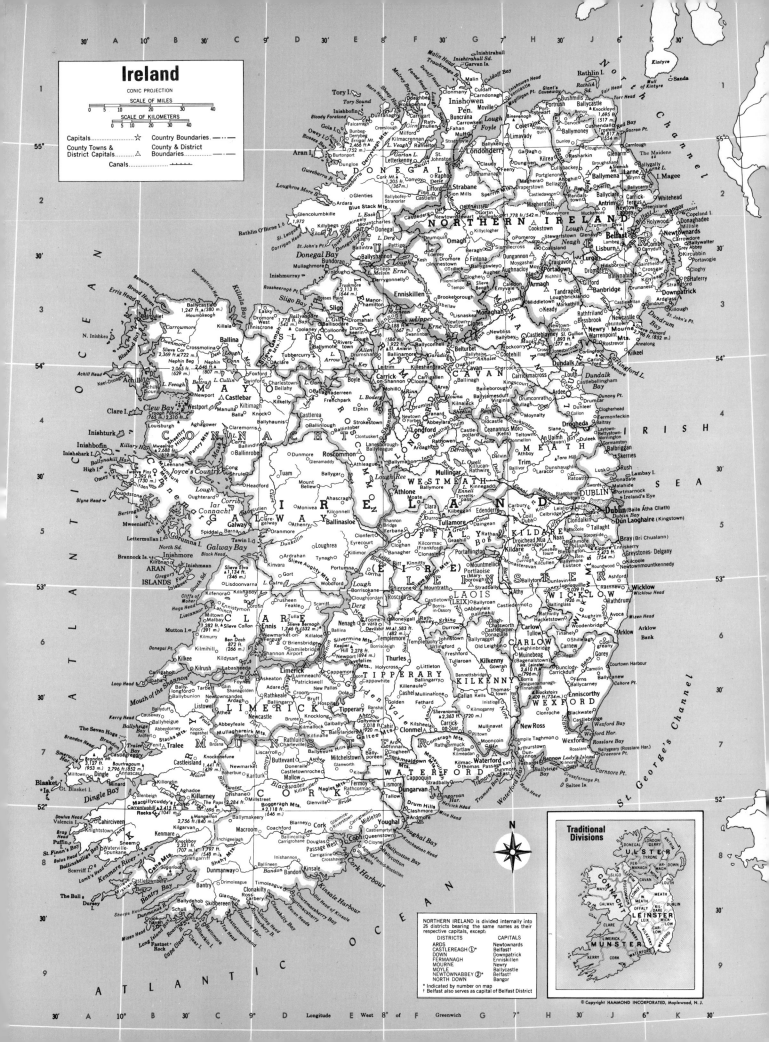

Ireland

CONIC PROJECTION

SCALE OF MILES

SCALE OF KILOMETERS

Capitals........................☆
County Towns & District Capitals............△
Canals..........................

Country Boundaries.......
County & District Boundaries.........

Traditional Divisions

NORTHERN IRELAND is divided internally into 26 districts bearing the same names as their respective capitals, except:

DISTRICTS	CAPITALS
ARDS	Newtownards
CASTLEREAGH ① *	Belfast†
DOWN	Downpatrick
FERMANAGH	Enniskillen
MOURNE	Newry
MOYLE	Ballycastle
NEWTOWNABBEY ② *	Belfast†
NORTH DOWN	Bangor

* Indicated by number on map
† Belfast also serves as capital of Belfast District

© Copyright HAMMOND INCORPORATED, Maplewood, N.J.

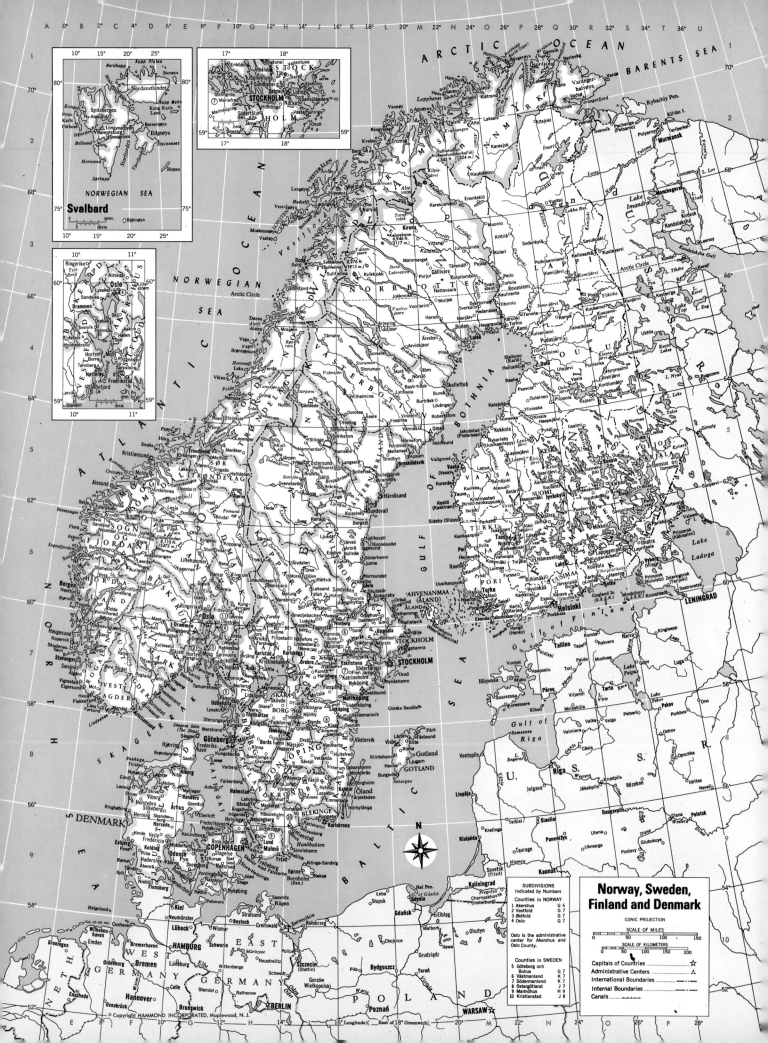

Svalbard

Norway, Sweden, Finland and Denmark

CONIC PROJECTION

SCALE OF MILES

SCALE OF KILOMETERS

SUBDIVISIONS
Indicated by Numbers

Counties in NORWAY

1	Akershus	G 6
2	Vestfold	G 7
3	Østfold	G 7
4	Oslo	G 7

Oslo is the administrative
center for Akershus and
Oslo County.

Counties in SWEDEN

5	Göteborg och Bohus	G 7
6	Västmanland	K 7
7	Södermanland	K 7
8	Östergötland	J 7
9	Malmöhus	H 9
10	Kristianstad	J 8

Capitals of Countries ☆
Administrative Centers △
International Boundaries
Internal Boundaries
Canals

© Copyright HAMMOND INCORPORATED, Maplewood, N.J.

AREA 125,053 sq. mi. (323,887 sq. km.)
POPULATION 4,092,000
CAPITAL Oslo
LARGEST CITY Oslo
HIGHEST POINT Glittertinden 8,110 ft. (2,472 m.)
MONETARY UNIT krone
MAJOR LANGUAGE Norwegian
MAJOR RELIGION Protestantism

AREA 173,665 sq. mi. (449,792 sq. km.)
POPULATION 8,320,000
CAPITAL Stockholm
LARGEST CITY Stockholm
HIGHEST POINT Kebnekaise 6,946 ft. (2,117 m.)
MONETARY UNIT krona
MAJOR LANGUAGE Swedish
MAJOR RELIGION Protestantism

AREA 130,128 sq. mi. (337,032 sq. km.)
POPULATION 4,788,000
CAPITAL Helsinki
LARGEST CITY Helsinki
HIGHEST POINT Haltiatunturi 4,343 ft. (1,324 m.)
MONETARY UNIT markka
MAJOR LANGUAGES Finnish, Swedish
MAJOR RELIGION Protestantism

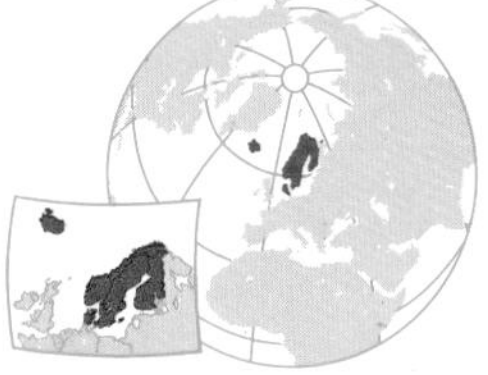

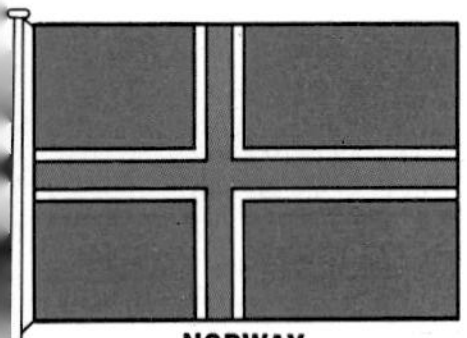

NORWAY

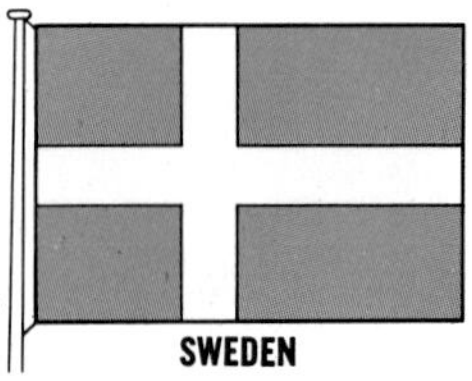

SWEDEN

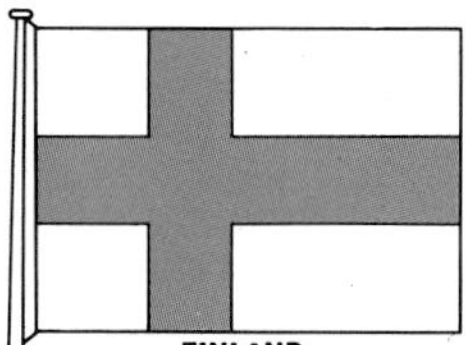

FINLAND

FINLAND

PROVINCES

venanmaa 22,380 ... L6
and (Ahvenanmaa) 22,380 ... L6
me 662,500 ... O6
ski-Suomi 241,770 ... O5
opio 252,023 ... P5
mi 346,478 ... Q6
ppi 196,792 ... P3
ikkeli 211,453 ... P6
ulu 406,309 ... P4
hjois-Karjala 179,065 ... Q5
rku ja Pori 697,988 ... N6
simaa 1,085,625 ... O6
asa 425,283 ... N5

CITIES and TOWNS

nekoski 10,725 ... O5
bo (Turku) 164,857 ... N6
avus 10,285 ... N5
rgaå 18,740 ... O6
enäs 7,391 ... N6
Espoo 117,090 ... O6
Forssa 18,442 ... N6
Haapajärvi 7,791 ... O5
Hämeenlinna 40,761 ... O6
Hamina 11,055 ... P6
Hangö 10,374 ... N7
Hanko (Hangö) 10,374 ... N7
Harjavalta 8,445 ... M6
Heinola 15,350 ... P6
Helsinki (cap.) 502,961 ... O6
Helsinki* 794,746 ... O6
Huutokoski† 6,458 ... P5
Hyvinkää 35,865 ... O6
Iisalmi 21,159 ... P5
Ikaalinen 8,364 ... N6
Imatra 35,590 ... Q6
Ivalo 2,661 ... P2
Jakobstad 20,397 ... N5
Jämsä 12,526 ... O6
Järvenpää 16,259 ... O6
Joensuu 41,429 ... R5
Jyväskylä 61,209 ... O5
Jyväskylä* 84,185 ... O5
Kajaani 20,583 ... P4
Kalajoki 3,624 ... N4
Kankaanpää 12,564 ... M6
Karhula 21,834 ... P6
Karis 8,152 ... N6
Karjaa (Karis) 8,152 ... N6
Karkkila 8,678 ... N6
Kauniainien 6,219 ... O6
Kauttua 3,297 ... M6
Kelloselkä† 8,200 ... Q3
Kemi 27,893 ... O4
Kemijärvi 12,951 ... P3
Kerava 19,966 ... O6
Kokemäki 10,188 ... N6
Kokkola 22,096 ... N5
Kotka 34,026 ... P6
Kotka* 60,235 ... P6
Kouvola 29,383 ... P6
Kouvola* 59,507 ... P6
Kristiinankaupunki (Kristinestad) 9,331 ... N5
Kristinestad 9,331 ... N5
Kuhmo 4,150 ... Q4
Kuopio 71,684 ... Q5
Kurikka 11,177 ... M5
Kuusamo 4,449 ... Q4
Kuusankoski 22,342 ... P6
Lahti 94,864 ... O6
Lahti* 112,129 ... O6
Lappeenranta 52,682 ... P6
Lapua 15,189 ... N5
Lieksa 20,274 ... R5
Loimaa 6,575 ... N6
Lovisa 8,674 ... P6
Maarianhamina (Mariehamn) 9,574 ... M7
Mänttä 7,910 ... O6
Mariehamn 9,574 ... M7
Mikkeli 27,112 ... P6
Naantali 7,814 ... M6
Nokia 22,308 ... N6
Nurmes 11,721 ... Q5
Nykarleby 7,408 ... N5
Oulainen 7,322 ... O4
Oulu 93,707 ... O4
Oulu* 103,044 ... O4
Outokumpu 10,736 ... Q5
Parainen 10,170 ... M6
Parkano 8,518 ... N6
Pieksämäki 12,923 ... P5
Pietarsaari (Jakobstad) 20,397 ... N5
Pori 80,343 ... M6
Pori* 86,635 ... M6
Posio† 6,205 ... Q3
Pudasjärvi† 12,594 ... P4
Raahe 15,379 ... O4
Raisio 14,271 ... M6
Rauma 29,081 ... M6
Riihimäki 24,106 ... O6
Rovaniemi 28,411 ... O3
Saarijärvi 2,714 ... O5
Salo 19,176 ... N6
Savonlinna 28,336 ... Q6
Seinäjoki 22,123 ... N5
Sodankylä 3,304 ... P3
Sotkamo 2,316 ... Q4
Suolahti 5,936 ... O5
Suonenjoki 9,286 ... P5
Tammisaari (Ekenäs) 7,391 ... N6
Tampere 168,118 ... N6
Tampere* 220,920 ... N6
Toijala 8,080 ... N6
Tornio 19,971 ... O4
Turku 164,857 ... N6
Turku* 217,423 ... N6
Turtola† 5,852 ... O3
Ulvila† 8,040 ... N6
Uusikaarlepyy (Nykarleby) 7,408 ... N5
Uusikaupunki 11,915 ... M6
Vaasa 54,402 ... M5
Vaasa* 58,224 ... M5
Valkeakoski 22,588 ... N6
Vammala 16,363 ... N6
Varkaus 24,450 ... Q5
Vasa (Vaasa) 54,402 ... M5
Vuotso† 10,186 ... P2
Ylivieska 10,827 ... O4

OTHER FEATURES

Åland (isls.) ... L6
Baltic (sea) ... K9
Bothnia (gulf) ... M5
Finland (gulf) ... P7
Hailuoto (isl.) ... O4
Haltiatunturi (mt.) ... M2
Hangöudd (prom.) ... N7
Haukivesi (lake) ... Q5
Iijoki (riv.) ... O4
Inari (lake) ... P2
Ivalojoki (riv.) ... P2
Juojärvi (lake) ... Q5
Kalajoki (riv.) ... O4
Kallavesi (lake) ... P5
Karlö (Hailuoto) (isl.) ... O4
Keitele (lake) ... O5
Kemijärvi (lake) ... Q3
Kemijoki (riv.) ... O3
Kiantajärvi (lake) ... Q4
Kilpisjärvi (lake) ... M2
Kitinen (riv.) ... P3
Kivijärvi (lake) ... O5
Koitere (lake) ... R5
Kuusamojärvi (lake) ... Q4
Längelmävesi (lake) ... O6
Lapland (reg.) ... O2
Lappajärvi (lake) ... O5
Lapuanjoki (riv.) ... N5
Lestijärvi (lake) ... O5
Lokka (res.) ... Q3
Muojärvi (lake) ... R4
Muonio (riv.) ... M2
Näsijärvi (lake) ... O6
Onkivesi (lake) ... P5
Orihvesi (lake) ... Q5
Oulujärvi (lake) ... P4
Oulujoki (riv.) ... O4
Ounasjoki (riv.) ... O3
Päijänne (lake) ... O6
Pielinen (lake) ... Q5
Puruvesi (lake) ... Q6
Puulavesi (lake) ... P5
Pyhäjärvi (lake) ... O5
Pyhäjärvi (lake) ... M6
Saimaa (lake) ... Q6
Siikajoki (riv.) ... O4
Simojärvi (lake) ... P3
Simojoki (riv.) ... O4
Tana (riv.) ... P2
Tornio (riv.) ... O3
Vallgrund (isl.) ... M5
Ylikitka (lake) ... Q3

NORWAY

COUNTIES

Akershus 355,196 ... G6
Aust-Agder 86,216 ... E7
Buskerud 209,684 ... F6
Finnmark 79,373 ... O2
Hedmark 183,465 ... G6
Hordaland 386,492 ... E6
Møre og Romsdal 231,944 ... E5
Nordland 243,233 ... J3
Nord-Trøndelag 122,886 ... H4
Oppland 178,259 ... F6
Oslo (city) 462,732 ... D3
Østfold 228,546 ... G7
Rogaland 287,653 ... E7
Sogn og Fjordane 103,135 ... E6
Sør-Trøndelag 241,361 ... G5
Telemark 158,853 ... F7
Troms 144,111 ... L2
Vest-Agder 131,659 ... E7
Vestfold 182,433 ... G7

CITIES and TOWNS

Ålesund 40,868 ... D5
Ålgård 2,322 ... D7
Alta 5,582 ... N2
Åndalsnes 2,574 ... F5
Årdalstangen 2,360 ... F6
Arendal 11,701 ... F7
Arendal* 21,228 ... F7
Årnes 2,267 ... G6
Askim 8,413 ... E4
Bamble† 7,031 ... F7
Barentsburg ... C2
Bergen 213,434 ... D6
Bodø 31,077 ... J3
Borge† 3,294 ... H2
Brønnøysund 3,130 ... G4
Dombås 1,114 ... F5
Drammen 50,777 ... C4
Drammen* 56,521 ... C4
Drøbak 4,538 ... D4
Eidsvoll 2,906 ... G6
Eigersund 11,379 ... D7
Elverum 7,391 ... G6
Farsund 8,908 ... E7
Flekkefjord 8,750 ... E7
Flora 8,822 ... D6
Fredrikstad 29,024 ... D4
Fredrikstad* 51,141 ... D4
Gjøvik 25,963 ... G6
Grimstad 13,091 ... F7
Halden 27,087 ... G7
Hamar 16,418 ... G6
Hamar* 25,138 ... G6
Hammerfest 7,610 ... N1
Hammerfest* 8,005 ... N1
Harstad 21,125 ... K2
Haugesund 27,386 ... D7
Haugesund* 29,277 ... D7
Hermansverk 706 ... E6
Holmestrand 8,246 ... C4
Holmsbu 273 ... D4
Honningsvag 3,780 ... O1
Horten 13,746 ... D4
Horten* 17,246 ... D4
Kirkenes 4,466 ... Q2
Kongsberg 19,854 ... F7
Kongsvinger 16,146 ... H6
Kopervik 4,221 ... D7
Kornsjø† 6,079 ... G7
Kragerø 5,249 ... F7
Kristiansand 59,488 ... F8
Kristiansund 18,847 ... E5
Kvinnherad† 2,898 ... E6
Larvik 9,097 ... C4
Larvik* 19,202 ... C4
Lenvik† 11,098 ... L2
Levanger 5,066 ... G5
Lillehammer 21,248 ... F6
Lillesand 3,028 ... F7
Lillestrøm† 11,550 ... E3
Longyearbyen ... D2
Lysaker† 81,612 ... D3
Mandal 11,579 ... E7
Meråker† 2,907 ... G5
Mo 21,033 ... J3
Molde 20,334 ... E5
Mosjøen 9,341 ... H4
Moss 25,786 ... D4
Moss* 27,430 ... D4
Mysen 3,760 ... G7
Namsos 11,452 ... G4
Narvik 19,582 ... K2
Nesttun† 11,519 ... D6
Nittedal† 8,889 ... D3
Notodden 12,970 ... F7
Nøtterøy 11,944 ... D4
Ny-Ålesund ... C2
Odda 7,401 ... E6
Oppdal 2,173 ... F5
Orkanger 3,685 ... F5
Oslo (cap.) 462,732 ... D3
Oslo* 645,413 ... D3
Porsgrunn 31,709 ... G7
Rakkestad 2,392 ... G7
Ringerike 30,156 ... C3
Risør 6,560 ... F7
Rjukan 5,334 ... F7
Røros 3,041 ... G5
Sandefjord 33,350 ... C4
Sandnes 33,934 ... D7
Sandvika† 34,337 ... C3
Sarpsborg 12,889 ... D4
Sarpsborg* 36,449 ... D4
Selje† 3,386 ... D5
Ski 9,081 ... D4
Skien 47,105 ... F7
Stavanger 86,639 ... D7
Stavern 2,604 ... D4
Steinkjer 20,553 ... G4
Stor-Elvdal† 2,993 ... G6
Sunndalsøra 5,114 ... F5
Sveagruva ... D2
Svolvaer 3,942 ... J2
Tønsberg 9,964 ... D4
Tønsberg* 36,374 ... D4
Tromsø 43,830 ... L2
Trondheim 134,910 ... F5
Ullensvang† 2,326 ... E6
Vadsø 6,019 ... Q1
Vardø 3,875 ... R1
Vik 1,019 ... E6
Volda 3,511 ... E5
Voss 5,944 ... E6

OTHER FEATURES

Alsten (isl.) ... H4
Andøya (isl.) ... J2
Barduelv (riv.) ... L2
Bellsund ... C2
Bjørnafjorden (fjord) ... D6
Bjornøya (isl.) ... D3
Boknafjord (fjord) ... D7
Bremanger (isl.) ... D6
Dønna (isl.) ... H3
Dovrefjell (hills) ... F5
Edgeøya (isl.) ... E2
Femundsjø (lake) ... G5
Folda (fjord) ... G4
Folda (fjord) ... J3
Frohavet (bay) ... F5
Frøya (isl.) ... F5
Glittertinden (mt.) ... F6
Hardangervidda (plat.) ... E6
Hardangerfjord (fjord) ... D7
Hinlopenstreten (str.) ... C1
Hinnøya (isl.) ... K2
Hitra (isl.) ... F5
Hopen (isl.) ... E2
Isfjorden (fjord) ... C2
Jostedalsbreen (glac.) ... E6
Kjölen (mts.) ... K3
Kongsfjorden (fjord) ... B2
Kvaløya (isl.) ... O1
Lågen (riv.) ... G6
Laksefjorden (fjord) ... P1
Langøy (isl.) ... J2
Lapland (reg.) ... K2
Leka (isl.) ... G4
Lindesnes (cape) ... E8
Lista (pen.) ... E7
Lofoten (isls.) ... H2
Lopphavet (bay) ... M1
Magerøya (isl.) ... P1
Moskenesøya (isl.) ... H3
Namsen (riv.) ... H4
Nordaustlandet (isl.) ... D1
Nordfjord (fjord) ... E6
Nordkapp (pt.) ... C1
Nordkinn (headland) ... Q1
Nordkinn (pen.) ... P1
North Cape (Nordkapp) (pt.) ... P1
Norwegian (sea) ... F3
Ofotfjorden (fjord) ... K2
Oslofjord (fjord) ... D4
Otra (riv.) ... E7
Otterøya (isl.) ... E5
Pasvikelv (riv.) ... Q2
Platen, Kapp (pt.) ... D1
Porsangen (fjord) ... O1
Rana (fjord) ... H3
Rauma (riv.) ... F5
Ringvassøy (isl.) ... L2
Romsdalsfjorden (fjord) ... E5
Saltfjorden (fjord) ... J3
Seiland (isl.) ... N1
Senja (isl.) ... K2
Skagerrak (str.) ... F8
Smøla (isl.) ... E5
Sognafjorden (fjord) ... D6
Sørkapp (pt.) ... C2
Sorøya (isl.) ... N1
Spitsbergen (isl.) ... C2
Storfjorden (fjord) ... D2
Sulitjelma (mt.) ... J3
Svalbard (isls.) ... C3
Tana (riv.) ... P1
Tanafjord (fjord) ... Q1
Tokke (riv.) ... F7
Trondheimsfjorden (fjord) ... G5
Tyrifjord (lake) ... C3
Vaerøy (isl.) ... H3
Vagåvatn (lake) ... F6
Vannøy (isl.) ... L1
Varangerhalvøya (pen.) ... Q1
Varangerfjord (fjord) ... Q2
Vega (isl.) ... G4
Vesterålen (isls.) ... J2
Vestfjord (fjord) ... H3
Vestvågøya (isl.) ... H3
Vikna (isls.) ... G4

SWEDEN

COUNTIES

Älvsborg 418,150 ... H7
Blekinge 155,391 ... J8
Gävleborg 294,595 ... K6
Göteborg och Bohus 714,660 ... G7
Gotland 54,447 ... L8
Halland 219,767 ... H8
Jämtland 133,559 ... J5
Jönköping 301,905 ... H8
Kalmar 240,768 ... K8
Kopparberg 281,082 ... J6
Kristianstad 272,090 ... J8

(continued on following page)

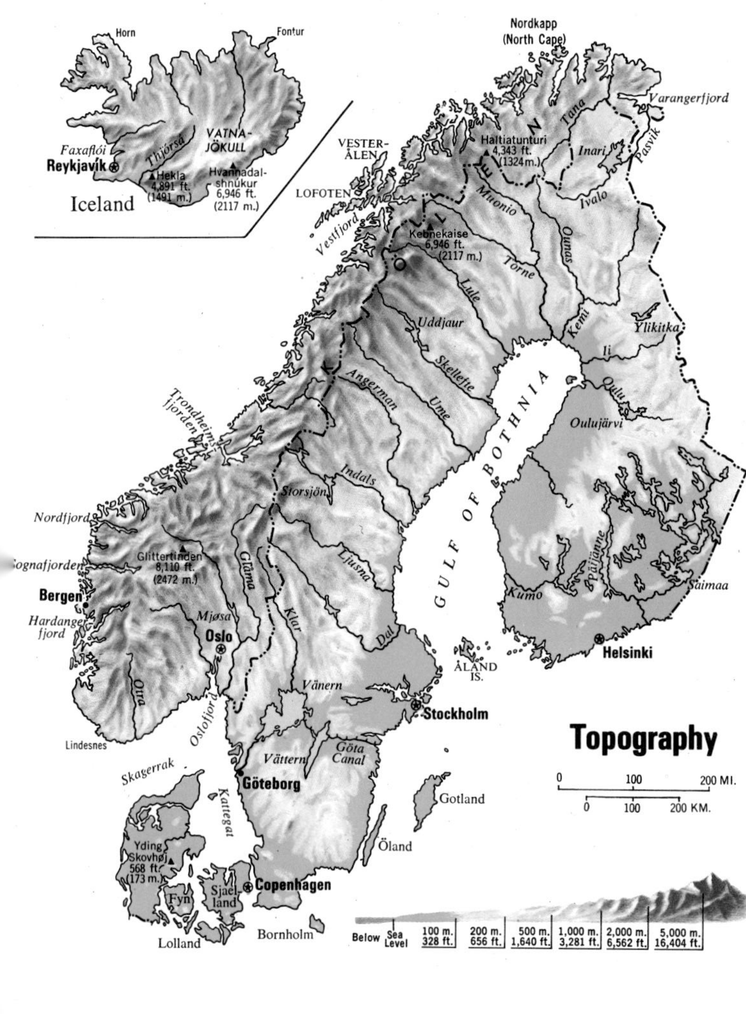

Horn
Fontur
Faxaflói
Reykjavík
Thjórsá
VATNA-JÖKULL
Hekla 4,891 ft. (1491 m.)
Hvannadal-shnúkur 6,946 ft. (2117 m.)
Iceland
Nordkapp (North Cape)
Varangerfjord
VESTER-ÅLEN
LOFOTEN
Vestfjord
Haltiatunturi 4,343 ft. (1324 m.)
Inari
Tana
Pasvik
Ivalo
Muonio
Ounas
Kebnekaise 6,946 ft. (2117 m.)
Torne
Lule
Kemi
Ylikitka
Uddjaur
Skellefte
Ii
Oulu
Ume
Ångerman
Oulujärvi
GULF OF BOTHNIA
Trondheimsfjorden
Storsjön
Indals
Nordfjord
Sognafjorden
Glittertinden 8,110 ft. (2472 m.)
Glåma
Ljusna
Päijänne
Saimaa
Bergen
Hardanger fjord
Mjøsa
Klar
Dal
Kumo
Oslo
Helsinki
ÅLAND IS.
Otra
Vänern
Oslofjord
Stockholm
Lindesnes
Vättern
Göta Canal
Topography
Skagerrak
Göteborg
Kattegat
Gotland
0 100 200 MI.
0 100 200 KM.
Öland
Yding Skovhøj 568 ft. (173 m.)
Fyn
Sjaelland
Copenhagen
Lolland
Bornholm
Below Sea Level
100 m. 328 ft.
200 m. 656 ft.
500 m. 1,640 ft.
1,000 m. 3,281 ft.
2,000 m. 6,562 ft.
5,000 m. 16,404 ft.

Norway, Sweden, Finland, Denmark and Iceland

(continued)

Kronoberg 169,454 J8
Malmöhus 740,137 H9
Norrbotten 264,215 L3
Örebro 273,994 J7
Östergötland 387,104 J7
Skaraborg 263,382 H7
Södermanland 252,030 K7
Stockholm 1,493,052 L7
Uppsala 229,879 K7
Värmland 284,442 H7
Västerbotten 236,367 K4
Västernorrland 268,202 K5
Västmanland 259,872 K7

CITIES and TOWNS

Åhus 6,125 J9
Alingsås 18,892 H7
Älmhult 7,390 H8
Alvesta 7,261 J8
Älvsbyn 4,707 M4
Åmål 9,556 H7
Ånge 3,760 J5
Ängelholm 16,016 H8
Arboga 11,819 J7
Arbrå 2,734 K6
Årjäng† 2,596 H7
Arvidsjaur 4,194 L4
Arvika 13,934 H7
Åseda 2,465 J8
Askim 17,609 G8
Åtvidaberg 8,436 K7
Avesta 19,095 J6
Bålsta 8,243 G1
Båstad 2,452 H8
Bengtsfors 3,535 H7
Boden 19,590 M4
Bollnäs 13,305 K6
Bollstabruk 3,548 L5
Borås 67,537 H8
Borås* 187,710 H8
Borgholm 2,789 K8
Borlänge 40,158 J6
Brunflo 3,460 J5
Dalby† 4,013 H6
Danderyd† 36,596 H1
Dannemora 291 K6
Edsbyn 4,388 J6
Eksjö 9,686 J8
Emmaboda 5,652 J8
Enköping 18,541 G1
Eskilstuna 66,409 K7
Eslöv 13,629 H9
Fagersta† 14,778 J6
Falkenberg 14,148 H8
Falköping 15,126 H7
Falun 30,073 J6
Färjestaden 2,995 K8
Filipstad 7,835 H7
Finspång 16,346 J7
Flen 6,770 K7
Forshaga 6,000 H7
Frösö 10,274 J5
Frövi 2,583 J7
Gällivare 8,669 M3
Gamleby 3,666 J8
Gävle 67,454 K6
Gimo 3,154 K6
Gislaved 8,564 H8
Gnesta 3,835 G2
Göteborg 444,540 G8
Göteborg* 690,767 G8
Hagfors 8,060 H6
Hällefors 7,862 J7
Hallsberg 6,799 J7
Hallstahammar 13,583 K7
Hallstavik 5,162 L6
Halmstad 49,558 H8
Haparanda 5,031 N4
Härnösand 18,971 L5
Hässleholm 16,813 H8
Hedemora 7,039 K6
Helsingborg 80,986 H8
Helsingborg* 215,894 H8
Hjo 4,615 J7
Hofors 11,459 K6
Höganäs 10,866 H8
Holmsund 5,467 M5
Hörnefors 2,441 L5
Huddinge 48,339 H1
Hudiksvall 15,004 K6
Hultsfred 5,763 K8
Husum 2,517 L5
Hyltebruk 3,469 H8
Iggesund 4,448 K6
Järna 6,237 G2
Jokkmokk 3,186 L3
Jönköping 78,650 H8
Jönköping* 131,499 H8
Kalix 7,668 N4
Kalmar 32,049 K8
Karlshamn 17,447 J8
Karlskoga† 35,425 J7
Karlskrona 33,414 J8
Karlstad 51,243 H7
Katrineholm 22,884 K7
Kinna 13,676 H8
Kiruna 25,410 L3
Kisa 4,323 J7
Köping 20,059 J7
Kopparberg 3,942 J7
Kramfors 7,719 L5
Kristianstad 30,780 J9
Kristinehamn 21,146 H7
Kumla 11,451 J7
Kungälv† 12,764 G8
Kungsbacka† 11,986 G8
Kvissleby 3,413 K5
Laholm 3,898 H8
Landskrona 29,486 H9
Långshyttan 2,744 K6
Laxå 5,166 J7
Leksand 4,410 J6
Lessebo 2,991 J8
Lidingö 30,098 H1
Lidköping 21,001 H7
Lindesberg 8,247 J7
Linköping 80,274 K7
Linköping* 132,839 K7
Ljungby 12,969 J8
Ljusdal 7,075 J6
Ljusne 3,578 K6
Ludvika 18,217 J6
Luleå 42,139 N4
Lund 55,047 H9
Lycksele 8,586 L4
Lysekil 7,815 G7
Malmberget 10,239 M3
Malmö 241,191 H9
Malmö* 453,339 H9
Malung 6,211 H6
Mariefred 2,553 F1
Mariestad 16,454 H7
Markaryd 4,266 H8
Märsta 17,066 K7
Marstrand 1,168 G8
Mellerud 3,579 H7
Mjölby 12,488 J7
Mölndal† 47,248 H8
Mönsterås 5,005 K8
Mora 8,772 J6
Motala 29,454 J7
Nacka 19,708 H1
Nässjö 18,634 J8
Nora 5,515 J7
Norberg 5,438 K6
Norrköping 85,244 K7
Norrköping* 163,206 K7
Norrtälje 12,784 L7
Nybro 13,010 J8
Nyköping 30,352 K7
Nynäshamn 11,070 L7
Ockelbo 2,810 K6
Olofström 10,096 J8
Örebro 117,877 J7
Örebro* 171,440 J7
Örnsköldsvik 29,514 L5
Orrefors 919 J8
Orsa 5,099 J6
Oskarshamn 19,021 K8
Östersund 40,056 J5
Östhammar 1,783 L6
Oxelösund 13,862 K7
Piteå 16,169 M4
Rättvik 4,087 J6
Rimbo 3,404 L7
Ronneby 12,086 J8
Säffle 11,428 H7
Sala 11,216 K7
Saltsjöbaden 8,113 J1
Sandviken 27,994 K6
Säter 4,297 J6
Sävsjö 4,913 J8
Sigtuna 4,780 H1
Simrishamn 5,834 J9
Skanör med Falsterbo 4,909 H9
Skara 10,138 H7
Skellefteå 29,353 M4
Skövde 29,945 H7
Skutskär 7,174 K6
Smedjebacken 8,418 J6
Söderhamn 14,673 K6
Söderköping 5,310 K7
Södertälje 58,408 G1
Sollefteå 8,923 K5
Sollentuna† 40,905 H1
Solna† 53,992 H1
Sölvesborg 7,292 J9
Stenungsund 8,361 G7
Stockholm (cap.) 665,550 G1
Stockholm* 1,357,183 G1
Storuman 2,587 K4
Storvik 2,748 K6
Strängnäs 10,255 F1
Strömstad 4,735 G7
Strömsund 4,119 K5
Sundbyberg† 27,058 G1
Sundsvall 52,268 K5
Sunne 4,273 H7
Surahammar 6,509 J7
Sveg 2,608 J5
Svenljunga 3,189 H8
Täby† 41,285 H1
Tibro 8,476 J7
Tidaholm 8,039 J7
Tierp 5,005 K6
Timrå 11,416 K5
Tomelilla 5,371 J9
Torsby 3,632 H6
Torshälla 8,231 K7
Tranås 14,854 J7
Trelleborg 22,559 H9
Trollhättan 42,499 H7
Trosa 3,128 K7
Uddevalla 32,700 G7
Ulricehamn 7,827 H8
Umeå 49,715 M5
Uppsala 101,850 K7
Uppsala* 157,202 L7
Vadstena 5,294 J7
Vaggeryd 3,974 J8
Valdemarsvik 3,558 K7
Vallentuna 10,477 H1
Vänersborg 20,510 G7
Vännäs 3,876 L5
Vansbro 2,708 H6
Vara 3,049 H7
Varberg 19,467 G8
Värnamo 15,726 J8
Västerås 98,858 K7
Västerås* 147,508 K7
Västerhaninge 14,125 H1
Västervik 21,239 K8
Vaxholm† 3,744 J1
Växjö 40,328 J8
Vetlanda 12,358 J8
Vilhelmina 4,060 K4
Vimmerby 7,405 J8
Virserum 2,495 J8
Visby 19,886 L8
Ystad 14,286 H9

OTHER FEATURES

Ångermanälven (riv.) K5
Åsnen (lake) J8
Baltic (sea) K9
Bolmen (lake) H8
Bothnia (gulf) N4
Dalälven (riv.) K6
Fårö (isl.) L8
Göta (canal) J7
Göta (riv.) H7
Gotland (isl.) L8
Gräsö (isl.) L6
Hanöbukten (bay) J9
Hjälmaren (lake) J7
Hoburgen (cliff) L8
Hornslandet (pen.) K6
Indalsälven (riv.) H5
Kalixälv (riv.) N3
Kalmarsund (sound) K8
Kattegat (str.) G8
Kebnekaise (mt.) L3
Kölen (mts.) K3
Klarälv (riv.) H6
Lapland (reg.) M2
Ljusnan (riv.) H5
Luleälv (riv.) M4
Mälaren (lake) G1
Muonioälv (riv.) M2
Öland (isl.) K8
Öresund (sound) H9
Ornö (isl.) J2
Österdalälven (riv.) H6
Piteälv (riv.) M4
Siljan (lake) J6
Skagerrak (str.) F8
Sommen (lake) J8
Stora Lulevatten (lake) L3
Storsjön (lake) J5
Sulitelma (mt.) K3
Torneälv (riv.) M3
Uddjaur (lake) L4
Umeälv (riv.) L4
Vänern (lake) H7
Västerdalälven (riv.) H6
Vättern (lake) J7

*City and suburbs.
†Population of commune.
†Population of parish.

DENMARK

COUNTIES

Århus 534,333 D5
Bornholm 47,241 F9
Copenhagen (commune) 622,612 F6
Faerøe Islands 41,969 B2
Frederiksberg (commune) 101,874 F6
Frederiksborg 260,825 E5
Fyn 433,765 D7
København (Copenhagen) (commune) 622,612 F6
Københaven 616,571 F6
Nordjylland 457,165 D4
Ribe 198,153 B7
Ringkøbing 242,006 B5
Roskilde 154,314 E6
Sønderjylland 238,502 C7
Storstrøm 252,780 E7
Vejle 306,809 C6
Vestsjaelland 259,484 E6
Viborg 221,002 C4

CITIES and TOWNS

Åbenrå 15,196 C7
Åbybro 2,897 C3
Åkirkeby 2,001 F9
Ålborg 154,582 D4
Ålestrup 1,926 C4
Århus 245,941 D5
Års 4,266 C4
Årup 1,675 D7
AErøskøbing 1,223 D8
Agerbaek 935 B6
Allingaåbro 1,385 D5
Allinge-Sandvig 1,991 F8
Ansager 1,157 B6
Arden 1,303 C4
Asaå 1,344 D3
Askov 904 C7
Asnaes 1,413 E6
Assens, Århus 1,341 D4
Assens, Fyn 5,139 D7
Augustenborg 2,628 D8
Auning 1,516 D5
Avlum 1,729 B5
Baelum 1,169 D4
Bagenkop 776 D8
Ballerup 50,673 F6
Bandholm 693 E8
Bedsted 965 B4
Birkerød 13,663 F6
Bjerringbro 4,761 C5
Bogense 2,861 D6
Bolderslev 774 C8
Børkop 1,410 C6
Borup 1,591 E7
Braedstrup 2,163 C6
Bramming 3,678 B7
Brande 4,784 B6
Bredebro 1,173 B7
Broager 2,143 C8
Brønderslev 10,247 C3
Brørup 2,584 C7
Brovst 4,200 C3
Bryrup 579 C5
Christiansfeld 1,994 C7
Copenhagen (cap.) 603,368 F6
Copenhagen* 1,327,940 F6
Dronninglund 4,661 D3
Dybvad 805 D3
Ebeltoft 3,017 D5
Egernsund 1,323 C8
Egtved 1,311 C6
Ejby 1,372 C7
Esbjerg 68,097 B7
Faåborg 6,495 D7
Fakse 2,720 F7
Fakse Ladeplads 1,799 F7
Farsø 2,821 C4
Farum 9,936 F6
Fjerritslev 2,134 C3
Fredensborg 4,709 F6
Fredericia 36,157 C6
Frederiksberg 101,874 F6
Frederikshavn 24,846 D3
Frederikssund 11,272 E6
Frederiksvaerk 8,903 E6
Fuglebjerg 1,094 E7
Gedser 1,200 F8
Gedsted 1,006 C4
Gelsted 1,307 C7
Gentofte 77,744 F6
Gilleleje 2,943 F5
Give 2,366 C6
Glamsbjerg 2,226 D7
Glostrup 28,326 F6
Glumsø 1,027 E7
Glyngøre 1,071 C4
Gørding 1,261 B7
Gørlev 1,542 E7
Graested 1,654 F5
Gram 2,061 C7
Graåsten 2,947 C8
Grenaå 12,569 D5
Grindsted 7,558 B6
Haårby 1,506 D7
Haderslev 20,042 C7
Hadsten 3,914 C5
Hadsund 3,652 D4
Hals 1,654 D3
Hammel 3,247 C5
Hammerum 3,227 C5
Hanstholm 1,716 B3
Harboør 1,359 B4
Haårlev 1,228 F7
Hasle 18
Haslev 6,925 E
Havdrup 1,833 F
Hedensted 2,659 C
Hellebaek 2,911 F
Helsinge 3,613 F
Helsingør 42,425 F
Herning 32,973 B
Hillerød 23,963 F
Hinnerup 2,061 D
Hirtshals 6,861 C
Hjallerup 1,573 C
Hjerm 647 B
Hjørring 19,692 C
Hobro 8,737 C
Højer 1,416 B
Højslev 1,641 C
Holbaek 19,485 E
Holeby 1,434 E
Holstebro 25,006 B
Holsted 1,390 B
Høng 2,488 E
Hornslet 2,561 D
Horsens 44,120 C
Hørsholm 19,346 F
Hørve 1,139 E
Hov 635 D
Humlum 546 B
Hundested 5,443 E
Hurup 2,287 B
Hvidbjerg 994 B
Hvide Sande 2,129 A
Ikast 9,222 C
Jelling 1,540 C
Jerslev 798 D
Juelsminde 1,991 D
Jyderup 2,901 E
Kalundborg 12,248 D
Karise 1,184 F
Karup 1,694 C
Kastrup† 17,391 F
Kerteminde 5,007 D
Kibaek 1,279 B
Kjellerup 3,245 C
Klitmøller 542 B
København (Copenhagen) (cap.) 603,368 F
Køge 18,608 F
Kolding 41,602 C
Kolind 1,036 D
Korsør 15,502 E
Kvaerndrup 891 D
Langaå 2,320 C
Lem 1,026 B
Lemvig 6,448 B
Løgstør 3,633 C
Løgumkloster 2,091 B
Lohals 580 D
Løjt Kirkeby 1,203 C
Løkken 1,345 C
Løsning 1,967 C
Lundby 747 E
Lunderskov 1,494 C
Lyngby 61,516 F
Malling 1,584 D
Mariager 1,692 D
Maribo 5,287 E
Marstal 4,124 D
Middelfart 13,315 C

Agriculture, Industry and Resources

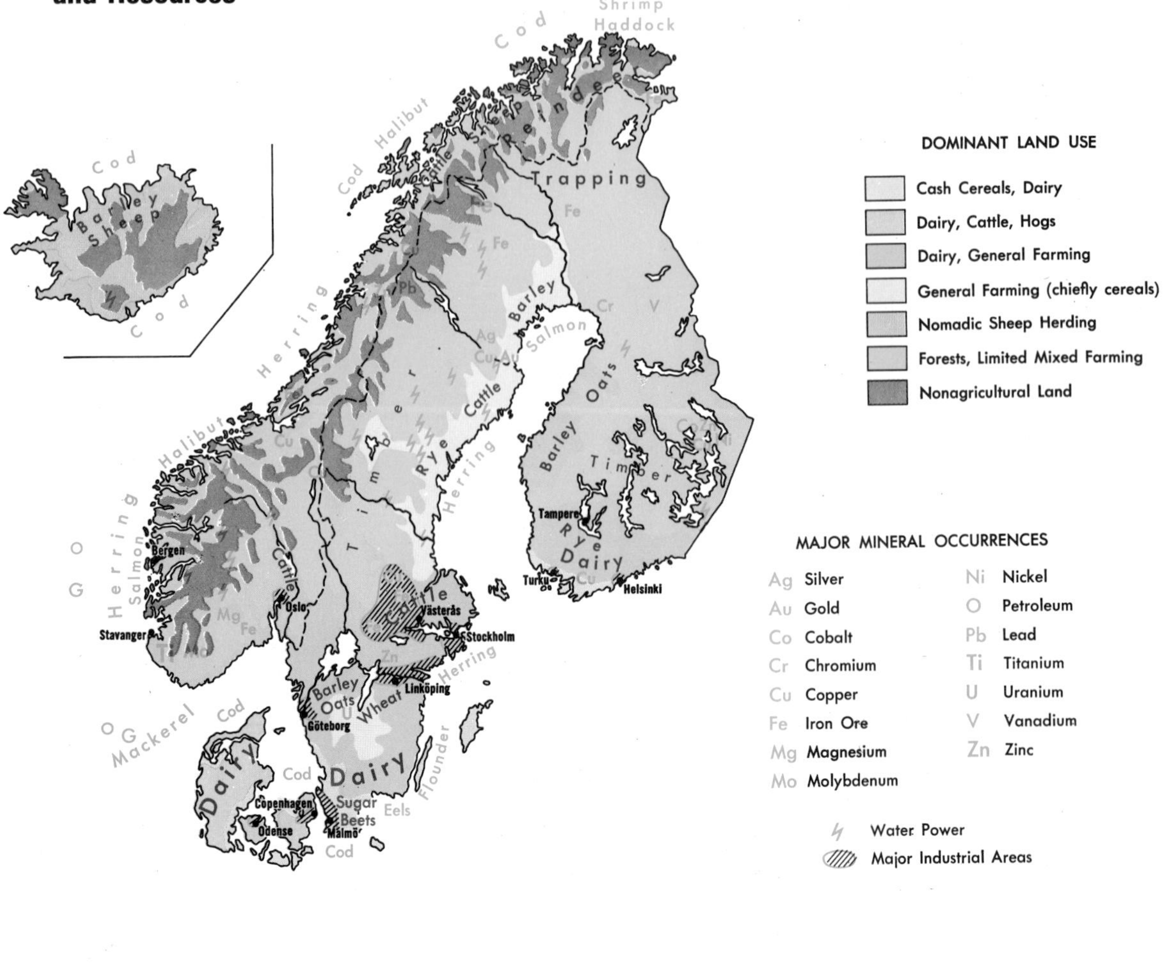

Shrimp
Haddock
Cod
Halibut
Reindeer
Trapping
Barley
Sheep
Herring
Salmon
Timber
Rye
Cattle
Oats
Dairy
Wheat
Mackerel
Sugar Beets
Eels
Flounder
Tampere
Turku
Helsinki
Bergen
Stavanger
Oslo
Västerås
Stockholm
Linköping
Göteborg
Copenhagen
Odense
Malmö
DOMINANT LAND USE
Cash Cereals, Dairy
Dairy, Cattle, Hogs
Dairy, General Farming
General Farming (chiefly cereals)
Nomadic Sheep Herding
Forests, Limited Mixed Farming
Nonagricultural Land
MAJOR MINERAL OCCURRENCES
Ag Silver
Au Gold
Co Cobalt
Cr Chromium
Cu Copper
Fe Iron Ore
Mg Magnesium
Mo Molybdenum
Ni Nickel
O Petroleum
Pb Lead
Ti Titanium
U Uranium
V Vanadium
Zn Zinc
Water Power
Major Industrial Areas

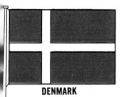

DENMARK

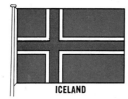

ICELAND

DENMARK
AREA 16,629 sq. mi. (43,069 sq. km.)
POPULATION 5,124,000
CAPITAL Copenhagen
LARGEST CITY Copenhagen
HIGHEST POINT Yding Skovhøj
568 ft. (173 m.)
MONETARY UNIT krone
MAJOR LANGUAGE Danish
MAJOR RELIGION Protestantism

ICELAND
AREA 39,768 sq. mi. (103,000 sq. km.)
POPULATION 228,785
CAPITAL Reykjavík
LARGEST CITY Reykjavík
HIGHEST POINT Hvannadalshnúkur
6,952 ft. (2,119 m.)
MONETARY UNIT króna
MAJOR LANGUAGE Icelandic
MAJOR RELIGION Protestantism

Jegeltender 711 .... B8
aestved 35,011 .... E7
laskov 16,393 .... E8
leksø 3,527 .... F9
ibe 2,796 .... C4
lordborg 4,132 .... B7
lordby, Ribe 2,084 .... B7
ørre Aby 2,165 .... C7
ørre Alslev 1,338 .... E8
ørre Broby 904 .... D7
ørre Nebel 901 .... B6
ørre Snede 1,461 .... C6
ørre Vorupør 441 .... B4
yborg 14,181 .... D7
ykøbing, Storstrøm 20,059 .... F8
ykøbing,
  Vestsjaelland 4,996 .... E6
ykøbing, Viborg 9,066 .... B4
ysted 1,229 .... E8
dder 6,617 .... D6
dense 168,178 .... D7
lgod 2,258 .... B6
rsted 1,093 .... B5
ster Vrå 906 .... C3
tterup 2,673 .... D7
rup 602 .... B6
åbe 3,584 .... A5
ingkøbing 6,298 .... E7
lingsted 14,076 .... E7
edby 5,296 .... E8
dding 2,102 .... B7
edekro 2,246 .... C7
dkaersbro 1,098 .... C5
edvig 1,115 .... C7
mø 816 .... B7
ne 1,523 .... D8
anne 14,736 .... F9
oslev 1,058 .... B4
dkøbing 747 .... B6
uds Vedby 1,071 .... E6
y 2,699 .... D5
yomgård 1,000 .... D5
æby 5,430 .... C3
askøbing 4,102 .... E8
kebjerg 29,015 .... C5
ndal 2,406 .... D3
kaelskør 4,585 .... E7
kaerbaek 2,483 .... B7
kagen 11,620 .... D2
kals 960 .... D3
kanderborg 11,344 .... D5
kårup 1,216 .... D7
ibby 1,549 .... E6
ive 17,015 .... C4
kjern 6,056 .... B5
kodborg 935 .... C7
kaerping 1,165 .... C4
agelse 26,851 .... E7
angerup 3,036 .... E6
edsted 1,105 .... B4
allested 960 .... D8
nderborg 24,526 .... C8
ønder Omme 1,393 .... C6
ønder 885 .... D7
øre 8,683 .... B5
øge 3,869 .... F8
enlille 1,014 .... E6
enstrup 1,245 .... D7
holm 1,224 .... C3
ore Heddinge 2,630 .... F7
øving 2,366 .... C4
randby 1,017 .... D3
truer 10,848 .... B4
Husavlk 1,193 .... C6
kanelø 1,193 .... E6
vendborg 24,203 .... D7
nerup 1,797 .... E6
arm 3,150 .... B6
raby 45,661 .... E6
hasted 30,608 .... F6
kem 511 .... D5
kyboron 2,425 .... A7
torup 11,252 .... B4
ryboron 2,425 .... B7
om 553 .... B5
inglev 1,531 .... C8
strup 762 .... B7
ftlund 2,147 .... B7
inslev 1,982 .... B5
ommerup 1,439 .... D7
onder 7,469 .... C6
ørring 1,537 .... C6
ustrup 794 .... B5
sdum 885 .... C7
fborg 1,377 .... B5
amdrup 3,111 .... C7
ole 11,615 .... B6
igen 6,213 .... C7
lule 43,976 .... B5
iholm 989 .... D5
iber Skerninge 603 .... D7
iestervig 747 .... B4
borg 27,441 .... C5
iby 1,549 .... E6
idebaek 2,248 .... B5
il 1,037 .... C6
idberg 1,500 .... B5
idnerup 2,284 .... B5
idjens 5,595 .... C7
iorbasse 791 .... B7
iordborg 11,639 .... E7

Vraå 2,652 .... C3

OTHER FEATURES

Ærø (isl.) D8
Als (isl.) C8
Amager (isl.) F6
Anholt (isl.) E4
Baagø (isl.) C7
Baltic (sea) E9
Bornholm (isl.) F9
Endelave (isl.) D6
Falster (isl.) E8
Fanø (isl.) B7
Fehmarn (str.) E8
Fejø (isl.) E8
Femø (isl.) E8
Frisian, North (isls.) B7
Fyn (isl.) D7
Gelsaa (riv.) C7
Gudenaa (riv.) C5
Isefjord (fjord) E6
Jutland (pen.) C5
Jylland (Jutland)
  (pen.) C5
Kattegat (str.) E4
Laesø (isl.) D3
Langeland (isl.) D8
Lille Baelt (chan.) C7
Limfjorden (fjord) C4
Løgster Bredning (fjord) C4
Lolland (isl.) E8
Møn (isl.) F8
Mors (isl.) B4
North (sea) B9
North Frisian (isls.) B7
Ømø (isl.) E7
Øresund (sound) F6
Rømø (isl.) B7
Samsø (isl.) D6
Sejerø (isl.) E6
Sjaelland (isl.) E6
Skagens Odde (cape) D2
Skagerrak (str.) C2
Skaw, The (Skagens Odde)
  (cape) D2
Storaa (riv.) B5
Store Baelt (chan.) D6
Susaa (riv.) E7
The Skaw (Skagens Odde)
  (cape) D2
Tranebjerg (mt.) C6
Yding Skovhøj (mt.) C6

FAEROE ISLANDS

CITIES and TOWNS

Klaksvlk 4,536 .... B2
Tórshavn (cap.), Faerøe
  Is. 11,618 .... A3

OTHER FEATURES

Faerøe (isls.) B2
Sandoy (isl.) B3
Streymoy (isl.) B3
Sudhuroy (isl.) B3

ICELAND

CITIES and TOWNS

Akranes 4,253 .... B1
Akureyri 10,755 .... C1
Hafnarfjordhur 9,696 .... B2
Husavlk 1,993 .... C1
Isafjordhur 2,680 .... B1
Keflavlk 5,663 .... B1
Kópavogur 11,165 .... B1
Nes (Neskaupstadhur) 1,552 .... D1
Neskaupstadhur 1,552 .... D1
Ólafsfjordhur 1,086 .... C1
Reykjavlk* (cap.) 81,693 .... B1
Reykjavlk* 98,521 .... B1
Saudhárkrokur 1,600 .... B1
Seydhisfjordhur 884 .... D1
Siglufjordhur 2,161 .... C1
Vestmannaeyjar 5,186 .... B2

OTHER FEATURES

Bjargtangar (pt.) A1
Breidhafjordhur (fjord) B1
Faxaflói (bay) B1
Fontur (pt.) D1
Gerpir (cape) D1
Grimsey (isl.) C1
Hekla (vol.) B1
Horn (cape) B1
Hunaflói (bay) B1
Hvannadalshnúkur (mt.) B1
North (Horn) cape B1
Reykjanesta (cape) A2
Surtsey (isl.) B2
Thjórsá (riv.) C1
Vatnajökull (glac.) C1

*City and suburbs.

Denmark and Iceland

CONIC PROJECTION

SCALE OF MILES

SCALE OF KILOMETERS

Capitals of Countries ____ ☆
Capitals of Counties (amter) ____ △
International Boundaries ____
Internal Boundaries ____

Denmark is divided into fourteen Counties plus Copenhagen and Frederiksberg communes.

Germany

CONIC PROJECTION

SCALE OF MILES

SCALE OF KILOMETERS

Capitals of Countries .... ☆
State and District Capitals .... ⊛
International Boundaries ....
State and District Boundaries ....
Canals ....

East Germany is divided into districts bearing the same name as their respective capitals.

© Copyright HAMMOND INCORPORATED, Maplewood, N.J.

AREA 95,985 sq. mi. (248,601 sq. km.)
POPULATION 61,658,000
CAPITAL Bonn
LARGEST CITY Berlin (West)
HIGHEST POINT Zugspitze 9,718 ft. (2,962 m.)
MONETARY UNIT Deutsche mark
MAJOR LANGUAGE German
MAJOR RELIGIONS Protestantism, Roman
    Catholicism

AREA 41,768 sq. mi. (108,179 sq. km.)
POPULATION 16,737,000
CAPITAL Berlin (East)
LARGEST CITY Berlin (East)
HIGHEST POINT Fichtelberg 3,983 ft. (1,214 m.)
MONETARY UNIT East German mark
MAJOR LANGUAGE German
MAJOR RELIGIONS Protestantism, Roman
    Catholicism

WEST GERMANY

EAST GERMANY

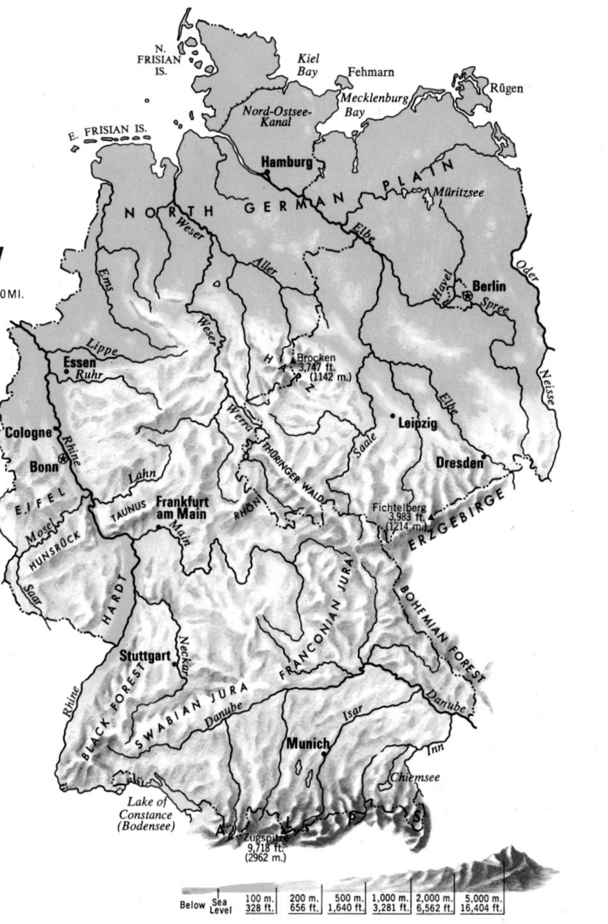

EAST GERMANY

DISTRICTS

Berlin 1,094,147	F4
Cottbus 872,242	F4
Dresden 1,845,459	E3
Erfurt 1,247,213	D3
Frankfurt 688,637	F2
Gera 738,847	E3
Halle 1,890,187	D3
Karl-Marx-Stadt 1,994,115	E3
Leipzig 1,457,817	E3
Magdeburg 1,297,881	D2
Neubrandenburg 628,686	E2
Potsdam 1,124,892	E2
Rostock 867,806	E1
Schwerin 592,334	D2
Suhl 550,497	D3

CITIES and TOWNS

Aken 11,742	D3
Altenburg 51,193	E3
Angermünde 11,786	E2
Anklam 19,099	E2
Annaberg-Buchholz 26,561	E3
Apolda 28,649	D3
Arnstadt 29,462	D3
Aschersleben 36,674	D3
Aue 32,622	E3
Auerbach 18,168	E3
Bad Doberan 12,541	D1
Bad Dürrenberg 15,192	D3
Bad Langensalza 166,282	D3
Bad Salzungen 17,277	D3
Barth 12,069	E1
Bautzen 45,851	F3
Bergen 13,244	E1
Berlin, East (cap.) 1,094,147	F4
Bernau bei Berlin 15,749	F2
Bernburg 44,428	D3
Bischofswerda 11,540	F3
Bitterfeld 27,062	E3
Blankenburg am Harz 18,784	D3
Boizenburg an der Elbe 12,428	D2
Borna 21,807	E3
Brandenburg 94,071	E2
Burg bei Magdeburg 29,027	D2
Calbe 15,976	D3
Chemnitz
(Karl-Marx-Stadt) 303,811	E3
Coswig, Dresden 22,149	E3
Coswig, Halle 12,473	E3
Crimmitschau 28,845	E3
Delitzsch 24,076	E3
Demmin 17,270	E2
Dessau 100,820	E3
Döbeln 27,824	E3
Dresden 507,692	E3
Eberbach 12,694	F3
Eberswalde-Finow 47,141	F2
Eilenburg 22,245	E3
Eisenach 49,954	D3
Eisenberg 13,450	D3
Eisenhüttenstadt 46,455	F2
Eisleben 29,797	D3
Erfurt 202,979	D3
Falkensee 25,295	E2
Falkenstein 14,367	E3
Finsterwalde 22,466	E3
Forst 28,084	F3
Frankfurt an der Oder 70,817	F2
Freiberg 50,815	E3
Freital 46,061	E3
Friedland	E2
Fürstenwalde 31,916	F2
Gardelegen 12,987	D2
Genthin 15,916	D2
Gera 113,108	E3
Glauchau 30,927	E3
Görlitz 84,658	F3
Gotha 59,243	D3
Greifswald 53,940	E1
Greiz 37,612	E3
Grevesmühlen 12,005	D2
Grimma 17,100	E3
Grimmen 14,571	E1
Grossenhain 18,712	E3
Grossräschen 12,889	E3
Guben
(Wilhelm-Pieck-Stadt) 32,731	F3
Güstrow 36,824	E2
Halberstadt 46,669	D3
Haldensleben 19,194	D2
Halle 241,425	D3
Halle-Neustadt 67,956	D3
Havelberg	D2
Heiligenstadt 21,315	D3
Heiligenstadt 13,931	D3
Hennigsdorf bei Berlin 24,853	E2
Hettstedt 20,291	D3
Hildburghausen 11,372	D3
Hoyerswerda 64,904	F3
Ilmenau 22,021	D3
Jena 99,431	D3
Johanngeorgenstadt 10,328	E3
Jüterbog 13,477	E3
Kamenz 18,221	F3
Karl-Marx-Stadt 303,811	E3
Kleinmachnow 14,059	E4
Klingenthal 13,614	E3
Königs Wusterhausen 11,825	E2

Köpenick 130,987	F4
Köthen 35,451	E3
Kühlungsborn	D1
Lauchhammer 26,939	E3
Leipzig 570,972	E3
Lichtenberg 192,063	F4
Limbach-Oberfrohna 25,706	E3
Löbau 18,077	F3
Lübben 14,224	F3
Lübbenau 22,350	F3
Luckenwalde 28,544	E2
Ludwigslust 13,280	D2
Magdeburg 276,089	D2
Markkleeberg 22,380	E3
Meerane 25,037	E3
Meiningen 26,134	D3
Meissen 43,561	E3
Merseburg 54,269	D3
Meuselwitz 13,585	E3
Mittweida 19,259	E3
Mühlhausen
(Thomas-Müntzer-Stadt) 44,106	D3
Nauen 11,940	E2
Naumburg 36,358	D3
Neubrandenburg 59,971	E2
Neuenhagen bei Berlin 12,603	F4
Neuruppin 24,888	E2
Neustrelitz 27,074	E2
Oelsnitz 15,084	E3
Oelsnitz im Erzgebirge 16,063	E3
Olbernhau 13,479	E3
Oranienburg 24,452	E2
Oschatz 18,974	E3
Oschersleben 17,377	D2
Pankow 136,527	F3
Parchim 22,927	D2
Pasewalk 15,099	F2
Peenemünde	E1
Perleberg 15,029	D2
Pirna 49,771	E3
Plauen 80,353	E3
Pössneck 18,648	D3
Potsdam 117,236	E2
Prenzlau 22,738	E2
Pritzwalk 11,887	D2
Quedlinburg 29,796	D3
Radeberg 18,528	E3
Radebeul 38,383	E3
Radeburg 17,334	E3
Rathenow 32,011	E2
Reichenbach 27,440	E3
Ribnitz-Damgarten 17,254	E1
Riesa 49,989	E3
Rochau 16,520	D2
Rostock 210,167	E1
Rudolstadt 31,698	D3
Saalfeld 33,648	D3
Sandwedel 21,741	D2
Sangerhausen 32,721	D3
Sassnitz 13,857	E1
Schkeuditz 15,585	E3
Schmalkalden 15,017	D3
Schmölln 13,406	E3
Schneeberg 20,376	E3
Schönebeck 45,197	D2
Schwedt 45,729	F2
Schwerin 104,984	D2
Sebnitz 13,470	F3
Senftenberg 29,953	F3
Sömmerda 20,712	D3
Sondershausen 23,383	D3
Sonneberg 29,193	D3
Spremberg 22,862	F3
Stassfurt 26,225	D3
Stendal 39,647	D2
Stralsund 72,167	E1
Strausberg 21,334	F2
Suhl 36,642	D3
Tangermünde 12,898	D2
Teltow 16,171	E4
Templin 11,718	E2
Thale 17,248	D3
Thomas-Müntzer-Stadt 44,106	D3
Torgau 21,613	E3
Torgelow 14,320	F2
Treptow 127,448	F4
Ueckermünde 11,423	F2
Waldheim 11,925	E3
Waltershausen 13,893	D3
Waren 22,921	E2
Weida 11,816	D3
Weimar 63,144	D3
Weissenfels 43,191	D3
Weissensee 78,451	F3
Weisswasser 25,910	F3
Werdau 22,249	E3
Wernigerode 34,658	D3
Wilhelm-Pieck-Stadt 32,731	F3
Wismar 56,765	D2
Wittenberg 51,364	E3
Wittenberge 32,907	D2
Wolfen 27,570	E3
Wolgast 16,384	F1
Wurzen 20,501	E3
Zehdenick 12,651	E2
Zeitz 44,582	E3
Zella-Mehlis 16,301	D3
Zerbst 19,356	E3
Zeulenroda 13,452	D3
Zittau 42,298	F3
Zwickau 123,069	E3

OTHER FEATURES

Altmark (reg.)	D2
Arkona (cape)	E1
Baltic (sea)	E1
Black Elster (riv.)	E3
Brandenburg (reg.)	E2
Elbe (riv.)	D2
Elde (riv.)	D2
Elster, Black (riv.)	E3
Elster, White (riv.)	E3
Erzgebirge (mts.)	E3
Fichtelberg (mt.)	E3
Harz (mts.)	D3
Havel (riv.)	E2
Lusatia (reg.)	F3
Mecklenburg (bay)	D1
Mecklenburg (reg.)	E2
Mulde (riv.)	E3
Neisse (riv.)	F3
Oder (riv.)	F2
Peene (riv.)	F2
Pomerania (reg.)	E2
Pomeranian (bay)	F1
Rhön (mts.)	D3
Rügen (isl.)	E1
Saale (riv.)	D3
Saxony (reg.)	E3
Spree (riv.)	F3
Spreewald (for.)	F3
Thüringer Wald (for.)	D3
Thuringia (reg.)	D3
Ucker (riv.)	E2
Unstrut (riv.)	D3
Usedom (isl.)	F1
Warnow (riv.)	D2
Werra (riv.)	D3
White Elster (riv.)	E3

WEST GERMANY

STATES

Baden-Württemberg 9,152,700	C4
Bavaria 10,810,400	D4
Berlin (West) (free
city) 1,984,800	E4
Bremen 716,800	C2
Hamburg 1,717,400	D2
Hesse 5,549,800	C3
Lower Saxony 7,238,500	C2
North
Rhine-Westphalia 17,129,600	B3
Rhineland-Palatinate 3,665,800	B4
Saarland 1,096,300	B4
Schleswig-Holstein 2,582,400	C1

CITIES and TOWNS

Aachen 242,453	B3
Aalen 64,735	D4
Ahaus 27,126	B2
Ahlen 54,214	B3
Ahrensburg 24,964	D2
Alfeld 24,273	C3
Alsdorf 47,473	B3
Altena 26,753	B3
Altona	C2
Alzey 15,190	C4
Amberg 46,934	D4
Andernach 27,132	B3
Ansbach 39,117	D4
Arnsberg 80,287	C3
Arolsen 15,619	C3
Aschaffenburg 55,398	C4
Augsburg 249,943	D4
Aurich 34,194	B2
Backnang 29,614	C4
Bad Berleburg 20,415	C3
Bad Driburg 17,478	C3
Bad Dürkheim 16,133	C4
Bad Ems 10,487	B3
Baden-Baden 49,718	C4
Bad Gandersheim 11,614	D3
Bad Harzburg 25,786	D3
Bad Hersfeld 29,248	C3
Bad Homburg vor der
Höhe 51,196	C3
Bad Honnef 20,903	B3
Bad Kissingen 22,279	D3
Bad Kreuznach 42,588	B4
Bad Lauterberg im Harz 14,715	D3
Bad Mergentheim 19,895	C4
Bad Münstereifel 14,340	B3
Bad Nauheim 25,916	C3
Bad Neuenahr-Ahrweiler 26,371	B3
Bad Oldesloe 19,640	D2
Bad Pyrmont 21,896	C3
Bad Reichenhall 13,048	E5
Bad Salzuflen 50,924	C3
Bad Schwartau 18,696	D2
Bad Segeberg 13,320	D2
Bad Tölz 12,458	D5
Bad Vilbel 25,012	C3
Bad Waldsee 14,296	C5
Bad Wildungen 15,418	C3
Bad Wimpfen 5,536	C4
Baiersbronn 14,845	C4
Balingen 29,310	C4
Bamberg 74,236	D4
Barsinghausen 32,873	C2
Bassum 14,113	C2
Bayreuth 67,035	D4
Bayrischzell 1,639	E5
Bebra 15,740	C3
Bendorf 15,943	B3
Bensheim 32,653	C4

Bentheim 13,681	B2
Berchtesgaden 8,558	E5
Bergisch Gladbach 99,517	B3
Berleburg (Bad
Berleburg) 20,415	C3
Berlin (West) 1,984,837	E4
Biberach an der Riss 28,891	C4
Bielefeld 316,058	C2
Bietigheim-Bissingen 34,042	C4
Bingen 24,541	B4
Birkenfeld 5,883	B4
Blaubeuren 11,652	C4
Böblingen 40,547	C4
Bocholt 65,460	B3
Bochum 414,842	B3
Bonn (cap.) 283,711	B3
Boppard 16,888	B3
Borghorst 17,238	B3
Borken 30,212	B3
Bornheim 32,847	B3
Bottrop 101,495	B3
Brake 18,089	C2
Bramsche 24,119	B2
Braunschweig
(Brunswick) 268,519	D2
Breisach am Rhein 9,230	B4
Bremen 572,969	C2
Bremerhaven 143,836	C2
Bremervörde 17,565	C2
Bretten 22,140	C4
Brilon 24,595	C3
Bruchsal 38,929	C4
Brühl 44,305	B3
Brunsbüttel 11,451	C2
Brunswick 268,519	D2
Buchholz in der
Nordheide 25,713	C2
Bückeburg 21,393	C2
Büdingen 16,845	C3
Bünde 40,021	C2
Büren 17,352	C3
Burg auf Fehmarn 5,874	D1
Burghausen 16,892	E4
Burgsteinfurt 31,367	B2
Butzbach 20,502	C3
Buxtehude 30,249	C2
Castrop-Rauxel 82,373	B3
Celle 74,347	D2
Cham 12,423	E4
Charlottenburg 201,732	E4
Clausthal-Zellerfeld 16,690	D3
Cloppenburg 19,757	B2
Coburg 46,244	D3
Coesfeld 30,617	B3
Cologne 1,013,771	B3
Cuxhaven 60,353	C1
Dachau 33,207	D4
Dahlem	E4
Darmstadt 137,018	C4
Deggendorf 25,307	E4
Delmenhorst 71,488	C2
Detmold 65,629	C3
Diepholz 14,201	C2
Dillenburg 16,648	C3
Dillingen 21,369	B4
Dillingen an der Donau 11,601	D4
Dingolfing 13,325	E4
Dinkelsbühl 10,034	D4
Donaueschingen 17,578	C5
Donauwörth 17,077	D4
Dorsten 65,718	B3
Dortmund 630,609	B3
Duderstadt 23,255	D3
Dudweiler 27,877	B4
Dülmen 35,635	B3
Düren 87,013	B3
Düsseldorf 664,336	B3
Eberbach 15,834	C4
Ebingen 22,594	C4
Eckernförde 22,938	D1
Ehingen 21,600	C4
Eichstätt 13,080	D4
Einbeck 29,821	C3
Eiserfeld 22,346	C3

Ellwangen 21,994	D4
Elmshorn 41,355	C2
Emden 53,509	B2
Emmendingen 24,722	B4
Emmerich 29,113	B3
Emsdetten 30,195	B2
Erlangen 100,671	D4
Eschwege 24,882	C3
Eschweiler 53,603	B3
Espelkamp 22,670	C2
Essen 677,568	B3
Esslingen am Neckar 95,298	C4
Ettlingen 35,159	C4
Euskirchen 43,558	B3
Eutin 17,701	D1
Fellbach 42,501	C4
Flensburg 93,213	C1
Forchheim 23,430	D4
Frankenberg-Eder 15,337	C3
Frankenthal 43,684	C4
Frankfurt am Main 636,157	C3
Frechen 41,453	B3
Freiburg im Breisgau 175,371	B5
Freising 31,524	D4
Freudenstadt 19,454	C4
Friedberg 24,762	C3
Friedrichshafen 51,544	C5
Fritzlar 15,079	C3
Fulda 58,976	C3
Fürstenfeldbruck 27,194	D4
Fürth 101,639	D4
Füssen 10,506	D5
Gaggenau 28,846	C4
Garbsen 56,337	C2
Garmisch-Partenkirchen 26,831	D5
Gatow	D2
Geesthacht 24,745	D2
Geislingen an der
Steige 28,693	C4
Geldern 24,082	B3
Gelnhausen 17,068	C3
Gelsenkirchen 322,584	B3
Georgsmarienhütte 30,259	B2
Geretsried 17,330	D5
Germersheim 12,041	C4
Gerolstein 5,400	B3
Gießen 76,533	C3
Gifhorn 31,635	D2
Glückstadt 12,159	C2
Goch 28,213	B3
Göppingen 15,980	C4
Göppingen 54,365	C4
Goslar 53,957	D3
Göttingen 123,797	D3
Greven 27,479	B2
Grevenbroich 56,392	B3
Griesheim 18,548	C4
Gronau 40,527	B2
Gummersbach 49,316	B3
Günzburg 13,528	D4
Gunzenhausen 13,565	D4
Gütersloh 77,128	C3
Haar 18,824	D4
Hagen 229,224	B3
Halberstadt 28,095	D3
Hamburg 1,717,383	D2
Hameln 61,066	C2
Hamm 172,210	B3
Hammelburg 12,350	C3
Hanau 86,676	C3
Hannover 552,955	C2
Harburg-Wilhelmsburg	C2
Hassloch 17,752	C4
Haunstetten 21,810	D4
Hechingen 15,926	C4
Heide 21,918	C1
Heidelberg 129,368	C4
Heidenheim an der Brenz 49,943	D4
Heilbronn 113,177	C4
Helmstedt 28,095	D2
Herford 64,385	C2
Herne 190,561	B3
Herrenberg 24,984	C4
Hersbruck 12,096	D4
Herten 68,246	B3
Hilden 55,848	B3
Hockenheim 16,890	C4
Hof 54,357	D3
Hofgeismar 13,380	C3
Holzminden 23,650	C3
Homburg 41,861	B4
Horn-Bad Meinberg 16,927	C3
Höxter 32,759	C3
Hückelhoven 34,865	B3
Hückeswagen 13,873	B3
Hürth 51,692	B3
Husum 24,984	C1
Ibbenbüren 42,202	B2
Idar-Oberstein 37,179	B4
Immenstadt im Allgäu 13,720	C5
Ingolstadt 88,500	D4
Iserlohn 96,174	B3
Isny im Allgäu 12,367	D5
Itzehoe 35,077	C2
Jever 12,096	B2
Jülich 31,564	B3
Kaiserslautern 100,886	B4
Karlsruhe 280,448	C4
Kassel 205,534	C3
Kaufbeuren 42,224	D5
Kehl 29,861	B4
Kelheim 11,996	D4
Kempten 56,944	D5
Kevelaer 20,971	B3
Kiel 262,164	D1
Kirchheim unter Teck 31,666	C4
Kitzingen 19,116	C4
Kleve 44,003	B3
Koblenz 118,394	B3
Köln (Cologne) 1,013,771	B3
Königswinter 34,586	B3
Konstanz 70,152	C5
Korbach 22,998	C3
Kornwestheim 27,271	C4
Krefeld 228,463	B3
Kreuztal 30,473	C3
Kronach 11,538	D3
Kulmbach 25,713	D3
Laatzen 43,724	C2
Lahnstein 19,725	B3
Lahr 35,570	B4
Lampertheim 31,993	C4
Landau in der Pfalz 37,661	C4
Landsberg am Lech 15,862	D4
Landshut 55,858	D4
Langen 31,038	C4
Langenfeld 47,092	B3
Langenhagen 47,092	C2
Lauenburg an der Elbe 11,077	D2
Lauf an der Pegnitz 19,443	D4
Lauingen 8,778	D4
Lauterbach 15,007	C3
Leer 32,785	B2
Lehrte 38,272	C2
Lemgo 39,664	C2
Lengerich 20,836	B2
Lichtenfels 13,719	D3
Limburg an der Lahn 28,606	C3
Lindau 23,930	C5

(continued on following page)

Topography

0   50   100 MI.

0   50   100 KM.

Below Sea Level	100 m. 328 ft.	200 m. 656 ft.	500 m. 1,640 ft.	1,000 m. 3,281 ft.	2,000 m. 6,562 ft.	5,000 m. 16,404 ft.

Germany Before World War I 1871-1914

Germany Between Wars 1919-1937

Occupied Germany 1945-1949

Lingen 43,785 .....B2	Oberpfalz 29,713 .....D4	Rastatt 38,030 .....C4	Schwetzingen 18,286 .....C4	Völklingen 47,271 .....B4	Ammersee (lake) D4	Lech (riv.) C5
Lippstadt 63,040 .....C3	Neumünster 84,777 .....C1	Rastede 16,905 .....C2	Seesen 23,577 .....D3	Waldkirch 19,009 .....B4	Amrum (isl.) C1	Leine (riv.) C2
Löhne 17,859 .....C3	Neunkirchen 54,992 .....B4	Ratingen 86,028 .....B3	Selb 16,723 .....E3	Waldkraiburg 20,140 .....E4	Baltrum (isl.) B2	Lippe (riv.) B3
Lohr am Main 16,435 .....C4	Neuss 148,198 .....B3	Ratzeburg 12,189 .....D2	Sennestadt 20,187 .....C3	Waldshut-Tiengen 22,046 .....C5	Bavarian (for.) E4	Main (riv.) C4
Lörrach 44,179 .....B5	Neustadt an der	Ravensburg 42,725 .....C5	Siegburg 34,943 .....B3	Walsrode 23,423 .....C2	Bavarian Alps (range) D5	Mecklenburg (bay) D1
Lübeck 232,270 .....D2	Weinstrasse 51,011 .....B4	Recklinghausen 122,437 .....B3	Siegen 115,552 .....C3	Wangen im Allgäu 23,127 .....C5	Black (for.) C4	Mosel (riv.) B4
Lüdenscheid 76,213 .....B3	Neustadt bei Coburg 12,665 .....D3	Regensburg 131,886 .....E4	Sigmaringen 15,437 .....C4	Warburg 22,150 .....C3	Bodensee (Constance) (lake) C5	Mosel (riv.) B4
Ludwigsburg 83,622 .....C4	Neustadt in Holstein 15,333 .....D1	Remagen 14,627 .....B4	Sindelfingen 54,134 .....C4	Warendorf 32,273 .....B3	Bohemian (for.) E4	Naab (riv.) D4
Ludwigshafen am Rhein 170,374 .....C4	Neu-Ulm 31,660 .....D4	Remscheid 133,145 .....B3	Singen 45,566 .....C5	Wedel 30,045 .....C2	Borkum (isl.) B2	Neckar (riv.) C4
Lüneburg 64,586 .....D2	Neuwied 62,029 .....B3	Rendsburg 34,407 .....C1	Soest 40,308 .....C3	Weiden in der Oberpfalz 42,697 .....D4	Breisgau (reg.) B5	Norderney (isl.) B2
Lünen 85,685 .....B3	Nienburg 30,978 .....C2	Reutlingen 95,289 .....C4	Solingen 171,810 .....B3	Weilburg 12,652 .....C3	Chiemsee (lake) E5	Nord-Ostsee (canal) C1
Mainz 183,880 .....C4	Norden 24,207 .....B2	Rheda-Wiedenbrück 37,371 .....C3	Soltau 19,949 .....C2	Weilheim in Oberbayern 15,347 .....D5	Constance (lake) C4	Nordstrand (isl.) C1
Mannheim 314,086 .....C4	Nordenham 31,457 .....C2	Rheine 71,539 .....B2	Sonthofen 17,821 .....D5	Weingarten 21,143 .....C5	Danube (riv.) C4	North (sea) C1
Marbach am Neckar 12,131 .....C4	Norderstedt 61,553 .....D2	Rheinfelden 27,500 .....B5	Springe 30,968 .....C3	Weinheim 41,005 .....C4	Donau (Danube) (riv.) C4	North Friesland (reg.) C1
Marburg an der Lahn 72,458 .....C3	Nordhorn 49,598 .....B2	Rietberg 22,421 .....C3	Speyer 44,471 .....C4	Weissenburg in Bayern 16,083 .....D4	East Friesland (reg.) B2	North Frisian (isls.) C1
Marktredwitz 16,404 .....E4	Nördlingen 16,480 .....D4	Rinteln 25,595 .....C2	Springe 30,968 .....C3	Wertheim 20,942 .....C4	East Frisian (isls.) B2	Oder (riv.) E2
Marl 91,930 .....B3	Northeim 32,665 .....C2	Stade 42,097 .....C2	Stadthagen 23,003 .....C3	Wesel 56,584 .....B3	Eder (res.) C3	Odenwald (for.) C4
Mayen 21,018 .....B3	Nürnberg 499,060 .....D4	Rosenheim 38,419 .....D5	Stadthagen 23,003 .....C3	Westerland 9,652 .....C1	Elbe (riv.) C2	Oker (riv.) D2
Mechernich 21,498 .....B3	Nürnberg (Nuremberg) 499,060 .....D4	Rotenburg 19,155 .....C2	Stolberg 57,379 .....B3	Westerstede 16,977 .....B2	Ems (riv.) B2	Pellworm (isl.) C1
Melle 41,339 .....C2	Nüftingen 34,333 .....C4	Rotenburg an der Fulda 14,438 .....C3	Straubing 43,774 .....E4	Wiehl 19,004 .....B3	Fehmarn (isl.) D1	Regen (riv.) E4
Melsungen 13,444 .....C3	Oberammergau 4,704 .....D5	Roth bei Nürnberg 17,782 .....D4	Stuttgart 600,421 .....C4	Wittingen 12,189 .....D2	Feldberg (mt.) C5	Regnitz (riv.) D4
Memmingen 34,612 .....D5	Oberhausen 237,147 .....B3	Rothenburg ob der	Sulzbach-Rosenberg 18,596 .....D4	Wittlich 15,321 .....B4	Fichtelgebirge (range) D3	Rhine (riv.) C4
Meppen 27,308 .....B2	Oberstdorf 11,687 .....D5	Tauber 11,609 .....D4	Tailfingen 17,278 .....C4	Witzenhausen 16,877 .....C3	Föhr (isl.) C1	Rhön (mts.) D3
Merzig 30,197 .....B4	Oberursel 39,802 .....C3	Rottenburg am Neckar	Tegel E3	Wolfenbüttel 51,386 .....D2	Franconian Jura (range) D4	Ruhr (riv.) B3
Meschede 32,472 .....C3	Offenbach am Main 115,251 .....C4	30,583 .....C4	Telgte 15,165 .....B3	Wolfsburg 126,298 .....D2	Frisian, East (isls.) B2	Saale (riv.) D3
Metzingen 19,224 .....C4	Offenburg 51,553 .....B4	Rottweil 24,534 .....C4	Tempelhof 159,730 .....E4	Worms 75,732 .....C4	Frisian, North (isls.) C1	Sauer (riv.) B4
Michelstadt 13,591 .....C4	Oldenburg 134,706 .....C2	Rüsselsheim 62,067 .....C4	Timmendorfer Strand 10,690 .....D1	Wunstorf 36,795 .....C2	Grosser Arber (mt.) E4	Schwarzwald (Black) (for.) C4
Minden 78,887 .....C2	Oldenburg in Holstein 9,201 .....D1	Saarbrücken 205,336 .....B4	Traunstein 14,088 .....E5	Wuppertal 405,369 .....B3	Halligen (isls.) C1	Schneeberg (mt.) D3
Mittenwald 8,831 .....D5	Opladen 42,789 .....B3	Saarlouis 39,974 .....B4	Travemünde D2	Würzburg 112,584 .....C4	Hardt (mts.) B4	Schwabian Jura (range) C4
Mölln 15,780 .....D2	Osnabrück 161,671 .....C2	Säckingen 13,956 .....C5	Treuchtlingen 11,939 .....D4	Xanten 15,688 .....B3	Harz (mts.) D3	Sylt (isl.) C1
Mönchengladbach 261,367 .....B3	Osterholz-Scharmbeck 22,734 .....C2	Sankt Goar 3,511 .....B4	Trier 100,338 .....B4	Zirndorf 13,661 .....D4	Hase (riv.) C2	Tauber (riv.) C4
Moosburg an der Isar 12,196 .....D4	Osterode am Harz 29,668 .....D3	Sankt Ingbert 43,263 .....B4	Troisdorf 56,402 .....B3	Zülpich 16,171 .....B3	Hegau (reg.) C5	Taunus (range) C3
Mosbach 23,663 .....C4	Paderborn 103,705 .....C3	Sankt Wendel 27,558 .....B4	Tübingen 71,348 .....C4	Zweibrücken 35,978 .....B4	Helgoland (isl.) B1	Tegernsee (lake) D5
Mühldorf am Inn 12,638 .....E4	Papenburg 27,039 .....B2	Saulgau 15,403 .....C4	Tuttlingen 32,342 .....C4	Zwischenahn 22,581 .....B2	Helgoland (bay) C1	Teutoburger Wald (for.) C2
Mülheim an der Ruhr 189,259 .....B3	Passau 50,920 .....E4	Schleswig 30,974 .....C1	Übach-Palenberg 22,403 .....B3		Hunsrück (mts.) B4	Vogelsberg (mts.) C3
Mülheim 12,183 .....B3	Peine 49,450 .....D2	Schlüchtern 13,801 .....C3	Überlingen 17,735 .....C5		Hunte (riv.) C2	Walchensee (lake) D5
München (Munich) 1,314,865 .....D4	Pfaffenhofen an der Ilm 13,684 .....D4	Schönberg 169,835 .....C4	Uelzen 37,550 .....D2		Iller (riv.) D5	Wangerooge (isl.) B2
Münden 27,018 .....C3	Pforzheim 108,635 .....C4	Schöningen 16,348 .....D2	Uetersen 16,330 .....C2		Inn (riv.) E4	Watzmann (mt.) E5
Munich 1,314,865 .....D4	Pfullingen 16,195 .....C4	Schramberg 19,677 .....C4	Ulm 98,237 .....C4		Isar (riv.) E4	Weser (riv.) C2
Münster 264,546 .....C3	Pinneberg 36,844 .....C2	Schwabach 33,136 .....D4	Uslar 17,251 .....C3		Juist (isl.) B2	Westerwald (for.) B3
Nagold 19,047 .....C4	Pirmasens 53,651 .....B4	Schwäbisch Gmünd 56,422 .....C4	Varel 24,435 .....C2	OTHER FEATURES	Kaiserstuhl (mt.) B4	Wümme (riv.) C2
Neckarsulm 20,112 .....C4	Plettenberg 29,273 .....B3	Schwäbisch Hall 32,129 .....C4	Vechta 21,786 .....C2		Kiel (bay) D1	Würmsee (Starnbergersee)
Neheim-Hüsten 36,373 .....C3	Porz am Rhein 74,915 .....B3	Schwalmstadt 17,800 .....C3	Verden 24,247 .....C2	Aller (riv.) C2	Kiel (Nord-Ostsee) (canal) C1	(lake) D5
Neuburg an der Donau 19,400 .....D4	Preetz 15,305 .....D1	Schwandorf in Bayern 22,547 .....E4	Viersen 84,220 .....B3	Allgäu (reg.) D5	Königssee (lake) E5	Zugspitze (mt.) D5
Neu-Isenburg 35,631 .....C3	Puttgarden D1	Schweinfurt 56,164 .....D3	Villingen-Schwenningen 80,646 .....C4	Altmühl (riv.) D4	Lahn (riv.) C3	
Neumarkt in der	Radolfzell 23,274 .....C5	Schwelm 31,850 .....B3			Langeoog (isl.) B2	

Agriculture, Industry and Resources

DOMINANT LAND USE

- Wheat, Sugar Beets
- Cereals (chiefly rye, oats, barley)
- Potatoes, Rye
- Dairy, Livestock
- Mixed Cereals, Dairy
- Truck Farming
- Grapes, Fruit
- Forests

MAJOR MINERAL OCCURRENCES

Ag	Silver	K	Potash
Ba	Barite	Lg	Lignite
C	Coal	Na	Salt
Cu	Copper	O	Petroleum
Fe	Iron Ore	Pb	Lead
G	Natural Gas	U	Uranium
Gr	Graphite	Zn	Zinc

⚡ Water Power
▨ Major Industrial Areas

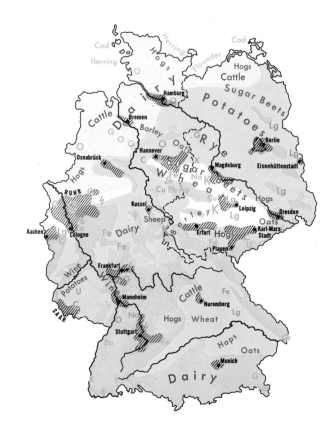

AREA 15,892 sq. mi. (41,160 sq. km.)
POPULATION 14,227,000
CAPITALS The Hague, Amsterdam
LARGEST CITY Amsterdam
HIGHEST POINT Vaalserberg 1,056 ft. (322 m.)
MONETARY UNIT guilder (florin)
MAJOR LANGUAGE Dutch
MAJOR RELIGIONS Protestantism, Roman Catholicism

AREA 11,781 sq. mi. (30,513 sq. km.)
POPULATION 9,855,110
CAPITAL Brussels
LARGEST CITY Brussels (greater)
HIGHEST POINT Botrange 2,277 ft. (694 m.)
MONETARY UNIT Belgian franc
MAJOR LANGUAGES French (Walloon), Flemish
MAJOR RELIGION Roman Catholicism

AREA 999 sq. mi. (2,587 sq. km.)
POPULATION 364,000
CAPITAL Luxembourg
LARGEST CITY Luxembourg
HIGHEST POINT Ardennes Plateau 1,825 ft. (556 m.)
MONETARY UNIT Luxembourg franc
MAJOR LANGUAGES Luxembourgeois (Letzeburgisch), French, German
MAJOR RELIGION Roman Catholicism

NETHERLANDS

BELGIUM

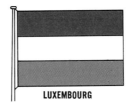
LUXEMBOURG

BELGIUM

PROVINCES

Antwerp 1,533,249	F6
Brabant 2,176,373	F7
East Flanders 1,310,117	D7
Hainaut 1,317,453	D7
Liège 1,008,905	H7
Limburg 652,547	G7
Luxembourg 217,310	G9
Namur 380,561	F8
West Flanders 1,054,429	B7

CITIES and TOWNS†

Aalst 46,659	D7
Aalter 9,173	C6
Aarlen (Arlon) 13,745	H9
Aarschot 12,474	F7
Aat (Ath) 11,842	D7
Aalken 8,677	G7
Alost (Aalst) 46,659	D7
Amay 7,617	G7
Andenne 8,091	G8
Anderlecht 103,796	B9

Anderlues 12,176	E8
Ans	H7
Antoing 3,426	C7
Antwerp 224,543	E6
Antwerp* (Antwerp) 224,543	E6
Antwerpen (Antwerp) 224,543	E6
Ardooie 7,081	C7
Arendonk 9,919	G6
Arlon 13,745	H9
As 5,496	H6
Asse 6,583	E7
Ath 11,842	D7
Attert	H9
Aubange 3,761	H9
Audenarde (Oudenaarde) 26,615	D7
Auderghem 34,546	C9
Auvelais 8,287	F8
Aywaille 3,850	H8
Baerle-Hertog	F6
Balen 15,110	G6
Basse-Sambre	F8
Bastenaken (Bastogne) 6,816	H9
Bastogne 6,816	H9
Beernem	C6
Beloeil	D7
Berchem 50,241	F6

Berchem-Sainte-Agathe 19,087	B9
Bergen (Mons) 59,362	E8
Beringen	G6
Bertogne	H8
Bertrix 4,562	G9
Beveren 15,913	E6
Bilzen 7,178	G7
Binche 10,098	E8
Blankenberge 13,969	C6
Bocholt 6,497	H6
Boom 16,584	E6
Borgerhout 49,002	E6
Borgloon 3,412	G7
Borgworm (Waremme) 10,956	G7
Bourg-Léopold (Leopoldsburg) 9,593	G6
Boussu 11,474	D8
Braine-l' Alleud 18,531	E7
Braine-le-Comte 11,957	D7
Brecht	F6
Bredene 9,244	B6
Bree 10,389	H6
Bruges 117,220	C6
Brugge (Bruges) 117,220	C6
Brussels (cap.)* 1,054,970	C9
Bruxelles (Brussels)	C9

(cap.)* 1,054,970	C9
Cerfontaine	E8
Charleroi 23,689	E8
Charleroi* 458,000	E8
Chastre	F7
Châtelet 14,752	E8
Chièvres 3,283	D7
Chimay 3,288	E8
Chiny	G9
Ciney 7,536	G8
Comblain-au-Pont 3,582	G8
Comines 8,192	B7
Courcelles 17,015	E8
Courtrai (Kortrijk) 44,961	C7
Couvin 4,234	F8
Damme	C6
De Haan	C6
Deinze 16,711	C7
Denderleeuw 9,925	E7
Dendermonde 22,119	E6
De Panne 6,985	B6
Dessel 7,505	G6
Destelbergen	D6
Deurne 80,766	F6
Diest 10,799	F7
Diksmuide 6,669	B6

Dilbeek 15,108	B9
Dilsen	H6
Dinant 9,747	G8
Dison 8,466	H7
Dixmude (Diksmuide) 6,669	B6
Doische	F8
Doornik (Tournai) 32,794	C7
Dour 10,059	D8
Drogenbos 4,840	B10
Duffel 13,802	F6
Durbuy	H8
Ecaussinnes 6,630	E7
Edingen (Enghien) 4,115	D7
Eeklo 19,144	D6
Éghezée	F7
Eigenbrakel (Braine-l'Alleud) 18,531	E7
Ekeren 27,648	E6
Ellezelles 3,556	D7
Enghien 4,115	D7
Erezée	E8
Erquelinnes 4,471	E8
Esneux 6,183	H7
Essen 10,795	F6
Estampuis	C7
Etterbeek 51,030	B9

Eupen 14,879	J7
Evere 26,957	C9
Evergem 12,886	D6
Farciennes	E8
Fernelmont	F7
Ferrières	H8
Filémalle 8,135	G7
Fleurus 8,523	F8
Florennes 4,107	F8
Forest 55,135	B9
Fosses-La-Ville 3,972	F8
Frameries 11,224	D8
Froidchapelle	E8
Furnes (Veurne) 9,946	B6
Ganshoren 21,147	B9
Geel 29,346	F6
Geldenaken (Jodoigne) 4,132	F7
Gembloux-sur-Orneau 11,249	F7
Genk 57,913	H7
Gent (Ghent) 148,860	D6
Geraardsbergen 17,533	D7
Gerpinnes	F8
Ghent 148,860	D6
Ghent* 477,000	D6
Gistel	B6
Gooik	C7
Gouvy	H8
Grammont (Geraardsbergen) 17,533	D7
Grez-Doiceau	F7
Grimbergen	E7
Haacht 4,436	F7
Habay	H9
Hal (Halle) 20,017	E7
Halen 5,322	G7
Halle 20,017	E7
Hamme 17,559	E6
Hamoir	G8
Hamont-Achel 6,893	H6
Hannut (Hannut) 7,232	G7
Hannut 7,232	G7
Harelbeke 18,498	C7
Hasselt 39,663	G7
Hastière	F8
Heist-Knokke 27,582	C6
Heist-op-den-Berg 13,472	F6
Hensies	D8
Herentals 18,639	F6
Herne	E7
Herselt 7,412	F6
Herstal 29,600	H7
Herve 4,118	H7
Heuvelland	B7
Hoboken 33,693	E6
Hoei (Huy) 12,736	G8
Hoeselt 6,884	G7
Honnelles	D8
Hoogstraten 4,381	F6
Hotton	H8
Huy 12,736	G8
Ichtegem	B6
Ieper 22,928	C7
Ingelmunster 10,245	C7
Ittre	E7
Ixelles 86,450	C9
Izegem 22,928	C7
Jabbeke	C6
Jemappes 18,632	D8
Jette 40,013	B9
Jodoigne 4,132	F7
Kalmthout 12,724	F6
Kapellen 13,352	F6
Kasterlee	F6
Kinrooi	H6
Knokke-Heist 27,582	C6
Koekelare 7,807	B6
Koekelberg 17,570	B9
Koksijde	B6
Kontich 14,432	E6
Kortemark 5,904	C6
Kortrijk 44,961	C7
Kraainem 11,390	C9
La Louvière 23,310	E8
La Louvière* 113,259	E8
Lanaken 8,659	H7
Landen 5,740	G7
Langemark-Poelkapelle 5,457	B7
Lasne	F7
Lede 10,316	D7
Léglise	H9
Leopoldsburg 9,593	G6
Le Roeulx	E8
Lessen (Lessines) 8,906	D7
Lessines 8,906	D7
Leuven 30,623	F7
Leuze-en-Hainaut 7,185	D7
Libin	G9
Libramont-Chevigny 2,975	G9
Lichtervelde 7,459	C6
Liedekerke 10,482	E7
Liège 145,573	H7
Liège* 622,000	H7
Lier 28,416	F6
Lierre (Lier) 28,416	F6
Limbourg 3,762	J7
Limburg (Limburg) 3,762	J7
Linkebeek 4,265	C10

Linter	G7
Lochristi	D6
Lokeren 26,740	D6
Lommel 21,984	G6
Lontzen	H9
Looz (Borgloon) 3,412	G7
Lo-Reninge	B7
Louvain (Leuven) 30,623	F7
Luik (Liège) 145,573	H7
Lummen	G7
Maaseik 8,622	H6
Maasmechelen	H7
Machelen 7,057	C9
Maldegem 14,474	C6
Malines (Mechelen) 65,466	F6
Malmédy 6,464	J8
Manage	E7
Manhay	H8
Marche-en-Famenne 4,567	G8
Marchin 4,206	G8
Mechelen 65,466	F6
Meerhout 8,567	G6
Meise	E7
Menen 22,037	C7
Menin (Menen) 22,037	C7
Merelbeke 13,837	D7
Merksem 39,768	E6
Merksplas 5,065	F6
Messancy 3,150	H9
Mettet 3,372	F8
Meulebeke 10,458	C7
Middelkerke	B6
Moeskroen (Mouscron) 37,311	C7
Mol 28,823	G6
Molenbeek-Saint-Jean 68,411	B9
Momignies	E8
Mons 59,362	E8
Montigny-le-Tilleul	B7
Moorslede	C7
Mortsel 28,012	E6
Mouscron 37,311	C7
Namen (Namur) 32,269	F8
Namur 32,269	F8
Nassogne	G8
Nazareth	D7
Neerpelt 8,771	G6
Neufchâteau 2,670	G9
Nevele	C7
Nieuport (Nieuwpoort) 8,273	B6
Nieuwpoort 8,273	B6
Nijvel (Nivelles) 16,126	E7
Ninove 12,428	D7
Nivelles 16,126	E7
Ohey	G8
Onhaye	F8
Oostende (Ostend) 71,227	B6
Oostkamp 8,999	C6
Opwijk 9,699	E7
Ostend 71,227	B6
Oudenaarde 26,615	D7
Oudenburg	B6
Oud-Turnhout 9,245	G6
Oupeye	H7
Overijse 16,181	F7
Overpelt 10,470	G6
Paliseul	G9
Peer 7,201	G6
Péruwelz 7,878	D7
Philippeville 2,076	F8
Plombières	H7
Pont-à-Celles	E8
Poperinge 12,671	B7
Profondeville	F8
Putte 6,953	F6
Quaregnon 17,688	D8
Quévy	D8
Quiévrain 5,510	D8
Raeren 3,655	J7
Ravels	G6
Rebecq 3,744	E7
Renaix (Ronse) 25,056	D7
Rendeux	H8
Retie 6,619	G6
Rochefort 4,357	G8
Roeselare 40,428	C7
Ronse 25,056	D7
Roulers (Roeselare) 40,428	C7
Rouvroy	G9
Ruislede	C6
Sainte-Ode	H8
Saint-Georges-sur-Meuse 6,003	G7
Saint-Gilles 55,055	B9
Saint-Hubert 3,001	G8
Saint-Josse-ten-Noode 23,633	C9
Saint-Nicolas	
Saint-Trond (Sint-Truiden) 21,473	G7
Saint-Vith (Sankt Vith) 3,001	J8
Sankt Vith 3,001	J8
Schaerbeek 118,950	C9
Schoten 29,914	E6
Seraing 40,545	G7
's-Gravenbrakel (Braine-le-Comte) 11,957	D7
Sint-Laureins	D6
Sint-Niklaas 49,214	E6

(continued on following page)

Agriculture, Industry and Resources

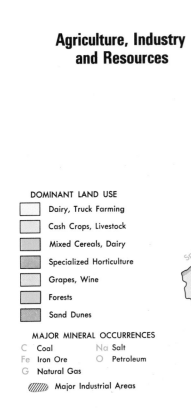

DOMINANT LAND USE

- Dairy, Truck Farming
- Cash Crops, Livestock
- Mixed Cereals, Dairy
- Specialized Horticulture
- Grapes, Wine
- Forests
- Sand Dunes

MAJOR MINERAL OCCURRENCES

C	Coal	Na	Salt
Fe	Iron Ore	O	Petroleum
G	Natural Gas		

Major Industrial Areas

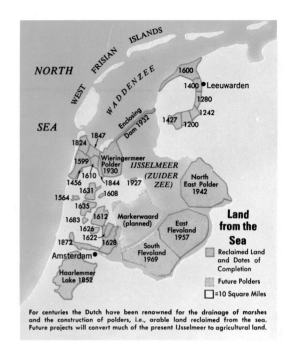

Netherlands, Belgium and Luxembourg

(continued)

Sint-Pieters-Leeuw 16,856 .... B9
Sint-Truiden 21,473 .... G7
Soignies 12,006 .... D7
Somme-Leuze G8
Spa 9,504 .... H8
Sprimont H8
Staden 5,499 .... B7
Stavelot 4,723 .... H8
Steenokkerzeel 4,037 .... C9
Stekene E6
Stoumont H8
Tamise (Temse) 14,950 .... E6
Tellin G8
Temse 14,950 .... E6
Tenneville H8
Termonde (Dendermonde) 22,119 .... E6
Tessenderlo 11,778 .... G6
Theux 5,316 .... H8
Thuin 5,777 .... E8
Tielt 14,077 .... C7
Tielt-Winge 3,743 .... F7
Tienen 24,134 .... F7
Tintigny G9
Tirlemont (Tienen) 24,134 .... F7
Tongeren 20,136 .... G7
Tongres (Tongeren) 20,136 .... G7
Torhout 15,156 .... C6
Tournai 32,794 .... C7
Trois-Ponts H8
Tubeke (Tubize) 11,507 .... E7
Tubize 11,507 .... E7
Turnhout 38,007 .... F6
Uccle 78,909 .... B9
Ukkel (Uccle) 78,909 .... B9
Vaux-sur-Sûre H9
Verviers 33,587 .... H7
Veurne 9,496 .... B6
Vielsalm 3,587 .... H8
Vilvoorde 34,633 .... F7
Vilvorde (Vilvoorde) 34,633 .... F7
Viroinval F8
Virton 3,558 .... H9
Visé 6,880 .... H7
Vleteren B7
Vorst (Forest) 55,135 .... B9
Vresse-sur-Semois F9
Waarschoot 7,905 .... D6
Wachtebeke D6
Waregem 17,725 .... C7
Waremme 10,956 .... G7
Waterloo 17,764 .... E7
Watermaal-Bosvoorde
(Watermael-Boitsfort C9
Watermael-Boitsfort 25,123 .... C9
Waver (Wavre) 11,767 .... F7
Wavre 11,767 .... F7
Wellin G8
Wemmel 12,631 .... B9
Wervik 12,672 .... B7
Westerlo 14,173 .... F6
Westmalle F6
Wetteren 20,816 .... D7
Wezembeek-Oppem 10,899 .... D9
Wezet (Visé) 6,880 .... H7
Willebroek 15,726 .... E6
Wilrijk 43,485 .... E6
Wingene 7,140 .... C6
Woluwe-Saint-Lambert 47,360 .... C9
Woluwe-Saint-Pierre 40,884 .... C9
Ypres (Ieper) 20,825 .... B7
Zaventem 10,625 .... C9
Zedelgem C6
Zeebrugge C6
Zele 18,585 .... E6
Zelzate 12,785 .... D6
Zemst E7
Zinnik (Soignies) 12,006 .... D7
Zonhoven 13,484 .... G6
Zottegem 21,461 .... D7
Zuienkerke C6

OTHER FEATURES

Albert, (canal) F6
Ardennes, (for.) F9
Botrange, (mt.) J8
Dender, (riv.) D7
Deûle, (riv.) B7
Dyle, (riv.) F7
Hohe Venn, (plat.) H8
Lesse, (riv.) F8
Lys, (riv.) B7
Mark, (riv.) F6
Meuse, (riv.) F8
Nethe, (riv.) F6
North, (sea) D4
Ourthe, (riv.) G8
Rupel, (riv.) F7
Sambre, (riv.) D8
Schelde (Scheldt), (riv.) C7
Scheldt, (riv.) C7
Schnee Eifel, (plat.) J8
Semois, (riv.) G9
Senne, (riv.) E7
Vaalserberg, (mt.) J7
Vesdre, (riv.) H7
Weisserstein, (mt.) J8
Yser, (riv.) B7
Zitterwald, (plat.) J8

LUXEMBOURG

CITIES and TOWNS

Clervaux 916 .... J8
Diekirch† 5,059 .... J9
Differdange 9,287 .... H9
Dudelange† 14,615 .... J10
Echternach† 3,792 .... J9
Esch-sur-Alzette† 27,574 .... J9
Ettelbruck† 5,990 .... J9
Grevenmacher† 2,918 .... J9
Luxembourg (cap.) 78,272 .... J9
Mamer 3,123 .... H9
Mersch 1,869 .... J9
Pétange 6,234 .... H9
Remich† 12,138 .... J9
Viandent† 1,520 .... J9
Wiltz 1,601 .... H9

OTHER FEATURES

Alzette, (riv.) J9
Clerf, (riv.) J8
Eisling, (mts.) H9
Mosel, (riv.) J9
Our, (riv.) J9
Sauer, (riv.) J9

NETHERLANDS

PROVINCES

Drenthe 405,924 .... K3
Flevoland G4
Friesland 560,614 .... H2
Gelderland 1,639,997 .... H4
Groningen 540,062 .... K2
Limburg 1,051,620 .... H6
North Brabant 1,967,261 .... F5
North Holland 2,295,875 .... F3
Overijssel 985,569 .... J4
South Holland 3,048,648 .... E5
Utrecht 867,909 .... G4
Zeeland 332,286 .... D6

CITIES and TOWNS†

Aalsmeer 20,779 .... F4
Aalten 17,486 .... K5
Aardenburg 3,869 .... C6
Akkrum 5,044 .... H2
Alkmaar 65,199 .... F3
Almelo 62,634 .... K4
Alphen aan de Rijn 46,065 .... F4
Amersfoort 87,784 .... G4
Amstelveen 71,803 .... B5
Amsterdam (cap.) 751,156 .... B4
Amsterdam* 987,205 .... B4
Andijk 5,301 .... G3
Apeldoorn 134,055 .... H4
Apeldoorn* 237,231 .... H4
Appingedam 13,295 .... K2
Arnhem 126,051 .... H4
Arnhem* 281,126 .... H4
Assen 43,783 .... K3
Asten 12,295 .... H6
Axel 12,072 .... D6
Baarle-Nassau 5,583 .... F6
Baarn 25,045 .... G4
Barneveld 34,189 .... H4
Bath E6
Beilen 12,948 .... K3
Bemmel 14,218 .... H5
Bergeijk 9,009 .... G6
Bergen 14,306 .... F3
Bergen op Zoom 40,770 .... E5
Bergum 28,047 .... H2
Berkel 9,367 .... F5
Berkhout 5,167 .... F3
Beverwijk 37,551 .... F4
Blerick J6
Bloemendaal 17,940 .... E4
Blokzijl H3
Bodegraven 15,848 .... F4
Bolsward 9,934 .... H2
Borculo 9,859 .... J4
Borger 12,017 .... K3
Borne 18,216 .... K4
Boskoop 12,985 .... F4
Boxmeer 12,662 .... H5
Boxtel 22,465 .... G5
Breda 118,086 .... F5
Breda* 151,182 .... F5
Breezand F3
Breskens C6
Brielle 10,620 .... E5
Brouwershaven 3,263 .... D5
Brummen 20,460 .... J4
Brunssum 26,116 .... J7
Buiksloot C4
Bussum 37,848 .... G4
Capelle 35,696 .... F5
Coevorden 13,089 .... K3
Colijnsplaat D5
Culemborg 17,682 .... G5
Cuyk 15,366 .... H5
Dalen 5,084 .... K3
De Bilt 32,588 .... G4
Dedemsvaart 12,975 .... J3
De Koog F2
Delft 86,103 .... E4
Delfzijl 23,316 .... K2
Den Burg 12,132 .... F2
Denekamp 11,533 .... L4
Den Helder 60,421 .... F3
Deurne 26,539 .... H6
Deventer 65,557 .... J4
Didam 14,263 .... J5
De Wijk 4,631 .... J3
Diemen 13,704 .... C5
Dieren J4
Diever 3,162 .... J3
Dinxperlo 7,296 .... K5
Dirksland 6,495 .... E5
Doesburg 9,759 .... J4
Doetinchem 34,915 .... J5
Dokkum 11,203 .... H2
Domburg 3,874 .... C5
Dongen 19,219 .... F5
Doorn 11,966 .... G4
Dordrecht 101,840 .... F5
Dordrecht* 186,793 .... F5
Drachten 45,390 .... J2
Driebergen 17,022 .... G4
Dronten 16,544 .... H3
Druten 11,113 .... H5
Echt 17,035 .... H6
Edam-Volendam 21,507 .... G4
Ede 79,897 .... H4
Egmond aan Zee 5,734 .... E3
Eindhoven 192,562 .... G6
Eindhoven* 358,234 .... G6
Elburg 18,082 .... H4
Elst 16,686 .... H5
Emmeloord 34,467 .... H3
Emmen 86,700 .... K3
Enkhuizen 13,430 .... G3
Enschede 141,597 .... K4
Enschede* 239,015 .... K4
Epe 32,267 .... H4
Erica K3
Ermelo 23,835 .... H4
Etten-Leur 26,167 .... F5
Europoort E5
Flushing 43,806 .... C6
Franeker 11,415 .... H2
Geertruidenberg 6,185 .... F5
Geldermalsen 8,952 .... G5
Geldrop 25,879 .... H6
Geleen 35,910 .... H7
Gemert 15,267 .... H5
Gendringen 19,086 .... J5
Genemuiden 6,058 .... H3
Gennep 14,773 .... H5
Giessendam-Hardinxveld 15,523 .... F5
Giethoorn J3
Gilze 19,603 .... F5
Goes 28,505 .... D6
Goirle 13,447 .... G5
Goor 11,435 .... K4
Gorinchem 28,337 .... G5
Gorredijk J2
Gouda 56,403 .... F4
Graauw E6
Gramsbergen 5,866 .... K3
Grave 9,492 .... H5
Groenlo 8,693 .... K4
Groesbeek 18,094 .... H5
Groningen 163,357 .... K2
Groningen* 201,662 .... K2
Grouw 8,567 .... H2
Haamstede 4,575 .... D5
Haarlem 164,672 .... F4
Haarlem* 232,048 .... F4
Haarlemmermeer
(Hoofddorp) 72,046 .... F4
Hague, The (cap.) 479,369 .... E4
Hague, The* 682,452 .... E4
Halfweg 4,456 .... B4
Hallum H2
Hardenberg 28,489 .... J3
Harderwijk 28,508 .... H4
Hardinxveld-Giessendam 15,523 .... G5
Harlingen 14,533 .... G2
Hasselt 5,817 .... J3
Hattem 11,074 .... H4
Heemskert 31,728 .... F3
Heemstede 27,376 .... F4
Heer H7
Heerde 16,833 .... H4
Heerenveen 34,948 .... H3
Heerhugowaard 26,019 .... F3
Heerlen 71,500 .... J7
Heesch 8,659 .... G5
Heiloo 20,524 .... F3
Hellendoorn 32,068 .... J4
Hellevoetsluis 14,186 .... E5
Helmond 59,249 .... H6
Hengelo, Gelderland 8,015 .... J4
Hengelo, Overijssel 72,281 .... K4
Heusden 5,542 .... G5
Hillegom 17,489 .... E4
Hilvarenbeek 8,408 .... G6
Hilversum 94,041 .... G4
Hilversum* 110,498 .... G4
Hippolytushoef 7,847 .... G3
Hoek D6
Hoek van Holland (Hook of
Holland) D4
Hoensbroek 22,441 .... H7
Holijsloot C4
Hollum H2
Holwerd H2
Hoofddorp
(Haarlemmermeer) 72,046 .... F4
Hoogeveen 42,673 .... J3
Hoogezand-Sappemeer 33,860 .... K2
Hoogkarspel 5,112 .... G3
Hook of Holland D4
Hoorn 24,609 .... G3
Horst 16,242 .... H6
Huissen 11,049 .... H5
Huizen 25,603 .... G4
Hulst 17,283 .... E6
IJmuiden 6,633 .... E4
IJsselstein 15,450 .... F4
Ilpendam 3,310 .... C4
Joure 14,329 .... H3
Kampen 29,488 .... H3
Katwijk aan Zee 37,437 .... E4
Kerkdriel 7,584 .... G5
Kerkrade 46,609 .... J7
Kesteren 8,257 .... G5
Klazienaveen 9,520 .... L3
Kollum 11,887 .... J2
Krimpen aan den IJssel 26,396 .... F5
Landsmeer 8,082 .... C4
Laren 13,615 .... G4
Leek 15,713 .... J2
Leerdam 15,030 .... F5
Leeuwarden 85,074 .... H2
Leiden 99,891 .... E4
Leiden* 167,554 .... E4
Lelystad H3
Lemmer 10,013 .... H3
Lisse 19,182 .... F4
Lith 5,088 .... G5
Lochem 17,274 .... J4
Lonneker K4
Loon op Zand 18,000 .... G5
Losser 20,688 .... L4
Maarssen 18,346 .... F4
Maasbree 9,462 .... H6
Maassluis 28,170 .... E5
Maastricht 111,044 .... H7
Maastricht* 145,862 .... H7
Margraten 3,318 .... H7
Medemblik 6,432 .... G3
Meerssen 8,414 .... H7
Meppel 21,057 .... J3
Middelburg 36,372 .... C6
Middelharnis 14,245 .... E5
Middenmeer F3
Millingen aan den Rijn 5,035 .... J5
Moerdijk F5
Monnickendam 8,127 .... C4
Montfoort 3,442 .... G4
Muiden 6,567 .... G4
Muntendam 4,147 .... K2
Naaldwijk 24,117 .... E4
Naarden 17,319 .... G4
Nagele H3
Neede 10,842 .... K4
Nes 3,012 .... H2
Nieuwegein 22,648 .... G4
Nieuwe-Pekela 5,086 .... L2
Nieuwkoop 8,923 .... F4
Nieuw-Schoonebeek 7,556 .... L3
Nijkerk 21,615 .... H4
Nijmegen 148,493 .... H5
Nijmegen* 213,981 .... H5
Noordwijk 22,386 .... E4
Norg 6,041 .... J2
Numansdorp 7,072 .... E5
Nunspeet 21,340 .... H4
Odoorn 11,973 .... K3
Oisterwijk 16,263 .... G5
Oldenzaal 26,624 .... K4
Olst 8,480 .... J4
Ommen 16,136 .... J3
Onstwedde K2
Oostburg 18,461 .... C6
Oosterhout 40,077 .... F5
Ooosterwolde 5,845 .... J2
Oostmahorn J2
Oostzaan 6,336 .... C4
Ootmarsum 3,901 .... K4
Oss 45,643 .... H5
Otterlo H4
Oud-Beijerland 14,251 .... E5
Ouddorp 9,091 .... D5
Oudenbosch 11,061 .... E5
Oude-Pekela 8,067 .... K2
Oudewater 6,870 .... F4
Purmerend 32,614 .... F4
Putten 18,243 .... H4
Raalte 23,598 .... J4
Renkum 34,547 .... H5
Reusel 6,901 .... G6
Rheden 49,755 .... J4
Rhenen 16,893 .... H5
Ridderkerk 45,069 .... F5
Rijnsburg 10,698 .... F4
Rijssen 20,008 .... J4
Rijswijk 54,123 .... E4
Roden 16,437 .... J2
Roermond 36,695 .... J6
Roosendaal 51,685 .... F5
Rotterdam 614,767 .... E5
Rotterdam* 1,016,505 .... E5
Rutten H3
Ruurlo 7,557 .... J4
Sappemeer-Hoogezand 33,860 .... K2
Schagen 13,929 .... F3
Scheveningen E4
Schiedam 78,068 .... E5
Schijndel 18,658 .... G5
Schiphol B5
Schoonhoven 10,753 .... F5
's Gravendeel 7,242 .... E5
's Gravenhage (The Hague)
(cap.) 479,369 .... E4
's Gravenhage* 682,452 .... E4
's Gravenzande 15,833 .... E4
's Heerenberg 18,326 .... J5
's Hertogenbosch 86,184 .... G5
Simpelveld 6,783 .... H7
Sint Annaland E5
Sint Jacobiparochie H2
Sittard 34,278 .... H6
Sliedrecht 21,839 .... F5
Slochteren 13,447 .... K2
Sloten, North Holland B5
Sloterdijk B4
Sluis 3,140 .... C6
Smilde 8,247 .... K3
Sneek 28,123 .... H2
Soest 40,165 .... G4
Soesterberg G4
Stadskanaal 13,946 .... L3
Staphorst 11,608 .... J3
Steenbergen 12,930 .... E5
Steenwijk 20,721 .... J3
Stiens 7,711 .... H2
Swifterbant H3
Tegelen 18,386 .... J6
Ter Apel L3
Termunten 4,803 .... K2
Terneuzen 33,731 .... D6
Tholen 17,213 .... E5
Tiel 24,974 .... G5
Tilburg 151,513 .... G5
Tilburg* 212,510 .... G5
Twello 22,542 .... J4
Uden 28,946 .... H5
Uithoorn 22,812 .... F4
Uithuizen 5,194 .... K2
Ulrum 3,665 .... J2
Urk 9,397 .... H3
Utrecht 250,887 .... G4
Utrecht* 464,357 .... G4
Vaals 11,057 .... H7
Vaassen 7,225 .... H4
Valkenswaard 27,121 .... H6
Veendam 26,168 .... K2
Veenendaal 35,845 .... G4
Veenhuizen J2
Veere 4,252 .... D5
Veghel 22,308 .... H5
Veldhoven 30,030 .... G6
Velp J5
Velsen 64,035 .... F4
Venlo 61,659 .... J6
Venraij 31,526 .... H6
Vianen 12,821 .... G5
Vlaardingen 78,311 .... E5
Vlagtwedde 16,719 .... L3
Vlijmen 13,515 .... G5
Vlissingen (Flushing) 43,806 .... C6
Volendam-Edam 21,507 .... G4
Voorburg 45,209 .... E4
Voorst 22,542 .... J4
Vorden 7,276 .... J4
Vriezenveen 16,025 .... K4
Vught 23,261 .... G5
Waalre 13,219 .... G6
Waalwijk 25,977 .... F5
Wageningen 28,659 .... H5
Wamel 8,979 .... H5
Warmenhuizen 3,818 .... F3
Weert 36,850 .... H6
Weesp 17,037 .... C5
West-Terschelling 4,542 .... G2
Wierden 20,618 .... K4
Wijhe 6,888 .... J4
Wijk bij Duurstede 7,927 .... G5
Wijk en Aalburg 9,266 .... F5
Winschoten 19,760 .... L2
Winsum 5,007 .... K2
Winterswijk 27,413 .... K5
Woensdrecht 9,101 .... E6
Woerden 22,064 .... F4
Wolvega 22,812 .... J3
Workum 4,135 .... G3
Zaandam (Zaanstad) 124,795 .... B4
Zaandam (Zaanstad)* 137,371 .... B4
Zaltbommel 8,010 .... G5
Zandvoort 16,289 .... E4
Zeist 58,630 .... G4
Zevenaar 26,560 .... J5
Zevenbergen 13,307 .... E5
Zierikzee 8,816 .... D5
Zundert 12,444 .... F6
Zutphen 29,188 .... J4
Zwartsluis 4,391 .... H3
Zwijndrecht 38,271 .... E5
Zwolle 77,826 .... J3

OTHER FEATURES

Alkmaardermeer (lake) F3
Ameland (isl.) H2
Bergumermeer (lake) J2
Beulaker Wijde (lake) H3
Borndiep (chan.) H2
De Fluessen (lake) G3
De Honte (bay) D6
De Peel (reg.) H6
De Twente (reg.) K4
De Zaan (riv.) B4
Dollard (bay) L2
Dommel (riv.) H6
Duiveland (isl.) D5
Eastern Scheldt (est.) D5
Eems (riv.) K2
Eijerlandsche Gat (str.) F2
Flevoland Polders 35,618 .... G4
Friesche Gat (chan.) J2
Frisian, West (isls.) G2
Galgenberg (hill) H4
Goeree (isl.) D5
Grevelingen (str.) E5
Griend (isl.) G2
Groninger Wad (sound) J2
Groote IJ Polder B4
Haarlemmermeer Polder 72,046 .... B5
Haringvliet (str.) E5
Het IJ (est.) C4
Hoek van Holland (cape) D5
Hondsrug (hills) K3
Houtrak Polder A4
Hunse (riv.) K3
IJmeer (bay) C4
IJssel (riv.) J4
IJsselmeer (lake) G3
Lauwers (chan.) J1
Lauwers Zee (bay) J2
Lek (riv.) F5
Lemelerberg (hill) J4
Lower Rhine (riv.) H5
Maas (riv.) G5
Mark (riv.) F6
Marken (isl.) G4
Markerwaard Polder G3
Marsdiep (chan.) F3
North (sea) E3
North Beveland (isl.) D5
North East Polder 34,467 .... H3
North Holland (canal) C4
North Sea (canal) F4
Old Rhine (riv.) E4
Oostzaan Polder 6,336 .... B4
Orange (canal) K3
Overflakkee (isl.) E5
Pinke Gat (chan.) H2
Regge (riv.) K4
Rhine (riv.) J5
Roer (riv.) J6
Rottumeplaat (isl.) J1
Rottumeroog (isl.) J1
Schiermonnikoog (isl.) J1
Schouwen (isl.) D5
Slotermeer (lake) H3
Sneekermeer (lake) H2
South Beveland (isl.) D6
Terschelling (isl.) G2
Texel (isl.) F2
Tjeukemeer (lake) H3
Tjonger (riv.) J3
Vaalserberg (mt.) J7
Vecht (riv.) F4
Vechte (riv.) J3
Veersche Meer (lake) D5
Veluwe (reg.) H4
Vlieland (isl.) F2
Vliestroom (str.) G2
Voorne (isl.) D5
Waal (riv.) G5
Waddenzee (sound) G2
Walcheren (isl.) C5
Wester Eems (chan.) K1
Western Scheldt (De Honte)
(bay) D6
West Frisian (isls.) F2
Westgat (chan.) F3
Wieringermeer Polder 11,870 .... G3
Wilhelmina (canal) G6
Willems (canal) G5

*City and suburbs.
†Population of cities in Belgium & Netherlands are communes

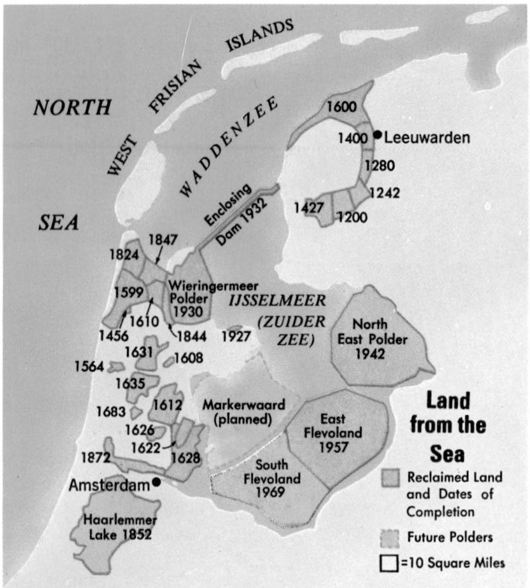

For centuries the Dutch have been renowned for the drainage of marshes and the construction of polders, i.e., arable land reclaimed from the sea. Future projects will convert much of the present IJsselmeer to agricultural land.

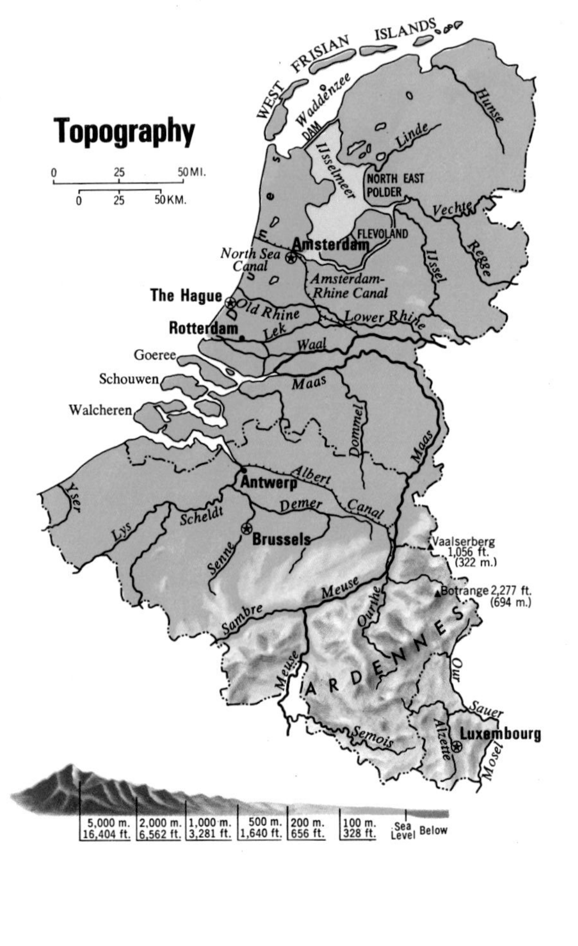

Netherlands,
Belgium and Luxembourg

CONIC PROJECTION

SCALE OF MILES

0 5 10   20   30   40

SCALE OF KILOMETRES

0 5 10 20   30   40   50

Capitals of Countries . . . . ★

Provincial Capitals . . . . △

International Boundaries . . . . . —·—·—

Provincial Boundaries . . . . . . —··—··—

Canals . . . .

© Copyright HAMMOND INCORPORATED, Maplewood, N.J.

AMSTERDAM

BRUSSELS

© Copyright HAMMOND INCORPORATED, Maplewood, N.J.

France

CONIC PROJECTION

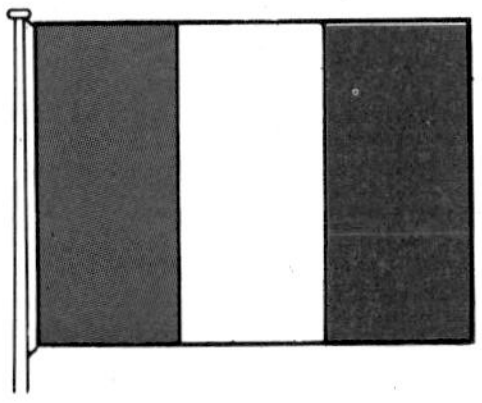

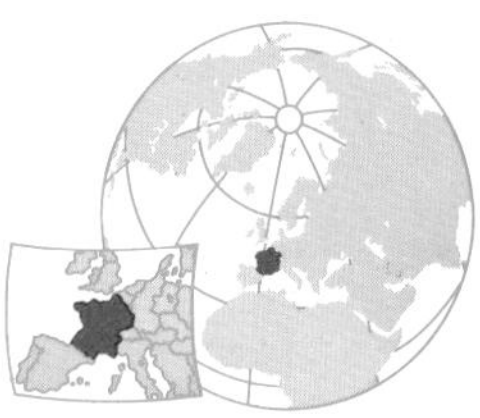

AREA 210,038 sq. mi. (543,998 sq. km.)
POPULATION 53,788,000
CAPITAL Paris
LARGEST CITY Paris
HIGHEST POINT Mont Blanc 15,771 ft. (4,807 m.)
MONETARY UNIT franc
MAJOR LANGUAGE French
MAJOR RELIGION Roman Catholicism

DEPARTMENTS

Ain 376,477 F4
Aisne 533,862 E3
Allier 378,406 E4
Alpes-de-Haute-Provence 112,178 G5
Alpes-Maritimes 816,681 G6
Ardèche 257,065 F5
Ardennes 309,306 F3
Ariège 137,857 D6
Aube 284,823 E3
Aude 272,366 E6
Aveyron 278,306 E5
Bas-Rhin 882,121 G3
Belfort (terr.) 128,125 G4
Bouches-du-Rhône 1,632,974 F6
Calvados 560,967 C3
Cantal 166,549 E5
Charente 337,064 D5
Charente-Maritime 497,859 C5
Cher 316,350 E4
Corrèze 240,363 D5
Corse du Sud 128,634 B6
Côte-d'Or 456,070 F4
Côtes-du-Nord 525,556 B3
Creuse 146,214 D4
Deux-Sèvres 335,829 C4
Dordogne 373,179 D5
Doubs 471,082 G4
Drôme 361,847 F5
Essonne 923,063 E3
Eure 422,952 D3
Eure-et-Loir 335,151 D3
Finistère 804,088 A3
Gard 494,575 F6
Gers 175,366 D6
Gironde 1,061,480 C5
Haute-Corse 161,208 B6
Haute-Garonne 777,431 D6
Haute-Loire 205,491 E5
Haute-Marne 212,304 F3
Hautes-Alpes 97,358 G5
Haute-Saône 222,254 G4
Haute-Savoie 447,795 G5
Hautes-Pyrénées 227,222 D6
Haute-Vienne 352,149 D5
Haut-Rhin 635,209 G4
Hauts-de-Seine 1,438,930 A2
Hérault 648,202 E6
Ille-et-Vilaine 702,199 C3
Indre 248,523 D4
Indre-et-Loire 478,601 D4
Isère 860,339 F5
Jura 238,856 F4
Landes 288,323 C5
Loire 742,396 F5
Loire-Atlantique 934,499 C4
Loiret 490,189 E4
Loir-et-Cher 283,686 D4
Lot 150,778 D5
Lot-et-Garonne 292,616 D5
Lozère 74,825 E5
Maine-et-Loire 629,849 C4
Manche 451,662 C3
Marne 530,399 F3
Mayenne 261,789 C3
Meurthe-et-Moselle 722,588 G3
Meuse 203,904 F3
Morbihan 563,588 B4
Moselle 1,006,373 G3
Nièvre 245,212 E4
Nord 2,510,738 E2
Oise 606,320 E3
Orne 293,523 C3
Paris (city) 2,299,830 B2
Pas-de-Calais 1,403,035 E2
Puy-de-Dôme 580,033 E5
Pyrénées-Atlantiques 534,748 C6
Pyrénées-Orientales 299,506 E6
Rhône 1,429,647 F5
Saône-et-Loire 569,810 F4
Sarthe 490,385 D3
Savoie 305,118 G5
Seine-et-Marne 755,762 E3
Seine-Saint-Denis 1,322,127 C1
Somme 538,462 E3
Tarn 338,024 E6
Tarn-et-Garonne 183,314 D5
Val-de-Marne 1,215,713 C1
Val-d'Oise 840,885 E3
Var 626,093 G6
Vaucluse 390,446 F6
Vendée 450,641 C4
Vienne 357,366 D4
Vosges 397,957 G3
Yonne 299,851 E4
Yvelines 1,082,255 D3

CITIES and TOWNS

Abbeville 25,252 D2
Agde 9,856 E6
Agen 33,763 D5
Aix-en-Provence 91,665 F6
Aix-les-Bains 21,884 G5
Ajaccio 47,065 B7
Albert 11,746 E2
Albertville 16,630 G5
Albi 43,942 E6
Alençon 32,917 D3
Alès 33,315 E5
Ambérieu-en-Bugey 9,294 F5
Amboise 10,498 D4
Amiens 129,453 D3
Ancenis 6,689 C4
Angers 136,603 C4
Angoulême 46,293 D5
Annecy 53,058 G5
Annonay 19,234 F5
Antibes 44,226 G6
Antony 57,450 B2
Apt 9,735 F6
Arcachon 13,856 C5
Argentan 16,063 D3
Argenteuil 101,542 A1
Arles 37,337 F6
Armentières 23,850 E2
Arras 45,804 F2
Asnières-sur-Seine 75,328 A1
Aubagne 26,145 F6
Aubenas 11,967 F5
Aubervilliers 72,859 B1
Auch 18,767 D6
Audincourt 18,570 G4
Aulnay-sous-Bois 77,982 B1
Auray 10,006 B4
Aurignac 744 D6
Aurillac 29,458 E5
Autun 19,441 F4
Auxerre 36,039 E4
Auxonne 6,414 F4
Avallon 8,518 E4
Avignon 73,482 F6
Avion 22,860 E2
Avranches 10,128 C3
Ax-les-Thermes 1,456 D6
Bagnères-de-Bigorre 9,080 D6
Bagnolet 35,858 B2
Bagnols-sur-Cèze 13,111 F5
Barbizon 1,189 E3
Barcelonnette 2,523 G5
Barfleur 701 C3
Bar-le-Duc 19,188 F3
Bar-sur-Aube 7,227 F3
Bastia 45,387 B6
Bayeux 13,381 C3
Bayonne 41,281 C6
Beaucaire 10,189 F6
Beaune 16,386 F4
Beauvais 53,493 E3
Belfort 54,469 G4
Belley 6,612 F5
Berck 14,104 D2
Bergerac 25,488 D5
Bernay 9,928 D3
Besançon 119,803 G4
Béthune 26,208 E2
Béziers 79,213 E6
Biarritz 27,453 C6
Blois 49,134 D4
Bobigny 43,041 B1
Bogny-sur-Meuse 6,845 F3
Bolbec 12,347 D3
Bondy 48,285 B1
Bonneville 6,717 G4
Bordeaux 220,830 C5
Boulogne-Billancourt 103,527 A2
Boulogne-sur-Mer 48,309 D2
Bourg-en-Bresse 40,052 F4
Bourges 75,200 E4
Bourgoin-Jallieu 18,504 F5
Bressuire 9,778 C4
Brest 163,940 A3
Briançon 8,523 G5
Brignoles 8,784 G6
Brioude 7,756 E5
Brive-la-Gaillarde 49,276 D5
Bruay-en-Artois 25,544 E2
Caen 116,987 C3
Cahors 19,288 D5
Calais 73,009 D2
Caluire-et-Cuire 43,024 F5
Cambrai 38,706 E2
Cannes 70,226 G6
Carcassonne 38,887 D6
Carmaux 11,970 E5
Carpentras 20,169 F5
Castelnaudary 8,947 E6
Castelsarrasin 6,562 D6
Castres 41,037 E6
Cavaillon 17,383 F6
Châlons-sur-Marne 50,870 F3
Chalon-sur-Saône 55,495 F4
Chambéry 52,286 F5
Chambord 166 D4
Chamonix-Mont-Blanc 6,246 G5
Champigny-sur-Marne 80,189 C2
Chantilly 10,517 E3
Charenton-le-Pont 20,383 B2
Charleville-Mézières 59,513 F3
Chartres 38,574 D3
Châteaubriant 12,417 C4
Château-du-Loir 5,598 D4
Châteaudun 14,634 D3
Château-Gontier 8,301 C4
Châteauroux 53,166 D4
Château-Thierry 13,379 E3
Châtellerault 33,811 D4
Châtillon 26,562 B2
Châtillon-sur-Seine 7,367 F4
Chatou 26,415 A1
Chaumont 26,568 F3
Chauny 14,324 E3
Chelles 24,192 C1
Cherbourg 31,333 C3
Chinon 5,378 D4
Choisy-le-Roi 38,629 B2
Cholet 49,887 C4
Clamart 52,881 A2
Clermont 7,834 E3
Clermont-Ferrand 153,379 E5
Clichy 47,731 B1
Cluny 4,335 F4
Cluses 12,713 G4
Cognac 21,567 C5
Colmar 58,585 G3
Colombes 83,241 A1
Commentry 8,074 E4
Commercy 6,918 F3
Compiègne 37,009 E3
Concarneau 15,096 A4
Cosne-Cours-sur-Loire 9,768 E4
Coudekerque-Branche 24,702 E2
Coulommiers 11,363 E3
Courbevoie 54,391 A1
Coutances 8,286 C3
Creil 31,893 E3
Crépy-en-Valois 10,661 E3
Créteil 58,665 B2
Cusset 13,672 E4
Dax 18,019 C6
Deauville 5,655 C3
Decazeville 9,318 E5
Decize 6,853 E4
Denain 26,096 E2
Dieppe 25,607 D3

Topography

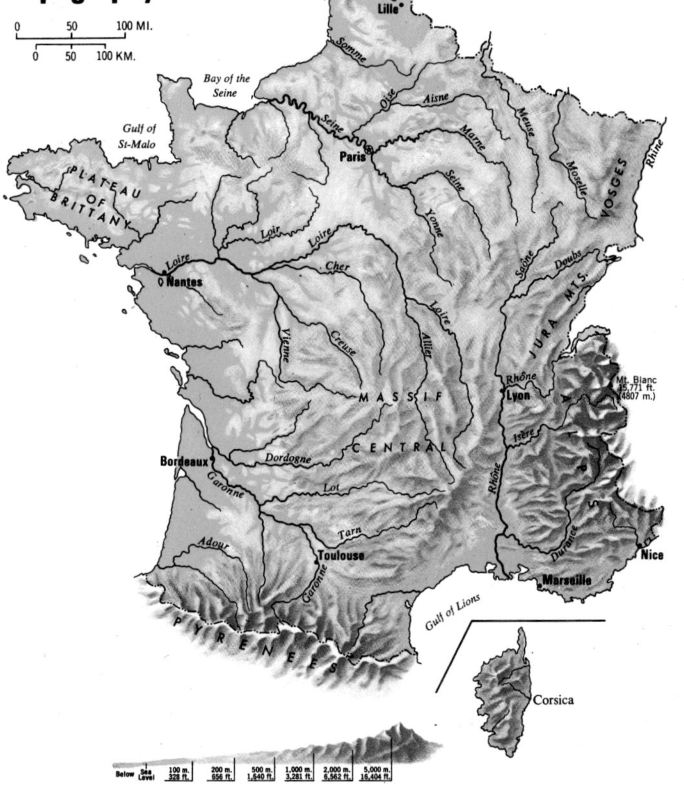
0 50 100 MI.
0 50 100 KM.
Lille
Somme
Bay of the Seine
Oise
Aisne
Seine
Meuse
Gulf of St-Malo
Marne
Paris
Rhine
PLATEAU OF BRITTANY
Moselle
VOSGES
Seine
Yonne
Loir
Loire
Loire
Cher
Saône
Doubs
Nantes
JURA MTS.
Vienne
Creuse
Allier
Loire
Rhône
Mt. Blanc 15,771 ft. (4807 m.)
MASSIF
Lyon
Isère
CENTRAL
Bordeaux
Dordogne
Garonne
Lot
Rhône
Tarn
Adour
Durance
Toulouse
Nice
Garonne
Marseille
Gulf of Lions
PYRENEES
Corsica
Below Sea Level
100 m. 328 ft.
200 m. 656 ft.
500 m. 1,640 ft.
1,000 m. 3,281 ft.
2,000 m. 6,562 ft.
5,000 m. 16,404 ft.

Historic Provinces

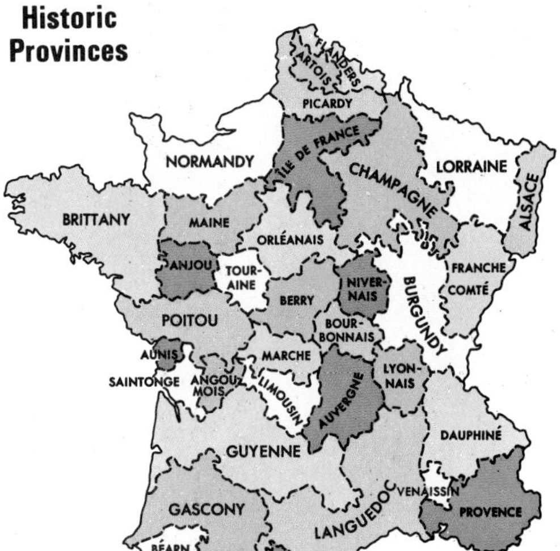
FLANDERS
ARTOIS
PICARDY
NORMANDY
ÎLE DE FRANCE
CHAMPAGNE
LORRAINE
ALSACE
BRITTANY
MAINE
ORLÉANAIS
ANJOU
TOUR-AINE
BERRY
NIVER-NAIS
BURGUNDY
FRANCHE COMTÉ
POITOU
BOUR-BONNAIS
AUNIS
MARCHE
LYON-NAIS
SAINTONGE
ANGOU-MOIS
LIMOUSIN
AUVERGNE
DAUPHINÉ
GUYENNE
VENAISSIN
GASCONY
LANGUEDOC
PROVENCE
BÉARN
FOIX
ROUSSILLON

A resident of the city of Caen thinks of himself as a Norman rather than as a citizen of the modern department of Calvados. In spite of the passing of nearly two centuries, the historic provinces which existed before 1790 command the local patriotism of most Frenchmen.

Digne 13,140 G5
Digoin 10,449 F4
Dijon 149,899 F4
Dinan 13,303 B3
Dinard 9,211 B3
Dôle 28,109 F4
Domrémy-la-Pucelle 190 F3
Douai 43,954 E2
Douarnenez 17,851 A3
Doullens 6,806 E2
Draguignan 19,653 G6
Drancy 64,258 B1
Dreux 31,503 D3
Dunkirk (Dunkerque) 78,171 E2
Elbeuf 18,642 D3
Épernay 29,286 E3
Épinal 39,000 G3
Épinay-sur-Seine 46,458 B1
Erstein 6,494 G3
Étampes 18,810 E3
Étaples 10,423 D2
Eu 8,349 D3
Évreux 46,181 D3
Évry 15,300 E3
Falaise 8,133 C3
Fécamp 20,835 D3
Figeac 8,675 D5
Firminy 23,776 F5
Flers 18,590 C3
Foix 9,569 D6
Fontainebleau 16,436 E3
Fontenay-le-Comte 12,301 C4
Fontenay-sous-Bois 46,200 C2
Forbach 24,812 G3
Fougères 26,260 C3
Fourmies 15,318 F2
Fréjus 27,805 G6
Gagny 36,714 C1
Gaillac 7,653 D6
Gap 24,962 G5
Gardanne 8,175 F6
Gennevillers 50,154 B1
Gentilly 16,843 B2
Gex 3,959 G4
Gien 13,817 E4
Gif 10,866 E3
Gisors 7,591 D3
Givet 7,787 F2
Givors 19,356 F5
Granville 12,869 C3
Grasse 24,260 G6
Graulhet 11,099 E6
Gray 8,718 F4
Grenoble 165,431 F5
Guebwiller 10,477 G4
Guéret 14,418 D4
Guingamp 9,269 B3
Guise 6,642 E3
Haguenau 23,023 G3
Harfleur 9,857 D3
Hautmont 19,130 F2
Hayange 8,479 F3
Hazebrouck 18,867 E2
Hendaye 9,404 C6
Hénin-Beaumont 26,296 E2
Hennebont 8,978 B4
Héricourt 8,481 G4
Hirson 11,909 F3
Honfleur 8,995 D3
Hyères 29,366 G6
Issoire 13,560 E5
Issoudun 15,065 D4
Issy-les-Moulineaux 47,355 A2
Istres 10,127 F6
Ivry-sur-Seine 62,804 B2
Joigny 10,825 E3
La Baule-Escoublac 13,854 B4
La Ciotat 29,290 F6
La Courneuve 37,917 B1
La Flèche 12,743 C4
La Grand-Combe 9,406 E5
L'Aigle 9,198 D3
Landerneau 13,983 B3
Langres 10,745 F4
Lannion 13,692 B3
Laon 27,420 E3
La Pallice C4
La Rochelle 72,936 C4
La Roche-sur-Yon 40,789 C4
La Seyne-sur-Mer 50,059 F6
Laval 50,734 C3
Lavelanet 9,278 E6
Le Blanc 7,431 D4
Le Blanc-Mesnil 49,062 B1
Le Bourget 10,520 B1
Le Cateau 8,680 E2
Le Chesnay 24,590 A2
Le Creusot 31,643 F4
Le Havre 216,917 C3
Le Mans 150,289 C3
Lens 39,973 E2
Le Puy 24,793 F5
Les Andelys 7,524 D3
Les Sables-d'Olonne 17,157 B4
Le Teil 7,993 F5
Le Tréport 6,463 D2
Levallois-Perret 52,460 A1
Lézignan-Corbières 6,929 E6
Libourne 21,265 C5
Liévin 33,040 E2
Lille 171,010 E2
Limoges 136,059 D5
Limoux 9,595 E6
Lisieux 24,972 D3
Livry-Gargan 32,879 C1
Lodève 7,131 E6
Longwy 20,107 F3
Lons-le-Saunier 20,897 F4
Lorient 68,655 B4
Loudéac 7,173 B3
Loudun 7,060 D4
Lourdes 17,685 C6
Louviers 17,919 D3
Luçon 8,834 C4
Lunel 12,392 E6
Lunéville 22,438 G3
Lure 8,538 G4
Luxeuil-les-Bains 10,061 G4
Lyon 454,265 F5
Mâcon 39,130 F4
Maisons-Alfort 53,963 B2
Maisons-Laffitte 23,465 A1
Malakoff 34,100 A2
Manosque 17,256 G6
Mantes-la-Jolie 42,403 D3
Marmande 13,223 C5
Marseille 901,421 F6
Martigues 26,850 F6
Maubeuge 34,152 F2
Mayenne 11,278 C3
Mazamet 13,148 E6
Meaux 41,831 E3
Mehun-sur-Yèvre 6,533 E4
Melun 36,913 E3
Mende 10,040 E5
Menton 24,736 G6
Metz 110,939 G3
Meudon 31,294 A2
Millau 20,401 E5
Mimizan 6,826 C5
Mirecourt 7,160 G3
Moissac 7,403 D5
Montargis 18,021 E3
Montauban 35,344 D5
Montbard 7,477 F4
Montbéliard 29,968 G4
Montbrison 9,945 E5
Montceau-les-Mines 28,093 F4
Mont-de-Marsan 24,812 C6
Mont-Dore 2,074 E5
Montélimar 25,422 F5
Montfort 2,701 C3
Montigny-les-Metz 24,208 G3
Montluçon 56,337 E4
Montmédy 1,859 F3
Montpellier 178,136 E6
Montreuil, Seine-Saint-Denis 96,441 B2
Montrouge 40,189 B2
Mont-Saint-Michel 88 C3
Morlaix 15,919 B3
Morteau 6,515 G4
Moulins 25,856 E4
Moyeuvre-Grande 12,448 G3
Mulhouse 116,494 G4
Muret 13,041 D6
Nancy 106,906 G3
Nanterre 94,441 A1
Nantes 252,537 C4
Narbonne 36,525 E6
Nemours 11,159 E3
Neufchâteau 8,582 F3
Neuilly-sur-Seine 65,941 A1
Nevers 45,122 E4
Nice 331,002 G6
Nîmes 123,914 F6
Niort 59,297 C4
Nogent-le-Rotrou 12,284 D3
Noisy-le-Sec 37,674 B1
Noyon 13,784 E3
Oloron-Sainte-Marie 11,616 C6
Orange 19,847 F5
Orléans 88,503 D3
Orly 26,090 B2
Orthez 9,639 C6
Oullins 27,731 F5
Oyonnax 22,548 F4
Pamiers 12,906 D6
Pantin 42,651 B1
Paray-le-Monial 11,523 F4
Paris (cap.) 2,291,554 B2
Parthenay 12,549 C4
Pau 81,560 C6
Périgueux 34,779 D5
Péronne 8,358 E3
Perpignan 101,198 E6
Pessac 50,333 C5
Pézenas 6,768 E6
Pithiviers 9,976 E3
Poitiers 78,739 D4
Pont-à-Mousson 14,461 G3
Pontarlier 17,778 G4
Pontivy 9,478 B3
Pont-l'Abbe 6,618 A4
Pontoise 26,702 E3
Port-de-Bouc 20,448 F6
Port-Saint-Louis-du-Rhône 9,649 F6
Port-Vendres 5,448 E6
Privas 9,385 F5
Provins 12,281 E3
Puteau 35,366 A2
Quimper 50,856 A4
Quimperlé 9,783 B4
Rambouillet 18,446 D3
Redon 9,528 C4
Reims 177,320 E3
Remiremont 10,250 G3
Rennes 194,094 C3

(continued on following page)

Rethel 8,189 .... F3
Révin 11,459 .... F3
Rezé 35,512 .... C4
Rive-de-Gier 17,369 .... F5
Roanne 54,999 .... E4
Rochechouart 2,953 .... D5
Rochefort 27,264 .... C4
Rodez 24,898 .... E5
Romans-sur-Isère 30,974 .... F5
Romilly-sur-Seine 17,276 .... F3
Romorantin-Lanthenay 15,727 .... D4
Roubaix 109,473 .... E2
Rouen 113,536 .... D3
Royan 17,978 .... C5
Rueil-Malmaison 62,504 .... A2
Sablé-sur-Sarthe 9,913 .... C4
Saint-Affrique 6,842 .... E5
Saint-Amand-Mont-Rond 11,896 .... E4
Saint-Brieuc 51,838 .... B3
Saint-Chamond 39,236 .... F5
Saint-Claude 12,651 .... F4
Saint-Cloud 28,052 .... A2
Saint-Denis 95,808 .... B1
Saint-Dié 22,834 .... G3
Saint-Dizier 36,377 .... F3
Sainte-Mère-Eglise 1,041 .... C3
Saintes 24,946 .... C5
Sainte-Savine 10,526 .... E3
Saint-Etienne 218,289 .... F5
Saint-Florent-sur-Cher 6,385 .... E4
Saint-Flour 6,900 .... E5
Saint-Gaudens 12,103 .... D6
Saint-Germain-en-Laye 35,351 .... A2
Saint-Gilles-Croix-de-Vie 6,569 .... B4
Saint-Girons 7,259 .... D6
Saint-Jean-d'Angély 8,801 .... C4
Saint-Jean-de-Luz 10,921 .... B6
Saint-Jean-de-Maurienne 9,525 .... G5
Saint-Jean-Pied-de-Port 1,725 .... C6
Saint-Junien 9,281 .... D5
Saint-Lô 21,670 .... C3
Saint-Malo 43,277 .... B3
Saint-Mandé 20,714 .... B2
Saint-Marcellin 6,768 .... F5
Saint-Maur-des-Fossés 80,797 .... B2
Saint-Mihiel 5,544 .... F3
Saint-Nazaire 65,228 .... B4
Saint-Omer 16,419 .... E2
Saint-Ouen 43,569 .... B1
Saint-Pol-de-Léon 6,571 .... A3
Saint-Quentin 69,956 .... E3
Saint-Raphaël 19,499 .... G6
Saint-Tropez 4,484 .... G6
Saint-Vallier 10,000 .... F5
Salon-de-Provence 31,783 .... F6
Sancerre 2,029 .... E4
Sarlat-La-Canéda 8,191 .... D5
Sarrebourg 12,442 .... G3
Sarreguemines 24,570 .... G3
Sartrouville 42,092 .... A1
Saumur 30,984 .... D4
Saverne 10,015 .... G3
Sceaux 19,651 .... A2
Sedan 23,867 .... F3
Sélestat 15,209 .... G3
Senlis 13,481 .... E3

Sens 25,621 .... E3
Sète 39,075 .... E6
Sèvres 21,100 .... A2
Sisteron 6,434 .... G5
Soissons 29,694 .... E3
Sotteville-lès-Rouen 30,393 .... D3
Stiring-Wendel 12,665 .... G3
Strasbourg 251,520 .... H3
Suresnes 37,456 .... A2
Tarare 11,931 .... F5
Tarascon 8,522 .... F6
Tarbes 54,286 .... D6
Thann 8,508 .... G4
Thiers 14,534 .... E5
Thionville 37,943 .... G3
Thonon-les-Bains 24,673 .... G4
Thouars 11,835 .... C4
Tonneins 7,256 .... D5
Toul 16,141 .... F3
Toulon 180,508 .... F6
Toulouse 371,143 .... D6
Tourcoing 102,092 .... E2
Tournon 8,568 .... F5
Tournus 7,284 .... F4
Tours 139,560 .... D4
Troyes 71,600 .... F3
Tulle 18,375 .... D5
Uckange 11,552 .... G3
Ussel 9,816 .... E5
Uzès 6,470 .... F5
Valence 67,101 .... F5
Valenciennes 41,976 .... E2
Vannes 36,722 .... B4
Vence 7,332 .... G6
Vendôme 17,828 .... D4
Vénissieux 74,264 .... F5
Verdun-sur-Meuse 22,889 .... F3
Vernon 21,184 .... D3
Versailles 93,359 .... A2
Vesoul 17,883 .... F4
Vichy 32,107 .... E4
Vienne 25,981 .... F5
Vierzon 33,057 .... E4
Villefranche 6,600 .... G6
Villefranche-de-Rouergue 10,848 .... E5
Villefranche-sur-Saône 29,996 .... F4
Villejuif 53,884 .... B2
Villemomble 28,684 .... C1
Villeneuve-Saint-Georges 31,378 .... B2
Villeneuve-sur-Lot 17,818 .... D5
Villeurbanne 115,913 .... F5
Vincennes 44,256 .... B2
Vire 12,832 .... C4
Vitré 10,989 .... C3
Vitry-le-François 19,075 .... F3
Vitry-sur-Seine 87,119 .... B2
Vizille 6,810 .... F5
Voiron 17,879 .... F5
Wissembourg 6,679 .... G3
Yvetot 10,088 .... D3

OTHER FEATURES

Adour (riv.) C6

Ain (riv.) F4
Aisne (riv.) E3
Ajaccio (gulf) B7
Allier (riv.) E5
Aube (riv.) F3
Auvergne (mts.) E5
Belle-Île (isl.) B4
Biscay (bay) B5
Blanc (mt.) G5
Bonifacio (str.) B7
Calais (Dover) (str.) D2
Causses (reg.) E5
Cévennes (mts.) E5
Charente (riv.) C5
Cher (riv.) D4
Corse (cape) B6
Corsica (isl.) B6
Côte-d'Or (mts.) F4
Cotentin (pen.) C3
Cottian Alps (range) G5
Creuse (riv.) D4
Dordogne (riv.) D5
Dore Alps (mts.) E5
Doubs (riv.) G4
Drôme (riv.) F5
Dronne (riv.) D5
Durance (riv.) F6
English (chan.) B3
Eure (riv.) D3
Faucilles (mts.) F3
Forez (mts.) E5
Fréjus (pass) G5
Gard (riv.) F5
Garonne (riv.) C5
Gave de Pau (riv.) C6
Geneva (lake) G4
Gers (riv.) D6
Gironde (riv.) C5
Graian Alps (range) A2
Groix (isl.) B4
Hague (cape) C3
Hérault (riv.) E6
Hyères (isls.) G6
Indre (riv.) D4
Isère (riv.) F5
Isle (riv.) D5
Langres (plat.) F4
Limousin (reg.) D5
Lions (gulf) F6
Little Saint Bernard (pass) G5
Loir (riv.) C4
Loire (riv.) E4
Lot (riv.) D5
Manche, La (English) (chan.) B3
Maritime Alps (range) G5
Marne (riv.) C2
Mayenne (riv.) C4
Mediterranean (sea) E7
Médoc (reg.) C5
Meuse (riv.) F3
Meuse (riv.) F3
Mont Cenis (tunnel) G5
Morvan (plat.) F4
Moselle (riv.) F3
Noirmoutier (isl.) B4
North (sea) E1
Oise (riv.) E3

Oléron (isl.) C5
Omaha (beach) C3
Orb (riv.) E6
Orne (riv.) D3
Ouessant (isl.) A3
Penmarch (pt.) A4
Perche (reg.) D3
Puy-de-Dôme (mt.) E5
Pyrenees (range) C6
Ré (isl.) C4
Rhine (riv.) G3
Rhône (riv.) F5
Risle (riv.) D3
Riviera (reg.) G6
Saint-Florent (gulf) B6
Saint-Malo (gulf) B3
Saône (riv.) F4
Sarthe (riv.) D4
Sein (isl.) A3
Seine (bay) D3
Seine (riv.) D3
Sologne (reg.) E4
Somme (riv.) D2
Tarn (riv.) E6
Ushant (Ouessant) (isl.) A3
Utah (beach) C3
Vaccarès (lag.) F6
Vienne (riv.) D4
Vilaine (riv.) C4
Vosges (mts.) G3
Yonne (riv.) E3

MONACO

CITIES and TOWNS

Monte Carlo 11,599 .... G6

* City and suburbs

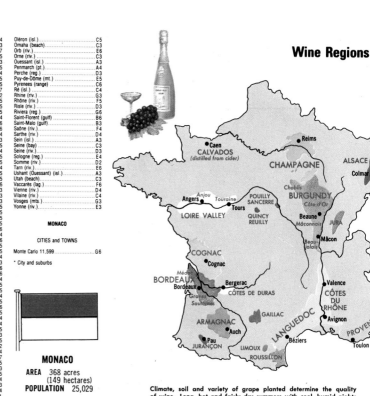

Wine Regions

Climate, soil and variety of grape planted determine the quality of wine. Long, hot and fairly dry summers with cool, humid nights constitute an ideal climate. The nature of the soil is such a determining influence that identical grapes planted in Bordeaux, Burgundy and Champagne, will yield wines of widely different types.

MONACO

AREA 368 acres
(149 hectares)
POPULATION 25,029

Agriculture, Industry and Resources

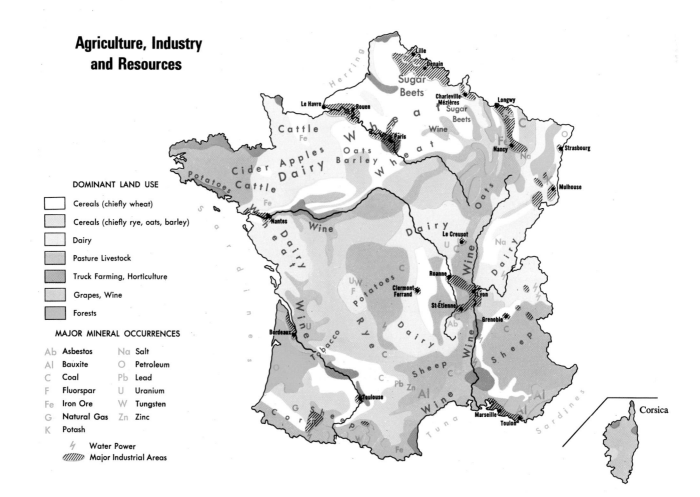

DOMINANT LAND USE

- Cereals (chiefly wheat)
- Cereals (chiefly rye, oats, barley)
- Dairy
- Pasture Livestock
- Truck Farming, Horticulture
- Grapes, Wine
- Forests

MAJOR MINERAL OCCURRENCES

- Ab Asbestos
- Al Bauxite
- C Coal
- F Fluorspar
- Fe Iron Ore
- G Natural Gas
- K Potash
- Na Salt
- O Petroleum
- Pb Lead
- U Uranium
- W Tungsten
- Zn Zinc
- ⚡ Water Power
- ▨ Major Industrial Areas

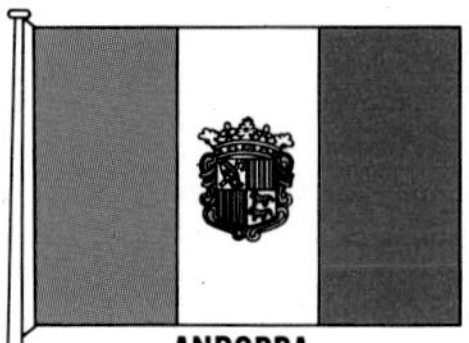
ANDORRA

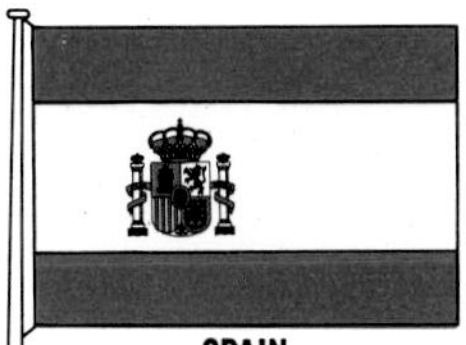
SPAIN

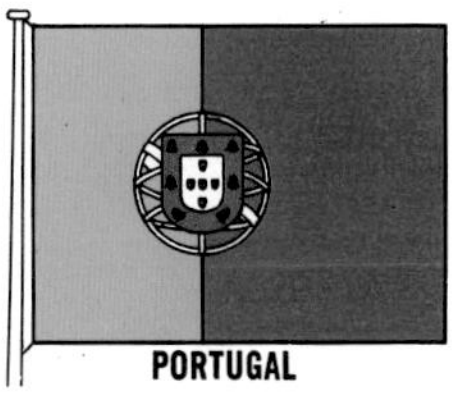
PORTUGAL

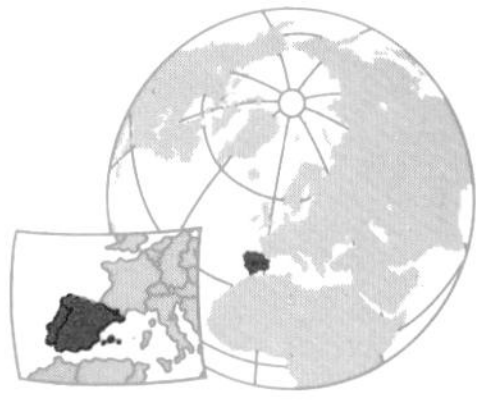

SPAIN

AREA 194,881 sq. mi. (504,742 sq. km.)
POPULATION 37,430,000
CAPITAL Madrid
LARGEST CITY Madrid
HIGHEST POINT Pico de Teide 12,172 ft. (3,710 m.) (Canary Is.); Mulhacén 11,411 ft. (3,478 m.) (mainland)
MONETARY UNIT peseta
MAJOR LANGUAGES Spanish, Catalan, Basque, Galician, Valencian
MAJOR RELIGION Roman Catholicism

PORTUGAL

AREA 35,549 sq. mi. (92,072 sq. km.)
POPULATION 9,933,000
CAPITAL Lisbon
LARGEST CITY Lisbon
HIGHEST POINT Malhão da Estrela 6,532 ft. (1,991 m.)
MONETARY UNIT escudo
MAJOR LANGUAGE Portuguese
MAJOR RELIGION Roman Catholicism

ANDORRA

AREA 188 sq. mi. (487 sq. km.)
POPULATION 31,000
CAPITAL Andorra la Vella
MONETARY UNITS French franc, Spanish peseta
MAJOR LANGUAGE Catalan
MAJOR RELIGION Roman Catholicism

GIBRALTAR

AREA 2.28 sq. mi. (5.91 sq. km.)
POPULATION 29,760
CAPITAL Gibraltar
MONETARY UNIT pound sterling
MAJOR LANGUAGES English, Spanish
MAJOR RELIGION Roman Catholicism

SPAIN

PROVINCES

Álava 204,323 ... E1
Albacete 335,026 ... E3
Alicante 920,105 ... F3
Almería 375,004 ... E4
Ávila 203,798 ... D2
Badajoz 687,599 ... C3
Baleares 558,287 ... H3
Barcelona 3,929,194 ... G2
Burgos 358,075 ... E1
Cáceres 457,777 ... C3
Cádiz 885,433 ... D4
Castellón 385,823 ... G2
Ciudad Real 507,650 ... D3
Córdoba 724,116 ... D3
Cuenca 247,158 ... E2
Gerona 414,397 ... H1
Granada 733,375 ... E4
Guadalajara 147,732 ... E2
Guipúzcoa 631,003 ... E1
Huelva 397,683 ... C4
Huesca 222,238 ... F1
Jaén 661,146 ... E4
La Coruña 1,004,188 ... B1
Las Palmas 579,710 ... C4
León 548,721 ... C1
Lérida 347,015 ... G2
Logroño 235,713 ... E1
Lugo 415,052 ... C1
Madrid 3,792,561 ... E2
Málaga 867,330 ... D4
Murcia 832,313 ... F4
Navarra 464,867 ... F1
Orense 413,733 ... C1
Oviedo 1,045,635 ... C1
Palencia 198,763 ... D1
Pontevedra 750,701 ... B1
Salamanca 371,607 ... C2
Santa Cruz de Tenerife 590,514 ... B5
Santander 467,138 ... D1
Segovia 162,770 ... D2
Sevilla 1,327,190 ... D4
Soria 114,956 ... E2
Tarragona 431,961 ... G2
Teruel 170,284 ... F2
Toledo 468,925 ... D3
Valencia 1,767,327 ... F3
Valladolid 412,572 ... D2
Vizcaya 1,043,310 ... E1
Zamora 251,934 ... D2
Zaragoza 760,186 ... F2

CITIES and TOWNS

Adra 10,851 ... E4
Aguilar 12,893 ... D4
Aguilas 15,525 ... F4
Alagón 5,114 ... F2
Alayor 5,124 ... J3
Albacete 82,607 ... F3
Albox 5,072 ... E4
Alburquerque 7,530 ... C3
Alcalá de Guadaira 28,781 ... D4
Alcalá de Henares 59,783 ... G4
Alcalá de los Gazules 5,262 ... D4
Alcalá la Real 9,849 ... E4
Alcanar 5,961 ... G2
Alcañiz 10,229 ... F2
Alcantarilla 19,895 ... F4
Alcaudete 8,557 ... E4
Alcázar de San Juan 24,620 ... E3
Alcira 30,493 ... F3
Alcora 6,711 ... F2
Alcoy 61,371 ... F3
Alfaro 8,766 ... F1
Algeciras 74,754 ... D4
Algemesí 21,158 ... F3
Alhama de Granada 6,148 ... E4
Alhama de Murcia 9,274 ... F4
Alicante 177,918 ... F3
Almadén 10,713 ... D3
Almagro 9,066 ... E3
Almansa 16,965 ... F3
Almendralejo 21,929 ... C3
Almería 104,008 ... E4
Almodóvar del Campo 7,310 ... D3
Almonte 9,960 ... C4
Almuñécar 7,812 ... E4
Álora 8,209 ... D4
Altea 7,262 ... G3
Amposta 11,767 ... G2
Andorra 6,485 ... F2
Andújar 25,962 ... D3
Antequera 28,039 ... D4
Aracena 5,390 ... C4
Aranda de Duero 18,183 ... E2
Aranjuez 28,559 ... E2
Archena 7,118 ... F3
Archidona 6,084 ... D4
Arcos de la Frontera 16,217 ... D4
Arenas de San Pedro 5,225 ... D2
Arenys de Mar 8,325 ... H2
Arévalo 5,807 ... D2
Argamasilla de Alba 6,192 ... E3
Arganda 11,876 ... G4
Arnedo 9,809 ... E1
Arrecife 21,310 ... C4
Arroyo de la Luz 8,130 ... C3
Artá 5,284 ... H3
Arucas 9,095 ... B5
Aspe 13,229 ... F3
Astorga 11,794 ... C1
Ávila de los Caballeros 30,958 ... D2
Avilés 67,186 ... C1
Ayamonte 9,897 ... C4
Ayora 5,249 ... F3
Azpeitia 7,835 ... E1
Azuaga 10,719 ... D3
Badajoz 80,793 ... C3
Badalona 162,888 ... H2
Baena 16,496 ... D4
Baeza 12,607 ... E4
Bailén 13,207 ... E3
Balaguer 11,676 ... G2
Bañolas 9,807 ... H1
Baracaldo 108,757 ... E1
Barbastro 13,243 ... F1
Barcarrota 5,012 ... C3
Barcelona 1,741,144 ... H2
Barcelona‡ 2,000,000 ... H2
Baza 14,290 ... E4
Beas de Segura 6,592 ... E3
Béjar 16,804 ... D2
Bélmez 5,161 ... D3
Benavente 11,779 ... D1
Benicarló 12,831 ... G2
Berga 11,163 ... G1
Berja 7,081 ... E4
Bermeo 16,714 ... E1
Betanzos 7,283 ... B1
Bilbao 393,179 ... E1
Bilbao‡ 450,000 ... E1
Binéfar 6,821 ... G2
Blanes 15,810 ... H2
Borjas Blancas 4,991 ... G2
Bujalance 8,236 ... D4
Bullas 8,131 ... F4
Burgos 118,366 ... E1
Burriana 21,298 ... G3
Cabeza del Buey 8,704 ... D3
Cabra 16,177 ... D4
Cáceres 53,108 ... C3
Cádiz 135,743 ... C4
Calahorra 16,315 ... E1
Calasparra 7,238 ... F3
Calatayud 16,524 ... F2
Calella 9,696 ... H2
Callosa de Ensarriá 5,701 ... G3
Calzada de Calatrava 5,751 ... E3
Campanario 7,722 ... D3
Campillos 7,014 ... D4
Campo de Criptana 12,604 ... E3
Candás 5,517 ... D1
Candeleda 5,153 ... D2
Cangas de Narcea 4,826 ... C1
Caniles 5,099 ... E4
Caravaca de le Cruz 10,411 ... E3
Carballo 5,542 ... B1
Carcagente 18,223 ... F3
Carmona 22,832 ... D4
Cartagena 52,312 ... F4
Caspe 8,766 ... G2
Cassá de la Selva 5,248 ... H2
Castellón de la Plana 79,773 ... G2
Castro del Río 10,087 ... D4
Castro-Urdiales 8,369 ... E1
Castuera 8,060 ... D3
Caudete 7,332 ... F3
Cazalla de la Sierra 5,382 ... D4
Cazorla 6,938 ... E4
Cehegín 9,661 ... F3
Cervera 5,693 ... G2
Ceuta 60,639 ... D5
Chiclana de la Frontera 22,986 ... C4
Chiva 5,394 ... F3
Ciempozuelos 9,185 ... F5
Cieza 22,929 ... F3
Ciudadela 13,701 ... H2
Ciudad Real 39,931 ... D3
Ciudad-Rodrigo 11,694 ... C2
Cocentaina 8,375 ... F3
Coín 14,190 ... D4
Colmenar de Oreja 4,930 ... G5
Colmenar Viejo 12,886 ... F4
Constantina 10,227 ... D4
Consuegra 10,026 ... E3
Córdoba 216,049 ... D4
Corella 5,850 ... F1
Coria 8,083 ... C3
Coria del Río 18,085 ... C4
Corral de Almaguer 8,006 ... E3
Crevillente 15,749 ... F3
Cuéllar 6,118 ... D2
Cuenca 33,980 ... E2
Cullera 15,128 ... F3
Daimiel 17,710 ... E3
Denia 14,514 ... G3
Dolores 5,420 ... F3
Don Benito 21,351 ... C3
Dos Hermanas 36,921 ... D4
Durango 20,403 ... E1
Écija 27,295 ... D4
Eibar 36,729 ... E1
Ejea de los Caballeros 9,766 ... F1
El Arahal 14,703 ... D4
Elche 101,271 ... F3
Elda 41,404 ... F3
Elizondo 2,516 ... F1
El Puerto de Santa María 36,451 ... C4
Espejo 5,925 ... D4
Estella 10,371 ... E1
Estepa 9,376 ... D4
Estepona 18,560 ... D4
Felanitx 9,100 ... H3
Ferrol del Caudillo 75,464 ... B1
Figueras 22,087 ... H1
Fraga 9,665 ... G2
Fregenal de la Sierra 6,826 ... C3
Fuengirola 20,597 ... D4
Fuente de Cantos 5,967 ... C3
Fuenterrabiá 2,350 ... E1
Fuentes de Andalucía 8,257 ... D4
Gandía 30,702 ... F3
Gerona 37,095 ... H2
Getafe 68,680 ... F4
Gijón 159,806 ... D1
Granada 185,799 ... E4
Granollers 30,066 ... H2
Guadalajara 30,924 ... E2
Guadix 15,311 ... E4
Guareña 7,706 ... C3
Guernica y Luno 12,046 ... E1
Haro 8,393 ... E1
Hellín 15,934 ... F3
Herencia 8,212 ... E3
Hinojosa del Duque 9,873 ... D3
Hortaleza ... G4
Hospitalet 241,978 ... H2
Huelma 5,260 ... E4
Huelva 96,689 ... C4
Huercal-Overa 5,158 ... F4
Huesca 33,076 ... F1
Huéscar 6,384 ... E4
Ibiza 16,943 ... G3
Igualada 27,941 ... G2
Inca 16,930 ... H3
Irún 38,014 ... F1
Iscar 5,192 ... D2
Isla Cristina 11,402 ... C4
Iznalloz 4,814 ... E4
Jaca 9,936 ... F1
Jaén 71,145 ... E4
Jaraíz de la Vera 6,379 ... D2
Játiva 20,934 ... F3
Jávea 6,228 ... G3
Jerez de la Frontera 112,411 ... C4
Jerez de los Caballeros 8,607 ... C3
Jijona 8,117 ... F3
Jódar 11,973 ... E4
Jumilla 16,407 ... F3
La Almunia de Doña Godina 4,835 ... F2
La Bañeza 8,480 ... C1
La Bisbal 6,374 ... H1
La Carolina 13,138 ... E3
La Coruña 184,372 ... B1
La Granja (San Ildefonso) 3,198 ... E2
La Guardia 4,967 ... B2
La Línea de la Concepción 51,021 ... D4
La Orotava 8,246 ... B4
La Palma del Condado 9,256 ... C4
La Puebla 9,923 ... H3
La Puebla de Montalbán 6,629 ... D3
La Rambla 6,525 ... D4
Laredo 9,114 ... E1
La Roda 11,460 ... E3
La Solana 13,894 ... E3
Las Palmas de Gran Canaria 260,368 ... B4
Las Pedroñeras 5,846 ... E3
La Unión 9,998 ... F4
Lebrija 15,081 ... D4
Leganés 57,537 ... F4
León 99,702 ... D1
Lérida 73,148 ... G2
Linares 45,330 ... E3
Liria 11,323 ... F3
Llerena 5,728 ... C3
Llivia 801 ... G1
Llodio 15,587 ... E1
Lluctmayor 9,630 ... H3
Logroño 83,117 ... E1
Loja 11,549 ... D4
Lora del Río 15,741 ... D4
Lorca 25,208 ... F4
Los Santos de Maimona 7,899 ... C3
Los Yébenes 5,477 ... E3
Lucena 21,527 ... D4
Lugo 53,504 ... C1
Madrid (cap.) 3,146,071 ... F4
Madrid‡ 3,500,000 ... F4
Madridejos 9,948 ... E3
Madroñera 5,397 ... D3
Mahón 17,802 ... J3
Málaga 334,988 ... D4
Málaga‡ 400,000 ... D4
Malagón 7,732 ... E3
Malpartida de Cáceres 5,054 ... C3
Manacor 20,266 ... H3
Mancha Real 7,547 ... E4
Manlleu 13,169 ... H1
Manresa 52,526 ... G2
Manzanares 15,024 ... E3
Marbella 19,648 ... D4
Marchena 16,227 ... D4
Marín 10,948 ... B1
Martos 16,395 ... E4
Mataró 73,129 ... H2
Medina del Campo 16,345 ... D2
Medina de Rioseco 4,874 ... D2
Medina-Sidonia 7,523 ... D4
Mérida 36,916 ... C3
Miajadas 8,042 ... D3
Mieres 22,790 ... D1
Minas de Ríotinto 3,939 ... C4
Miranda de Ebro 29,355 ... E1
Moguer 7,629 ... C4
Mollerusa 6,685 ... G2
Monesterio 5,923 ... C3
Monforte 14,002 ... C1
Monóvar 9,071 ... F3
Montehermoso 5,952 ... C2
Montellano 6,658 ... D4
Montijo 11,931 ... C3
Montilla 18,670 ... D4
Montoro 9,295 ... D3
Monzón 14,089 ... G2
Mora 10,523 ... E3
Moratalla 5,101 ... E3
Morón de la Frontera 25,662 ... D4
Mota del Cuervo 5,130 ... E3
Motril 25,121 ... E4
Mula 9,168 ... F3
Munera 5,003 ... E3
Murcia 102,242 ... F4
Navalcarnero 6,212 ... F4
Navalmoral de la Mata 9,650 ... D3
Nerja 7,413 ... E4
Nerva 10,830 ... C4
Novelda 16,867 ... F3
Nules 9,027 ... F3
Ocaña 5,603 ... E3
Oliva 16,717 ... F3
Oliva de la Frontera 8,560 ... C3
Olivenza 7,616 ... C3
Olot 18,062 ... H1
Olvera 9,825 ... D4
Onda 13,012 ... F3
Onteniente 23,685 ... F3
Orense 63,542 ... C1
Orihuela 17,610 ... F3
Osuna 17,384 ... D4
Oviedo 130,021 ... C1
Padul 6,377 ... E4
Palafrugell 10,421 ... H2
Palamós 7,679 ... H2
Palencia 58,327 ... D2
Palma 191,416 ... H3
Palma del Río 15,075 ... D4
Pamplona 142,686 ... F1
Pego 8,861 ... F3
Peñafiel 4,794 ... E2
Peñaranda de Bracamonte 6,094 ... D2
Peñarroya-Pueblonuevo 15,649 ... D3
Pinos-Puente 7,634 ... E4
Plasencia 26,897 ... C2
Pola de Lena 5,760 ... D1
Pollensa 7,625 ... H3
Ponferrada 22,838 ... C1
Pontevedra 27,118 ... B1
Porcuna 8,169 ... D4
Port-Bou 2,230 ... H1
Portugalete 45,589 ... E1
Posadas 7,245 ... D4
Pozoblanco 13,280 ... D3
Pozuelo de Alarcón 14,041 ... D2
Priego de Córdoba 12,676 ... D4
Puente-Genil 22,888 ... D4
Puertollano 50,609 ... D3
Puerto Real 13,993 ... D4
Puigcerdá 4,418 ... G1
Quesada 6,965 ... E4
Quintana de la Serena 5,171 ... D3
Quintanar de la Orden 7,764 ... E3
Reinosa 10,863 ... D1
Requena 9,836 ... F3
Reus 47,240 ... G2
Ripoll 9,283 ... H1
Ronda 22,094 ... D4
Roquetas 5,617 ... G2
Rosas 5,448 ... H1
Rota 20,021 ... C4
Rute 8,294 ... D4
Sabadell 148,223 ... H2
Sagunto 17,052 ... F3
Salamanca 125,132 ... D2
Sallent 7,118 ... H2
Salobreña 5,961 ... E4
Salt 5,572 ... H1
Sama 9,863 ... D1
San Carlos de la Rápita 8,946 ... G2
San Clemente 6,016 ... E3
San Feliu de Guíxols 12,006 ... H2
San Fernando 59,309 ... C4
San Ildefonso 3,198 ... E2

Agriculture, Industry and Resources

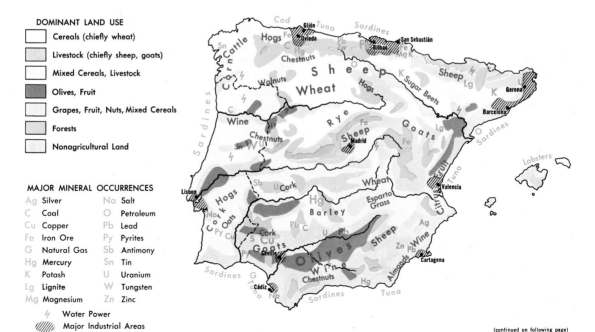

DOMINANT LAND USE

- Cereals (chiefly wheat)
- Livestock (chiefly sheep, goats)
- Mixed Cereals, Livestock
- Olives, Fruit
- Grapes, Fruit, Nuts, Mixed Cereals
- Forests
- Nonagricultural Land

MAJOR MINERAL OCCURRENCES

Ag	Silver	Na	Salt
C	Coal	O	Petroleum
Cu	Copper	Pb	Lead
Fe	Iron Ore	Py	Pyrites
G	Natural Gas	Sb	Antimony
Hg	Mercury	Sn	Tin
K	Potash	U	Uranium
Lg	Lignite	W	Tungsten
Mg	Magnesium	Zn	Zinc

Water Power
Major Industrial Areas

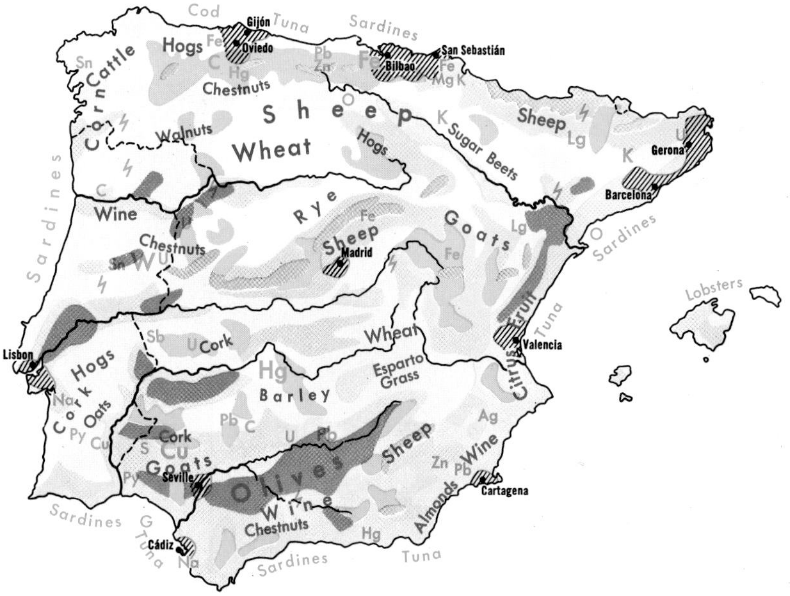

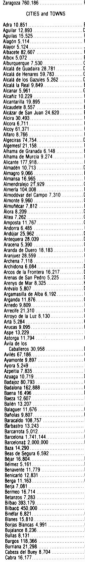

(continued on following page)

San Lorenzo de El
  Escorial 8,098 .... E2
Sanlúcar de Barrameda 29,483 ... C4
Sanlúcar la Mayor 6,121 .... C4
San Roque 8,224 .... D4
San Sebastián 159,557 .... F1
Santa Cruz de la Palma 10,393 .. B4
Santa Cruz de Mudela 6,354 ..... E3
Santa Cruz de Tenerife 74,910 .. B4
Santa Eugenia 5,946 .... B1
Santa Fé 8,990 .... E4
Santander 130,019 .... D1
Santiago 51,620 .... B1
Santo Domingo de la
  Calzada 5,638 .... E1
Santoña 9,546 .... E1
San Vicente de
  Alcántara 7,006 .... C3
Saragossa 449,319 .... F2
Saragossa† 500,000 .... F2
Segorbe 6,962 .... F3
Segovia 41,880 .... D2
Seo de Urgel 6,604 .... G1
Seville 511,447 .... D4
Seville† 560,000 .... D4
Sitges 8,906 .... G2
Socuéllamos 12,610 .... E3
Sóller 6,470 .... H3
Solsona 5,346 .... G2
Sonseca 6,594 .... D3
Soria 24,744 .... E2
Sotrondio 5,914 .... D1
Sueca 20,019 .... F3
Tabernes de Valldigna 13,962 ... F3
Tafalla 8,858 .... F1
Talavera de la Reina 39,889 .... D2
Tarancón 8,238 .... E3
Tarazona 11,067 .... E2
Tarazona de la Mancha 5,952 .... E3
Tarifa 9,201 .... D4
Tarragona 53,548 .... G2
Tàrrega 9,036 .... G2
Tauste 6,832 .... F2
Telde 13,257 .... B5
Teruel 20,614 .... F2

Tobarra 5,887 .... F3
Toledo 43,905 .... D3
Tolosa 15,164 .... F1
Tomelloso 26,041 .... E3
Tordesillas 5,815 .... D2
Toro 8,455 .... D2
Torredonjimeno 12,507 .... D4
Torrejón de Ardoz 21,081 ...... G4
Torrelavega 19,933 .... D1
Torremolinos 20,484 .... D4
Torrente 38,397 .... F3
Torrevieja 9,431 .... F4
Torrijos 6,362 .... D3
Torrox 5,583 .... E4
Tortosa 20,030 .... G2
Totana 12,714 .... F4
Trigueros 6,280 .... C4
Trujillo 9,024 .... D3
Tudela 20,942 .... E1
Úbeda 28,306 .... E3
Utiel 9,168 .... E3
Utrera 28,287 .... D4
Valdemoro 6,263 .... F4
Valdepeñas 24,018 .... E3
Valencia 626,675 .... F3
Valencia† 700,000 .... F3
Valencia de Alcántara 5,963 ... C3
Valladolid 227,511 .... D2
Vall de Uxó 23,976 .... F3
Vallecas G4
Valls 14,189 .... G2
Valverde del Camino 10,566 .... C4
Vejer de la Frontera 6,184 .... C4
Vélez-Málaga 20,794 .... E4
Vendrell 7,951 .... G2
Vera 4,903 .... F4
Vergara 11,541 .... E1
Vicálvaro G4
Vich 23,449 .... H2
Vigo 114,526 .... B1
Vilafranca del
  Penadés 16,875 .... G2
Villacañas 9,883 .... E3
Villacarrillo 9,452 .... E3
Villafranca de los

Barros 12,610 .... C3
Villagarcía 6,601 .... B1
Villajoyosa 12,573 .... F3
Villanueva de Córdoba 11,270 .. D3
Villanueva del Arzobispo 8,076 . E3
Villanueva de la Serena 16,687 . D3
Villanueva de los
  Infantes 7,8,154 .... E3
Villanueva y Geltrú 35,714 .... G2
Villarreal de los
  Infantes 29,482 .... F3
Villarrobledo 19,698 .... E3
Villarrubia de los Ojos 9,144 . E3
Villaverde F4
Villena 23,483 .... F3
Vinaroz 13,727 .... G2
Vitoria 124,791 .... E1
Yecla 19,352 .... F3
Zafra 11,583 .... C3
Zalamea de la Serena 6,017 .... D3
Zamora 48,791 .... D2
Zaragoza (Saragossa) 449,319 .. F2

OTHER FEATURES

Alborán (isl.) E5
Alcaraz, Sierra de (range) E3
Alcudia (bay) H3
Almanzor (mt.) D3
Almanzora (riv.) F4
Andalusia (reg.) C4
Aneto (peak) G1
Aragón (reg.) F2
Arosa, Ría de (est.) B1
Asturias (reg.) C1
Balaitous (mt.) F1
Balearic (Baleares)
  (isls.) H3
Barbate (riv.) D4
Biscay (bay) E1
Cabrera (isl.) H3
Cádiz (gulf) C4
Cala Burras (pt.) H3
Canary (isls.) B4
Cantabrian (range) C1
Catalonia (reg.) G2

Cinca (riv.) G2
Columbretes (isls.) G3
Costa Brava (reg.) H2
Costa de Sola (Costa del Sol)
  (reg.) D4
Creus (cape) H1
Cuenca, Sierra de (range) F3
Demanda, Sierra de la (range) . E1
Douro (riv.) C2
Duero (Douro) (riv.) C2
Ebro (riv.) E2
Eresma (riv.) D2
Esla (riv.) D1
Estats (peak) G1
Estremadura (reg.) C3
Finisterre (cape) B1
Formentera (isl.) G3
Formentor (cape) H2
Fuerteventura (isl.) B4
Galicia (reg.) B1
Gata (cape) F4
Gata (mts.) C2
Genil (riv.) D4
Gibraltar (str.) D5
Gomera (isl.) B5
Gran Canaria (isl.) B5
Gredos, Sierra de (range) D3
Guadalimar (riv.) E3
Guadalquivir (riv.) D3
Guadarrama, Sierra de (range) . E2
Guadarrama (riv.) E2
Guadiana (riv.) D3
Güdar, Sierra de (range) F2
Henares (riv.) G4
Hierro (isl.) A5
Ibiza (isl.) G3
Jalón (riv.) E2
Jarama (riv.) E2
Júcar (riv.) F3
Lanzarote (isl.) C4
La Palma (isl.) A4
León (reg.) C1
Llobregat (riv.) H2
Majorca (isl.) H3
Mallorca (Majorca)
  (isl.) H3

Mancha, La (reg.) E3
Manzanares (riv.) F4
Marismas, Las (marsh) C4
Mar Menor (lag.) F4
Mayor (cape) F1
Menorca (Minorca) (isl.) J2
Miño (riv.) B1
Moncayo, Sierra de (range) J2
Montserrat (mt.) G2
Morena, Sierra (range) E3
Mulhacén (mt.) E4
Murcia (reg.) F4
Nao (cape) G3
Navia (riv.) C1
Nevada, Sierra (mts.) E4
New Castile (reg.) E3
Odiel (riv.) C4
Old Castile (reg.) D2
Órbigo (riv.) D1
Palos (cape) F4
Peñalara (mt.) D2
Peñas (cape) D1
Penibética, Sistema (range) ... E4
Perdido (mt.) G1
Pyrenees (range) F1

Rosas (gulf) H1
San Jorge (gulf) G2
Segura (riv.) F3
Sil (riv.) C1
Tajo (Tagus) (riv.) D3
Teide, Pico de (peak) B5
Tenerife (isl.) B5
Ter (riv.) H1
Tinto (riv.) C4
Toledo (mts.) E3
Tortosa (cape) G2
Trafalgar (cape) D4
Turia (riv.) F3
Urgel, Llanos de (plain) G2
Valencia (gulf) G3
Valencia, Albufera de (lag.) .. G3
Vascongadas (reg.) E1

PORTUGAL

DISTRICTS

Aveiro 545,230 .... B2

Beja 204,440 .... C3
Braga 609,415 .... B2
Bragança 180,395 .... C2
Castelo Branco 254,355 .... C3
Coimbra 399,380 .... B2
Évora 226,840 .... C3
Faro 268,040 .... B4
Guarda 270,720 .... C2
Leiria 376,940 .... B3
Lisbon 1,568,020 .... A3
Oporto (Porto)
  1,309,560 .... B2
Portalegre 145,545 .... C3
Porto 1,309,560 .... B2
Santarém 427,995 .... B3
Setúbal 469,555 .... B3
Viana do Castelo
  250,510 .... B2
Vila Real 265,605 .... B2
Viseu 410,795 .... C2

CITIES and TOWNS

Abrantes 11,775 .... B3
Águeda 9,343 .... B2
Albufeira 7,479 .... B4
Alcácer do Sal 13,187 .... B3
Alcântara 23,699 .... A1

Topography

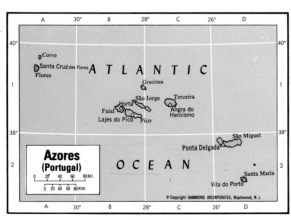

Azores (Portugal)

AZORES

INTERNAL DIVISIONS

Angra do Heroísmo
  (dist.) 83,500 .... C1
Horta (dist.) 38,700 .... A1
Ponta Delgada (dist.) 153,700 . D2

CITIES and TOWNS

Angra do Heroísmo 13,795 ...... C1
Horta 6,145 .... B1
Lajes do Pico 2,147 .... B1
Ponta Delgada 20,195 .... C2
Santa Cruz das Flores 1,880 ... A1
Vila do Porto 4,149 .... D2

OTHER FEATURES

Azores (isls.) A2
Corvo (isl.) A1
Faial (isl.) A1
Flores (isl.) A1
Graciosa (isl.) C1
Pico (isl.) B1
Santa Maria (isl.) D2
São Jorge (isl.) B1
São Miguel (isl.) C1
Terceira (isl.) C1

© Copyright HAMMOND INCORPORATED, Maplewood, N.J.

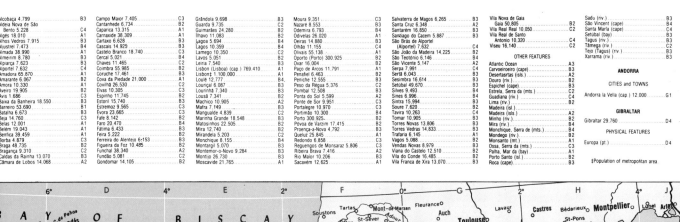

Alcobaça 4,799	B3	Campo Maior 7,405	C3
Aldeia Nova de São Bento 5,228	C4	Cantanhede 6,734	B2
Algés 18,010	A1	Caparica 13,315	A1
Alhos Vedros 7,915	B3	Cartaxo 38,309	B3
Aljustrel 7,473	B4	Cartaxo 6,628	B3
Almada 38,990	A1	Cascais 14,925	A1
Almeirim 8,780	B3	Castelo Branco 18,740	C2
Alpiarça 7,623	A1	Cercal 5,021	B4
Alportel 7,632	C4	Chaves 11,465	C2
Amadora 65,870	A1	Coimbra 55,985	B2
Amarante 6,067	B2	Coruche 17,461	B3
Amora 10,330	A1	Cova da Piedade 21,000	A1
Aveiro 19,905	B2	Covilhã 26,530	C2
Avis 1,686	B3	Espinho 11,745	B2
Baixa da Banheira 18,550	A1	Estoril 15,740	A1
Barreiro 53,690	B1	Estremoz 9,565	C3
Batalha 6,673	B3	Évora 23,665	C3
Beja 14,760	C3	Fafe 8,142	B2
Belas 12,001	A1	Faro 20,470	B4
Belém 19,043	A1	Fátima 6,433	B3
Benfica 39,459	A1	Feira 5,222	B2
Borba 4,878	C3	Ferreira do Alentejo 6,153	B3
Braga 48,735	B2	Figueira da Foz 10,485	B2
Bragança 9,310	C2	Funchal 38,340	A2
Caldas da Rainha 13,070	B3	Fundão 5,081	C2
Câmara de Lobos 14,068	A2	Gondomar 14,105	B2

Grândola 9,698	B3	Moura 9,351	C3
Guarda 9,735	C2	Nazaré 8,553	B3
Guimarães 24,280	B2	Odemira 6,793	B4
Ílhavo 11,083	B2	Odivelas 26,020	A1
Lagoa 5,694	B4	Oeiras 14,880	A1
Lagos 14,920	B4	Olhão 11,155	C4
Lamego 10,350	C2	Olivais 55,138	A1
Lavos 5,051	B2	Oporto (Porto) 300,925	B2
Leiria 7,540	B3	Ovar 16,004	B2
Lisbon (Lisboa) (cap.) 769,410	A1	Paço de Arcos 11,791	A1
Lisbon† 1,100,000	A1	Penafiel 6,463	B2
Loulé 12,777	B4	Peniche 12,555	A3
Lourical 6,697	B3	Peso da Régua 5,376	C2
Lourinhã 7,340	A3	Pombal 12,508	B3
Lousã 7,341	B2	Ponta do Sol 5,599	A2
Machico 10,905	A2	Ponte de Sor 9,951	B3
Mafra 7,149	A3	Portalegre 10,970	C3
Mangualde 4,839	C2	Portimão 10,300	C4
Marinha Grande 18,548	B3	Porto 300,925	B2
Matosinhos 22,505	B2	Póvoa de Varzim 17,415	B2
Mira 6,433	B2	Proença-a-Nova 4,792	B3
Mirandela 5,203	C2	Queluz 25,845	A1
Monção 8,555	B2	Redondo 6,858	C3
Monchique 5,070	B4	Reguengos de Monsaraz 5,806	C3
Montargil 5,070	B3	Ribeira Brava 7,416	A2
Montemor-o-Novo 9,284	B3	Rio Maior 10,206	A1
Montijo 26,730	A1		
Moscavide 21,765	A1	Sacavém 12,625	A1

Salvaterra de Magos 6,265	B3	Vila Nova de Gaia 50,805	B2
Santa Cruz 6,348	A2	Vila Real 60,050	C2
Santarém 16,850	B3	Vila Real de Santo António 10,320	C4
Santiago do Cacem 5,887	B3	Viseu 16,140	C2
São Brás de Alportel 7,632	C4		
São João da Madeira 14,225	B2	**OTHER FEATURES**	
São Teotónio 6,146	B4	Atlantic Ocean	A3
São Vicente 5,147	A2	Carvoeiroro (cape)	B3
Serpa 7,991	C3	Desertartas (isls.)	B4
Sertã 6,043	B3	Douro (riv.)	B2
Sesimbra 16,614	A3	Espichel (cape)	A3
Setúbal 49,670	B3	Estrela, Serra da (mts.)	C2
Silves 9,493	B4	Guadiana (riv.)	C4
Sines 6,996	B4	Lima (riv.)	B2
Soure 7,620	B2	Madeira (isl.)	A2
Tavira 10,263	C4	Madeira (isls.)	A2
Tomar 10,905	B3	Minho (riv.)	B2
Torres Novas 13,806	B3	Mira (riv.)	B4
Torres Vedras 14,833	A3	Monchique, Serra de (mts.)	B4
Trafaria 6,145	A1	Mondego (riv.)	B2
Vagos 5,088	B2	Monsanto (riv.)	C2
Vendas Novas 8,979	B3	Odsa, Serra da (mts.)	C3
Viana do Castelo 12,510	B2	Porto Santo (isl.)	A2
Vila do Conde 16,485	B2	Roca (cape)	B3
Vila Franca de Xira 13,070	B3		

Sado (riv.)	B3
São Vincent (cape)	B4
Santa Maria (cape)	C4
Setubal (bay)	B3
Tagus (riv.)	B3
Tâmega (riv.)	C2
Tejo (Tagus) (riv.)	B3
Xarrama (riv.)	B3

ANDORRA

CITIES and TOWNS

Andorra la Vella (cap.) 12,000 ... G1

GIBRALTAR

Gibraltar 29,760 ... D4

PHYSICAL FEATURES

Europa (pt.) ... D4

‡Population of metropolitan area.

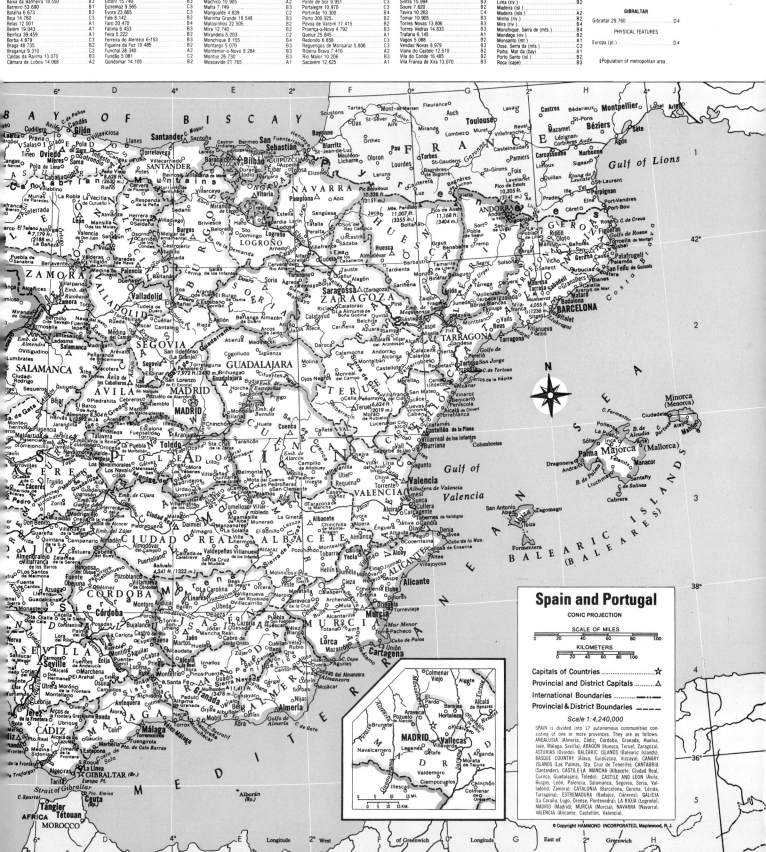

Spain and Portugal

CONIC PROJECTION

SCALE OF MILES

0 20 40 60 80 100

KILOMETERS

0 20 40 60 80 100

Capitals of Countries ....☆
Provincial and District Capitals ....△
International Boundaries ....▬▬▬
Provincial & District Boundaries .....▬ ▬ ▬

Scale 1:4,240,000

SPAIN is divided into 17 autonomous communities consisting of one or more provinces. They are as follows: ANDALUSIA (Almería, Cádiz, Córdoba, Granada, Huelva, Jaén, Málaga, Sevilla); ARAGÓN (Huesca, Teruel, Zaragoza); ASTURIAS (Oviedo); BALEARIC ISLANDS (Balearic Islands); BASQUE COUNTRY (Álava, Guipúzcoa, Vizcaya); CANARY ISLANDS (Las Palmas, Sta. Cruz de Tenerife); CANTABRIA (Santander); CASTILE-LA MANCHA (Albacete, Ciudad Real, Cuenca, Guadalajara, Toledo); CASTILE AND LEON (Ávila, Burgos, León, Palencia, Salamanca, Segovia, Soria, Valladolid, Zamora); CATALONIA (Barcelona, Gerona, Lérida, Tarragona); ESTREMADURA (Badajoz, Cáceres); GALICIA (La Coruña, Lugo, Orense, Pontevedra); LA RIOJA (Logroño); MADRID (Madrid); MURCIA (Murcia); NAVARRA (Navarra); VALENCIA (Alicante, Castellón, Valencia).

© Copyright HAMMOND INCORPORATED, Maplewood, N.J.

VATICAN CITY

AREA 108.7 acres (44 hectares)
POPULATION 728

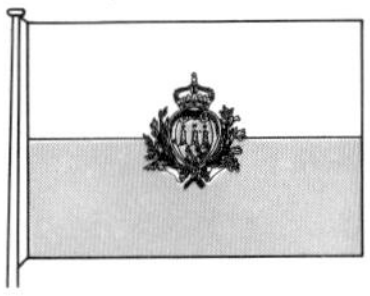

SAN MARINO

AREA 23.4 sq. mi. (60.6 sq. km.)
POPULATION 19,149

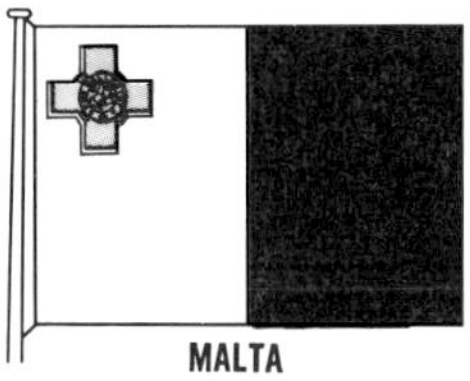

MALTA

AREA 122 sq. mi. (316 sq. km.)
POPULATION 343,970
CAPITAL Valletta
LARGEST CITY Sliema
HIGHEST POINT 787 ft. (240 m.)
MONETARY UNIT Maltese lira
MAJOR LANGUAGES Maltese, English
MAJOR RELIGION Roman Catholicism

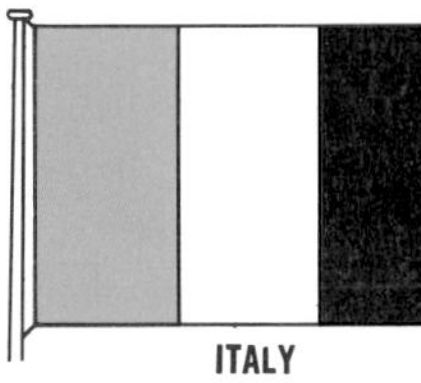

ITALY

AREA 116,303 sq. mi. (301,225 sq. km.)
POPULATION 57,140,000
CAPITAL Rome
LARGEST CITY Rome
HIGHEST POINT Dufourspitze (Mte. Rosa) 15,203 ft. (4,634 m.)
MONETARY UNIT lira
MAJOR LANGUAGE Italian
MAJOR RELIGION Roman Catholicism

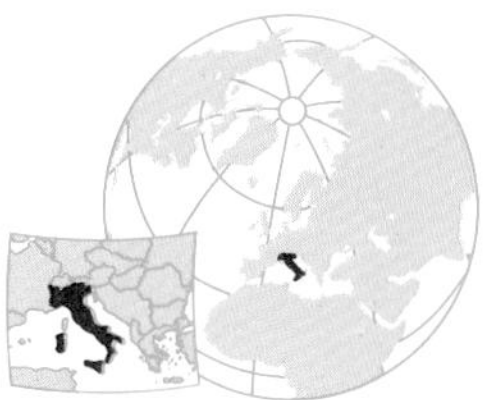

ITALY

REGIONS

Abruzzi 1,166,664 D3
Aosta 109,150 A2
Apulia (Puglia) 3,582,787 F4
Basilicata 603,064 F4
Calabria 1,988,051 F5
Campania 5,059,348 E4
Emilia-Romagna 3,846,755 C2
Friuli-Venezia Giulia 1,213,532 D1
Latium (Lazio) 4,689,482 D3
Liguria 1,853,578 B2
Lombardy 8,543,657 B2
Marche 1,359,907 D3
Molise 319,807 E4
Piedmont 4,432,313 A2
Sardinia 1,473,800 B4
Sicily 4,680,715 D6
Trentino-Alto Adige 841,886 C1
Tuscany 3,473,097 C3
Umbria 775,783 D3
Veneto 2,109,502 D3

PROVINCES

Agrigento 454,045 D6
Alessandria 483,183 B2
Ancona 416,611 D3
Aosta 109,150 A2
Arezzo 306,340 C3
Ascoli Piceno 340,758 D3
Asti 218,547 B2
Avellino 427,509 E4
Bari 1,351,288 F4
Belluno 221,155 D1
Benevento 286,499 E4
Bergamo 829,019 B2
Bologna 918,844 C2
Bolzano-Bozen 414,041 C1
Brescia 957,686 C2
Brindisi 366,027 G4
Cagliari 802,888 B5
Caltanissetta 282,069 D6
Campobasso 227,641 E4
Caserta 677,959 E4
Catania 938,273 E6
Catanzaro 718,069 F5
Chieti 351,567 E3
Como 720,463 B2
Cosenza 691,659 F5
Cremona 334,281 B2
Cuneo 540,504 A2
Enna 202,131 E6
Ferrara 383,639 C2
Florence 1,146,367 C3
Foggia 657,292 E4
Forlì 565,470 D2
Frosinone 422,630 D4
Genoa 1,087,973 B2
Gorizia 142,412 D2
Grosseto 216,315 C3
Imperia 225,127 B3
Isernia 92,166 E4
L'Aquila 293,066 D3
La Spezia 244,435 B2
Latina 376,238 D4
Lecce 696,503 G4
Leghorn 335,265 C3
Lucca 380,356 C3
Macerata 286,155 D3
Mantua 376,892 C2
Massa-Carrara 200,955 C2
Matera 194,629 F4
Messina 654,703 E5
Milan 3,903,685 B2
Modena 553,852 C2
Naples 2,709,929 E4
Novara 496,811 B2
Nuoro 273,021 B4
Padua 762,998 C2
Palermo 1,124,015 D5
Parma 395,497 C2
Pavia 526,389 B2
Perugia 552,936 D3
Pesaro e Urbino 316,383 D3
Pescara 264,981 E3
Piacenza 284,881 B2
Pisa 375,933 C3
Pistoia 254,335 C2
Pordenone 253,906 D2
Potenza 408,435 E4
Ragusa 255,047 E6
Ravenna 351,876 D2
Reggio di Calabria 578,323 E5
Reggio nell'Emilia 392,696 C2
Rieti 143,162 D3
Rome 3,490,377 F6
Rovigo 251,908 C2
Salerno 957,452 E4
Sassari 397,891 B4
Savona 296,043 B2
Siena 257,221 C3
Sondrio 169,149 B1
Syracuse 365,039 E6
Taranto 511,677 F4
Teramo 257,080 D3
Terni 222,847 D3
Trapani 405,393 D5
Trento 427,845 C1
Treviso 668,620 D2
Trieste 300,304 E2
Turin 2,287,016 A2
Udine 516,910 D1
Varese 725,823 B2
Venice 807,251 D2
Vercelli 406,252 B2
Verona 733,595 C2
Vicenza 677,884 C2
Viterbo 257,075 C3

CITIES and TOWNS

Acireale 34,081 E6
Acqui Terme 20,099 B2
Acri 8,150 F5
Adrano 31,988 E6
Adria 11,951 D2
Agira 11,262 E6
Agnone 3,965 E4
Agrigento 40,513 D6
Agropoli 9,413 E4
Alassio 13,512 A2
Alatri 5,710 D4
Alba 23,522 B2
Albano Laziale 15,561 F7
Albenga 13,397 B3
Albino 8,837 B2
Alcamo 41,448 D6
Alessandria 78,644 B2
Alghero 28,454 B4
Altamura 44,879 F4
Amalfi 4,205 E4
Amantea 6,132 E5
Amelia 4,331 D3
Ancona 88,427 D3
Andria 76,405 F4
Anguillara Sabazia 3,241 F6
Anzio 14,966 D4
Aosta 35,053 A2
Aprilia 18,412 D4
Aragona 11,213 D6
Arezzo 56,693 C3
Argenta 6,682 D2
Ariano Irpino 9,796 E4
Ariccia 7,287 F7
Artena 5,034 F7
Ascoli Piceno 43,041 D3
Assisi 4,630 D3
Asti 62,277 B2
Atessa 3,079 E3
Atri 4,686 D3
Augusta 32,501 E6
Avellino 44,750 E4
Aversa 46,536 E4
Avezzano 26,456 D3
Avigliano 5,400 E4
Avola 29,089 E6
Bagheria 32,465 D5
Barcellona Pozzo di Gotto 25,280 E5
Bari 339,110 F4
Barletta 75,116 F4
Bassano del Grappa 33,002 C2
Bellagio 3,258 B2
Belluno 22,180 D1
Benevento 48,523 E4
Bergamo 127,553 B2
Biancavilla 18,743 E6
Biella 46,453 B2
Bisceglie 45,014 F4
Bitonto 39,714 F4
Bitti 4,606 B4
Bologna 493,282 C2
Bolzano (Bolzen) 102,806 C1
Bondeno 7,451 C2
Bonorva 5,232 B4
Bordighera 8,994 A3
Borgo 4,013 C1
Borgomanero 16,655 B2
Bôrgo San Lorenzo 7,699 C2
Bosa 8,045 B4
Boves 3,896 A2
Bra 18,399 A2
Bracciano 7,681 C3
Brescia 189,092 C2
Bressanone 12,261 C1
Brindisi 76,612 G4
Bronte 17,823 E6
Brunico 5,175 D1
Budrio 5,635 C2
Busto Arsizio 72,400 B2
Cagli 4,356 D3
Cagliari 211,015 B5
Caltagirone 34,444 E6
Caltanissetta 52,838 D6
Camaiore 8,578 C3
Camerino 4,644 D3
Campobasso 35,551 E4
Campo Tures 1,325 C1
Canicatti 28,761 E6
Canosa di Puglia 30,263 E4
Cantù 28,617 B2
Capua 13,938 E4
Caravaggio 11,298 B2
Carbonia 23,031 B5
Carini 14,255 D5
Carloforte 6,671 B5
Carmagnola 16,469 A2
Carpi 41,789 C2
Carrara 56,236 C2
Casale Monferrato 35,156 B2
Casalmaggiore 6,374 C2
Cascina-Navacchio 28,263 C3
Caserta 51,621 E4
Cassano allo Ionio 9,661 F5
Cassino 14,747 D4
Castelfranco Veneto 16,042 D2
Castel Gandolfo 2,965 F7
Castellammare del Golfo 13,144 D5
Castellammare di Stabia 64,341 E4
Castel San Pietro Terme 6,985 C2
Castelvetrano 29,167 D6
Castiglion Fiorentino 3,797 C3
Castrovillari 15,207 F5
Catania 403,390 E6
Catanzaro 52,054 F5
Caulonia 3,402 F5
Cava de'Tirreni 33,868 E4
Cavarzere 7,917 D2
Cecina 19,415 C3
Cefalù 11,043 E5
Ceglie Messapico 17,512 F4
Celano 9,531 D3
Cerignola 44,648 E4
Cernobbio 8,026 B2
Cerveteri 5,239 E6
Cesano 2,883 F6
Cesena 49,915 D2
Cesenatico 12,805 D2
Chiari 12,017 C2
Chiavari 29,950 B2
Chieri 27,548 A2
Chieti 31,895 E3
Chioggia 24,044 D2
Chivasso 21,369 A2
Ciampino 36,728 F7
Cittadella 9,321 C2
Città di Castello 18,880 C3
Cittanova 11,045 F5
Cividale del Friuli 8,345 D1
Civitavecchia 41,305 C3
Clusone-Fiorine 6,428 C2
Codroipo 6,117 D2
Colle di Val d'Elsa 8,657 C3
Comacchio 10,437 D2
Comiso 24,508 E6
Como 73,257 B2
Conegliano 28,635 D2
Conversano 16,805 F4
Corato 38,163 F4
Cori 6,829 F7
Corigliano Calabro 14,518 F5
Corleone 11,057 D6
Correggio 11,415 C2
Cortina d'Ampezzo 7,285 D1
Cortona 3,482 C3
Cosenza 94,565 F5
Courmayeur 1,401 A2
Crema 26,061 B2
Cremona 75,988 B2
Crotone 44,081 F5
Cuneo 41,633 A2
Cuorgnè 6,752 A2
Desenzano del Garda 14,624 C2
Diano Marina 6,001 B3
Domodossola 18,562 A1
Dorgali 6,714 B4
Eboli 19,787 E4
Edolo 3,707 C1
Empoli 30,526 C3
Enna 27,351 E6
Este 12,992 C2
Fabriano 18,355 D3
Faenza 36,241 D2
Fano 31,238 D3
Fasano 21,247 F4
Favara 27,940 D6
Feltre 11,806 C1
Fermo 17,521 D3
Ferrandina 8,372 F4
Ferrara 97,507 C2
Fidenza 18,064 B2
Fiesole 3,772 C3
Finale Emilia 7,474 C2
Finale Ligure 11,461 B2
Firenze (Florence) 441,654 C3
Fiumicino 13,180 F7
Florence 441,654 C3
Floridia 16,562 E6
Foggia 136,436 E4
Foligno 26,887 D3
Fondi 16,472 D4
Forlì 83,303 D2
Formia 18,978 D4
Fossano 15,857 A2
Fossombrone 5,882 D3
Francavilla Fontana 30,347 F4
Frascati 14,217 F7
Frosinone 34,066 D4
Gaeta 21,973 D4
Galatina 22,137 G4
Galatone 13,880 F4
Gallarate 43,773 B2
Gallipoli 16,878 F4
Garessio 3,359 A2
Gela 66,845 E6
Gemona 6,863 D1
Genoa 787,011 B2
Genova (Genoa) 787,011 B2
Genzano di Roma 14,147 F7
Giarre 18,233 E6
Gioia del Colle 23,299 F4
Gioiosa Ionica 3,811 F5
Giovinazzo 17,768 F4
Giulianova 17,926 E3
Gorizia 35,912 D2
Gravina in Puglia 32,006 F4
Grosseto 48,309 C3
Grottaferrata 10,639 F7
Grottaglie 23,556 F4
Guardiagrele 4,122 E3
Guastalla 7,639 C2
Gubbio 12,371 D3
Guidonia 8,413 F6
Iglesias 24,472 B5
Imola 42,111 C2
Imperia 37,585 B3
Isernia 12,290 E4
Ivrea 26,530 B2
Jesi 33,011 D3
Ladispoli 6,625 E6
Lagonegro 5,613 E4
La Maddalena 10,405 B4
Lanciano 19,652 E3
Lanusei 5,508 B5
Lanuvio 2,970 F7
L'Aquila 36,233 D3
Larino 5,166 E4
La Spezia 121,254 B2
Latina 53,003 D4
Lauria 4,927 E4
Lavello 11,486 E4
Lecce 80,114 G4
Lecco 53,165 B2
Leghorn 170,369 C3
Legnago 15,534 C2
Lendinara 7,079 C2
Lentini 31,429 E6
Leonforte 16,317 E6
Lerici 5,407 B2
Licata 40,997 D6
Lido di Ostia 61,492 F7
Lido di Venezia 18,794 D2
Lipari 3,886 E5
Livigno 2,135 C1
Livorno (Leghorn) 170,369 C3
Lodi 42,489 B2
Lonigo 6,368 C2
Lucca 54,280 C3
Lucera 29,355 E4
Lugo 19,497 D2
Macerata 33,470 D3
Macomer 9,433 B4
Maglie 13,326 G4
Manduria 25,194 F4
Manfredonia 44,463 F4
Mantua 59,529 C2
Marino 12,135 F7
Marsala 34,150 D6
Marsciano 5,372 D3
Martina Franca 31,811 F4
Massa 56,591 C2
Massafra 22,610 F4
Massa Marittima 6,438 C3
Matera 43,026 F4
Mazara del Vallo 37,441 D6
Mazzarino 14,981 E6
Melfi 13,355 E4
Menfi 12,386 D6
Merano 30,951 C1
Mesagne 26,955 G4
Messina 203,937 E5
Mestre 184,818 D2
Milan 1,724,557 B2
Milazzo 18,576 E5
Minturno 2,428 D4
Mirandola 11,551 C2
Mira Taglio 10,194 D2
Mistretta 6,631 E6
Modena 149,029 C2
Modica 31,074 E6
Mola di Bari 23,778 F4
Molfetta 63,250 F4
Moncalieri 49,953 A2
Mondovì Breo 12,524 A2
Monfalcone 29,589 D2
Monopoli 29,776 F4
Monreale 19,348 D5
Monselice 9,047 C2
Montalto Uffugo 3,173 E5
Montebelluna 9,573 D2
Montefiascone 6,885 D3
Montepulciano 4,069 C3
Monterotondo 15,869 F6
Monte Sant'Angelo 17,756 F4
Montevarchi 16,849 C3
Monza 110,735 B2
Mortara 13,929 B2
Naples 1,214,775 E4
Nardò 24,142 F4
Narni 6,213 D3
Naro 13,171 D6
Nettuno 20,927 D4
Nicastro 27,206 F5
Nicosia 13,982 E6
Niscemi 23,925 E6
Nizza Monferrato 7,532 B2
Nocera Inferiore 44,415 E4
Noto 21,606 E6
Novara 92,634 B2
Novi Ligure 29,944 B2
Nuoro 30,551 B4
Olbia 20,998 B4
Oliena 7,030 B4
Orbetello 6,884 C3
Oristano 20,966 B5
Ortona 11,966 E3
Orvieto 8,813 D3
Osimo 12,034 D3
Ostia Antica 2,583 F7
Ostuni 27,241 F4
Otranto 3,707 G4
Ozieri 9,149 B4
Pachino 20,427 E6
Padua 210,950 C2
Palazzolo Acreide 8,981 E6
Palermo 556,374 D5
Palestrina 9,239 F7
Palma di Montechiaro 22,381 D6
Palmi 14,405 E5
Palombara Sabina 5,292 F6
Pantelleria 3,116 C6
Paola 11,330 E5
Parma 151,967 C2
Partanna 10,303 D6
Partinico 25,447 D6
Paterno 41,504 E6
Patti 7,500 E5
Pavia 80,639 B2
Pavullo nel Frignano 5,026 C2
Penne 5,889 D3
Pergine Valsugana 6,248 C1
Pergola 3,866 D3
Perugia 65,975 D3
Pesaro 72,104 D3
Pescara 125,391 E3
Pescia 9,918 C3
Piacenza 100,001 B2
Piazza Armerina 21,754 E6
Pietrasanta 6,620 B3
Pinerolo 33,935 A2
Piombino 35,641 C3
Piove di Sacco 7,035 C2
Pisa 91,156 C3
Pisticci 11,239 F4
Pistoia 55,403 C2
Poggibonsi 21,271 C3
Pomezia 11,915 F7
Pont Canavese 4,075 A2
Pontecorvo 5,986 D4
Pontinia 3,166 D4
Pontremoli 5,222 B2
Popoli 5,372 E3
Pordenone 43,230 D2
Portocivitanova 25,773 D3
Porto Empedocle 15,986 D6
Portoferraio 7,579 C3
Portofino 720 B2
Portogruaro 12,258 D2
Portomaggiore 6,343 C2
Porto Recanati 5,389 D3
Porto Torres 15,422 B4
Potenza 46,869 E4
Pozzallo 12,199 E6
Pozzuoli 53,546 D4
Prato 108,385 C3
Prima Porta 11,393 F6
Priverno 9,950 D4
Putignano 19,290 F4
Quartu Sant'Elena 29,715 B5
Ragusa 55,751 E6
Rapallo 22,272 B2
Ravenna 75,153 D2
Recanati 10,176 D3
Reggio di Calabria 110,291 E5
Reggio nell'Emilia 102,337 C2
Rho 39,206 B2
Riesi 15,855 E6
Rieti 26,775 D3
Rimini 101,579 D2
Rionero in Vulture 11,230 E4
Riva del Garda 8,513 C2
Roccastrada 2,629 C3
Rome (cap.) 2,535,018 F6
Ronciglione 5,900 C3
Rossano 12,119 F5
Rovereto 26,827 C2
Rovigo 31,124 C2
Ruvo di Puglia 23,133 F4

(continued on following page)

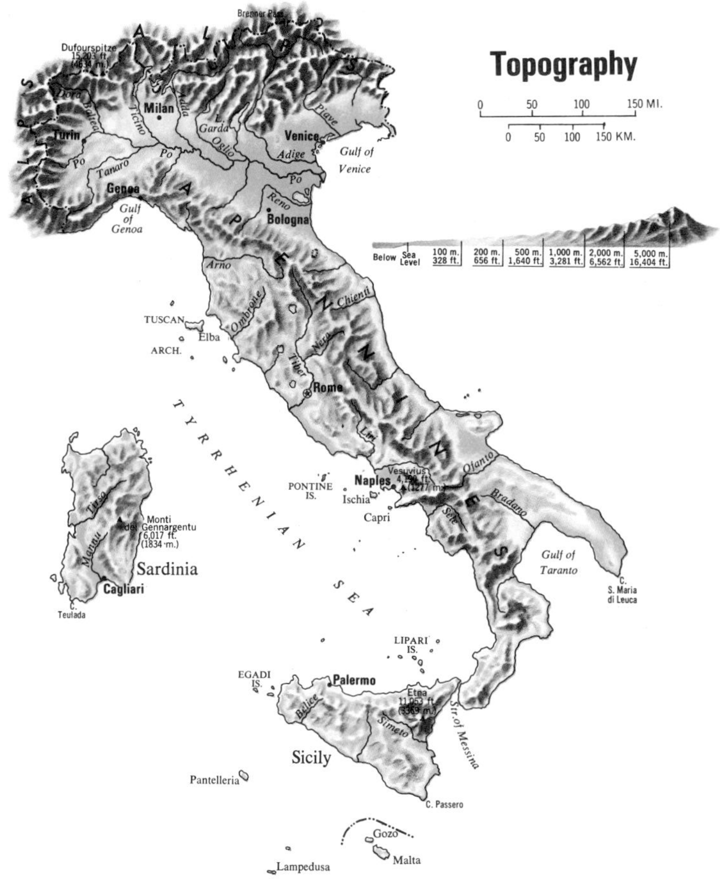
Topography
0 50 100 150 MI.
0 50 100 150 KM.
Below Sea Level
100 m. 328 ft.
200 m. 656 ft.
500 m. 1,640 ft.
1,000 m. 3,281 ft.
2,000 m. 6,562 ft.
5,000 m. 16,404 ft.
Brenner Pass
Dufourspitze
Milan
Turin
Po
Tanaro
Ticino
Adda
Garda
Oglio
Venice
Adige
Piave
Gulf of Venice
Genoa
Gulf of Genoa
Reno
Bologna
Arno
Chienti
Ombrone
Tiber
TUSCAN ARCH.
Elba
Rome
TYRRHENIAN SEA
PONTINE IS.
Naples
Vesuvius
Ischia
Capri
Sele
Ofanto
Bradano
Gulf of Taranto
C. S. Maria di Leuca
Sardinia
Monti del Gennargentu
6,017 ft.
(1834 m.)
Cagliari
C. Teulada
LIPARI IS.
EGADI IS.
Palermo
Etna
Str. of Messina
Sicily
Pantelleria
C. Passero
Gozo
Malta
Lampedusa

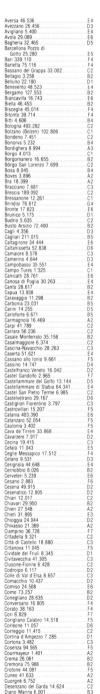

Sabaudia 4.501 .... D4
Saint Vincent 3.737 .... A2
Sala Consilina 8.177 .... E4
Salemi 10.180 .... D6
Salerno 146.534 .... E4
Salsomaggiore Terme 13.677 .... B2
Saluzzo 13.929 .... A2
Sambiase 10.567 .... F5
San Bartolomeo in Galdo 6.943 .... E4
San Benedetto del
Tronto 40.108 .... E3
San Cataldo 19.609 .... D6
San Giovanni in Fiore 16.116 .... F5
San Giovanni in
Persiceto 12.151 .... C2
San Marco in Lamis 15.817 .... E4
San Miniato 3.245 .... C3
Sannicandro Garganico 17.939 .... E4
San Remo 47.684 .... A3
Sansepolcro 11.443 .... C3
San Severino Marche 6.447 .... D3
San Severo 49.622 .... E4
Santa Maria Capua
Vetere 31.077 .... E4
Sant' Elpidio a Mare 4.446 .... E3
Santeramo in Colle 19.758 .... F4
San Vito 3.901 .... B5
San Vito al Tagliamento 6.328 .... D2
San Vito dei Normanni 18.447 .... F4
San Vito Romano 3.256 .... F6
Saronno 32.477 .... B2
Sarroch 3.560 .... B5
Sassari 94.312 .... B4
Sassuolo 33.451 .... C2
Savigliano 14.036 .... A2
Savona 76.274 .... B2
Schio 27.890 .... C2
Sciacca 29.803 .... D6
Scicli 18.405 .... E6
Segni 7.193 .... F7
Senigallia 25.413 .... D3
Sesto Fiorentino 41.636 .... C3
Sestri Levante 18.331 .... B2
Settebagni 5.022 .... F6
Sezze 7.043 .... F5
Siderno 8.023 .... F5
Siena 56.539 .... C3
Siniscola 6.149 .... B4
Sinnai 8.499 .... B5
Siracusa (Syracuse) 93.006 .... E6
Sondrio 19.724 .... B1
Sora 14.031 .... E4
Soresina 9.300 .... C2
Sorrento 13.078 .... E4
Sorso 10.741 .... B4
Spoleto 18.013 .... D3
Squinzano 14.053 .... G4
Stresa 3.758 .... B2
Sulmona 18.221 .... D3
Susa 5.773 .... A2
Suzzara 12.013 .... C2
Syracuse 93.006 .... E6
Taormina 6.696 .... E6
Taranto 205.158 .... F4
Tarquinia 10.300 .... C3
Taurianova 12.198 .... E5
Tempio Pausania 10.382 .... B4
Teramo 31.163 .... D3
Termini Imerese 24.085 .... D5
Termoli 13.986 .... E3
Terni 75.873 .... D3
Terracina 24.092 .... D4
Terralba 8.551 .... B5
Tirano 7.413 .... C1
Tivoli 28.393 .... F6
Todi 5.705 .... D3
Tolentino 11.642 .... D3
Torino (Turin) 1.181.698 .... A2
Torre Annunziata 71.068 .... E4
Torre del Greco 74.752 .... E4
Torremaggiore 16.171 .... E4
Tortona 24.165 .... B2
Trani 40.508 .... F4
Trapani 90.305 .... D5
Trento 64.272 .... C1
Treviglio 21.920 .... B2
Treviso 87.447 .... D2
Tricase 10.481 .... G5
Trieste 257.259 .... E2
Trino 6.722 .... B2
Turin 1.181.698 .... A2
Udine 97.544 .... D2
Umbertide 6.640 .... D3
Urbino 7.735 .... D3
Valdagno 20.342 .... C2
Valenza 20.533 .... B2
Valmontone 6.543 .... F7
Varallo Pombia 3.118 .... B2
Varazze 11.676 .... B2
Varese 65.978 .... B2
Vasto 17.295 .... E3
Velletri 22.020 .... F7
Venafro 5.156 .... E4
Venezia (Venice) 108.082 .... D2
Venice 108.082 .... D2
Venosa 10.993 .... E4
Ventimiglia 20.343 .... A3
Verbania 29.994 .... B2
Vercelli 54.934 .... B2
Veroli 2.793 .... D4
Verona 227.032 .... C2
Viadana 6.667 .... C2
Viareggio 49.965 .... C3
Vibo Valentia 16.005 .... F5
Vicenza 99.451 .... C2
Vicovaro 3.005 .... D3
Vigevano 62.855 .... B2
Villacidro 12.651 .... B5
Villafranca di Verona 11.762 .... C2
Viterbo 39.291 .... C3
Vittoria 43.673 .... E6
Vittorio Veneto 25.476 .... D1
Vizzini 8.583 .... E6
Voghera 37.316 .... B2
Volterra 10.732 .... C3
Zagarolo 4.232 .... F7

OTHER FEATURES

Adda (riv.) B2
Adige (riv.) C2
Adriatic (sea) E3
Alicudi (isl.) E5
Apennines, Central (range) D3
Apennines, Northern (range) C2
Apennines, Southern (range) E4
Arno (riv.) C3
Asinara (isl.) B3
Bernina, Piz (peak) B1
Blanc (mt.) A2
Bolsena (lake) C3
Bonifacio (str.) B4
Bracciano (lake) C3
Brenner (pass) C1
Capraia (isl.) B3
Capri (isl.) E4
Carbonara (cape) B5
Carnic Alps (range) D1
Castellammare (gulf) D5
Circeo (cape) D4
Como (lake) B1
Cottian Alps (range) A2
Dolomite Alps (range) C1
Dora Baltea (riv.) A2
Dora Riparia (riv.) A2
Egadi (isls.) C6
Elba (isl.) C3
Etna (vol.) E6
Favignana (isl.) D6

Filicudi (isl.) E5
Gaeta (gulf) D4
Garda (lake) C2
Gennargentu, Monti del (mt.) B5
Genoa (gulf) B2
Giannutri (isl.) C3
Giglio (isl.) C3
Gorgona (isl.) B3
Graian Alps (range) A2
Gran Paradiso (mt.) A2
Great Saint Bernard (pass) A2
Ionian (sea) F6
Ischia (isl.) D4
Julian Alps (range) D1
Lampedusa (isl.) D7
Lepontine Alps (range) B1
Levanzo (isl.) D5
Ligurian (sea) B3
Linosa (isl.) D7
Lipari (isl.) E5
Lipari (isls.) E5
Maggiore (lake) B1
Manfredonia (gulf) F4
Marettimo (isl.) C6
Maritime Alps (range) A2
Marmolada (mt.) C1
Mediterranean (sea) B5
Messina (str.) E6
Metauro (riv.) D3
Mincio (riv.) C2
Montecristo (isl.) C3
Nera (riv.) D3
Ombrone (riv.) C3
Oglio (riv.) C2
Oristano (gulf) B5
Orosei (gulf) B4
Ortles (range) C1
Otranto (str.) G5
Ötztal Alps (range) C1
Panarea (isl.) E5
Panaro (riv.) C2
Pantelleria (isl.) D6
Pelagie (isls.) D7
Pennine Alps (range) A2
Pianosa (isl.) C3
Piave (riv.) D2
Po (riv.) C2
Pompeii (ruins) E4
Pontine (isls.) D4
Ponza (isl.) D4
Rosa (mt.) A1
Salina (isl.) E5
Salso (riv.) D6
San Pietro (isl.) B5
Santa Maria di Leuca (cape) G5
Sant' Antioco (pen.) B5
Sant' Eufemia (gulf) F5
Sardinia (isl.) B4
Sicily (isl.) E6
Sicily (str.) D6
Simplon (tunnel) A1
Spartivento (cape) B5
Spartivento (cape) F5
Squillace (gulf) F5
Stromboli (isl.) E5
Taganaro (riv.) B2
Tanaro (riv.) B2
Taranto (gulf) F4
Testa del Gargano (cape) F4
Tiber (riv.) D3
Trasimeno (lake) D3
Tremiti (isls.) E3
Tuscan (arch.) B3
Tyrrhenian (sea) C4
Ustica (isl.) D5
Vaticano (cape) E5
Venice (gulf) D2
Ventotene (isl.) D4

Vesuvius (vol.) E4
Viso (mt.) A2
Volturno (riv.) E4
Vulcano (isl.) E5

MALTA

CITIES and TOWNS

Sliema 20.095 .... E7
Valletta (cap.) 14.042 .... E7
Victoria 5.249 .... E6

SAN MARINO

CITIES and TOWNS

San Marino (cap.) 4.628 .... D3
San Marino* 5.410 .... D3

VATICAN CITY

Vatican City 728 .... B6

*City and suburbs.

Agriculture, Industry and Resources

DOMINANT LAND USE

Wheat, Rice, Dairy

Pasture Livestock

Cereals, Livestock

Fruit, Truck and Mixed Farming

Grapes, Wine

Forests

Nonagricultural Land

MAJOR MINERAL OCCURRENCES

Ab	Asbestos	K	Potash	Pb	Lead
Al	Bauxite	Lg	Lignite	Py	Pyrites
C	Coal	Mr	Marble	S	Sulfur
Fe	Iron Ore	Na	Salt	Sb	Antimony
G	Natural Gas	O	Petroleum	Zn	Zinc
Hg	Mercury				

⚡ Water Power

▨ Major Industrial Areas

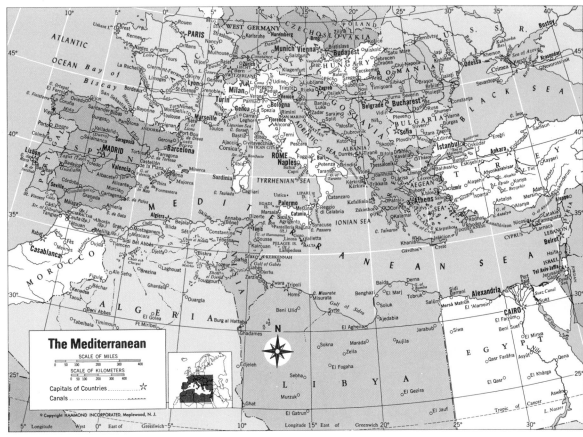

The Mediterranean

SCALE OF MILES
0 50 100 200 300 400

SCALE OF KILOMETERS
0 50 100 200 300 400

Capitals of Countries .... ☆

Canals

© Copyright HAMMOND INCORPORATED, Maplewood, N. J.

SWITZERLAND
AREA 15,943 sq. mi. (41,292 sq. km.)
POPULATION 6,365,960
CAPITAL Bern
LARGEST CITY Zürich
HIGHEST POINT Dufourspitze
(Mte. Rosa) 15,203 ft. (4,634 m.)
MONETARY UNIT Swiss franc
MAJOR LANGUAGES German, French,
Italian, Romansch
MAJOR RELIGIONS Protestantism,
Roman Catholicism

LIECHTENSTEIN
AREA 61 sq. mi. (158 sq. km.)
POPULATION 25,220
CAPITAL Vaduz
LARGEST CITY Vaduz
HIGHEST POINT Grauspitze 8,527 ft.
(2,599 m.)
MONETARY UNIT Swiss franc
MAJOR LANGUAGE German
MAJOR RELIGION Roman Catholicism

SWITZERLAND

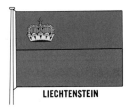

LIECHTENSTEIN

Languages

German
French
Italian
Romansch

Switzerland is a multilingual nation with four official languages. 70% of the people speak German, 19% French, 10% Italian and 1% Romansch.

SWITZERLAND

CANTONS

Aargau 442,400 ....F2
Appenzell, Ausser
  Rhoden 46,700 ....H2
Appenzell, Inner Rhoden 13,500 ..H2
Baselland 219,500 ....E2
Baselstadt 209,700 ....E1
Bern 920,900 ....D2
Fribourg 181,600 ....D3
Geneva (Genève) 338,600 ....B4
Glarus 35,700 ....H3
Graubünden (Grisons) 164,300 ....H3
Grisons (Graubünden) 164,300 ....H3
Jura 67,200 ....D2
Lucerne (Luzern) 292,900 ....F2
Luzern 292,900 ....F2
Neuchâtel 162,200 ....C3
Nidwalden 26,900 ....F3
Obwalden 25,400 ....F3
Sankt Gallen 385,000 ....H2
Schaffhausen 69,300 ....G1
Schwyz 93,100 ....G2
Soleure (Solothurn) 221,800 ....E2
Solothurn 221,800 ....E2
Thurgau 183,500 ....H1
Ticino 264,400 ....G4
Uri 34,000 ....G3
Valais 214,000 ....D4
Vaud 523,500 ....B3
Zug 73,600 ....G2
Zürich 1,117,300 ....G2

CITIES and TOWNS

Aadorf 3,022 ....G2
Aarau 16,881 ....F2
Aarau* 51,800 ....F2

Aarberg 3,122 ....D2
Aarburg 5,943 ....F2
Adelboden 3,326 ....E3
Adliswil 15,920 ....F2
Aeschi bei Spiez 1,402 ....E3
Affoltern am Albis 7,363 ....F2
Affoltern im Emmental 1,223 ....E2
Aigle 6,532 ....C4
Airolo 2,140 ....G3
Alle 1,615 ....D2
Allschwil 17,638 ....D1
Alpnach 3,277 ....F3
Altdorf 8,647 ....G3
Altstätten 9,084 ....J2
Amriswil 7,601 ....H1
Andelfingen 1,453 ....G1
Andermatt 1,589 ....G3
Appenzell 5,217 ....H2
Arbedo-Castione 2,456 ....G4
Ardon 12,227 ....H1
Arbon* 15,400 ....H1
Ardon 1,498 ....D4
Arosa 2,717 ....J3
Arth 7,580 ....F2
Ascona 4,086 ....G4
Attalens 1,116 ....C3
Au 4,944 ....J2
Aubonne 1,983 ....B4
Avenches 2,235 ....D3
Baar 14,074 ....F2
Baden 14,115 ....F2
Baden* 66,800 ....F2
Bad Ragaz 3,713 ....H2
Balerna 3,885 ....G5
Balsthal 5,607 ....E2
Bäretswil 2,733 ....G2
Basel 199,600 ....E1
Basel* 379,700 ....E1
Bassecourt 2,985 ....D2
Bätterkinden 1,757 ....E2

Bauma 3,159 ....G2
Beatenberg 1,263 ....E3
Beinwil am See 2,520 ....F2
Belfaux 1,075 ....D3
Bellinzona 16,979 ....H4
Bellinzona* 31,000 ....H4
Belp 6,981 ....D3
Berg 1,039 ....H1
Bern (cap.) 154,700 ....D3
Bern* 265,300 ....D3
Beromünster 1,552 ....F2
Bettlach 4,046 ....D2
Bex 5,069 ....D4
Biasca 4,696 ....H4
Biberist 7,769 ....D2
Biel 63,400 ....D2
Biel**89,900 ....D2
Bière 1,252 ....B3
Binningen 15,344 ....D1
Bischofszell 4,233 ....H1
Blumenstein 1,049 ....E3
Bodio 1,425 ....G4
Bolligen 26,121 ....D3
Boltigen 1,519 ....D3
Bonaduz 1,289 ....H3
Boncourt 1,528 ....C2
Bönigen 1,738 ....E3
Boswil 1,904 ....F2
Boudry 4,372 ....C3
Bourg Saint-Pierre 236 ....D5
Breil-Brigels 1,215 ....H3
Breitenbach 2,455 ....E2
Bremgarten 4,873 ....F2
Brienz 2,796 ....F3
Brig 5,191 ....F4
Brissago 2,120 ....G4
Brittnau 2,888 ....E2
Broc 1,842 ....D3
Brugg 8,635 ....F2
Brusio 1,344 ....K4
Bubendorf 2,070 ....E2
Bubikon 3,244 ....G2
Buchs 8,454 ....H2
Bülach 11,043 ....G1
Bulle 7,556 ....D3
Buochs 3,232 ....F3
Büren an der Aare 3,085 ....D2
Burgdorf 15,888 ....E2
Burgdorf* 18,400 ....E2
Bürglen, Thurgau 1,920 ....H1
Bürglen, Uri 3,401 ....G3
Bussigny-près-Lausanne 4,509 ....B3
Bütschwil 3,270 ....H2
Carouge 14,055 ....B4
Castagnola 4,430 ....G4
Cazis 1,687 ....H3
Cernier 1,717 ....C2
Chalais 1,651 ....E4
Cham 8,209 ....F2
Chamoson 2,049 ....D4
Charmey 1,155 ....D3
Château-d'Oex 3,203 ....C3
Châtel-Saint-Denis 2,842 ....C3
Chêne-Bougeries 8,670 ....B4
Chavornay 1,521 ....C3
Chexbres 1,607 ....C3
Chippis 1,561 ....E4
Chur 32,400 ....J3
Churwalden 1,052 ....J3
Claro 1,143 ....G4
Collombey-Muraz 2,279 ....C4
Collonge-Bellerive 3,541 ....B4
Conthey 4,259 ....D4
Coppet 1,097 ....B4
Corcelles-près-Payerne 1,256 ....C3
Corgémont 1,645 ....D2
Cossonay 1,529 ....B3
Courgenay 1,954 ....D2
Courrendlin 2,656 ....D2
Courroux 1,788 ....D2
Courtelary 1,462 ....C2
Courtételle 1,864 ....D2
Couvet 3,481 ....C3
Cully 1,535 ....C4
Davos 10,238 ....J3
Degersheim 3,400 ....H2
Delémont 11,797 ....D2
Derendingen 4,917 ....E2
Dielsdorf 2,691 ....F1
Diemtigen 1,913 ....D3
Diepoldsau 3,311 ....J2
Diessenhofen 2,532 ....G1
Dietikon 22,705 ....F2
Disentis-Muster 2,319 ....G3
Domat-Ems 5,701 ....H3
Dombresson 1,109 ....C2
Dornach 5,258 ....E2
Döttingen 3,380 ....F1
Dübendorf 19,639 ....G2
Düdingen 4,932 ....D3
Dürnten 4,820 ....G2
Dürrenroth 1,084 ....E2
Ebnat-Kappel 5,131 ....H2
Echallens 1,643 ....C3
Ecublens 6,379 ....B3
Egg 5,250 ....G2
Eggiwil 2,391 ....E3
Eglisau 2,160 ....G1
Egnach 3,466 ....H1

Agriculture, Industry and Resources

DOMINANT LAND USE

Cereals, Dairy
Pasture Livestock
General Farming, Livestock
Fruit, Truck, Mixed Farming
Forests
Nonagricultural Land

⚡ Water Power
Major Industrial Areas

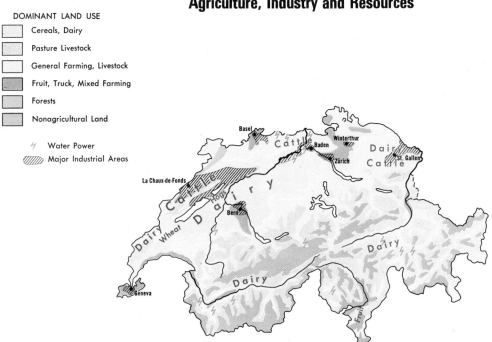

(continued on following page)

Switzerland and Liechtenstein

(continued)

Topography

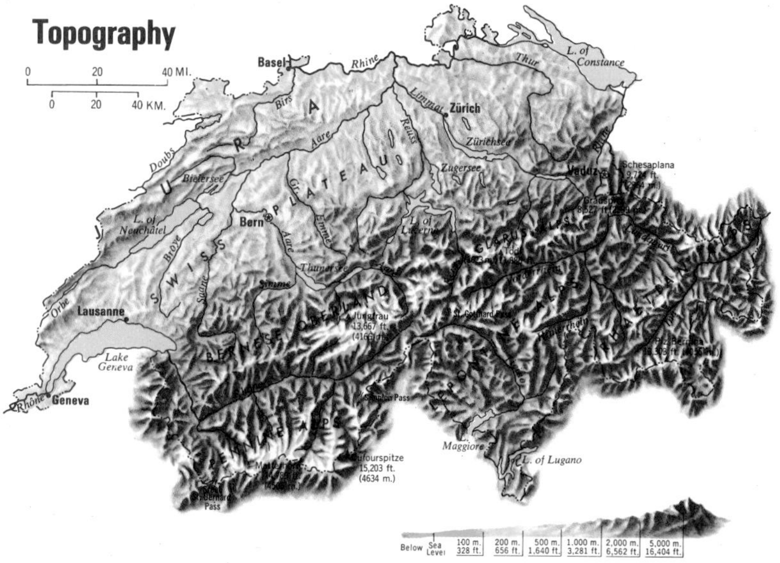

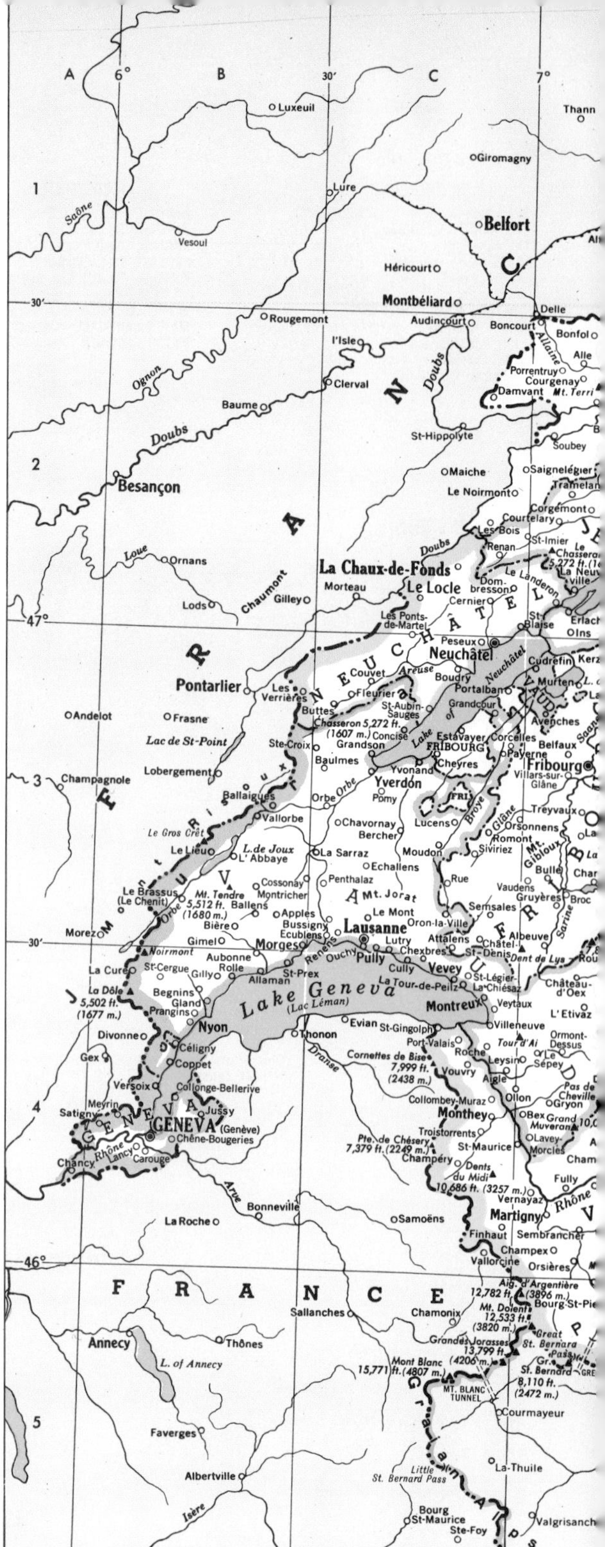

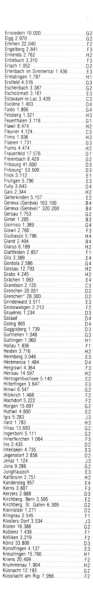

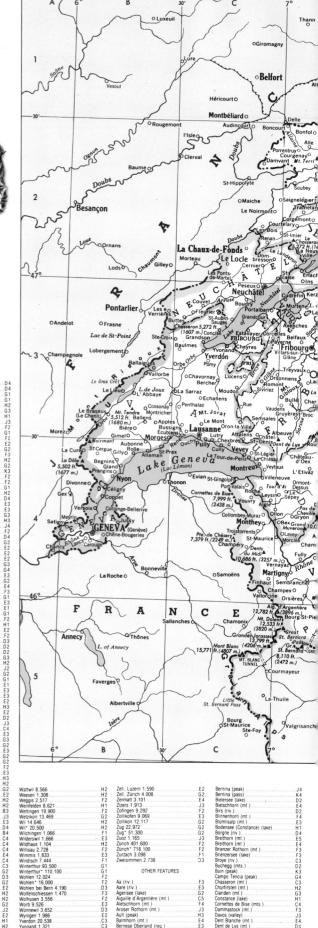

Einsiedeln 10,020	G2
Elgg 2,970	G2
Emmen 22,040	F2
Engelberg 2,841	F3
Ennenda 2,762	H2
Entlebuch 3,310	F3
Erlach 1,052	D2
Erlenbach im Simmental 1,436	E3
Ermatingen 1,787	H1
Erstfeld 4,516	G3
Eschenbach 3,387	G2
Escholzmatt 3,161	E3
Estavayer-le-Lac 3,439	C3
Evolène 1,403	D4
Faido 1,866	G4
Felsberg 1,321	H3
Feuerthalen 3,118	G1
Flawil 8,474	H2
Fleurier 4,124	C3
Flims 1,936	H3
Flüelen 1,731	G3
Flums 4,474	H2
Frauenfeld 17,576	G1
Freienbach 8,429	G2
Fribourg 41,600	D3
Fribourg* 53,500	D3
Frick 3,112	E1
Frutigen 5,796	E3
Fully 3,643	D4
Gais 2,344	H2
Gelterkinden 5,157	E2
Geneva (Genève) 163,100	B4
Geneva (Genève)* 320,200	B4
Gersau 1,753	G2
Gimel 1,205	B3
Giornico 1,389	G4
Giswil 2,760	F3
Giubiasco 5,796	H4
Gland 2,404	B4
Glarus 6,189	H2
Glattfelden 2,857	F1
Glis 3,389	E4
Gordola 2,586	G4
Gossau 12,793	H2
Grabs 4,245	H2
Grächen 1,063	E4
Grandson 2,135	C3
Grenchen 20,051	D2
Grenchen* 28,300	D2
Grindelwald 3,511	E3
Grosswangen 2,213	F2
Gruyères 1,234	D3
Gstaad	D4
Gsteig 865	D4
Guggisberg 1,739	D3
Gurtnellen 1,048	G3
Guttingen 1,060	H1
Hallau 1,836	F1
Heiden 3,716	H2
Heimberg 3,046	E3
Hérémence 1,484	D4
Hergiswil 4,364	F3
Herisau 14,597	H2
Herzogenbuchsee 5,140	E2
Hilterfingen 3,647	E3
Hinwil 6,547	G2
Hitzkirch 1,468	F2
Hochdorf 5,222	F2
Horgen 15,691	G2
Huttwil 4,800	E2
Igis 5,283	J3
Ilanz 1,783	H3
Illnau 13,693	G2
Ingenbohl 5,111	G2
Innertkirchen 1,064	F3
Ins 2,435	D2
Interlaken 4,735	E3
Jegenstorf 2,858	D2
Jenaz 1,124	J3
Jona 9,286	G2
Jungfraujoch	E3
Kaltbrunn 2,751	H2
Kandersteg 957	E4
Kerns 3,807	F3
Kerzers 2,688	D3
Kirchberg, Bern 3,595	E2
Kirchberg, St. Gallen 6,309	G2
Kleinlützel 1,271	D2
Klingnau 2,545	F1
Klosters Dorf 3,534	J3
Kloten 16,388	G2
Koblenz 1,439	F1
Kölliken 3,219	F2
Köniz 33,800	D3
Konolfingen 4,137	E3
Kreuzlingen 15,760	H1
Kriens 20,409	F2
Krummenau 1,904	H2
Küsnacht 12,193	G2
Küssnacht am Rigi 7,956	F2
Küttigen 4,181	F2
L'Abbaye 1,319	B3
La Chaux-de-Fonds 42,500	C2
Lachen 4,914	G2
Lancy 20,523	B4
La Neuveville 3,917	D2
Langenthal 13,077	E2
Langenthal* 22,100	E2
Langnau am Albis 4,879	G2
Langnau in Emmental 8,950	E3
La Roche 1,069	D3
La Sarraz 1,190	C3
La Tour-de-Peilz 8,864	C4
Läufelfingen 1,243	E2
Laufen 4,723	D2
Laufenburg 2,128	F1
Laupen 2,139	D3
Lauperswil 2,542	E3
Lausanne 136,100	C3
Lausanne* 228,700	C3
Lauterbrunnen 3,431	E3
Le Brassus 5,465	B3
Le Châble 4,541	D4
Le Chenit (Le Brassus) 5,465	B3
Le Landeron 2,768	C2
Le Locle 14,452	C2
Le Mont-sur-Lausanne 2,692	C3
Lengau 4,736	D2
Lenk 1,876	D4
Le Noirmont 1,516	C2
Lens 2,052	D4
Lenzburg 7,594	F2
Les Bois 1,110	C2
Les Ponts-de-Martel 1,327	C2
Leuk 2,796	E4
Leukerbad 1,056	E4
Leysin 2,752	C4
Liechtensteig 2,131	H2
Liestal 12,500	E2
Liestal-Sissach* 40,800	E2
Linthal 1,458	H3
Littau 13,495	F2
Locarno 14,143	G4
Locarno* 39,200	G4
Lodrino 1,075	G4
Lotzwil 2,323	E2
Lucens 2,144	C3
Lucerne 70,200	F2
Lucerne* 158,600	F2
Lugano 22,280	G4
Lugano* 64,200	G4
Lungern 1,813	F3
Luthern 1,706	E2
Lutry 4,994	C3
Lützelflüh 3,842	E3
Luzern (Lucerne) 70,200	F2
Lyss 8,131	D2
Maienfeld 1,542	J2
Malans 1,294	J3
Malleray 1,969	D2
Malters 5,100	F2
Malvaglia 1,099	H4
Männedorf 7,419	G2
Marbach 1,265	E3
Martigny 10,478	C4
Meilen 9,881	G2
Meiringen 3,759	F3
Melide 1,315	G5
Mellingen 3,211	F2
Mels 5,969	H2
Mendrisio 6,223	G5
Menzingen 3,483	G2
Menznau 2,185	E2
Mesocco 1,376	H4
Meyrin 14,255	B4
Minusio 5,027	G4
Möhlin 6,003	E1
Mollis 2,628	H2
Montana 1,725	D4
Monthey 10,114	C4
Montreux 20,421	C4
Morges 11,931	B3
Morges* 17,200	B3
Moudon 3,773	C3
Moutier 8,794	D2
Müllheim 1,620	G1
Mümliswil-Ramiswil 2,702	E2
Münchenbuchsee 6,459	E2
Münsingen 8,350	E3
Muotathal 2,763	G3
Muri 4,853	F2
Muri bei Bern 3,057	E3
Mürren	E3
Murten 4,256	D3
Muttenz 15,518	E1
Näfels 3,739	H2
Naters 5,517	E4
Nebikon 1,378	F2
Nendaz 4,051	D4
Nesslau 1,934	H2
Netstal 2,771	H2
Neuchâtel 38,400	C3
Neuchâtel* 61,700	C3
Neuenegg 3,452	D3
Neuhausen am Rheinfall 12,103	G1
Neunkirch 1,239	F1
Nidau 7,962	D2
Niederbipp 3,293	E2
Niederurnen 3,354	G2
Nunningen 1,450	E2
Nyon 11,424	B4
Oberägeri 2,992	G2
Oberburg 3,015	E2
Oberdiessbach 2,145	E3
Oberdorf 1,953	E2
Oberriet 6,123	J2
Obersiggenthal 6,623	F1
Oberzwil 4,659	H2
Oensingen 3,387	E2
Oftringen 9,189	E2
Ollon 4,470	D4
Olten 21,209	E2
Olten* 49,000	E2
Opfikon 11,115	G2
Orbe 4,522	C3
Orsières 2,470	D4
Ouchy	C4
Paradiso 3,101	G5
Payerne 6,899	C3
Penthalaz 1,701	C3
Péry 1,486	D2
Peseux 5,578	C3
Pfaffnau 2,584	E2
Pieterlen 3,485	D2
Plaffeien 1,448	D3
Pontresina 1,646	J3
Porrentruy 7,827	C2
Port-Valais 1,363	C4
Poschiavo 3,563	J4
Prangins 1,466	B4
Pratteln 15,127	E1
Pully 15,917	C4
Quinto 1,490	G3
Rafz 2,215	G1
Ramsen 1,217	G1
Rapperswil 8,713	G2
Raron 1,257	E4
Regensdorf 8,566	F2
Reichenbach im Kandertal 2,900	E3
Reiden 3,275	F2
Reinach in Aargau 5,862	F2
Reinach in Baselland 13,419	E2
Renan 1,094	C2
Renens 17,391	C3
Rheinau 2,075	G1
Rheineck 3,275	J2
Rheinfelden 6,866	E1
Richterswil 7,380	G2
Riehen 21,026	E1
Riggisberg 2,193	E3
Riva San Vitale 1,607	G5
Rivera 1,146	G4
Roggwil 3,403	E2
Rolle 3,658	B4
Romanshorn 8,329	H1
Romont 3,276	C3
Rorschach 11,963	H2
Rorschach* 24,200	H2
Rosenlaui	F3
Rothrist 5,883	E2
Roveredo 2,037	H4
Rüeggisberg 1,857	E3
Rumlang 5,677	G2
Rüschegg 1,346	D3
Ruswil 4,756	F2
Rüthi 1,493	J2
Rüti, Zürich 9,546	G2
Saanen 5,840	D4
Sachseln 3,059	F3
Saignelégier 1,745	D2
Saint-Aubin-Sauges 2,058	C3
Saint-Blaise 2,586	D2
Sainte-Croix 6,240	B3
Saint-Imier 6,740	D2
Saint-Légier-La Chiésaz 2,230	C4
Saint-Martin 1,120	E4
Saint-Maurice 3,808	C4
Saint Moritz 5,699	J3
Saint Niklaus 2,043	E4
Saint-Prex 2,306	B4
Saint Stephan 1,213	D3
Saint-Ursanne 1,073	D2
Samedan 2,574	J3
Sankt Gallen 81,900	H2
Sankt Gallen* 90,400	H2
Sankt Margrethen 5,101	J2
Sargans 4,058	H2
Sarnen 6,952	F3
Satigny 1,877	A4
Savièse 3,585	D4
Saxon 2,409	D4
Schaffhausen 36,800	G1
Schaffhausen* 55,800	G1
Schänis 2,355	H2
Schattdorf 3,292	G3
Scherzingen 1,420	H1
Schiers 2,342	J3
Schinznach-Dorf 1,154	F2
Schleitheim 1,544	G1
Schlieren 11,869	F2
Schönenwerd 4,793	E2
Schübelbach 4,395	G2
Schüpfheim 3,773	F3
Schwanden 2,823	H2
Schwyz 12,194	G2
Scuol 1,686	K3
Sempach 1,619	F2
Seon 3,628	F2
Seuzach 3,258	G1
Sevelen 2,742	H2
Sierre 11,017	D4
Signau 2,642	E3
Sigriswil 3,540	E3
Silenen 2,338	G3
Sils im Domleschg 762	H3
Silvaplana 714	J4
Sins 2,435	F2
Sion 21,925	D4
Sirnach 3,706	G2
Sissach 4,938	E2
Solothurn (Soleure) 17,708	E2
Solothurn* 35,600	E2
Somvix 1,555	G3
Sonvico 1,129	G4
Spiez 9,911	E3
Stäfa 9,937	G2
Stalden 1,121	E4
Stans 5,180	F3
Steckborn 3,752	G1
Steffisburg 12,621	E3
Stein 1,763	E1
Stein am Rhein 2,751	G1
Suhr 7,223	F2
Sulgen 1,834	H1
Sumiswald 5,334	E2
Sursee 7,052	F2
Tafers 2,021	D3
Täuffelen 1,761	D2
Tavannes 3,869	D2
Tavetsch 1,273	G3
Teufen 5,300	H2
Thal 4,919	J2
Thalwil 13,591	G2
Thayngen 3,640	G1
Therwil 5,412	E1
Thun 37,000	E3
Thun* 63,600	E3
Thunstetten 2,483	E2
Thusis 2,381	H3
Trachselwald 1,199	E2
Tramelan 5,549	D2
Trimmis 1,109	J3
Troistorrents 2,208	C4
Trub 1,833	E3
Trun 1,607	G3
Turbenthal 2,939	G2
Uetendorf 3,132	E3
Unterägeri 4,671	G2
Unteriberg 1,344	G2
Unterkulm 2,596	F2
Unterseen 4,192	E3
Untervaz 1,230	H3
Urnäsch 2,313	H2
Uster 21,819	G2
Utzenstorf 3,193	E2
Uznach 3,984	H2
Uzwil 9,133	H2
Vallorbe 4,028	B3
Vaz-Obervaz 2,003	J3
Vechigen 3,595	E3
Vernayaz 1,356	D4
Versoix 5,627	B4
Vevey 17,957	C4
Vevey-Montreux* 62,300	C4
Villeneuve 3,705	C4
Visp 5,252	E4
Vouvry 1,851	C4
Vuadens 1,278	C3
Wädenswil 15,695	G2
Wahlern 4,832	D3
Wald 8,185	G2
Waldenburg 1,449	E2
Waldkirch 2,669	H2
Walenstadt 3,446	H2
Wallisellen 10,415	G2
Walzenhausen 2,082	J2
Wangen an der Aare 2,013	E2
Wängi 2,730	H1
Wartau 3,604	H2
Wattwil 8,566	H2
Weesen 1,308	H2
Weggis 2,517	F2
Weinfelden 8,621	H1
Wettingen 19,900	F2
Wetzikon 13,469	G2
Wil 14,646	H2
Wil* 20,500	H2
Wilchingen 1,066	F1
Wilderswil 1,666	E3
Wildhaus 1,104	H2
Willisau 2,728	F2
Wimmis 1,833	E3
Windisch 7,444	F1
Winterthur 93,500	G1
Winterthur* 110,100	G1
Wohlen 12,024	F2
Wohlen* 16,000	F2
Wohlen bei Bern 4,190	D3
Wolfenschiessen 1,470	F3
Wolhusen 3,556	F2
Worb 9,526	E3
Wünnewil 3,652	D3
Wynigen 1,986	E2
Yverdon 20,538	C3
Yvonand 1,321	C3
Zell, Luzern 1,590	E2
Zell, Zürich 4,008	G2
Zermatt 3,101	E4
Zizers 1,913	J3
Zofingen 9,292	F2
Zollikofen 9,069	E3
Zollikon 12,117	G2
Zug 22,972	G2
Zug* 51,300	G2
Zuoz 1,165	J3
Zürich 401,600	F2
Zürich* 718,100	F2
Zurzach 3,098	F1
Zweisimmen 2,738	D3

OTHER FEATURES

Aa (riv.)	F3
Aare (riv.)	E3
Ägerisee (lake)	G2
Aiguille d'Argentière (mt.)	C5
Aletschhorn (mt.)	F4
Aroser Rothorn (mt.)	J3
Ault (peak)	H3
Balmhorn (mt.)	E4
Bernese Oberland (reg.)	E3
Bernina (peak)	J4
Bernina (pass)	K4
Bielersee (lake)	D2
Bietschhorn (mt.)	E4
Birs (riv.)	D2
Blinnenhorn (mt.)	F4
Blümlisalp (mt.)	E3
Bodensee (Constance) (lake)	H1
Borgne (riv.)	D4
Breithorn (mt.)	E5
Breithorn (mt.)	E4
Brienzer Rothorn (mt.)	F3
Brienzersee (lake)	F3
Broye (riv.)	C3
Buchegg (mts.)	D2
Buin (peak)	K3
Campo Tencia (peak)	G4
Chasseron (mt.)	C3
Churfirsten (mt.)	H2
Clariden (mt.)	G3
Constance (lake)	H1
Cornettes de Bise (mts.)	C4
Dammastock (mt.)	F3
Davos (valley)	J3
Dent Blanche (mt.)	E4
Dent de Lys (mt.)	D4

Switzerland and Liechtenstein
CONIC PROJECTION

Dent de Ruth (mt.)	D3
Dent d'Hérens (mt.)	E5
Dents du Midi (mt.)	C4
Diablerets (mt.)	D4
Doldenhorn (mt.)	E4
Dolent (mt.)	C5
Dom (mt.)	E5
Doubs (riv.)	C2
Drance (riv.)	D4
Dufourspitze (mt.)	E5
Emmental (riv.)	E3
Engadine (valley)	K3
Err (peak)	J3
Finsteraarhorn (mt.)	E3
Finstermünz (pass)	K3
Fletschhorn (mt.)	F4
Fluchthorn (mt.)	K3
Flüela (pass)	J3
Furka (pass)	F3
Generoso (mt.)	H5
Geneva (lake)	C4
Glärnisch (mt.)	G3
Glarus Alps (mts.)	H3
Grand Combin (mt.)	D5
Grande Dixence (dam)	D4
Grand Muveran (mt.)	D4

Grauehörner (mts.)	H3
Great Saint Bernard (mt.)	D5
Great Saint Bernard (pass)	D5
Greifensee (lake)	F2
Greina (pass)	G3
Grimsel (pass)	F3
Gross Emme (riv.)	E2
Gross Litzner (mt.)	K3
Hinterrhein (riv.)	H3
Hochwang (mt.)	J3
Hohenstollen (mt.)	F3
Hörnli (mt.)	G2
Inn (riv.)	K3
Jorat (mt.)	D4
Jungfrau (mt.)	E3
Jura (mts.)	B3
Kaiseregg (mt.)	D3
Kesch (peak)	J3
La Dôle (mt.)	B4
Landquart (riv.)	J3
Le Chasseral (mt.)	C3
Le Gros Crêt (mt.)	B3
Léman (Geneva) (lake)	C4
Leone (mt.)	F4
Lepontine Alps (range)	G4
Limmat (riv.)	F2

Linard (peak)	K3
Linden (mts.)	F2
Linth (riv.)	G3
Lötschberg (tunnel)	E3
Lower Engadine (valley)	K3
Lucerne (lake)	F3
Lugano (lake)	H5
Madrisahorn (mt.)	J3
Maggia (riv.)	G4
Maggiore (lake)	G5
Männlifluh (mt.)	E3
Marmontana (mt.)	H4
Matterhorn (mt.)	E5
Mauvoisin (dam)	D4
Moësa (riv.)	H4
Morat (lake)	D3
Muota (riv.)	G3
Murg (riv.)	G2
Murtaröl (peak)	K3
Muttler (peak)	K3
Naafkopf (mt.)	J3
Napf (mt.)	E3
National Park	K3
Neuchâtel (lake)	C3
Noirmont (mt.)	B4
Oberalp (pass)	G3

Oberalpstock (mt.)	G3
Ochsen (mt.)	D3
Ofen (pass)	K3
Ofenhorn (mt.)	F3
Orbe (riv.)	C3
Pennine Alps (range)	D5
Pilatus (mt.)	F3
Plessur (riv.)	J3
Poschiavo (valley)	K4
Pragel (pass)	G3
Quaternals (peak)	J4
Reuss (riv.)	F2
Rhätikon (mts.)	J3
Rheinwaldhorn (mt.)	G4
Rhine (riv.)	G4
Rhône (riv.)	D4
Rimpfischhorn (mt.)	E4
Ringelspitz (mt.)	H3
Risoux (mt.)	B3
Rosa (mt.)	E4
Rosstock (mt.)	G3
Rothorn (mt.)	E4
Saane (Sarine) (riv.)	D3
Saint Gotthard (pass)	G3

Saint Gotthard (tunnel)	G3
San Bernardino (pass)	H3
Säntis (mt.)	H2
Sarine (Saane) (riv.)	D3
Sarnen (lake)	F3
Schesaplana (mt.)	J3
Scherhorn (mt.)	G3
Schreckhorn (mt.)	F3
Schwarzhorn (mt.)	E4
Schwarzhorn (mt.)	G3
Seez (riv.)	H3
Sempach (lake)	F2
Septimer (pass)	J4
Sesvenna (peak)	K3
Sihlsee (lake)	G3
Silvretta (mt.)	J3
Simme (riv.)	D3
Simplon (pass)	F4
Simplon (tunnel)	F4
Sonnenhorn (mt.)	F4
Splügen (pass)	H3
Stockhorn (mt.)	E3
Sulzfluh (mt.)	J3
Susten (pass)	G3
Sustenhorn (mt.)	G4
Tamaro (mt.)	G4

Tamina (riv.)	H3
Tendre (peak)	B3
Terri (peak)	G3
Thunersee (lake)	E3
Thur (riv.)	G1
Ticino (riv.)	F3
Titlis (mt.)	F3
Tödi (mt.)	G3
Toggenburg (dist.)	H2
Töss (riv.)	G1
Tour (mt.)	C4
Umbrail (peak)	K3
Untersee (lake)	F1
Unterwalden (reg.)	F3
Upper Engadine (valley)	J4
Urirotstock (mt.)	F3
Vadret (peak)	J3
Valsermein (mt.)	H3
Vanil Noir (mt.)	D3
Velan (mt.)	D5
Visp (riv.)	E4
Vorab (mt.)	H3

Weisshorn (mt.)	J3
Weissmies (mt.)	F4
Wetterhorn (mt.)	F3
Wildhorn (mt.)	D4
Wildstrubel (mt.)	E4
Zellersee (lake)	G1
Zugersee (lake)	F2
Zürichsee (lake)	F2

LIECHTENSTEIN

CITIES and TOWNS

Schaan 4,552	H2
Triesen 2,971	H2
Vaduz (cap.) 4,614	H2

OTHER FEATURES

Grauspitz (mt.)	J2
Ochsenkopf (mt.)	J2
Rhätikon (mt.)	J2
Rhine (riv.)	J2

*City and suburbs

AUSTRIA

PROVINCES

Burgenland 272,119	D3
Carinthia 525,728	B3
Lower Austria 1,414,161	C3
Salzburg 401,766	B3
Styria 1,192,442	C3
Tirol 540,771	A3
Upper Austria 1,223,444	B2
Vienna (city) 1,614,841	D2
Vorarlberg 271,473	A3

CITIES and TOWNS†

Admont 3,126	C3
Allentsteig 2,783	C2
Altheim 4,766	B2
Althofen 3,886	C3
Amstetten 13,330	C2
Andau 3,058	D3
Arnoldstein 6,740	B3
Aspang Markt 2,316	C3
Attnang-Puchheim 7,837	B2
Bad Aussee 5,039	B3
Baden 22,631	D2
Badgastein 5,228	B3
Bad Goisern 6,360	B3
Bad Hofgastein 5,525	B3
Bad Ischl 12,060	B3
Bad Leonfelden 2,712	C2
Bad Sankt-Leonhard im Lavanttal 4,882	C3
Berndorf 8,371	D2
Bischofshofen 9,417	B3
Bludenz 12,050	A3
Bramberg am Wildkogel 3,129	B3
Braunau am Inn 16,432	B2
Bregenz 22,839	A3
Bruck an der Leitha 7,506	D2
Bruck an der Mur 16,359	C3
Deutsch Feistritz 3,820	C3
Deutschkreutz 3,673	D3
Deutsch Landsberg 6,614	C3
Deutsch Wagram 4,481	D2
Dornbirn 33,810	A3
Ebenthal 2,272	C3
Ebensee 9,413	B3
Eferding 3,014	C2
Eggenburg 3,730	C2
Ehrwald 2,198	A3
Horn 6,264	C3
Hüttenberg 3,251	C3
Imst 5,855	A3
Innsbruck 115,800	A3
Innsbruck* 167,200	A3
Jenbach 5,868	A3
Jennersdorf 4,210	C3
Judenburg 11,346	C3
Kapfenberg 26,001	C3
Kappl 2,156	A3
Kaprun 2,604	B3
Kindberg 6,128	C3
Kirchdorf an der Krems 3,471	C3
Kitzbühel 7,995	B3
Klagenfurt 74,326	C3
Klagenfurt* 112,600	C3
Klosterneuburg 21,912	D2
Knittelfeld 14,517	C3
Koflach 12,612	C3
Königswiesen 2,921	C2
Korneuburg 8,892	D2
Kössen 2,764	B3
Kötschach-Mauthen 3,740	B3
Krems an der Donau 21,733	C2
Kufstein 12,766	B3
Kundl 3,020	A3
Laa an der Thaya 5,455	D2
Laakirchen 7,664	B3
Lambach 3,301	C2
Landeck 7,388	A3
Längenfeld 2,838	A3
Langenlois 4,957	C2
Langenwang 4,071	C3
Lavamünd 4,120	C3
Leibnitz 6,646	C3
Lenzing 5,385	B3
Leoben 35,153	C3
Lienz 11,696	B3
Lezen 6,244	C3
Lilienfeld 3,126	C3
Linz 203,990	C2
Linz* 356,500	C2
Lustenau 15,239	A3
Mannersdorf am Leithagebirge 4,012	D3
Marchegg 2,678	D2
Mariazell 2,298	C3
Matrei in Osttirol 4,003	B3
Mattersburg 5,417	D3
Mattighofen 4,344	B2
Mauerkirchen 2,237	B2
Mautern in Steiermark 2,536	C3
Sankt Valentin 8,715	C2
Sankt Veit an der Glan 11,047	C3
Sankt Wolfgang im Salzkammergut 2,746	B3
Scharding 5,874	B2
Scheibbs 4,419	C2
Schladming 3,460	B3
Schrems 3,393	C2
Schruns 3,607	A3
Schwarzach im Pongau 3,616	B3
Schwaz 10,253	A3
Schwechat 14,997	D2
Schwertberg 3,881	C2
Sierning 8,162	C2
Sillian 1,988	B3
Solbad Hall in Tirol 12,335	A3
Spital am Pyhrn 2,315	C3
Spittal an der Drau 13,690	B3
Steinach 2,698	A3
Steyr 40,578	C2
Stockerau 12,634	D2
Strassburg 2,850	C3
Tamsweg 5,060	B3
Ternitz 10,287	C3
Traiskirchen 8,878	D2
Traun 20,843	C2
Trieben 4,639	C3
Trofaiach 8,731	C3
Tulln 7,705	D2
Velden am Wörthersee 7,306	C3
Vienna (cap.) 1,700,000	D2
Vienna* 1,858,700	D2
Vöcklabruck 10,627	B2
Voitsberg 11,094	C3
Völkermarkt 10,772	C3
Vordernberg 2,508	C3
Waidhofen an der Thaya 4,200	C2
Waidhofen an der Ybbs 5,218	C3
Weitensfeld-Flattnitz 5,206	B3
Weitra 3,250	C2
Weiz 8,241	C3
Wels 47,279	C2
Weyer Markt 2,518	C3
Wien (Vienna) (cap.) 1,700,000	D2
Wiener Neustadt 34,774	D3
Wildon 2,002	C3
Wilhelmsburg 6,307	C2
Wolfsberg 31,176	C3
Wörgl 7,811	A3
Ybbs an der Donau 6,422	C2
Zams 3,120	A3
Zell am See 7,456	B3
Zell am Ziller 1,882	A3
Zeltweg 8,431	C3
Zirl 4,157	A3
Zistersdorf 3,412	D2
Zwettl-Niederösterreich 11,624	C2

OTHER FEATURES

Allgäu Alps (mts.)	A3
Bavarian Alps (mts.)	A3
Bodensee (Constance) (lake)	A3
Brenner (pass)	A3
Carnic Alps (mts.)	B3
Constance (lake)	A3
Danube (riv.)	C2
Donau (Danube) (riv.)	D2
Drau (riv.)	C3
Enns (riv.)	C3
Grossglockner (mt.)	B3
Hohe Tauern (range)	B3
Inn (riv.)	A3
Karawanken (range)	C3
March (riv.)	D2
Mühlviertel (reg.)	C2
Mur (riv.)	C3
Neusiedler See (lake)	D3
Nieder Tauern (range)	B3
Ötztal Alps (mts.)	A3
Raab (riv.)	C3
Rhine (riv.)	A3
Salzach (riv.)	B2
Salzkammergut (reg.)	B3
Semmering (pass)	C3
Thaya (riv.)	C2
Traun (riv.)	C2
Wildspitze (mt.)	A3
Zugspitze (mt.)	A3

CZECHOSLOVAKIA

REPUBLICS

Czech Socialist Rep. 9,964,338	B1
Slovak Socialist Rep. 4,670,409	E2

REGIONS

Bratislava (city) 333,000	D2
Jihočeský 662,002	D2
Jihomoravský 1,966,850	D2
Praha (city) 1,161,200	C1
Severočeský 1,122,035	C1
Severomoravský 1,849,286	D2
Středočeský 1,193,041	C1
Středoslovenský 1,436,351	C2
Východočeský 1,214,581	C1
Východoslovenský 1,298,481	F2
Západočeský 865,094	C1
Západoslovenský 1,610,542	D2

CITIES and TOWNS

Aš 120,000	B1
Austerlitz (Slavkov)	D2
Banovce nad Bebravou 11,400	E2
Banská Bystrica 53,000	E2
Banská Štiavnica 7,486	E2
Bardějov 17,400	F2
Benešov 11,100	C2
Beroun 17,600	C2
Bílina 17,800	D1
Blansko 13,800	D2
Boskovice 8,531	D2
Brandýs nad Labem-Stará Boleslav 333,000	C1
Bratislava 333,000	D3
Břeclav 21,100	D2
Brezno 14,800	E2
Brno 335,700	D2
Bruntál 12,300	D2
Bystřice pod Hostýnem 6,681	D2
Čadca 16,800	E2
Čáslav 6,591	D3
Čáslav 10,200	C2
Česká Lípa 18,600	C1
Česká Třebová 14,700	C2
České Budějovice 80,800	C2
Český Brod 6,640	C1
Český Krumlov 9,900	C2
Český Těšín 17,200	E2
Cheb 27,000	B1
Chocen 8,198	C2
Chodov 14,400	B1
Chomutov 44,200	B1
Chotěboř 6,692	C2
Chrudim 18,800	C2
Detva 13,100	E2
Dobříš 6,378	C2
Dobruška 5,779	D1
Dolný Kubín 9,900	E2
Domažlice 9,100	B2
Dubnica nad Váhom 11,300	E2
Duchcov 9,712	B1
Dunajská Streda 13,000	D3
Dvory nad Žitavou 5,847	E3
Dvůr Králové nad Labem 16,800	C1
Falknov (Sokolov) 23,900	B1
Fiľakovo 7,822	E2
Frenštát pod Radhoštěm 8,516	E2
Frýdek-Místek 43,800	E2
Frýdlant v Čechách 5,948	C1
Frýdlant nad Ostravicí 6,250	E2
Galanta 12,300	D3
Gottwaldov 84,300	D2
Handlová 16,200	E2
Havľov 85,000	E2
Havlíčkův Brod 19,200	C2
Hlinsko 8,890	C2
Hlohovec 15,200	D3
Hlučín 15,300	E2
Hnúšťa-Likier	E2
Hodonín 22,600	D2
Holešov 9,091	D2
Holič 7,602	D2
Holice 6,151	C1
Horažďovice	B2
Hořice v Podkrkonoší 7,715	C1
Horná Štubňa	E2
Horní Benešov	C2
Horní Libina	C2
Hofovice 5,665	C2
Horšovský Týn	B2
Hostinné	C1
Hradec Králové 85,600	C1
Hranice 13,300	E2
Hrinová 7,800	E2
Hronov 9,767	D1
Hrušovany	E2
Humenné 22,200	F2
Humpolec 7,810	C2
Hurbanovo	E3
Hustopeče	D2
Ilava	E2
Ivančice 7,314	D2

Topography

0 50 100 MI.	
0 50 100 KM.	

| 5,000 m. 16,404 ft. | 2,000 m. 6,562 ft. | 1,000 m. 3,281 ft. | 500 m. 1,640 ft. | 200 m. 656 ft. | 100 m. 328 ft. | Sea Level | Below |

Eisenerz 11,563	C3
Eisenkappel-Vellach 3,761	C3
Eisenstadt 10,059	D3
Enns 9,622	C2
Feldbach 3,887	C3
Feldkirch 21,214	A3
Feldkirchen in Kärnten 11,188	B3
Ferlach 7,621	C3
Fieberbrunn 3,651	B3
Fohnsdorf 11,169	C3
Frankenmarkt 2,960	B3
Frauenkirchen 2,749	D3
Freistadt 5,956	C2
Freidberg 2,504	C3
Friesach 7,257	C3
Frohnleiten 5,081	C3
Fulpmes 2,553	A3
Fürstenfeld 6,054	C3
Gaming 4,181	C3
Gänserndorf 4,211	D2
Gleisdorf 4,921	C3
Gloggnitz 7,078	C3
Gmünd, Carinthia 2,267	B3
Gmünd, Lower Austria 6,323	C2
Gmunden 12,270	B3
Golling an der Salzach 3,089	B3
Götzis 7,931	A3
Gratwein 2,747	C3
Graz 251,900	C3
Graz* 314,200	C3
Grein 2,767	C2
f21Grieskirchen 4,519	B2
Grosssiegharts 3,288	C2
Grünburg 3,773	C2
Güssing 3,675	D3
Haag 5,060	C2
Hainburg an der Donau 6,009	D2
Hainfeld 3,897	C3
Hallein 14,371	B3
Hallstatt 1,313	B3
Hartberg 5,702	C3
Haslach an der Mühl 2,636	C2
Heidenreichstein 4,340	C2
Heiligenblut 1,324	B3
Hermagor-Preseggersee 7,531	B3
Herzogenburg 7,299	C2
Hohenau an der March 3,591	D2
Hohenberg 2,016	C3
Hohenems 11,487	A3
Hollabrunn 6,563	C2
Hopfgarten in Nordtirol 4,784	B3
Mauthausen 4,419	C2
Mauthen-Kötschach 3,750	B3
Mayrhofen 3,174	A3
Melk 5,108	C2
Mistelbach an der Zaya 6,306	D2
Mittersill 4,361	B3
Mödling 18,712	D2
Mondsee 2,141	B3
Murau 2,710	B3
Mürzzuschlag 11,564	C3
Neuberg an der Mürz 2,183	C3
Neumarkt am Wallersee 3,267	B3
Neunkirchen 9,102	C3
Neusiedl am See 3,999	D3
Neustift im Stubaital 2,789	A3
Ober Grafendorf 4,109	C2
Oberndorf bei Salzburg 3,293	B3
Obervellach 2,420	B3
Oberwart 5,661	C3
Paternion 5,805	B3
Perg 4,872	C2
Peuerbach 2,161	B2
Pfunds 2,043	A3
Pinkafeld 4,610	C3
Pöchlarn 3,990	C2
Portschach am Wörthersee 2,511	B3
Poysdorf 5,774	D2
Pregarten 3,249	C2
Raabs an der Thaya 4,194	C2
Radenthein 6,847	B3
Radkersburg 2,000	C3
Radstadt 3,585	B3
Rankweil 8,440	A3
Rechnitz 3,412	D3
Reichenau an der Rax 4,053	C3
Retz 4,780	C2
Ried im Innkreis 10,534	B2
Rottenmann 4,781	C3
Saalfelden am Steinernen Meer 10,172	B3
Salzburg 122,100	B3
Salzburg* 213,430	B3
Sankt Aegyd am Neuwalde 3,165	C3
Sankt Anton am Arlberg 2,086	A3
Sankt Johann in Tirol 5,942	B3
Sankt Michael in Obersteiermark 3,717	C3
Sankt Michael im Lungau 2,839	B3
Sankt Paul im Lavanttal 6,721	C3
Sankt Pölten 43,300	C2

AREA 32,375 sq. mi. (83,851 sq. km.)
POPULATION 7,507,000
CAPITAL Vienna
LARGEST CITY Vienna
HIGHEST POINT Grossglockner
12,457 ft. (3,797 m.)
MONETARY UNIT schilling
MAJOR LANGUAGE German
MAJOR RELIGION Roman Catholicism

AREA 49,373 sq. mi. (127,876 sq. km.)
POPULATION 15,276,799
CAPITAL Prague
LARGEST CITY Prague
HIGHEST POINT Gerlachovka 8,707 ft.
(2,654 m.)
MONETARY UNIT koruna
MAJOR LANGUAGES Czech, Slovak
MAJOR RELIGIONS Roman Catholicism,
Protestantism

AREA 35,919 sq. mi. (93,030 sq. km.)
POPULATION 10,709,536
CAPITAL Budapest
LARGEST CITY Budapest
HIGHEST POINT Kékes 3,330 ft.
(1,015 m.)
MONETARY UNIT forint
MAJOR LANGUAGE Hungarian
MAJOR RELIGIONS Roman Catholicism,
Protestantism

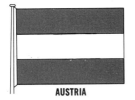
AUSTRIA

CZECHOSLOVAKIA

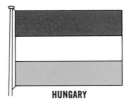
HUNGARY

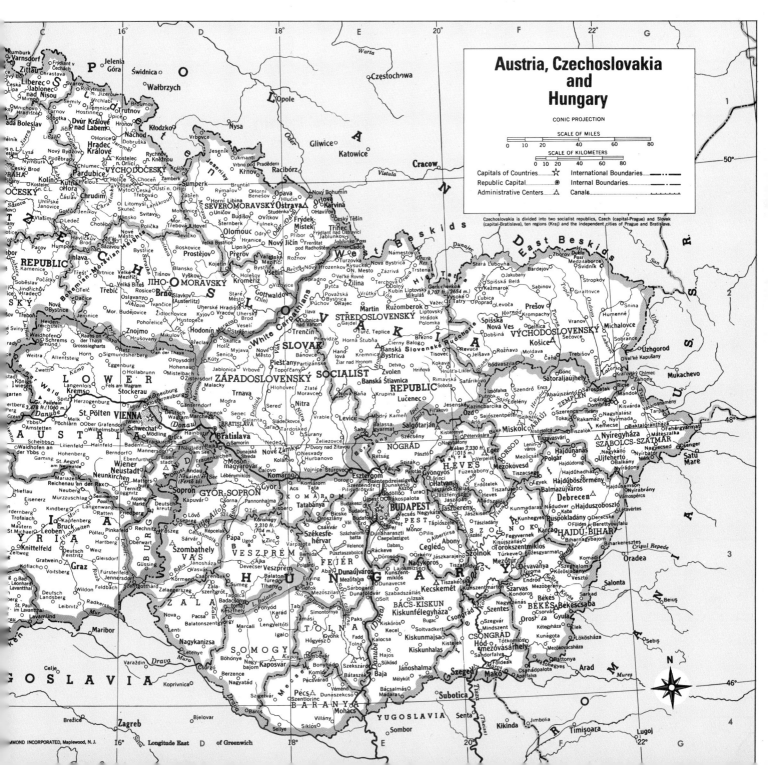

Austria, Czechoslovakia and Hungary

(continued)

Jablonec nad Nisou 36,300 .... C1
Jablonica D2
Jablunkov 9,405 .... E2
Jáchymov B1
Jakubany F2
Jaroměř 11,600 .... C1
Jelšava F2
Jemnice C2
Jeseník 10,900 .... D1
Jesenské F2
Jevíčko D2
Jičín 13,200 .... C1
Jihlava 44,500 .... C2
Jilemnice C1
Jindřichův Hradec 15,700 .... C2
Jiřkov 11,400 .... B1
Kadaň 18,100 .... B1
Kamenice C2
Kaplice C2
Karlovy Vary 43,300 .... B1
Karviná 79,100 .... E2
Kdyně B2
Kežmarok 11,000 .... F2
Kladno 61,200 .... B1
Klatovy 18,500 .... B2
Kojetín 5,852 .... D2
Kokava nad Rimavicou 5,391 .... E2
Kolárovo 10,500 .... D3
Kolín 29,100 .... C1
Komárno 28,200 .... D3
Košice 169,100 .... F2
Kostelec nad Orlicí 5,575 .... D1
Kráľovský Chlmec 5,329 .... G2
Kralupy nad Vltavou 16,900 .... C1
Kraslice 6,733 .... B1
Kremnica 5,941 .... E2
Krnov 25,000 .... D1
Kroměříž 23,200 .... D2
Krompachy 6,332 .... F2
Krupina 6,627 .... E2
Krupka 8,301 .... B1
Kutná Hora 19,200 .... C2
Kyjov 10,700 .... D2
Kynšperk 5,524 .... B1
Kysucké Nové Mesto 11,700 .... E2
Lanškroun 8,683 .... D2
Levice 19,000 .... E2
Levoča 10,100 .... F2
Libáň C1
Liberec 75,600 .... C1
Nové Město na Moravě 6,581 .... D2
Nové Město nad Váhom 15,900 .... D2
Nové Strašecí B1
Nové Zámky 27,300 .... D3
Nový Bohumín 16,700 .... E2
Nový Bor 7,621 .... C1
Nový Bydžov 6,824 .... C1
Nový Hrozenkov E2
Nový Jičín 21,400 .... E2
Nymburk 13,600 .... C1
Nýřany 6,204 .... B2
Nýrsko B2
Odry D2
Olomouc 82,800 .... D2
Opava 53,800 .... E2
Orlová 25,500 .... E2
Ostrava 293,500 .... E2
Ostrov 18,200 .... B1
Pardubice 78,500 .... C1
Partizánske 15,100 .... E2
Pelhřimov 11,900 .... C2
Pezinok 13,100 .... D2
Piešťany 25,400 .... D2
Písek 25,100 .... C2
Plzeň 155,000 .... B2
Počátky C2
Podbořany B1
Poděbrady 13,400 .... C1
Pohořelice D2
Polička 6,529 .... D2
Polná C2
Polomka E2
Poprad 25,800 .... F2
Považská Bystrica 19,300 .... E2
Prachatice 7,900 .... B2
Prague (Praha) (cap.) 1,161,200 .... C1
Přelouč 6,251 .... C1
Přerov 43,500 .... D2
Prešov 61,000 .... F2
Přeštice B2
Příbor 7,726 .... E2
Příbram 31,300 .... B2
Prievidza 30,900 .... E2
Prostějov 44,200 .... D2
Protivín C2
Púchov 9,306 .... E2
Radnice B2
Rajec E2
Rakovník 14,200 .... B1
Štúrovo 8,287 .... E3
Šumperk 25,900 .... D1
Šurany 6,693 .... E2
Sušice 10,300 .... B2
Svárov C1
Svidník 4,600 .... F2
Svitavy 15,000 .... D2
Tábor 28,100 .... C2
Tachov 11,400 .... B2
Telč 5,285 .... C2
Teplice 52,300 .... B1
Tišnov 8,263 .... D2
Topoľčany 17,500 .... D2
Třebíč 23,900 .... C2
Trebišov 13,700 .... F2
Třeboň 6,068 .... C2
Trenčín 38,800 .... E2
Třešť 5,053 .... C2
Třinec 32,000 .... E2
Trnava 48,600 .... D2
Trutnov 24,500 .... D1
Turnov 13,600 .... C1
Turzovka 6,107 .... E2
Uherské Hradiště 32,100 .... D2
Uherský Brod 12,800 .... D2
Uničov 10,800 .... D2
Úpice 6,323 .... C1
Ústí nad Labem 74,900 .... C1
Ústí nad Orlicí 13,700 .... D2
Valašské Meziříčí 19,400 .... D2
Varnsdorf 14,700 .... C1
Važec E2
Vejprty B1
Velká Bíteš D2
Velká Bystřice D2
Veľké Kapušany G2
Velké Meziříčí 7,590 .... D2
Veľké Rovné E2
Veselí nad Lužnicí C2
Veselí nad Moravou 11,500 .... D2
Vimperk 5,749 .... B2
Vítkov 5,138 .... D2
Vizovice D2
Vlašim 8,873 .... C2
Vodňany 5,620 .... C2
Vojnice E3
Volary B2
Volyně B2
Votice C2
Jablunka (pass) E2
Jeseníky (mts.) D1
Jihlava (riv.) D2
Krušné Hory (Erzgebirge) (mts.) B1
Labe (riv.) C1
Lipno (res.) C2
Lužnice (riv.) C2
Moldau (Vltava) (riv.) C2
Morava (riv.) D2
Nitra (riv.) E2
Oder (Odra) (riv.) D2
Ohře (riv.) B1
Ondava (riv.) F2
Orava (riv.) E2
Orlická (res.) C2
Sázava (riv.) C2
Slovenské Rudohorie (mts.) E2
Sudeten (mts.) C1
Svitava (riv.) D2
Svratka (riv.) D2
Tatra, High (mts.) E2
Torysa (riv.) F2
Úhlava (riv.) B2
Váh (riv.) D2
Vltava (riv.) C2
White Carpathians (mts.) E2

HUNGARY

COUNTIES

Bács-Kiskun 568,532 .... E3
Baranya 434,030 .... E4
Békés 436,987 .... F3
Borsod-Abaúj-Zemplén 808,924 .... F2
Budapest (city) 2,060,170 .... E3
Csongrád 456,862 .... F3
Fejér 421,568 .... E3
Győr-Sopron 428,476 .... D3
Hajdú-Bihar 552,417 .... F3
Heves 350,874 .... F3
Komárom 321,579 .... E3
Nógrád 239,907 .... E3
Pest 973,486 .... E3
Somogy 360,308 .... D3
Szabolcs-Szatmár 593,746 .... G3
Szolnok 446,379 .... F3
Tolna 266,414 .... E3
Vas 285,527 .... D3
Csenger 4,792 .... G3
Csepel 71,693 .... E3
Csepreg 4,079 .... D3
Csongrád 22,202 .... E3
Csorna 12,131 .... D3
Csorvás 6,826 .... F3
Csurgó 5,463 .... D3
Dabas 13,075 .... E3
Debrecen 192,484 .... F3
Derecske 9,579 .... F3
Dévaványa 11,208 .... F3
Devecser 5,482 .... D3
Dombóvár 19,917 .... E3
Dombrád 6,328 .... F2
Dömsöd 6,545 .... E3
Dorog 10,754 .... E3
Dunaföldvár 10,318 .... E3
Dunaharaszti 15,788 .... E3
Dunakeszi 25,187 .... E3
Dunaszekcső 2,999 .... E3
Dunaújváros 60,694 .... E3
Dunavecse 4,521 .... E3
Edelény 9,559 .... F2
Eger 61,283 .... F3
Egyek 7,956 .... F3
Elek 6,032 .... F3
Enes 2,565 .... F2
Endrőd 8,136 .... F3
Enying 7,518 .... E3
Érd 41,210 .... E3
Erdőtelek 4,250 .... F3
Esztergom 30,476 .... E3
Fadd 4,805 .... E3
Fegyvernek 8,421 .... F3
Fehérgyarmat 6,729 .... G3
Földeák 3,855 .... F3
Földes 5,293 .... F2
Fonyód 3,957 .... D3
Füzesabony 6,965 .... F3
Füzesgyarmat 7,097 .... F3
Gödöllő 28,057 .... E3
Gönc 2,875 .... F2
Gyoma 10,392 .... F3
Gyöngyös 36,927 .... E3
Gyönk 2,507 .... E3
Győr 123,618 .... D3
Gyula 34,514 .... F3
Hajdúböszörmény 32,145 .... F3
Hajdúdorog 10,118 .... F3
Hajdúhadház 13,626 .... F3
Körmend 11,787 .... D3
Körösladány 6,565 .... F3
Kőszeg 12,705 .... D3
Kunágota 4,622 .... F3
Kunhegyes 10,116 .... F3
Kunmadaras 7,343 .... F3
Kunszentmárton 11,103 .... F3
Kunszentmiklós 7,952 .... E3
Lajosmizse 12,872 .... E3
Lébénymiklós 6,190 .... D3
Lengyeltóti 3,389 .... D3
Leninváros 18,667 .... F3
Lenti 8,106 .... D3
Létavértes 9,106 .... G3
Letenye 4,395 .... D3
Lökösháza 2,514 .... F3
Lőrinci 10,679 .... E3
Madaras 4,519 .... E3
Makó 29,943 .... F3
Mándok 5,093 .... G2
Marcali 12,485 .... D3
Mátészalka 17,709 .... G3
Mélykút 7,640 .... E3
Mérk 3,211 .... G3
Mezőberény 12,702 .... F3
Mezőcsát 6,729 .... F3
Mezőfalva 5,008 .... E3
Mezőhegyes 8,631 .... F3
Mezőkovácsháza 7,473 .... F3
Mezőkövesd 18,435 .... F3
Mezőszilas 2,792 .... E3
Mezőtúr 22,018 .... F3
Mindszent 8,730 .... F3
Miskolc 206,727 .... F2
Mohács 21,385 .... E4
Monor 16,838 .... E3
Mór 12,066 .... E3
Mosonmagyaróvár 29,732 .... D3
Nádudvar 9,447 .... F3
Nagyatád 12,946 .... D3
Nagybajom 4,402 .... D3
Nagyecsed 8,225 .... G3
Nagyhalász 6,437 .... F2
Nagykálló 11,282 .... F3
Nagykanizsa 48,494 .... D3
Nagykáta 11,922 .... E3
Nagykőrös 27,900 .... E3
Nagyszénás 7,124 .... F3
Nyírábrány 4,509 .... G3
Nyíradony 7,146 .... G3
Szarvas 20,598 .... F3
Szécsény 5,690 .... E2
Százhalombatta 13,963 .... E3
Szeged 171,342 .... E3
Szeghalom 9,736 .... F3
Szegvár 6,395 .... F3
Székesfehérvár 103,197 .... E3
Szekszárd 34,592 .... E3
Szendrő 4,098 .... F2
Szentendre 16,844 .... E3
Szentes 35,326 .... F3
Szentgotthárd 5,837 .... D3
Szentlőrinc 3,926 .... E3
Szerencs 8,612 .... F2
Szigetvár 12,114 .... D3
Szikszó 6,419 .... F2
Szil 2,073 .... D3
Szolnok 75,203 .... F3
Szombathely 82,830 .... D3
Tab 3,922 .... E3
Tamási 7,602 .... E3
Tápiószele 5,575 .... E3
Tapolca 17,161 .... D3
Tarpa 3,436 .... G2
Tata 24,114 .... E3
Tatabánya 75,942 .... E3
Tét 4,441 .... D3
Tiszacsege 6,263 .... F3
Tiszaföldvár 12,560 .... F3
Tiszafüred 12,259 .... F3
Tiszakécske 12,378 .... E3
Tiszalök 6,230 .... F2
Tiszavasvári 13,292 .... F3
Tokaj 4,845 .... F2
Tolna 8,997 .... E3
Tompa 5,365 .... E3
Törökszentmiklós 25,551 .... F3
Tótkomlós 8,803 .... F3
Tura 8,235 .... E3
Túrkeve 11,393 .... F3
Újfehértó 14,412 .... F3
Újpest 80,384 .... E3
Újszász 7,098 .... F2
Vác 34,837 .... E3
Vál 2,488 .... E3
Vámospércs 5,213 .... F3
Várpalota 28,293 .... E3
Vásárosnamény 8,637 .... G2
Vasvár 4,275 .... D3
Vecsés 19,193 .... E3

Agriculture, Industry and Resources

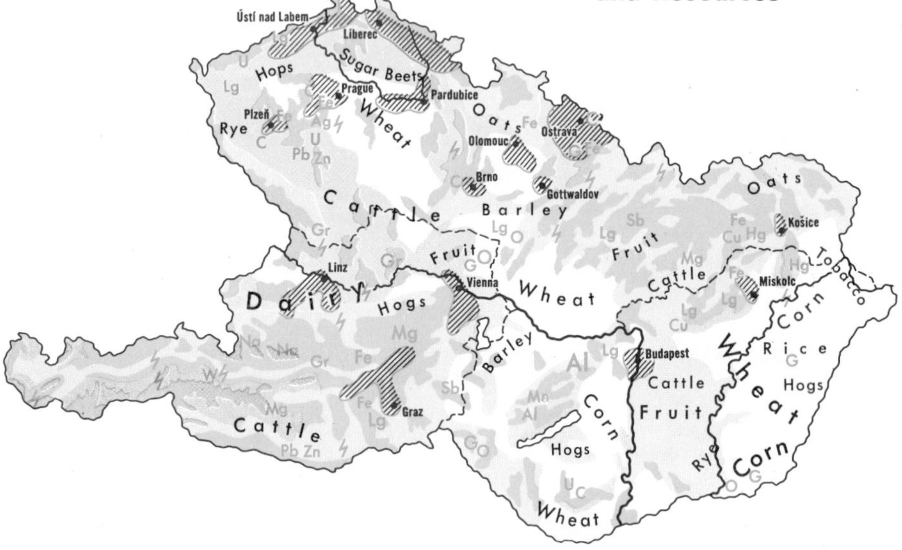

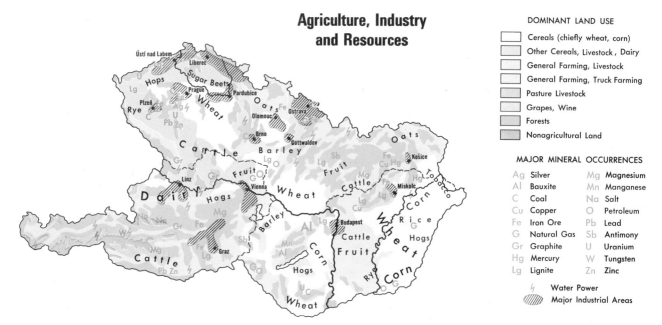

DOMINANT LAND USE

- Cereals (chiefly wheat, corn)
- Other Cereals, Livestock, Dairy
- General Farming, Livestock
- General Farming, Truck Farming
- Pasture Livestock
- Grapes, Wine
- Forests
- Nonagricultural Land

MAJOR MINERAL OCCURRENCES

Ag	Silver	Mg	Magnesium
Al	Bauxite	Mn	Manganese
C	Coal	Na	Salt
Cu	Copper	O	Petroleum
Fe	Iron Ore	Pb	Lead
G	Natural Gas	Sb	Antimony
Gr	Graphite	U	Uranium
Hg	Mercury	W	Tungsten
Lg	Lignite	Zn	Zinc

- Water Power
- Major Industrial Areas

Lidice C1
Lipník nad Bečvou 7,358 .... D2
Liptovský Mikuláš 19,400 .... E2
Litoměřice 19,700 .... C1
Litomyšl 8,112 .... D2
Litovel 5,805 .... D2
Litvínov 23,300 .... B1
Lomnice C2
Louny 15,200 .... B1
Lovosice 9,323 .... C1
Ľubica F2
Lučenec 23,300 .... E2
Lysá nad Labem 9,920 .... C1
Malacky 13,200 .... D2
Mariánské Lázně 14,600 .... B2
Martin 47,800 .... E2
Medzilaborce F2
Mělník 17,800 .... C1
Michalovce 23,600 .... G2
Mikulov 6,267 .... D2
Milevsko 7,091 .... C2
Mimoň 6,773 .... C1
Mladá Boleslav 36,900 .... C1
Mladá Vožice C2
Mnichovo Hradiště 5,239 .... C1
Modra 7,219 .... D2
Modrý Kameň 6,200 .... E2
Mohelnice 6,050 .... D2
Moldava nad Bodvou 5,397 .... F2
Moravská Třebová 9,052 .... D2
Moravské Budějovice 5,576 .... D2
Most 59,400 .... B1
Myjava 6,657 .... D2
Náchod 19,300 .... D1
Námestovo E2
Neded D2
Nejdek 8,187 .... B1
Nepomuk B2
Nesvady 5,453 .... E3
Netolice C2
Nitra 50,000 .... E2
Nová Baňa 6,218 .... E2
Nová Bystrica E2
Nová Bystřice C2
Nové Hrady C2
Nové Město na Moravě 6,581 .... D2
Revúca 5,901 .... F2
Říčany u Prahy 8,407 .... C2
Rimavská Sobota 5,800 .... E2
Rokycany 12,800 .... B2
Rokytnice nad Jizerou C1
Rosice D2
Roudnice nad Labem 11,800 .... C1
Rožňava 12,400 .... F2
Rožnov pod Radhoštěm 11,600 .... E2
Rumburk C1
Ružomberok 22,600 .... E2
Rychnov nad Kněžnou 7,500 .... D1
Rýmařov 7,522 .... D2
Sabinov 5,473 .... F2
Šafárikovo F2
Šahy 5,049 .... E2
Šaľa 15,200 .... D2
Samorín 8,287 .... D2
Sečovce 5,744 .... F2
Sedlčany C2
Semily 8,200 .... C1
Senec 8,544 .... D2
Senica 12,300 .... D2
Sereď 12,500 .... D2
Skalica 11,100 .... D2
Skuteč D2
Sládečkovce 5,598 .... D2
Slaný 13,200 .... C1
Slavkov D2
Snina 10,900 .... G2
Soběslav 6,140 .... C2
Sobotka C1
Sobrance G2
Sokolov 23,900 .... B1
Spišská Belá F2
Spišská Nová Ves 26,100 .... F2
Stará Ľubovňa 5,800 .... F2
Staré Město 6,293 .... D2
Šternberk 13,700 .... D2
Stod B2
Strakonice 19,000 .... B2
Strážnice 5,482 .... D2
Stříbro B2
Stropkov 5,645 .... F2
Studénka 9,744 .... D2
Vráble E2
Vracov D2
Vranov nad Teplou 14,700 .... F2
Vrbno pod Pradědem 5,594 .... D1
Vrbovce D1
Vrbové D2
Vrchlabí 11,700 .... C1
Vrútky 5,756 .... E2
Vsetín 24,100 .... D2
Vyškov 15,100 .... D2
Vysoké Mýto 8,830 .... D2
Vysoké Tatry F2
Vyšší Brod C2
Zábřeh 11,300 .... D2
Žamberk 5,040 .... D1
Žatec 17,400 .... B1
Zázrivá E2
Zbiroh B2
Zborov F2
Žďár nad Sázavou 17,800 .... C2
Želiezovce 5,478 .... E2
Žiar nad Hronom 14,800 .... E2
Židlochovice D2
Žilina 56,000 .... E2
Zlaté Moravce 10,300 .... E2
Zlín (Gottwaldov) 84,300 .... D2
Žlutice B1
Znojmo 28,500 .... D2
Zvolen 29,000 .... E2

OTHER FEATURES

Berounka (riv.) C2
Beskids, East (mts.) F1
Beskids, West (mts.) E2
Bohemian (for.) B2
Bohemian-Moravian Heights (hills) C2
Danube (riv.) C2
Dunajec (riv.) F2
Dyje (riv.) D2
Erzgebirge (mts.) B1
Gerlachovka (mt.) E2
Hornád (riv.) F2
Hron (riv.) E2
Ipeľ (riv.) E2
Veszprém 386,740 .... D3
Zala 316,610 .... D3

CITIES and TOWNS

Aba 4,271 .... E3
Abádszalók 6,386 .... F3
Abaújszántó 4,209 .... F2
Abony 15,624 .... E3
Ács 8,423 .... E3
Ajka 29,601 .... D3
Albertirsa 11,252 .... E3
Alsózsolca 5,045 .... F2
Arló 4,203 .... F2
Aszód 6,218 .... E3
Bácsalmás 9,025 .... E3
Badacsonytomaj 2,933 .... D3
Baja 38,456 .... E3
Baktalórántháza 3,736 .... G2
Balassagyarmat 18,534 .... E2
Balatonfüred 12,599 .... D3
Balkány 7,667 .... G3
Balmazújváros 17,371 .... F3
Barcs 11,448 .... D4
Bátaszék 7,274 .... E3
Battonya 9,324 .... F3
Békés 22,287 .... F3
Békéscsaba 67,266 .... F3
Berettyóújfalu 16,406 .... F3
Berzence 3,406 .... D3
Bicske 10,720 .... E3
Biharkeresztes 4,788 .... F3
Biharnagybajom 4,093 .... F3
Böhönye 3,215 .... D3
Bonyhád 14,841 .... E3
Budafok 40,623 .... E3
Budaörs 13,958 .... E3
Budakeszi 10,429 .... E3
Budapest (cap.) 2,060,170 .... E3
Bugak 4,989 .... E3
Cegléd 40,567 .... E3
Celldömölk 12,533 .... D3
Cigánd 4,767 .... F2
Csabrendek 3,045 .... D3
Csákvár 5,238 .... E3
Csanádpalota 4,642 .... F3
Hajdúnánás 18,146 .... F3
Hajdúsámson 7,492 .... F3
Hajdúszoboszló 23,374 .... F3
Hajós 5,113 .... E3
Hatvan 24,790 .... E3
Heves 10,943 .... F3
Hódmezővásárhely 54,481 .... F3
Hőgyész 3,534 .... E3
Ibrány 7,037 .... F2
Izsák 7,686 .... E3
Izsófalva 6,816 .... F2
Jánoshalma 12,534 .... E3
Jánosháza 3,274 .... D3
Jászapáti 10,424 .... E3
Jászárokszállás 10,139 .... E3
Jászberény 31,347 .... E3
Jászfényszaru 6,869 .... E3
Jászkarajenő 4,101 .... E3
Jászkisér 6,816 .... F3
Jászladány 7,823 .... F3
Kaba 6,654 .... F2
Kalocsa 18,613 .... E3
Kaposvár 72,330 .... D3
Kapuvár 11,243 .... D3
Karád 2,754 .... D3
Karcag 25,264 .... F3
Kazincbarcika 37,481 .... F2
Kecel 10,493 .... E3
Kecskemét 91,929 .... E3
Kemecse 4,583 .... F2
Keszthely 21,671 .... D3
Kétegyháza 4,728 .... F3
Kisbér 4,562 .... D3
Kiskőrös 15,499 .... E3
Kiskunfélegyháza 35,339 .... E3
Kiskunhalas 30,552 .... E3
Kiskunmajsa 14,439 .... E3
Kispest 65,106 .... E3
Kistelek 8,544 .... E3
Kisterenye 6,844 .... E2
Kisújszállás 13,699 .... F3
Kisvárda 17,828 .... G2
Komádi 8,765 .... F3
Komárom 19,955 .... E3
Komló 30,301 .... E3
Kondoros 7,319 .... F3
Nyírbátor 13,388 .... G3
Nyíregyháza 108,156 .... F3
Nyírmada 4,744 .... F2
Örkény 5,013 .... E3
Orosháza 36,243 .... F3
Oroszlány 20,604 .... E3
Ózd 48,521 .... F2
Pacsa 1,984 .... D3
Paks 19,514 .... E3
Pannonhalma 3,731 .... D3
Pápa 32,202 .... D3
Pásztó 7,962 .... E3
Pécs 168,788 .... E3
Pécsvárad 3,672 .... E3
Pétervására 2,753 .... F3
Pilis 9,055 .... E3
Pilisvörösvár 10,217 .... E3
Polgár 9,429 .... F3
Polgárdi 5,767 .... E3
Püspökladány 15,730 .... F3
Pusztaszabolcs 5,794 .... E3
Putnok 7,103 .... F2
Ráckeve 7,534 .... E3
Rajka 2,448 .... D3
Rakamaz 5,407 .... F2
Rákospalota 60,983 .... E3
Répcelak 1,997 .... D3
Ricse 2,992 .... G2
Sajószentpéter 13,992 .... F2
Salgótarján 49,320 .... E2
Sándorfalva 5,949 .... F3
Sárbogárd 11,178 .... E3
Sarkad 11,937 .... F3
Sárospatak 15,316 .... F2
Sárvár 15,126 .... D3
Sátoraljaújhely 19,252 .... F2
Sellye 2,804 .... D4
Siklós 10,567 .... E4
Simontornya 4,892 .... E3
Siófok 20,084 .... E3
Solt 6,911 .... E3
Soltvadkert 7,934 .... E3
Sopron 53,930 .... D3
Sükösd 4,430 .... E3
Sümeg 6,229 .... D3
Szabadszállás 8,223 .... E3
Velence 3,463 .... E3
Vémend 2,293 .... E3
Verpelét 4,622 .... F2
Veszprém 54,898 .... D3
Vésztő 9,815 .... F3
Villány 2,764 .... E4
Záhony 3,049 .... G2
Zalaegerszeg 39,671 .... D3
Zalaszentgrót 5,346 .... D3
Zirc 5,980 .... D3

OTHER FEATURES

Bakony (mts.) D3
Balaton (lake) D3
Berettyó (riv.) F3
Bükk (mts.) F2
Csepelsziget (isl.) E3
Danube (riv.) E3
Dráva (riv.) D3
Duna (Danube) (riv.) E3
Fertő tó (Neusiedler See) (lake) D3
Great Alföld (plain) F3
Hernád (riv.) F2
Kapos (riv.) D3
Kékes (mt.) E3
Körös (riv.) F3
Maros (riv.) F3
Mátra (mts.) E3
Mecsek (mts.) D3
Mura (riv.) D3
Rába (riv.) D3
Sajó (riv.) F2
Sárviz csatorna (canal) E3
Sió csatorna (canal) E3
Szentendreisziget (isl.) E3
Tisza (riv.) F3
Zala (riv.) D3

*City and suburbs.
†Population of Austrian cities are communes.

YUGOSLAVIA

AREA 98,766 sq. mi. (255,804 sq. km.)
POPULATION 22,471,000
CAPITAL Belgrade
LARGEST CITY Belgrade
HIGHEST POINT Triglav 9,393 ft. (2,863 m.)
MONETARY UNIT Yugoslav dinar
MAJOR LANGUAGES Serbo-Croatian, Slovenian,
  Macedonian, Montenegrin, Albanian
MAJOR RELIGIONS Eastern Orthodoxy,
  Roman Catholicism, Islam

ALBANIA

AREA 11,100 sq. mi. (28,749 sq. km.)
POPULATION 2,590,600
CAPITAL Tiranë
LARGEST CITY Tiranë
HIGHEST POINT Korab 9,026 ft. (2,751 m.)
MONETARY UNIT lek
MAJOR LANGUAGE Albanian
MAJOR RELIGIONS Islam, Eastern Orthodoxy,
  Roman Catholicism

ROMANIA

AREA 91,699 sq. mi. (237,500 sq. km.)
POPULATION 22,048,305
CAPITAL Bucharest
LARGEST CITY Bucharest
HIGHEST POINT Moldoveanul 8,343 ft.
  (2,543 m.)
MONETARY UNIT leu
MAJOR LANGUAGES Romanian, Hungarian
MAJOR RELIGION Eastern Orthodoxy

BULGARIA

AREA 42,823 sq. mi. (110,912 sq. km.)
POPULATION 8,862,000
CAPITAL Sofia
LARGEST CITY Sofia
HIGHEST POINT Musala 9,597 ft. (2,925 m.)
MONETARY UNIT lev
MAJOR LANGUAGE Bulgarian
MAJOR RELIGION Eastern Orthodoxy

GREECE

AREA 50,944 sq. mi. (131,945 sq. km.)
POPULATION 9,599,000
CAPITAL Athens
LARGEST CITY Athens
HIGHEST POINT Olympus 9,570 ft. (2,917 m.)
MONETARY UNIT drachma
MAJOR LANGUAGE Greek
MAJOR RELIGION Eastern (Greek) Orthodoxy

BULGARIA

GREECE

YUGOSLAVIA

ALBANIA

ROMANIA

Agriculture, Industry and Resources

DOMINANT LAND USE

- ⬜ Cereals (chiefly wheat, corn)
- ⬜ Mixed Farming, Horticulture
- ⬜ Pasture Livestock
- ⬜ Tobacco, Cotton
- ⬜ Grapes, Wine
- ⬜ Forests
- ⬜ Nonagricultural Land

MAJOR MINERAL OCCURRENCES

Ab	Asbestos	Mg	Magnesium
Ag	Silver	Mn	Manganese
Al	Bauxite	Mr	Marble
C	Coal	Na	Salt
Cr	Chromium	Ni	Nickel
Cu	Copper	O	Petroleum
Fe	Iron Ore	Pb	Lead
G	Natural Gas	Sb	Antimony
Hg	Mercury	U	Uranium
Lg	Lignite	Zn	Zinc

⚡ Water Power
▨ Major Industrial Areas

ALBANIA

CITIES and TOWNS

Berat 25,700	D5
Çorovodë	E5
Burrel	D5
Delvinë 6,000	D6
Durrës (Durazzo) 53,800	D5
Elbasan 41,700	E5
Ersekë	D5
Fier 23,000	D5
Gjirokastër 17,100	D5
Kavajë 18,700	D5
Korçë 47,300	E5
Krujë 7,900	D5
Kuçovë (Stalin) 14,000	D5
Kukës 6,100	E4
Leskovik	E5
Lezhë	D5
Lushnjë 18,900	D5
Memaliaj	D5
Peqin	D5
Përmet	D5
Peshkopi 6,600	E5
Pogradec 10,100	E5
Pukë	E4
Sarandë 8,700	D6
Shëngjin	D5
Shijak 6,200	D5
Shkodër 55,300	D5
Stalin 14,000	D5
Tepelenë	D5
Tiranë (Tirana)	
(cap.) 171,300	E5
Vlorë 50,000	D5

OTHER FEATURES

Adriatic (sea)	B4
Drin (riv.)	E4
Korab (mt.)	E5
Otranto (str.)	D5
Prespa (lake)	E5
Sazan (isl.)	D5
Scutari (lake)	D4
Vijosë (riv.)	D5

BULGARIA

CITIES and TOWNS

Akhtopol 938	H4
Alfatar 3,249	H4
Ardino 5,080	G5
Asenovgrad 43,049	G5
Aytos 20,967	H4
Balchik 11,070	H4
Bansko 10,011	F5
Belogradchik 6,892	F4
Berkovitsa 16,253	F4
Blagoevgrad 50,043	F5
Botevgrad 17,789	F4
Bregovo 5,567	F3
Breznik 4,699	F4
Burgas 144,449	H4
Byala 10,564	G4
Byala Slatina 15,788	F4
Chirpan 20,595	G4
Devin 7,120	G5
Dimitrovgrad 45,596	G4
Dobrich (Tolbukhin) 86,184	H4
Dryanovo 9,804	G4
Elena 7,008	G4
Elin Pelin 5,499	F4
Elkhovo 12,397	H4
Gabrovo 75,034	G4
General-Toshevo 8,928	H4
Godech 5,225	F4
Gorna Oryakhovitsa 34,157	G4
Gotse Delchev 17,015	F5
Grudovo 9,871	H4
Ikhtiman 11,482	F4
Isperikh 10,500	H4
Ivaylovgrad 3,900	H5
Karapelit	H4
Karlovo 25,472	G4
Karnobat 21,480	H4
Kavarna 10,872	H4
Kazanlŭk 53,607	G4
Kharmanli 19,240	H5
Khaskovo 75,031	G4
Kotel 8,229	H4
Krumovgrad 5,211	G5
Kubrat 9,826	H4
Kula 5,667	F4
Kŭrdzhali 47,757	G5
Kyustendil 48,239	F4
Lom 30,538	F4
Lovech 43,858	G4

Lukovit 10,400	G4
Malko Tŭrnovo 4,233	H4
Maritsa 8,664	H4
Michurin 4,434	H4
Mikhaylovgrad 40,064	F4
Momchilgrad 8,185	G5
Nesebŭr 6,768	H4
Nikopol 5,563	G4
Nova Zagora 21,872	G4
Novi Pazar 15,751	H4
Omurtag 9,067	H4
Oryakhovo 14,012	F4
Panagyurishte 20,649	F4
Pazardzhik 65,577	G4
Pernik 87,432	F4
Peshtera 16,882	G4
Petrich 24,381	F5
Pirdop 8,248	G4
Pleven 107,567	G4
Plovdiv 300,242	G4
Pomorie 11,960	H4
Popina	H3
Popovo 19,428	H4
Provadiya 15,143	H4
Radomir 10,436	F4
Razgrad 42,486	H4
Rázlog 13,690	F5
Rositsa	H4
Ruse 160,351	H4
Samokov 25,763	F4
Sandanski 19,003	F5
Sevlievo 24,421	G4
Shabla 4,471	J4
Shumen 83,525	H4
Silistra 58,270	H3
Simeonovgrad (Maritsa) 8,664	G4
Sliven 90,137	H4
Smolyan 29,032	G5
Smyadovo 5,020	H4
Sofia (cap.) 965,728	F4
Sozopol 3,877	H4
Stanke Dimitrov 42,034	F4
Stara Zagora 122,200	G4
Svilengrad 15,150	G5
Svishtov 29,412	G4
Teteven 12,555	G4
Tolbukhin 86,184	H4
Topolovgrad 7,230	H4
Troyan 23,692	G4
Trŭn 3,435	F4
Tŭrgovishte 38,796	H4
Tutrakan 11,447	H4
Varna 251,654	J4
Veliko Tŭrnovo 56,497	G4
Vidin 53,030	F4
Vratsa 61,265	F4
Yambol 75,861	H4
Zimnitsa	H4
Zlatograd 7,732	G5

OTHER FEATURES

Balkan (mts.)	F4
Black (sea)	J4
Danube (riv.)	H4
Dunav (Danube) (riv.)	H4
Emine (cape)	H4
Iskŭr (riv.)	F4
Kaliakra (cape)	J4
Maritsa (riv.)	G4
Mesta (riv.)	F5
Midzhur (mt.)	F4
Musala (mt.)	F4
Osŭm (riv.)	G4
Rhodope (mts.)	F5
Rujen (mt.)	F4
Struma (riv.)	F5
Timok (riv.)	F3
Tundzha (riv.)	H4
Vit (riv.)	G4

GREECE

REGIONS

Aegean Islands 417,813	G6
Athens, Greater 2,566,775	F7
Áyion Óros (aut.	
dist.) 1,732	G5
Central Greece and	
Euboea 966,543	F6
Crete 456,642	G8
Epirus 310,334	E6
Ionian Islands 184,443	D6
Macedonia 1,888,952	E5
Pelopónnisos 986,912	F7
Thessaly 659,913	F6
Thrace 329,582	G5

CITIES and TOWNS

Agrínion 30,973	E6
Aíyina 5,704	F7

Aíyion 18,829	F6
Alexandroúpolis 22,995	H5
Alivérion 4,414	G6
Almirós 5,680	F6
Amaliás 14,177	E7
Amfilokhía 4,668	E6
Ámfissa 6,605	F6
Andíssa 1,762	H6
Andravídha 3,046	E6
Ándros 1,827	G7
Áno Víannos 1,431	G8
Andýía 2,750	G8
Ardhéa 3,555	F5
Areópolis 674	F7
Argalastí 1,621	F6
Árgos 18,890	F7
Argostólion 7,060	E6
Arkhángelos 3,016	J7
Árnaia 2,424	F5
Árta 19,498	E6
Astipálaia 787	H7
Atalándi 4,581	F6
Athens (cap.) 867,023	F7
Athens* 2,566,775	F7
Ayía 3,241	F6
Áyios Kírikos 1,083	H7
Áyios Matthaíos 1,596	D6
Áyios Nikólaos 5,002	G8
Candia (Iráklion) 77,506	G8
Canea (Khaniá) 40,564	G8
Corinth 20,773	F6
Delfí 1,185	F6
Delviнákion 1,067	E6
Dhidhimótikhon 8,388	H5
Dhíkaia 1,222	H5
Dhimitsána 996	F7
Dhomokós 1,991	F6
Dráma 29,692	F5
Édhessa 13,967	F5
Elassón 7,200	F6
Eleftheroúpolis 4,888	G5
Ermoúpolis 13,502	G7
Fársala 6,967	F6
Filiátes 2,579	E6
Filiátrá 5,919	E7
Filíppiás 3,248	E6
Flórina 11,164	E5
Gargalánoi 5,888	E7
Grevená 8,106	E5
Ídhra 2,381	F7
Ierápetra 7,055	G8
Igoumenítsa 4,109	E6
Ioánnina 40,130	E6
Íos 1,270	G7
Iráklion 77,506	G8
Ístaia 4,059	F6
Itháki 2,293	E6
Kalámai 39,133	F7
Kalampáka 5,453	E6
Kalávrita 1,948	F6
Kálimnos 6,492	H7
Kándanos 403	F8
Kardhítsa 25,685	E6
Kariá 1,350	E6
Kariaí 301	G5
Káristos 3,550	G6
Kárpathos 1,363	H8
Karpenísion 4,414	E6
Kastéllion	
(Kíssamos) 2,996	F8
Kastéllion 1,152	G8
Kastoría 15,407	E5
Katákolon 690	E7
Katerini 28,808	F5
Kaválla 46,234	G5
Kéa 693	G7
Kérkira 28,630	D6
Khálkis 36,300	F6
Khaniá 40,564	G8
Khíos 24,084	G6
Khóra Sfakíon 246	G8
Kiáton 7,392	F6
Kilkís 10,538	F5
Klmí 2,772	F6
Kiparissía 3,882	E7
Kíssamos 2,996	F8
Kíthira 349	F7
Komotiní 28,896	G5
Kónitsa 3,150	E5
Koropí 9,367	G7
Kos 7,828	H7
Kozáni 23,240	E5
Kranídhion 3,657	F7
Lagkadás 1,350	F5
Lamía 37,872	F6
Langadhás 6,707	F5
Langádhia	F7
Lárisa 72,336	F6
Lávrion 8,283	G7
Leonídhion 3,181	F7
Levkádhia 15,445	E6
Levkás 6,818	E6
Limenária 1,507	G5

(continued on following page)

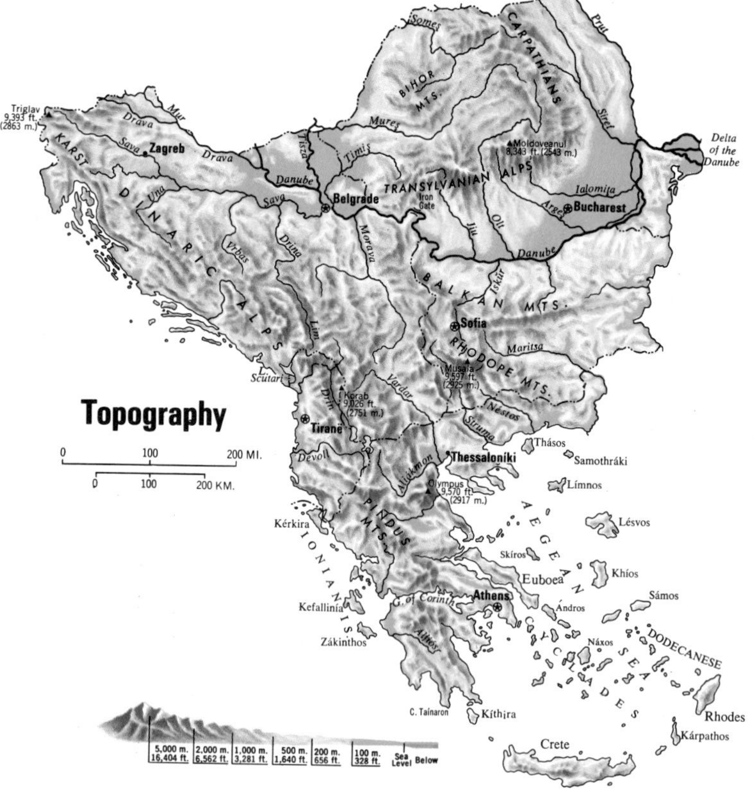
Triglav 9,393 ft. (2863 m.)
KARST
Mur
Drava
Sava
Zagreb
Drava
DINARIC ALPS
Una
Vrbas
Drina
Lim
Scutari
Someş
Mureş
BIHOR MTS.
CARPATHIANS
Siret
Prut
Tisza
Timiş
Moldoveanul 8,343 ft. (2543 m.)
TRANSYLVANIAN ALPS
Ialomiţa
Argeş
Olt
Jiu
Bucharest
Danube
Delta of the Danube
Belgrade
Iron Gate
Morava
BALKAN MTS.
Iskŭr
Sofia
RHODOPE MTS.
Maritsa
Musala 9,597 ft. (2925 m.)
Vardar
Korab 9,026 ft. (2751 m.)
Drin
Tiranë
Nestos
Struma
Devoll
Thásos
Samothráki
Thessaloníki
Aliákmon
Olympus 9,570 ft. (2917 m.)
Límnos
PINDUS MTS.
Kérkira
IONIAN SEA
AEGEAN SEA
Lésvos
Skíros
Khíos
Euboea
G. of Corinth
Athens
Kefallinía
Sámos
Ándros
Zákinthos
Alfiós
Náxos
CYCLADES
DODECANESE
C. Taínaron
Kíthira
Rhodes
Kárpathos
Crete
5,000 m. 16,404 ft.
2,000 m. 6,562 ft.
1,000 m. 3,281 ft.
500 m. 1,640 ft.
200 m. 656 ft.
100 m. 328 ft.
Sea Level
Below
0
100
200 MI.
100
200 KM.

Topography

Límni 2,394 F6
Líndos 700 J7
Litókhoron 5,561 F5
Lixoúrion 3,364 E6
Loutrá Aidhipsoú 2,195 F6
Marathón 1,976 G6
Megalópolis 3,357 E7
Mégara 17,294 F6
Meligalá 1,724 F7
Mesolóngion 11,614 E6
Messíni 6,625 E7
Métsovon 2,823 E6
Mikínai 390 F7
Mílos 850 G7
Mírina 3,982 G6
Míthimna 1,414 G6
Mitilíni 23,426 H6
Moírai 2,948 G8
Moláoi 2,484 F7
Monólithos 247 H7
Moúdhros 1,024 G6
Náousa 17,375 F5
Návpaktos 8,170 F6
Návplion 9,281 F7
Náxos 2,892 G7
Neápolis 3,070 F7
Neméa 4,356 F7
Néon Karlóvasi 4,401 H7
Nestórion 1,143 E5
Nigríta 7,301 F5
Oinóí 188 F6
Orestías 10,727 H5
Paramithía 2,747 E6
Pátrai 111,607 E6
Pérdika 1,198 E6
Péta 2,116 E6
Pílos 2,258 E7
Piraiévs (Piraeus) 187,362 F7
Pírgos 20,599 E7
Piryí 1,455 G6
Píthion 1,047 H5
Plomárion 4,353 H6
Políkastron 5,279 F5
Polikhnitos 4,152 G6
Políyiros 3,707 F5
Póros 4,051 F7
Préveza 11,439 E6
Psakhná 4,650 F6
Psári 622 E7
Ptolemaís 16,588 E5
Réthimnon 14,969 G8
Rhodes (Ródhos) 32,092 J7
Salamís 18,256 F6
Salonika
(Thessaloníki) 345,799 F5
Sámi 957 E6
Sámos 5,146 H7
Samothráki 508 G5
Sápai 2,456 G5
Sérrai 39,897 F5
Sérvia 3,834 F5
Siátista 4,852 E5
Sidhirókastron 6,363 F5
Sími 2,344 H7
Sitía 6,167 H8
Skíathos 3,707 F6
Skíros 1,925 G6
Skópelos 2,545 F6
Souflíon 5,637 H5
Sparta 10,549 F7
Spétsai 3,427 F7
Spíli 789 G8
Stavrós 1,700 F5
Stilís 4,427 F6
Thásos 2,052 G5
Thessaloníki 345,799 F5
Thessaloníki* 482,361 F5
Thíra 1,322 G7
Thívai 15,971 F6
Timbákion 3,229 G8
Tínos 3,423 G7
Tírnavos 10,451 F6
Tríkkala 34,794 E6
Trípolis 20,209 F7
Vámos 652 F8
Vartholomión 3,015 E7
Vathí 2,491 H7
Velvendós 4,063 F5
Vérroia 29,528 F5
Vólos 51,290 F6
Vónitsa 3,324 E6
Vrondádhes 4,253 G6
Xánthi 24,867 G5
Yerolimín 73 F7
Yiannitsá 18,151 F5
Yíthion 4,915 F7
Zákinthos 9,339 E7
Zante (Zákinthos) 9,339 E7

OTHER FEATURES

Aegean (sea) G6
Akrítas (cape) E7
Aktí (pen.) G5
Amorgós (isl.) G7
Anáfi (isl.) G7
Andikíthira (isl.) F8
Ándros (isl.) G7
Árda (riv.) G5
Argolís (gulf) F7
Astipálaia (isl.) H7
Áthos (mt.) G5
Áyios Evstrátios
(isl.) G6
Áyios Yeóryios (cape) G5
Cephalonia (Kefallinía)
(isl.) E6
Corfu (Kérkira) (isl.) D6
Corinth (gulf) F6
Crete (isl.) G8
Crete (sea) G7
Cyclades (isls.) G7
Día (isl.) G8
Dodecanese (isls.) H8
Euboea (Évvoia)
(isl.) G6
Évros (riv.) H5
Évvoia (isl.) G6
Gávdhos (isl.) F8
Ídhi (mt.) G8
Ikaría (isl.) G7
Ionian (sea) D7
Íos (isl.) G7
Itháki (Ithaca) (isl.) E6
Kafirévs (cape) G6
Kálimnos (isl.) H7
Kárpathos (isl.) H8
Kásos (isl.) H8
Kassándra (pen.) F6
Kéa (isl.) G7
Kefallinía (isl.) E6
Kérkira (isl.) D6
Khálki (isl.) H7
Khaniá (gulf) G8
Khíos (isl.) G6
Kímolos (isl.) G7
Kiparissía (gulf) E7
Kíthira (isl.) F7
Kíthnos (isl.) G7
Kos (isl.) H7
Kriós (cape) F8
Kríti (Crete) (isl.) G8
Lakonía (gulf) F7
Léros (isl.) H7
Lésvos (isl.) G6
Levítha (isl.) H7
Levkás (isl.) E6
Límnos (isl.) G6
Maléa (cape) F7
Matapan (Taínaron) (cape) F7
Merabéllou (gulf) H8
Mesará (gulf) G8
Messíni (gulf) E7
Míkonos (isl.) G7
Mílos (isl.) G7
Mirtóön (sea) F7
Náxos (isl.) G7
Néstos (riv.) G5
Nísiros (isl.) H7
Northern Sporades (isls.) F6
Olympia (isls.) E7
Olympus (mt.) F5
Parnassus (mt.) F6
Páros (isl.) G7
Pátmos (isl.) H7
Paxoí (isl.) D6
Pindus (mts.) E6
Piniós (riv.) E6
Prespa (lake) E5
Psará (isl.) G6
Psevdhókavos (cape) G6
Rhodes (isl.) H7
Rhodope (mts.) G5
Salonika (Thermaic) (gulf) F6
Sámos (isl.) H7
Samothráki (isl.) G5
Saría (isl.) H8
Saronic (gulf) F7
Sérifos (isl.) G7
Sídheros (cape) H8
Sífnos (isl.) G7
Sími (isl.) H7
Síros (isl.) G7
Sithoniá (pen.) F5
Skíros (isl.) G6
Spátha (cape) F8
Strimón (gulf) G5
Strofádhes (isls.) E7
Taínaron (cape) F7
Thásos (isl.) G5
Thermaic (gulf) F6
Thíra (isl.) G7
Tílos (isl.) H7
Tínos (isl.) G7
Toronaic (gulf) F5
Vardar (riv.) E5
Voïvís (lake) F6
Vólvi (lake) F5
Voúxa (cape) F8
Zákinthos (Zante)
(isl.) E7

ROMANIA

CITIES and TOWNS

Aiud 25,173 F2
Alba Iulia 44,552 F2
Alexandria 38,296 G3
Anina 11,594 E3
Arad 161,568 E2
Babadag 8,423 J3
Bacău 131,413 H2
Baia de Aramă 5,065 F3
Baia Mare 112,893 F2
Băile Herculane 4,606 F3
Băileşti 21,246 F3
Balş 16,091 G3
Beiuş 9,992 F2
Bereşti Tîrg H2
Bicaz 9,490 G2
Bîrlad 59,059 H2
Bistriţa 47,562 G2
Bivolari H2
Blaj 21,678 F2
Borşa 25,287 G2
Botoşani 69,881 H2
Brad 18,391 F2
Brăila 203,983 H3
Braşov 259,108 G3
Bucharest (Bucureşti)
(cap.) 1,832,015 G3
Bucharest* 1,960,097 G3
Buhuşi 20,204 H2
Buzău 106,738 H3
Buziaş 8,310 E3
Calafat 16,421 F3
Călăraşi 58,960 H3
Caracal 31,159 G3
Caransebeş 27,429 F3
Carei 24,496 F2
Cernavodă 14,686 J3
Chişineu Criş 9,344 E2
Cîmpeni 7,722 F2
Cîmpia Turzii 23,745 F2
Cîmpina 33,259 H3
Cîmpulung 33,448 G3
Cîmpulung Moldovenesc 19,270 G2
Cisnădie 21,114 G3
Cluj-Napoca 274,095 F2
Cogealac J3
Comaneşti 18,177 H2
Constanţa 279,308 J3
Corabia 20,454 G4
Costeşti 10,446 G3
Craiova 220,893 F3
Cujmir F3
Curtea de Argeş 23,555 G3
Dăbuleni F4
Dăeni J3
Darabani 12,207 H1
Dej 35,396 F2
Deta 6,956 E3
Deva 68,290 F3
Dorohoi 23,121 H2
Drăgăneşti Olt 11,606 G3
Drăgăşani 16,290 F3
Drobeta-Turnu Severin 80,114 F3
Făgăraş 34,762 G3
Fălciu J2
Fălticeni 22,463 H2
Făurei 3,620 H3
Feteşti 28,730 H3
Focşani 62,275 H3
Folteşti H3
Găeşti 13,384 G3
Galaţi 252,884 H3
Gheorghe Gheorghiu-Dej 41,297 H2
Gheorghieni 20,592 G2
Gherla 19,303 G2
Giurgiu 53,241 G3
Haţeg 9,706 F3
Hîrlău 8,135 H2
Hîrşova 8,434 J3
Huedin 8,557 F2
Hunedoara 83,159 F3
Huşi 24,329 J2
Iaşi 262,493 H2
Ineu 10,414 E2
Isaccea 5,283 J3
Jibou F2
Jimbolia 15,325 E3
Lipova 12,427 E2
Luduş 15,771 G2
Lugoj 48,558 F3
Lupeni 28,251 F3
Mangalia 27,263 J4
Medgidia 43,691 J3
Mediaş 68,442 G2
Miercurea Ciuc 38,097 G2
Mizil 14,294 H3
Mociu G2
Moineşti 21,015 H2
Moldova Nouă 18,498 E3
Moreni 17,743 G3
Nădlac 8,407 E2
Năsăud 8,646 G2
Negreşti 7,435 H2
Ocna Mureş 16,381 G2
Odobeşti 8,440 H3
Odorheiu Secuiesc 33,392 G2
Olteniţa 25,536 H3
Oradea 175,400 E2
Orăştie 18,769 F3
Oraviţa 13,628 E3
Orşova 14,873 F3
Panciu 7,772 H3
Paşcani 26,937 H2
Pătulele F3
Pechea H3
Pecica E2
Periam E2
Petrila 25,087 F3
Petroşeni 42,316 F3
Piatra Neamţ 84,192 G2
Pincota 7,494 E2
Piteşti 125,029 G3
Pleniţa F3
Ploieşti 207,009 H3
Poenari Burchi G3
Poiana Mare F4
Pucioasa 14,056 G3
Rădăuţi 24,222 G2
Reghin 31,948 G2
Reşiţa 90,698 E3
Rîmnicu Sărat 29,815 H3
Rîmnicu Vîlcea 75,070 G3
Roman 56,466 H2
Roşiori de Vede 28,832 G3
Săcele 29,391 G3
Salonta 19,698 E2
Satu Mare 108,152 F2
Săveni 7,913 H1
Sebeş 27,448 F3
Sebiş 6,401 F2
Segarcea 8,783 F3
Sfîntu Gheorghe 51,210 G3
Sfîntu Gheorghe J3
Sibiu 156,854 G3
Sighetu Marmaţiei 38,879 F2
Sighişoara 32,296 G2
Şimleul Silvaniei 14,780 F2
Sinaia 14,215 G3
Sînnicolaul Mare 13,565 E2
Siret 6,677 G1
Slănic 8,017 G3
Slatina 54,954 G3
Slobozia 35,207 H3
Solca 4,835 G2
Sovata 10,745 G2
Ştefăneşti H2
Strehaia 11,431 F3
Suceava 66,857 G2
Sulina 5,240 J3
Tăşnad 10,441 F2
Techirghiol 11,228 J3
Tecuci 37,928 H3
Timişoara 281,320 E3
Tinca F2
Tîrgovişte 71,533 G3
Tîrgu Cărbuneşti 7,536 F3
Tîrgu Frumos 6,428 H2
Tîrgu Jiu 70,629 F3
Tîrgu Mureş 129,284 G2
Tîrgu Neamţ 15,756 G2
Tîrgu Ocna 12,960 H2
Tîrgu Secuiesc 18,265 H2
Tîrnăveni 27,799 F2
Topliţa 14,347 G2
Tulcea 67,091 J3
Turda 57,972 F2
Turnu Măgurele 30,003 G4
Urlaţa 10,900 H3
Urziceni 13,500 H3
Vasile Roaită J3
Vaslui 44,134 H2
Vatra Dornei 16,748 G2
Videle 11,323 G3
Vişeul de Sus 20,697 F2
Viziru H3
Zalău 36,158 F2
Zărneşti 23,378 G3
Zimnicea 15,111 G4

OTHER FEATURES

Argeş (riv.) G3
Bîrlad (riv.) H2
Black (sea) J4
Brăila (marshes) H3
Buzău (riv.) H3
Carpathian (mts.) G2
Crişul Alb (riv.) F2
Crişul Repede (riv.) F2
Danube (delta) J3
Danube (riv.) H4
Ialomiţa (marshes) J3
Ialomiţa (riv.) H3
Jijia (riv.) H2
Jiu (riv.) F3
Moldoveanul (mt.) G3
Mureş (riv.) E2
Olt (riv.) G3
Peleaga (mt.) F3
Pietrosul (mt.) G2
Prut (riv.) J2
Siret (riv.) H2
Someş (riv.) F2
Timiş (riv.) E3
Tîrnava Mare (riv.) G2
Transylvanian Alps (mts.) G3

YUGOSLAVIA

INTERNAL DIVISIONS

Bosnia and Hercegovina
(rep.) 3,710,965 C3
Croatia (rep.) 4,396,397 C3
Kosovo (aut. reg.) 1,240,919 E4
Macedonia (rep.) 1,623,598 E5
Montenegro (rep.) 527,207 D4
Serbia (rep.) 8,401,673 E3
Slovenia (rep.) 1,697,068 B2
Vojvodina (aut.
prov.) 1,953,980 D3

CITIES and TOWNS

Aleksinac 11,943 E4
Apatin 17,501 D3
Arendjelovac 15,659 E3
Bačka Topola 16,028 D3
Bakar B3
Banja Luka 85,786 C3
Bar 3,594 D4
Bečej 26,616 E3
Bela Crkva 11,137 E3
Belgrade (cap.) 727,945 E3
Beli Manastir 7,325 D3
Beograd (Belgrade)
(cap.) 727,945 E3
Berovo 5,053 F5
Bihać 24,155 B3
Bijeljina 24,888 D3
Bijelo Polje 9,298 D4
Bileća 4,083 D4
Biograd 3,595 B4
Bitola 64,467 E5
Bjelovar 21,019 C3
Blato 5,591 C4
Bled 4,710 A2
Bor 27,520 E3
Bosanska Dubica 9,191 C3
Bosanska Gradiška 9,742 C3
Bosanska Kostajnica 2,535 B3
Bosanska Krupa 8,947 C3
Bosanski Brod 10,113 D3
Bosanski Novi 9,861 C3
Bosanski Petrovac 4,113 C3
Bosanski Šamac 4,949 D3
Brčko 25,575 D3
Brežice 3,271 B3
Budva 2,483 D4
Bugojno 9,079 C3
Čačak 38,890 E4
Čakovec 11,766 C2
Čapljina 4,677 C4
Caribrod (Dimitrovgrad) 5,449 F4
Cazin 1,213 B3
Celje 30,827 B2
Cetinje 12,089 D4
Ćuprija 17,691 E4
Daruvar 8,478 C3
Debar 8,597 E5
Derventa 11,887 C3
Dimitrovgrad 5,449 F4
Djakovica 29,499 E4
Djakovo 15,833 D3
Doboj 18,073 C3
Donji Vakuf 4,928 C3
Drvar 6,237 C3
Dubrovnik 31,213 C4
Fiume (Rijeka) 128,883 B3
Foča 9,370 D4
Gacko 1,641 D4
Gevgelija 9,319 F5
Glamoč 2,627 C3
Gnjilane 21,359 E4
Gornji Milanovac 11,114 D3
Gornji Vakuf 2,429 C4
Gospić 8,238 B3
Gostivar 18,805 E5
Gračac 3,228 B3
Gračanica 9,302 D3
Gradačac 7,571 D3
Grubišno Polje 2,771 C3
Gusinje 2,616 D4
Herceg Novi 6,645 D4
Ivangrad 11,373 E4
Ivanjica 5,719 E4
Jajce 9,221 C3
Jesenice 16,163 A2
Kanjiža 11,348 D2
Karlovac 47,046 B3
Kavadarci 17,974 E5
Kičevo 14,189 E5
Kikinda 37,392 E3
Kladanj 3,255 D3
Ključ 3,466 C3
Knin 7,279 C3
Knjaževac 11,734 F4
Kočani 16,611 F5
Kočevje 7,277 B3
Kolašin 2,111 D4
Konjic 9,161 D4
Koper 16,683 A3
Koprivnica 16,398 C2
Kosovska Mitrovica 42,526 E4
Kostajnica 9,161 C3
Kotor 5,728 D4
Kragujevac 72,080 E3
Kraljevo 28,065 E4
Kranj 26,341 B2
Križevci 8,501 C2
Krk 1,500 B3
Krško 4,451 B3
Kruševac 29,902 E4
Kulen Vakuf 1,078 B3
Kumanovo 44,791 E4
Kutina 10,892 C3
Leskovac 46,050 E4
Livno 7,223 C4
Ljubinje 785 D4
Ljubljana 169,064 B3
Ljubuški 2,891 C4
Loznica 13,513 D3
Maglaj 5,869 D3
Makarska 6,589 C4
Maribor 94,976 B2
Modriča 7,406 D3
Mostar 47,821 D4
Murska Sobota 9,665 C2
Našice 5,836 C3
Negotin 11,325 F3
Nevesinje 3,077 D4
Nikšić 28,940 D4
Nin 1,782 B3
Niš 128,231 F4
Nova Gorizia A2
Nova Gradiška 11,765 C3
Novi 2,682 B3
Novi Pazar 28,696 E4
Novi Sad 143,591 D3
Novo Mesto 9,553 B3
Novska 5,168 C3
Ogulin 9,975 B3
Ohrid 26,352 E5
Omiš 3,515 C4
Opatija 9,238 A3
Osijek 94,989 D3
Pag 2,318 B3
Pančevo 53,979 E3
Paraćin 21,555 E4
Peć 41,783 E4
Petrinja 12,296 B3
Piran 5,485 A3
Pirot 29,658 F4
Plav 3,072 D4
Pljevlja 14,459 D4
Ploče 4,257 C4
Pola (Pula) 47,117 A3
Poreč 4,512 A3
Postojna 6,085 B3
Požarevac 33,336 E3
Preševo 7,634 E4
Priboj 12,556 D4
Prijedor 22,379 C3
Prijepolje 7,960 D4
Prilep 48,045 E5
Priština 71,264 E4
Prizren 41,875 E4
Prokuplje 20,617 E4
Prozor 1,420 C4
Ptuj 9,245 C2
Pula 47,117 A3
Rab 1,675 B3
Radoviš 9,373 F5
Ragusa (Dubrovnik) 31,213 C4
Raška 3,935 E4
Ravne na Koroškem 6,529 B2
Rijeka 128,883 B3
Rogatica 4,801 D4
Rovinj 8,998 A3
Rožaj E4
Ruma 24,180 D3
Šabac 43,539 D3
Samobor 7,821 B3
Sanski Most 8,718 C3
Sarajevo 245,058 D4
Senj 4,927 B3
Senta 24,694 D3
Šibenik 29,619 C4
Šid 11,867 D3
Sinj 4,705 C4
Sisak 37,215 C3
Sjenica 9,118 E4
Škofja Loka 4,971 A2
Skopje 308,117 E5
Skradin 893 B4
Slavonska Požega 18,160 C3
Slavonski Brod 38,829 D3
Smederevo 39,200 E3
Smederevska Palanka 18,837 E3
Sombor 44,210 D3
Split 150,739 C4
Srebrenica 3,101 D3
Sremska Mitrovica 32,569 D3
Štip 27,218 F5
Stolac 3,862 D4
Ston 407 C4
Struga 11,369 E5
Strumica 22,770 F5
Subotica 89,476 D2
Surdulica 7,048 F4
Svetozarevo 27,812 E4
Svilajnac 7,848 E3
Teslić 4,940 C3
Tetovo 35,293 E5
Titograd 54,639 D4
Titovo Užice 35,465 D4
Titov Veles 35,583 E5
Travnik 12,745 C3
Trbovlje 16,393 B2
Trebinje 3,553 D4
Trogir 6,162 C4
Trstenik 7,167 E4
Tržič 4,435 B2
Tuzla 53,836 D3
Ub 3,785 E3
Ulcinj 7,472 D5
Umag 3,228 A3
Uroševac E4
Valjevo 26,655 D3
Varaždin 34,662 B2
Vareš 7,632 D3
Velenje 11,225 B2
Velika Plana E3
Veliki Bečkerek
(Zrenjanin) 60,201 E3
Vinkovci 29,257 D3
Virovitica 16,389 C3
Višegrad 4,753 D4
Visoko 9,365 D4
Vlasenica 4,033 D3
Vranje 25,909 F4
Vrbas 22,502 D3
Vršac 33,573 E3
Vučitrn 11,701 E4
Vukovar 29,500 D3
Žabljak 1,023 D4
Zadar 43,588 B3
Zagreb 561,773 C3
Zaječar 27,724 E4
Zara (Zadar) 43,588 B3
Zenica 49,522 C3
Žepče 3,177 D3
Zrenjanin 60,201 E3
Zvornik 8,498 D3

OTHER FEATURES

Adriatic (sea) B4
Bobotov Kuk (mt.) D4
Bosna (riv.) D3
Brač (isl.) C4
Cazma (riv.) C3
Cres (isl.) B3
Čvrsnica (mt.) C4
Dalmatia (reg.) C4
Danube (riv.) E3
Dinaric Alps (mts.) B3
Drava (riv.) C3
Drina (riv.) D3
Dugi Otok (isl.) B3
Hvar (isl.) C4
Ibar (riv.) E4
Istria (pen.) A3
Kamenjak (cape) A3
Kladovo F3
Korab (mt.) E5
Korčula (isl.) C4
Kornat (isl.) B4
Krk (isl.) B3
Kupa (riv.) B3
Kvarner (gulf) B3
Lastovo (Lagosta) (isl.) C4
Lim (riv.) D4
Lošinj (isl.) B3
Midzhur (mt.) F4
Mljet (isl.) C4
Morava (riv.) E3
Mur (riv.) B2
Neretva (riv.) D4
Ohrid (lake) E5
Pag (isl.) B3
Palagruža (Pelagosa) (isl.) C4
Prespa (lake) E5
Rab (isl.) B3
Rujen (mt.) F4
Sava (riv.) D3
Scutari (lake) D4
Slavonia (reg.) C3
Šolta (isl.) C4
Tara (riv.) D4
Timok (riv.) F3
Tisa (riv.) E3
Triglav (mt.) A2
Una (riv.) C3
Vardar (riv.) E5
Vis (isl.) C4
Vrbas (riv.) C3
Žirje (isl.) B4

*City and suburbs.

The Balkan States

CONIC PROJECTION

SCALE OF MILES

0 25 50 75 100 125 150 175

SCALE OF KILOMETERS

0 25 50 75 100 125 150 175

Capitals of Countries .... ☆
Administrative Centers .... △
International Boundaries ___.___.___
Major Internal Boundaries ___ ___ ___
Minor Internal Boundaries ....
Canals _____

BULGARIA and GREECE are divided into counties and departments, respectively. Because of the scale no attempt has been made to delimit and name these subdivisions; their administrative centers have, however, been designated.

The larger divisions named in Greece are well-known geographical regions, without administrative function.

ROMANIA consists of thirty-nine counties and three cities of regional status, Bucharest, Constanța and Petroșeni. Scale does not permit delimiting these counties.

ALBANIA is divided into twenty-seven districts. Scale does not permit the delimitation of these divisions.

YUGOSLAVIA is a federation of six republics. The Serbian republic includes an autonomous province (Vojvodina), and an autonomous region (Kosovo).

© Copyright HAMMOND INCORPORATED, Maplewood, N. J.

Topography

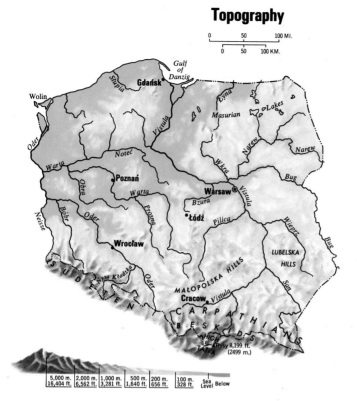

0   50   100 MI.

0   50   100 KM.

| 5,000 m. 16,404 ft. | 2,000 m. 6,562 ft. | 1,000 m. 3,281 ft. | 500 m. 1,640 ft. | 200 m. 656 ft. | 100 m. 328 ft. | Sea Level | Below |

PROVINCES

Biata Podlaska 283,200 ....F3
Białystok 613,800 ....F2
Bielsko 765,500 ....D4
Bydgoszcz 982,100 ....C2
Chełm 221,000 ....F3
Ciechanów 398,500 ....E2
Cracow (Kraków) 1,097,600 ....E4
Cracow (city) 651,300 ....E4
Częstochowa 723,200 ....D3
Elblag 419,800 ....D1
Gdańsk 1,312,300 ....D1
Gorzów 428,700 ....B2
Jelenia Góra 483,400 ....B3
Kalisz 640,300 ....D3
Katowice 3,439,700 ....D3
Kielce 1,030,400 ....E3
Konin 423,700 ....D2
Koszalin 428,500 ....C1
Krosno 418,000 ....E4
Legnica 405,600 ....C4
Leszno 340,600 ....C3
Łódź 1,063,700 ....D3
Łódź (city) 777,800 ....D3
Łomza 320,600 ....F2
Lublin 875,300 ....F3

Nowy Sącz 600,300 ....E4
Olsztyn 654,400 ....E2
Opole 961,600 ....C3
Ostrołęka 360,700 ....E2
Piła 414,000 ....C2
Piotrków 581,900 ....D3
Płock 479,700 ....D2
Poznań 1,156,500 ....C2
Przemyśl 373,100 ....F4
Radom 674,400 ....E3
Rzeszów 602,200 ....F4
Siedlce 602,100 ....F3
Sieradz 388,000 ....D3
Skierniewice 388,300 ....E3
Słupsk 352,900 ....C1
Suwałki 412,700 ....F1
Szczecin 841,400 ....B2
Tarnobrzeg 532,200 ....E3
Tarnów 573,900 ....E4
Toruń 580,500 ....D2
Wałbrzych 709,600 ....C3
Warsaw 2,117,700 ....E2
Warsaw (city) 1,377,100 ....E2
Wrocław 1,014,600 ....C3
Włocławek 478,000 ....D2
Zamość 472,300 ....F3
Zielona Góra 575,000 ....B3

CITIES and TOWNS

Aleksandrów Kujawski 9,600 ....
Aleksandrów
  Łódzki 14,400 ....
Allenstein (Olsztyn) 94,119 ....
Andrespol 12,400 ....
Andrychów 14,300 ....
Augustów 19,784 ....
Auschwitz
  (Oświęcim) 39,600 ....
Bartoszyce 15,500 ....
Beuthen (Bytom) 186,993 ....
Biała Podlaska 26,100 ....
Białogard 20,500 ....
Białystok 166,619 ....
Bielawa 30,900 ....
Bielsko-Biała 105,601 ....
Bielsk Podlaski 14,000 ....
Będzin 42,787 ....
Bilgoraj 12,888 ....
Blonie 12,500 ....
Bochnia 14,500 ....
Bogatynia 11,800 ....
Boguszów-Gorce 11,900 ....
Bolesławiec 30,500 ....

Agriculture, Industry and Resources

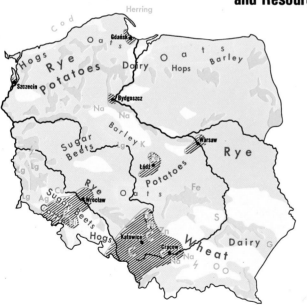

MAJOR MINERAL OCCURRENCES

Ag Silver
C   Coal
Cu Copper
Fe Iron Ore
G   Natural Gas
K   Potash
Lg Lignite

Na Salt
Ni Nickel
O   Petroleum
Pb Lead
S   Sulfur
Zn Zinc

⚡ Water Power
▨ Major Industrial Areas

DOMINANT LAND USE

☐ Cereals (chiefly wheat)

▨ Rye, Oats, Barley, Potatoes

☐ General Farming, Livestock

▨ Forests

Poland 1938

0   50   100
MILES

Poland 1945

0   50   100
MILES

AREA 120,725 sq. mi. (312,678 sq. km.)
POPULATION 35,815,000
CAPITAL Warsaw
LARGEST CITY Warsaw
HIGHEST POINT Rysy 8,199 ft.
(2,499 m.)
MONETARY UNIT zloty
MAJOR LANGUAGE Polish
MAJOR RELIGION Roman Catholicism

Braniewo 12.100	D1
Breslau (Wrocław) 461.900	C3
Brieg (Brzeg) 30.780	C3
Brodnica 17.300	D2
Brzeg 30.780	C3
Brzeg Dolny 10.800	C3
Brzesko 9.701	E3
Busko Zdrój 11.100	E3
Bydgoszcz 280.460	C2
Bytom 186.993	A4
Bytów 10.642	C1
Chełm 38.789	F2
Chełmno 17.906	D2
Chełmża 14.200	D2
Chodzież 21.200	C2
Chojnice 23.500	C2
Chojnów 11.000	B3
Chorzów 151.338	A4
Choszczno 9.800	B2
Chrzanów 29.300	E3
Ciechanów 28.500	E2
Cieplice	
Śląskie-Zdrój 15.400	D4
Cieszyn 25.234	D4
Cracow 651.300	E3
Czechowice-Dziedzice 25.400	D4
Czeladź 31.843	B4
Częstochowa 187.613	D3
Dąbrowa Górnicza 61.660	B3
Danzig (Gdańsk) 364.285	D1
Darłowo 11.200	C1
Dębica 22.900	E3
Dęblin 14.600	E3
Dębno 10.700	B2
Działdowo 10.100	E2
Dzierżoniów 32.800	C3
Elbing (Elbląg) 89.835	D1
Ełk 27.188	F2
Gdańsk 364.285	D1
Gdynia 190.125	D1
Giżycko 18.200	F1
Gliwice (Gleiwitz) 170.912	A4
Głogów (Glogau) 20.226	C3
Głowno 12.800	D3
Głubczyce 11.300	C3
Głuchołazy 13.200	C3
Gniezno 50.643	C2
Goleniów 16.200	B2
Gorlice 15.200	E4
Gorzów Wielkopolski 74.267	B2
Gostyń 13.000	C3
Gostynin 12.000	D2
Grajewo 13.300	F2
Grodzisk Mazowiecki 20.400	E2
Grójec 10.300	E3
Grudziądz 75.511	D2
Grünberg (Zielona Góra) 59.700	B3
Gryfice 13.200	B2
Guben (Gubin) 14.600	B3
Hajnówka m4.345	F2
Hindenburg (Zabrze) 199.400	A4
Hirschberg (Jelenia Góra) 55.720	B3
Hrubieszów 14.999	F3
Iława 16.400	D2
Inowrocław 54.817	D2

Jarocin 18.100	C3
Jarosław 29.000	F4
Jasło 17.025	E4
Jastrzębie Zdrój 34.400	D3
Jaworzno 63.271	B4
Jędrzejów 13.264	E3
Jelenia Góra 55.720	B3
Kalisz 81.227	D3
Kamienna Góra 21.000	C3
Kartuzy 10.558	C1
Katowice 303.264	B4
Kędzierzyn-Koźle 45.600	C3
Kępno 10.151	C3
Kętrzyn 19.300	E1
Kielce 125.952	E3
Kłobuck 12.600	D3
Kłodzko 26.000	C3
Kluczbork 18.000	D3
Knurów 28.400	A4
Koło 13.100	D2
Kołobrzeg 25.419	B1
Konin 40.600	D2
Konstantynów	
Łódzki 12.800	D3
Kościan 18.700	C3
Kościerzyna 18.914	C1
Koslin (Koszalin) 64.414	C1
Kostrzyn 11.200	B2
Koszalin 64.414	C1
Kraków (Cracow) 651.300	E4
Krapkowice 13.800	C3
Kraśnik Fabryczny 14.600	F3
Krasnystaw 12.495	F3
Krosno 26.500	E4
Krotoszyn 21.900	C3
Krynica 10.200	E4
Küstrin 11.200	B2
Kutno 30.000	D2
Kwidzin 23.104	D2
Łańcut 12.049	F3
Landsberg (Gorzów Wielkopolski) 74.267	B2
Łazíska Górne 10.800	A4
Łębork 25.000	C1
Łęczyca 13.900	D2
Legionowo 20.800	E2
Legnica 75.843	C3
Leszczyny 12.200	A4
Leszno 33.890	C3
Libiąż 10.600	D3
Lidzbark Warmiński 12.900	E1
Liegnitz (Legnica) 75.843	C3
Lipno 10.900	D2
Łódź 777.800	D3
Łomża 25.500	F2
Łowicz 20.400	D2
Luban 17.200	B3
Lubartów 10.000	F3
Lubin 28.400	C3
Lubliniec 19.800	D3
Lubón 16.400	C2
Lubsko 12.600	B3
Łuków 15.500	F3
Malbork (Marienburg) 30.900	D1

Międzyrzec Podlaski 13.500	F3
Międzyrzecz 14.900	B2
Mielec 26.800	E3
Mików 21.300	B4
Minsk Mazowiecki 24.200	E2
Mława 20.007	E2
Mońki 9.560	F2
Morąg 9.681	D2
Mrągowo 13.400	E2
Myślenice 12.100	D4
Mysłowice 44.737	C4
Myszków 18.000	D3
Nakło nad Notecią 16.800	C2
Namysłów 11.076	C3
Neisse (Nysa) 31.837	C3
Nidzica 9.642	E2
Nowa Ruda 18.100	C3
Nowa Sól 33.300	B3
Nowy Dwór Mazowiecki 16.900	E2
Nowy Sącz 41.103	E4
Nowy Targ 21.900	E4
Nysa 31.837	C3
Oborniki 10.200	C2
Oława 17.746	C3
Oleśnica 27.500	C3
Olkusz 15.800	D3
Olsztyn 94.119	E2
Opoczno 12.168	E3
Opole 86.510	C3
Oppeln 86.510	C3
Orzesze 9.600	A4
Ostróda 21.300	D2
Ostrołęka 21.981	E2
Ostrów Mazowiecka 15.000	E2
Ostrów Wielkopolski 49.530	C3
Ostrowiec	
Świętokrzyski 49.958	E3
Oświęcim 39.600	D3
Otwock 39.863	E2
Ozorków 18.200	D3
Pabianice 62.275	D3
Piekary Śląskie 36.300	B4
Piła 43.778	C2

Pionki 13.600	E3
Piotrków Trybunalski 59.683	D3
Pisz 11.100	F2
Pleszew 13.348	C3
Płock 71.727	D2
Płońsk 11.619	E2
Police 12.700	B2
Poznań 469.085	C2
Prudnik 20.300	C3
Pruszcz Gdański 13.000	D1
Pruszków 42.961	E2
Przasnysz 11.100	E2
Przemyśl 53.228	F4
Puck 9.500	D1
Puławy 34.800	E3
Pułtusk 12.600	E2
Rabka 10.700	D4
Raciborz 40.418	C3
Radom 158.640	E3
Radomsko 31.179	D3
Ratibor (Raciborz) 40.418	C3
Rawa Mazowiecka 9.800	E3
Rawicz 14.100	C3
Ruda Śląska 142.407	B4
Rumia 23.300	D1
Rybnik 43.415	D3
Rypin 10.029	D2
Rzeszów 82.192	F4
Sandomierz 16.800	E3
Sanok 21.600	F4
Schneidemühl (Piła) 36.600	C2
Schwiebittz	
(Świdnica) 47.542	C3
Siedlce 38.983	F2
Siemianowice	
Śląskie 57.278	B4
Sieradz 18.500	D3
Sierpc 12.000	D2
Skarżysko-Kamienna 39.194	E3
Skawina 15.900	D4
Skierniewice 25.590	E2
Sławno 10.700	C1
Słubice 12.000	B2
Słupsk 68.311	C1

Sochaczew 20.500	E2
Sokółka 10.023	F2
Sokołów Podlaski 9.569	F2
Sopot 47.573	D1
Sosnowiec 144.652	B4
Śrem 15.600	C2
Środa Śląska 10.259	C3
Środa Wielkopolska 14.800	C2
Stalowa Wola 29.768	F3
Starachowice 42.807	E3
Stargard Szczeciński 44.400	B2
Starogard Gdański 33.400	D2
Stary Sącz 57.400	D1
Stettin (Szczecin) 337.294	B2
Stolp (Słupsk) 68.311	C1
Strzegom 14.000	C3
Strzelce Opolskie 14.700	D3
Strzelin 9.800	C3
Sulechów 10.200	B2
Suwałki 25.360	F1
Swarzędz 12.100	C2
Świdnica 47.542	C3
Świdnik 31.900	F3
Świdwin 12.500	B2
Świebodzice 18.500	C3
Świebodzin 14.900	B2
Świecie 17.900	D2
Świętochłowice 57.633	A4
Świnoujście	
(Świnemünde) 27.900	B1
Szamotuły 14.600	C2
Szczecin 337.204	B2
Szczecinek 28.600	C2
Szczytno 17.371	E2
Sztrotowa 11.200	D3
Tarnobrzeg 18.800	E3
Tarnów 85.514	E4
Tarnowskie Góry 34.200	A3
Tczew 40.794	D1
Tomaszów Lubelski 12.329	F3
Tomaszów Mazowiecki 54.911	E3
Toruń 129.152	D2
Trzcianka 10.900	C2
Trzebinia-Siersza	

Turek 18.500	D2
Tychy 71.384	B4
Ustka 9.900	C1
Wąbrzeźno 11.800	D2
Wadowice 11.800	D4
Wągrowiec 15.600	C2
Wałbrzych 125.048	C3
Wałcz 18.900	C2
Wałdenburg (Wałbrzych) 125.048	C3
Warsaw (Warszawa) (cap.) 1.377.100	E2
Wejherowo 33.600	D1
Wieliczka 13.600	D3
Wieluń 14.300	D3
Wisła 9.800	D4
Włocławek 77.169	D2
Wodzisław Śląski 25.600	D4
Wolin 35.458	B2
Wołomin 24.000	E2
Wołów 10.500	C3
Wrocław 523.318	C3
Września 17.800	C2
Wschowa 10.000	C3
Wyszków	E2
Wyszków 12.000	E2
Ząbkowice Śląskie 13.800	C3
Zabrze 197.214	A4
Zagań 21.400	B3
Zakopane 27.039	E4
Zambrów 14.082	F2
Zamość 34.234	F3
Zary 28.300	B3
Zawiercie 39.410	D3
Zduńska Wola 29.066	D3
Zgierz 42.838	D3
Zgorzelec 28.400	B3
Ziębice 9.700	C3
Zielona Góra 73.156	B3
Złocieniec 10.100	C2
Złotoryja 12.200	C3
Złotów 11.600	C2
Znin 9.600	C2
Żyrardów 33.196	E2

Żywiec 22.400	D4

OTHER FEATURES

Baltic (sea)	B1
Beskids (range)	D4
Brda (riv.)	C2
Brynica (riv.)	A3
Bug (riv.)	F2
Danzig (Gdańsk) (gulf)	E4
Dukla (pass)	E4
Dunajec (riv.)	E4
Gwda (riv.)	C2
Hel (spit)	D1
High Tatra (range)	E4
Kłodnica (riv.)	A4
Łyna (riv.)	E2
Mamry, Jezioro (lake)	E1
Masurian (lkes)	E2
Narew (riv.)	E2
Neisse (riv.)	B3
Notec (riv.)	C2
Nysa Kłodzka (riv.)	C3
Nysa Łużycka (Neisse) (riv.)	B3
Oder (riv.)	B2
Orava (riv.)	D4
Pilica (riv.)	D3
Pomeranian (bay)	B1
Prosna (riv.)	C3
Rysy (riv.)	E4
San (riv.)	F3
Słupia (riv.)	C1
Śniardwy, Jezioro (lake)	E2
Sudeten (range)	B3
Uznam (Usedom) (isl.)	B1
Vistula (riv.)	D1
Warmia (reg.)	D1
Warta (riv.)	D2
Wieprz (riv.)	F3
Wisła (Vistula) (riv.)	D2
Wkra (riv.)	E2
Wolin (Wollin) (isl.)	B2

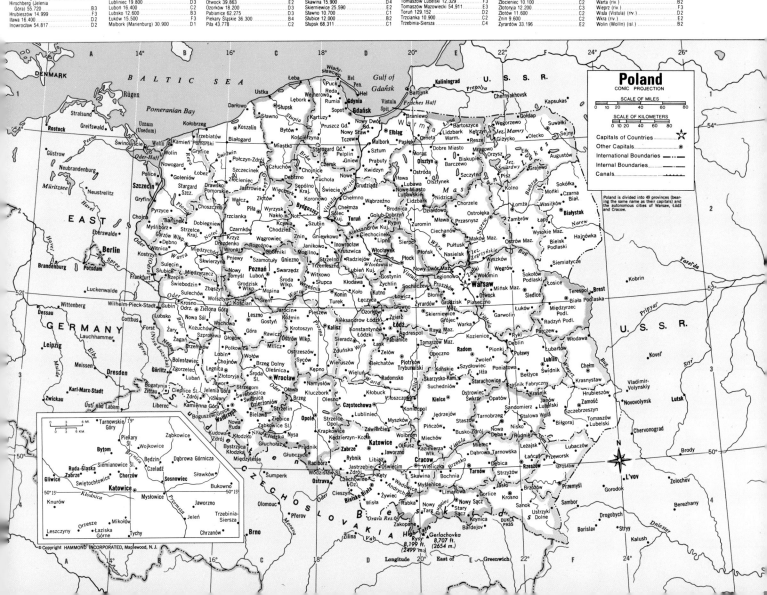

Poland
CONIC PROJECTION

SCALE OF MILES
0 10 20 40 60 80

SCALE OF KILOMETERS
0 10 20 40 60 80

★ Capitals of Countries
◉ Other Capitals
International Boundaries
Internal Boundaries
Canals

Poland is divided into 49 provinces (bearing the same name as their capitals) and the autonomous names of Warsaw, Łódź and Cracow.

UNION REPUBLICS

Armenian S.S.R. 3,031,000 .... E6
Azerbaidzhan S.S.R. 6,028,000 ... E5
Estonian S.S.R. 1,466,000 .... C4
Georgian S.S.R. 5,015,000 .... D5
Kazakh S.S.R. 14,684,000 .... G5
Kirgiz S.S.R. 3,529,000 .... H5
Latvian S.S.R. 2,521,000 .... C4
Lithuanian S.S.R. 3,398,000 ..... C4
Moldavian S.S.R. 3,947,000 ...... C5
Russian S.F.S.R. 137,551,000 .... D4
Tadzhik S.S.R. 3,801,000 .... H6
Turkmen S.S.R. 2,759,000 .... F6
Ukrainian S.S.R. 49,755,000 ..... C5
Uzbek S.S.R. 15,391,000 .... G5
White Russian S.S.R. 9,560,000 .. C4

INTERNAL DIVISIONS

Abkhaz A.S.S.R. 505,000 .... E5
Adygey Aut. Obl. 405,000 .... D5
Adzhar A.S.S.R. 354,000 .... E5
Aginsk Buryat Aut. Okr. 69,000 .. M4
Bashkir A.S.S.R. 3,849,000 ...... F4
Buryat A.S.S.R. 900,000 .... M4
Chechen-Ingush
    A.S.S.R. 1,154,000 .... E5
Chukchi Aut. Okr. 133,000 ...... R3
Chuvash A.S.S.R. 1,292,000 ..... E4
Dagestan A.S.S.R. 1,628,000 .... E5
Evenki Aut. Okr. 16,000 .... K3
Gorno-Altay Aut. Obl. 172,000 .. J4
Gorno-Badakhshan Aut.
    Obl. 127,000 .... H6
Jewish Aut. Obl. 190,000 .... O5
Kabardin-Balkar

Kalmuck A.S.S.R. 294,000 .... E6
Karachay-Cherkess Aut.
    Obl. 368,000 .... E5
Karakalpak A.S.S.R. 904,000 .... G5
Karelian A.S.S.R. 736,000 ...... D3
Khakass Aut. Obl. 500,000 ..... J4
Khanty-Mansi Aut. Okr. 569,000 . H3
Komi A.S.S.R. 1,119,000 .... F3
Komi-Permyak Aut. Okr. 173,000 . F4
Koryak Aut. Okr. 34,000 .... R3
Mari A.S.S.R. 703,000 .... E4
Mordvinian A.S.S.R. 991,000 .... E4
Nagorno-Karabakh Aut.
    Obl. 161,000 .... E6
Nakhichevan A.S.S.R. 239,000 ... E6
Nenets Aut. Okr. 47,000 .... F3
North Ossetian
    A.S.S.R. 597,000 .... E5
South Ossetian Aut.
    Obl. 98,000 .... E5
Tatar A.S.S.R. 3,436,000 .... F4
Taymyr Aut. Okr. 44,000 .... K2
Tuvinian A.S.S.R. 267,000 ...... K4
Udmurt A.S.S.R. 1,494,000 ...... F4
Ust-Ordynskiy Buryat Aut.
    Okr. 133,000 .... L4
Yakut A.S.S.R. 839,000 .... N3
Yamal-Nenets Aut. Okr. 158,000 . H3

CITIES and TOWNS

Abakan 128,000 .... K4
Abay 34,245 .... K5
Abaza 15,202 .... J4
Achinsk 117,000 .... K4

Agata K3
Aginskoye 7,922 .... M4
Akmolinsk
    (Tselinograd) 234,000 ..... H4
Aksay 10,010 .... F4
Aktash J4
Aktyubinsk 191,000 .... F4
Aldan 17,689 .... N4
Aleksandrovsk-Sakhalinskiy
    20,342 .... P5
Alekseyevka 18,041 .... E4
Aleysk 32,487 .... J4
Alga 12,000 .... F4
Aliskerovo R3
Allakh-Yun O3
Alma-Ata 910,000 .... H5
Almaznyy M3
Ambarchik R3
Amderma F3
Amursk 24,010 .... O4
Anadyr 7,703 .... S3
Andizhan 230,000 .... H5
Angarsk 239,000 .... L4
Angren H5
Anzhero-Sudzhensk
    105,000 .... J4
Aral'sk 37,722 .... G5
Archangel (Arkhangel'sk)
    385,000 .... E3
Arkalyk 15,108 .... G4
Armavir 162,000 .... E5
Arsen'yev 60,000 .... O5
Artem 69,000 .... O5
Artemovskiy M4
Arys 26,414 .... G5
Arzamas 93,000 .... E4
Asbest 79,000 .... G4
Ashkhabad 312,000 .... F6

Asino 29,395 .... J4
Astrakhan 461,000 .... F5
Atbasar 37,228 .... G4
Atka Q3
Ayaguz 35,827 .... J5
Ayan O4
Aykhal M3
Bagdanin M4
Baku* 1,022,000 .... F5
Baku* 1,550,000 .... F5
Balakovo 152,000 .... E4
Balashov 93,000 .... E4
Baley 27,215 .... M4
Balkhash 78,000 .... H5
Balykshi 22,397 .... F5
Bam N4
Barabinsk 37,274 .... H4
Baranovichi
    131,000 .... C4
Barnaul 533,000 .... J4
Batagay 10,000 .... O3
Batumi 123,000 .... E5
Baykit K3
Baykonur G5
Bayram-Ali 31,987 .... G6
Belgorod 240,000 .... D4
Belogorsk 63,000 .... N4
Belomorsk 16,595 .... D3
Beloretsk 71,000 .... F4
Belovo 112,000 .... J4
Berdichev 80,000 .... C5
Berdsk 67,000 .... J4
Bereznik 185,000 .... F4
Berezovo 6,000 .... G3
Beringovskiy T3
Bikin 17,473 .... O5
Bira O5

Birobidzhan 69,000 .... O5
Biruni G5
Biysk 212,000 .... J4
Blagoveshchensk
    172,000 .... N4
Bobruysk 192,000 .... C4
Bodaybo 19,000 .... M4
Borisoglebsk 68,000 .... E4
Borzya 27,815 .... M4
Bratsk 214,000 .... L4
Brest 177,000 .... C4
Brindakit O4
Bryansk 394,000 .... D4
Bugul'ma 80,000 .... F4
Bukachacha 10,000 .... M4
Bukhara 185,000 .... G5
Bulun N2
Buzuluk 76,000 .... F4
Chadan K4
Chapayevsk 85,000 .... F4
Chara M4
Chardzhou 140,000 .... G6
Charsk 10,100 .... J5
Cheboksary 308,000 .... E4
Chegdomyn 16,499 .... O4
Chelkar 19,377 .... F5
Chelyabinsk 1,030,000 .... G4
Cheremkhovo 77,000 .... L4
Cherepovets 266,000 .... D4
Cherkessk 91,000 .... E5
Chernenko E4
Chernigov 238,000 .... D4
Chernogorsk 71,000 .... K4
Chernovtsy 219,000 .... C5
Chernyshevsk 10,000 .... M4
Chersky Q3
Chimbay 18,899 .... G5
Chimkent 322,000 .... H5
Chirchik 132,000 .... H5

Chita 303,000 .... M4
Chokurdakh P2
Chumikan O4
Dal'negorsk 33,506 .... O5
Dal'nerechensk 28,224 .... O5
Daugavpils 116,000 .... C4
Denau G6
Dikson J2
Dimitrovgrad 106,000 .... F4
Dnepropetrovsk 1,066,000 .... D5
Donetsk 1,021,000 .... D5
Drogobych 66,000 .... C5
Druzhba P3
Druzhina P3
Dudinka 19,701 .... J3
Dushanbe 494,000 .... G6
Dzerzhinsk 257,000 .... E4
Dzhalal-Abad 55,000 .... H5
Dzhalinda N4
Dzhambul 264,000 .... H5
Dzhelinda M2
Dzhetygara 32,169 .... G4
Dzhezkazgan 89,000 .... G5
Dzhusaly 20,658 .... G5
Egvekinot S3
Ekibastuz 66,000 .... H4
Ekimchan O4
El'dikan O3
Elista 70,000 .... E5
Emba 17,820 .... F5
Engel's 161,000 .... E4
Ervian 1,019,000 .... E5
Evensk Q3
Fergana 176,000 .... H5
Fort-Shevchenko 12,000 ...... F5
Frolovo 33,398 .... E5
Frunze 533,000 .... H5

Gasan-Kuli F6
Gol'chikha J3
Gomel 383,000 .... C4
Gor'kiy 1,344,000 .... E4
Gorno-Altaysk 34,413 .... J4
Gornyak 16,643 .... F4
Grodno 195,000 .... C4
Groznyy 375,000 .... E5
Gubakha 33,243 .... F4
Gulistan 30,879 .... H5
Gur'yev 131,000 .... F5
Gusinoozersk
    10,000 .... L4
Gyda H2
Igarka 15,624 .... J3
Igrim G3
Ilanskiy 22,852 .... K4
Indiga E3
Inta 51,000 .... G3
Iolotan 10,000 .... G6
Irkutsk 550,000 .... L4
Ishim 63,000 .... G4
Isil'kul' 25,958 .... H4
Iul'tin T3
Ivano-Frankovsk
    150,000 .... C5
Ivanovo 465,000 .... E4
Ivdel 15,308 .... F4
Izhevsk 549,000 .... F4
Izmail 83,000 .... C5
Kachug L4
Kagan 34,117 .... G5
Kalachinsk 20,809 .... H4
Kalakan M4
Kalinin 412,000 .... D4
Kaliningrad 355,000 .... B4
Kalmykovo F5
Kaluga 265,000 .... D4
Kamen'-na-Obi 35,604 .... H4

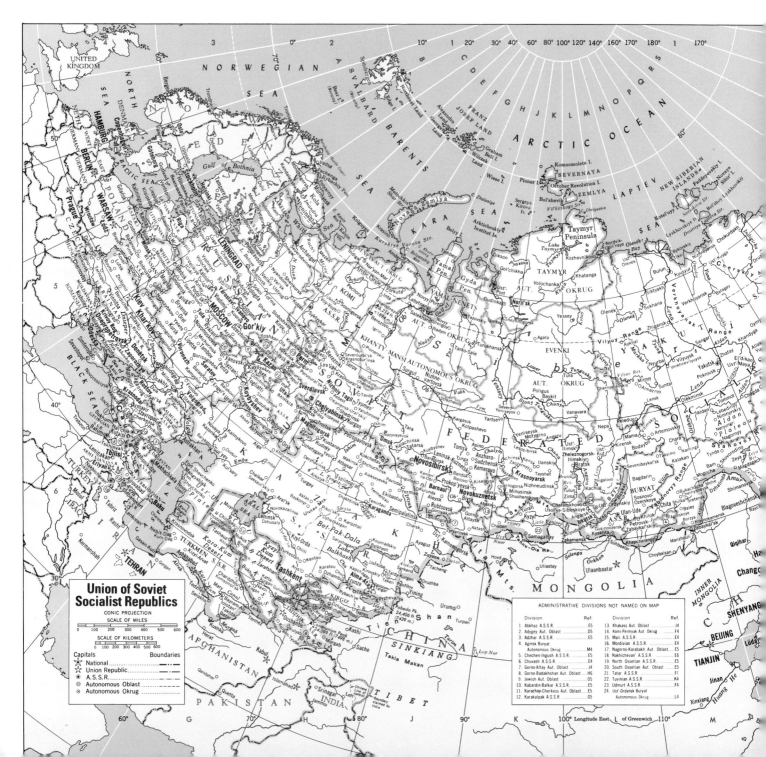

Union of Soviet Socialist Republics

CONIC PROJECTION
SCALE OF MILES
0   100 200 300 400 500 600
SCALE OF KILOMETERS
0 100 200 300 400 500 600

Capitals	Boundaries
★ National	
⊛ Union Republic	
⊙ A.S.S.R.	
⊚ Autonomous Oblast	
⊙ Autonomous Okrug	

ADMINISTRATIVE DIVISIONS NOT NAMED ON MAP

Division	Ref.	Division	Ref.
1. Abkhaz A.S.S.R.	E5	13. Khakass Aut. Oblast	J4
2. Adygey Aut. Oblast	D5	14. Komi-Permyak Aut. Okrug	F4
3. Adzhar A.S.S.R.	E5	15. Mari A.S.S.R.	E4
4. Aginsk Buryat		16. Mordivian A.S.S.R.	E4
Autonomous Okrug	M4	17. Nagorno-Karabakh Aut. Oblast	E5
5. Chechen-Ingush A.S.S.R.	E5	18. Nakhichevan' A.S.S.R.	E5
6. Chuvash A.S.S.R.	E4	19. North Ossetian A.S.S.R.	E5
7. Gorno-Altay Aut. Oblast	J4	20. South Ossetian Aut. Oblast	E5
8. Gorno-Badakhshan Aut. Oblast	H6	21. Tatar A.S.S.R.	F4
9. Jewish Aut. Oblast	O5	22. Tuvinian A.S.S.R.	K4
10. Kabardin-Balkar A.S.S.R.	E5	23. Udmurt A.S.S.R.	F4
11. Karachay-Cherkess Aut. Oblast	E5	24. Ust-Ordynsk Buryat	
12. Karakalpak A.S.S.R.	G5	Autonomous Okrug	L4

AREA 8,649,490 sq. mi. (22,402,179 sq. km.)
POPULATION 262,436,227
CAPITAL Moscow
LARGEST CITY Moscow
HIGHEST POINT Communism Peak 24,599 ft. (7,498 m.)
MONETARY UNIT ruble
MAJOR LANGUAGES Russian, Ukrainian, White Russian, Uzbek, Azerbaidzhani, Tatar, Georgian, Lithuanian, Armenian, Yiddish, Latvian, Mordvinian, Kirgiz, Tadzhik, Estonian, Kazakh, Moldavian (Romanian), German, Chuvash, Turkmenian, Bashkir
MAJOR RELIGIONS Eastern (Russian) Orthodoxy, Islam, Judaism, Protestantism (Baltic States)

Kamenskoye	R3	Kavalerovo 16.415	O5			
Kamensk-Ural'skiy 187.000	G4	Kazan' 993.000	F4			
Kamyshin 112.000	E4	Kem' 21.025	D3			
Kandalaksha 42.656	C3	Kemerovo 471.000	J4			
Kansk 101.000	K4	Kentau 52.000	G5			
Kapchagay	H5	Kerki 10.000	G6			
Kara	G3	Kerki 10.000	O5			
Karaganda 572.000	H5	Khabarovsk 528.000	O5			
Karasuk 22.637	H4	Khanty-Mansiysk 24.754	H3			
Karatau 26.962	H5	Khar kov 1.444.000	D4			
Karazhal 17.702	H5	Khatanga	L2			
Kargasok	J4	Kherson 319.000	D5			
Karpinsk	F4	Khilok 17.000	M4			
Karshi 108.000	G6	Khiva 24.139	F5			
Kartaly 42.801	F5	Khodzheyli 36.435	F5			
Katangli	P4	Kholmsk 37.412	P5			
Kattakurgan 53.000	G5	Khorog 12.295	H6			
Kaunas 370.000	C4	Kiev 2.144.000	D4			

UNION REPUBLICS

	AREA (sq. mi.)	AREA (sq. km.)	POPULATION	CAPITAL and LARGEST CITY
RUSSIAN S.F.S.R.	6,592,812	17,075,400	137,551,000	Moscow 7,831,000
KAZAKH S.S.R.	1,048,300	2,715,100	14,684,000	Alma-Ata 910,000
UKRAINIAN S.S.R.	233,089	603,700	49,755,000	Kiev 2,144,000
TURKMEN S.S.R.	188,455	488,100	2,759,000	Ashkhabad 312,000
UZBEK S.S.R.	173,591	449,600	15,391,000	Tashkent 1,780,000
WHITE RUSSIAN S.S.R.	80,154	207,600	9,560,000	Minsk 1,262,000
KIRGIZ S.S.R.	76,641	198,500	3,529,000	Frunze 533,000
TADZHIK S.S.R.	55,251	143,100	3,801,000	Dushanbe 494,000
AZERBAIDZHAN S.S.R.	33,436	86,600	6,028,000	Baku 1,022,000
GEORGIAN S.S.R.	26,911	69,700	5,015,000	Tbilisi 1,066,000
LITHUANIAN S.S.R.	25,174	65,200	3,398,000	Vilna 481,000
LATVIAN S.S.R.	24,595	63,700	2,521,000	Riga 835,000
ESTONIAN S.S.R.	17,413	45,100	1,466,000	Tallinn 430,000
MOLDAVIAN S.S.R.	13,012	33,700	3,947,000	Kishinev 503,000
ARMENIAN S.S.R.	11,506	29,800	3,031,000	Erivan 1,019,000

Kirensk 10.000	L4	Krasnokamsk 56,000	F4	Leninakan 207.000	E5	Mezen	E3	Navoi 84.000	G6
Kirov 390.000	E4	Krasnotur insk 61.000	G3	Leningrad 4.073.000	D4	Miass 150.000	G4	Nazyvayevsk 15.792	H4
Kirovabad 232.000	E5	Krasnoural'sk 39.743	G4	Leningrad* 4.588.000	D4	Michurinsk 101.000	E4	Nebit-Dag 71.000	F6
Kirovograd 237.000	D5	Krasnovodsk 53.000	F5	Leninogorsk 54.000	J5	Milerovo 34.627	E5	Nefteyugansk 52.000	H3
Kirovskiy	H5	Krasnoyarsk 796.000	K4	Leninsk	C4	Minsk 1.262.000	C4	Nel'kan	O4
Kiselevsk 122.000	J4	Kremenchug 210.000	D5	Leninsk-Kuznetskiy 132.000	J4	Minsk* 1.276.000	C4	Nepa	L4
Kishinev 503.000	C5	Krivoy Rog 650.000	D5	Leninskoye	E6	Minusinsk 56.000	K4	Neryungri	N4
Kizel 46.264	F4	Kudymkar 26.350	F4	Lenkoran' 35.505	E6	Mirnyy 23.826	M3	Nevel'sk 20.726	P5
Kizyl-Arvat 21.671	F6	Kul'sary 16.427	F5	Lensk 16.758	M3	Mogilev 290.000	D4	Nikolayev 440.000	D5
Klaipeda 176.000	B4	Kulunda 15.264	H4	Lesosibirsk	K4	Mogocha 17.884	N4	Nikolayevsk-na-Amure	
Kokand 153.000	H5	Kulyab 55.000	H6	Lesozavodsk 34.957	O5	Molodechno 73.000	C4	30.082	P4
Kokchetav 103.000	H4	Kum-Dag 10.000	F6	Liepaja 108.000	B4	Monchegorsk 51.000	C3	Nikol'skoye	R4
Kolomna 147.000	E4	Kungur 80.000	F4	Lipetsk 396.000	E4	Moscow (cap.) 7.831.000	D4	Nizhneudinsk 39.743	K4
Kolpashevo 24.911	J4	Kupino 20.799	H4	Luga 31.905	D4	Moscow* 8.011.000	D4	Nizhnevartovsk	
Komsomol'sk 15.385	G4	Kurgan 310.000	G4	Lutsk 137.000	C4	Motygino 10.000	K4	109.000	H3
Komsomol'sk-na-Amure 264.000	O4	Kurgan-Tyube 34.620	H6	L'vov 667.000	C4	Mozyr' 73.000	D4	Nizhneyansk	O3
Kondopoga 27.908	D3	Kursk 375.000	D4	Lys va 75.000	F4	Murgab	H6	Nizhniy Tagil 398.000	G4
Kopeysk 146.000	G4	Kushka	G6	Magadan 121.000	P4	Murmansk 381.000	D3	Nordvik-Ugol'naya	M2
Korf	R3	Kustanay 165.000	G4	Magadagachi 15.059	N4	Murmansk (cap) 7.831.000	D3	Noril'sk 180.000	J3
Korsakov 38.210	P5	Kutaisi 194.000	E5	Magnitogorsk 406 000	G4	Muynak 12.000	F5	Novaya Kazanka	F5
Koslan	E3	Kuybyshev 1.216.000	F4	Makhachkala 251.000	E5	Mys Shmidta	T3	Novgorod 186.000	D4
Kostroma 255.000	E4	Kuybyshev 40.166	H4	Makinsk 22.850	H4	Nadym	H3	Novoaltaysk 34.815	G5
Kotlas 61.000	E3	Kyakhta 15.316	L4	Mama	M4	Nagornyy	N4	Novokuznetsk 541.000	J4
Kovel' 33.351	C4	Kyysyur	N2	Mariupol' 503.000	D5	Nakhichevan' 33.279	E6	Novomoskovsk 147.000	E4
Kovrov 143.000	E4	Kyzyl 66.000	K4	Markovo	S3	Nakhodka 133.000	O5	Novorossiysk 159.000	D5
Kozhevnikovo	L2	Kyzyl-Orda 156.000	G5	Mary (Merv) 74.000	G6	Nal'chik 207.000	E5	Novosibirsk 1.312.000	J4
Krasino	E5	Labytnangi	G3	Maykop 128.000	D5	Namangan 227.000	H5	Novozybkov 34.433	D4
Krasnodar 560.000	E5	Lebedinyy	N4	Mednogorsk 38.024	F4	Naminga	M4	Novyy Port	G3
Krasnokamensk 51.000	M4	Leninabad 130.000	G5	Medvezh'yegorsk 17.465	D3	Nar'yan-Mar 16.864	F3	Novyy Uzen' 18.073	F5
						Naryn 21.098	H5	Novyy Urengoy	H3

Topography

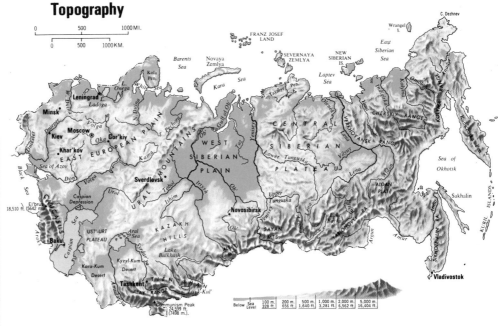

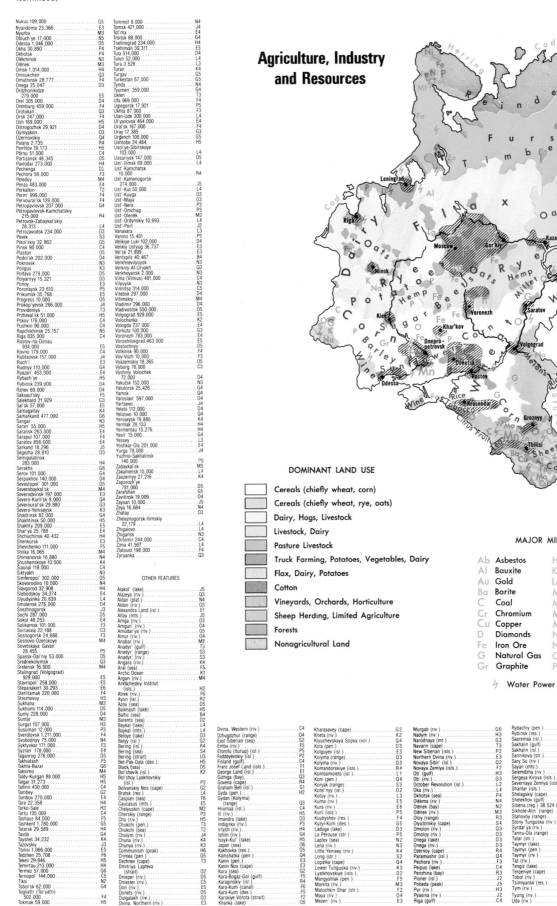

Agriculture, Industry and Resources

Nukus 109,000 ... G5
Nyandoma 23,366 ... E3
Nyurba ... M3
Obluch'ye 17,000 ... N5
Odessa 1,046,000 ... D5
Okha 30,890 ... P4
Okhotsk ... N3
Olëkminsk ... N3
Olënek ... M3
Omsk 1,014,000 ... H4
Omsukchan ... Q3
Omutninsk 28,777 ... F4
Onega 25,047 ... D3
Ordzhonikidze 279,000 ... E5
Orel 305,000 ... D4
Orenburg 459,000 ... F4
Orotukan ... P3
Orsk 247,000 ... F4
Osh 169,000 ... H5
Ostrogozhsk 29,921 ... E4
Oymyakon ... O3
Ozernovskiy ... R4
Palana 2,735 ... R4
Panfilov 19,173 ... H5
Pärnu 51,000 ... C4
Partizansk 48,345 ... O5
Pavlodar 273,000 ... H4
Pechenga ... D2
Pechora 56,000 ... F3
Peleduy ... M4
Penza 483,000 ... E4
Perkatkin ... T2
Perm' 999,000 ... F4
Pervoural'sk 129,000 ... F4
Petropavlovsk 207,000 ... G4
Petropavlovsk-Kamchatskiy 215,000 ... R4
Petrovsk-Zabaykal'sky 28,313 ... L4
Petrozavodsk 234,000 ... D3
Pevek ... S3
Pikol'skiy 32,862 ... G5
Pinsk 90,000 ... C4
Plastun ... O5
Podol'sk 202,000 ... D4
Pokrovsk ... N3
Poligus ... K3
Poltava 279,000 ... D5
Polyarnyy 15,321 ... D3
Ponoy ... E3
Poronaysk 23,610 ... P5
Prikumsk 33,768 ... E5
Progress 10,000 ... O5
Prokop'yevsk 266,000 ... J4
Provideniya ... T3
Przheval'sk 51,000 ... H5
Pskov 176,000 ... C4
Pushkin 90,000 ... C4
Raychikhinsk 25,157 ... N5
Ryazan' 453,000 ... E4
Rybach'ye ... H5
Rybinsk 239,000 ... D4
Rzhev 69,000 ... D4
Saksaul'sky ... F5
Salekhard 21,929 ... G3
Sal'sk 57,000 ... E5
Samagaltay ... K4
Samarkand 477,000 ... G6
Sangar ... N3
Saran' 55,000 ... H5
Saransk 263,000 ... E4
Sarapul 107,000 ... F4
Saratov 856,000 ... E4
Sarkand 18,296 ... H5
Segezha 28,810 ... D3
Semipalatinsk 283,000 ... H4
Serakhs ... G6
Serov 101,000 ... G4
Serpukhov 140,000 ... D4
Sevastopol' 301,000 ... D5
Severobaykal'sk ... M4
Severodvinsk 197,000 ... E3
Severo-Kuril'sk 8,000 ... Q4
Severoural'sk 29,880 ... G3
Severo-Yeniseysk ... K3
Shadrinsk 82,000 ... G4
Shakhtinsk 50,000 ... H5
Shakhty 209,000 ... E5
Shar'ya 25,788 ... E4
Shchuchinsk 40,432 ... H4
Shenkursk ... E3
Shevchenko 111,000 ... F5
Shilka 16,065 ... M4
Shimanovsk 16,880 ... N4
Shushenskoye 10,000 ... K4
Siauliai 118,000 ... C4
Siktyakh ... N3
Simferopol' 302,000 ... D5
Skovorodino 10,000 ... N4
Slavgorod 32,908 ... H4
Slobodskoy 34,374 ... F4
Slyudyanka 20,639 ... L4
Smolensk 276,000 ... D4
Snezhnogorsk ... J3
Sochi 287,000 ... D5
Sokol 48,253 ... E4
Solikamsk 101,000 ... F3
Sortavala 22,188 ... C4
Sosnogorsk 24,688 ... F3
Sosnovo-Ozerskoye ... M4
Sovetskaya Gavan' 28,455 ... P5
Spassk-Dal'niy 53,000 ... O5
Srednekolymsk ... Q3
Sretensk 16,000 ... M4
Stalingrad (Volgograd) 929,000 ... E5
Stavropol' 258,000 ... E5
Stepanakert 30,293 ... E6
Sterlitamak 220,000 ... F4
Strezhevoy ... H3
Sukhana ... M3
Sukhumi 114,000 ... E5
Sumy 228,000 ... D4
Suntar ... M3
Surgut 107,000 ... H3
Susuman 12,000 ... P3
Sverdlovsk 1,211,000 ... F4
Svobodnyy 75,000 ... N4
Syktyvkar 171,000 ... F3
Syzran' 178,000 ... E4
Taganrog 276,000 ... D5
Takhiatash ... F5
Takhta-Bazar ... G6
Taksimo ... M4
Taldy-Kurgan 88,000 ... H5
Talgar 31,273 ... H5
Tallinn 430,000 ... C4
Tambey ... G2
Tambov 270,000 ... E4
Tara 22,358 ... H4
Tarko-Sale ... H3
Tartu 105,000 ... C4
Tashauz 84,000 ... F5
Tashkent 1,780,000 ... G5
Tatarsk 29,589 ... H4
Tavda ... G4
Tayshet 34,232 ... K4
Tazovskiy ... J3
Tbilisi 1,066,000 ... E5
Tedzhen 25,708 ... F6
Tekeli 29,846 ... H5
Temirtau 213,000 ... H4
Termez 57,000 ... G6
Ternopol' 144,000 ... C5
Tiksi ... N2
Tobol'sk 62,000 ... G4
Togliatti (Tol'yatti) 502,000 ... F4
Tokmak 59,000 ... H5

Tommot 8,000 ... N4
Tomsk 421,000 ... J4
Tot'ma ... E4
Troitsk 88,000 ... G4
Tselinograd 234,000 ... H4
Tskhinvali 30,311 ... E5
Tula 514,000 ... D4
Tulun 52,000 ... L4
Tura 3,528 ... L3
Turgay ... G5
Turkestan 67,000 ... G5
Tynda ... N4
Tyumen' 359,000 ... G4
Uelen ... T3
Ufa 969,000 ... F4
Uglegorsk 17,921 ... P5
Ukhta 87,000 ... F3
Ulan-Ude 300,000 ... L4
Ul'yanovsk 464,000 ... E4
Ural'sk 167,000 ... F4
Uray 17,385 ... G3
Urgench 100,000 ... F5
Ushtobe 24,484 ... H5
Usol'ye-Sibirskoye 103,000 ... L4
Ussuriysk 147,000 ... O5
Ust'-Ilimsk 69,000 ... L4
Ust'-Kamchatsk 10,000 ... R4
Ust'-Kamenogorsk 274,000 ... J5
Ust'-Kut 50,000 ... L4
Ust'-Kuyga ... O3
Ust'-Maya ... O3
Ust'-Nera ... P3
Ust'-Omchug ... P3
Ust'-Olenëk ... M2
Ust'-Ordynskiy 10,693 ... L4
Ust'-Port ... J2
Vanavara ... L3
Vel'sk ... E3
Velikiye Luki 102,000 ... D4
Velikiy Ustyug 36,737 ... E3
Vel'sk 21,899 ... E3
Ventspils 40,467 ... B4
Verkhnevilyuysk ... N3
Verkniy At-Uryakh ... Q3
Verkhoyansk 2,000 ... N3
Vilna (Vilnius) 481,000 ... C4
Vilyuysk ... N3
Vinnitsa 314,000 ... D5
Vitebsk 297,000 ... D4
Vitimskiy ... M4
Vladimir 296,000 ... D4
Vladivostok 550,000 ... O5
Volgograd 929,000 ... E5
Volochanka ... K2
Vologda 237,000 ... E4
Vorkuta 100,000 ... G3
Voronezh 783,000 ... E4
Voroshilovgrad 463,000 ... E5
Vostochnyy ... O5
Votkinsk 10,000 ... F3
Voy-Vozh 10,000 ... F3
Vyazemskiy 18,365 ... O5
Vyborg 76,000 ... C3
Vyshniy Volochek 72,000 ... D4
Yakutsk 152,000 ... N3
Yalutorsk 25,426 ... G4
Yamsk ... Q3
Yaroslavl' 597,000 ... D4
Yartsevo ... J4
Yelets 112,000 ... D4
Yelizovo 10,000 ... Q4
Yeniseysk 19,880 ... K4
Yermak 28,133 ... H4
Yermentau 15,276 ... H4
Yessil' 15,000 ... G4
Yessey ... L3
Yoshkar-Ola 201,000 ... E4
Yurga 78,000 ... J4
Yuzhno-Sakhalinsk 140,000 ... P5
Zabaykal'sk ... M5
Zakamensk 10,000 ... L4
Zaozernyy 27,216 ... K4
Zaporozh'ye 781,000 ... D5
Zarafshan ... G4
Zavitinsk 19,009 ... N4
Zaysan 10,000 ... J5
Zeya 16,684 ... N4
Zhatay ... O3
Zheleznogorsk-Ilimskiy 22,179 ... L4
Zhigalovo ... L4
Zhigansk ... N3
Zhitomir 244,000 ... C4
Zima 41,567 ... L4
Zlatoust 198,000 ... F4
Zyryanka ... Q3

OTHER FEATURES

Alakol' (lake) ... J5
Alazeya (riv.) ... Q3
Aldan (plat.) ... N4
Aldan (riv.) ... O3
Alexandra Land (isl.) ... E1
Altai (mts.) ... J5
Amga (riv.) ... O3
Amgun' (riv.) ... O4
Amur'ya (riv.) ... G4
Amur (riv.) ... O4
Anabar (riv.) ... M2
Anadyr' (gulf) ... T3
Anadyr' (range) ... S3
Anadyr' (riv.) ... S3
Angara (riv.) ... K4
Aral (sea) ... F5
Arctic Ocean ... K1
Argun (riv.) ... M4
Arkticheskiy Institut (isls.) ... H2
Atrek (riv.) ... F6
Ayon (isl.) ... R2
Azov (sea) ... D5
Balkhash (lake) ... H5
Baltic (sea) ... B4
Barents (sea) ... D2
Baykal (lake) ... L4
Baykal (mts.) ... L4
Beloye (lake) ... D3
Belyy (isl.) ... G2
Bering (isl.) ... R4
Bering (sea) ... S4
Bering (strait) ... U3
Bet-Pak-Dala (des.) ... H5
Black (sea) ... D5
Bol'shevik (isl.) ... K2
Bol'shoy Lyakhovskiy (isl.) ... P2
Bolvanskiy Nos (cape) ... G2
Bratsk (res.) ... L4
Caspian (sea) ... F6
Caucasus (mts.) ... E5
Chelyuskin (cape) ... M2
Cherskiy (range) ... P3
Chu (riv.) ... H5
Chukchi (pen.) ... T3
Chukchi (sea) ... T2
Chulym (riv.) ... J4
Chuna (riv.) ... K4
Chunya (riv.) ... K3
Communism (peak) ... H6
Crimea (pen.) ... D5
Dezhnev (cape) ... T3
Dmitriya Lapteva (strait) ... O2
Dnieper (riv.) ... D5
Dniester (riv.) ... C5
Don (riv.) ... E5
Donets (riv.) ... E5
Dulgalakh (riv.) ... O3
Dvina, Northern (riv.) ... E3

Dvina, Western (riv.) ... C4
Dzhugdzhur (range) ... O4
East Siberian (sea) ... S2
Emba (riv.) ... F5
Etorofu (Iturup) (isl.) ... P5
Faddeyevskiy (isl.) ... P2
Finland (gulf) ... C4
Franz Josef Land (isls.) ... F1
George Land (isl.) ... E1
Gizhiga (bay) ... Q3
Govena (cape) ... R4
Graham Bell (isl.) ... G1
Gyda (pen.) ... H2
Gydan (Kolyma) (range) ... Q3
Hiiumaa (isl.) ... C4
Ili (riv.) ... H5
Imandra (lake) ... D3
Indigirka (riv.) ... P2
Irtysh (riv.) ... H4
Ishim (riv.) ... G4
Issyk-Kul' (lake) ... H5
Japan (sea) ... O6
Kakhovka (res.) ... D5
Kamchatka (pen.) ... Q4
Kanin (pen.) ... E3
Kanin Nos (cape) ... E3
Kara (sea) ... G2
Kara-Bogaz-Gol (gulf) ... F5
Kara-Kum (des.) ... F6
Kara-Kum (canal) ... F6
Karskiye Vorota (strait) ... F2
Khanka (lake) ... O5

Kharasavey (cape) ... G2
Kheta (riv.) ... K2
Klyuchevskaya Sopka (vol.) ... Q4
Kola (pen.) ... D3
Kolguyev (isl.) ... E3
Kolyma (range) ... Q3
Kolyma (riv.) ... Q3
Komandorskiye (isls.) ... R4
Komsomolets (isl.) ... L1
Koni (pen.) ... Q4
Koryak (range) ... R4
Kotel'nyy (isl.) ... O2
Kotuy (riv.) ... L3
Kuma (riv.) ... E5
Kura (riv.) ... E5
Kuril (isls.) ... P5
Kuybyshev (res.) ... F4
Kyzyl-Kum (des.) ... G5
Ladoga (lake) ... D3
La Pérouse (str.) ... P5
Laptev (sea) ... N2
Lena (riv.) ... N3
Little Yenisey (riv.) ... K4
Long (str.) ... S2
Lopatka (cape) ... Q4
Lower Tunguska (riv.) ... K3
Lyatkhovskiye (isls.) ... P2
Mangyshlak (pen.) ... F5
Markha (riv.) ... M3
Matochkin Shar (str.) ... F2
Maya (riv.) ... O4
Mezen (riv.) ... E3

Murgab (riv.) ... G6
Nadym (riv.) ... H3
Narodnaya (mt.) ... G3
Navarin (cape) ... T3
New Siberian (isls.) ... P2
Northern Dvina (riv.) ... E3
Novaya Sibir' (isl.) ... Q2
Novaya Zemlya (isls.) ... F2
Ob' (gulf) ... H3
Ob' (riv.) ... G4
October Revolution (isl.) ... L1
Oka (riv.) ... L4
Okhotsk (sea) ... P4
Olëkma (riv.) ... N4
Olënek (bay) ... N2
Olënek (riv.) ... M3
Oloy (riv.) ... R3
Olyutorskiy (cape) ... S4
Omolon (riv.) ... Q3
Omoloy (riv.) ... N2
Onega (lake) ... D3
Onega (riv.) ... D3
Ozernoy (gulf) ... R4
Paramushir (isl.) ... Q4
Pechora (riv.) ... F3
Peipus (lake) ... C4
Penzhina (bay) ... R3
Penzhina (riv.) ... R3
Pioner (isl.) ... K2
Pobeda (peak) ... H5
Pur (riv.) ... H3
Pyasina (riv.) ... J2
Riga (gulf) ... C4

Rybachiy (pen.) ... D2
Rybinsk (res.) ... D4
Saaremaa (isl.) ... B4
Sakhalin (gulf) ... P4
Sakhalin (isl.) ... P4
Sannikova (str.) ... O2
Sary Su (riv.) ... H5
Sayan (mts.) ... K4
Selemdzha (riv.) ... N4
Sergeya Kirova (isls.) ... J2
Severnaya Zemlya (isls.) ... L1
Shantar (isl.) ... O4
Shelagskiy (cape) ... R2
Shelekhov (gulf) ... Q3
Siberia (reg.) 38,524,000 ... M3
Sikhote-Alin' (range) ... O5
Stanovoy (range) ... N4
Stony Tunguska (riv.) ... K3
Syrdar'ya (riv.) ... G5
Tannu-Ola (range) ... K5
Tatar (str.) ... P4
Taymyr (lake) ... K2
Taymyr (pen.) ... L2
Taymyr (riv.) ... K2
Taz (riv.) ... J3
Tengiz (lake) ... G4
Terpeniye (cape) ... P5
Tobol (riv.) ... G4
Tsimlyansk (res.) ... E5
Tym (riv.) ... J3
Tyung (riv.) ... M3
Uda (riv.) ... O4

Ulutau (mts.) ... G5
Ural (mts.) ... F4
Ural (riv.) ... F5
Urup (isl.) ... P5
Ussuri (riv.) ... O5
Ust'-Urt (plat.) ... F5
Vakh (riv.) ... H3
Velikaya (riv.) ... C4
Verkhoyansk (range) ... N3
Vil'kitskogo (str.) ... K1
Vilyuy (range) ... L3
Vilyuy (res.) ... M3
Vilyuy (riv.) ... M3
Vitim (riv.) ... M4
Volga (riv.) ... E4
Western Dvina (riv.) ... C4
White (sea) ... D3
Wiese (isl.) ... H1
Wilczek Land (isl.) ... G1
Wrangel (isl.) ... S2
Yablonovyy (range) ... M4
Yamal (pen.) ... G2
Yana (riv.) ... N2
Yelizavety (cape) ... P4
Yenisey (riv.) ... J3
Yenisey (gulf) ... J2
Zaysan (lake) ... J5
Zeya (riv.) ... N4
Zhelaniye (cape) ... G1

*City, and suburbs

DOMINANT LAND USE

- Cereals (chiefly wheat, corn)
- Cereals (chiefly wheat, rye, oats)
- Dairy, Hogs, Livestock
- Livestock, Dairy
- Pasture Livestock
- Truck Farming, Potatoes, Vegetables, Dairy
- Flax, Dairy, Potatoes
- Cotton
- Vineyards, Orchards, Horticulture
- Sheep Herding, Limited Agriculture
- Forests
- Nonagricultural Land

MAJOR MINERAL OCCURRENCES

Ab	Asbestos	Hg	Mercury	Pb	Lead
Al	Bauxite	K	Potash	Pe	Peat
Au	Gold	Lg	Lignite	Pt	Platinum
Ba	Barite	Mg	Magnesium	S	Sulfur, Pyrites
C	Coal	Mi	Mica	Tc	Talc
Cr	Chromium	Mn	Manganese	Ti	Titanium
Cu	Copper	Mo	Molybdenum	U	Uranium
D	Diamonds	Na	Salt	V	Vanadium
Fe	Iron Ore	Ni	Nickel	W	Tungsten
G	Natural Gas	O	Petroleum	Zn	Zinc
Gr	Graphite	P	Phosphates		

⚡ Water Power   ▨ Major Industrial Areas

Agriculture, Industry and Resources

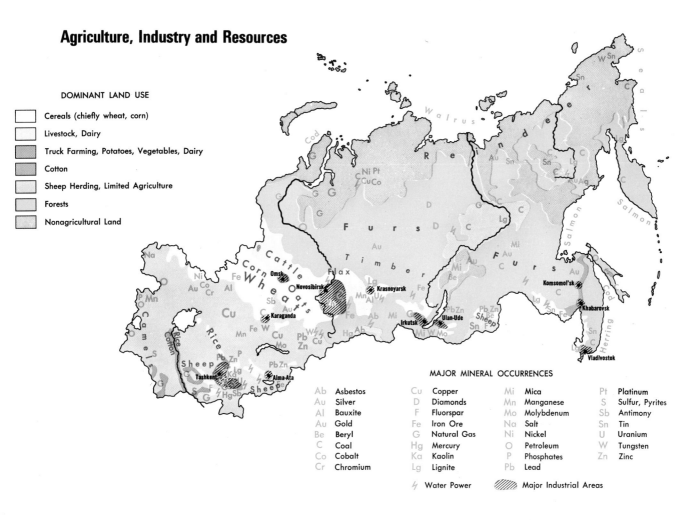

DOMINANT LAND USE

- Cereals (chiefly wheat, corn)
- Livestock, Dairy
- Truck Farming, Potatoes, Vegetables, Dairy
- Cotton
- Sheep Herding, Limited Agriculture
- Forests
- Nonagricultural Land

MAJOR MINERAL OCCURRENCES

Ab	Asbestos	Cu	Copper	Mi	Mica	Pt	Platinum
Au	Silver	D	Diamonds	Mn	Manganese	S	Sulfur, Pyrites
Al	Bauxite	F	Fluorspar	Mo	Molybdenum	Sb	Antimony
Au	Gold	Fe	Iron Ore	Na	Salt	Sn	Tin
Be	Beryl	G	Natural Gas	Ni	Nickel	U	Uranium
C	Coal	Hg	Mercury	O	Petroleum	W	Tungsten
Co	Cobalt	Ka	Kaolin	P	Phosphates	Zn	Zinc
Cr	Chromium	Lg	Lignite	Pb	Lead		

⚡ Water Power ▨ Major Industrial Areas

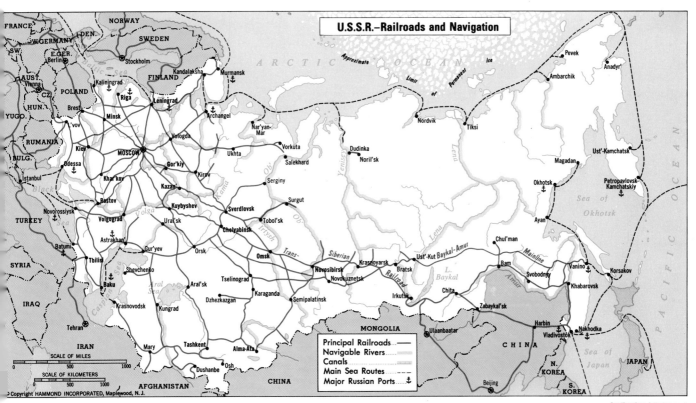

U.S.S.R.–Railroads and Navigation

- Principal Railroads ————
- Navigable Rivers ————
- Canals ————
- Main Sea Routes -----
- Major Russian Ports ⚓

SCALE OF MILES
0 500 1000

SCALE OF KILOMETERS
0 500 1000

© Copyright HAMMOND INCORPORATED, Maplewood, N.J.

(continued on following page)

Union of Soviet Socialist Republics
European Part

CONIC PROJECTION

SCALE OF MILES

0 50 100   200   300

SCALE OF KILOMETERS

0 50 100   200   300

National Capitals .... ☆
Capitals of Union Republics .... ⬡
Administrative Centers .... △
International boundaries ....
Union Republic boundaries ....
A.S.S.R., Oblast, Kray boundaries ....
Autonomous Oblast boundaries ....
Autonomous Okrug boundaries ....

The government of the United States has not recognized the incorporation of Estonia, Latvia and Lithuania into the Soviet Union.

Administrative Divisions bear same names as their respective Capitals or Centers, except:

Abkhaz A.S.S.R.	Sukhumi	F6
Adygey Aut. Oblast	Maykop	F6
Adzhar A.S.S.R.	Batumi	F6
Bashkir A.S.S.R.	Ufa	J4
Chechen-Ingush A.S.S.R.	Groznyy	G6
Chuvash A.S.S.R.	Cheboksary	G3
Crimean Oblast	Simferopol'	D6
Dagestan A.S.S.R.	Makhachkala	G6
Kabardin-Balkar A.S.S.R.	Nal'chik	F6
Kalmuck A.S.S.R.	Elista	F5
Karachay-Cherkess Aut. Obl.	Cherkessk	F6
Karelian A.S.S.R.	Petrozavodsk	D2
Komi A.S.S.R.	Syktyvkar	H2
Komi-Permyak Aut. Okrug	Kudymkar	H3
Mari A.S.S.R.	Yoshkar-Ola	G3
Mordvinian A.S.S.R.	Saransk	G4
Nagorno-Karabakh Aut. Obl.	Stepanakert	G7
Nenets Aut. Okrug	Nar'yan-Mar	H1
North Ossetian A.S.S.R.	Ordzhonikidze	F6
South Ossetian Aut. Obl.	Tskhinvali	F6
Tatar A.S.S.R.	Kazan'	G3
Trans-Carpathian Oblast	Uzhgorod	B5
Udmurt A.S.S.R.	Izhevsk	H3
Volyn Oblast	Lutsk	C4

© Copyright HAMMOND INCORPORATED, Maplewood, N.J.

U.S.S.R. — EUROPEAN

UNION REPUBLICS

Armenian S.S.R. 3,031,000 .... F6
Azerbaidzhan S.S.R. 6,028,000 .... G6
Estonian S.S.R 1,466,000 .... C3
Georgian S.S.R. 5,015,000 .... F6
Latvian S.S.R 2,521,000 .... B3
Lithuanian S.S.R. 3,398,000 .... B3
Moldavian S.S.R. 3,947,000 .... C5
Russian S.F.S.R. 137,551,000 .... F3
Ukrainian S.S.R. 49,755,000 .... D5
White Russian S.S.R. 9,560,000 .... C4

INTERNAL DIVISIONS

Abkhaz A.S.S.R. 505,000 .... F6
Adygey Aut. Obl. 405,000 .... F6
Adzhar A.S.S.R. 354,000 .... F6
Bashkir A.S.S.R. 3,849,000 .... J4
Chechen-Ingush A.S.S.R. 1,154,000 .... G6
Chuvash A.S.S.R. 1,292,000 .... G3
Crimean Oblast 2,183,000 .... D6
Dagestan A.S.S.R. 1,628,000 .... G6
Kabardin-Balkar A.S.S.R. 674,000 .... F6
Kalmuck A.S.S.R. 294,000 .... F5
Karachay-Cherkess Aut. Obl. 368,000 .... F6
Karelian A.S.S.R. 736,000 .... D2
Komi A.S.S.R. 1,119,000 .... H2
Komi-Permyak Aut. Okr. 173,000 .... H3
Mari A.S.S.R. 703,000 .... G3
Mordvinian A.S.S.R. 991,000 .... G4
Nagorno-Karabakh Aut. Obl. 161,000 .... G7
Nakhichevan' A.S.S.R. 239,000 .... F7
Nenets Aut. Okr. 47,000 .... H1
North Ossetian A.S.S.R. 597,000 .... F6
South Ossetian Aut. Obl. 98,000 .... F6
Tatar A.S.S.R. 3,436,000 .... G3
Trans-Carpathian Oblast 1,155,000 .... B5
Udmurt A.S.S.R. 1,494,000 .... H3
Volyn Oblast 1,015,000 .... C4

CITIES and TOWNS

Abdulino 26,010 .... H4
Agdam 21,277 .... G6
Agryz 19,267 .... H3
Akhaltsikhe 18,972 .... F6
Akhtubinsk 43,466 .... G5
Akhty G6
Akhtyrka 41,354 .... E4
Akkerman (Belgorod-Dnestrovskiy) 32,928 .... D5
Alagir 18,161 .... F6
Alatyr' 43,499 .... G4
Alaverdi 21,311 .... F6
Aleksandriya 82,000 .... D5
Aleksandrovsk 18,286 .... J3
Alekseyevka 25,562 .... E4
Aleksin 67,000 .... E4
Ali-Bayramly 33,828 .... G7
Al'met'yevsk 110,000 .... H3
Alushta 22,016 .... D6
Amderma K1
Anapa 29,900 .... E6
Apatity 62,000 .... D1
Apsheronsk 32,867 .... F6
Archangel (Arkhangel'sk) 385,000 .... F2
Armavir 162,000 .... F5
Arzamas 93,000 .... F3
Astara G7
Astrakhan' 461,000 .... G5
Atkarsk 28,881 .... G4
Azov 75,000 .... E5
Bakhchisaray 15,912 .... D6
Baku 1,022,000 .... H6
Balakhna 36,542 .... F3
Balaklava D6
Balakovo 152,000 .... G4
Balashov 93,000 .... F4
Baltiysk 20,300 .... A4
Baranovichi 131,000 .... C4
Barysh 20,792 .... G4
Bataysk 90,000 .... E5
Batumi 123,000 .... F6
Belaya Tserkov' 151,000 .... C5
Belebey 32,460 .... H4
Belev 17,733 .... E4
Belgorod 240,000 .... E4
Belgorod-Dnestrovskiy 32,928 .... D5
Belomorsk 16,595 .... D2
Belorechensk 35,970 .... E6
Beloretsk 71,000 .... J4
Belozersk E3
Bel'tsy 125,000 .... C5
Belush'ya Guba H1
Bendery 101,000 .... C5
Berdichev 80,000 .... C5
Berdyansk 122,000 .... E5
Beregovo 27,308 .... B5
Berezniki 185,000 .... J3
Beslan 26,893 .... F6
Bezhetsk 30,030 .... E3
Birsk 29,607 .... J3
Bobrov 17,977 .... F4
Bobruysk 192,000 .... C4
Bologoye 33,949 .... D3
Bor 63,000 .... F3
Borislav 33,800 .... B5
Borisoglebsk 68,000 .... F4
Borisov 112,000 .... C4
Borovichi 60,000 .... D3
Brest 177,000 .... B4
Bryansk 394,000 .... D4
Bugul'ma 80,000 .... H4
Buguruslan 54,000 .... H4
Buturlinovka 21,643 .... F4
Buy 29,946 .... F3
Buynaksk 37,946 .... G6
Buzuluk 76,000 .... H4
Bykhov 17,371 .... C4
Cēsis 17,696 .... C3
Chadyr-Lunga 20,474 .... C5
Chapayevsk 85,000 .... G4
Chaykovskiy 48,034 .... H3
Cheboksary 308,000 .... G3
Cherepovets 266,000 .... E3
Cherkassy 228,000 .... D5
Cherkessk 91,000 .... F6
Chernigov 238,000 .... D4
Chernobyl' C4
Chernovtsy 219,000 .... C5
Chernushka 21,106 .... J3
Chervonograd 55,000 .... B4
Chiatura 25,474 .... F6
Chistopol' 64,000 .... H3
Chortkov 19,183 .... B5
Chudovo D3
Chusovoy 56,000 .... J3
Danilov 17,500 .... E3
Dankov 20,030 .... E4
Daugavpils 116,000 .... C3
Davlekanovo 20,123 .... H4
Derbent 70,000 .... G6
Dimitrovgrad 106,000 .... G4
Dneprodzerzhinsk 250,000 .... D5
Dnepropetrovsk 1,066,000 .... D5
Dobrush 16,809 .... D4
Dobryanka 18,349 .... J3
Donetsk 1,021,000 .... E5
Drogobych 66,000 .... B5
Dubna 55,000 .... E3
Dubna E4
Dubno 25,442 .... C4
Dvinsk (Daugavpils) 116,000 .... C3
Dyat'kovo 26,825 .... D4
Dzerzhinsk 257,000 .... F3
Dzhankoy 43,459 .... D5
Dzhul'fa G7
Echmiadzin 31,819 .... F6
Elektrostal' 139,000 .... E3
Elista 70,000 .... F5
El'ton G5
Engel's 161,000 .... G4
Erivan 1,019,000 .... F6
Fastov 51,000 .... C4
Feodosiya 76,000 .... D5
Frolovo 33,398 .... F5
Furmanov 40,155 .... F3
Gagra 23,025 .... E6
Galich 19,374 .... F3
Gandzha (Kirovabad) 232,000 .... G6
Gatchina 75,000 .... C3
Gay 28,250 .... J4
Gaysin 23,741 .... C5
Gdov C3
Gelendzhik 29,086 .... E6
Genichesk 20,031 .... E5
Georgiu-Dezh 52,000 .... E4
Glazov 81,000 .... H3
Glubokoye C3
Glukhov 27,096 .... D4
Gomel' 383,000 .... D4
Gori 56,000 .... F6
Gorki 22,117 .... D4
Gor'kiy 1,344,000 .... F3
Gorlovka 336,000 .... E5
Gorodets 34,229 .... F3
Gremikha E1
Gremyachinsk 29,975 .... J3
Grodno 195,000 .... B4
Groznyy 375,000 .... G6
Gryazi 41,292 .... F4
Gubakha 33,243 .... J3
Gubkin 65,000 .... E4
Gudauta F6
Gudermes 32,445 .... G6
Gukovo 68,000 .... F5
Gus'-Khrustal'nyy 72,000 .... F3
Imishli 17,839 .... G7
Inta 51,000 .... K1
Inza 19,060 .... G4
Ishimbay 57,000 .... J4
Ivano-Frankovsk 150,000 .... B5
Ivanovo 465,000 .... E3
Izberbash 17,299 .... G6
Izhevsk 549,000 .... H3
Izmail 83,000 .... C5
Izyum 61,000 .... E5
Jēkabpils 22,440 .... C3
Jelgava 68,000 .... B3
Jurmala 61,000 .... B3
Kadiyevka (Stakhanov) 108,000 .... E5
Kafan 29,916 .... G7
Kagul 26,249 .... C5
Kakhovka 28,472 .... D5
Kalach 18,475 .... F4
Kalach-na-Donu 20,795 .... F5
Kalinin 412,000 .... E3
Kaliningrad, Kaliningrad 355,000 .... B4
Kaliningrad, Moscow Oblast 133,000 .... E3
Kalinkovichi 23,918 .... C4
Kaluga 265,000 .... E4
Kalush 60,000 .... B5
Kamenets-Podol'skiy 81,000 .... C5
Kamenka 30,067 .... F4
Kamensk-Shakhtinskiy 72,000 .... F5
Kamyshin 112,000 .... F4
Kanash 40,682 .... G3
Kandalaksha 42,656 .... D1
Kapsukas 28,763 .... B4
Karachayevsk F6
Karachev 15,972 .... E4
Kashin 17,678 .... E3
Kasimov 33,066 .... F4
Kaspiysk 38,990 .... G6
Kaunas 370,000 .... B4
Kazan' 993,000 .... G3
Kazatin 26,649 .... C5
Kem' 21,025 .... D2
Kerch' 157,000 .... E5
Keret' D1
Khachmas 22,313 .... G6
Khadyzhensk 17,856 .... E6
Khar'kov 1,444,000 .... E5
Khasavyurt 65,000 .... G6
Khashuri 24,469 .... F6
Kherson 319,000 .... D5
Khmel'nitskiy 172,000 .... C5
Khotin 10,319 .... C5
Khust 23,810 .... B5
Khvalynsk 16,249 .... G4
Kiev 2,144,000 .... D4
Kiliya 24,276 .... C5
Kimovsk 44,490 .... E4
Kimry 58,000 .... E3
Kinel' 39,373 .... H4
Kineshma 101,000 .... F3
Kirishi 27,252 .... D3
Kirov, Kaluga 29,355 .... D4
Kirov, Kirov 390,000 .... G3
Kirovabad 232,000 .... G6
Kirovakan 146,000 .... G6
Kirovo-Chepetsk 71,000 .... H3
Kirovograd 237,000 .... D5
Kirovsk 38,484 .... D1
Kirsanov 21,795 .... F4
Kishinev 503,000 .... C5
Kislovodsk 101,000 .... F6
Kizel 46,264 .... J3
Kizlyar 29,745 .... G6
Klaipeda 176,000 .... B3
Klintsy 67,000 .... D4
Kobrin 24,935 .... B4
Kobuleti 18,051 .... F6
Kohtla-Järve 73,000 .... C3
Kolomiya 52,000 .... B5
Kolomna 147,000 .... E4
Kolpino 114,000 .... D3
Kommunarsk 120,000 .... E5
Komrat 21,369 .... C5
Komsomol'skiy 17,078 .... K1
Kondopoga 27,908 .... D2
Königsberg (Kaliningrad) 355,000 .... B4
Konotop 82,000 .... D4
Konstantinovka 112,000 .... E5
Korenovsk 26,323 .... E5
Korosten' 65,000 .... C4
Korostyshev 21,153 .... C4
Koryazhma 33,230 .... G2
Kostopol' 17,548 .... C4
Kostroma 255,000 .... F3
Kotel'nich 29,196 .... G3
Kotel'nikovo 19,063 .... F5
Kotlas 61,000 .... G2
Kotovo 20,553 .... G4
Kotovsk, Odessa 36,463 .... C5
Kotovsk, Tambov 33,347 .... F4
Kovel' 33,351 .... C4
Kovrov 143,000 .... F3
Kovylkino 17,300 .... F4
Kramatorsk 178,000 .... E5
Krasnoarmeysk 60,000 .... G4
Krasnodar 560,000 .... E6
Krasnograd 18,386 .... E5
Krasnokamsk 56,000 .... H3
Krasnoslobodsk 17,749 .... G5
Krasnovishersk J2
Krasnyy Kut 17,087 .... G4
Krasnyy Luch 106,000 .... E5
Krasnyy Sulin 41,684 .... F5
Kremenchug 210,000 .... D5
Krichev 25,682 .... D4
Krivoy Rog 650,000 .... D5
Krolevets 18,307 .... D4
Kronshtadt 39,477 .... C3
Kropotkin 70,000 .... F5
Krymsk 41,430 .... E5
Kuba 18,871 .... G6
Kudymkar 26,350 .... H3
Kulebaki 46,252 .... F3
Kumertau 52,000 .... J4
Kunda C3
Kungur 80,000 .... J3
Kupyansk 30,055 .... E5
Kuressaare 12,140 .... B3
Kursk 375,000 .... E4
Kutaisi 194,000 .... F6
Kuvandyk 22,914 .... J4
Kuybyshev 1,216,000 .... H4
Kuznetsk 94,000 .... G4
Kuzomen' E1
Labinsk 54,000 .... F6
Lakhdenpokh'ya C2
Lebedin 29,240 .... D4
Leninakan 207,000 .... F6
Leningrad 4,073,000 .... C3
Leningrad* 4,588,000 .... C3
Leninogorsk 54,000 .... H4
Lenkoran' 35,505 .... G7
L'gov 25,110 .... E4
Lida 66,000 .... C4
Liepāja 108,000 .... B3
Likhoslavl' E3
Lipetsk 396,000 .... E4
Lisichansk 119,000 .... E5
Livny 37,290 .... E4
Lodeynoye Pole 19,632 .... D2
Lozovaya 53,000 .... E5
Lubny 54,000 .... D4
Luga 31,905 .... C3
Lutsk 137,000 .... B4
L'vov (Lwów) 667,000 .... B5
Lys'va 75,000 .... J3
Lyubertsy 160,000 .... E3
Lyubotin 33,324 .... E4
Lyudinovo 33,871 .... D4
Makeyevka 436,000 .... E5
Makhachkala 251,000 .... G6
Makharadze 21,679 .... F6
Malaya Vishera 15,381 .... D3
Malgobek 20,548 .... F6
Manturovo 21,510 .... F3
Marganets 50,000 .... E5
Mariupol' 503,000 .... E5
Marks 17,132 .... G4
Maykop 128,000 .... F6
Mednogorsk 38,024 .... J4
Medvezh'yegorsk 17,465 .... D2
Melenki 18,545 .... F3
Meleuz 24,851 .... J4
Melitopol' 161,000 .... D5
Memel (Klaipeda) 176,000 .... B3
Merefa 29,985 .... E5
Mezen' F1
Michurinsk 101,000 .... F4
Mikhaylovka 58,000 .... F4
Millerovo 34,627 .... F5
Mineral'nye Vody 67,000 .... F6
Mingechaur 60,000 .... G6
Minsk 1,262,000 .... C4
Minsk* 1,276,000 .... C4
Mirgorod 28,407 .... D5
Mogilev 290,000 .... C4
Mogilev-Podol'skiy 26,051 .... C5
Molodechno 73,000 .... C4
Molotov (Perm') 999,000 .... J3
Monchegorsk 51,000 .... D1
Morshansk 44,245 .... F4
Moscow (Moskva) (cap.) 7,831,000 .... E3
Moscow* 8,011,000 .... E3
Mozhaysk 20,321 .... E3
Mozhga 38,930 .... H3
Mozyr' 73,000 .... C4
Mtsensk 27,833 .... E4
Mukachevo 72,000 .... B5
Murmansk 381,000 .... D1
Murom 114,000 .... F3
Mytishchi 141,000 .... E3
Nakhichevan' 33,279 .... F7
Nal'chik 207,000 .... F6
Narva 73,000 .... C3
Nar'yan-Mar 16,864 .... H1
Neftekamsk 70,000 .... J3
Nelidovo 29,813 .... D3
Nerekhta 25,722 .... F3
Nevel' 17,804 .... D3
Nevinnomyssk 104,000 .... F6
Nezhin 70,000 .... D4
Nikel' 21,299 .... C1
Nikolayev 440,000 .... D5
Nikol'sk 20,740 .... G4
Nikopol' 146,000 .... D5
Nizhnekamsk 134,000 .... H3
Nizhniy Lomov 17,460 .... F4
Nizhniy Novgorod (Gor'kiy) 1,344,000 .... F3
Nosovka 19,430 .... D4
Novaya Kakhovka 52,000 .... D5
Novgorod 186,000 .... D3
Novgorod-Severskiy D4
Novoanninskiy 20,461 .... F4
Novocherkassk 183,000 .... F5
Novograd-Volynskiy 41,194 .... C4
Novogrudok 19,374 .... C4
Novokuybyshevsk 109,000 .... G4
Novomoskovsk 147,000 .... E4
Novopolotsk 67,000 .... C3
Novorossiysk 159,000 .... E6
Novoshakhtinsk 104,000 .... E5
Novotroitsk 95,000 .... J4
Novoukrainka 19,554 .... D5
Novouzensk G4
Novovolynsk 41,187 .... B4
Novovyatsk 26,408 .... G3
Novozybkov 34,433 .... D4
Nurlat 17,533 .... H4
Nyandoma 23,366 .... F2
Nytva 17,491 .... H3
Nyuvchim H2
Obninsk 73,000 .... E3
Ochamchira 18,718 .... F6
Odessa 1,046,000 .... D5
Oktyabr'sk 33,981 .... G4
Oktyabr'skiy 88,000 .... H4
Okulovka 19,194 .... D3
Olenegorsk 21,485 .... D1
Olonets D2
Omutninsk 28,777 .... H3
Onega 25,047 .... E2
Ordzhonikidze 279,000 .... F6
Orel 305,000 .... E4
Orenburg 459,000 .... J4
Orgeyev 25,798 .... C5
Orsha 112,000 .... C4
Orsk 247,000 .... J4
Osa 15,038 .... J3
Osipenko (Berdyansk) 122,000 .... E5
Osipovichi 19,705 .... C4
Ostashkov 23,419 .... D3
Ostrogozhsk 29,921 .... E4
Ostrov 22,369 .... C3
Otradnyy 44,426 .... H4
Panevežys 102,000 .... B3
Pärnu 51,000 .... C3
Pavlograd 107,000 .... E5
Pavlovo 68,000 .... F3
Pechenga D1
Pechora 56,000 .... J1
Penza 483,000 .... G4
Perm' 999,000 .... J3
Pervomaysk 72,000 .... D5
Petrokrepost' D3
Petrovsk 30,953 .... G4
Petrozavodsk 234,000 .... D2
Petsamo (Pechenga) D1
Pinsk 90,000 .... C4
Podol'sk 202,000 .... E3
Podporozh'ye 21,545 .... D2
Pokhvistnevo 26,125 .... H4
Polonnoye 22,484 .... C4
Polotsk 71,000 .... C3
Poltava 279,000 .... D5
Polyarnyy 15,321 .... D1
Ponoy F1
Poti 45,979 .... F6
Povenets E2
Povorino 20,591 .... F4
Prikumsk 35,768 .... F6
Priluki 65,000 .... D4
Primorsk C2
Primorsko-Akhtarsk 25,981 .... E5
Priozersk 16,652 .... D2
Privolzhskiy 23,041 .... G4
Priyutovo 21,051 .... H4
Prokhladnyy 40,074 .... F6
Pskov 176,000 .... C3
Pugachev 33,963 .... G4
Pushkin 90,000 .... C3
Pyatigorsk 110,000 .... F6
Rabocheostrovsk D1
Rakhov B5
Rakvere 17,891 .... C3
Rasskazovo 40,038 .... F4
Razdan 26,833 .... G6
Rechitsa 60,000 .... C4
Reni 19,625 .... C5
Revel (Tallinn) 430,000 .... B3
Rēzekne 30,803 .... C3
Riga 835,000 .... B3
Romny 53,000 .... D4
Roslavl' 56,000 .... D4
Rossosh' 36,438 .... E4
Rostov 30,815 .... E3
Rostov-na-Donu 934,000 .... F5
Rovno 179,000 .... C4
Rtishchevo 37,146 .... F4
Rubezhnoye 66,000 .... E5
Rustavi 129,000 .... G6
Ruzayevka 41,084 .... F4
Ryazan' 453,000 .... E4
Ryazhsk 25,425 .... F4
Rybinsk 239,000 .... E3
Rybnitsa 32,266 .... C5
Rzhev 69,000 .... D3
Safonovo 53,000 .... D3
Saki 24,208 .... D5
Salavat 137,000 .... H4
Sal'sk 57,000 .... F5
Sal'yany 24,228 .... G7
Samara (Kuybyshev) 1,216,000 .... H4
Sambor 29,253 .... B5
Saransk 263,000 .... G4
Sarapul 107,000 .... H3
Saratov 856,000 .... G4
Sasovo 27,228 .... F4
Segezha 28,810 .... D2
Semenov 23,633 .... F3
Semiluki 18,221 .... E4
Sengiley G4
Serdobol' (Sortavala) 22,188 .... D2
Serdobsk 33,783 .... F4
Sergach 22,509 .... F3
Serpukhov 140,000 .... E4
Sevastopol' 301,000 .... D6
Severodonetsk 113,000 .... E5
Severodvinsk 197,000 .... E2
Severomorsk 50,000 .... D1
Shakhty 209,000 .... F5
Shakhun'ya 20,009 .... G3
Shar'ya 25,788 .... G3
Shchekino 70,000 .... E4
Shchigry 17,133 .... E4
Sheki 43,158 .... G6
Shemakha 17,986 .... G6
Shepetovka 38,707 .... C4
Shostka 82,000 .... D4
Shpola 19,806 .... D5
Shumerlya 33,816 .... G3
Shuya 72,000 .... F3
Šiauliai 118,000 .... B3
Sibay 37,656 .... J4
Simferopol' 302,000 .... D6
Skadovsk D5
Skopin 24,429 .... F4
Slantsy 41,146 .... C3
Slavuta 25,573 .... C4
Slavyansk 140,000 .... E5
Slavyansk-na-Kubani 54,000 .... E5
Slobodskoy 34,374 .... H3
Slonim 30,279 .... B4
Slutsk 35,609 .... C4
Smela 62,000 .... D5
Smolensk 276,000 .... D4
Sochi 287,000 .... E6
Sokol 48,243 .... F3
Soligorsk 65,000 .... C4
Solikamsk 101,000 .... J3
Sol'-Iletsk 22,227 .... J4
Sorochinsk 23,235 .... H4
Soroki 21,924 .... C5
Sortavala 22,188 .... D2
Sosnogorsk 24,688 .... H2
Sovetsk (Tilsit) 38,456 .... B4
Sovetsk 17,027 .... G3
Stakhanov 108,000 .... E5
Stalingrad (Volgograd) 929,000 .... F5
Staraya Russa 34,577 .... D3
Staryy Oskol 115,000 .... E4
Stavropol' 258,000 .... F5
Stepanakert 30,293 .... G7
Sterlitamak 220,000 .... J4
Stupino 70,000 .... E4
Sudak E6
Sukhumi 114,000 .... F6
Sumgait 190,000 .... G6
Sumy 228,000 .... E4
Svetlogorsk 55,000 .... C4
Svetlograd 40,265 .... F5
Syktyvkar 171,000 .... H2
Syzran' 178,000 .... G4
Taganrog 276,000 .... E5
Tallinn 430,000 .... B3
Tambov 270,000 .... F4
Tartu 105,000 .... C3
Taurage 19,461 .... B3
Tbilisi 1,066,000 .... F6
Telavi 21,179 .... G6
Telšiai 20,220 .... B3
Temryuk 23,172 .... E5
Ternopol' 144,000 .... C5
Teykovo 41,607 .... E3
Tiflis (Tbilisi) 1,066,000 .... F6
Tighina (Bendery) 101,000 .... C5
Tikhoretsk 64,000 .... F5
Tikhvin 59,000 .... D3
Tilsit (Sovetsk) 38,456 .... B4
Timashevsk 29,055 .... E5
Tiraspol' 139,000 .... D5
Togliatti (Tol'yatti) 502,000 .... G4
Tokmak 59,000 .... E5
Toropets 16,863 .... D3
Torzhok 45,443 .... D3
Troitsko-Pechorsk J2
Tskhinvali 30,311 .... F6
Tuapse 60,000 .... E6
Tula 514,000 .... E4
Tutayev 16,839 .... E3
Tuymazy 37,021 .... H4
Tver (Kalinin) 412,000 .... E3
Tyrnyauz 18,253 .... F6
Uchaly 21,808 .... J4
Ufa 969,000 .... J4
Uglich 35,463 .... E3
Ukmerge 21,663 .... C3
Ul'yanovsk 464,000 .... G4
Uman' 79,000 .... D5
Unecha 21,749 .... D4
Ungeny 17,228 .... C5
Uryupinsk 38,192 .... F4
Usinsk J1
Usman' 20,150 .... E4
Uvarovo 24,946 .... F4
Uzhgorod 91,000 .... B5
Uzlovaya 65,000 .... E4
Valga 16,795 .... C3
Valmiera 20,331 .... C3
Valuyki 29,093 .... E4
Vasil'kov 26,741 .... D4
Velikiye Luki 102,000 .... D3
Velikiy Ustyug 36,737 .... F2
Vel'sk 21,899 .... F2
Ventspils 40,467 .... B3
Vereshchagino 23,585 .... H3
Vichuga 52,000 .... F3
Viipuri (Vyborg) 76,000 .... C2
Vileyka C4
Vilna (Vilnius) 481,000 .... C4
Vinnitsa 314,000 .... C5
Vinogradov 20,580 .... B5
Vitebsk 297,000 .... C3
Vladimir 296,000 .... F3
Vladimir-Volynskiy 28,412 .... B4
Volgodonsk 91,000 .... F5
Volgograd 929,000 .... F5
Volkhov 47,025 .... D3
Volkovysk 28,266 .... B4
Vologda 237,000 .... F3
Vol'sk 66,000 .... G4
Volzhsk 52,000 .... G3
Volzhskiy 209,000 .... G5
Vorkuta 100,000 .... K1
Voronezh 783,000 .... E4
Voroshilovgrad 463,000 .... E5
Voskresensk 76,000 .... E3
Votkinsk 90,000 .... H3
Voznesensk 36,457 .... D5
Vyatskiye Polyany 32,729 .... H3
Vyaz'ma 52,000 .... D3
Vyborg 76,000 .... C2
Vyksa 54,000 .... F3
Vyshniy Volochek 72,000 .... D3
Yalta 80,000 .... D6
Yanaul 20,115 .... J3
Yaroslavl' 597,000 .... E3
Yartsevo 36,662 .... D3
Yefremov 53,000 .... E4
Yelabuga 31,728 .... H3
Yelets 112,000 .... E4
Yenakiyevo 114,000 .... E5
Yershov 21,731 .... G4
Yessentuki 78,000 .... F6
Yevlakh 29,462 .... G6
Yevpatoria 93,000 .... D5
Yeysk 71,000 .... E5
Yoshkar-Ola 201,000 .... G3
Yur'yevets 20,144 .... F3
Zagorsk 107,000 .... E3
Zapolyarnyy 22,084 .... D1
Zaporozh'ye 781,000 .... E5
Zelenodol'sk 85,000 .... G3
Zelenokumsk 29,691 .... F6
Zernograd 20,324 .... F5
Zhdanov 503,000 .... E5
Zheleznodorozhnyy 76,000 .... H2
Zheleznogorsk 65,000 .... E4
Zhigulevsk 52,130 .... G4
Zhitomir 244,000 .... C4
Zhlobin 25,359 .... D4
Zhmerinka 36,195 .... C5
Zhodino 22,083 .... C4
Zhovtnevoye 31,102 .... D5
Znamenka 27,393 .... D5
Zolotonosha 27,639 .... D5
Zugdidi 39,896 .... F6
Zuyevka 17,001 .... H3

OTHER FEATURES

Apsheron (pen.) H6
Araks (riv.) G7
Azov (sea) E5
Baltic (sea) B3
Barents (sea) E1
Belaya (riv.) H3
Beloye (lake) E2
Black (sea) D6
Bug (riv.) B4
Bug (riv.) D5
Caspian (sea) G6
Caucasus (mts.) F6
Crimea (pen.) D5
Desna (riv.) D4
Dnieper (riv.) D5
Dniester (riv.) C5
Don (riv.) F5
Donets (riv.) E5
Dvina (bay) E2
Dvina, Northern (riv.) F2
Dvina, Western (riv.) C3
Dykh-Tau (mt.) F6
El'brus (mt.) F6
Finland (gulf) C3
Hiiumaa (isl.) B3
Il'men' (lake) D3
Imandra (lake) D1
Kakhovka (res.) D5
Kama (riv.) H2
Kandalaksha (gulf) D1
Kanin (pen.) G1
Kara (sea) K1
Karskiye Vorota (str.) J1
Kazbek (mt.) F6
Khoper (riv.) F4
Kola (pen.) E1
Kolguyev (isl.) G1
Kuban' (riv.) E5
Kura (riv.) G6
Kuybyshev (res.) G4
Ladoga (lake) D2
Lapland (reg.) D1
Mezen' (riv.) G1
Moksha (riv.) F4
Narodnaya (mt.) J1
Niemen (riv.) B4
Novaya Zemlya (isls.) H1
Oka (riv.) F4
Onega (bay) E2
Onega (lake) E2
Onega (riv.) E2
Pechora (riv.) H1
Peipus (lake) C3
Pripet (marshes) C4
Pripyat' (riv.) C4
Prut (riv.) C5
Riga (gulf) B3
Rybachiy (pen.) D1
Rybinsk (res.) E3
Saaremaa (isl.) B3
Samara (riv.) H4
Sevan (lake) G6
Seym (riv.) D4
Sura (riv.) G4
Svir' (riv.) D2
Timan (ridge) G1
Tsil'ma (riv.) H1
Tsimlyansk (res.) F5
Tuloma (riv.) D1
Ural (mts.) J2
Ural (riv.) J4
Usa (riv.) K1
Valday (hills) D3
Vaygach (isl.) K1
Velikaya (riv.) C3
Volga (riv.) G5
Volga-Don (canal) F5
Volgograd (res.) G5
Volkhov (riv.) D3
Vorskla (riv.) E4
Vyatka (riv.) H3
Vychegda (riv.) G2
Vyg (lake) E2
White (sea) E1
Yamantau (mt.) J4
Yugorskiy (pen.) K1

*City and suburbs.

ESTONIA

LATVIA

LITHUANIA

The government of the United States has not recognized the incorporation of Estonia, Latvia and Lithuania into the Soviet Union, nor does it recognize other post-war territorial changes shown on this map. The flags shown here were the official flags of the independent Baltic States prior to 1939.

© Copyright HAMMOND INCORPORATED, Maplewood, N. J.

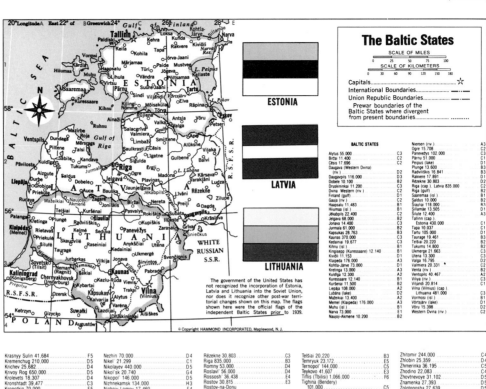

The Baltic States

SCALE OF MILES 0 25 50 75 100
SCALE OF KILOMETERS 0 30 60 90 120 150 180

Capitals .... ☆
International Boundaries .... —··—
Union Republic Boundaries .... —·—
Prewar boundaries of the Baltic States where divergent from present boundaries ....

BALTIC STATES

Alytus 55,000 .... C3
Biržai 11,400 .... C2
Cēsis 17,696 .... C2
Daugava (Western Dvina) (riv.) D2
Daugavpils 116,000 .... D3
Dobele 10,100 .... B2
Druskininkai 11,200 .... C3
Dvina Western (riv.) C2
Finland (gulf) D1
Gauja (riv.) C2
Haapsalu 11,483 .... B1
Hiiumaa (isl.) B1
Jēkabpils 22,400 .... C2
Jelgava 68,000 .... B2
Jonava 14,400 .... C3
Jurmala 61,000 .... B2
Kapsukas 28,763 .... B3
Kaunas 370,000 .... C3
Kedainiai 19,677 .... C3
Kihnu (isl.) B1
Kingisepp (Kuressaare) 12,140 .... B1
Kiviõli 11,153 .... D1
Klaipeda 176,000 .... A3
Kohtla-Järve 73,000 .... D1
Kretinga 13,000 .... A3
Kuldīga 12,300 .... A2
Kuressaare 12,140 .... B1
Kuršenai 11,500 .... B2
Liepāja 108,000 .... A2
Lubāna (lake) D2
Mažeikiai 13,400 .... A2
Memel (Klaipeda) 176,000 .... A3
Muhu (isl.) B1
Narva 73,000 .... E1
Naujoji-Akmene 10,200 .... B2
Niemen (riv.) A3
Ogre 15,708 .... C2
Panevežys 102,000 .... C3
Pärnu 51,000 .... C1
Peipus (lake) D1
Plunge 13,600 .... B3
Radviliškis 16,841 .... B3
Rakvere 17,891 .... D1
Rēzekne 30,803 .... D2
Riga (cap.), Latvia 835,000 .... C2
Riga (gulf) B2
Saaremaa (isl.) B1
Saldus 10,000 .... B2
Šiauliai 118,000 .... B3
Sillamäe 13,505 .... D1
Šilute 12,400 .... A3
Tallinn (cap.), Estonia 430,000 .... C1
Tapa 10,037 .... C1
Tartu 105,000 .... D1
Taurage 19,461 .... B3
Telšiai 20,220 .... B2
Tukums 14,800 .... B2
Ukmerge 21,663 .... C3
Utena 13,300 .... C3
Valga 16,795 .... D2
Valmiera 20,331 .... C2
Venta (riv.) B2
Ventspils 40,467 .... A2
Viliya (riv.) C3
Viljandi 20,814 .... C1
Vilna (Vilnius) (cap.), Lithuania 481,000 .... C3
Vormosi (isl.) B1
Võrtsjärv (lake) D1
Võru 15,398 .... D2
Western Dvina (riv.) C2

ALGERIA
AREA 919,591 sq. mi. (2,381,740 sq. km.)
POPULATION 17,422,000
CAPITAL Algiers
LARGEST CITY Algiers
HIGHEST POINT Tahat 9,852 ft. (3,003 m.)
MONETARY UNIT Algerian dinar
MAJOR LANGUAGES Arabic, Berber, French
MAJOR RELIGION Islam

ANGOLA
AREA 481,351 sq. mi. (1,246,700 sq. km.)
POPULATION 7,078,000
CAPITAL Luanda
LARGEST CITY Luanda
HIGHEST POINT Mt. Moco 8,593 ft. (2,620 m.)
MONETARY UNIT kwanza
MAJOR LANGUAGES Mbundu, Kongo, Lunda, Portuguese
MAJOR RELIGIONS Tribal religions, Roman Catholicism

BENIN
AREA 43,483 sq. mi. (112,620 sq. km.)
POPULATION 3,338,240
CAPITAL Porto-Novo
LARGEST CITY Cotonou
HIGHEST POINT Atakora Mts. 2,083 ft. (635 m.)
MONETARY UNIT CFA franc
MAJOR LANGUAGES Fon, Somba, Yoruba, Bariba, French, Mina, Dendi
MAJOR RELIGIONS Tribal religions, Islam, Roman Catholicism

BOTSWANA
AREA 224,764 sq. mi. (582,139 sq. km.)
POPULATION 819,000
CAPITAL Gaborone
LARGEST CITY Francistown
HIGHEST POINT Tsodilo Hill 5,922 ft. (1,805 m.)
MONETARY UNIT pula
MAJOR LANGUAGES Setswana, Shona, Bushman, English, Afrikaans
MAJOR RELIGIONS Tribal religions, Protestantism

BURKINA FASO
AREA 105,869 sq. mi. (274,200 sq. km.)
POPULATION 6,908,000
CAPITAL Ouagadougou
LARGEST CITY Ouagadougou
HIGHEST POINT 2,352 ft. (717 m.)
MONETARY UNIT CFA franc
MAJOR LANGUAGES Mossi, Lobi, French, Samo, Gourounsi
MAJOR RELIGIONS Islam, tribal religions, Roman Catholicism

BURUNDI
AREA 10,747 sq. mi. (27,835 sq. km.)
POPULATION 4,021,910
CAPITAL Bujumbura
LARGEST CITY Bujumbura
HIGHEST POINT 8,858 ft. (2,700 m.)
MONETARY UNIT Burundi franc
MAJOR LANGUAGES Kirundi, French, Swahili
MAJOR RELIGIONS Tribal religions, Roman Catholicism, Islam

CAMEROON
AREA 183,568 sq. mi. (475,441 sq. km.)
POPULATION 8,503,000
CAPITAL Yaoundé
LARGEST CITY Douala
HIGHEST POINT Cameroon 13,350 ft. (4,069 m.)
MONETARY UNIT CFA franc
MAJOR LANGUAGES Fang, Bamileke, Fulani, Duala, French, English
MAJOR RELIGIONS Tribal religions, Christianity, Islam

CAPE VERDE
AREA 1,557 sq. mi. (4,033 sq. km.)
POPULATION 324,000
CAPITAL Praia
LARGEST CITY Praia
HIGHEST POINT 9,281 ft. (2,829 m.)
MONETARY UNIT Cape Verde escudo
MAJOR LANGUAGE Portuguese
MAJOR RELIGION Roman Catholicism

CENTRAL AFRICAN REPUBLIC
AREA 242,000 sq. mi. (626,780 sq. km.)
POPULATION 2,284,000
CAPITAL Bangui
LARGEST CITY Bangui
HIGHEST POINT Gao 4,659 ft. (1,420 m.)
MONETARY UNIT CFA franc
MAJOR LANGUAGES Banda, Gbaya, Sangho, French
MAJOR RELIGIONS Tribal religions, Christianity, Islam

CHAD
AREA 495,752 sq. mi. (1,283,998 sq. km.)
POPULATION 4,309,000
CAPITAL N'Djamena
LARGEST CITY N'Djamena
HIGHEST POINT Emi Koussi 11,204 ft. (3,415 m.)
MONETARY UNIT CFA franc
MAJOR LANGUAGES Arabic, Bagirmi, French, Sara, Massa, Moudang
MAJOR RELIGIONS Islam, tribal religions

COMOROS
AREA 719 sq. mi. (1,862 sq. km.)
POPULATION 290,000
CAPITAL Moroni
LARGEST CITY Moroni
HIGHEST POINT Karthala 7,746 ft. (2,361 m.)
MONETARY UNIT CFA franc
MAJOR LANGUAGES Arabic, French, Swahili
MAJOR RELIGION Islam

CONGO
AREA 132,046 sq. mi. (342,000 sq. km.)
POPULATION 1,537,000
CAPITAL Brazzaville
LARGEST CITY Brazzaville
HIGHEST POINT Leketi Mts. 3,412 ft. (1,040 m.)
MONETARY UNIT CFA franc
MAJOR LANGUAGES Kikongo, Bateke, Lingala, French
MAJOR RELIGIONS Christianity, tribal religions, Islam

DJIBOUTI
AREA 8,880 sq. mi. (23,000 sq. km.)
POPULATION 386,000
CAPITAL Djibouti
LARGEST CITY Djibouti
HIGHEST POINT Moussa Ali 6,768 ft. (2,063 m.)
MONETARY UNIT Djibouti franc
MAJOR LANGUAGES Arabic, Somali, Afar, French
MAJOR RELIGIONS Islam, Roman Catholicism

EGYPT
AREA 386,659 sq. mi. (1,001,447 sq. km.)
POPULATION 41,572,000
CAPITAL Cairo
LARGEST CITY Cairo
HIGHEST POINT Jeb. Katherina 8,651 ft. (2,637 m.)
MONETARY UNIT Egyptian pound
MAJOR LANGUAGE Arabic
MAJOR RELIGIONS Islam, Coptic Christianity

EQUATORIAL GUINEA
AREA 10,831 sq. mi. (28,052 sq. km.)
POPULATION 244,000
CAPITAL Malabo
LARGEST CITY Malabo
HIGHEST POINT 9,868 ft. (3,008 m.)
MONETARY UNIT CFA franc
MAJOR LANGUAGES Fang, Bubi, Spanish
MAJOR RELIGIONS Tribal religions, Christianity

ETHIOPIA
AREA 471,776 sq. mi. (1,221,900 sq. km.)
POPULATION 31,065,000
CAPITAL Addis Ababa
LARGEST CITY Addis Ababa
HIGHEST POINT Ras Dashan 15,157 ft. (4,620 m.)
MONETARY UNIT birr
MAJOR LANGUAGES Amharic, Gallinya, Tigrinya, Somali, Sidamo, Arabic, Ge'ez
MAJOR RELIGIONS Coptic Christianity, Islam

GABON
AREA 103,346 sq. mi. (267,666 sq. km.)
POPULATION 551,000
CAPITAL Libreville
LARGEST CITY Libreville
HIGHEST POINT Ibounzi 5,165 ft. (1,574 m.)
MONETARY UNIT CFA franc
MAJOR LANGUAGES Fang and other Bantu languages, French
MAJOR RELIGIONS Tribal religions, Christianity, Islam

GAMBIA
AREA 4,127 sq. mi. (10,689 sq. km.)
POPULATION 601,000
CAPITAL Banjul
LARGEST CITY Banjul
HIGHEST POINT 100 ft. (30 m.)
MONETARY UNIT dalasi
MAJOR LANGUAGES Mandingo, Fulani, Wolof, English, Malinke
MAJOR RELIGIONS Islam, tribal religions, Christianity

GHANA
AREA 92,099 sq. mi. (238,536 sq. km.)
POPULATION 11,450,000
CAPITAL Accra
LARGEST CITY Accra
HIGHEST POINT Togo Hills 2,900 ft. (884 m.)
MONETARY UNIT cedi
MAJOR LANGUAGES Twi, Fante, Dagbani, Ewe, Ga, English, Hausa, Akan
MAJOR RELIGIONS Tribal religions, Christianity, Islam

GUINEA
AREA 94,925 sq. mi. (245,856 sq. km.)
POPULATION 5,143,284
CAPITAL Conakry
LARGEST CITY Conakry
HIGHEST POINT Nimba Mts. 6,070 ft. (1,850 m.)
MONETARY UNIT syli
MAJOR LANGUAGES Fulani, Mandingo, Susu, French
MAJOR RELIGIONS Islam, tribal religions

GUINEA-BISSAU
AREA 13,948 sq. mi. (36,125 sq. km.)
POPULATION 777,214
CAPITAL Bissau
LARGEST CITY Bissau
HIGHEST POINT 689 ft. (210 m.)
MONETARY UNIT Guinea-Bissau escudo
MAJOR LANGUAGES Balante, Fulani, Crioulo, Mandingo, Portuguese
MAJOR RELIGIONS Islam, tribal religions, Roman Catholicism

IVORY COAST
AREA 124,504 sq. mi. (322,465 sq. km.)
POPULATION 7,920,000
CAPITAL Yamoussoukro
LARGEST CITY Abidjan
HIGHEST POINT 5,745 ft. (1,751 m.)
MONETARY UNIT CFA franc
MAJOR LANGUAGES Bale, Bete, Senufu, French, Dioula
MAJOR RELIGIONS Tribal religions, Islam

KENYA
AREA 224,960 sq. mi. (582,646 sq. km.)
POPULATION 15,327,061
CAPITAL Nairobi
LARGEST CITY Nairobi
HIGHEST POINT Kenya 17,058 ft. (5,199 m.)
MONETARY UNIT Kenya shilling
MAJOR LANGUAGES Kikuyu, Luo, Kavirondo, Kamba, Swahili, English
MAJOR RELIGIONS Tribal religions, Christianity, Hinduism, Islam

LESOTHO
AREA 11,720 sq. mi. (30,355 sq. km.)
POPULATION 1,339,000
CAPITAL Maseru
LARGEST CITY Maseru
HIGHEST POINT 11,425 ft. (3,482 m.)
MONETARY UNIT loti
MAJOR LANGUAGES Sesotho, English
MAJOR RELIGIONS Tribal religions, Christianity

LIBERIA
AREA 43,000 sq. mi. (111,370 sq. km.)
POPULATION 1,873,000
CAPITAL Monrovia
LARGEST CITY Monrovia
HIGHEST POINT Wutivi 5,584 ft. (1,702 m.)
MONETARY UNIT Liberian dollar
MAJOR LANGUAGES Kru, Kpelle, Bassa, Vai, English
MAJOR RELIGIONS Christianity, tribal religions, Islam

LIBYA
AREA 679,358 sq. mi. (1,759,537 sq. km.)
POPULATION 2,856,000
CAPITAL Tripoli
LARGEST CITY Tripoli
HIGHEST POINT Bette Pk. 7,500 ft. (2,286 m.)
MONETARY UNIT Libyan dinar
MAJOR LANGUAGES Arabic, Berber
MAJOR RELIGION Islam

MADAGASCAR
AREA 226,657 sq. mi. (587,041 sq. km.)
POPULATION 8,742,000
CAPITAL Antananarivo
LARGEST CITY Antananarivo
HIGHEST POINT Maromokotro 9,436 ft. (2,876 m.)
MONETARY UNIT Madagascar franc
MAJOR LANGUAGES Malagasy, French
MAJOR RELIGIONS Tribal religions, Roman Catholicism, Protestantism

MALAWI
AREA 45,747 sq. mi. (118,485 sq. km.)
POPULATION 5,968,000
CAPITAL Lilongwe
LARGEST CITY Blantyre
HIGHEST POINT Mulanje 9,843 ft. (3,000 m.)
MONETARY UNIT Malawi kwacha
MAJOR LANGUAGES Chichewa, Yao, English, Nyanja, Tumbuka, Tonga, Ngoni
MAJOR RELIGIONS Tribal religions, Islam, Christianity

MALI

AREA 464,873 sq. mi. (1,204,021 sq. km.)
POPULATION 6,906,000
CAPITAL Bamako
LARGEST CITY Bamako
HIGHEST POINT Hombori Mts. 3,789 ft. (1,155 m.)
MONETARY UNIT Mali franc
MAJOR LANGUAGES Bambara, Senufu, Fulani, Soninke, French
MAJOR RELIGIONS Islam, tribal religions

MAURITANIA

AREA 419,229 sq. mi. (1,085,803 sq. km.)
POPULATION 1,634,000
CAPITAL Nouakchott
LARGEST CITY Nouakchott
HIGHEST POINT 2,972 ft. (906 m.)
MONETARY UNIT ouguiya
MAJOR LANGUAGES Arabic, Wolof, Tukolor, French
MAJOR RELIGION Islam

AFRICA

AREA 11,707,000 sq. mi. (30,321,130 sq. km.)
POPULATION 469,000,000
LARGEST CITY Cairo
HIGHEST POINT Kilimanjaro 19,340 ft. (5,895 m.)
LOWEST POINT Lake Assal, Djibouti -512 ft. (-156 m.)

MAURITIUS

AREA 790 sq. mi. (2,046 sq. km.)
POPULATION 959,000
CAPITAL Port Louis
LARGEST CITY Port Louis
HIGHEST POINT 2,711 ft. (826 m.)
MONETARY UNIT Mauritian rupee
MAJOR LANGUAGES English, French, French Creole, Hindi, Urdu
MAJOR RELIGIONS Hinduism, Christianity, Islam

MAYOTTE

AREA 144 sq. mi. (373 sq. km.)
POPULATION 47,300
CAPITAL Dzaoudzi

RÉUNION

AREA 969 sq. mi. (2,510 sq. km.)
POPULATION 491,000
CAPITAL St-Denis

MOROCCO

AREA 172,414 sq. mi. (446,550 sq. km.)
POPULATION 20,242,000
CAPITAL Rabat
LARGEST CITY Casablanca
HIGHEST POINT Jeb. Toubkal 13,665 ft. (4,165 m.)
MONETARY UNIT dirham
MAJOR LANGUAGES Arabic, Berber, French
MAJOR RELIGIONS Islam, Judaism, Christianity

MOZAMBIQUE

AREA 303,769 sq. mi. (786,762 sq. km.)
POPULATION 12,130,000
CAPITAL Maputo
LARGEST CITY Maputo
HIGHEST POINT Mt. Binga 7,992 ft. (2,436 m.)
MONETARY UNIT metical
MAJOR LANGUAGES Makua, Thonga, Shona, Portuguese
MAJOR RELIGIONS Tribal religions, Roman Catholicism, Islam

NAMIBIA (SOUTH-WEST AFRICA)

AREA 317,827 sq. mi. (823,172 sq. km.)
POPULATION 1,200,000
CAPITAL Windhoek
LARGEST CITY Windhoek
HIGHEST POINT Brandberg 8,550 ft. (2,606 m.)
MONETARY UNIT rand
MAJOR LANGUAGES Ovambo, Hottentot, Herero, Afrikaans, English
MAJOR RELIGIONS Tribal religions, Protestantism

NIGER

AREA 489,189 sq. mi. (1,267,000 sq. km.)
POPULATION 5,098,427
CAPITAL Niamey
LARGEST CITY Niamey
HIGHEST POINT Banguezane 6,234 ft. (1,900 m.)
MONETARY UNIT CFA franc
MAJOR LANGUAGES Hausa, Songhai, Fulani, French, Tamashek, Djerma
MAJOR RELIGIONS Islam, tribal religions

NIGERIA

AREA 357,000 sq. mi. (924,630 sq. km.)
POPULATION 82,643,000
CAPITAL Lagos
LARGEST CITY Lagos
HIGHEST POINT Dimlang 6,700 ft. (2,042 m.)
MONETARY UNIT naira
MAJOR LANGUAGES Hausa, Yoruba, Ibo, Ijaw, Fulani, Tiv, Kanuri, Ibibio, English, Edo
MAJOR RELIGIONS Islam, Christianity, tribal religions

RWANDA

AREA 10,169 sq. mi. (26,337 sq. km.)
POPULATION 4,819,317
CAPITAL Kigali
LARGEST CITY Kigali
HIGHEST POINT Karisimbi 14,780 ft. (4,505 m.)
MONETARY UNIT Rwanda franc
MAJOR LANGUAGES Kinyarwanda, French, Swahili
MAJOR RELIGIONS Tribal religions, Roman Catholicism, Islam

SÃO TOMÉ AND PRÍNCIPE

AREA 372 sq. mi. (963 sq. km.)
POPULATION 85,000
CAPITAL São Tomé
LARGEST CITY São Tomé
HIGHEST POINT Pico 6,640 ft. (2,024 m.)
MONETARY UNIT dobra
MAJOR LANGUAGES Bantu languages, Portuguese
MAJOR RELIGIONS Tribal religions, Roman Catholicism

SENEGAL

AREA 75,954 sq. mi. (196,720 sq. km.)
POPULATION 5,508,000
CAPITAL Dakar
LARGEST CITY Dakar
HIGHEST POINT Futa Jallon 1,640 ft. (500 m.)
MONETARY UNIT CFA franc
MAJOR LANGUAGES Wolof, Peul (Fulani), French, Mende, Mandingo, Dida
MAJOR RELIGIONS Islam, tribal religions, Roman Catholicism

SEYCHELLES

AREA 145 sq. mi. (375 sq. km.)
POPULATION 63,000
CAPITAL Victoria
LARGEST CITY Victoria
HIGHEST POINT Morne Seychellois 2,993 ft. (912 m.)
MONETARY UNIT Seychellois rupee
MAJOR LANGUAGES English, French, Creole
MAJOR RELIGION Roman Catholicism

SIERRA LEONE

AREA 27,925 sq. mi. (72,325 sq. km.)
POPULATION 3,470,000
CAPITAL Freetown
LARGEST CITY Freetown
HIGHEST POINT Loma Mts. 6,390 ft. (1,947 m.)
MONETARY UNIT leone
MAJOR LANGUAGES Mende, Temne, Vai, English, Krio (pidgin)
MAJOR RELIGIONS Tribal religions, Islam, Christianity

SOMALIA

AREA 246,200 sq. mi. (637,658 sq. km.)
POPULATION 3,645,000
CAPITAL Mogadishu
LARGEST CITY Mogadishu
HIGHEST POINT Surud Ad 7,900 ft. (2,408 m.)
MONETARY UNIT Somali shilling
MAJOR LANGUAGES Somali, Arabic, Italian, English
MAJOR RELIGION Islam

SOUTH AFRICA

AREA 455,318 sq. mi. (1,179,274 sq. km.)
POPULATION 23,771,970
CAPITALS Cape Town, Pretoria
LARGEST CITY Johannesburg
HIGHEST POINT Injasuti 11,182 ft. (3,408 m.)
MONETARY UNIT rand
MAJOR LANGUAGES Afrikaans, English, Xhosa, Zulu, Sesotho
MAJOR RELIGIONS Protestantism, Roman Catholicism, Islam, Hinduism, tribal religions

SUDAN

AREA 967,494 sq. mi. (2,505,809 sq. km.)
POPULATION 18,691,000
CAPITAL Khartoum
LARGEST CITY Khartoum
HIGHEST POINT Jeb. Marra 10,073 ft. (3,070 m.)
MONETARY UNIT Sudanese pound
MAJOR LANGUAGES Arabic, Dinka, Nubian, Beja, Nuer
MAJOR RELIGIONS Islam, tribal religions

SWAZILAND

AREA 6,705 sq. mi. (17,366 sq. km.)
POPULATION 547,000
CAPITAL Mbabane
LARGEST CITY Manzini
HIGHEST POINT Emlembe 6,109 ft. (1,862 m.)
MONETARY UNIT lilangeni
MAJOR LANGUAGES siSwati, English
MAJOR RELIGIONS Tribal religions, Christianity

TANZANIA

AREA 363,708 sq. mi. (942,003 sq. km.)
POPULATION 17,527,560
CAPITAL Dar es Salaam
LARGEST CITY Dar es Salaam
HIGHEST POINT Kilimanjaro 19,340 ft. (5,895 m.)
MONETARY UNIT Tanzanian shilling
MAJOR LANGUAGES Nyamwezi-Sukuma, Swahili, English
MAJOR RELIGIONS Tribal religions, Christianity, Islam

TOGO

AREA 21,622 sq. mi. (56,000 sq. km.)
POPULATION 2,472,000
CAPITAL Lomé
LARGEST CITY Lomé
HIGHEST POINT Agou 3,445 ft. (1,050 m.)
MONETARY UNIT CFA franc
MAJOR LANGUAGES Ewe, French, Twi, Hausa
MAJOR RELIGIONS Tribal religions, Roman Catholicism, Islam

TUNISIA

AREA 63,378 sq. mi. (164,149 sq. km.)
POPULATION 6,367,000
CAPITAL Tunis
LARGEST CITY Tunis
HIGHEST POINT Jeb. Chambi 5,066 ft. (1,544 m.)
MONETARY UNIT Tunisian dinar
MAJOR LANGUAGES Arabic, French
MAJOR RELIGION Islam

UGANDA

AREA 91,076 sq. mi. (235,887 sq. km.)
POPULATION 12,630,076
CAPITAL Kampala
LARGEST CITY Kampala
HIGHEST POINT Margherita 16,795 ft. (5,119 m.)
MONETARY UNIT Ugandan shilling
MAJOR LANGUAGES Luganda, Acholi, Teso, Nyoro, Soga, Nkole, English, Swahili
MAJOR RELIGIONS Tribal religions, Christianity, Islam

WESTERN SAHARA

AREA 102,703 sq. mi. (266,000 sq. km.)
POPULATION 76,425
HIGHEST POINT 2,700 ft. (823 m.)
MAJOR LANGUAGE Arabic
MAJOR RELIGION Islam

ZAIRE

AREA 905,063 sq. mi. (2,344,113 sq. km.)
POPULATION 28,291,000
CAPITAL Kinshasa
LARGEST CITY Kinshasa
HIGHEST POINT Margherita 16,795 ft. (5,119 m.)
MONETARY UNIT zaire
MAJOR LANGUAGES Tshiluba, Mongo, Kikongo, Kingwana, Zande, Lingala, Swahili, French
MAJOR RELIGIONS Tribal religions, Christianity

ZAMBIA

AREA 290,586 sq. mi. (752,618 sq. km.)
POPULATION 5,679,808
CAPITAL Lusaka
LARGEST CITY Lusaka
HIGHEST POINT Sunzu 6,782 ft. (2,067 m.)
MONETARY UNIT Zambian kwacha
MAJOR LANGUAGES Bemba, Tonga, Lozi, Luvale, Nyanja, English
MAJOR RELIGIONS Tribal religions

ZIMBABWE

AREA 150,803 sq. mi. (390,580 sq. km.)
POPULATION 7,360,000
CAPITAL Harare
LARGEST CITY Harare
HIGHEST POINT Mt. Inyangani 8,517 ft. (2,596 m.)
MONETARY UNIT Zimbabwe dollar
MAJOR LANGUAGES English, Shona, Ndebele
MAJOR RELIGIONS Tribal religions, Protestantism

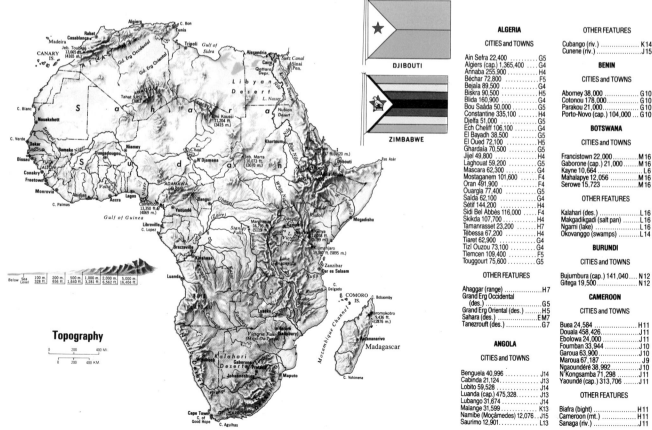

Topography

Below Sea Level | 100 m. 328 ft. | 200 m. 656 ft. | 500 m. 1,640 ft. | 1,000 m. 3,281 ft. | 2,000 m. 6,562 ft. | 5,000 m. 16,404 ft.

0   200   400 MI.
0   200   400 KM.

DJIBOUTI

ZIMBABWE

ALGERIA

CITIES and TOWNS

Ain Sefra 22,400 .... G5
Algiers (cap.) 1,365,400 ...... H4
Annaba 255,900 .... H4
Béchar 72,800 .... F5
Bejaïa 89,500 .... G4
Biskra 90,500 .... H5
Blida 160,900 .... G4
Bou Saâda 50,000 .... G5
Constantine 335,100 .... H4
Djelfa 51,000 .... G5
Ech Cheliff 106,100 .... G4
El Bayadh 38,500 .... G5
El Oued 72,100 .... H5
Ghardaïa 70,500 .... G5
Jijel 49,800 .... H4
Laghouat 59,200 .... G5
Mascara 62,300 .... G4
Mostaganem 101,600 .... F4
Oran 491,900 .... F4
Ouargla 77,400 .... G5
Saïda 62,100 .... F4
Sétif 144,200 .... H4
Sidi Bel Abbès 116,000 .... F4
Skikda 107,700 .... H4
Tamanrasset 23,200 .... H7
Tébessa 67,200 .... H4
Tiaret 62,900 .... G4
Tizi Ouzou 73,100 .... G4
Tlemcen 109,400 .... F5
Touggourt 75,600 .... G5

OTHER FEATURES

Ahaggar (range) H7
Grand Erg Occidental
 (des.) G5
Grand Erg Oriental (des.) H5
Sahara (des.) EM7
Tanezrouft (des.) G7

ANGOLA

CITIES and TOWNS

Benguela 40,996 .... J14
Cabinda 21,124 .... J13
Lobito 59,528 .... J14
Luanda (cap.) 475,328. .... J13
Lubango 31,674 .... J14
Malange 31,599 .... K13
Namibe (Moçâmedes) 12,076... J15
Saurimo 12,901. .... L13

OTHER FEATURES

Cubango (riv.) K14
Cunene (riv.) J15

BENIN

CITIES and TOWNS

Abomey 38,000 .... G10
Cotonou 178,000 .... G10
Parakou 21,000 .... G10
Porto-Novo (cap.) 104,000 .... G10

BOTSWANA

CITIES and TOWNS

Francistown 22,000 .... M16
Gaborone (cap.) 21,000 .... M16
Kayne 10,664 .... L6
Mahalapye 12,056 .... M16
Serowe 15,723 .... M16

OTHER FEATURES

Kalahari (des.) L16
Makgadikgadi (salt pan) L16
Ngami (lake) L16
Okovanggo (swamps) L14

BURUNDI

CITIES and TOWNS

Bujumbura (cap.) 141,040 ..... N12
Gitega 19,500 .... N12

CAMEROON

CITIES and TOWNS

Buea 24,584 .... H11
Douala 458,426. .... J11
Ebolowa 24,000 .... J11
Foumban 33,944 .... J10
Garoua 63,900 .... J10
Maroua 67,187 .... J9
Ngaoundéré 38,992 .... J10
N'Kongsamba 71,298 .... J11
Yaoundé (cap.) 313,706 ...... J11

OTHER FEATURES

Biafra (bight) H11
Cameroon (mt.) H11
Sanaga (riv.) J11

CENTRAL AFRICAN REPUBLIC

CITIES and TOWNS

Bambari 31,285 .... L10
Bangassou 21,773 .... L10
Bangui (cap.) 279,792 .... K11
Berberati 27,285. .... K11
Bossangoa 25,150 .... K11
Bouar 29,528 .... K11

OTHER FEATURES

Lobaye (riv.) K10
Shinko (riv.) L10

CHAD

CITIES and TOWNS

Abéché 28,100 .... L9
Bongor 14,300 .... K9
Faya-Largeau 6,800 .... K8
Moundou 39,600 .... K10
N'Djamena (cap.) 179,000 .... K9

OTHER FEATURES

Baguirmi (reg.) K9
Chad (lake) K9
Emi Koussi (mt.) L8
Ennedi (plat.) L8
Sahara (des.) EM7
Shari (riv.) K9
Sudan (reg.) EM9
Tibesti (mts.) K7
Wadai (reg.) L9

COMOROS

CITIES and TOWNS

Moroni (cap.) 12,000 .... P14

OTHER FEATURES

Mwali (isl.) P14
Njazidja (isl.) P14
Nzwani (isl.) P14

CONGO

CITIES and TOWNS

Brazzaville (cap.) 298,967 .... J12
Impfondo K11
Ouesso K11

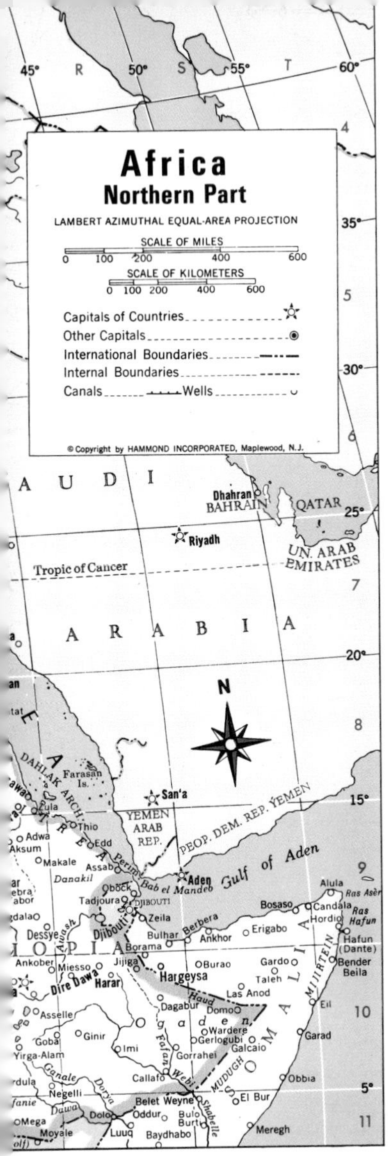
Africa
Northern Part
LAMBERT AZIMUTHAL EQUAL-AREA PROJECTION
SCALE OF MILES
0 100 200 400 600
SCALE OF KILOMETERS
0 100 200 400 600
Capitals of Countries
Other Capitals
International Boundaries
Internal Boundaries
Canals
Wells
© Copyright by HAMMOND INCORPORATED, Maplewood, N.J.
45° 50° 55° 60°
35° 30° 25° 20° 15° 5°
SAUDI ARABIA
Dhahran
BAHRAIN
QATAR
Riyadh
U.N. ARAB EMIRATES
Tropic of Cancer
Farasan Is.
San'a
YEMEN ARAB REP.
PEOP. DEM. REP. YEMEN
Gulf of Aden
Aden
Bab el Mandeb
Assab
Makale
Adwa
Aksum
Danakil
Tadjoura
Obock
DJIBOUTI
Djibouti
Zeila
Bulhar
Berbera
Erigabo
Bosaso
Candala
Alula
Hordio
Ras Hafun
Hafun (Dante)
Bender Beila
Dessye
Ankober
Miesso
Dire Dawa
Harar
Jijiga
Hargeysa
Burao
Gardo
Taleh
Las Anod
Dagabur
Domo
Eil
Asselle
Ginir
Goba
Imi
Wardere
Gerlogubi
Galcaio
Garad
Yirga-Alam
Gorrahei
Callafo
Obbia
Negelli
Belet Weyne
Bulo Burti
El Bur
Dolo
Oddur
Mega
Moyale
Luuq
Baydhabo
Meregh

FLAGS OF AFRICA

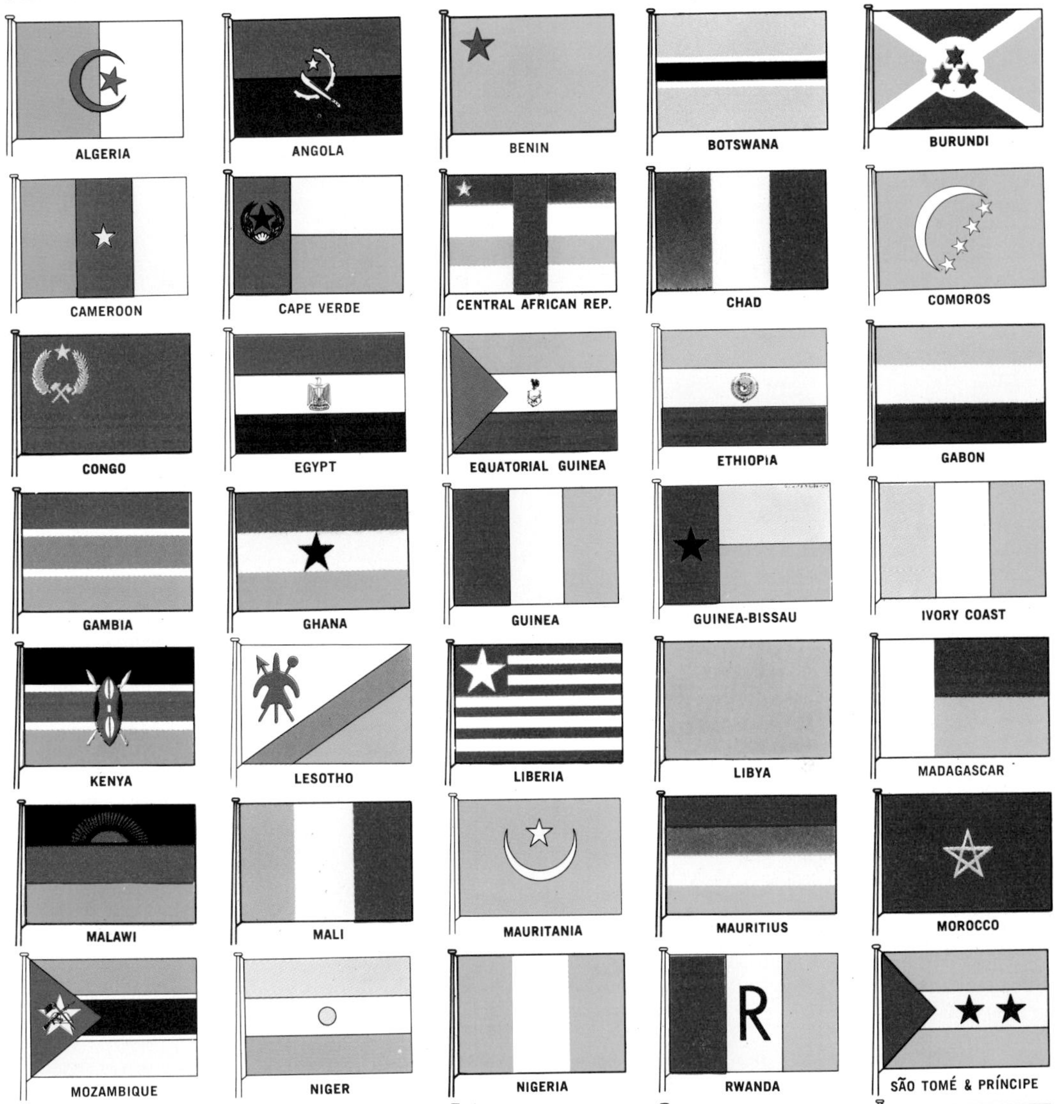
ALGERIA
ANGOLA
BENIN
BOTSWANA
BURUNDI
CAMEROON
CAPE VERDE
CENTRAL AFRICAN REP.
CHAD
COMOROS
CONGO
EGYPT
EQUATORIAL GUINEA
ETHIOPIA
GABON
GAMBIA
GHANA
GUINEA
GUINEA-BISSAU
IVORY COAST
KENYA
LESOTHO
LIBERIA
LIBYA
MADAGASCAR
MALAWI
MALI
MAURITANIA
MAURITIUS
MOROCCO
MOZAMBIQUE
NIGER
NIGERIA
RWANDA
R
SÃO TOMÉ & PRÍNCIPE

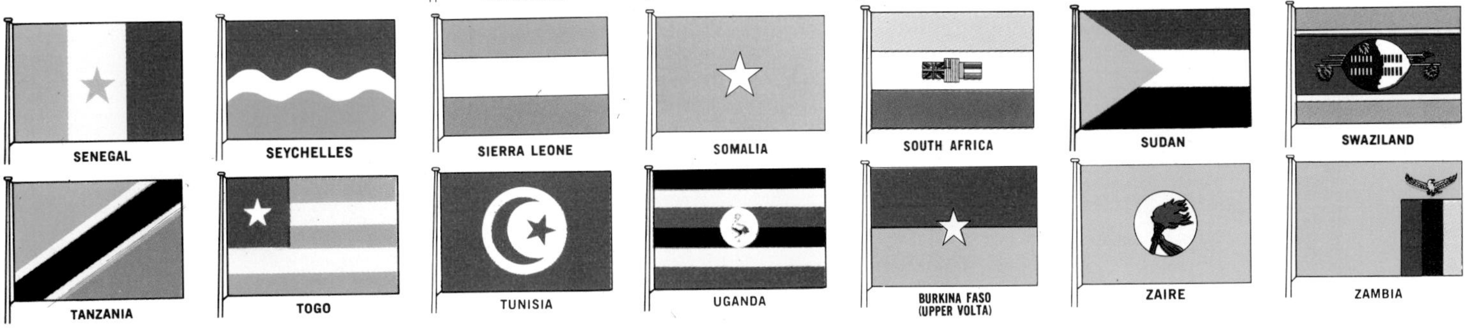
SENEGAL
SEYCHELLES
SIERRA LEONE
SOMALIA
SOUTH AFRICA
SUDAN
SWAZILAND
TANZANIA
TOGO
TUNISIA
UGANDA
BURKINA FASO (UPPER VOLTA)
ZAIRE
ZAMBIA

Pointe-Noire 141,700 .... J12

OTHER FEATURES

Congo (riv.) K12
Ubangi (riv.) K11

DJIBOUTI

CITIES and TOWNS

Djibouti (cap.) 96,000 .... P9
Obock P9

EGYPT

CITIES and TOWNS

Alexandria 2,318,655 .... M5
Aswân 144,377 .... N7
Asyût 213,983 .... N6
Beni Suef 118,148 .... N6
Cairo (cap.) 5,084,463 .... N5
Damietta (Dumyat) 93,546 .... N5
El A'lamein M5
El Faiyûm 167,081 .... M6
El Khârga 26,375 .... N6
El Minya 146,423 .... M6
Ismailia 145,978 .... N5
Luxor 92,748 .... N6
Mersá Matrûh 27,857 .... M5
Port Said 262,620 .... N5
Qena 94,013 .... N6
Sidi Barrani 1,574 .... M5
Suez 194,001 .... N6
Tanta 284,636 .... N5

OTHER FEATURES

Aqaba (gulf) O6
Arabian (des.) N6
Aswân (dam) N7
Banas (cape) O7
Farâfra (oasis) M6
Khârga (oasis) N6
Libyan (des.) M6
Nasser (lake) N7
Nile (riv.) N7
Qattara (depr.) M5
Sahara (des.) EM7
Sinai (pen.) N6
Siwa (oasis) M6
Suez (canal) N5
Suez (gulf) N6

EQUATORIAL GUINEA

CITIES and TOWNS

Bata 270,241 .... H11
Malabo (cap.) 37,237 .... A3

OTHER FEATURES

Annobón (isl.) G12
Bioko (Fernando Po)
(isl.) H11
Elobey (isl.) H11
Rlo Muni (terr.) 203,000 .... J11

ETHIOPIA

CITIES and TOWNS

Addis Ababa (cap.)
1,196,300 .... O10
Adwa 16,400 .... O9
Aksum 12,800 .... O9
Asmara 393,800 .... O9
Assab 16,000 .... P9
Debra Markos 30,260 .... O9
Dessye 49,750 .... O9
Dire Dawa 63,700 .... P10
Gondar 38,600 .... O9
Harar 48,440 .... P10
Jimma 47,360 .... O10
Makale 30,780 .... P9
Massawa 19,800 .... O8
Soddu 11,900 .... O10
Yirga-Alam 14,500 .... O10

OTHER FEATURES

Abay (Blue Nile) (riv.) O9
Dahlak (arch.) P8
Danakil (reg.) P9
Dashan, Ras (mt.) O9
Eritrea (reg.) O8
Mandeb, Bab el (str.) R9
Ogaden (reg.) P10
Tana (lake) O9

GABON

CITIES and TOWNS

Franceville 9,345 .... J12
Lambaréné 17,770 .... H12
Libreville (cap.) 105,080 ...... H11
Mouila 15,016 .... J12
Oyem 12,455 .... J11
Port-Gentil 48,190 .... H12
Tchibanga 14,001 .... J12

OTHER FEATURES

Lopez (cape) H12
Ogooué (riv.) J12

GAMBIA

CITIES and TOWNS

Banjul (Bathurst)
(cap.) 39,476 .... C9
Georgetown 2,510 .... C9

GHANA

CITIES and TOWNS

Accra (cap.) 564,194 .... G11
Axim 8,107 .... F11
Cape Coast 51,653 .... F11
Ho 24,199 .... G10
Keta 14,446 .... G10
Koforidua 46,235 .... F10
Kumasi 260,286 .... F10
Obuasi 31,005 .... F10
Oda 20,957 .... F10
Sekondi 33,713 .... F11
Sekondi-Takoradi*
160,868 .... F11
Takoradi 58,161 .... F11
Tamale 83,653 .... F10
Tarkwa 14,702 .... F10
Tema 60,767 .... G10
Wa 21,374 .... F9
Winneba 30,778 .... F11
Yendi 22,072 .... F10

OTHER FEATURES

Ashanti (reg.) F10
Volta (riv.) F10

GUINEA

CITIES and TOWNS

Beyla E10
Conakry (cap.)* 525,671 .... D10
Dabola D9
Kankan 85,310 .... E9
Kindia 79,861 .... D9
Labé 79,670 .... D9
N'Zérékoré 23,000 .... E10
Siguiri E9

GUINEA-BISSAU

CITIES and TOWNS

Bissau (cap.) 109,486 .... D9
Bolama○ 9,133 .... D9
Cacheu○ 15,194 .... C9

IVORY COAST

CITIES and TOWNS

Abidjan 685,828 .... E10
Agboville 27,192 .... F10
Bingerville 18,218 .... F10
Bondoukou 19,111 .... F10
Bouaké 173,248 .... F10
Dabou 23,870 .... F11
Daloa 60,958 .... E10
Dimbokro 30,986 .... F10
Ferkessédougou 25,307 .... E10
Gagnoa 42,362 .... E10
Grand-Bassam 25,808 .... F11
Katiola 21,559 .... E10
Korhogo 47,657 .... E10
Man 50,315 .... E10
Port-Bouet 72,616 .... F11
Sassandra 9,404 .... E11
Yamoussoukro (cap) 50,000 ...... E10

OTHER FEATURES

Cavally (riv.) E10
Sassandra (riv.) E10

KENYA

CITIES and TOWNS

Eldoret 18,196 .... O11
Kisumu 32,431 .... N12
Lamu 7,403 .... P12
Malindi 10,757 .... P12
Mombasa 247,073 .... P12
Nairobi (cap.) 509,286 .... O12
Nakuru 47,151 .... O11
Nanyuki 11,624 .... O11

OTHER FEATURES

Elgon (mt.) N11
Kenya (mt.) O12
Turkana (Rudolf) (lake) O11

LESOTHO

CITIES and TOWNS

Maseru (cap.) 71,500 .... M17

LIBERIA

CITIES and TOWNS

Buchanan 23,999 .... D10
Greenville 8,462 .... E11
Harper 10,627 .... E11
Marshall D10

(continued on following page)

Agriculture, Industry and Resources

DOMINANT LAND USE

- Cereals, Horticulture, Livestock
- Cash Crops, Mixed Cereals
- Cotton, Cereals
- Diversified Tropical Crops
- Plantation Agriculture
- Oases
- Pasture Livestock
- Nomadic Livestock Herding
- Forests
- Nonagricultural Land

MAJOR MINERAL OCCURRENCES

Ab	Asbestos	Mi	Mica
Ag	Silver	Mn	Manganese
Al	Bauxite	Na	Salt
Au	Gold	O	Petroleum
Be	Beryl	P	Phosphates
C	Coal	Pb	Lead
Co	Cobalt	Pt	Platinum
Cr	Chromium	Sb	Antimony
Cu	Copper	Sn	Tin
D	Diamonds	So	Soda Ash
Fe	Iron Ore	Ti	Titanium
G	Natural Gas	U	Uranium
Gp	Gypsum	V	Vanadium
Gr	Graphite	W	Tungsten
K	Potash	Zn	Zinc

Water Power

Major Industrial Areas

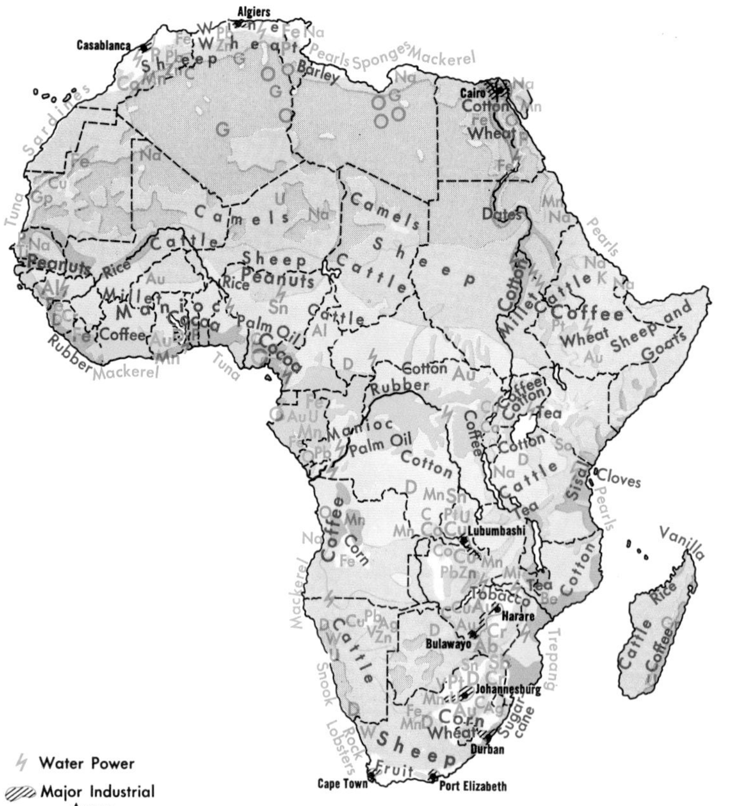

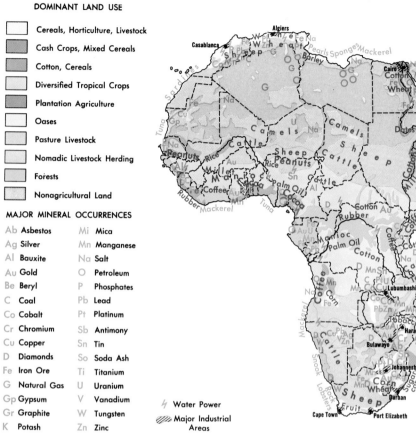

Monrovia (cap.) 166,507 D10

OTHER FEATURES

Palmas (cape) E11

LIBYA

CITIES and TOWNS

Ajedabia○ 53,170 L5
Baida○ 59,765 L5
Benghazi○ 286,943 K5
Brak○ 12,507 J6
Derna○ 44,145 L5
El Azizia○ 34,077 J5
El Jauf○ 6,481 L7
El Marj (Barce)○ 55,444 L5
Ghadames○ 6,172 J6
Gharian○ 65,224 J5
Ghat○ 6,924 J6
Homs○ 66,890 J5
Misurata○ 102,439 K5
Murzuk○ 22,185 J6
Nalut○ 23,535 J5
Sebha○ 35,879 K6
Shahat○ 17,157 L5
Syrte○ 22,797 K5
Tobruk○ 58,384 L5
Tripoli (cap.)○ 550,438 J5
Ubari○ 19,132 J6
Waddan○ 5,347 K6
Zella○ 72,092 K6
Zliten○ 58,981 K5
Zwara○ 15,078 J5

OTHER FEATURES

Cyrenaica (reg.) L6
Fezzan (reg.) J6
Idehan (des.) J6
Kufra (oasis) L7
Sahara (des.) EM7
Sidra (gulf) L5
Tripolitania (reg.) J5

MADAGASCAR

CITIES and TOWNS

Ambanja 12,258 R14
Ambatondrazaka 18,044 R15
Ambilobe 9,415 R14
Ambositra 16,780 R16
Antalaha 17,541 S14
Antananarivo 451,808 R15
Antsirabe 32,979 R16
Antsiranana (Diego-Suarez) 40,443 R14
Arivonimamo 8,497 R15
Faradofay (Fort-Dauphin) 13,805 R17
Farafangana 10,817 R16
Fenoarivo 7,696 R16
Fianarantsoa 68,054 R16
Maevatanana 7,197 R15
Maintirano 6,375 P15
Majunga 65,864 R15
Manakara 19,768 R16
Mananjary 14,638 R16
Marovoay 20,253 R15
Moramanga 10,806 R15
Morondava 19,061 P16
Sambava 6,215 S14
Tamatave 77,395 S15
Toliara 45,676 P16

OTHER FEATURES

Bobaomby (Amber) (cape) S15
Mozambique (chan.) O16
Nossi-Bé (isl.) R14
Tsiafajavona (mt.) R15
Vohimena (Ste Marie) (cape) P17

MALAWI

CITIES and TOWNS

Blantyre 222,153 N15
Karonga 11,873 N13
Lilongwe (cap.) 102,924 N14
Nkhotakota 10,312 N14
Zomba 21,000 N15

OTHER FEATURES

Nyasa (lake) N14
Shire (riv.) N15

MALI

CITIES and TOWNS

Bamako (cap.) 404,022 E9
Bougouni 17,246 E9
Djenné 10,251 F9
Gao 30,714 G8
Goundam 10,262 F8
Kati 24,991 E9
Kayes 44,736 D9
Kita 17,538 E9
Koulikoro 16,376 E9
Koutiala 27,497 F9
Mopti 53,885 F9
Nioro 11,617 E8
San 22,962 F9
Ségou 64,890 E9
Sikasso 47,030 E9
Timbuktu 20,483 F8

OTHER FEATURES

Adrar des Iforas (plat.) G7
Niger (riv.) G9
Sahara (des.) EM7

MAURITANIA

CITIES and TOWNS

Atar 16,326 D7
Bir Mogreïn D6
Bogué 8,056 D8
Boutilimit 7,261 D8
Fdérik 2,160 D7
Kaédi 20,248 D8
Kiffa 10,629 D8
Néma 8,232 E8
Nouadhibou 21,961 C7
Nouakchott (cap.) 134,986 C8
Rosso 16,466 C8
Tidjikja 7,870 D8

OTHER FEATURES

Adrar (reg.) D7
Blanc (cape) C7
Hodh (reg.) E8
Sahara (des.) EM7
Senegal (riv.) D8
Tagant (reg.) D8

MAURITIUS

CITIES and TOWNS

Curepipe 52,709 S19
Mahébourg 15,463 T19
Port Louis (cap.) 141,022 S19

MAYOTTE

CITIES AND TOWNS

Mamoutzou (cap.) 196 R14

MOROCCO

CITIES and TOWNS

Agadir 61,192 D5
Al Hoceima 18,686 F4
Casablanca 1,506,373 E5
El Jadida 55,501 E5
Essaouira 30,061 D5
Fès 325,327 F5
Kenitra 139,206 E5
Khenifra 25,526 F5
Larache 45,710 E4
Marrakech 332,741 E5
Meknès 248,369 E5
Ouezzane 33,267 E5
Oujda 175,532 F5
Rabat (cap.) 367,620 E5
Safi 129,113 E5
Salé 155,557 E5
Settat 42,325 E5
Tangier (Tanger) 187,894 E4
Taroudant 22,272 E5
Taza 55,157 F5
Tétouan 139,105 F4

OTHER FEATURES

Atlas (mts.) E5
Beddouza, Ras el (cape) E5
Draa, Wadi (dry riv.) E6
Juby (cape) D5

MOZAMBIQUE

CITIES and TOWNS

Bartolomeu Dias○ 6,102 O16
Beira 46,293 O15
Caia 1,363 N15
Chibuto 23,763 N16
Chimoio 4,507 N15
Homoíne 1,122 O16
Ibo 1,015 P14
Inhambane 4,975 O16
Magude 1,502 N16
Maniamba 7,634 O14
Maputo (cap.) 755,300 N17
Marromeu 1,330 O15
Massangena○ 3,301 N16
Meconta 1,051 O14
Moçambique 1,730 P15
Mocímboa da Praia 935 P14
Mocuba 2,293 O15
Nacala 4,601 P14
Nampula 23,072 P15
Pemba 3,629 P14
Quelimane 10,522 O15
Songo 1,350 N15
Tete 4,549 N15
Vila de Sena○ 21,074 N15
Xai-Xai 5,234 N16

OTHER FEATURES

Angoche (isl.) O16
Delagoa (bay) N17
Delgado (cape) P14
Mozambique (chan.) O16
Nyasa (chan.) N14
Rovuma (riv.) O14
Save (riv.) N16

NAMIBIA

CITIES and TOWNS

Bethanie 1,207 K17
Gobabis 4,428 K16
Grootfontein 4,627 K15
Karasburg 2,693 K17
Karibib 1,653 K16
Keetmanshoop 10,297 K17
Lüderitz 6,642 J17
Mariental 4,629 K16
Omaruru 2,783 K16
Oranjemund 2,594 K17
Otjiwarongo 8,018 K16
Outjo 2,545 K15
Rehoboth 5,363 K16
Swakopmund 5,681 J16
Tsumeb 12,338 K15
Usakos 2,334 K16
Windhoek (cap.) 61,369 K16

OTHER FEATURES

Caprivi Strip (reg.) L15
Cubango (riv.) K15
Cunene (riv.) J15
Damaraland (reg.) K16
Etosha Pan (salt pan) J15
Fish (riv.) K17
Fria (cape) J15
Great Namaland (reg.) K17
Kalahari (des.) L16
Namib (des.) J15
Okovanggo (riv.) K15
Orange (riv.) K17
Ovamboland (reg.) K15

NIGER

CITIES and TOWNS

Agadès 11,000 H8
Bilma J8
Birni-N'Konni 10,000 H9
Gaya 5,000 G9
Iférouane J9
Maradi 45,852 H9
N'Guigmi J9
Niamey (cap.) 225,314 G9
Tahoua 31,265 H9
Zinder 58,436 H9

OTHER FEATURES

Air (mts.) H8
Djado (plat.) J7
Niger (riv.) G9
Sahara (des.) EM7
Ténéré (des.) J8

NIGERIA

CITIES and TOWNS

Aba 177,000 H10
Abeokuta 253,000 G10
Benin City 136,000 H10
Bonny H11
Calabar 103,000 H10
Enugu 187,000 H10
Ibadan 847,000 G10
Ife 176,000 G10
Ilorin 282,000 G10
Kaduna 202,000 H9
Kano 399,000 H9
Katsina 109,424 H9
Lagos (cap.) 1,060,848 G10
Maiduguri 189,000 J9
Ogbomosho 432,000 H10
Onitsha 220,000 H10
Oshogbo 282,000 H10
Oyo 152,000 G10
Port Harcourt 242,000 H11
Sokoto H9
Yola J10
Zaria 224,000 H9

OTHER FEATURES

Adamawa (reg.) J10
Benin (bight) G11
Benue (riv.) H10
Chad (lake) K9
Gongola (riv.) J9
Kaduna (riv.) H9
Niger (riv.) G9

RÉUNION

CITIES and TOWNS

Le Port 21,564 P20
Le Tampon 17,089 P20
Saint-Denis (cap.) 80,075 P19
Saint-Louis 10,252 P20
Saint-Pierre 21,817 P20

OTHER FEATURES

Bassas da India (isl.) O16
Europa (isl.) P16
Glorioso (isls.) R14
Juan de Nova (isl.) P15
Piton des Neiges (mt.) P20

RWANDA

CITIES and TOWNS

Kigali (cap.) 117,749 N12

SÃO TOMÉ AND PRÍNCIPE

CITIES and TOWNS

São Tomé (cap.) 7,681 H11

OTHER FEATURES

Príncipe (isl.) H11
São Tomé (isl.) H11

SENEGAL

CITIES and TOWNS

Dagana 10,506 D8
Dakar (cap.) 798,792 C9
Diourbel 50,618 C9
Kaolack 106,899 C9
Louga 35,063 C8
Matam 10,002 D8
M'Bour 37,663 C9
Saint-Louis 88,404 C8
Tambacounda 25,147 D9
Thiès 117,333 C9
Ziguinchor 72,726 C9

OTHER FEATURES

Senegal (riv.) D8
Verde (cape) C9

SEYCHELLES

OTHER FEATURES

Aldabra (isls.) P13
Assumption (isl.) R14
Cerf (isl.) S13
Cosmoledo (isls.) R13
Farquhar (isl.) S14
Providence (isl.) S13
Saint Pierre 47

SIERRA LEONE

CITIES and TOWNS

Bo 42,216 D10
Bonthe 6,230 D10
Freetown (cap.) 274,000 D10
Makeni 28,684 D10

OTHER FEATURES

Sherbro (isl.) D10

SOMALIA

CITIES and TOWNS

Afmadu 2,580 P11
Barawa (Brava) 6,167 P11
Baydhabo 14,962 P11
Belet Weyne 11,426 P11
Berbera 12,219 R9
Borama 3,244 P9
Bosaso R9
Brava 6,167 P11
Bulo Burti 5,247 P11
Burao 12,617 R10
Chisimayu 17,872 P12
Eil S10
Erigabo 4,279 R9
Galcaio R10
Giohar 13,156 R11
Hargeysa 40,254 P10
Jilib 3,232 P11
Las Anod 2,441 R10
Marka 17,708 R11
Mogadishu (cap.) 371,000 R11
Oddur P11
Zeila 1,226 P9

OTHER FEATURES

Asèr, Ras (cape) S9
Chiambone, Ras (cape) P12
Giuba (Juba) (riv.) P11
Mijirtein (reg.) R10
Mudugh (reg.) R10
Wabi Shabelle (riv.) R11

SOUTH AFRICA

INTERNAL DIVISIONS

Bophuthatswana (aut. rep.) 1,200,000 L17
Cape (prov.) 5,543.506 L18
Ciskei (aut. rep.) M18
Natal (prov.) 5,722,215 N17
Orange Free State (prov.) 1,833,216 M17
Transkei (aut. rep.) 2,000,000 M18
Transvaal (prov.) 10,673,033 M16
Venda (aut. rep.) 450,000 N16

CITIES and TOWNS

Aliwal North 12,311 M18
Beaufort West 17,862 L18
Bellville 49,026 G19
Benoni□ 164,543 M17
Bethlehem 29,918 M17
Bisho M18
Bloemfontein□ 182,329 L17
Calvinia 6,386 K18
Cape Town (cap.)□ 833,731 F19
Ceres 9,230 H18
Cradock 20,822 M18
De Aar 18,057 L18
Durban□ 975,494 N18
East London□ 126,671 M18
George 24,625 L18
Germiston□ 293,257 M17
Goodwood 31,592 G19
Graaff-Reinet 22,392 L18
Grahamstown 41,302 M18
Johannesburg□ 1,417,818 M17
Kimberley 105,258 L17
King William's Town 15,798 M18
Knysna 13,479 L18
Kraaifontein 10,286 G19
Kroonstad 51,988 M17
Ladysmith 28,920 N17
Louis Trichardt 8,906 M16
Malmesbury 9,314 G18
Messina 21,121 M16
Middelburg, C. of G.H. 11,121 M18
Middelburg, Transv. 26,942 N17
Mmabatho L17
Moorreesburg 4,945 K18
Mossel Bay 17,574 L18
Newcastle 14,407 N17
Oudtshoorn 26,907 L18
Paarl 49,244 H19
Parow 60,768 G19
Pietermaritzburg□ 174,179 N17
Pietersburg 27,174 N16
Pinelands 11,769 G19
Port Elizabeth□ 413,961 M18
Port Nolloth 2,893 K17
Port Shepstone 5,581 N18
Potchefstroom 57,443 M17
Pretoria (cap.)□ 573,283 M17
Prieska 8,521 L17
Queenstown 39,304 M18
Richards Bay 598 N17
Saldanha 4,994 K18
Simonstown 12,137 F19
Somerset West 11,828 G19
Stellenbosch 29,955 G19
Strand 24,503 G19
Thohoyandou N16
Uitenhage 70,517 M18
Umtata 25,216 M18
Upington 28,632 L17
Vryburg 16,916 L17
Walvis Bay 21,725 J16
Wellington 17,092 H18
Worcester 41,198 H18

OTHER FEATURES

Agulhas (cape) K19
Algoa (bay) M18
Cape (pt.) F20
False (bay) G20
Good Hope (cape) F20
Hangklip (cape) G20
Kalahari (des.) L16
Limpopo (riv.) N16
Maclear (cape) F20
Molopo (riv.) L17
Nossob (riv.) L17
Orange (riv.) K17

Robben (isl.) F19
Saint Helena (isl.) K18
Sandown (bay) G20
Table (bay) F19
Table (mt.) F19
Vaal (riv.) M17
Zululand☐ 756,707 ...... N17

SUDAN

CITIES and TOWNS

Atbara 66,000 .... N8
Dongola 6,000 .... M8
Ed Damazin 12,000 ...... N9
Ed Dueim 27,000 .... N9
El Fasher 52,000 .... M9
El Geneina 33,000 .... L9
El Obeid 90,000 .... N9
En Nahud 23,000 .... M9
Gedaref 92,000 .... O9
Juba 57,000 .... N10
Kadugli 18,000 .... M9
Kassala 99,000 .... O8
Khartoum (cap.) 334,000 . N8
Khartoum North 151,000 . N8
Kosti 57,000 .... N9
Malakal 35,000 .... N10
Nyala 60,000 .... L9
Omdurman 299,000 .... N8
Port Sudan 133,000 ...... O8
Wadi Halfa N7
Wad Medani 107,000 ..... N9
Wau 53,000 .... N10

OTHER FEATURES

Arab, Bahr el (riv.) M10
Atbara (riv.) O8
Blue Nile (riv.) N9
Gezira, El (reg.) N9
Meroe (ruin) N8
Nasser (lake) N7
Nile (riv.) N7
Nubian (des.) N7
Sahara (des.) EM7
Sobat (riv.) N10
Sudan (reg.) FM9
White Nile (riv.) N10

SWAZILAND

CITIES and TOWNS

Mbabane (cap.) 23,109 .. N17

TANZANIA

CITIES and TOWNS

Arusha 55,281 .... O12
Bagamoyo 5,112 .... O13
Bukoba 20,430 .... N12
Chake Chake 4,862 ...... P13
Dar es Salaam
(cap.) 757,346 .... P1
Dodoma 45,703 .... N13
Geita 3,066 .... O13
Iringa 57,182 .... O13
Kigoma-Ujiji 50,044 ...... N12
Kilosa 4,458 .... O13
Kilwa Kivinje 2,790 ...... P13
Kondoa 4,514 .... O12
Lindi 27,308 .... O14
Lushoto 1,803 .... O14
Mbeya 76,606 .... N13
Morogoro 61,890 .... O13
Moshi 52,223 .... O12
Mtwara-Mikindani 48,510 . P14
Musoma 32,658 .... N12
Mwadui 7,383 .... N12
Mwanza 110,611 .... N12
Nachingwea 3,751 .... O14
Pangani 2,955 .... O13
Shinyanga 21,703 .... N12
Singida 29,252 .... N12
Songea 17,954 .... O14
Tabora 67,392 .... N12
Tanga 103,409 .... O13
Zanzibar 110,669 .... P13

OTHER FEATURES

Great Ruaha (riv.) O13
Kilimanjaro (mt.) O12
Mafia (isl.) P13
Natron (lake) O12
Nyasa (lake) N14
Pangani (riv.) O12
Pemba (isl.) P13
Rufiji (riv.) O13
Rukwa (lake) N13

Tanganyika (lake) N13
Victoria (lake) N12
Zanzibar (isl.) P13

TOGO

CITIES and TOWNS

Anécho 10,889 .... G10
Kpalimé 19,801 .... G10
Lomé (cap.) 148,443 ..... G10
Sokodé 29,623 .... G10

TUNISIA

CITIES and TOWNS

Bizerte 62,856 .... J4
Gabès 40,585 .... H5
Gafsa 42,225 .... H4
Kairouan 54,546 .... H4
Mahdia 25,711 .... J4
Menzel Bourguiba 42,111 . H4
Moknine 26,035 .... J4
Sfax 171,297 .... J5
Sousse 69,530 .... J4
Tunis (cap.) 550,404 ..... J4

OTHER FEATURES

Bon (cape) J4
Djerba (isl.) J5
Djerid, Shott el (salt lake) . H5
Gabès (gulf) J5

UGANDA

CITIES and TOWNS

Arua 10,837 .... N11
Entebbe 21,096 .... N12
Jinja 52,509 .... N11
Kabale 8,234 .... N12
Kampala (cap.) 478,895 . N11
Mbarara 16,078 .... N12
Soroti 8,130 .... N11

OTHER FEATURES

Albert (lake) M11
Edward (lake) M12
Kioga (lake) N11
Ruwenzori (range) N11
Victoria (lake) N12

BURKINA FASO (UPPER VOLTA)

CITIES and TOWNS

Bobo Dioulasso 115,063 . F9
Koudougou 36,838 .... F9
Ouagadougou (cap.) 172,661 . F9
Ouahigouya 25,690 ...... F9

OTHER FEATURES

Black Volta (riv.) F9
Red Volta (riv.) F9

Sudan (reg.) FM9
White Volta (riv.) F9

WESTERN SAHARA

CITIES and TOWNS

Dakhla C7
Laayoune 24,519 .... D6

OTHER FEATURES

Blanc (cape) C7
Bojador (cape) C6

ZAIRE

CITIES and TOWNS

Aketi 17,200 .... L11
Bandundu☐ K12
Beni 22,800 .... M11
Boma 61,100 .... J13
Bukavu 134,861 .... M12
Bumba 34,700 .... L11
Bunia 28,800 .... N11
Butembo 27,800 .... M11
Demba 22,000 .... L13
Dilolo 14,000 .... L13
Gemena 37,300 .... L11
Goma 48,600 .... M12
Ilebo 32,200 .... L12
Isiro 49,300 .... M11
Kalemie 62,300 .... M13

Kamina 56,300 .... L13
Kananga 428,960 .... L13
Kasongo 37,800 .... M12
Kikwit 111,960 .... K13
Kinshasa (cap.) 1,323,039 . K12
Kisangani 229,596 .... M11
Kolwezi 81,600 .... L14
Lubumbashi 318,000 ..... M14
Luebo 21,800 .... L13
Manono 44,500 .... M13
Matadi 110,436 .... J13
Mbandaka 107,910 ...... K11
Mbanza-Ngungu 55,800 . K11
Mbuji-Mayi 256,154 ..... L13
Mwene Ditu 71,200 ...... L13
Panda-Likasi 146,394 ... M14
Port Kioga 42,800 .... L12
Tshikapa 38,900 .... L13
Virunga 21,900 .... M13
Watsa 21,300 .... M11
Yangambi 22,600 .... L11

OTHER FEATURES

Albert (lake) M11
Aruwimi (riv.) M11
Bomu (riv.) L11
Boyoma (Stanley) (falls) . M11
Congo (riv.) K12
Edward (lake) M12
Kasai (riv.) K12
Kivu (reg.) M12
Lualaba (riv.) M13
Luapula (riv.) M14

Lulua (riv.) L13
Mweru (lake) M13
Ruwenzori (range) N11
Stanley (falls) M11
Stanley Pool (lake) K12
Tanganyika (lake) N13
Uangi (riv.) K11
Uele (riv.) L11
Zaire (Congo) (riv.) K12

ZAMBIA

CITIES and TOWNS

Broken Hill (Kabwe) 143,635 . M14
Choma 17,943 .... M14
Kabwe 143,635 .... M14
Kasama 38,093 .... N13
Livingstone 71,987 .... M15
Lusaka (cap.) 538,469 ... M15
Mazabuka 29,602 .... M15
Mongu 24,919 .... L15
Mpika 25,880 .... N14
Ndola 282,439 .... M14
Senanga 7,204 .... L15
Solwezi 15,032 .... M14

OTHER FEATURES

Bangweulu (lake) N14
Kafue (riv.) M15
Kariba (lake) M15
Mweru (lake) M13
Victoria (falls) M15

Zambezi (riv.) M15

ZIMBABWE

CITIES and TOWNS

Bulawayo 359,000 .... M16
Chegutu 12,000 .... M15
Chinhoyi 25,000 .... M15
Gwaai○ 2,710 .... M15
Gwelo 68,000 .... M15
Harare (cap.) 601,000 ... M15
Hwange 33,000 .... M15
Kadoma 32,000 .... M15
Kariba 3,943 .... M15
Matopos○ 11,330 .... M16
Mutare 61,000 .... M15
Nyanda 22,000 .... M15
Salisbury (Harare)
(cap.) 601,000 .... M15
Shurugwi 8,387 .... M15

OTHER FEATURES

Kariba (lake) M15
Limpopo (riv.) N16
Victoria (falls) M15
Zambezi (riv.) M15

*City and suburbs.
○Population of sub-district or division.
☐Population of urban area.

Asia

LAMBERT AZIMUTHAL EQUAL-AREA PROJECTION

SCALE OF MILES

0 100 200 400 600 800 1000 1200

SCALE OF KILOMETERS

0 200 400 600 800 1000 1200

Capitals of Countries .... ⊛

Other Capitals .... ⊛

International Boundaries ....

Other Boundaries..........................

Canals ....

Scale 1:46,500,000

© Copyright HAMMOND INCORPORATED, Maplewood, N.J.

Population Distribution

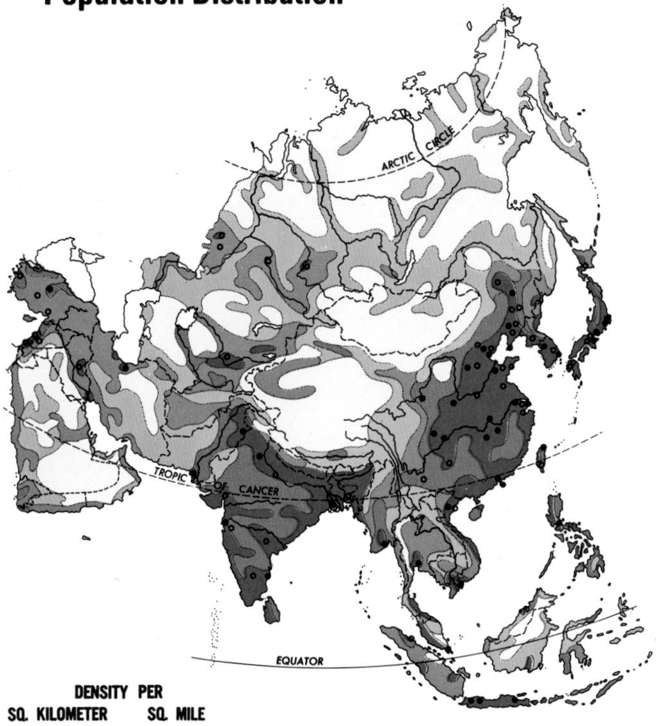

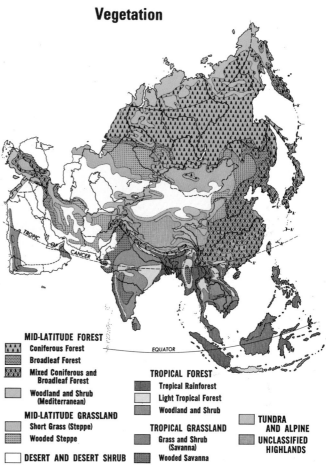

DENSITY PER

SQ. KILOMETER	SQ. MILE
Over 100	Over 260
50-100	130-260
10-50	25-130
1-10	3-25
Under 1	Under 3

• Cities with over 2,000,000 inhabitants (including suburbs)

○ Cities with over 1,000,000 inhabitants (including suburbs)

AREA 17,128,500 sq. mi. (44,362,815 sq. km.)
POPULATION 2,633,000,000
LARGEST CITY Tokyo
HIGHEST POINT Mt. Everest 29,028 ft. (8,848 m.)
LOWEST POINT Dead Sea -1,296 ft. (-395 m.)

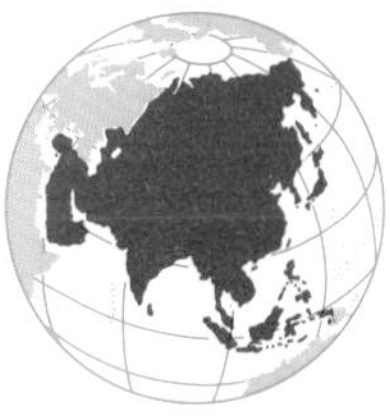

Vegetation

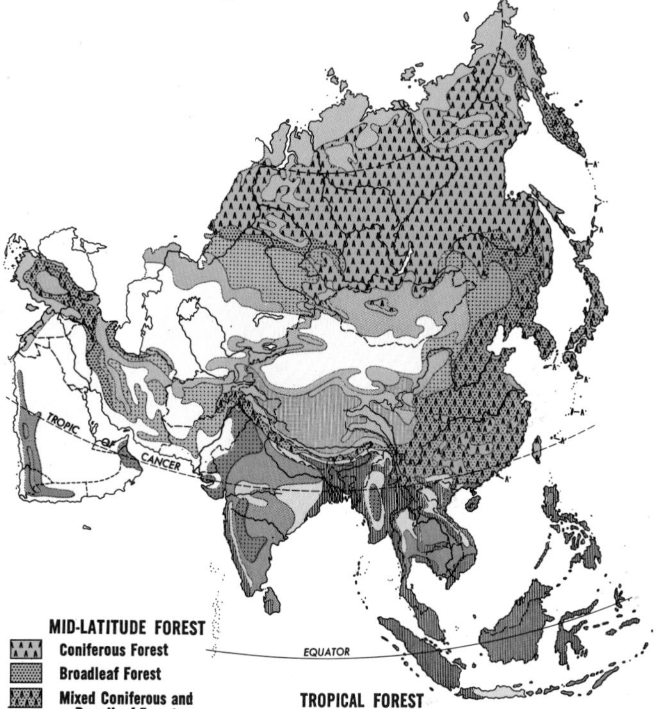

MID-LATITUDE FOREST
- Coniferous Forest
- Broadleaf Forest
- Mixed Coniferous and Broadleaf Forest
- Woodland and Shrub (Mediterranean)

MID-LATITUDE GRASSLAND
- Short Grass (Steppe)
- Wooded Steppe

DESERT AND DESERT SHRUB

TROPICAL FOREST
- Tropical Rainforest
- Light Tropical Forest
- Woodland and Shrub

TROPICAL GRASSLAND
- Grass and Shrub (Savanna)
- Wooded Savanna

TUNDRA AND ALPINE

UNCLASSIFIED HIGHLANDS

Abadan, Iran F 6
Abu Dhabi (cap.), U.A.E. G 7
Adana, Turkey E 6
Aden (cap.), P.D.R. Yemen F 8
Aden (gulf) F 8
Afghanistan H 6
Agra, India J 7
Ahmadabad, India J 7
Aleppo, Syria E 6
Al Kuwait (cap.), Kuwait F 7
Alma-Ata, U.S.S.R. J 5
Altai (mts.) K 5
Altun Shan (range), China K 6
Amman (cap.), Jordan E 6
Amudar'ya (riv.), U.S.S.R. H 5
Amur (riv.) P 5
Andaman (isls.), India L 8
Ankara (cap.), Turkey E 5
Aqaba (gulf) E 7
Arabian (sea) H 8
Araks (riv.) F 6
Aral (sea), U.S.S.R. G 5
Ararat (mt.), Turkey F 6
Arctic (ocean) C 1
Asahikawa, Japan P 5
Ashkhabad, U.S.S.R. G 6
Baghdad (cap.), Iraq F 6
Bahawalpur, Pakistan J 7
Bahrain G 7
Bali (isl.), Indonesia N1 0
Balkhash (lake), U.S.S.R. J 5
Bandar Seri Begawan (cap.), Brunei N 9
Bandung, Indonesia M10
Bangalore, India J 8
Bangkok (cap.), Thailand M 8
Bangladesh L 7
Basra, Iraq F 6
Baykal (lake), U.S.S.R. N 4
Beijing (cap.), China N 5
Beirut (cap.), Lebanon E 6
Bengal (bay) K 8
Bering (sea) V 4
Bering (strait) W 3
Bhutan L 7
Black (sea) E 5
Blagoveshchensk, U.S.S.R. O 4
Bombay, India J 8
Bonin (isls.), Japan E 7
Borneo (isl.) N 9
Brahmaputra (riv.) L 7
British Indian Ocean Territory J10
Brunei N 9
Bukhara, U.S.S.R. H 5
Burma L 7
Calcutta, India K 7
Cambodia M 8
Cannanore (isls.), India H 8
Canton, China N 7
Caspian (sea) G 5
Celebes (isl.), Indonesia N10
Chang Jiang (Yangtze) (riv.), China N 6
Chelyabinsk, U.S.S.R. H 4
Chengdu, China M 6
China L 6
Chittagong, Bangladesh L 7
Chongqing, China M 7
Christmas (isl.), Australia M11
Chukchi (pen.), U.S.S.R. V 3
Cocos (isls.), Australia L11
Colombo (cap.), Sri Lanka J 9
Comorin (cape), India J 9
Cyprus E 6
Dacca (Dhaka) (cap.), Bangladesh L 7
Dalian, China O 6
Damascus (cap.), Syria E 6
Da Nang, Vietnam M 8
Delhi, India J 7
Dhahran, Saudi Arabia F 7
Dhaka (cap.), Bangladesh L 7
Diego Garcia (isl.), Br. Ind. Ocean Terr. J10
Doha (cap.), Qatar G 7
Dushanbe, U.S.S.R. H 6
East China (sea) O 7
Euphrates (riv.) F 6
Everest (mt.) K 7
Frunze, U.S.S.R. J 5
Fukuoka, Japan O 6
Ganges (riv.) K 7
George Town, Malaysia M 9
Gobi (des.) M 5
Great Khingan (range), China O 5
Great Wall (ruins), China N 5
Guangzhou (Canton), China N 7
Hadhramaut (reg.), P.D.R. Yemen F 8
Hainan (isl.), China N 8
Haiphong, Vietnam M 7
Hakodate, Japan R 5
Halmahera (isl.), Indonesia O 9
Hangzhou, China N 6
Hanoi (cap.), Vietnam M 7
Harbin, China O 5
Herat, Afghanistan H 6
Himalaya (mts.) L 7
Hindu Kush (mts.) J 6
Hiroshima, Japan P 6
Ho Chi Minh City, Vietnam M 8
Hokkaido (isl.), Japan R 5
Hong Kong N 7
Honshu (isl.), Japan P 6
Huang He (Hwang Ho) (riv.), China N 6
Hue, Vietnam M 8
Hyderabad, India J 8
Hyderabad, Pakistan H 7
Inch'ŏn, S. Korea O 6
India J 7
Indian (ocean) H10
Indonesia M10
Indus (riv.) H 7
Inner Mongolia (reg.), China N 5
Iran G 7
Iraq F 6
Irkutsk, U.S.S.R. M 4
Irrawaddy (riv.), Burma L 7
Irtysh (riv.), U.S.S.R. J 4
Isfahan, Iran G 6
Islamabad (cap.), Pakistan J 6
Israel E 6
Izmir, Turkey D 6
Jaipur, India J 7
Jakarta (cap.), Indonesia M10
Japan R 6
Japan (sea) P 6
Java (isl.), Indonesia M10
Jerusalem (cap.), Israel E 6
Jidda, Saudi Arabia E 7
Jordan E 6
Kabul (cap.), Afghanistan H 6
Kamchatka (pen.), U.S.S.R. S 4
Kanpur, India K 7
Kara (sea), U.S.S.R. H 2
Karachi, Pakistan H 7
Karakorum (ruins), Mongolia M 5
Kathmandu (cap.), Nepal K 7
Kazakh, S.S.R., U.S.S.R. H 5
Kerman, Iran G 6
Khabarovsk, U.S.S.R. P 5
Khyber (pass) J 6
Kirgiz S.S.R., U.S.S.R. J 5
Kistna (riv.), India J 8
Kitakyushu, Japan P 6
Kobe, Japan P 6
Kolyma (range), U.S.S.R. S 3
Krasnoyarsk, U.S.S.R. L 4
Kuala Lumpur (cap.), Malaysia M 9
Kunlun (range), China K 6
Kunming, China M 7
Kuril (isls.), U.S.S.R. R 5
Kuwait F 7
Kyoto, Japan P 6
Kyushu (isl.), Japan P 6
Lahore, Pakistan J 6
Lanzhou, China M 6
Laos M 8
Laptev (sea), U.S.S.R. O 2
Latakia, Syria E 6
Lebanon E 6
Lena (riv.), U.S.S.R. O 3
Leyte (isl.), Philippines O 8
Lhasa, China L 7
Lucknow, India K 7
Luzon (isl.), Philippines O 8
Macau N 7
Madras, India K 8
Magnitogorsk, U.S.S.R. H 4
Makassar (str.), Indonesia N10
Malacca (str.) M 9
Malaya (reg.), Malaysia M 9
Malaysia M 9
Maldives J 9
Male (cap.), Maldives J 9
Mandalay, Burma L 7
Manila (cap.), Philippines N 8
Mecca (cap.), Saudi Arabia F 7
Medan, Indonesia L 9
Medina, Saudi Arabia F 7
Mekong (riv.) M 8
Mindanao (isl.), Philippines O 9
Molucca (isls.), Indonesia O10
Mongolia M 5
Mosul, Iraq F 6
Muscat (cap.), Oman G 7
Mysore, India J 8
Nagasaki, Japan O 6
Nagoya, Japan P 6
Naha, Japan O 7
Nanjing, China N 6
Nepal K 7
New Delhi, India J 7
New Guinea (isl.) P10
Nicosia (cap.), Cyprus E 6
North Korea O 5
Novosibirsk, U.S.S.R. J 4
Ob' (riv.), U.S.S.R. H 3
Okhotsk (sea), U.S.S.R. R 4
Okinawa (isls.), Japan O 7
Oman G 8
Omsk, U.S.S.R. J 4
Osaka, Japan P 6
Pacific (ocean) T 5
Pakistan H 7
Pamir (plat.) J 6
Peking (Beijing) (cap.), China N 5
Persian (gulf) G 7
Philippines O 8
Phnom Penh (cap.), Cambodia M 8
Poona, India J 8
Pusan, S. Korea O 6
P'yongyang (cap.), N. Korea O 6
Qatar G 7
Rangoon (cap.), Burma L 8
Rawalpindi, Pakistan J 6
Red (sea) E 7
Riyadh (cap.), Saudi Arabia F 7
Russian Soviet Federated Socialist Republic, U.S.S.R. L 3
Ryukyu (isls.), Japan O 7
Sabah (reg.), Malaysia N 9
Saigon (Ho Chi Minh City), Vietnam M 8
Sakhalin (isl.), U.S.S.R. R 4
Salween (riv.) L 8
Samarkand, U.S.S.R. H 6
San'a (cap.), Yemen Arab Rep. F 8
Sapporo, Japan P 5
Sarawak (reg.), Malaysia N 9
Saudi Arabia F 7
Seoul (cap.), S. Korea O 6
Severnaya Zemlya (isls.), U.S.S.R. M 1
Shanghai, China O 6
Shikoku, Japan P 6
Siberia (reg.), U.S.S.R. M 4
Singapore M 9
Sinkiang (reg.), China K 5
Socotra (isl.), P.D.R. Yemen G 8
South China (sea) N 8
South Korea O 6
Sri Lanka K 9
Sulu (sea), Philippines N 9
Sumatra (isl.), Indonesia L 9
Sunda (str.), Indonesia M10
Surabaya, Indonesia N10
Sverdlovsk, U.S.S.R. H 4
Syrdar'ya (riv.), U.S.S.R. H 5
Syria E 6
Tabriz, Iran F 6
Tadzhik S.S.R., U.S.S.R. H 6
Taipei (cap.), Taiwan O 7
Taiwan (isl.) N 7
Ta'izz, Yemen Arab Rep. F 8
Takla Makan (des.), China K 6
Tashkent, U.S.S.R. H 5
Taymyr (pen.), U.S.S.R. L 2
Tehran (cap.), Iran G 6
Tel Aviv-Jaffa, Israel E 6
Thailand M 8
Tianjin, China N 6
Tibet (reg.), China K 6
Tien Shan (range) K 5
Tigris (riv.) F 6
Timor (isl.), Indonesia O 10
Tokyo (cap.), Japan R 6
Tonkin (gulf) M 8
Turkey E 6
Turkmen S.S.R., U.S.S.R. G 6
Ulaanbaatar (cap.), Mongolia M 5
Union of Soviet Socialist Republics L 3
United Arab Emirates G 7
Ural (mts.), U.S.S.R. G 4
Urmia (lake), Iran F 6
Ürümqi, China K 5
Uzbek S.S.R., U.S.S.R. H 5
Varanasi, India K 7
Verkhoyansk, U.S.S.R. P 3
Vientiane (cap.), Laos M 8
Vietnam M 8
Vladivostok, U.S.S.R. P 5
Wŏnsan, N. Korea O 6
Wuhan, China N 6
Xi'an, China M 6
Yakutsk, U.S.S.R. O 3
Yalu (riv.) O 5
Yangtze (riv.), China N 6
Yellow (sea) O 6
Yemen Arab Republic F 8
Yemen, People's Democratic Republic of F 8
Yenisey (riv.), U.S.S.R. K 3
Yogyakarta, Indonesia M10
Yokohama, Japan R 6
Zhengzhou, China S 3

| SAUDI ARABIA | KUWAIT | YEMEN ARAB REPUBLIC | BAHRAIN | QATAR | OMAN | PEOPLE'S DEM. REP. OF YEMEN |

AFGHANISTAN

CITIES and TOWNS

Anar Darreh	H3	Balkh	J2	Farsi	J3	Jorm	K2	Lashkar Gah 26.646	H3	Qalat 5.946	J3	Sheberghan 54.870	H2
Andkhvoy	H2	Bamian 7.355	J3	Feyzabad 10.142	K2	Kabul (cap) 905.108	J3	Mar uf	J3	Qale h-ye Now 5.340	H3	Shindand	H3
Aqcheh	J2	Baraki Barak	J3	Gardez 11.415	J3	Kalat (Qalat) 5.946	J3	Mazar-e Sharif 122.567	J2	Qale h-ye Panjeh	K2	Spin Buldak	J3
Aybak 33.016	J2	Belcheragh	H2	Gereshk	J3	Kandahar (Qandahar) 178.409	J3	Meymaneh 54.954	H2	Qandahar 178.409	J3	Tagab	H3
Baghlan 75.130	J2	Chahar Borjak	H3	Ghazni 30.425	J3	Khanabad	J2	Mirabad	H3	Qoruoz 107.191	J3	Talogan 46.202	J2
		Charikar 25.093	J3	Ghurian	H3	Khugiani	J3	Moqor	J3	Rostaq	J2	Teyvareh	H3
		Dowlat Yar	J3	Gizab	J3	Kowst	J3	Now Zad	H3	Rudbar	J2	Tulak	H3
		Dowlatabad	J2	Hazar Qadam	J3	Kuhestan	J2	Owbeh	H3	Sakhar	J3	Zaranj 6.477	H3
		Dowshi	H3	Herat 163.960	H3	Landay	J3	Panjab	J3	Sar-e Pol	J2	Zibak	K2
		Farah 18.797	H3	Jalalabad 56.384	K3	Lash-e Joveyn	H3	Pol-e Khomri	J2	Shah Juy	J3		

UNITED ARAB EMIRATES

OTHER FEATURES

Farah Rud (riv.) H3
Gowd-e Zerreh (depr.) H4
Harirud (riv.) H3
Helmand (riv.) J3
Hindu Kush (mts.) J2
Kabul (riv.) K3
Konar (riv.) K2
Lurah (riv.) J3

Margow, Dasht-e (des.) H3
Murghab (riv.) H2
Namaksar (salt lake) H3
Paropamisus (mts.) H3
Rigestan (reg.) H3

BAHRAIN

CITIES and TOWNS

Manama (cap.) 88,785 ....F4
Muharraq 37,732 ....F4

GAZA STRIP

CITIES and TOWNS

Gaza* 118,272 ....B3

IRAN

CITIES and TOWNS

Abadan 296,081 ....E3
Abadeh 16,000 ....F3
Abarqu 8,000 ....F3
Ahvaz 329,006 ....E3

Amol 68,782 ....F2
Anar 463 ....G3
Anarak 2,038 ....F3
Arak 114,507 ....E3
Ardabil 147,404 ....E2
Ardestan 5,868 ....F3
Asterabad (Gorgan) 88,348 .....F2
Babol 67,790 ....F2
Bafq 5,000 ....G3
Baft 6,000 ....G4

(continued on following page)

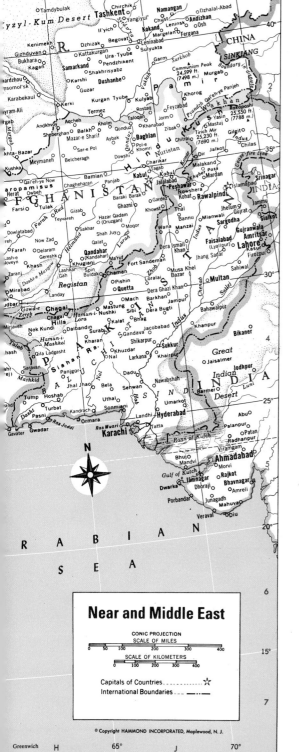

SAUDI ARABIA

AREA 829,995 sq. mi.
(2,149,687 sq. km.)
POPULATION 8,367,000
CAPITAL Riyadh
MONETARY UNIT Saudi riyal
MAJOR LANGUAGE Arabic
MAJOR RELIGION Islam

KUWAIT

AREA 6,532 sq mi. (16,918 sq. km.)
POPULATION 1,355,827
CAPITAL Al Kuwait
MONETARY UNIT Kuwaiti dinar
MAJOR LANGUAGE Arabic
MAJOR RELIGION Islam

YEMEN ARAB REPUBLIC

AREA 77,220 sq. mi. (200,000 sq. km.)
POPULATION 6,456,189
CAPITAL San'a
MONETARY UNIT Yemeni rial
MAJOR LANGUAGE Arabic
MAJOR RELIGION Islam

BAHRAIN

AREA 240 sq. mi. (622 sq. km.)
POPULATION 358,857
CAPITAL Manama
MONETARY UNIT Bahraini dinar
MAJOR LANGUAGE Arabic
MAJOR RELIGION Islam

QATAR

AREA 4,247 sq. mi. (11,000 sq. km.)
POPULATION 220,000
CAPITAL Doha
MONETARY UNIT Qatari riyal
MAJOR LANGUAGE Arabic
MAJOR RELIGION Islam

OMAN

AREA 120,000 sq. mi. (310,800 sq. km.)
POPULATION 891,000
CAPITAL Muscat
MONETARY UNIT Omani rial
MAJOR LANGUAGE Arabic
MAJOR RELIGION Islam

PEOPLE'S DEM. REP. OF YEMEN

AREA 111,101 sq. mi. (287,752 sq. km.)
POPULATION 1,969,000
CAPITAL Aden
MONETARY UNIT Yemeni dinar
MAJOR LANGUAGE Arabic
MAJOR RELIGION Islam

UNITED ARAB EMIRATES

AREA 32,278 sq. mi. (83,600 sq. km.)
POPULATION 1,040,275
CAPITAL Abu Dhabi
MONETARY UNIT dirham
MAJOR LANGUAGE Arabic
MAJOR RELIGION Islam

Near and Middle East

CONIC PROJECTION
SCALE OF MILES
SCALE OF KILOMETERS

Capitals of Countries .... ☆
International Boundaries ___ ___ ___

Topography

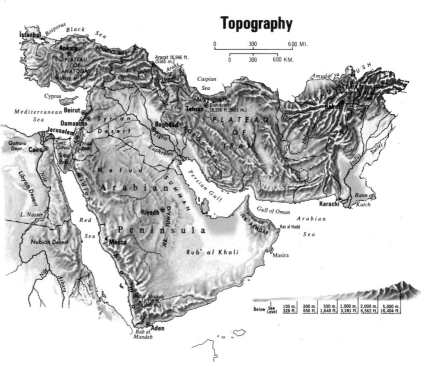

Below Sea Level | 100 m. 328 ft. | 200 m. 656 ft. | 500 m. 1,640 ft. | 1,000 m. 3,281 ft. | 2,000 m. 6,562 ft. | 5,000 m. 16,404 ft.

(continued)

Bakhtaran 290,861 E3
Bam 22,000 G4
Bampur 1,585 H4
Bandar 'Abbas 89,103 G4
Bandar-e Anzali (Enzeli) 55,978 E2
Bandar-e Khomeyni 6,000 E3
Bandar-e Lengeh 4,920 F4
Bandar-e Rig 1,889 F4
Bandar-e Torkeman 13,000 F2
Bejestan 3,823 G3
Birjand 25,854 G3
Bojnurd 31,248 G2
Borazjan 20,000 F4
Borujerd 100,103 E3
Bushehr 57,681 F4
Chah Bahar 1,800 H4
Chalus 15,000 F2
Damghan 13,000 F2
Darab 13,000 G4
Dasht-e Azadegan 21,000 E3
Dashtiari H4
Dezful 110,287 E3
Dezh Shahpur 1,384 E2
Emamshahr 30,767 G2
Enzeli 55,978 E2
Estahbanat 18,187 F4
Fahrej (Iranshahr)5,000 H4
Fasa 19,000 F4
Ferdows 11,000 G3
Gach Saran F3
Garmsar 4,723 F2
Golpayegan 20,515 F3
Gonabad 8,000 G3
Gorgan 88,348 F2
Hamadan 155,846 E3
Iranshahr 5,000 H4
Isfahan 671,825 F3
Jahrom 38,236 F4
Kangan 2,682 F4
Kangavar 9,414 E3
Kashan 84,545 F3
Kashmar 17,000 G2
Kazerun 51,309 F4
Kerman 140,309 G3
Khash 7,439 H4
Khorramabad 104,928 E3
Khorramshahr 146,709 E3
Khvoy 70,040 E2
Lar 22,000 F4
Mahabad 28,610 E2
Maragheh 60,820 E2
Marand 24,000 E2
Meshed 670,180 H2
Mianeh 28,447 E2
Minab 4,228 G2
Mirjaveh 11,000 H4
Nahavand 24,000 E3
Na'in 5,925 F3
Najafabad 76,236 F3
Nasratabad (Zabol) 20,000 H3
Natanz 4,370 F3
Nehbandan 2,130 G3
Neyshabur 59,101 G2
Nikshahr H4
Pahlevi (Enzeli) 55,978 E2
Qasr-e Qand 1,879 H4
Qayen 6,000 G3
Qazvin 138,527 E2
Qom 246,831 F3
Quchan 29,133 G2
Qum (Qom) 246,831 F3
Rafsanjan 21,000 G3
Rasht 187,203 E2
Ravar 5,074 G3
Rey 102,825 F2
Reza'iyeh (Urmia) 163,991 D2
Sabzevar 69,174 G2
Sabzvaran 7,000 G4
Sai'dabad 20,000 G4
Sanandaj 95,834 E2
Saqqez 17,000 E2
Saravan H4
Sari 70,936 F2
Saveh 17,565 F2
Semnan 31,058 F2
Shahdad 2,777 G3
Shahreza 34,220 F3
Shiraz 416,408 F4
Shirvan 11,000 G2
Shustar 24,000 E3
Sirjan (Sai'dabad) 20,000 G4
Tabas 10,000 G3
Tabas-Masina (Tabas) 466 H3
Tabriz 598,576 E2
Tarom 394 G4
Tehran (cap.) 4,496,159 F2
Tonekabon 12,000 F2
Torbat-e Heydariyeh 30,106 G2
Torbat-e Jam 13,000 H2
Torud 721 F2
Turan G2
Turbat-i-Shaikh Jam 13,000 H2
Urmia 163,991 D2
Yazd 135,978 F3
Yazdan H3
Zabol 20,000 H3
Zahedan 92,628 H4
Zanjan 99,967 E2
Zarand 5,000 G3

OTHER FEATURES

Araks (riv.) E2
Atrek (riv.) G2
Bazman, Kuh-e (mt.) H4
Damavand (mt.) F2
Dez (riv.) E3
Elburz (mts.) F2
Gavkhuni (lake) F3
Gorgan (riv.) F2
Halil (riv.) G4
Jaz Murian, Hamun-e (marsh) G4
Karun (riv.) E3
Kavir, Dasht-e (salt des.) G3
Kavir-e Namak (salt des.) G3
Lut, Dasht-e (des.) G3
Maidani, Ras (cape) G4
Mand Rud (riv.) F4
Mashkid (riv.) H4
Mehran (riv.) F4
Namak, Daryacheh-ye (salt lake) F3
Namaksar (salt lake) H3
Namakzar-e Shahdad (salt lake) G3
Oman (gulf) G5
Persian (gulf) F4
Qeys (isl.) F4
Qezel Owzan (riv.) E2
Qeshm (isl.) G4
Safidar, Kuh-e (mt.) F4
Shaikh Shua'ib (isl.) F4
Shir Kuh (mt.) F3
Taftan, Kuh-e (mt.) H4
Talab (riv.) H4
Tashk (lake) F4
Urmia (lake) E2
Zagros (mts.) E3

IRAQ

CITIES and TOWNS

Al'Aziziya 7,450 E3
Al Falluja 38,072 D3
Al Fatha† 15,329 D2
Al Musaiyib 15,955 D3
Al Qurna 5,638 E3
'Amadiya 2,578 D2
'Amara 64,847 E3
'Ana 15,729 D3
An Najaf 128,096 D3
An Nasiriya 60,405 E3
Arbela (Erbil) 90,320 D2
Ar Rahhaliya 1,579 D3
As Salman 3,584 E3
Baghdad (cap.) 502,503 E3
Baghdad* 1,745,328 E3
Baq'uba 34,575 D3
Basra 313,327 E3
Erbil 90,320 D2
Habbaniya 14,405 D3
Haditha 6;870 D3
Hai 16,988 E3
Hilla 84,717 D3
Hit 9,131 D3
Karbal'a 83,301 D3
Khanaqin 23,522 D3
Kirkuk 167,413 D2
Kirkuk* 176,794 D2
Kut 42,116 E3
Maidan 354 E3
Mosul 315,157 D2
Qala' Sharqat 2,434 D2
Ramadi 28,723 D3
Rutba 5,091 D3
Samarra 24,746 D3
Samawa 33,473 D3
Shithatha 2,326 D3
Sulaimaniya 86,822 E2
Tikrit 9,921 D3

OTHER FEATURES

'Aneiza, Jebel (mt.) C3
'Ara'r, Wadi (dry riv.) D3
Batin, Wadi al (dry riv.) E4
Euphrates (riv.) E3
Hauran, Wadi (dry riv.) D3
Mesopotamia (reg.) D3
Syrian (El Hamad) (des.) D3
Tigris (riv.) E3

KUWAIT

CITIES and TOWNS

Al Kuwait (cap.) 181,774 E4
Mina al Ahmadi E4
Mina Saud E4

OTHER FEATURES

Bubiyan (isl.) E4
Persian (gulf) F4

OMAN

CITIES and TOWNS

Adam G5
Buraimi G5
Dhank G5
Ibra G5
I'bri G5
Juwara G6
Kamil G5
Khaluf G5
Khasab G4
Manah G5
Masqat (Muscat) (cap.) 7,500 G5
Matrah 15,000 G5
Mina al Fahal G5
Murbat G6
Muscat (cap.) 7,500 G5
Nizwa G5
Quryat G5
Raysut (Risut) F6
Salala 4,000 F6
Sarur G5
Shinas G5
Sohar G5
Sur G5
Suwaiq G5

OTHER FEATURES

Akhdar, Jebel (range) G5
Batina (reg.) G5
Dhofar (reg.) F6
Hadd, Ras al (cape) G5
Jibsh, Ras (cape) G5
Kuria Muria (isls.) G6
Madraka, Ras (cape) G6
Masira (gulf) G6
Masira (isl.) G5
Musandam, Ras (cape) G4
Nus, Ras (cape) G6
Oman (gulf) G5
Oman (reg.) G5
Ruus al Jibal (dist.) G4
Sauqira (bay) G6
Sauqira, Ras (cape) G6
Sham, Jebel (mt.) G5
Sharbatat, Ras (cape) G6

QATAR

CITIES and TOWNS

Doha (cap.) 150,000 F4
Dukhan F4
Umm Sai'd F5

OTHER FEATURES

Persian (gulf) F4
Rakan, Ras (cape) F4

SAUDI ARABIA

CITIES and TOWNS

Aba as Sau'd 47,501 D6
'Abaila F5
Abha 30,150 D6
Abqaiq E4
Abu 'Arish D6
Abu Hadriya E4
'Ain al Mubarrak C5
Al 'Ain C4
Al-'Ala C4
Al 'Auda E4
Al Birk D6
Al Hilla E5
Al Lidam D5
Al Lith C5
Al Muadhdam C4
'Anaiza D4
Artawiya E4
'Ashaira D5
Ayun D4
Badr C5
Buraida 69,940 D4
Dam D5
Dammam 127,844 F4
Dar al Hamra C4
Dhaba C4
Dhahran E4
Dharma E5
Dilam E5
Doqa D6
Duwadami D5
Er Ras D4
Faid D4
Gail E5
Haddar E5
Hadiya C4
Hafar al Batin E4
Hail 40,502 D4
Hamar E5
Hamda D6
Hanakiya D5
Haql C4
Harad E5
Haraja D6
Hariq E5
Hofuf 101,271 E4
Jabrin E5
Jauf C4
Jidda 561,104 C5
Jizan (Qizan) 32,812 D6
Jubail F4
Jubba D4
Junaina D5
Kaf C3
Khaibar, 'Asir D5
Khaibar, Hejaz C4
Khamis Mushait 49,581 D6
Khay D6
Khurma D5
Laila E5
Majmaa' D4
Maqna C4
Marib E6
Mastaba C5
Mastura C5
Mecca (cap.) 366,801 C5
Medain Salih C4
Medina 198,186 D5
Mendak D5
Mina Sau'd E4
Mubarraz 54,325 E4
Mudhnib D4
Muwailih C4
Najran (Aba as Sau'd) 47,501 D6
Nisab D4
O'qair E4
Qadhima C5
Qafar D4
Qasr al Haiyanya D4
Qatif E4
Qizan 32,812 D6
Qunfidha D6
Qusaiba D4
Rabigh C5
Ra's al Khafji E4
Ras Tanura F4
Riyadh (cap.) 666,840 E5
Rumah E4
Sabya D6
Sakaka D4
Salwa F5
Shaqra D4
Shuqaiq D6
Sufeina D5
Sulaiyil E5
Taif 204,857 D5
Taima C4
Tamra E5
Tathlith D6
Tebuk (Tabuk) 74,825 C4
Truba D4
Turaba D5
Umm Lajj C4
Wejh C4
Yamama E5
Yenbo C5
Zahran D6
Zalim D5
Zilfi E4

OTHER FEATURES

Abu-Mad, Ras (cape) C5
'Aneiza, Jebel (mt.) C3
'Aqaba (gulf) C4
Arafat, Jebel (mt.) D5
'Ara'r, Wadi (dry riv.) D3
Arma (plat.) E4
Aswad, Ras al (cape) C5
Bahr es Safi (des.) E6
Barida, Ras (cape) C5
Bisha, Wadi (dry riv.) D5
Dahana (des.) E4
Dawasir, Wadi (dry riv.) E5
Dawasir, Hadhb (range) D5
Farasan (isls.) D6
Hatiba, Ras (cape) C5
Jafura (des.) F5
Mashabi (isl.) C4
Midian (dist.) C4
Mishaa'b, Ras (cape) E4
Nefud (des.) D4
Nefud Dahi (des.) D5
Persian (gulf) F4
Ranya, Wadi (dry riv.) D5
Red (sea) C5
Rima, Wadi (dry riv.) D4
Rimal, Ar (des.) F5
Rub al Khali (des.) F5
Safaniya, Ras (cape) E4
Salma, Jebel (mts.) D4
Shaibara (isl.) C4
Shammar, Jebel (plat.) D4
Sirhan, Wadi (dry riv.) C3
Subh, Jebel (mt.) C5
Summan (plat.) E4
Tihama (reg.) C5
Tiran (isl.) C4
Tiran (str.) C4
Tuwaiq, Jebel (range) E5

UNITED ARAB EMIRATES

CITIES and TOWNS

Abu Dhabi (cap.) 347,000 F5
'AJman G4
'Aradah F5
Buraimi G5
Dubai F4
Fujairah G4
Jebel Dhanna F5
Ras al Khaimah G4
Ruwais F5
Sharjah F4
Umm al Qaiwain G4

OTHER FEATURES

Das (isl.) F4
Oman (gulf) G5
Yas (isl.) F5
Zirko (isl.) F5

WEST BANK

CITIES and TOWNS

Hebron 38,309 C3

OTHER FEATURES

Dead (sea) C3

YEMEN ARAB REP.

CITIES and TOWNS

'Amran D6
Bait al Faqih D7
Dhamar 19,467 D7
El Beida 5,975 E7
Hajja 5,814 D6
Harib E7
Hodeida 80,314 D7
Huth D6
Ibb 19,066 D7
Luhaiya D6
Marib 292 D6
Mocha D7
Saa'da 4,252 D6
Sana' (cap.) 134,588 D6
Sheikh Sai'd D7
Tai'zz 78,642 D7
Yarim D7
Zabid D7

OTHER FEATURES

Hanish (isls.) D7
Manar, Jebel (mt.) D7
Mandeb, Bab el (str.) D7
Red (sea) C5
Sabir, Jebel (mt.) D7
Tihama (reg.) C5
Zuqar (isl.) D7

YEMEN, PEOPLE'S DEM. REPUBLIC OF

CITIES and TOWNS

Aden (cap.) 240,370 E7
Ahwar E7
Balhaf E7
Bir 'Ali E7
Damqut F6
Ghaida F6
Habban E7
Hadibu F7
Hajarain E6
Haura E7
Hureidha E6
I'rqa E7
Lahej E7
Leijun E6
Lodar E7
Madinat ash Shab' E7
Meifa E7
Mukalla 45,000 E7
Nisab E7
Nuqub E6
Qishn F6
Riyan E7
Saihut F6
Seiyun 20,000 E6
Shabwa E6
Shibam E6
Shihr E7
Shuqra E7
Tarim E6
Yeshbum E7
Zinjibar E7

OTHER FEATURES

Fartak, Ras (cape) F6
Hadhramaut (dist.) E7
Hadhramaut, Wadi (dry riv.) F7
Kamaran (isl.) D6
Perim (isl.) D7
Socotra (isl.) F7

*City and suburbs.

Agriculture, Industry and Resources

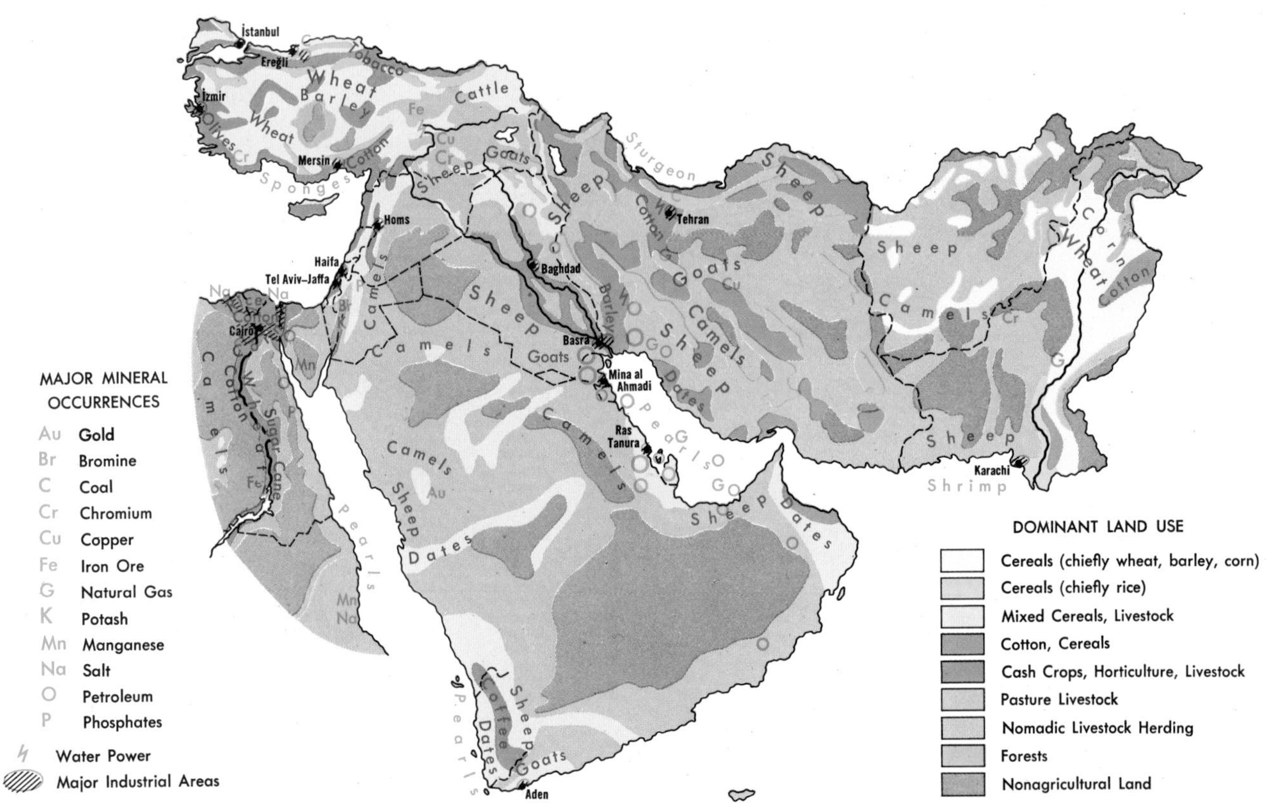
MAJOR MINERAL OCCURRENCES
Au Gold
Br Bromine
C Coal
Cr Chromium
Cu Copper
Fe Iron Ore
G Natural Gas
K Potash
Mn Manganese
Na Salt
O Petroleum
P Phosphates
Water Power
Major Industrial Areas
DOMINANT LAND USE
Cereals (chiefly wheat, barley, corn)
Cereals (chiefly rice)
Mixed Cereals, Livestock
Cotton, Cereals
Cash Crops, Horticulture, Livestock
Pasture Livestock
Nomadic Livestock Herding
Forests
Nonagricultural Land
İstanbul
Ereğli
İzmir
Mersin
Homs
Haifa
Tel Aviv–Jaffa
Cairo
Baghdad
Tehran
Basra
Mina al Ahmadi
Ras Tanura
Karachi
Aden
Wheat
Barley
Tobacco
Cattle
Olives
Sponges
Cotton
Goats
Sheep
Sturgeon
Camels
Dates
Corn
Pearls
Shrimp
Sugar Cane
Coffee

TURKEY

SYRIA

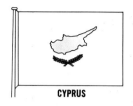
LEBANON

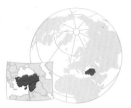
CYPRUS

TURKEY
AREA 300,946 sq. mi.
(779,450 sq. km.)
POPULATION 45,217,556
CAPITAL Ankara
LARGEST CITY Istanbul
HIGHEST POINT Ararat 16,946 ft.
(5,165 m.)
MONETARY UNIT Turkish lira
MAJOR LANGUAGE Turkish
MAJOR RELIGION Islam

SYRIA
AREA 71,498 sq. mi. (185,180 sq. km.)
POPULATION 8,979,000
CAPITAL Damascus
LARGEST CITY Damascus
HIGHEST POINT Hermon 9,232 ft.
(2,814 m.)
MONETARY UNIT Syrian pound
MAJOR LANGUAGES Arabic, French,
Kurdish, Armenian
MAJOR RELIGIONS Islam, Christianity

LEBANON
AREA 4,015 sq. mi. (10,399 sq. km.)
POPULATION 3,161,000
CAPITAL Beirut
LARGEST CITY Beirut
HIGHEST POINT Qurnet es Sauda
10,131 ft. (3,088 m.)
MONETARY UNIT Lebanese pound
MAJOR LANGUAGES Arabic, French
MAJOR RELIGIONS Christianity, Islam

CYPRUS
AREA 3,473 sq. mi. (8,995 sq. km.)
POPULATION 629,000
CAPITAL Nicosia
LARGEST CITY Nicosia
HIGHEST POINT Troödos 6,406 ft. (1,953 m.)
MONETARY UNIT Cypriot pound
MAJOR LANGUAGES Greek, Turkish, English
MAJOR RELIGIONS Eastern (Greek) Orthodoxy,
Islam

CYPRUS

CITIES and TOWNS

Dhali 2,970	E5
Episkopi 2,150	E5
Famagusta 38,960	E5
Ktima	E5
Kyrenia 3,892	E5
Kythrea 3,400	E5
Lapithos 3,600	E5
Larnaca 19,608	E5
Lefka 3,650	E5
Limassol 79,641	E5
Morphou 9,040	E5
Nicosia (cap.) 115,718	E5
Paphos 8,984	E5
Polis 2,200	E5
Rizokarpasso 3,600	E5
Yialousa 2,750	E5

OTHER FEATURES

Andreas (cape)	F5
Arnauti (cape)	E5
Gata (cape)	E5
Greco (cape)	F5
Kormakiti (cape)	E5
Troodos (mt.)	E5

LEBANON

CITIES and TOWNS

A'leih 18,630	F6
Amyun 7,926	F6
Baa'lbek 15,560	G5
Batrun 5,976	F5
Beirut (cap.) 474,870	F6
Beirut* 938,940	F6
Hermil 2,652	G5
Merj U'yun 9,318	F6
Rashaiya 6,731	F6
Rayak 1,480	G6
Saida 32,200	F6
Sidon (Saida) 32,200	F6
Sur 16,483	F6
Tripoli (Tarabulus) 127,611	F5

Tyre (Sur) 16,483	F6
Zahle 53,121	F6
Zegharta 18,210	G5

OTHER FEATURES

Lebanon (mts.)	F6
Leontes (Litani) (riv.)	F6
Litani (riv.)	F6
Sauda, Qurnet es (mt.)	G5

SYRIA

PROVINCES

Aleppo 1,316,872	G4
Damascus 1,457,934	G6
Deir ez Zor 292,780	H5
Dera' 230,481	G6
El Quneitra 16,490	G6
Es Suweida 139,650	G6
Hama 514,748	G5
Haseke 468,506	J4
Homs 546,176	G5
Idlib 383,695	G5
Latakia 389,552	F5
Rashid 243,736	G5
Tartus 302,065	F5

CITIES and TOWNS

Abu Kemal 6,907	J5
A'in el A'rab 4,529	H4
Aleppo 639,428	G4
Azaz 13,923	G4
Baniyas 8,537	F5
Busra	G6
Damascus (cap.) 836,668	G6
Damascus* 923,253	G6
Deir ez Zor 66,164	H5
Dera' 27,651	G6
Dimashq (Damascus)
(cap.) 836,668	G6
Duma 30,050	G6
El Bab 27,366	G4
El Haseke 32,746	J4
El Ladhiqiya (Latakia) 125,716	F5
El Quryatein	G5
El Quneitra 17,752	G6
El Rashid 37,151	H5

En Nebk 16,334	G5
Es Suweide 29,524	G6
Et Tell el Abyad	H4
Haffe 4,656	G5
Haleb (Aleppo) 639,428	G4
Hama 137,421	G5
Harim 6,837	G4
Homs 215,423	G5
Idlib 34,515	G5
Izra 3,226	G6
Jeble 15,715	F5
Jerablus 8,610	G4
Jisr esh Shughur 13,131	G5
Latakia 125,716	F5
Masyaf 7,058	G5
Membij 13,796	G4
Meskene	H5
Meyadin 12,515	J5
Qala'n es Salihiye	J5
Qamishliye 31,448	J4
Quteife 4,993	G6
Raqqa (El Rashid) 37,151	H5
Sabkha 3,375	H5
Safita 9,650	G5
Selemiya 21,677	G5
Tadmur 10,670	H5
Tartus 29,842	F5
Telkalakh 6,242	K4
Zebdani 10,010	G6

OTHER FEATURES

A'mrit (ruins)	F5
Arwad (Ruad) (isl.)	F5
A'si (Orontes) (riv.)	G5
Druz, Jebel ed (mts.)	G6
El Furat (riv.)	H4
Euphrates (El Furat) (riv.)	H4
Hermon (mt.)	F6
Khabur (riv.)	J5
Orontes (riv.)	G5
Palmyra (Tadmor) (ruins)	H5
Ruwaq, Jebel er (mts.)	G5

TURKEY

PROVINCES

Adana 1,240,475	F4

Adiyaman 346,892	H4
Afyonkarahisar 579,171	D3
Agri 330,201	K3
Amasya 322,806	F2
Ankara 2,585,293	E3
Antalya 669,357	C4
Artvin 228,026	J2
Aydin 609,869	B4
Balikesir 789,255	B3
Bilecik 137,120	D2
Bingöl 210,804	J3
Bitlis 218,305	J3
Bolu 428,704	D2
Burdur 222,896	C4
Bursa 961,639	C2
Çanakkale 369,385	B2
Çankiri 265,468	E2
Çorum 547,580	F2
Denizli 560,916	C4
Diyarbakir 651,233	H4
Edirne 340,732	B2
Elazig 417,924	H3
Erzincan 283,683	H3
Erzurum 746,666	J3
Eskişehir 495,097	D3
Gaziantep 715,939	G4
Giresun 463,587	H2
Gümüşhane 293,673	H2
Hakkâri 126,036	K4
Hatay 744,113	G4
İçel 714,817	F4
Isparta 322,685	D4
İstanbul 3,904,588	C2
İzmir 1,673,966	B3
Kahramanmaraş 641,480	G4
Kars 707,398	K2
Kastamonu 438,243	E2
Kayseri 676,809	F3
Kirklareli 268,399	C2
Kirşehir 232,653	F3
Kocaeli 477,736	D2
Konya 1,422,461	E4
Kütahya 470,423	C3
Malatya 574,558	G3
Manisa 872,375	B3
Mardin 519,687	J4
Mugla 400,796	C4
Muş 267,203	J3
Nevşehir 249,308	F3
Niğde 463,121	F4

Ordu 664,290	G2
Rize 336,278	J2
Sakarya 495,649	D2
Samsun 906,381	F2
Siirt 381,503	J4
Sinop 267,605	F2
Sivas 741,713	G3
Tekirdağ 319,987	B2
Tokat 599,166	G2
Trabzon 719,008	H2
Tunceli 164,591	H3
Urfa 597,277	H4
Uşak 229,679	C3
Van 386,314	K3
Yozgat 500,371	F3
Zonguldak 836,156	D2

CITIES and TOWNS

Acigöl 3,934	F3
Açipayam 5,046	C4
Adalia (Antalya) 130,774	D4
Adana 475,384	F4
Adapazari 114,130	D2
Adilcevaz 9,022	K3
Adiyaman 43,782	H4
Afyonkarahisar 60,150	D3
Ağlasun 4,288	D4
Ağli 3,399	E2
Ağri (Karaköse) 35,284	K3
Ahlat 7,995	J3
Akçaabat 10,756	H2
Akçadağ 7,366	G3
Akçakoca 9,066	D2
Akdağmadeni 7,909	F3
Akhisar 53,357	B3
Aksaray 45,564	F3
Akşehir 35,544	D3
Akseki 5,141	D4
Akviran 3,799	E4
Akyazi 12,438	D2
Alaca 12,552	F2
Alacaham 2,321	G3
Alaçam 10,013	F2
Alanya 18,520	D4
Alaşehir 23,243	C3
Alexandretta
(İskenderun) 107,437	G4
Aliağa 5,727	B3

Alibeyköyü 33,387	D6
Almus 4,225	G2
Alpu 3,718	D3
Altindağ 512,392	E2
Altinova 6,980	B3
Altintaş 3,386	C3
Altinözü 5,158	G4
Alucra 7,070	H2
Amasra 4,369	E2
Amasya 41,496	G2
Anamur 21,475	E4
Andirin 5,018	G4
Ankara (cap.) 1,701,004	E3
Antakya 77,518	G4
Antalya 130,774	D4
Beyşehir 15,060	D4
Beytüşşebap 2,766	K4
Biga 15,188	B2
Bigadiç 7,535	C3
Bilecik 11,269	D2
Bingöl (Çapakçur) 22,047	J3
Birecik 20,104	H4
Bismil 12,775	J4
Bitlis 25,054	J3
Bodrum 7,858	B4
Boğazliyan 10,329	F3
Bolu 32,812	D2
Bolvadin 29,218	D3
Bor 16,560	F4
Borçka 4,636	J2
Boronva 45,096	B3
Boyabat 13,139	F2
Bozdoğan 7,218	C4
Bozkir 5,294	E4
Bozkurt 2,948	F2
Bozova 5,462	H4
Bozüyük 15,197	C3
Bucak 15,090	D4
Bulancak 14,153	H2
Bulanik 8,296	K3
Buldan 11,115	C3
Bünyan 12,277	G3
Burdur 36,633	D4
Burhaniye 12,800	B3
Bursa 346,103	C2
Büyükada	D6
Büyükdere	D5
Çal 3,274	C3
Çal 2,450	K2
Çaldiran 3,366	K3

Araç 3,594	E2
Aralik 4,155	L3
Arapkir 8,436	H3
Ardahan 16,285	K2
Ardeşen 7,980	J2
Ardanuç 2,942	J2
Arguvan 2,461	H3
Arhavi 6,311	J2
Arpaçay 2,651	K2
Arsin 6,557	H2
Artova 2,813	G2
Artvin 13,390	J2
Aşkale 10,817	J3

Avanos 8,635	F3
Ayancik 7,202	F2
Ayaş 4,575	E2
Aybasti 13,180	G2
Aydin 59,579	B4
Aydincik 6,739	E4
Ayrancı 2,664	E4
Ayvacik 3,120	B3
Ayvalik 18,041	B3
Azdavay 3,120	E2
Babaeski 17,090	B2
Bafra 34,288	F2
Bahçe 10,212	G4
Bakirköy 200,942	D6
Baklan 3,327	C4
Bala 4,107	E3
Balikesir 99,443	B3
Balya 2,362	B3
Banaz 6,264	C3
Bandirma 45,752	B2
Bartin 18,409	E2

Başkale 8,558	K3
Başmakçı 5,925	C4
Batman 64,384	J4
Bayat 4,671	F2
Bayburt 20,156	J2
Bayindir 14,078	B3
Baykan 2,690	J3
Bayramiç 6,385	B3
Bergama 29,749	B3
Beşiktaş 174,931	D6
Beşiri 4,165	J4
Beşni 16,313	H4
Beykoz 76,804	D5
Beyoğlu 230,532	D6
Beypazari 14,963	D2

(continued on following page)

Agriculture, Industry and Resources

DOMINANT LAND USE

- ☐ Cereals (chiefly wheat, barley), Livestock
- ☐ Cash Crops, Horticulture, Livestock
- ☐ Pasture Livestock
- ☐ Nomadic Livestock Herding
- ☐ Forests
- ☐ Nonagricultural Land

MAJOR MINERAL OCCURRENCES

Ab	Asbestos		Na	Salt
Al	Bauxite		O	Petroleum
C	Coal		P	Phosphates
Cr	Chromium		Pb	Lead
Cu	Copper		Py	Pyrites
Fe	Iron Ore		Sb	Antimony
Hg	Mercury		Zn	Zinc
Mg	Magnesium			

⚡ Water Power
▨ Major Industrial Areas

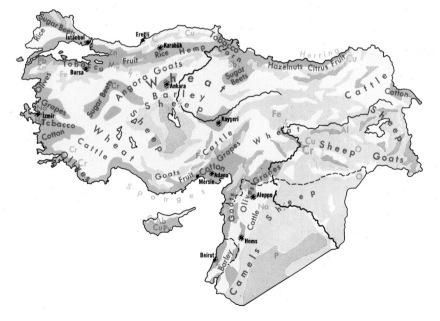

Çalköy 3.002	C3		Demirkent 4.204	E4		Erzincan 60.351	H3
Çamardı 2.419	E4		Demirköy 4.257	B2		Erzurum 162.973	J3
Çameli 2.502	C4		Denizli 106.902	C4		Eskimalatya 10.182	H3
Çamlıdere 4.386	E2		Derecik 4.188	H2		Eskipazar 2.865	D3
Çan 11.797	B6		Derik 13.292	J4		Eskişehir 259.952	D3
Çanakkale 30.788	B6		Deretmili 5.618	F2		Esme 7.828	C4
Çandır 6.986	F2		Develi 17.323	F3		Espiye 8.168	H2
Çankaya 895.005	E3		Devrek 9.164	D2		Eynesil 6.081	H2
Çankırı 28.512	E2		Devrekâni 4.014	E2		Eyüp 95.486	D6
Çapakçur 22.047	J3		Dicle 5.247	J3		Eziberder 3.631	H2
Çardak 4.232	C6		Didik 6.916	B3		Fatih 504.127	D6
Çarşamba 23.973	G2		Dinar 19.873	C4		Fatsa 19.758	G2
Çatak 2.366	K4		Dirmil 3.476	C4		Feke 5.576	F4
Çatalca 2.366	C2		Diyadin 5.094	K3		Fethiye 12.700	C4
Çatalzeytin 2.271	F1		Diyarbakır 169.535	H4		Fevzipaşa 5.495	G4
Çay 12.200	D3		Doğanbey 3.077	D4		Fındıklı 5.008	J2
Çaycuma 8.118	E2		Doğanhisar 9.487	D3		Finike 4.200	D4
Çayeli 13.480	J2		Doğanşehir 10.280	G3		Foça 4.829	B3
Çayıralan 8.071	F3		Döğer 3.478	D2		Gallipoli 13.466	C5
Çayırlı 4.580	J2		Doğubeyazıt 17.612	K3		Gaziantep 300.882	G4
Çekerek 3.796	F2		Domaniç 2.729	C3		Gazipaşa 6.696	E4
Çelikhan 5.066	H3		Dörtyol 19.390	F4		Gökçe 4.470	D6
Çemişkezek 3.048	H3		Dumlu 4.206	J3		Gölbaşı 33.110	G4
Çerkeş 3.780	E2		Durağan 3.259	F2		Gedis 10.649	C3
Çerkezköy 8.428	C2		Dursunbey 8.615	C3		Gelibolu (Gallipoli) 13.466	C5
Çermik 9.749	H3						

Çeşme 5.284	B3		Düzce 32.129	D2		Gemerek 5.769	G3
Çetinkaya 3.616	G3		Eceabat 3.642	B6		Gemlik 20.704	C3
Ceyhan 62.909	F4		Edirne 63.001	B2		Genç 7.671	J3
Ceylânpınar 20.171	H4		Edremit 26.110	B3		Genzin 4.925	J3
Çiçekdağı 3.203	F2		Eflâni 3.793	D3		Gerciş 4.393	J4
Çide 3.520	E1		Eğridir 9.799	D4		Gerede 8.259	E2
Çifteler 8.163	D3		Elazığ 131.415	H3		Gerger 2.773	H3
Çihanbeyli 10.079	E3		Elbistan 26.048	G3		Germecik 10.558	B4
Çıldır 2.260	K2		Eleşkirt 8.202	K3		Gerze 7.313	F1
Çimin 5.341	H3		Elmalı 10.184	C4		Gevaş 6.333	K3
Çine 11.308	B4		Emet 6.239	C3		Geyve 7.806	D2
Çivril 7.721	C4		Emirdağ 13.184	D3		Giresun 38.236	H2
Çizre 15.557	K4		Emirgazi 5.244	E4		Gökçe 4.470	D6
Çölemerik 11.735	K4		Enez 2.486	B2		Göksun 10.481	G3
Çorlu 40.134	C2		Erbaa 20.315	G2		Gölbaşı 15.103	G4
Çorum 64.652	F2		Erciş 22.351	K3		Gölcük 33.279	C2
Çubuk 23.351	E2		Erdek 8.685	B3		Göle 7.680	K2
Çukur 5.479	F3		Erdemli 19.936	E4		Gölhisar 7.095	C4
Çukurca 3.019	K4		Ereğli 45.992	D2		Gölköy 10.022	G3
Çumra 19.225	E3		Ereğli 50.354	E4		Gölmarmara 11.982	B3
Çüngüş 2.616	H3		Ergani 21.936	H3		Gölpazarı 5.002	D2
Daday 2.528	E1		Erkilet 3.924	F3		Gönen 16.091	B3
Darende 8.055	G3		Ermenak 13.464	E4		Gördes 7.909	C3
Dazkırı 3.912	D4		Eruh 5.340	K4		Gövce 8.079	C3
Delice 3.462	F2		Erzin 15.314	G4		Göynücek 2.600	F2
Demirci 15.016	C3					Göynük 2.519	D2

Güdül 4.746	E2
Gülnar 6.188	E4
Gülşehir 6.188	F3
Gümüş 3.066	F2
Gümüşhacıköy 12.789	F2
Gümüşhane 11.166	H2
Güney 7.154	C4
Gürün 9.138	G3
Hacıbektaş 5.032	F3
Hacılar 15.622	F3
Hadim 10.467	E4
Hafik 5.398	G3
Hakkâri (Çölemerik) 11.735	K4
Halfeti 3.689	G4
Hamur 2.267	K3
Hanak 2.581	K2
Hani 7.559	H3
Harput 3.231	H3
Haruniye 12.837	G4
Hassa 10.926	G4
Hatay (Antakya) 77.518	G4
Havran 7.552	B3
Havsa 4.298	B2
Havza 15.341	F2
Haymana 6.123	E3

Hayrabolu 12.331	B2
Hazro 4.896	J3
Hekimhan 11.818	G3
Hendek 15.291	D2
Hilvan 6.473	H4
Hinis 10.226	J3
Hisarönü 4.485	E2
Hizan 2.545	K3
Hopa 9.089	J2
Horasan 7.724	K2
Hozat 5.796	H3
İçel (Mersin) 152.236	F4
İdil 4.862	J4
İğdir 29.542	K2
İliğin 6.624	K3
İlğin 11.830	D3
İlica 8.947	J3
İmranli 5.667	H2
İncesu 7.089	F3
İnebolu 6.824	E2
İnegöl 37.805	C2
İnönü 4.152	D3
İpsala 6.829	B2
İpsile 2.328	G2
İskenderun 107.437	G4
İskilip 16.588	F2
İslahiye 20.683	G4
Isparta 62.870	J3
İspir 3.929	J2
İstanbul 2.547.364	D6
İvrindi 3.730	B3
İzmir 636.834	B3
İzmit 165.483	C2
İznik 11.614	C2
Kadıköy 354.957	D6
Kadınhanı 11.802	E3
Kadirli 34.779	F4
Kağıthane 164.448	D6
Kağızman 11.517	K2
Kâhta 15.602	H4
Kalan 11.637	H3
Kale 3.399	C4
Kalecik 4.707	E2
Kaman 16.516	E3
Kandıra 10.187	D2
Kangal 5.937	G3
Karabük 69.182	E2
Karacabey 21.648	C3
Karahallı 5.539	C3
Karaisalı 2.316	F4
Karakoçan 5.604	H3
Karaköse (Ağrı) 35.284	K3

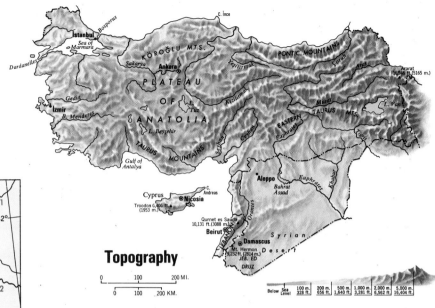

Topography

0   100   200 MI.

0   100   200 KM.

| Below Sea Level | 100 m. 328 ft. | 200 m. 656 ft. | 500 m. 1,640 ft. | 1,000 m. 3,281 ft. | 2,000 m. 6,562 ft. | 5,000 m. 16,404 ft. |

Karaman 43.759	E4
Karamanli 5.904	C4
Karapinar 19.589	E4
Karasi 11.600	D2
Karataş 5.598	F4
Karayaka 4.242	G2
Karayazi 3.595	J3
Kargı 5.021	F2
Karlıova 3.631	J3
Kars 54.892	K2
Karşıyaka 171.600	B3
Kartal 53.073	D6
Kaş 2.493	C4
Kastamonu 29.993	F2
Kavak, Çanakkale 3.932	C5
Kavak, Samsun 3.964	G2
Kayseri 207.037	F3
Kazanlı 4.461	F4
Kazımkarabekir 4.086	E4
Keban 5.800	H3
Keçiborlu 7.096	C3
Keles 2.423	C3
Kelkit 6.928	H2
Kemah 3.038	H3
Kemaliye 3.014	H3
Kemalpaşa 7.572	J2
Kemerburgaz 7.234	D5
Kemithisar 6.205	F4
Kepsut 4.700	C3
Keşan 27.088	B2
Keşap 5.264	H2
Keskin 10.540	E3
Kiği 5.598	J3
Kilimli 26.649	D2
Kilis 54.055	G4
Kınık 11.785	B3
Kiraz 5.284	C3
Kırıkhan 38.118	G4
Kırıkkale 137.874	E3
Kırkağaç 15.078	B3
Kırklareli 33.265	B2
Kırşehir 41.415	F3
Kızılcahamam 7.050	E2
Kızılhisar 11.011	C3
Kızıltepe 21.531	J4
Kızılviran 3.260	J3
Kocaeli (İzmit) 165.483	D2
Koçarli 5.182	B4
Konya 246.727	E4
Korkuteli 10.334	C4
Köyceğiz 4.612	C4
Koyulhisar 3.861	G2
Kozaklı 6.200	F3
Kozan 32.045	F4
Kozlu 27.322	D2
Kozluk 6.197	J3
Küçükçekmece 56.411	D6
Kula 10.807	C3
Kula 4.474	J3
Kulu 11.707	E3
Kumkale 1.752	B6
Kumluca 7.704	C4
Kurşunlu 6.562	E2
Kurtalan 7.001	J3
Kuşadası 10.269	B4
Kütahya 82.442	C3
Kuyucak 6.039	C4
Lâdik 6.785	G2
Lâpseki 3.727	C6
Lice 8.625	J3
Lüleburgaz 32.401	C2
Maden 15.151	H3
Mağara 4.314	C3
Mahmudiye 5.240	D3
Malatya 154.505	H4
Malazgirt 13.094	J3
Malkara 14.399	B2
Maltepe 66.343	D6
Manavgat 10.804	D4
Manisa 78.114	B3
Manyas 4.410	B3
Maraş (Kahramanmaraş) 135.782	G4
Mardin 36.629	J4
Marmaris 5.596	C4
Mazgirt 3.141	H3
Mazıdağı 4.842	J4
Meçitözü 6.066	F2
Menemen 18.464	B3
Mengen 2.459	D2
Menç 3.922	B2
Mersin 152.236	F4
Merzifon 30.801	F2
Mesudiye 4.294	F4
Midyat 16.905	J4
Midye 2.003	C2
Mihalıççık 4.004	D3
Milâs 17.929	B4
Mucur 9.398	F3
Mudanya 8.399	C2
Mudurnu 3.905	D2

Muğla 24.178	C4
Muradiye 6.334	K3
Muş 27.761	J3
Mustafakemalpaşa 27.706	C3
Mut 11.466	E4
Mutki 2.815	J3
Muttalip 3.917	D3
Nallıhan 7.883	D2
Narman 4.607	J2
Nazilli 52.176	C4
Nevşehir 30.203	F3
Niğde 31.844	F3
Niksar 19.156	G2
Nizip 36.190	G4
Nurhak 5.330	G4
Nusaybin 23.684	J4
Ödemiş 37.364	C3
Of 10.376	J2
Oğuzeli 7.194	G4
Oltu 10.093	J2
Ömerli 4.738	J4
Ordu 47.481	G2
Orhaneli 3.335	C3
Orhangazi 12.181	C2
Orta 3.596	E2
Ortaca 8.604	C4
Ortakaravıran 3.856	E4
Ortaköy, Çorum 2.657	F2
Ortaköy, Niğde 6.371	F3
Osmancık 11.921	F2
Osmaneli 4.789	D2
Osmaniye 61.581	F4
Ovacık, Tunceli 2.248	H3
Özalp 4.188	K3
Palu 5.489	H3
Pasinler 14.267	J2
Patnos 15.918	K3
Pazar, Rize 8.856	J2
Pazar, Tokat 4.412	G3
Pazarcık 15.943	G4
Pazaryeri 5.633	C2
Pera (Beyoğlu) 230.532	D6
Perşembe 6.701	G2
Pertek 4.176	H3
Pervari 4.126	K4
Pınarbaşı 9.503	G3
Pınarhisar 10.523	B2
Polatlı 35.267	E3
Posof 2.209	J2
Pozantı 5.408	F4
Pülümür 3.442	H3
Puturge 4.878	H3
Refahiye 6.570	H3
Reşadiye 9.022	G2
Reyhanlı 25.749	G4
Rize 36.044	J2
Sabanözü 3.442	E2
Safranbolu 14.793	E2
Şaimbeyli 3.622	G4
Sakarya (Adapazarı) 114.130	D2
Salihli 45.514	C3
Samandağ 22.540	F4
Samsat 2.083	H4
Samsun 168.478	F2
Sandıklı 13.181	D3
Sapanca 9.040	D2
Saraçhane 3.919	C3
Saraköy 10.513	C4
Sarayönü 8.946	E3
Sarıgöl 6.979	C3
Sarıkamış 21.262	K2
Sarıkaya 5.160	F3
Sarıköy 4.695	B2
Sarıoğlan 3.245	F3
Sarıyer 79.329	D5
Şarkî 3.591	G3
Şarkikaraağaç 4.772	D3
Şarkışla 12.763	G3
Şarköy 5.396	B2
Sason 3.211	J3
Savaştepe 7.179	B3
Şavşat 3.078	K2
Şavur 4.983	J4
Seben 2.471	D2
Şebinkarahisar 10.214	H2
Şefaatli 6.769	F3
Şehitler 6.484	B3
Selçuk 12.251	B3
Selendi 4.457	C3
Selim 3.569	K2
Selimiye 2.989	B4
Senirkent 8.247	D3
Şenkaya 3.190	K2
Şereflikoçhisar 20.523	E3
Serik 14.161	D4
Seydişehir 25.651	D3
Seyitgazi 2.819	D3
Siirt 35.654	J3
Şile 4.062	D2
Silifke 19.257	E4
Silivri 8.525	C2
Silopi 4.460	K4

Silvan 29.599	J3
Simav 11.601	C3
Sincanlı 3.847	D3
Sindirgi 7.818	C3
Sinop 16.098	F2
Şiran 5.048	H2
Şırnak 10.587	K4
Şirvan 5.166	K3
Sivas 149.201	G3
Sivaslı 4.394	C3
Siverek 40.990	H4
Sivrihisar 8.713	D3
Smyrna (İzmir) 636.834	B3
Söğüt 5.829	D3
Söke 35.407	B4
Solhan 7.014	J3
Soma 23.713	B3
Sorgun 14.081	F3
Suşehri 8.154	H2
Sulakyurt 4.311	E2
Sultandağı 4.017	D3
Sultanhani 5.112	E3
Suluova 21.278	F2
Sungurlu 21.641	F2
Sürmene 8.096	J2
Sürüç 20.395	H4
Suşehri 10.863	H2
Susurluk 14.000	C3
Susuz 5.006	K2
Sütçüler 2.721	D4
Tarsus 102.186	F4
Taşkent 7.098	E4
Taşlıçay 8.146	K3
Taşoya 6.516	H4
Tatvan 29.271	C4
Tavas 9.728	C4
Tavşanlı 19.575	C3
Tefenni 4.280	C4
Tekirdağ 41.257	B2
Tercan 6.068	H3
Terme 15.660	G2
Tire 30.694	B3
Tirebolu 7.385	H2
Tokat 48.588	G2
Tomarza 6.448	F3
Tömük 7.660	F4
Tonya 10.544	H2
Torbalı 17.237	B3
Tortum 4.110	J2
Torul 3.221	H2
Tosya 17.515	F2
Trabzon 97.210	H2
Trabzon (Trabzon) 97.210	H2
Tunceli (Kalan) 11.637	H3
Turgutlu 47.009	B3
Turhal 39.170	G2
Türkeli 2.194	F2
Türkoğlu 9.207	G4
Tutak 4.325	K3
Tuzluca 5.209	K3
Tuzlukçu 4.613	D3
Ula 5.117	C4
Ulaş 2.449	G3
Ulubey 4.214	C3
Uluborlu 10.016	C3
Uludere 4.050	K4
Ulukışla 6.336	F4
Umurbey 2.754	C6
Ünye 23.366	G2
Urfa 132.934	H4
Ürgüp 6.758	F3
Urla 13.903	B3
Uşak 58.578	C3
Yaprak 3.020	G4
Yatağan 4.903	C4
Yayladağı 4.471	F5
Yenice, Çanakkale 4.004	B3
Yenice, İçel 4.106	F4
Yenice, Zonguldak 5.791	E2
Yenicekoba 5.740	E3
Yenikoy, İstanbul	D6
Yenimahalle 198.643	D3
Yenişehir 15.188	C2
Yerküy 19.927	F3
Yeşilköy	D6
Yeşilhisar 10.409	F3
Yeşilköy	B3
Yeşilova, Burdur 3.685	C4
Yeşilova, Niğde 5.237	E3

Yeşilyurt 7.451	H3
Yildizeli 7.043	G3
Yozgat 32.501	F3
Yüksekova 7.329	L4
Yumurtalık 2.442	F4
Yunak 6.187	D3
Yusufeli 3.050	J2
Zara 10.376	G3
Zeytinburnu 123.548	D6
Zeytindağ 3.517	B3
Zile 32.157	F3
Zivarik 2.703	E3
Zonguldak 90.221	D2

OTHER FEATURES

Abydos (ruins)	B6
Acı (lake)	C4
Adalar (isl.)	D6
Aegean (sea)	A3
Ağrı, Büyük (Ararat) (mt.)	L3
Akdağ (mt.)	C4
Aladağ (mt.)	F4
Alexandretta (gulf)	F4
Amanos (mts.)	G4
Anamur (cape)	E5
Anatolia (reg.)	D3
Ankara (riv.)	D3
Antalya (gulf)	D4
Anti-Taurus (mts.)	G3
Araks (riv.)	K2
Ararat (mt.)	L3
Arpa (riv.)	K2
Baba (cape)	A3
Batı Fırat (riv.)	H3
Beyşehir (lake)	D4
Black (sea)	E1
Bosporus (str.)	D6
Boccaada (isl.)	A3
Burgaz (isl.)	D6
Büyük Ağrı (Ararat) (mt.)	L3
Çanakkale Boğazı (Dardanelles) (str.)	B6
Çandarlı (gulf)	B3
Çanik (mts.)	G2
Ceyhan (riv.)	F4
Cilo Dağı (mt.)	K4
Dardanelles (str.)	B6
Dicle (riv.)	J4
Eastern Taurus (mts.)	J3
Ephesus (ruins)	B3
Erciyas Dağı (mt.)	F3
Ergene (riv.)	B2
Euphrates (Fırat) (riv.)	G4
Fırat (riv.)	G4
Gediz (riv.)	C4
Gelidonya (cape)	D4
Gökçeada (isl.)	A2
Göksu (riv.)	E4
Helles (cape)	B6
Heybeli (isl.)	D6
İlium (ruins)	B6
İmroz (Gökçeada) (isl.)	A2
İnce (cape)	F1
İstranca (mts.)	B2
Kaçkar Dağı (mt.)	J2
Karadeniz Boğazı (Bosporus) (str.)	C2
Karasu-Aras (mts.)	J3
Kerme (gulf)	B4
Keşiş Tepesi (mt.)	H3
Kızılırmak (riv.)	F2
Koca (riv.)	C2
Köroğlu (mts.)	D2
Küre (mts.)	E2
Mandalya (gulf)	B4
Marmara (isl.)	B2
Marmara (sea)	C2
Menderes, Büyük (riv.)	C4
Menç (riv.)	B2
Murat (riv.)	H3
Pontic (mts.)	H2
Porsuk (riv.)	D3
Prinkipo (Adalar) (isl.)	D6
Sakarya (riv.)	D2
Saros (gulf)	B2
Seyhan (riv.)	F4
Sinop (cape)	F1
Sultan (mts.)	D3
Süphan Dağı (mt.)	J3
Taurus (mts.)	E4
Tigris (Dicle) (riv.)	J4
Troy (İlium) (ruins)	B6
Tuz (lake)	E3
Van (lake)	K3
Yeşilırmak (riv.)	G2

• City and suburbs

Turkey, Syria, Lebanon and Cyprus

© Copyright HAMMOND INCORPORATED, Maplewood, N.J.

SCALE OF MILES

0 25 50 75 100 125 150

SCALE OF KILOMETERS

0 25 50 75 100 125 150

Capitals of Countries .... ☆   Capitals of Provinces .... △

Provincial Boundaries _____

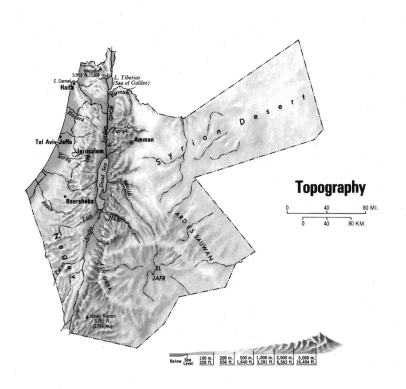

Topography

ISRAEL

DISTRICTS

Central 572,300 ....B3
Haifa 480,600 ....C2
Jerusalem 338,600 ....B4
Northern 473,700 ....C2
Southern 351,300 ....B5
Tel Aviv 905,100 ....B3

CITIES and TOWNS

Acre 34,400 ....C2
Afiqim 1,243 ....D2
'Afula 17,400 ....C2
Ahuzzam 407 ....B4
Akko (Acre) 34,400 ....C2
Arad 5,400 ....C5
'Arrabe 6,000 ....C2
Ashdod 40,500 ....B4
Ashdot Yaa'qov 1,197 ....D2
Ashqelon 43,100 ....A4
Atlit 1,516 ....C2
Avihayil 579 ....B3
Bat Shelomo 218 ....B2
Bat Yam 124,100 ....B3
Be'eri 390 ....A5
Be'er Menuha D5
Beersheba (Be'er
  Sheva) 101,000 ....B5
Be'er Tuveya 602 ....B4
Beit Guvrin B4
Bene Beraq 74,100 ....B3
Bet Qama 228 ....B4
Bet She'an 11,300 ....D3
Bet Shemesh 10,100 ....B4
Binyamina 2,701 ....B2
Carmiel C2
Dafna 577 ....D1
Daliyat al-Karmel 6,200 ....B2
Dan 498 ....D1
Dimona 23,700 ....D4
Dor 195 ....B2
E'in Gedi C5
E'in Harod 1,372 ....C2
Elat D6
Elath (Elat) 12,800 ....D6
El 'Auja D5
Elyakim 568 ....C2
Elyashiv 435 ....B3
Even Yehuda 3,464 ....B3
Gal'on 356 ....B4
Gat 430 ....B4
Gedera 5,400 ....B4
Gerofit D5
Gesher 360 ....C2
Gesher Haziv 238 ....C1
Gevara'm 283 ....B4
Gilat 561 ....B5
Ginnosar 473 ....D2
Giv'atayim 48,500 ....B3
Giva't Brenner 1,505 ....B4
Giv'at Hayyim 1,360 ....B3
Habonim 189 ....B2
Hadera 31,900 ....B3
Haifa 227,800 ....B2
Haifa* 367,400 ....B2
Hatseva D5
Hazerim 127 ....B5

Hazor Hagelilit D2
Helez 466 ....B4
Herzeliyya 41,200 ....B3
Hod Hasharon 13,500 ....B3
Hodiyya 400 ....B4
Holon 121,200 ....B3
Iksal 2,156 ....C2
Jerusalem (cap.) 376,000 ....C4
Jish 1,498 ....C1
Kafar Kanna 5,200 ....C2
Kafr Yasif 2,975 ....C1
Karkur-Pardes Hanna 13,600 ....C2
Kefar Blum 565 ....D1
Kefar Gila'di 701 ....C1
Kefar Ruppin 306 ....D3
Kefar Sava 26,500 ....B3
Kefar Vitkin 808 ....B3
Kefar Zekhariya 420 ....B4
Kinneret 909 ....D2
Lod (Lydda) 30,500 ....B4
Lydda 30,500 ....B4
Magen 149 ....A5
Maa'lot-Tarshiha C1
Malkiya D1
Mash 'Abbe Sade 238 ....B6
Mavqi'm 177 ....B4
Megiddo C2
Metula 261 ....D1
Migdal 688 ....C2
Migdal Ha E'meq C2
Mikhmoret 608 ....B3
Mishmar Hanegev 336 ....B5
Mishmar Hayarden D1
Mivtahim 398 ....A5
Mizpe Ramon 331 ....C5
Moza Ilit 219 ....C4
Mughar 4,010 ....C2
Muqeible 459 ....C2
Nahariyya 24,000 ....C1
Nazareth 33,300 ....C2
Nazerat I'lit C2
Negba 453 ....B4
Nes Ziyyona 11,700 ....B4
Netanya 70,700 ....B3
Netivot B5
Nevatim 436 ....B5
Newe Yam 211 ....B2
Newe Zohar C5
Nir Yitzhaq 209 ....A5
Nizzanim 479 ....B4
Ofaqim B5
Omer B5
Oron C6
Or Yehuda B3
Pardes Hanna-Karkur 13,600 ....B2
Peduyim 361 ....B5
Petah Tiqwa 112,000 ....B3
Qadima 2,937 ....B3
Qalansuwa B3
Qedma 157 ....B4
Qiryat Atta C2
Qiryat Bialik 18,000 ....C2
Qiryat Gat 19,200 ....B4
Qiryat Mal'akhi B4
Qiryat Motzkin 17,600 ....C2
Qiryat Shemona 15,200 ....C1
Qiryat Tivo'n 9,800 ....C2
Qiryat Yam 19,800 ....C2
Raa'nana 14,900 ....B3
Ramat Gan 120,900 ....B3

Ramat Hasharon 20,100 ....B3
Rame 2,986 ....C1
Ramla 34,100 ....B4
Rehovot 39,200 ....B4
Rei'm 155 ....A5
Revadim 175 ....B4
Revivim 258 ....B5
Rishon Le Ziyyon 51,900 ....B4
Rosh Ha 'Ayin B3
Rosh Pinna 700 ....D2
Ruhama 497 ....B4
Saa'd 418 ....A5
Safad (Zefat) 13,600 ....C2
Sakhnin 8,400 ....C2
Sede Boger D5
Sederot B4
Sedom C5
Sedot Yam 511 ....B3
Shave Ziyyon 269 ....C1
Shefara'm 11,800 ....C2
Shefayim 614 ....B3
Shoval 393 ....B5
Tayibe 11,700 ....B3
Tel Aviv-Jaffa 343,300 ....B3
Tel Aviv-Jaffa* 1,219,900 ....B3
Tiberias 23,800 ....C2
Tirat Hakarmel 14,400 ....B2
Tirat Zevi 353 ....D3
Tur'an 2,304 ....C2
Umm el Fahm 13,300 ....C2
Urim 203 ....A5
Uzza 487 ....B4
Yad Mordekhai 416 ....A4
Yagur 1,266 ....C2
Yahav D5
Yavne 10,100 ....B4
Yavne'el 1,580 ....D2
Yehud 8,900 ....B3
Yeroham 5,800 ....B5
Yesodot 293 ....B4
Yesud Hamaa'la 428 ....D1
Yiftah D1
Yirka 2,715 ....C1
Yotvata D6
Zavdi'el 396 ....B4
Ze'elim 148 ....A5
Zefat 13,600 ....C2
Zikhron Yaa'qov 6,500 ....B2
Zippori 241 ....C2

OTHER FEATURES

Aqaba (gulf) D6
'Araba, Wadi (valley) D5
Besor (dry riv.) B5
Carmel (cape) B2
Carmel (mt.) C2
Dead (sea) C4
Galilee, Sea of (Tiberias)
  (lake) D2
Galilee (reg.) C2
Gerar (dry riv.) B5
Hadera (dry riv.) B3
Haniqra, Rosh (cape) C1
Jordan (riv.) C1
Judaea (reg.) B4
Lakhish (dry riv.) B4
Meiron (mt.) C1
Negev (reg.) D5

Archaeological Sites in Palestine

■ Major Excavations

Miles 0 10 20 30

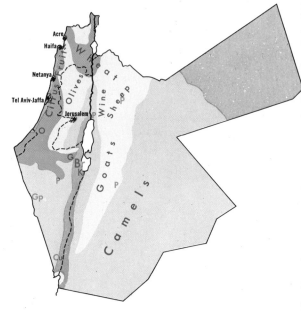

Agriculture, Industry and Resources

DOMINANT LAND USE

☐ Cereals, Livestock

■ Cash Crops, Horticulture

☐ Nomadic Livestock Herding

☐ Nonagricultural Land

MAJOR MINERAL OCCURRENCES

Br Bromine   K Potash

Cu Copper   O Petroleum

G Natural Gas   P Phosphates

Gp Gypsum

▨ Major Industrial Areas

© Copyright HAMMOND INCORPORATED

ISRAEL

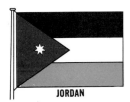

JORDAN

ISRAEL

AREA 7,847 sq. mi. (20,324 sq. km.)
POPULATION 3,878,000
CAPITAL Jerusalem
LARGEST CITY Tel Aviv-Jaffa
HIGHEST POINT Meiran 3,963 ft.
(1,208 m.)
MONETARY UNIT shekel
MAJOR LANGUAGES Hebrew, Arabic
MAJOR RELIGIONS Judaism, Islam,
Christianity

JORDAN

AREA 35,000 sq. mi.
(90,650 sq. km.)
POPULATION 2,152,273
CAPITAL Amman
LARGEST CITY Amman
HIGHEST POINT Jeb. Ramm 5,755 ft.
(1,754 m.)
MONETARY UNIT Jordanian dinar
MAJOR LANGUAGE Arabic
MAJOR RELIGION Islam

IRAN

INTERNAL DIVISIONS

Azerbaijan, East (prov.) 3,194,543 ....E1
Azerbaijan, West (prov.) 1,404,875 ....D1
Bakhtaran (prov.) 1,016,199 ....E3
Bakhtiari (governorate) 394,300 ....F4
Boyer Ahmediyeh and Kohkiluyeh (governorate) 244,750 ....G5
Bushehr 345,427 ....G6
Central (Markazi) (prov.) 6,921,283 ....G3
Esfahan (Isfahan) (prov.) 1,974,938 ....H4
Fars (prov.) 2,020,947 ....H6
Gilan (prov.) 1,577,800 ....F2
Hamadan (governorate) 1,086,512 ....F3
Hormozgan (prov.) 463,419 ....J7
Ilam (governorate) 244,222 ....F4
Kerman (prov.) 1,088,045 ....K6
Khorasan (prov.) 3,266,650 ....K3
Khuzestan (prov.) 2,176,612 ....F5
Kordestan (Kurdistan) (prov.) 781,889 ....E3
Lorestan (Luristan) (governorate) 924,848 ....F4
Mazandaran (prov.) 2,384,226 ....H2
Semnan (governorate) 485,875 ....J3
Sistan and Baluchestan (prov.) 659,297 ....M6
Yazd (governorate) 356,218 ....J5
Zanjan (governorate) 579,000 ....F2

CITIES and TOWNS

Abadan 296,081 ....F5
Abadeh 16,000 ....H5
Abarqu 8,000 ....H5
Abhar 24,000 ....F2
Abu Jari 24,195 ....E1
Ahar 24,000 ....E1
Amol 68,782 ....H2
Anarak 2,038 ....H4
Andimeshk 16,000 ....F4
Aradan 8,978 ....H3
Arak 114,507 ....F3
Ardabil 147,404 ....F1
Ardestan 5,868 ....H4
Asterabad (Gorgan) 88,348 ....J2
Babol 67,790 ....H2
Babol Sar 7,237 ....H2
Baft 6,000 ....K6
Bakhtaran 290,861 ....E3
Bam 22,000 ....L6
Bandar 'Abbas 89,103 ....J7
Bandar-e Anzali (Enzeli) 55,978 ....F2
Bandar-e Deylam 3,691 ....G5
Bandar-e Khomeyni 6,000 ....G5
Bandar-e Lengeh 4,920 ....J7
Bandar-e Mas hur 17,000 ....F5
Bandar-e Rig 1,889 ....G6
Bandar-e Torkeman 13,000 ....H2
Bandar Shahpur 6,000 ....F5
Bastak 2,473 ....J7
Bastam 3,296 ....J2
Behbehan 39,874 ....G5
Behshahr 26,032 ....H2

Bejestan 3,823 ....K3
Bijar 12,000 ....E3
Birjand 25,854 ....L4
Bojnurd 31,248 ....K2
Borazjan 20,000 ....G6
Bostan 4,619 ....F4
Bowkan 9,000 ....E2
Bushehr (Bushire) 57,681 ....G6
Chalus 15,000 ....G2
Damavand 5,319 ....H3
Damghan 13,000 ....J3
Darab 13,000 ....J6
Daran 4,609 ....G4
Darreh Gaz 21,000 ....L2
Dasht-e Azadegan 21,000 ....F5
Dehkhvaregan 6,000 ....D2
Delijan 6,000 ....G3
Dezful 110,287 ....F4
Duzdab (Zahedan) 92,628 ....M6
Emamshahr 30,767 ....J2
Enzeli 55,978 ....F2
Esfahan (Isfahan) 671,820 ....G4
Eslamabad 12,000 ....E3
Estahbanat 18,187 ....H6
Evaz 6,064 ....J7
Ezna 5,000 ....F4
Fahrej (Iranshahr) 5,000 ....M7
Fariman 8,000 ....L3
Farrashband 3,532 ....H6
Fasa 19,000 ....H6
Ferdows 11,000 ....L3
Firuzabad 8,718 ....H6
Firuzkuh 6,000 ....H3
Fowman 9,000 ....F2
Gach Saran G5

Ganaveh 9,000 ....G6
Garmsar 4,723 ....H3
Gavater M8
Ghaemshahr 63,289 ....H2
Golpayegan 20,515 ....G4
Golshan (Tabas) 10,000 ....L4
Gomishan 6,000 ....J2
Gonabad 8,000 ....L3
Gonbad-e Kavus 59,868 ....J2
Gonbadli 531 ....M2
Gorgan (Gurgan) 88,348 ....J2
Haft Gel 10,000 ....F5
Hamadan 155,846 ....F3
Hashtgar 5,000 ....G3
Hormoz 2,569 ....J7
Huzgan 4,172 ....J6
Ilam 15,000 ....E4
Iranshahr 5,000 ....M7
Isfahan 671,825 ....G4
Jahrom 38,236 ....H6
Jajarm 3,641 ....K2
Jask 1,078 ....K8
Kalaleh 4,043 ....J2
Kangan 2,682 ....G7
Kangavar 9,414 ....F3
Kashan 84,545 ....G3
Kashmar 17,000 ....L3
Kazerun 51,309 ....G6
Kazvin (Qazvin) 138,527 ....F2
Kerman 140,309 ....K5
Khaf 5,000 ....L3
Khalkhal 5,422 ....F2
Khash 7,439 ....M6
Khiyav 9,000 ....F1
Khoman 3,054 ....F2
Khomeinishar 46,836 ....G4

Khorramabad 104,928 ....F4
Khorramshahr 146,709 ....F5
Khvaf 5,000 ....L3
Khvonsar 10,947 ....G4
Khvor 2,912 ....J4
Khvoy (Khoi) 70,040 ....D1
Kord Kuy 9,855 ....J2
Lahijan 25,725 ....G2
Lar 22,000 ....J7
Mahabad 28,610 ....D2
Mahallat 12,000 ....G4
Mahan 8,000 ....K6
Maku 7,000 ....D1
Malamir (Izeh) 1,983 ....F5
Malayer 28,434 ....F3
Maragheh 60,820 ....E2
Marand 24,000 ....D1
Marv Dasht 25,498 ....H6
Mashhad (Meshed) 670,180 ....L2
Masjed Soleyman 77,161 ....F5
Medishahr 9,000 ....H3
Mehran 664 ....E4
Meshed 670,180 ....L2
Meshed-i-Sar (Babol) 7,000 ....H2
Meybod 15,000 ....J4
Miandowab 19,000 ....E2
Mianeh 28,447 ....E2
Minab 7,000 ....K7
Mirjaveh 11,000 ....N6
Naft-e Shah 3,043 ....D4
Nahavand 24,000 ....F3
Na'in 5,925 ....H4
Nasratabad (Zabol) 20,000 ....M5
Natanz 4,370 ....J6
Neyriz 16,114 ....J6
Neyshabur 59,101 ....L2

Nishapur (Neyshabur) 59,101 ....L2
Nosratabad 20,000 ....L6
Now Shahr 8,000 ....G2
Orumiyeh (Urmia) 163,991 ....D1
Oshnoviyeh 5,000 ....D2
Pahlevi (Enzeli) 55,978 ....F2
Pazanan 81 ....F5
Qasr-e Shirin 15,094 ....E3
Qayen 6,000 ....L4
Qom (Qom) 246,831 ....G3
Qorveh 2,929 ....F3
Quchan 29,133 ....L2
Qum 246,831 ....G3
Rafsanjan 21,000 ....K5
Ramhormoz 9,000 ....F5
Rasht 187,203 ....F2
Ravar 5,074 ....K5
Resht (Rasht) 187,203 ....F2
Rey 102,825 ....G3
Reza'iyeh (Urmia) 163,991 ....D1
Rigan 8,255 ....L6
Rud Sar 7,460 ....G2
Sabzevar 69,174 ....K2
Sabzvaran 7,000 ....K6
Saeendey 4,195 ....E2
Sai' dabad 20,000 ....J2
Sakht-Sar 12,000 ....G2
Salmas 13,161 ....D1
Sanandaj 95,834 ....E3
Saqqez 17,000 ....E2
Sarab 16,000 ....E1
Sarakhs 3,461 ....N2
Sari 70,936 ....H2
Savanat (Estahbanat) 18,187 ....G3
Saveh 17,565 ....G3
Semnan 31,058 ....H3

Shadegan 6,000 ....F5
Shahdad 2,777 ....K6
Shahistan (Saravan) 4,012 ....N7
Shahreza 34,220 ....G4
Shahrud (Emamshahr) 30,767 ....J2
Sharafkhaneh 1,260 ....D1
Shiraz 416,408 ....H6
Shirvan 11,000 ....K2
Shush 1,433 ....F5
Shushtar 24,000 ....F5
Sinneh (Sanandaj) 95,834 ....E3
Sirjan (Sa'idabad) 20,000 ....K5
Sivand 1,811 ....H5
Songor 10,433 ....E3
Sufian 2,914 ....D1
Sultanabad (Kashmar) 17,000 ....L3
Tabas 10,000 ....L4
Tabriz 598,576 ....E1
Taft 7,000 ....J5
Tajrish 157,486 ....G3
Takestan 13,485 ....F2
Tehran (cap.) 4,496,159 ....G3
Torbat-e Heydariyeh 30,106 ....L3
Torbat-e Jam 13,000 ....M3
Tun (Ferdows) 11,000 ....L4
Turbat-i-Shaikh Jam 13,000 ....M3
Tuysarkan 12,000 ....F3
Urmia 163,991 ....D1
Varamin 11,183 ....G3
Yazd (Yezd) 135,978 ....J5
Yazd-e Khvasat 3,544 ....H5
Zabedan 92,628 ....M6
Zabol 20,000 ....M5
Zanjan 99,967 ....F2
Zarand 5,000 ....K6
Zarqam 7,000 ....H6
Zenjan (Zanjan) 99,967 ....F2

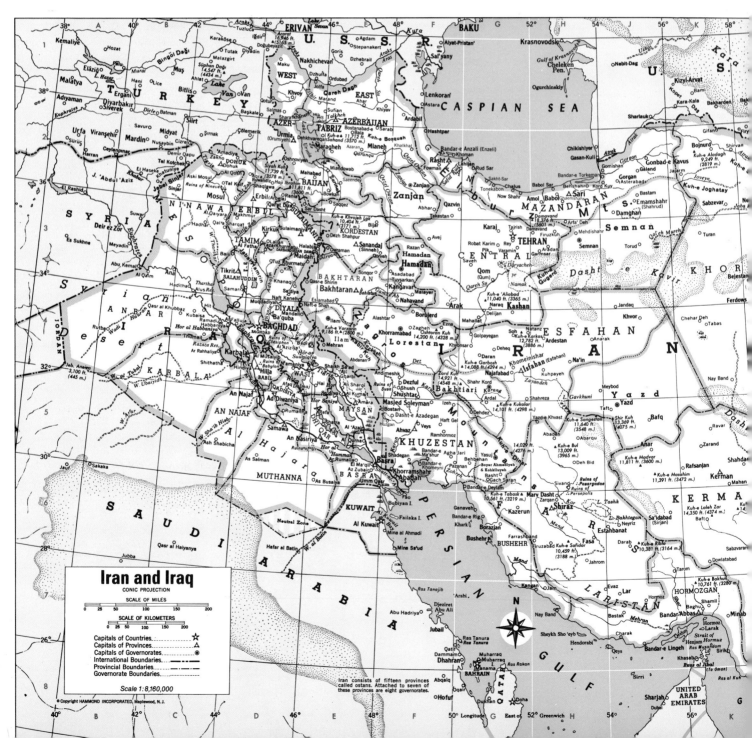

Iran and Iraq

CONIC PROJECTION

SCALE OF MILES
0   25   50   100   150   200

SCALE OF KILOMETERS
0   25 50   100   150   200

Capitals of Countries ....★
Capitals of Provinces ....△
Capitals of Governorates ....◉
International Boundaries ....
Provincial Boundaries ....
Governorate Boundaries ....

Scale 1:8,160,000

Iran consists of fifteen provinces called ostans. Attached to seven of these provinces are eight governorates.

OTHER FEATURES

Aji Chai (riv.)	E1
A'rabi (isl.)	G7
Araks (Aras) (riv.)	E1
Atrak (Atrek) (riv.)	J2
Bakhtegan (lake)	J6
Baluchistan (reg.)	M7
Bampur (riv.)	M7
Behistun (ruins)	E3
Caspian (sea)	G1
Damavand (Demavend) (mt.)	H3
Dez (riv.)	F4
Elburz (mts.)	G2
Farsi (isl.)	G7
Gorgan (riv.)	J2
Kanun (riv.)	F5
Karkheh (riv.)	E4
Kashaf Rud (riv.)	M2
Khark (Kharg) (isl.)	G6
Kuh (cape)	K8
Kurang (riv.)	G4
Laristan (reg.)	J7
Makran (reg.)	M8
Mand Rud (riv.)	G6
Mehran (riv.)	J7
Namaksar (lake)	M4
Nezwar (mt.)	H3
Oman (gulf)	M8
Pasargadae (ruins)	H5
Persepolis (ruins)	H6
Persian (gulf)	F6
Qareh (riv.)	E1
Qareh Su (riv.)	G3
Qeshm (isl.)	J7
Qezel Owzam (riv.)	F2
Safid Rud (riv.)	F2
Shaikh Shua'ib (isl.)	H7
Shelagh (riv.)	M5
Shirvan (riv.)	E3
Shur (riv.)	J7
Siah Kuh (mt.)	L3
Silup (riv.)	M8
Susa (ruins)	F4
Talab (riv.)	N6
Tashk (lake)	J6
Urmia (lake)	D2
Zagros (mts.)	E4
Zarineh (riv.)	E2
Zilbir (riv.)	D1
Zohreh (riv.)	F5

IRAQ
GOVERNORATES

Anbar	B4
An Najaf	C5
Babil	D4
Baghdad	D4
Basra	E5
Dhi Qar	E5
Diyala	D3
Dohuk	C2
Erbil	D2
Karbala	B4
Maysan	E4
Muthanna	D5
Ninawa	B3
Qadisiya	D4
Salahuddin	D3
Sulaimaniya	D3
Tamin	D3
Wasit	D4

CITIES and TOWNS

Ad Diwaniya 60,553	D5
A'faq 5,390	D4
Al A'ziziya 7,450	D4
Al Falluja 38,072	C4
Al Fathat 15,329	D4
A'li Gharbi 15,456	E4
A'li Sharqi 8,398	E4
Al Kufa 30,862	D4
Al Musaiyib 15,955	D4
Al Q'aim 3,372	B3
Al Qaiyara 3,060	C3
Al Qosh 3,863	C2
Al Qurna 5,638	E5
A'mara 2,578	C2
A'mara 64,847	E5
A'na 15,729	B3
An Najaf 128,096	D4
An Nasiriya 60,405	D5
A'qra 8,659	D2
Arbela (Erbil) 90,320	D2
Aski Mosul 643	C2
As Salman 1,789	D5
Az Zubair 41,408	E5
Badra 3,564	D4
Baghdad (cap.) 502,503	D4
Baghdad* 1,745,328	D4
Baiji 15,785	C3
Baq'uba 34,575	D4
Basra 313,327	E5
Dohuk 16,998	C2
Erbil 90,320	D2
Fao 15,399	F6
Habbaniya 14,405	C4
Haditha 6,870	C3
Hai 16,988	E4
Halabja 11,206	D3
Hilla 84,717	D4
Hindiya 16,436	C4
Hit 9,131	C4
Karbal'a 83,301	D3
Khanaqin 23,522	D3
Kifri 8,500	D3
Kirkuk 167,413	D3
Kirkuk* 176,794	D3
Kubaisa 4,023	C4
Kut 42,116	D4
Makhmur 2,556	C3
Mandali 11,262	D4
Mosul 315,157	C2
Muqdadiyah 12,181	D4
Naft Kaneh	D3
Na'maniya 11,943	D4
Qal'at Diza 6,250	D2
Ramadi 28,723	C4
Rania 4,090	D2
Refai' 7,681	E5
Rumaitha 10,222	D5
Rutba 5,091	B4
Ruwandiz 5,801	D2
Sad'iya 5,285	D3
Samarra 24,746	C3
Samawa 33,473	D5
Shaikh Saa'd 2,958	E4
Shaqlawa 6,814	D2
Shatra 18,822	E5
Sinjar 7,942	B2
Sulaimaniya 86,822	D3
Tal Kaif 7,482	C2
Taza Khurmatu 2,681	C3
Tikrit 9,921	C3
Tuz Khurmatu 13,860	D3
Zakho 14,790	C2

OTHER FEATURES

Adhaim (riv.)	D3
Aneiza, Jebel (mt.)	A4
A'rab, Shatt al- (riv.)	F5
A'ra'r, Wadi (dry riv.)	B5
Babylon (ruins)	D4
Batin, Wadi al (dry riv.)	E6
Ctesiphon (ruins)	D4
Darbandikhan (dam)	D3
Euphrates (riv.)	E4
Great Zab (riv.)	C2
Hauran, Wadi (dry riv.)	B4
Little Zab (riv.)	C3
Mesopotamia (reg.)	B3
Nineveh (ruins)	C2
Sad'iya, Hor (lake)	E4
Saniya, Hor (lake)	E5
Shai'b Hisb, Wadi (dry riv.)	C5
Sinjar, Jebel (mts.)	B2
Siyah Kuh (mts.)	B2
Syrian (des.)	B4
Tigris (riv.)	E4
Ubaiyidh, Wadi (dry riv.)	B5
Ur (ruins)	E5

*City and suburbs.
†Population of commune.

IRAN

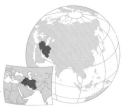

IRAQ

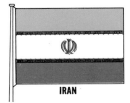

AREA 636,293 sq. mi. (1,648,000 sq. km.)
POPULATION 37,447,000
CAPITAL Tehran
LARGEST CITY Tehran
HIGHEST POINT Damavand 18,376 ft. (5,601 m.)
MONETARY UNIT Iranian rial
MAJOR LANGUAGES Persian, Azerbaijani, Kurdish
MAJOR RELIGION Islam

AREA 172,476 sq. mi. (446,713 sq. km.)
POPULATION 12,767,000
CAPITAL Baghdad
LARGEST CITY Baghdad
HIGHEST POINT Haji Ibrahim 11,811 ft. (3,600 m.)
MONETARY UNIT Iraqi dinar
MAJOR LANGUAGES Arabic, Kurdish
MAJOR RELIGION Islam

Topography

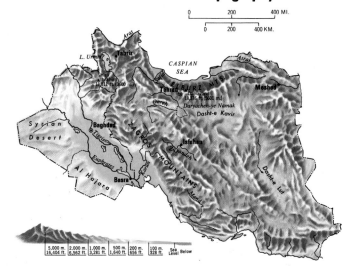

Agriculture, Industry and Resources

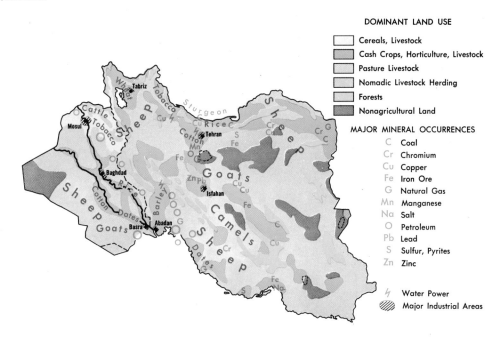

DOMINANT LAND USE

- Cereals, Livestock
- Cash Crops, Horticulture, Livestock
- Pasture Livestock
- Nomadic Livestock Herding
- Forests
- Nonagricultural Land

MAJOR MINERAL OCCURRENCES

- C Coal
- Cr Chromium
- Cu Copper
- Fe Iron Ore
- G Natural Gas
- Mn Manganese
- Na Salt
- O Petroleum
- Pb Lead
- S Sulfur, Pyrites
- Zn Zinc

⚡ Water Power
▨ Major Industrial Areas

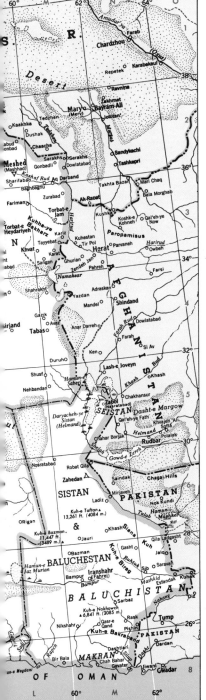

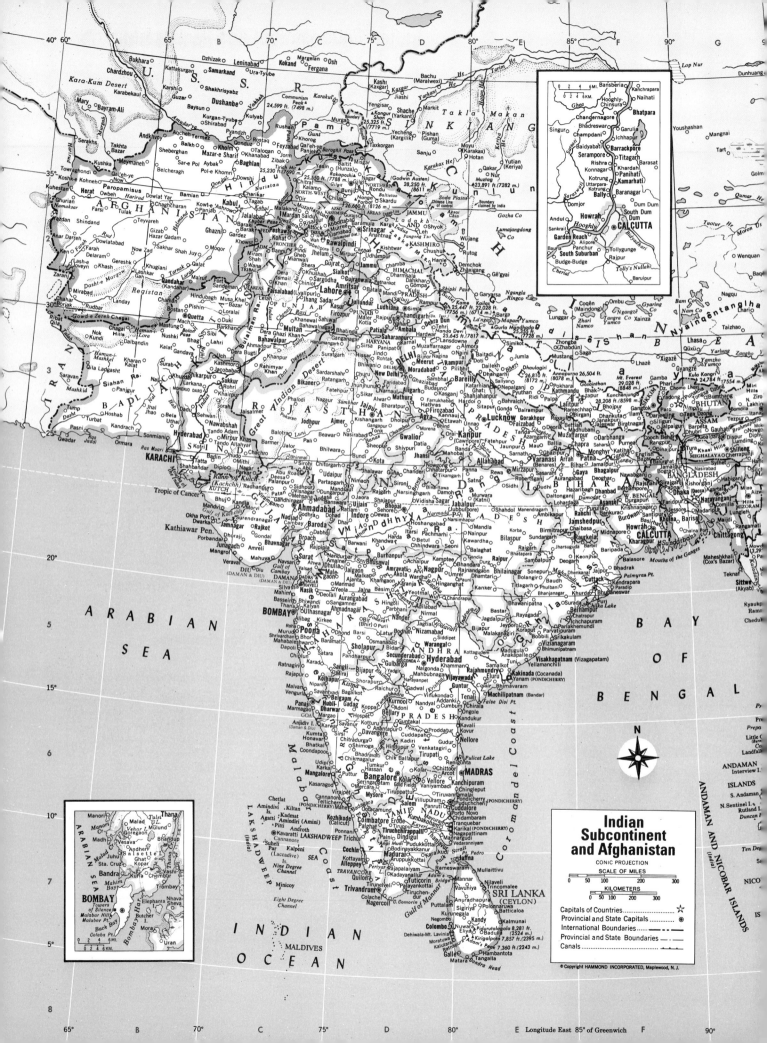

Indian Subcontinent and Afghanistan

CONIC PROJECTION

SCALE OF MILES

KILOMETERS

Capitals of Countries .... ☆
Provincial and State Capitals .... ◉
International Boundaries ....
Provincial and State Boundaries ....
Canals ....

© Copyright HAMMOND INCORPORATED, Maplewood, N.J.

INDIA

AREA 1,269,339 sq. mi. (3,287,588 sq. km.)
POPULATION 683,810,051
CAPITAL New Delhi
LARGEST CITY Calcutta (greater)
HIGHEST POINT Nanda Devi 25,645 ft. (7,817 m.)
MONETARY UNIT Indian rupee
MAJOR LANGUAGES Hindi, English, Bihari, Telugu,
Marathi, Bengali, Tamil, Gujarati, Rajasthani,
Kanarese, Malayalam, Oriya, Punjabi, Assamese,
Kashmiri, Urdu
MAJOR RELIGIONS Hinduism, Islam, Christianity,
Sikhism, Buddhism, Jainism, Zoroastrianism, Animism

PAKISTAN

AREA 310,403 sq. mi. (803,944 sq. km.)
POPULATION 83,782,000
CAPITAL Islamabad
LARGEST CITY Karachi
HIGHEST POINT K2 (Godwin Austen)
28,250 ft. (8,611 m.)
MONETARY UNIT Pakistani rupee
MAJOR LANGUAGES Urdu, English, Punjabi,.
Pushtu, Sindhi, Baluchi, Brahui
MAJOR RELIGIONS Islam, Hinduism, Sikhism,
Christianity, Buddhism

SRI LANKA (CEYLON)

AREA 25,332 sq. mi.
(65,610 sq. km.)
POPULATION 14,850,001
CAPITAL Colombo
LARGEST CITY Colombo
HIGHEST POINT Pidurutalagala
8,281 ft. (2,524 m.)
MONETARY UNIT Sri Lanka rupee
MAJOR LANGUAGES Sinhala, Tamil,
English
MAJOR RELIGIONS Buddhism,
Hinduism, Christianity, Islam

AFGHANISTAN

AREA 250,775 sq. mi.
(649,507 sq. km.)
POPULATION 15,540,000
CAPITAL Kabul
LARGEST CITY Kabul
HIGHEST POINT Nowshak
24,557 ft. (7,485 m.)
MONETARY UNIT afghani
MAJOR LANGUAGES Pushtu, Dari,
Uzbek
MAJOR RELIGION Islam

NEPAL

AREA 54,663 sq. mi.
(141,577 sq. km.)
POPULATION 14,179,301
CAPITAL Kathmandu
LARGEST CITY Kathmandu
HIGHEST POINT Mt. Everest
29,028 ft. (8,848 m.)
MONETARY UNIT Nepalese rupee
MAJOR LANGUAGES Nepali,
Maithili, Tamang, Newari, Tharu
MAJOR RELIGIONS Hinduism,
Buddhism

MALDIVES

AREA 115 sq. mi. (298 sq. km.)
POPULATION 143,046
CAPITAL Male
LARGEST CITY Male
HIGHEST POINT 20 ft. (6 m.)
MONETARY UNIT Maldivian rufiyaa
MAJOR LANGUAGE Divehi
MAJOR RELIGION Islam

BHUTAN

AREA 18,147 sq. mi.
(47,000 sq. km.)
POPULATION 1,298,000
CAPITAL Thimphu
LARGEST CITY Thimphu
HIGHEST POINT Kula Kangri
24,784 ft. (7,554 m.)
MONETARY UNIT ngultrum
MAJOR LANGUAGES Dzongka,
Nepali
MAJOR RELIGIONS Buddhism,
Hinduism

BANGLADESH

AREA 55,126 sq. mi.
(142,776 sq. km.)
POPULATION 87,052,024
CAPITAL Dhaka
LARGEST CITY Dhaka
HIGHEST POINT Keokradong
4,034 ft. (1,230 m.)
MONETARY UNIT taka
MAJOR LANGUAGES Bengali,
English
MAJOR RELIGIONS Islam,
Hinduism, Christianity

INDIA

PAKISTAN

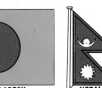

SRI LANKA (CEYLON)

BHUTAN

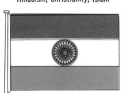

AFGHANISTAN

MALDIVES

BANGLADESH

NEPAL

AFGHANISTAN

CITIES and TOWNS

Bala Murghab 10,000........ A1
Balkh 15,000................. B1
Chahardeh.................... B2
Girishk 10,000............... A2
Kabul (cap.) 318,094....... B2
Kabul* 534,350............. B2
Kuhsan...................... A2
Kushk 10,000............... A1
Landi Muhammad Amin
  Khan 1,000............... A2
Panjao 3,000................ B2
Qaleh-i-Kang 17,400....... A2
Sabzawar 5,000............ A2
Shindand
  (Sabzawar) 5,000........ A2
Taiwara 5,000.............. A2

OTHER FEATURES

Farah Rud (riv.)............. A2
Hari Rud (riv.).............. A1
Helmand (riv.).............. B2
Hindu Kush (mts.).......... B1
Jam (mt.)................... A2
Kabul (riv.)................. C2
Kunar (riv.)................. C1
Kunduz (riv.)............... B1
Lora (riv.).................. B2
Margo, Dasht-i- (des.)..... A2
Namaksar (salt lake)....... A2
Paropamisus (range)....... A2
Registan (reg.)............. B2

BANGLADESH

CITIES and TOWNS

Chittagong 416,733.......... G4
Cox's Bazar (Maheshkhali) ... G4
Dhaka (Dacca) (cap.)
  1,310,976.................. G4
Dhaka (Dacca) ☐ 2,539,991 . G4
Habiganj..................... G4
Jamalpur.................... F4
Khulna 436,000.............. F4
Kishorganj................... G4
Madaripur................... G4
Maheshkhali................. G4
Narayanganj 176,879........ G4
Nawabganj................... F4
Noakhali 19,874............. G4
Rangamati 6,416............. G4

OTHER FEATURES

Bengal, Bay of (sea)........ F5
Brahmaputra (riv.).......... G3

Ganges (riv.)............... F3
Sundarbans (reg.).......... F4

BHUTAN

CITIES and TOWNS

Bumthang 10,000............ G3
Punakha 12,000............. G3
Taga Dzong 18,000.......... G3
Tongsa Dzong 2,500........ G3

OTHER FEATURES

Chomo Lhari (mt.).......... F3
Himalaya (mts.)............ E2
Kula Kangri (mt.).......... G3

INDIA

INTERNAL DIVISIONS

Andaman and Nicobar Isls.
  (terr.) 115,133 .... G6
Andhra Pradesh
  (state) 43,502,708 .... D5
Arunachal Pradesh
  (terr.) 467,511 .... G3
Assam (state) 14,625,152 .. G3
Bihar (state) 56,353,369 ... F4
Chandigarh
  (terr.) 257,251 .... D2
Dadra and Nagar Haveli
  (terr.) 74,170 .... C4
Daman and Diu
  (terr.) 857,771 .... C4
Delhi (terr.) 4,065,698 ..... D3
Gujarat (state) 26,697,475 .. C4
Haryana (state) 10,036,808 . D3
Himachal Pradesh
  (state) 3,460,434 .... D2
Jammu and Kashmir
  (state) 4,616,632 .... D2
Karnataka
  (state) 29,299,014 ...... D6
Kerala (state) 21,347,375 .. D6
Lakshadweep
  (terr.) 31,810 .... C6
Madhya Pradesh
  (state) 41,654,119 ...... D4
Maharashtra
  (state) 50,412,235 ...... C5
Manipur (state) 1,072,753 .. G4
Meghalaya
  (state) 1,011,699 .... G3
Mizoram (terr.) 332,390 .... G4
Nagaland
  (state) 516,449 .... G3

(continued on following page)

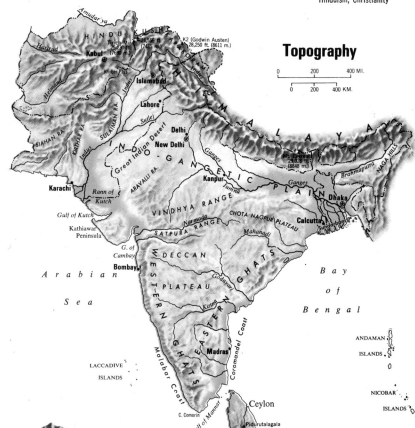

Topography

0   200   400 MI.

0   200   400 KM.

| 5,000 m. | 2,000 m. | 1,000 m. | 500 m. | 200 m. | 100 m. | Sea | Below |
| 16,404 ft. | 6,562 ft. | 3,281 ft. | 1,640 ft. | 656 ft. | 328 ft. | Level | |

Orissa (state) 21,944,615... E5
Pondicherry (terr.) 471,707 ... E6
Punjab (state) 13,551,060.. D2
Rajasthan (state) 25,765,806 ... C3
Sikkim (state) 209,843 ... F3
Tamil Nadu (state) 41,199,168 ... D6
Tripura (state) 1,556,342 ... G4
Uttar Pradesh (state) 88,341,144 ... D3
West Bengal (state) 44,312,011 ... F4

CITIES and TOWNS

Abu 9,840 ... C4
Agra 591,917 ... D3
Agra□ 634,622 ... D3
Ahmadabad 1,591,832 ... C4
Ahmadabad□ 1,741,522 ... C4
Ajanta ... D4
Ajmer 262,851 ... C3
Akola 168,438 ... D4
Alibag 11,913 ... C5
Aligarh 252,314 ... D3
Allahabad 490,622 ... E3
Allahabad□ 513,036 ... E3
Alleppey 160,166 ... D7
Almora 19,671 ... D3
Ambikapur 23,087 ... E4
Amravati 193,800 ... D4
Amritsar 407,628 ... C2
Amritsar□ 458,029 ... C2
Asansol 155,968 ... F4
Aurangabad, Maharashtra 150,483 ... D5
Baltit ... C1
Bandra ... B7
Bangalore 1,540,741 ... D6
Bangalore□ 1,653,779 ... D6
Bareilly 296,248 ... D3
Baroda 466,696 ... C4
Baroda□ 467,487 ... C4
Barwani 22,099 ... D4
Belgaum 192,427 ... C5
Benares (Varanasi) 583,856 ... E3
Bhagalpur 172,202 ... F4
Bhatpara 204,750 ... F1
Bhavnagar 225,358 ... C4
Bhawanipatna 22,808 ... E5
Bhilai 157,173 ... E4
Bhopal 298,022 ... D4
Bikaner 188,518 ... C3
Bombay (Greater)* 5,970,575 ... B7
Bunji ... C1
Calcutta 3,148,746 ... F2
Calcutta□ 7,031,382 ... F2
Calicut (Kozhikode) 333,979 ... D6
Cawnpore (Kanpur) 1,154,388 ... E3
Chamba 11,814 ... D2
Chanderi 10,294 ... D4
Chandigarh 218,743 ... D2
Chembur ... B7
Chilas ... C1
Chushul ... D2
Cocanada (Kakinada) 164,200 ... E5
Cochin 439,066 ... D6
Coimbatore 356,368 ... D6
Coimbatore□ 736,203 ... D6
Colachel 18,819 ... D7
Cuttack 194,068 ... F4
Dehra Dun 166,073 ... D2
Delhi 3,287,883 ... D3
Delhi□ 3,647,023 ... D3
Dhanbad□ 434,031 ... F4
Dharmsala 10,939 ... D2
Dharwar-Hubli 379,166 ... C5
Diphu 10,200 ... G3
Dispur 1,725 ... G3
Dungarpur 19,773 ... C4
Durgapur 206,638 ... F4
Dwarka 17,801 ... B4
Gangtok 12,000 ... F3
Garden Reach 154,913 ... F2
Gaya 179,884 ... F4
Gilgit ... C1
Gorakhpur 230,911 ... E3
Goregaon ... B7
Guntur 269,991 ... D5
Gwalior 384,772 ... D3
Gwalior□ 406,140 ... D3
Haflong 5,197 ... G3
Honavar 12,444 ... C6
Howrah 737,877 ... F2
Hubli-Dharwar 379,166 ... C5
Hunza (Baltit) ... C1
Hyderabad 1,607,396 ... D5
Hyderabad□ 1,796,339 ... D5
Ichchapuram 15,850 ... F5
Indore 543,381 ... D4
Indore□ 560,936 ... D4
Itanagar⊙ 18,787 ... G3
Jabalpur 426,224 ... D4
Jabalpur□ 534,845 ... D4
Jaipur 615,258 ... D3
Jaipur□ 636,768 ... D3
Jaisalmer 16,578 ... C3
Jajpur 16,707 ... F4
Jalor 15,478 ... C3
Jammu 155,338 ... D2
Jamnagar 214,816 ... B4
Jamnagar□ 227,640 ... B4
Jamshedpur 341,576 ... F4
Jamshedpur□ 456,146 ... F4
Jhansi 173,292 ... D3
Jodhpur 317,612 ... C3
Jubbulpore (Jabalpur) 426,224 ... D4
Juhu ... B7
Jullundur 296,106 ... D2
Kakinada 164,200 ... E5
Kamarhati 169,404 ... F1
Kandla 17,995 ... C4
Kanpur 1,154,388 ... E3
Kanpur□ 1,275,242 ... E3
Kargil 2,390 ... D2
Katarnian Ghat ... E3
Kavaratti 4,420 ... C6
Kendrapara 20,079 ... F4
Kohima 21,545 ... G3
Kolhapur 259,050 ... C5
Koraput 21,505 ... E5
Kota 212,991 ... D3
Kozhikode 333,979 ... D6
Kumta 19,112 ... C6
Kurla ... B7
Leh 5,519 ... D2
Lucknow 749,239 ... E3
Lucknow□ 813,982 ... E3
Ludhiana 397,850 ... D2
Ludhiana□ 401,176 ... D2
Madras 2,469,449 ... E6
Madras□ 3,169,930 ... E6
Madurai 549,114 ... D7
Madurai□ 711,501 ... D7
Mahabaleshwar 7,318 ... C5
Mahe 8,972 ... D6
Malad ... B6
Malegaon 191,847 ... C4
Malvan 17,579 ... C5
Mandi 16,849 ... D2
Mandla 24,406 ... E4
Mangalore 165,174 ... C6
Meerut 270,993 ... D3
Mercara 19,357 ... D6
Mirpur ... C2
Moradabad 258,590 ... D3
Mulund ... B6
Muzaffarabad ... C2
Mysore 355,685 ... D6
Nagar ... D1
Nagpur 866,076 ... D4
Nagpur□ 930,459 ... D4
Nahan 16,017 ... D2
Naini Tal 23,986 ... D3
Nasik 176,091 ... C5
New Delhi (cap.) 301,801 ... D3
Okha Port 10,687 ... B4
Pachmarhi 1,212 ... D4
Panna 22,316 ... E4
Pasighat 5,116 ... G3
Patna 473,001 ... F3
Patna□ 491,217 ... F3
Poona 856,105 ... C5
Poona□ 1,135,034 ... C5
Porto Novo 17,412 ... E6
Raipur 174,518 ... E4
Rajahmundry 165,912 ... E5
Rajapur 9,017 ... C5
Rajkot 300,612 ... C4
Rameswaram 16,755 ... D7
Rampur, Uttar Pradesh 161,417 ... D3
Ranchi 175,934 ... F4
Raxaul 12,064 ... E3
Sadiya⊙ 64,252 ... H3
Saharanpur 225,396 ... D3
Salem 308,716 ... D6
Salem□ 416,440 ... D6
Santa Cruz ... B7
Sarnath ... E3
Secunderabad 250,636 ... D5
Seringapatam 14,100 ... D6
Sholapur 398,361 ... D5
Sidhi 8,341 ... E4
Silvassa ... C4
Sirohi 18,774 ... C4
Skardu ... D1
South Suburban 272,600 ... F2
Srinagar 403,413 ... D2
Srinagar□ 423,253 ... D2
Sundargarh 17,244 ... E4
Surat 471,656 ... C4
Surat□ 493,001 ... C4
Tehri 5,480 ... D2
Thana 170,675 ... B6
Tiruchchirappalli 307,400 ... D6
Tiruchchirappalli□ 464,624 ... D6
Tiruchendur 18,126 ... D7
Tollygunge ... F2
Tranquebar 17,318 ... E6
Trivandrum 409,627 ... D7
Trombay ... B7
Tura 15,489 ... G3
Tuticorin 155,310 ... D7
Udaypur 161,278 ... C4
Udhampur 16,392 ... D2
Ujjain 203,278 ... D4
Ulhasnagar 168,462 ... C5
Varanasi 583,856 ... E3
Varanasi□ 606,721 ... E3
Vellore□ 178,554 ... D6
Vengurla 11,805 ... C5
Vijayawada 317,258 ... D5
Visakhapatnam 352,504 ... E5
Vizagapatam (Visakhapatnam) 352,504 ... E5
Warangal 207,520 ... D5
Yanam 8,291 ... E5
Yasin ... C1

OTHER FEATURES

Abor (hills) ... G3
Adam's Bridge (sound) ... D7
Agatti (isl.) ... C6
Amindiri (isl.) ... C6
Amindivi (isls.) ... C6
Amini (Amindiri) (isl.) ... C6
Andaman (isls.) ... G6
Andaman (sea) ... G6
Androth (isl.) ... C6
Anjidiv (Angedeva) (isl.) ... C6
Arabian (sea) ... B5
Back (bay) ... B7
Baltistan (reg.) ... D1
Bengal, Bay of (sea) ... F5
Berar (reg.) ... D4
Brahmaputra (riv.) ... G3
Butcher (isl.) ... B7
Cambay (gulf) ... C4
Cannanore (isls.) ... C6
Car Nicobar (isl.) ... G7
Chambal (riv.) ... D3
Chenab (riv.) ... C2
Chetlat (isl.) ... C6
Chilka (lake) ... F5
Coco (chan.) ... G6
Colaba (pt.) ... B7
Comorin (cape) ... D7
Coromandel Coast (reg.) ... E6
Daman (dist.) ... C4
Damodar (riv.) ... F4
Deccan (plat.) ... D6
Diu (dist.) ... C4
Eastern Ghats (mts.) ... D6
Elephanta (isl.) ... B7
Ganga (Ganges) (riv.) ... F3
Ganges, Mouths of the (delta) ... F4
Ganges (riv.) ... F3
Ghaghra (riv.) ... E3
Goa (dist.) ... C5
Godavari (riv.) ... D5
Godwin Austen (K2) (mt.) ... D1
Golconda (ruins) ... D5
Great (chan.) ... G7
Great Indian (des.) ... C3
Great Nicobar (isl.) ... G7
Himalaya (mts.) ... D2
Hindu Kush (mts.) ... C1
Hooghly (riv.) ... F2
Indus (riv.) ... B3
Jhelum (riv.) ... C2
Jumna (riv.) ... E3
K2 (mt.) ... D1
Kachchh (gulf) ... B4
Kachchh (Kutch), Rann of (salt marsh) ... B4
Kadmat (isl.) ... C6
Kalpeni (isl.) ... C7
Kamet (mt.) ... D2
Kanchenjunga (mt.) ... F3
Karakoram (mts.) ... D1
Kaveri (riv.) ... D6
Khasi (hills) ... G3
Kiltan (isl.) ... C6
Kistna (Krishna) (riv.) ... D5
Krishna (Kistna) (riv.) ... D5
Kunlun (range) ... D1
Kutch (Kachchh) (gulf) ... B4
Kutch, Rann of (salt marsh) ... B4
Laccadive (Cannanore) (isls.) ... C6
Ladakh (reg.) ... D2
Little Andaman (isl.) ... G6
Little Nicobar (isl.) ... G7
Mahanadi (riv.) ... E4
Malabar (hill) ... B7
Malabar Coast (reg.) ... C6
Mannar (gulf) ... D7
Middle Andaman (isl.) ... G6
Minicoy (isl.) ... C7
Miri (hills) ... G3
Mishmi (hills) ... H3
Nancowry (isl.) ... G7
Nanda Devi (mt.) ... D2
Nanga Parbat (mt.) ... D1
Narmada (riv.) ... D4
Nicobar (isls.) ... G7
North Andaman (isl.) ... G6
Palk (strait) ... D7
Penganga (riv.) ... D5
Periyar (lake) ... D7
Pitti (isl.) ... C6
Pulicat (lake) ... E6
Rakaposhi (mt.) ... C1
Salsette (isl.) ... B7
Sambhar (lake) ... C3
Satpura (range) ... D4
Shipki (pass) ... D2
South Andaman (isl.) ... G6
Sundarbans (reg.) ... F4
Sutlej (riv.) ... C3
Ten Degree (chan.) ... G7
Towers of Silence ... B7
Travancore (reg.) ... D7
Tungabhadra (riv.) ... D5
Vindhya (range) ... D4
Western Ghats (mts.) ... C5
Zaskar (mts.) ... D2

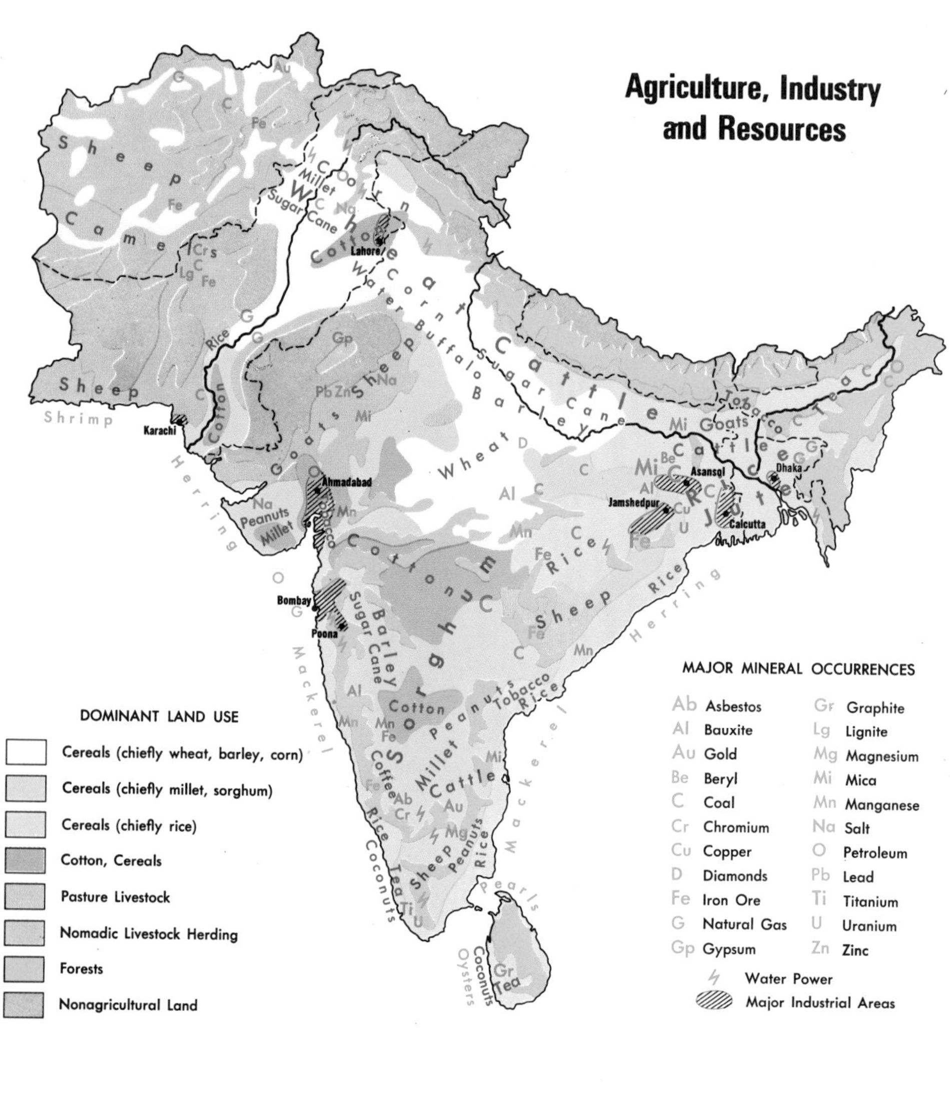
Agriculture, Industry and Resources
DOMINANT LAND USE
Cereals (chiefly wheat, barley, corn)
Cereals (chiefly millet, sorghum)
Cereals (chiefly rice)
Cotton, Cereals
Pasture Livestock
Nomadic Livestock Herding
Forests
Nonagricultural Land
MAJOR MINERAL OCCURRENCES
Ab Asbestos
Al Bauxite
Au Gold
Be Beryl
C Coal
Cr Chromium
Cu Copper
D Diamonds
Fe Iron Ore
G Natural Gas
Gp Gypsum
Gr Graphite
Lg Lignite
Mg Magnesium
Mi Mica
Mn Manganese
Na Salt
O Petroleum
Pb Lead
Ti Titanium
U Uranium
Zn Zinc
Water Power
Major Industrial Areas
Lahore
Karachi
Ahmadabad
Bombay
Poona
Jamshedpur
Asansol
Calcutta
Dhaka
Shrimp
Herring
Mackerel
Pearls
Oysters
Coconuts

MALDIVES

Maldives 136,000 ... C7

NEPAL

CITIES and TOWNS

Dhangarhi ... E3
Jumla⊙ 122,753 ... E3
Kathmandu⊙ 353,752 ... E3
Lalitpur⊙ 154,998 ... E3
Mukhtinath ... E3
Mustang⊙ 26,944 ... E3
Nepalganj 23,523 ... E3
Pokhara 20,611 ... E3
Pyuthan⊙ 137,338 ... E3
Ridi ... E3
Sallyana⊙ 141,457 ... E3

OTHER FEATURES

Annapurna (mt.) ... E3
Bheri (riv.) ... E3
Dhaulagiri (mt.) ... E3
Everest (mt.) ... F3
Himalaya (mts.) ... D2
Kanchenjunga (mt.) ... F3

PAKISTAN

PROVINCES

Azad Kashmir ... C2
Baluchistan 2,409,000 ... B3
Federal Administrated Tribal Areas ... C2
Islamabad District 235,000 ... C2
Northern Areas ... D1
North-West Frontier 10,909,000 ... C2
Punjab 37,374,000 ... C2
Sind 13,965,000 ... B3

CITIES and TOWNS

Abbottabad 47,011 ... C2
Bahawalpur 133,956 ... C3
Bahawalpur* 181,000 ... C3
Baltit ... C1
Campbellpore 19,041 ... C2
Chiniot 69,124 ... C2
Dera Ghazi Khan 71,429 ... C3
Dera Ismail Khan 59,892 ... C2
Faisalabad 822,263 ... C2
Gujranwala 360,419 ... C2
Gujrat 100,581 ... C2
Hunza (Baltit) ... C1
Hyderabad 628,310 ... B3
Islamabad (cap.) 77,318 ... C2
Jacobabad 57,292 ... B3
Jhang Sadar 135,722 ... C2
Jhelum 63,653 ... C2
Karachi 3,498,634 ... B4
Karachi* 3,650,000 ... B4
Khanewal 67,617 ... C2
Kohat 64,634 ... C2
Lahore 2,165,372 ... C2
Larkana 71,943 ... B3
Lyallpur (Faisalabad) 822,263 ... C2
Mardan 115,218 ... C2
Mardan* 131,000 ... C2
Multan 542,195 ... C2
Multan* 723,000 ... C2
Nagar ... D1
Nal ... B3
Nawabshah 80,779 ... B3
Nowshera 56,117 ... C2
Peshawar 268,366 ... C2
Peshawar* 331,000 ... C2
Quetta 156,000 ... B2
Rahimyar Khan 74,407 ... C3
Rahimyar Khan* 130,000 ... C3
Rawalpindi 615,392 ... C2
Sahiwal 106,213 ... C2
Sargodha 201,407 ... C2
Sargodha* 225,000 ... C2
Shikarpur 70,301 ... B3
Sialkot 203,779 ... C2
Sukkur 158,876 ... B3
Tando Adam 31,246 ... B3

OTHER FEATURES

Arabian (sea) ... B5
Bolan (pass) ... B3
Chagai (hills) ... A3
Chenab (riv.) ... C2
Hindu Kush (mts.) ... B1
Indus (riv.) ... B3
Jhelum (riv.) ... C2
Khyber (pass) ... C2
Kunar (riv.) ... C1
Kutch, Rann of (salt marsh) ... B4
Mashkel (riv.) ... A3
Mohenjo Daro (ruins) ... B3
Muari, Ras (cape) ... B4
Ravi (riv.) ... C2
Siahan (range) ... A3
Sulaiman (range) ... C3.
Sutlej (riv.) ... C3
Talab (riv.) ... A3
Taxila (ruins) ... C2
Tirich Mir (mt.) ... C1
Zhob (riv.) ... B2

SRI LANKA (CEYLON)

CITIES and TOWNS

Colombo (cap.) 618,000 ... D7
Colombo* 852,098 ... D7
Hambantota 6,908 ... E7
Kalmunai 19,176 ... E7
Mannar 11,157 ... E7
Mullaittivu 4,930 ... E7
Nuwara Eliya 16,347 ... E7
Polonnaruwa 9,551 ... E7
Puttalam 17,982 ... D7
Sigiriya 1,446 ... E7
Vavuniya 15,639 ... E7

OTHER FEATURES

Adam's (peak) ... E7
Adam's Bridge (shoals) ... D7
Dondra (head) ... E7
Kirigalpota (mt.) ... E7
Mannar (gulf) ... D7
Palk (str.) ... D7
Pedro (pt.) ... E6
Pidurutalagala (mt.) ... E7

*City and suburbs.
⊙Population of district.
□Population of urban areas.

AREA 145,730 sq. mi. (377,441 sq. km.)
POPULATION 117,057,485
CAPITAL Tokyo
LARGEST CITY Tokyo
HIGHEST POINT Fuji 12,389 ft. (3,776 m.)
MONETARY UNIT yen
MAJOR LANGUAGE Japanese
MAJOR RELIGIONS Buddhism, Shintoism

AREA 46,540 sq. mi. (120,539 sq. km.)
POPULATION 17,914,000
CAPITAL P'yŏngyang
LARGEST CITY P'yŏngyang
HIGHEST POINT Paektu 9,003 ft. (2,744 m.)
MONETARY UNIT won
MAJOR LANGUAGE Korean
MAJOR RELIGIONS Confucianism, Buddhism, Ch'ondogyo

AREA 38,175 sq. mi. (98,873 sq. km.)
POPULATION 37,448,836
CAPITAL Seoul
LARGEST CITY Seoul
HIGHEST POINT Halla 6,398 ft. (1,950 m.)
MONETARY UNIT won
MAJOR LANGUAGE Korean
MAJOR RELIGIONS Confucianism, Buddhism, Ch'ondogyo, Christianity

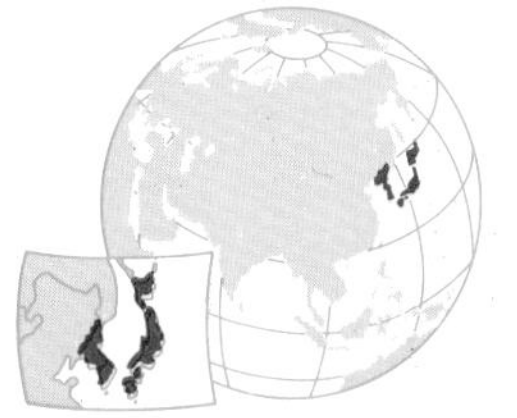

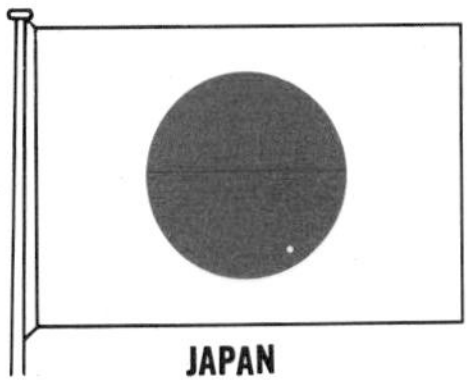

JAPAN

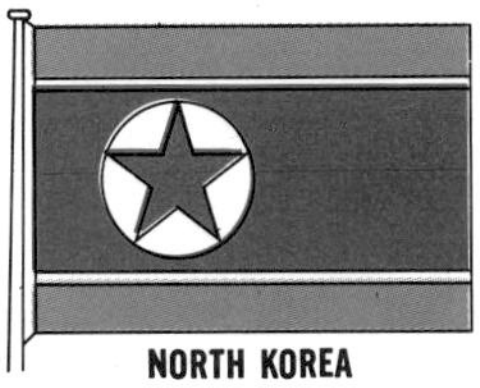

NORTH KOREA

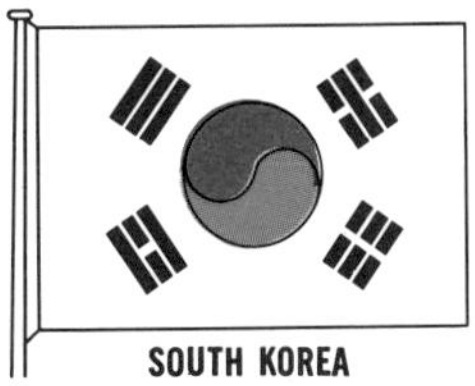

SOUTH KOREA

JAPAN

PREFECTURES

Aichi 5,923,569 H6
Akita 1,232,481 J4
Aomori 1,468,646 K3
Chiba 4,149,147 P2
Ehime 1,465,215 F7
Fukui 773,599 G5
Fukuoka 4,292,963 D7
Fukushima 1,970,616 K5
Gifu 1,867,978 H6
Gumma 1,756,480 J5
Hiroshima 2,646,324 E6
Hokkaido 5,338,206 K2
Hyogo 4,992,140 H7
Ibaraki 2,342,198 K5
Ishikawa 1,069,872 H5
Iwate 1,385,563 K4
Kagawa 961,292 G6
Kagoshima 1,723,902 E8
Kanagawa 6,397,748 O2
Kochi 808,397 F7
Kumamoto 1,715,273 E7
Kyoto 2,424,856 J7
Miė 1,626,002 H6
Miyagi 1,955,267 K4
Miyazaki 1,085,055 E8
Nagano 2,017,564 J5
Nagasaki 1,571,912 D7
Nara 1,077,491 J8
Niigata 2,391,938 J5
Oita 1,190,314 E7
Okayama 1,814,305 F6
Okinawa 1,042,572 N6
Osaka 8,278,925 J8
Saga 837,674 E7
Saitama 4,821,340 O2
Shiga 985,621 J7
Shimane 768,886 F6
Shizuoka 3,308,799 H6
Tochigi 1,698,003 K5
Tokushima 805,166 G7
Tokyo 11,673,554 O2
Tottori 581,311 G6
Toyama 1,070,791 H5
Wakayama 1,072,118 G6
Yamagata 1,220,302 K4
Yamaguchi 1,555,218 E6
Yamanashi 783,050 J6

CITIES and TOWNS

Abashiri 43,825 M1
Ageo 146,358 O2
Aikawa 13,546 H4
Aizuwakamatsu 108,650 J5
Ajigasawa 18,086 J3
Akashi 234,905 H8
Aki 24,480 F7
Akita 261,246 J4
Akkeshi 16,778 M2
Akune 30,295 E7
Amagasaki 545,783 H8
Amagi 42,725 E7
Anan 60,439 G7
Aomori 264,222 K3
Asahi 34,028 K6
Asahikawa 320,526 L2
Ashibetsu 36,520 L2
Ashikaga 162,359 J5
Ashiya 76,211 H8
Atami 51,437 J6
Atsugi 108,955 O2
Awaji 9,623 H8
Ayabe 43,490 G6
Beppu 133,894 E7
Bibai 38,416 L2
Biratori 9,331 L2
Chiba 659,356 P2
Chichibu 61,798 J5
Chigasaki 152,023 O3
Chitose 61,031 K2
Chofu 175,924 O2
Choshi 90,374 K6
Daito 110,829 J8
Ebetsu 77,624 K2
Eniwa 39,884 K2
Esashi, Hokkaido 10,172 L1
Esashi, Hokkaido 14,409 J3
Esashi, Iwate 36,336 K4
Fuchu, Hiroshima 50,217 F6
Fuchu, Tokyo 182,474 O2
Fuji 199,195 J6
Fujieda 90,358 J6
Fujisawa 265,975 O3
Fukagawa 36,000 L2
Fukuchiyama 60,003 G6
Fukue 32,018 D7
Fukui 231,364 G5
Fukuoka 1,002,201 D7
Fukushima 246,531 K5
Fukuyama 329,714 F6
Funabashi 423,101 P2
Furukawa 54,356 K4
Gifu 408,707 H6
Gobo 30,272 G7
Gose 37,554 J8
Gosen 39,376 J5
Goshogawara 49,040 K3
Gotsu 27,992 F6
Habikino 94,160 J8
Haboro 13,624 K1
Hachinohe 224,366 K3
Hachioji 322,580 O2
Hadano 103,663 O3
Hagi 52,724 E6
Hakodate 307,453 K3
Hakui 28,726 H5
Hamada 50,316 E6
Hamamatsu 468,884 H6
Hanamaki 65,826 K4
Hanno 55,926 O2
Haramachi 43,483 K5
Hayama 24,026 O3
Higashiosaka 524,750 J8
Hikone 85,066 H6
Himeji 436,086 G6
Himi 61,789 H5
Hino 126,847 O2
Hirakata 297,618 J7
Hirara 29,301 L7
Hirata 30,942 F6
Hiratsuka 195,635 O3
Hiroo 11,399 L2
Hirosaki 164,911 K3
Hiroshima 852,611 E6
Hitachi 202,383 K5
Hitachiota 35,322 K5
Hitoyoshi 41,118 E7
Hofu 105,540 E6
Hondo 40,432 E7
Honjo 40,488 J4
Hyuga 53,448 E7
Ibaraki 210,286 J7
Ibusuki 32,339 E8
Ichihara 194,068 P3
Ichikawa 319,291 P2
Ichinohe 21,433 K3
Ichinomiya 238,463 H6
Ichinoseki 59,122 K4
Ide 9,112 J7
Iida 77,112 H6
Iizuka 75,417 E7
Ikeda, Hokkaido 12,306 L2
Ikeda, Osaka 100,268 H7
Ikoma 48,848 J8
Ikuno 6,658 G6
Imabari 119,726 F6
Imari 60,913 D7
Imazu 11,519 G6
Ina 54,468 H6
Isahaya 73,341 D7
Ise 104,957 H6
Ishigaki 34,657 L7
Ishige 19,220 P2
Ishinomaki 115,085 K4
Ishioka 43,679 K5
Itami 171,978 H7
Ito 68,072 J6
Itoigawa 36,646 H5
Itoman 39,363 N6
Iwaizumi 20,219 K4
Iwaki 330,213 K5
Iwakuni 111,069 E6
Iwami 16,063 G6
Iwamizawa 72,305 L2
Iwanai 25,823 K2
Iwasaki 4,437 J3
Iwata 67,665 H6
Iwatsuki 83,825 O2
Iyo 27,805 F7
Izuhara 18,460 D6
Izumi 118,237 J8
Izumiotsu 66,250 J8
Izumisano 86,139 G6
Izumo 71,568 F6
Joetsu 123,418 H5
Joyo 58,923 J7
Kadoma 143,238 J7
Kaga 61,599 H5
Kagoshima 456,827 E8
Kaizuka 79,506 H8
Kakogawa 169,293 G6
Kamaishi 68,981 L4
Kamakura 165,552 O3
Kameoka 58,184 J7
Kamiisco 27,229 K3
Kaminoyama 37,858 J4
Kamiyaku 8,668 E8
Kamo 8,953 J7
Kanazawa 395,263 H5
Kanonji 44,131 F6
Kanoya 67,951 E8
Kanuma 81,799 J5
Karatsu 75,224 D7
Kaseda 24,969 D8
Kashihara 95,701 J8
Kashiwa 203,065 P2
Kashiwara 63,586 J8
Kashiwazaki 80,351 J5
Kasugai 213,857 H6
Kasukabe 121,639 O2
Katsuta 79,996 K5
Katsuura 26,755 K6
Kawachinagano 66,936 J8
Kawagoe 225,465 O2
Kawaguchi 345,538 J6
Kawanishi 115,773 H7
Kawasaki 1,014,951 O2
Kesennuma 66,616 K4
Kikonai 10,034 K3
Kimitsu 76,016 O3
Kiryu 134,239 J5
Kisarazu 96,840 P3
Kishiwada 174,952 J8
Kitaibaraki 44,332 K5
Kitakami 48,759 K4
Kitakata 37,471 J5
Kitakyushu 1,058,058 E6
Kitami 91,519 L2
Kizu 11,890 J7
Kobayashi 38,325 E8
Kobe 1,360,605 H7
Kochi 280,962 F7
Kodaira 156,181 O2
Kofu 193,879 J6
Koga 55,973 J5
Koganei 102,714 O2
Kokubu 31,660 E8
Komagane 30,318 H6
Komatsu 100,273 H5
Koriyama 264,628 K5
Koshigaya 195,917 P2
Koyama 16,394 E8
Kubohama 17,817 F7
Kuji 38,122 K3
Kuki 45,797 O2
Kumagaya 131,485 J5
Kumamoto 488,166 E7
Kumano 27,026 G7
Kumiyama 11,540 J7
Kurashiki 392,755 F6
Kurayoshi 50,785 F6
Kure 242,655 F6
Kuroiso 42,349 K5
Kurume 204,474 E7
Kushikino 30,456 E8
Kushima 30,038 E8
Kushimoto 18,997 G7
Kushiro 206,840 M2
Kyonan 13,067 O3
Kyoto 1,461,059 J7
Machida 255,305 O2
Maebashi 250,241 J5
Maihara 12,845 G6
Maizuru 97,780 G6
Makubetsu 18,444 L2
Makurazaki 29,685 O3
Mashike 9,312 K2
Masuda 50,734 E6
Matsubara 132,662 H8
Matsue 127,440 F6
Matsumae 18,307 J3
Matsumoto 185,595 H5
Matsusaka 108,893 H6
Matsuto 36,170 H5
Matsuyama 367,323 F7
Mihara 83,679 F6
Miki 53,731 H7
Mikuni 21,602 G5
Minamata 36,782 E7
Minobu 10,345 J6
Minoo 79,621 J7
Misawa 37,437 K3
Mitaka 164,950 O2
Mito 197,953 K5
Mitsukaido 38,820 P2
Miura 47,888 O3
Miyako 61,912 L4
Miyakonojo 118,289 E8
Miyazaki 234,347 E8
Miyazu 30,194 G6
Miyoshi 37,193 F6
Mizusawa 52,266 K4
Mobara 64,942 K6
Mombetsu 32,825 L1
Monbetsu 15,029 L2
Mooka 47,345 K5
Mori 17,030 K2
Moriguchi 178,383 J7
Morioka 216,223 K4
Motobu 17,823 N6
Muko 45,886 J7
Murakami 32,939 J4
Muroran 158,715 K2
Muroto 26,660 G7
Musashino 139,508 O2
Mutsu 44,646 K3
Nachikatsuura 23,596 H7
Nagahama, Ehime 13,144 F7
Nagahama, Shiga 54,064 H6
Nagano 306,637 J5
Nagaoka, Kyoto 65,557 J7
Nagaoka, Niigata 171,742 J5
Nagaokakyo 65,557 J7
Nagasaki 450,194 D7
Nagato 27,327 E6
Nago 45,210 N6
Nagoya 2,079,740 H6
Naha 295,006 N6
Nakaminato 33,147 K5
Nakamura 34,437 F7
Nakasato 14,248 K3
Nakatsu 59,111 E7
Nanao 49,493 H5
Nankoku 42,832 F7
Nara 257,538 J8
Narashino 117,852 P2
Nayoro 35,145 L1
Naze 46,359 O5
Nemuro 45,817 M2
Neyagawa 254,311 J7
Nichinan 52,171 E8
Niigata 423,188 J5
Niihama 131,712 F6
Niimi 30,014 F6
Niitsu 58,970 J5
Nishinomiya 400,622 H8

(continued on following page)

Agriculture, Industry and Resources

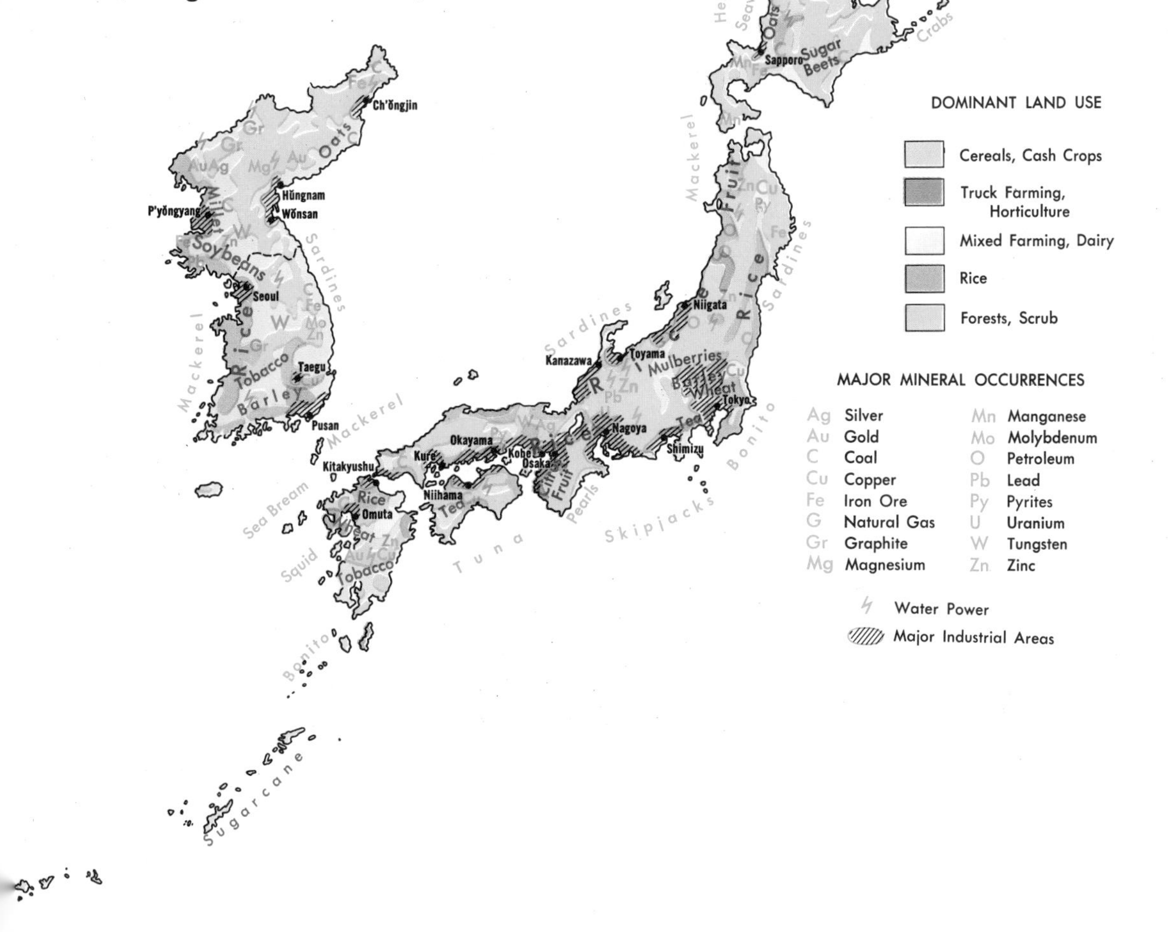
Ch'ŏngjin
Hŭngnam
Wŏnsan
P'yŏngyang
Seoul
Taegu
Pusan
Sapporo
Niigata
Toyama
Kanazawa
Tokyo
Nagoya
Shimizu
Kobe
Osaka
Okayama
Kure
Kitakyushu
Niihama
Omuta
Oats
Soybeans
Rice
Tobacco
Barley
Sugar Beets
Fruit
Mulberries
Wheat
Tea
Salmon
Herring
Seaweed
Crabs
Mackerel
Sardines
Sea Bream
Squid
Bonito
Tuna
Skipjacks
Pearls
Sugarcane
DOMINANT LAND USE
Cereals, Cash Crops
Truck Farming, Horticulture
Mixed Farming, Dairy
Rice
Forests, Scrub
MAJOR MINERAL OCCURRENCES
Ag Silver
Au Gold
C Coal
Cu Copper
Fe Iron Ore
G Natural Gas
Gr Graphite
Mg Magnesium
Mn Manganese
Mo Molybdenum
O Petroleum
Pb Lead
Py Pyrites
U Uranium
W Tungsten
Zn Zinc
Water Power
Major Industrial Areas

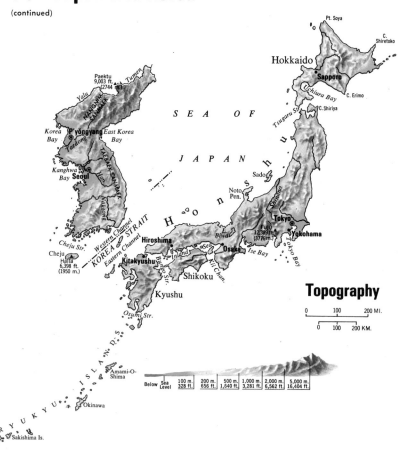

Hokkaido

Sapporo

SEA OF JAPAN

Honshu

Fuji 12,389 ft. (3776 m.)

Tokyo

Yokohama

Hiroshima

Osaka

Kitakyushu

Shikoku

Kyushu

Paektu 9,003 ft. (2744 m.)

P'yŏngyang

East Korea Bay

Korea Bay

Seoul

Kanghwa Bay

KOREA STRAIT

Cheju Str.

Cheju Halla 6,398 ft. (1950 m.)

RYUKYU ISLANDS

Amami-O-Shima

Okinawa

Sakishima Is.

Topography

Scale: 0 100 200 MI. / 0 100 200 KM.

| Below Sea Level | 100 m. 328 ft. | 200 m. 656 ft. | 500 m. 1,640 ft. | 1,000 m. 3,281 ft. | 2,000 m. 6,562 ft. | 5,000 m. 16,404 ft. |

Nishinoomote 24,266 .... E8
Nobeoka 134,521 .... E7
Noboribetsu 50,885 .... K2
Noda 78,193 .... P2
Nogata 58,551 .... E7
Nose 9,749 .... J7
Noshiro 59,215 .... J3
Noto 15,815 .... H5
Numata 45,255 .... J6
Numazu 199,325 .... J6
Obama 33,890 .... G6
Obihiro 141,774 .... L2
Oda 37,449 .... F6
Odate 71,828 .... K3
Odawara 173,519 .... J6
Ofunato 39,632 .... K4
Oga 39,619 .... J4
Ogaki 140,424 .... H6
Oga 4,717 .... J5
Ohata 12,632 .... K3
Oita 320,237 .... E7
Ojiya 44,375 .... J5
Okawa 50,395 .... E7
Okaya 61,776 .... J5
Okayama 513,471 .... F6
Okazaki 234,510 .... H6
Omagari 40,581 .... K4
Omiya 327,698 .... O2
Omu 7,407 .... L1
Omura, Bonin Is. 1,507 .... M3
Omura, Nagasaki 60,919 .... E7
Omuta 165,969 .... E7
Onagawa 16,945 .... K4
Ono 41,918 .... H6
Onoda 43,804 .... E6
Onomichi 102,951 .... F6
Osaka 2,778,987 .... J8
Ota 110,723 .... J5
Otaru 184,406 .... K2
Otawara 42,332 .... K5
Otofuke 26,933 .... L2
Otsu 191,481 .... J7
Owase 31,797 .... H5
Oyabe 35,791 .... H5
Oyama 120,264 .... J5
Ozu 37,294 .... F7
Rausu 8,249 .... M1
Rikuzentakata 29,439 .... K4
Rumoi 36,882 .... K2
Ryotsu 22,110 .... J4
Ryugasaki 40,565 .... P2
Sabae 57,252 .... H5
Saga 152,258 .... E7
Sagamihara 377,398 .... O2
Saigo 14,409 .... F5
Saiki 52,863 .... E7
Saito 37,054 .... E7
Sakado 51,232 .... O2
Sakai, Ibaraki 24,347 .... P1
Sakai, Osaka 750,688 .... J8
Sakaide 67,624 .... G6
Sakaiminato 35,821 .... F6
Sakata 97,723 .... J4
Saku 56,143 .... J5
Sakurai 54,043 .... J8
Sanda 35,261 .... H7
Sanjo 81,806 .... J5
Sapporo 1,240,613 .... L1
Saruhfutsu 3,552 .... L1
Sasebo 250,729 .... D7
Satte 43,083 .... O1
Sawara 43,807 .... K6
Sayama 98,548 .... O2
Sendai, Kagoshima 61,788 .... E8
Sendai, Miyagi 615,473 .... K4
Setouchi 15,290 .... O5
Settsu 76,704 .... J7
Shari 15,996 .... M2
Shibata 74,025 .... J5
Shibushi 30,028 .... M2
Shimabara 45,179 .... E7
Shimamoto 22,404 .... J7

Shimizu 243,049 .... J6
Shimoda 31,700 .... J6
Shimonoseki 266,593 .... E6
Shinjo 33,023 .... H7
Shinjo 42,227 .... H5
Shiogama 59,235 .... K4
Shirakawa 42,685 .... K5
Shiranuka 14,897 .... M2
Shiroishi 40,862 .... K4
Shizunai 24,833 .... L2
Shizuoka 446,952 .... H6
Shobara 23,867 .... F6
Soka 167,177 .... O2
Soma 37,551 .... K5
Sonobe 17,902 .... J7
Suita 300,956 .... J7
Sukagawa 54,922 .... K5
Sukumo 25,340 .... F7
Sumoto 44,137 .... G6
Sunagawa 28,023 .... K2
Suzuka 141,829 .... H6
Tachikawa 138,129 .... O2
Tagawa 61,464 .... E7
Tajimi 68,901 .... H6
Takaishi 66,824 .... J7
Takamatsu 298,999 .... F6
Takaoka 169,621 .... H5
Takarazuka 162,624 .... H7
Takasaki 211,348 .... J5
Takatsuki 330,570 .... J7
Takayama 60,504 .... H5
Takefu 65,012 .... G6
Takikawa 50,090 .... K2
Tanabe, Kyoto 30,022 .... J7
Tanabe, Wakayama 66,999 .... G7
Tateyama 56,139 .... K6
Tendo 48,082 .... K4
Tenri 62,909 .... J8
Teshio 6,509 .... K1
Toba 25,791 .... H6
Tobetsu 17,351 .... K2
Togane 33,406 .... K6
Toi 6,983 .... J6
Tojo 13,796 .... F6
Tokamachi 50,211 .... J5
Tokorozawa 196,870 .... O2
Tokushima 239,281 .... G7
Tokuyama 106,967 .... E6
Tokyo (cap.) 8,646,520 .... O2
Tokyo* 11,673,554 .... O2
Tomakomai 132,477 .... K2
Tomiyama 7,389 .... O3
Tondabayashi 91,393 .... J8
Tosa 30,679 .... F7
Tosashimizu 24,856 .... E7
Tosu 50,733 .... E7
Tottori 122,312 .... G6
Toyama 290,143 .... H5
Toyohashi 284,585 .... H6
Toyonaka 398,384 .... J7
Toyooka 46,210 .... G6
Toyota 248,774 .... H6
Tsu 139,538 .... H6
Tsubame 43,265 .... J5
Tsuchiura 104,028 .... J5
Tsuruga 60,205 .... H6
Tsuruoka 95,932 .... J4
Tsuyama 79,907 .... F6
Ueda 105,151 .... J5
Ugo 21,956 .... J4
Uji 133,405 .... J7
Ujiie 20,213 .... J4
Urakawa 20,213 .... L2
Urawa 331,145 .... O2
Ushibuka 24,250 .... D7

Usuki 39,163 .... F7
Utsunomiya 344,420 .... K5
Uwajima 70,428 .... F7
Wajima 33,234 .... H5
Wakasa 6,989 .... G6
Wakayama 389,717 .... G6
Wakkanai 55,464 .... K1
Warabi 76,311 .... O2
Yaizu 94,102 .... J6
Yakumo 19,260 .... J2
Yamaguchi 106,099 .... E6
Yamato 145,881 .... O2
Yamatokoriyama 71,001 .... J8
Yamatotakada 58,637 .... J8
Yao 261,639 .... J8
Yatsushiro 103,691 .... E7
Yawata 50,132 .... J7
Yawatahama 45,259 .... F7
Yoichi 25,816 .... K2
Yokawa 8,015 .... H7
Yokkaichi 247,001 .... H6
Yokohama 2,621,771 .... O3
Yokota 389,557 .... E6
Yokote 43,030 .... K4
Yonago 118,332 .... F6
Yonezawa 91,974 .... K5
Yono 71,549 .... O2
Yubari 50,131 .... L2
Yubetsu 6,693 .... L1
Yukuhashi 53,750 .... E7
Yuzawa 38,005 .... K4
Zushi 58,181 .... O3

OTHER FEATURES

Abashiri (riv.) M1
Agano (riv.) J5
Akan National Park M2
Amakusa (isls.) D7
Amami (isl.) N5
Amami-O-Shima (isl.) N5
Ara (riv.) O2
Asahi (mt.) J4
Asama (mt.) J5
Ashizuri (cape) F7
Aso (mt.) E7
Aso National Park E7
Atsumi (bay) H6
Awa (isl.) J4
Awaji (isl.) G6
Bandai (mt.) K5
Bandai-Asahi National Park J4
Biwa (lake) H6
Bonin (isls.) M3
Boso (pen.) P2
Bungo (strait) E7
Chichi (isl.) M3
Chichibu-Tama National Park J6
Chokai (mt.) J4
Chubu-Sangaku National Park H5
Dadai (isl.) D7
Dai (mt.) F6
Daio (cape) H6
Daisen (mt.) F6
Daisen-Oki National Park F6
Daisetsu (mt.) L2
Daisetsu-Zan National Park L2
Dogo (isl.) F5
Dozen (isls.) F5
East China (sea) D8
Edo (riv.) P2
Erimo (cape) L3
Esan (pt.) K3
Fuji (mt.) J6
Fuji (riv.) J6
Fuji-Hakone-Izu National Park J6
Gassan (mt.) J4
Goto (isls.) D7
Habomai (isls.) N2

Hachiro (lag.) J3
Haha (isl.) M3
Hakken (mt.) H6
Haku (mt.) H5
Hakusan National Park H5
Harima (sea) G6
Hida (riv.) H6
Hodaka (mt.) H5
Hokkaido (isl.) L2
Honshu (isl.) J5
Ie (isl.) N6
Iheya (isl.) N6
Iki (isl.) D7
Ina (riv.) J6
Inawashiro (lake) K5
Inubo (cape) K6
Iriomote (isl.) K7
Iro (cape) J6
Ise (bay) H6
Ise-Shima National Park H6
Ishigaki (isl.) L7
Ishikari (bay) K2
Ishikari (riv.) K2
Ishizuchi (mt.) F7
Iwaki (mt.) K3
Iwate (mt.) K3
Iyo (isl.) J6
Iyo (sea) E7
Izu (isls.) J6
Izu (pen.) J6
Japan (sea) G4
Joshinetsu-Kogen National Park J5
Kagoshima (bay) E8
Kamui (cape) K2
Kariba (mt.) K2
Kasumiga (lag.) K5
Kazan-retto (Volcano) (isls.) M4
Kerama (isls.) M6
Kii (chan.) G7
Kii (pen.) H6
Kikai (isl.) O5
Kino (riv.) G6
Kirishima-Yaku National Park E7
Kita Iwo (isl.) M4
Kitakami (riv.) K4
Komaga (mt.) J5
Koshiki (isl.) D8
Kuchino (isl.) O4
Kume (isl.) M6
Kunashiri (isl.) N1
Kutcharo (lake) M1
Kyushu (isl.) E7
Meakan (mt.) M2
Minami Iwo (isl.) M5
Miura (pen.) O3
Miyako (isl.) L7
Miyako (isls.) L7
Mogami (riv.) K4
Motsuta (cape) J2
Muko (isl.) M3
Muko (riv.) H7
Muroto (pt.) G7
Mutsu (bay) K3
Nampo-Shoto (isls.) M3
Nansei Shoto (Ryukyu) (isls.) M6
Nantai (mt.) J5
Nasu (mt.) K5
Nemuro (strait) M1
Nii (isl.) J6
Nikko National Park J5
Nishino (isl.) M3
Nojima (cape) J6
Nonappu (pt.) N2
Noto (pen.) H5
Oani (riv.) K3
Obitsu (riv.) P3
Oga (pen.) J4
Ogasawara-gunto (Bonin) (isls.) M3

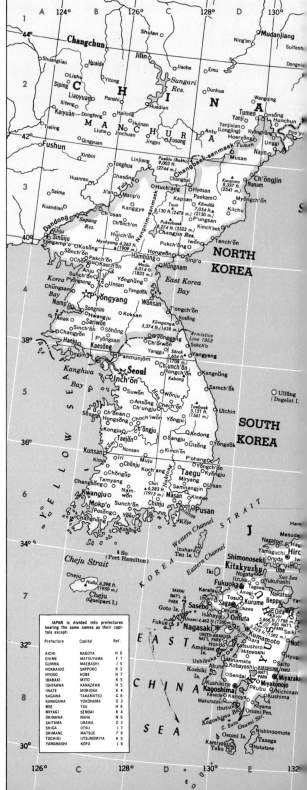

Okhotsk (sea) M1
Oki (isls.) F5
Okinawa (isl.) N6
Okinawa (isls.) N6
Okinoerabu (isl.) N5
Okushiri (isl.) J2
Oma (cape) K3
Omono (riv.) J4
Ono (riv.) E7
Ontake (mt.) H6
Osaka (bay) H8
O-Shima (isl.) J6
Osumi (isls.) E8
Osumi (pen.) E8
Osumi (str.) E8
Otakine (mt.) K5
Rikuchu-Kaigan National Park L4
Rishiri (isl.) K1
Ryukyu (isls.) L7
Sado (isl.) J4
Sagami (bay) O3
Sagami (riv.) J6
Sagami (sea) J6
Saikai National Park D7
Sakishima (isls.) K7

San'in Kaigan National Park G6
Sata (cape) E8
Setonaikai National Park G7
Shikoku (isl.) F7
Shikotan (isl.) N2
Shikotsu (lake) K2
Shikotsu-Toya National Park K3
Shimane (pen.) F5
Shimokita (pen.) K3
Shinano (riv.) J5
Shiono (cape) H7
Shiragami (cape) J3
Shirane (mt.) J5
Shirane (mt.) H6
Shiretoko (cape) M1
Shiriya (cape) K3
Soya (pt.) L1
Suo (sea) E7
Suruga (bay) J6
Suwanose (isl.) O4
Suzu (pt.) H5
Takeshima (isls.) F5
Tama (riv.) O2
Tanega (isl.) E8
Tappi (cape) K3

Korea Map

| 124° A | B 126° | C 128° | D 130° |

Changchun, Mudanjiang, Jilin, Shulan, Ning'an, Suifenc, Dongni, Shuangliao, Huaide, Jiaohe, Emu, Wangqing, Siping, Yitong, Panshi, Dunhua, Yanji (Longjing), Onsŏng, Hunchun, Liaoyuan, Xifeng, Hailong, Huinan, Yanjixian (Longjing), Kyŏnghŭng, Pos'y, Tieling, Jinchuan, Fusong, Tumen, Yanji, Unggi, Qinyuan, Xinbin, Linjiang, Paektu (Baktu), 9,003 ft. (2744 m.), Musan, Ch'ŏngjin, Fushun, Huanren, Chasŏng, Hyesan, 8,337 ft. (2541 m.), Nanam, Kanggye, Paekam, Kilchu, Kuandian, Ji'an, Yalu, Kōmdŏk, 7,054 ft. (2150 m.), Dandong, Supung Res., Ch'osan, Kanggye, Myohyang, 6,263 ft. (1909 m.), Changjin Res., Kimch'aek, Sinŭiju, Huich'ŏn, 6,274 ft. (2522 m.), Iwŏn, Tanch'ŏn, Sŏnch'ŏn, Pakch'ŏn, Modo, Hongwŏn, Sinp'o, NORTH KOREA, Yongamp'o, Kusŏng, Kilju, Kaech'ŏn, Hamhŭng, Hŭngnam, Chŏngju, Sunch'ŏn, Yŏnghŭng, Korea Bay, Chŭngsan, Anju, Unsan, East Korea Bay, Namp'o, P'yŏngyang, Songnim, Koksan, Wŏnsan, T'ongch'ŏn, Sariwŏn, Haeju, P'yŏngsan, Ch'ŏrwŏn, Yangyang, 5,374 ft. (1638 m.), Kangwŏn, Kaesŏng, Armistice Line 1953, Kangnŭng, Panmunjŏm, Ch'unch'ŏn, Kebong, Seoul, Inch'ŏn, Wŏnju, Ullŭng (Dagelet I.), Suwŏn, Ansŏng, Wŏnju, Ch'ungju, Samch'ŏk, Ch'ŏnan, Hongsŏng, Ch'ŏngju, Yŏngju, Ulchin, SOUTH KOREA, Kongju, Taejŏn, Sangju, Ŭisŏng, Andong, P'ohang, Kunsan, Iri, Chŏnju, Nonsan, Kimch'ŏn, Yŏngch'ŏn, 5,121 ft. (1561 m.), Kŭmje, Muju, Taegu, Kyŏngju, Ulsan, Chŏngŭp, Namwŏn, Chinju, Kwangju, Nam-wŏn, Chiri, 6,283 ft. (1915 m.), Masan, Samnangjin, Mokp'o, Posŏng, Sunch'ŏn, Pusan, Chang-hŭng, Kŏje, Koch'ang, Cheju Strait, (Port Hamilton), Cheju, Halla 6,398 ft. (1950 m.), Cheju (Quelpart I.), Tsu Is., Kita Iwo, Tsushima, Shimonoseki, Kitakyushu, Fukuoka, Iizuka, Ube, Hagi, Karatsu, Sasebo, Nagasaki, Kurume, Oita, Beppu, Kumamoto, Miyazaki, Kagoshima, Miyakonojo

EAST CHINA SEA

JAPAN is divided into prefectures bearing the same names as their capitals except:

Prefecture	Capital	Ref.
AICHI	NAGOYA	H 6
EHIME	MATSUYAMA	F 7
GUMMA	MAEBASHI	J 5
HOKKAIDO	SAPPORO	K 2
HYOGO	KOBE	H 7
IBARAKI	MITO	K 5
ISHIKAWA	KANAZAWA	H 5
IWATE	MORIOKA	K 4
KAGAWA	TAKAMATSU	G 6
KANAGAWA	YOKOHAMA	J 6
MIE	TSU	H 6
MIYAGI	SENDAI	K 4
OKINAWA	NAHA	N 6
SAITAMA	URAWA	O 2
SHIGA	OTSU	J 7
SHIMANE	MATSUE	F 6
TOCHIGI	UTSUNOMIYA	J 5
YAMANASHI	KOFU	J 6

Tarama (isl.) L7
Tazawa (lake) K4
Teshio (riv.) L1
Teshio (riv.) L1
Tobi (isl.) J4
Tokachi (riv.) L2
Tokachi (riv.) L2
Tokara (isls.) O5
Tokuno (isl.) O5
Tokyo (bay) O2
Tone (riv.) K6
Tosa (bay) F7
Towada (lake) K3
Towada-Hachimantai National
    Park K3
Toya (lake) K2
Toyama (bay) H5
Tsu (isls.) D6
Tsugaru (str.) K3
Tsurugi (mt.) G7
Uchiura (bay) K2
Unzen (mt.) D7
Unzen-Amakusa National Park D7
Volcano (isls.) M4
Wakasa (bay) G6

Yaeyama (isls.) K7
Yaku (isl.) E8
Yodo (riv.) J7
Yonaguni (isl.) K7
Yoron (isl.) N6
Yoshino (riv.) G6
Yoshino-Kumano National Park H7
Zao (mt.) K5

KOREA (NORTH)
CITIES and TOWNS

Ch'ŏngjin 306,000 . . . . E3
Chŏngju B4
Haeju 140,000 . . . . B4
Hamhŭng 484,000 . . . . C4
Heijo (P'yŏngyang) C4
P'yŏngyang (cap.) 1,250,000 . . . . . . B4
Sariwŏn B4
Sinŭiju 300,000 . . . . B3
Songnim B4
Wŏnsan 275,000 . . . . C4

OTHER FEATURES

Baktu (Paektu) (mt.) C3
Changjin (res.) C3
East Korea (bay) D4
Japan (sea) D4
Kanghwa (bay) B5
Kŏmdŏk (mt.) D3
Kŭmgang (mt.) D4
Hyesan D3
Iwŏn D3

Kaech'ŏn B4
Kaesŏng 175,000 . . . . C4
Kanggye C3
Kapsan D3
Kilchu D3
Manp'ojaek 100,000 . . . . C3
Najin E3
Namp'o 140,000 . . . . B4
Onsŏng E2
P'anmunjŏm C4
Sariwŏn C4
Tumen (riv.) D2
Tuun (mt.) C3
Yalu (riv.) C3
Yellow (sea) B6

Kwanmo (mt.) D3
Myohyang (mt.) C3
Nangnim-sanmaek (range) C3
Paektu (mt.) C3
Puksubaek (mt.) C3

KOREA (SOUTH)
CITIES and TOWNS

Andong 95,364 . . . . D5
Ansŏng 27,723 . . . . C5
Changhŭng 22,227 . . . . C6
Changsŏng 26,266 . . . . C6
Chech'ŏn 74,239 . . . . D5
Cheju 135,081 . . . . C7
Chinhae 103,640 . . . . D6

Chinju 154,646 . . . . D6
Choch'iwŏn 29,198 . . . . C5
Ch'ŏnan 96,766 . . . . C5
Ch'ŏngju 192,707 . . . . C5
Chŏngŭp 54,864 . . . . C6
Chŏnju 311,393 . . . . C5
Ch'ŏrwŏn 8,180 . . . . C4
Ch'unch'ŏn 140,530 . . . . D4
Ch'ungju 105,274 . . . . D5
Hongch'ŏn 29,499 . . . . D5
Hwach'ŏn 26,995 . . . . C4
Inch'ŏn 800,007 . . . . C5
Iri 117,155 . . . . C5
Kangnŭng 84,981 . . . . D5
Kimch'ŏn 67,078 . . . . D5
Kimje 221,414 . . . . C5
Kimhae 203,428 . . . . D6
Koch'ang 23,721 . . . . C6
Kohŭng 217,446 . . . . C6
Kŏnju 39,756 . . . . C5
Kunsan 154,780 . . . . C5
Kwangju 607,011 . . . . C6
Kyŏngju 108,431 . . . . D5
Masan 371,917 . . . . D6
Miryang 42,951 . . . . D6

Mokp'o 192,958 . . . . C6
Muju 18,130 . . . . C5
Namwŏn 50,857 . . . . C6
Nonsan 226,429 . . . . C5
P'anmunjŏm C5
P'ohang 134,418 . . . . D5
Posŏng 20,256 . . . . C6
Pusan 2,453,173 . . . . D6
Samch'ŏk 42,526 . . . . D5
Samnangjin 19,374 . . . . D6
Sangju 52,839 . . . . D5
Seoul (cap.) 6,889,502 . . . . C5
Sokch'o 71,387 . . . . D4
Sŏsan 38,081 . . . . C5
Sunch'ŏn 108,063 . . . . C6
Suwŏn 224,145 . . . . C5
Taegu 1,310,768 . . . . D6
Taejŏn 506,708 . . . . C5
Tamyang 15,494 . . . . C6
Ŭisŏng 26,480 . . . . D5
Ŭlchin 27,607 . . . . D5
Ulsan 252,570 . . . . D6
Wŏnju 120,276 . . . . D5
Yanggu 277,986 . . . . C4
Yangyang 10,819 . . . . D4

Yŏngch'ŏn 50,765 . . . . D6
Yŏngdŏk 18,671 . . . . D5
Yŏngju 70,793 . . . . D5
Yŏsu 130,623 . . . . C6

OTHER FEATURES

Cheju (isl.) C7
Cheju (str.) C7
Chiri (mt.) C6
Dagelet (Ullŭng) (isl.) E5
East China (sea) C8
Halla (mt.) C7
Han (riv.) C5
Japan (sea) G4
Kanghwa (bay) B5
Kebang (mt.) D5
Kŏje (isl.) D6
Korea (str.) D6
Korea (str.) C5
Kŭm (riv.) C5
Port Hamilton (So) (isl.) C7
Quelpart (Cheju) (isl.) C7
So (isl.) C6

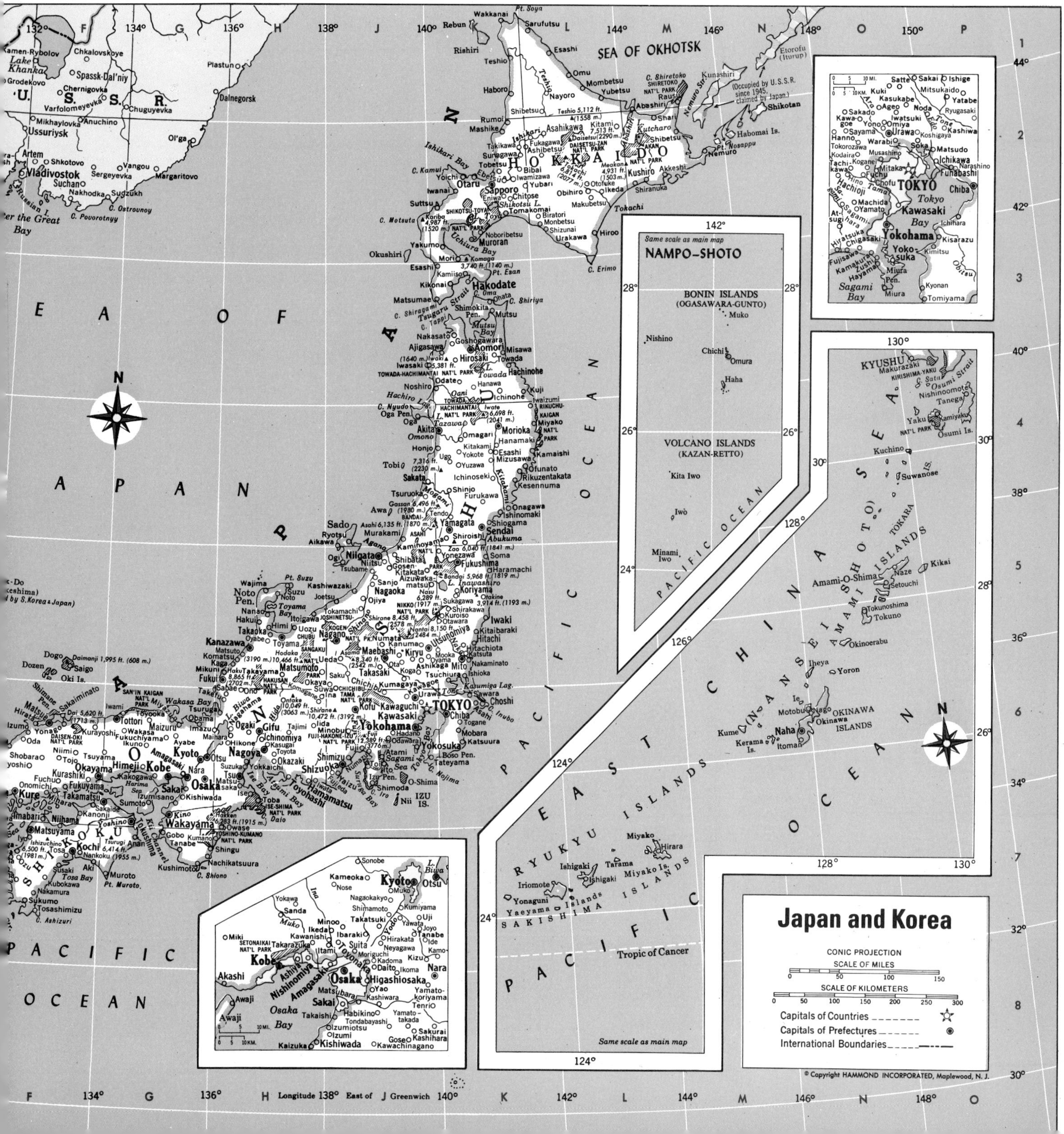

Japan and Korea

CONIC PROJECTION

SCALE OF MILES

0 50 100 150

SCALE OF KILOMETERS

0 50 100 150 200 250 300

Capitals of Countries _____ ☆
Capitals of Prefectures _____ ◉
International Boundaries _____

NAMPO-SHOTO

Same scale as main map

BONIN ISLANDS
(OGASAWARA-GUNTO)

VOLCANO ISLANDS
(KAZAN-RETTO)

KYUSHU

CHINA (MAINLAND)

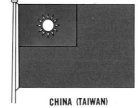

CHINA (TAIWAN)

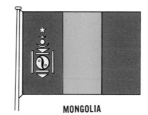

MONGOLIA

CHINA (MAINLAND)
AREA 3,691,000 sq. mi. (9,559,690 sq. km.)
POPULATION 958,090,000
CAPITAL Beijing
LARGEST CITY Shanghai
HIGHEST POINT Mt. Everest 29,028 ft.
(8,848 m.)
MONETARY UNIT yuan
MAJOR LANGUAGES Chinese, Chuang, Uigur,
Yi, Tibetan, Miao, Mongol, Kazakh
MAJOR RELIGIONS Confucianism, Buddhism,
Taoism, Islam

Topography

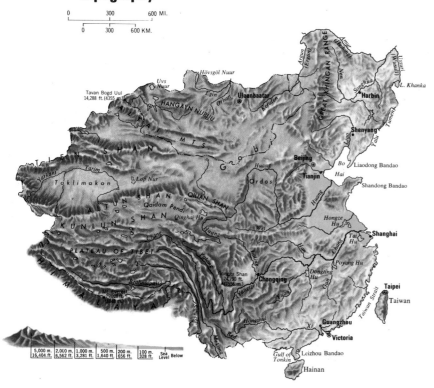

On this map Chinese place-names have been rendered according to the Pinyin spelling system within the area controlled by the People's Republic of China. Alphabetically listed below are selected Chinese place-names spelled in the traditional manner, followed by the equivalent Pinyin form.

Amoy (Hsiamen)	Xiamen	Kirin	Jilin	Sian	Xi'an
Anhwei	Anhui	Kiukiang	Jiujiang	Siangtan	Xiangtan
Canton		Kwangsi	Guangxi	Sining	Xining
(Kwangchow)	Guangzhou	Chuang	Zhuang	Sinkiang-	
Chefoo (Yentai)	Yantai	Kwangchow	Guangzhou	Uighur	Xinjiang Uygur
Chekiang	Zhejiang	Kweichow	Guizhou	Soochow	Suzhou
Chengchow	Zhengzhou	Kweilin	Guilin	Swatow	Shantou
Chengteh	Chengde	Kweiyang	Guiyang	Szechwan	Sichuan
Chengtu	Chengdu	Lanchow	Lanzhou	Tachai	Dazhai
Chinchow	Jinzhou	Liuchow	Liuzhou	Tatung	Datong
Chungking	Chongqing	Loyang	Luoyang	Tibet	Xizang
Fukien	Fujian	Lüta	Dalian	Tientsin	Tianjin
Hangchow	Hangzhou	Mutankiang	Mudanjiang	Tsinan	Jinan
Heilungkiang	Heilongjiang	Nanking	Nanjing	Tsinghai	Qinghai
Hofei	Hefei	Ningpo	Ningbo	Tsingtao	Qingdao
Honan	Henan	Ningsia Hui	Ningxia Huizu	Tsining	Jining
Hopei	Hebei	Paoting	Baoding	Tsitsihar	Qiqihar
Huhehot	Hohhot	Paotow	Baotou	Tzepo	Zibo
Hwainan	Huainan	Peking	Beijing	Urumchi	Ürümqi
Inner Mongolia	Nei Monggol	Pengpu	Bengbu	Wusih	Wuxi
Kansu	Gansu	Shansi	Shanxi	Yenan	Yan'an
Kiangsi	Jiangxi	Shantung	Shandong	Yinchwan	Yinchuan
Kiangsu	Jiangsu	Shensi	Shaanxi		
Kingtehchen	Jingdezhen	Shihkiachwang	Shijiazhuang		

CHINA†
PROVINCES

Anhui (Anhwei) 47,130,000 .... J5
Fujian (Fukien) 24,500,000 .... J6
Gansu (Kansu) 18,730,000 .... E3
Guangdong (Kwangtung)
55,930,000 .... H7
Guangxi Zhuangzu (Kwangsi
Chuang Autonomous Reg.)
34,020,000 .... G7
Guizhou (Kweichow)
26,860,000 .... G6
Heilongjiang
(Heilungkiang) 33,760,000 .... K2
Hebei (Hopei) 50,570,000 .... J4
Henan (Honan) 70,660,000 ...... H5
Hubei (Hupei) 45,750,000 ...... H5
Hunan 51,660,000 .... H6
Jiangsu (Kiangsu) 58,340,000 .. K5
Jiangxi (Kiangsi) 31,830,000 .... J6
Jilin (Kirin) 24,740,000 .... L3
Liaoning 37,430,000 .... K3
Nei Monggol (Inner Mongolian
Aut. Reg.) 8,900,000 .... H3
Ningxia Huizu (Ningsia Hui Aut.
Reg.) 3,660,000 .... F3
Qinghai (Tsinghai) 3,650,000 .... E4
Shaanxi (Shensi) 27,790,000 .... G5
Shanxi (Shansi) 24,340,000 ...... H4
Shandong
(Shantung) 71,600,000 ...... J4
Sichuan
(Szechwan) 97,070,000 ...... F5
Taiwan 16,609,961 .... K7
Xinjiang Uygur (Sinkiang-Uigur
Aut. Reg.) 12,330,000 .... B3
Xizang (Tibet Aut.
Reg.) 1,790,000 .... B5
Yunnan 30,920,000 .... F7
Zhejiang
(Chekiang) 37,510,000 ...... K6

CITIES AND TOWNS

Aihui (Aigun) (Heihe) L1
Amoy (Xiamen) 400,000 .... J7
Anqing (Anking) 160,000 .... J5

Anshan 1,500,000 .... K3
Anyang 225,000 .... H4
Aqsu (Aksu) B3
Baoding (Paoting) 350,000 ...... J4
Baoji (Paoki) 275,000 .... G5
Baoshan E7
Baotou (Paotow) 800,000 ...... G3
Bei'an (Pehan) 130,000 .... L2
Beihai (Pakhoi) 175,000 .... G7
Beijing (Peking) (cap.)
⊙8,500,000 .... J3
Bengbu (Pengpu) 400,000 ...... J5
Benxi (Penki) 750,000 .... K3
Canton (Guangzhou)
2,300,000 .... H7
Chamdo (Qamdo) E5
Changchun 1,500,000 .... K3
Changde (Changteh) 225,000 .. H6
Changhua 137,236 .... K7
Changsha 850,000 .... H6
Changzhi (Changchih) H4
Changzhou (Changchow)
400,000 .... K5
Chankiang (Zhanjiang)
220,000 .... H7
Chao'an (Chaochow) J7
Charkhlia (Ruoqiang) C4
Chefoo (Yantai) 180,000 .... K4
Chengchow (Zhengzhou)
1,500,000 .... H5
Chengde (Chengteh) 200,000 .. J3
Chengdu (Chengtu)
2,000,000 .... F5
Cherchen (Qiemo) C4
Chiai 238,713 .... K7
Chinchow (Jinzhou) 750,000 .. K3
Chinkiang (Zhenjiang)
250,000 .... J5
Chinwangtao (Qinhuangdao)
400,000 .... K4
Chongqing (Chungking)
3,500,000 .... G6
Chüanchow (Quanzhou)
130,000 .... J6
Chuchow (Zhuzhou) 350,000 .. H6
Chuguchak (Tacheng) B2
Chungshan (Tangshan)
135,000 .... H7

Dali E6
Dalian 1,480,240 .... K4
Dandong (Tantung) 450,000 .... K3
Datong (Tatung) 300,000 .... H3
Erenhot H3
Foshan (Fatshan) H7
Fushun 1,700,000 .... K3
Fuxin (Fusin) 350,000 .... K3
Fuzhou (Foochow) 900,000 .... J6
Ganzhou (Kanchow) 135,000 .. H6
Garyarsa (Gartok) B5
Gejiu (Kokiu) 250,000 .... F7
Golmud (Golmo) D4
Guangzhou (Canton)
2,300,000 .... H7
Guilin (Kweilin) 225,000 .... G6
Guiyang (Kweiyang) 1,500,000 G6
Gulja (Yining) 160,000 .... B3
Gyangzê C6
Haikou (Hoihow) 500,000 ...... H8
Hailar J2
Hami (Kumul) D3
Handan (Hantan) 500,000 ...... H4
Hangzhou (Hangchow)
1,100,000 .... J5
Hanzhong (Hanchung)
120,000 .... G5
Harbin 2,750,000 .... L2
Hefei (Hofei) 400,000 .... J5
Hegang (Hokang) 3,530,000 .... L1
Heihe (Aihui) (Aigun) L1
Hengyang 310,000 .... H6
Hohhot (Huhehot) 700,000 .... H3
Horqin Youyi Qianqi (Ulanhot)
110,000 .... K2
Hotan B4
Huainan 350,000 .... J5
Huangshi 200,000 .... J5
Ichang (Yichang) 150,000 ...... H5
Ichun (Yichun) 200,000 .... L2
Ipin (Yibin) 275,000 .... F6
Jiamusi (Kiamusze) 275,000 .... M2
Ji'an (Kian) 100,000 .... J6
Jiangmen (Kongmoon)
150,000 .... H7
Jiaozuo (Tsiaotso) 300,000 .... H4
Jilin (Kirin) 1,200,000 .... L3
Jinan (Tsinan) 1,500,000 ...... J4

Jingdezhen (Kingtehchen)
300,000 .... J6
Jining (Tsining) 160,000 .... H3
Jinshi (Tsingshih) 100,000 ...... H6
Jinzhou (Chinchow) 750,000 .. K3
Jiujiang (Kiukiang) 120,000 .... J6
Jixi (Kisi) 350,000 .... M2
Juichin (Ruijin) J6
Kaifeng (Kaifeng) 330,000 ...... H5
Kalgan (Zhangjiakou)
1,000,000 .... J3
Kanchow (Ganzhou) 135,000 .. H6
Kaohsiung 1,028,334 .... J7
Karakax (Kara Kash) (Moyu) .. A4
Karghalik (Yecheng) A4
Kashi (Kashgar) 175,000 .... A4
Kaxgar (Kashi) 175,000 .... A4
Keelung 342,604 .... K6
Keriya (Yutian) B4
Khotan (Hotan) B4
Kiamusze (Jiamusi) 275,000 .. M2
Kian (Ji'an) 100,000 .... J6
Kingtehchen (Jingdezhen)
300,000 .... J6
Kirin (Jilin) 1,200,000 .... L3
Kisi (Jixi) 350,000 .... M2
Kiukiang (Jiujiang) 120,000 .... J6
Kokiu (Gejiu) 250,000 .... F7
Kongmoon (Jiangmen) 150,000 H7
Kuldja (Yining) 160,000 .... B3
Kunming 1,700,000 .... F6
Kwangchow (Canton)
2,300,000 .... H7
Kweilin (Guilin) 225,000 .... G6
Kweisui (Hohhot) 700,000 ...... H3
Kweiyang (Guiyang) 1,500,000 G6
Lanzhou (Lanchow) 1,500,000 F4
Leshan (Loshan) 250,000 ...... F6
Lhasa 175,000 .... D6
Lhazê (Lhatse) C6
Lianyungang (Lienyünkang)
300,000 .... J5
Liaoyang 250,000 .... K3
Liaoyuan 300,000 .... K3
Linqing (Lintsing) J4
Liuzhou (Liuchow) 250,000 .... G7
Lopnur (Lop Nur) C3
Lüda (Dalian) 1,480,240 .... K4

(continued on following page)

CHINA (TAIWAN)

AREA 13,971 sq. mi. (36,185 sq. km.)
POPULATION 16,609,961
CAPITAL Taipei
LARGEST CITY Taipei
HIGHEST POINT Yü Shan 13,113 ft. (3,997 m.)
MONETARY UNIT new Taiwan yüan (dollar)
MAJOR LANGUAGES Chinese, Formosan
MAJOR RELIGIONS Confucianism, Buddhism,
Taoism, Christianity, tribal religions

MONGOLIA

AREA 606,163 sq. mi. (1,569,962 sq. km.)
POPULATION 1,594,800
CAPITAL Ulaanbaatar
LARGEST CITY Ulaanbaatar
HIGHEST POINT Tabun Bogdo 14,288 ft.
(4,355 m.)
MONETARY UNIT tughrik
MAJOR LANGUAGES Khalkha Mongolian,
Kazakh (Turkic)
MAJOR RELIGION Buddhism

HONG KONG

AREA 403 sq. mi. (1,044 sq. km.)
POPULATION 5,022,000
CAPITAL Victoria
MONETARY UNIT Hong Kong dollar
MAJOR LANGUAGES Chinese, English
MAJOR RELIGIONS Confucianism, Buddhism,
Christianity

MACAU

AREA 6 sq. mi. (16 sq. km.)
POPULATION 271,000
CAPITAL Macau
MONETARY UNIT pataca
MAJOR LANGUAGES Chinese, Portuguese
MAJOR RELIGIONS Confucianism, Buddhism,
Taoism, Christianity

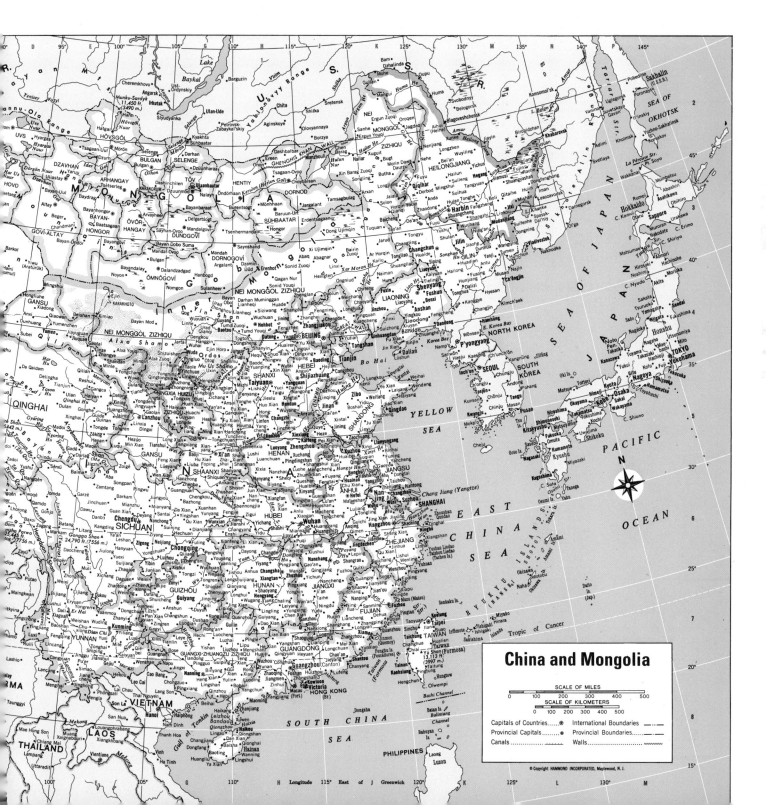

China and Mongolia

SCALE OF MILES
0   100   200   300   400   500
SCALE OF KILOMETERS
0 100 200 300 400 500

Capitals of Countries......⊛   International Boundaries _____
Provincial Capitals........◉   Provincial Boundaries_____
Canals ....   Walls ....~~~~~~~~

© Copyright HAMMOND INCORPORATED, Maplewood, N.J.

Luoyang (Loyang) 750,000 ....H5
Lüshun K4
Luzhou (Luchol) 225,000 .....G6
Ma'anshan J5
Manzhouli (Manchouli) J2
Maoming (Mowming) H7
Mengzi F7
Mianyang G5
Minfeng (Niya) B4
Moyu (Karakax) A4
Mudanjiang
  (Mutankiang) 400,000 ......M3
Mukden (Shenyang) 3,750,000 K3
Nanchang 900,000 ....J6
Nanchong (Nanchung) 275,000 G5
Nanjing (Nanking) 2,000,000 .J5
Nanning 375,000 ....G7
Nanping J6
Nantong 300,000 ....K5
Nanyang H5
Neijiang (Neikiang) 240,000 .G6
Nenjiang L2
Ningbo (Ningpo) 350,000 .....K6
Ningsia (Yinchuan,
  Yinchwan) 175,000 ....G4
Paicheng (Baicheng) K2
Pakhoi (Beihai) 175,000 .....G7
Paoki (Baoji) 275,000 ....G5
Paoting (Baoding) 350,000 ...J4
Paotow (Baotou) 800,000 .....G3
Pehan (Bei'an) 130,000 ......L2
Peking (Beijing)
  (cap.)○ 8,500,000 ....J3
Pengpu (Bengbu) 400,000 .....J5
Penki (Benxi) 750,000 ....K3
Pingdingshan H5
Pingliang G4
Pingtung 165,360 ....K7
Pingxiang, Guangxi
  Zhuangzu G7
Pingxiang, Jiangxi H6
Piqan (Shanshan) D3
Qamdo E5
Qarkilik (Ruoqiang) C4
Qiemo (Qarqan) C4
Qingdao (Tsingtao) 1,900,000 K4
Qingjiang 110,000 ....J5
Qinhuangdao
  (Chinwangtao) 400,000 .....K4
Qiqihar
  (Tsitsihar) 1,500,000 .....K2
Qitai C3

Qoqek (Tacheng) B2
Quanzhou
  (Chüanchow) 130,000 ....J7
Ruijin (Juichin) J6
Ruoqiang (Qarkilik) C4
Shache (Yarkand) A4
Shanghai○ 10,980,000 ....K5
Shangqui (Shangkiu) 250,000 .J5
Shangrao (Shangjao) 100,000 .J6
Shangshui 100,000 ....J5
Shanshan (Piqan) D3
Shantou (Swatow) 400,000 ....J7
Shaoguan (Shiukwan) 125,000 H7
Shaoxing (Shaohing) 225,000 .K5
Shaoyang 275,000 ....H6
Shashi 125,000 ....H5
Shenyang (Mukden) 3,750,000 K3
Shigatse (Xigazê) C6
Shihezi (Shihhotzu) C3
Shijiazhuang
  (Shihkiachwang) 1,500,000 .J4
Shiyan H5
Shizuishan (Shihsuishan) G4
Shuangcheng L2
Shuangyashan 150,000 ....M2
Siakwan (Xiaguan) E6
Sian (Xi'an) 1,900,000 ......G5
Siangfan (Xiangfan) 150,000 .H5
Siangtan (Xiangtan) 300,000 .H6
Sienyang (Xianyang) 125,000 G5
Simao (Fusingchen) F7
Sinchu 208,038 ....K7
Singtai (Xingtai) H4
Sining (Xining) 250,000 .....F4
Sinsiang (Xinxiang) 300,000 .H4
Sinyang (Xinyang) 125,000 ...H5
Siping (Szeping) 180,000 ....K3
Soche (Shache) A4
Suao K7
Süchow (Xuzhou) 1,500,000 ...J5
Suifenhe M3
Suihua L2
Suining G6
Suzhou (Soochow) 1,300,000 ..K5
Swatow (Shantou) 400,000 ....J7
Tacheng (Qoqek) B2
Tai'an J4
Taichung 565,255 ....K7
Tainan 541,390 ....J7
Taipei 2,108,193 ....K7
Taitung K7
Taiyuan 2,725,000 ....H4

Taizhou (Taichow) 275,000 ...K5
Tali (Dali) E6
Tangshan 1,200,000 ....J4
Tantung (Dandong) 450,000 ...K3
Tao'an K2
Taoyuan 105,841 ....K6
Tatung (Datong) 300,000 .....H3
Tehchow (Dezhou) J4
Tianjin (Tientsin)○ 7,210,000 J4
Tianshui 100,000 ....F5
Tieling K3
Tientsin (Tianjin)○ 7,210,000 J4
Tingtai (Xingtai) H4
Tongchuan (Tungchwan) G5
Tonghua (Tunghwa) 275,000 ...L3
Tongjiang (Tungkiang) M2
Tongliao K3
Tongling J5
Tsiaotso (Jiaozuo) 300,000 ..H4
Tsinan (Jinan) 1,500,000 ....J4
Tsingkiang
  (Qingjiang) 110,000 ....J5
Tsingshih (Jinshi) 100,000 ..H6
Tsingtao (Qingdao) 1,900,000 K4
Tsining (Jining) 160,000 ....H3
Tsitsihar
  (Qiqihar) 1,500,000 ....K2
Tsunyi (Zunyi) 275,000 ......G6
Tumen M3
Tunxi (Tunki) J5
Turpan (Turfan) C3
Tzekung (Zigong) 350,000 ....F6
Tzepo (Zibo) 1,750,000 ......J4
Uch Turfan (Wushi) A3
Ulanhot (Horqin Youyi
  Qianqi) 100,000 ....K3
Ulughchat (Wuqia) A4
Ürümqi
  (Urumchi) 500,000 ....C3
Usu B3
Wanxian (Wanhsien) 175,000 ..G5
Weifang 260,000 ....J4
Weihai (Weihaiwei) K4
Wenzhou 250,000 ....J6
Wuda G4
Wuhan 4,250,000 ....H5
Wuhu 300,000 ....J5
Wuqi G4
Wuqia (Wuqia) A4
Wushi A4
Wuxi (Wusih) 900,000 ....K5
Wuxing (Wuhing) 160,000 .....K5
Wuzhong (Wuchung) G4

Wuzhou (Wuchow) 150,000 .....H7
Xiaguan (Siakwan) E6
Xiamen (Amoy) 400,000 ....J7
Xi'an (Sian) 1,900,000 ......G5
Xiangfan (Siangfan) 150,000 .H5
Xiangtan (Siangtan) 300,000 .H6
Xianyang (Sienyang) 125,000 G5
Xiapu (Siapu) K6
Xichang (Sichang) F6
Xigazê (Shigatse) C6
Xingtai (Singtai) H4
Xining (Sining) 250,000 .....F4
Xinxiang (Sinsiang) 300,000 .H4
Xinyang (Sinyang) 125,000 ...H5
Xuzhou (Süchow) 1,500,000 ...J5
Ya'an 100,000 ....F6
Yadong C6
Yan'an (Yenan) G4
Yanji (Yenki) 130,000 ....L3
Yangquan
  (Yangchuan) 350,000 ....H4
Yangzhou (Yangchow)
  210,000 ....J5
Yantai (Chefoo) 180,000 .....K4
Yarkand (Shache) A4
Ya Xian G8
Yecheng A4
Yenan (Yan'an) G4
Yibin (Ipin) 275,000 ....F6
Yichang (Ichang) 150,000 ....H5
Yichun 200,000 ....L2
Yinchuan (Ningsia) 175,000 ..G4
Yingkou 215,000 ....K3
Yining 160,000 ....B3
Yiyang H4
Yuci (Yütze) H4
Yuli (Lopnur) C3
Yumen 325,000 ....E4
Yungkia (Wenzhou) 250,000 ..J6
Yutian B4
Zhangjiakou
  (Kalgan) 1,000,000 ....J3
Zhangzhou (Changchow) J7
Zhanjiang
  (Chankiang) 220,000 ....H7
Zhaoqing H7
Zhengzhou
  (Chengchow) 1,500,000 .....H5
Zhenjiang
  (Chinkiang) 250,000 ....J5
Zhongshan
  (Chungshan) 135,000 ....H7

Zhuzhou (Chuchow) 350,000 ...H6
Zibo (Tzepo) 1,750,000 ......J4
Zigong (Tzekung) 350,000 ....F6
Zunyi (Tsunyi) 275,000 ......G6

OTHER FEATURES

Altun Shan (range) C4
Alxa Shamo (des.) F4
Amur (Heilong Jiang) (riv.) L2
A'nyêmaqên Shan (mts.) E5
Argun' (Ergun He) (riv.) K1
Bashi (chan.) K7
Bayan Har Shan (range) E5
Bo Hai (gulf) J4
Bosten (Bagrax) Hu (lake) ...C3
Chang Jiang (Yangtze) (riv.) E5
Da Hingan Ling (range) J3
Dian Chi (lake) F7
Dongsha (isl.) J7
Dongting Hu (riv.) H6
East China (sea) L6
Ergun He (Argun') (riv.) K1
Er Hai (lake) F6
Everest (mt.) C6
Formosa (Taiwan) (str.) J7
Gangdisê Shan (range) B5
Ghenghis Khan Wall (ruin) ...H2
Gobi (des.) G3
Grand (canal) J4
Great Wall (ruins) G4,J
Gurla Mandhada (mt.) B5
Hainan (isl.) H8
Hangzhou Wan (bay) K5
Heilong Jiang (Amur) (riv.) .L2
Himalaya (mts.) C6
Hotan He (riv.) B4
Huang He (Yellow) (riv.) J4
Hulun Nur (lake) J2
Inner Mongolia (reg.) H3
Jinmen (Quemoy) (isl.) J7
Jinsha Jiang (Yangtze) (riv.) E5
Junggar Pendi (desert
  basin) C2
Karakhoto (ruins) F3
Karamiran Shankou (pass) C4
Keriya Shankou (pass) B4
Khanka (lake) M3
Kongur Shan (mt.) A4
Kunlun Shan (range) B4
Kuruktag Shan (range) C4

Lancang Jiang (riv.) F7
Leizhou Bandao (pen.) G7
Liaodong Bandao (pen.) K3
Liao He (riv.) K3
Lop Nor (Lop Nur) (lake) D3
Manas He (riv.) C3
Mazu (Matsu) (isl.) K6
Mekong (Lancang Jiang)
  (riv.) F7
Muztag (mt.) B4
Muztagata (mt.) A3
Nam Co (lake) D5
Namzha Parwa (mt.) E5
Nan Ling (mts.) H6
Nu Jiang (riv.) E5
Nyainqêntanglha Shan
  (range) D5
Olwanpi (cape) K7
Ordos (reg.) G4
Penghu (Pescadores) (isls.) .J7
Pobeda (peak) A3
Poyang Hu (lake) J6
Pratas (Dongsha) (isl.) J7
Qaidam Pendi (basin) D4
Qarqan He (riv.) C4
Qilian Shan (range) E4
Qinghai Hu (lake) E4
Qiongzhou Haixia (str.) G7
Quemoy (Jinmen) (isl.) J7
Salween (Nu Jiang) (riv.) ...E5
Siling Co (lake) C5
Songhua Jiang (Sungari)
  (riv.) M2
South China (sea) J7
Tai Hu (lake) K5
Taiwan (Formosa) (str.) J7
Taizhou (Tachen) (isls.) K6
Takla Makan (Taklimakan Shamo)
  (des.) B4
Tanggula Shan (range) D5
Tangra Yumco (lake) C5
Tarim Pendi (basin) B4
Tian Shan (range) B3
Tibet (reg.) B5
Tongtian He (Zhi Qu) (riv.) .D5
Tonkin (gulf) G7
Tumen (riv.) L3
Ulu Muztag (mt.) C4
Ussuri (Wusuli Jiang) (riv.) M2
Wei He (riv.) G5
Wusuli Jiang (Ussuri) (riv.) M2

Xiang Jiang (riv.) H6
Xi Jiang (riv.) H6
Yalong Jiang (riv.) F6
Yalu (riv.) K3
Yangtze (Chang Jiang) (riv.) E5
Yarkant He (riv.) A4
Yellow (Huang He) (riv.) J4
Yellow (sea) K4
Yü Shan (mt.) K7

HONG KONG

CITIES and TOWNS

Kowloon* 2,378,480 ....H7
Victoria (cap.)* 1,026,870 ..H7

MACAU (MACAO)

CITIES and TOWNS

Macau (Macao (cap.) 226,880 .H7

MONGOLIA

CITIES and TOWNS

Tamsagbulag J2
Ulaanbaatar (Ulan Bator)
  (cap.) 345,000 ....G2

OTHER FEATURES

Altai (mts.) C2
Dzavhan Gol (riv.) D2
Hangayn Nuruu (mts.) E2
Har Us Nuur (lake) D2
Herlen Gol (Kerulen)
  (riv.) H2
Hovd Gol (riv.) D2
Hövsgöl Nuur (lake) F1
Hyargas Nuur (lake) D2
Karakorum (ruins) F2
Kerulen (riv.) F2
Munku-Sardyk (mt.) F1
Orhon Gol (riv.) F2
Selenge Mörön (riv.) G1
Tannu-Ola (range) D1
Tavan Bogd Uul (mt.) C2
Uvs Nuur (lake) D1

○Population of municipality.   *City and suburbs   †Populations of mainland cities excluding Peking (Beijing), Shanghai and Tianjin (Tientsin), courtesy of Kingsley Davis, Office of Int'l Population and Urban Research, Institute of Int'l Studies, Univ. of California.

Agriculture, Industry and Resources

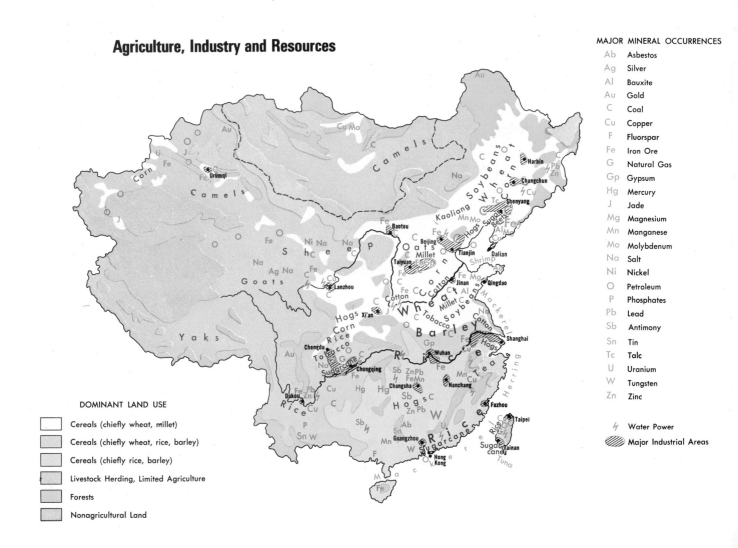

MAJOR MINERAL OCCURRENCES

Ab	Asbestos
Ag	Silver
Al	Bauxite
Au	Gold
C	Coal
Cu	Copper
F	Fluorspar
Fe	Iron Ore
G	Natural Gas
Gp	Gypsum
Hg	Mercury
J	Jade
Mg	Magnesium
Mn	Manganese
Mo	Molybdenum
Na	Salt
Ni	Nickel
O	Petroleum
P	Phosphates
Pb	Lead
Sb	Antimony
Sn	Tin
Tc	Talc
U	Uranium
W	Tungsten
Zn	Zinc

⚡ Water Power

▨ Major Industrial Areas

DOMINANT LAND USE

☐ Cereals (chiefly wheat, millet)

▧ Cereals (chiefly wheat, rice, barley)

▧ Cereals (chiefly rice, barley)

▨ Livestock Herding, Limited Agriculture

▨ Forests

▨ Nonagricultural Land

BURMA

THAILAND

LAOS

CAMBODIA

VIETNAM

MALAYSIA

SINGAPORE

BURMA
AREA   261,789 sq. mi. (678,034 sq. km.)
POPULATION   32,913,000
CAPITAL   Rangoon
LARGEST CITY   Rangoon
HIGHEST POINT   Hkakabo Razi 19,296 ft.
   (5,881 m.)
MONETARY UNIT   kyat
MAJOR LANGUAGES   Burmese, Karen, Shan,
   Kachin, Chin, Kayah, English
MAJOR RELIGIONS   Buddhism, tribal religions

THAILAND
AREA   198,455 sq. mi. (513,998 sq. km.)
POPULATION   46,455,000
CAPITAL   Bangkok
LARGEST CITY   Bangkok
HIGHEST POINT   Doi Inthanon 8,452 ft.
   (2,576 m.)
MONETARY UNIT   baht
MAJOR LANGUAGES   Thai, Lao, Chinese,
   Khmer, Malay
MAJOR RELIGIONS   Buddhism, tribal religions

LAOS
AREA   91,428 sq. mi. (236,800 sq. km.)
POPULATION   3,721,000
CAPITAL   Vientiane
LARGEST CITY   Vientiane
HIGHEST POINT   Phou Bia 9,252 ft. (2,820 m.)
MONETARY UNIT   kip
MAJOR LANGUAGE   Lao
MAJOR RELIGIONS   Buddhism, tribal religions

CAMBODIA
AREA   69,898 sq. mi. (181,036 sq. km.)
POPULATION   5,200,000
CAPITAL   Phnom Penh
LARGEST CITY   Phnom Penh
HIGHEST POINT   5,948 ft. (1,813 m.)
MONETARY UNIT   riel
MAJOR LANGUAGE   Khmer (Cambodian)
MAJOR RELIGION   Buddhism

VIETNAM
AREA   128,405 sq. mi. (332,569 sq. km.)
POPULATION   52,741,766
CAPITAL   Hanoi
LARGEST CITY   Ho Chi Minh City (Saigon)
HIGHEST POINT   Fan Si Pan 10,308 ft.
   (3,142 m.)
MONETARY UNIT   dong
MAJOR LANGUAGES   Vietnamese, Thai,
   Muong, Meo, Yao, Khmer, French,
   Chinese, Cham
MAJOR RELIGIONS   Buddhism, Taoism,
   Confucianism, Roman Catholicism,
   Cao-Dai

MALAYSIA
AREA   128,308 sq. mi. (332,318 sq. km.)
POPULATION   13,435,588
CAPITAL   Kuala Lumpur
LARGEST CITY   Kuala Lumpur
HIGHEST POINT   Mt. Kinabalu 13,455 ft.
   (4,101 m.)
MONETARY UNIT   ringgit
MAJOR LANGUAGES   Malay, Chinese, English,
   Tamil, Dayak, Kadazan
MAJOR RELIGIONS   Islam, Confucianism,
   Buddhism, tribal religions, Hinduism,
   Taoism, Christianity, Sikhism

SINGAPORE
AREA   226 sq. mi. (585 sq. km.)
POPULATION   2,413,945
CAPITAL   Singapore
LARGEST CITY   Singapore
HIGHEST POINT   Bukit Timah 581 ft. (177 m.)
MONETARY UNIT   Singapore dollar
MAJOR LANGUAGES   Chinese, Malay, Tamil,
   English, Hindi
MAJOR RELIGIONS   Confucianism, Buddhism,
   Taoism, Hinduism, Islam, Christianity

Topography

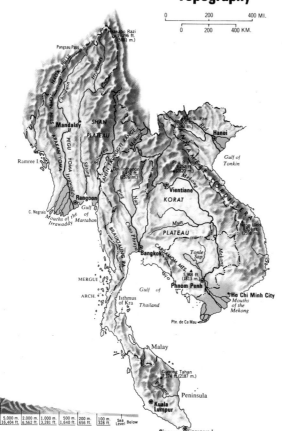

BURMA

INTERNAL DIVISIONS

Arakan (state) 1,710,913	B3
Chin (state) 323,094	B2
Irrawaddy (div.) 4,152,521	B3
Kachin (state) 735,144	C1
Karen (state) 865,218	C3
Kayah (state) 126,492	C3
Magwe (div.) 2,632,144	B2
Mandalay (div.) 3,662,312	B2
Mon (state) 1,313,111	C3
Pegu (div.) 3,174,109	C3
Rangoon (div.) 3,186,886	C3
Sagaing (div.) 3,115,502	B1
Shan (state) 3,178,214	C2
Tenasserim (div.) 717,607	C4

CITIES and TOWNS

Akyab (Sittwe) 42,329	B2
Allanmyo 15,580	B3
Amarapura 11,268	B2
Amherst 6,000	C3
An	B3
Anin	C4
Bassein 126,045	B3
Bhamo 9,821	C1
Chauk 24,466	B2
Danubyu	B3
Falam	B2
Fort Hertz (Putao)	C1
Gawai	C1
Gokteik	C2
Gwa	B3
Gyobingauk 9,922	C3
Haka	B2
Henzada 61,972	B3
Hmawbi 23,032	C3
Homalin	B1
Hsenwi	C2
Hsipaw	C2
Htawgaw	C1
Insein 143,625	C3
Kamaing	C1
Karathuri	C5
Katha 7,648	C1
Kawludo	C3
Kawthaung 1,520	C5
Keng Hkam	C2
Keng Tung	C2
Koma	C2
Kunlong	C2
Kyaikto 13,154	C3
Kya-in Seikkyi	C3
Kyangin 6,073	B3
Kyaukme	C2
Kyaukpadaung 5,480	B2
Kyaukpyu 7,335	B3
Kyaukse 8,659	C2
Labutta 12,982	B3
Lai-hka	C2
Lamu	B3
Lashio	C2
Lenya	C5
Letpadan 15,896	C3
Lewe	C3
Loi-kaw	C3
Lonton	B1
Magwe 13,270	B2
Maingkwan	C1
Maliwun	C5
Mandalay 418,008	C2
Man Hpang	C2
Martaban 5,661	C3
Ma-ubin 23,362	B3
Maungdaw 3,772	B2
Mawkmai	C2
Mawlaik 2,993	B2
Mawlu	C1
Maymyo 22,287	C2
Meiktila 19,474	C2
Mergui 33,697	C4
Minbu 9,096	B2

Minhla 6,470	B3
Mogaung 2,920	C1
Mogok 8,334	C2
Mohnyin	C1
Möng Hsat	C2
Möng Maü	C3
Möng Mit	C2
Möng Pan	C2
Möng Si	C2
Möng Ton	C2
Möng Tung	C2
Monywa 26,279	B2
Moulmein 171,977	C3
Mudon 20,136	C3
Myanaung 11,155	B3
Myaungmya 24,532	B3
Myingyan 36,439	B2
Myitkyina 12,382	C1
Myohaung 6,534	B3
Naba	B1
Namhkam	C2
Namlan	C2
Namtu	C2
Natmauk	B2
Okkan 14,443	B3
Okpo 12,155	C3
Pakokku 30,943	B2
Palaw 5,596	C4
Paletwa	B2
Pantha	B2
Papun	C3
Pasawng	C3
Paungde 17,286	B3
Pegu 47,378	C3
Prome (Pye) 36,997	B3
Putao	C1
Pyapon 19,174	B3
Pye 36,997	B3
Pyinmana 22,025	C3
Pyu 10,443	C3
Rangoon (cap.) 1,586,422	C3
Rangoon* 2,055,365	C3
Rathedaung 2,969	B2
Sadon	C1
Sagaing 15,382	B2
Samka	C2
Sandoway 5,172	B3
Shingbwiyang	B1
Shwebo 17,827	B2
Shwenyaung	C2
Singkaling Hkamti	B1
Singu 4,027	C2
Sinlumkaba	C1
Sittwe 42,329	B2
Sumprabum	C1
Syriam 15,296	C3
Taungdwingyi 16,233	C2
Taunggyi	C2
Tavoy 40,312	C4
Tharrawaddy 8,977	C3
Thaton 38,047	C3
Thaungdut	B1
Thayetmyo 11,649	B3
Thazi 7,531	C2
Thongwa 10,829	C3
Toungoo 31,589	C3
Wakema 20,716	B3
Yamethin 11,167	C2
Yandoon 15,245	B3
Ye 12,852	C4
Yenangyaung 24,416	B2
Yesagyo 7,880	B2
Ye-u 5,307	B2
Ywathit	C3
Zadi	C4
Zalun 899	B3

OTHER FEATURES

Amya (pass)	C4
Andaman (sea)	B4
Arakan Yoma (mts.)	B3
Ataran (riv.)	C4
Bengal, Bay of (sea)	B3
Bentick (isl.)	C5

(continued on following page)

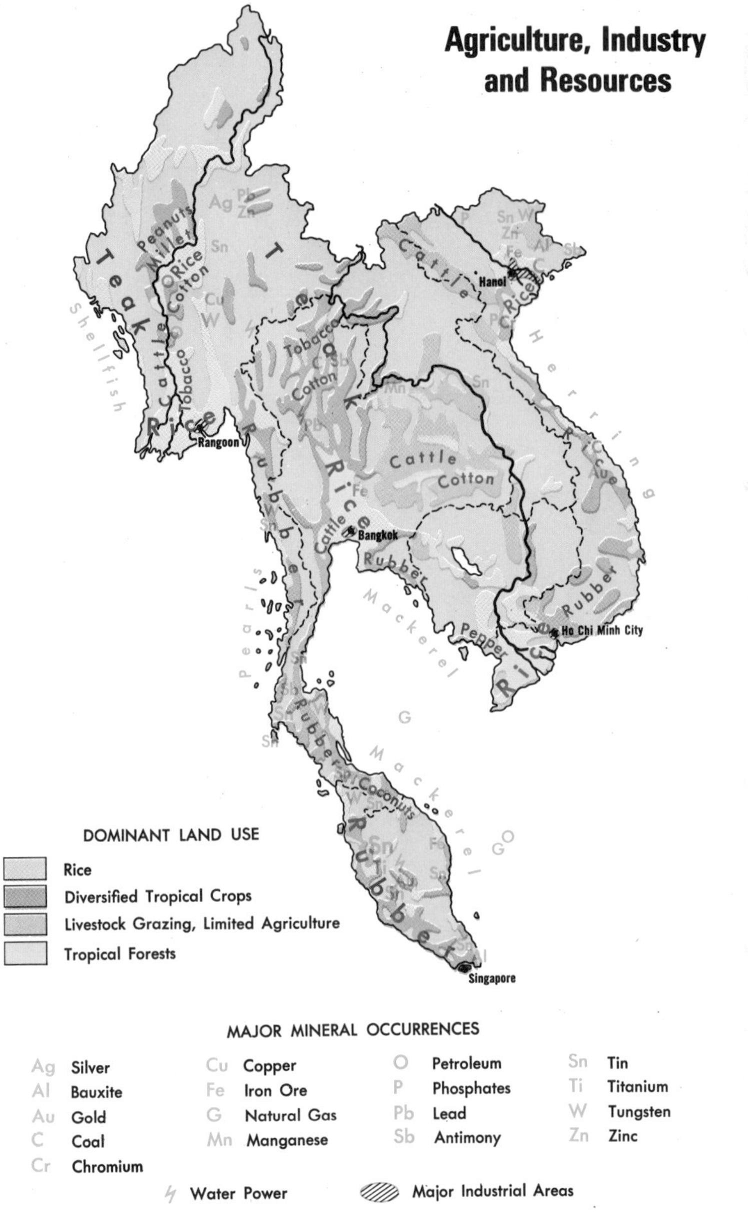
Agriculture, Industry and Resources
Teak
Peanuts
Millet
Rice
Cotton
Tobacco
Cattle
Shellfish
Rubber
Pearls
Mackerel
Herring
Coconuts
Pepper
Rangoon
Bangkok
Hanoi
Ho Chi Minh City
Singapore
DOMINANT LAND USE
Rice
Diversified Tropical Crops
Livestock Grazing, Limited Agriculture
Tropical Forests
MAJOR MINERAL OCCURRENCES
Ag Silver
Al Bauxite
Au Gold
C Coal
Cr Chromium
Cu Copper
Fe Iron Ore
G Natural Gas
Mn Manganese
O Petroleum
P Phosphates
Pb Lead
Sb Antimony
Sn Tin
Ti Titanium
W Tungsten
Zn Zinc
Water Power
Major Industrial Areas

Bilauktaung (range) C4
Chaukan (pass) C1
Cheduba (isl.) B3
Chin (hills) B2
Chindwin (riv.) B2
Coco (chan.) B4
Combermere (bay) B3
Daung Kyun (isl.) C4
Dawna (range) C3
Great Coco (isl.) B4
Great Tenasserim (riv.) C4
Heinze Chaung (bay) C4
Heywood (chan.) B3
Hka, Nam (riv.) C2
Hkakabo Razi (mt.) C1
Indawgyi (lake) C1
Inle (lake) C2
Irrawaddy (riv.) B3
Irrawaddy, Mouths of the (delta) B4
Kadan Kyun (isl.) C4
Kaladan (riv.) B2
Kalegauk (isl.) C4
Khao Luang (mt.) C5
Lanbi Kyun (isl.) C5
Launglon Bok (isls.) C4
Loi Leng (mt.) C2
Manipur (riv.) B2
Martaban (gulf) C4
Mekong (riv.) D2
Mergui (arch.) C5
Mon (riv.) B2
Mu (riv.) B2
Negrais (cape) B3
Pakchan (riv.) C5
Pangsau (pass) C1
Pawn, Nam (riv.) C2
Pegu Yoma (mts.) B3
Preparis (isl.) B4
Ramree (isl.) B3
Salween (riv.) C3
Shan (plat.) C2
Sittang (riv.) C3
Taungthonton (mt.) B1
Tavoy (pt.) C4
Tenasserim (isl.) C4
Teng, Nam (riv.) C2
Three Pagodas (pass) C4
Victoria (mt.) B2

CAMBODIA (KAMPUCHEA)

CITIES and TOWNS

Batdambang (Battambang) D4
Choam Khsant E4
Kampong Cham E4
Kampong Chhnang D4
Kampong Khleang E4
Kampong Saom D5
Kampong Spoe E5
Kampong Thum E4
Kampong Trabek E5
Kampot E5
Kaoh Nhek E4
Kracheh E4
Krong Kaoh Kong D4
Krong Keb E5
Kulen E4
Lumphat E4
Moung Roessei D4
Pailin D4
Paoy Pet D4
Phnom Penh (cap.) c. 300,000 E5
Phnum Tbeng Meanchey E4
Phsar Ream D5
Phumi Banam E5
Phumi Phsar E4
Phumi Prek Kak E4
Phumi Samraong D4
Pouthisat D4
Prek Pouthi E5
Prey Veng E5
Pursat (Pouthisat) D4
Rovieng Tbong E4
Sambor E4
Senmonoron E4
Siempang E4
Siemreab D4
Sisophon D4
Sre Ambel D5
Sre Khtum E4
Stoeng Treng E4
Suong E5
Svay Rieng E5
Takev E5
Virochey E4

OTHER FEATURES

Angkor Wat (ruins) E4
Dangrek (mts.) D4
Drang, Ia (riv.) E4
Joncs (plain) E5
Khong, Se (riv.) E4
Kong, Kaoh (isl.) D5
Mekong (riv.) E4
Rung, Kaoh (isl.) D5
San, Se (riv.) E4
Sen, Stoeng (riv.) E4
Srepok (riv.) E4
Tang, Kaoh (isl.) D5
Thailand (gulf) D5
Tonle Sap (lake) D4
Wai, Poulo (isls.) D5

LAOS

CITIES and TOWNS

Attapu 2,750 E4
Ban Khon E4
Ban Lahanam E3
Borikan D3
Champasak 3,500 E4
Dônghén E3
Khamkeut⊙ 31,206 E3
Louang Namtha 1,459 D2
Louangphrabang 7,596 D3
Muang Hinboun 1,750 E3
Muang Kènthao D3
Muang Khammoun 5,500 E3
Muang Không 1,750 E4
Muang Khôngxédôn 2,000 E4
Muang Khoua D2
Muang May E4
Muang Ou Tai D2
Muang Paktha D2
Muang Phin E3
Muang Tahoi E3
Muang Vapi E4
Muang Xaignabouri (Sayaboury) 2,500 D3
Mounlapamôk E4
Napè E3
Nong Het E3
Pakxé 8,000 E4
Phiafai⊙ 17,216 E4
Phôngsali 2,500 D2
San Nua (Sam Neua) 3,000 E2
Saravan 2,350 E4
Savannakhét 8,500 E3
Sayaboury (Muang Xaignabouri) 2,500 D3
Thakhek (Muang Khammouan) 5,500 E3
Tourakom D3
Viangchan (Vientiane) 132,253 D3
Vientiane (cap.) 132,253 D3
Xiangkhoang 3,500 D3

OTHER FEATURES

Bolovens (plat.) E4
Hou, Nam (riv.) D2
Jars (plain) D3
Mekong (riv.) D3
Ou, Nam (riv.) D2
Phou Bia (mt.) D3
Phou Cô Pi (mt.) E3
Phou Loi (mt.) D2
Rao Co (mt.) E3
Se Khong (riv.) E4
Tha, Nam (riv.) D2
Xianghoang (plat.) D3

MALAYA, MALAYSIA*

STATES

Federal Territory 937,875 D7
Johor (Johore) 1,601,504 D7
Kedah 1,102,200 D6
Kelantan 877,575 D6
Melaka 453,153 D7
Negeri Sembilan 563,955 D7
Pahang 770,644 D7
Perak 1,762,288 D6
Perlis 147,726 D6
Pinang (Penang) 911,586 D6
Selangor 1,467,441 D7
Terengganu 542,280 D6

CITIES and TOWNS

Alor Gajah 2,222 D7
Alor Setar 66,260 D6
Bandar Maharani (Muar) 61,218 D7
Bandar Penggaram (Batu Pahat) 53,291 D7
Batu Gajah 10,692 D6
Batu Pahat 53,291 D7
Bentong 22,683 D7
Butterworth 61,187 D6
Chukai 12,514 D6
Gemas 5,214 D7
George Town (Pinang) 269,603 C6
Ipoh 247,953 D6
Johor Baharu (Johore Bharu) 136,234 F5
Kampar 26,591 D6
Kangar 8,758 D6
Kelang 113,611 D7
Keluang 43,272 D7
Kota Baharu 55,124 D6
Kota Tinggi 8,725 F5
Kuala Dungun 17,560 D6
Kuala Lipis 9,270 D6
Kuala Lumpur (cap.) 451,977 D7
Kuala Lumpur* 937,875 D7
Kuala Pilah 12,508 D7
Kuala Rompin 1,384 D7
Kuala Selangor 3,132 D7
Kuala Terengganu 53,320 D6
Kuantan 43,358 D7
Kulai 11,841 F5
Lumut 3,255 D6
Malacca (Melaka) 87,160 D7
Mawai F5
Melaka 87,160 D7
Mersing 18,246 E7
Muar 61,218 D7
Pekan 4,682 D7
Pekan Nanas 9,003 E5
Pinang (George Town) 269,603 C6
Pontian Kechil 8,349 E5
Port Dickson 10,300 D7
Port Kelang D7
Port Weld 3,233 D6
Raub 18,433 D7
Segamat 17,796 D7
Seremban 80,921 D7
Sungai Petani 35,959 C6
Taiping 54,645 D6
Tanah Merah 7,012 D6
Telok Anson 44,524 D6
Tumpat 10,673 D6

OTHER FEATURES

Aur, Pulau (isl.) E7
Belumut, Gunong (mt.) D7
Gelang, Tanjong (pt.) D6
Johor, Sungai (riv.) F5
Johore (str.) E6
Kelantan, Sungai (riv.) D6
Langkawi, Pulau (isl.) C6
Ledang, Gunong (mt.) D7
Lima, Pulau (isl.) F6
Malacca (str.) D7
Malay (pen.) D6
Pahang, Sungai (riv.) D7
Pangkor, Pulau (isl.) D6
Perak, Gunong (mt.) D6
Perhentian, Kepulauan (isls.) D6
Pulai, Sungai (riv.) E5
Ramunia, Tanjong (pt.) F6
Redang, Pulau (isl.) D6
Sedili Kechil, Tanjong (pt.) F5
Tahan, Gunong (mt.) D6
Temiang, Bukit (mt.) D6
Tenggol, Pulau (isl.) D6
Tinggi, Pulau (isl.) E7

SINGAPORE

CITIES and TOWNS

Jurong 50,974 E6
Nee Soon 37,641 F6
Serangoon 89,558 F6
Singapore (cap.) 2,413,945 F6

OTHER FEATURES

Keppel (harb.) F6
Main (str.) F6
Singapore (str.) F6
Tekong Besar, Pulau (isl.) F6

THAILAND (SIAM)

CITIES and TOWNS

Ang Thong 7,267 C4
Ayutthaya (Phra Nakhon Si Ayutthaya) 37,213 D4
Ban Aranyaprathet 12,276 D4
Bangkok (cap.) 1,867,297 D4
Bangkok* 2,495,312 D4
Bang Lamung D4
Bang Saphan C5
Ban Kantang 9,247 C6
Ban Kapong C5
Ban Khlong Yai D5
Ban Kui Nua D4
Ban Ngon D3
Ban Pak Phanang 13,590 D5
Banphot Phisai C3
Ban Pua D3
Ban Sattahip D4
Ban Tha Uthen D3
Bua Chum D4
Buriram 16,431 D4
Chachoengsao 22,106 D4
Chai Badan D4
Chai Buri D3
Chainat 9,944 D4
Chaiya C5
Chaiyaphum 12,540 D4
Chang Khoeng C3
Chanthaburi 15,479 D4
Chiang Dao C3
Chiang Khan D3
Chiang Mai 83,729 C3
Chiang Rai 13,927 C3
Chiang Saen C2
Chon Buri 39,367 D4
Chumphon 11,643 C5
Den Chai C3
Hat Yai 47,953 C6
Hot C3
Hua Hin 21,426 D4
Kalasin 14,960 D3
Kamphaeng Phet 12,378 C3
Kanchanaburi 16,397 C4
Khanu C3
Khemmarat E4
Khon Kaen 29,431 D3
Khorat (Nakhon Ratchasima) 66,071 D4
Krabi 8,764 C5
Krung Thep (Bangkok) (cap.) 1,867,297 D4
Kumphawapi D3
Lae D3
Lampang 40,100 C3
Lamphun 11,309 C3
Lang Suan 4,020 C5
Loei 10,137 D3
Lom Sak 10,597 D3
Lop Buri 23,112 D4
Mae Hong Son 3,981 C3
Maha Sarakham 19,707 D3
Mukdahan E3
Nakhon Nayok 8,185 D4
Nakhon Pathom 34,300 C4
Nakhon Phanom 20,385 D3
Nakhon Ratchasima 66,071 D4
Nakhon Sawan 46,853 D4
Nakhon Si Thammarat 40,671 D5
Nan 17,738 D3
Nang Rong D4
Narathiwat 21,256 D6
Ngao D3
Nong Khai 21,150 D3
Pattani 21,938 D6
Phanat Nikhom 10,514 D4
Phangnga 5,738 C5
Phatthalung 13,336 D6
Phayao 20,346 C3
Phet Buri 27,755 C4
Phetchabun 6,240 D3
Phichai D3
Phichit 10,814 D3
Phitsanulok 33,883 D3
Phon Phisai D3
Phrae 17,555 D3
Phra Nakhon Si Ayutthaya 37,213 D4
Phuket 34,362 C6
Phutthaisong D4
Prachin Buri 14,167 D4
Prachuap Khiri Khan 9,075 D5
Pran Buri D4
Rahaeng (Tak) 16,317 C3
Ranong 10,301 C5
Rat Buri 32,271 C4
Rayong 14,846 D4
Roi Et 20,242 D4
Rong Kwang D3
Sakon Nakhon 18,943 E3
Samut Prakan 46,632 D4
Samut Sakhon 33,619 D4
Samut Songkhram 23,574 C4
Sara Buri 25,025 D4
Satun 7,315 C6
Sawankhalok 8,387 C3
Selaphum E3
Sing Buri 9,050 D4
Singora (Songkhla) 41,193 D6
Sisaket 13,662 E4
Songkhla 41,193 D6
Sukhothai 15,488 D3
Suphan Buri 18,768 C4
Surat Thani 24,923 C5
Surin 16,342 D4
Suwannaphum D4
Tak 16,317 C3
Takua Pa 7,825 C5
Thoen C3
Thon Buri 628,015 D4
To Mo D6
Trang 32,985 C6
Trat 7,917 D4
Ubon 40,650 E4
Udon Thani 56,218 D3
Uthai Thani 10,525 C4
Uttaradit 12,022 D3
Warin Chamrap 21,520 E4
Yala 30,051 D6
Yasothon 12,079 D4

OTHER FEATURES

Amya (pass) C4
Bilauktaung (range) C4
Chang, Ko (isl.) D4
Chao Phraya, Mae Nam (riv.) D4
Chi, Mae Nam (riv.) D3
Dangrek (Dong Rak) (mts.) D4
Doi Inthanon (mt.) C3
Doi Pha Hom Pok (mt.) C2
Doi Pia Fai (mt.) D4
Kao Prawa (mt.) C3
Khao Luang (mt.) C5
Khwae Noi, Mae Nam (riv.) C4
Kra (isth.) C5
Kut, Ko (isl.) D5
Laem Pho (cape) D6
Laem Talumphuk (cape) D5
Lanta, Ko (isl.) C6
Luang (mt.) C5
Mae Klong, Mae Nam (riv.) C4
Mekong (riv.) E3
Mun, Mae Nam (riv.) D4
Nan, Mae Nam (riv.) D3
Nong Lahan (lake) D3
Pakchan (riv.) C5
Pa Sak, Mae Nam (riv.) D4
Phangan, Ko (isl.) D5
Phuket, Ko (isl.) C5
Ping, Mae Nam (riv.) C3
Samui (str.) D5
Samui, Ko (isl.) D5
Siam (Thailand) (gulf) D5
Tao, Ko (isl.) C5
Tapi, Mae Nam (riv.) C5
Terutao, Ko (isl.) C6
Tha Chin, Mae Nam (riv.) C4
Thale Luang (lag.) D6
Thalu, Ko (isls.) C5
Three Pagodas (pass) C4
Wang, Mae Nam (riv.) C3

VIETNAM

CITIES and TOWNS

An Loc (Binh Long) 15,276 E5
An Nhon F4
An Tuc (An Khe) F4
Ap Long Ha F5
Ap Vinh Hao F5
Bac Can E2
Bac Giang E2
Bac Lieu 53,841 E5
Bac Ninh 22,560 E2
Ba Don E3
Bai Thuong E3
Ban Me Thuot 68,771 F4
Bao Ha D2
Bao Lac E2
Bien Hoa 87,135 E5
Binh Long (An Loc) 15,276 E5
Binh Son F4
Bo Duc E4
Bong Son (Hoai Nhon) F4
Cam Ranh 118,111 F5
Can Tho 182,424 E5
Cao Bang E2
Cao Lanh 16,482 E5
Chau Phu 37,175 E5
Chu Lai F4
Con Cuong E3
Cua Rao E3
Da Lat 105,072 F5
Dam Doi E5
Da Nang 492,194 E3
Dien Bien Phu D2
Dong Hoi E3
Duong Dong D5
Gia Dinh E5
Go Cong 33,191 E5
Ha Giang E2
Haiphong* 1,279,067 E2
Hanoi (cap.)* 2,570,905 E2
Ha Tien E5
Ha Tinh E3
Hau Bon E4
Hoa Binh E2
Hoa Da F5
Hoai Nhon F4
Ho Chi Minh City (Saigon)* 3,419,678 E5
Hoi An 45,059 F4
Hoi Xuan E2
Hon Chong E5
Hon Gai 100,000 E2
Hue 209,043 E3
Huong Khe E3
Ke Bao E2
Khanh Hoa F4
Khanh Hung 59,015 E5
Khe Sanh E3
Kien Hung E5
Kontum 33,554 E4
Lac Giao (Ban Me Thuot) 68,771 E4
Lai Chau D2
Lang Son 15,071 E2
Lao Cai E2
Loc Ninh E5
Long Xuyen 72,658 E5
Mo Duc F4
Mong Cai E2
Muong Khuong E2
My Tho 119,892 E5
Nam Dinh E2
Nghia Lo D2
Nha Trang 216,227 F4
Ninh Binh E3
Phan Rang 33,377 F5
Phan Thiet 80,122 F5
Phu Cuong 28,267 E5
Phu Lang Thuong (Bac Giang) E2
Phuc Loi E3
Phu Dien E3
Phu Ly E2
Phu My F4
Phu Qui E3
Phu Rieng E5
Phu Tho 10,888 E2
Phu Vinh 48,485 E5
Pleiku 23,720 E4
Quang Nam E4
Quang Ngai 14,119 F4
Quang Tri 15,874 E3
Quang Yen E2
Quan Long 59,331 E5
Qui Nhon 213,757 F4
Rach Gia 104,161 E5
Ron E3
Sa Dec 51,867 E5
Saigon (Ho Chi Minh City)* 3,419,678 E5
Song Cau F4
Son Ha F4
Son La D2
Son Tay 19,213 E2
Tam Ky 38,532 F4
Tam Quan F4
Tan An 38,082 E5
Tay Ninh 22,957 E5
Thai Binh 14,739 E2
Thai Nguyen E2
Thanh Hoa 31,211 E3
Thanh Tri E5
That Khe E2
Tien Yen E2
Tra Vinh (Phu Vinh) 48,485 E5
Truc Giang 68,629 E5
Trung Khanh Phu E2
Tuyen Quang E2
Tuy Hoa 63,552 F4
Van Hoa E2
Van Ninh F4
Van Yen E2
Vinh 43,954 E3
Vinh Long 30,667 E5
Vinh Yen E2
Vu Liet E3
Vung Tau 108,436 E5
Xuan Loc
Yen Bai

OTHER FEATURES

Bach Long Vi, Dao (isl.)
Ba Den, Nui (mt.)
Bai Bung, Mui (Ca Mau) (pt.)
Black (riv.)
Ca Mau (Mui Bai Bung) (pt.)
Cam Ranh, Vinh (bay)
Cat Ba, Dao (isl.)
Chon May, Vung (bay)
Cu Lao, Hon (isls.)
Deux Frères, Les (isls.)
Dinh, Mui (cape)
Fan Si Pan (mt.)
Ia Drang (riv.)
Joncs (plain)
Kontum (plat.)
Khoai, Hon (isl.)
Lang Bian, Nui (mts.)
Lay, Mui (cape)
Mekong, Mouths of the (delta)
Nam Tram, Mui (cape)
Nightingale (Bach Long Vi) (isl.)
Panjang, Hon (Hon Tho Chau) (isl.)
Phu Quoc, Dao (isl.)
Rao Co (mt.)
Red (riv.)
Se San (riv.)
Sip Song Chau Thai (mts.)
Song Ba (riv.)
Song Ca (riv.)
Song Cai (riv.)
South China (sea)
Tonkin (gulf)
Varella, Mui (cape)
Wai, Poulo (isls.)
Yang Sin, Chu (mt.)

*See Southeast Asia, p. 84 for other part of Malaysia.

*City and suburbs.
⊙Population of district.

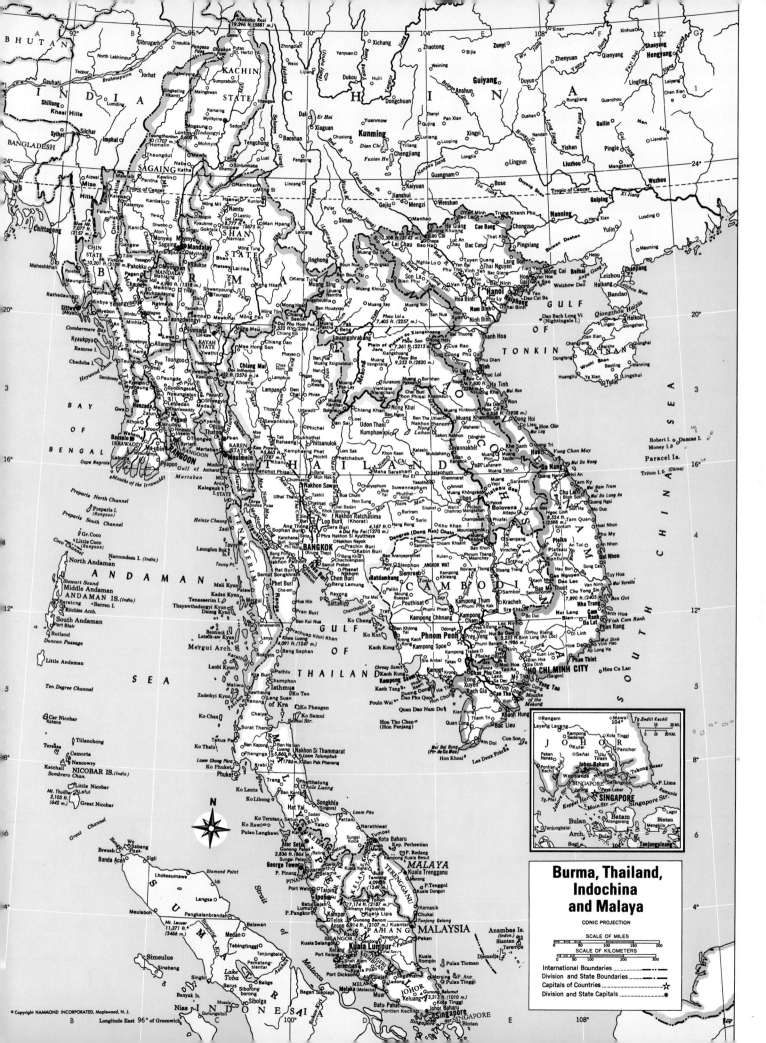

PHILIPPINES

AREA 115,707 sq. mi. (299,681 sq. km.)
POPULATION 48,098,460
CAPITAL Manila
LARGEST CITY Manila
HIGHEST POINT Apo 9,692 ft. (2,954 m.)
MONETARY UNIT peso
MAJOR LANGUAGES Pilipino (Tagalog), English, Spanish, Bisayan, Ilocano, Bikol
MAJOR RELIGIONS Roman Catholicism, Islam, Protestantism, tribal religions

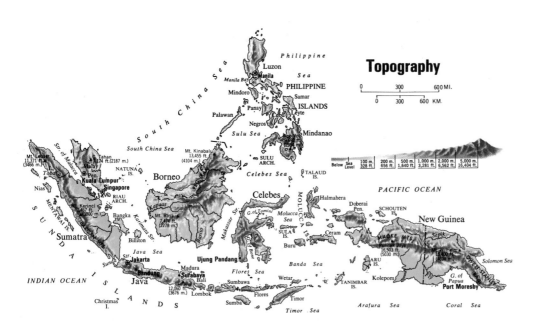

Topography

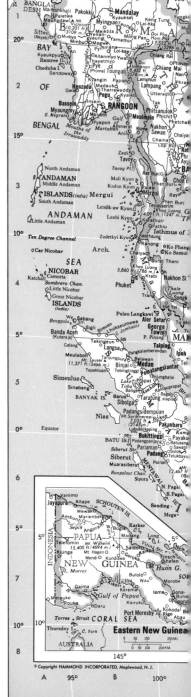

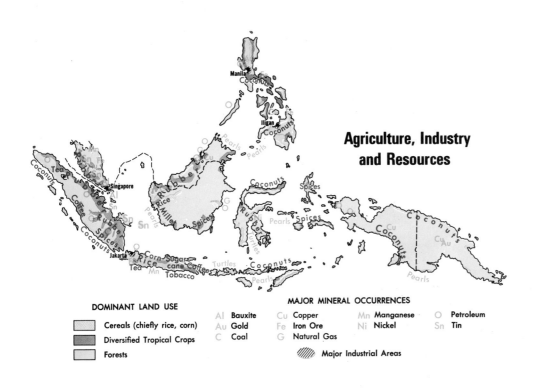

Agriculture, Industry and Resources

DOMINANT LAND USE

Cereals (chiefly rice, corn)
Diversified Tropical Crops
Forests

MAJOR MINERAL OCCURRENCES

Al Bauxite	Cu Copper	Mn Manganese	O Petroleum
Au Gold	Fe Iron Ore	Ni Nickel	Sn Tin
C Coal	G Natural Gas		

Major Industrial Areas

AUSTRALIA

AREA 2,966,136 sq. mi. (7,682,3...
POPULATION 14,576,330
CAPITAL Canberra
LARGEST CITY Sydney
HIGHEST POINT Mt. Kosciusko 7...
(2,228 m.)
LOWEST POINT Lake Eyre -39 ft.
MONETARY UNIT Australian doll...
MAJOR LANGUAGE English
MAJOR RELIGIONS Protestantism
Roman Catholicism

AUSTRALIA

STATES and TERRITORIES

Ashmore and Cartier Is., Terr.
of.................................C 2
Australian Capital Territory
221,609 ....H 7
Coral Sea Islands Territory ...H 2
New South Wales 5,126,217...H 6
Norfolk Island 2,175 ....L 5
Northern Territory 123,324 ....E 3
Queensland 2,295,123.........G 4
South Australia 1,285,033.....F 6
Tasmania 418,957 ....H 8
Victoria 3,832,443...............G 7
Western Australia 1,273,624...B 5

CITIES and TOWNS

Adelaide (cap.), S. Aust.
882,520 ....D 8
Albany, W. Aust. 15,222......B 6
Albury, N.S.W. 35,072 ....H 7
Alice Springs, N. Terr. 18,395..E 4
Altona, Vic. 30,909 ....J 3
Ararat, Vic. 8,336 ....J 6
Armidale, N.S.W. 18,922......J 6
Ashfield, N.S.W. 41,253........K 4
Auburn, N.S.W. 46,622 ....K 4
Ayr, Queens. 8,787..............H 4
Bairnsdale, Vic. 9,459 ....H 7
Ballarat, Vic. 35,681............G 7
Bankstown, N.S.W. 152,636...K 4
Bathurst, N.S.W. 19,640 ....H 6
Bega, N.S.W. 4,388 ....J 7
Bendigo, Vic. 31,841 ....G 7
Blackall, Queens. 1,609........H 4
Blacktown, N.S.W. 181,139...K 4

INDONESIA

AREA 788,430 sq. mi. (2,042,034 sq. km.)
POPULATION 147,490,298
CAPITAL Jakarta
LARGEST CITY Jakarta
HIGHEST POINT Puncak Jaya 16,503 ft.
(5,030 m.)
MONETARY UNIT rupiah
MAJOR LANGUAGES Bahasa Indonesia,
Indonesian and Papuan languages,
English
MAJOR RELIGIONS Islam, tribal religions,
Christianity, Hinduism

BRUNEI

AREA 2,226 sq. mi. (5,765 sq. km.)
POPULATION 192,832
CAPITAL Bandar Seri Begawan
LARGEST CITY Bandar Seri Begawan
HIGHEST POINT Pagon 6,070 ft. (1,850 m.)
MONETARY UNIT Brunei Dollar
MAJOR LANGUAGES Malay, English, Chinese
MAJOR RELIGIONS Islam, Buddhism,
Christianity, tribal religions

PAPUA NEW GUINEA

AREA 183,540 sq. mi. (475,369 sq. km.)
POPULATION 3,010,727
CAPITAL Port Moresby
LARGEST CITY Port Moresby
HIGHEST POINT Mt. Wilhelm 15,400 ft.
(4,694 m.)
MONETARY UNIT kina
MAJOR LANGUAGES pidgin English,
Hiri Motu, English
MAJOR RELIGIONS Tribal religions,
Christianity

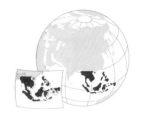

DOMINANT LAND US...

- Cereals (chiefly wheat),
- Dairy, Truck Farming
- Cash Crops, Horticulture
- Pasture Livestock
- Range Livestock
- Forests
- Nonagricultural Land

MAJOR

Ab	Asbestos	G	Natur...
Ag	Silver	Gp	Gypsu...
Al	Bauxite	Lg	Lignite
Au	Gold	Ls	Limest...
C	Coal	Mg	Magn...
Cu	Copper	Mi	Mica
D	Diamonds	Mn	Mang...
Fe	Iron Ore		

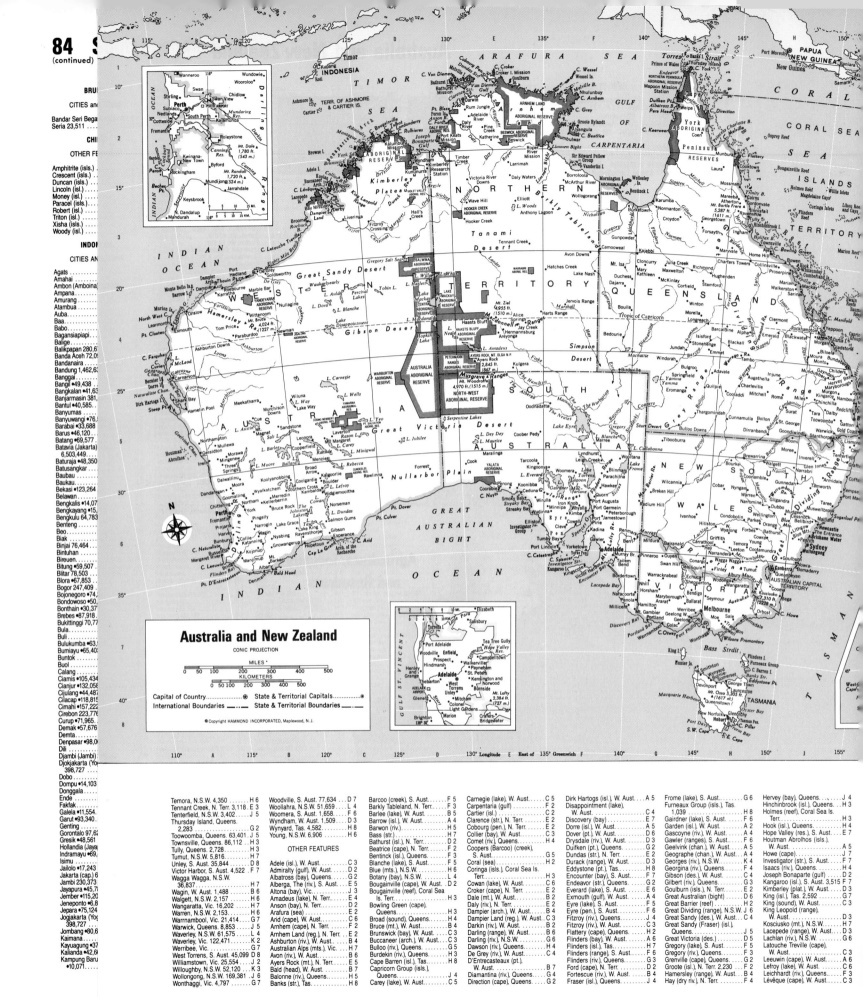

Australia and New Zealand

CONIC PROJECTION

MILES
0 50 100   200   300   400   500

KILOMETERS
0 50 100   200   300   400   500

Capital of Country .... ⊛   State & Territorial Capitals .... ◉
International Boundaries ------   State & Territorial Boundaries _____

® Copyright HAMMOND INCORPORATED, Maplewood, N.J.

BRU...

CITIES and...

Bandar Seri Bega...
Seria 23,511 ...

CHI...

OTHER FE...

Amphitrite (isls.) .
Crescent (isls.) .
Duncan (isls.) .
Lincoln (isls.) .
Money (isl.) .
Paracel (isls.) .
Robert (isl.) .
Triton (isl.) .
Xisha (isls.) .
Woody (isl.) .

INDO...

CITIES AN...

Agats ...
Amahai ...
Ambon (Amboina) .
Ampana ...
Amurang ...
Atambua ...
Auba ...
Baa ...
Babo ...
Bagansiapiapi...
Balige ...
Balikpapan 280,6...
Banda Aceh 72,0...
Bandanaira ...
Bandung 1,462,6...
Banggai ...
Bangil •49,438 ...
Bangkalan •41,63...
Banjarmasin 381,...
Bantul •40,585...
Banyumas ...
Banyuwangi •76,...
Barabai •33,688 ...
Barus •46,120...
Batang •69,577...
Batavia (Jakarta)
6,503,449...
Baturaja •48,350...
Batusangkar ...
Baubau ...
Baukau ...
Bekasi •123,264...
Belawan ...
Bengkalis •14,07...
Bengkayang •15,...
Bengkulu 64,783...
Benteng ...
Beo ...
Biak ...
Binjai 76,464 ...
Bintuhan ...
Bireuen ...
Bitung •59,507 ...
Blitar 78,503 ...
Blora •67,853 ...
Bogor 247,409 ...
Bojonegoro •74,...
Bondowoso •50,...
Bonthain •30,37...
Brebes •87,918...
Bukittinggi 70,77...
Bula ...
Buli ...
Bulukumba •63,...
Bumiayu •65,40...
Buntok ...
Buol ...
Calang ...
Ciamis •105,434...
Cianjur •132,058...
Cijulang •44,487...
Cilacap •118,815...
Cimahi •157,222...
Cirebon 223,776...
Curup •71,965...
Demak •57,676...
Demta...
Denpasar •98,0...
Dili ...
Djambi (Jambi) ...
Djokjakarta (Yo...
398,727 ...
Dobo ...
Dompu •14,103...
Donggala ...
Ende ...
Fakfak ...
Galela •11,554...
Garut •93,340...
Genting ...
Gorontalo •57,6...
Gresik •48,561...
Hollandia (Jaya...
Indramayu •69,...
Isimu ...
Jailolo •17,243...
Jakarta (cap.) 6...
Jambi 230,373...
Jayapura •45,7...
Jember •115,20...
Jeneponto •6,8...
Jepara •75,124...
Jogjakarta (Yog...
398,727...
Jombang •80,6...
Kaimana ...
Kayuagung •37...
Kalianda •42,6...
Kampung Baru
•10,071...

Temora, N.S.W. 4,350 ...... H 6	Woodville, S. Aust. 77,634 ... D 7	Barcoo (creek), S. Aust. .... F 5
Tennant Creek, N. Terr. 3,118 .. E 3	Woollahra, N.S.W. 51,659 ... L 4	Barkly Tableland, N. Terr. ... F 3
Tenterfield, N.S.W. 3,402 ... J 5	Woomera, S. Aust. 1,658 ... F 6	Barlee (lake), W. Aust. ..... B 5
Thursday Island, Queens.	Wyndham, W. Aust. 1,509 ... D 3	Barrow (isl.), W. Aust. ..... A 4
2,283 .... G 2	Wynyard, Tas. 4,582 .... H 8	Barwon (riv.) .... H 5
Toowoomba, Queens. 63,401 .. J 5	Young, N.S.W. 6,906 .... H 6	Bass (str.) .... H 7
Townsville, Queens. 86,112 .. H 3		Bathurst (isl.), N. Terr. ..... D 2
Tully, Queens. 2,728 .... H 3	**OTHER FEATURES**	Beatrice (cape), N. Terr. ... F 2
Tumut, N.S.W. 5,816 .... H 6		Bentinck (isl.), Queens. .... F 3
Unley, S. Aust. 35,844 ...... D 8	Adele (isl.), W. Aust. .... C 3	Blanche (lake), S. Aust. .... F 5
Victor Harbor, S. Aust. 4,522 . F 7	Admiralty (gulf), W. Aust. ... D 2	Blue (mts.), N.S.W. .... H 6
Wagga Wagga, N.S.W.	Albatross (bay), Queens. ... G 2	Botany (bay), N.S.W. ...... L 4
36,837 .... H 7	Alberga, The (riv.), S. Aust. . E 5	Bougainville (cape), W. Aust. D 2
Wagin, W. Aust. 1,488 ...... B 6	Altona (bay), Vic. .... J 3	Bougainville (reef), Coral Sea
Walgett, N.S.W. 2,157 ...... H 5	Amadeus (lake), N. Terr. ... E 4	Is. Terr. .... H 3
Wangaratta, Vic. 16,202 .... H 7	Anson (bay), N. Terr. ...... D 2	Bowling Green (cape),
Warren, N.S.W. 2,153 .... H 6	Arafura (sea) .... E 2	Queens. .... H 3
Warrnambool, Vic. 21,414 ... G 7	Arid (cape), W. Aust. ...... C 6	Broad (sound), Queens. .... H 4
Warwick, Queens. 8,853 .... J 5	Arnhem (cape), N. Terr. .... E 2	Bruce (mt.), W. Aust. ...... B 4
Waverley, Vic. 61,575 ...... L 4	Arnhem Land (reg.), N. Terr. E 2	Brunswick (bay), W. Aust. .. C 3
Waverley, Vic. 122,471 ..... K 2	Ashburton (riv.), W. Aust. .. A 4	Buccaneer (arch.), W. Aust. . C 3
West Torrens, S. Aust. 45,099 D 8	Australian Alps (mts.), Vic. . H 7	Bulloo (riv.), Queens. ...... G 5
Williamstown, Vic. 25,554 ... J 2	Avon (riv.), W. Aust. ...... B 6	Burdekin (riv.), Queens. .... H 3
Willoughby, N.S.W. 52,120 .. K 3	Ayers Rock (mt.), N. Terr. .. E 5	Cape Barren (isl.), Tas. .... H 8
Wollongong, N.S.W. 169,381 . J 6	Bald (head), W. Aust. ...... B 7	Capricorn Group (isls.),
Wonthaggi, Vic. 4,797 ...... H 8	Balonne (riv.), Queens. .... H 5	Queens. .... J 4
	Banks (str.), Tas. .... H 8	Carey (lake), W. Aust. ..... C 5

Carnegie (lake), W. Aust. ... C 5	Dirk Hartogs (isl.), W. Aust. . A 5	Frome (lake), S. Aust. ...... G 6
Carpentaria (gulf) .... F 2	Disappointment (lake),	Furneaux Group (isls.), Tas.
Cartier (isl.) .... C 2	W. Aust. .... C 4	1,039 .... H 8
Clarence (str.), N. Terr. .... E 2	Discovery (bay), S. Aust. ... F 7	Gairdner (lake), S. Aust. ... F 6
Cobourg (pen.), N. Terr. .... E 2	Dorre (isl.), W. Aust. ...... A 5	Garden (isl.), W. Aust. ..... A 2
Collier (bay), W. Aust. ..... C 3	Dover (isl.), W. Aust. ...... D 6	Gascoyne (riv.), W. Aust. ... A 4
Comet (riv.), Queens. ...... H 4	Drysdale (riv.), W. Aust. ... D 3	Gawler (ranges), S. Aust. .. E 6
Coopers (Barcoo) (creek),	Duifken (pt.), Queens. ..... G 2	Geelvink (chan.), W. Aust. . A 5
S. Aust. .... G 5	Dundas (str.), N. Terr. ..... E 2	Geographe (chan.), W. Aust. A 5
Coral (sea) .... H 3	Durack (range), W. Aust. ... D 3	Georges (riv.), N.S.W. ..... K 4
Coringa (isls.), Coral Sea Is.	Eddystone (pt.), Tas. ...... H 8	Georgina (riv.), Queens. ... F 4
Terr. .... H 3	Encounter (bay), S. Aust. ... F 7	Gibson (des.), W. Aust. .... C 4
Cowan (lake), W. Aust. .... C 6	Endeavor (str.), Queens. ... G 2	Gilbert (riv.), Queens. ..... G 3
Croker (isl.), N. Terr. ...... E 2	Everard (lake), S. Aust. .... E 6	Goulburn (isls.), N. Terr. ... E 2
Dale (mt.), W. Aust. .... B 2	Exmouth (gulf), W. Aust. ... A 4	Great Australian (bight) .... D 6
Daly (riv.), N. Terr. .... E 2	Eyre (lake), S. Aust. ...... F 5	Great Barrier (reef) .... H 3
Dampier (arch.), W. Aust. .. B 4	Eyre (pen.), S. Aust. ...... F 6	Great Dividing (range), N.S.W. J 6
Dampier Land (reg.), W. Aust. C 3	Fitzroy (riv.), Queens. ..... J 4	Great Sandy (des.), W. Aust. C 4
Darkin (riv.), W. Aust. ..... B 2	Fitzroy (riv.), W. Aust. ..... C 3	Great Sandy (Fraser) (isl.) .. J 4
Darling (range), W. Aust. ... B 6	Flattery (cape), Queens. ... H 2	Great Victoria (des.) ...... D 5
Darling (riv.), N.S.W. ...... G 6	Flinders (bay), W. Aust. .... A 6	Gregory (lake), S. Aust. .... F 5
Dawson (riv.), Queens. .... H 4	Flinders (range), S. Aust. ... F 6	Gregory (riv.), Queens. .... F 3
De Grey (riv.), W. Aust. .... C 4	Flinders (riv.), Queens. .... G 3	Grenville (cape), Queens. .. G 2
D'Entrecasteaux (pt.),	Ford (cape), N. Terr. ...... D 2	Groote (isl.), N. Terr. 2,230 . F 2
W. Aust. .... B 7	Fortescue (riv.), W. Aust. .. B 4	Hamersley (range), W. Aust. B 4
Diamantina (riv.), Queens. .. G 4	Fraser (isl.), Queens. ...... J 4	Hay (dry riv.), N. Terr. ..... F 4
Direction (cape), Queens. .. G 2		

Hervey (bay), Queens. ..... J 4
Hinchinbrook (isl.), Queens. . H 3
Holmes (reef), Coral Sea Is.
Terr. .... H 3
Hook (isl.), Queens. .... H 4
Hope Valley (res.), S. Aust. . E 7
Houtman Abrolhos (isls.),
W. Aust. .... A 5
Howe (cape) .... J 7
Investigator (str.), S. Aust. . F 7
Isaacs (riv.), Queens. ..... H 4
Joseph Bonaparte (gulf) ... D 2
Kangaroo (isl.), S. Aust. 3,515 F 7
Kimberley (plat.), W. Aust. .. D 3
King (isl.), Tas. 2,592 ...... G 7
King (sound), W. Aust. ..... C 3
King Leopold (range),
W. Aust. .... D 3
Kosciusko (mt.), N.S.W. .... H 7
Lacepede (range), W. Aust. . C 3
Lachlan (riv.), N.S.W. ...... G 6
Latouche Treville (cape),
.... C 3
Leeuwin (cape), W. Aust. ... A 6
Lefroy (lake), W. Aust. ..... C 5
Leichhardt (riv.), Queens. .. F 3
Lévêque (cape), W. Aust. ... C 3

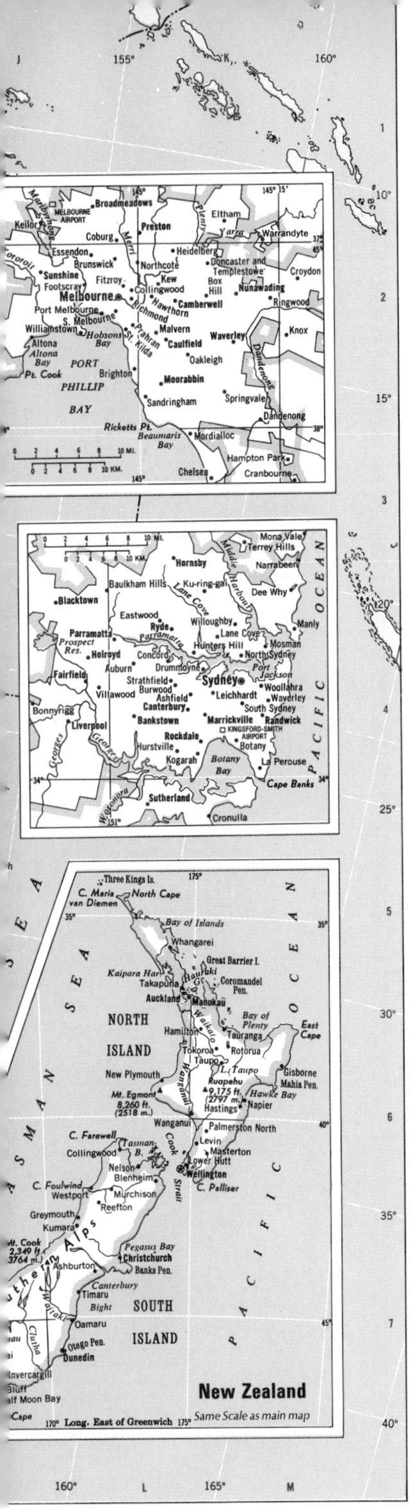

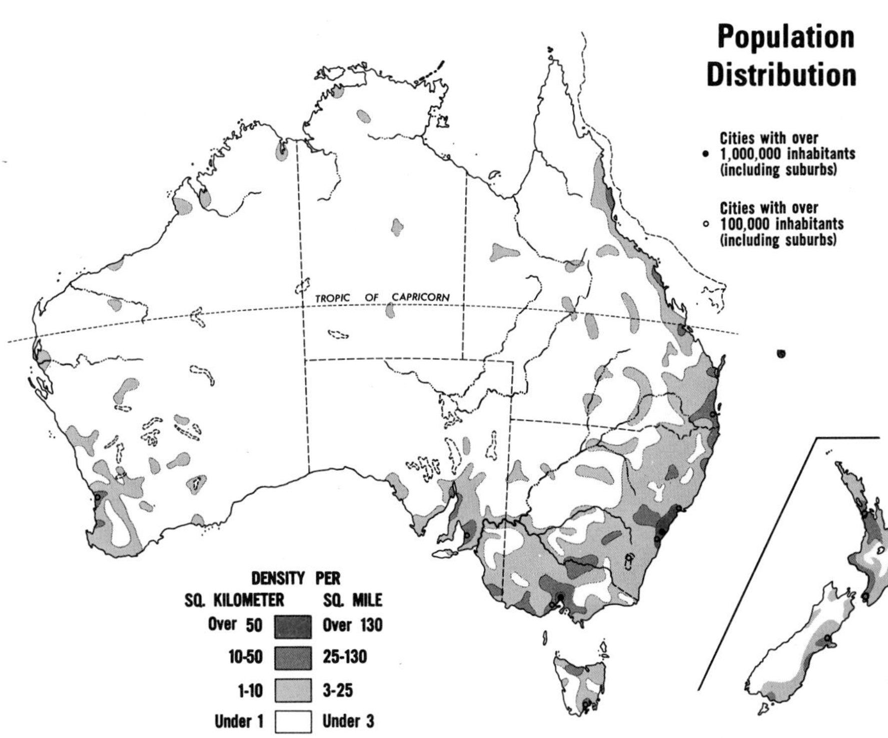

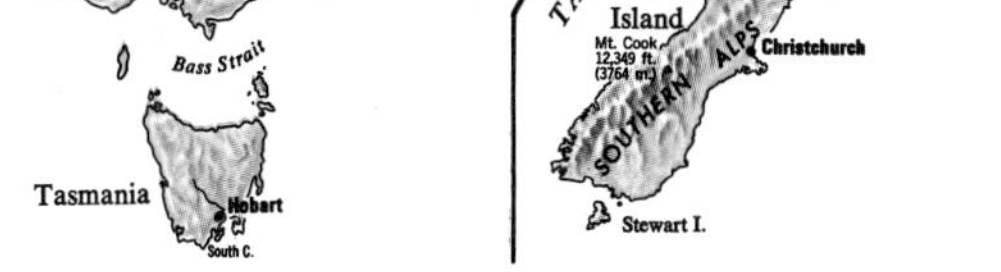

Population Distribution

- • Cities with over 1,000,000 inhabitants (including suburbs)
- ○ Cities with over 100,000 inhabitants (including suburbs)

DENSITY PER

SQ. KILOMETER	SQ. MILE
Over 50	Over 130
10-50	25-130
1-10	3-25
Under 1	Under 3

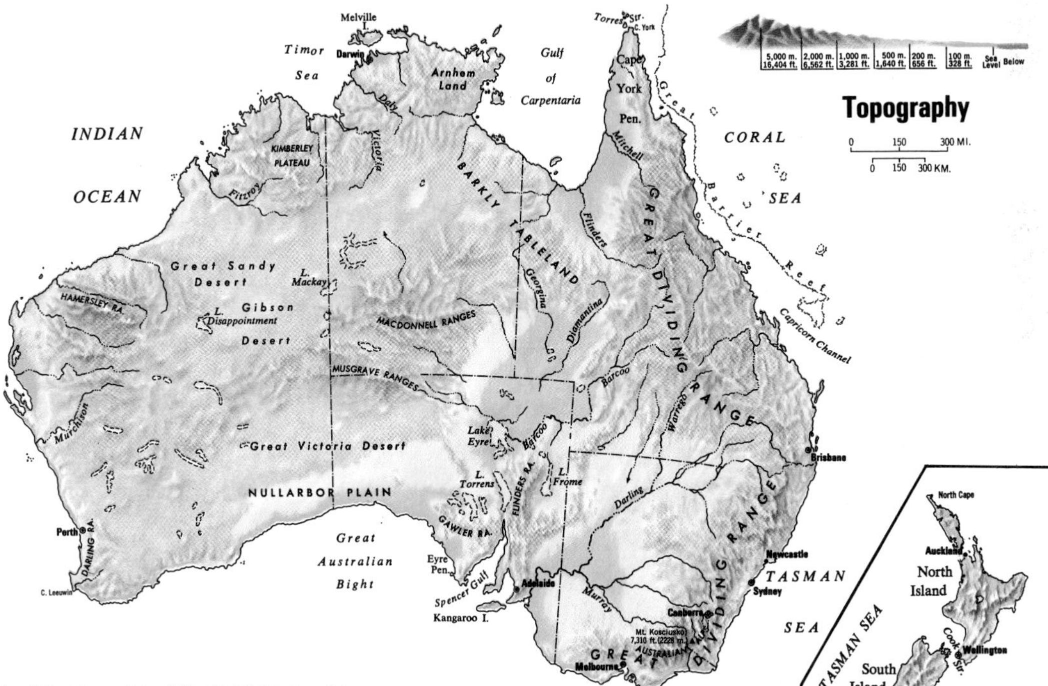

Topography

5,000 m. 16,404 ft. 2,000 m. 6,562 ft. 1,000 m. 3,281 ft. 500 m. 1,640 ft. 200 m. 656 ft. 100 m. 328 ft. Sea Level Below

0   150   300 MI.
0   150   300 KM.

New Zealand — Same Scale as main map

Lihou (cays), Coral Sea Is. Terr. . . . . J 3
Limmen Bight (riv.), N. Terr. F 3
Little Para (riv.), S. Aust. . . . D 7
Lofty (mt.), S. Aust. . . . . E 8
Londonderry (cape), W. Aust. D 2
Macdonald (lake), W. Aust. . . D 4
Macdonnell (ranges), N. Terr. E 4
Mackay (lake), N. Terr. . . . . . D 4
Macquarie (harb.), Tas. . . . . G 8
Macumba (riv.), S. Aust. . . . . F 5
Magdelaine (cays), Coral Sea Is. Terr. . . . . H 3
Main Barrier (range), N.S.W. . G 6
Manifold (cape), Queens. . . . . J 4
Margaret (riv.), W. Aust. . . . D 3
Maurice (lake), S. Aust. . . . . E 5
Melville (bay), N. Terr. . . . . . F 2
Melville (cape), Queens. . . . . G 2
Melville (isl.), N. Terr. . . . . . E 2
Mitchell (riv.), Queens. . . . . . G 3
Montague (sound), W. Aust. . . C 2
Monte Bello (isls.), W. Aust. . A 4
Moore (lake), W. Aust. . . . . . B 5
Moreton (isl.), Queens. . . . . . J 5
Mornington (isl.), Queens. . . F 3
Murchison (riv.), W. Aust. . . . B 5

Murray (riv.) . . . . G 6
Murrumbidgee (riv.), N.S.W. . H 6
Musgrave (range), S. Aust. . . E 5
Naturaliste (cape), W. Aust. . D 7
Naturaliste (chan.), W. Aust. . A 5
Norman (riv.), Queens. . . . . . G 3
North West (cape), W. Aust. . A 4
Nullarbor (plain) . . . . D 6
Onkaparinga (riv.), S. Aust. . . D 8
Ord (riv.), W. Aust. . . . . D 3
Ossa (mt.), Tas. . . . . H 8
Oyster (bay), Tas. . . . . H 8
Paroo (riv.), N.S.W. . . . . G 5
Pera (head), Queens. . . . . . . G 2
Peron (cape), W. Aust. . . . . . A 2
Pillar (cape), Tas. . . . . H 8
Plenty (riv.) Vic. . . . . K 2
Port Davey (inlet), Tas. . . . . G 8
Port Phillip (bay), Vic. . . . . . K 3
Prince of Wales (isl.), Queens. G 2
Princess Charlotte (bay), Queens. . . . . G 2
Recherche (arch.), W. Aust. . . C 6
Roebuck (bay), W. Aust. . . . . C 3
Roper (riv.), N. Terr. . . . . . . E 3
Ruihieres (cape), W. Aust. . . D 2
Saint Vincent (gulf), S. Aust. . D 8

Sandy (cape), Queens. . . . . . J 4
Shark (bay), W. Aust. . . . . . . A 5
Simpson (des.), N. Terr. . . . . F 4
Sir Edward Pellew Group (isls.), N. Terr. . . . . F 3
South West (cape), Tas. . . . . G 7
Spencer (cape), S. Aust. . . . . F 7
Spencer (gulf), S. Aust. . . . . F 6
Steep (pt.), W. Aust. . . . . . . A 5
Sturt (des.), Queens. . . . . . . G 5
Talbot (cape), W. Aust. . . . . D 2
Tasman (pen.), Tas. . . . . H 8
Tasman (sea) . . . . J 7
Thomson (riv.), Queens. . . . . G 4
Torrens (lake), S. Aust. . . . . F 6
Torrens (riv.) . . . . E 7
Torres (str.), Queens. . . . . . . G 2
Trinity (bay), Queens. . . . . . H 3
Van Diemen (cape), N. Terr. . E 2
Van Diemen (gulf), N. Terr. . . E 2
Victoria (riv.), N. Terr. . . . . . E 3
Warrego (riv.), Queens. . . . . H 5
Wellesley (isls.), Queens. . . . F 3
Wells (lake), W. Aust. . . . . . C 5
Wessel (cape), N. Terr. . . . . . F 2
Wessel (isls.), N. Terr. . . . . . F 2

Whitsunday (isl.), Queens. . . . H 4
Willis (isls.), Coral Sea Is. Terr. . . . . J 3
Wilsons (prom.), Vic. . . . . . . H 7
Wooramel (riv.), W. Aust. . . . A 5
York (cape), Queens. . . . . . . G 2
York (sound), W. Aust. . . . . . C 2
Yorke (pen.), S. Aust. . . . . . F 7

NEW ZEALAND

CITIES and TOWNS

Ashburton 14,151 . . . . K 7
Auckland 144,963 . . . . L 6
Blenheim 17,849 . . . . L 7
Bluff 2,720 . . . . K 8
Christchurch 164,680 . . . . . . L 7
Dunedin 77,176 . . . . K 8
Gisborne 29,986 . . . . L 6
Greymouth 8,103 . . . . K 7
Hamilton 91,109 . . . . L 6
Hastings 36,083 . . . . L 6
Invercargill 49,446 . . . . K 8
Levin 14,652 . . . . L 6
Lower Hutt 63,245 . . . . L 6

Manukau 159,362 . . . . L 6
Masterton 18,785 . . . . L 6
Napier 48,314 . . . . L 6
Nelson 33,304 . . . . L 7
New Plymouth 44,095 . . . . . L 6
Oamaru 13,043 . . . . K 8
Palmerston North 60,105 . . . L 6
Rotorua 38,157 . . . . L 6
Takapuna 64,844 . . . . L 6
Taupo 13,651 . . . . L 6
Tauranga 37,099 . . . . L 6
Timaru 28,412 . . . . K 7
Tokoroa 18,713 . . . . L 6
Wanganui 37,012 . . . . L 6
Wellington (cap.) 135,688 . . . L 7
Westport 4,686 . . . . K 7

Whangarei 36,550 . . . . L 5

OTHER FEATURES

Alps, Southern (mts.) . . . . . . K 7
Canterbury (bight) . . . . L 7
Clutha (riv.) . . . . K 8
Cook (str.) . . . . L 6
East (cape) . . . . L 6
Egmont (mt.) . . . . L 6
Foveaux (str.) . . . . K 8
Great Barrier (isl.) . . . . L 6
Hauraki (gulf) . . . . L 6
Hawke (bay) . . . . L 6
Islands (bay) . . . . L 5

Marie van Diemen (cape) . . . K 5
North (isl.) 2,322,989 . . . . . . K 6
Otego (pen.) . . . . K 8
Pegasus (bay) . . . . L 7
Plenty (bay) . . . . L 6
Ruapehu (mt.) . . . . L 6
South (cape) . . . . K 8
South (isl.) 3,175,737 . . . . . . L 7
Stewart (isl.) . . . . K 8
Tasman (bay) . . . . L 7
Three Kings (isl.) . . . . K 5
Waikato (riv.) . . . . L 6
West (cape) . . . . K 8

*Population of metropolitan area.
†Population of urban area.

FIJI
AREA 7,055 sq. mi. (18,272 sq. km.)
POPULATION 588,068
CAPITAL Suva
LARGEST CITY Suva
HIGHEST POINT Tomaniivi 4,341 ft.
(1,323 m.)
MONETARY UNIT Fijian dollar
MAJOR LANGUAGES Fijian, Hindi, English
MAJOR RELIGIONS Protestantism, Hinduism

KIRIBATI
AREA 291 sq. mi. (754 sq. km.)
POPULATION 56,213
CAPITAL Bairiki (Tarawa)
HIGHEST POINT (on Banaba I.) 285 ft. (87 m.)
MONETARY UNIT Australian dollar
MAJOR LANGUAGES I-Kiribati, English
MAJOR RELIGIONS Protestantism, Roman
Catholicism

NAURU
AREA 7.7 sq. mi. (20 sq. km.)
POPULATION 7,254
CAPITAL Yaren (district)
MONETARY UNIT Australian dollar
MAJOR LANGUAGES Nauruan, English
MAJOR RELIGION Protestantism

SOLOMON ISLANDS
AREA 11,500 sq. mi. (29,785 sq. km.)
POPULATION 221,000
CAPITAL Honiara
HIGHEST POINT Mount Popomanatseu
7,647 ft. (2,331 m.)
MONETARY UNIT Solomon Islands dollar
MAJOR LANGUAGES English, pidgin English,
Melanesian dialects
MAJOR RELIGIONS Tribal religions,
Protestantism, Roman Catholicism

TONGA
AREA 270 sq. mi. (699 sq. km.)
POPULATION 90,128
CAPITAL Nuku'alofa
LARGEST CITY Nuku'alofa
HIGHEST POINT 3,389 ft. (1,033 m.)
MONETARY UNIT pa'anga
MAJOR LANGUAGES Tongan, English
MAJOR RELIGION Protestantism

TUVALU
AREA 9.78 sq. mi. (25.33 sq. km.)
POPULATION 7,349
CAPITAL Fongafale (Funafuti)
HIGHEST POINT 15 ft. (4.6 m.)
MONETARY UNIT Australian dollar
MAJOR LANGUAGES English, Tuvaluan
MAJOR RELIGION Protestantism

Abaiang (atoll) 3,296 .... H 5
Abemama (atoll) 2,300 .... H 5
Adamstown (cap.), Pitcairn Is.
54 .... N 8
Admiralty (isls.) .... E 6
Agaña (cap.), Guam 896 ...... E 4
Agrihan (isl.) .... E 4
Ailinglapalap (atoll) 1,385 .... G 5
Ailuk (atoll) 413 .... H 4
Aitutaki (atoll) 2,348 .... K 7
Alofi (cap.), Niue 960 .... K 7
Alotau 4,310. .... E 7
Ambrym (isl.) 6,324 .... G 7
American Samoa 32,297 .... J 7
Anaa (atoll) 444. .... M 7
Angaur (isl.) 243 .... D 5
Apataki (atoll). .... M 7
Apia (cap.), W. Samoa 33,100 .. J 7
Arno (atoll) 1,487 .... H 5
Arorae (atoll) 1,626. .... H 6
Atafu (atoll) 577. .... J 6
Atiu (isl.) 1,225 .... L 8
Austral (isls.) 5,208. .... L 8
Avarua (cap.), Cook Is. .... L 8
Babelthuap (isl.) 10,391. ..... D 5
Bairiki (cap.), Kiribati 1,777 ... H 5
Baker (isl.) .... J 5
Banaba (isl.) 2,314 .... G 6
Banks (isls.) 3,158 .... G 7
Belau 12,116. .... D 5
Belep (isls.) 624 .... G 7
Bellona (reefs) .... G 8
Beru (atoll) 2,318 .... H 6
Bikini (atoll) .... G 4
Bismarck (arch.) 218,339 ..... E 6
Bonin (isls.) 1,879 .... E 3
Bora-Bora (isl.) 2,572. .... L 7
Bougainville (isl.) 71,761 ..... F 6
Bounty (isls.) .... H 10
Bourail 3,149. .... G 8
Butaritari (atoll) 2,971 .... H 5
Capitol Hill (cap.), No.
Marianas 592 .... E 4
Caroline (isls.). .... M 7
Caroline (isls.). .... E 5
Chichi (isl.) 1,879 .... E 3
Choiseul (isl.) 10,349. .... F 6
Christmas (Kiritimati) (isl.)
674 .... L 5
Cook (isls.) 17,695. .... K 7
Coral (sea) .... F 7
Danger (Pukapuka) (atoll)
797 .... K 7
Daru 7,127. .... E 7
Disappointment (isls.) 373. ... N 7
Ducie (isl.) .... O 8
Easter (isl.) 1,598 .... Q 8
Ebon (atoll) 887. .... G 5
Efate (isl.) 18,038. .... G 7
Enderbury (isl.) .... J 6
Enewetak (Eniwetok) (atoll)
542 .... G 4
Erromanga (isl.) 945. .... H 7
Espiritu Santo (isl.) 16,220 ... E 7
Fais (isl.) 207. .... E 5
Fakaofo (atoll) 654 .... J 6
Fanning (Tabuaeran) (isl.) 340 L 5
Faraulep (atoll) 132. .... E 5
Fatuhiva (isl.) 386. .... N 7
Fiji 588,068 .... H 8
Flint (isl.) .... L 7
Fly (riv.) .... E 6
Fongafale (cap.), Tuvalu ...... H 6
French Polynesia 137,382. .... L 8
Funafuti (atoll) 2,120 .... H 6
Futuna (Hoorn) (isls.) 3,173 .. J 7
Gambier (isls.) 556. .... N 8
Gardner (Nukumaroro)(isl.). ... J 6
Gilbert (isls.) 47,711. .... H 6
Greenwich (Kapingamarangi)
(atoll) 508 .... F 5
Guadalcanal (isl.) 46,619 ..... F 7
Guam (isl.) 105,979. .... E 4
Hall (isls.) 647. .... F 5
Hawaiian (isls.) 964,691. ..... J 3
Henderson (isl.) .... O 8
Hivaoa (isl.) 1,159. .... N 6
Honiara (cap.), Solomon Is.
14,942 .... F 6
Hoorn (isls.) 3,173 .... J 7
Howland (isl.) .... J 5
Huahine (isl.) 3,140 .... L 7
Hull (Orona)(isl.). .... J 6
Huon (gulf) .... E 6
Ifalik (atoll) 389 .... E 5
Iwo (isl.) .... E 3
Jaluit (atoll) 1,450 .... G 5
Jarvis (isl.) .... K 6
Johnston (atoll) 327 .... K 4
Kadavu (Kandavu) (isl.) 8,699 H 7
Kanton (atoll) .... K 6
Kapingamarangi (atoll) 508. ... F 5
Kavieng 4,633 .... E 6
Kermadec (isls.). .... J 9
Kieta 3,491. .... F 6
Kimbe 4,662. .... E 6
Kingman (reef) .... K 5
Kiribati 57,500. .... H 6
Kiritimati (isl.) 674. .... L 5
Kolonia (cap.), Micronesia
5,549 .... F 5
Koror (cap.), Belau 6,222. .... D 5
Kosrae (isl.) 5,491 .... G 5
Kwajalein (atoll) 6,624 .... G 5
Lae 61,617. .... E 6
Lau Group (isls.) 14,452 ..... J 7
Lavongai (isl.). .... F 6
Lifu (isl.) 7,585. .... K 8
Line (isls.). .... K 5
Little Makin (atoll) 1,445 ..... H 5
Lord Howe (Ontong Java) (isl.)
1,082 .... G 6
Lord Howe (isl.) 287 .... G 9
Lorengau 3,986. .... E 6
Louisiade (arch.). .... F 7
Loyalty (isls.) 14,518 .... G 8
Luganville 4,935. .... G 7
Madang 21,335 .... E 6

Majuro (atoll) (cap.), Marshall
Is. 8,583. .... H 5
Makin (Butaritari) (atoll) 2,971 H 5
Malaita (isl.) 50,912 .... G 6
Malden (isl.) .... L 6
Malekula (isl.) 15,931. .... G 7
Maloelap (atoll) 763 .... H 5
Mangaia (isl.) 1,364 .... L 8
Mangareva (isl.) 556. .... N 8
Manihiki (atoll) 405. .... K 7
Manra (isl.) .... K 6
Manua (isls.) 1,459 .... J 7
Manus (isl.) 25,844. .... E 6
Marcus (isl.) .... F 3
Maré (isl.) 4,156 .... G 8
Marianas, Northern 16,780 ... E 4
Mariana Trench .... E 4
Marquesas (isls.) 5,419 ...... N 6
Marshall Islands 30,873. ...... G 4
Marutea (atoll) .... N 7
Mata Utu (cap.), Wallis and
Futuna 558 .... J 7
Mauke (isl.) 684 .... L 8
Melanesia (reg.). .... E 4
Micronesia (reg.). .... E 4
Micronesia, Federated States
of 73,160 .... F 5
Midway (isls.) 453. .... J 3
Mili (atoll) 763 .... H 5
Moen (atoll) 10,351. .... F 5

Moorea (isl.) 5,788 .... L 7
Mururoa (isl.). .... M 8
Nadi 6,938. .... H 7
Namonuito (atoll) 783. .... E 5
Namorik (atoll) 617. .... G 5
Nanumea (atoll) 844. .... H 6
Nauru 7,254. .... G 6
Ndeni (isl.) 4,854. .... G 7
New Britain (isl.) 148,773 .... F 6
New Caledonia 133,233 ...... G 8
New Caledonia (isl.)
118,715 .... G 8
New Georgia (isl.) 16,472 .... F 6
New Guinea (isl.) .... D 6
New Ireland (isl.) 65,657 ..... F 6
Ngatik (atoll) 560. .... F 5
Ngulu (atoll) 21. .... D 5
Niuatoputapu (isl.) 1,650 ..... J 7
Niue (isl.) 3,578. .... K 7
Niutao (atoll) 866. .... H 6
Nomoi (isls.) 1,879. .... F 5
Nonouti (atoll) 2,223. .... H 6
Norfolk Island (terr.) 2,175. ... G 8
Northern Marianas 116,780 ... E 4
Nouméa (cap.), New Caled.
56,078 .... G 8
Nui (atoll) 603 .... H 6
Nuku'alofa (cap.), Tonga
18,356 .... J 8
Nukuhiva (isl.) 1,484. .... M 6

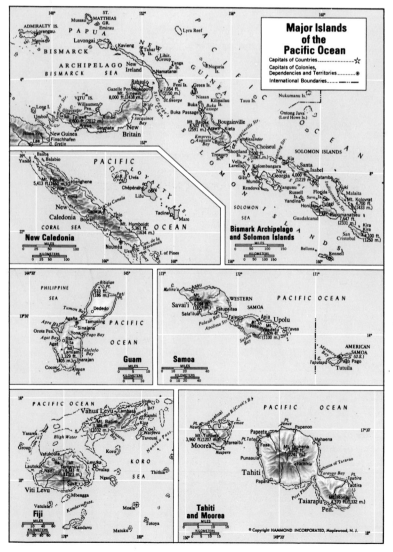

Major Islands of the Pacific Ocean
Capitals of Countries .... ☆
Capitals of Colonies,
Dependencies and Territories .... ⊛
International Boundaries .... —·—·—

® Copyright HAMMOND INCORPORATED, Maplewood, N. J.

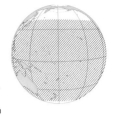

Nukumaroro (isl.) .... J 6
Ocean (Banaba) (isl.) 2,314 ... G 6
Oeno (isl.) .... O 8
Onotoa (atoll) 1,997 .... H 6
Ontong Java (isl.) 1,082 ..... G 6
Orona (isl.) .... J 6
Pacific Islands, Terr. of the
  132,929 .... F 5
Pagan (isl.) .... E 4
Pago Pago (cap.) Amer.
  Samoa 3,075 .... J 7
Palmyra (atoll) .... K 5
Papeete (cap.) Fr. Poly.
  22,967 .... M 7
Papua (gulf) .... E 6
Papua New Guinea
  3,010,727 .... E 6
Peleliu (isl.) 609. .... D 5
Penrhyn (Tongareva) (atoll)
  608 .... L 6
Phoenix (isls.) .... J 6
Pines (isl.) 1,095. .... H 7
Pitcairn (isl.) 54 .... O 8
Polynesia (reg.) .... K 7
Pohnpei (Ponape)(isl.)
  19,935 .... F 5
Popondetta 6,429 .... E 6
Port Moresby (cap.), Papua
  N.G. 123,624 .... E 6
Pukapuka (atoll) 797 .... K 7

Pulap (atoll) 427 .... E 5
Puluwat (atoll) 441 .... E 5
Rabaul 14,954 .... F 6
Raiatea (isl.) 2,517 .... L 7
Raivavae (isl.) 1,023. ..... M 8
Rakahanga (atoll) 269 ..... K 7
Ralik Chain (isls.) .... G 5
Rangiroa (atoll) .... M 7
Rapa (isl.) 398. .... M 8
Rarotonga (isl.) 9,477 ..... L 8
Ratak Chain (isls.) .... G 5
Reao (atoll) 424. .... N 7
Rennell (isl.) 1,132 .... F 7
Rikitea .... N 8
Rimatara (isl.) 813 .... L 8
Rongelap (atoll) 235. ...... G 5
Rota (isl.) 1,261. .... E 4
Rotuma (isl.) 2,805. .... H 7
Rurutu (isl.) 1,555. .... L 8
Saipan (isl.) 14,549. ...... E 4
Sala y Gómez (isl.) .... P 8
Samarai 869 .... G 7
Samoa (isls.) .... J 7
San Cristobal (isl.) 11,212. . G 7
Santa Cruz (isls.) 5,421. ... G 7
Santa Isabel (isl.) 10,420. .. G 6
Savai'i (isl.) 43,150 .... J 7
Senyavin (isls.) 20,035. .... F 5
Society (isls.) 117,703 ..... L 7
Solomon (isls.) .... F 6

Solomon (sea) .... F 6
Solomon Islands 221,000. ... G 6
Starbuck (isl.) .... L 6
Suva (cap.), Fiji 63,628. ... H 7
Swains (isl.) 27 .... K 7
Sydney (Manra)(isl.) ...... K 6
Tabiteuea (atoll) 3,942. ... H 6
Tabuaeran (isl.) 340 ...... L 5
Tahaa (isl.) 3,513 .... L 7
Tahiti (isl.) 95,604 .... L 7
Takaroa (atoll) 337 .... M 7
Tanna (isl.) 15,715 .... H 7
Tarawa (atoll) 17,129 ..... H 5
Tasman (sea) .... J 8
Teraina (isl.) 458 .... L 5
Tinian (isl.) 866 .... E 4
Tokelau (isl.) 1,575 ...... J 6
Tonga 90,128. .... J 8
Tongareva (atoll) 608 ..... L 6
Tongatapu (isl.) 57,130 ... J 8
Torres (isls.) 325 .... G 7
Torres (strait) .... D 6
Trobriand (isls.) .... F 6
Truk (isls.) 37,488. .... F 5
Tuamotu (arch.) 9,052 ..... M 7
Tubuai (Austral) (isls.)
  5,208 .... M 8
Tubuai (isl.) 1,419. .... M 8
Tutuila (isl.) 30,538 ...... J 7
Tuvalu 7,349. .... H 6

Uapou (isl.) 1,563 .... M 6
Ujelang (atoll) 309 .... F 5
Ulithi (atoll) 710 .... D 4
Upolu (isl.) 114,620 ...... J 7
Uturoa 2,517 .... L 7
Uvéa (isl.) 2,777 .... H 6
Vaitupu (isl.) 1,273 ...... H 6
Vanikoro (isl.) 267. ...... G 7
Vanimo 3,071. .... E 6
Vanua Levu (isl.) 103,122 .. H 7
Vanuatu 112,596. .... G 7

Vila (cap.), Vanuatu
  4,729 .... G 7
Viti Levu (isl.) 445,422 ... H 7
Volcano (isls.) .... E 3
Vostok (isl.) .... L 7
Wake (isl.) 302. .... G 4
Wallis (isls.) 6,019. ...... J 7
Wallis and Futuna 9,192 ... J 7
Washington (Teraina) (isl.)
  458 .... L 5
Wau 2,349. .... E 6

Western Samoa 158,130 .... J 7
Wewak 19,890. .... E 6
Woleai (atoll) 638 .... E 5
Wotje (atoll) 535 .... H 5
Yap (isl.) 6,670. .... D 5

*City and suburbs.
●Population of urban area.

VANUATU

AREA 5,700 sq. mi. (14,763 sq. km.)
POPULATION 112,596
CAPITAL Vila
HIGHEST POINT Mt. Tabwemasana
  6,165 ft. (1,879 m.)
MONETARY UNIT vatu
MAJOR LANGUAGES Bislama, English,
  French
MAJOR RELIGIONS Christian, animist

WESTERN SAMOA

AREA 1,133 sq. mi. (2,934 sq. km.)
POPULATION 158,130
CAPITAL Apia
LARGEST CITY Apia
HIGHEST POINT Mt. Silisili 6,094 ft.
  (1,857 m.)
MONETARY UNIT tala
MAJOR LANGUAGES Samoan, English
MAJOR RELIGIONS Protestantism,
  Roman Catholicism

Pacific Ocean

LAMBERT AZIMUTHAL EQUAL-AREA PROJECTION

®Copyright HAMMOND INCORPORATED, Maplewood, N.J.

NAUTICAL MILES

STATUTE MILES

KILOMETERS

Capitals of Countries .... ☆
Capitals of Colonies,
  Dependencies, States and Territories .. ★
Administrative Centers .... ⊛

International Boundaries ....
Internal Boundaries ....
Railroads ....
Distances Between Points ___ 5444 ___
                              (nautical miles)

South America — Northern Part

LAMBERT AZIMUTHAL EQUAL-AREA PROJECTION

SCALE OF MILES
0 100 200 300 400 500

SCALE OF KILOMETRES
0 100 200 300 400 500

Capitals of Countries .... ☆
Other Capitals .... △
International Boundaries .... — — —
Other Boundaries .... — · · —

© Copyright HAMMOND INCORPORATED, Maplewood, N.J.

ARGENTINA

PROVINCES

Buenos Aires 10,796,036	H 11
Catamarca 206,204	G 9
Chaco 692,410	H 9
Chubut 262,196	G 12
Córdoba 2,407,135	H 10
Corrientes 657,716	J 9
Distrito Federal 2,908,001	J 10
Entre Ríos 902,241	J 10
Formosa 292,479	H 8
Jujuy 408,514	G 8
La Pampa 207,132	G 11
La Rioja 163,342	G 9
Mendoza 1,187,305	G 10
Misiones 579,579	K 9
Neuquén 241,904	G 11
Río Negro 383,896	G 12
Salta 662,369	G 8
San Juan 469,973	G 10
San Luis 212,837	G 10
Santa Cruz 114,479	G 13
Santa Fe 2,457,188	H 9
Santiago del Estero 652,318	H 9
Tierra del Fuego, Antártida, e Islas del Atlántico Sur 29,451	G 14
Tucumán 968,066	G 9

CITIES and TOWNS

Azul 43,582	J 11
Bahía Blanca *220,765	H 11
Balcarce 28,985	J 11
Bell Ville 26,559	H 10
Bolívar 16,382	H 11
Buenos Aires (cap.) *9,927,404	H 10
Campana 51,498	J 10
Catamarca *88,432	H 9
Chivilcoy 43,779	H 11
Comodoro Rivadavia 96,865	G 13
Concepción del Uruguay 46,065	J 10
Concordia 93,618	J 10
Córdoba *982,018	G 10
Corrientes 179,590	J 9
Cruz del Eje 23,473	H 10
Curuzú Cuatiá 24,955	J 9
Embarcación 9,016	G 8
Esperanza 22,838	H 10
Formosa 95,067	J 9
Gaimán 2,651	G 12
Gastre	G 12
General Alvear 21,250	G 11
General Pico 30,180	H 11
General Roca 38,296	G 11
Godoy Cruz 141,553	G 10
Goya 47,357	J 9
Jachal 8,832	G 10
Jujuy 124,487	G 8
La Plata *560,341	J 11
La Rioja 66,826	G 9
Liberador General San Martín 30,814	H 8
Lincoln 19,009	H 11
Maquinchao 1,295	G 12
Mar del Plata 407,024	J 11
Mendoza *596,796	G 10
Mercedes 50,856	G 10

Miramar 15,473	J 11
Necochea 50,939	J 11
Neuquén 90,037	G 11
Olavarría 63,686	H 11
Paraná 159,581	J 10
Pehuajó 25,613	H 11
Pergamino 68,989	H 10
Plaza Huincul 7,988	G 11
Posadas 139,941	J 9
Presidencia Roque Sáenz Peña 49,261	J 9
Puerto Madryn 20,709	G 12
Punta Alta 54,375	H 11
Rafaela 53,152	H 10
Rawson 12,981	H 12
Reconquista 32,442	J 9
Resistencia *218,438	J 9
Rinconada	G 8
Río Cuarto 110,148	H 10
Río Gallegos 43,479	G 14
Río Grande 13,271	G 14
Rivadavia	H 8
Rosario *954,606	H 10
Rosario de la Frontera 13,531	H 9
Salta 260,323	G 8
San Antonio de los Cobres 2,357	G 8
San Carlos de Bariloche 48,222	F 12
San Francisco *58,616	H 10
San Juan *290,479	G 10
San Luis 70,632	G 10
San Miguel de Tucumán *496,914	H 9
San Nicolás 96,313	J 10

San Rafael 7,047	G 10
Santa Cruz 2,353	G 14
Sante Fe 287,240	H 10
Santa Rosa 51,689	H 11
Santiago del Estero 148,357	H 9
Tandil 78,821	J 9
Tartagal 31,367	H 8
Trelew 52,073	G 12
Trenque Lauquen 22,504	H 11
Tres Arroyos 42,118	H 11
Ushuaia 10,988	G 14
Valchecta 2,994	G 12
Venado Tuerto 46,775	H 10
Viedma 24,338	H 12
Villa Dolores 21,508	G 10
Villa María *67,490	H 10

OTHER FEATURES

Aconcagua (mt.)	G 10
Andes de Patagonia (mts.)	F 14
Argentino (lake)	F 14
Bermejo (riv.)	H 9
Colorado (riv.)	H 11
Estados, Los (isl.)	H 14
Gran Chaco (reg.)	H 8
Iguassú (falls)	K 9
Magellan (str.)	G 14
Maipo (mt.)	G 10
Nahuel Huapi (lake)	F 12
Negro (riv.)	H 11
Ojos del Salado (mt.)	G 9
Pampas (plain)	H 11
Patagonia (reg.)	G 12
Plata, Río de la (est.)	J 11
Salado (riv.)	G 11

Salado (riv.)	H 9
San Antonio (cape)	J 11
San Martín (lake)	F 13
San Matías (gulf)	H 12
Staten (Los Estados) (isl.)	H 14
Tierra del Fuego (isl.)	G 14
Tres Puntas (cape)	H 13
Uruguay (riv.)	J 9
Valdés (pen.)	H 12

BOLIVIA

CITIES and TOWNS

Cochabamba 204,684	G 7
Guaqui 2,084	G 7
Guayamerín 1,470	G 6
Huanchaca	G 8
La Paz (cap.) 635,283	G 7
Oruro 124,213	G 7
Potosí 77,397	G 7
Puerto Suárez 1,159	J 7
Santa Cruz 254,682	H 7
Sucre (cap.) 63,625	G 7
Tarija 38,916	H 8

OTHER FEATURES

Abuná (riv.)	G 6
Beni (riv.)	G 6
Desaguadero (riv.)	G 7
Grande (riv.)	H 7
Guaporé (riv.)	H 6
Illampu (mt.)	G 7
Mamoré (riv.)	H 6
Poopó (lake)	G 7

Real, Cordillera (mts.)	G 7
Titicaca (lake)	F 7

BRAZIL

STATES

Acre 301,605	F 5
Alagoas 1,987,581	N 5
Amapá (terr.) 175,634	K 3
Amazonas 1,432,066	G 5
Bahia 9,474,263	M 6
Ceará 5,294,876	N 5
Distrito Federal 1,177,393	L 7
Espírito Santo 2,023,821	M 8
Goiás 3,865,482	L 6
Maranhão 4,002,599	L 5
Mato Grosso 1,141,661	J 6
Mato Grosso do Sul 1,370,333	J 7
Minas Gerais 13,390,805	M 7
Pará 3,411,868	K 4
Paraíba 2,772,600	N 5
Paraná 7,630,466	K 8
Pernambuco 6,147,102	N 5
Piauí 2,140,066	M 5
Rio de Janeiro 11,297,327	M 8
Rio Grande do Norte 1,899,720	N 5
Rio Grande do Sul 7,777,212	K 9
Rondônia 492,810	H 6
Roraima (terr.) 79,153	H 3
Santa Catarina 3,628,751	K 9
São Paulo 25,040,698	L 8
Sergipe 1,141,834	N 6

CITIES and TOWNS

Alagoinhas 76,377	N 6
Alcobaça 3,430	N 7
Alegrete 54,786	J 9
Amapá 2,676	J 3
Amarante 6,848	M 5
Anápolis 160,520	L 7
Andradina 42,036	K 8
Aracaju 288,106	N 6
Araçatuba 1,113,486	K 8
Araguari 73,302	L 7
Arapiraca 84,133	N 6
Araraquara 47,202	L 8
Araxá 51,339	L 7
Bacabal 43,229	L 5
Bagé 66,743	K 10
Bahia (Salvador) 1,496,276	N 6
Barbacena 69,675	M 8
Barcelos 1,846	H 4
Barra do Garças	K 7
Barretos 65,294	L 8
Baurú 178,861	L 8
Bebedouro 39,070	L 8
Belém 758,117	L 4
Belo Horizonte 2,541,788	M 7
Benjamin Constant 6,563	G 4
Blumenau 144,819	L 9
Boa Vista 43,131	H 3
Borba 5,366	J 4
Botucatu 56,316	L 8
Bragança 1,208	L 4
Brasília (cap.) 411,305	L 7
Brejo 5,859	M 5
Brumado 24,663	M 6

(continued on following page)

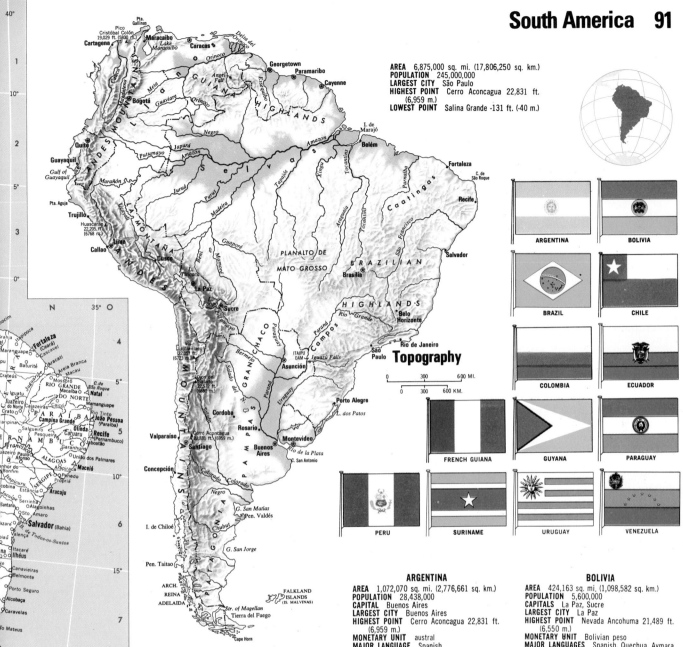

AREA 6,875,000 sq. mi. (17,806,250 sq. km.)
POPULATION 245,000,000
LARGEST CITY São Paulo
HIGHEST POINT Cerro Aconcagua 22,831 ft.
(6,959 m.)
LOWEST POINT Salina Grande -131 ft. (-40 m.)

Topography

0   300   600 MI.
0   300   600 KM.

ARGENTINA   BOLIVIA

BRAZIL   CHILE

COLOMBIA   ECUADOR

FRENCH GUIANA   GUYANA   PARAGUAY

PERU   SURINAME   URUGUAY   VENEZUELA

ARGENTINA
AREA 1,072,070 sq. mi. (2,776,661 sq. km.)
POPULATION 28,438,000
CAPITAL Buenos Aires
LARGEST CITY Buenos Aires
HIGHEST POINT Cerro Aconcagua 22,831 ft.
(6,959 m.)
MONETARY UNIT austral
MAJOR LANGUAGE Spanish
MAJOR RELIGION Roman Catholicism

BOLIVIA
AREA 424,163 sq. mi. (1,098,582 sq. km.)
POPULATION 5,600,000
CAPITALS La Paz, Sucre
LARGEST CITY La Paz
HIGHEST POINT Nevada Ancohuma 21,489 ft.
(6,550 m.)
MONETARY UNIT Bolivian peso
MAJOR LANGUAGES Spanish, Quechua, Aymara
MAJOR RELIGION Roman Catholicism

BRAZIL
AREA 3,284,426 sq. mi. (8,506,663 sq. km.)
POPULATION 119,098,992
CAPITAL Brasília
LARGEST CITY São Paulo (greater)
HIGHEST POINT Pico da Neblina 9,889 ft.
(3,014 m.)
MONETARY UNIT cruzeiro
MAJOR LANGUAGE Portuguese
MAJOR RELIGION Roman Catholicism

CHILE
AREA 292,257 sq. mi. (756,946 sq. km.)
POPULATION 11,275,440
CAPITAL Santiago
LARGEST CITY Santiago
HIGHEST POINT Ojos del Salado 22,572 ft.
(6,880 m.)
MONETARY UNIT Chilean escudo
MAJOR LANGUAGE Spanish
MAJOR RELIGION Roman Catholicism

COLOMBIA
AREA 439,513 sq. mi. (1,138,339 sq. km.)
POPULATION 27,520,000
CAPITAL Bogotá
LARGEST CITY Bogotá
HIGHEST POINT Pico Cristóbal Colón
19,029 ft. (5,800 m.)
MONETARY UNIT Colombian peso
MAJOR LANGUAGE Spanish
MAJOR RELIGION Roman Catholicism

ECUADOR
AREA 109,483 sq. mi. (283,561 sq. km.)
POPULATION 8,354,000
CAPITAL Quito
LARGEST CITY Guayaquil
HIGHEST POINT Chimborazo 20,561 ft.
(6,267 m.)
MONETARY UNIT sucre
MAJOR LANGUAGES Spanish, Quechua
MAJOR RELIGION Roman Catholicism

FRENCH GUIANA
AREA 35,135 sq. mi. (91,000 sq. km.)
POPULATION 73,022
CAPITAL Cayenne
LARGEST CITY Cayenne
HIGHEST POINT 2,723 ft. (830 m.)
MONETARY UNIT French franc
MAJOR LANGUAGE French
MAJOR RELIGIONS Roman Catholicism,
Protestantism

GUYANA
AREA 83,000 sq. mi. (214,970 sq. km.)
POPULATION 820,000
CAPITAL Georgetown
LARGEST CITY Georgetown
HIGHEST POINT Mt. Roraima 9,094 ft.
(2,772 m.)
MONETARY UNIT Guyana dollar
MAJOR LANGUAGES English, Hindi
MAJOR RELIGIONS Christianity, Hinduism,
Islam

PARAGUAY
AREA 157,047 sq. mi. (406,752 sq. km.)
POPULATION 2,973,000
CAPITAL Asunción
LARGEST CITY Asunción
HIGHEST POINT Amambay Range
2,264 ft. (690 m.)
MONETARY UNIT guaraní
MAJOR LANGUAGES Spanish, Guaraní
MAJOR RELIGION Roman Catholicism

PERU
AREA 496,222 sq. mi. (1,285,215 sq. km.)
POPULATION 17,031,221
CAPITAL Lima
LARGEST CITY Lima
HIGHEST POINT Huascarán 22,205 ft.
(6,768 m.)
MONETARY UNIT sol
MAJOR LANGUAGES Spanish, Quechua, Aymara
MAJOR RELIGION Roman Catholicism

SURINAME
AREA 55,144 sq. mi. (142,823 sq. km.)
POPULATION 354,860
CAPITAL Paramaribo
LARGEST CITY Paramaribo
HIGHEST POINT Julianatop 4,200 ft. (1,280 m.)
MONETARY UNIT Suriname guilder
MAJOR LANGUAGES Dutch, Hindi, Indonesian
MAJOR RELIGIONS Christianity, Islam,
Hinduism

URUGUAY
AREA 72,172 sq. mi. (186,925 sq. km.)
POPULATION 2,899,000
CAPITAL Montevideo
LARGEST CITY Montevideo
HIGHEST POINT Mirador Nacional 1,644 ft.
(501 m.)
MONETARY UNIT Uruguayan peso
MAJOR LANGUAGE Spanish
MAJOR RELIGION Roman Catholicism

VENEZUELA
AREA 352,143 sq. mi. (912,050 sq. km.)
POPULATION 14,313,000
CAPITAL Caracas
LARGEST CITY Caracas
HIGHEST POINT Pico Bolívar 16,427 ft.
(5,007 m.)
MONETARY UNIT Bolívar
MAJOR LANGUAGE Spanish
MAJOR RELIGION Roman Catholicism

Cáceres 33,472	J 7	Cruzeiro do Sul 11,189	F 5	Jacobina 26,723	N 6	Paracatu 29,911	L 7	Presidente Prudente 127,623	K 8	São Leopoldo 94,864	K 9	Vitória da Conquista 125,717	N 7

Cachoeira do Sul 59,967....K 10
Cachoeira de Itapemirim
84,994...............N 8
Caicó 30,777.............N 5
Cajazeiras 30,834.........N 5
Campina Grande 222,229...N 5
Campinas 566,517.........L 8
Campo Grande 282,844....K 8
Campos 174,218...........M 7
Cananéia 5,581............L 8
Caratinga 39,621..........M 7
Caravelas 3,704...........N 7
Caruaru 137,636..........N 5
Cataguases 40,659........M 8
Catalão 30,516...........L 7
Catanduva 64,813.........L 8
Caxias 56,755............M 4
Caxias do Sul 198,824....K 9
Ceará (Fortaleza) 648,815..N 4
Codajás 4,923............H 4
Codó 11,593..............N 4
Colatina 61,057..........M 7
Conceição................J 5
Conselheiro Lafaiete 66,262..M 8
Corumbá 66,014..........J 7
Crateús 29,905...........N 5
Crato 49,244.............N 5
Cruz Alta 53,315.........K 9

Cuiabá 167,894...........J 7
Curitiba †843,733........K 9
Diamantina 20,197........M 7
Divinópolis 108,344......L 8
Erexim 46,927...........K 9
Feira de Santana 225,003..N 6
Floriano 35,761..........M 5
Florianópolis 153,547.....L 9
Fonte Boa 3,278.........G 4
Fortaleza 648,815........N 4
Foz do Iguaçu 93,619.....K 9
Franca 143,630...........L 8
Garanhuns 64,854........N 5
Governador Valadares
173,699..............M 7
Guarapuava 17,189.......K 9
Humaitá.................H 5
Iguatu 39,611...........N 5
Ilhéus 71,240............N 6
Ipiaú 27,384............N 6
Itabuna 129,938.........M 6
Itajaí 78,867............L 9
Itajubá 53,506...........L 8
Itapetinga 36,897........M 7
Itaqui 23,136...........J 9
Jaboatão 67,120.........O 5
Jacarèzinho 92,364.......K 8

Januária 20,484..........M 6
Jaú 59,522..............L 8
Jequié 84,792...........M 6
João Pessoa 290,424.....O 5
Joinvile 217,074.........L 9
Juazeiro 60,940.........M 5
Juazeiro do Norte 125,248..M 5
Juiz de Fora 299,728.....M 8
Jundiaí 210,015.........L 8
Limeira 137,812.........L 8
Lins 44,633.............L 8
Londrina 258,054........K 8
Macapá 89,081...........K 3
Macau 17,543...........N 4
Maceió 376,479..........N 5
Manaus 613,068.........H 4
Manicoré 9,532..........H 5
Maracaju 9,699..........K 8
Marília 103,904..........K 8
Maringá 158,047.........K 8
Mato Grosso............J 6
Montes Claros 151,881...M 7
Mossoró 118,007........N 5
Natal 376,552...........O 5
Niterói 386,185.........M 8
Olinda 266,392..........N 5
Ouro Preto 27,821.......M 8

Paraíba (João Pessoa)
290,424.............O 5
Paranaguá 68,366........L 9
Paranaíba 21,305.........M 4
Passo Fundo 103,121.....K 9
Passos 56,998...........L 8
Patrocínio 29,520........L 7
Paulo Afonso 62,066.....N 5
Pedreiras 30,843.........L 4
Pelotas 197,092.........K 10
Penedo 27,064...........N 6
Pernambuco (Recife)
1,184,215...........O 5
Pesqueira 27,864.........N 5
Petrolina 73,436.........M 5
Petrópolis 149,427.......M 8
Picos 33,098............M 5
Piracicaba 179,395.......L 8
Pirapora 31,533.........L 7
Piripiri 29,497...........M 4
Poços de Caldas 81,448...L 8
Ponta Grossa 171,111....K 9
Porto Alegre 1,108,883...K 10
Pôrto Esperança 410.....J 7
Pôrto Nacional 19,052....L 6
Porto Seguro 5,007......N 7
Porto Velho 101,644.....H 5
Presidente Epitácio 23,406..K 8

Presidente Prudente 127,623..K 8
Propriá 19,034..........N 6
Recife 1,184,215.........O 5
Ribeirão Preto 300,704...L 8
Rio Branco 87,462.......G 5
Rio Grande 124,706......K 10
Rio Grande do Sul.......
Rio Pardo 18,370........K 9
Rio Verde 47,639........K 7
Salgueiro 25,915........N 5
Salvador 1,496,276......N 6
Santa Maria 151,202.....K 9
Santana do Livramento
58,165..............K 10
Santarém 101,534.......J 4
Santo Amaro 29,627......N 6
Santo Ângelo 50,161.....K 9
Santo Antônio do Platina
21,284..............K 8
Santos 411,023..........L 8
São Bernardo do Campo
381,261.............L 8
São Gonçalo 221,278.....P 13
São João da Bôa Vista
45,712..............L 8
São João del Rei 53,401...M 8
São José do Rio Preto
171,982.............K 8

São Luís 182,466........M 4
São Martinho............J 5
São Mateus 22,522......N 7
São Paulo 7,033,529.....L 8
Sena Madureira 6,666....G 5
Senhor do Bonfim 33,811..N 6
Serra do Navio 415.......K 3
Sobral 69,072...........M 4
Sorocaba 254,718.......L 8
Taguatinga 480,109......L 7
Taubaté 155,371.........L 8
Tefé 14,670.............G 4
Teófilo Otoni 83,108.....M 7
Teresina 339,264........M 4
Tocantinópolis 8,427.....L 5
Três Lagoas 45,171......K 8
Tubarão 64,585.........L 9
Tutóia 4,766............M 4
Uaupés.................G 4
Uberaba 180,296........L 7
Uberlândia 230,400......L 7
União da Vitória 22,682...K 9
Uruguaiana 79,059.......J 9
Vacaria 37,370..........K 9
Valença 29,904.........N 6
Varginha 57,448.........M 8
Vila Velha Argolas 74,166..N 8
Vitória 144,143.........N 8

São Leopoldo 94,864.....K 9
Vitória da Conquista 125,717..N 7
Volta Redonda 177,772...M 8
Xique-Xique 17,625......N 6

OTHER FEATURES
Abuná (riv.).............J
Acaraí, Serra do (mts.)....J
Acre (riv.).............G
Amazon (Amazonas) (riv.)..G
Apiacás, Serra dos (mts.)..J
Araguaia (riv.)..........J
Aripuanã (riv.)..........H
Bandeira, Pico de (mt.)...M
Braço Maior do Araguaia
(riv.)...............K
Braço Menor do Araguaia
(riv.)...............K
Branco (riv.)...........J
Caatingas (for.)........M
Campos (plain)..........K
Carajás, Serra dos (mts.)..J
Carinhanha (riv.).......L
Caviana (isl.)..........K
Corcovado (mt.)........O
Frio (isl.).............L
Gradaús, Serra dos (mts.)..K
Grande, Rio (riv.)......L
Gurupi, Serra do (mts.)...L
Iguassú (falls).........K
Itaipu (res.)...........K
Itapecuru (riv.)........M
Japurá (riv.)...........H
Javari (riv.)...........G
Jequitinhonha (riv.).....M
Juruá (riv.)...........G
Madeira (riv.)..........H
Mantiqueira, Serra da (mts.)..L
Mar, Serra de (mts.).....L
Marajó (isl.)...........K
Mato Grosso, Planalto de
(plat.)..............K
Neblina, Pico da (peak)...G
Negro (riv.)...........J
Nhamundá (riv.).........J
Oyapock (riv.)..........K
Pacaraimã, Serra (mts.)...J
Paraguai (riv.).........J
Parecis, Serra dos (mts.)..J
Parnaíba (riv.).........M
Patos (lag.)...........K
Roncador, Serra do (mts.)..K
Roosevelt (riv.)........H
Santa Catarina (isl.)....L
São Francisco (riv.).....M
São João de Merití (riv.)..M
São Roque (cape).......M
São Sebastião (isl.).....L
São Torré (cape).......M
Selvas (for.)..........F–J
Sertao (reg.)..........M
Solimões (riv.).........H
Tapajós (riv.)..........J
Teles Pires (riv.).......J
Tocantins (riv.)........L
Todos-os-Santos (bay)....N
Tumucumaque, Serra (mts.)..J
Urubupunga (dam)........K
Uruguai (riv.)..........K
Xingu (riv.)...........J

CHILE

CITIES and TOWNS
Antofagasta 125,100.....F
Arauco 5,400...........F
Arica 87,700...........F
Calama 45,900..........F
Calbuco △21,673........F
Cauquenes 20,200.......F
Cerro Manantiales.......G
Chañaral △36,949.......F
Chillán 128,515.........F
Chuquicamata 22,100....F
Concepción 206,226.....F
Copiapó 45,200.........F
Coquimbo 73,953........F
Corral △5,533..........F
Curepto △13,020........F
Illapel 12,200..........F
Iquique 645,000........F
La Serena 99,908.......F
La Unión 15,200........F
Linares 37,900.........F
Los Ángeles 49,500.....F
Los Vilos △10,453......F
Lota 48,100...........F
Maullín △14,544........G
Mulchén 13,700........F
Ollagüe..............F
Osorno 68,800.........F
Ovalle 31,700.........F
Parral 17,000.........F
Puerto Montt 119,059...F
Punta Arenas 2,140.....F
Quirihue △11,178......F
San Fernando 23,600....F
Santiago (cap.) 3,614,947..F
Talca 133,160.........F
Talcahuano 148,300.....F
Tarapacá..............G
Temuco 197,232.......F
Tocopilla 22,000.......F
Valdivia 115,536.......F
Vallenar 26,800........F
Valparaíso 271,580.....F
Villarrica 25,091.......F
Viña del Mar 281,361...F

OTHER FEATURES
Andes (mts.)..........F
Atacama (des.).........F
Chiloé (isl.) 119,286....E
Corcovado (gulf).......G
Coronados (gulf).......G
Horn (cape)...........G
Llullaillaco (vol.)......G

Agriculture, Industry and Resources

MAJOR MINERAL OCCURRENCES

Al	Bauxite
Ag	Silver
Au	Gold
Be	Beryl
C	Coal
Cr	Chromium
Cu	Copper
D	Diamonds
Em	Emeralds
Fe	Iron Ore
G	Natural Gas
Hg	Mercury
Id	Iodine
Mi	Mica
Mn	Manganese
Mo	Molybdenum
N	Nitrates
Na	Salt
Ni	Nickel
O	Petroleum
P	Phosphates
Pb	Lead
Pt	Platinum
Q	Quartz Crystal
S	Sulfur
Sb	Antimony
Sn	Tin
U	Uranium
V	Vanadium
W	Tungsten
Zn	Zinc

⚡ Water Power

▨ Major Industrial Areas

DOMINANT LAND USE

- Wheat, Livestock
- Wheat, Corn, Livestock
- Cereals, Livestock
- Diversified Tropical Crops (chiefly plantation agriculture)
- Truck Farming, Horticulture, Special Crops
- Upland Cultivated Areas
- Intensive Livestock Ranching
- Upland Livestock Grazing, Limited Agriculture
- Extensive Livestock Ranching
- Forests
- Nonagricultural Land

...pa (riv.) .... F 8
...agellan (str.) .... E 14
...aipo (mt.) .... O 10
...avarino (isl.) .... G 14
"Higgins (lake) .... F 13
...jos del Salado (mt.) .... G 9
...enas (gulf) .... E 13
...aitao (pen.) .... E 13
...erra del Fuego (isl.) .... G 14

COLOMBIA
CITIES and TOWNS
...rauca 7,613 .... F 2
...arrancabermeja 87,191 .... F 2
...arranquilla 661,009 .... F 1
...ogotá (cap.) 2,696,270 .... E 3
...olívar .... E 3
...ucaramanga 291,661 .... F 2
...uenaventura 115,770 .... E 3
...uga 71,016 .... E 3
...artagena 292,512 .... E 1
...niquinirá 21,727 .... F 1
...agué 42,546 .... F 1
El Banco 20,756 .... F 2
...acativá 27,892 .... F 3
...orencia 31,817 .... E 3
...agué 176,223 .... E 3
...iales 30,871 .... E 3
...agangué 34,396 .... E 2
...anizales 199,904 .... E 2
...edellín 1,070,924 .... E 2
...itú 1,637 .... F 3
...ocoa 6,221 .... E 3
...ontería 89,583 .... E 2
...eiva 105,476 .... E 3
...amco 38,742 .... F 2
...njá 51,620 .... F 2
...llavicencio 82,869 .... E 2
...arumal 21,333 .... E 2

OTHER FEATURES
...to Ritacuva (mt.) .... F 2
...paporis (riv.) .... F 3
...rauca (riv.) .... G 2
...aquetá (riv.) .... F 4
...asanare (riv.) .... F 2
...auca (riv.) .... E 2
...entral, Cordillera (mts.) .... E 2
...uainía (riv.) .... G 3
...aviare (riv.) .... F 3
...ila (riv.) .... E 3
...rida (riv.) .... G 3
...agdalena (riv.) .... F 2
...rinoco (riv.) .... G 2
...utumayo (riv.) .... E 3
...ima (mt.) .... E 3
...aupés (riv.) .... F 3
...chada (riv.) .... F 3

ECUADOR
CITIES and TOWNS
...mbato 77,955 .... E 4
...abahoyo 28,914 .... D 7
...aquerizo Moreno 1,311 .... D 7
...uenca 104,470 .... E 4
...smeraldas 60,364 .... D 3
...uayaquil 823,219 .... D 4
...arra 41,335 .... E 3
...bijapa 19,996 .... E 4
...atacunga 21,921 .... E 4
...oja 47,697 .... E 4
...acas 1,934 .... E 4
...achala 69,170 .... D 4
...anta 64,519 .... D 4
...asaje 20,790 .... E 4
...ortoviejo 59,550 .... D 7
...uerto Villamil .... E 4
...uito (cap.) 599,828 .... E 4
...obamba 58,087 .... E 4
...anta Elena 7,687 .... D 4
...anta Rosa 19,696 .... E 4
...na .... E 4
...cán 24,398 .... E 3

OTHER FEATURES
...himborazo (mt.) .... E 4
...otopaxi (mt.) .... E 4
...uayaquil (gulf) .... D 4
...orona (riv.) .... E 4
...apo (riv.) .... E 4
...ccidental, Cordillera (mts.) .... E 4
...astaza (riv.) .... E 4
...eal, Cordillera (mts.) .... E 4
...antiago (riv.) .... E 4

FALKLAND ISLANDS
CITIES and TOWNS
...anley (cap.) .... J 14

OTHER FEATURES
East Falkland (isl.) .... J 14
Falkland (sound) .... H 14
West Falkland (isl.) .... H 14

FRENCH GUIANA
CITIES and TOWNS
Cayenne (cap.) 37,097 .... K 2
Guisanbourg .... K 3
Iracoubo 483 .... K 2
Mana 623 .... K 2
Saint-Georges 921 .... K 3
St-Laurent du Maroni 5,042 .... K 2

OTHER FEATURES
Devils (isl.) .... K 2
Maroni (riv.) .... K 2
Oyapock (riv.) .... K 3

GUYANA
CITIES and TOWNS
Corriverton ●10,502 .... J 2
Georgetown (cap.) 63,184 .... J 2
Morawhanna ●292 .... J 2
New Amsterdam 17,782 .... J 2

OTHER FEATURES
Courantyne (riv.) .... J 3
Cuyuni (riv.) .... H 2
Essequibo (riv.) .... J 3
Kaieteur (falls) .... J 3
Mazaruni (riv.) .... H 2
Roraima (mt.) .... H 2
Rupununi (riv.) .... J 3

PARAGUAY
CITIES and TOWNS
Asunción (cap.) 387,676 .... J 9
Concepción 19,392 .... J 8
Encarnación 23,343 .... J 8
Fuerte Olimpo 3,063 .... H 8
Mariscal Estigarribia 3,150 .... H 8
Puerto Casado 4,078 .... J 8
Puerto Guaraní 302 .... J 8
Puerto Sastre 160 .... J 8
Villarrica 17,687 .... J 8

OTHER FEATURES
Gran Chaco (reg.) .... H 8
Itaipú (res.) .... K 8
Paraguay (riv.) .... J 8
Paraná (riv.) .... K 9
Pilcomayo (riv.) .... H 8

PERU
CITIES and TOWNS
Arequipa 447,431 .... F 7
Ayacucho 68,535 .... F 6
Cajamarca 60,280 .... E 5
Callao 441,374 .... E 6
Cañete 15,277 .... E 6
Catacaos 30,927 .... D 5
Cerro de Pasco 71,558 .... E 6
Chiclayo 280,244 .... E 5
Chimbote 216,406 .... E 5
Chincha Alta 37,475 .... E 6
Coracora 4,598 .... F 7
Cusco 181,604 .... F 6
Huacho 43,402 .... E 6
Huancavelica 20,889 .... E 6
Huancayo 165,132 .... F 6

Huánuco 52,628 .... E 6
Huaráz 45,116 .... E 5
Ica 111,087 .... E 6
Ilo 31,549 .... F 7
Iquitos 173,629 .... F 4
Jauja 14,630 .... E 6
Juliaca 77,976 .... F 6
La Oroya 33,305 .... E 6
Lima (cap.) 375,957 .... E 6
Machupicchu 544 .... F 6
Matarani .... F 7
Mollendo 21,206 .... F 7
Moquegua 21,488 .... F 7
Nazca 22,756 .... F 6
Pacasmayo 17,588 .... D 5
Paita 18,749 .... D 5
Pisco 53,414 .... E 6
Piura 186,354 .... D 5
Pucallpa 91,953 .... E 5
Puerto Maldonado 12,609 .... G 6
Puno 66,477 .... F 7
Sullana 80,947 .... D 4
Supe 10,061 .... E 6
Tacna 92,862 .... F 7
Talara 55,122 .... D 4
Tarma 34,369 .... E 6
Trujillo 354,557 .... E 5
Tumbes 48,187 .... D 4

OTHER FEATURES
Aguja (pt.) .... D 5
Altiplano (plat.) .... F 6
Apurímac (riv.) .... F 6
Central, Cordillera (mts.) .... E 5
Huascarán (mt.) .... E 5
Madre de Dios (riv.) .... G 6
Marañón (riv.) .... E 4
Misti, El (mt.) .... F 7
Montaña, La (reg.) .... F 5
Napo (riv.) .... F 4

Occidental, Cordillera (mts.) .. F 6
Oriental, Cordillera (mts.) ..... E 5
Paracas (pen.) .... E 6
Putumayo (riv.) .... F 4
Real, Cordillera (mts.) .... F 6
Sechura (bay) .... D 5
Titicaca (lake) .... F 7
Ucayali (riv.) .... E 5
Urubamba (riv.) .... F 6
Vilcanota (mt.) .... F 6

SURINAME
CITIES and TOWNS
Albina 1,000 .... K 3
Groningen 600 .... J 2
Moengo 2,100 .... K 3
Nieuw-Nickerie 7,400 .... J 2
Paramaribo (cap.) ●67,905 .... K 2
Totness 1,300 .... J 2

OTHER FEATURES
Coeroeni (riv.) .... J 3
Tapanahoni (riv.) .... J 3

URUGUAY
CITIES and TOWNS
Artigas 29,256 .... J 10
Canelones 15,938 .... J 10
Colonia 16,895 .... J 10
Durazno 25,811 .... J 10
Florida 25,030 .... J 10
Fray Bentos 19,569 .... J 10
Maldonado 22,159 .... K 11
Melo 38,260 .... K 10
Mercedes 34,667 .... J 10
Minas 35,433 .... K 10

Montevideo (cap.) 1,173,254 . J 11
Paysandú 62,412 .... J 10
Rivera 49,013 .... J 10
Rocha 21,612 .... K 10
Salto 72,948 .... J 10
Tacuarembó 34,152 .... J 10
Treinta y Tres 25,757 .... K 10
Trinidad 17,598 .... J 10

OTHER FEATURES
Mirim (lag.) .... K 10
Negro (riv.) .... J 10
Plata, Río de la (est.) .... J 11
Uruguay (riv.) .... J 9

VENEZUELA
CITIES and TOWNS
Barcelona 78,201 .... H 2
Barinas 56,329 .... G 2
Barquisimeto 330,815 .... F 2
Bruzual 941 .... G 2
Calabozo 37,282 .... G 2
Caracas (cap.) 1,035,499 ..... G 1
Carora 36,115 .... F 1
Carúpano 50,935 .... H 1
Ciudad Bolívar 103,728 ..... H 2
Ciudad Piar 3,965 .... H 2
Coro 68,701 .... G 1
Cumaná 119,751 .... H 1
El Tigre 49,801 .... H 2
El Tocuyo 19,351 .... G 2
Guanare 34,148 .... G 2
La Guaira 20,344 .... G 1
Los Teques 63,170 .... G 1
Maracaibo 651,574 .... F 1
Maracay 255,134 .... G 1
Maturín 98,188 .... H 2

Mérida 74,214 .... F 2
Puerto Ayacucho 10,417 ..... G 2
Puerto Cabello 72,103 .... G 1
Puerto La Cruz 63,276 .... H 1
San Carlos 21,029 .... G 2
San Cristóbal 151,717 ..... F 2
San Felipe 43,801 .... G 1
San Fernando 38,960 .... G 2
Trujillo 25,921 .... F 2
Tucacas 4,780 .... G 1
Tucupita 21,417 .... H 2
Valencia 367,171 .... G 2
Valera 76,740 .... F 2
Valle de la Pascua 36,809 .. G 2
Villa de Cura 27,832 .... G 2

OTHER FEATURES
Angel (fall) .... H 2
Arauca (riv.) .... G 2
Apure (riv.) .... F 2
Bolívar (riv.) .... F 2
Caroní (riv.) .... H 3
Casiquiare, Brazo (riv.) ..... G 3
Maracaibo (lake) .... F 2
Margarita (isl.) .... H 1
Mérida (mts.) .... F 2
Orinoco (riv.) .... G 2
Paraguana (pen.) .... F 1
Paria (gulf) .... H 1
Serpents Mouth (str.) .... H 2
Tortuga, La (isl.) .... G 1
Venezuela (gulf) .... F 1

*City and suburb.
†Population of metropolitan area.
△Population of commune.
●Population of district, sub-district or division.

South America
Southern Part
LAMBERT AZIMUTHAL EQUAL-AREA PROJECTION

SCALE OF MILES
0 100 200 300 400 500

SCALE OF KILOMETERS

Capitals of Countries .... ☆
Other Capitals .... △
International Boundaries ....
Other Boundaries ....

© Copyright HAMMOND INCORPORATED, Maplewood, N.J.

ATLANTIC OCEAN
PACIFIC OCEAN
DRAKE PASSAGE
Tropic of Capricorn

North America

LAMBERT AZIMUTHAL EQUAL-AREA PROJECTION

MILES
0 100 200 400 600 800

KILOMETERS
0 100 200 400 600 800

Capitals of Countries .... ●
Other Capitals .... ⊛
International Boundaries .... ——
Other Boundaries........................... ——

® Copyright HAMMOND INCORPORATED, Maplewood, N.J.

Population Distribution

AREA 9,363,000 sq. mi.
(24,250,170 sq. km.)
POPULATION 370,000,000
LARGEST CITY New York
HIGHEST POINT Mt. McKinley 20,320 ft.
(6,194 m.)
LOWEST POINT Death Valley -282 ft.
(-86 m.)

Vegetation

DENSITY PER

SQ. KILOMETER	SQ. MILE
Over 100	Over 260
50-100	130-260
10-50	25-130
1-10	3-25
Under 1	Under 3

● Cities with over 2,000,000 inhabitants (including suburbs)

○ Cities with over 1,000,000 inhabitants (including suburbs)

MID-LATITUDE FOREST

Coniferous Forest

Broadleaf Forest

Mixed Coniferous and Broadleaf Forest

Woodland and Shrub (Mediterranean)

MID-LATITUDE GRASSLAND

Short Grass (Steppe)

Tall Grass (Prairie)

TROPICAL FOREST

Tropical Rainforest

Light Tropical Forest

TROPICAL GRASSLAND

Wooded Savanna

DESERT AND DESERT SHRUB

TUNDRA AND ALPINE

PERMANENT ICE

Acapulco de Juárez, Mex. H8
Alaska (pen.), Alaska C4
Albany (cap.), N.Y. L5
Albuquerque, N. Mex. H6
Amarillo, Texas H6
Anchorage, Alaska D3
Antigua (isl.) M8
Arctic (ocean) B2
Arkansas (riv.), U.S. J6
Athabasca (lake), Can. H4
Atlanta (cap.), Ga. K6
Augusta (cap.), Maine M5
Austin (cap.), Texas J6
Baffin (isl.), N.W.T. L2
Bahamas L7
Baltimore, Md. L6
Barbados N8
Barrow (pt.), Alaska C2
Beaufort (sea) D2
Belize K8
Belmopan (cap.), Belize K8
Bering (str.) B3
Bermuda (isls.) M6
Birmingham, Ala. K6
Bismarck (cap.), N. Dak. H5
Boise (cap.), Idaho G5
Boston (cap.), Mass. L5
Buffalo, N.Y. L5
Calgary (cap.), Alta. G4
California (gulf), Mex. G7
Canada G4
Canaveral (cape), Fla. L7
Caribbean (sea) K8
Carson City (cap.), Nev. G6
Cascade (range), U.S. F5
Charleston, S.C. L6
Charleston (cap.), W. Va. K6
Charlotte, N.C. K6
Charlottetown (cap.), P.E.I. M5
Chattanooga, Tenn. K6
Cheyenne (cap.), Wyo. H5
Chicago, Ill. K5
Chihuahua, Mex. H7
Cincinnati, Ohio K6
Ciudad Juárez, Mex. H6
Cleveland, Ohio K5
Clipperton (isl.) G9
Coast (ranges), U.S. F5
Cocos (isl.), C. Rica K9
Cod (cape), Mass. M5

Colorado (riv.), U.S. G6
Columbia (cap.), S.C. K6
Columbia (riv.), U.S. F5
Columbus (cap.), Ohio K6
Concord (cap.), N.H. L5
Costa Rica K8
Cuba L7
Dallas, Texas J6
Denver (cap.), Colo. H6
Des Moines (cap.), Iowa J5
Detroit, Mich. K5
Dominica M8
Dominican Republic L8
Dover (cap.), Del. L6
Duluth, Minn. J5
Edmonton, Alta. G4
Ellesmere (isl.), N.W.T. K1
El Paso, Texas H6
El Salvador J8
Erie (lake) K5
Fairbanks, Alaska D3
Farewell (cape), Greenl. P4
Florida (strs.) K7
Fort Worth, Texas J6
Frankfort (cap.), Ky. K6
Fraser (riv.), Br. Col. F4
Fredericton, N. Br. M5
Fresno, Calif. G6
Godthåb (Nuuk) (cap.), Greenl. N3
Grand Bahama (isl.), Bahamas L7
Grand Rapids, Mich. K5
Great Bear (lake), N.W.T. F3
Great Falls, Mont. G5
Great Salt (lake), Utah G6
Great Slave (lake), N.W.T. H3
Greenland P2
Greenland (sea) T2
Grenada M8
Guadalajara, Mex. H7
Guadeloupe (isl.) M8
Guantánamo, Cuba L7
Guatemala J8
Guatemala (cap.), Guat. J8
Haiti L8
Halifax (cap.), N.S. M5
Hamilton, Ont. L5
Harrisburg (cap.), Pa. L5
Hartford (cap.), Conn. L5
Hatteras (cape), N.C. L6

Havana (cap.), Cuba K7
Helena (cap.), Mont. G5
Hispaniola (isl.) L7
Honduras K8
Houston, Texas J7
Hudson (bay), Can. K3
Huron (lake) K5
Indianapolis (cap.), Ind. K5
Inuvik, N.W.T. E3
Jackson (cap.), Miss. K6
Jacksonville, Fla. K6
Jamaica L8
James (bay), Can. K4
Jefferson City (cap.), Mo. J6
Juan de Fuca (str.) F5
Julianehåb (Qaqortoq), Greenl. P3
Kansas City, Mo. J6
Ketchikan, Alaska E4
Key West, Fla. K7
Kingston (cap.), Jamaica L8
Knoxville, Tenn. K6
Kodiak (isl.), Alaska C4
Labrador (reg.), Newf. M4
Lansing (cap.), Mich. K5
Lesser Antilles (isls.) M8
Lincoln (cap.), Nebr. J5
Little Rock (cap.), Ark. J6
London, Ont. K5
Los Angeles, Calif. G6
Louisville, Ky. K6
Lower California (pen.), Mex. G7
Mackenzie (riv.), N.W.T. F3
Macon, Ga. K6
Madison (cap.), Wis. J5
Managua (cap.), Nic. K8
Manitoba (lake), Man. H4
Martinique (isl.) M8
Mazatlán, Mex. H7
McKinley (mt.), Alaska C3
Mead (lake), U.S. G6
Medicine Hat, Alta. H4
Memphis, Tenn. K6
Mendocino (cape), Calif. F5
Mérida, Mex. J7
Mexico H7
Mexico (gulf) K7
Mexico City (cap.), Mex. J7
Miami, Fla. K7

Michigan (lake), U.S. K5
Milwaukee, Wis. K5
Minneapolis, Wis. J5
Mississippi (riv.), U.S. J5
Missouri (riv.) J5
Mobile, Ala. K6
Monterrey, Mex. J7
Montgomery (cap.), Ala. K6
Montpelier (cap.), Vt. L5
Montréal, Que. L5
Moose Jaw, Sask. H4
Nares (str.) L2
Nashville (cap.), Tenn. K6
Nassau (cap.), Bahamas L7
Nelson (riv.), Man. J4
Netherlands Antilles M8
Newfoundland (isl.), Can. M4
New Orleans, La. K7
New York, N.Y. L5
Nicaragua K8
Nome, Alaska B3
Norfolk, Va. L6
North Bay, Ont. L5
North Saskatchewan (riv.), Can. G4
Nuuk (cap.), Greenl. N3
Oakland, Calif. F6
Oaxaca, Mex. J8
Ohio (riv.), U.S. K6
Oklahoma City (cap.), Okla. J6
Olympia (cap.), Wash. F5
Omaha, Nebr. J5
Ontario (lake) L5
Ottawa (cap.), Can. L5
Panama K9
Panama (canal), Pan. L9
Panamá (cap.), Pan. L9
Parry (chan.), N.W.T. G2

Peace (riv.), Can. G4
Pensacola, Fla. K6
Philadelphia, Pa. L6
Phoenix (cap.), Ariz. G6
Pierre (cap.), S. Dak. J5
Pittsburgh, Pa. K5
Port-au-Prince (cap.), Haiti L8
Portland, Maine M5
Portland, Oreg. F5
Providence (cap.), R.I. L5
Prudhoe (bay), Alaska D2
Puebla, Mex. J8
Puerto Rico M8
Qaanaaq, Greenl. M2
Quebec (cap.), Que. L5
Queen Charlotte (isls.), Br. Col. E4
Queen Elizabeth (isls.), N.W.T. G2
Raleigh (cap.), N.C. L6
Red (riv.) J5
Red (riv.), U.S. J6
Regina (cap.), Sask. H4
Reno, Nev. G6
Richmond (cap.), Va. L6
Rio Grande (riv.) H7
Rochester, N.Y. L5
Rocky (mts.) F4
Sable (cape), N.S. M5
Sacramento (cap.), Calif. F6
Saint Augustine, Fla. K7
Saint John (riv.), N. Br. M5
St. John's (cap.), Newf. N5
Saint Kitts and Nevis M8
Saint Lawrence (gulf) M5
Saint Lawrence (riv.) L5

Saint Louis, Mo. K6
Saint Lucia M8
Saint Paul (cap.), Minn. J5
Saint Pierre and Miquelon (isls.) N5
Saint Vincent and The Grenadines M8
Salem (cap.), Oreg. F5
Salt Lake City (cap.), Utah G6
Saltillo, Mex. H7
San Antonio, Texas J7
San Diego, Calif. G6
San Francisco, Calif. F6
San José (cap.), C. Rica K9
San Juan (cap.), P. Rico M8
San Salvador (cap.), El Salv. J8
Santa Fe (cap.), N. Mex. H6
Santiago de Cuba, Cuba L8
Santo Domingo (cap.), Dom. Rep. L8
Saskatoon, Sask. H4
Sault Ste. Marie, Ont. K5
Savannah, Ga. K6
Seattle, Wash. F5
Shreveport, La. J6
Sierra Madre Occidental (mts.), Mex. H7
Sierra Nevada (range), Calif. F6
Sioux City, Iowa J5
Sioux Falls, S. Dak. J5
Snake (riv.), U.S. G5
South Saskatchewan (riv.), Can. G4
Springfield (cap.), Ill. J6

Sudbury, Ont. K5
Superior (lake) K5
Sverdrup (isls.), N.W.T. J2
Tacoma, Wash. F5
Tallahassee (cap.), Fla. K6
Tampa, Fla. K7
Tampico, Mex. J7
Tegucigalpa (cap.), Hond. K8
Thule (Qaanaaq), Greenl. M2
Thunder Bay, Ont. K5
Toledo, Ohio K5
Topeka (cap.), Kansas J6
Toronto (cap.), Ont. K5
Trenton (cap.), N.J. L5
Trinidad and Tobago N8
Tucson, Ariz. G6
Tulsa, Okla. J6
United States H5
Vancouver, Br. Col. F4
Vancouver (isl.), Br. Col. F5
Veracruz, Mex. J8
Victoria (cap.), Br. Col. F5
Victoria (isl.), N.W.T. G2
Virgin Islands (isls.) M8
Washington, D.C. (cap.), U.S. L6
West Indies (isls.) M7
Whitehorse (cap.), Yukon E3
Wichita, Kansas J6
Windward (passg.) L8
Winnipeg (cap.), Man. J5
Woods (lake) J5
Yellowknife, N.W.T. G3
Yucatán (pen.), Mex. K7
Yukon (riv.) C3

Abitibi (lake), Ont. .... H 6
Aklavik, N.W.T. 721 .... C 2
Albany (riv.), Ont. .... H 5
Alberta (prov.) 2,237,724 ..... E 5
Amherst, N.S. 9,684 .... K 6
Amos, Que. 9,421 .... J 6
Anticosti (isl.), Que. .... K 6
Athabasca (lake) .... F 4
Athabasca (riv.), Alta. .... E 4
Axel Heiburg (isl.), N.W.T. .... N 3
Baffin (reg.), N.W.T. 8,300 .... C 1
Baffin (bay), N.W.T. .... J 1
Baffin (isl.), N.W.T. .... J 1
Baker Lake, N.W.T. 954 .... G 3
Banff Nat'l Park, Alta. .... E 5
Banks (isl.), N.W.T. .... D 1
Bathurst, N. Br. 15,705 .... K 6
Belle Isle (str.), Newf. .... L 5
Bonavista, Newf. 4,460 .... L 6
Boothia (pen.), N.W.T. .... G 1
Brandon, Man. 36,242 .... F 6
British Columbia (prov.)
      2,744,467 .... D 4
Cabot (str.) .... K 6
Calgary, Alta. 592,743 .... E 5
Cambridge Bay, N.W.T. 815 ..... F 2
Campbellton, N. Br. 9,818 ..... K 6
Camrose, Alta. 12,570 .... E 5
Cape Breton (isl.), N.S. ...... K 6
Cartwright, Newf. 658 .... L 5
Channel-Port aux Basques,
      Newf. 5,988 .... L 6
Charlottetown (cap.), P.E.I.
      15,282 .... K 6
Chatham, N. Br. 6,779 .... K 6

Chesterfield Inlet, N.W.T. 249 . G 3
Chibougamau, Que. 10,732 ...... J 6
Chicoutimi, Que. 60,064 .... J 6
Chidley (cape), Newf. .... K 3
Chilliwack, Br. Col. 40,642 ... D 6
Churchill, Man. 1,186 .... G 4
Coast (mts.) .... C 4
Coppermine, N.W.T. 809 .... E 2
Corner Brook, Newf. 24,339 .... K 6
Cornwall, Ont. 46,144 .... J 7
Cranbrook, Br. Col. 15,915 .... E 6
Cree (lake), Sask. .... F 4
Dartmouth, N.S. 62,277 .... K 7
Dauphin, Man. 8,971 .... F 5
Davis (str.), N.W.T. .... K 2
Dawson, Yukon 697 .... C 3
Devon (isl.), N.W.T. .... M 3
Drumheller, Alta. 6,508 .... E 5
Edmonton (cap.), Alta.
      532,246 .... E 5
Edmundston, N. Br. 12,044 ..... K 6
Ellesmere (isl.), N.W.T. ...... N 3
Eskimo Point, N.W.T. 1,022 .... G 3
Estevan, Sask. 9,174 .... F 6
Finlay (riv.), Br. Col. .... D 4
Flin Flon, Man.-Sask. 8,261 ... F 4
Fogo (isl.), Newf. .... L 6
Fort-Chimo, Que. .... K 4
Fort Frances, Ont. 8,906 ...... G 6
Fort Franklin, N.W.T. 521 ..... D 2
Fort-George, Que. 2,222 .... J 5
Fort McMurray, Alta. 31,000 ... E 4
Fort McPherson, N.W.T. 632 .... C 2
Fort Nelson, Br. Col. 3,724 ... D 4
Fort Providence, N.W.T. 605 ... E 3

Fort Saskatchewan, Alta.
      12,169 .... E 5
Fort Simpson, N.W.T. 980 ...... D 3
Fort Smith (reg.) N.W.T.
Fort Smith, N.W.T. 2,298 ...... E 3
Foxe (basin), N.W.T. .... J 2
Franklin (dist.), N.W.T. ...... J 1
Fraser (riv.), Br. Col. .... D 5
Fredericton, N. Br. 43,723 .... K 6
Frobisher Bay, N.W.T. 2,333 ... K 3
Fundy (bay) .... K 7
Gander, Newf. 10,404 .... L 6
Gaspé, Que. 17,261 .... K 6
Georgian (bay), Ont. .... H 6
Geraldton, Ont. 2,956 .... H 6
Glace Bay, N.S. 21,466 .... L 6
Goose Bay, Newf. 7,103 .... K 5
Gouin (res.), Que. .... J 6
Grand Falls, Newf. 8,765 ...... L 6
Grande Prairie, Alta. 24,263 .. E 4
Great Bear (lake), N.W.T. ..... D 2
Great Slave (lake), N.W.T. .... E 3
Guelph, Ont. 71,207 .... H 7
Halifax (cap.), N.S. 114,594 .. K 7
Hamilton, Ont. 306,434 .... H 7
Harbour Grace, Newf. 2,988 .... L 6
Havre-St-Pierre, Que. 3,200 ... K 5
Hay River, N.W.T. 2,863 .... E 3
Hearst, Ont. 5,533 .... H 6
Hecate (str.), Br. Col. .... C 5
Hull, Que. 56,225 .... J 6
Inuvik (reg.), N.W.T. 7,485 ... D 2
Inuvik, N.W.T. 3,147 .... C 2
Iroquois Falls, Ont. 6,339 .... H 6

Jasper Nat'l Park, Alta. ...... E 5
Jonquière, Que. 60,354 .... J 6
Juan de Fuca (str.), Br. Col. . D 6
Kamloops, Br. Col. 64,048 ..... D 5
Kane (basin), N.W.T. .... N 3
Kapuskasing, Ont. 12,014 ...... H 6
Keewatin (reg.), N.W.T. 4,327 . G 2
Kelowna, Br. Col. 59,196 ...... E 6
Kenora, Ont. 9,817 .... G 6
Kingston, Ont. 52,616 .... J 7
Kirkland Lake, Ont. 12,219 .... H 6
Kitikmeot (reg.), N.W.T. 3,245 . F 1
Kitimat, Br. Col. 12,462 ...... D 5
Kluane (lake), Yukon .... C 3
Kootenay (lake), Br. Col. ..... E 6
Labrador (reg.), Newf. .... K 4
Lacombe, Alta. 5,591 .... E 5
Lake Harbour, N.W.T. 252 ...... J 3
Lake Louise, Alta. 355 .... E 5
Lancaster (sound), N.W.T. ..... H 1
Leduc, Alta. 12,471 .... E 5
Lesser Slave (lake), Alta. .... E 4
Lethbridge, Alta. 54,072 ...... E 6
Liard (riv.) .... D 3
Lloydminster, Alta.-Sask.
      15,031 .... E 5
Logan (mt.), Yukon .... B 3
London, Ont. 254,280 .... H 7
Lunenburg, N.S. 3,014 .... K 7
Mackenzie (dist.), N.W.T. ..... E 2
Mackenzie (riv.), N.W.T. ...... C 2
Magdalen (isls.), Que. .... K 6
Manicouagan (riv.), Que. ...... K 5
Manitoba (lake), Man. .... G 5
Manitoba (prov.) 1,026,241 .... G 5

Manitoulin (isl.), Ont. .... H 6
Maple Creek, Sask. 2,470 ...... F 6
Marathon, Ont. 2,271 .... H 6
Mayo, Yukon 398 .... C 3
M'Clintock (chan.), N.W.T. .... F 1
Medicine Hat, Alta. 40,380 .... E 5
Melville, Sask. 5,092 .... F 5
Melville (isl.), N.W.T. .... E 1
Merritt, Br. Col. 6,110 .... D 5
Minto (lake), Que. .... J 5
Mistassibi (riv.), Que. .... J 5
Mistassini (lake), Que. .... J 5
Moncton, N. Br. 54,743 .... K 6
Mont-Joli, Que. 6,359 .... K 6
Mont-Laurier, Que. 8,405 ...... J 6
Montréal, Que. 980,354 .... J 7
Moose Jaw, Sask. 33,941 .... F 6
Moosonee, Sask. 2,579 .... F 5
Moosonee, Ont. 1,433 .... H 5
Morden, Man. 4,579 .... G 6
Nain, Newf. 938 .... K 4
Nanaimo, Br. Col. 47,069 ...... D 6
Nares (str.), N.W.T. .... N 3
Nelson, Br. Col. 9,143 .... E 6
Nelson (riv.), Man. .... G 4
New Brunswick (prov.)
      696,423 .... K 6
Newfoundland (isl.) .... L 6
Newfoundland (prov.) 567,681 .. L 5
New Westminster, Br. Col.
      38,550 .... D 6
Niagara Falls, Ont. 70,960 .... J 7
Norman Wells, N.W.T. 420 ...... D 2
North Battleford, Sask.
      14,030 .... F 5

North Bay, Ont. 51,268 .... J 6
North Magnetic Pole .... F 1
North Saskatchewan (riv.) ..... E 5
N. Vancouver, Br. Col. 33,952 . D 6
Northwest Territories 45,741 .. E 2
Nova Scotia (prov.) 847,422 ... K 7
Okanagan (lake), Br. Col. ..... D 6
Ontario (prov.) 8,625,107 ..... H 6
Ottawa (cap.), Canada
      295,163 .... J 6
Ottawa (riv.) .... J 6
Owen Sound, Ont. 19,883 .... H 7
Pangnirtung, N.W.T. 839 .... K 2
Parry (chan.), N.W.T. .... E-H 1
Parry Sound, Ont. 6,124 .... J 6
Peace (riv.), Alta. .... E 4
Peace River, Alta. 5,907 ...... E 4
Peel (riv.) .... C 2
Pelly (riv.), Yukon .... C 3
Pembroke, Ont. 14,026 .... J 6
Péribonca (riv.), Que. .... J 5
Peterborough, Ont. 60,620 ..... J 7
Pond Inlet, N.W.T. 705 .... J 1
Portage la Prairie, Man.
      13,086 .... G 5
Port Radium, N.W.T. 56 .... E 2
Poste-de-la-Baleine, Que.
      435 .... J 4
Povungnituk, Que. .... J 4
Prince Albert, Sask. 31,380 ... F 5
Prince Albert Nat'l Park, Sask. F 5
Prince Edward Island (prov.)
      122,506 .... K 6
Prince George, Br. Col.
      67,559 .... D 5

Prince Patrick (isl.), N.W.T. . M 3
Prince Rupert, Br. Col. 16,197 . C 5
Québec (prov.) 6,438,403 ...... J 5
Québec (cap.), Que. 166,474 ... J 6
Queen Charlotte (isls.), Br.
      Col. .... C 5
Queen Elizabeth (isls.),
      N.W.T. .... M 3
Quesnel, Br. Col. 8,240 .... D 5
Race (cape), Newf. .... L 6
Rainy (lake), Ont. .... G 6
Rainy River, Ont. 1,061 .... G 6
Rankin Inlet, N.W.T. 1,109 .... G 3
Ray (cape), Newf. .... L 6
Red Deer, Alta. 46,393 .... E 5
Regina (cap.), Sask. 162,613 .. F 5
Reindeer (lake) .... F 4
Revelstoke, Br. Col. 5,544 .... E 5
Riding Mountain Nat'l Park,
      Man. .... F 5
Rimouski, Que. 29,120 .... K 6
Rivière-du-Loup, Que. 13,459 .. K 6
Roberval, Que. 11,429 .... J 6
Robson (mt.), Br. Col. .... D 5
Rocky (mts.) .... D 5
Rocky Mountain House, Alta.
      4,698 .... E 5
Rouyn, Que. 17,224 .... J 6
Sable (cape), N.S. .... K 7
Sable (isl.), N.S. .... L 7
Saint Elias (mt.), Yukon ...... B 3
Saint John, N. Br. 80,521 ..... K 6
St. John's (cap.), Newf.
      83,770 .... L 6
Saint Lawrence (riv.) .... K 6

AREA 3,851,787 sq. mi. (9,976,139 sq. km.)
POPULATION 24,343,181
CAPITAL Ottawa
LARGEST CITY Montréal
HIGHEST POINT Mt. Logan 19,524 ft. (5,951 m.)
MONETARY UNIT Canadian dollar
MAJOR LANGUAGES English, French
MAJOR RELIGIONS Protestantism, Roman Catholicism

Population Distribution

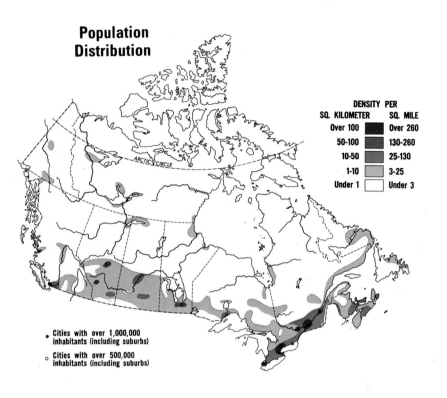

DENSITY PER	
SQ. KILOMETER	SQ. MILE
Over 100	Over 260
50-100	130-260
10-50	25-130
1-10	3-25
Under 1	Under 3

● Cities with over 1,000,000 inhabitants (including suburbs)

○ Cities with over 500,000 inhabitants (including suburbs)

Vegetation

MID-LATITUDE FOREST
Coniferous Forest
Broadleaf Forest
Mixed Coniferous and Broadleaf Forest

MID-LATITUDE GRASSLAND
Short Grass (Steppe)
Tall Grass (Prairie)

DESERT AND DESERT SHRUB
TUNDRA AND ALPINE
PERMANENT ICE

Saint Pierre & Miquelon (isls.)
6,041 .... L 6
Sarnia, Ont. 50,892 .... H 7
Saskatchewan (prov.) 968,313 F 5
Saskatchewan (riv.)......... F 5
Saskatoon, Sask. 154,210 .. H 5
Sault Sainte Marie, Ont.
82,697 .... H 6
Schefferville, Que. 1,997.... K 5
Selkirk, Man. 10,037 .... G 5
Sept-Iles (Seven Is.), Que.
29,262 .... K 5
Shawinigan, Que. 23,011 .... J 6
Sherbrooke, Que. 74,075 .... J 7
Sioux Lookout, Ont. 3,074... G 5
Skeena (riv.), Br. Col....... D 5
Slave (riv.) .... E 3
Smallwood (res.), Newf. ... K 5
Southampton (isl.), N.W.T. .. H 2
Stettler, Alta. 5,136 .... E 5
Stewart (riv.), Yukon ...... C 3
Stikine (riv.), Br. Col....... C 4
Sudbury, Ont. 91,829 ...... H 6
Swift Current, Sask. 14,747 .. F 5
Sydney, N.S. 29,444....... K 6
Terrace, Br. Col. ○10,914.... D 5
The Pas, Man. 6,390 .... F 5
Thompson, Man. 14,288 .... G 4
Thunder Bay, Ont. 112,486... H 6
Timmins, Ont. 46,114....... H 6
Toronto (cap.), Ont. 599,217 . H 7
Trail, Br. Col. 9,599 .... E 6
Trois-Rivières, Que. 50,466... J 6
Truro, N.S. 12,552......... K 6
Tuktoyaktuk, N.W.T. 772..... C 2

Val-d'Or, Que. 21,371........ J 6
Vancouver, Br. Col. 414,281 . D 6
Vancouver (isl.), Br. Col...... D 6
Vanderhoof, Br. Col. 2,323.... D 5
Vegreville, Alta. 5,251 ...... E 5
Vernon, Br. Col. 19,987 ...... E 5
Victoria (cap.), Br. Col. 64,379 D 6
Victoria (isl.), N.W.T........ E 1
Wabush, Newf. 3,155........ K 5
Waterton-Glacier International
Peace Park, Alta. .... E 6
Wetaskiwin, Alta. 9,597 ...... E 5
Weyburn, Sask. 9,523 ...... F 6
Whitehorse (cap.), Yukon
14,814 .... C 3
Williams Lake, Br. Col. 8,362 . D 5
Williston (lake), Br. Col...... D 4
Windsor, N.S. 3,646 .... K 7
Windsor, Ont. 192,083...... H 7
Winnipeg (cap.), Man.
564,473 .... G 6
Winnipeg (lake), Man....... G 5
Winnipegosis (lake), Man.... F 5
Wood Buffalo Nat'l Park, Alta. E 4
Woods (lake) .... G 6
Wrigley, N.W.T. 137......... D 3
Yarmouth, N.S. 7,475....... K 7
Yellowknife (cap.), N.W.T.
9,483 .... E 3
Yoho Nat'l Park, Br. Col...... E 5
York Factory, Man. .... G 4
Yorkton, Sask. 15,339 ...... F 5
Yukon Territory 23,153....... C 3

○Population of municipality.

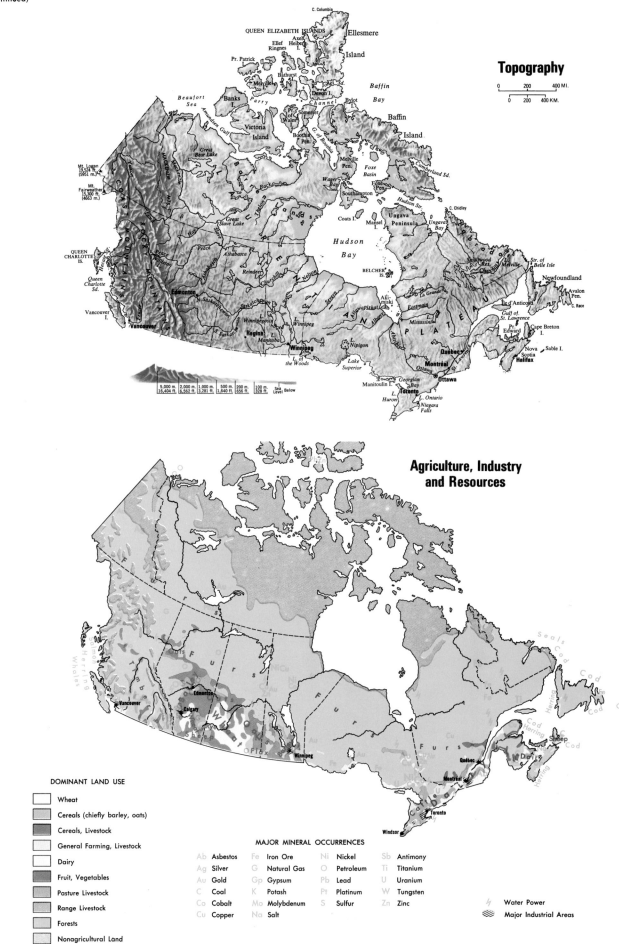

Topography

0   200   400 MI.

0   200   400 KM.

C. Columbia
QUEEN ELIZABETH ISLANDS — Ellesmere
Axel — Island
Ellef Heiberg
Ringnes
Pr. Patrick
Melville — Bathurst
Banks — Parry — Devon I. — Bylot — Baffin Bay
I. — Channel
Beaufort Sea — Pr. of Wales — Baffin
Amundsen Gulf — Prince of Somerset — Island
Victoria — Boothia
Island — Pen. — G. of Boothia
Melville Pen.
Mt. Logan — Great Bear Lake — Wager Bay — Foxe Basin
19,524 ft. — Foxe
(5951 m.) — Coats I. — Pen.
Mt. Fairweather — Great Slave Lake — Mansel — Ungava — C. Chidley
15,300 ft. — Peace — Athabasca — Peninsula — Ungava Bay
(4663 m.) — Reindeer L. — Hudson — Smallwood Res. — Melville — Str. of Belle Isle
QUEEN CHARLOTTE IS. — Peace — Churchill — Bay — Churchill — Newfoundland
Queen Charlotte Sd. — Nelson — Avalon Pen.
Edmonton — N. Saskatchewan — Severn — Grande — C. Race
Vancouver I. — Saskatchewan — Winnipegosis — Eastmain — Mistassini — Île d'Anticosti
Vancouver — Saskat. — L. — Attawapiskat — Gulf of St. Lawrence
Regina — L. Manitoba — L. Winnipeg — Albany — Pr. Edward — Cape Breton I.
Winnipeg — Nova Scotia — Sable I.
L. of the Woods — L. Nipigon — Québec — Halifax
Lake Superior — Montréal — Ottawa
Manitoulin I. — Georgian Bay — Ottawa
Toronto — L. Ontario
L. Huron — Niagara Falls

5,000 m. | 2,000 m. | 1,000 m. | 500 m. | 200 m. | 100 m. | Sea | Below
16,404 ft. | 6,562 ft. | 3,281 ft. | 1,640 ft. | 656 ft. | 328 ft. | Level

Agriculture, Industry and Resources

Edmonton
Vancouver — Calgary
Winnipeg — Québec
Montréal
Toronto
Windsor

DOMINANT LAND USE

- Wheat
- Cereals (chiefly barley, oats)
- Cereals, Livestock
- General Farming, Livestock
- Dairy
- Fruit, Vegetables
- Pasture Livestock
- Range Livestock
- Forests
- Nonagricultural Land

MAJOR MINERAL OCCURRENCES

Ab	Asbestos	Fe	Iron Ore	Ni	Nickel
Ag	Silver	G	Natural Gas	O	Petroleum
Au	Gold	Gp	Gypsum	Pb	Lead
C	Coal	K	Potash	Pt	Platinum
Co	Cobalt	Mo	Molybdenum	S	Sulfur
Cu	Copper	Na	Salt		

Sb	Antimony
Ti	Titanium
U	Uranium
W	Tungsten
Zn	Zinc

⚡ Water Power

▨ Major Industrial Areas

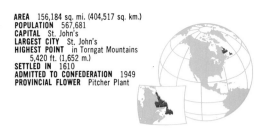

AREA 156,184 sq. mi. (404,517 sq. km.)
POPULATION 567,681
CAPITAL St. John's
LARGEST CITY St. John's
HIGHEST POINT in Torngat Mountains
 5,420 ft. (1,652 m.)
SETTLED IN 1610
ADMITTED TO CONFEDERATION 1949
PROVINCIAL FLOWER Pitcher Plant

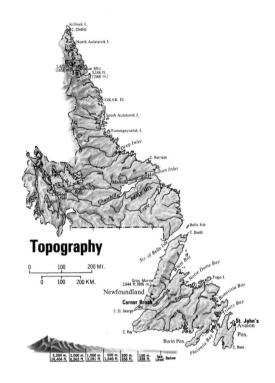

Topography

Newfoundland
Corner Brook

Agriculture, Industry and Resources

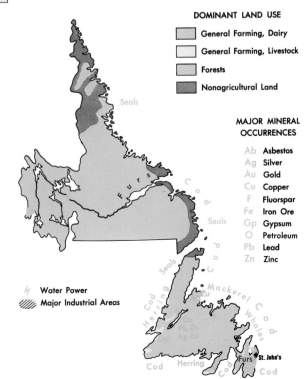

DOMINANT LAND USE

General Farming, Dairy
General Farming, Livestock
Forests
Nonagricultural Land

MAJOR MINERAL OCCURRENCES

Ab	Asbestos
Ag	Silver
Au	Gold
Cu	Copper
F	Fluorspar
Fe	Iron Ore
Gp	Gypsum
O	Petroleum
Pb	Lead
Zn	Zinc

Water Power
Major Industrial Areas

Newfoundland
SCALE
0 10 20 40 60 80 100 MI.
0 10 20 40 60 80 100 KM.
Provincial Capital..........⊛
Provincial Boundaries..........─ ─ ─

© Copyright by HAMMOND INCORPORATED, Maplewood, N.J.

CITIES and TOWNS

Arnold's Cove 1,124 .... C 4
Badger 1,090 .... B 3
Baie Verte 2,491 .... B 3
Battle Harbour .... C 1
Bay Bulls 1,081 .... D 4
Bay de Verde 786 .... D 3
Bay Roberts 4,512 .... D 4
Belleoram 565 .... C 4
Bishop's Falls 4,395 .... C 3
Bonavista 4,460 .... D 3
Botwood 4,074 .... C 3
Buchans 1,655 .... B 3
Burgeo 2,504 .... B 4
Burin 2,904 .... C 4
Carbonear 5,335 .... D 4
Carmanville 966 .... C 3
Cartwright 658 .... E 2
Catalina 1,162 .... D 3
Channel-Port aux Basques
 5,988 .... A 4
Clarenville 2,878 .... C 3
Corner Brook 24,339 .... A 3
Cow Head 695 .... A 3
Cox's Cove 980 .... B 3
Deer Lake 4,348 .... B 3
Dunville 1,817 .... D 4
Englee 998 .... C 2
Ferryland 795 .... D 4
Fleur de Lys 616 .... C 2
Fogo 1,105 .... C 3
Fortune 2,473 .... C 4
Gander 10,404 .... C 3
Garnish 761 .... C 4
Glovertown 2,165 .... C 3
Goose Bay-Happy Valley
 (Goose Airport) 7,103 .... D 2
Goulds 4,242 .... D 4
Grand Bank 3,901 .... B 4

Grand Falls 8,765 .... C 3
Hampden 838 .... B 3
Harbour Breton 2,461 .... B 4
Harbour Grace 2,988 .... D 4
Hare Bay 1,520 .... C 3
Holyrood 1,789 .... D 4
Joe Batt's Arm-Barr'd Islands
 1,155 .... D 3
King's Point 825 .... B 3
Labrador City 11,538 .... C 2
Lamaline 548 .... C 4
Lark Harbour 783 .... A 3
La Scie 1,422 .... C 3
Lawn 999 .... C 4
Lewisporte 3,963 .... C 3
Lourdes 932 .... A 3
Lumsden 645 .... D 3
Marystown 6,299 .... C 4
Milltown-Head of Bay d'Espoir
 1,376 .... C 4
Mount Pearl 11,543 .... D 4
Nain 938 .... D 1
Norris Arm 1,216 .... C 3
Norris Point 1,033 .... B 3
Pasadena 2,685 .... B 3
Placentia 2,204 .... D 4
Port au Choix 1,311 .... B 2
Port Blandford 702 .... C 3
Port Hope Simpson 581 .... E 2
Port Saunders 769 .... B 2
Pouch Cove 1,522 .... D 4
Ramea 1,386 .... B 4
Rigolet 271 .... D 2
Robert's Arm 1,005 .... C 3
Roddickton 1,142 .... B 2
Rose Blanche-Harbour le Cou
 975 .... A 4
Saint Alban's 1,968 .... B 4
Saint Anthony 3,017 .... C 2
Saint George's 1,756 .... A 3
St. John's (cap.) 83,770 .... D 4

St. John's *154,820 .... D 4
Saint Lawrence 2,012 .... C 4
Saint Lunaire-Griquet 1,010 .... C 2
Saint Vincent's-St. Stephens-
 Peter's River 796 .... D 4
Seal Cove 751 .... B 2
Shoal Cove 223 .... B 2
Springdale 3,501 .... B 3
Stephenville 8,876 .... A 3
Stephenville Crossing
 2,172 .... A 3
Summerford 1,198 .... C 3
Sunnyside 703 .... C 4
Terrenceville 796 .... C 4
Torbay 3,394 .... D 4
Trepassey 1,473 .... D 4
Trout River 759 .... A 3
Twillingate 1,506 .... C 3
Victoria 1,870 .... D 4
Wabana 4,254 .... D 4
Wesleyville 1,225 .... D 3
Windsor 5,747 .... C 3

OTHER FEATURES

Ashuanipi (lake) .... C 2
Atikonak (lake) .... C 2
Avalon (pen.) .... D 4
Bell (isl.) .... C 1
Belle (isl.) .... B 2
Belle Isle (str.) .... B 2
Bonavista (bay) .... D 3
Bonne (bay) .... A 3
Cabot (str.) .... A 4
Chidley (cape) .... D 1
Churchill (riv.) .... D 2
Conception (bay) .... D 4
Exploits (riv.) .... B 3
Fogo (isl.) .... C 3
Fortune (bay) .... C 4

Grand (lake) .... B 3
Grey (isls.) .... C 2
Gros Morne Nat'l Park .... B 3
Hamilton (inlet) .... E 2
Hamilton (sound) .... D 3
Hare (bay) .... C 2
Hermitage (bay) .... B 4
Humber (riv.) .... B 3
Ingornachoix (bay) .... A 2
Killinek (isl.) .... D 1
Labrador (reg.) .... D 1
Long Range (mts.) .... A 4
Mealy (mts.) .... A 1
Meelpaeg (lake) .... B 3
Melville (lake) .... E 2
Menihek (lakes) .... C 2
Newfoundland (isl.) .... B 2
New World (isl.) .... D 1
North Aulatsivik (isl.) .... D 1
Notre Dame (bay) .... C 3
Pistolet (bay) .... C 2
Placentia (bay) .... C 4
Ponds (isl.) .... D 1
Port au Port (pen.) .... A 3
Race (cape) .... D 4
Random (isl.) .... D 3
Ray (cape) .... A 4
Red Indian (lake) .... B 3
Saint George's (bay) .... A 3
Saint John (cape) .... C 2
Saint Lawrence (gulf) .... A 3
Saint Mary's (bay) .... D 4
Sandy (lake) .... B 3
Smallwood (res.) .... D 1
South Aulatsivik (isl.) .... D 1
Terra Nova Nat'l Park .... D 3
Torngat (mts.) .... D 1
Trinity (bay) .... D 3
White (bay) .... B 2

*Population of metropolitan area.

NOVA SCOTIA

COUNTIES

Annapolis 22,522	C 4
Antigonish 18,110	F 3
Cape Breton 127,035	H 3
Colchester 43,224	E 3
Cumberland 35,231	D 3
Digby 21,689	C 4
Guysborough 12,752	F 3
Halifax 288,126	E 4
Hants 33,121	D 4
Inverness 22,337	G 2
Kings 49,739	D 4
Lunenburg 45,746	D 4
Pictou 50,350	F 3
Queens 13,126	D 4
Richmond 12,284	H 3
Shelburne 17,328	C 5
Victoria 8,432	H 2
Yarmouth 26,290	C 5

CITIES and TOWNS

Alder Point 651	H 2
Aldershot	D 3
Amherst◎ 9,684	D 3
Annapolis Royal◎ 631	C 4
Antigonish◎ 5,205	F 3
Arichat 824	H 3
Aylesford 744	D 3
Baddeck◎ 972	H 2
Barrington Passage 722	C 5
Bear River-Sissiboo 854	C 4
Beaverbank 1,322	E 4
Berwick 1,699	D 4
Bridgetown 1,047	C 4
Bridgewater 6,669	D 4
Brookfield 619	E 3
Brooklyn 1,269	D 4
Cambridge Station 799	D 3
Canning 763	D 3
Canso 1,255	H 3
Centreville 765	C 4
Chéticamp 1,022	G 2

Chester 1,131	D 4
Chester Basin 639	D 4
Church Point 318	C 4
Clark's Harbour 1,059	C 5
Coldbrook Station 617	D 3
Cow Bay 670	E 4
Dartmouth 62,277	E 4
Debert 618	E 3
Digby◎ 2,558	C 4
Dominion 2,856	J 2
Donkin 873	J 2
Ellershouse-Hartville 662	D 4
Elmsdale 1,172	E 4
Enfield 1,510	E 4
Fall River 1,897	E 4
Falmouth 1,110	D 3
Glace Bay 21,466	J 2
Guysborough◎ 496	G 3
Halifax (cap.)◎ 114,594	E 4
Halifax ★277,727	E 4
Hantsport 1,395	D 3
Herring Cove 1,323	E 4
Hilden 1,262	E 3

Ingonish 471	H 2
Inverness 2,013	G 2
Judique 925	G 3
Kentville◎ 4,974	D 3
Kingston 1,612	C 4
Lakeside 936	E 4
Lantz 1,172	E 4
Liverpool◎ 3,304	C 5
Lockeport 929	C 5
Louisbourg 1,410	J 3
Louisdale 979	G 3
Lower West Pubnico 790	C 5
Lunenburg◎ 3,014	D 4
Mahone Bay 1,228	D 4
Meteghan 890	B 4
Middleton 1,834	C 4
Milford Station 748	E 3
Milton 1,678	D 4
Mount Uniacke 1,145	E 4
Mulgrave 1,099	G 3
Musquodoboit Harbour 936	E 4
New Glasgow 10,464	F 3
New Victoria 1,374	H 2

New Waterford 8,808	J 2
North Sydney 7,820	H 2
Oxford 1,470	D 3
Parrsboro 1,799	D 3
Pictou◎ 4,628	F 3
Porters Lake 893	E 4
Port Hastings 312	G 3
Port Hawkesbury 3,850	G 3
Port Hood◎ 701	G 2
Port Morien 717	J 2
Port Williams 1,227	D 3
Prospect 693	E 4
Pugwash 648	D 3
Reserve Mines 2,472	H 2
River Hébert 835	D 3
Saint Peters 669	H 3
Sandy Point 691	C 5
Scotchtown 2,037	H 2
Sheet Harbour 819	F 4
Shelburne◎ 2,303	C 5
Shubenacadie 984	E 3
Springhill 4,896	D 3
Stellarton 5,435	F 3

Stewiacke 1,174	E 3
Sydney◎ 29,444	H 2
Sydney Mines 8,501	H 2
Terence Bay 960	E 4
Thorburn 1,014	F 3
Three Mile Plains 1,355	D 4
Timberlea 1,159	E 4
Trenton 3,154	F 3
Truro◎ 12,552	E 3
Waterville 687	D 3
Waverley 1,699	E 4
Wedgeport 827	C 5
Western Shore 1,712	D 4
Westmount 3,097	H 2
Westville 4,522	F 3
Wileville 746	D 4
Windsor◎ 3,646	D 3
Wolfville 3,235	D 3
Yarmouth◎ 7,475	B 5

OTHER FEATURES

Advocate (bay)	D 3

Ainslie (lake)	G 2
Amet (sound)	E 3
Andrew (isl.)	G 2
Annapolis (basin)	C 4
Annapolis (riv.)	C 4
Antigonish (harb.)	G 3
Argos (cape)	G 3
Aspy (bay)	H 2
Avon (riv.)	D 4
Baccaro (pt.)	C 5
Baddeck (riv.)	H 2
Barachois (isl.)	G 4
Barren (isl.)	G 4
Barrington (bay)	C 5
Bedford (basin)	E 4
Berry (head)	B 4
Boularderie (isle)	H 2
Bras d'Or (lake)	H 2
Brier (isl.)	B 4
Breton (cape)	J 3
Canso (cape)	H 3
Canso (str.)	G 3
Cap d'Or (cape)	D 3

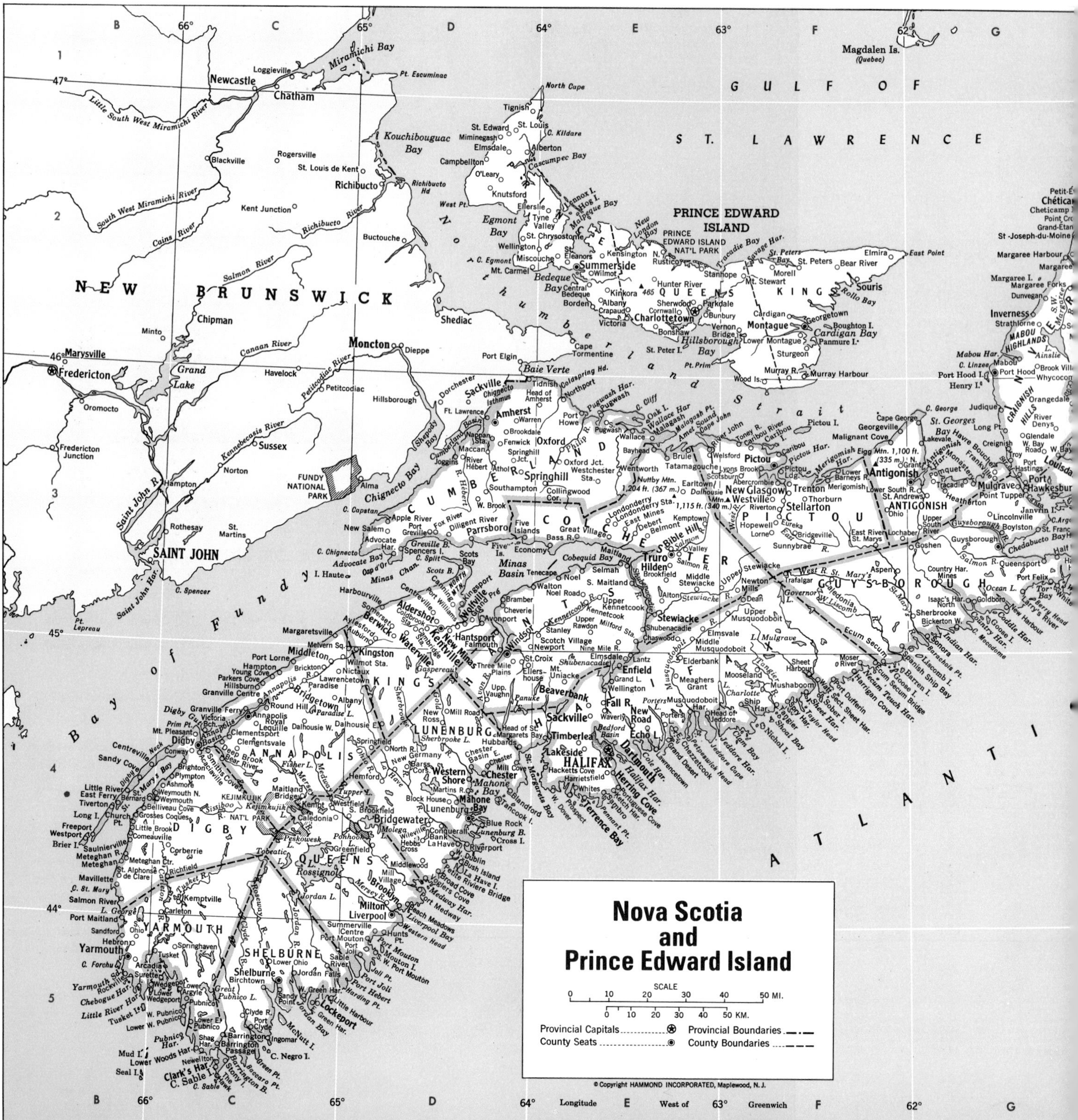

Cape Breton (isl.) .... J 2
Cape Breton Highlands Nat'l
  Park .... H 2
Cape Negro (isl.) .... C 5
Cape Sable (isl.) .... C 5
Capstan (cape) .... D 3
Caribou (isl.) .... F 3
Carleton (riv.) .... C 4
Charlotte (lake) .... F 4
Chebogue (harb.) .... B 5
Chedabucto (bay) .... G 3
Chéticamp (isl.) .... G 2
Chignecto (bay) .... D 3
Chignecto (cape) .... C 3
Chignecto (isth.) .... D 3
Clam (bay) .... F 4
Cliff (cape) .... E 3
Clyde (riv.) .... C 5
Cobequid (bay) .... E 3
Coddle (harb.) .... G 3
Coldspring (head) .... E 3
Cole (harb.) .... E 4
Country (harb.) .... G 3

Craignish (hills) .... G 3
Cross (isl.) .... D 4
Cumberland (basin) .... D 3
Dalhousie (mt.) .... E 3
Dauphin (cape) .... H 2
Digby Gut (chan.) .... C 4
Digby Neck (pen.) .... B 4
East (bay) .... H 3
East (riv.) .... F 3
East Bay (hills) .... H 3
Egmont (cape) .... H 2
Eigg (mt.) .... F 3
Fisher (lake) .... C 4
Five (isls.) .... D 3
Forchu (bay) .... H 3
Forchu (cape) .... B 5
Framboise Cove (bay) ...... H 3
Fundy (bay) .... C 3
Gabarus (bay) .... H 3
Gabarus (cape) .... J 3
Gaspereau (lake) .... D 4
George (cape) .... G 3
George (lake) .... B 5

Gold (riv.) .... D 4
Goose (isl.) .... F 4
Goose (isl.) .... G 3
Governor (island) .... F 3
Great Bras d'Or (chan.) ..... H 2
Great Pubnico (lake) .... C 5
Green (pt.) .... C 5
Greville (bay) .... D 3
Guysborough (riv.) .... G 3
Halifax (harb.) .... E 4
Harding (pt.) .... D 5
Haute (isl.) .... C 3
Hébert (riv.) .... D 3
Henry (isl.) .... G 3
Indian (harb.) .... G 3
Ingonish North (bay) .... H 2
Janvrin (isl.) .... G 3
Jeddore (harb.) .... F 4
John (cape) .... E 3
Joli (pt.) .... D 5
Jordan (bay) .... C 5
Jordan (lake) .... C 4
Jordan (riv.) .... C 5
Kejimkujik (lake) .... C 4
Kejimkujik Nat'l Park .... C 4
Kennetcook (riv.) .... D 3
La Have (isl.) .... D 4
La Have (riv.) .... D 4
Linzee (cape) .... G 2
Liscomb (isl.) .... G 3
Little River (harb.) .... B 5
Liverpool (bay) .... D 5
Lomond, Loch (lake) .... H 3
Long (isl.) .... B 4
Louisbourg Nat'l Hist. Park .. J 3
Lunenburg (bay) .... D 4
Mabou (harb.) .... G 2
Mabou Highlands (hills) ..... G 2
Madame (isl.) .... H 3
Mahone (bay) .... D 4
Malagash (pt.) .... E 3
Margaree (isl.) .... F 4
McNutt (isl.) .... C 5
Medway (harb.) .... D 4
Medway (riv.) .... C 4
Merigomish (harb.) .... F 3
Mersey (riv.) .... C 4
Michaud (pt.) .... H 3
Minas (basin) .... D 3
Minas (chan.) .... D 3
Mira (bay) .... J 2
Mira (riv.) .... H 3
Mocodome (cape) .... G 3
Molega (lake) .... D 4
Morien (cape) .... J 2
Mouton (isl.) .... D 5
Mud (isl.) .... B 5
Mulgrave (lake) .... F 3
Musquodoboit (riv.) .... E 4
Necum Teuch (harb.) .... F 4
Nichol (isl.) .... F 4
North (cape) .... H 1
North (mt.) .... D 3
North Aspy (riv.) .... H 2
North Bay Ingonish (bay) ... H 2
North East Margaree (riv.) .. H 2
Northumberland (str.) .... E 2
Nuttby (mt.) .... E 3
Oak (isl.) .... E 3
Ocean (lake) .... D 4
Ohio (riv.) .... D 4
Panuke (lake) .... C 4
Paradise (lake) .... E 4
Pennant (pt.) .... C 4
Percé (cape) .... J 2
Peskowesk (lake) .... C 4
Petit-de-Grat (isl.) .... H 3
Petpeswick (head) .... E 3
Philip (riv.) .... F 3
Pictou (harb.) .... F 3
Pictou (isl.) .... F 3
Pleasant (bay) .... D 4
Ponhook (lake) .... D 4
Porters (lake) .... E 4
Port Hebert (harb.) .... D 5
Port Hood (isl.) .... G 2
Port Joli (harb.) .... D 5
Port Mouton (harb.) .... D 5
Poulet Cove (bay) .... H 2
Prim (pt.) .... C 4
Pubnico (harb.) .... C 5
Pugwash (harb.) .... E 3
Roseway (riv.) .... C 4
Rossignol (lake) .... C 4
Sable (cape) .... C 5
Sable (isl.) .... J 5
Saint Andrews (chan.) ...... H 2
Saint Anns (bay) .... H 2
Saint Georges (bay) .... G 3
Saint Lawrence (bay) .... H 1
Saint Lawrence (cape) ...... H 1
Saint Margarets (bay) .... E 4
Saint Mary (cape) .... B 4
Saint Marys (bay) .... B 4
Saint Mary's (riv.) .... F 3
Saint Paul (isl.) .... H 1
Saint Peters (bay) .... H 3

PRINCE EDWARD ISLAND

AREA 2,184 sq. mi. (5,657 sq. km.)
POPULATION 122,506
CAPITAL Charlottetown
LARGEST CITY Charlottetown
HIGHEST POINT 465 ft. (142 m.)
SETTLED IN 1720
ADMITTED TO CONFEDERATION 1873
PROVINCIAL FLOWER Lady's Slipper

NOVA SCOTIA

AREA 21,425 sq. mi. (55,491 sq. km.)
POPULATION 847,442
CAPITAL Halifax
LARGEST CITY Halifax
HIGHEST POINT Cape Breton Highlands
  1,747 ft. (532 m.)
SETTLED IN 1605
ADMITTED TO CONFEDERATION 1867
PROVINCIAL FLOWER Trailing Arbutus or
  Mayflower

Topography

0   30   60 MI.
0   30   60 KM.

Salmon (riv.) .... E 3
Salmon (riv.) .... G 3
Scatarie (isl.) .... J 2
Scots (bay) .... D 3
Seall (isl.) .... B 5
Sheet (harb.) .... F 4
Sherbrooke (lake) .... D 4
Sherbrooke (riv.) .... D 4
Shoal (bay) .... F 4
Shubenacadie (lake) .... E 4
Shubenacadie (riv.) .... E 3
Sissiboo (riv.) .... C 4
Smoky (cape) .... H 2
Sober (isl.) .... F 4
South West Margaree (riv.) .. G 2
Split (cape) .... D 3
Spry (harb.) .... F 4
Stewiacke (riv.) .... E 3
Sydney (harb.) .... H 2
Tangier (head) .... F 4
Taylor (head) .... F 4
Tobeatic (lake) .... C 4
Tor (bay) .... G 3
Tupper (lake) .... D 4
Tusket (isl.) .... B 5

Tusket (riv.) .... C 4
Verte (bay) .... D 2
Wallace (harb.) .... E 3
West (bay) .... G 3
West (pt.) .... H 5
West (riv.) .... F 3
Western (head) .... D 5
West Liscomb (riv.) .... F 3
West Saint Mary's (riv.) .... G 3
Whitehaven (harb.) .... G 3
Yarmouth (sound) .... B 5

PRINCE EDWARD ISLAND

COUNTIES

Kings 19,215 .... F 2
Prince 42,821 .... D 2
Queens 60,470 .... E 2

CITIES and TOWNS

Alberton 1,020 .... E 2
Bunbury 1,024 .... E 2
Charlottetown (cap.)⊛ 15,282 . E 2

Cornwall 1,838 .... E 2
Georgetown⊛ 737 .... F 2
Kensington 1,143 .... E 2
Miscouche 752 .... D 2
Montague 1,957 .... F 2
Murray Harbour 443 .... F 2
North Rustico 688 .... D 2
O'Leary 736 .... D 2
Parkdale 2,018 .... E 2
Saint Edward 650 .... D 2
Saint Eleanors 2,716 ...... E 2
Sherwood 5,681 .... E 2
Souris 1,413 .... F 2
Summerside⊛ 7,828 .... E 2
Tignish 982 .... D 2
Wilmot 1,563 .... E 2

OTHER FEATURES

Bedeque (bay) .... E 2
Boughton (isl.) .... F 2
Cardigan (bay) .... F 2
Cascumpeque (bay) .... D 2
East (pt.) .... G 2
Egmont (bay) .... D 2

Egmont (cape) .... D 2
Hillsborough (bay) .... E 2
Hog (isl.) .... E 2
Kildare (cape) .... E 2
Lennox (isl.) .... E 2
Malpeque (bay) .... E 2
New London (bay) .... E 1
North (pt.) .... E 1
Northumberland (str.) ...... D 2
Panmure (isl.) .... F 2
Prim (pt.) .... E 2
Prince Edward Island Nat'l
  Park .... E 2
Rollo (bay) .... F 2
Saint Lawrence (gulf) ...... F 2
Saint Peters (bay) .... F 2
Saint Peters (isl.) .... E 2
Savage (harb.) .... E 2
Tracadie (bay) .... F 2
West (pt.) .... D 2
Wood (isls.) .... F 3

⊛County seat.
*Population of metropolitan area.

Agriculture, Industry and Resources

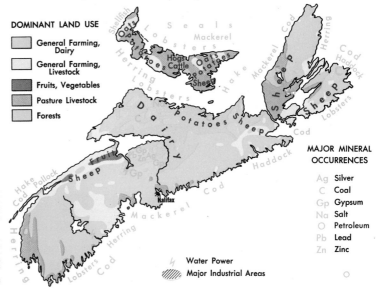

DOMINANT LAND USE

- General Farming, Dairy
- General Farming, Livestock
- Fruits, Vegetables
- Pasture Livestock
- Forests

MAJOR MINERAL OCCURRENCES

Ag Silver
C   Coal
Gp Gypsum
Na Salt
O   Petroleum
Pb Lead
Zn Zinc

Water Power
Major Industrial Areas

COUNTIES

Albert 23,632 .... F 3
Carleton 24,659 .... C 2
Charlotte 26,571 .... C 3
Gloucester 86,156 .... E 1
Kent 30,799 .... E 2
King's 51,114 .... E 3
Madawaska 34,892 .... B 1
Northumberland 54,134 ..... D 2
Queen's 12,485 .... D 3
Restigouche 40,593 .... C 1
Saint John 86,148 .... E 3
Sunbury 21,012 .... D 3
Victoria 20,815 .... C 1
Westmorland 107,640 .... F 2
York 74,213 .... C 3

CITIES and TOWNS

Acadie Siding 64 .... E 2
Acadieville 176 .... E 2
Adamsville 94 .... E 2
Albert Mines 120 .... F 3
Alcida 174 .... E 1
Aldouane 64 .... E 2
Allardville 478 .... E 1
Alma 329 .... F 3
Anagance 114 .... E 3
Anse-Bleue 562 .... E 1

Apohaqui 341 .... E 3
Argyle 63 .... C 2
Armstrong Brook 191 .... E 1
Aroostook 403 .... C 2
Arthurette 178 .... C 2
Astle 201 .... D 2
Atholville 1,694 .... D 1
Aulac 113 .... F 3
Back Bay 455 .... D 3
Baie-Sainte-Anne 709 ...... F 1
Baie-Verte 175 .... F 2
Bairdsville 81 .... C 2
Baker Brook 527 .... B 1
Balmoral 1,823 .... D 1
Barachois 686 .... F 2
Barnaby River 38 .... E 2
Barnettville 117 .... E 2
Bartibog Bridge 122 .... E 1
Bas-Caraquet 1,859 .... F 1
Bass River 112 .... E 2
Bath 794 .... C 2
Bathurst⊛ 15,705 .... E 1
Bayfield 81 .... G 2
Bayside .... C 3
Beaubois 211 .... E 2
Beaver Brook Station 95 ... E 2
Beaver Harbour 316 .... D 3
Beechwood 111 .... C 2
Beersville 52 .... E 2
Belledune 690 .... E 1

Bellefleur 83 .... C 1
Bellefond 243 .... E 1
Belleisle Creek 145 .... E 3
Benjamin River 171 .... D 1
Ben Lomond .... E 3
Benton 101 .... C 3
Beresford 3,652 .... E 1
Berry Mills 238 .... E 2
Bertrand 1,268 .... E 1
Berwick 129 .... E 3
Black Point 131 .... D 1
Black River 150 .... E 1
Blacks Harbour 1,356 ...... D 3
Blackville 892 .... E 2
Blissfield 119 .... D 2
Bloomfield Ridge 153 ...... D 2
Bloomfield Station 62 ..... E 3
Boiestown 299 .... D 2
Bonny River 153 .... D 3
Bosse 193 .... B 1
Bourgeois 215 .... F 2
Brantville 1,066 .... E 1
Breau-Village 293 .... F 2
Brest 94 .... E 1
Brewers Mills 199 .... C 2
Briggs Corner 89 .... D 2
Bristol 824 .... C 2
Brockway (Lower Brockway-
  Brockway) 97 .... C 3

Browns Flat 295 .... D 3
Buctouche 2,476 .... F 2
Burnsville 156 .... E 1
Burton⊛ 291 .... D 3
Burtts Corner 484 .... D 2
Cambridge-Narrows 433 ..... E 3
Campbellton 9,818 .... D 1
Canaan 115 .... E 2
Canaan Forks 78 .... E 2
Canaan Road 86 .... E 2
Canterbury 474 .... C 3
Cap-Bateau 417 .... F 1
Cape Tormentine 229 .... G 2
Cap Lumière 262 .... F 2
Cap-Pelé 2,199 .... F 2
Caraquet 4,315 .... E 1
Carlingford 229 .... C 2
Carlisle 75 .... C 2
Caron Brook 171 .... B 1
Carrolls Crossing 119 ..... D 2
Castalia 145 .... D 4
Central-Saint-Simon (St.
  Simon) 991 .... E 1
Centreville 577 .... C 2
Chance Harbour 63 .... D 3
Charlo 1,603 .... D 1
Chatham 6,779 .... E 1
Chatham Head .... E 1
Chipman 1,829 .... E 2

Clair 915 .... B 1
Clarendon 80 .... D 3
Cliffordvale (Limestone-
  Cliffordvale) 69 .... C 2
Clifton 194 .... E 1
Coal Branch 90 .... E 2
Coal Creek 61 .... E 2
Cocagne Cape 278 .... F 2
Cocagne-Cocagne Sud 600 ... F 2
Codys 125 .... E 3
Coldstream 217 .... C 2
Coles Island 160 .... E 3
College Bridge 536 .... F 3
Collette 198 .... E 2
Connell 58 .... C 2
Connors 96 .... B 1
Cork 54 .... D 3
Cornhill 111 .... E 3
Coughlan 30 .... E 1
Cross Creek 192 .... D 2
Cumberland Bay 231 .... E 2
Dalhousie⊛ 4,958 .... D 1
Dalhousie Junction 105 .... D 1
Darlington 749 .... D 1
Daulnay 398 .... E 1
Dawsonville 278 .... C 1
Debec 200 .... C 2
Dieppe 8,511 .... F 2
Dipper Harbour 166 .... D 3
Doaktown 1,009 .... D 2

Dorchester⊛ 1,101 .... F 3
Dorchester Crossing 605 ... F 2
Douglastown 1,091 .... E 1
Drummond 849 .... C 1
Duguayville 337 .... E 1
Dumfries 150 .... C 3
Dupuis Corner 303 .... F 2
Durham Bridge 255 .... D 2
East Riverside-Kingshurst
  989 .... E 3
Edmundston⊛ 12,044 .... B 1
Eel River Bridge 377 ...... F 1
Eel River Crossing 1,431 .. D 1
Elgin 301 .... E 3
Enniskillen 63 .... D 3
Escuminac 194 .... F 1
Evandale 58 .... D 3
Evangeline 356 .... F 1
Everett 48 .... C 1
Fairfield 250 .... E 3
Fairhaven 142 .... C 4
Fairisle 415 .... E 1
Fairvale 3,960 .... E 3
Ferry Road 325 .... E 1
Fielding 197 .... C 2
Five Fingers 189 .... C 1
Flatlands 249 .... D 1
Florenceville 709 .... C 2
Forest City 25 .... C 3
Fosterville 58 .... C 3

Four Falls 69 .... C 2
Fredericton (cap.)⊛ 43,723 . D 3
Fredericton Junction 711 .. D 3
Gagetown⊛ 618 .... D 3
Gardner Creek 56 .... E 3
Geary 654 .... D 3
Germantown 62 .... F 3
Gillespie 96 .... C 2
Glassville 147 .... C 2
Glencoe 147 .... D 1
Glenlivet 284 .... C 1
Gloucester Junction 36 .... E 1
Gondola Point 3,076 .... E 3
Grafton 385 .... C 2
Grand Bay 3,173 .... E 3
Grande-Anse 817 .... E 1
Grand Falls 6,203 .... C 1
Grand Falls Hill 152 ..... C 1
Grand Harbour 614 .... D 4
Gray Rapids 266 .... D 2
Hammondvale 72 .... E 3
Hampstead 87 .... D 3
Hampton⊛ 3,141 .... E 3
Harcourt 127 .... E 2
Hardwicke 114 .... F 1
Hardwood Ridge 191 .... D 2
Hartland 846 .... C 2
Harvey, Albert 58 .... F 3
Harvey, York 356 .... D 3
Hatfield Point 176 .... E 3

New Brunswick

SCALE
0 5 10   20   30   40 MI.
0 5 10   20   30   40 KM.

Provincial Capitals .... ⊛
County Seats .... ⊛
International Boundaries ... ___ ___
Provincial Boundaries .... _____
County Boundaries .... ___ ___

© Copyright HAMMOND INCORPORATED, Maplewood, N.J.

avelock 439 E 3
ayesville 107 D 2
azeldean 108 C 2
ead of Millstream 61 E 3
illman 69 C 2
illsborough 1,239 F 3
olmesville 146 C 2
oltville 222 D 2
oneydale 77 C 3
opewell Cape® 144 F 3
opewell Hill 172 F 3
oward 77 E 2
owland Ridge 55 C 2
oyt 114 D 3
kerman 396 F 1
shtown 605 F 2
land View 240 D 3
acksonville 363 C 2
acquet River 778 E 1
aneville 204 E 1
eanne Mance 89 E 1
emseg 228 D 3
olicure 96 F 3
uniper 525 C 2
edgwick 1,222 C 1
eenan Siding 86 E 2
ent Junction 112 E 2
ent Lake 57 E 2
eswick 260 D 3
ilburn 134 C 2
illam 60 E 2
ingsclear 250 D 3
ngsley 145 D 2
rkland 69 C 3
nowlesville 82 C 2
ouchibouguac 213 F 2
ac Baker 292 B 1
agacéville 227 E 1
ake George 170 C 3
aketon 81 E 2
akeville 201 C 2
ambertville 109 C 3
amèque 1,571 F 1
andry 281 E 1
aplante 197 E 1
avillette 576 E 1
awrence Station 229 C 3
eech 584 E 1
eger Brook F 2
egerville 184 F 2
e Goulet 1,173 F 1
eonardville 158 C 4
epreau 208 D 3
evesque 77 C 1
ttle Cape 513 F 2
ttle Shippegan 131 F 1
oggieville 781 E 1
orne 937 D 1
Lower Coverdale 616 F 2
Lower Derby 206 E 2
Lower Durham 52 D 2
Lower Hainesville 66 C 2
Lower Kars 30 E 3
Lower Millstream 184 E 3
Lower Sapin F 2
Lower Southampton C 3
Ludlow 100 D 2
Maces Bay 182 D 3
Madran 247 E 1
Magaguadavic 126 C 3
Maisonnette 757 E 1
Malden 93 G 2
Manners Sutton 159 D 3
Manuels 332 F 1
Mapleview 65 C 2
Marcelville 61 E 2
Martin 104 C 1
Maugerville 249 D 3
Maxwell 64 C 3
McAdam 1,837 C 3
McGivney 156 D 2
McKendrick 608 D 1
McNamee 147 D 2
Meductic 234 C 3
Melrose 121 F 2
Memramcook 276 F 2
Menneval 110 C 1
Midgic Station 208 F 3
Mill Cove 253 D 3
Millerton 130 E 2
Millville 309 C 2
Minto 3,399 D 2
Miscou Centre 554 F 1
Miscou Harbour 106 F 1
Mispec 180 E 3
Moncton 54,743 F 2
Moores Mills 117 C 3
Morrisdale 202 D 3
Moulin-Morneault 459 B 1
Murray Corner 233 G 2
Nackawic 1,357 C 2
Napadogan 103 D 2
Nash Creek 235 D 1
Nashwaak Bridge 142 D 2
Nashwaak Village 258 D 2
Nauwigewauk 139 E 3
Neguac 1,755 E 1
Nelson-Miramichi 1,452 E 2
Newcastle® 6,284 E 2
Newcastle Creek 210 D 2
New Denmark 112 C 1
New Jersey 65 E 1
New Market 143 D 3
New Maryland 485 D 3
New River Beach 33 D 3
Newtown 154 E 3
New Zion 171 D 2
Nicholas Denys 170 D 1
Nictau 30 C 1
Nigadoo 1,075 E 1
Noinville 50 E 2
Nordin 393 E 1
North Head 661 D 4
Norton 1,372 E 3
Notre-Dame 344 F 2
Oak Bay 183 C 3
Oak Point 83 D 3
Oromocto 9,064 D 3
Paquetville 626 E 1
Peel 117 C 2
Pelletier Mills 88 B 1
Pennfield D 3
Penniac 179 D 2
Penobsquis 259 E 3
Perth-Andover® 1,872 C 2
Petitcodiac 1,401 E 3
Petite-Rivière-de-l'Île 549 F 1
Petit Rocher 1,860 E 1
Petit Rocher Sud E 1
Pigeon Hill 595 F 1
Plaster Rock 1,222 C 2
Pocologan 150 D 3
Point de Bute 155 F 3
Pointe-du-Chêne 482 F 2
Pointe-Sapin 331 F 2
Pointe-Verte 1,335 E 1
Pollett River 73 E 3
Pontgrave 229 F 1
Pont-Lafrance 875 E 1
Pont-Landry 444 F 1
Port Elgin 504 F 2
Prime 89 B 1
Prince of Wales 138 D 3
Prince William 225 C 3
Quarryville 205 E 2
Queenstown 112 D 3
Quispamsis 6,022 E 3
Red Bank 141 E 2
Renforth 1,490 E 3
Renous 192 E 2
Rexton 928 F 2
Richardsville D 1
Richibucto® 1,722 E 2
Richibucto Village 442 F 2
Richmond Corner 84 C 2
Riley Brook 126 C 1
Ripples 233 D 3
River de Chute 22 C 2
River Glade 268 E 3
Riverside-Albert 478 F 3
Riverview 14,907 F 2
Rivière-du-Portage 661 F 1
Rivière Verte 1,054 B 1
Robertville 733 E 1
Robichaud 485 F 2
Robinsonville 206 C 1
Rogersville 1,237 E 2
Rollingdam 65 C 3
Rosaireville 86 E 2
Rothesay 1,764 E 3
Rowena 73 C 2
Roy 173 F 2
Royal Road 41 D 2
Rusagonis 231 D 3
Sackville 5,654 F 3
Saint Almo 17 C 2
Saint-André 385 C 1
Saint Andrews® 1,760 C 3
Saint-Antoine 1,217 F 2
Saint Arthur 369 D 1
Saint-Basile 3,214 B 1
Saint-Charles 355 F 2
Saint Croix 86 C 3
Sainte-Anne 329 E 1
Sainte-Anne-de-Kent 337 F 2
Sainte-Anne-de-Madawaska 1,332 B 1
Saint-Édouard-de-Kent 157 F 2
Sainte-Marie-de-Kent 283 F 2
Sainte-Marie-sur-Mer 539 F 1
Sainte-Rose-Gloucester 410 F 1
Saint-François-de-Madawaska 753 B 1
Saint George 1,163 D 3
Saint Hilaire 244 B 1
Saint-Ignace 96 F 2
Saint-Isidore 794 E 1
Saint-Jacques 2,297 B 1
Saint-Jean-Baptiste-de-Restigouche 228 C 1
Saint John® 80,521 E 3
Saint-Joseph 630 F 3
Saint-Joseph-de-Madawaska 173 B 1
Saint-Léolin 799 E 1
Saint Leonard 1,566 C 1
Saint-Louis-de-Kent 1,166 F 2
Saint Margarets 63 E 2
Saint Martin de Restigouche 124 C 1
Saint Martins 530 E 3
Saint-Paul 365 E 2
Saint Quentin 2,334 C 1
Saint-Raphaël-sur-Mer 562 F 1
Saint Sauveur 252 E 1
Saint Stephen 5,120 C 3
Saint Wilfred E 1
Salisbury 1,672 E 2
Salmon Beach 277 E 1
Salmon Creek 38 E 2
Saumarez 690 E 1
Scoudouc 207 F 2
Seal Cove 548 D 4
Shannon 39 E 3
Shediac 4,285 F 2
Shediac Bridge 441 F 2
Sheffield 112 D 3
Sheila 1,172 F 1
Shemogue 199 F 2
Shepody 86 F 3
Shippegan 2,471 F 1
Siegas 227 C 1
Sillikers 292 E 2
Simonds 221 C 2
Sisson Ridge 170 C 2
Six Roads 239 F 1
Smiths Creek 163 E 3
Somerville 326 C 2
South Branch 86 F 2
Springfield, King's 116 E 3
Springfield, York 130 C 2
Stanley 432 D 2
Stickney 232 C 2
Storeytown 140 D 2
Sunny Corner 405 E 2
Sunnyside 87 D 1
Sussex 3,972 E 3
Sussex Corner 1,023 E 3
Tabusintac 231 E 1

AREA 28,354 sq. mi. (73,437 sq. km.)
POPULATION 696,403
CAPITAL Fredericton
LARGEST CITY Saint John
HIGHEST POINT Mt. Carleton 2,690 ft. (820 m.)
SETTLED IN 1611
ADMITTED TO CONFEDERATION 1867
PROVINCIAL FLOWER Purple Violet

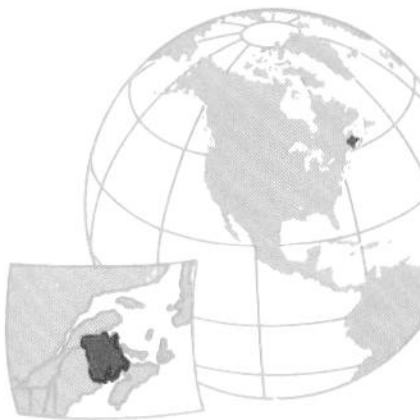

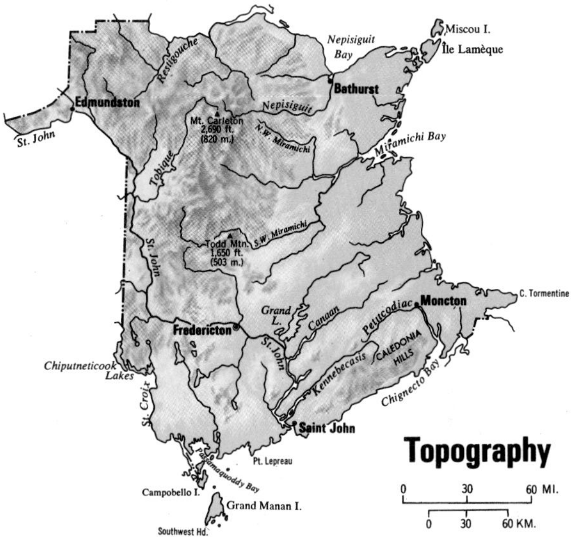

Topography

0 30 60 MI.
0 30 60 KM.

5,000 m. 16,404 ft. | 2,000 m. 6,562 ft. | 1,000 m. 3,281 ft. | 500 m. 1,640 ft. | 200 m. 656 ft. | 100 m. 328 ft. | Sea Level | Below

Taxis River 118 D 2
Tay Creek 161 D 2
Taymouth 301 D 2
Temperance Vale 357 C 2
The Range 58 E 2
Thibault 306 C 1
Tide Head 952 D 1
Tilley 95 C 2
Tobique Narrows 140 C 2
Tracadie 2,452 F 1
Tracy 636 D 3
Turtle Creek 81 F 3
Tweedside 87 C 3
Upham 107 E 3
Upper Blackville 60 E 2
Upper Buctouche 158 F 2
Upper Gagetown 236 D 3
Upper Hainesville 189 C 2
Upper Kent 203 C 2
Upper Maugerville 543 D 3
Upper Mills 153 C 3
Upper Rockport 18 F 3
Upper Sheila 706 E 1
Upper Woodstock 257 C 2
Upsalquitch 112 D 1
Val-Comeau 534 F 1
Val d'Amour 462 D 1
Val Doucet 505 E 1
Verret 637 B 1
Village-Saint-Laurent 187 E 1
Waasis 264 D 3
Wapske 195 C 2
Waterford 120 E 3
Waterville 181 C 2
Waweig C 3
Wayerton 188 E 1
Weaver 86 E 2
Weldon 227 F 3
Welsford 230 D 3
Welshpool 260 D 4
Westfield 1,100 D 3
West Quaco 48 E 3
White Head 185 D 4
White Rapids 238 E 2
Whitney 216 E 2
Wickham 72 D 3
Wicklow 143 C 2
Williamsburg 258 D 2
Williamstown 156 C 2
Willow Grove 509 E 3
Wilmot 57 C 3
Wilson Point 45 F 1
Wilsons Beach 844 D 4
Windsor 43 C 2
Wirral 110 D 3
Woodstock® 4,649 C 2
Woodwards Cove 146 D 4
Youngs Cove 65 E 3
Zealand 458 D 2

OTHER FEATURES

Bald (mt.) C 1
Bartibog (riv.) E 1
Bay du Vin (riv.) E 2
Big Tracadie (riv.) E 1
Buctouche (harb.) F 2
Buctouche (riv.) F 2
Campobello (isl.) D 4
Canaan (riv.) E 2
Carleton (mt.) D 1
Chaleur (bay) E 1
Chignecto (bay) F 3
Chiputneticook (lakes) C 3
Cocagne (isl.) F 2
Cumberland (basin) F 3
Deer (isl.) D 4
Digdeguash (riv.) C 3
Escuminac (bay) F 1
Escuminac (pt.) F 1
Fundy (bay) E 3
Fundy Nat'l Park E 3
Gaspereau (riv.) D 2
Grand (bay) D 3
Grand (lake) C 3
Grand (lake) D 3
Grand Manan (chan.) C 4
Grand Manan (isl.) D 4
Grande (riv.) C 1
Green (riv.) B 1
Hammond (riv.) E 3
Harvey (lake) C 3
Heron (isl.) D 1
Kedgwick (riv.) C 1
Kennebecasis (riv.) E 3
Keswick (riv.) C 2
Kouchibouguac (bay) F 2
Kouchibouguacis (riv.) E 2
Kouchibouguac Nat'l Park F 2
Lamèque (isl.) F 1
Lepreau (riv.) D 3
Little (riv.) D 2
Long (isl.) D 3
Long Reach (inlet) D 3
Maces (bay) D 3
Mactaquac (lake) C 3
Madawaska (riv.) B 1
Magaguadavic (lake) C 3
Magaguadavic (riv.) C 3
Miramichi (bay) E 1
Miscou (isl.) F 1
Miscou (pt.) F 1
Mount Carleton Prov. Park D 1
Musquash (harb.) D 3
Nashwaak (riv.) D 2
Nepisiguit (bay) E 1
Nepisiguit (riv.) D 1
Nerepis (riv.) D 3
Northern (head) D 4
North Sevogle (riv.) D 1
Northumberland (str.) F 2
Northwest Miramichi (riv.) D 1
Oromocto (lake) C 3
Oromocto (riv.) D 3
Passamaquoddy (bay) C 3
Patapédia (riv.) C 1
Petitcodiac (riv.) F 3
Pokemouche (riv.) E 1
Pokesudie (isl.) F 1
Pollett (riv.) E 3
Quaco (head) E 3
Renous (riv.) D 2
Restigouche (riv.) C 1
Richibucto (harb.) F 2
Richibucto (riv.) E 2
Roosevelt Campobello Int'l Park D 4
Saint Croix (riv.) C 3
Saint Francis (riv.) A 1
Saint John (harb.) E 3
Saint John (riv.) C 2
Saint Lawrence (gulf) F 1
Salisbury (bay) F 3
Salmon (riv.) C 1
Salmon (riv.) E 2
Shediac (isl.) F 2
Shepody (bay) F 3
Shippegan (bay) E 1
Shippegan Gully (str.) F 1
South Sevogle (riv.) D 1
Southwest (head) D 4
Southwest Miramichi (riv.) D 2
Spear (cape) G 2
Spednik (lake) C 3
Spencer (cape) E 3
Tabusintac (riv.) E 1
Tabusintac Gully (str.) F 1
Tetagouche (riv.) D 1
Tobique (riv.) C 2
Upsalquitch (riv.) D 1
Utopia (lake) D 3
Verte (bay) G 2
Washademoak (lake) E 3
West (isls.) D 4
White Head (isl.) D 4

®County seat.

Agriculture, Industry and Resources

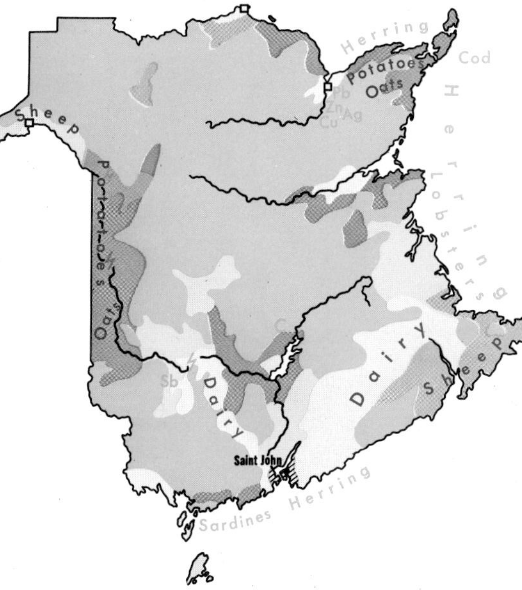

DOMINANT LAND USE

- Cereals, Livestock
- Dairy
- Potatoes
- General Farming, Livestock
- Pasture Livestock
- Forests

MAJOR MINERAL OCCURRENCES

Ag Silver | Pb Lead
C Coal | Sb Antimony
Cu Copper | Zn Zinc

Water Power
Major Industrial Areas

Topography

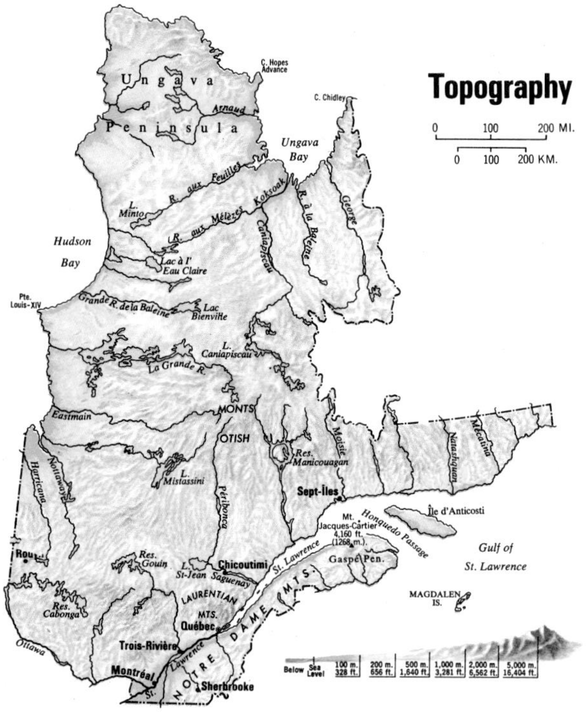
Ungava Peninsula
Ungava Bay
Hudson Bay
C. Hopes Advance
C. Chidley
L. Minto
Lac à l'Eau Claire
Grande R. de la Baleine
Lac Bienville
Caniapiscau
La Grande R.
Eastmain
MONTS
OTISH
Res. Manicouagan
L. Mistassini
Sept-Îles
Île d'Anticosti
Mt. Jacques-Cartier 4,160 ft. (1268 m.)
Gulf of St. Lawrence
Gaspé Pen.
MAGDALEN IS.
Chicoutimi
St-Jean
Saguenay
Res. Gouin
Res. Cabonga
LAURENTIAN MTS.
Québec
Trois-Rivières
Montréal
Sherbrooke
NOTRE DAME MTS.
Ottawa
0 100 200 MI.
0 100 200 KM.
Below Sea Level 100 m. 328 ft. 200 m. 656 ft. 500 m. 1,640 ft. 1,000 m. 3,281 ft. 2,000 m. 6,562 ft. 5,000 m. 16,404 ft.

COUNTIES

Argenteuil 32,454 .... C 4
Arthabaska 59,277 .... E 4
Bagot 26,840 .... E 4
Beauce 73,427 .... G 3
Beauharnois 54,034 .... C 4
Bellechasse 23,559 .... G 3
Berthier 31,096 .... C 3
Bonaventure 40,487 .... C 2
Brome 17,436 .... E 4
Chambly 307,090 .... J 4
Champlain 119,595 .... E 2
Charlevoix-Est 17,448 ...... G 2
Charlevoix-Ouest 14,172 .... G 2
Châteauguay 59,968 .... D 4
Chicoutimi 174,441 .... G 1
Compton 20,536 .... F 4
Deux-Montagnes 71,252 ...... C 4
Dorchester 33,949 .... C 3
Drummond 69,770 .... E 4
Frontenac 26,814 .... G 4
Gaspé-Est 41,173 .... D 1
Gaspé-Ouest 18,943 .... C 1
Gatineau 54,229 .... B 3
Hull 131,213 .... B 4
Huntingdon 16,953 .... C 4
Iberville 23,180 .... D 4
Île-de-Montréal 1,760,122 .. H 4
Île-Jésus 268,335 .... H 4
Joliette 60,384 .... C 3
Kamouraska 28,642 .... H 2
Labelle 34,395 .... B 3
Lac-Saint-Jean-Est 47,891 .. F 1
Lac-Saint-Jean-Ouest 62,952 . E 1
Laprairie 105,962 .... H 4
L'Assomption 109,705 .... D 4
Lévis 94,104 .... J 3
L'Islet 22,062 .... G 2
Lotbinière 29,653 .... F 3
Maskinongé 20,763 .... D 3
Matane 29,955 .... B 1
Matapédia 23,715 .... B 2
Mégantic 57,892 .... F 3
Missisquoi 36,161 .... D 4
Montcalm 27,557 .... C 3
Montmagny 25,622 .... G 3
Montmorency No. 1 23,048 ... F 2
Montmorency No. 2 6,436 .... G 3
Napierville 13,562 .... D 4
Nicolet 33,513 .... E 3
Papineau 37,975 .... B 4
Pontiac 20,283 .... A 3
Portneuf 58,843 .... E 3
Québec 458,980 .... F 3
Richelieu 53,058 .... D 4
Richmond 40,871 .... E 4
Rimouski 69,099 .... J 1
Rivière-du-Loup 41,250 ..... H 2
Rouville 42,391 .... D 4
Saguenay 115,881 .... H 1
Saint-Hyacinthe 55,888 ..... D 4
Saint-Jean 55,576 .... D 4
Saint-Maurice 107,703 ...... D 3
Shefford 70,733 .... E 4
Sherbrooke 115,983 .... E 4
Soulanges 15,429 .... C 4
Stanstead 38,186 .... F 4
Témiscouata 52,570 .... J 2
Terrebonne 193,865 .... H 4
Vaudreuil 50,043 .... C 4
Verchères 63,353 .... J 4
Wolfe 15,635 .... F 4
Yamaska 14,797 .... E 3

CITIES and TOWNS

Acton Vale 4,371 .... E 4
Albanel 992 .... E 1
Alma◎ 26,322 .... F 1
Amqui◎ 4,048 .... B 2
Ancienne-Lorette 12,935 .... H 3
Angers .... B 4
Anjou 37,346 .... H 4
Annaville 712 .... E 3
Armagh 878 .... G 3
Arthabaska◎ 6,827 .... F 3
Arvida .... F 1
Asbestos 7,967 .... F 4
Ascot Corner 847 .... F 4
Audet 760 .... G 4
Ayer's Cliff◎ 810 .... E 4
Aylmer 26,695 .... B 4
Baie-Comeau 12,866 .... A 1
Baie-d'Urfé 3,674 .... G 4
Baie-Saint-Paul◎ 3,961 ..... G 2
Baie-Trinité 749 .... B 1
Beaconsfield 19,613 .... H 4
Beauceville 4,302 .... G 3
Beauharnois◎ 7,025 .... D 4
Beaumont 791 .... F 3
Beauport 60,447 .... J 3
Beaupŕe 2,740 .... G 2
Bécancour◎ 10,247 .... E 3
Bedford◎ 2,832 .... E 4
Beebe Plain 1,072 .... E 4
Bélair (Val-Bélair) 12,695 . H 3
Beloeil 17,540 .... D 4
Bernierville 2,120 .... F 3
Berthier-en-Bas 562 .... G 3
Berthierville◎ 4,049 .... D 3
Bic 2,994 .... J 1
Biencourt 824 .... J 2
Black Lake 5,148 .... F 3
Blainville 14,682 .... H 4
Boischatel 3,345 .... J 3
Bois-des-Filion 4,943 ...... H 4
Bolduc 1,565 .... G 4
Bonaventure 1,371 .... C 2
Boucherville 29,704 .... J 4
Bromont 2,731 .... E 4
Bromptonville 3,035 .... F 4
Brossard 52,232 .... H 4
Brownsburg 2,875 .... C 4
Buckingham 7,992 .... B 4
Cabano 3,291 .... J 2
Cacouna 1,160 .... H 2
Calumet 729 .... C 4
Candiac 8,502 .... J 4
Cap-à-l'Aigle 819 .... G 2
Cap-Chat 3,464 .... B 1
Cap-de-la-Madeleine 32,626 . E 3
Caplan-Rivière Caplan 1,139 . C 2
Cap-Saint-Ignace 1,485 ..... G 2
Cap-Santé◎ 671 .... F 3
Carignan 4,544 .... J 4
Carleton 2,710 .... C 2
Causapscal 2,501 .... B 2
Chambly 12,190 .... J 4
Chambord 961 .... E 1
Chandler 3,946 .... D 2
Charlemagne 4,827 .... H 4
Charlesbourg 68,326 .... J 3
Charny 8,240 .... J 3
Châteauguay 36,928 .... H 4
Château-Richer◎ 3,628 ...... F 3
Chénéville 633 .... B 4
Chicoutimi◎ 60,064 .... G 1
Chicoutimi-Jonquière *135,172 ... G 1
Chute-aux-Outardes 2,280 ... A 1
Clermont 3,621 .... G 2
Coaticook 6,271 .... F 4
Coleraine 1,660 .... F 4
Compton 728 .... F 4
Contrecoeur 5,449 .... D 4
Cookshire◎ 1,480 .... F 4
Coteau-du-Lac 1,247 .... C 4
Coteau-Landing◎ 1,386 ...... C 4
Côte-Saint-Luc 27,531 ...... H 4
Courcelles 608 .... G 4
Courville .... J 3
Cowansville 12,240 .... E 4
Crabtree 1,950 .... D 4
Danville 2,200 .... E 4
Daveluyville 1,257 .... E 3
Deauville 942 .... E 4
Dégelis 3,477 .... J 2
Delisle 4,011 .... F 1
Delson 4,935 .... H 4
Desbiens 1,541 .... E 1
Deschaillons-sur-Saint-Laurent 950 ... E 3
Deschambault 977 .... E 3
Deschênes .... B 4
Deux-Montagnes 9,944 .... H 4
Didyme 667 .... E 1
Disraëli 3,181 .... F 4
Dolbeau 8,766 .... E 1
Dollard-des-Ormeaux 39,940 . H 4
Donnacona 5,731 .... F 3
Dorion 5,749 .... C 4
Dorval 17,727 .... H 4
Dosquet 703 .... F 3
Douville .... D 4
Drummondville◎ 27,347 ...... E 4
Drummondville-Sud 9,220 .... E 4
Dunham 2,887 .... E 4
Durham-Sud 1,045 .... E 4
East Angus 4,016 .... F 4
East Broughton 1,397 .... F 3
East Broughton Station 1,302 . F 3
Eastman 612 .... E 4
Entrelacs 1,735 .... C 3
Farnham 6,498 .... E 4
Ferme-Neuve 2,266 .... B 3
Forestville 4,271 .... H 1
Frampton 684 .... G 3
Francoeur 1,422 .... F 3
Gaspé 17,261 .... D 1
Gatineau 74,988 .... B 4
Giffard .... J 3
Girardville 1,128 .... E 1
Gracefield 869 .... A 3
Granby 38,069 .... E 4
Grand'Mère 15,442 .... E 3
Grande-Rivière 4,420 .... D 2
Grandes-Bergeronnes 748 .... H 1
Grande-Vallée 700 .... D 1
Greenfield Park 18,527 ..... J 4
Grenville 1,417 .... C 4
Gros-Morne 672 .... C 1
Hampstead 7,598 .... H 4
Ham-Sud◎ 62 .... F 4
Hauterive 13,995 .... A 1
Hébertville 2,515 .... F 1
Hébertville-Station 1,442 .. F 1
Hemmingford 737 .... D 4
Henryville 595 .... D 4
Howick 639 .... D 4
Hudson 4,414 .... C 4
Hull◎ 56,225 .... B 4
Huntingdon◎ 3,018 .... C 4
Île-Perrot 5,945 .... G 4
Iberville◎ 8,587 .... D 4
Inverness◎ 329 .... F 3
Joliette◎ 16,987 .... D 3
Jonquière 60,354 .... F 1
Jonquière-Chicoutimi *135,172 ... F 1
Kingsey Falls 818 .... E 4
Kirkland 10,476 .... H 4
Knowlton (Lac-Brome)◎ 4,316 ... E 4
La Baie 20,935 .... G 1
Labelle 1,534 .... C 3
Lac-à-la-Croix 1,017 .... F 1
Lac-Alouette-Lac-Brière 1,356 D 4
Lac-au-Saumon 1,332 .... B 2
Lac-aux-Sables 838 .... E 3
Lac-Beaufort .... F 3
Lac-Bouchette 1,703 .... E 1
Lac-Carré 717 .... C 3
Lac-des-Écorces 766 .... B 3
Lac-Drolet 1,120 .... G 4
Lac-Etchemin 2,729 .... G 3
Lachenaie 8,631 .... D 4
Lachine 37,521 .... H 4
Lachute◎ 11,729 .... C 4
Lac-Mégantic◎ 6,119 .... G 4
Lacolle 1,319 .... D 4
Lac-Saint-Charles 5,837 .... H 3
Lafontaine 4,799 .... C 4
La Guadeloupe 1,692 .... F 4
La Malbaie◎ 4,030 .... G 2
Lambton 1,559 .... F 4
L'Annonciation 2,384 .... C 3
Lanoraie (Lanoraie-d'Autry) 1,613 ... D 4
La Pêche 4,977 .... B 4
La Pérade 1,039 .... E 3
La Pocatière 4,560 .... H 2
La Prairie◎ 10,627 .... J 4
La Providence .... E 4
Larouche 662 .... F 1
La Salle 76,299 .... H 4
L'Ascension 1,287 .... F 1
L'Assomption◎ 4,844 .... D 4
La Station-du-Coteau 892 ... C 4
Laterrière 788 .... F 1
La Tuque 11,556 .... E 2
Laurentides 1,947 .... D 4
Laurier-Station 1,123 ...... F 3
Laurierville 939 .... F 3
Lauzon 13,362 .... J 3
Laval 268,335 .... H 4
Lavaltrie 2,053 .... D 4
L'Avenir 1,116 .... E 4
Lawrenceville 562 .... E 4
Le Moyne 6,137 .... J 4
L'Épiphanie 2,971 .... D 4
Léry 2,239 .... H 4
Lévis 17,895 .... J 3
Lennoxville 3,922 .... F 4
Les Méchins 803 .... B 1
Linière 1,168 .... G 3
L'Islet 1,070 .... G 2
L'Islet-sur-Mer 774 .... G 2
L'Isle-Verte 1,142 .... G 1
Longueuil◎ 124,320 .... J 4
Loretteville◎ 15,060 .... H 3
Lorraine 6,881 .... H 4
Louiseville◎ 3,735 .... E 3
Luceville 1,524 .... J 1
Lyster 830 .... F 3
Magog 13,604 .... E 4
Maniwaki◎ 5,424 .... B 3
Manseau 626 .... E 3
Maple Grove 2,009 .... H 4
Maria 1,178 .... C 2
Marieville◎ 4,877 .... D 4
Mascouche 20,345 .... H 4
Maskinongé 1,005 .... E 3
Masson 4,264 .... B 4
Massueville 671 .... E 4
Matane◎ 13,612 .... B 1
Matapédia 586 .... B 2
Melocheville 1,892 .... C 4
Mercier 6,352 .... H 4
Metabetchouan 3,406 .... F 1
Mirabel◎ 14,080 .... H 4
Mistassini 6,682 .... E 1
Montauban 557 .... E 3
Mont-Carmel 807 .... H 2
Montcerf 570 .... A 3
Montebello 1,229 .... B 4
Mont-Joli 6,359 .... J 1
Mont-Laurier◎ 8,405 .... B 3
Mont-Louis 756 .... C 1
Montmagny◎ 12,405 .... G 3
Montréal◎ 980,354 .... H 4
Montréal *2,828,349 .... H 4
Montréal-Est 3,778 .... J 4
Montréal-Nord 94,914 .... H 4
Mont-Rolland 1,517 .... C 4
Mont-Royal 19,247 .... H 4
Mont-Saint-Hilaire 10,066 .. D 4
Morin Heights 592 .... C 4
Murdochville 3,396 .... C 1
Nantes 1,167 .... F 4

Agriculture, Industry and Resources

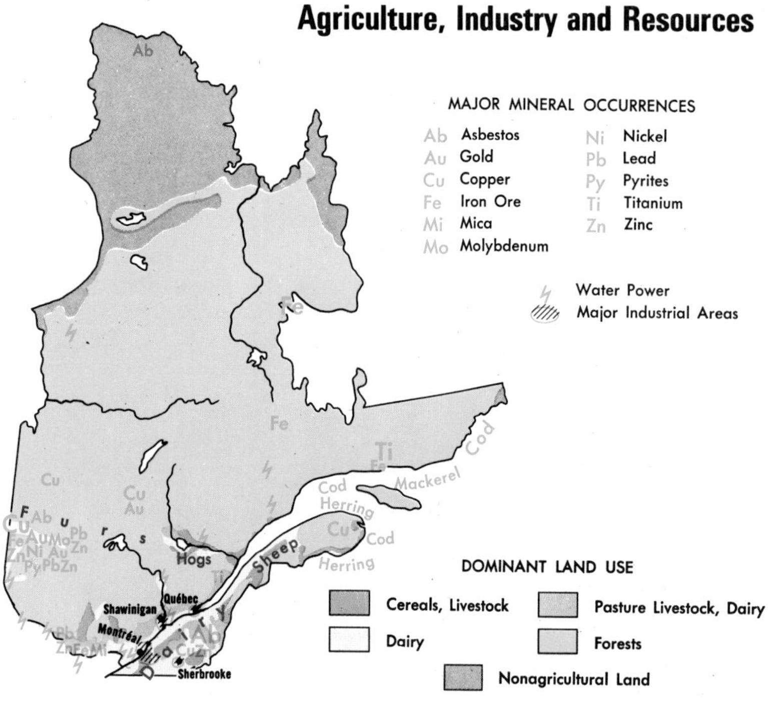
MAJOR MINERAL OCCURRENCES
Ab Asbestos
Au Gold
Cu Copper
Fe Iron Ore
Mi Mica
Mo Molybdenum
Ni Nickel
Pb Lead
Py Pyrites
Ti Titanium
Zn Zinc
Water Power
Major Industrial Areas
DOMINANT LAND USE
Cereals, Livestock
Pasture Livestock, Dairy
Dairy
Forests
Nonagricultural Land
Cod
Mackerel
Herring
Sheep
Hogs
Québec
Shawinigan
Montréal
Sherbrooke

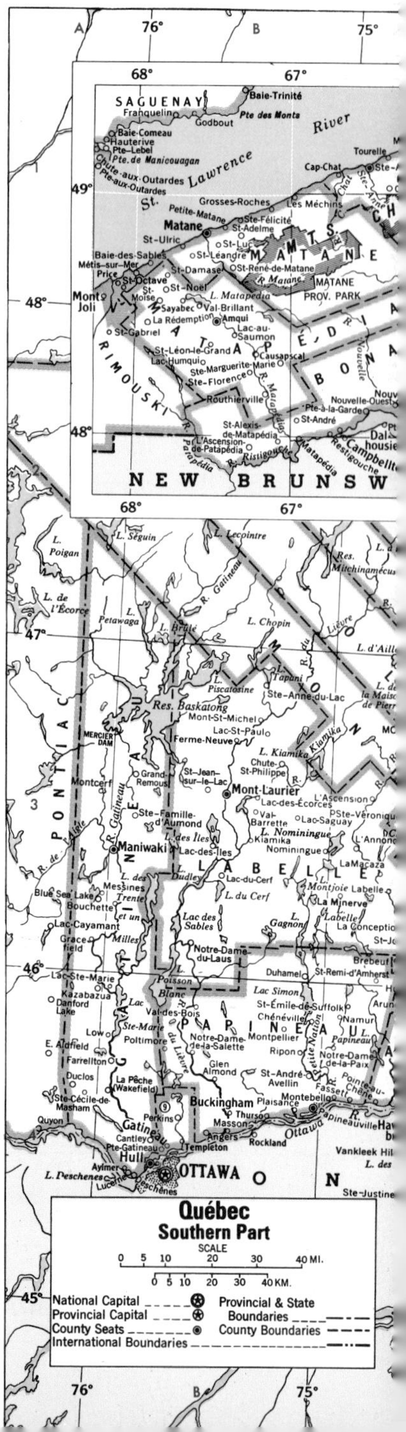
Québec
Southern Part
SCALE
0 5 10 20 30 40 MI.
0 5 10 20 30 40 KM.
National Capital
Provincial Capital
County Seats
International Boundaries
Provincial & State Boundaries
County Boundaries
OTTAWA
Hull
Gatineau
Buckingham
Maniwaki
Mont-Laurier
Matane
Mont-Joli
Baie-Comeau
Baie-Trinité
Cap-Chat
SAGUENAY
MATANE
RIMOUSKI
NEW BRUNSWICK
PONTIAC
LABELLE
PAPINEAU
GATINEAU
76°
75°
68°
67°

Napierville⊙ 2,343 .... D 4
Neuville 996................ F 3
New Carlisle⊙ 1,292......... D 2
New Richmond 4,257......... C 2
Nicolet 4,880 .... E 3
Nominingue 881 .... B 3
Normandin 4,041 .... E 1
North Hatley 689............ F 4
Notre-Dame-de-la-Doré 1,064 E 1
Notre-Dame-des-Laurentides . H 3
Notre-Dame-des-Prairies 6,150 .... D 3
Notre-Dame-du-Bon-Conseil 1,089 .... E 4
Notre-Dame-du-Lac⊙ 2,258 .. J 2
Nouvelle 669 .... C 2
Oka 1,538................... C 4
Omerville 1,398............. E 4
Ormstown 1,659 .... D 4
Orsainville .... H 3
Otis 673 .... G 1
Otterburn Park 4,268 .... D 4
Outremont 24,338............ H 4
Pabos 1,295................. D 2
Pabos-Mills 1,565 .... D 2
Papineauville⊙ 1,481 .... C 4
Paspébiac 1,914 .... D 2
Percé⊙ 4,839................ D 1
Petit-Cap 1,023 .... D 1
Petite-Matane 1,065......... B 1
Petit-Saguenay (Saint-François-d'Assise) 804 .... G 1
Pierrefonds 38,390 .... H 4
Pierreville 1,212 .... E 3
Pincourt 8,750.............. D 4
Pintendre 1,849............. J 3
Plaisance 748 .... B 4
Plessisville 7,249 .... F 3
Pohénégamooke 3,702 ...... H 2
Pointe-à-la-Croix 1,481 ...... C 2
Pointe-au-Père 796.......... J 1
Pointe-au-Pic 1,054 .... G 2
Pointe-aux-Outardes 1,056... A 1
Pointe-aux-Trembles 36,270 .. J 4
Pointe-Calumet 2,935 .... G 4
Pointe-Claire 24,571......... H 4
Pointe-du-Lac 5,359......... E 3
Pointe-Gatineau .... B 4
Pointe-Lebel 1,573 .... A 1
Pont-Rouge 3,580............ F 3
Port-Alfred 8,621............ G 1
Portneuf 1,333.............. F 3
Portneuf-sur-Mer (Rivière-Portneuf-sur-Mer) 1,255 ... H 1
Price 2,273................. A 1
Princeville 4,023 .... F 3
Proulxville 588............. E 3
Québec (cap.) 166,474 ...... H 3
Québec *576,075 .... H 3
Quyon 744 .... A 4
Rawdon 2,958 .... D 3
Repentigny 34,419 .... J 4
Richelieu 1,832............. D 4
Richmond⊙ 3,568............ E 4
Rigaud 2,268............... C 4
Rimouski⊙ 29,120 .... J 1
Rimouski-Est 2,506 .... J 1
Ripon 620.................. B 4
Rivière-à-Pierre 615 .... E 3
Rivière-au-Renard 2,211 ..... D 1
Rivière-Bleue 1,690 .... J 2
Rivière-Bois-Clair 604 .... F 3
Rivière-du-Loup⊙ 13,459..... H 2
Rivière-du-Moulin .... G 1
Rivière-Éternité 659 .... G 1
Rivière-Portneuf-Portneuf-sur-Mer 1,255 .... H 1
Robertsonville 1,987 .... F 3
Roberval⊙ 11,429............ E 1
Rock Island 1,179............ E 4
Rosemère 7,778 .... H 4
Rougemont 972.............. D 4
Roxboro 6,292.............. H 4
Roxton Falls 1,245 .... E 4
Sacré-Coeur-de-Saguenay 1,678 .... H 1
Saint-Adelme 618........... B 1
Saint-Adelphe 1,159......... E 3
Saint-Adolphe-d'Howard 1,686..................... C 4
Saint-Adrien 597............ F 4
Saint-Agapitville 2,954....... F 3
Saint-Aimé-des-Lacs 861 .... G 2
Saint-Alban 673............. E 3
Saint-Alexandre-de-Kamouraska 1,048........ H 2
Saint-Alexis-des-Monts 1,984. D 3
Saint-Amable 2,424 .... J 4
Saint-Ambroise 3,606........ F 1
Saint-Anaclet 1,377 .... J 1
Saint-André-Avellin 1,312 .... B 4
Saint-André-Est 1,293 .... C 4
Saint-Anselme 1,808 .... F 3
Saint-Antoine 7,012 .... H 4
Saint-Antonin 941........... H 2
Saint-Aubert 884............ G 2
Saint-Augustin-de-Québec 2,475 .... E 3
Saint-Basile-Sud 1,719 ...... F 3
Saint-Basile-le-Grand 7,658 .. J 4
Saint-Benjamin 1,027........ G 3
Saint-Bernard 585 .... F 3
Saint-Bernard-sur-Mer 711 ... G 2
Saint-Boniface-de-Shawinigan 3,164 .... D 3
Saint-Bruno 2,580........... F 1
Saint-Bruno-de-Montarville 22,880 .... J 4
Saint-Camille-de-Bellechasse 1,744 .... G 3
Saint-Casimir 1,133 .... E 3
Saint-Césaire 2,935 .... D 4
Saint-Charles 1,019 .... G 3
Saint-Charles-de-Mandeville 1,392 .... D 3
Saint-Chrysostome 1,018 .... D 4
Saint-Côme 660 .... D 3
Saint-Constant 9,938 .... H 4
Saint-Cyprien 860........... J 2
Saint-Cyrille 1,041 .... E 4
Saint-Damien-de-Buckland 1,522 .... G 3
Saint-David 5,380........... J 3
Saint-David-de-Falardeau 1,876 .... F 1
Saint-Denis 861 .... D 4

AREA 594,857 sq. mi. (1,540,680 sq. km.)
POPULATION 6,438,403
CAPITAL Québec
LARGEST CITY Montréal
HIGHEST POINT Mont D'Iberville 5,420 ft. (1,652 m.)
SETTLED IN 1608
ADMITTED TO CONFEDERATION 1867
PROVINCIAL FLOWER White Garden Lily

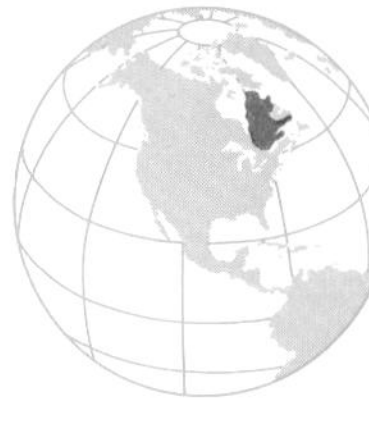

Saint-Dominique 2,068 ...... E 4
Saint-Donat-de-Montcalm 1,521 .... C 3
Sainte-Adèle 4,675.......... C 4
Sainte-Agathe 709 .... F 3
Sainte-Agathe-des-Monts 5,641 .... C 3
Sainte-Anne-de-Beaupré 3,292 .... F 2
Sainte-Anne-de-Bellevue 3,981 .... H 4
Sainte-Anne-des-Monts⊙ 6,062 .... C 1
Sainte-Anne-des-Plaines 4,258 .... H 4
Sainte-Anne-du-Lac 686 ..... B 3
Sainte-Aurélie 1,045......... G 3
Sainte-Blandine 849......... J 1
Sainte-Catherine 1,474 ...... F 3
Sainte-Claire 1,566.......... G 3
Sainte-Croix⊙ 1,814......... F 3
Sainte-Félicité 711 .... B 1
Sainte-Foy 68,883 .... H 3
Sainte-Geneviève 2,573 ..... H 4
Sainte-Geneviée-de-Batiscan⊙ 356 .... E 3
Sainte-Hélène-de-Bagot 1,328.................... E 4
Sainte-Hénédine⊙ 639....... F 3
Sainte-Julie-de-Verchères 14,243 .... J 4
Sainte-Julienne⊙ 750........ D 4
Sainte-Justine 1,080 .... G 3
Saint-Élie 639 .... E 3
Saint-Elzéar 743 .... F 3
Sainte-Marie 8,937.......... G 3
Sainte-Martine⊙ 2,196....... D 4
Saint-Émile 5,216........... H 3
Sainte-Monique 705......... F 1
Sainte-Pétronille 982 .... J 3
Sainte-Perpétue-de-L'Islet 1,232 .... H 2
Saint-Éphrem-de-Tring 973 ... G 3
Saint-Épiphane 647 .... H 2
Sainte-Pudentienne 866 ..... E 4
Sainte-Rosalie 2,862 .... E 4
Saint-Esprit 1,068........... D 4
Sainte-Thérèse 18,750....... H 4
Sainte-Thérèse-Ouest (Boisbriand) 13,471 .... H 4
Sainte-Thècle 1,703 .... E 3
Saint-Étienne-de-Grès 845 ... E 3
Saint-Étienne-de-Lauzon 1,218 .... J 3

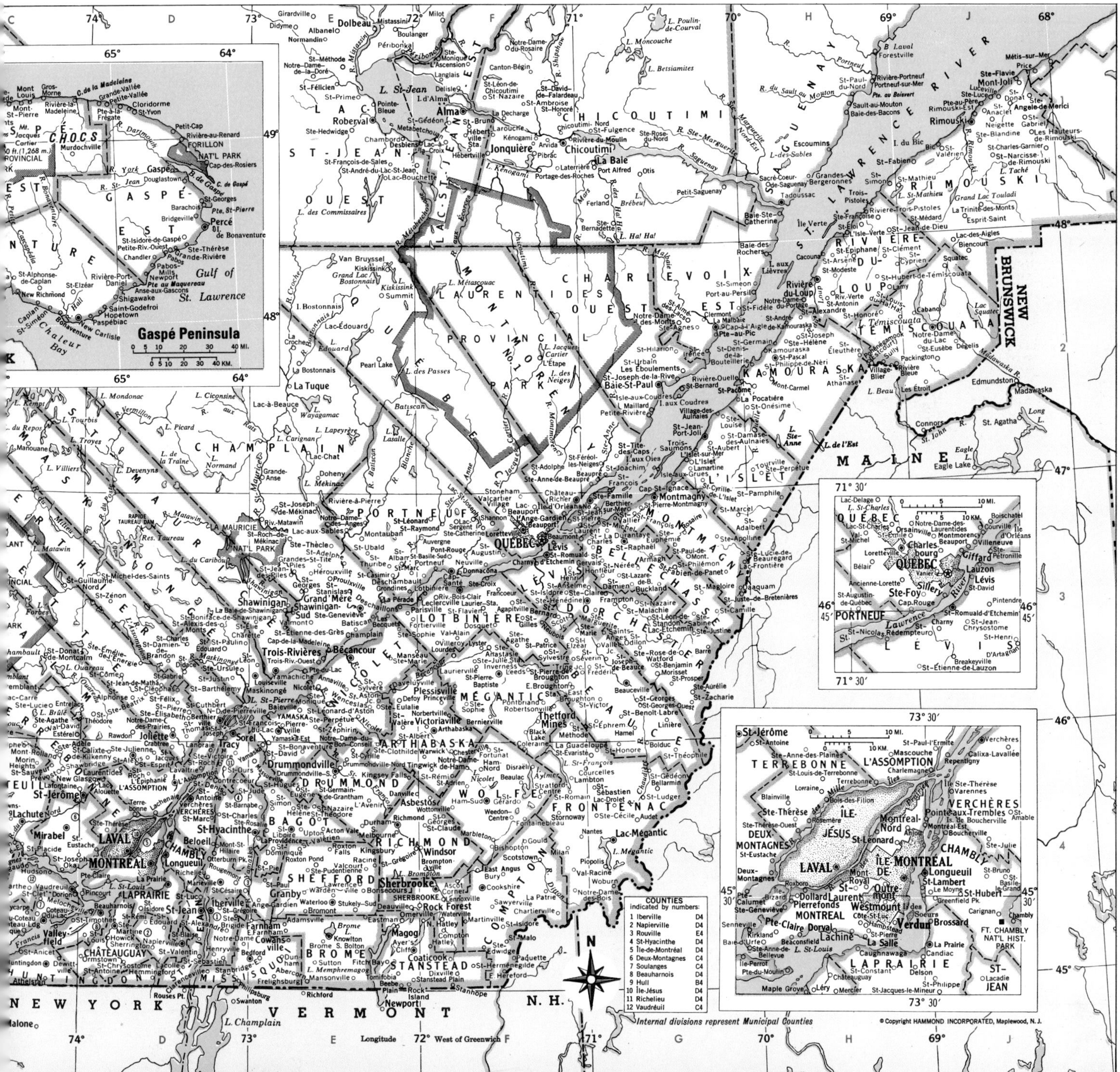

Gaspé Peninsula
Gulf of St. Lawrence
Chaleur Bay
NEW BRUNSWICK
MAINE
NEW YORK
VERMONT
N.H.
ST. LAWRENCE RIVER
Québec
Montréal
Trois-Rivières
Sherbrooke
Chicoutimi
Rimouski
COUNTIES indicated by numbers:
1 Iberville D4
2 Napierville D4
3 Rouville E4
4 St-Hyacinthe D4
5 Île-de-Montréal D4
6 Deux-Montagnes C4
7 Soulanges C4
8 Beauharnois C4
9 Hull B4
10 Île-Jésus D4
11 Richelieu D4
12 Vaudreuil C4
Longitude 72° West of Greenwich
Internal divisions represent Municipal Counties
© Copyright HAMMOND INCORPORATED, Maplewood, N. J.

Saint-Eustache 29,716......H 4
Saint-Fabien 1,361......J 1
Saint-Félicien 9,058......E 1
Saint-Félix-de-Valois 1,462...D 3
Saint-Ferréol-les-Neiges
　1,758......G 2
Saint-Flavien 734......F 3
Saint-François-de-Sales 831..E 1
Saint-François-du-Lac® 942...E 3
Saint-Fulgence 950......G 1
Saint-Gabriel 3,161......D 3
Saint-Gabriel-de-Rimouski
　779......J 1
Saint-Gédéon, Frontenac
　1,569......G 4
Saint-Gédéon, Lac-St-Jean-E.
　1,000......F 1
Saint-Georges, Beauce
　10,342......G 3
Saint-Georges, Champlain
　3,344......E 3
Saint-Georges-Ouest 6,378...G 3
Saint-Germain-de-Grantham
　1,373......E 4
Saint-Gervais 973......F 3
Saint-Gilles 912......F 3
Saint-Grégoire (Mont-St-
　Grégoire) 740......D 4
Saint-Henri 1,970......F 3
Saint-Honoré, Beauce 1,116..G 4
Saint-Honoré, Chicoutimi
　1,790......F 1
Saint-Hubert 60,573......J 4
Saint-Hubert-de-Témiscouata
　871......J 2
Saint-Hyacinthe® 38,246.....D 4
Saint-Isidore 811......E 4
Saint-Isidore-de-Laprairie 769 D 4
Saint-Jacques 2,152......D 3
Saint-Jacques-le-Mineur
　1,203......H 4
Saint-Jean-Chrysostome
　6,930......J 3
Saint-Jean-de-Dieu 1,377....J 1
Saint-Jean-de-Matha 931.....D 3
Saint-Jean-Port-Joli 1,813...G 2
Saint-Jean-sur-Richelieu®
　35,640......D 4
Saint-Jérôme 25,123......H 4
Saint-Joachim 1,139......F 3
Saint-Joseph-de-Beauce
　3,216......G 3
Saint-Joseph-de-Sorel 2,545..D 3
Saint-Jovite 3,841......C 3
Saint-Lambert 20,557......J 4
Saint-Laurent 65,900......H 4

Saint-Lazare 731......G 3
Saint-Léonard 79,429......H 4
Saint-Léonard-d'Aston 992...E 3
Saint-Léon-de-Chicoutimi 749 F 1
Saint-Léon-de-Standon 816...F 4
Saint-Léonard-le-Grand 722..B 2
Saint-Liboire® 746......E 4
Saint-Louis-de-Gonzague
　615......D 4
Saint-Louis-de-Terrebonne
　14,172......H 4
Saint-Louis-du-Ha! Ha! 809..J 2
Saint-Luc 8,815......D 4
Saint-Luc-de-Matane 598....B 1
Saint-Marc-des-Carrières
　2,822......E 3
Saint-Méthode-de-Frontenac
　925......F 3
Saint-Michel-de-Bellechasse
　963......G 3
Saint-Michel-des-Saints
　1,584......D 3
Saint-Nazaire-de-Chicoutimi
　962......F 1
Saint-Nérée 970......G 3
Saint-Nicolas 5,074......H 3
Saint-Noël 666......B 1
Saint-Odilon 580......G 3
Saint-Omer 718......C 2
Saint-Ours 625......D 4
Saint-Pacôme 1,998......G 2
Saint-Pamphile 3,428......H 3
Saint-Pascal 2,763......H 2
Saint-Paul-de-Montminy 602..G 3
Saint-Paulin 663......D 3
Saint-Paul-l'Ermite (Le
　Gardeur) 8,312......J 4
Saint-Philippe-de-Néri 715...H 2
Saint-Pie 1,725......E 4
Saint-Pierre 5,305......H 4
Saint-Pierre-d'Orléans 880...G 3
Saint-Polycarpe 602......C 4
Saint-Prime 2,522......E 1
Saint-Prosper-de-Dorchester
　2,150......G 3
Saint-Raphaël® 1,346......G 3
Saint-Raymond 3,605......F 3
Saint-Rédempteur 4,463.....J 3
Saint-Régis 1,370......C 4
Saint-Rémi 5,146......D 4
Saint-Roch-de-l'Achigan
　1,160......D 4
Saint-Roch-de-Richelieu®
　1,650......D 3
Saint-Romuald-d'Etchemin®
　9,849......J 3

Saint-Sauveur-des-Monts
　2,348......C 4
Saint-Siméon 1,152......G 2
Saint-Simon 602......H 1
Saint-Stanislas 1,443......E 3
Saint-Sylvère 1,006......E 3
Saint-Timothée 2,113......D 4
Saint-Tite 3,031......E 3
Saint-Tite-des-Caps 626.....G 2
Saint-Ubald 1,605......E 3
Saint-Ulric 792......B 1
Saint-Urbain-de-Charlevoix
　1,079......G 2
Saint-Victor 1,104......G 3
Saint-Zacharie 1,284......G 3
Saint-Zotique 1,774......C 4
Sault-au-Mouton 828......H 1
Sawyerville 939......F 4
Sayabec 1,721......B 2
Scotstown 762......F 4
Senneville 1,221......H 4
Shannon 3,488......F 3
Shawbridge 942......C 4
Shawinigan 23,011......E 3
Shawinigan-Sud 11,325......E 3
Shawville 1,608......A 4
Sherbrooke® 74,075......E 4
Sherrington 614......D 4
Sillery 12,825......J 3
Sorel® 20,347......D 4
Squatec 1,000......J 2
Stanstead Plain 1,093......F 4
Sutton 1,599......E 4
Tadoussac® 900......H 1
Templeton......B 4
Terrebonne 11,769......H 4
Thetford Mines 19,965......F 3
Thurso 2,780......B 4
Tourelle (Tourelle-Grand-
　Tourelle) 942......C 1
Tourville 659......H 2
Tracy 12,843......D 3
Tring-Jonction 1,315......F 3
Trois-Pistoles 4,445......H 1
Trois-Rivières 50,466......E 3
Trois-Rivières *111,453......E 3
Trois-Rivières-Ouest 13,107..E 3
Upton 926......E 4
Val-Barrette 609......B 3
Val-Brillant 687......B 1
Valcourt 2,601......E 4
Val-David 2,336......C 3
Valleyfield (Salaberry-de-
　Valleyfield) 29,574......C 4
Vanier 10,725......J 3

Varennes 8,764......J 4
Vaudreuil® 7,608......C 4
Verchères 4,473......J 4
Verdun 61,287......H 4
Victoriaville 21,838......F 3
Villeneuve......J 3
Warwick 2,847......E 4
Waterloo® 4,664......E 4
Waterville 1,397......E 4
Weedon-Centre 1,263......F 4
Westmount 20,480......H 4
Wickham 2,043......E 4
Windsor 5,233......E 4
Wottonville 673......F 4
Yamachiche® 1,258......E 3

OTHER FEATURES

Alma (isl.)......F 1
Aylmer (lake)......F 4
Baskatong (res.)......B 3
Batiscan (riv.)......E 2
Bécancour (riv.)......E 3
Bonaventure (isl.)......D 1
Bonaventure (riv.)......C 2
Brome (lake)......E 4
Brompton (lake)......E 4
Cascapédia (riv.)......C 1
Chaleur (bay)......C 2
Champlain (lake)......D 4
Chaudière (riv.)......F 3
Chic-Chocs (mts.)......C 1
Chicoutimi (riv.)......F 1
Coudres (isl.)......G 2
Deschênes (lake)......B 4
Deux Montagnes (lake)......C 4
Ditton (riv.)......F 4
Forillon Nat'l Park......D 1
Fort Chambly Nat'l Hist. Park..J 4
Gaspé (bay)......D 2
Gaspé (cape)......D 2
Gaspé (pen.)......D 2
Gaspésie Prov. Park......C 1
Gatineau (riv.)......B 3
Îles (lake)......B 3
Jacques-Cartier (mt.)......C 1
Jacques-Cartier (riv.)......F 1
Kénogami (lake)......F 1
Kiamika (lake)......B 3
La Maurice Nat'l Park......D 3
Laurentides Prov. Park......F 2
Lièvre (riv.)......B 4
Lièvres (isl.)......H 2
Maskinongé (riv.)......D 3
Matane (riv.)......B 1
Matane Prov. Park......B 1

Matapédia (riv.)......B 2
Mégantic (lake)......G 4
Memphremagog (lake)......E 4
Mercier (dam)......A 3
Métabetchouane (riv.)......F 1
Mille Îles (riv.)......H 4
Montmorency (riv.)......F 3
Mont-Tremblant Prov. Park...C 3
Nicolet (riv.)......E 3
Nominingue (lake)......B 3
Nord (riv.)......C 4
Orléans (isl.)......F 3
Ottawa (riv.)......B 4
Ouareau (riv.)......D 3
Ouelle (riv.)......H 2
Patapédia (riv.)......B 2
Péribonca (riv.)......F 1
Petite Nation (riv.)......B 4
Prairies (riv.)......H 4
Rimouski (riv.)......J 1
Ristigouche (riv.)......B 2
Saguenay (riv.)......G 1
Sainte-Anne (lake)......F 3
Sainte-Anne (riv.)......G 2
Saint-François (lake)......E 4
Saint-François (riv.)......E 4
Saint-Jean (lake)......E 1
Saint Lawrence (gulf)......D 2
Saint Lawrence (riv.)......H 1
Saint-Louis (lake)......H 4
Saint-Maurice (riv.)......E 3
Saint-Pierre (lake)......E 3
Shawinigan (riv.)......E 3
Shipshaw (riv.)......F 1
Soeurs (isl.)......H 4
Témiscouata (lake)......H 2
Tremblant (lake)......C 3
Trente et un Milles (lake)....B 3
Verte (isl.)......H 1
Yamaska (riv.)......E 4
York (riv.)......D 1

®County seat.
*Population of metropolitan area.

QUÉBEC, NORTHERN

INTERNAL DIVISIONS

Abitibi (county) 93,529......B 2
Abitibi (terr.)......B 3
Berthier (county) 31,096......C 3
Bonaventure (county) 40,487.D 3
Champlain (county) 119,595..C 3
Charlevoix-Est (co.) 17,448...C 3

Charlevoix-Ouest (county)
　14,172......C 3
Chicoutimi (county) 174,441..C 3
Gaspé-Est (county) 41,173...E 3
Gaspé-Ouest (county) 18,943 D 3
Gatineau (county) 54,229....B 3
Joliette (county) 60,384......C 3
Lac-Saint-Jean-Est (county)
　47,891......C 3
Lac-Saint-Jean-Ouest
　(county) 62,952......C 3
Maskinongé (county) 20,763..C 3
Matane (county) 29,955......D 3
Matapédia (county) 23,715...D 3
Mistassini (terr.)......B 3
Montcalm (county) 27,557...B 3
Montmorency No. 1 (county)
　23,048......C 3
Nouveau-Québec (terr.)......E 1
Pontiac (county) 20,283......B 3
Portneuf (county) 58,843....C 3
Québec (county) 458,980....C 3
Rimouski (county) 69,099....D 3
Saguenay (county) 115,881..D 2
Saint-Maurice (co.) 107,703..C 3
Témiscamingue (co.) 52,570..B 3

CITIES and TOWNS

Alma® 26,322......C 3
Amos® 9,421......B 3
Baie-Comeau 12,866......D 3
Baie-du-Poste 1,690......C 2
Chicoutimi® 60,064......C 3
Gaspé 17,261......D 3
Hauterive 13,995......D 3
Jonquière 60,354......C 3
Lévis 17,895......C 3
La Tuque 11,556......C 3
Manicouagan......D 2
Maniwaki® 5,424......B 3
Matane® 13,612......D 3
Mistassini (Baie-du-Poste)
　1,690......C 2
Mont-Laurier® 8,405......C 3
Montmagny 12,405......C 3
New Carlisle® 781......E 3
Nouveau-Comptoir......B 2
Percé® 4,839......D 3
Port-Cartier-Ouest......D 3
Port-Menier® 275......D 3
Povungnituk 745......E 1
Québec (cap.)® 166,474....C 3
Rimouski® 29,120......D 3
Rivière-au-Tonnerre 480.....D 2
Rivière-du-Loup 13,459......D 3

Rouyn 17,224......B 3
Sept-Îles 29,262......D 2
Seven Islands (Sept-Îles)
　29,262......D 2
Shawinigan 23,011......C 3
Tadoussac 900......C 3
Val d'Or 21,371......B 3
Ville-Marie 2,651......B 3

OTHER FEATURES

Allard (lake)......E 2
Anticosti (isl.)......E 3
Baleine, Grand Rivière de la
　(riv.)......B 1
Bell (riv.)......B 3
Betsiamites (riv.)......C 2
Bienville (lake)......C 2
Broadback (riv.)......B 2
Cabonga (res.)......B 3
Caniapiscau (riv.)......C 1
Eastmain (riv.)......B 2
Eau Claire (lake)......C 1
Feuilles (riv.)......C 1
Gaspésie Prov. Park......F 2
George (riv.)......D 1
Gouin (res.)......B 3
Grande Rivière, La (riv.).....B 2
Honguedo (passage)......E 3
Hudson (bay)......A 1
Hudson (str.)......C 1
Jacques-Cartier (passage)...E 3
James (bay)......A 2
Koksoak (riv.)......D 1
Laurentides Prov. Park......C 3
Louis-XIV (pt.)......B 2
Manicouagan (res.)......D 2
Minto (lake)......C 1
Mistassini (riv.)......C 2
Mistassini (lake)......C 2
Moisie (riv.)......D 2
Natashquan (riv.)......E 2
Nottaway (riv.)......B 2
Nouveau-Québec (crater)....F 1
Otish (mts.)......C 2
Ottawa (riv.)......B 3
Péribonca (riv.)......C 2
Plétipi (lake)......C 2
Saguenay (riv.)......C 3
Saint-Jean (lake)......C 3
Saint Lawrence (gulf)......D 3
Saint Lawrence (riv.)......D 3
Ungava (pen.)......E 1

®County seat.
*Population of metropolitan area.

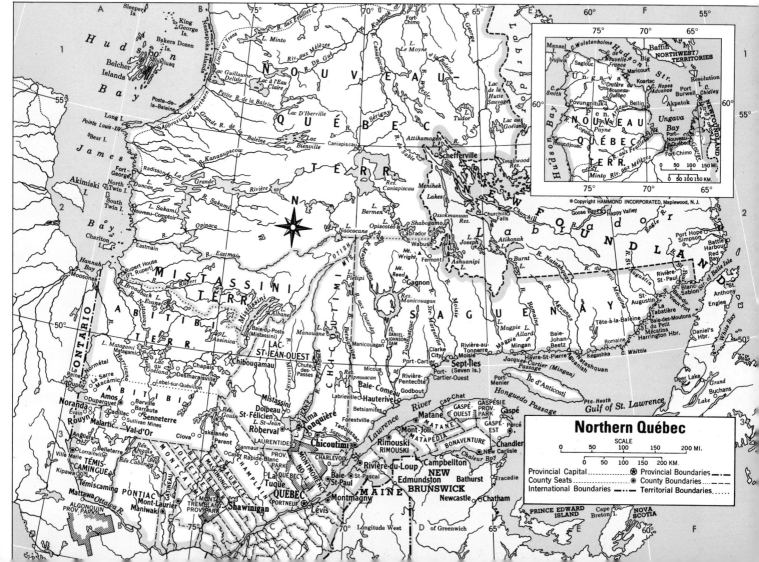

Northern Québec

SCALE
0　50　100　150　200 MI.
0　50　100　150　200 KM.

Provincial Capital ....★
County Seats ....◉
International Boundaries ...▬ ▬ ▬
Provincial Boundaries ▬ · ▬ · ▬
County Boundaries ▬ ─ ▬ ─ ▬
Territorial Boundaries ....

© Copyright HAMMOND INCORPORATED, Maplewood, N. J.

ONTARIO, NORTHERN

INTERNAL DIVISIONS

Algoma (terr. dist.) 133,553...D 3
Cochrane (terr. dist.) 96,875...D 2
Kenora (terr. dist.) 59,421...C 2
Manitoulin (terr. dist.) 11,001...D 3
Nipissing (terr. dist.) 80,268...E 3
Parry Sound (terr. dist.) 33,528...E 3
Rainy River (terr. dist.) 22,798 B 3
Renfrew (county) 87,484...E 3
Sudbury (reg. munic.) 159,779...D 3
Sudbury (terr. dist.) 27,068...D 3
Thunder Bay (terr. dist.) 153,997...C 3
Timiskaming (terr. dist.) 41,288...D 3

CITIES and TOWNS

Chalk River 1,010...E 3
Elliot Lake 16,723...D 3
Fort Albany 482...D 2
Fort Frances 8,906...B 3
Kapuskasing 12,014...D 3
Kenora 9,817...B 3
Kirkland Lake 12,219...D 3
Moose Factory 1,452...D 2
Moosonee 1,433...D 2
Nickel Centre 12,318...D 3
North Bay 51,268...E 3
Pembroke 14,026...E 3
Sault Sainte Marie 82,697...D 3
Sudbury 91,829...D 3
Thunder Bay 112,486...C 3
Timmins 46,114...D 3
Valley East 20,433...D 3

OTHER FEATURES

Abitibi (lake)...E 3
Abitibi (riv.)...D 2
Albany (riv.)...C 2
Algonquin Prov. Park...E 3
Asheweig (riv.)...C 2
Attawapiskat (lake)...C 2
Attawapiskat (riv.)...C 2
Basswood (lake)...B 3
Berens (riv.)...A 2
Big Trout (lake)...B 2
Black Duck (riv.)...C 1
Bloodvein (riv.)...A 2
Caribou (isl.)...C 3

Cobham (riv.)...A 2
Eabamet (lake)...C 2
Ekwan (riv.)...C 2
English (riv.)...B 2
Fawn (riv.)...C 2
Finger (lake)...B 2
Georgian (bay)...D 3
Hannah (bay)...D 2
Henrietta Maria (cape)...D 1
Hudson (bay)...D 1
Huron (lake)...D 2
James (bay)...D 2
Kapiskau (riv.)...D 2
Kapuskasing (riv.)...D 3
Kenogami (riv.)...C 2
Kesagami (riv.)...E 2
Lake of the Woods (lake)...B 3
Lake Superior Prov. Park...D 3
Little Current (riv.)...C 2
Long (lake)...C 3
Manitoulin (isl.)...D 3
Mattagami (riv.)...D 2
Michipicoten (riv.)...D 3
Mille Lacs (lake)...B 3
Missinaibi (lake)...D 2
Missinaibi (riv.)...D 2
Missisa (lake)...C 2
Nipigon (lake)...C 3
Nipissing (lake)...E 3
North (chan.)...D 3
North Caribou (lake)...B 2
Nungesser (lake)...B 2
Ogidaki (mt.)...D 3
Ogoki (riv.)...C 2
Opazatika (riv.)...D 2
Opinnagau (riv.)...D 2
Otoskwin (riv.)...C 2
Ottawa (riv.)...E 3
Pipestone (riv.)...B 2
Polar Bear Prov. Park...D 1
Pukaskwa Prov. Park...C 3
Quetico Prov. Park...B 3
Rainy (lake)...B 3
Red (lake)...B 2
Sachigo (riv.)...B 2
Saganaga (lake)...B 3
Saint Ignace (isl.)...C 3
Saint Joseph (isl.)...D 3
Sandy (lake)...B 2
Savant (lake)...B 2
Seine (riv.)...B 2
Seul (lake)...B 2
Severn (lake)...B 2
Severn (riv.)...B 2
Shamattawa (riv.)...C 2
Shibogama (lake)...C 2

Sibley Prov. Park...C 3
Slate (isls.)...C 3
Stout (lake)...B 2
Superior (lake)...D 3
Sutton (lake)...D 2
Sutton (riv.)...D 1
Timagami (lake)...E 3
Timiskaming (lake)...E 3
Trout (lake)...B 2
Wabuk (pt.)...D 1
Winisk (lake)...C 2
Winisk (riv.)...C 2
Winnipeg (riv.)...A 2
Woods (lake)...B 3

ONTARIO

INTERNAL DIVISIONS

Algoma (terr. dist.) 133,553...J 5
Brant (county) 104,427...D 4
Bruce (county) 60,020...C 3
Cochrane (terr. dist.) 96,875...J 4
Dufferin (county) 31,145...D 3
Dundas (county) 18,946...J 2
Durham (reg. munic.) 283,639 F 3
Elgin (county) 69,707...C 5
Essex (county) 312,467...B 5
Frontenac (county) 108,133...H 3
Glengarry (county) 20,254...K 2
Grenville (county) 27,176...J 2
Grey (county) 73,824...D 3
Haldimand-Norfolk (reg. munic.) 89,456...E 5
Haliburton (county) 11,361...F 2
Halton (reg. munic.) 253,883...E 4
Hamilton-Wentworth (reg. munic.) 411,445...D 4
Hastings (county) 106,883...G 3
Huron (county) 56,127...C 4
Kenora (terr. dist.) 59,421...G 5
Kent (county) 107,022...B 5
Lambton (county) 123,445...B 5
Lanark (county) 45,676...H 3
Leeds (county) 53,765...H 3
Lennox and Addington (county) 33,040...G 3
Manitoulin (terr. dist.) 11,001...B 2
Middlesex (county) 318,184...C 4
Muskoka (dist. munic.) 38,370...E 3
Niagara (reg. munic.) 368,288 E 4
Nipissing (terr. dist.) 80,268...E 3
Northumberland (county) 64,966...G 3

Ottawa-Carleton (reg. munic.) 546,849...J 2
Oxford (county) 85,920...D 4
Parry Sound (terr. dist.) 33,528...D 2
Peel (reg. munic.) 490,731...E 4
Perth (reg. munic.) 66,096...C 4
Peterborough (county) 102,452...F 3
Prescott (county) 30,365...K 2
Prince Edward (county) 22,336...G 3
Rainy River (terr. dist.) 22,798 G 5
Renfrew (county) 87,484...G 2
Russell (county) 22,412...J 2
Simcoe (county) 225,071...E 3
Stormont (county) 61,927...K 2
Sudbury (reg. munic.) 159,779...K 6
Sudbury (terr. dist.) 27,068...J 5
Thunder Bay (terr. dist.) 153,997...H 5
Timiskaming (terr. dist.) 41,288...K 5
Toronto (metro. munic.) 2,137,395...K 4
Victoria (county) 47,854...F 3
Waterloo (reg. munic.) 305,496...D 4
Wellington (county) 129,432...D 4
York (county) 252,053...E 4

CITIES and TOWNS

Ailsa Craig 765...C 4
Ajax 25,475...E 4
Alban 342...D 2
Alexandria 3,271...K 2
Alfred 1,057...K 2
Alliston 4,712...E 3
Alvinston 736...B 5
Almonte 3,855...H 2
Amherstburg 5,685...A 5
Amherst View 6,110...H 3
Ancaster 14,428...D 4
Angus 3,085...E 3
Apsley 264...F 3
Arkona 473...C 4
Armstrong 378...H 4
Arnprior 5,828...H 2
Aroland 291...H 4
Arthur 1,700...D 4
Astorville 340...E 1
Athens 948...J 3
Atherley 366...E 3
Atikokan 4,452...G 5

Atwood 723...D 4
Aurora 16,267...J 3
Avonmore 273...K 2
Aylmer 5,254...C 5
Bala 577...E 2
Bancroft 2,329...G 2
Barrie 38,423...E 3
Barry's Bay 1,216...G 2
Batawa 430...G 3
Bath 1,071...H 3
Bayfield 649...C 4
Beachburg 682...H 2
Beachville 917...D 4
Beardmore 583...H 5
Beaverton 1,952...E 3
Beeton 1,989...E 3
Belle River 3,568...B 5
Belleville 34,881...G 3
Belmont 831...C 5
Bethany 365...F 3
Bewdley 508...F 3
Binbrook 306...E 4
Blackstock 720...F 3
Blenheim 4,044...C 5
Blind River 3,444...J 5
Bloomfield 718...G 4
Blyth 926...C 4
Bobcaygeon 1,625...F 3
Bonfield 540...E 1
Bothwell 915...C 5
Bourget 1,057...K 2
Bracebridge 9,063...E 2
Bradford 7,370...E 3
Braeside 492...H 2
Brampton 149,030...J 4
Brantford 74,315...D 4
Bridgenorth 1,633...F 3

Brigden 635...B 5
Brighton 3,147...G 3
Britt 419...D 2
Brockville 19,896...J 3
Bruce Mines 635...J 5
Brussels 962...C 4
Burford 1,461...D 4
Burgessville 302...D 4
Burk's Falls 922...E 2
Burlington 114,853...E 4
Cache Bay 665...D 1
Caesarea 551...F 3
Calabogie 256...H 2
Caledon 26,645...E 4
Callander 1,158...E 1
Cambridge 77,183...D 4
Campbellford 3,409...G 3
Cannington 1,623...E 3
Capreol 3,845...K 5
Caramat 265...H 5
Cardinal 1,753...J 2
Carleton Place 5,626...H 2
Carlisle 781...D 4
Carlsbad Springs 616...J 2
Carp 707...H 2
Cartier 590...J 5
Casselman 1,675...J 2
Castleton 346...F 3
Chalk River 1,010...G 1
Chapleau 3,243...J 5
Charing Cross 443...B 5
Chatham 40,952...B 5
Chatsworth 383...D 3
Cherry Valley 289...G 4
Chesley 1,840...C 3
Chesterville 1,430...J 2
Chute-à-Blondeau 365...K 2
City View...J 2
Clarence Creek 796...J 2
Clarksburg 508...D 3

Clifford 645...D 4
Clinton 3,081...C 4
Cobalt 1,759...K 5
Cobden 997...H 2
Coboconk 426...F 3
Cobourg 11,385...F 4
Cochrane 4,848...J 5
Colborne 1,796...G 4
Colchester 711...B 6
Coldwater 964...E 3
Collingwood 12,064...D 3
Comber 667...B 5
Conestogo 295...D 4
Consecon 295...G 3
Cookstown 918...E 3
Cornwall 46,144...K 2
Cottam 404...B 5
Courtland 647...D 5
Courtright 1,024...B 5
Crediton 370...C 4
Creemore 1,182...D 3
Crysler 540...J 2
Cumberland 518...J 2
Cumberland Beach-Bramshot-
Buena Vista 674...E 3
Dashwood 472...C 4
Deep River 5,095...G 1
Delaware 481...C 5
Delhi 4,043...D 5
Delta 360...H 3
Deseronto 1,740...G 3
Douglas 363...H 2
Drayton 809...D 4
Dresden 2,550...B 5
Drumbo 476...D 4
Dryden 6,640...G 4
Dublin 295...C 4
Dubreuilville 988...J 5
Dundalk 1,250...D 3
Dundas 19,586...D 4
Dungannon 284...C 4
Dunnville 11,353...E 5
Durham 2,458...D 3
Dutton 1,115...C 5
Earlton 1,028...K 5
East York 101,974...J 4
Echo Bay 786...J 5
Eden Mills 318...D 4
Eganville 1,245...G 2
Egmondville 465...C 4
Elgin 327...H 3
Elk Lake 526...K 5
Elliot Lake 16,723...B 1
Elmira 7,063...D 4
Elmvale 1,183...E 3
Elmwood 364...C 3
Elora 2,666...D 4
Embro 727...D 4
Embrun 1,883...J 2
Emeryville-Puce 1,611...F 5
Emo 762...F 5
Englehart 1,689...K 5
Enterprise 357...H 3
Erieau 430...C 5
Erin 2,313...D 4
Espanola 5,836...J 5
Essex 6,295...B 5
Etobicoke 298,713...J 4
Everett 570...E 3
Exeter 3,732...C 4
Fauquier 561...J 5
Fenelon Falls 1,701...F 3
Fergus 6,064...D 4
Field 462...J 5
Finch 353...J 2
Fingal 380...C 5
Fitzroy Harbour 446...H 2
Flesherton 565...D 3
Foleyet 484...J 5
Fordwich 365...C 4
Forest 2,671...C 4
Formosa 393...C 3
Fort Erie 24,096...E 5
Fort Frances 8,906...F 5
Foxboro 597...G 3
Frankford 1,919...G 3
Fraserdale 303...J 5
Freelton 307...D 4
Gananoque 4,863...H 3
Garden Village 270...E 1
Geraldton 2,956...H 5
Glencoe 1,694...C 5
Glen Miller 639...G 3
Glen Robertson 378...K 2
Glen Walter 710...K 2
Goderich 7,322...C 4
Gogama 652...J 5
Goodwood 335...E 3
Gore Bay 777...B 2
Gorrie 468...C 4
Grafton 409...G 4
Grand Bend 680...C 4
Grand Valley 1,226...D 4
Granton 315...C 4
Gravenhurst 8,532...E 3
Greely 567...J 2
Green Valley 459...K 2
Grimsby 15,797...E 4
Guelph 71,207...D 4

AREA 412,580 sq. mi. (1,068,582 sq. km.)
POPULATION 8,625,107
CAPITAL Toronto
LARGEST CITY Toronto
HIGHEST POINT in Timiskaming Dist.
  2,275 ft. (693 m.)
SETTLED IN 1749
ADMITTED TO CONFEDERATION 1867
PROVINCIAL FLOWER White Trillium

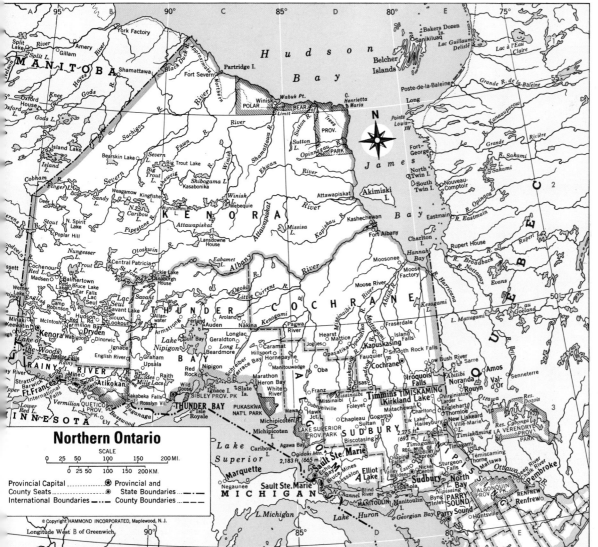

(continued on following page)

Haileybury⊙ 4,925 ....K 5	Iroquois 1,211 ....J 3	Lisle 265 ....E 3	Maynooth 277 ....G 2	Napanee 4,803 ....G 3	Ottawa⊙ (cap.), Canada	Port Rowan 811 ....D 5
Haldimand 16,866 ......E 5	Iroquois Falls 6,339 ....J 5	Listowel 5,026 ....D 4	McGregor 1,145 ....B 5	Navan 419 ....J 2	295,163 ....J 2	Port Stanley 1,891 ....D 5
Haliburton 1,443 ......F 2	Johnstown 789 ....J 3	Little Britain 265 ......F 3	McKerrow 260 ....C 1	Neustadt 511 ....D 3	Ottawa-Hull *717,978 ...J 2	Pottageville 266 ......J 3
Halton Hills 35,190 ...E 4	Kakabeka Falls 300 ....G 5	Little Current 1,507 ...B 2	Meaford 4,367 ....D 3	Newboro 260 ....H 3	Otterville 776 ....D 5	Powassan 1,169 ....E 1
Hamilton 306,434 .....E 4	Kanata 19,728 ....J 2	London 254,280 ......C 5	Melbourne 346 ....C 5	Newburgh 617 ....H 3	Owen Sound⊙ 19,883 ...D 3	Prescott 4,670 ....J 2
Hamilton *542,095 ....E 4	Kapuskasing 12,014 ...H 5	London *283,668 .....C 5	Merlin 745 ....B 5	Newbury 441 ....C 5	Paincourt 414 ....B 5	Princeton 462 ....D 5
Hanover 6,316 ....C 3	Kars 449 ....J 2	Longlac 2,431 ....H 5	Merrickville 984 .....J 3	Newcastle 32,229 .....F 4	Paisley 1,039 ....C 3	Puce-Emeryville 1,611 ...B 5
Harriston 1,954 ......D 4	Kearney 538 ....E 2	Long Sault 1,227 .....K 2	Metcalfe 687 ....J 2	New Hamburg 3,923 ...D 4	Pakenham 367 ....H 2	Rainy River 1,061 .....F 5
Harrow 2,274 ....C 5	Keene 353 ....F 3	L'Orignale 1,819 .....K 2	Midhurst 1,457 ....E 3	New Liskeard 5,551 ...K 5	Palmerston 1,989 .....D 4	Ramore 382 ....K 5
Harrowsmith 599 .....H 3	Keewatin 1,863 ....F 4	Lucan 1,616 ....C 4	Midland 12,132 ....D 3	Newmarket⊙ 29,753 ...E 3	Paris 7,485 ....D 4	Rayside-Balfour 15,017 ...K 5
Harwood 332 ....F 3	Kemptville 2,362 .....J 2	Lucknow 1,088 ....C 4	Mildmay 928 ....C 3	Niagara Falls 70,960 ...E 4	Parkhill 1,358 ....C 4	Red Rock 1,260 ....K 5
Hastings 975 ....F 3	Kenora⊙ 9,817 ....F 4	Lyn 518 ....J 3	Milford Bay 401 ......E 2	Niagara-on-the-Lake 12,186 ...E 4	Parry Sound⊙ 6,124 ...E 2	Renfrew 8,283 ....H 2
Havelock 1,385 ....F 3	Killaloe Station 634 ...G 2	Lynden 451 ....D 4	Millbank 337 ....D 4	Nickel Centre 12,318 ...D 1	Pefferlaw 857 ....E 3	Richards Landing 405 ...J 5
Hawkesbury 9,877 ....K 2	Killarney 433 ....C 2	Lynhurst 685 ....C 5	Millbrook 927 ....F 3	Nipigon 2,377 ....H 5	Pelham 11,104 ....E 4	Richmond 2,880 ......J 2
Hawkestone 275 ......E 3	Kincardine 5,778 .....C 3	MacGregor's Bay 861 ...E 2	Milton 28,067 ....E 4	Nobel 386 ....D 2	Pembroke⊙ 14,026 ....G 2	Richmond Hill 37,778 ...J 5
Hawk Junction 349 ...J 5	Kingsville 5,134 ......B 6	MacTier 647 ....E 2	Milverton 1,463 ......C 4	Noelville 702 ....D 1	Penetanguishene 5,315 ...D 3	Ridgetown 3,062 ......C 5
Hearst 5,533 ....J 4	Kinmount 262 ....E 2	Madawaska 264 ....F 2	Minaki 319 ....F 4	North Bay⊙ 51,268 ...E 1	Perth⊙ 5,655 ....H 3	Ripley 591 ....C 3
Hensall 973 ....C 4	Kirkland Lake 12,219 ...K 5	Madoc 1,249 ....F 3	Mindemoya 376 ....B 2	North Gower 838 ......J 2	Petawawa 5,520 ....G 2	River Valley 275 .....D 1
Hepworth 393 ....C 3	Kitchener⊙ 139,734 ...D 4	Maitland 667 ....J 3	Minden⊙ 838 ....F 3	North York 559,521 ...J 4	Peterborough⊙ 60,620 ...F 3	Rockcliffe Park 1,869 ...J 2
Hickson 263 ....D 4	Kitchener *287,801 ...D 4	Mallorytown 368 .....J 3	Mississauga 315,056 ...J 4	Norwich 2,117 ....D 5	Petrolia 4,234 ....B 5	Rockland 3,961 ....J 2
Highgate 435 ....C 5	Komoka 1,152 ....C 4	Manitouwadge 3,155 ...H 5	Mitchell 2,777 ....C 4	Norwood 1,278 ....F 3	Pickering 37,754 .....K 4	Rockwood 1,068 ......D 4
Hillsburgh 1,065 .....D 4	Lakefield 2,374 ......F 3	Manitowaning 518 ....C 2	Monkton 520 ....C 4	Nottawa 360 ....D 3	Picton⊙ 4,361 ....G 3	Rodney 1,007 ....C 5
Hillsdale 370 ....E 3	Lanark 753 ....H 3	Manotick-Hillside Gardens	Moonbeam 838 ....J 5	Oakville 75,773 ......E 4	Plantagenet 870 ......K 2	Rosslyn Village 362 ...K 5
Holland Landing 2,771 ...E 4	Lancaster 637 ....K 2	2,694 ....J 2	Mooretown 344 ....B 5	Oakwood 404 ....F 3	Plattsville 495 ....D 4	Round Lake Centre 255 ...G 2
Honey Harbour 505 ...E 2	Langton 348 ....D 5	Marathon 2,271 ......H 5	Moose Creek 393 .....K 2	Odessa 849 ....H 3	Point Edward 2,383 ...B 5	Russell 1,099 ....J 2
Hornepayne 1,848 ....J 5	Lansdowne 540 ....H 3	Markdale 1,289 ......D 3	Morewood 264 ....J 2	Oil City 266 ....B 5	Pontypool 759 ....F 3	Ruthven 649 ....B 6
Hudson 515 ....G 4	Larder Lake 1,084 ....K 5	Markham 37,037 .....K 4	Morpeth 284 ....C 5	Oil Springs 627 ......B 5	Port Burwell 655 .....B 5	Saint Albert 254 .....J 2
Huntsville 11,467 ....E 2	Latchford 397 ....K 5	Markstay 444 ....D 1	Mount Albert 1,165 ...E 3	Omemee 819 ....F 3	Port Carling 629 .....E 2	Saint Catharines⊙ 124,018 ...E 4
Huron Park 1,104 ....C 4	Leamington 12,528 ...B 5	Marmora 1,304 ....G 3	Mount Brydges 1,557 ...C 5	Onaping Falls 6,198 ...J 5	Port Colborne 19,225 ...E 5	Saint Catharines-Niagara
Ignace 2,499 ....G 5	Limoges 930 ....J 2	Martintown 388 ......K 2	Mount Forest 3,474 ...D 3	Opasatika 413 ....J 5	Port Elgin 6,131 ......C 3	*304,353 ....E 4
Ilderton 301 ....C 4	Lincoln 14,196 ....E 4	Massey 1,274 ....C 1	Mount Hope 557 ......E 4	Orangeville⊙ 13,740 ...D 4	Port Franks 547 ......C 4	Saint Charles 382 ....D 1
Ingersoll 8,494 ......D 4	Linden Beach 579 ....B 6	Matachewan 444 .....K 5	Munster 1,531 ....J 2	Orillia 23,955 ....E 3	Port Hope 9,992 ......F 4	Saint Clair Beach 2,845 ...B 5
Ingleside 1,400 ......J 2	Lindsay⊙ 13,596 .....F 3	Matheson 966 ....K 5	Nakina 936 ....H 4	Osgoode 1,138 ....J 2	Port Lambton 921 ....B 5	Saint Clements 890 ...D 4
Innerkip 715 ....D 4	Linwood 450 ....D 4	Mattawa 2,652 ....F 1	Nanticoke⊙ 19,816 ...E 5	Oshawa 117,519 ......F 4	Port McNicoll 1,883 ...E 3	Saint-Eugène 470 ....K 2
Inverhuron 438 ......C 3	Lion's Head 467 ......C 2	Mattice 803 ....J 5		Oshawa *154,217 .....F 4	Port Perry 4,712 .....E 3	Saint George 865 ....D 4
Iron Bridge 821 ......A 1		Maxville 836 ....K 2				Saint Isidore de Prescott 746 ...K 2

Saint Jacobs 1,189 . . . . D 4
Saint Mary's 4,883 . . . . C 4
Saint Thomas® 28,165 . . . . D 5
Saint Williams 442 . . . . D 5
Salem 825 . . . . D 4
Sarnia® 50,892 . . . . B 5
Sauble Beach 729 . . . . C 3
Sault Sainte Marie® 82,697 . . J 5
Scarborough 443,353 . . . . K 4
Schomberg 923 . . . . J 3
Schreiber 1,968 . . . . D 4
Scotland 600 . . . . D 4
Seaforth 2,114 . . . . C 4
Searchmont 384 . . . . J 5
Sebringville 579 . . . . C 4
Seeleys Bay 503 . . . . H 3
Shakespeare 602 . . . . C 4
Shallow Lake 418 . . . . C 3
Shannonville 314 . . . . G 3
Shanty Bay 358 . . . . E 3
Sharbot Lake 495 . . . . H 3
Shedden 292 . . . . C 5
Shelburne 2,862 . . . . D 5
Simcoe® 14,326 . . . . D 5
Sioux Lookout 3,074 . . . . G 4
Sioux Narrows 394 . . . . F 5
Smithfield 349 . . . . G 3
Smiths Falls 8,831 . . . . H 3
Smithville 1,936 . . . . E 5
Smooth Rock Falls 2,352 . . . . J 5
Sombra 420 . . . . B 5
Southampton 2,830 . . . . C 3
South Mountain 285 . . . . J 3
South River 1,109 . . . . E 2
Spanish 1,063 . . . . J 5
Sparta 283 . . . . C 5

Spencerville 438 . . . . J 3
Springfield 555 . . . . C 5
Springford 309 . . . . D 5
Stayner 2,530 . . . . E 3
Stirling 1,638 . . . . G 3
Stittsville 2,652 . . . . J 2
Stoney Creek 36,762 . . . . E 4
Stoney Point 1,090 . . . . B 5
Straffordville 752 . . . . D 5
Stratford® 26,262 . . . . C 4
Strathroy 8,748 . . . . C 4
Sturgeon Falls 6,045 . . . . E 1
Sudbury® 91,829 . . . . K 5
Sudbury *149,923 . . . . K 5
Sunderland 703 . . . . E 3
Sundridge 734 . . . . E 2
Sydenham 595 . . . . H 3
Tamworth 402 . . . . H 3
Tara 687 . . . . C 3
Tavistock 1,885 . . . . D 4
Tecumseh 6,364 . . . . B 5
Teeswater 1,026 . . . . C 3
Terrace Bay 2,639 . . . . H 5
Thamesford 1,920 . . . . C 4
Thamesville 961 . . . . C 4
Thedford 694 . . . . C 4
Thessalon 1,620 . . . . J 5
Thornbury 1,435 . . . . D 3
Thorndale 581 . . . . C 4
Thornton 414 . . . . E 3
Thorold 15,412 . . . . E 4
Thunder Bay® 112,486 . . . . . . H 5
Thunder Bay *121,379 . . . . . . H 5
Tilbury 4,298 . . . . B 5
Tillsonburg 10,487 . . . . D 5
Timmins 46,114 . . . . K 5

Tiverton 806 . . . . C 3
Tobermory 282 . . . . C 2
Toronto (cap.)® 599,217 . . . . K 4
Toronto *2,998,947 . . . . K 4
Tottenham 3,022 . . . . E 3
Trenton 15,085 . . . . G 3
Trout Creek 652 . . . . E 2
Turkey Point 407 . . . . D 5
Tweed 1,574 . . . . G 3
Udora 375 . . . . E 3
Union 485 . . . . C 5
Uxbridge 4,209 . . . . E 3
Valley East 10,433 . . . . J 5
Vanier 18,792 . . . . J 2
Vankleek Hill 1,774 . . . . K 2
Vars 527 . . . . J 2
Vaughan 29,674 . . . . J 4
Vermilion Bay 505 . . . . G 4
Verner 1,076 . . . . D 1
Vernon 303 . . . . J 2
Verona 754 . . . . H 3
Victoria Harbour 1,125 . . . . . . E 3
Vienna 369 . . . . D 5
Virginiatown 1,010 . . . . K 5
Vittoria 420 . . . . D 5
Wabigoon 268 . . . . G 5
Walden 10,139 . . . . J 5
Waikerton® 4,682 . . . . C 3
Wallaceburg 11,506 . . . . B 5
Wardsville 450 . . . . C 5
Warkworth 618 . . . . G 3
Warren 579 . . . . D 1
Warsaw 314 . . . . F 3
Wasaga Beach 4,705 . . . . D 3
Washago 569 . . . . E 3
Waterloo 49,428 . . . . D 4
Watford 1,402 . . . . C 5
Waubaushene 878 . . . . E 3
Wawa 4,206 . . . . J 5
Webbwood 519 . . . . C 1
Welcome 293 . . . . F 3
Welland 454,448 . . . . E 5
Wellesley 997 . . . . D 4
Wellington 1,082 . . . . G 4
Wendover 326 . . . . J 2
West Lorne 1,258 . . . . C 5
Westmeath 262 . . . . H 2
Westport 621 . . . . H 3
Wheatley 1,638 . . . . B 5
Whitby® 36,698 . . . . F 4
Whitchurch-Stouffville 13,557 . J 3
White River △1,006 . . . . J 5
Whitney 766 . . . . F 2
Wiarton 2,074 . . . . C 3
Wikwemikong 1,030 . . . . J 5
Williamsburg 407 . . . . J 3
Williamsford 256 . . . . H 3
Williamstown 328 . . . . K 2
Winchester 2,001 . . . . J 3
Windsor® 192,083 . . . . B 5
Windsor *246,110 . . . . B 5
Wingham 2,897 . . . . C 4
Wolfe Island 271 . . . . H 3
Woodstock® 26,603 . . . . D 4
Woodville 575 . . . . F 3
Wroxeter 350 . . . . C 4
Wyoming 1,682 . . . . B 5
Yarker 319 . . . . H 3
York 134,617 . . . . J 4
Zephyr 330 . . . . E 3
Zurich 795 . . . . C 4

OTHER FEATURES

Abitibi (riv.) . . . . J 5
Algonquin Prov. Park . . . . . . F 2
Amherst (isl.) . . . . H 3
Balsam (lake) . . . . F 3
Barrie (isl.) . . . . B 1
Bays (lake) . . . . F 2
Big Rideau (lake) . . . . H 3
Black (riv.) . . . . E 3
Bruce (pen.) . . . . C 2
Buckhorn (lake) . . . . F 3
Cabot (head) . . . . C 2
Charleston (lake) . . . . J 3
Christian (isl.) . . . . D 3
Clear (lake) . . . . F 3
Cockburn (isl.) . . . . A 2
Couchiching (lake) . . . . E 3
Croker (cape) . . . . D 3

Don (riv.) . . . . J 4
Doré (lake) . . . . G 2
Douglas (pt.) . . . . C 3
Erie (lake) . . . . E 5
Flowerpot (isl.) . . . . C 2
French (riv.) . . . . D 1
Georgian (bay) . . . . D 2
Georgian Bay Is.
 Nat'l Park . . . . C 2, D 3
Georgina (isl.) . . . . E 3
Grand (riv.) . . . . D 4
Humber (riv.) . . . . J 3
Hurd (cape) . . . . C 2
Huron (lake) . . . . B 3
Ipperwash Prov. Park . . . . . . C 4
Joseph (lake) . . . . E 2
Killarney Prov. Park . . . . C 1
Killbear Point Prov. Park . . . . D 2
Lake of the Woods (lake) . . . . F 5

Lake Superior Prov. Park . . . . J 5
Lonely (isl.) . . . . C 2
Long (pt.) . . . . D 5
Long Point (bay) . . . . D 5
Madawaska (riv.) . . . . G 2
Magnetawan (riv.) . . . . D 2
Main (chan.) . . . . C 2
Manitou (lake) . . . . B 1
Manitoulin (isl.) . . . . B 2
Mattagami (riv.) . . . . J 5
Michipicoten (isl.) . . . . H 5
Missinaibi (riv.) . . . . J 5
Mississagi (riv.) . . . . A 1
Mississippi (lake) . . . . H 2
Muskoka (lake) . . . . E 2
Niagara (riv.) . . . . E 4
Nipigon (lake) . . . . H 5
Nipissing (lake) . . . . E 1
North (chan.) . . . . A 1
Nottawasaga (bay) . . . . D 3
Ogidaki (mt.) . . . . J 5
Ontario (lake) . . . . G 4
Opeongo (lake) . . . . F 2
Ottawa (riv.) . . . . H 2
Owen (sound) . . . . D 3
Panache (lake) . . . . C 1
Parry (isl.) . . . . D 2
Parry (sound) . . . . D 2
Pelee (pt.) . . . . B 6
Petre (pt.) . . . . G 4
Point Pelee Nat'l Park . . . . . . B 5
Presqu'ile Prov. Park . . . . . . G 3
Pukaskwa Prov. Park . . . . . . H 5
Quetico Prov. Park . . . . G 5

Rainy (lake) . . . . G 5
Rice (lake) . . . . F 3
Rideau (lake) . . . . H 3
Rondeau Prov. Park . . . . C 5
Rosseau (lake) . . . . E 2
Saint Clair (lake) . . . . B 5
Saint Clair (riv.) . . . . B 5
Saint Lawrence (lake) . . . . . . K 3
Saint Lawrence (riv.) . . . . J 3
Saint Lawrence Is. Nat'l Park . J 3
Saugeen (riv.) . . . . C 3
Scugog (lake) . . . . F 3
Seul (lake) . . . . G 4
Severn (riv.) . . . . E 3
Sibley Prov. Park . . . . H 5
Simcoe (lake) . . . . E 3
South (bay) . . . . C 2
Spanish (riv.) . . . . C 1
Stony (lake) . . . . G 3
Superior (lake) . . . . H 5
Sydenham (riv.) . . . . B 5
Thames (riv.) . . . . B 5
Theano (pt.) . . . . J 5
Thousand (isls.) . . . . H 3
Timagami (lake) . . . . K 5
Trout (lake) . . . . E 1
Vernon (lake) . . . . E 2
Walpole (isl.) . . . . B 5
Welland (canal) . . . . E 5
Woods (lake) . . . . F 5

®County seat.
*Population of metropolitan area.
△Population of town or township.

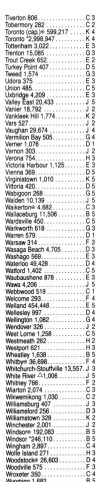

Ontario
Southern Part

SCALE
0 10 20 30 40 50 MI.
0 10 20 30 40 50 KM.

® National Capital . . . . . . ⊛
® Provincial Capital . . . . . ⊛
® County Seats . . . . ⊙
International
Boundaries

Provincial & State
 Boundaries
County Boundaries
Canals

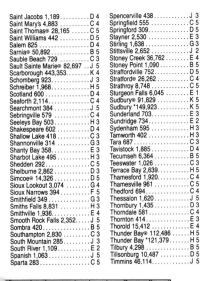

Topography

0   100   200 MI.
0   100   200 KM.

Below Sea Level | 100 m. 328 ft. | 200 m. 656 ft. | 500 m. 1,640 ft. | 1,000 m. 3,281 ft. | 2,000 m. 6,562 ft. | 5,000 m. 16,404 ft.

Agriculture, Industry and Resources

DOMINANT LAND USE

- Cereals, Cash Crops, Livestock
- Dairy
- General Farming, Livestock
- Fruits, Vegetables
- Pasture Livestock
- Forests
- Nonagricultural Land

MAJOR MINERAL OCCURRENCES

Ab Asbestos
Ag Silver
Au Gold
Co Cobalt
Cu Copper
Fe Iron Ore
G   Natural Gas
Gr Graphite

Mg Magnesium
Mr Marble
Na Salt
Ni Nickel
Pb Lead
Pt Platinum
U   Uranium
Zn Zinc

⚡ Water Power
▨ Major Industrial Areas

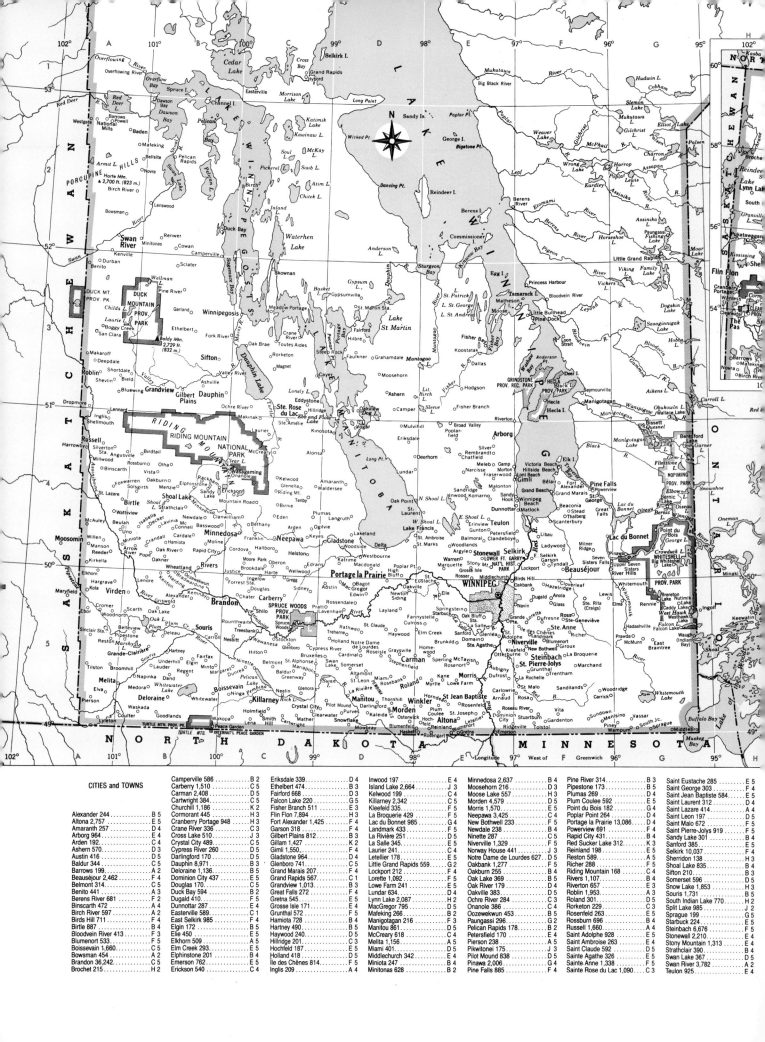

CITIES and TOWNS

Alexander 244 .... B 5
Altona 2,757 .... E 5
Amaranth 257 .... D 4
Arborg 964 .... E 3
Arden 192 .... C 4
Ashern 570 .... D 3
Austin 416 .... C 5
Baldur 344 .... C 5
Barrows 199 .... A 2
Beauséjour 2,462 .... E 4
Belmont 314 .... C 5
Benito 441 .... A 3
Berens River 681 .... F 2
Binscarth 472 .... A 4
Birch River 597 .... B 3
Birds Hill 711 .... F 4
Birtle 887 .... B 4
Bloodvein River 413 .... F 3
Blumenort 533 .... F 5
Boissevain 1,660 .... B 5
Bowsman 454 .... A 3
Brandon 36,242 .... C 5
Brochet 215 .... H 2

Camperville 586 .... B 2
Carberry 1,510 .... C 5
Carman 2,408 .... D 5
Cartwright 384 .... C 5
Churchill 1,186 .... K 2
Cormorant 445 .... H 3
Cranberry Portage 948 .. H 3
Crane River 336 .... C 3
Cross Lake 510 .... J 3
Crystal City 489 .... C 5
Darlingford 170 .... D 5
Dauphin 8,971 .... B 3
Deloraine 1,136 .... B 5
Dominion City 437 ...... E 5
Douglas 170 .... C 5
Duck Bay 594 .... B 2
Dugald 410 .... E 4
Dunnottar 287 .... E 4
Easterville 589 .... C 1
East Selkirk 985 .... E 4
Elgin 172 .... B 5
Elie 450 .... E 4
Elkhorn 509 .... A 5
Elm Creek 293 .... D 5
Elphinstone 201 .... C 4
Emerson 762 .... E 5
Erickson 540 .... C 4

Eriksdale 339 .... D 4
Ethelbert 474 .... B 3
Fairford 668 .... D 3
Falcon Lake 220 .... G 5
Fisher Branch 511 ...... E 3
Flin Flon 7,894 .... H 3
Fort Alexander 1,425 ... F 4
Garson 318 .... F 4
Gilbert Plains 812 ..... B 3
Gillam 1,092 .... K 2
Gimli 1,550 .... F 4
Gladstone 964 .... D 4
Glenboro 741 .... C 5
Grand Marais 207 .... F 4
Grand Rapids 567 .... C 1
Grandview 1,013 .... B 3
Great Falls 272 .... F 4
Gretna 545 .... E 5
Grosse Isle 171 .... E 4
Grunthal 517 .... F 5
Hamiota 728 .... B 4
Hartney 490 .... B 5
Haywood 240 .... D 5
Hillridge 201 .... C 3
Hochfeld 187 .... E 5
Holland 448 .... D 5
Île des Chênes 814 ..... E 4
Inglis 209 .... A 4

Inwood 197 .... E 4
Island Lake 2,664 ...... J 3
Kelwood 199 .... C 4
Killarney 2,342 .... C 5
Kleefeld 335 .... F 5
La Broquerie 429 .... F 5
Lac du Bonnet 985 ...... G 4
Landmark 433 .... F 5
La Rivière 251 .... D 5
La Salle 345 .... E 5
Laurier 241 .... C 4
Letellier 178 .... E 5
Little Grand Rapids 559 G 2
Lockport 212 .... F 4
Lorette 1,092 .... F 5
Lowe Farm 241 .... D 5
Lundar 634 .... D 4
Lynn Lake 2,087 .... H 2
MacGregor 795 .... D 5
Manigotagan 216 .... F 3
Manitou 861 .... D 5
McCreary 618 .... C 4
Melita 1,156 .... A 5
Miami 401 .... D 5
Middlechurch 342 .... F 5
Miniota 247 .... B 4
Minitonas 628 .... B 2

Minnedosa 2,637 .... B 4
Moosehorn 216 .... D 3
Moose Lake 557 .... H 3
Morden 4,579 .... D 5
Morris 1,570 .... E 5
Neepawa 3,425 .... C 4
New Bothwell 233 .... F 5
Newdale 238 .... B 4
Ninette 287 .... C 5
Niverville 1,329 .... F 5
Norway House 441 .... J 3
Notre Dame de Lourdes 627 D 5
Oakbank 1,277 .... F 4
Oakburn 255 .... B 4
Oak Lake 369 .... B 5
Oak River 179 .... B 4
Oakville 383 .... D 5
Ochre River 284 .... C 3
Onanole 386 .... C 4
Oozewekwun 453 .... B 4
Paungassi 296 .... G 2
Pelican Rapids 178 ..... B 2
Petersfield 170 .... E 4
Pikwitonei 175 .... J 3
Pilot Mound 838 .... D 5
Pine Falls 885 .... F 4

Pine River 314 .... B 3
Pipestone 173 .... B 5
Plumas 269 .... D 4
Plum Coulee 592 .... E 5
Point du Bois 182 ...... G 4
Poplar Point 264 .... D 4
Portage la Prairie 13,086 D 4
Powerview 691 .... F 4
Rapid City 431 .... B 4
Red Sucker Lake 312 .... K 3
Reinland 198 .... E 5
Reston 589 .... B 5
Richer 288 .... F 5
Riding Mountain 168 .... B 4
Rivers 1,107 .... B 4
Riverton 657 .... E 3
Roblin 1,953 .... A 3
Roland 301 .... D 5
Rorketon 229 .... C 3
Rosenfeld 263 .... E 5
Rossburn 696 .... B 4
Russell 1,660 .... A 4
Saint Adolphe 928 ...... E 5
Saint Ambroise 263 ..... E 4
Saint Claude 592 .... D 5
Sainte Agathe 326 ...... E 5
Sainte Anne 1,338 ...... F 5
Sainte Rose du Lac 1,090 C 3

Saint Eustache 285 ..... E 5
Saint George 303 .... F 4
Saint Jean Baptiste 584 E 5
Saint Laurent 312 ...... D 4
Saint Lazare 414 .... A 4
Saint Leon 259 .... D 5
Saint Malo 672 .... F 5
Saint Pierre-Jolys 919 . F 5
Sandy Lake 301 .... B 4
Sanford 385 .... E 5
Selkirk 10,037 .... F 4
Sherridon 138 .... H 3
Shoal Lake 835 .... B 4
Sifton 210 .... B 3
Somerset 596 .... D 5
Snow Lake 1,853 .... H 3
Souris 1,731 .... B 5
South Indian Lake 770 .. H 2
Split Lake 985 .... J 2
Sprague 199 .... G 5
Starbuck 224 .... E 5
Steinbach 6,676 .... F 5
Stony Mountain 1,313 ... E 4
Stonewall 2,210 .... E 4
Strathclair 390 .... B 4
Swan Lake 367 .... D 5
Swan River 3,782 .... A 2
Teulon 925 .... E 4

Manitoba
Northern Part

0 40 80 120 MI.

0 40 80 120 KM.

Manitoba
Southern Part

SCALE

0 5 10   20   40   60 MI.

0 5 10 20   40   60 KM.

Provincial Capital .... ⊛
International Boundaries —·—·—
Provincial Boundaries ———

© Copyright HAMMOND INCORPORATED, Maplewood, N.J.

The Pas 6,390 .... H 3
Thicket Portage 195 .... J 3
Thompson 14,288 .... J 2
Treherne 743 .... D 5
Tyndall 421 .... F 4
Virden 2,940 .... A 5
Vita 364 .... F 5
Wabowden 655 .... J 3
Wallace Lake ●2,044 .... G 3
Wanless 193 .... H 3
Warren 459 .... E 4
Waskada 239 .... B 5
Wawanesa 492 .... C 5
Whitemouth 320 .... G 5
Whitewater ●856 .... B 5
Winkler 5,046 .... E 5
Winnipeg (cap.) 564,473 .... E 5
Winnipeg *584,842 .... E 5
Winnipeg Beach 565 .... F 4
Winnipegosis 855 .... B 3
Woodlands 185 .... E 4
Wooodridge 170 .... G 5
York Landing 229 .... J 2

OTHER FEATURES

Aikens (lake) .... G 3
Anderson (lake) .... D 2
Anderson (pt.) .... F 3
Armit (lake) .... A 2
Assapan (riv.) .... G 2
Assiniboine (riv.) .... C 5
Assinika (lake) .... G 2
Assinika (riv.) .... G 2
Atim (lake) .... C 2
Baldy (mt.) .... B 3
Basket (lake) .... C 3
Beaverhill (lake) .... J 3
Berens (isl.) .... E 2
Berens (riv.) .... F 2
Bernic (lake) .... G 5
Big Sand (lake) .... H 2
Bigstone (lake) .... J 3
Bigstone (pt.) .... E 3
Bigstone (riv.) .... H 3
Birch (isl.) .... C 2
Black (isl.) .... F 3
Black (riv.) .... F 4
Bloodvein (riv.) .... F 3
Bonnet (lake) .... G 4
Buffalo (bay) .... G 5
Burntwood (riv.) .... J 2
Caribou (riv.) .... J 1
Carroll (lake) .... G 3
Cedar (lake) .... B 1
Channel (isl.) .... B 2
Charron (lake) .... A 2
Childs (lake) .... A 3
Chitek (lake) .... C 2
Churchill (cape) .... K 2
Churchill (riv.) .... J 2
Clear (lake) .... C 4
Clearwater Lake Prov. Park .. H 3
Cobham (riv.) .... G 1
Cochrane (riv.) .... H 1
Commissioner (isl.) .... E 2
Cormorant (lake) .... H 3
Cross (bay) .... C 1
Cross (lake) .... J 3
Crowduck (lake) .... G 4
Dancing (pt.) .... D 2
Dauphin (lake) .... C 3
Dauphin (riv.) .... D 3
Dawson (bay) .... B 2
Dog (lake) .... D 3
Dogskin (lake) .... G 3
Duck Mountain Prov. Park .. B 3
Eardley (lake) .... F 2

East Shoal (lake) .... E 4
Ebb and Flow (lake) .... C 3
Egg (isl.) .... E 3
Elbow (lake) .... G 4
Elk (isl.) .... F 4
Elliot (lake) .... G 2
Etawney (lake) .... J 2
Etomami (riv.) .... F 2
Falcon (lake) .... G 5
Family (lake) .... G 3
Fisher (bay) .... E 3
Fisher (riv.) .... E 3
Fishing (lake) .... G 2
Flintstone (lake) .... G 4
Fox (lake) .... K 2
Gammon (riv.) .... G 3
Garner (lake) .... G 4
Gem (lake) .... G 4
George (isl.) .... E 2
George (lake) .... G 4
Gilchrist (creek) .... F 2
Gilchrist (lake) .... G 2
Gods (lake) .... K 3
Gods (riv.) .... K 3
Granville (lake) .... H 2
Grass (riv.) .... J 2
Grass River Prov. Park ...... H 3
Grindstone Prov. Rec. Park .. F 3
Gunisao (lake) .... J 3
Gypsum (lake) .... D 3
Harrop (lake) .... G 2
Harte (mt.) .... A 2
Hayes (riv.) .... K 3
Hecla (isl.) .... F 3
Hecla Prov. Park .... F 3
Hobbs (lake) .... G 3
Horseshoe (lake) .... G 2
Hubbart (pt.) .... K 2
Hudson (bay) .... J 1
Hudwin (lake) .... G 1
Inland (lake) .... C 2
International Peace Garden .. B 5
Island (lake) .... K 3
Katimik (lake) .... C 2
Kawinaw (lake) .... C 2
Kinwow (bay) .... B 2
Kississing (lake) .... H 3
Knee (lake) .... J 3
Lake of the Woods (lake) ... H 5
La Salle (riv.) .... E 5
Laurie (lake) .... A 3
Leaf (riv.) .... F 2
Lewis (lake) .... F 3
Leyond (riv.) .... G 2
Little Birch (lake) .... E 3
Lonely (lake) .... C 3
Long (lake) .... G 4
Long (pt.) .... D 1
Long (pt.) .... D 4
Manigotagan (lake) .... G 4

Manigotagan (riv.) .... G 3
Manitoba (lake) .... D 4
Mantagao (riv.) .... E 3
Marshy (lake) .... B 5
McKay (lake) .... C 2
McPhail (riv.) .... F 2
Minnedosa (riv.) .... B 4
Moar (lake) .... G 2
Molson (lake) .... J 3
Moose (isl.) .... E 3
Morrison (lake) .... C 1
Mossy (riv.) .... C 3
Mukutawa (lake) .... G 2
Mukutawa (riv.) .... E 1
Muskeg (bay) .... G 6
Nejanilini (lake) .... J 1
Nelson (riv.) .... J 2
Nopiming Prov. Park .... G 4
Northern Indian (lake) ...... J 2
North Knife (lake) .... J 2
North Seal (riv.) .... H 2
North Shoal (lake) .... E 4
Nueltin (lake) .... H 1
Oak (lake) .... B 5
Obukowin (lake) .... G 3
Oiseau (lake) .... G 4
Oiseau (riv.) .... G 4
Overflow (bay) .... A 1
Overflowing (riv.) .... A 1
Owl (riv.) .... K 2
Oxford (lake) .... J 3
Paint (lake) .... J 2
Palsen (riv.) .... G 2
Pelican (bay) .... B 2
Pelican (lake) .... B 2
Pelican (lake) .... C 5
Pembina (hills) .... D 5
Pembina (riv.) .... C 5
Peonan (pt.) .... D 3
Pickerel (lake) .... C 2
Pigeon (riv.) .... F 2
Pipestone (creek) .... A 5
Plum (creek) .... B 5
Plum (lake) .... B 5
Poplar (riv.) .... E 2
Porcupine (hills) .... A 3
Portage (bay) .... D 3
Punk (isl.) .... E 2
Quesnel (lake) .... G 4
Rat (riv.) .... F 5
Red (riv.) .... F 4
Red Deer (lake) .... A 2
Red Deer (riv.) .... A 2
Reindeer (isl.) .... D 3
Reindeer (lake) .... H 2
Riding (mt.) .... B 4
Riding Mountain Nat'l Park .. B 4
Rock (lake) .... C 5
Ross (isl.) .... J 3
Sagemace (bay) .... B 3

Saint Andrew (lake) .... E 3
Saint George (lake) .... E 3
Saint Martin (lake) .... D 3
Saint Patrick (lake) .... E 3
Sale (riv.) .... E 5
Sandy (isls.) .... D 2
Sasaginnigak (lake) .... G 3
Seal (riv.) .... J 2
Selkirk (isl.) .... C 1
Setting (lake) .... H 3
Shoal (lake) .... G 5
Shoal (riv.) .... B 2
Sipiwesk (lake) .... J 3
Sisib (lake) .... C 2
Sleeve (lake) .... E 3
Slemon (lake) .... G 1
Snowshoe (lake) .... G 4
Soul (lake) .... C 2
Souris (riv.) .... B 5
Southern Indian (lake) ...... H 2
South Knife (riv.) .... J 2
South Seal (riv.) .... J 2
Split (lake) .... J 2
Spruce (isl.) .... B 1
Spruce Woods Prov. Park ... C 5
Stevenson (lake) .... J 3
Sturgeon (bay) .... E 3
Swan (lake) .... B 2
Swan (lake) .... D 5
Swan (riv.) .... A 3
Tadoule (lake) .... J 2
Tamarack (isl.) .... F 3
Tatnam (cape) .... K 2
Traverse (bay) .... F 4
Turtle (mts.) .... B 5
Turtle (riv.) .... C 3
Turtle Mountain Prov. Park ... B 5
Valley (riv.) .... B 3
Vickers (lake) .... F 3
Viking (lake) .... G 3
Wanipigow (riv.) .... G 3
Washow (bay) .... F 3
Waterhen (lake) .... C 2
Weaver (lake) .... F 2
Wellman (lake) .... B 3
West Hawk (lake) .... G 5
West Shoal (lake) .... E 4
Whitemouth (lake) .... G 5
Whitemouth (riv.) .... G 5
Whiteshell Prov. Park .... G 4
Whitewater (lake) .... B 5
Wicked (pt.) .... D 2
Winnipeg (lake) .... E 2
Winnipeg (riv.) .... G 4
Winnipegosis (lake) .... C 2
Woods (lake) .... H 5
Wrong (lake) .... F 2

*Population of metropolitan area.
●Population of rural municipality.

AREA 250,999 sq. mi. (650,087 sq. km.)
POPULATION 1,026,241
CAPITAL Winnipeg
LARGEST CITY Winnipeg
HIGHEST POINT Baldy Mtn. 2,729 ft.
(832 m.)
SETTLED IN 1812
ADMITTED TO CONFEDERATION 1870
PROVINCIAL FLOWER Prairie Crocus

Topography

0   75   150 MI.

0   75   150 KM.

Below Sea Level 100 m. 328 ft. 200 m. 656 ft. 500 m. 1,640 ft. 1,000 m. 3,281 ft. 2,000 m. 6,562 ft. 5,000 m. 16,404 ft.

Agriculture, Industry and Resources

DOMINANT LAND USE

Cereals (chiefly barley, oats)

Cereals, Livestock

Dairy

Livestock

Forests

Nonagricultural Land

MAJOR MINERAL OCCURRENCES

Au Gold
Co Cobalt
Cu Copper
Na Salt

Ni Nickel
O Petroleum
Pb Lead
Pt Platinum
Zn Zinc

  Water Power

  Major Industrial Areas

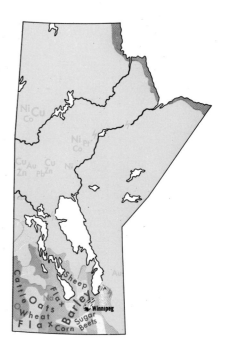

Topography

0 60 120 MI.
0 60 120 KM.

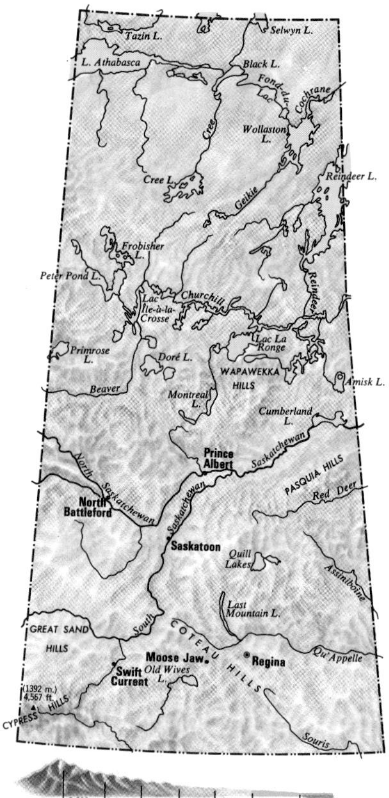

CITIES and TOWNS

Abbey 218 C 5
Aberdeen 496 E 3
Abernethy 300 H 5
Air Ronge 557 M 3
Alameda 318 J 6
Alida 169 K 6
Allan 871 E 4
Alsask 652 B 4
Annaheim 209 G 3
Antelope •231 C 5
Arborfield 439 H 2
Archerwill 286 H 3
Arcola 493 J 6
Arlington Beach •432 F 4
Asquith 507 D 3
Assiniboia 2,924 E 6
Avonlea 442 G 5
Baildon •799 F 5
Balcarres 739 H 5
Balgonie 777 G 5
Batoche E 3
Battleford 3,565 C 3
Beauval 606 L 3
Beechy 279 D 5
Bengough 536 F 6
Bethune 369 F 5
Bienfait 835 J 6
Biggar 2,561 C 3
Big River 819 D 2
Birch Hills 957 F 3
Bjorkdale 269 H 3
Blaine Lake 653 D 3
Borden 197 D 3
Brabant Lake 245 M 3
Bradwell 168 E 4
Bredenbury 467 K 5
Briercrest 151 F 5
Broadview 840 J 5
Brock 184 C 4
Browning •687 J 6
Bruno 772 F 3
Buchanan 392 J 4
Buffalo Gap •598 F 6
Buffalo Narrows 1,088 L 3
Burstall 550 B 5
Cabri 632 C 5
Cadillac 173 D 6
Calder 164 K 4
Cana •1,238 J 5
Candle Lake 219 F 2
Cando 163 C 3
Canoe Lake 182 L 3
Canora 2,667 J 4
Canwood 340 E 2
Carievale 246 K 6
Carlyle 1,074 J 6
Carnduff 1,043 K 6
Carrot River 1,169 H 2
Central Butte 548 E 5
Ceylon 184 G 6
Chaplin 389 E 5
Chitek Lake 170 D 2
Choiceland 543 G 2
Christopher Lake 227 F 2
Churchbridge 972 J 5
Clavet 234 E 4
Climax 293 C 6
Cochin 221 C 2
Codette 236 H 2
Coleville 383 B 4
Colonsay 594 F 4
Connaught Heights •982 G 3
Conquest 256 D 4
Consul 153 B 6
Coronach 1,032 F 6
Craik 565 F 4
Craven 206 G 5
Creelman 184 H 6
Creighton 1,636 N 4
Cudworth 947 F 3
Cumberland House 831 J 2
Cupar 669 G 5
Cut Knife 624 B 3
Dalmeny 1,064 E 3
Davidson 1,166 E 4
Debden 403 E 2
Delisle 980 D 4
Denare Beach 592 M 4
Denzil 199 B 3
Deschambault Lake 386 M 3
Dinsmore 398 D 4
Dodsland 272 C 4
Domremy 209 F 3
Drake 211 G 4
Duck Lake 699 E 3
Dundurn 531 E 4
Dysart 275 H 5
Earl Grey 303 G 5
Eastend 723 C 6
Eatonia 528 B 4
Ebenezer 164 J 4
Edam 384 C 2
Edenwold 143 G 5
Elbow 313 E 4
Eldorado 229 L 2
Elfros 199 H 4
Elrose 624 D 4
Elstow 143 E 4
Endeavour 199 J 3
Englefeld 271 G 3
Erwood 149 J 3
Esterhazy 3,065 K 5
Estevan 9,174 J 6
Eston 1,413 C 4
Eyebrow 168 E 5
Fillmore 396 H 6
Fleming 141 K 5
Flin Flon 367 N 4
Foam Lake 1,452 H 4
Fond du Lac 494 L 2
Fort Qu'Appelle 1,827 H 5
Fox Valley 380 B 5
Francis 182 H 5
Frobisher 166 J 6
Frontier 619 C 6
Gainsborough 308 K 6
Gerald 197 K 5
Glaslyn 430 C 2
Glenavon 284 J 5
Glen Ewen 168 K 6
Goodsoil 263 L 4
Govan 394 G 4
Grand Coulee 208 G 5
Gravelbourg 1,338 E 6
Grayson 264 J 5
Green Acres 139 F 2
Green Lake 634 L 4
Grenfell 1,307 J 5
Guernsey 198 F 4
Gull Lake 1,095 C 5
Hafford 557 D 3
Hague 625 E 3
Hanley 484 E 4
Harris 259 D 4
Hawarden 137 E 4
Hearts Hill •552 B 3
Hepburn 411 E 3
Herbert 1,019 D 5
Hodgeville 329 E 5
Holdfast 297 F 5
Hudson Bay 2,361 J 3
Humboldt 4,705 F 3
Hyas 165 J 4
Île-à-la-Crosse 1,035 L 3
Imperial 501 F 4
Indian Head 1,889 H 5
Invermay 353 J 4
Ituna 870 H 4
Jansen 223 G 4
Jasmin •14 H 4
Kamsack 2,688 K 4
Kelliher 397 H 4
Kelvington 1,054 H 3
Kenaston 345 E 4
Kennedy 275 J 5
Kerrobert 1,141 C 4
Kincaid 256 D 6
Kindersley 3,969 B 4
Kinistino 783 F 3
Kipling 1,016 J 5
Kisbey 228 J 6
Kronau 154 G 5
Kyle 516 C 5
Lac Pelletier •586 C 6
Lafleche 583 E 6
Laird 233 E 3
Lake Lenore 361 G 3
La Loche 1,632 L 3
Lampman 651 J 6
Lancer 156 C 5
Landis 277 C 3
Lang 219 G 6
Langenburg 1,324 K 5
Langham 1,151 E 3
Lanigan 1,732 F 4
La Ronge 2,579 L 3
Lashburn 813 B 2
Leader 1,108 B 5
Leask 478 E 2
Lebret 274 H 5
Lemberg 414 H 5
Leoville 393 D 2
Leroy 504 G 4
Lestock 402 G 4
Limerick 164 E 6
Lintlaw 234 H 3
Lipton 364 H 5
Lloydminster 6,034 A 2
Loon Lake 369 B 1
Loreburn 201 E 4
Lucky Lake 333 D 5
Lumsden 1,303 G 5
Luseland 704 B 3
Macdowall 171 E 2
Macklin 976 A 3
Macoun 190 H 6
Maidstone 1,001 B 2
Mankota 375 D 6
Manor 368 K 6
Maple Creek 2,470 B 6
Marcelin 238 E 3
Margo 153 H 4
Marriott •627 D 4
Marsden 229 B 3
Marshall 453 B 2
Martensville 1,966 E 3
Maryfield 431 K 6
Maymont 212 D 3
McLean 189 G 5
Meacham 178 F 3
Meadow Lake 3,857 C 1
Meath Park 262 F 2
Medstead 163 C 2
Melfort 6,010 G 3
Melville 5,092 J 5
Meota 235 C 2
Mervin 155 C 2
Midale 564 H 6
Middle Lake 275 F 3
Milden 251 D 4
Milestone 602 G 5
Montmartre 544 H 5
Montreal Lake 448 F 1
Moose Jaw 33,941 F 5
Moose Range •679 H 2
Moosomin 2,579 K 5
Morse 416 D 5
Mortlach 293 E 5
Mossbank 464 E 6
Muenster 385 F 3
Naicam 886 G 3
Neilburg 354 B 3
Neuanlage 144 E 3
Neudorf 425 J 5
Neuhorst 146 E 3
Nipawin 4,376 H 2
Nokomis 524 F 4
Norquay 552 J 4
North Battleford 14,030 C 3
North Portal 164 J 6
Odessa 232 H 5
Ogema 441 G 6
Osler 527 E 3
Outlook 1,976 E 4
Oxbow 1,191 J 6
Paddockwood 211 F 2
Pangman 227 G 6
Paradise Hill 421 B 2
Patuanak 173 L 3
Paynton 210 B 2
Pelican Narrows 331 N 3
Pelly 391 K 4
Pennant 202 C 5
Pense 472 G 5
Perdue 407 D 3
Pierceland 425 K 4
Pilger 150 F 3
Pilot Butte 1,255 G 5
Pine House 612 M 3
Plenty 175 C 4
Plunkett 150 F 4
Ponteix 769 D 6
Porcupine Plain 937 H 3
Preeceville 1,243 J 4
Prelate 317 B 5
Prince Albert 31,380 F 2
Prud'homme 222 F 3
Punnichy 394 G 4
Qu'Appelle 653 H 5
Quill Lake 514 G 3
Quinton 169 G 4
Rabbit Lake 159 D 2
Radisson 439 D 3
Radville 1,012 G 6
Rama 133 H 4
Raymore 635 G 4
Redvers 859 K 6
Regina (cap.) 162,613 G 5
Regina *164,313 G 5
Regina Beach 603 F 5
Rhein 271 J 4
Richmound 188 B 5
Riverhurst 193 E 5
Rocanville 934 K 5
Roche Percé 142 J 6
Rockglen 511 F 6
Rosetown 2,664 D 4
Rose Valley 538 H 3
Rosthern 1,609 E 3
Rouleau 443 G 5
Saint Benedict 157 F 3
Saint Brieux 401 G 3
Saint Louis 448 F 3
Saint Philips •538 K 4
Saint Walburg 802 B 2
Saltcoats 549 J 4
Sandy Bay 756 N 3
Saskatoon 154,210 E 3
Saskatoon *154,210 E 3
Sceptre 169 B 5
Scott 203 C 3
Sedley 373 H 5
Semans 344 G 4
Shaunavon 2,112 C 6
Sheho 285 H 4
Shell Lake 220 D 2
Shellbrook 1,228 E 2
Simpson 231 F 4
Sintaluta 215 H 5
Smeaton 246 G 2
Southey 697 G 5
Spalding 337 G 3
Spiritwood 926 D 2
Springside 533 J 4
Spy Hill 354 K 5
Star City 527 G 3
Stenen 143 J 4
Stockholm 391 J 5
Stonehenge •701 F 6
Storthoaks 142 K 6
Stoughton 716 J 6
Strasbourg 842 G 4
Sturgis 789 J 4
Swift Current 14,747 D 5
Tantallon 196 K 5
Theodore 473 J 4
Timber Bay 152 F 1
Tisdale 3,107 H 3
Togo 181 K 4
Tompkins 275 C 5
Torch River •2,440 G 2
Torquay 311 H 6
Tramping Lake 178 B 3
Tugaske 175 E 5
Turnor Lake 166 L 3
Turtleford 505 B 2
Unity 2,408 B 3
Uranium City 2,507 L 2
Val Marie 236 D 6
Vanguard 292 D 6
Vanscoy 298 D 4
Vibank 369 H 5
Viscount 386 F 4
Vonda 313 F 3
Wadena 1,495 H 4
Wakaw 1,030 F 3
Waldeck 292 D 5
Waldheim 758 E 3
Walpole •711 K 6
Wapella 487 K 5
Warman 2,076 E 3
Waseca 169 B 2
Waskesiu Lake 176 E 2
Watrous 1,830 F 4
Watson 901 G 3
Wawota 622 J 6
Weldon 279 F 2
Welwyn 170 K 5
Weyburn 9,523 H 6
White City 602 G 5
White Fox 394 H 2
Whitewood 1,003 J 5
Wilcox 202 G 5
Wilkie 1,501 C 3
Willow Bunch 494 F 6
Willow Creek •1,218 B 6
Windthorst 254 J 5
Wiseton 195 D 4
Wishart 212 H 4
Wollaston Lake 248 N 2
Wolseley 904 H 5
Wymark 162 D 5
Wynyard 2,147 G 4
Yarbo 158 K 5
Yellow Grass 477 H 6
Yorkton 15,339 J 4
Young 456 F 4
Zenon Park 273 H 2

OTHER FEATURES

Allan (hills) E 4
Amisk (lake) M 4
Antelope (lake) C 5
Antler (riv.) K 6
Arm (riv.) F 5
Assiniboine (riv.) J 3
Athabasca (lake) L 2
Bad (lake) C 4
Bad (hills) C 4
Basin (lake) F 3
Batoche Nat'l Hist. Site E 3
Battle (creek) B 6
Battle (riv.) B 3
Bear (hills) C 4
Beaver (hills) H 4
Beaver (riv.) L 4
Beaverlodge (lake) L 2
Big Muddy (lake) G 6
Bigstick (lake) B 5
Birch (lake) C 2
Bitter (lake) B 5
Black (lake) M 2
Boundary (plat.) B 6
Brightsand (lake) B 2
Bronson (lake) B 2

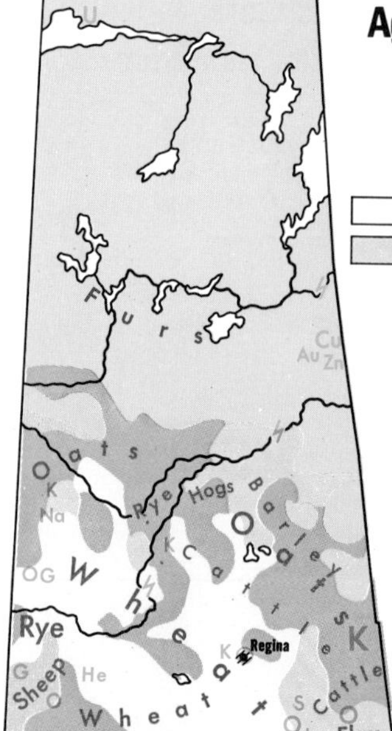

Agriculture, Industry and Resources

DOMINANT LAND USE

Wheat
Cereals (chiefly barley, oats)
Cereals, Livestock
Livestock
Forests

MAJOR MINERAL OCCURRENCES

Au Gold
Cu Copper
G Natural Gas
He Helium
K Potash
Lg Lignite
Na Salt
O Petroleum
S Sulfur
U Uranium
Zn Zinc

Water Power
Major Industrial Areas

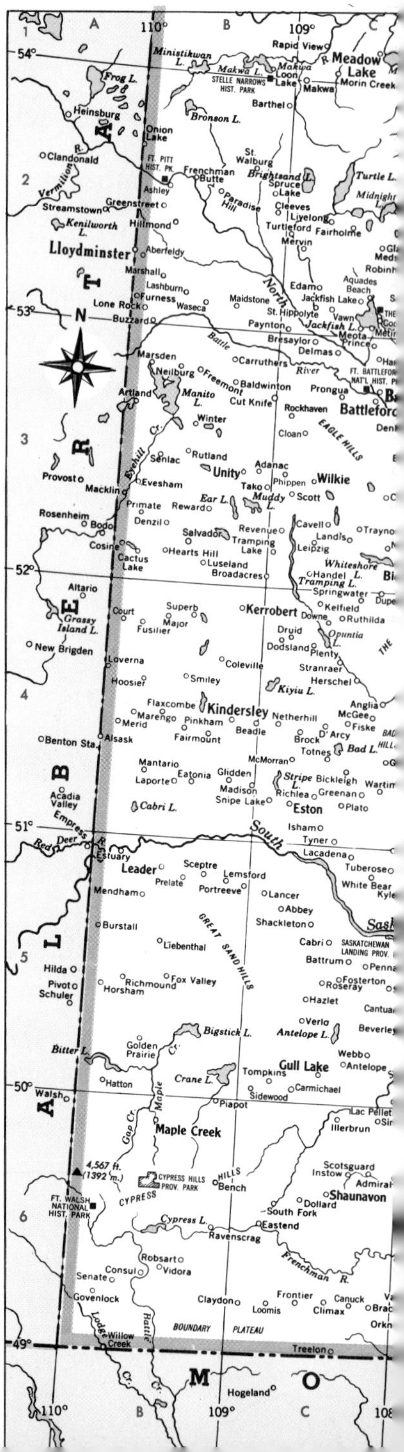

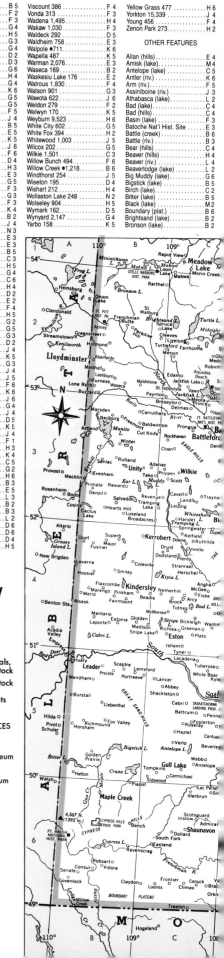

Buffalo Pound Prov. Park .... F 5
Cabri (lake) .... B 4
Cactus (hills) .... F 5
Candle (lake) .... F 2
Cannington Manon Hist. Park . J 6
Canoe (lake) .... L 3
Carrot (riv.) .... J 2
Chaplin (lake) .... E 5
Chipman (riv.) .... M 2
Chitek (lake) .... D 2
Churchill (riv.) .... M 3
Clearwater (riv.) .... L 3
Cochrane (riv.) .... N 2
Coteau (hills) .... D 4
Cowan (lake) .... D 2
Crane (lake) .... B 5
Crean (lake) .... E 1
Cree (lake) .... L 3
Cree (riv.) .... M 2
Cumberland (lake) .... J 1
Cypress (hills) .... B 6
Cypress (lake) .... B 6
Cypress Hills Prov. Park ... B 6
Danielson Prov. Park ...... E 4
Delaronde (lake) .... E 1
Diefenbaker (lake) .... E 4
Doré (lake) .... L 3
Douglas Prov. Park .... E 4
Duck Lake Hist. Park ...... E 3
Duck Mountain Prov. Park .. K 4
Eagle (hills) .... C 3
Eaglehill (creek) .... D 4

Ear (lake) .... B 3
Echo Valley Prov. Park ..... G 5
Etomami (riv.) .... J 3
Eyebrow (lake) .... E 5
Eyehill (creek) .... B 3
Fife (lake) .... E 6
File (hills) .... H 5
Fir (riv.) .... J 2
Fond du Lac (riv.) .... J 2
Forrest (lake) .... L 3
Fort Battleford Nat'l Park .. C 3
Fort Carlton Hist. Park ..... E 3
Fort Pitt Hist. Park .... B 2
Fort Walsh Nat'l Hist. Park . A 6
Foster (lake) .... M 3
Frenchman (riv.) .... C 6
Frobisher (lake) .... L 3
Gap (creek) .... B 6
Gardiner (dam) .... D 4
Geikie (riv.) .... M 3
Good Spirit (lake) .... J 4
Goodspirit Lake Prov. Park . J 4
Great Sand (hills) .... B 5
Green (lake) .... D 1
Greenwater Lake Prov. Park . H 3
Haultain (riv.) .... L 3
Île-à-la-Crosse (lake) ..... L 3
Ironspring (creek) .... G 3
Jackfish (lake) .... C 2
Katepwa Prov. Park .... H 5
Kingsmere (lake) .... E 1
Kiyiu (lake) .... C 4

Lac La Ronge Prov. Park ... M 3
Lanigan (creek) .... F 4
Last Mountain (lake) ...... F 4
Leaf (lake) .... J 2
Leech (lake) .... J 2
Lenore (lake) .... G 3
Little Manitou (lake) ...... E 5
Lodge (creek) .... B 6
Long (lake) .... H 6
Loon (creek) .... G 4
Makwa (lake) .... B 1
Makwa (riv.) .... B 1
Manito (lake) .... B 3
Maple (creek) .... B 5
McFarlane (riv.) .... L 2
Meadow (lake) .... C 1
Meadow Lake Prov. Park .. C 1
Meeting (lake) .... D 2
Midnight (lake) .... B 2
Ministikwan (lake) .... B 1
Missouri Coteau (hills) .... D 5
Montreal (lake) .... F 1
Moose (mt.) .... J 6
Moose Jaw (riv.) .... E 5
Moose Mountain (creek) .. J 6
Moose Mountain Prov. Park . J 6
Mossy (riv.) .... H 1
Muddy (lake) .... B 3
Mudjatik (riv.) .... L 3
Nipawin Prov. Park .... G 1
North Saskatchewan (riv.) . D 3
Notukeu (creek) .... D 6

Oldman (riv.) .... L 2
Old Wives (lake) .... E 5
Opuntia (lake) .... C 4
Overflowing (riv.) .... K 2
Pasquia (hills) .... J 2
Pasquia (riv.) .... J 2
Pelican (lake) .... E 3
Peter Pond (lake) .... L 3
Pheasant (hills) .... J 5
Pine Lake Prov. Park ...... E 4
Pinto (lake) .... D 6
Pipestone (creek) .... K 6
Pipestone (riv.) .... L 2
Ponass (lakes) .... J 3
Poplar (riv.) .... K 3
Porcupine (hills) .... K 3
Primrose (lake) .... L 3
Primrose Lake Air Weapons
  Range .... L 3
Prince Albert Nat'l Park ... E 1
Qu'Appelle (riv.) .... J 5
Quill (lakes) .... G 4
Red Deer (lake) .... A 5
Red Deer (riv.) .... K 3
Reindeer (lake) .... M 2
Reindeer (riv.) .... N 3
Riou (lake) .... M 2
Rivers (lake) .... E 3
Ronge, La (lake) .... M 3
Rowans Ravine Prov. Park . F 4
St. Victor Petroglyphs Hist.
  Park .... E 6

Saskatchewan (riv.) ...... H 2
Saskatchewan Landing Prov.
  Park .... C 5
Saskeram (riv.) .... K 2
Scott (lake) .... M 2
Selwyn (lake) .... M 2
Souris (riv.) .... H 6
South Saskatchewan (riv.) . C 5
Steele Narrows Hist. Park .. B 2
Stripe (lake) .... C 4
Sturgeon (riv.) .... E 2
Swan (lake) .... J 3
Swift Current (creek) ..... D 5
Tazin (lake) .... L 2
The Battlefords Prov. Park . C 2

Thickwood (hills) .... D 2
Thunder (hills) .... L 4
Tobin (lake) .... H 2
Torch (riv.) .... H 2
Touchwood (hills) .... G 4
Tramping (lake) .... C 3
Trout (lake) .... M 2
Turtle (lake) .... C 2
Twelvemile (lake) .... E 6
Vermilion (hills) .... E 5
Wapawekka (hills) ...... M 4
Waskana (creek) .... G 5
Waskesiu (lake) .... E 2
Watham (riv.) .... M 3
Weed (hills) .... J 5

White Fox (riv.) .... G 2
White Gull (creek) .... G 2
Whiteshore (lake) .... C 3
Whiteswan (lakes) ...... F 1
William (riv.) .... L 2
Willow Bunch (lake) ..... F 6
Witchekan (lake) .... D 2
Wollaston (lake) .... N 2
Wood (mt.) .... E 6
Wood (riv.) .... E 6
Wood Mountain Hist. Park . E 6

*Population of metropolitan area.
•Population of rural municipality.

AREA 251,699 sq. mi. (651,900 sq. km.)
POPULATION 968,313
CAPITAL Regina
LARGEST CITY Regina
HIGHEST POINT Cypress Hills 4,567 ft.
  (1,392 m.)
SETTLED IN 1774
ADMITTED TO CONFEDERATION 1905
PROVINCIAL FLOWER Prairie Lily

© Copyright HAMMOND INCORPORATED, Maplewood, N. J.

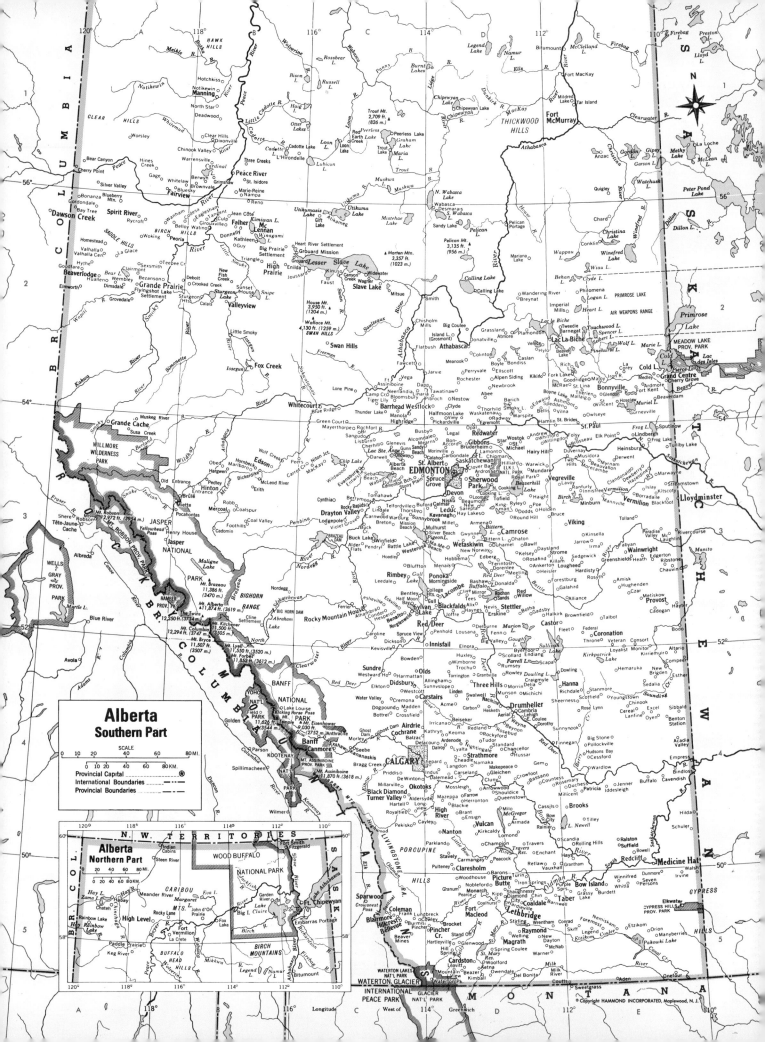

Alberta
Southern Part

SCALE
0 10 20   40   60   80 MI.
0 10 20 40   60   80 KM.

Provincial Capital .... ⊛
International Boundaries ____ — ____ —
Provincial Boundaries ____ — ·· — ·· —

Alberta
Northern Part

0 20 40 60 80 MI.
0 20 40 60 80 KM.

© Copyright HAMMOND INCORPORATED, Maplewood, N.J.

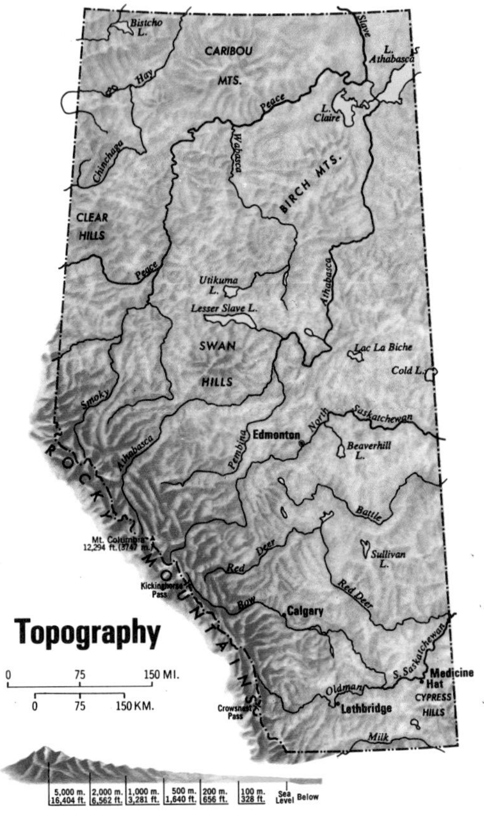
Topography
CARIBOU MTS.
BIRCH MTS.
CLEAR HILLS
SWAN HILLS
Bistcho L.
L. Athabasca
L. Claire
Utikuma L.
Lesser Slave L.
Lac La Biche
Cold L.
Beaverhill L.
Sullivan L.
Edmonton
Calgary
Lethbridge
Medicine Hat
CYPRESS HILLS
Mt. Columbia 12,294 ft. (3747 m.)
Kickinghorse Pass
Crowsnest Pass
Slave
Peace
Hay
Chinchaga
Wabasca
Athabasca
Smoky
Pembina
North Saskatchewan
Battle
Red Deer
Bow
Oldman
S. Saskatchewan
Milk
0 75 150 MI.
0 75 150 KM.
5,000 m. 16,404 ft.
2,000 m. 6,562 ft.
1,000 m. 3,281 ft.
500 m. 1,640 ft.
200 m. 656 ft.
100 m. 328 ft.
Sea Level
Below

AREA 255,285 sq. mi. (661,185 sq. km.)
POPULATION 2,237,724
CAPITAL Edmonton
LARGEST CITY Edmonton
HIGHEST POINT Mt. Columbia 12,294 ft. (3,747 m.)
SETTLED IN 1861
ADMITTED TO CONFEDERATION 1905
PROVINCIAL FLOWER Wild Rose

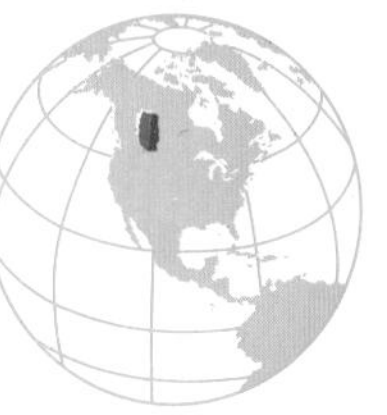

CITIES and TOWNS

Acme 457	D 4
Airdrie 8,414	D 4
Alberta Beach 485	C 3
Alix 837	D 3
Andrew 548	D 3
Antler Lake 334	D 3
Ardmore 224	E 2
Arrowwood 156	D 4
Athabasca 1,731	D 2
Banff 4,208	C 4
Barnwell 359	D 5
Barons 315	D 4
Barrhead 3,736	C 2
Bashaw 875	D 3
Bassano 1,200	D 4
Bawlf 350	D 3
Beaumont 2,638	D 3
Beaverlodge 1,937	A 2
Beiseker 580	D 4
Bentley 823	C 3
Berwyn 557	B 1
Big Valley 360	D 3
Black Diamond 1,444	C 4
Blackfalds 1,488	D 3
Blackfoot 220	E 3
Blackie 298	D 4
Bon Accord 1,376	D 3
Bonnyville 4,454	E 2
Bowden 989	C 4
Bow Island 1,491	E 5
Boyle 638	D 2
Bragg Creek 505	C 4
Breton 552	C 3
Brooks 9,421	E 4
Bruce 88	E 3
Bruderheim 1,136	D 3
Burdett 220	E 5
Calgary 592,743	C 4
Calgary *592,743	C 4
Calmar 1,003	D 3
Camrose 12,570	D 3
Canmore 3,484	C 4
Carbon 434	D 4
Cardston 3,267	D 5
Carmangay 266	D 4
Caroline 436	C 3
Carseland 484	D 4
Carstairs 1,587	D 4
Castor 1,123	D 3
Cereal 249	E 4
Champion 339	D 4
Chauvin 298	E 3
Chipman 266	D 3
Clairmont 469	A 2
Claresholm 3,493	D 4
Clive 364	D 3
Clyde 364	D 2
Coaldale 4,579	D 5
Coalhurst 882	D 5
Cochrane 3,544	C 4
Cold Lake 2,110	E 2
College Heights 267	D 3
Consort 632	E 3
Cooking Lake 218	D 3
Coronation 1,309	E 3
Coutts 400	D 5
Cowley 304	D 5
Cremona 382	C 4
Crossfield 1,217	C 4
Daysland 679	D 3
Delburne 574	D 3
Desmarais 260	D 2
Devon 3,885	D 3
Didsbury 3,095	C 4
Donalda 280	D 3
Donnelly 336	B 2
Drayton Valley 5,042	C 3
Drumheller 6,508	D 4
Duchess 429	E 4
East Coulee 218	D 4
Eckville 870	C 3
Edgerton 387	E 3
Edmonton (cap.) 532,246	D 3
Edmonton *657,057	D 3
Edmonton Beach 280	C 3
Edson 5,835	B 3
Elk Point 1,022	E 3
Elnora 249	D 3
Entwistle 462	C 3
Erskine 259	D 3
Evansburg 779	C 3
Exshaw 353	C 4
Fairview 2,869	A 1
Falher 1,102	B 2
Faust 399	C 2
Foremost 568	E 5
Forestburg 924	E 3
Fort Assiniboine 207	C 2
Fort Chipewyan 944	C 5
Fort Macleod 3,139	D 5
Fort McKay 267	E 1
Fort McMurray 31,000	E 1
Fort Saskatchewan 12,169	D 3
Fort Vermilion 752	B 5
Fox Creek 1,978	B 2
Fox Lake 634	B 5
Gibbons 2,276	D 3
Gift Lake 428	C 2
Girouxville 325	B 2
Gleichen 381	D 4
Glendon 430	E 2
Glenwood 259	D 5
Grand Centre 3,146	E 2
Grande Cache 4,523	A 3
Grande Prairie 24,263	A 2
Granum 399	D 5
Grimshaw 2,316	B 1
Grouard Mission 221	C 2
Hanna 2,806	E 4
Hardisty 641	E 3
Hay Lakes 302	D 3
Heisler 212	D 3
High Level 2,194	A 5
High Prairie 2,506	B 2
High River 4,792	D 4
Hines Creek 575	A 1
Hinton 8,342	B 3
Holden 430	D 3
Hughenden 267	E 3
Hythe 639	A 2
Innisfail 5,247	D 3
Innisfree 255	E 3
Irma 474	E 3
Irricana 558	D 4
Irvine 360	E 5
Jasper 3,269	B 3
John d'Or Prairie 437	B 5
Joussard 330	B 2
Killam 1,005	E 3
Kinuso 285	C 2
Kitscoty 497	E 3
Lac La Biche 2,007	E 2
Lacombe 5,591	D 3
La Crete 479	B 5
Lake Louise 355	B 4
Lamont 1,563	D 3
Leduc 12,471	D 3
Legal 1,022	D 3
Lethbridge 54,072	D 5
Linden 407	D 4
Little Buffalo Lake 253	B 1
Lloydminster 8,997	E 3
Longview 301	C 4
Lougheed 226	E 3
Lundbreck 244	C 5
Magrath 1,576	D 5
Manning 1,173	B 1
Mannville 788	E 3
Marlboro 211	B 3
Marwayne 500	E 3
Mayerthorpe 1,475	C 3
McLennan 1,125	B 2
Medicine Hat 40,380	E 4
Milk River 894	D 5
Millet 1,120	D 3
Mirror 507	D 3
Monarch 212	D 5
Morinville 4,657	D 3
Morrin 244	D 4
Mundare 604	D 3
Myrnam 397	E 3
Nacmine 369	D 4
Nampa 334	B 1
Nanton 1,641	D 4
New Norway 291	D 3
New Sarepta 417	D 3
Nobleford 534	D 5
North Calling Lake 234	D 2
Okotoks 3,847	C 4
Olds 4,813	D 4
Onoway 621	C 3
Oyen 975	E 4
Peace River 5,907	B 1
Penhold 1,531	D 3
Picture Butte 1,404	D 5
Pincher Creek 3,757	D 5
Plamondon 259	D 2
Pollockville 19	E 4
Ponoka 5,221	D 3
Provost 1,645	E 3
Rainbow Lake 504	A 5
Ralston 357	E 4
Raymond 2,837	D 5
Redcliff 3,876	E 4
Red Deer 46,393	D 3
Redwater 1,932	D 3
Rimbey 1,685	C 3
Robb 230	B 3
Rockyford 329	D 4
Rocky Mountain House 4,698	C 3
Rosemary 328	E 4
Rycroft 649	A 2
Ryley 483	D 3
Saint Albert 31,996	D 3
Saint Paul 4,884	E 3
Sangudo 398	C 3
Sedgewick 879	E 3
Sexsmith 1,180	A 2
Shaughnessy 270	D 5
Sherwood Park 29,285	D 3
Slave Lake 4,506	C 2
Smith 216	D 2
Smoky Lake 1,074	D 2
Spirit River 1,104	A 2
Spruce Grove 10,326	D 3
Standard 379	D 4
Stavely 504	D 4
Stettler 5,136	D 3
Stirling 688	D 5
Stony Plain 4,839	C 3
Strathmore 2,986	D 4
Strome 281	E 3
Sundre 1,742	C 4
Swan Hills 2,497	C 2
Sylvan Lake 3,779	C 3
Taber 5,988	E 5
Thorhild 576	D 2
Thorsby 737	C 3
Three Hills 1,787	D 4
Tilley 345	E 4
Tofield 1,504	D 3
Trochu 880	D 4
Turner Valley 1,311	C 4
Two Hills 1,193	E 3
Valleyview 2,061	B 2
Vauxhall 1,049	D 4
Vegreville 5,251	E 3
Vermilion 3,766	E 3
Veteran 314	E 3
Viking 1,232	E 3
Vilna 345	E 2
Vulcan 1,489	D 4
Wabamun 662	C 3
Wabasca 701	D 2
Wainwright 4,266	E 3
Warburg 501	C 3
Warner 477	D 5
Waskatenau 290	D 2
Wembley 1,169	A 2
Westlock 4,424	C 2
Wetaskiwin 9,597	D 3
Whitecourt 5,585	C 2
Wildwood 441	C 3
Willingdon 366	E 3
Youngstown 297	E 4

OTHER FEATURES

Abraham (lake)	B 3
Alberta (mt.)	B 3
Assiniboine (mt.)	C 4
Athabasca (lake)	C 5
Athabasca (riv.)	D 1
Banff Nat'l Park	B 4
Battle (riv.)	D 3
Bear (lake)	A 2
Beaver (riv.)	E 2
Beaverhill (lake)	D 3
Behan (lake)	E 2
Belly (riv.)	D 5
Berland (riv.)	A 3
Berry (creek)	E 4
Biche (lake)	E 2
Big (isl.)	B 5
Big Horn (dam)	B 3
Bighorn (range)	B 3
Birch (hills)	A 2
Birch (lake)	E 3
Birch (mts.)	B 5
Birch (riv.)	B 5
Bison (lake)	B 1
Bittern (lake)	D 3
Botha (riv.)	B 1
Bow (riv.)	D 4
Boyer (riv.)	A 5
Brazeau (mt.)	B 3
Brazeau (riv.)	B 3
Buffalo (lake)	D 3
Buffalo Head (hills)	B 5
Burnt (lakes)	C 1
Cadotte (lake)	B 1
Cadotte (riv.)	B 1
Calling (lake)	D 2
Canal (creek)	E 5
Cardinal (lake)	B 1
Caribou (mts.)	B 5
Chinchaga (riv.)	A 5
Chip (lake)	C 3
Chipewyan (lake)	D 1
Chipewyan (riv.)	D 1
Christina (lake)	E 2
Christina (riv.)	E 1
Claire (lake)	B 5
Clear (hills)	A 1
Clearwater (riv.)	C 4
Clearwater (riv.)	E 1
Clyde (lake)	E 2
Cold (lake)	E 2
Columbia (mt.)	B 3
Crowsnest (pass)	C 5
Cypress (hills)	E 5
Cypress Hills Prov. Park	E 5
Dillon (riv.)	E 2
Dowling (lake)	D 4
Dunkirk (riv.)	D 1
Eisenhower (mt.)	C 4
Elbow (riv.)	C 4
Elk Island Nat'l Park	D 3
Ells (riv.)	D 1
Etzikom Coulee (riv.)	E 5
Eva (lake)	B 5
Farrell (lake)	D 4
Firebag (riv.)	E 1
Forbes (mt.)	B 4
Freeman (riv.)	C 2
Frog (lake)	E 3
Garson (lake)	E 1
Gipsy (lake)	E 1
Gordon (lake)	E 1
Gough (lake)	D 3
Graham (lake)	C 1
Gull (lake)	C 3
Haig (lake)	B 1
Hawk (hills)	B 1
Hay (lake)	A 5
Hay (riv.)	A 5
Heart (lake)	E 2
Highwood (riv.)	C 4
House (mt.)	C 2
House (riv.)	D 2
Iosegun (lake)	B 2
Iosegun (riv.)	B 2
Jackfish (riv.)	B 5
Jasper Nat'l Park	A 3
Kakwa (riv.)	A 2
Kickinghorse (pass)	B 4
Kimiwan (lake)	B 2
Kirkpatrick (lake)	E 4
Kitchener (mt.)	B 3
Legend (lake)	D 1
Lesser Slave (lake)	C 2
Liége (riv.)	D 1
Little Bow (riv.)	D 4
Little Cadotte (riv.)	B 1
Little Smoky (riv.)	B 2
Livingstone (range)	C 4
Logan (lake)	E 2
Loon (lake)	C 1
Loon (riv.)	C 1
Lubicon (lake)	C 1
Lyell (mt.)	B 4
MacKay (riv.)	D 1
Maligne (lake)	B 3
Margaret (lake)	B 5
Marie (lake)	E 2
Marion (lake)	D 3
Marten (mt.)	C 2
McClelland (lake)	E 1
McGregor (lake)	D 4
McLeod (riv.)	B 3
Meikle (riv.)	A 1
Mikkwa (riv.)	B 5
Milk (riv.)	D 5
Mistehae (lake)	C 2
Muriel (lake)	E 2
Muskwa (lake)	C 1
Muskwa (riv.)	C 1
Namur (lake)	D 1
Newell (lake)	E 4
Nordegg (riv.)	C 3
North Saskatchewan (riv.)	E 3
North Wabasca (lake)	D 1
Notikewin (riv.)	A 1
Oldman (riv.)	D 5
Otter (lakes)	B 1
Pakowki (lake)	E 5
Panny (riv.)	C 1
Peace (riv.)	B 1
Peerless (lake)	C 1
Pelican (lake)	D 2
Pelican (mts.)	D 2
Pembina (riv.)	C 3
Pigeon (lake)	D 3
Pinehurst (lake)	E 2
Porcupine (hills)	C 4
Primrose (lake)	E 2
Rainbow (lake)	A 5
Red Deer (lake)	D 3
Red Deer (riv.)	D 4
Richardson (riv.)	C 5
Rocky (mts.)	B-C 4
Rosebud (riv.)	D 4
Russell (lake)	C 1
Saddle (hills)	A 2
Sainte Anne (lake)	C 3
Saint Mary (res.)	D 5
Saint Mary (riv.)	D 5
Saulteaux (riv.)	C 2
Seibert (lake)	E 2
Simonette (riv.)	A 2
Slave (riv.)	C 5
Smoky (riv.)	A 2
Snake Indian (riv.)	A 3
Snipe (lake)	B 2
Sounding (creek)	E 4
South Saskatchewan (riv.)	E 4
South Wabasca (lake)	D 2
Spencer (lake)	E 2
Spray (mts.)	C 4
Sturgeon (lake)	B 2
Sullivan (lake)	D 3
Swan (hills)	C 2
Swan (riv.)	C 2
Temple (mt.)	B 4
The Twins (mt.)	B 3
Thickwood (hills)	D 1
Touchwood (lake)	E 2
Travers (res.)	D 4
Trout (mt.)	C 1
Trout (riv.)	C 1
Utikuma (lake)	C 2
Utikuma (riv.)	C 1
Utikumasis (lake)	C 2
Vermilion (riv.)	E 3
Wabasca (riv.)	C 1
Wallace (mt.)	C 2
Wapiti (riv.)	A 2
Wappau (lake)	E 2
Watchusk (lake)	E 1
Waterton-Glacier Int'l Peace Park	C 5
Waterton Lakes Nat'l Park	C 5
Whitemud (riv.)	A 1
Wildhay (riv.)	B 3
Willmore Wilderness Prov. Park	A 3
Winagami (lake)	B 2
Winefred (lake)	E 2
Winefred (riv.)	E 2
Wolf (lake)	E 2
Wolverine (riv.)	B 1
Wood Buffalo Nat'l Park	B 5
Yellowhead (pass)	A 3
Zama (lake)	A 5

*Population of metropolitan area.

Agriculture, Industry and Resources

DOMINANT LAND USE

- Wheat
- Cereals (chiefly barley, oats)
- Cereals, Livestock
- Dairy
- Pasture Livestock
- Range Livestock
- Forests
- Nonagricultural Land

MAJOR MINERAL OCCURRENCES

- C Coal
- O Petroleum
- G Natural Gas
- S Sulfur
- Na Salt
- Water Power
- Major Industrial Areas

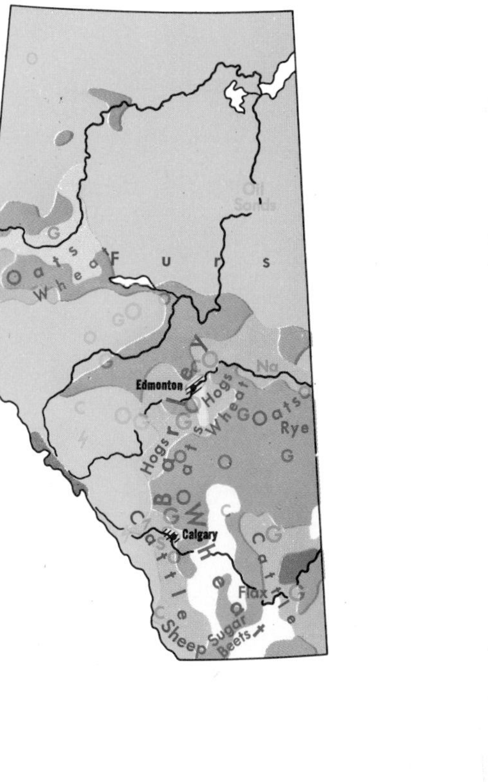
Furs
Oats
Wheat
Oil Sands
Edmonton
Calgary
Hogs
Oats
Wheat
Rye
Cattle
Sheep
Sugar Beets
Flax
Na

Topography

0   100   200 MI.

0   100   200 KM.

Mt. Fairweather 15,300 ft. (4663 m.)

Mt. Robson 12,972 ft. (3954 m.)

Mt. Waddington 13,104 ft. (3994 m.)

Prince Rupert

Graham I.

QUEEN CHARLOTTE ISLANDS

Moresby I.

Hecate Strait

QUEEN CHARLOTTE SOUND

Prince George

Kicking Horse Pass

Crowsnest Pass

Vancouver

Kelowna

Island

Vancouver

Victoria

| Below Sea Level | 100 m. 328 ft. | 200 m. 656 ft. | 500 m. 1,640 ft. | 1,000 m. 3,281 ft. | 2,000 m. 6,562 ft. | 5,000 m. 16,404 ft. |

CITIES and TOWNS

Abbotsford 12,745 .... L 3
Alert Bay 626 .... D 5
Armstrong 2,683 .... H 5
Ashcroft 2,156 .... G 5
Ashton Creek 452 .... H 5
Balfour 472 .... J 5
Barlow 441 .... F 3
Barrière 1,370 .... H 4
Blueberry Creek 635 .... J 5
Blue River 384 .... H 4
Boston Bar 498 .... G 5
Bowen Island 1,125 .... K 3
Brackendale 1,719 .... F 5
Burnaby ○136,494 .... K 3
Burns Lake 1,777 .... D 3
Cache Creek 1,308 .... G 5
Campbell River 15,370 ..... E 5
Canal Flats 919 .... K 5
Canyon 698 .... J 5
Cassiar 1,045 .... K 2
Castlegar 6,902 .... J 5

Cawston 785 .... H 5
Central Saanich ○9,890 .... K 3
Chase 1,777 .... H 5
Chemainus 2,069 .... J 3
Cherry Creek 450 .... G 5
Chetwynd 2,553 .... G 2
Chilliwack ○40,642 .... M 3
Clearwater 1,461 .... G 4
Clinton 804 .... G 4
Coldstream ○6,450 .... H 5
Comox 6,607 .... H 2
Coquitlam ○61,077 .... K 3
Courtenay 8,992 .... E 5
Cranbrook 15,915 .... K 5
Creston 4,190 .... J 5
Crofton 1,303 .... J 3
Cultus Lake 481 .... M 3
Cumberland 1,947 .... E 5
Dawson Creek 11,373 ..... G 2
Delta ○74,692 .... K 3
Duncan 4,228 .... J 3
Elkford 3,126 .... K 5
Enderby 1,816 .... H 5
Erickson 972 .... J 5

Errington 609 .... J 3
Esquimalt ○15,870 .... K 4
Falkland 478 .... H 5
Fernie 5,444 .... K 5
Forest Grove 444 .... G 4
Fort Fraser 574 .... E 3
Fort Langley 2,326 ..... L 3
Fort Nelson 3,724 ...... M 2
Fort Saint James 2,284 .. E 3
Fort Saint John 13,891 .. G 2
Fraser Lake 1,543 ...... E 3
Fruitvale 1,904 .... J 5
Gabriola 1,627 .... J 3
Galiano 826 .... K 3
Ganges 1,118 .... K 3
Gibsons 2,594 .... K 3
Gold River 2,225 ..... D 5
Golden 3,476 .... J 4
Grand Forks 3,486 .... H 6
Granisle 1,430 .... D 3
Greenwood 856 .... H 5
Hagensborg 350 ...... D 4
Harrison Hot Springs 569 . M 3
Hatzic 1,055 .... L 3

Hazelton 393 .... D 2
Hedley 426 .... G 5
Holberg 444 .... C 5
Honeymoon Bay 474 ..... J 3
Hope 3,205 .... M 3
Hornby Island 474 ..... H 2
Horsefly 430 .... G 4
Houston 1,714 .... D 3
Hudson Hope 984 ...... F 2
Invermere 1,969 ...... J 5
Kaleden 998 .... H 5
Kamloops 64,048 ..... G 5
Kaslo 854 .... J 5
Kelowna 59,196 ...... H 5
Kent ○3,394 .... M 3
Keremeos 830 .... G 5
Kimberley 7,375 ..... K 5
Kitimat 12,462 ...... C 3
Kitsault 554 .... C 2
Kitwanga 369 .... D 2
Lac La Hache 647 .... G 4
Ladysmith 4,558 .... J 3
Lake Cowichan 2,391 .. J 3
Langley 15,124 ..... L 3
Lantzville 969 ..... J 3
Likely 425 .... G 4
Lillooet 1,725 ..... G 5
Lion's Bay 1,078 ... K 3
Logan Lake 2,637 ... G 5
Lumby 1,266 .... H 5
Lytton 428 .... G 5
Mackenzie 5,797 .... F 2
Mackenzie ○5,890 ... F 2
Malakwa 392 .... H 5
Maple Bay 393 ..... K 3
Maple Ridge ○32,232 . L 3
Masset 1,569 ...... B 3
Matsqui ○42,001 ... L 3
Mayne 546 .... K 3
McBride 641 ...... G 3
Merritt 6,110 .... G 5
Midway 633 ...... H 6
Mill Bay 583 .... K 3
Mission ○20,056 .. L 3
Mission City 9,948 . L 3
Montrose 1,229 ... J 5
Nakusp 1,495 ..... J 5
Nanaimo 47,069 ... J 3
Naramata 876 ..... H 5
Nelson 9,143 ..... J 5
New Denver 642 ... J 5
New Hazelton 792 . D 2
New Westminster 38,550 . K 3
Nicomen Island 360 . L 3
Nootka .... D 5
North Cowichan ○18,210 . J 3
North Pender Island 906 . K 3
North Saanich ○6,117 . K 3
North Vancouver 33,952 . K 3
North Vancouver ○65,367 . K 3
Oak Bay ○16,990 .. K 4
Okanagan Falls 1,030 . H 5
Okanagan Landing 834 . H 5
Okanagan Mission .. H 5
Old Barkerville 11 . G 3
Oliver 1,893 ..... H 5
One Hundred Mile House
  1,925 .... G 4
Osoyoos 2,738 .... H 5
Oyama 430 .... H 5
Parksville 5,216 .. J 3
Peachland ○2,865 . G 5

Penticton 23,181 .... H 5
Pitt Meadows ○6,209 .... L 3
Port Alberni 19,892 .... H 3
Port Alice 1,668 ...... L 3
Port Clements 380 ..... B 3
Port Coquitlam 27,535 .. L 3
Port Edward 989 ...... B 3
Port Hardy ○3,778 .... D 5
Port McNeill 2,474 ... D 5
Port Moody 14,917 ... L 3
Pouce-Coupé 821 ..... G 2
Powell River ○13,423 . E 5
Prince George 67,559 . F 3
Prince Rupert 16,197 . B 3
Princeton 3,051 ..... G 5
Qualicum Beach 2,844 . J 3
Queen Charlotte 1,070 . A 3
Quesnel 8,240 ...... F 4
Radium Hot Springs 419 . J 5
Revelstoke 5,544 .... J 5
Richmond ○96,154 ... K 3
Roberts Creek 926 ... J 3
Robson 1,008 ...... J 5
Rossland 3,967 .... H 6
Royston 754 ...... H 2
Saanich ○78,710 ... K 3
Salmo 1,169 ..... J 5
Salmon Arm 1,946 .. H 5
Salmon Arm ○10,780 . H 5
Saltair 1,356 .... J 3
Sandspit 794 .... B 3
Sayward 482 ..... D 5
Sechelt 1,096 ... J 3
Shawnigan Lake 419 . J 3
Shoreacres 555 .. J 5
Sicamous 1,057 .. H 5
Sidney 7,946 .... K 3
Slocan 351 ..... J 5
Slocan Park 414 .. J 5
Smithers 4,570 .. D 2
Sointula 567 ... D 5
Sooke 852 ..... J 4
Sorrento 659 ... H 5
South Hazelton 500 . D 2
South Wellington 620 . J 3
Spallumcheen 4,213 . H 5
Sparwood 3,267 ... K 5
Sproat Lake 440 .. H 3
Squamish 1,590 ... F 5
Stewart ○1,456 ... C 2
Summerland ○7,473 . G 5
Surrey ○147,138 .. K 3
Tahsis 1,739 .... D 5
Taylor 966 ..... G 2
Telkwa 840 .... D 2
Terrace 8,893 ... C 3
Terrace ○10,914 . C 3
Thornhill 4,281 . C 3
Thrums 360 .... J 5
Tofino 705 .... E 5
Trail 9,599 ... J 6
Ucluelet 1,593 . E 6
Union Bay 601 .. H 2
Valemount 1,130 . H 4
Vancouver 414,281 . K 3
Vancouver (Greater)
  *1,169,831 ... K 3
Vanderhoof 2,323 . E 3
Vavenby 479 .... H 4
Vernon 19,987 ... H 5
Victoria (cap.) 64,379 . K 4
Victoria *233,481 .. K 4
Warfield 1,969 ... J 5
Wasa 345 ..... J 5
Wells 417 .... G 3
Westbank 1,271 . H 5
West Vancouver ○35,728 . K 3
Westwold 409 ... H 5
Whistler ○1,365 . G 5
White Rock 13,550 . K 3
Williams Lake 8,362 . F 4
Wilson Creek 611 . J 2
Windermere 611 .. J 2
Winlaw 435 ..... K 5
Woss Lake 395 .. D 5
Wynndel 566 ... J 5
Yarrow 1,201 ... M 3
Youbou 965 .... J 3

OTHER FEATURES

Adams (lake) .... H 4
Adams (riv.) .... H 4
Alberni (inlet) ...... J 3
Alsek (riv.) .... H 1
Aristazabal (isl.) ... C 4
Assiniboine (mt.) .... K 5
Atlin (lake) .... J 1
Azure (lake) ...... G 4
Babine (lake) ..... E 3
Babine (riv.) ..... D 2
Banks (isl.) ..... B 3
Barkley (sound) ... E 6
Beale (cape) ..... E 6
Beatton (riv.) ... G 1
Bella Coola (riv.) . D 4
Bennett, W.A.C. (dam) . F 2
Birkenhead Lake Prov. Park . F 5
Bowron Lake Prov. Park . G 3
Bowser (lake) .... D 2
Brooks (pen.) .... D 5
Browning Entrance (str.) . B 3
Bryce (mt.) ..... J 4
Bugaboo Glacier Prov. Park . J 5
Bulkley (riv.) ... D 2
Burke (chan.) ... D 4
Burnaby (isl.) .. B 4
Bute (inlet) .... D 4
Caamaño (sound) . C 4
Calvert (isl.) .. C 4
Canim (lake) ... G 4
Canoe (riv.) .. H 4
Cariboo (mts.) . G 3
Carpenter (lake) . F 5
Carp Lake Prov. Park . F 3
Cassiar (mts.) . K 2
Castle (mt.) .. A 2

Cathedral Prov. Park ..... H 5
Charlotte (lake) .... E 4
Chatham (sound) .... B 3
Chehalis (lake) ...... L 3
Chilcotin (riv.) ..... E 4
Chilko (lake) ...... F 4
Chilko (riv.) ..... F 4
Chilkoot (pass) .... J 1
Chuchi (lake) ..... E 2
Churchill (peak) .. L 2
Clayoquot (sound) . D 5
Clearwater (lake) . G 4
Clearwater (riv.) . G 4
Coast (mts.) ..... D 3
Columbia (lake) .. K 5
Columbia (mt.) ... J 4
Columbia (riv.) .. J 5
Cook (cape) ..... C 5
Cowichan (lake) . J 3
Crowsnest (pass) . K 5
Cypress Prov. Park . K 3
Dean (chan.) .... D 4
Dean (riv.) .... D 4
Dease (lake) ... K 2
Dease (riv.) ... K 2
Devils Thumb (mt.) . K 2
Dixon Entrance (chan.) . A 3
Douglas (chan.) .. C 3
Duncan (riv.) ... J 5
Dundas (isl.) ... B 3
Elk (riv.) ..... K 5
Elk Lakes Prov. Park . K 5
Eutsuk (lake) .. D 3

Fairweather (mt.) ...... H 1
Finlay (riv.) .... E 1
Fitzhugh (sound) ..... D 4
Flathead (riv.) ..... K 6
Flores (isl.) ...... D 5
Fontas (riv.) ..... M 2
Forbes (mt.) ..... J 4
Fort Nelson (riv.) . M 2
François (lake) ... D 3
Fraser (lake) ... E 3
Fraser (riv.) ... F 4
Fraser Reach (chan.) . C 3
Galiano (isl.) ... K 3
Gardner (canal) .. C 3
Garibaldi Prov. Park . F 5
Georgia (str.) .. J 3
Germansen (lake) . E 2
Gil (isl.) ..... C 3
Glacier Nat'l Park . J 3
Golden Ears Prov. Park . L 2
Gordon (riv.) ... J 3
Graham (isl.) .. A 3
Graham Reach (chan.) . C 3
Grenville (chan.) . C 3
Halfway (riv.) .. F 1
Hamber Prov. Park . H 4
Harrison (lake) .. M 2
Hawkesbury (isl.) . C 3
Hazelton (mts.) . C 2
Hecate (str.) ... B 3
Hobson (lake) .. G 4
Homathko (riv.) . E 4
Horsefly (lake) . G 4

Agriculture, Industry and Resources

DOMINANT LAND USE

- Cereals, Livestock
- Dairy
- Fruits, Vegetables
- Pasture Livestock
- Forests
- Nonagricultural Land

MAJOR MINERAL OCCURRENCES

Ab	Asbestos	Gp	Gypsum
Ag	Silver	Mo	Molybdenum
Au	Gold	Ni	Nickel
C	Coal	O	Petroleum
Cu	Copper	Pb	Lead
Fe	Iron Ore	S	Sulfur
G	Natural Gas	Sn	Tin
		Zn	Zinc

⚡ Water Power

▨ Major Industrial Areas

Kitimat

Vancouver

Victoria

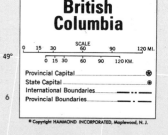

British Columbia

SCALE

0 15 30   60   90   120 MI.

0 15 30   60   90   120 KM.

Provincial Capital .... ✬
State Capital .... ✫
International Boundaries ... ———
Provincial Boundaries ..... ———

© Copyright HAMMOND INCORPORATED, Maplewood, N.J.

Howe (sound)	K 2	Louise (isl.)	B 4	Nootka (sound)	D 5	Quesnel (riv.)	F 4	
Hunter (isl.)	C 4	Lower Arrow (lake)	H 5	North Thompson (riv.)	G 4	Rivers (inlet)	D 4	
Inklin (riv.)	A 1	Lyell (isl.)	B 4	Observatory (inlet)	C 2	Robson (mt.)	H 3	
Inzana (lake)	E 3	Lyell (mt.)	J 4	Okanagan (lake)	H 5	Rocky (mts.)	F 2	
Isaac (lake)	G 3	Mabel (lake)	H 5	Okanagan Mtn. Prov. Park	H 5	Roderick (isl.)	C 4	
Iskut (riv.)	B 2	Mahood (lake)	G 4	Okanogan (riv.)	H 6	Rose (pt.)	B 3	
Jervis (inlet)	E 5	Malaspina (str.)	J 2	Omineca (mts.)	E 2	Saint James (cape)	B 4	
John Jay (mt.)	G 5	Manning Prov. Park	G 5	Omineca (riv.)	E 2	Salmon (riv.)	F 3	
Johnstone (str.)	D 5	Masset (inlet)	A 3	Ootsa (lake)	D 3	Salmon Arm (inlet)	J 2	
Juan de Fuca (str.)	J 4	McCauley (isl.)	B 3	Owikeno (lake)	D 4	San Juan (riv.)	J 3	
Kates Needle (mt.)	A 1	McGregor (riv.)	G 3	Pacific Rim Nat'l Park	E 6	Schoen Lake Prov. Park	E 5	
Kechika (riv.)	L 2	Meziadin (lake)	C 2	Parsnip (riv.)	F 3	Scott (cape)	C 5	
Kenney (dam)	E 3	Milbanke (sound)	C 4	Peace (riv.)	G 2	Scott (isls.)	C 5	
Kettle (riv.)	H 5	Moberly (lake)	F 2	Pend Oreille (riv.)	J 6	Seechelt (inlet)	J 2	
Kicking Horse (pass)	J 4	Monashee (mts.)	H 4	Petitot (riv.)	M 2	Seechelt (pen.)	J 2	
King (isl.)	D 4	Moresby (isl.)	B 4	Pinchi (lake)	E 3	Selkirk (mts.)	J 4	
Klinaklini (riv.)	E 4	Morice (lake)	D 3	Pine (riv.)	G 2	Seymour (inlet)	D 4	
Kloch (lake)	E 2	Morice (riv.)	D 3	Pitt (riv.)	C 3	Sheslay (riv.)	J 2	
Knight (inlet)	E 5	Mount Assiniboine Prov. Park	K 5	Pitt (lake)	L 2	Shuswap (lake)	H 4	
Knox (cape)	A 3	Mount Edziza Prov. Park and		Porcher (isl.)	B 3	Sikanni Chief (riv.)	F 1	
Kokanee Glacier Prov. Park	J 5	Rec. Area.	B 1	Portland (canal)	B 2	Silver Star Prov. Park	H 5	
Koocanusa (lake)	K 6	Mount Revelstoke Nat'l Park	H 4	Portland (inlet)	C 3	Sir Sandford (mt.)	H 4	
Kootenay (lake)	J 5	Mount Robson Prov. Park	H 3	Price (riv.)	G 6	Skagit (riv.)	G 6	
Kootenay (riv.)	J 5	Muncho Lake Prov. Park	L 2	Princess Royal (isl.)	C 3	Skeena (mts.)	C 2	
Kootenay Nat'l Park	J 4	Murray (riv.)	G 3	Principe (chan.)	C 3	Skeena (riv.)	C 3	
Kotcho (lake)	M 2	Murtle (lake)	H 4	Prophet (riv.)	M 2	Skidegate (inlet)	B 3	
Kotcho (riv.)	M 2	Muskwa (riv.)	M 2	Purcell (mts.)	J 5	Slocan (lake)	J 5	
Kunghit (isl.)	B 4	Nanika (dam)	D 3	Quatsino (sound)	C 5	Smith (sound)	C 4	
Kyuquot (sound)	D 5	Nass (riv.)	C 2	Queen Charlotte (isls.)	B 3	South Bentinck Arm (inlet)	D 4	
Langara (isl.)	A 3	Nation (riv.)	F 2	Queen Charlotte (sound)	C 4	Stave (lake)	L 3	
Laredo (sound)	C 4	Nechako (riv.)	E 3	Queen Charlotte (str.)	D 5	Stephens (isl.)	B 3	
Liard (riv.)	L 2	Nitinat (lake)	H 3	Queens (sound)	C 4	Stikine (riv.)	B 1	
Lillooet (riv.)	F 5	Nootka (isl.)	D 5	Quesnel (lake)	G 4	Stone Mountain Prov. Park	L 2	

Strathcona Prov. Park	E 5	Three Guardsmen (mt.)	H 1
Stuart (lake)	E 3	Thutade (lake)	D 2
Sustut (riv.)	D 2	Tiedemann (mt.)	E 4
Tagish (lake)	J 1	Toad (riv.)	L 2
Tahtsa (lake)	D 3	Toba (inlet)	E 5
Takla (lake)	D 2	Tochcha (lake)	E 3
Taku (riv.)	J 2	Top Of The World Prov. Park	K 5
Tatlatui (lake)	D 2	Trembleur (lake)	E 3
Tatlayoko (lake)	E 4	Troitsa (lake)	D 3
Tchentlo (lake)	E 2	Tumeka (lake)	C 1
Teslin (lake)	K 1	Turnagain (riv.)	K 2
Tetachuck (lake)	E 3	Tuya (riv.)	K 2
Texada (isl.)	J 2	Tweedsmuir Prov. Park	D 3
Tezzeron (lake)	E 3	Upper Arrow (lake)	H 5
Thompson (riv.)	G 5	Valdes (isl.)	K 3

Vancouver (isl.)	D 5
Virago (sound)	A 3
Waddington (mt.)	E 4
Wapiti (riv.)	H 3
Wells Gray Prov. Park	H 4
West Road (riv.)	E 3
Whitesail (lake)	D 3
Williston (lake)	F 2
Work (chan.)	C 3
Yellowhead (pass)	H 4
Yoho Nat'l Park	J 4

AREA 366,253 sq. mi. (948,596 sq. km.)
POPULATION 2,744,467
CAPITAL Victoria
LARGEST CITY Vancouver
HIGHEST POINT Mt. Fairweather 15,300 ft.
    (4,663 m.)
SETTLED IN 1806
ADMITTED TO CONFEDERATION 1871
PROVINCIAL FLOWER Dogwood

*Population of metropolitan area.
○Population of municipality.

118 Mexico

Topography

0   150   300 MI.
0   150   300 KM.

Tijuana
Ciudad Juárez
Sierra Madre Occidental
Bolsón de Mapimí
Monterrey
Falcon Res.
Rio Grande
C. San Lucas
Islas Marías
León
Guadalajara
C. Corrientes
L. de Chapala
IS. REVILLAGIGEDO
Mexico City
Popocatépetl 17,887 ft. (5451 m.)
Citlaltépetl 18,855 ft. (5747 m.)
Yucatán Pen.
Bay of Campeche
Lag. de Términos
Sierra Madre del Sur
Acapulco
Isthmus of Tehuantepec
Gulf of Tehuantepec

5,000 m. 16,404 ft. | 2,000 m. 6,562 ft. | 1,000 m. 3,281 ft. | 500 m. 1,640 ft. | 200 m. 656 ft. | 100 m. 328 ft. | Sea Level | Below

---

STATES

Aguascalientes 504,300 .... H6
Baja California 1,227,400 .... B1
Baja California Sur 221,000 .... C3
Campeche 371,800 .... O7
Chiapas 2,097,500 .... N8
Chihuahua 1,935,100 .... F2
Coahuila 1,561,000 .... H3
Colima 339,400 .... G7
Distrito Federal 9,377,300 .... L1
Durango 1,160,300 .... G4
Guanajuato 3,045,600 .... J6
Guerrero 2,174,200 .... J8
Hidalgo 1,518,200 .... K6
Jalisco 4,296,500 .... H6
México 7,542,300 .... K7
Michoacán 3,049,400 .... H7
Morelos 931,400 .... K7
Nayarit 729,500 .... G6
Nuevo León 2,463,500 .... J4
Oaxaca 2,517,500 .... L8
Puebla 3,285,300 .... K7
Querétaro 730,900 .... J6
Quintana Roo 209,900 .... P7
San Luis Potosí 1,669,900 .... J5
Sinaloa 1,882,200 .... F4
Sonora 1,498,100 .... D2
Tabasco 1,150,000 .... N7
Tamaulipas 1,924,900 .... K4
Tlaxcala 548,500 .... N1
Veracruz 5,263,800 .... L7
Yucatán 1,034,300 .... P6
Zacatecas 1,144,700 .... H5

CITIES and TOWNS

Acala 11,483 .... N8
Acámbaro 32,257 .... J7
Acaponeta 11,844 .... G6
Acapulco de Juárez 309,254 .... K8
Acatlán de Osorio 7,624 .... K7
Acatzingo de Hidalgo 6,905 .... N2
Aconchi 1,596 .... D2
Actopan, Hidalgo 11,037 .... K6
Actopan, Veracruz 2,265 .... Q1
Agua Dulce 21,060 .... M7
Agualeguas 2,502 .... J3
Agua Prieta 20,754 .... E1
Aguascalientes 181,277 .... H6
Aguililla 5,715 .... H7
Ahome 4,182 .... E4
Ahuacatitlán 4,436 .... L1
Ahuacatlán 5,350 .... G6
Ahumada 6,466 .... F1
Ajalpan 8,238 .... L7
Álamo 9,954 .... L6
Álamos 4,269 .... E3
Aldama, Chihuahua 6,047 .... G2
Aldama, Tamaulipas 3,033 .... K5
Aljojuca 3,204 .... O1
Allende, Coahuila 11,076 .... J2
Allende, Nuevo León 9,914 .... J4
Almoloya del Río 3,714 .... K1
Altamira 6,053 .... L5
Altar 2,519 .... D1
Altepexi 6,661 .... L7
Alto Lucero 3,698 .... P1
Altotonga 6,754 .... P1
Alvarado 15,592 .... M7
Amatlán de los Reyes 3,664 .... P2
Amealco 2,960 .... K6
Ameca 21,018 .... H6
Amecameca de Juárez 16,276 .... L1
Amozoc de Mota 9,203 .... N2
Anáhuac, Chihuahua 10,886 .... F2
Anáhuac, Nuevo León 8,168 .... J3
Angostura 4,104 .... E4
Antiguo Morelos 1,569 .... K5
Apan 13,705 .... M1
Apatzingán de la
  Constitución 44,849 .... H7
Apizaco 21,189 .... N1
Aquiles Serdán 2,565 .... G2
Aramberri 1,786 .... J4
Arandas 18,934 .... H6
Arcelia 10,024 .... J7
Ario de Rosales 8,774 .... H7
Arizpe 1,736 .... D1
Armería 10,616 .... G7
Arriaga 13,193 .... N8
Arteaga 5,324 .... H7
Ascensión 4,104 .... E1
Asunción Nochixtlán 3,235 .... L8
Atlixco 41,967 .... M2
Atotonilco el Alto 16,271 .... H6
Atoyac de Álvarez 8,874 .... J8
Autlán de Navarro 20,398 .... G7
Axochiapan 8,283 .... M2
Ayutla de los Libres 3,618 .... K8
Azcapotzalco 534,554 .... L1
Azoyú 3,446 .... K8
Bacadéhuachi 1,514 .... E2

Bacalar 2,121 .... P7
Bachíniva 1,809 .... F2
Bácum 2,668 .... D3
Bahía Tortugas 1,457 .... B3
Balancán de
  Domínguez 3,669 .... O8
Bamoa 5,866 .... E4
Banderilla 3,488 .... P2
Baviácora 2,049 .... E2
Benjamín Hill 5,366 .... D1
Bernardino de Sahagún 12,327 .... N1
Boca del Río 2,354 .... Q2
Bolonchén de Rejón 2,342 .... O7
Buenaventura 3,924 .... F2
Burgos 673 .... K4
Cabo San Lucas 1,534 .... C5
Cacahoatán 5,079 .... N9
Cadereyta Jiménez 13,586 .... K4
Calkiní 6,870 .... O6
Calnali 3,318 .... K6
Calpulalpan 8,659 .... M1
Calvillo 6,453 .... H6
Campeche 69,506 .... O7
Cananea 17,518 .... D1
Canatlán 5,983 .... G6
Cancún 326 .... Q6
Candela 1,689 .... J3
Candelaria 1,982 .... O7
Canitas de Felipe
  Pescador 4,885 .... H5
Capulhuac de Mirafuentes 8,289 .... K1
Cárdenas 2,804 .... D2
Cárdenas, San Luis
  Potosí 12,020 .... K6
Cárdenas, Tabasco 15,643 .... N8
Carichic 1,520 .... F3
Castaños 8,996 .... J3
Catemaco 11,786 .... M7
Ceballos 2,937 .... H3
Cedral 4,057 .... J5
Celaya 79,977 .... J6
Celestún 1,490 .... O6
Cerritos 10,421 .... J5
Cerro Azul 20,259 .... L6
Chahuites 5,218 .... M8
Chalchihuites 1,894 .... G5
Chalco de Díaz
  Covarrubias 12,172 .... M1
Champotón 6,606 .... O7
Charcas 10,491 .... J5
Chetumal 23,685 .... Q7
Chiapa de Corzo 8,571 .... N8
Chiautempan 12,327 .... N1
Chietla 4,602 .... M2
Chignahuapan 3,805 .... N1
Chihuahua 327,313 .... F2
Chilapa de Álvarez 9,204 .... K8
Chilpancingo de los
  Bravos 36,193 .... K8
China, Nuevo León 4,958 .... K4
Chocomán 5,114 .... P2
Choix 2,503 .... E3
Chumatlán 9,451 .... G7
Cintalapa de Figueroa 12,036 .... N8
Ciudad Acuña (Villa
  Acuña) 30,276 .... J2
Ciudad Altamirano 8,694 .... J7
Ciudad Camargo,
  Tamaulipas 5,953 .... K3
Ciudad Camargo,
  Chihuahua 24,030 .... G3
Ciudad Camargo,
  Tamaulipas 5,953 .... K3
Ciudad del Carmen 34,656 .... N7
Ciudad Delicias 52,446 .... G2
Ciudad del Maíz 5,241 .... K5
Ciudad de Río Grande 11,651 .... H5
Ciudad Guerrero 3,110 .... F2
Ciudad Guzmán 48,166 .... H7
Ciudad Hidalgo, Chiapas 4,105 .... N9
Ciudad Hidalgo,
  Michoacán 24,692 .... J7
Ciudad Juárez 424,135 .... F1
Ciudad Lerdo 19,803 .... H4
Ciudad Madero 115,302 .... L5
Ciudad Mante 51,247 .... K5
Ciudad Obregón 144,795 .... E3
Ciudad Miguel Alemán 11,259 .... K3
Ciudad Río Bravo 38,696 .... K3
Ciudad Satélite 35,083 .... L1
Ciudad Serdán 9,581 .... O2
Ciudad Valles 47,587 .... K5
Ciudad Victoria 83,897 .... K5
Coalcomán de Matamoros 4,875 .... H7
Coatepec 21,542 .... P1
Coatepelco 5,268 .... L2
Coatzacoalcos 69,753 .... M7
Coatzingo 3,038 .... M2
Cocorit 4,478 .... E3
Colima 58,450 .... H7
Colón 3,346 .... J6
Colotlán 6,135 .... H5
Comala 5,462 .... G7
Comalcalco 14,963 .... N7

Comitán de
  Domínguez 21,249 .... O8
Compostela 9,801 .... G6
Concepción del Oro 8,144 .... J4
Concordia 3,947 .... G5
Contla 7,517 .... N1
Copala 3,783 .... K8
Coquimatlán 6,212 .... G7
Córdoba 78,495 .... P2
Cosalá 2,279 .... F4
Cosamaloapan de Carpio 19,766 .... M7
Cosautlán de Carvajal 2,039 .... P2
Coscomatepec de Bravo 6,023 .... P2
Cosío 2,680 .... H5
Costa Rica 11,795 .... F4
Cotija de la Paz 9,178 .... H7
Coyoacán 339,446 .... L1
Coyotepec 8,888 .... L1
Coyuca de Benítez 6,328 .... J8
Coyuca de Catalán 2,926 .... J7
Coyutla 3,726 .... L6
Cozumel 5,858 .... Q6
Creel 2,449 .... E3
Cuatrociénagas de
  Carranza 5,523 .... H3
Cuauhtémoc 26,369 .... F2
Cuautepec de Hinojosa 5,501 .... K6
Cuautitlán de Romero
  Rubio 11,439 .... L1
Cuautla Morelos 13,946 .... L2
Cuencamé de Ceniceros 3,774 .... H4
Cuernavaca 239,813 .... L2
Cuicatlán 2,733 .... L8
Cuitlahuac 4,813 .... P2
Culiacán 228,001 .... F4
Cumpas 2,395 .... E2
Cunduacán 4,397 .... N7
Dimas 2,194 .... F4
Doctor Arroyo 4,290 .... K5
Dolores Hidalgo de la Independencia
  Naci 16,849 .... J6
Durango 182,633 .... G4
Dzibalchén 1,917 .... P7
Dzidzantún 7,064 .... P6
Dzitbalché 4,393 .... P6
Ébano 17,489 .... L6
Ecatepec de Morelos 11,899 .... L1
Ejutla de Crespo 5,263 .... L8
Eldorado 8,115 .... E4
El Fuerte 7,179 .... E3
El Porvenir 3,030 .... G1
El Potosí 2,032 .... J4
El Salto 7,818 .... G5
El Zacatón 2,686 .... J5
Empalme 24,927 .... D3
Encarnación de Díaz 10,474 .... H6
Ensenada 77,687 .... A1
Escalón 2,998 .... G3
Escárcega 7,248 .... O7
Escuinapa de Hidalgo 16,442 .... G5
Escuintla 4,111 .... N9
Esperanza, Puebla 4,258 .... O2
Esperanza, Sonora 11,762 .... L3
Espita 5,394 .... Q6
Esqueda 1,458 .... E1
Etchojoa 4,398 .... E3
Ezequiel Montes 3,139 .... K6
Fortín de las Flores 9,358 .... P2
Francisco I. Madero 12,613 .... H4
Fresnillo de González
  Echeverría 44,475 .... H5
Frontera 10,066 .... N7
Galeana, Nuevo León 3,429 .... J4
General Bravo 3,486 .... J4
General Terán 5,354 .... K4
Gómez Farías 3,030 .... F2
Gómez Palacio 79,650 .... H4
Gregorio 6,440 .... J5
Guadalajara 1,478,383 .... H6
Guadalupe, Nuevo León 51,899 .... K4
Guadalupe, Zacatecas 13,246 .... H5
Guadalupe Bravo 3,333 .... F1
Guadalupe Victoria,
  Durango 7,931 .... H4
Guadalupe Victoria,
  Puebla 3,946 .... O1
Guamúchil 17,151 .... E4
Guanajuato 36,809 .... J6
Guasave 57,492 .... D3
Gustavo Díaz Ordaz 10,154 .... K3
Gutiérrez Zamora 9,099 .... L6
Halachó 4,804 .... O6
Hecelchakán 4,279 .... O6
Hermosillo 232,691 .... D2
Heroica Caborca 20,771 .... C1
Heroica Nogales 52,108 .... D1
Hidalgo, Tamaulipas 2,450 .... K4
Hidalgo del Parral
  (Parral) 57,619 .... G3
Hopelchén 3,699 .... P7
Huajuapan de León 13,822 .... L8

Huamantla 15,565 .... N1
Huaquechula 2,294 .... M2
Huatabampo 18,506 .... D3
Huatusco de Chicuellar 9,501 .... P2
Huauchinango 16,826 .... L6
Huautla de Jiménez 6,132 .... L7
Huehuetlán el Chico 2,667 .... M2
Huejotzingo 8,552 .... M1
Huejutla 6,854 .... K6
Huetamo 9,333 .... J7
Hueyotlipan de Hidalgo 2,353 .... M1
Huimanguillo 7,075 .... N8
Huitzilán 3,573 .... M1
Huitzuco de los Figueroa 9,406 .... K7
Huixcolotla 4,037 .... N2
Huixtepec 5,927 .... L8
Huixtla 15,737 .... N9
Hunucmá 8,020 .... P6
Ignacio de la Llave 3,962 .... Q2
Iguala de la
  Independencia 45,355 .... K7
Imuris 1,958 .... D1
Irapuato 135,596 .... J6
Isla, Veracruz 8,075 .... M7
Isla Mujeres 2,663 .... Q6
Ixmiquilpan 6,048 .... K6
Ixtapa 14,254 .... J8
Ixtapalapa 522,095 .... L1
Ixtenco 5,035 .... N1
Ixtepec 14,025 .... M8
Ixtlán del Río 10,986 .... G6
Izamal 7,818 .... P6
Izúcar de Matamoros 21,164 .... M2
Jala 4,535 .... G6
Jalacingo 3,427 .... P1
Jalapa Enríquez 161,352 .... P1
Jalpa 9,904 .... H6
Jalpa de Méndez 4,785 .... N7
Jalpan 1,878 .... K6
Jáltipan de Morelos 15,170 .... M8
Jantetelco 2,015 .... L2
Jaumave 3,072 .... K5
Jerez de García
  Salinas 20,325 .... H5
Jico 7,269 .... P1
Jilotepec de Abasolo 4,252 .... K7
Jiménez, Chihuahua 18,095 .... G3
Joachín 3,918 .... L2
Jojutla de Juárez 14,438 .... L2
Jonacatepec 3,468 .... L2
Jonuta 2,746 .... N7
José Cardel 5,396 .... Q1
Juan Aldama 9,667 .... H4
Juchipila 6,328 .... H6
Juchitán de Zaragoza 30,218 .... M8
Kantunikín 1,970 .... Q6
La Barca 18,055 .... H6
La Barra de Navidad 1,829 .... G7
La Concordia 3,559 .... N8
La Cruz, Sinaloa 4,218 .... F5
Lagos de Moreno 33,782 .... J6
La Huerta 4,328 .... G7
La Paz, Baja California
  Sur 46,011 .... D5
La Paz, San Luis
  Potosí 3,735 .... J6
La Piedad Cavadas 34,963 .... H6
Las Choapas 20,166 .... M7
Las Hadas G7
Las Nieves 2,668 .... G3
Las Rosas 7,658 .... N8
León 468,887 .... J6
Lerdo de Tejada 11,628 .... M8
Lerma 4,158 .... O7
Libres 4,893 .... O1
Linares 24,456 .... K4
Llera de Canales 3,564 .... K5
Loma Bonita 15,804 .... M7
Loreto, Baja California 2,570 .... D4
Loreto, Zacatecas 7,132 .... J5
Los Mochis 67,953 .... E3
Los Reyes de Salgado 19,452 .... H7
Macuspana 12,293 .... N8
Madera 9,759 .... E2
Magdalena de Kino 10,281 .... D1
Maltrata 5,457 .... O2
Manzanillo 20,777 .... G7
Mapastepec 5,457 .... N9
Mapimí 2,737 .... G4
Martínez de la Torre 17,203 .... L6
Mascota 5,674 .... G6
Matamoros, Coahuila 15,125 .... H4
Matamoros, Tamaulipas 165,124 .... L4
Matehuala 28,799 .... J5
Matías Romero 13,200 .... M8
Maxcanú 6,505 .... O6
Mazatlán 147,010 .... F5
Melchor Múzquiz 18,868 .... H3
Melchor Ocampo del
  Balsas 4,766 .... H8
Mérida 233,912 .... P6
Metepec 4,625 .... M2
Metlatonoc 1,870 .... K8

(Index, right column)

Mexicali 317,228 .... B1
Mexico City (cap.) 9,377,300 .... L1
Mexico City* 13,993,866 .... L1
Miacatlán 3,980 .... K2
Mier 5,636 .... K3
Miguel Auza 9,303 .... H4
Minatitlán 68,397 .... M8
Mineral del Monte 8,887 .... K6
Miquihuana 1,971 .... J5
Misantla 8,799 .... P1
Miahuatlán de Porfirio
  Díaz 5,714 .... L8
Mocorito 3,993 .... F4
Moctezuma, San Luis
  Potosí 1,734 .... J5
Moctezuma, Sonora 2,700 .... E2
Monclova 78,134 .... J3
Montemorelos 18,642 .... K4
Monterrey 1,006,221 .... J4
Monterrey* 1,923,402 .... J4
Morelia 199,099 .... J7
Morelos 4,241 .... H4
Morelos Cañada 2,288 .... O2
Moroleón 25,620 .... J6
Motozintla de Mendoza 4,682 .... N9

Motul de Felipe Carillo
  Puerto 12,949 .... P6
Muna 5,491 .... P6
Naco 3,580 .... D1
Nacozari 2,976 .... E1
Nadadores 2,461 .... H3
Naica 7,190 .... G2
Namiquipa 4,875 .... F2
Nanacamilpa 6,356 .... M1
Naolinco de Victoria 4,365 .... P1
Naranjos 14,732 .... L6
Naucalpan de Juárez 9,425 .... L1
Nautla 1,935 .... L6
Nava 4,097 .... J2
Navojoa 43,817 .... D3
Navolato 12,799 .... E4
Nazas 2,881 .... G4
Netzahualcóyotl 580,436 .... L1
Nieves 3,966 .... H5
Nochistlán 8,780 .... H6
Nogales 14,254 .... P2
Nombre de Dios 3,188 .... G5
Nopalucan de la Granja 3,002 .... O1
Nueva Casas Grandes 20,023 .... F1
Nueva Ciudad Guerrero 3,300 .... K3

Nueva Italia de Ruiz 14,718 .... J7
Nueva Rosita 34,706 .... J3
Nuevo Ideal 5,252 .... G4
Nuevo Laredo 184,622 .... J2
Oaxaca de Juárez 114,948 .... L8
Ocampo, Coahuila 1,613 .... H3
Ocampo, Tamaulipas 4,801 .... K5
Ocosingo 2,946 .... O8
Ocotlán 35,361 .... H6
Ocotlán de Morelos 5,882 .... L8
Ojinaga 12,757 .... G2
Ojocaliente 7,582 .... H5
Ometepec 7,342 .... K8
Oriental 6,009 .... O1
Orizaba 105,150 .... P2
Otumba de Gómez
  Farías 3,198 .... M1
Oxkutzcab 8,182 .... P6
Ozuluama 2,851 .... L6
Ozumba de Alzate 6,876 .... M1
Pachuca de Soto 83,892 .... K6
Padilla 4,581 .... K5
Palenque 2,595 .... O8
Palizada 2,332 .... O7
Palomas 2,129 .... F1

Mexico
CONIC PROJECTION
SCALE OF MILES
0   100   200
SCALE OF KILOMETERS
0   100   200   300

National Capitals .... ★   State Capitals .... ★
International Boundaries .... ＿ ･ ＿   State Boundaries .... ＿＿

© Copyright HAMMOND INCORPORATED, Maplewood, N.J.

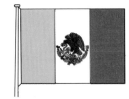

Panabá 3,056	P6
Pánuco 14,277	K6
Papanoa 3,033	J8
Papantla de Olarte 26,773	L6
Paraíso 7,561	N7
Parral 57,619	G3
Parras de la Fuente 18,207	H4
Paso de Ovejas 4,371	O2
Pátzcuaro 17,299	J7
Pedro Montoya 4,563	K6
Pénjamo 9,245	J6
Peñón Blanco 2,726	H4
Pericos 4,445	F4
Perote 12,742	O1
Petatlán 9,419	J8
Peto 8,362	P6
Pichucalco 4,615	N8
Piedras Negras, Coahuila 41,033	J2
Piedras Negras, Veracruz 4,099	Q2
Pijijiapan 5,053	N9
Pitiquito 2,268	D1
Potam 2,825	D3
Poza Rica de Hidalgo 152,276	L6
Praxedis G. Guerrero 2,399	G1
Profesor Rafael Ramírez 5,338	O1
Progreso 17,518	P6
Puebla de Zaragoza 465,985	N2
Puente de Ixtla 10,435	K2
Puerto Ángel 1,489	L9
Puerto Escondido 3,845	L9
Puerto Juárez 100	Q6
Puerto Madero 1,908	N9
Puerto Peñasco 8,452	C1
Puerto Vallarta 24,155	G6
Purificación 3,311	G7
Puruándiro 9,956	J7
Putla de Guerrero 3,572	L8
Quechola 3,374	O2
Querétaro 142,448	J6
Ramos Arizpe 6,205	J4
Rayón, San Luis Potosí 4,451	K6
Rayón, Sonora 1,283	D2
Reynosa 181,646	K3
Rincón de Romos 8,348	H5
Ríoverde 16,804	J6
Rodeo 2,584	G4
Rosamorada 2,635	G5

(continued on following page)

AREA 761,601 sq. mi. (1,972,546 sq. km.)
POPULATION 67,395,826
CAPITAL Mexico City
LARGEST CITY Mexico City
HIGHEST POINT Citlaltépetl 18,855 ft. (5,747 m.)
MONETARY UNIT Mexican peso
MAJOR LANGUAGE Spanish
MAJOR RELIGION Roman Catholicism

States Indicated by Numbers

1 Tlaxcala	6 Querétaro
2 Morelos	7 Guanajuato
3 Distrito Federal	8 Aguascalientes
4 México	9 Nayarit
5 Hidalgo	10 Colima

Rosario, Sinaloa 10,276 ....G5
Rosario, Sonora 1,887 ....E3
Ruiz 8,954 ....G6
Sabancuy 1,819 ....O7
Sabinas 20,538 ....J3
Sabinas Hidalgo 17,439 ....J3
Sahuaripa 4,710 ....E2
Sahuayo de Díaz 28,727 ....H7
Sain Alto 3,628 ....H5
Salamanca 61,039 ....J6
Salina Cruz 22,004 ....M9
Salinas 7,471 ....J5
Saltillo 200,712 ....J4
Salvatierra 18,975 ....J6
San Andrés Tuxtla 24,267 ....M7
San Blas, Nayarit 3,443 ....G6
San Blas, Sinaloa 6,222 ....J3
San Buenaventura 9,188 ....J3
San Carlos, Coahuila 1,960 ....J2
San Cristóbal de las
  Casas 25,700 ....N8
San Felipe, Baja
  California 160 ....B1
San Felipe, Guanajuato 10,129 ....J6
San Fernando,
  Tamaulipas 27,656 ....L4
San Francisco del Oro 12,116 ....F3
San Francisco del
  Rincón 27,079 ....H6
San Gabriel Ehilac 6,707 ....K7
San Ignacio, Sinaloa 1,804 ....F5
San Jerónimo de
  Juárez 5,204 ....J8
San José del Cabo 2,571 ....D5
San Juan 15,422 ....J6
San Juan de los Lagos 19,570 ....H6
San Juan Xiutetelco 3,306 ....O1
San Luis de la Paz 12,654 ....J6
San Luis del Cordero 2,203 ....H4
San Luis Potosí 271,123 ....J5
San Luis Río Colorado 49,990 ....B1
San Marcos 5,861 ....K8
San Martín de las
  Pirámides 4,575 ....M1
San Martín Texmelucan 23,355 ....M1
San Miguel de Allende 24,286 ....J6
San Nicolás de los
  Garza 28,803 ....J3
San Pedro de las
  Colonias 26,882 ....H4
San Pedro Pochutla 4,395 ....L9
San Rafael 8,974 ....O1
San Salvador el Seco 7,729 ....O1
Santa Ana 7,020 ....D1
Santa Ana Chiautempan
  (Chiautémpan) 12,327 ....N1
Santa Bárbara 16,978 ....F3
Santa Clara 3,449 ....H4
Santa María del Oro 4,231 ....G3
Santa María del Río 4,972 ....J6
Santa María del Tule 1,674 ....L8
Santander Jiménez 3,586 ....K4
Santa Rosalía 7,356 ....C3
Santiago Ixcuintla 17,321 ....G6
Santiago Jamiltepec 5,280 ....K8
Santiago Juxtlahuaca 2,923 ....K8
Santiago Miahuatlán 4,917 ....O2
Santiago Papasquiaro 6,636 ....F4
Santiago Pinotepa
  Nacional 9,382 ....K8
Santiago Tuxtla 9,426 ....M7
Saucillo 8,467 ....G2
Sayula 14,339 ....H7
Sayula de Alemán 4,896 ....M8
Seybaplaya 4,439 ....O7
Silao 31,825 ....J6
Simojovel de Allende 3,779 ....N8
Sinaloa de Leyva 1,998 ....E4
Soledad de Doblado 6,612 ....O2
Soledad Díez

Gutiérrez 9,622 ....J5
Sombrerete 11,077 ....H5
Sonoyta 2,463 ....C1
Sotuta 3,772 ....P6
Tabasco 3,197 ....H6
Tacámbaro de Codallos 9,695 ....J7
Tacotalpa 2,019 ....N8
Tala 15,744 ....H6
Talpa de Allende 4,264 ....L8
Tamazulápan del Progreso 2,870 ....L8
Tamazunchale 12,302 ....K6
Tamiahua 6,264 ....L6
Tampico 212,188 ....L5
Tamulín 7,251 ....K6
Tantoyuca 11,902 ....L6
Tapachula 60,620 ....N9
Taxco de Alarcón 27,089 ....K7
Tayoltita 2,697 ....G4
Teapa 6,534 ....N8
Tecamachalco 3,319 ....O2
Tecate 14,738 ....A1
Tecomán 31,625 ....H7
Tecpan de Galeana 8,095 ....J8
Tecuala 12,461 ....G5
Tehuacán 47,497 ....L7
Tehuantepec 16,179 ....M8
Tekax de Álaro
  Obregón 10,326 ....P6
Telóloapan 10,335 ....K7
Temax 4,915 ....P6
Temósachic 1,738 ....E2
Tenabo 3,278 ....P6
Tenancingo de Degollado 12,807 ....K7
Tenango de Río Blanco 12,302 ....O2
Tenosique de Pino
  Suárez 11,393 ....O8
Teocaltiche 13,745 ....H6
Teocelo 4,572 ....P1
Teotihuacán de Arista 2,238 ....L1
Teotitlán del Camino 3,106 ....L8
Tepache 1,591 ....E2
Tepalcingo 5,968 ....M2
Tepatitlán de Morelos 29,292 ....H6
Tepeaca 7,466 ....N2
Tepeapulco 7,027 ....M1
Tepehuanes 2,531 ....G4
Tepeji del Río 10,365 ....L1
Tepexi de Rodríguez 2,618 ....N2
Tepic 108,924 ....G6
Tepoztlán 6,851 ....L1
Tequixquitla 4,825 ....O1
Terán 5,215 ....N8
Terrenate 1,515 ....N1
Texcoco de Mora 18,044 ....M1
Tezuitlán 23,948 ....O1
Tezonapa 3,506 ....P2
Tezontepec 2,762 ....M1
Ticul 14,341 ....P6
Tierra Blanca 22,727 ....L7
Tila 2,633 ....N8
Tijuana 363,154 ....A1
Tixtla de Guerrero 10,334 ....K8
Tizayuca 6,262 ....L1
Tizimín 18,343 ....Q6
Tlachichuca 3,721 ....O1
Tlacolula de Matamoros 8,300 ....L8
Tlacotepec de Mejía 1,595 ....P1
Tlahualilo de Zaragoza 8,951 ....H4
Tlalancaleca 5,090 ....M1
Tlalixcoyán 3,211 ....Q2
Tlalmanalco de
  Velásquez 5,744 ....L1
Tlalnepantla de
  Comonfort 45,575 ....L1
Tlalpan 130,719 ....L1
Tlaltenango de Sánchez
  Román 15,611 ....H6
Tlaltizapán 6,384 ....L2
Tlapacoyan 13,172 ....P1
Tlapa de Comonfort 6,676 ....K8

Tlaquepaque 59,760 ....G6
Tlatlauquitepec 4,299 ....O1
Tlaquiltenango 8,625 ....L2
Tlaxcala de Xicotencatl 9,972 ....N1
Tultepec 8,321 ....L1
Tuxpan, Jalisco 14,693 ....H7
Tuxpan, Nayarit 20,322 ....G6
Tuxpan de Rodríguez
  Cano 33,901 ....L6
Tuxtepec 17,701 ....L7
Tuxtla Gutiérrez 66,851 ....N8
Tzucabab 4,876 ....P7
Umán 8,371 ....P6
Unión de Tula 6,399 ....H7
Unión Hidalgo 8,658 ....M8
Ures 3,681 ....D2

Úrsulo Galván 2,637 ....Q1
Uruapan del Progreso 108,124 ......H7
Valladolid 14,663 ....P6
Valle de Allende 4,973 ....G3
Valle de Bravo 7,628 ....J7
Valle Hermoso 19,278 ....L4
Vanegas 2,042 ....J5
Venado 2,790 ....J5
Venustiano Carranza 23,624 ....N8
Veracruz 255,646 ....Q1
Vicam 4,104 ....D3
Vicente Guerrero,
  Durango 8,451 ....G4
Victor Rosales 7,629 ....H5
Viesca 2,923 ....H4

Villa Acuña 30,276 ....J2
Villa Cuauhtémoc 6,611 ....L5
Villa de Cos 1,850 ....H5
Villa de Guadelupe
  Hidalgo 88,537 ....L1
Villa Frontera 25,761 ....J3
Villa García 2,765 ....J5
Villahermosa 133,181 ....N8
Villa Hidalgo 2,126 ....E1
Villaldama 2,350 ....J3
Villa Matamoros 1,998 ....G3
Villanueva 5,995 ....H5
Villa Vicente Guerrero 18,280 ....N1
Xaltocan 2,524 ....N1
Xicotencatl 6,374 ....K5
Xicotepec de Juárez 12,656 ....L6
Xochihuehuetlán 3,268 ....K8
Xochimilco 116,493 ....L1
Xochitlán 3,312 ....N2
Yajalón 4,506 ....N8
Yanga 3,843 ....P2
Yaqui 8,061 ....D3
Yautepec 15,761 ....L2
Yavaros 1,959 ....E3
Yécora 2,816 ....E2
Yecuatla 2,816 ....P1
Yehualtepec 2,558 ....O2
Zaachila 7,270 ....L8
Zacapoaxtla 4,527 ....O1
Zacapu 31,989 ....J7
Zacatepec 16,839 ....L2
Zacatecas 50,251 ....H5
Zacatelco 14,117 ....N1
Zacatlán 7,909 ....O1
Zacoalco de Torres 11,343 ....H6
Zamora de Hidalgo 5,775 ....H7
Zaragoza, Coahuila 6,797 ....J2
Zaragoza, Chihuahua 3,984 ....F1
Zaragoza, Puebla 4,754 ....O1
Zempoala 5,064 ....O1
Zihuatanejo 4,879 ....J8
Zimatlán de Álvarez 5,746 ....L8
Zitácuaro 36,911 ....J7
Zongolica 2,378 ....P2
Zumpango de Ocampo 12,923 ....L1
Zumpango del Río 8,162 ....J8

Falcón (res.) ....K
Falso (cape) ....D
Fuerte (riv.) ....E
Giganta, Sierra de la (mts.) ....D
Grande (riv.) ....E
Grande (riv.) ....N
Grande de Santiago (riv.) ....N
Grijalva (riv.) ....N
Guzmán (lake) ....F
Herrero (pt.) ....P
Hondo (riv.) ....P
Jesús Máría (reef) L
La Boquilla (res.) ....F
La Paz (bay) ....D
Lobos (cape) C
Lobos (pt.) C
Lower California (pen.) C
Madre (lag.) L
Madre del Sur, Sierra (mts.) ....J
Madre Occidental, Sierra
  (mts.) F3
Madre Oriental, Sierra (mts.) ....J
Magdalena (bay) C
Maldonado (pt.) ....K
Mapimí (depr.) ....G
Marla Cleófas (isl.) ....G
Marla Madre (isl.) ....G
Marla Magdalena (isl.) ....G
Mexico (gulf) ....N
Mezquital (riv.) ....G
Mita (pt.) ....G
Mita (ruin) ....P
Moctezuma (riv.) ....K
Monserrate (isl.) ....D
Montague (isl.) ....B
Muerto, Mar (lag.) ....N
Nauhcampatépetl (mt.) ....O
Nayarit, Sierra (mts.) J5
Nazas (riv.) ....G
Nuevo, Bajo (reef) ....O
Orizaba (Citlaltépetl)
  (mt.) O2
Palenque (ruin) ....N
Palmito de la Virgen
  (isl.) ....F
Palmito Verde (isl.) ....F
Pánuco (riv.) ....K
Paricutín (vol.) ....J
Pátzcuaro (lake) ....J
Pérez (isl.) ....P
Petacalco (bay) ....J
Popocatépetl (mt.) ....N
Ramos (riv.) ....G
Revillagigedo (isls.) C
Roca Partida (isl.) C
Sabinas (riv.) ....J
San Antonio (res.) L
San Benedicto (isl.) C
San Benito (isl.) ....B
San Jorge (bay) ....D
San José (isl.) ....D
San Lázaro (cape) C
San Lucas (cape) ....E
San Marcos (isl.) C
San Rafael (reef) ....N
Santa Ana (reef) ....N
Santa Catalina (isl.) ....D
Santa Cruz (isl.) ....D
Santa Eugenia (pt.) ....B
Santa Margarita (isl.) C
Santa Marla (isl.) ....F
Santa Marla (riv.) ....F
Santiaguillo (lake) ....G
Sebastián Vizcaíno (bay) C
Socorro (isl.) C
Sonora (riv.) ....D
Superior (lag.) ....M
Teacapán (inlet) ....M
Tehuantepec (gulf) ....M
Teotihuacán (ruin) ....M
Términos (lag.) ....O
Tiburón (isl.) C
Triángulo Este (isl.) ....N
Triángulo Oeste (isl.) ....N
Tula (riv.) ....K
Urique (riv.) ....F
Usumacinta (riv.) ....N
Uxmal (ruin) ....P
Valsequillo (res.) ....N
Verde (riv.) ....H
Verde (riv.) ....F
Yaqui (riv.) ....E

OTHER FEATURES

Agiobampo (bay) E3
Aguanaval (riv.) H4
Amistad (res.) J2
Ángel de la Guarda (isl.) C2
Antigua (riv.) Q1
Arena (pt.) E5
Arenas (cay) O5
Atoyac (riv.) N2
Atoyac (riv.) Q2
Babia (riv.) P7
Bacalar (lake) P7
Ballenas (bay) C3
Balsas (riv.) J7
Banderas (bay) G6
Bavispe, Río de (riv.) E1
Bianco (riv.) Q2
Bravo (Grande) (riv.) G2
Burro (mts.) J2
California (gulf) D3
Campeche (bank) P5
Campeche (bay) N7
Candelaria (riv.) O8
Carmen (isl.) D3
Casas Grandes (riv.) F1
Catoche (cape) Q6
Cedros (isl.) B2
Cerralvo (isl.) E4
Chamela (bay) G7
Chapala (lake) H6
Chetumal (bay) P8
Chichén-Itzá (ruin) P6
Citlaltépetl (mt.) O2
Clarión (isl.) B7
Colorado (riv.) B1
Conchos (riv.) F2
Corrientes (cape) F6
Coyuca (riv.) J8
Creciente (isl.) D5
Cuitzeo (lake) J7
Delgada (pt.) P6
Dzibilchaltún (ruin) P6
El Infiernillo (res.) O2
Espíritu Santo (isl.) D4

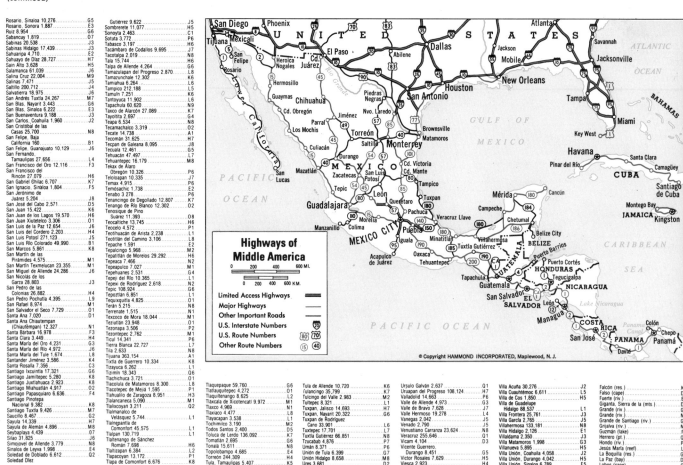

Highways of
Middle America

0   200   400   600 MI.

0   200   400   600 KM.

Limited Access Highways
Major Highways
Other Important Roads
U.S. Interstate Numbers
U.S. Route Numbers
Other Route Numbers

© Copyright HAMMOND INCORPORATED, Maplewood, N.J.

Agriculture, Industry and Resources

DOMINANT LAND USE

- Wheat, Livestock
- Cereals (chiefly corn), Livestock
- Diversified Tropical Cash Crops
- Cotton, Mixed Cereals
- Livestock, Limited Agriculture
- Range Livestock
- Forests
- Nonagricultural Land

MAJOR MINERAL OCCURRENCES

Ag	Silver	G	Natural Gas	O	Petroleum
Au	Gold	Gr	Graphite	Pb	Lead
C	Coal	Hg	Mercury	S	Sulfur
Cu	Copper	Mn	Manganese	Sb	Antimony
F	Fluorspar	Mo	Molybdenum	Sn	Tin
Fe	Iron Ore	Na	Salt	W	Tungsten
				Zn	Zinc

Water Power

Major Industrial Areas

GUATEMALA

AREA 42,042 sq. mi. (108,889 sq. km.)
POPULATION 7,262,419
CAPITAL Guatemala
LARGEST CITY Guatemala
HIGHEST POINT Tajumulco 13,845 ft.
  (4,220 m.)
MONETARY UNIT quetzal
MAJOR LANGUAGES Spanish, Quiché
MAJOR RELIGION Roman Catholicism

BELIZE

AREA 8,867 sq. mi. (22,966 sq. km.)
POPULATION 144,857
CAPITAL Belmopan
LARGEST CITY Belize City
HIGHEST POINT Victoria Peak 3,681 ft. (1,122 m.)
MONETARY UNIT Belize dollar
MAJOR LANGUAGES English, Spanish, Mayan
MAJOR RELIGIONS Roman Catholicism, Protestantism

EL SALVADOR

AREA 8,260 sq. mi. (21,393 sq. km.)
POPULATION 4,813,000
CAPITAL San Salvador
LARGEST CITY San Salvador
HIGHEST POINT Santa Ana 7,825 ft.
  (2,385 m.)
MONETARY UNIT colón
MAJOR LANGUAGE Spanish
MAJOR RELIGION Roman Catholicism

HONDURAS

AREA 43,277 sq. mi. (112,087 sq. km.)
POPULATION 3,691,000
CAPITAL Tegucigalpa
LARGEST CITY Tegucigalpa
HIGHEST POINT Las Minas 9,347 ft.
  (2,849 m.)
MONETARY UNIT lempira
MAJOR LANGUAGE Spanish
MAJOR RELIGION Roman Catholicism

NICARAGUA

AREA 45,698 sq. mi. (118,358 sq. km.)
POPULATION 2,703,000
CAPITAL Managua
LARGEST CITY Managua
HIGHEST POINT Cerro Mocotón 6,913 ft.
  (2,107 m.)
MONETARY UNIT córdoba
MAJOR LANGUAGE Spanish
MAJOR RELIGION Roman Catholicism

COSTA RICA

AREA 19,575 sq. mi. (50,700 sq. km.)
POPULATION 2,245,000
CAPITAL San José
LARGEST CITY San José
HIGHEST POINT Chirripó Grande
  12,530 ft. (3,819 m.)
MONETARY UNIT colón
MAJOR LANGUAGE Spanish
MAJOR RELIGION Roman Catholicism

PANAMA

AREA 29,761 sq. mi. (77,082 sq. km.)
POPULATION 1,830,175
CAPITAL Panamá
LARGEST CITY Panamá
HIGHEST POINT Vol. Baru 11,401 ft.
  (3,475 m.)
MONETARY UNIT balboa
MAJOR LANGUAGE Spanish
MAJOR RELIGION Roman Catholicism

Agriculture, Industry and Resources

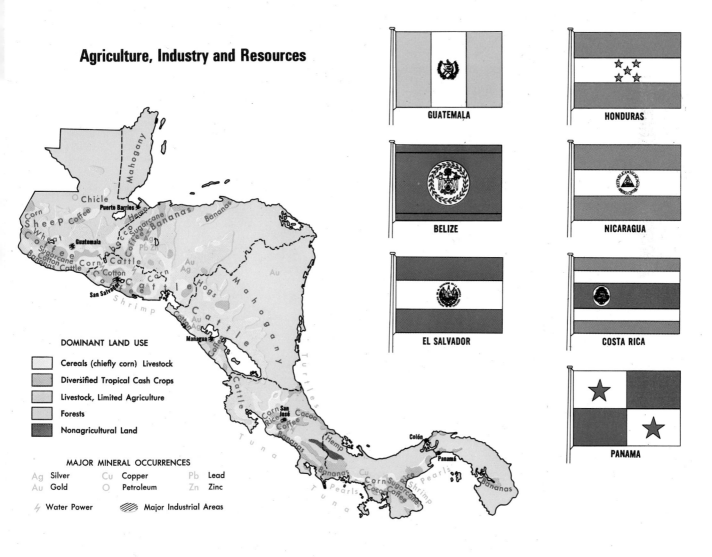

DOMINANT LAND USE

- Cereals (chiefly corn) Livestock
- Diversified Tropical Cash Crops
- Livestock, Limited Agriculture
- Forests
- Nonagricultural Land

MAJOR MINERAL OCCURRENCES

Ag Silver   Cu Copper   Pb Lead
Au Gold   O   Petroleum   Zn Zinc

⚡ Water Power   ▨ Major Industrial Areas

BELIZE

CITIES and TOWNS

Belize City 39,887 ....C2
Belize City* 50,925 ....C2
Belmopan (cap.) 2,932 ....C2
Corozal Town 6,862 ....C1
Hattieville 904 ....C2

Libertad 856 ....C1
Orange Walk Town 8,441 ....C1
Punta Gorda 2,219 ....C2
San Ignacio 5,606 ....C2
Stann Creek Town 6,627 ....C2

OTHER FEATURES

Ambergris (cay) D1
Belize (riv.) C2

Bokel (cay) D2
Glover (reef) D2
Half Moon (cay) D2
Hondo (riv.) C1
Honduras (gulf) D2
Mauger (cay) D2
New (riv.) C2
Saint Georges (cay) D2
Sarstún (riv.) C3
Turneffe (isls.) D2

COSTA RICA

CITIES and TOWNS

Alajuela 33,122 ....E6
Atenas 1,726 ....E6
Bagaces 2,129 ....E5
Boruca⊙ 1,892 ....F6

Buenos Aires⊙ 302 ....F6
Cañas 6,053 ....E5
Cartago 21,753 ....F6
Ciudad Quesada 9,754 ....E5
Esparta 4,699 ....E5
Filadelfia 2,958 ....E5
Golfito 6,962 ....F6
Grecia 8,355 ....E5
Guácimo 1,168 ....F5
Guápiles 3,524 ....F5

Heredia 22,700 ....E5
Las Juntas 1,129 ....E5
Liberia 10,802 ....E5
Limón 29,621 ....F6
Miramar 1,673 ....E5
Nicoya 7,474 ....E5
Orotina 3,170 ....E5
Palmares 3,083 ....E5
Paraíso 8,446 ....F6
Puerto Cortés 2,070 ....F6

Puntarenas 26,331 ....E6
Quepos 2,155 ....E6
San José (cap.) 215,441 ....F5
San José* 391,107 ....F5
San Marcos 917 ....E6
San Ramón 9,245 ....E5
Santa Cruz 5,777 ....E5
Santo Domingo 5,148 ....F6
Siquirres 4,361 ....F5
Turrialba 12,151 ....F6

(continued on following page)

OTHER FEATURES

Blanca (pt.) F5
Blanco (cape) E6
Blanco (peak) F6
Burica (pt.) F6
Cahuita (pt.) F6
Carreta (pt.) F6
Chirripó Grande (mt.) F6
Coronada (bay) F6
Cuilapa Miravalles (vol.) E5
Dulce (gulf) F6
Góngora (mt.) E5
Guionos (pt.) E5
Irazú (mt.) F6
Judas (pt.) E6
Llerena (pt.) F6
Matapalo (cape) E6
Nicoya (gulf) E6
Nicoya (pen.) E6
Papagayo (gulf) E6
Salinas (bay) D5
San Juan (riv.) E5
Santa Elena (cape) D5

Talamanca (range) F6
Velas (cape) D5

EL SALVADOR

CITIES and TOWNS

Acajutla 8,598 .... B4
Ahuachapán 17,242 .... B4
Atiquizaya 7,035 .... C3
Chalatenango 7,633 .... C3
Chinameca 6,303 .... C4
Cojutepeque 20,615 .... C4
Estanzuelas 2,548 .... C4
Ilobasco 6,572 .... C4
Intipucá 3,469 .... D4
Jucuarán 1,443 .... C4
La Libertad C4
La Palma 1,998 .... C3
La Unión 17,207 .... D4
Metapán 7,704 .... C3
Nueva San Salvador 35,106 .... C4
Puerto de la Concordia C4
San Francisco Gotera 4,725 .... C4

San Miguel 59,304 .... D4
Santa Ana 96,306 .... C4
Santa Rosa de Lima 5,707 .... D4
San Vicente 18,872 .... C4
Sensuntepeque 7,226 .... C4
Sonsonate 33,562 .... C4
Suchitoto 5,540 .... C4
Texistepeque 1,722 .... C3
Usulután 19,616 .... C4
Zacatecoluca 15,718 .... C4

OTHER FEATURES

Fonseca (gulf) D4
Güija (lake) C3
Lempa (riv.) C4
Remedios (pt.) B4
Santa Ana (mt.) C4

GUATEMALA

CITIES and TOWNS

Amatitlán 15,251 .... B3

Antigua 17,994 .... B3
Asunción Mita 7,477 .... C3
Cahabón 1,344 .... C3
Chajul 4,329 .... B3
Champerico 5,722 .... A3
Chichicastenango 2,635 .... B3
Chimaltenango 12,860 .... B3
Chiquimula 16,126 .... C3
Coatepeque 15,979 .... A3
Cobán 11,418 .... B3
Comalapa 10,980 .... B3
Cubulco 2,021 .... B3
Cuilapa 4,287 .... C3
Cuilco 862 .... A3
Dolores 973 .... C2
El Estor 2,324 .... C3
El Progreso 4,009 .... B3
Escuintla 33,205 .... B3
Flores 1,477 .... C2
Gualán 5,169 .... C3
Guatemala (cap.) 700,538 .... B3
Huehuetenango 12,570 .... A3
Ipala 3,386 .... C3
Iztapa 1,237 .... B4

Jacaltenango 4,517 .... B3
Jalapa 13,788 .... B3
Jutiapa 8,210 .... B3
La Gomera 2,394 .... B3
La Libertad 908 .... B2
Livingston 2,898 .... C3
Los Amates 1,383 .... C3
Masagua 1,178 .... B3
Mazatenango 23,285 .... B3
Momostenango 5,210 .... B3
Morales 2,113 .... C3
Ocós 741 .... A3
Panzós 1,643 .... C3
Puerto Barrios 22,598 .... C3
Quezaltenango 53,021 .... B3
Quezaltepeque 2,222 .... C3
Rabinal 4,625 .... B3
Retalhuleu 19,060 .... A3
Río Hondo 1,416 .... C3
Sacapulas 1,439 .... B3
Salamá 5,529 .... B3
San Andrés 1,066 .... B2
San Felipe 3,210 .... A3
San José 9,402 .... B4
San Luis 1,136 .... C2

San Luis Jilotepeque 6,055 .... C3
San Marcos 5,700 .... A3
San Martín Jilotepeque 3,770 .... B3
San Mateo Ixtatán 1,834 .... A3
San Pedro Carchá 4,465 .... B3
Santa Cruz del Quiché 7,651 .... B3
Santa Rosa de Lima 1,161 .... B3
Sololá 3,960 .... B3
Tacaná 1,280 .... A3
Tejutla 1,205 .... A3
Tikal C2
Totonicapán 8,568 .... B3
Zacapa 12,688 .... C3

OTHER FEATURES

Atitlán (lake) B3
Atitlán (vol.) B3
Azul (riv.) C2
Chixoy (riv.) B3
Güija (lake) C3
Honduras (gulf) D2
Izabal (lake) C3
Minas (mts.) C3
Motagua (riv.) C3

Pasión (riv.) B2
Petén-Itzá (lake) C2
San Pedro (riv.) B2
Sarstún (riv.) C3
Tacaná (vol.) A3
Tres Puntas (cape) C3
Usumacinta (riv.) B2

HONDURAS

CITIES and TOWNS

Amapala 2,274 .... D4
Brus Laguna 933 .... E3
Catacamas 9,134 .... E3
Cedros 917 .... D3
Choloma 961 .... D3
Choluteca 26,152 .... D4
Comayagua 15,941 .... D3
Corquín 2,629 .... C3
Danlí 10,825 .... D3
El Dulce Nombre 1,297 .... E3

Central America
CONIC PROJECTION
SCALE OF MILES
0   25   50   100   150
SCALE OF KILOMETERS
0   25   50   100   150

Capitals of Countries .... ☆
International Boundaries ....
Canals ....

© Copyright HAMMOND INCORPORATED, Maplewood, N.J.

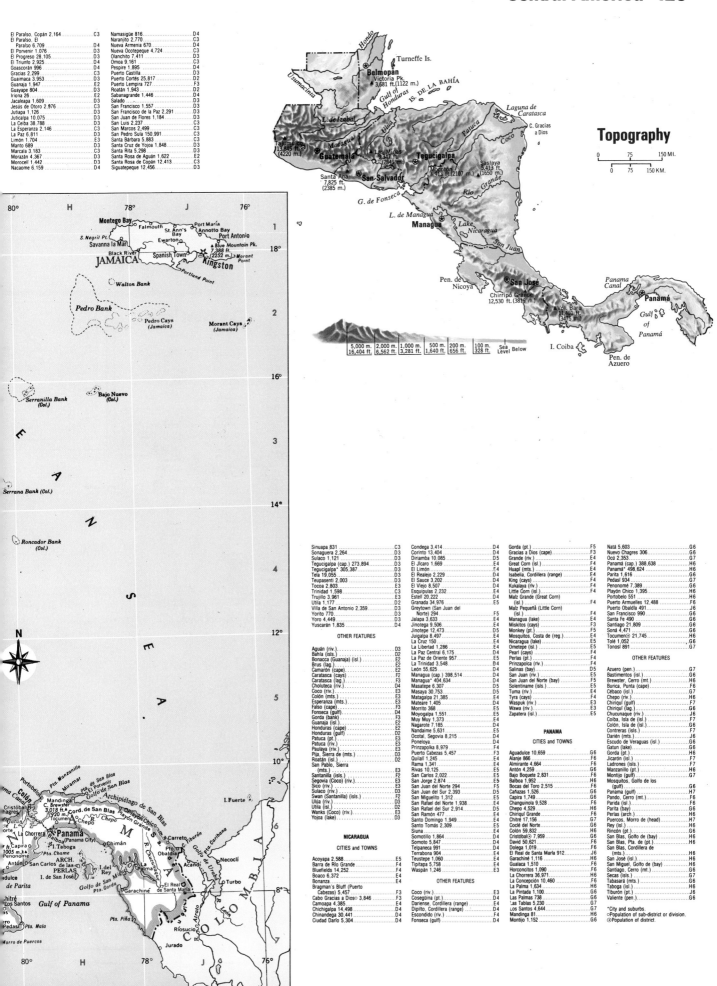

El Paraíso, Copán 2,164 ....C3
El Paraíso, El
 Paraíso 6,709 ....D4
El Porvenir 1,076 ....D3
El Progreso 28,105 ....D3
El Triunfo 2,925 ....D4
Goascorán 996 ....D4
Gracias 2,299 ....C3
Guaimaca 3,953 ....D3
Guanaja 1,947 ....E2
Guayape 804 ....D3
Iriona 26 ....E2
Jacaleapa 1,609 ....D3
Jesús de Otoro 2,976 ....C3
Jutiapa 1,126 ....D3
Juticalpa 10,075 ....D3
La Ceiba 38,788 ....D2
La Esperanza 2,146 ....D3
La Paz 6,811 ....D3
Limón 1,704 ....E3
Manto 689 ....D3
Marcala 3,183 ....C3
Morazán 4,367 ....D3
Morocelí 1,442 ....D3
Nacaome 6,159 ....D4

Namasigüe 816 ....D4
Naranjito 2,770 ....D4
Nueva Armenia 670 ....D4
Nueva Ocotepeque 4,724 ....C3
Olanchito 7,411 ....D3
Omoa 9,161 ....C3
Pespire 1,895 ....D4
Puerto Castilla D2
Puerto Cortés 25,817 ....D2
Puerto Lempira 727 ....F3
Roatán 1,943 ....D2
Sabanagrande 1,446 ....D4
Salado D3
San Francisco 1,557 ....D3
San Francisco de la Paz 2,291 ....D3
San Juan de Flores 1,184 ....D3
San Luis 2,237 ....C3
San Marcos 2,499 ....C3
San Pedro Sula 150,991 ....C3
Santa Bárbara 5,883 ....C3
Santa Cruz de Yojoa 1,848 ....D3
Santa Rita 5,298 ....D3
Santa Rosa de Aguán 1,622 ....E2
Santa Rosa de Copán 12,413 ....C3
Siguatepeque 12,456 ....D3

Topography

0   75   150 MI.
0   75   150 KM.

5,000 m. | 2,000 m. | 1,000 m. | 500 m. | 200 m. | 100 m. | Sea
16,404 ft. | 6,562 ft. | 3,281 ft. | 1,640 ft. | 656 ft. | 328 ft. | Level Below

Sinuapa 831 ....C3
Sonaguera 2,264 ....D3
Sulaco 1,121 ....D3
Tegucigalpa (cap.) 273,894 ....D3
Tegucigalpa* 305,387 ....D3
Tela 19,055 ....D3
Teupasenti 2,003 ....D3
Tocoa 2,803 ....E3
Trinidad 1,598 ....C3
Utila 1,177 ....D2
Villa de San Antonio 2,359 ....D3
Yorito 770 ....D3
Yoro 4,449 ....D3
Yuscarán 1,835 ....D4

OTHER FEATURES

Aguán (riv.) D3
Bahía (isls.) D2
Bonacca (Guanaja) (isl.) E2
Brus (lag.) E2
Camarón (cape) E2
Caratasca (cays) F2
Caratasca (lag.) F2
Choluteca (riv.) D4
Coco (riv.) E3
Colón (mts.) E3
Esperanza (mts.) D3
Falso (cape) F3
Fonseca (gulf) D4
Gorda (bank) F3
Guanaja (isl.) E2
Honduras (cape) E2
Honduras (gulf) D2
Patuca (pt.) E3
Patuca (riv.) E3
Paulaya (riv.) E3
Pija, Sierra de (mts.) D3
Roatán (isl.) D2
Santilla (isls.) F2
Segovia (Coco) (riv.) E3
Sulaco (riv.) D3
Swan (Santanilla) (isls.) F2
Ulúa (riv.) D3
Utila (isl.) D2
Wanks (Coco) (riv.) E3

NICARAGUA

CITIES and TOWNS

Acoyapa 2,588 ....E5
Barra de Río Grande F4
Bluefields 14,252 ....F4
Boaco 6,372 ....E4
Bonanza E3
Bragman's Bluff (Puerto
 Cabezas) 5,457 ....F3
Cabo Gracias a Dios 3,846 ....F3
Camoapa 4,385 ....E4
Chichigalpa 14,498 ....D4
Chinandega 30,441 ....D4
Ciudad Darío 5,304 ....D4

Condega 3,414 ....D4
Corinto 13,404 ....D4
Diriamba 10,085 ....D5
El Jícaro 1,669 ....E4
El Limón E4
El Realejo 2,229 ....D4
El Sauce 3,202 ....D4
El Viejo 8,507 ....D4
Esquipulas 2,232 ....E4
Granada 34,976 ....E5
Estelí 20,222 ....D4
Greytown (San Juan del
 Norte) 294 ....F5
Jalapa 3,633 ....E4
Jinotega 9,506 ....E4
Jinotepe 12,473 ....D5
Juigalpa 8,497 ....E4
La Cruz 150 ....E4
La Libertad 1,286 ....E4
La Paz Central 6,175 ....D4
La Paz de Oriente 957 ....E5
La Trinidad 3,548 ....D4
León 55,625 ....D4
Managua (cap.) 398,514 ....D4
Managua* 404,634 ....D4
Masatepe 6,307 ....D5
Masaya 30,753 ....D5
Matagalpa 21,385 ....E4
Mateare 1,405 ....D4
Morrito 368 ....E5
Moyogalpa 1,551 ....E5
Muy Muy 1,373 ....E4
Nagarote 7,185 ....D4
Nandaime 5,631 ....E5
Ocotal, Segovia 8,215 ....D4
Poneloya D4
Prinzapolka 8,979 ....F4
Puerto Cabezas 5,457 ....F3
Quilalí 1,245 ....E4
Rama 1,341 ....E4
Rivas 10,125 ....E5
San Carlos 2,022 ....E5
San Jorge 2,874 ....E5
San Juan del Norte 294 ....F5
San Juan del Sur 2,393 ....D5
San Miguelito 1,312 ....E5
San Rafael del Norte 1,938 ....E4
San Rafael del Sur 2,914 ....D5
San Ramón 477 ....E4
Santo Domingo 1,949 ....E4
Santo Tomás 2,309 ....E4
Siuna E4
Somotillo 1,864 ....D4
Somoto 5,847 ....D4
Telpaneca 991 ....D4
Terrabona 904 ....E4
Teustepe 1,060 ....E4
Tipitapa 5,758 ....D4
Waspán 1,246 ....E3

OTHER FEATURES

Coco (riv.) E3
Coseguina (vol.) D4
Dariense, Cordillera (range) E4
Dipilto, Cordillera (range) D4
Escondido (riv.) E4
Fonseca (gulf) D4

Gorda (pt.) F5
Gracias a Dios (cape) F3
Grande (riv.) E4
Great Corn (isl.) F4
Huapí (mts.) E4
Isabella, Cordillera (range) E4
King (cays) F4
Kukalaya (riv.) F4
Little Corn (isl.) F4
Maíz Grande (Great Corn)
 (isl.) F4
Maíz Pequeña (Little Corn)
 (isl.) F4
Managua (lake) E4
Miskitos (cays) F3
Monkey (pt.) F4
Mosquitos, Costa de (reg.) E4
Nicaragua (lake) E5
Ometepe (isl.) E5
Pearl (cays) F4
Perlas (pt.) F4
Prinzapolca (riv.) F4
Salinas (bay) D5
San Juan (riv.) E5
San Juan del Norte (bay) F5
Solentiname (isls.) E5
Tuma (riv.) E4
Tyra (cays) F4
Waspuk (riv.) E3
Wawa (riv.) E3
Zapatera (isl.) E5

PANAMA

CITIES and TOWNS

Aguadulce 10,659 ....G6
Alanje 866 ....F6
Almirante 4,664 ....F6
Antón 4,259 ....G6
Bajo Boquete 2,831 ....F6
Balboa 1,952 ....H6
Bocas del Toro 2,515 ....F6
Cañazas 1,749 ....G6
Changuinola 9,528 ....F6
Chepo 4,529 ....H6
Chiriquí Grande F6
Chitré 17,156 ....G7
Coclé del Norte G6
Colón 59,832 ....H6
Cristóbal⊙ 7,959 ....H6
David 50,621 ....F6
Dolega 1,019 ....F6
El Real de Santa María 912 ....J6
Garachiné 1,116 ....H6
Gualaca 1,510 ....F6
Horconcitos 1,090 ....F6
La Chorrera 36,971 ....H6
La Concepción 10,460 ....F6
La Palma 1,634 ....H6
La Pintada 1,100 ....G6
Las Tablas 738 ....G7
Las Tablas 5,230 ....G7
Mandinga 81 ....H6
Montijo 1,152 ....G6

Natá 5,603 ....G6
Nuevo Chagres 306 ....G6
Ocú 2,353 ....G7
Panamá (cap.) 388,638 ....H6
Panamá* 498,624 ....H6
Parita 1,616 ....G6
Pedasí 934 ....G7
Penonomé 7,389 ....G6
Playón Chico 1,395 ....H6
Portobelo 551 ....H6
Puerto Armuelles 12,488 ....F6
Puerto Obaldía 491 ....J6
San Francisco 990 ....G6
Santa Fe 490 ....G6
Santiago 21,809 ....G6
Soná 4,471 ....G6
Tocumen⊙ 21,745 ....H6
Tolé 1,052 ....G6
Tonosí 891 ....G7

OTHER FEATURES

Azuero (pen.) G7
Bastimentos (isl.) G6
Brewster, Cerro (mt.) H6
Burica, Punta (cape) F6
Cébaco (isl.) G7
Chepo (riv.) H6
Chiriquí (gulf) F6
Chiriquí (lag.) F6
Chucunaque (riv.) J6
Coiba, Isla de (isl.) F7
Colón, Isla de (isl.) G6
Contreras (isls.) F7
Darién (gulf) J6
Escudo de Veraguas (isl.) G6
Gatún (lake) G6
Jicarón (isl.) F7
Ladrones (isls.) F6
Manzanillo (isl.) H6
Montijo (gulf) G7
Mosquitos, Golfo de los
 (gulf) G6
Panamá (gulf) H7
Pando, Cerro (mt.) F6
Parida (isl.) F6
Parita (bay) G6
Perlas (arch.) H6
Puercos, Morro de (head) H7
Rey (isl.) H6
Rincón (pt.) H6
San Blas, Golfo de (bay) H6
San Blas, Pta. de (pt.) H6
San Blas, Cordillera de
 (mts.) H6
San José (isl.) H6
San Miguel, Golfo de (bay) H6
Santiago, Cerro (mt.) G7
Secas (isls.) F6
Tabasará (mts.) G6
Taboga (isl.) H6
Tiburón (pt.) J6
Valiente (pen.) G6

*City and suburbs.
⊙Population of sub-district or division.
⊙Population of district.

BAHAMAS · **CUBA** · **HAITI** · **DOMINICAN REPUBLIC** · **JAMAICA**

BAHAMAS

AREA 5,382 sq. mi. (13,939 sq. km.)
POPULATION 209,505
CAPITAL Nassau
LARGEST CITY Nassau
HIGHEST POINT Mt. Alvernia 206 ft. (63 m.)
MONETARY UNIT Bahamian dollar
MAJOR LANGUAGE English
MAJOR RELIGIONS Roman Catholicism, Protestantism

CUBA

AREA 44,206 sq. mi. (114,494 sq. km.)
POPULATION 9,706,369
CAPITAL Havana
LARGEST CITY Havana
HIGHEST POINT Pico Turquino 6,561 ft. (2,000 m.)
MONETARY UNIT Cuban peso
MAJOR LANGUAGE Spanish
MAJOR RELIGION Roman Catholicism

JAMAICA

AREA 4,411 sq. mi. (11,424 sq. km.)
POPULATION 2,161,000
CAPITAL Kingston
LARGEST CITY Kingston
HIGHEST POINT Blue Mountain Peak 7,402 ft. (2,256 m.)
MONETARY UNIT Jamaican dollar
MAJOR LANGUAGE English
MAJOR RELIGIONS Protestantism, Roman Catholicism

GRENADA

AREA 133 sq. mi. (344 sq. km.)
POPULATION 103,103
CAPITAL St. George's
LARGEST CITY St. George's
HIGHEST POINT Mt. St. Catherine 2,757 ft. (840 m.)
MONETARY UNIT East Caribbean dollar
MAJOR LANGUAGES English, French patois
MAJOR RELIGIONS Roman Catholicism, Protestantism

DOMINICA

AREA 290 sq. mi. (751 sq. km.)
POPULATION 74,089
CAPITAL Roseau
HIGHEST POINT Morne Diablotin 4,747 ft. (1,447 m.)
MONETARY UNIT Dominican dollar
MAJOR LANGUAGES English, French patois
MAJOR RELIGIONS Roman Catholicism, Protestantism

SAINT VINCENT AND THE GRENADINES

AREA 150 sq. mi. (388 sq. km.)
POPULATION 124,000
CAPITAL Kingstown
HIGHEST POINT Soufrière 4,000 ft. (1,219 m.)
MONETARY UNIT East Caribbean dollar
MAJOR LANGUAGE English
MAJOR RELIGIONS Protestantism, Roman Catholicism

HAITI

AREA 10,694 sq. mi. (27,697 sq. km.)
POPULATION 5,009,000
CAPITAL Port-au-Prince
LARGEST CITY Port-au-Prince
HIGHEST POINT Pic La Selle 8,793 ft. (2,680 m.)
MONETARY UNIT gourde
MAJOR LANGUAGES Creole French, French
MAJOR RELIGION Roman Catholicism

TRINIDAD AND TOBAGO

AREA 1,980 sq. mi. (5,128 sq. km.)
POPULATION 1,067,108
CAPITAL Port of Spain
LARGEST CITY Port of Spain
HIGHEST POINT Mt. Aripo 3,084 ft. (940 m.)
MONETARY UNIT Trinidad and Tobago dollar
MAJOR LANGUAGES English, Hindi
MAJOR RELIGIONS Roman Catholicism, Protestantism, Hinduism, Islam

DOMINICAN REPUBLIC

AREA 18,704 sq. mi. (48,443 sq. km.)
POPULATION 5,647,977
CAPITAL Santo Domingo
LARGEST CITY Santo Domingo
HIGHEST POINT Pico Duarte 10,417 ft. (3,175 m.)
MONETARY UNIT Dominican peso
MAJOR LANGUAGE Spanish
MAJOR RELIGION Roman Catholicism

BARBADOS

AREA 166 sq. mi. (430 sq. km.)
POPULATION 248,983
CAPITAL Bridgetown
LARGEST CITY Bridgetown
HIGHEST POINT Mt. Hillaby 1,104 ft. (336 m.)
MONETARY UNIT Barbadian dollar
MAJOR LANGUAGE English
MAJOR RELIGION Protestantism

SAINT LUCIA

AREA 238 sq. mi. (616 sq. km.)
POPULATION 115,783
CAPITAL Castries
HIGHEST POINT Mt. Gimie 3,117 ft. (950 m.)
MONETARY UNIT East Caribbean dollar
MAJOR LANGUAGES English, French patois
MAJOR RELIGIONS Roman Catholicism, Protestantism

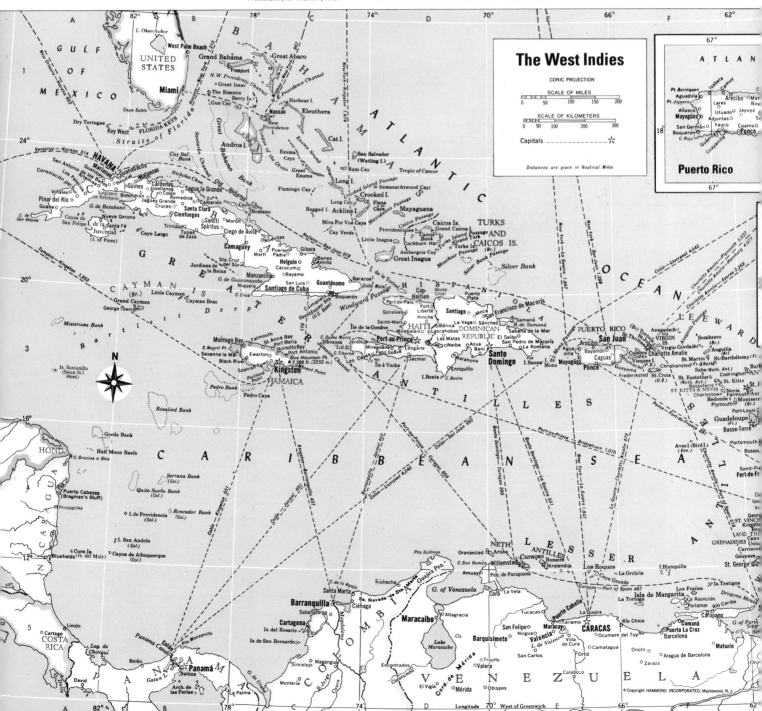

The West Indies

CONIC PROJECTION

SCALE OF MILES
0 50 100 150 200

SCALE OF KILOMETERS
0 50 100 200 300

Capitals ············· ☆

Distances are given in Nautical Miles

Puerto Rico

© Copyright HAMMOND INCORPORATED, Maplewood, N.J.

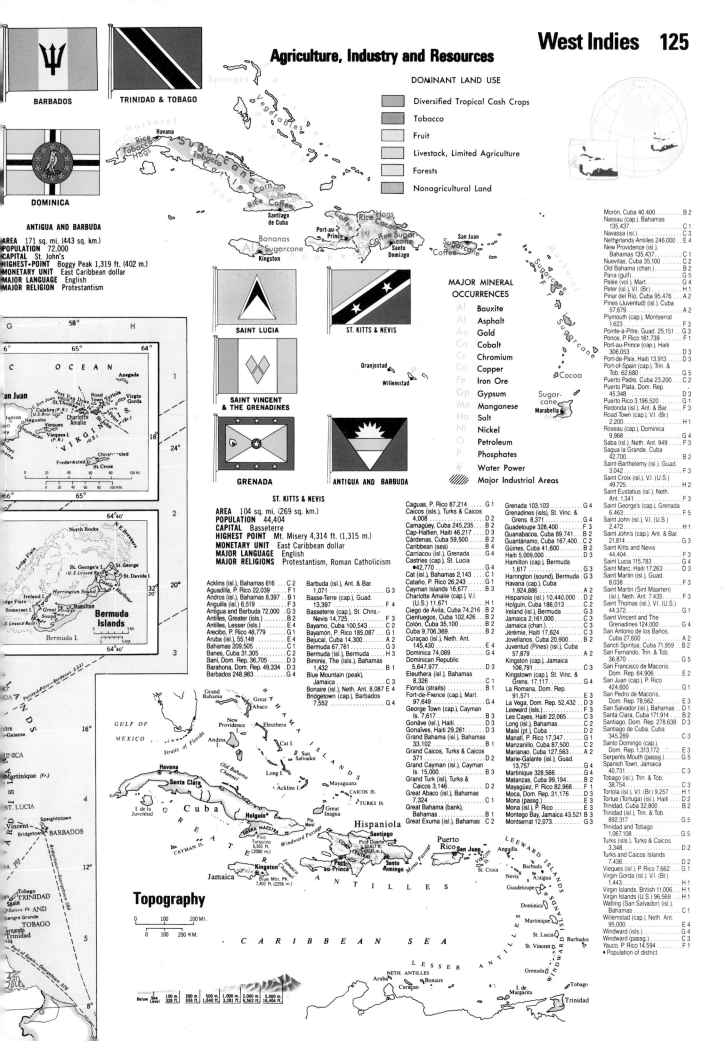

Agriculture, Industry and Resources

DOMINANT LAND USE

- Diversified Tropical Cash Crops
- Tobacco
- Fruit
- Livestock, Limited Agriculture
- Forests
- Nonagricultural Land

BARBADOS

TRINIDAD & TOBAGO

DOMINICA

ANTIGUA AND BARBUDA
AREA 171 sq. mi. (443 sq. km.)
POPULATION 72,000
CAPITAL St. John's
HIGHEST POINT Boggy Peak 1,319 ft. (402 m.)
MONETARY UNIT East Caribbean dollar
MAJOR LANGUAGE English
MAJOR RELIGION Protestantism

SAINT LUCIA

ST. KITTS & NEVIS

SAINT VINCENT & THE GRENADINES

GRENADA

ANTIGUA AND BARBUDA

MAJOR MINERAL OCCURRENCES

Al	Bauxite
At	Asphalt
Au	Gold
Co	Cobalt
Cr	Chromium
Cu	Copper
Fe	Iron Ore
Gp	Gypsum
Mn	Manganese
Na	Salt
Ni	Nickel
O	Petroleum
P	Phosphates
⚡	Water Power
▨	Major Industrial Areas

ST. KITTS & NEVIS
AREA 104 sq. mi. (269 sq. km.)
POPULATION 44,404
CAPITAL Basseterre
HIGHEST POINT Mt. Misery 4,314 ft. (1,315 m.)
MONETARY UNIT East Caribbean dollar
MAJOR LANGUAGE English
MAJOR RELIGIONS Protestantism, Roman Catholicism

Acklins (isl.), Bahamas 616 ... C 2
Aguadilla, P. Rico 22,039 ... F 1
Andros (isl.), Bahamas 8,397 ... B 1
Anguilla (isl.) 6,519 ... F 3
Antigua and Barbuda 72,000 ... G 3
Antilles, Greater (isls.) ...
Antilles, Lesser (isls.) ... E 4
Arecibo, P. Rico 48,779 ... G 1
Aruba (isl.), 55,148 ... E 4
Bahamas 209,505 ... C 1
Banes, Cuba 31,305 ... D 3
Baní, Dom. Rep. 36,705 ... D 3
Barahona, Dom. Rep. 49,334 ... D 3
Barbados 248,983 ... G 4
Barbuda (isl.), Ant. & Bar. 1,071 ... G 3
Basse-Terre (cap.), Guad. 13,397 ... F 4
Basseterre (cap.), St. Chris.-Nevis 14,725 ... F 3
Bayamo, Cuba 100,543 ... C 2
Bayamón, P. Rico 185,087 ... G 1
Bejucal, Cuba 14,300 ... A 2
Bermuda 67,761 ... G 3
Bermuda (isl.), Bermuda ... H 3
Biminis, The (isls.), Bahamas 1,432 ... B 1
Blue Mountain (peak), Jamaica ... C 3
Bonaire (isl.), Neth. Ant. 8,087 ... E 4
Bridgetown (cap.), Barbados 7,552 ... G 4

Caguas, P. Rico 87,214 ... G 1
Caicos (isls.), Turks & Caicos 4,008 ... D 2
Camagüey, Cuba 245,235 ... B 2
Cap-Haïtien, Haiti 46,217 ... D 3
Cárdenas, Cuba 59,500 ... B 2
Caribbean (sea) ... B 4
Carriacou (isl.), Grenada ... G 4
Castries (cap.), St. Lucia •42,770 ... G 4
Cat (isl.), Bahamas 2,143 ... C 1
Cataño, P. Rico 26,243 ... G 1
Cayman Islands 16,677 ... B 3
Charlotte Amalie (cap.), V.I. (U.S.) 11,671 ... H 1
Ciego de Ávila, Cuba 74,216 ... B 2
Cienfuegos, Cuba 102,426 ... B 2
Colón, Cuba 35,100 ... B 2
Cuba 9,706,369 ... B 2
Curaçao (isl.), Neth. Ant. 145,430 ... E 4
Dominica 74,089 ... G 4
Dominican Republic 5,647,977 ... D 3
Eleuthera (isl.), Bahamas 8,326 ... C 1
Florida (straits) ... B 1
Fort-de-France (cap.), Mart. 97,649 ... G 4
George Town (cap.), Cayman Is. 7,617 ... B 3
Gonâve (isl.), Haiti ... D 3
Gonaïves, Haiti 29,261 ... D 3
Grand Bahama (isl.), Bahamas 33,102 ... B 1
Grand Caicos, Turks & Caicos 371 ... D 2
Grand Cayman (isl.), Cayman Is. 15,000 ... B 3
Grand Turk (isl), Turks & Caicos 3,146 ... D 2
Great Abaco (isl.), Bahamas 7,324 ... C 1
Great Bahama (bank), Bahamas ... B 1
Great Inagua (isl.), Bahamas ... C 2
Great Exuma (isl.), Bahamas ... C 2

Grenada 103,103 ... G 4
Grenadines (isls), St. Vinc. & Grens. 8,371 ... G 4
Guadeloupe 328,400 ... F 3
Guanabacoa, Cuba 89,741 ... B 2
Guantánamo, Cuba 167,400 ... C 2
Güines, Cuba 41,600 ... A 2
Haiti 5,009,000 ... D 3
Hamilton (cap.), Bermuda 1,617 ... G 3
Harrington (sound), Bermuda . G 3
Havana (cap.), Cuba 1,924,886 ... A 2
Hispaniola (isl.) 10,440,000 ... C 2
Holguín, Cuba 186,013 ... C 2
Ireland (isl.), Bermuda ... G 3
Jamaica 2,161,000 ... C 3
Jamaica (chan.) ... C 3
Jérémie, Haiti 17,624 ... C 3
Jovellanos, Cuba 20,900 ... B 2
Juventud (Pines) (isl.), Cuba 57,879 ... A 2
Kingston (cap.), Jamaica 106,791 ... C 3
Kingstown (cap.), St. Vinc. & Grens. 17,117 ... G 4
La Romana, Dom. Rep. 91,571 ... E 3
La Vega, Dom. Rep. 52,432 ... D 3
Leeward (isls.) ... E 3
Les Cayes, Haiti 22,065 ... C 3
Long (isl.), Bahamas ... C 2
Maisí (pt.), Cuba ... D 2
Manatí, P. Rico 17,347 ... G 1
Manzanillo, Cuba 87,500 ... C 2
Marianao, Cuba 127,563 ... A 2
Marie-Galante (isl.), Guad. 13,757 ... G 4
Martinique 328,566 ... G 4
Matanzas, Cuba 99,194 ... B 2
Mayagüez, P. Rico 82,968 ... F 1
Moca, Dom. Rep. 31,176 ... D 3
Mona (passg.) ... E 3
Mona (isl.), P. Rico ... E 3
Montego Bay, Jamaica 43,521 ... B 3
Montserrat 12,073 ... G 3

Morón, Cuba 40,400 ... B 2
Nassau (cap.), Bahamas 135,437 ... C 1
Navassa (isl.) ... C 3
Netherlands Antilles 246,000 ... E 4
New Providence (isl.), Bahamas 135,437 ... C 1
Nuevitas, Cuba 35,100 ... C 2
Old Bahama (chan.) ... B 2
Paria (gulf) ... G 5
Pelée (vol.), Mart. ...
Peter (isl.), V.I. (Br.) ... H 1
Pinar del Río, Cuba 95,476 ... A 2
Pines (Juventud) (isl.), Cuba 57,879 ... A 2
Plymouth (cap.), Montserrat 1,623 ... F 3
Pointe-à-Pitre, Guad. 25,151 ... G 3
Ponce, P. Rico 161,739 ... F 1
Port-au-Prince (cap.), Haiti 306,053 ... D 3
Port-de-Paix, Haiti 13,913 ... D 3
Port-of-Spain (cap.), Trin. & Tob. 62,680 ... G 5
Puerto Padre, Cuba 23,200 ... C 2
Puerto Plata, Dom. Rep. 45,348 ... D 3
Puerto Rico 3,196,520 ... G 1
Redonda (isl.), Ant. & Bar. ... F 3
Road Town (cap.), V.I. (Br.) 2,200 ... H 1
Roseau (cap.), Dominica 9,968 ... G 4
Saba (isl.), Neth. Ant. 949 ... F 3
Sagua la Grande, Cuba 42,700 ... B 2
Saint-Barthélemy (isl.), Guad. 3,042 ... F 3
Saint Croix (isl.), V.I. (U.S.) 49,725 ... H 2
Saint Eustatius (isl.), Neth. Ant. 1,341 ... F 3
Saint George's (cap.), Grenada 6,463 ... F 5
Saint John (isl.), V.I. (U.S.) 2,472 ... H 1
Saint John's (cap.), Ant. & Bar. 21,814 ... G 3
Saint Kitts and Nevis 44,404 ... F 3
Saint Lucia 115,783 ... G 4
Saint Marc, Haiti 17,263 ... D 3
Saint Martin (isl.) 8,038 ... F 3
Saint Martin (Sint Maarten) (isl.), Neth. Ant. 7,435 ... F 3
Saint Thomas (isl.), V.I. (U.S.) 44,372 ... G 1
Saint Vincent and The Grenadines 124,000 ... G 4
San Antonio de los Baños, Cuba 27,600 ... A 2
Sancti Spíritus, Cuba 71,959 ... B 2
San Fernando, Trin. & Tob. 36,870 ... G 5
San Francisco de Macorís, Dom. Rep. 64.906 ... E 2
San Juan (cap.), P. Rico 424,600 ... G 1
San Pedro de Macorís, Dom. Rep. 78,562 ... E 3
San Salvador (isl.), Bahamas . D 1
Santa Clara, Cuba 171,914 ... B 2
Santiago, Dom. Rep. 278,638 ... D 3
Santiago de Cuba, Cuba 345.289 ... C 3
Santo Domingo (cap.), Dom. Rep. 1,313,172 ... E 3
Serpents Mouth (passg.) ... G 5
Spanish Town, Jamaica 40,731 ... C 3
Tobago (isl.), Trin. & Tob. 38.754 ... G 5
Tortola (isl.), V.I. (Br.) 9,257 ... H 1
Tortue (Tortuga) (isl.), Haiti ... D 2
Trinidad, Cuba 32.800 ... B 2
Trinidad (isl.), Trin. & Tob. 892,317 ... G 5
Trinidad and Tobago 1,067,108 ... G 5
Turks (isls.), Turks & Caicos 3,348 ... D 2
Turks and Caicos Islands 7,436 ... D 2
Vieques (isl.), P. Rico 7,662 ... G 1
Virgin Gorda (isl.), V.I. (Br.) 1,443 ... H 1
Virgin Islands, British 11,006 ... H 1
Virgin Islands (U.S.) 96,569 ... H 1
Watling (San Salvador) (isl.), Bahamas ... C 1
Willemstad (cap.), Neth. Ant. 95,000 ... E 4
Windward (isls.) ... G 4
Windward (passg.) ... C 3
Yauco, P. Rico 14,594 ... F 1
• Population of district.

Bermuda Islands

Topography

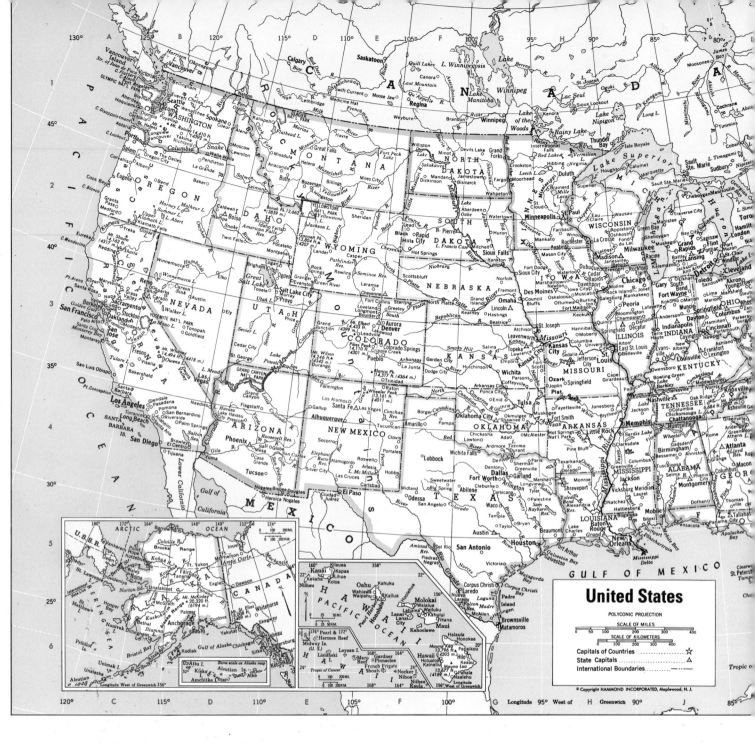

United States — POLYCONIC PROJECTION

Akron, Ohio‡ 660.328 ..... K2
Alabama (state) 3.890.061 ..... J4
Alaska (state) 400.481 ..... D6
Alaska (gulf), Alaska D6
Alaska (range), Alaska C5
Albany, N.Y.‡ 795.019 ..... M2
Albuquerque, N. Mex‡ 454.499 ..... E3
Aleutian (isls.), Alaska .....
Anchorage, Alaska‡ 173.017 ..... D6
Annapolis (cap.), Md. 31.740 ..... L3
Ann Arbor, Mich‡ 264.748 ..... K2
Appalachian (mts.) .....
Appleton, Wis 291.325 ..... J2
Arizona (state) 2.717.866 ..... D4
Arkansas (state) 2.285.513 ..... H3
Arkansas (riv.) H3
Atlanta (cap.), Ga‡ 2.029.618 ..... K4
Atlantic City, N.J.‡ 194.119 ..... M3
Attu (isl.), Alaska D6
Augusta, Ga‡ 327.372 ..... K4
Augusta (cap.), Maine 21.819 ..... N2
Austin (cap.), Texas‡ 536.450 ..... G4
Bakersfield, Calif ‡ 403.089 ..... C3
Baltimore, Md.‡ 2.174.023 ..... L3
Baton Rouge (cap.).
  La ‡ 493.973 ..... H4
Beaumont, Texas‡ 375.497 ..... H4
Bering (sea), Alaska C5
Bering (str.), Alaska C5
Bighorn (riv.) E2
Binghamton, N.Y‡ 301.336 ..... L2
Birmingham, Ala ‡ 847.360 ..... J4
Bismarck (cap.).
  Dak ‡ 79.988 ..... G1
Bitterroot (range) D1
Black Hills (mts.) F2
Boise (cap.), Idaho‡ 173.076 ..... C2
Borah (peak), Idaho D2

Boston (cap.), Mass.‡ 2.763.357 ..... M2
Bridgeport, Conn ‡ 395.455 ..... M2
Brazos (riv.), Texas G4
Brooks (range), Alaska C5
Buffalo, N.Y ‡ 1.242.573 ..... L2
California (state) 23.668.562 ..... B3
Canadian (riv.) F3
Canaveral (Kennedy) (cape).
Cape Fear (riv.), N.C. L4
Carson City (cap.).
  Nev. 32.022 ..... C3
Cascade (range) B1
Cedar Rapids, Iowa‡ 169.775 ..... H2
Champlain (lake) M2
Charleston, S.C.‡ 430.301 ..... L4
Charleston, W.
  Va ‡ 269.595 ..... K3
Charlotte, N.C ‡ 637.218 ..... K3
Chattahoochee (riv.) K4
Chattanooga, Tenn ‡ 426.540 ..... J3
Chesapeake (bay) L3
Cheyenne (cap.), Wyo. 47.283 ..... F2
Chicago, Ill ‡ 7.102.328 ..... J2
Cimarron (riv.) G3
Cincinnati, Ohio‡ 1.401.403 ..... K3
Cleveland, Ohio‡ 1.898.720 ..... K2
Coast (ranges) B2
Cod (cape), Mass. N2
Colorado (state) 2.888.834 ..... E3
Colorado (riv.) D4
Colorado (riv.), Texas G4
Colorado Springs.
  Colo ‡ 317.458 ..... F3
Columbia (cap.), S.C.‡ 408.176 ..... K4
Columbia (riv.) B1
Columbus, Ga ‡ 239.196 ..... K4

Columbus (cap.), Ohio‡ 1.093.293 ..... K3
Concord (cap.), N.H. 30.400 ..... M2
Connecticut (state) 3.107.576 ..... M2
Connecticut (riv.) M2
Corpus Christi. Texas‡ 326.228 ..... G5
Cumberland (riv.) J3
Dallas, Texas‡ 2.905.350 ..... G4
Davenport, Iowa‡ 383.958 ..... H2
Dayton, Ohio‡ 830.070 ..... K3
Death Valley (depr.), Calif. C3
Delaware (state) 595.225 ..... L3
Delaware (bay) M3
Denver (cap.), Colo ‡ 1.619.921 ..... F3
Des Moines (cap.).
  Iowa‡ 338.048 ..... H2
Detroit, Mich ‡ 4.352.762 ..... K2
District of Columbia 637.651 ..... L3
Dover (cap.), Del. 23.512 ..... L3
Duluth, Minn ‡ 266.650 ..... H1
Durham, N.C ‡ 530.673 ..... L3
Elbert (mt.). Colo. E3
El Paso, Texas‡ 479.899 ..... E4
Erie, Pa ‡ 279.780 ..... K2
Eugene, Oreg ‡ 275.226 ..... B2
Evansville, Ind ‡ 309.408 ..... J3
Everglades, The (swamp).
  Fla K5
Fayetteville, N.C ‡ 247.160 ..... L3
Flint, Mich ‡ 521.589 ..... K2
Florida (state) 9.739.992 ..... K5
Florida (keys). Fla. K6
Fort Smith. Ark ‡ 203.269 ..... H3
Fort Wayne, Ind ‡ 382.961 ..... J2
Fort Worth. Texas 385.141 ..... G4
Frankfort (cap.). Ky. 25.973 ..... K3
Fresno. Calif ‡ 515.013 ..... C3
Galveston, Texas‡ 195.940 ..... H5
Gary. Ind ‡ 642.781 ..... J2

Georgia (state) 5.464.265 ..... K4
Gila (riv.) D4
Glacier Nat'l Park. Mont. D1
Golden Gate (chan.). Calif. B3
Grand Canyon Nat'l Park,
  Ariz D3
Grand Rapids, Mich ‡ 601.680 ..... K2
Great Salt (lake). Utah D2
Greensboro, N.C ‡ 827.385 ..... L3
Greenville, S.C ‡ 568.758 ..... K4
Hamilton, Ohio‡ 258.787 ..... K3
Harrisburg (cap.), Pa.‡ 446.072 ..... L2
Hartford (cap.), Conn.‡ 726.114 ..... M2
Hatteras (cape), N.C. M3
Havasu (lake) D4
Hawaii (state) 965.000 ..... F5
Hawaii (isl.), Hawaii F6
Helena (cap.), Mont. 23.938 ..... D1
Honolulu (cap.).
  Hawaii 762.874 ..... F5
Houston, Texas‡ 2.905.350 ..... G5
Huntington, W. Va.‡ 311.350 ..... K3
Huntsville, Ala ‡ 308.593 ..... J4
Huron (lake). Mich. K2
Idaho (state) 943.935 ..... C2
Illinois (state) 11.418.461 ..... J3
Indiana (state) 5.490.179 ..... J3
Aleutian (isls.), Alaska D6
Iowa (state) 2.913.387 ..... H2
Jackson (cap.), Miss ‡ 320.425 ..... J4
Jacksonville, Fla ‡ 737.519 ..... K4
Jefferson City (cap.).
  Mo. 33.619 ..... H3

Kans.-Mo ‡ 1.327.020 ..... G3
Kentucky (state) 3.661.433 ..... J3
Kentucky (lake) J3
Knoxville, Tenn ‡ 476.517 ..... K3
Lancaster, Pa ‡ 362.346 ..... L2
Lansing (cap.), Mich ‡ 476.517 ..... K2
Las Vegas, Nev ‡ 461.816 ..... C3
Lexington, Ky ‡ 318.136 ..... K3
Lima, Ohio‡ 218.244 ..... K2
Lincoln (cap.), Nebr.‡ 192.884 ..... G2
Little Rock (cap.).
  Ark ‡ 393.494 ..... H4
Long (isl.), N.Y M2
Long Beach, Calif. 361.334 ..... C4
Los Angeles, Calif ‡ 7.477.657 ..... C4
Louisiana (state) 4.203.972 ..... H4
Louisville, Ky ‡ 906.240 ..... J3
Lowell, Mass ‡ 233.410 ..... M2
Lubbock, Texas‡ 211.651 ..... F4
Macon, Ga ‡ 254.623 ..... K4
Madison (cap.), Wis ‡ 323.545 ..... H2
Maine (state) 1.124.660 ..... N1
Maryland (state) 4.216.446 ..... L3
Massachusetts (state) 5.737.037 ..... M2
Maui (isl.), Hawaii F5
Mauna Kea (mt.). Hawaii F6
Mauna Loa (mt.). Hawaii F6
May (cape). N.J. M3
McKinley (mt.). Alaska D5
Mendocino (cape). Calif. A2
Mexico (gulf) .....
Miami, Fla ‡ 1.625.979 ..... K5
Michigan (state) 9.258.344 ..... J2
Michigan (lake) J2
Milwaukee, Wis ‡ 1.397.143 ..... J2
Minneapolis, Minn ‡ 2.114.256 ..... H1

Minnesota (state) 4.077.148 ..... H1
Mississippi (state) 2.520.638 ..... J4
Mississippi (riv.) H4
Missouri (state) 4.917.444 ..... H3
Missouri (riv.) G2
Mitchell (mt.). N.C. K3
Mobile, Ala ‡ 442.819 ..... J4
Montana (state) 786.690 ..... E1
Montgomery (cap.).
  Ala ‡ 272.687 ..... J4
Nantucket (isl.). Mass. N2
Nashville (cap.).
  Tenn ‡ 850.505 ..... J3
Nebraska (state) 1.570.006 ..... F2
Nevada (state) 799.184 ..... C3
Newark, N.J ‡ 1.965.304 ..... M2
New Hampshire (state) 920.610 ..... M2
New Jersey (state) 7.364.158 ..... M2
New Mexico (state) 1.299.968 ..... E4
New Orleans, La ‡ 1.186.725 ..... H5
Newport News, Va ‡ 364.449 ..... L3
New York (state) 17.557.288 ..... L2
New York, N.Y ‡ 9.119.737 ..... M2
Norfolk, Va ‡ 806.691 ..... L3
North Carolina
  (state) 5.874.429 ..... L3
North Dakota (state) 652.695 ..... F1
Ohio (state) 10.797.419 ..... K2
Oklahoma (state) 3.025.266 ..... G3
Oklahoma City (cap.).
  Okla ‡ 834.088 ..... G3
Olympia (cap.). Wash ‡ 124.264 ..... B1
Omaha, Nebr ‡ 570.399 ..... G2
Ontario (lake). N.Y L2

Oregon (state) 2.632.663 ..... B2
Orlando, Fla ‡ 700.699 ..... K5
Ozark (mts.) H3
Paterson, N.J ‡ 447.585 ..... M2
Pennsylvania (state) L2
Pensacola, Fla ‡ 289.782 ..... J4
Peoria, Ill ‡ 365.864 ..... J2
Philadelphia, Pa ‡ 4.716.818 ..... M2
Phoenix (cap.), Ariz ‡ 1.508.030 ..... D4
Pierre (cap.), S. Dak. 11.793 ..... F2
Pikes (peak). Colo. F3
Pittsburgh, Pa ‡ 2.263.894 ..... L2
Platte (riv.). Nebr. G2
Portland, Maine ‡ 183.625 ..... N2
Portland, Oreg ‡ 1.242.187 ..... B1
Potomac (riv.) L3
Providence (cap.).
  R.I ‡ 919.216 ..... M2
Racine, Wis ‡ 173.132 ..... J2
Raleigh (cap.), N.C ‡ 530.673 ..... L3
Rainier (mt.). Wash. B1
Reading, Pa ‡ 312.509 ..... L2
Red (riv.) H4
Red River of the North G1
Richmond (cap.), Va ‡ 632.015 ..... L3
Rio Grande (riv.) F5
Roanoke, Va ‡ 224.477 ..... L3
Rochester, N.Y ‡ 971.079 ..... L2
Rocky (mts.) E3
Sacramento (cap.).
  Calif ‡ 1.014.002 ..... B3
Saginaw, Mich ‡ 224.548 ..... K2
Saint Clair (lake). Mich. K2
Saint Lawrence (riv.). N.Y N1
Saint Louis, Mo ‡ 2.355.276 ..... H3

AREA 3,623,420 sq. mi.
(9,384,658 sq. km.)
POPULATION 226,504,825
CAPITAL Washington
LARGEST CITY New York
HIGHEST POINT Mt. McKinley 20,320 ft.
(6,194 m.)
MONETARY UNIT U.S. dollar
MAJOR LANGUAGE English
MAJOR RELIGIONS Protestantism,
Roman Catholicism, Judaism

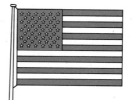

Population Distribution

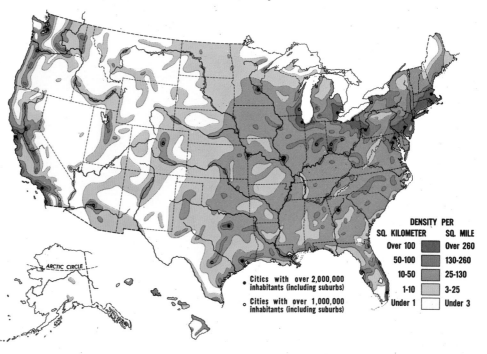

DENSITY PER

SQ. KILOMETER	SQ. MILE
Over 100	Over 260
50-100	130-260
10-50	25-130
1-10	3-25
Under 1	Under 3

● Cities with over 2,000,000
inhabitants (including suburbs)

○ Cities with over 1,000,000
inhabitants (including suburbs)

Vegetation

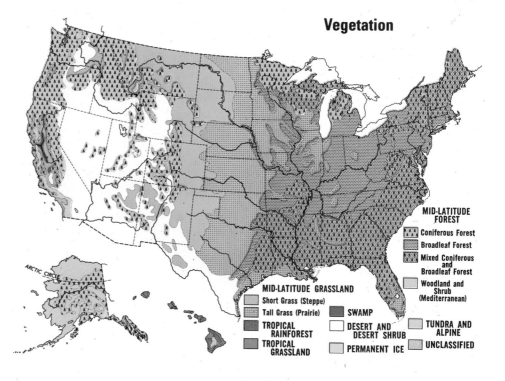

MID-LATITUDE
FOREST

- Coniferous Forest
- Broadleaf Forest
- Mixed Coniferous and Broadleaf Forest
- Woodland and Shrub (Mediterranean)

MID-LATITUDE GRASSLAND
- Short Grass (Steppe)
- Tall Grass (Prairie)

TROPICAL RAINFOREST

TROPICAL GRASSLAND

- SWAMP
- DESERT AND DESERT SHRUB
- PERMANENT ICE

- TUNDRA AND ALPINE
- UNCLASSIFIED

Saint Paul (cap.).
  Minn. 270,230 .... H1
Sakakawea (lake), N. Dak F1
Salem (cap.), Oreg.‡ 249,895 ... B1
Salinas, Calif.‡ 290,444 .... B3
Salt Lake City (cap.).
  Utah‡ 936,255 .... D2
Salton Sea (lake), Calif C4
San Antonio, Texas‡ 1,071,954 .. G5
San Bernardino,
  Calif.‡ 1,557,080 .... C4
San Diego, Calif.‡ 1,861,846 ... C4
San Francisco, Calif.‡ 325,721 . B3
San Joaquin (riv.), Calif C3
San Jose, Calif.‡ 1,295,071 .... B3
Santa Ana, Calif.‡ 1,931,570 ... C4
Santa Barbara, Calif.‡ 298,660 . C4
Santa Fe (cap.), N.
  Mex. 48,899 .... E3
Savannah, Ga.‡ 228,178 .... K4
Scranton, Pa. 88,117 .... L2
Seattle, Wash.‡ 1,606,765 ...... B1
Shasta (mt.), Calif B2
Shreveport, La.‡ 376,646 .... H4
Sierra Nevada (mts.) B3
Snake (riv.) C1
South Bend, Ind.‡ 280,772 ...... J2
Spokane, Wash.‡ 341,835 .... C1
South Carolina
  (state) 3,119,208 .... K4
South Dakota (state) 690,178 ... F2
Springfield (cap.),
  Ill.‡ 187,338 .... H3
Springfield, Mass.‡ 530,668 .... M2
Springfield, Mo.‡ 207,704 ...... H3
Springfield, Ohio‡ 183,885 ..... K2
Stockton, Calif.‡ 347,342 ...... B3
Superior (lake) J1
Syracuse, N.Y.‡ 642,375 .... L2

Tacoma, Wash.‡ 485,643 .... B1
Tahoe (lake) C3
Tallahassee (cap.).
  Fla.‡ 159,542 .... K4
Tampa, Fla.‡ 1,569,492 .... K5
Tennessee (state) 4,590,750 .... J3
Terre Haute, Ind.‡ 176,583 ..... J3
Texas (state) 14,228,383 .... G4
Toledo, Ohio‡ 791,599 .... K2
Topeka (cap.), Kans.‡ 185,442 .. G3
Trenton (cap.), N.J.‡ 307,863 .. M2
Tucson, Ariz.‡ 531,263 .... D4
Tulsa, Okla.‡ 689,628 .... G3
Utah (state) 1,461,037 .... D3
Utica, N.Y.‡ 320,180 .... M2
Vermont (state) 511,456 .... M2
Virginia (state) 5,346,279 ..... L3
Wabash (riv.) J3
Washington (state) 4,130,163 ... B1
Washington, D.C. (cap.).
  U.S.‡ 3,060,240 .... L3
Waterbury, Conn.‡ 228,059 ...... M2
Waterloo, Iowa 75,985 .... H2
West Palm Beach, Fla.‡ 573,125 . K5
West Virginia (state) 1,949,644 . K3
Wheeling, W. Va.‡ 185,566 ...... K2
Whitney (mt.), Calif C3
Wichita, Kans.‡ 411,313 .... G3
Wilkes-Barre, Pa. 51,551 .... L2
Wilmington, Del.‡ 524,108 ...... M3
Wisconsin (state) 4,705,335 .... J2
Woods (lake), Minn G1
Worcester, Mass.‡ 372,940 ...... M2
Wyoming (state) 470,816 .... E2
Yellowstone Nat'l Park, Wyo D2
York, Pa.‡ 381,255 .... L3
Yosemite Nat'l Park, Calif C3
Youngstown, Ohio‡ 531,350 ...... K2
Yukon (riv.), Alaska C5

‡ Population of metropolitan area.

Topography

Agriculture, Industry and Resources

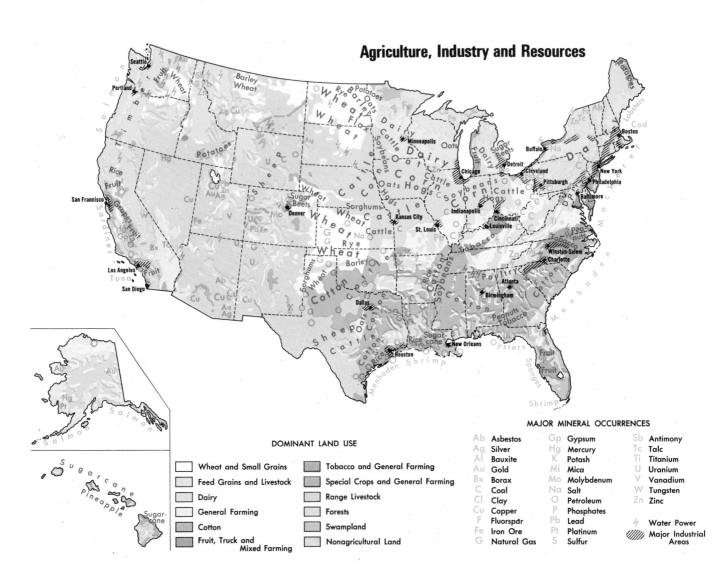

DOMINANT LAND USE

- Wheat and Small Grains
- Feed Grains and Livestock
- Dairy
- General Farming
- Cotton
- Fruit, Truck and Mixed Farming
- Tobacco and General Farming
- Special Crops and General Farming
- Range Livestock
- Forests
- Swampland
- Nonagricultural Land

MAJOR MINERAL OCCURRENCES

Ab	Asbestos	Gp	Gypsum	Sb	Antimony
Ag	Silver	Hg	Mercury	Tc	Talc
Al	Bauxite	K	Potash	Ti	Titanium
Au	Gold	Mi	Mica	U	Uranium
Bx	Borax	Mo	Molybdenum	V	Vanadium
C	Coal	Na	Salt	W	Tungsten
Cl	Clay	O	Petroleum	Zn	Zinc
Cu	Copper	P	Phosphates		
F	Fluorspar	Pb	Lead	⚡	Water Power
Fe	Iron Ore	Pt	Platinum	▨	Major Industrial Areas
G	Natural Gas	S	Sulfur		

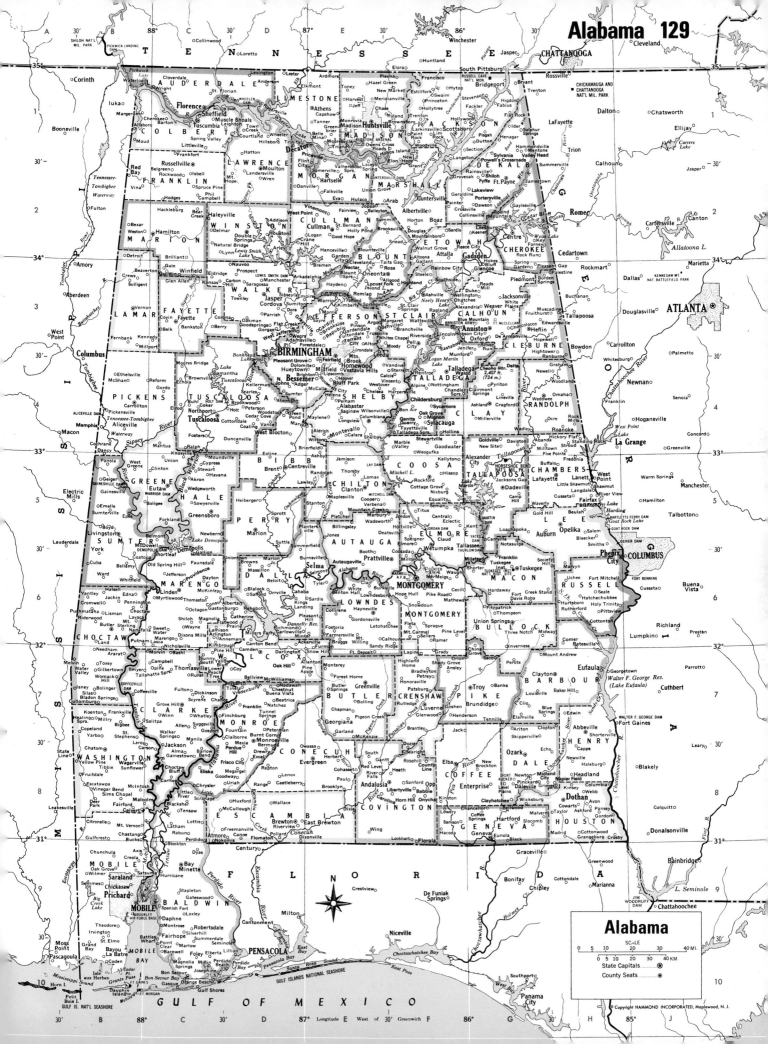

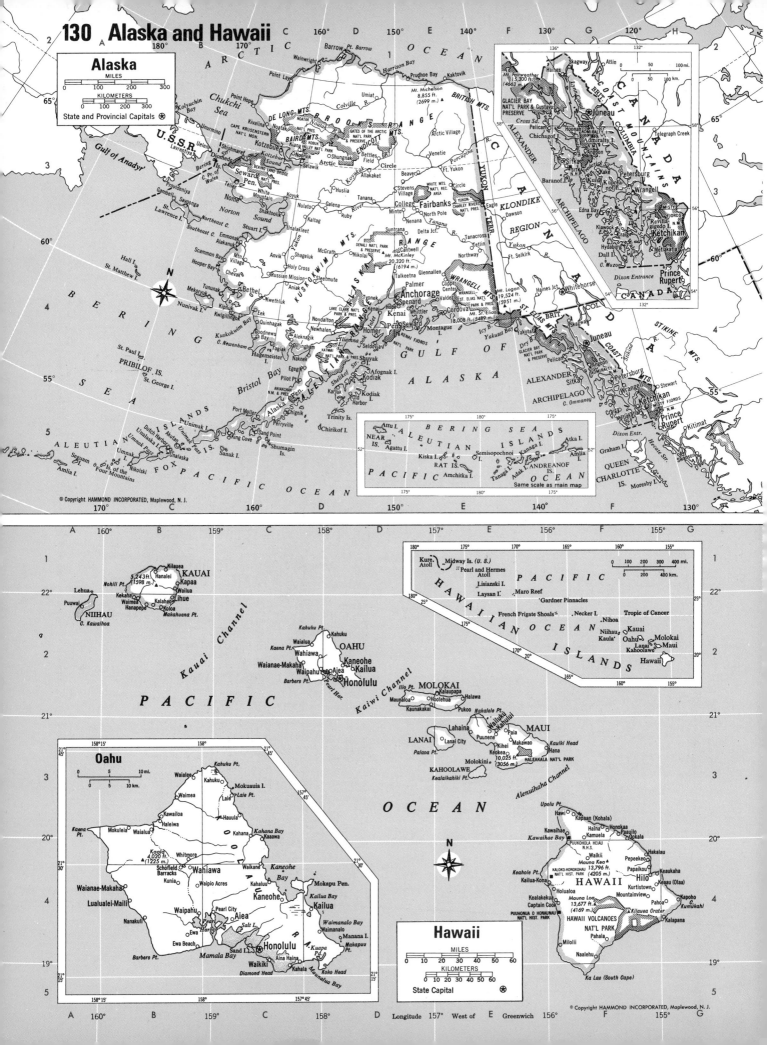

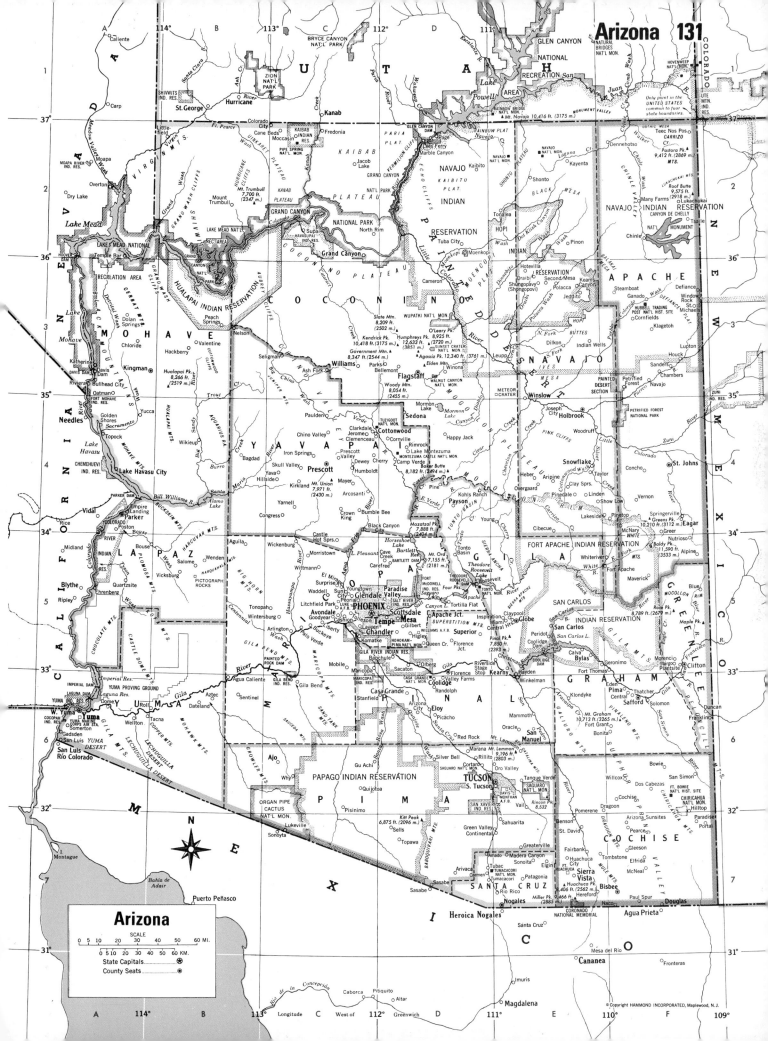

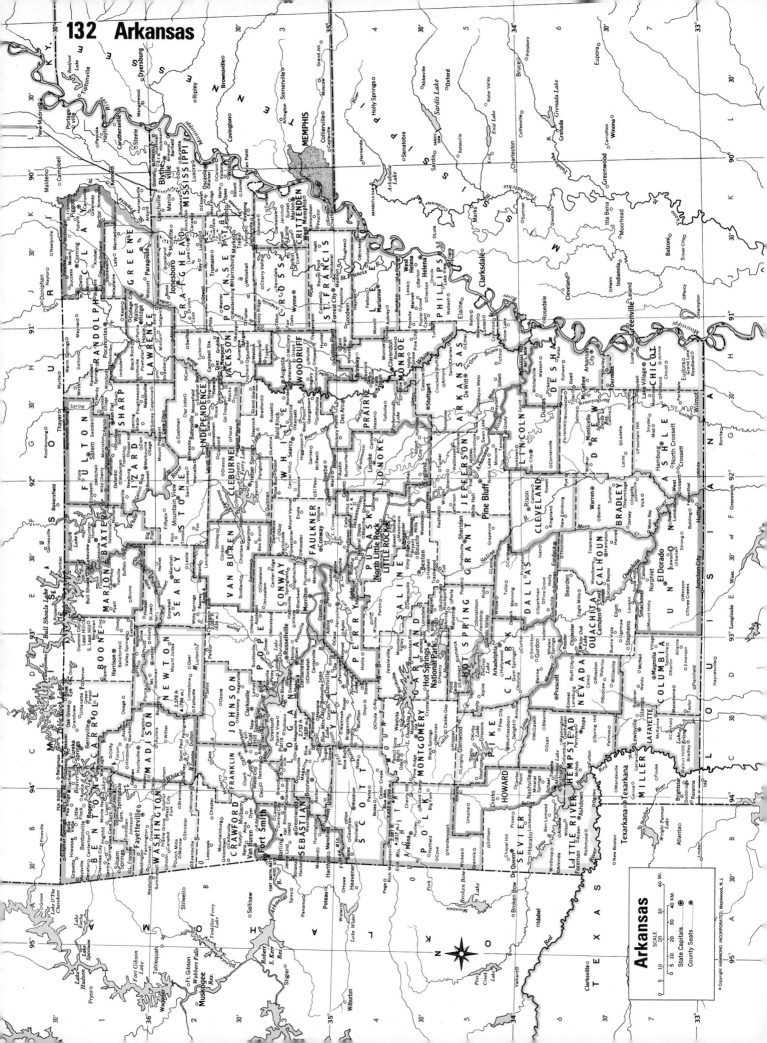

Arkansas

SCALE
0 5 10   20   30   40 MI.
0 5 10 20 30 40 KM.

State Capitals........⊛
County Seats..........◉

© Copyright HAMMOND INCORPORATED, Maplewood, N.J.

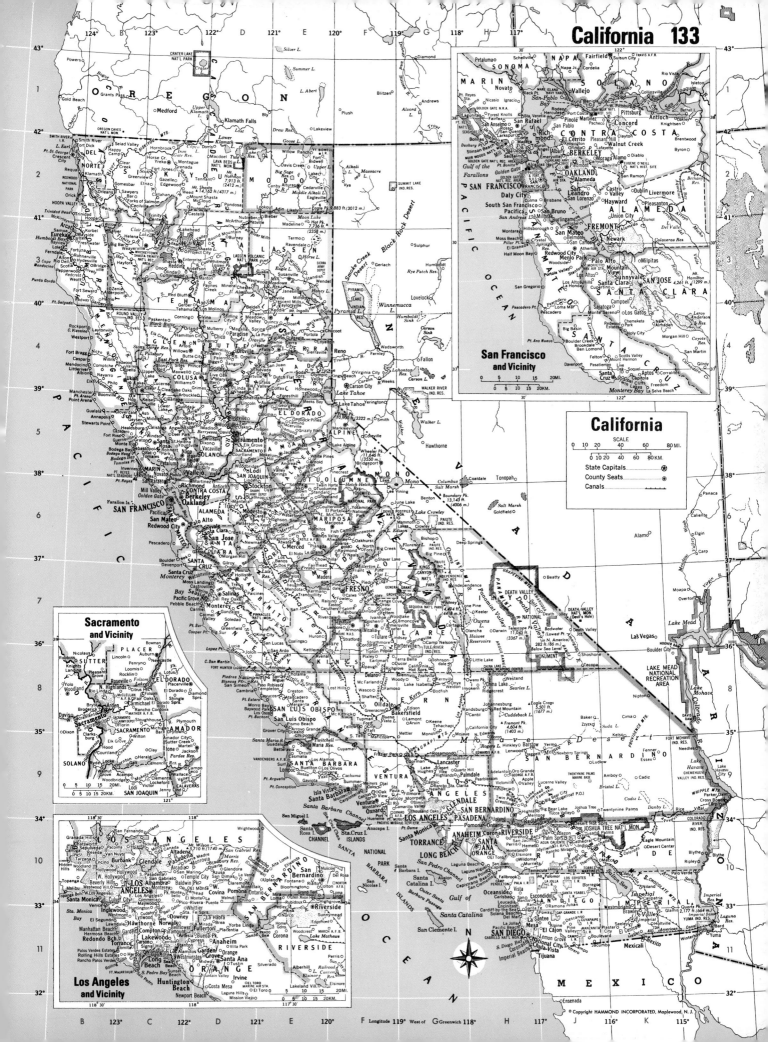

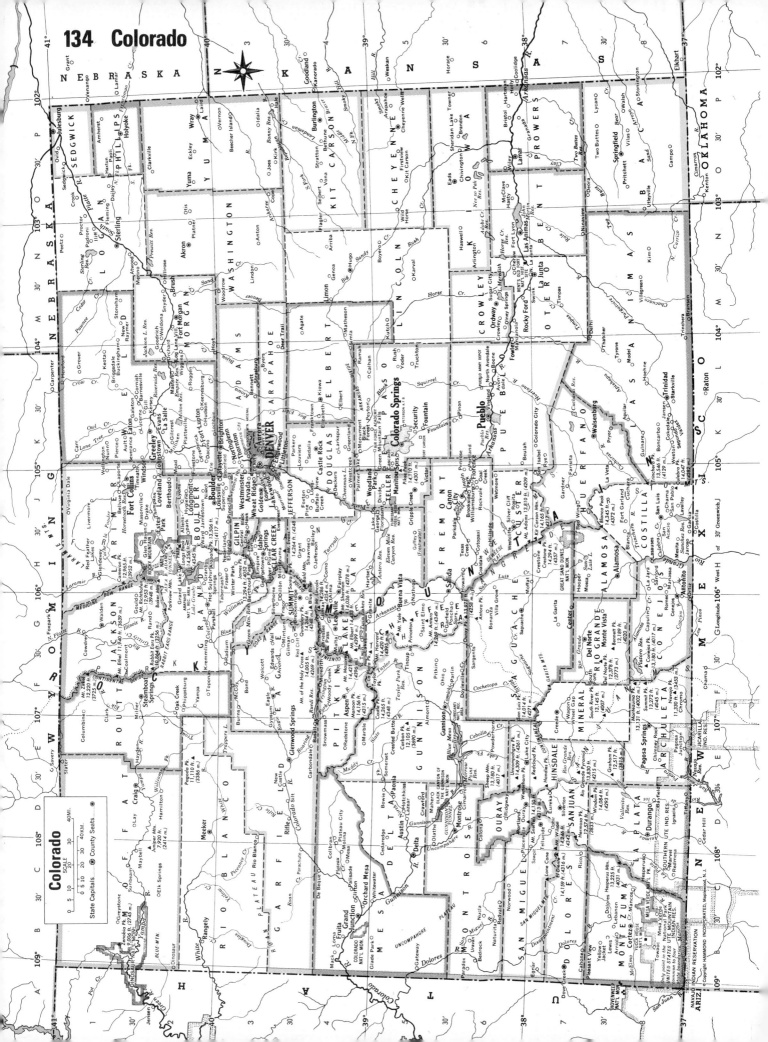

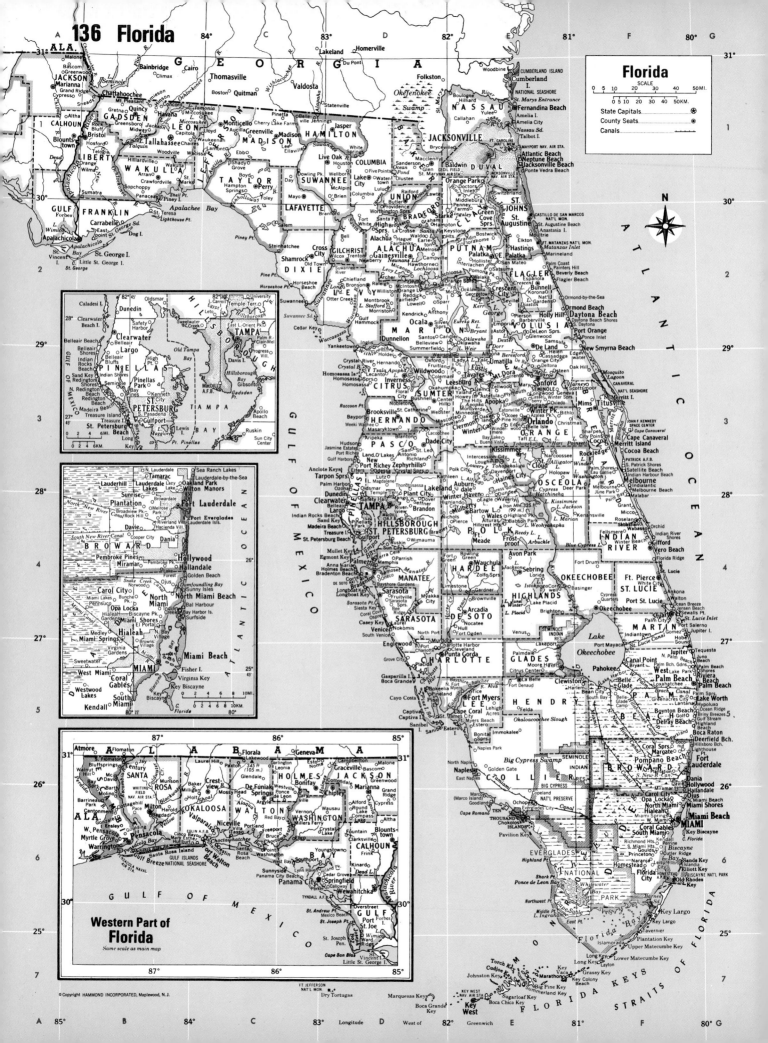

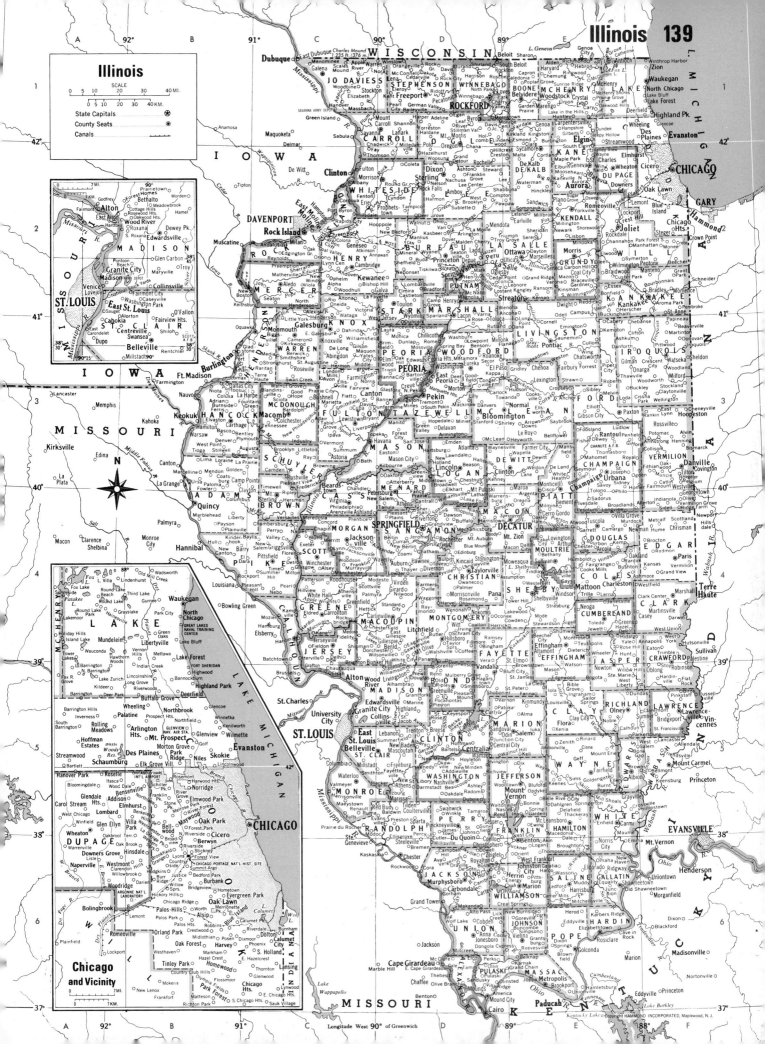

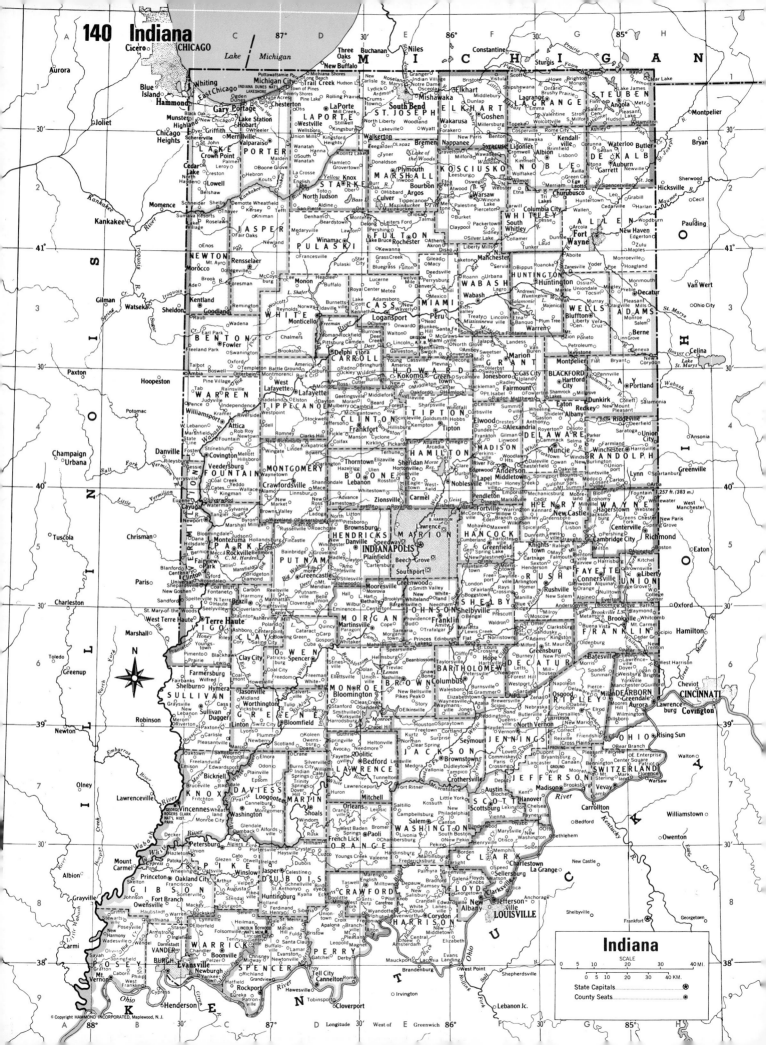

Indiana

SCALE

0 5 10   20   30   40 MI.

0 5 10   20   30   40 KM.

State Capitals .... ⊛

County Seats .... ◉

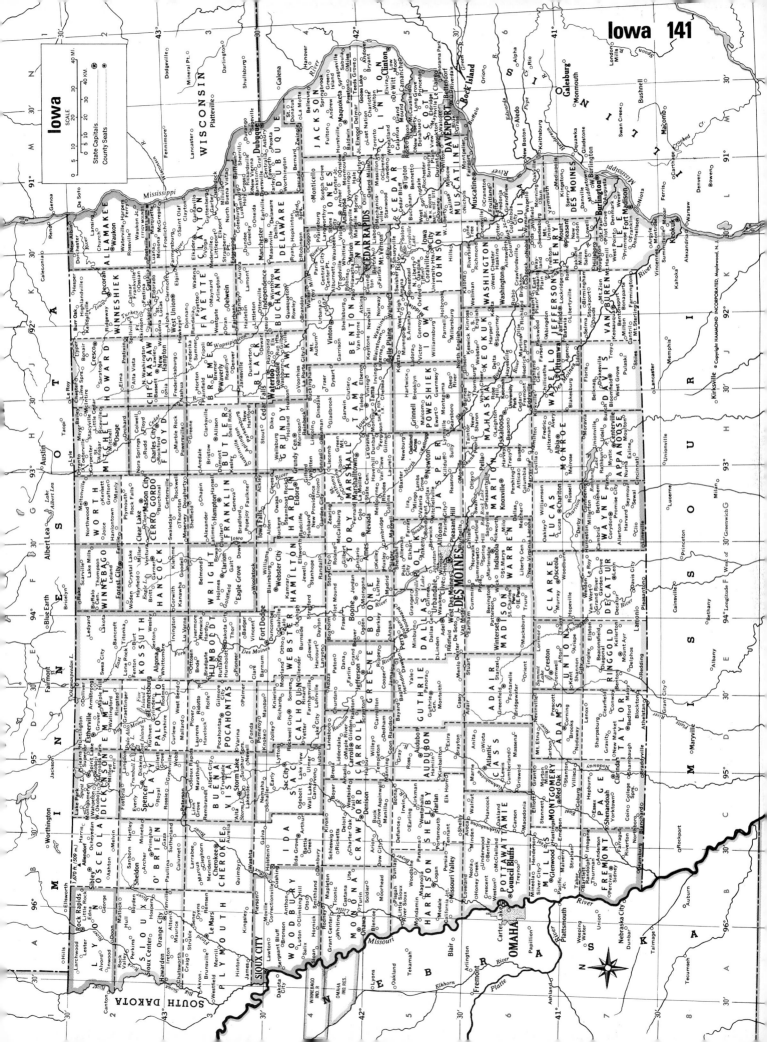

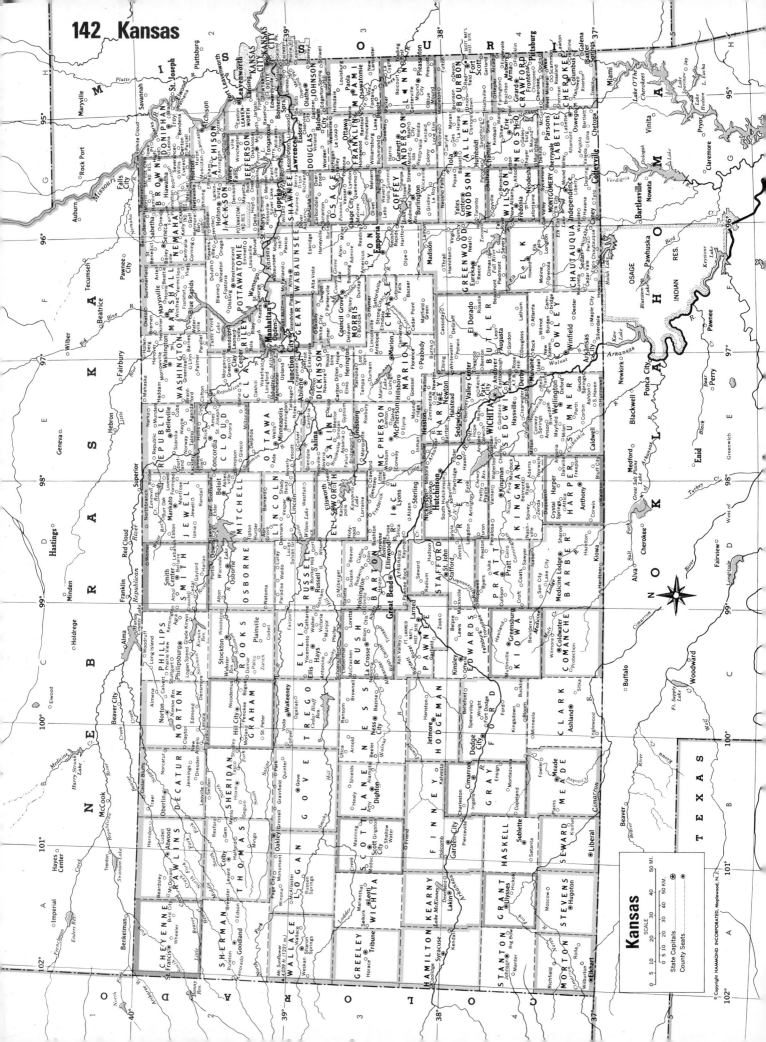

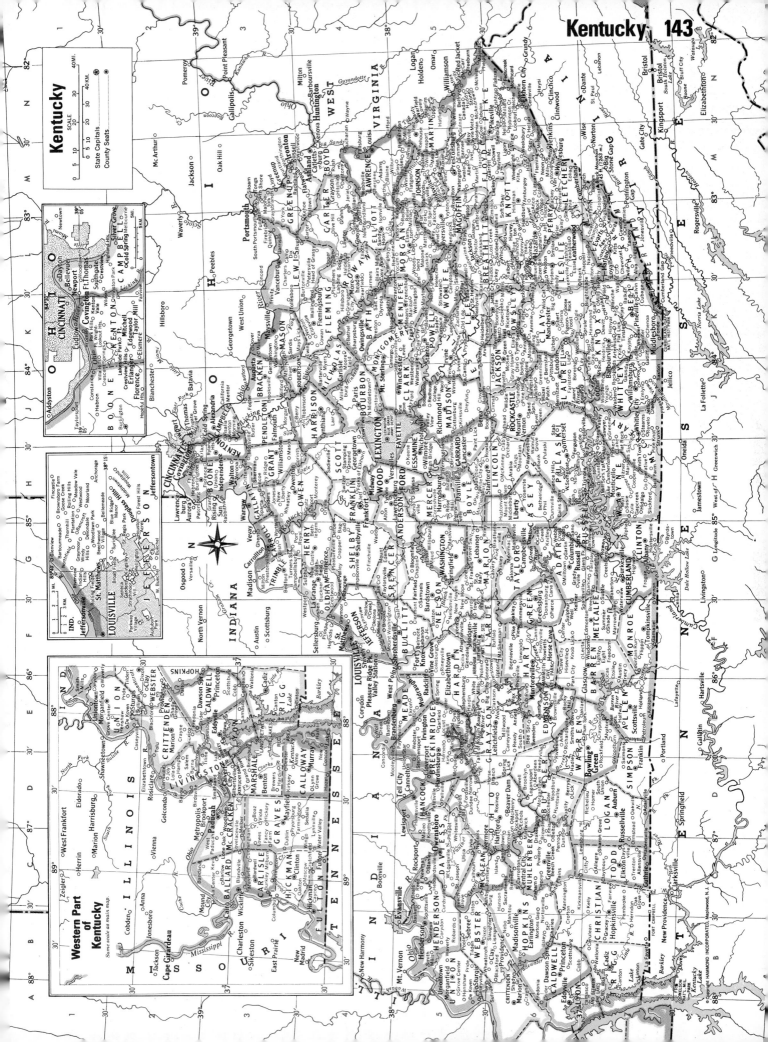

New Orleans, Baton Rouge and Vicinity

GULF OF MEXICO

Louisiana

SCALE

State Capitals

Parish Seats

Canals

© Copyright HAMMOND INCORPORATED, Maplewood, N.J.

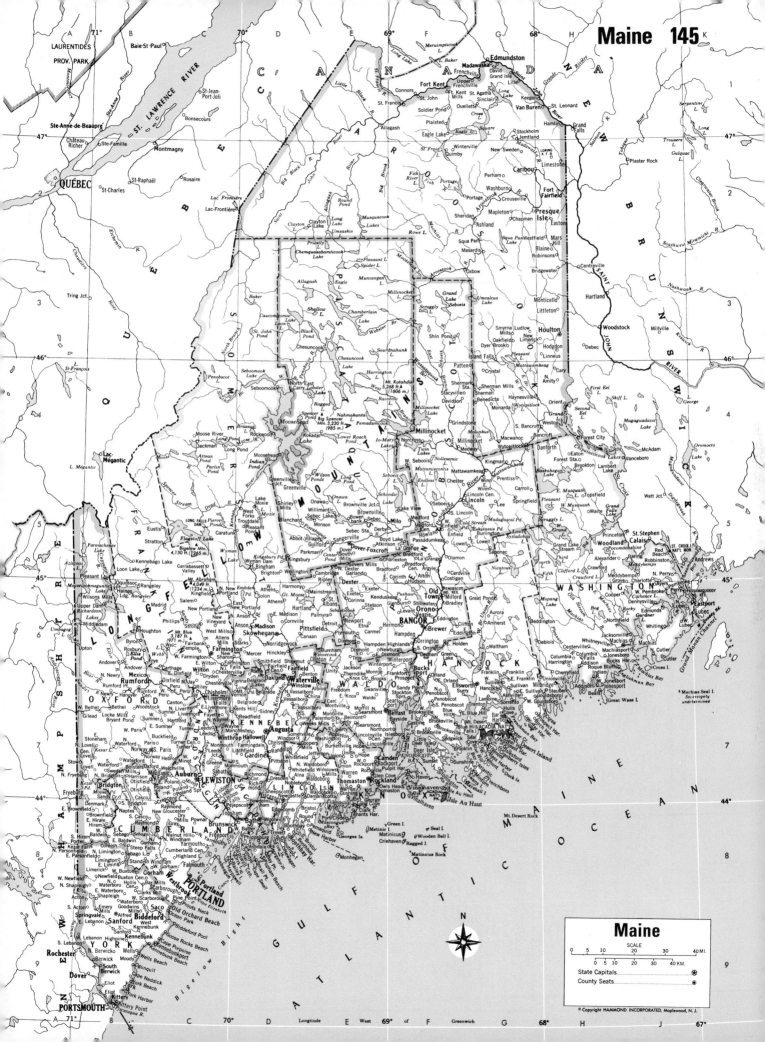

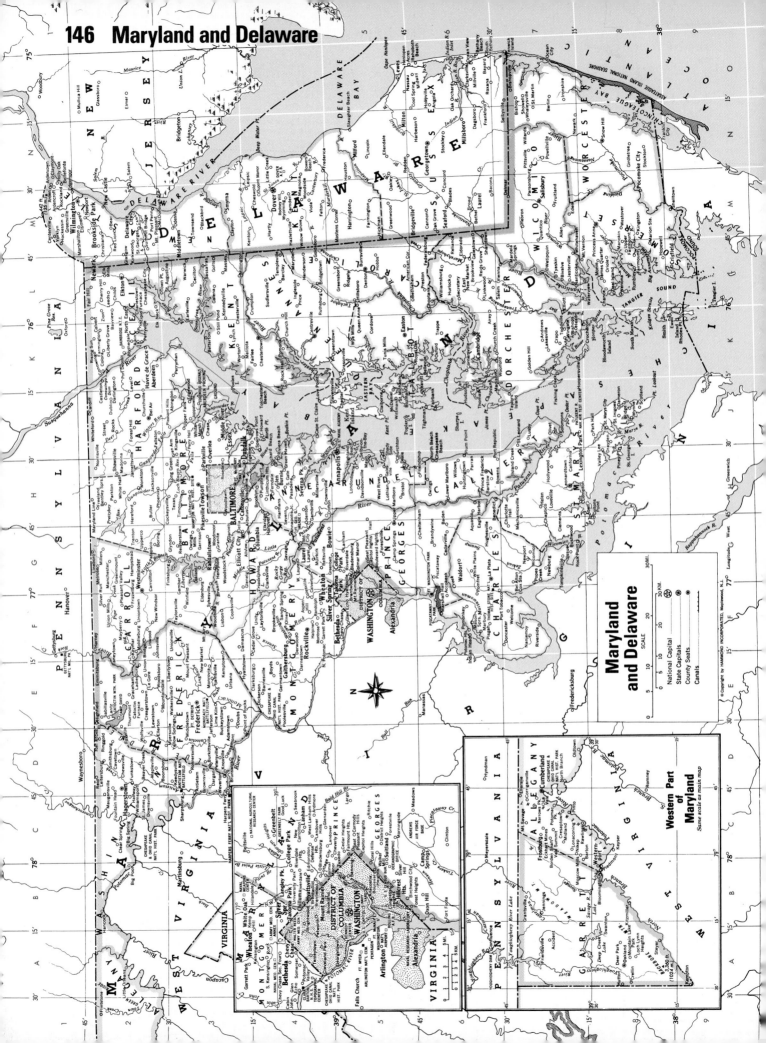

Maryland and Delaware

SCALE

National Capital
State Capitals
County Seats
Canals

© Copyright by HAMMOND INCORPORATED, Maplewood, N.J.

Western Part of Maryland

Same scale as main map

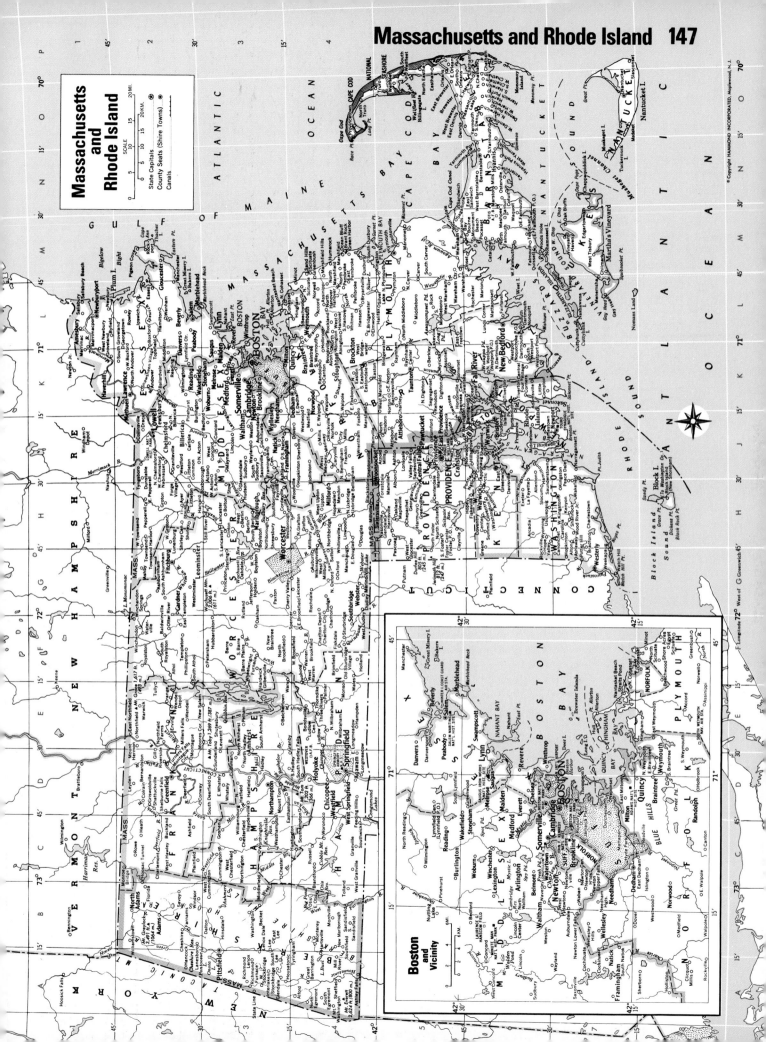

Michigan

SCALE

0 5 10 20 30 40 50 MI.

0 5 10 20 30 40 50 KM.

State Capitals..............⊛

County Seats...............◉

Canals.....................

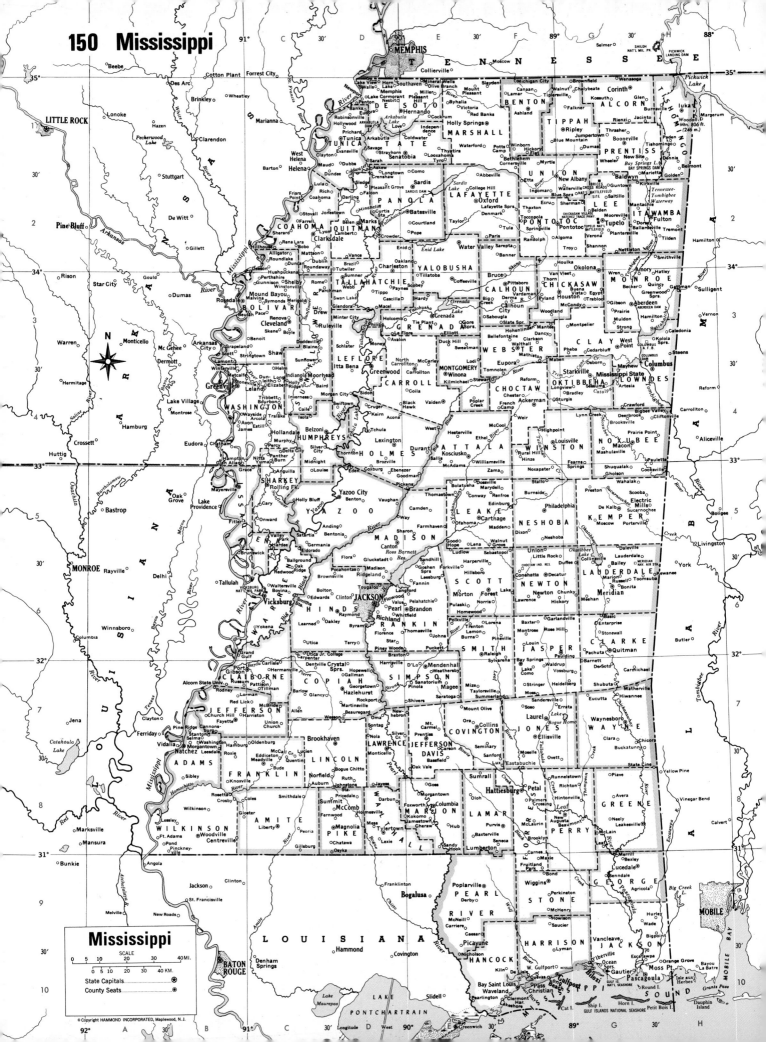

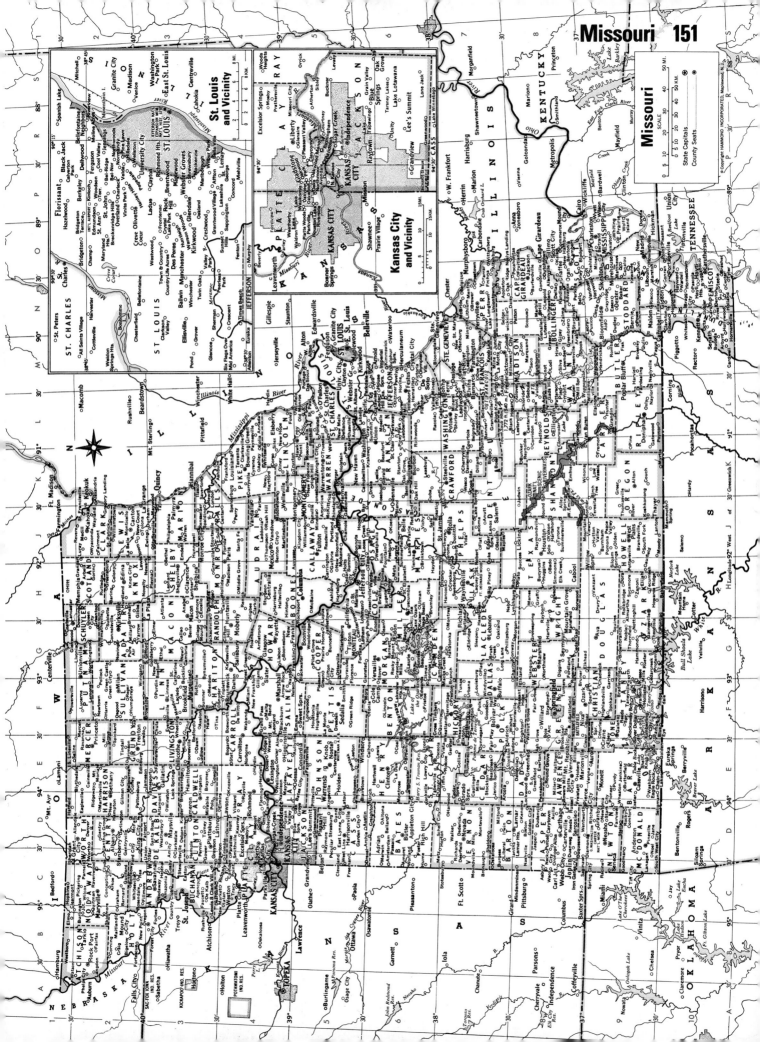

St. Louis and Vicinity

Kansas City and Vicinity

Missouri

SCALE
State Capitals
County Seats

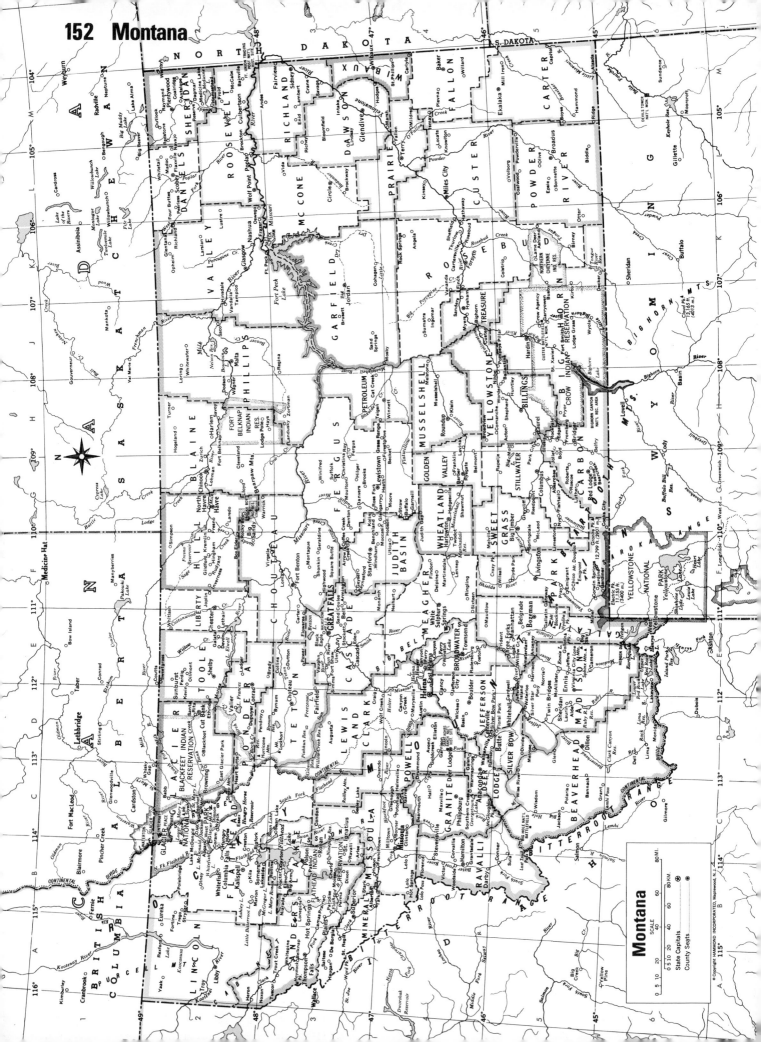

Montana
SCALE
0 5 10 20   40   60   80 MI.
0 5 10 20   40   60   80 KM.

⊛ State Capitals
◉ County Seats

© Copyright HAMMOND INCORPORATED, Maplewood, N.J.

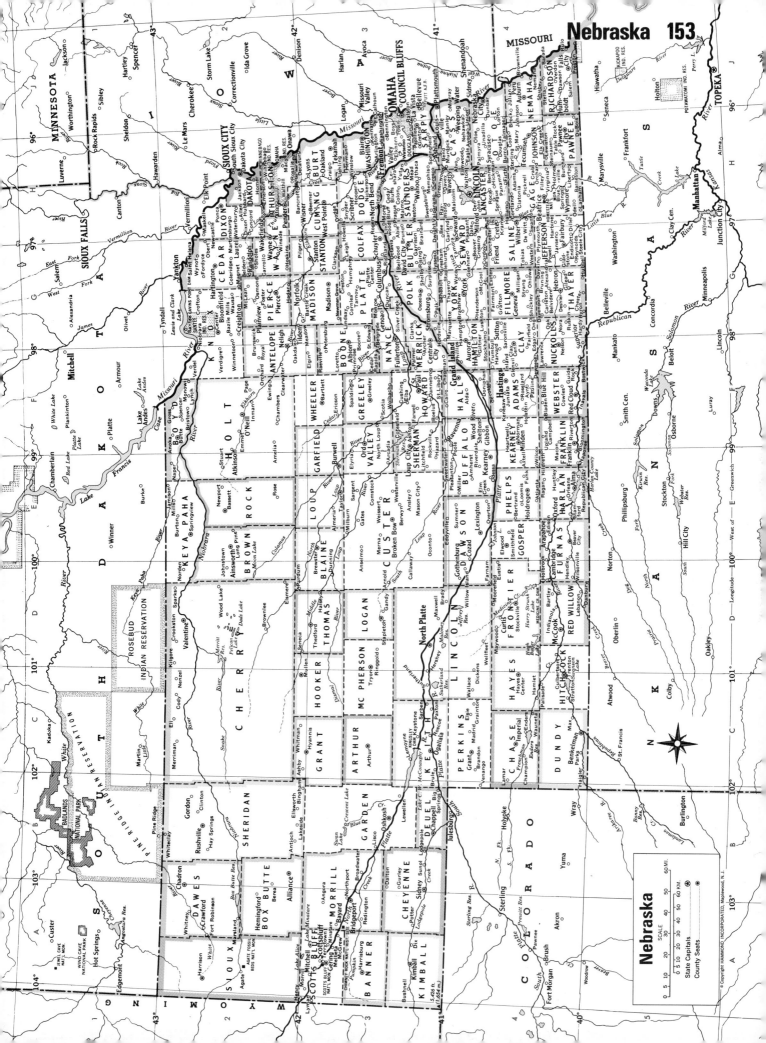

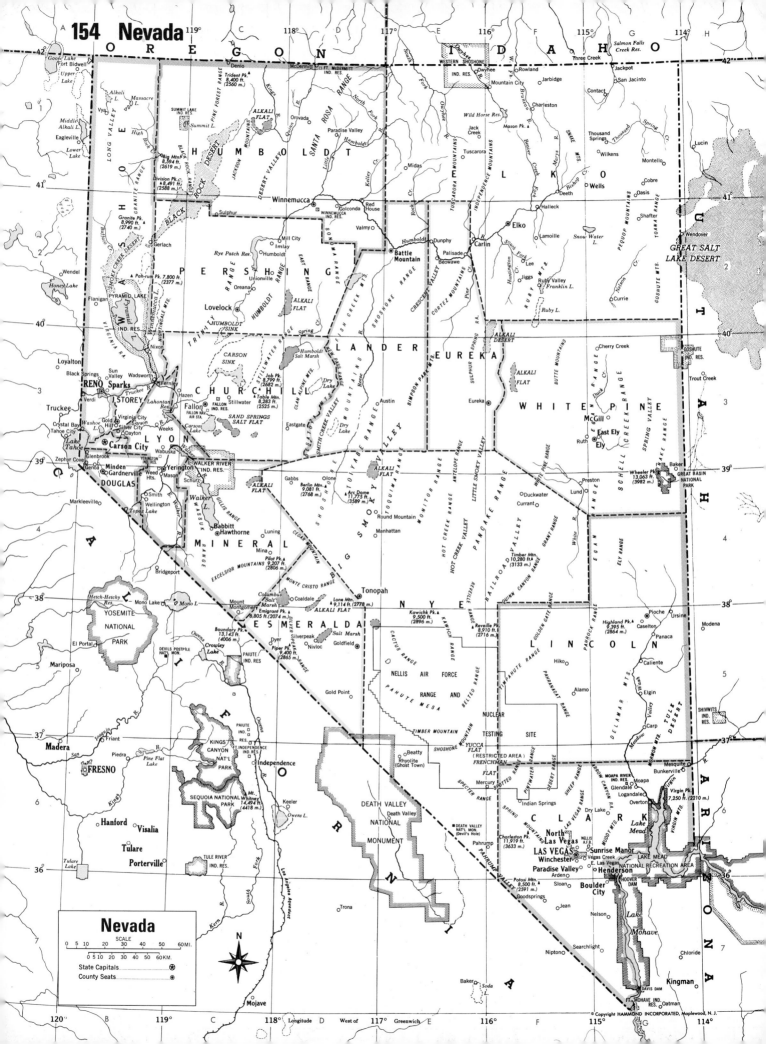

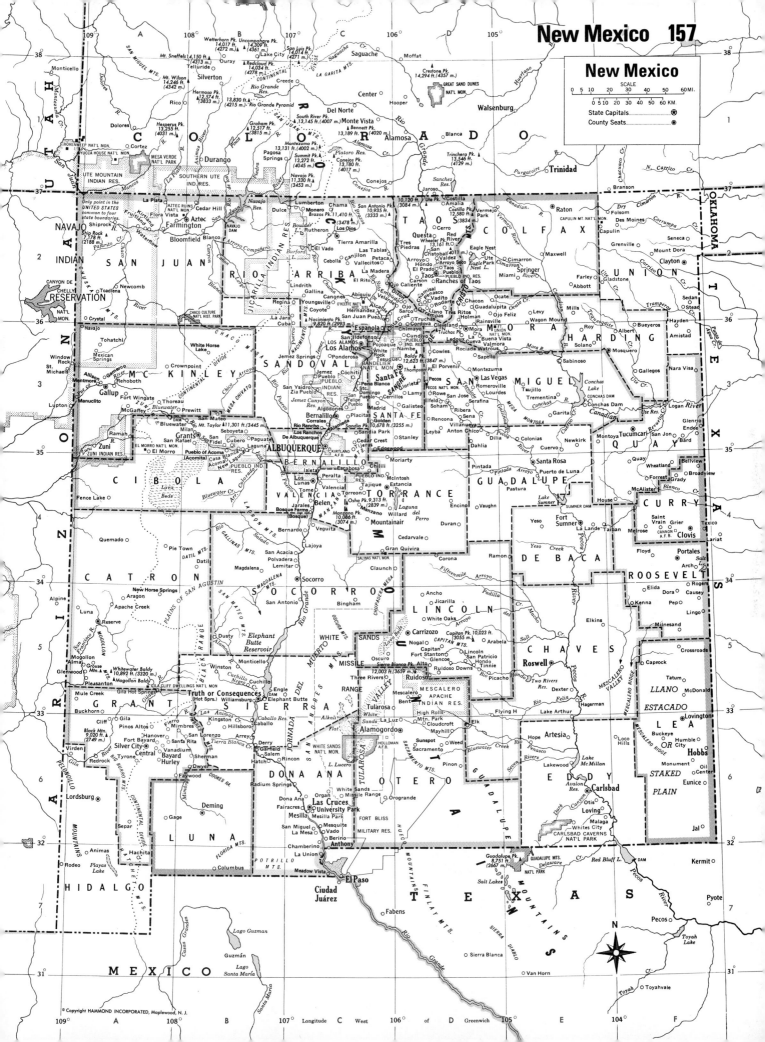

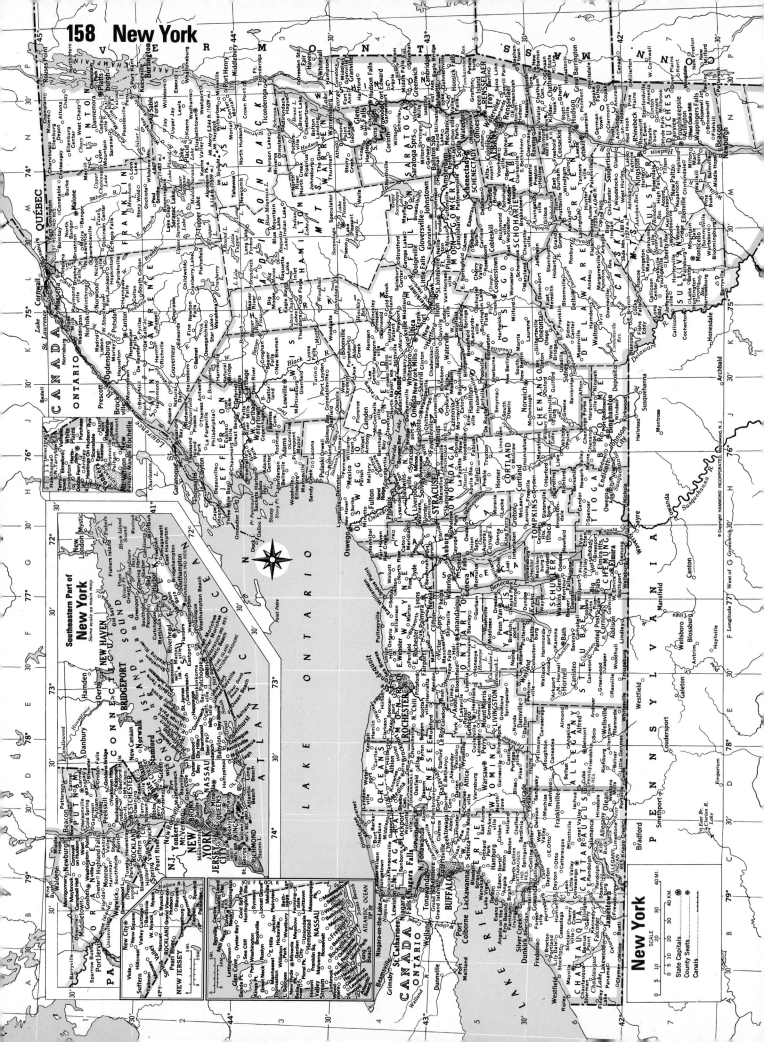

New York

SCALE

| 10 | 20 | 30 | 40 MI. |

| 0 5 10 | 20 | 30 | 40 KM. |

State Capitals .... ⊛
County Seats .... ⊙
Canals ....

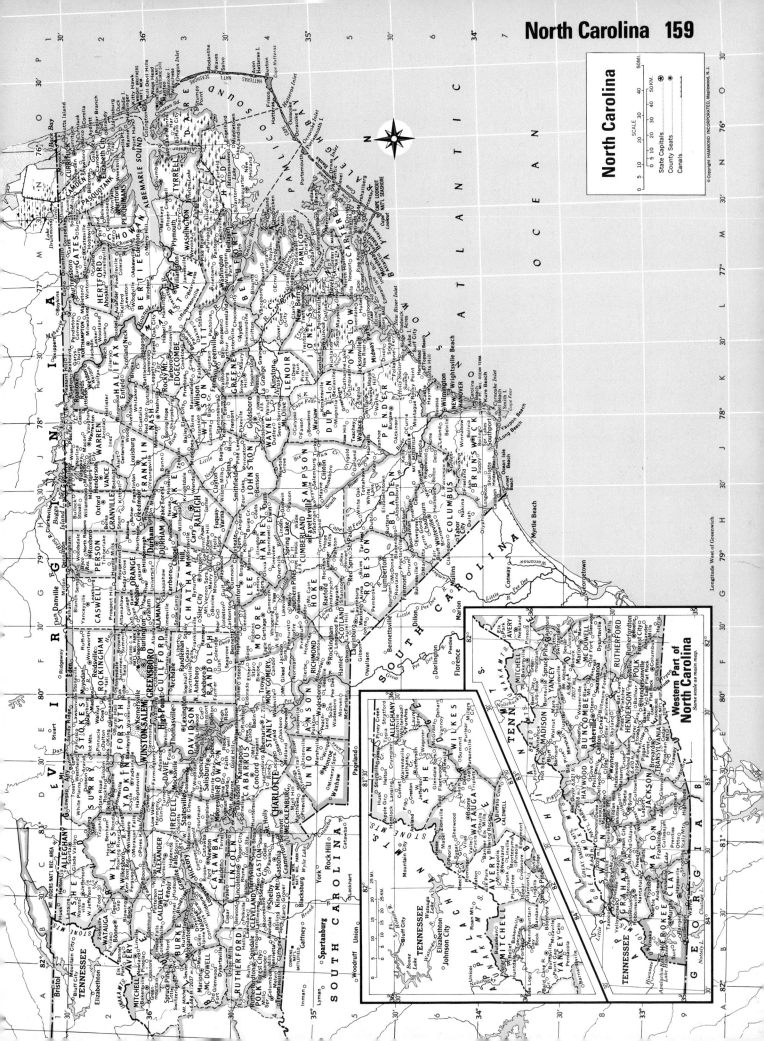

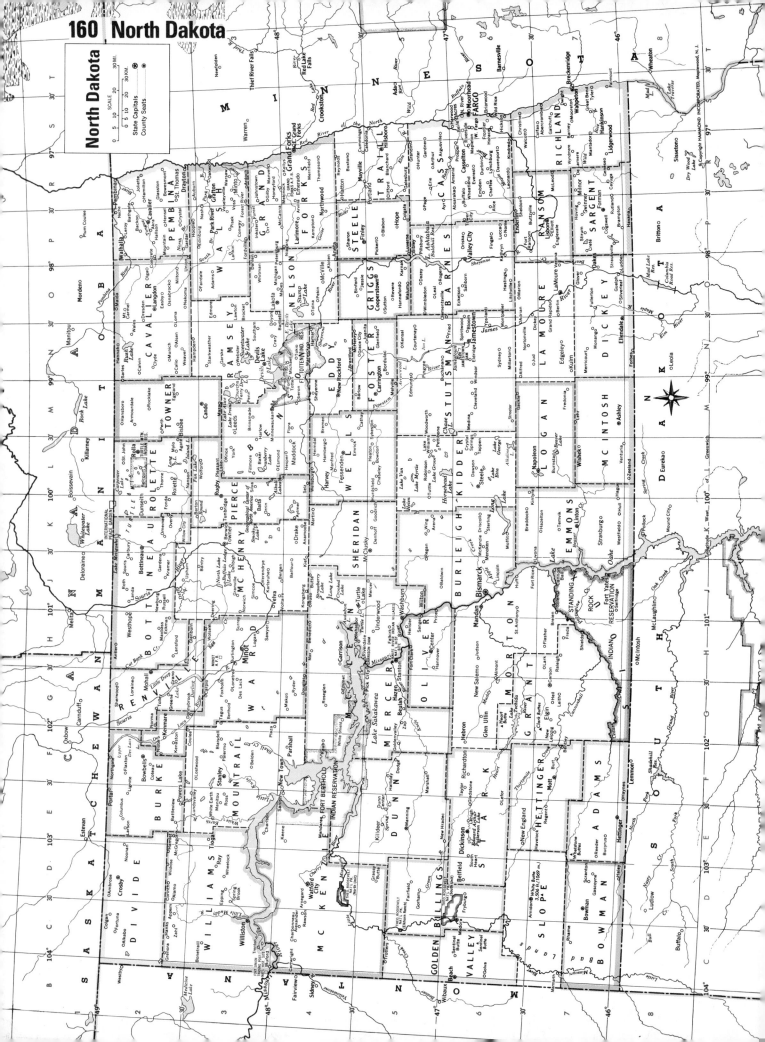

North Dakota

SCALE

State Capitals ⊛
County Seats ⊙

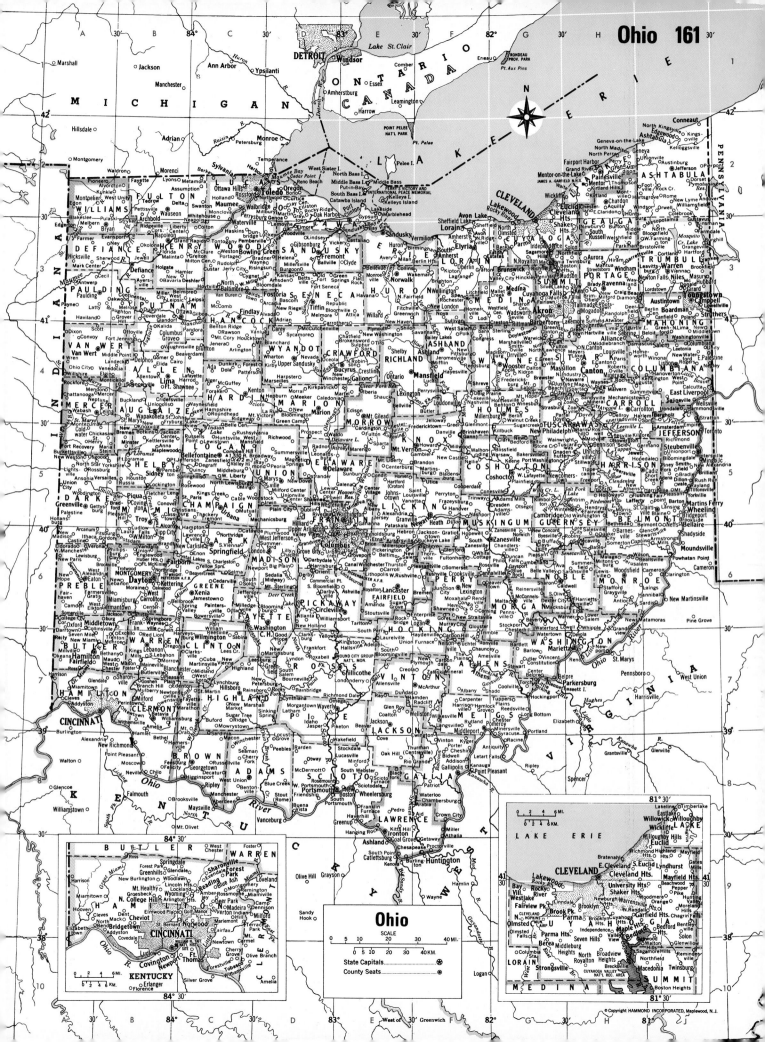

Ohio 161

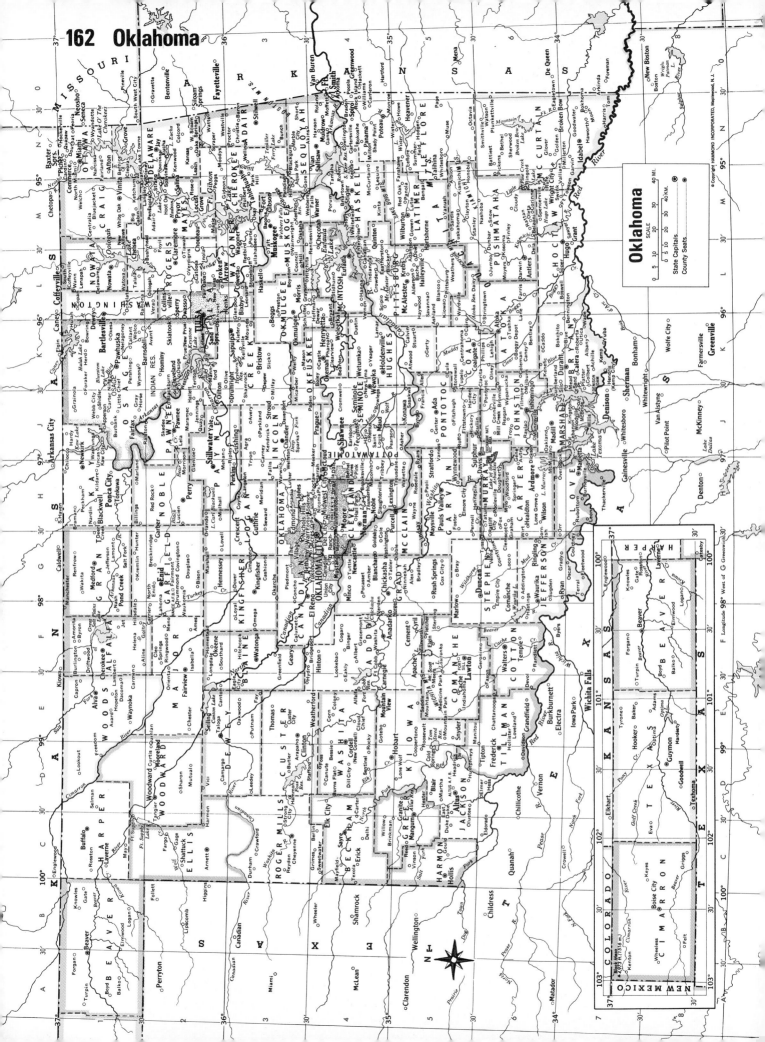

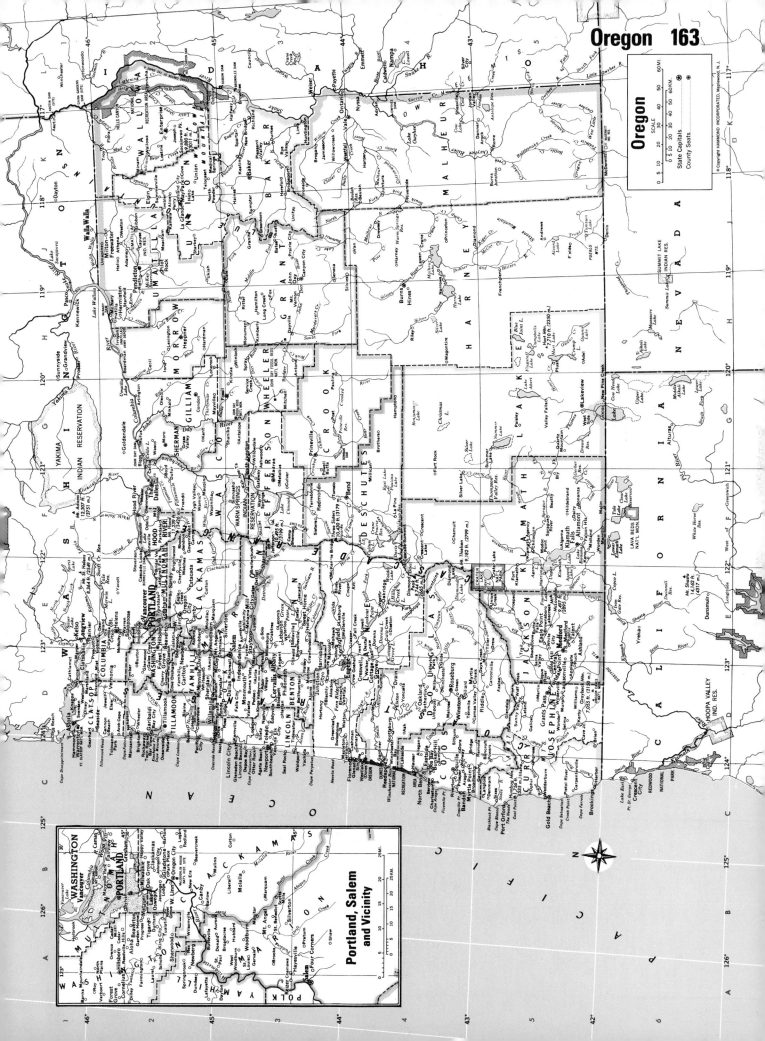

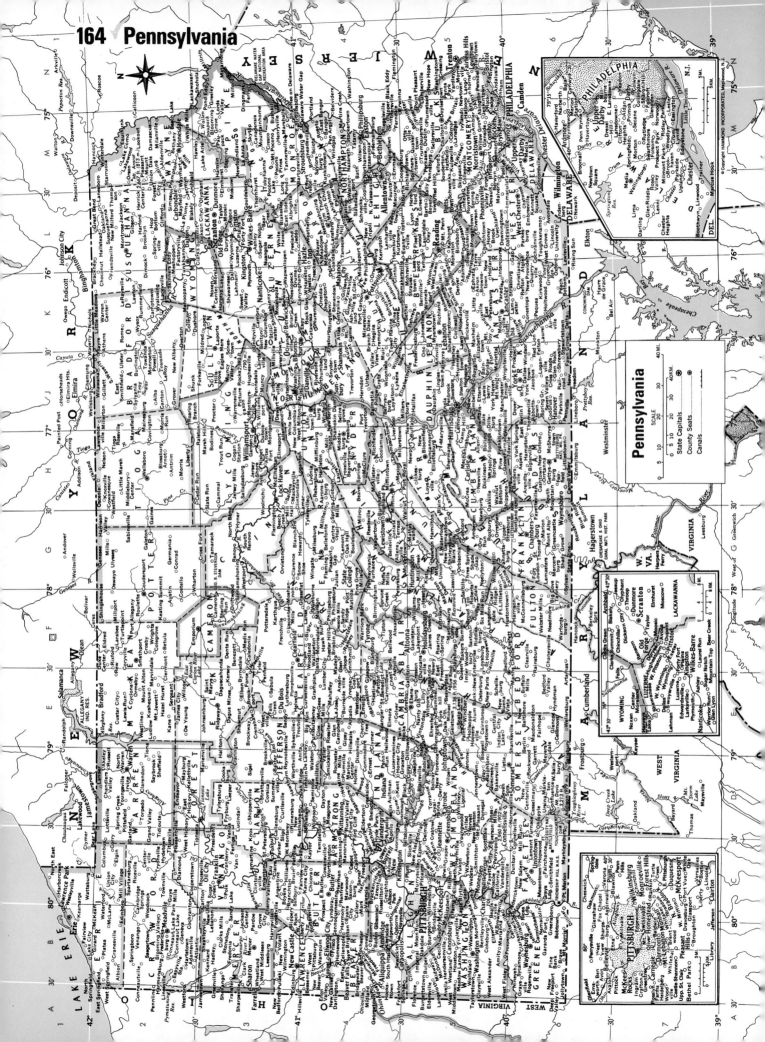

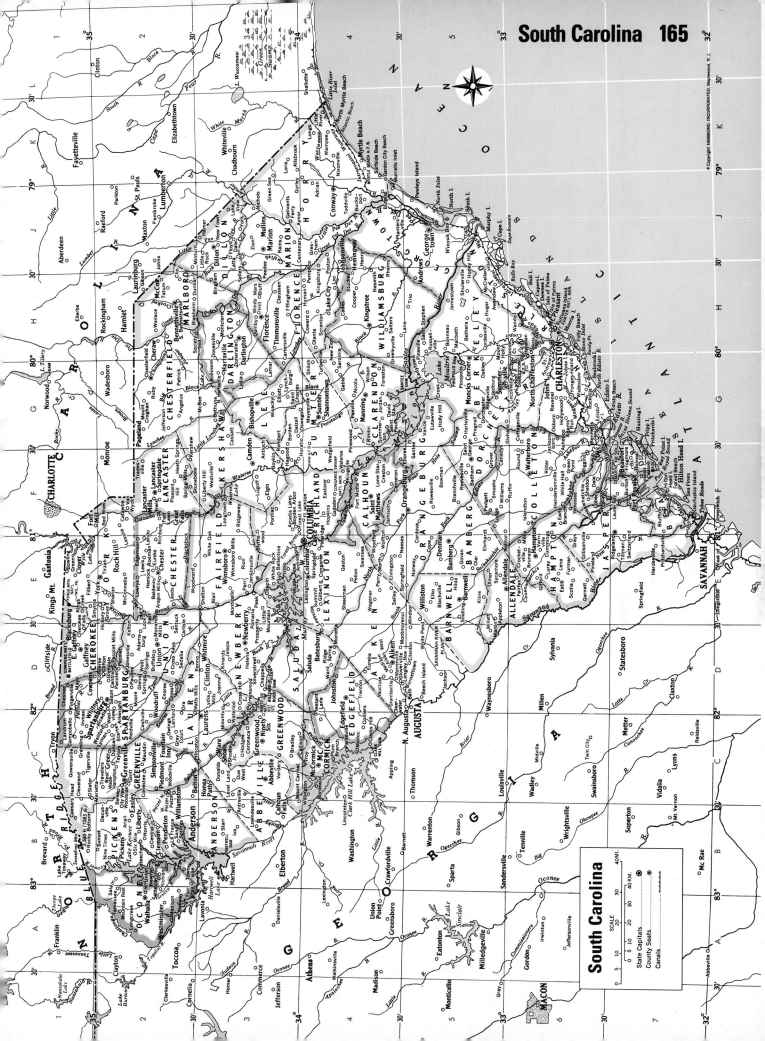

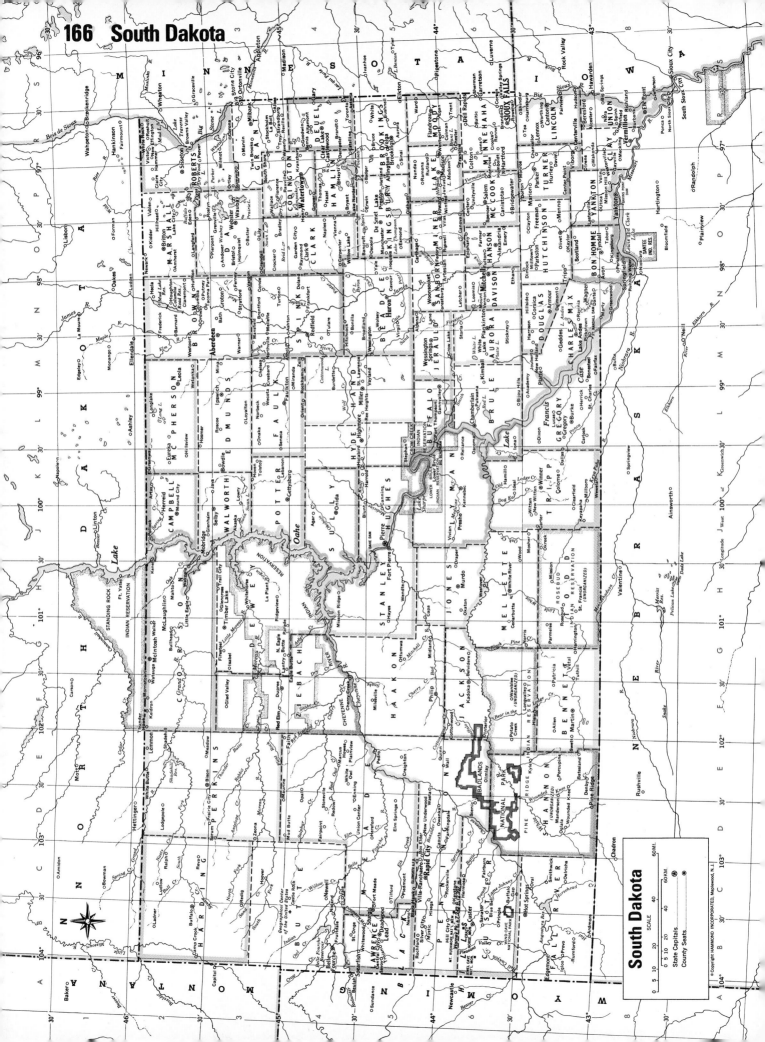

South Dakota

SCALE

0   5 10   20   40   60 MI.
0   5 10   20   40   60 KM.

⊛ State Capitals
o   County Seats

©Copyright HAMMOND INCORPORATED, Maplewood, N.J.

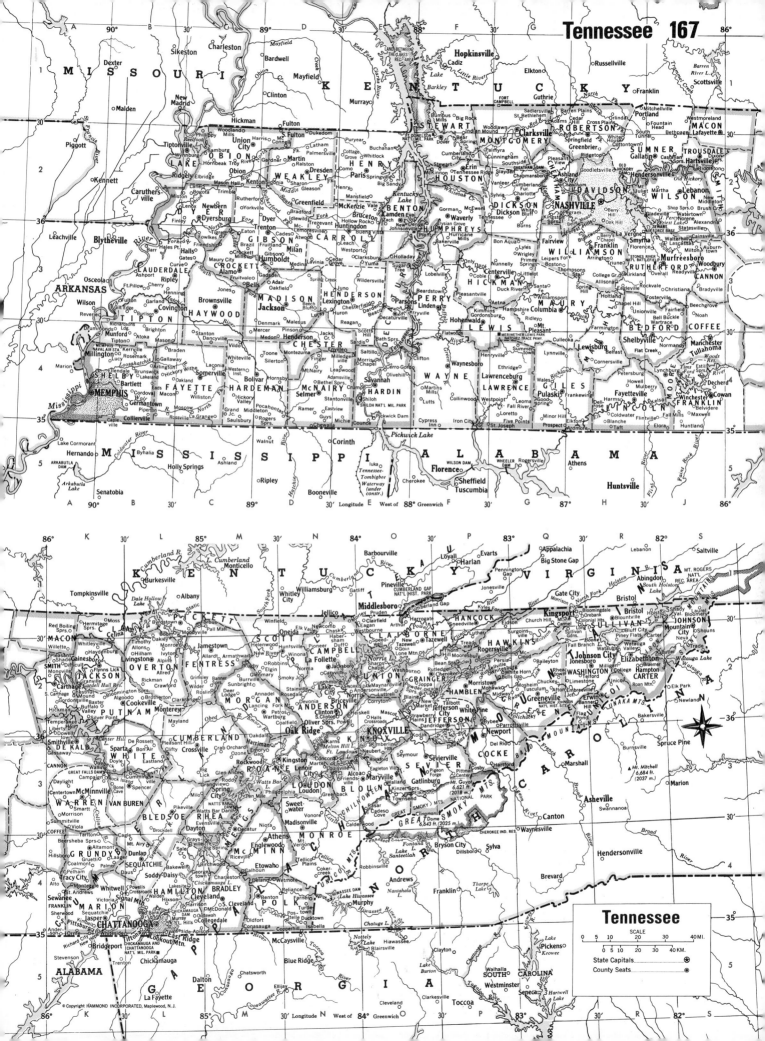

Tennessee

SCALE
0 5 10 20 30 40 MI.
0 5 10 20 30 40 KM.

State Capitals............⊛
County Seats.............◉

© Copyright HAMMOND INCORPORATED, Maplewood, N.J.

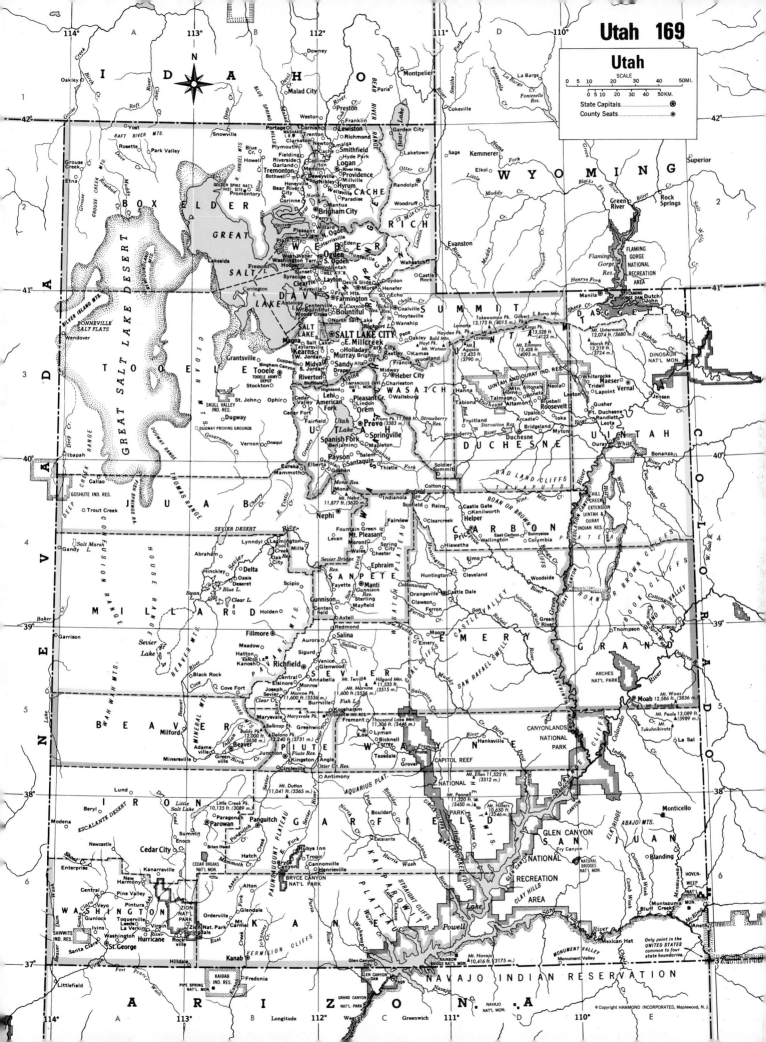

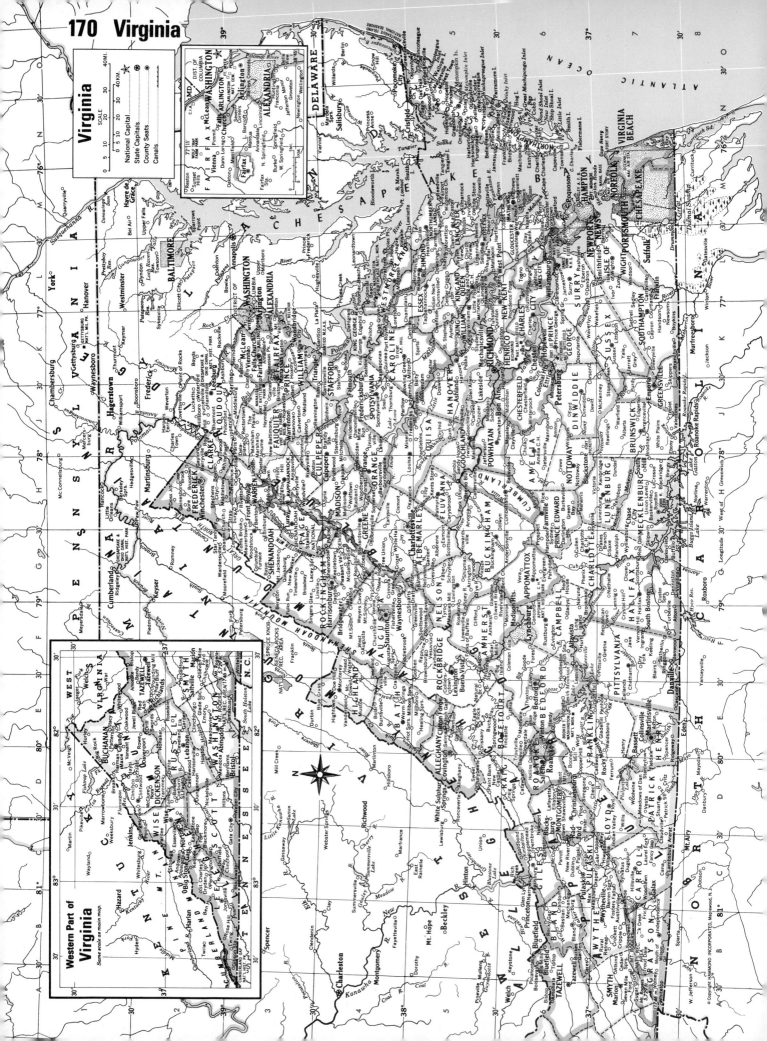

170 Virginia

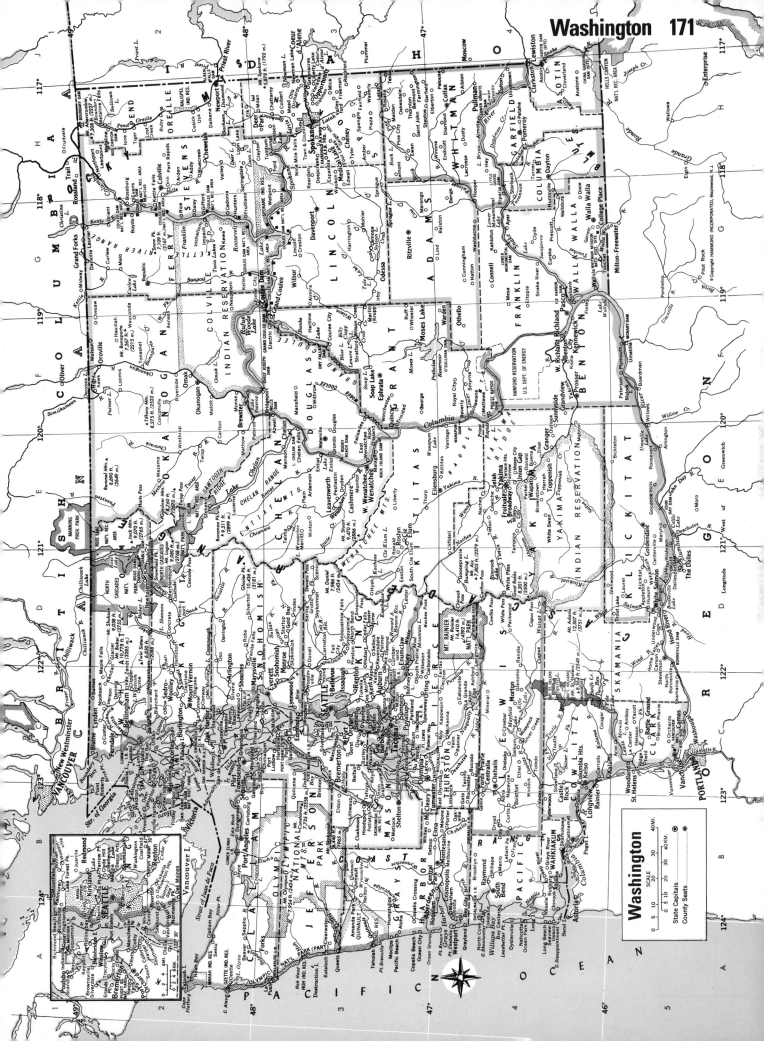

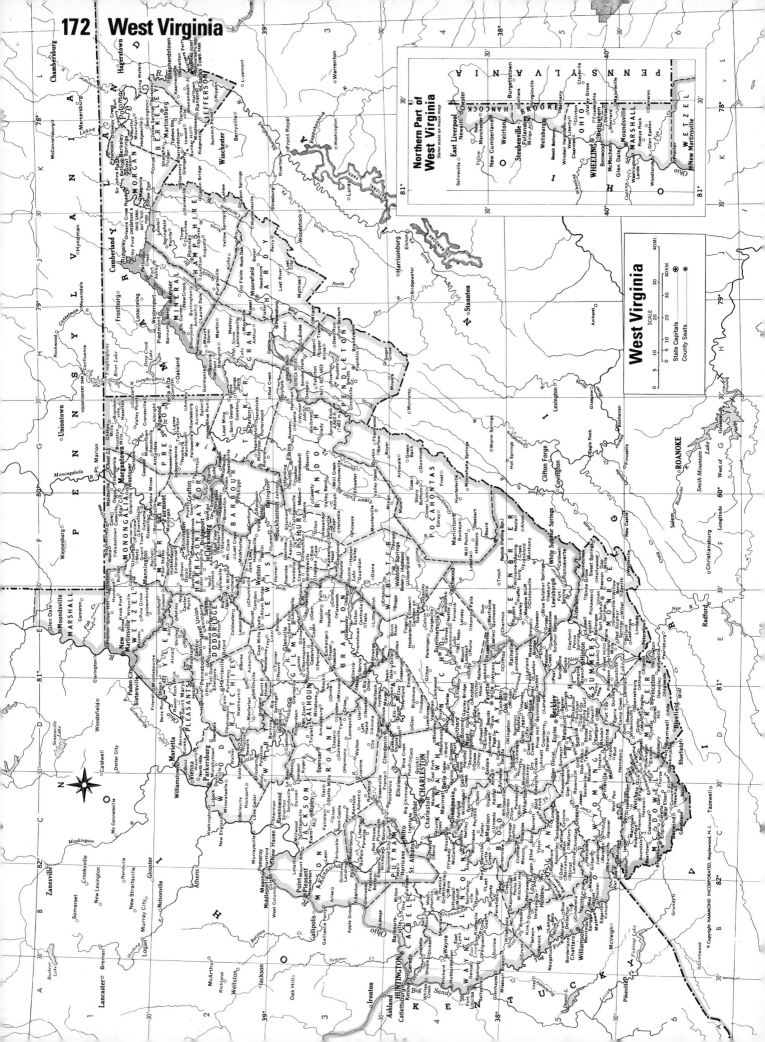

Northern Part of West Virginia
Same scale as main map

West Virginia

SCALE

| 0 5 10 20 30 40 MI. |
| 0 5 10 20 30 40 KM. |

⊛ State Capitals
● County Seats

© Copyright HAMMOND INCORPORATED, Maplewood, N.J.

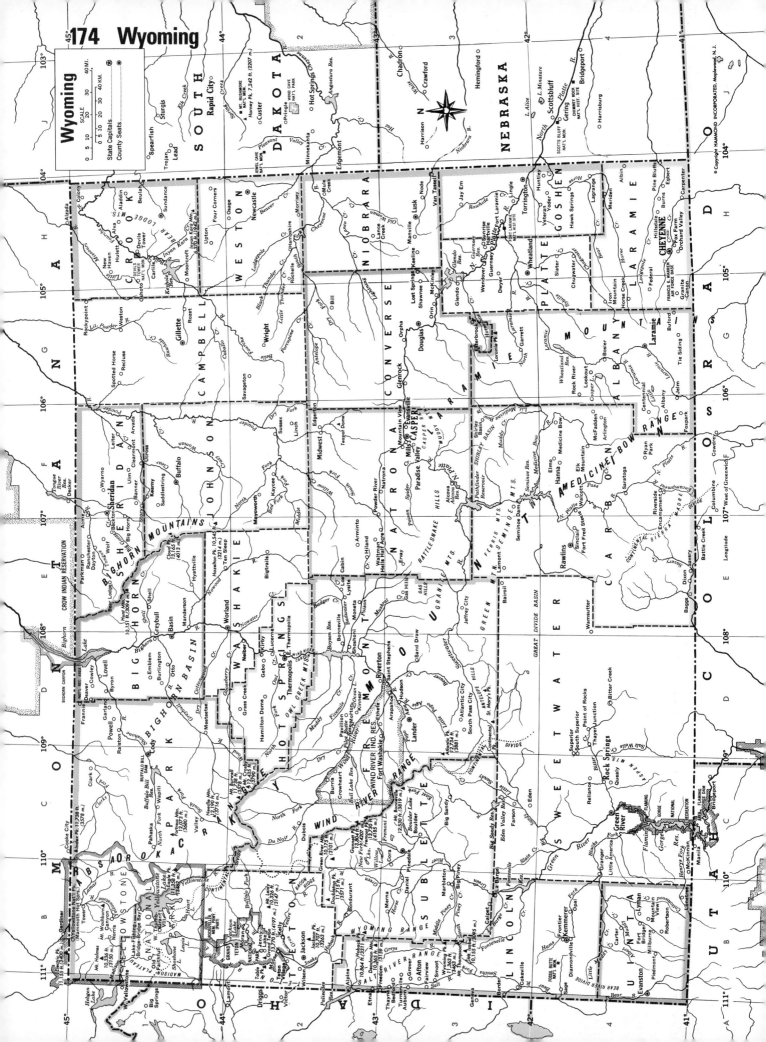

	LAND AREA IN SQUARE MILES	POPULATION 1980	CAPITAL	LARGEST CITY	STATE FLOWER	STATE BIRD
Alabama	51,705	3,893,888	Montgomery	Birmingham	Camellia	Yellowhammer
Alaska	591,004	401,851	Juneau	Anchorage	Forget-me-not	Willow Ptarmigan
Arizona	114,000	2,718,425	Phoenix	Phoenix	Saguaro Cactus Blossom	Cactus Wren
Arkansas	53,187	2,286,435	Little Rock	Little Rock	Apple Blossom	Mockingbird
California	158,706	23,667,565	Sacramento	Los Angeles	Golden Poppy	California Valley Quail
Colorado	104,091	2,889,735	Denver	Denver	Rocky Mountain Columbine	Lark Bunting
Connecticut	5,018	3,107,576	Hartford	Bridgeport	Mountain Laurel	Robin
Delaware	2,044	594,317	Dover	Wilmington	Peach Blossom	Blue Hen Chicken
Florida	58,664	9,746,342	Tallahassee	Jacksonville	Orange Blossom	Mockingbird
Georgia	58,910	5,463,105	Atlanta	Atlanta	Cherokee Rose	Brown Thrasher
Hawaii	6,471	964,691	Honolulu	Honolulu	Hibiscus	Nene (Hawaiian Goose)
Idaho	83,564	944,038	Boise	Boise	Syringa	Mountain Bluebird
Illinois	56,345	11,426,596	Springfield	Chicago	Native Violet	Cardinal
Indiana	36,185	5,490,260	Indianapolis	Indianapolis	Peony	Cardinal
Iowa	56,275	2,913,808	Des Moines	Des Moines	Wild Rose	Eastern Goldfinch
Kansas	82,277	2,364,236	Topeka	Wichita	Sunflower	Western Meadowlark
Kentucky	40,409	3,660,257	Frankfort	Louisville	Goldenrod	Cardinal
Louisiana	47,752	4,206,312	Baton Rouge	New Orleans	Magnolia	Eastern Brown Pelican
Maine	33,265	1,125,027	Augusta	Portland	White Pine Cone and Tassel	Chickadee
Maryland	10,460	4,216,975	Annapolis	Baltimore	Black-eyed Susan	Baltimore Oriole
Massachusetts	8,284	5,737,037	Boston	Boston	Mayflower	Chickadee
Michigan	58,527	9,262,078	Lansing	Detroit	Apple Blossom	Robin
Minnesota	84,402	4,075,970	St. Paul	Minneapolis	Pink and White Lady's-Slipper	Common Loon
Mississippi	47,689	2,520,638	Jackson	Jackson	Magnolia	Mockingbird
Missouri	69,697	4,916,759	Jefferson City	St. Louis	Hawthorn	Bluebird
Montana	147,046	786,690	Helena	Billings	Bitterroot	Western Meadowlark
Nebraska	77,355	1,569,825	Lincoln	Omaha	Goldenrod	Western Meadowlark
Nevada	110,561	800,493	Carson City	Las Vegas	Sagebrush	Mountain Bluebird
New Hampshire	9,279	920,610	Concord	Manchester	Purple Lilac	Purple Finch
New Jersey	7,787	7,364,823	Trenton	Newark	Purple Violet	Eastern Goldfinch
New Mexico	121,593	1,302,981	Santa Fe	Albuquerque	Yucca	Road Runner
New York	49,108	17,558,072	Albany	New York	Rose	Bluebird
North Carolina	52,669	5,881,813	Raleigh	Charlotte	Flowering Dogwood	Cardinal
North Dakota	70,702	652,717	Bismarck	Fargo	Wild Prairie Rose	Western Meadowlark
Ohio	41,330	10,797,624	Columbus	Cleveland	Scarlet Carnation	Cardinal
Oklahoma	69,956	3,025,290	Oklahoma City	Oklahoma City	Mistletoe	Scissor-tailed Flycatcher
Oregon	97,073	2,633,149	Salem	Portland	Oregon Grape	Western Meadowlark
Pennsylvania	45,308	11,863,895	Harrisburg	Philadelphia	Mountain Laurel	Ruffed Grouse
Rhode Island	1,212	947,154	Providence	Providence	Violet	Rhode Island Red
South Carolina	31,113	3,121,833	Columbia	Columbia	Carolina (Yellow) Jessamine	Carolina Wren
South Dakota	77,116	690,768	Pierre	Sioux Falls	Pasqueflower	Ring-necked Pheasant
Tennessee	42,144	4,591,120	Nashville	Memphis	Iris	Mockingbird
Texas	266,807	14,229,288	Austin	Houston	Bluebonnet	Mockingbird
Utah	84,899	1,461,037	Salt Lake City	Salt Lake City	Sego Lily	Sea Gull
Vermont	9,614	511,456	Montpelier	Burlington	Red Clover	Hermit Thrush
Virginia	40,767	5,346,818	Richmond	Norfolk	Dogwood	Cardinal
Washington	68,139	4,132,180	Olympia	Seattle	Western Rhododendron	Willow Goldfinch
West Virginia	24,231	1,950,279	Charleston	Charleston	Big Rhododendron	Cardinal
Wisconsin	56,153	4,705,521	Madison	Milwaukee	Wood Violet	Robin
Wyoming	97,809	469,557	Cheyenne	Casper	Indian Paintbrush	Meadowlark

Acquisitions of Territory

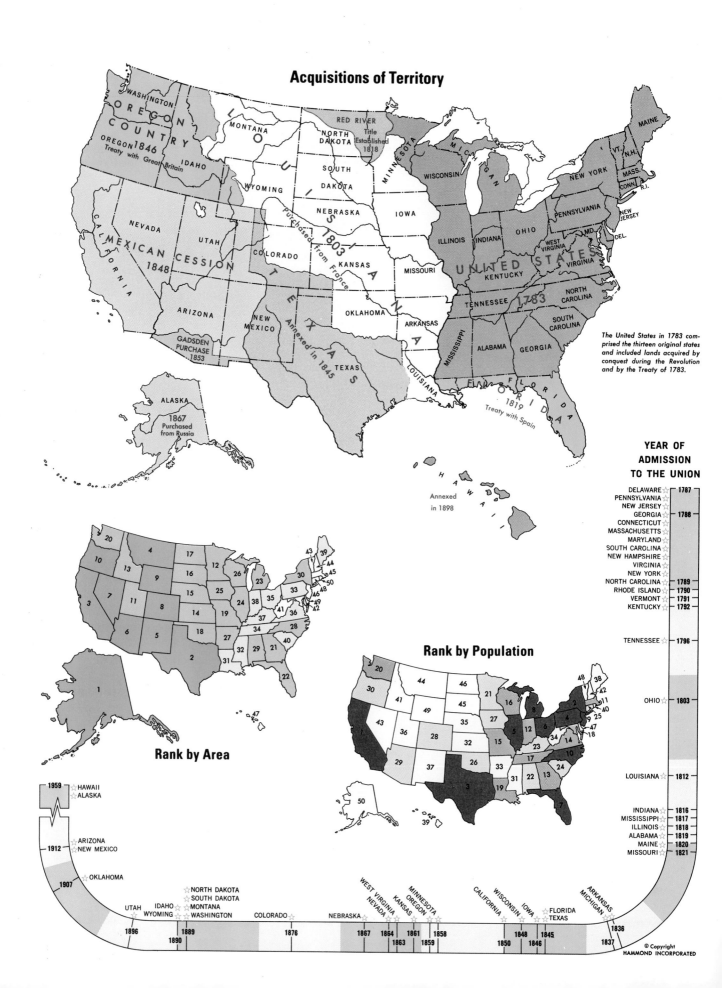

OREGON COUNTRY 1846 Treaty with Great Britain

RED RIVER Title Established 1818

MEXICAN CESSION 1848

LOUISIANA Purchased 1803 from France

UNITED STATES 1783

TEXAS Annexed in 1845

GADSDEN PURCHASE 1853

FLORIDA 1819 Treaty with Spain

ALASKA 1867 Purchased from Russia

HAWAII Annexed in 1898

The United States in 1783 comprised the thirteen original states and included lands acquired by conquest during the Revolution and by the Treaty of 1783.

YEAR OF ADMISSION TO THE UNION

DELAWARE ☆	1787
PENNSYLVANIA ☆	
NEW JERSEY ☆	
GEORGIA ☆	1788
CONNECTICUT ☆	
MASSACHUSETTS ☆	
MARYLAND ☆	
SOUTH CAROLINA ☆	
NEW HAMPSHIRE ☆	
VIRGINIA ☆	
NEW YORK ☆	
NORTH CAROLINA ☆	1789
RHODE ISLAND ☆	1790
VERMONT ☆	1791
KENTUCKY ☆	1792
TENNESSEE ☆	1796
OHIO ☆	1803
LOUISIANA ☆	1812
INDIANA ☆	1816
MISSISSIPPI ☆	1817
ILLINOIS ☆	1818
ALABAMA ☆	1819
MAINE ☆	1820
MISSOURI ☆	1821

Rank by Area

Rank by Population

1959 ☆HAWAII ☆ALASKA

1912 ☆ARIZONA ☆NEW MEXICO

1907 ☆OKLAHOMA

1896 ☆UTAH

1890 ☆IDAHO ☆WYOMING

1889 ☆NORTH DAKOTA ☆SOUTH DAKOTA ☆MONTANA ☆WASHINGTON

1876 ☆COLORADO

1867 ☆NEBRASKA ☆NEVADA

1864 ☆KANSAS

1863 ☆WEST VIRGINIA

1861 ☆OREGON

1859 ☆MINNESOTA

1858 ☆CALIFORNIA

1850 ☆WISCONSIN

1848 ☆IOWA

1846 ☆FLORIDA ☆TEXAS

1845 ☆ARKANSAS ☆MICHIGAN

1837

1836

© Copyright HAMMOND INCORPORATED

This index, arranged in strict alphabetical order, includes grand divisions, countries, states, colonial possessions, major geographical areas, cities, towns and other features (both physical and man-made). Page number and index keys are given for the map on which they are shown at the largest scale. Note that inset maps continue the sequence of the keys from the main map. Population figures, where available, are also included for countries, some internal political divisions, islands and island groups, and for cities and towns. An asterisk preceding the population denotes that it represents an area larger than the city proper (i.e., metropolitan area, municipality, etc.).

LIST OF ABBREVIATIONS

A.F.B.	Air Force Base
Afghan.	Afghanistan
Ala.	Alabama
Alg.	Algeria
Alta.	Alberta
Ant. & Barb.	Antigua & Barbuda
Antarc.	Antarctica
arch.	archipelago
Arg.	Argentina
Ariz.	Arizona
Ark.	Arkansas
A.S.S.R.	Autonomous Soviet Socialist Republic
Austr.	Australia
aut.	autonomous
Bah.	Bahamas
Bang.	Bangladesh
Belg.	Belgium
Bol.	Bolivia
Bots.	Botswana
Braz.	Brazil
Br., Brit.	British
Br. Col.	British Columbia
Bulg.	Bulgaria
Burk. Faso	Burkina Faso
Calif.	California
Camb.	Cambodia
Can.	Canada
cap.	capital
Cent. Afr. Rep.	Central African Republic
chan.	channel
Chan. Is.	Channel Islands
Col.	Colombia
Colo.	Colorado
Conn.	Connecticut
C. Rica	Costa Rica
Czech.	Czechoslovakia
D.C.	District of Columbia
Del.	Delaware
Dem.	Democratic
Den.	Denmark
depr.	depression
des.	desert
dist.	district
Dom. Rep.	Dominican Republic
E.	East, Eastern
Ecua.	Ecuador
E. Ger.	East Germany
El Sal.	El Salvador
Eng.	England
Equat. Guin.	Equatorial Guinea
est.	estuary
Eth.	Ethiopia
Fed.	Federal, Federated
Fin.	Finland
Fla.	Florida
for.	forest
Fr.	France, French
Fr. Poly.	French Polynesia
Ft.	Fort
Ga.	Georgia
Ger.	Germany
Greenl.	Greenland
Gt.	Great
Guad.	Guadeloupe
Guat.	Guatemala
Guy.	Guyana
har., harb.	harbor
Hond.	Honduras
Hung.	Hungary
isl., isls.	isle, island, islands
Ill.	Illinois
Ind.	Indiana
Indon.	Indonesia
Int'l	International
Ire.	Ireland
Isr.	Israel
isth.	isthmus
Iv. Coast	Ivory Coast
Jam.	Jamaica
Kans.	Kansas
Ky.	Kentucky
La.	Louisiana
Leb.	Lebanon
Lux.	Luxembourg
Madag.	Madagascar
Man.	Manitoba
Mass.	Massachusetts
Maur.	Mauritania
Md.	Maryland
Mex.	Mexico
Mich.	Michigan
Minn.	Minnesota
Miss.	Mississippi
Mo.	Missouri
Mong.	Mongolia
Mont.	Montana
Mor.	Morocco
Moz.	Mozambique
mt., mtn., mts.	mount, mountain, mountains
N., No.	North, Northern
N. Amer.	North America
Nat'l Pk.	National Park
N. Br.	New Brunswick
N.C.	North Carolina
N. Dak.	North Dakota
Nebr.	Nebraska
Neth.	Netherlands
Neth. Ant.	Netherlands Antilles
Nev.	Nevada
Newf.	Newfoundland
N.H.	New Hampshire
Nic.	Nicaragua
N. Ire.	Northern Ireland
N.J.	New Jersey
N. Korea	North Korea
N. Mex.	New Mexico
Nor.	Norway
N.S.	Nova Scotia
N.W.T.	Northwest Territories (Canada)
N.Y.	New York
N.Z.	New Zealand
Okla.	Oklahoma
Ont.	Ontario
Oreg.	Oregon
Pa.	Pennsylvania
Pak.	Pakistan
Pan.	Panama
Papua N.G.	Papua New Guinea
Par.	Paraguay
P.D.R. Yemen	People's Democratic Republic of Yemen
P.E.I.	Prince Edward Island
pen.	peninsula
Phil.	Philippines
Pk.	Park
plat.	plateau
Pol.	Poland
Port.	Portugal, Portuguese
P. Rico	Puerto Rico
prom.	promontory
prov.	province, provincial
pt., pte.	point, pointe
Que.	Québec
reg.	region
Rep.	Republic
res.	reservoir
R.I.	Rhode Island
riv.	river
Rom.	Romania
S.	South, Southern
sa.	serra, sierra
S. Africa	South Africa
S. Amer.	South America
São T. & Pr.	São Tomé & Príncipe
Sask.	Saskatchewan
S.C.	South Carolina
Scot.	Scotland
S. Dak.	South Dakota
Sen.	Senegal
Sing.	Singapore
S. Korea	South Korea
S. Leone	Sierra Leone
Sol. Is.	Solomon Islands
Sp.	Spain, Spanish
S.S.R.	Soviet Socialist Republic
St., Ste.	Saint, Sainte
St. Chris. & Nevis	St. Christopher & Nevis
str.	strait
St. Vinc. & Grens.	Saint Vincent & The Grenadines
Switz.	Switzerland
Tanz.	Tanzania
Tenn.	Tennessee
terr.	territory
Thai.	Thailand
Trin. & Tob.	Trinidad & Tobago
Tun.	Tunisia
U.A.E.	United Arab Emirates
U.K.	United Kingdom
Urug.	Uruguay
U.S.	United States
U.S.S.R.	Union of Soviet Socialist Republics
Va.	Virginia
Ven., Venez.	Venezuela
V.I. (Br.)	Virgin Islands (British)
V.I. (U.S.)	Virgin Islands (U.S.)
Viet.	Vietnam
vol.	volcano
Vt.	Vermont
W.	West, Western
Wash.	Washington
W. Ger.	West Germany
W. Indies	West Indies
Wis.	Wisconsin
W. Samoa	Western Samoa
W. Va.	West Virginia
Wyo.	Wyoming
Yugo.	Yugoslavia
Zim.	Zimbabwe

A

	Pop.	Key	Pg.
Aachen, W. Ger.	242,453	B 3	20
Aare (riv.), Switz.		E 3	37
Aba, Nigeria	177,000	H 10	54
Abadan, Iran	296,081	F 5	68
Abakan, U.S.S.R.	128,000	K 4	46
Abeokuta, Nigeria	253,000	G 10	54
Aberdeen, Md.	11,533	K 2	146
Aberdeen, Scot.	210,362	F 3	13
Aberdeen, S. Dak.	25,851	M 3	166
Aberdeen, Wash.	18,739	B 3	171
Abidjan, Iv. Coast	685,828	E 10	54
Abilene, Kans.	6,572	E 3	142
Abilene, Texas	98,315	E 5	168
Abington, Pa.	59,084	M 5	164
Abitibi (riv.), Ont.		J 5	108
Abraham Lincoln Birthplace Nat'l Hist. Site, Ky.		F 5	143
Abruzzi (reg.), Italy		D 3	32
Abu Dhabi (cap.), U.A.E.	347,000	F 5	60
Acadia Nat'l Pk., Maine		G 7	145
Acapulco, Mex.	309,254	K 8	119
Accra (cap.), Ghana	564,194	G 11	54
Achinsk, U.S.S.R.	117,000	K 4	46
Aconcagua (mt.), Arg.		G 10	93
Acre (riv.), Braz.		G 6	90
Acre, Isr.	34,400	C 2	67
Ada, Okla.	15,902	J 5	162
Adamawa (reg.), Africa		J 10	54
Adams Nat'l Hist Site, Mass.		D 7	147
Adamstown (cap.), Pitcairn	54	N 8	89
Adana, Turkey	475,384	F 4	64
Addis Ababa (cap.), Eth.	1,196,300	O 10	54
Addison, Ill.	29,759	B 5	139
Adelaide, Austr.	882,520	D 8	86
Aden (cap.), P.D.R. Yemen	240,370	E 7	60
Adige (riv.), Italy		C 2	32
Adirondack (mts.), N.Y.		M 3	158
Admiralty (isls.), Papua N.G.		E 6	89
Adrar (reg.), Maur.		D 7	54
Adrian, Mich.	21,186	F 7	148
Adriatic (sea), Europe		F 4	6
Aegean (sea)		G 6	43
Afars & Issas, see Djibouti			
Afghanistan	15,540,000	A 2	70
Africa	469,000,000		52-57
Agadir, Morocco	61,192	D 5	54
Agaña (cap.), Guam	896	E 4	89
Agate Fossil Beds Natl Mon., Nebr.		A 2	153
Agawam, Mass.	26,271	D 4	147
Ageo, Japan	146,358	O 2	75
Agra, India	591,917	D 3	70
Aguascalientes, Mex.	181,277	H 6	119
Ahaggar (mts.), Alg.		H 7	54
Ahmadabad, India	1,591,832	C 4	70
Ahwaz (Ahvaz), Iran	329,006	F 5	68
Aiea, Hawaii	32,879	C 4	130
Aiken, S.C.	14,978	D 4	165
Air (mts.), Niger		H 8	54
Air Force Acad., Colo.	8,655	K 5	134
Aix-en-Provence, France	91,655	F 6	26
Ajaccio, France	47,056	B 7	26
Ajmer, India	262,851	C 3	70
Akashi, Japan	234,905	H 8	75
Akita, Japan	261,246	J 4	75
Akola, India	168,436	D 4	70
Akron, Ohio	237,177	G 3	161
Aktyubinsk, U.S.S.R.	191,000	F 4	46
Alabama (riv.), Ala.		C 8	129
Alabama (state), U.S.	3,893,888		129
Alameda, Calif.	63,852	J 2	133
Alamogordo, N. Mex.	24,024	C 6	157
Alamosa, Colo.	6,830	H 8	156
Aland (isls.), Fin.		L 6	16
Alaska (gulf) Alaska		K 3	130
Alaska (state), U.S.	401,851		130
Albacete, Spain	82,607	F 3	31
Albania	2,590,600	E 5	43
Albany, Ga.	74,550	D 7	137
Albany (cap.), N.Y.	101,727	N 5	158
Albany, Oreg.	26,678	D 3	163
Albert (Mobutu Sese Seko) (lake), Africa		M 11	57
Alberta (prov.), Can.	2,237,724		114
Albert Lea, Minn.	19,200	E 7	149
Alborg, Den.	154,582	D 4	19
Albuquerque, N. Mex.	331,767	C 3	157
Alderney (isl.), Chan. Is.	1,686	E 8	11
Aleppo, Syria	639,428	C 4	64
Aleutian (isls.), Alaska		D 4	130
Alexandria, Egypt	2,318,655	M 5	54
Alexandria, La.	51,565	E 4	144
Alexandria, Va.	103,217	N 3	170
Algeria	17,422,000	F 6	54
Algiers (cap.), Alg.	1,365,400	G 4	54
Alhambra, Calif.	64,615	C 10	133
Alicante, Spain	177,918	F 3	30
Aligarh, India	252,314	D 3	70
Al Kuwait (cap.), Kuwait	181,774	E 4	60
Allahabad, India	440,622	E 3	70
Allen Park, Mich.	34,196	B 7	148
Allentown, Pa.	103,758	L 4	164
Allepey-Cochin, India	160,166	D 7	70
Alliance, Ohio	24,315	H 4	161
Alma-Ata, U.S.S.R.	910,000	H 5	46
Almería, Spain	104,008	E 4	30
Alps (mts.), Europe		E 4	6
Altadena, Calif.	40,983	C 10	133
Altai (mts.), Asia		J 5	46
Alton, Ill.	34,171	A 2	139
Altoona, Pa.	57,078	F 4	164
Altun Shan (Altyn Tagh) (mts.), China		C 4	77
Altus, Okla.	23,101	D 5	162
Amagasaki, Japan	545,783	H 8	75
Amana, Iowa	300	K 5	141
Amarillo, Texas	149,230	C 2	168
Amazon (riv.), S. Amer.		J 4	90
American Fork, Utah	12,693	C 3	169
American Samoa	32,297	J 7	89
Americus, Ga.	16,120	D 6	137
Ames, Iowa	45,775	F 4	141
Amherst, N.S.	9,684	D 3	100
Amherst, Mass.	33,229	E 3	147
Amiens, France	129,453	D 3	26
Amistad Nat'l Rec. Area, Texas		D 8	168
Amman (cap.), Jordan	1,711,850	D 4	67
Amoy, see Xiamen, China			
Amravati, India	193,800	D 4	70
Amritsar, India	407,628	C 2	70
Amsterdam (cap.), Neth.	751,156	B 4	25
Amsterdam, N.Y.	21,872	M 5	158
Amudar'ya (riv.), Asia		G 5	46
Amur (riv.), Asia		D 4	46
Anaconda-Deer Lodge Co., Mont.	12,518	C 4	152
Anadyr', U.S.S.R.	7,703	S 3	46
Anaheim, Calif.	219,494	D 11	133
Anchorage, Alaska	174,431	J 2	130
Ancona, Italy	88,427	D 3	32
Andalusia (reg.), Spain		C 4	31
Andaman (isls.), India		G 6	70
Anderson, Ind.	64,695	F 4	140
Anderson, S.C.	27,965	B 2	165
Andes (mts.), S. Amer.		F 10	93
Andizhan, U.S.S.R.	230,000	H 5	46
Andorra	31,000	G 1	31
Andorra la Vella (cap.), Andorra	12,000	G 1	31
Andover, Mass.	26,370	K 2	147
Andrew Johnson, Nat'l Hist. Site, Tenn.		Q 2	167
Andrews A.F.B., Md.	10,064	C 5	146
Andropov, U.S.S.R.	239,000	E 3	50
Andros (isl.), Bah.	8,397	B 1	124
Angara (riv.), U.S.S.R.		K 4	46
Angarsk, U.S.S.R.	239,000	L 4	46
Angel (falls), Ven.		H 2	90
Angers, France	136,603	C 4	26
Angkor Wat (ruins), Camb.		D 4	81
Angola	7,078,000	K 4	57
Anguilla (isl.)	6,519	F 3	124
Ankara (cap.), Turkey	1,701,064	E 3	64
Ankeny, Iowa	15,429	F 5	141
Ann (cape), Mass.		M 2	147
Annaba, Alg.	255,900	H 4	54
An Najaf, Iraq	128,096	D 5	68
Annandale, Va.	49,524	N 3	170
Annapolis (cap.), Md.	31,740	H 5	146
Annapolis Royal, N.S.	631	C 4	100
Annapurna (mt.), Nepal		E 3	70
Ann Arbor, Mich.	107,966	F 6	148
Anniston, Ala.	29,523	G 3	129
Anqing, China	160,000	J 5	77
Anshan, China	1,500,000	K 3	77
Ansonia, Conn.	19,039	C 3	135
Antakya, Turkey	77,518	G 4	64
Antananarivo (cap.), Madag.	451,808	R 15	57
Antarctica			5
Antibes, France	44,236	G 6	26
Anticosti (isl.), Que.		E 3	106
Antietam Nat'l Battlfld., Md.		H 3	146
Antigua and Barbuda	72,000	G 3	124
Antilles (isls.), W. Indies		B-F 2-4	124
Antioch, Calif.	42,683	L 1	133
Antofagasta, Chile	125,100	F 8	90
Antsiranana (Diégo-Suarez), Madag.	40,443	R 14	57
Antwerp, Belg.	224,543	E 6	25
Anyang, China	225,000	H 4	77
Aomori, Japan	264,202	K 3	75
Apalachee (bay), Fla.		B 2	136
Apennines (mts.), Italy		B-F 2-5	32
Apia (cap.), W. Samoa	33,100	J 7	89
Apostle Is. Nat'l Lakeshore, Wis.		C 1	173
Appalachian (mts.), U.S.		K 3	126
Appleton, Wis.	58,913	J 7	173
Appomattox Court House Nat'l Hist. Pk., Va.		F 6	170
Aqaba (gulf), Asia		C 4	60

	Pop.	Key	Pg.
Arabian (sea), Asia		H 8	58
Arabian (des.), Egypt		N 6	54
Aracaju, Braz.	288,106	N 6	90
Arad, Rom.	161,568	E 2	43
Arafura (sea)		D 6	89
Aragón (reg.), Spain		F 2	31
Aral (sea), U.S.S.R.		F 5	46
Aran (isls.), Ire.	1,499	B 5	15
Ararat (mt.), Turkey		L 3	64
Arcadia, Calif.	45,994	C 10	133
Archangel, U.S.S.R.	385,000	F 2	50
Arches Nat'l Pk., Utah		E 5	169
Arctic Ocean			4
Ardabil, Iran	147,404	F 1	68
Ardennes (for.), Belg.		F 9	25
Ardmore, Okla.	23,689	H 6	162
Arecibo, P. Rico	48,779	G 1	124
Arequipa, Peru	447,431	F 7	90
Argenteuil, France	101,542	A 1	26
Argentina	28,438,000		93
Argonne Nat'l Lab., Ill.		B 6	139
Árgos, Greece	18,890	F 7	43
Arhus, Den.	245,941	D 5	19
Arica, Chile	87,700	F 7	90
Arizona (state), U.S.	2,718,425		131
Arkadelphia, Ark.	10,005	D 5	132
Arkansas (riv.), U.S.		H 3	126
Arkansas (state), U.S.	2,286,435		132
Arkansas Post Nat'l Mem., Ark.		H 5	132
Arles, France	37,337	F 6	26
Arlington, Mass.	48,219	C 6	147
Arlington, Texas	160,123	F 2	168
Arlington, Va.	152,599	O 3	170
Arlington Heights, Ill.	66,116	B 5	139
Armagh, N. Ire.	13,606	H 3	15
Armavir, U.S.S.R.	162,000	F 5	50
Armenian S.S.R., U.S.S.R.	3,031,000	F 6	50
Arnhem, Neth.	281,126	H 4	25
Arno (riv.), Italy		C 3	32
Arran (isl.), Scot.		C 5	13
Arthabaska, Que.	6,827	F 3	105
Aruba (isl.)	55,148	E 4	124
Arvada, Colo.	84,576	J 3	134
Asahikawa, Japan	320,526	L 2	75
Asansol, India	155,968	F 4	70
Asbury Park, N.J.	17,015	F 3	156
Ascension (isl.), St. Helena	719		1
Ashanti (reg.), Ghana		F 10	54
Ashdod, Isr.	40,500	B 4	67
Ashikaga, Japan	162,359	J 5	75
Asheville, N.C.	53,583	E 8	159
Ashkhabad, U.S.S.R.	312,000	F 2	46
Ashland, Ky.	27,064	M 4	143
Ashland, Oreg.	14,943	E 5	163
Ashtabula, Ohio	23,449	J 2	161
Asia	2,633,000,000		58
Asmara, Eth.	393,800	O 9	54
Aspen, Colo.	3,678	F 4	134
Aspen Hill, Md.	47,455	F 4	146
Assam (state), India		G 3	70
Assateague Isl. Nat'l Seashore, U.S.		O 4	170
Astoria, Oreg.	9,998	O 1	163
Astrakhan', U.S.S.R.	461,000	G 5	50
Asturias (reg.), Spain		C 1	31
Asunción (cap.), Par.	387,676	J 9	90
Aswân, Egypt	144,377	N 7	54
Asyût, Egypt	213,983	N 6	54
Atacama (des.), Chile		G 8	93
Atchison, Kans.	11,407	G 2	142
Athabasca (lake), Can.		F 4	96
Athens, Ga.	42,549	F 3	137
Athens (cap.), Greece	867,023	F 7	43
Athens, Ohio	19,743	F 7	161
Áthos (mt.), Greece		G 5	43
Atka (isl.), Alaska		M 4	130
Atlanta (cap.), Ga.	425,022	K 1	137
Atlantic City, N.J.	40,199	E 5	156
Atlantic Ocean			5
Atlas (mts.), Africa		E 5	54
Atsugi, Japan	108,955	O 2	75
Attleboro, Mass.	34,196	J 5	147
Attu (isl.), Alaska		J 2	130
Auburn, Ala.	28,471	H 5	129
Auburn, Maine	23,128	C 7	145
Auburn, N.Y.	32,548	G 5	158
Auburn, Wash.	26,417	C 3	171
Auckland, N.Z.	144,963	L 6	87
Augsburg, W. Ger.	243,943	D 4	20
Augusta, Ga.	47,532	J 4	137
Augusta (cap.), Maine	21,819	D 7	145
Aurangabad, India	150,483	D 5	70
Aurora, Colo.	158,588	K 3	134
Aurora, Ill.	81,293	E 2	139
Aurora, Ohio	8,177	H 3	161
Aurora, Minn.	23,020	E 7	149
Auschwitz, see Oświęcim, Poland			
Austin (cap.), Texas	354,496	G 7	168
Australia	14,576,330		86
Australian Alps (mts.), Austr.		H 7	86
Australian Cap. Terr., Austr.	221,609	H 7	86
Austria	7,507,000		39
Auvergne (mts.), France		E 5	26
Avalon (pen.), Newf.		D 4	99
Avignon, France	73,482	F 6	26
Avon (riv.), Eng.		F 7	11
Ayers Rock (mt.), Austr.		E 5	86
Azerbaidzhan S.S.R., U.S.S.R.	6,028,000	G 6	50
Azores (isls.), Port.			30
Azov (sea), U.S.S.R.		C 5	50
Aztec Ruins Nat'l Mon., N. Mex.		A 2	157
Azusa, Calif.	29,380	D 10	133

B

	Pop.	Key	Pg.
Bab el Mandeb (str.)		D 7	60
Bacău, Rom.	131,413	H 2	43
Bacolod, Phil.	262,415	G 3	83
Badalona, Spain	162,888	H 2	31
Baden-Baden, W. Ger.	49,718	C 4	20
Badlands Nat'l Pk., S. Dak.		E 6	166
Baffin (isl.), N.W.T.		J 1	96
Baghdad (cap.), Iraq	502,503	D 4	68
Bahamas	209,505	C 1	124
Bahawalpur, Pak.	133,956	C 3	70
Bahia (Salvador), Braz.	1,496,276	N 6	90
Bahía Blanca, Arg.	*220,765	H 11	90
Bahrain	358,857	F 4	60
Bairiki (cap.), Kiribati	1,777	H 5	89
Bakersfield, Calif.	105,735	G 8	133
Bakhtaran, Iran	290,861	E 3	68
Baku, U.S.S.R.	1,022,000	H 6	50
Balakovo, U.S.S.R.	152,000	G 4	50
Baldwin, N.Y.	31,630	B 4	158
Baldwin Park, Calif.	50,554	D 10	133
Balearic (isls.), Spain		H 3	31
Bali (isl.), Indon.	2,074,438	F 7	83
Balikpapan, Indon.	280,675	F 6	83
Balkan (mts.), Bulg.		G 4	43
Balkhash (lake), U.S.S.R.		H 5	46
Baltic (sea), Europe		F 3	6
Baltimore, Md.	786,755	H 3	146
Baluchistan (reg.), Pak.		B 3	70
Bamako (cap.), Mali	404,022	E 9	54
Banaba (isl.), Kiribati	2,314	G 7	89
Banda (sea), Indon.		H 7	83
Bandar Seri Begawan, (cap.), Brunei	63,868	E 4	83
Bandelier Nat'l Mon., N. Mex.		C 3	157
Bandung, Indon.	1,462,637	H 2	83
Banff Nat'l Pk., Alta.		B 4	114
Bangalore, India	1,540,741	D 6	70
Bangkok (cap.), Thai.	2,495,312	D 4	81
Bangladesh	87,052,024	G 4	70
Bangor, Maine	31,643	F 6	145
Bangui (cap.), Cent. Afr. Rep.	279,792	K 10	54
Banja Luka, Yugo.	85,786	C 3	43
Banjarmasin, Indon.	381,286	E 6	83
Banjul (cap.), Gambia	39,476	C 9	54
Banks (isl.), N.W.T.		D 1	96
Baoding, China	350,000	J 4	77
Baoji, China	275,000	G 5	77
Baotou, China	800,000	G 3	77
Baranovichi, U.S.S.R.	131,000	C 4	50
Barbados	248,983	G 4	124
Barberton, Ohio	29,751	G 4	161
Barbuda (isl.), see Antigua & Barbuda			
Barcelona, Spain	1,741,144	H 2	31
Barcelona, Ven.	78,201	G 2	90
Bareilly, India	296,248	D 3	70
Barents (sea), Europe		J 1	6
Bar Harbor, Maine	4,124	G 7	145
Bari, Italy	339,110	F 4	32
Barnaul, U.S.S.R.	533,000	J 4	46
Barnet, Eng.	305,200	H 7	11
Barnstable, Mass.	30,898	N 6	147
Barquisimeto, Ven.	330,815	F 2	90
Barranquilla, Col.	661,009	F 1	90
Barre, Vt.	9,824	C 3	155
Barrie, Ont.	38,423	E 3	108
Barrow (pt.), Alaska		G 1	130
Barstow, Calif.	17,690	H 9	133
Bartlesville, Okla.	34,568	K 1	162
Basel, Switz.	199,600	E 1	37
Basildon, Eng.	135,720	J 8	11
Basra, Iraq	313,327	E 5	68
Bassein, Burma	126,045	B 3	81
Basse-Terre (cap.), Guad.	13,397	F 4	124
Basseterre (cap.), St. Chris. & Nevis	14,725	F 3	124
Bastrop, La.	15,527	G 1	144
Bath, Eng.	83,100	E 6	11
Bathurst (Banjul) (cap.), Gambia	39,476	C 9	54
Bathurst, N. Br.	15,705	E 1	102
Bathurst (isl.), N.W.T.		M 3	96
Batna, Alg.	112,100	F 1	54
Baton Rouge (cap.), La.	219,419	K 2	144
Battle Creek, Mich.	35,724	D 6	148
Batumi, U.S.S.R.	123,000	F 6	50
Bat Yam, Isr.	124,100	B 3	67
Bavaria (state), W. Ger.		D 4	20
Bayamón, P. Rico	185,087	D 4	124
Bay City, Mich.	41,593	F 5	148
Bayeux, France	13,381	C 3	26
Baykal (lake), U.S.S.R.		L 4	46
Baykonur, U.S.S.R.		G 5	46
Bayonne, N.J.	65,047	B 2	156
Bayreuth, W. Ger.	67,035	D 4	20
Baytown, Texas	56,923	L 2	168
Bear (lake), U.S.		G 7	138
Bearpaw (mts.), Mont.		G 2	152
Beatrice, Nebr.	12,891	H 4	153
Beaufort (sea), N. Amer.		D 2	94
Beaufort, S.C.	8,634	F 7	165
Beaumont, Texas	118,102	K 7	168
Beaverhead (mts.), Idaho		E 4	138
Beaverton, Oreg.	30,582	A 2	163
Beckley, W. Va.	20,492	D 5	172
Beersheba, Isr.	101,000	B 5	67
Beihai, China	175,000	G 7	77
Beijing (Peking) (cap.), People's Rep. of China	*8,500,000	J 3	77
Beirut (cap.), Leb.	474,800	F 6	64
Belau (Palau)	12,116	D 5	89
Belém, Braz.	758,117	L 4	90
Belfast, Maine	6,243	F 7	145
Belfast (cap.), N. Ire.	353,700	J 2	15
Belgaum, India	192,427	C 5	70
Belgium	9,855,110		25
Belgorod, U.S.S.R.	240,000	E 4	50
Belgrade (cap.), Yugo.	727,945	E 3	43
Belize	144,857	C 2	122
Belize City, Belize	39,887	C 2	122
Bellary, India	125,183	D 5	70
Belleville, Ill.	41,580	B 3	139
Belleville, N.J.	35,367	B 2	156
Belleville, Ont.	34,881	G 3	108
Bellevue, Nebr.	21,813	J 3	153
Bellevue, Wash.	73,903	B 2	171
Bellflower, Calif.	53,441	C 11	133
Bellingham, Wash.	45,791	C 2	171
Bellingshausen (sea), Antarc.		C 14	5
Belmont, Mass.	26,100	C 6	147
Belmopan (cap.), Belize	144,857	C 2	122
Belo Horizonte, Braz.	*2,541,788	M 7	90
Beloit, Wis.	35,207	H 10	173
Beltsville, Md.	12,760	C 3	146
Bemidji, Minn.	10,949	D 3	149
Benares, see Varanasi, India			
Bend, Oreg.	17,263	F 3	163
Bengal (bay), Asia		K 8	58
Bengbu, China	400,000	J 5	77
Benghazi, Libya	286,943	K 5	54
Benguela, Angola	40,996	J 14	54
Benin	3,338,240	G 10	54
Bennington, Vt.	15,815	A 6	155
Benoni, S. Africa	*151,294	M 17	57
Benton, Ark.	17,717	E 4	132
Benton Harbor, Mich.	14,707	C 6	148
Bent's Old Fort Nat'l Hist. Site, Colo.		M 6	134
Benxi, China	750,000	K 3	77
Beppu, Japan	133,894	E 7	75
Berchtesgaden, W. Ger.	8,558	E 5	20
Berea, Ky.	8,226	J 5	143
Berezniki, U.S.S.R.	185,000	J 3	50
Bergamo, Italy	127,553	B 2	32
Bergen, Nor.	213,434	D 6	16
Bering (sea)		S 4	46
Bering (str.)		U 3	46
Berkeley, Calif.	103,328	J 2	133
Berkshire (hills), Mass.		B 4	147
Berlin, N.H.	13,084	E 3	155
Berlin, East (cap.), E. Ger.	1,094,147	F 4	20
Berlin, West, W. Ger.	1,983,837	E 4	20
Bermuda	67,761	H 3	124
Bern (cap.), Switz.	154,700	D 3	37
Berwyn, Ill.	46,849	B 6	139
Besançon, France	119,803	G 4	26
Bessemer, Ala.	31,729	D 4	129
Bethany, Okla.	22,130	G 3	162
Bethel, Conn.	16,004	B 3	135
Bethel Park, Pa.	34,755	B 7	164
Bethesda, Md.	62,736	A 4	146
Bethlehem, West Bank	14,439	C 4	67
Bethlehem, Pa.	70,419	M 4	164
Bettendorf, Iowa	27,381	N 5	141
Beverly, Mass.	37,655	E 5	147
Beverly Hills, Calif.	32,367	B 10	133
Bhagalpur, India	172,202	F 4	70
Bhavnagar, India	225,358	C 4	70
Bhilainagar, India	157,173	E 4	70
Bhopal, India	298,022	D 4	70
Bhutan	1,298,000	G 3	70
Bialystok, Pol.	166,619	F 2	45
Biarritz, France	27,453	C 6	26
Biddeford, Maine	19,638	B 9	145
Bielefeld, W. Ger.	316,058	C 2	20
Bielsko-Biala, Poland	105,601	D 4	45
Big Bend Nat'l Pk., Texas		A 8	168
Bighorn (riv.), U.S.		E 2	126
Big Spring, Texas	24,804	C 5	168
Bikaner, India	188,518	C 3	70
Bikini (atoll), Marshall Is.		G 4	89
Bilbao, Spain	393,170	E 1	31
Billerica, Mass.	36,727	J 2	147
Billings, Mont.	66,842	H 5	152
Biloxi, Miss.	49,311	G 10	150
Biminis, The (isls.), Bah.	1,432	B 1	124
Binghamton, N.Y.	55,860	J 6	158
Bioko (isl.), Equat. Guin.		H 11	54
Birkenhead, Eng.	135,750	G 2	11
Birmingham, Ala.	284,413	D 3	129
Birmingham, Eng.	1,058,800	F 5	11
Birmingham, Mich.	21,689	B 6	148
Bisbee, Ariz.	7,154	F 7	131
Biscay (bay), Europe		D 4	6
Biscayne Nat'l Pk., Fla.		F 6	136
Bisho, S. Africa		M 18	57
Bismarck (cap.), N. Dak.	44,485	J 6	160
Bismarck (arch.), Papua N.G.	218,339	E 6	89
Bissau (cap.), Guinea-Bissau	109,486	D 9	54
Bitterroot (range), U.S.		D 1	126
Biysk, U.S.S.R.	212,000	J 4	46
Bizerte, Tun.	62,856	J 4	54
Black (sea)		H 4	6
Black (for.), W. Ger.		C 4	20
Black Canyon of the Gunnison Nat'l Mon., Colo.		D 5	134
Blackfoot, Idaho	10,065	F 6	138
Black Hills (mts.), U.S.		F 2	126
Blackpool, Eng.	149,000	G 1	11
Blacksburg, Va.	30,638	D 6	170
Bladensburg, Md.	7,691	C 4	146
Blagoveshchensk, U.S.S.R.	172,000	N 4	46
Blanc (mt.), Europe		E 4	6
Blanca (peak), Colo.		H 7	134
Blantyre, Malawi	222,153	N 15	57
Blida, Alg.	160,900	G 4	54
Block (isl.), R.I.		H 8	147
Bloemfontein, S. Africa	149,836	L 17	57
Bloomfield, N.J.	47,792	B 2	156
Bloomington, Ill.	44,189	D 3	139
Bloomington, Ind.	52,044	D 6	140
Bloomington, Minn.	81,831	G 6	149
Blue (mts.), Oreg.		J 3	163
Bluefield, W. Va.	16,060	D 6	172
Blue Nile (riv.), Africa		N 9	54
Blue Springs, Mo.	25,927	R 6	151
Blytheville, Ark.	23,844	L 2	132
Bobo-Dioulasso, Burk. Faso	115,063	F 9	54
Bobruysk, U.S.S.R.	192,000	C 4	50
Boca Raton, Fla.	49,505	F 5	136
Bochum, W. Ger.	414,852	B 3	20
Bogalusa, La.	16,976	L 5	144
Bogor, Indon.	247,409	H 2	83
Bogotá (cap.), Col.	2,696,270	F 3	90
Bo Hai (gulf), China		J 4	77
Bohemia (for.), Czech.		B 2	39
Boise (cap.), Idaho	102,160	B 6	138
Bolívar (mt.), Ven.		F 2	90
Bolivia	5,600,000	G 7	90
Bologna, Italy	493,282	C 2	32
Bolton, Eng.	154,480	H 2	11
Bolzano, Italy	102,806	C 1	32
Bombay, India	*5,970,575	B 7	70
Bon (cape), Tun.		J 4	54
Bonaire (isl.), Neth. Ant.	8,087	E 4	124
Bonin (isls.), Japan	1,879	M 3	75
Bonn (cap.), W. Ger.	283,711	B 3	20
Bonneville (dam), U.S.		E 2	163
Booker T. Washington Nat'l Mon., Va.		E 6	170
Boone, Iowa	12,602	F 4	141
Bophuthatswana (aut rep.), S. Africa		L 17	57
Bora Bora (isl.), Fr. Poly.	2,579	L 7	89
Borah (peak), Idaho		E 5	138
Bordeaux, France	220,830	C 5	26
Borger, Texas	15,837	C 2	168

	Pop.	Key	Pg.
Borisov, U.S.S.R.	112,000	C 4	50
Borneo (isl.), Asia		E 5	83
Bornholm (isl.), Den.		F 8	19
Bosnia-Hercegovina (rep.), Yugo.		C 3	43
Bosporus (str.), Turkey		C 2	64
Bossier City, La.	50,817	C 1	144
Boston (cap.), Mass.	562,994	D 7	147
Botany (bay), Austr.		L 4	86
Bothnia (gulf), Europe		M 5	16
Botswana	819,000	L 16	57
Bouaké, Iv. Coast	173,248	F 10	54
Bougainville (isl.), Papua N.G	71,761	F 6	89
Boulder, Colo.	76,685	J 2	134
Boulder City, Nev.	9,590	G 7	154
Boulogne, France	48,309	D 2	26
Bountiful, Utah	32,877	C 3	169
Bourges, France	75,200	E 4	26
Bournemouth, Eng.	144,100	F 7	11
Bowie, Md.	33,695	G 4	146
Bowie, Texas	5,610	G 4	168
Bowling Green, Ky.	40,450	D 7	143
Bowling Green, Ohio	25,728	C 3	161
Boynton Beach, Fla.	35,624	F 5	136
Bozeman, Mont.	21,645	E 5	152
Bradenton, Fla.	30,170	D 4	136
Bradford, Eng.	458,900	J 1	11
Brahmaputra (riv.), Asia		G 3	70
Brăila, Rom.	203,983	H 3	43
Braintree, Mass.	36,337	D 8	147
Brandenburg (reg.), E. Ger.		E 2	20
Branford, Conn.	23,363	D 3	135
Brantford, Ont.	74,315	D 4	108
Brasília (cap.), Braz.	411,305	L 7	90
Braşov, Rom.	259,108	G 3	43
Bratislava, Czech.	333,000	D 2	39
Bratsk, U.S.S.R.	214,000	L 4	46
Brattleboro, Vt.	11,886	B 6	155
Brazil	119,098,992		90,93
Brazos (riv.), Texas		H 7	168
Brazzaville (cap.), Congo	298,967	J 12	57
Breda, Neth.	118,086	F 5	25
Bremen, W. Ger.	572,969	C 2	20
Bremerhaven, W. Ger.	143,836	C 2	20
Bremerton, Wash.	36,208	A 2	171
Brenner (pass), Europe		A 3	39
Brentwood, N.Y.	44,321	E 2	158
Brescia, Italy	189,092	C 2	32
Breslau, see Wroclaw, Poland			
Brest, France	163,940	A 3	26
Brest, U.S.S.R.	177,000	B 4	50
Brezhnev, U.S.S.R.	301,000	H 3	50
Breton (sound), La.		M 7	144
Brices Cross Roads Nat'l Battlfld. Site, Miss.		G 2	150
Brick, N.J.	53,629	E 3	156
Bridgeport, Conn.	142,546	C 4	135
Bridgeton, N.J.	18,795	C 5	156
Bridgetown (cap.), Barbados	7,552	G 4	124
Brigham City, Utah	15,596	C 2	169
Brighton, Eng.	156,500	G 7	11
Brindisi, Italy	76,612	G 4	32
Brisbane, Austr.	942,836	K 3	86
Bristol (bay), Alaska		F 3	130
Bristol, Conn.	57,370	D 2	135
Bristol, Eng.	416,300	E 6	11
Bristol, R.I.	20,128	J 6	147
Bristol, Tenn.	23,986	R 1	167
Bristol (chan.), U.K.		C 6	11
Bristol, Va.	19,042	D 3	170
British Columbia (prov.), Can.	2,744,467		117
British Indian Ocean Terr.	2,000	J 10	58
Brno, Czech.	335,700	D 2	39
Brocton, Mass.	95,172	K 4	147
Broken Arrow, Okla.	35,761	L 2	162
Broken Hill, Austr.	26,913	G 6	86
Bromley, Eng.	299,100	H 8	11
Bronx (borough), N.Y.	1,168,972	C 2	158
Brookfield, Wis.	34,035	K 1	173
Brookhaven, Nat'l Lab., N.Y.		E 2	158
Brookings, S. Dak.	14,951	R 5	166
Brookline, Mass.	55,062	C 7	147
Brooklyn (borough), N.Y.	2,230,936	C 2	158
Brooklyn Center, Minn.	31,230	G 5	149
Brooklyn Park, Minn.	43,332	G 5	149
Brooks (range), Alaska		G 1	130
Brownsville, Texas	84,997	G 12	168
Brownwood, Texas	19,396	F 6	168
Bruges, Belg.	117,220	C 6	25
Brunei	192,832	E 4	83
Brunswick, Ga.	17,605	K 8	137
Brunswick, Maine	17,366	C 8	145
Brunswick, W. Ger.	268,519	D 2	20
Brussels (cap.), Belg.	*1,054,970	C 9	25
Bryan, Texas	44,337	H 7	168
Bryansk, U.S.S.R.	394,000	D 4	50

	Pop.	Key	Pg.
Bryce Canyon Nat'l Pk., Utah		B 6	169
Bucaramanga, Col.	291,661	F 2	90
Bucharest (cap.), Rom.	1,832,015	G 3	43
Budapest (cap.), Hung.	2,060,170	E 3	39
Buena Park, Calif.	64,165	D 11	133
Buenaventura, Col.	115,770	E 3	90
Buenos Aires (cap.), Arg.	*9,927,404	H 10	93
Buffalo, N.Y.	357,870	B 5	158
Bug (riv.), Europe		F 2	45
Bujumbura (cap.), Burundi	141,040	N 12	57
Bukavu, Zaire	134,861	M 12	57
Bukhara, U.S.S.R.	185,000	G 5	46
Bulawayo, Zim.	359,000	M 16	57
Bulgaria	8,862,000	G 4	43
Burbank, Calif.	84,625	C 10	133
Burdwan, India	143,318	F 4	70
Burgas, Bulg.	144,449	H 4	43
Burgos, Spain	118,366	E 1	31
Burkina Faso	6,908,000	F 9	54
Burlingame, Calif.	26,173	J 2	133
Burlington, Iowa	29,529	L 7	141
Burlington, N.J.	10,246	D 3	156
Burlington, N.C.	37,266	F 2	159
Burlington, Ont.	114,853	E 4	108
Burlington, Vt.	37,712	A 3	155
Burma	32,913,000	B 2	81
Burnsville, Minn.	35,674	E 6	149
Bursa, Turkey	346,103	C 2	64
Burundi	4,021,910	M 12	57
Butler, Pa.	17,026	C 4	164
Butte-Silver Bow Co., Mont.	37,205	D 5	152
Butuan, Phil.	172,489	H 4	83
Buzzards (bay), Mass.		L 7	147
Bydgoszcz, Pol.	280,460	C 2	45
Byelorussia, see White Russian S.S.R., U.S.S.R.			
Bytom, Pol.	186,193	A 3	45

C

	Pop.	Key	Pg.
Cabinda (dist.), Angola		H 13	57
Cabot (str.), Can.		K 6	96
Cabrillo Nat'l Mon., Calif.		H 11	133
Cádiz, Spain	135,743	C 4	31
Caen, France	116,987	C 3	26
Cagayan de Oro, Phil.	227,312	G 4	83
Cagliari, Italy	211,015	B 5	32
Cahokia, Ill.	18,904	A 3	139
Caicos (isls.), Turks & Caicos Is.	4,008	D 2	124
Cairo (cap.), Egypt	5,084,463	N 5	54
Cairo, Ill.	5,931	D 6	139
Calabria (reg.), Italy		F 5	32
Calais, France	73,009	D 2	26
Calais, Maine	4,262	J 5	145
Calcasieu (lake), La.		D 7	144
Calcutta, India	3,148,746	F 2	70
Caldwell, Idaho	17,699	B 6	138
Calgary, Alta.	*592,743	C 4	114
Cali, Col.	898,253	E 3	90
Calicut (Kozhikode), India	333,979	D 6	70
California (gulf), Mex.		D 3	119
California (state), U.S.	23,667,565		133
Callao, Peru	447,374	E 6	90
Calumet City, Ill.	39,697	C 6	139
Camagüey, Cuba	245,235	B 2	124
Cambodia	5,200,000	E 4	81
Cambridge, Eng.	106,400	G 5	11
Cambridge, Md.	11,703	K 6	146
Cambridge, Mass.	15,322	C 7	147
Camden, Ark.	15,356	E 6	132
Camden, N.J.	84,910	B 3	156
Camden, S.C.	7,462	F 3	165
Cameroon	8,503,000	J 11	54
Campania (reg.), Italy		E 4	32
Campeche (bay), Mex.		N 7	119
Campina Grande, Braz.	222,229	N 5	90
Campinas, Braz.	566,517	L 8	93
Camp Lejeune, N.C.	30,764	L 5	159
Campobello (isl.), N. Br.		D 4	102
Campo Grande, Braz.	282,844	K 8	90
Campos, Braz.	174,218	M 8	90
Camp Pendleton, Calif.	10,017	H 10	133
Cam Ranh, Viet.	118,111	F 5	81
Cam Ranh (bay), Viet.		F 5	81
Canada	24,343,181		96
Canadian (riv.), U.S.		F 3	126
Canary (isls.), Spain		B 4	31
Canaveral (cape), Fla.		F 3	136
Canberra (cap.), Austr.	*220,822	H 7	86
Cannanore (isls.), India		C 6	70
Cannes, France	70,226	G 6	26
Cantabrian (mts.), Spain		C 1	31
Canterbury, Eng.	115,600	H 6	11
Can Tho, Viet.	182,424	E 5	81

	Pop.	Key	Pg.
Canton (Guangzhou), China	2,300,000	H 7	77
Canton (isl.), Kiribati		J 6	89
Canton, Ohio	93,077	H 4	161
Canyon de Chelly Nat'l Mon., Ariz.		F 2	131
Canyonlands Nat'l Pk., Utah		D 5	169
Cape (prov.), S. Africa		L 18	57
Cape Breton (isl.), N.S.		J 2	100
Cape Cod Nat'l Seashore, Mass.		P 5	147
Cape Coral, Fla.	32,103	E 5	136
Cape Girardeau, Mo.	34,361	O 8	151
Cape Hatteras Nat'l Seashore, N.C.		O 4	159
Cape Lookout Nat'l Seashore, N.C.		N 5	159
Cape May, N.J.	4,853	D 5	156
Cape Town (cap.), S. Africa	697,514	F 19	57
Cape Verde	324,000		1
Cape York (pen.), Austr.		G 2	86
Capitol Reef Nat'l Pk., Utah		C 5	169
Capri (isl.), Italy		E 4	32
Caprivi Strip (reg.), Namibia		L 15	57
Capulin Mtn. Nat'l Mon., N. Mex.		E 2	157
Caracas (cap.), Ven.	1,035,499	G 1	90
Carbondale, Ill.	26,414	D 6	139
Carcassonne, France	38,887	D 6	26
Cardiff (cap.), Wales	281,500	B 7	11
Caribbean (sea)			124
Caribou, Maine	9,916	G 2	145
Carlisle, Pa.	18,314	H 5	164
Carl Sandburg Home Nat'l Hist Site, N.C.		E 9	159
Carlsbad, N. Mex.	25,496	E 6	157
Carlsbad Caverns Nat'l Pk., N. Mex.		E 6	157
Carmel, Calif.	4,707	D 7	133
Carmel (mt.), Isr.		C 2	67
Carmichael, Calif.	43,108	C 8	133
Caroline (isls.), Micronesia		E-F 5	89
Carpathians (mts.), Europe		G 4	6
Carpinteria, Calif.	10,835	F 9	133
Carrara, Italy	56,236	C 2	32
Carrizo (mts.), Ariz.		G 2	131
Carrollton, Texas	40,595	G 2	168
Carson, Calif.	81,221	C 11	133
Carson (sink), Nev.		C 3	154
Carson City (cap.), Nev.	32,022	B 3	154
Cartagena, Col.	292,512	E 1	90
Cartagena, Spain	52,312	F 4	31
Casablanca, Mor.	1,506,373	E 5	54
Casa Grande, Ariz.	14,971	D 6	131
Casa Grande Ruins Nat'l Mon., Ariz.		D 6	131
Cascade (range), U.S.		B 1	126
Casper, Wyo.	51,016	F 3	174
Caspian (sea)		F 6	46
Castile (reg.), Spain		D-E 2	31
Castillo de San Marcos Nat'l Mon., Fla.		E 2	136
Castries (cap.), St. Lucia	42,770	G 4	124
Castro Valley, Calif.	44,011	K 2	133
Catalonia (reg.), Spain		G 2	31
Catania, Italy	403,390	E 6	32
Catonsville, Md.	33,208	H 3	146
Catskill, N.Y.	4,718	N 6	158
Catskill (mts.), N.Y.		L 6	158
Caucasus (mts.), U.S.S.R.		E 5	46
Cawnpore, see Kanpur, India			
Cayenne (cap.), Fr. Guiana	37,079	K 2	90
Cayman Islands	16,677	B 3	124
Cebu, Phil.	490,281	G 3	83
Cedar Breaks Nat'l Mon., Utah		B 6	169
Cedar City, Utah	10,972	A 6	169
Cedar Falls, Iowa	36,322	H 3	141
Cedar Rapids, Iowa	110,243	K 5	141
Celebes (sea), Asia		G 5	83
Celebes (isl.), Indon.	7,732,383	G 6	83
Central African Republic	2,284,000	K 10	54
Central America	21,000,000		122
Centralia, Ill.	15,126	D 5	139
Centralia, Wash.	11,555	C 4	177
Cerritos, Calif.	53,020	C 11	133
Ceylon (Sri Lanka)	14,850,000	E 7	70
Chaco, Gran (reg.), S. Amer.		H 9	90
Chaco Culture Nat'l Hist. Pk., N. Mex.		B 2	157
Chad	4,309,000	K 8	54
Chad (lake), Africa		K 9	54
Chagos (arch.), Br. Ind. Oc. Terr.		J 10	58
Chambersburg, Pa.	16,174	G 6	164
Chambly, Que.	12,190	J 4	105
Champaign, Ill.	58,133	E 3	139
Champlain (lake), N. Amer.		A 2	155
Chandigarh, India	218,743	D 2	70
Chandler, Ariz.	29,673	D 5	131
Changchun, China	1,500,000	K 3	77
Changhua, China	137,236	K 7	77

	Pop.	Key	Pg.
Chang Jiang (Yangtze) (riv.), China		K 5	77
Changsha, China	850,000	H 6	77
Changzhou, China	400,000	K 5	77
Channel Islands	133,000	E 8	11
Channel Is. Nat'l Pk., Calif.		F 10	133
Chapel Hill, N.C.	32,421	G 3	157
Chardzhou, U.S.S.R.	140,000	G 6	46
Charleston, S.C.	69,510	G 6	165
Charleston (cap.), W. Va.	63,968	D 4	172
Charles Town, W. Va.	2,857	L 2	172
Charlotte (hbr.), Fla.		D 5	136
Charlotte, N.C.	314,447	D 4	159
Charlotte Amalie (cap.), V.I. (U.S.)	11,671	F 3	124
Charlottesville, Va.	39,916	G 4	170
Charlottetown (cap.), P.E.I.	15,282	E 2	100
Chartres, France	38,574	D 3	26
Château-Thierry, France	13,370	E 3	26
Chatham, N. Br.	6,779	E 1	102
Chattahoochee, Fla.	5,332	B 1	136
Chattahoochee (riv.), U.S.		K 4	126
Chattanooga, Tenn.	169,558	K 4	167
Chautauqua, N.Y.	300	A 6	158
Cheboksary, U.S.S.R.	308,000	G 3	50
Cheboygan, Mich.	5,106	E 3	148
Cheektowaga, N.Y.	109,442	C 5	158
Chefoo, see Yantai, China			
Chehalis, Wash.	6,100	C 4	171
Cheju, S. Korea	135,081	C 7	74
Cheju (isl.), S. Korea		C 7	74
Chelan (lake), Wash.		E 2	171
Chelmsford, Mass.	31,174	J 2	147
Chelsea, Mass.	25,431	D 6	147
Chelyabinsk, U.S.S.R.	1,030,000	G 4	46
Chelyuskin (cape), U.S.S.R.		L 2	46
Chemnitz, see Karl-Marx-Stadt, E. Ger.			
Chengde, China	200,000	J 3	77
Chengdu (Chengtu), China	2,000,000	F 5	77
Cherbourg, France	31,333	C 3	26
Cherepovets, U.S.S.R.	266,000	E 3	50
Cherkassy, U.S.S.R.	228,000	D 5	50
Chernenko, U.S.S.R.		K 4	46
Chernigov, U.S.S.R.	238,000	D 4	50
Chenovtsy, U.S.S.R.	219,000	C 5	50
Cherry Hill, N.J.	68,785	B 3	156
Cherry Point Marine Air Sta., N.C.		M 5	159
Chesapeake (bay), U.S.		L 3	126
Chesapeake, Va.	114,486	M 7	170
Chesapeake & Ohio Canal Hist. Pk., U.S.		K 2	170
Cheshire, Conn.	21,788	D 2	135
Chester, Eng.	117,000	G 2	11
Chester, Pa.	45,794	L 7	164
Chevy Chase, Md.	12,232	A 4	146
Cheyenne (riv.), U.S.		F 2	126
Cheyenne (cap.), Wyo.	47,283	H 4	174
Chiai, China	238,713	K 7	77
Chiba, Japan	659,356	P 2	75
Chicago, Ill.	3,005,072	C 5	139
Chicago Heights, Ill.	37,026	C 6	139
Chicago Portage Nat'l Hist Site, Ill.		B 6	139
Chichagof (isl.), Alaska		M 3	130
Chichén-Itzá (ruins), Mex.		P 6	119
Chickamauga & Chattanooga Nat'l Mil. Pk., Ga.		B 1	137
Chickasha, Okla.	15,828	G 4	162
Chiclayo, Peru	280,244	E 5	90
Chico, Calif.	26,603	D 4	133
Chicopee, Mass.	55,112	D 4	147
Chicoutimi, Que.	60,064	G 1	105
Chihuahua, Mex.	327,313	F 2	119
Chile	11,275,440	F 8	90
		F 8-14	93
Chillicothe, Ohio	23,420	E 7	161
Chillum, Md.	32,775	B 4	146
Chimborazo (mt.), Ecua.		E 4	90
Chimbote, Peru	216,406	E 5	90
Chimkent, U.S.S.R.	322,000	H 5	46
Chimney Rock Nat'l Hist. Site, Nebr.		A 3	153
China, People's Rep. of	958,090,000		77
China, Rep. of (Taiwan)	16,609,961	K 7	77
Chinju, S. Korea	154,646	D 6	74
Chino, Calif.	40,165	D 10	133
Chirchik, U.S.S.R.	132,000	H 5	46
Chiricahua Nat'l Mon., Ariz.		F 6	131
Chita, U.S.S.R.	303,000	M 4	46
Chittagong, Bang.	889,760	G 4	70
Chofu, Japan	175,924	O 2	75
Chŏngjin, N. Korea	306,000	E 3	74
Ch'ŏngju, S. Korea	192,707	C 5	74
Chongqing (Chunkgking), China	3,500,000	G 6	77
Chorzów, Poland	151,338	B 4	45

	Pop.	Key	Pg.
Christchurch, N.Z.	164,680	L 7	87
Christmas (isl.), Austr.		M11	58
Christmas (isl.), Kiribati	674	L 5	89
Chukchi (pen.), U.S.S.R.		T 3	46
Chula Vista, Calif.	83,927	J 11	133
Ch'unch'ŏn, S.Korea	140,530	D 5	74
Churchill, Man.	1,186	K 2	110
Churchill (falls), Newf.		D 2	99
Cicero, Ill.	61,232	B 5	139
Cimarron (riv.), U.S.		G 3	126
Cincinnati, Ohio	385,457	B 9	161
Cirebon, Indon.	223,776	H 2	83
Citlaltépetl (mt.), Mex.		O 2	119
Citrus Heights, Calif.	85,911	C 8	133
Ciudad Bolívar, Ven.	103,728	H 2	90
Ciudad Juárez, Mex.	424,135	F 1	119
Ciudad Madero, Mex.	115,302	L 5	119
Ciudad Obregón, Mex.	144,795	E 3	119
Claremont, Calif.	30,950	D10	133
Claremont, N.H.	14,557	C 5	155
Claremore, Okla.	12,085	M 2	162
Clarksburg, W. Va.	22,371	F 2	172
Clarksdale, Miss.	21,137	D 2	150
Clarksville, Tenn.	54,777	G 1	167
Clayton, Mo.	14,273	P 3	151
Clearwater, Fla.	85,528	B 2	136
Clearwater (mts.), Idaho		C 3	138
Clermont-Ferrand, France	153,379	E 5	26
Cleveland, Ohio	573,822	H 9	161
Cleveland, Tenn.	26,415	M 4	167
Cleveland Heights, Ohio	56,438	H 9	161
Clifton, N.J.	74,388	B 2	156
Clinton, Iowa	32,828	N 5	141
Clovis, Calif.	33,021	F 7	133
Clovis, N. Mex.	31,194	F 4	157
Cluj-Napoca, Rom.	274,095	F 2	43
Coast (ranges), U.S.		B 2	126
Cóbh, Ire.	6,076	E 8	15
Cochabamba, Bol.	204,684	G 7	90
Cochin-Allepey, India	439,066	D 6	70
Cod (cape), Mass.		O 4	147
Cody, Wyo.	6,790	D 1	174
Coeur d'Alene, Idaho	20,054	B 2	138
Coffeyville, Kans.	15,185	G 4	142
Cohoes, N.Y.	18,144	N 5	158
Coimbatore, India	356,368	D 6	70
College Park, Ga.	24,632	K 2	137
College Park, Md.	23,614	C 4	146
College Station, Texas	37,272	H 7	168
Cologne, W. Ger.	1,013,771	B 3	20
Colombia	27,520,000	F 3	90
Colombo (cap.), Sri Lanka	618,000	D 7	70
Colón, Pan.	59,832	H 6	122
Colorado (riv.), Texas		F 7	168
Colorado (riv.), U.S.		D 4	126
Colorado (state), U.S.	2,889,735		134
Colorado Nat'l Mon., Colo.		B 4	134
Colorado Springs, Colo.	214,821	K 5	134
Columbia, Md.	52,518	G 4	146
Columbia, Mo.	62,061	H 5	151
Columbia (riv.), N. Amer.		F 5	94
Columbia (cap.), S.C.	101,208	F 4	165
Columbia, Tenn.	26,571	G 3	167
Columbus, Ga.	169,441	C 6	137
Columbus, Ind.	30,614	E 6	140
Columbus, Miss.	27,383	H 3	150
Columbus (cap.), Ohio	565,032	E 6	161
Colville (riv.), Alaska		H 1	130
Communism (peak), U.S.S.R.		H 6	46
Como (lake), Italy		H 4	37
Comorin (cape), India		D 7	70
Comoros	290,000	P14	57
Compiègne, France	37,009	E 3	26
Compton, Calif.	81,286	C11	133
Conakry (cap.), Guinea,	*525,671	D10	54
Concepción, Chile	206,226	F11	93
Conception (bay), Newf.		D 4	99
Concord, Calif.	103,255	K 1	133
Concord, Mass.	16,293	B 6	147
Concord (cap.), N.H.	30,400	D 5	155
Concord, N.C.	16,942	D 4	159
Congo	1,537,000	K12	57
Congo (riv.), Africa		K12	57
Congo, Democratic Rep. of the, see Zaire			
Connecticut (riv.), U.S.		M 2	126
Connecticut (state), U.S.	3,107,576		135
Constance (lake), Europe		H 1	37
Constanța, Rom.	279,308	J 3	43
Constantine, Alg.	335,100	H 4	54
Conway, Ark.	20,375	F 3	132
Cook (inlet), Alaska		H 3	130
Cook (mt.), N.Z.		K 7	87
Cook (str.), N.Z.		L 6	87
Cook Islands	17,695	K 7	89
Coon Rapids, Minn.	35,826	G 5	149

	Pop.	Key	Pg.
Cooperstown, N.Y.	2,342	L 5	158
Coos Bay, Oreg.	14,424	C 4	163
Copenhagen (cap.), Den.	603,368	E 6	19
Copper (riv.), Alaska		K 2	130
Coral (sea)		F 7	89
Coral Gables, Fla.	43,241	B 5	136
Coral Springs, Fla.	37,349	F 5	136
Córdoba, Arg.	*982,018	G10	93
Córdoba, Spain	216,049	D 4	31
Corfu, see Kérkira, Greece			
Corinth, Greece	20,773	F 7	43
Cork, Ire.	128,645	E 8	15
Corner Brook, Newf.	24,339	A 3	99
Corning, N.Y.	12,953	F 6	158
Cornwall, Ont.	46,144	K 2	108
Coro, Ven.	68,701	G 1	90
Coromandel (coast), India		E 6	70
Corona, Calif.	37,791	E11	133
Coronado Nat'l Mem., Ariz.		E 7	131
Corpus Christi, Texas	231,999	G10	168
Corsica (isl.), France		B 6	26
Corsicana, Texas	21,712	H 5	168
Cortland, N.Y.	20,138	H 5	158
Corvallis, Oreg.	40,960	D 3	163
Coshocton, Ohio	13,405	G 5	161
Costa Brava (reg.), Spain		H 2	31
Costa Mesa, Calif.	82,562	D11	133
Costa Rica	2,245,000	E 5	122
Côte-d'Or (mts.), France		F 4	26
Cotentin (pen.), France		C 3	26
Cotonou, Benin	178,000	G10	54
Coulee Dam Nat'l Rec. Area, Wash.		G 2	171
Council Bluffs, Iowa	56,449	B 6	141
Coventry, Eng.	336,800	F 5	11
Coventry, R.I.	27,065	H 6	147
Covina, Calif.	33,751	D10	133
Covington, Ky.	49,563	K 1	143
Cowpens Nat'l Battlfld. Site, S.C.		D 1	165
Cozumel (isl.), Mex.		Q 6	119
Cracow, Pol.	650,300	E 4	45
Craiova, Rom.	220,893	F 3	43
Cranbrook, Br. Col.	15,915	K 5	117
Cranford, N.J.	24,573	E 2	156
Cranston, R.I.	71,992	J 5	147
Crater Lake Nat'l Pk., Oreg.		E 5	163
Craters of the Moon Nat'l Mon., Idaho		E 6	138
Crawfordsville, Ind.	13,325	D 4	140
Crete (isl.), Greece		G 8	43
Crimea (pen.), U.S.S.R.		D 5	50
Croatia (rep.), Yugo.		C 3	43
Crowley, La.	16,036	F 6	144
Croydon, Eng.	330,600	H 8	11
Crystal, Minn.	25,543	G 5	149
Cuba	9,706,369	B 2	124
Cucamonga, Calif.	55,250	E10	133
Cúcuta, Col.	219,772	F 2	90
Cuenca, Ecua.	104,470	E 4	90
Cuernavaca, Mex.	239,813	L 2	119
Cuiabá, Braz.	167,894	J 7	90
Culebra (isl.), P. Rico	1,265	G 1	124
Culiacán, Mex.	228,001	F 4	119
Cullman, Ala.	13,084	E 2	129
Culver City, Calif.	38,139	B10	133
Cumaná, Ven.	119,751	H 1	90
Cumberland, Md.	25,933	D 7	146
Cumberland (riv.), U.S.		J 3	126
Cumberland Gap Nat'l Hist. Pk., U.S.		O 1	167
Cumberland Isl. Nat'l Seashore, Ga.		K 9	137
Cupertino, Calif.	34,265	K 3	133
Curaçao (isl.), Neth. Ant.	145,430	E 4	124
Curecanti Nat'l Rec. Area, Colo.		F 6	134
Curitiba, Braz.	*843,733	K 9	93
Cusco, Peru	181,604	F 6	90
Custer Battlfld. Nat'l Mon., Mont.		J 5	152
Cuttack, India	194,068	F 4	70
Cuyahoga Falls, Ohio	43,890	G 3	161
Cyclades (isls.), Greece		G 7	43
Cypress, Calif.	40,391	D11	133
Cyprus	629,000	E 5	64
Cyrenaica (reg.), Libya		L 6	54
Czechoslovakia	15,276,799		39
Czech Socialist Rep., Czech.		B 1	39
Czestochowa, Pol.	187,613	D 3	45

D

	Pop.	Key	Pg.
Dacca (Dhaka)(cap.), Bang.	1,679,572	G 4	70
Dachau, W. Ger.	33,207	D 4	20
Daito (isls.), Japan		M 6	77
Dakar (cap.), Sen.	798,792	C 9	54
Da Lat, Viet.	105,072	F 5	81
Dalhousie, N. Br.	4,958	D 1	102
Dalian, China	4,000,000	K 4	77
Dallas, Texas	904,078	G 2	168
Dalton, Ga.	20,939	C 1	137
Daly City, Calif.	78,519	H 2	133
Damanhur, Egypt	188,927	B 3	60
Damascus (cap.), Syria	836,668	G 6	64
Damavand (mt.), Iran		H 2	68
Damietta, Egypt	93,546	N 5	54
Da Nang, Viet.	492,194	E 3	81
Danbury, Conn.	60,470	B 3	135
Dandong, China	450,000	K 3	77
Danube (riv.), Europe		G 4	6
Danvers, Mass.	24,100	D 5	147
Danville, Ill.	38,985	F 3	139
Danville, Va.	45,642	E 7	170
Danzig (Gdańsk)(gulf), Pol.		D 1	45
Daqing, China	758,430	L 2	77
Darby, Pa.	11,513	M 7	164
Dardanelles (str.), Turkey		B 6	64
Dar es Salaam (cap.), Tanz.	757,346	P13	57
Darien, Conn.	18,892	B 4	135
Darién (mts.), Pan.		J 6	122
Darjeeling, India	42,873	F 3	70
Darling (riv.), Austr.		G 6	86
Darmstadt, W. Ger.	137,018	C 4	20
Dartmouth, Mass.	23,966	K 6	147
Dartmouth, N.S.	62,277	E 4	100
Darwin, Austr.	56,482	E 2	86
Datong, China	300,000	H 3	77
Davao, Phil.	610,375	H 4	83
Davenport, Iowa	103,264	M 5	141
Davis (sea), Antarc.		C 5	88
Davis, Calif.	36,640	B 8	133
Davis (str.), N. Amer.		N 3	94
Dawson, Yukon	697	C 3	96
Dawson Creek, Br. Col.	11,373	G 2	117
Dayton, Ohio	193,444	B 6	161
Daytona Beach, Fla.	54,176	F 2	136
Dead (sea), Asia		C 4	67
Dearborn, Mich.	90,660	B 7	148
Dearborn Heights, Mich.	67,706	B 7	148
Death Valley (depr.), Calif.		H 7	133
Death Valley Nat'l Mon., U.S.		H 7	133
Debrecen, Hung.	192,484	F 3	39
Decatur, Ala.	42,002	D 1	129
Decatur, Ga.	18,404	K 1	137
Decatur, Ill.	94,081	E 4	139
Deccan (plat.), India		D 5-6	70
Dedham, Mass.	25,298	C 7	147
Deerfield, Ill.	17,430	B 5	139
Deerfield Beach, Fla.	39,193	F 5	136
Defiance, Ohio	16,810	B 3	161
Dehiwala-Mt. Lavinia, Sri Lanka	154,785	D 7	70
Dehra Dun, India	166,073	D 2	70
De Kalb, Ill.	33,099	E 2	139
De Land, Fla.	15,354	E 2	136
Delaware, Ohio	18,780	E 5	161
Delaware (bay), U.S.		M 3	126
Delaware (riv.), U.S.		D 3	156
Delaware (state), U.S.	594,317		146
Delaware Water Gap Nat'l Rec. Area, U.S.		C 1	156
Del City, Okla.	28,523	G 4	162
Delhi, India	3,287,883	D 3	70
Delray Beach, Fla.	34,325	F 5	136
Del Rio, Texas	30,034	D 8	168
Denali Nat'l Pk., Alaska		K 2	130
Denmark	5,124,000		19
Denmark (str.)		B 2	6
Denton, Texas	48,063	G 4	168
Denver (cap.), Colo.	492,365	K 3	134
Denville, N.J.	14,380	E 2	156
Depew, N.Y.	19,819	C 5	158
Derby, Conn.	12,346	C 3	135
Derby, Eng.	213,700	F 5	11
De Ridder, La.	11,057	D 5	144
Derry, N.H.	18,875	E 6	155
Des Moines (cap.), Iowa	191,003	G 5	141
De Soto Nat'l Mem., Fla.		D 4	136
Des Plaines, Ill.	53,568	B 5	139
Dessau, E. Ger.	100,820	E 3	20
Detroit, Mich.	1,203,339	B 7	148
Devil's (isl.), Fr. Guiana		K 2	90
Devils Postpile Nat'l Mon., Calif.		F 6	133
Devils Tower Nat'l Mon., Wyo.		H 1	174
Devon (isl.), N.W.T.		M 3	96
Dhaka (cap.), Bang.	1,679,572	G 4	70
Dhaulagiri (mt.), Nepal		E 3	70
Dhulia, India	137,129	C 4	70
Diamond (head), Hawaii		C 4	130
Dickinson, N. Dak.	15,924	E 6	160
Diego Garcia (isls.), Br. Ind. Oc. Terr.		J 10	58
Dien Bien Phu, Viet.		D 2	81
Dieppe, France	25,607	D 3	26
Dijon, France	149,899	F 4	26
Dinaric Alps (mts.), Yugo.		B 3	43
Dinosaur Nat'l Mon., U.S.		B 2	134
Diomede (isls.)		E 1	130
Dire Dawa, Eth.	56,700	P10	54
Disappointment (cape), Wash.		A 4	171
District of Columbia, U.S.	638,432	B 5	146
Dixon, Ill.	15,701	D 2	139
Dixon Entrance (str.), N. Amer.		E 4	94
Diyarbakir, Turkey	169,535	H 4	64
Djakarta, see Jakarta, Indon.			
Djibouti	386,000	P 9	54
Djibouti (cap.), Djibouti	96,000	P 9	54
Djokjakarta, see Yogyakarta, Indon.			
Dneprodzerzhinsk, U.S.S.R.	250,000	D 5	50
Dnepropetrovsk, U.S.S.R.	1,066,000	D 5	50
Dnieper (riv.), U.S.S.R.		D 5	50
Dniester (riv.), U.S.S.R.		C 5	50
Dobbs Ferry, N.Y.	10,053	H 1	158
Dodecanese (isls.), Greece		H 8	43
Dodge City, Kans.	18,001	B 4	142
Doha (cap.), Qatar	150,000	F 4	60
Dolomite Alps (mts.), Italy		C 1	32
Dominica	74,089	G 4	124
Dominican Republic	5,647,977	D 3	124
Don (riv.), U.S.S.R.		E 5	50
Dondra (head), Sri Lanka		E 7	70
Donegal, Ire.	1,725	F 2	15
Donets (riv.), U.S.S.R.		D 5	50
Donetsk, U.S.S.R.	1,021,000	D 5	50
Dordogne (riv.), France		D 5	26
Dordrecht, Neth.	101,840	F 5	25
Dornbirn, Austria	33,810	A 3	39
Dortmund, W. Ger.	630,609	B 3	20
Dothan, Ala.	48,750	H 8	129
Douala, Cameroon	458,426	J 11	54
Douglas, Ariz.	13,058	F 7	131
Douglas (cap.), I. of Man	20,389	C 3	11
Dover (cap.), Del.	23,507	M 4	146
Dover, Eng.	34,160	J 6	11
Dover (str.), Europe		J 7	11
Dover, N.H.	22,377	F 5	155
Dover, N.J.	14,681	D 2	156
Downers Grove, Ill.	42,572	A 6	139
Downey, Calif.	82,602	C11	133
Drake (passage)		C15	88
Dráva (riv.), Europe		D 3	39
Dresden, E. Ger.	507,972	E 3	20
Duarte, Calif.	16,766	D10	133
Dubai, U.A.E.		F 4	60
Dublin, Ga.	16,083	G 5	137
Dublin (cap.), Ire.	567,866	K 5	15
Dubrovnik, Yugo.	31,213	C 4	43
Dubuque, Iowa	62,321	M 3	141
Dudley, Eng.	187,110	E 5	11
Dufourspitze (mt.), Switz.		E 5	37
Duisburg, W. Ger.	591,635	B 3	20
Duluth, Minn.	92,811	F 4	149
Dumont, N.J.	18,334	C 1	156
Duncan, Okla.	22,517	G 5	162
Dundalk, Md.	71,293	J 3	146
Dundee, Scot.	194,732	F 4	13
Dunedin, Fla.	30,203	B 2	136
Dunedin, N.Z.	77,176	L 7	87
Dunkirk (Dunkerque), France	78,171	E 2	26
Dunkirk, N.Y.	15,310	B 5	158
Dunmore, Pa.	16,781	F 7	164
Durango, Colo.	11,649	D 8	134
Durango, Mex.	182,633	G 1	119
Durant, Okla.	11,972	K 6	162
Durban, S. Africa	736,852	J 17	57
Durgapur, India	206,638	F 4	70
Durham, Eng.	88,800	J 3	11
Durham, N.H.	10,652	F 5	155
Durham, N.C.	100,538	H 2	159
Dushanbe, U.S.S.R.	494,000	G 6	46
Düsseldorf, W. Ger.	664,336	B 3	20
Dvina, Northern (riv.), U.S.S.R.		E 3	50
Dvina, Western (riv.), U.S.S.R.		C 4	50
Dzaoudzi (cap.), Mayotte	196	R14	57
Dzerzhinsk, U.S.S.R.	257,000	F 3	50
Dzhambul, U.S.S.R.	264,000	H 5	46

E

	Pop.	Key	Pg.
Eagle Pass, Texas	21,407	D 9	168
Ealing, Eng.	293,800	H 8	11
East Aurora, N.Y.	6,803	C 5	158
East Brunswick, N.J.	37,711	E 3	156
East Chicago, Ind.	39,786	C 1	140
East China (sea), Asia		L 6	77
East Cleveland, Ohio	36,957	H 9	161

	Pop.	Key	Pg.
East Detroit, Mich.	38,280	B 6	148
Easter (isl.), Chile	1,598	Q 8	89
Eastern Ghats (mts.), India		D-F 4-6	70
East Frisian (isls.), W. Ger.		B 2	20
East Greenwich, R.I.	10,211	H 6	147
East Hampton, Conn.	8,572	E 2	135
East Hartford, Conn.	52,563	E 1	135
East Haven, Conn.	25,028	D 3	135
Eastlake, Ohio	22,104	J 8	161
East Lansing, Mich.	51,392	E 6	148
East Liverpool, Ohio	16,687	J 4	161
East London, S. Africa,	*126,671	M18	57
East Meadow, N.Y.	39,317	B 3	158
East Moline, Ill.	20,907	C 2	139
Easton, Pa.	26,027	M 4	164
East Orange, N.J.	77,690	B 2	156
East Peoria, Ill.	22,385	D 3	139
East Point, Ga.	37,486	K 2	137
East Providence, R.I.	50,980	J 5	147
East St. Louis, Ill.	55,200	A 2	139
East Siberian (sea), U.S.S.R.		R 2	46
Eau Claire, Wis.	51,569	D 6	173
Ebro (riv.), Spain		G 2	31
Ecorse, Mich.	14,447	B 7	148
Ecuador	8,354,000	E 4	90
Eden, N.C.	15,572	F 1	159
Eden Prairie, Minn.	16,623	G 6	149
Edenton, N.C.	5,367	M 2	159
Edgewood, Md.	19,455	J 3	146
Edina, Minn.	46,073	G 5	149
Edinburg, Texas	24,075	F 11	168
Edinburgh (cap.), Scot.	470,085	D 1	13
Edison, N.J.	70,193	E 2	156
Edison Nat'l Hist. Site., N.J.		A 2	156
Edmond, Okla.	34,637	H 3	142
Edmonds, Wash.	27,679	C 3	171
Edmonton (cap.), Alta.	*657,057	D 3	114
Edmundston, N. Br.	12,044	B 1	102
Edwards (plat.), Texas		C 7	168
Edwards A.F.B., Calif.	8,554	H 9	133
Edwardsville, Ill.	12,480	B 2	139
Eel (riv.), Calif.		B 4	133
Effigy Mounds, Nat'l Mon., Iowa		L 2	141
Effingham, Ill.	11,270	E 4	139
Eglin A.F.B., Fla.	7,574	C 6	136
Egmont (mt.), N.Z.		L 6	87
Egypt	41,572,000	M 6	54
		A 4	60
Eielson A.F.B., Alaska	5,232	K 1	130
Eindhoven, Neth.	192,565	G 6	25
El 'Alamein, Egypt		M 5	54
El Asnam, Alg.	106,100	G 4	54
Elat (Elath), Isr.	12,800	D 5	67
Elazig, Turkey	131,415	H 3	64
Elba (isl.), Italy		C 3	32
Elbe (riv.), Ger.		D 2	20
Elbert (mt.), Colo.		G 4	134
El'brus (mt.), U.S.S.R.		F 6	50
Elburz (mts.), Iran		G 2	68
El Cajon, Calif.	73,892	J 11	133
El Centro, Calif.	23,996	K 11	133
El Dorado, Ark.	25,270	E 7	132
Elektrostal', U.S.S.R.	139,000	E 3	50
Elephanta (isl.), India		B 7	70
Elephant Butte (res.), N. Mex.		B 5	157
Eleuthera (isl.), Bah.	8,326	C 1	124
El Faiyûm, Egypt	167,081	M 6	54
Elgin, Ill.	63,981	E 1	139
Elizabeth, N.J.	106,201	B 2	157
Elizabeth City, N.C.	14,004	N 2	159
El Karnak, Egypt		B 4	60
Elk Grove Village, Ill.	28,907	B 5	139
Elkhart, Ind.	41,305	F 1	140
Ellensburg, Wash.	11,752	E 3	171
Ellesmere (isl.), N.W.T.		N 3	96
El Mansûra, Egypt	257,866	B 3	60
Elmendorf A.F.B., Alaska		J 2	130
Elmhurst, Ill.	44,276	B 5	139
El Minya, Egypt	146,143	B 4	60
Elmira, N.Y.	35,327	G 6	158
El Monte, Calif.	79,494	D 10	133
El Morro Nat'l Mon., N. Mex.		A 3	157
Elmwood Park, Ill.	24,016	B 5	139
El Paso, Texas	425,259	A 10	168
El Reno, Okla.	15,486	F 3	162
El Salvador	4,813,000	C 4	122
Elyria, Ohio	57,538	F 3	161
Emmaus, Pa.	11,001	M 4	164
Emporia, Kans.	25,287	F 3	142
Endicott, N.Y.	14,457	H 6	158
Enewetak (atoll)	542	G 4	89
Enfield, Conn.	42,695	E 1	135
Enfield, Eng.	260,900	H 7	11
England	46,220,955		11
Englewood, Colo.	30,021	K 3	134
Englewood, N.J.	23,701	C 2	156
English (chan.), Europe		D 8	11
Enid, Okla.	50,363	G 2	162
Enschede, Neth.	141,597	K 4	25
Entebbe, Uganda	21,096	N 12	57
Enugu, Nigeria	187,000	H 10	54
Enzeli (Bandar-e Anzali), Iran	55,978	F 2	68
Ephrata, Pa.	11,095	K 5	164
Equatorial Guinea	244,000	H 11	57
Erbil, Iraq	90,320	D 2	68
Erfurt, E. Ger.	202,979	D 3	20
Erie (lake), N. Amer.		K 5	94
Erie, Pa.	119,123	B 1	164
Eritrea (reg.), Eth.		O 8	54
Erivan, U.S.S.R.	1,019,000	F 6	50
Erzgebirge (mts.), Europe		E 3	20
Erzurum, Turkey	162,973	J 3	64
Escalante (des.), Utah		A 6	169
Escanaba, Mich.	14,355	C 3	148
Escondido, Calif.	64,355	J 10	133
Eskişehir, Turkey	259,952	D 3	64
Espiritu Santo (isl.), Vanuatu	16,220	G 7	89
Essen, W. Ger.	677,568	B 3	20
Essex, Md.	39,614	J 3	146
Essex, Vt.	14,392	A 2	155
Estonian S.S.R., U.S.S.R.	1,466,000	C 1	51
Ethiopia	31,065,000	O 9	54
Etna (vol.), Italy		E 6	32
Eton, Eng.	4,950	G 8	11
Etosha (salt pan), Namibia		J 15	57
Euboea (Évvoia) (isl.), Greece		G 6	43
Euclid, Ohio	59,999	J 9	161
Eugene, Oreg.	105,624	D 3	163
Eunice, La.	12,749	F 6	144
Euphrates (riv.), Asia		D 4	68
Eureka, Calif.	24,153	A 3	133
Europe	676,000,000		6
Evans (mt.), Colo.		H 3	134
Evanston, Ill.	73,706	B 5	139
Evansville, Ind.	130,496	C 9	140
Everest (mt.), Asia		F 3	70
Everett, Mass.	37,195	D 6	147
Everett, Wash.	54,413	C 3	171
Everglades Nat'l Pk., Fla.		F 6	136
Évvoia (isl.), Greece		G 6	43
Ewa Beach, Hawaii	14,369	B 4	130
Exeter, Eng.	93,300	D 7	11
Exeter, N.H.	11,024	F 6	155
Eyre (lake), Austr.		F 5	86
Ez Zarqa', Jordan	263,400	E 3	67

F

	Pop.	Key	Pg.
Faeroe (isls.), Den.	41,969	B 2	19
Fairbanks, Alaska	22,645	K 1	130
Fairborn, Ohio	29,702	B 6	161
Fairfax, Va.	19,390	M 3	170
Fairfield, Calif.	58,099	K 1	133
Fairfield, Conn.	54,849	B 4	135
Fairfield, Ohio	30,777	A 7	161
Fair Lawn, N.J.	32,229	B 1	156
Fairmont, W. Va.	23,863	F 2	172
Fairweather (mt.), N. Amer.		L 3	130
Faisalabad, Pak.	822,263	C 2	70
Falcon (res.), N. Amer.		E 11	168
Falkland Islands	1,813	H 14	93
Fall River, Mass.	92,574	K 6	147
Falmouth, Mass.	23,640	M 6	147
Famagusta, Cyprus	38,960	F 5	64
Fanning (Tabuaeran) (isl.), Kiribati	340	L 5	89
Farewell (cape), Greenl.		O 4	94
Farallon (isls.), Calif.		B 6	133
Fargo, N. Dak.	61,383	S 6	160
Faribault, Minn.	16,241	E 6	149
Farmington, N. Mex.	31,222	A 2	157
Farmington Hills, Mich.	58,056	F 6	148
Faro, Port.	20,470	B 4	30
Farrukhabad (Fatehgarh), India	102,768	D 3	70
Fayetteville, Ark.	36,608	B 1	132
Fayetteville, N.C.	59,507	H 4	159
Fear (cape), N.C.		K 7	159
Fergana, U.S.S.R.	176,000	H 5	46
Fergus Falls, Minn.	12,519	B 4	149
Ferrara, Italy	97,507	C 2	32
Fès, Mor.	325,327	F 5	54
Fezzan (reg.), Libya		J 6	54
Fianarantsoa, Madag.	68,054	R 16	57
Fiji	588,068	H 8	89
Findlay, Ohio	35,594	C 3	161
Finisterre (cape), Spain		B 1	31
Finland	4,788,000		16
Finland (gulf), Europe		G 3	6
Finlay (riv.), Br. Col.		E 1	117
Fire Isl. Nat'l Seashore, N.Y.		F 2	158
Firenze (Florence), Italy	441,654	C 3	32
Fitchburg, Mass.	39,580	G 2	147
Fiume, see Rijeka, Yugo.			
Fiumicino, Italy	13,180	F 7	32
Flagstaff, Ariz.	34,743	D 3	131
Flaming Gorge (res.), U.S.		C 4	174
Flanders (provs.), Belg.		C-D 7	25
Flathead (lake), Mont.		C 3	152
Flattery (cape), Wash.		A 2	171
Flensburg, W. Ger.	92,313	C 1	20
Flint, Mich.	159,611	F 5	148
Floral Park, N.Y.	16,805	A 3	158
Florence, Ala.	37,029	C 1	129
Florence, Italy	441,654	C 3	32
Florence, Ky.	15,586	J 2	129
Florence, S.C.	29,176	H 3	165
Flores (isl.), Indon.	860,328	G 7	83
Florianópolis, Braz.	153,547	L 9	93
Florida (bay), Fla.		F 6	136
Florida (state), U.S.	4,788,000		136
Florissant, Mo.	55,372	P 2	151
Florissant Fossil Beds Nat'l Mon., Colo.		J 5	134
Flushing, Neth.	43,806	C 6	25
Foggia, Italy	136,436	E 4	32
Folkestone, Eng.	45,610	J 6	11
Fond du Lac, Wis.	35,863	K 8	173
Fongafale (cap.), Tuvalu		H 6	89
Fonseca (gulf), Cent. Amer.		O 4	122
Fontainebleau, France	16,436	E 3	26
Fontana, Calif.	37,107	E 10	133
Foochow, see Fuzhou, China			
Forlì, Italy	83,303	D 2	32
Formosa (Taiwan) (isl.), China	16,609,961	K 7	77
Fortaleza, Braz.	648,815	N 4	90
Ft. Belvoir, Va.	7,726	K 3	170
Ft. Benning, Ga.		B 6	137
Ft. Bliss, Texas	12,687	A 2	168
Ft. Bowie Nat'l Hist. Site, Ariz.		F 6	131
Ft. Bragg, N.C.	37,834	H 4	159
Ft. Campbell, U.S.		C 7	143
Ft. Caroline Nat'l Mem., Fla.		E 1	136
Ft. Clatsop Nat'l Mem., Oreg.		C 1	163
Ft. Collins, Colo.	65,092	J 1	134
Ft. Davis Nat'l Hist. Site, Texas		D 11	168
Ft.-de-France (cap.), Martinique	97,649	G 4	124
Ft. Dodge, Iowa	29,423	E 3	141
Ft. Donelson Nat'l Mil. Pk., Tenn.		F 2	167
Ft. Frederica Nat'l Mon., Ga.		K 8	137
Ft. George G. Meade, Md.	14,083	G 4	146
Forth (firth), Scot.		F 4	13
Ft. Jefferson Nat'l Mon., Fla.		C 7	136
Ft. Knox, Ky.	31,055	F 5	143
Ft. Laramie Nat'l Hist. Site, Wyo.		H 3	174
Ft. Larned Nat'l Hist. Site, Kans.		C 3	142
Ft. Lauderdale, Fla.	153,279	C 4	136
Ft. Lee, N.J.	32,449	C 2	156
Ft. Lee, Va.	9,784	K 6	170
Ft. Leonard Wood, Mo.	21,262	H 7	151
Ft. Macleod, Alta.	3,139	D 5	114
Ft. Madison, Iowa	13,520	L 7	141
Ft. Matanzas Nat'l Mon., Fla.		E 2	136
Ft. McHenry Nat'l Mon., Md.		H 3	146
Ft. McMurray, Alta.	31,000	E 1	114
Ft. Myers, Fla.	36,638	E 5	136
Ft. Peck Lake (res.), Mont.		K 3	152
Ft. Pierce, Fla.	33,802	F 4	136
Ft. Point Nat'l Hist. Site, Calif.		J 2	133
Ft. Pulaski Nat'l Mon., Ga.		L 6	137
Ft. Raleigh Nat'l Hist. Site, N.C.		O 3	159
Ft. Riley, Kans.	18,233	F 2	142
Ft. Sill, Okla.	15,924	F 5	162
Ft. Smith, Ark.	71,626	B 3	132
Ft. Smith, N.W.T.	2,298	E 3	96
Ft. Sumter Nat'l Mon., S.C.		H 6	165
Ft. Thomas, Ky.	16,012	L 1	143
Ft. Union Nat'l Mon., N. Mex.		E 3	157
Ft. Union Trading Post Nat'l Hist. Site, N. Dak.		B 3	160
Ft. Vancouver Nat'l Hist. Site, Wash.		C 5	171
Ft. Walton Beach, Fla.	20,829	C 6	136
Ft. Wayne, Ind.	172,028	G 2	140
Ft. Worth, Texas	385,164	F 2	168
Fostoria, Ohio	15,743	D 3	161
Fountain Valley, Calif.	55,080	D 11	133
Foxe (basin), N.W.T.		J 2	96
Framingham, Mass.	65,113	A 7	147
France	53,788,000		26
Francis Case (lake), S. Dak.		L 7	166
Francistown, Botswana	22,000	M 16	57
Frankfort, Ind.	15,168	E 4	140
Frankfort (cap.), Ky.	25,973	H 4	143
Frankfurt-am-Main, W. Ger.	636,157	C 3	20
Frankfurt-an-der-Oder, E. Ger.	70,817	F 2	20
Franklin D. Roosevelt (lake), Wash.		G 2	171
Franz Josef Land (isls.), U.S.S.R.		E-G 1	46
Fraser (riv.), Br. Col.		F 4	117
Fraser, Mich.	14,560	B 6	148
Fredericia, Den.	36,157	C 6	19
Frederick, Md.	28,086	E 3	146
Fredericksburg, Va.	15,322	J 4	170
Fredericton (cap.), N. Br.	43,723	D 3	102
Frederiksberg, Den.	101,874	F 6	19
Frederikshavn, Den.	24,846	D 3	19
Freeport, Ill.	26,266	D 1	139
Freeport, N.Y.	38,272	B 4	158
Freetown (cap.), S. Leone	274,000	D 10	54
Freiburg im Breisgau, W. Ger.	175,371	B 5	20
Fremantle, Austr.	22,484	B 2	86
Fremont, Calif.	131,945	K 3	133
Fremont, Nebr.	23,979	H 3	153
French Guiana	73,022	K 3	90
French Polynesia	137,382	M 8	89
Fresno, Calif.	217,289	F 7	133
Fribourg, Switz.	41,600	D 3	37
Fridley, Minn.	30,228	G 5	149
Friedrichshafen, W. Ger.	51,544	C 5	20
Friesland (prov.), Neth.		G 1	25
Frobisher Bay, N.W.T.	2,333	K 2	96
Front Royal, Va.	11,126	H 3	170
Frunze, U.S.S.R.	533,000	H 5	46
Fujairah, U.A.E.		G 4	61
Fuji (mt.), Japan		J 6	75
Fujian (Fukien) (prov.), China		J 6	77
Fujisawa, Japan	265,975	O 3	75
Fukui, Japan	231,634	G 5	75
Fukuoka, Japan	1,002,201	D 7	75
Fukushima, Japan	246,531	K 5	75
Fukuyama, Japan	329,714	F 6	75
Fullerton, Calif.	102,034	D 11	133
Fulton, Mo.	11,046	J 5	151
Funabashi, Japan	423,101	P 2	75
Funchal, Port.	38,340	A 2	32
Fundy (bay), N. Amer.		E 3	102
Fundy Nat'l Pk., N. Br.		E 3	102
Fürth, W. Ger.	101,639	D 4	20
Fushun, China	1,700,000	K 3	77
Füssen, W. Ger.	10,506	D 5	20
Fuxin, China	350,000	K 3	77
Fuzhou, China	900,000	J 6	77

G

	Pop.	Key	Pg.
Gabès (gulf), Tun.		J 5	54
Gabon	551,000	J 12	57
Gaborone (cap.), Bots.	21,000	L 16	57
Gadsden, Ala.	47,565	G 2	129
Gaffney, S.C.	13,453	D 1	165
Gafsa, Tun.	42,225	H 5	54
Gainesville, Fla.	81,371	D 2	136
Gainesville, Ga.	15,280	E 2	137
Gaithersburg, Md.	26,424	F 4	146
Galápagos (isls.), Ecua.		J 9	94
Galaţi, Rom.	252,884	H 3	43
Galesburg, Ill.	35,305	C 3	139
Galicia (reg.), Spain		B 1	31
Galilee (reg.), Isr.		C 2	67
Gallatin, Tenn.	17,191	H 2	167
Galle, Sri Lanka	72,720	D 7	70
Gallipoli, Turkey	13,466	A 1	64
Gallup, N. Mex.	18,167	A 3	157
Galveston, Texas	61,902	L 3	168
Galway, Ire.	27,726	C 5	15
Gambia	601,000	C 9	54
Gander, Newf.	10,404	C 3	99
Ganges (riv.), Asia		F 3	70
Gangtok, India	12,000	F 3	70
Garda (lake), Italy		C 2	32
Garden City, Kans.	18,256	B 4	142
Garden City, N.Y.	22,927	B 3	158
Garden Grove, Calif.	123,307	D 11	133
Garfield, N.J.	26,803	B 2	156
Garfield Heights, Ohio	34,938	J 9	161
Garland, Texas	138,857	H 2	168
Garmisch-Partenkirchen, W. Ger.	26,831	D 5	20
Garonne (riv.), France		C 5	26
Gary, Ind.	151,953	C 1	140
Gaspé (pen.), Que.		D 2	105
Gastonia, N.C.	47,333	C 4	159
Gates of the Arctic Nat'l Pk., Alaska		D 2	130
Gateway Nat'l Rec. Area, U.S.		D 3	158
Gauhati, India	123,783	G 3	70
Gaya, India	179,884	F 4	70

	Pop.	Key	Pg.
Gaza Strip, Egypt		A 5	67
Gaziantep, Turkey	300,882	G 4	64
Gdańsk, Pol.	364,385	D 1	45
Gdańsk (gulf), Pol.		D 1	45
Gdynia, Pol.	190,125	D 1	45
Gejiu, China	250,000	F 7	77
Gelsenkirchen, W. Ger.	322,584	B 3	20
General Grant Grove Section, Kings Canyon Nat'l Pk., Calif.		G 7	133
Geneva (lake), Europe		C 4	37
Geneva, N.Y.	15,133	G 5	158
Geneva, Switz.	163,100	B 4	37
Genoa (Genova), Italy	787,011	B 2	32
George Rogers Clark Nat'l Hist. Pk., Ind.		B 7	140
Georgetown (cap.), Cayman Is.	7,617	A 3	124
Georgetown (cap.), Guyana	63,184	J 2	90
George Town (Pinang), Malaysia	269,603	C 6	81
George Washington Birthplace Nat'l Mon., Va.		L 4	170
George Washington Carver Nat'l Mon., Mo.		D 9	151
Georgia (str.), Br. Col.		E 5	117
Georgia (state), U.S.	5,463,105		137
Georgian (bay), Ont.		C-D 2	108
Georgian S.S.R., U.S.S.R.	5,015,000	D 5	50
Geraldton, Austr.	20,895	A 5	86
Germany, East	16,737,000		20
Germany, West	61,658,000		20
Gettysburg, Pa.	7,194	H 6	164
Ghana	11,450,000	F 10	54
Ghazni, Afghan.	30,425	B 2	70
Ghent, Belg.	148,860	D 6	25
Gibraltar	29,760	D 4	31
Gibraltar (str.)		D 5	31
Gibson (des.), Austr.		D 4	86
Gifu, Japan	408,707	H 6	75
Gijón, Spain	159,806	D 1	31
Gila (riv.), U.S.		B 6	131
Gila Cliff Dwellings Nat'l Mon., N. Mex.		A 5	157
Gilbert Is. (Kiribati)	47,711	H 6	89
Gillette, Wyo.	12,134	G 1	174
Gironde (riv.), France		C 5	26
Giza, Egypt	1,246,713	B 4	60
Glace Bay, N.S.	21,466	J 2	100
Glacier Bay Nat'l Pk., Alaska		M 3	130
Glacier Nat'l Pk., Br. Col.		J 4	117
Glacier Nat'l Pk., Mont.		C 2	152
Glasgow, Scot.	880,617	B 2	13
Glassboro, N.J.	14,574	C 4	156
Glastonbury, Conn.	24,327	E 2	135
Glen Burnie, Md.	37,263	H 4	146
Glen Canyon Nat'l Rec. Area, U.S.		D 6	169
Glen Cove, N.Y.	24,618	A 3	158
Glendale, Ariz.	97,172	C 5	131
Glendale, Calif.	139,060	C 10	133
Glens Falls, N.Y.	15,897	N 4	158
Glenview, Ill.	32,060	B 5	139
Gliwice, Pol.	170,912	A 4	45
Gloucester, Eng.	91,600	E 6	11
Gloucester, Mass.	27,768	M 2	147
Gloversville, N.Y.	17,836	M 4	158
Goa (dist.), India		C 5	70
Gobi (des.), Asia		G 3	77
Godavari (riv.), India		D 5	70
Godhavn (Qeqertarsuaq), Greenl.	1,012	C 12	4
Godthab (Nuuk) (cap.), Greenl.	9,561	C 12	4
Godwin Austen (K2) (mt.), India		D 1	70
Goiânia, Braz.	703,263	L 7	90
Golan Heights, Syria		D 1	67
Golconda (ruins), India		D 5	70
Gold Coast, Austr.	135,437	J 5	86
Golden, Colo.	12,237	J 3	134
Golden Gate Nat'l Rec. Area, Calif.		H 2	133
Golden Spike Nat'l Hist. Site, Utah		B 2	169
Golden Valley, Minn.	22,775	G 5	149
Goldsboro, N.C.	31,871	K 4	159
Gomel', U.S.S.R.	383,000	D 4	50
Gonâve (isl.), Haiti		D 3	124
Gondar, Eth.	38,600	O 9	54
Good Hope (cape), S. Africa		C 20	57
Goose (lake), U.S.		G 5	163
Goose Bay-Happy Valley, Newf.	7,103	D 2	99
Gorakhpur, India	230,911	E 3	70
Gorham, Maine	10,101	C 8	145
Gor'kiy, U.S.S.R.	1,344,000	F 3	50
Gorlovka, U.S.S.R.	336,000	E 5	50
Goshen, Ind.	19,665	F 1	140
Göta (canal), Sweden		J 7	16
Göteborg, Sweden	444,540	G 8	16
Gotland (isl.), Sweden		D 3	16
Göttingen, W. Ger.	123,797	D 3	20
Gouda, Neth.	56,403	F 4	25
Granada, Spain	185,799	E 4	31
Gran Canaria (isl.), Spain		B 5	30
Gran Chaco (reg.), S. Amer.		H 9	93
Grand (canal), China		J 4	77
Grand Bahama (isl.), Bah.	33,102	B 1	124
Grand Canyon Nat'l Pk., Ariz.		C 2	131
Grand Cayman (isl.), Cayman Is.	15,000	B 3	124
Grande (riv.), Bol.		H 7	90
Grande, Rio (riv.), N. Amer.		H 7	94
Grande Prairie, Alta.	24,263	A 2	114
Grand Forks, N. Dak.	43,765	R 4	160
Grand Island, Nebr.	33,180	F 4	153
Grand Junction, Colo.	27,956	B 4	134
Grand Manan (isl.), N. Br.		D 4	102
Grand Portage Nat'l Mon., Minn.		G 2	149
Grand Prairie, Texas	71,462	G 2	168
Grand Rapids, Mich.	181,843	D 5	148
Grand Teton Nat'l Pk., Wyo.		B 2	174
Granite City, Ill.	36,815	A 2	139
Grants, N. Mex.	11,439	B 3	157
Grants Pass, Oreg.	15,032	D 5	163
Grasse, France	24,260	G 6	26
Gravesend, Eng.	53,500	J 8	11
Graz, Austria	251,900	C 3	39
Great Abaco (isl.), Bah.	7,324	C 1	124
Gt. Australian (bight), Austr.		D-E 6	86
Gt. Barrier (reef), Austr.		H-J 2-3	86
Gt. Bear (lake), N.W.T.		D 2	99
Great Bend, Kans.	16,608	D 3	142
Great Britain & Northern Ireland (United Kingdom)	55,672,000		8
Gt. Dividing (range), Austr.		H-J 4-5	86
Gt. Eastern Erg (des.), Africa		H 5	54
Gt. Exuma (isl.), Bah.		C 2	124
Great Falls, Mont.	56,725	E 3	152
Gt. Inagua (isl.), Bah.	939	D 2	124
Gt. Salt (lake), Utah		B 2-3	169
Gt. Sand Dunes Nat'l Mon., Colo.		H 7	134
Gt. Sandy (des.), Austr.		C 4	86
Gt. Slave (lake), N.W.T.		E 3	96
Gt. Smoky (mts.), U.S.		C 8	159
Gt. Smoky Mts. Nat'l Pk., Tenn.		C 8	159
Gt. Victoria (des.), Austr.		D-E 5	86
Gt. Wall (ruins), China		G 4	77
Gt. Western Erg (des.), Alg.		G 5	54
Greece	9,599,000		43
Greece, N.Y.	16,177	E 4	158
Greeley, Colo.	53,006	K 2	134
Green (riv.), U.S.		D 3	126
Green (mts.), Vt.		B1-4	155
Green Bay, Wis.	87,899	K 6	173
Greeneville, Tenn.	14,097	Q 2	167
Greenfield, Mass.	18,436	D 2	147
Greenfield, Wis.	31,467	L 2	173
Greenland	49,773	B 12	4
Greenland (sea)		B 10	4
Greensboro, N.C.	155,642	F 2	159
Greensburg, Pa.	17,558	D 5	164
Greenville, Miss.	40,613	B 4	150
Greenville, N.C.	35,740	L 3	159
Greenville, S.C.	581,242	C 2	165
Greenwich, Conn.	59,578	A 4	135
Greenwich, Eng.	207,200	H 8	11
Greenwood, Miss.	20,115	D 4	150
Greenwood, S.C.	21,613	C 3	165
Grenada	103,103	G 4	124
Grenadines (isls.), W. Indies		G 4	124
Grenoble, France	165,431	F 5	26
Gresham, Oreg.	33,005	B 2	163
Gretna, La.	20,615	O 4	144
Griffin, Ga.	20,728	D 4	137
Grodno, U.S.S.R.	195,000	B 4	50
Groningen, Neth.	163,357	K 2	25
Grosse Pointe Woods, Mich.	18,886	B 6	148
Grossglockner (mt.), Austria		B 3	39
Groton, Conn.	10,086	G 3	135
Groznyy, U.S.S.R.	375,000	G 6	50
Guadalajara, Mex.	1,478,383	H 6	119
Guadalajara, Spain	30,924	E 2	31
Guadalcanal (isl.), Sol. Is.	46,619	F 7	89
Guadalquivir (riv.), Spain		C 4	31
Guadalupe (mts.), U.S.		D 6	157
Guadalupe Mts. Nat'l Pk., Texas		C 10	168
Guadeloupe	328,400	F 3	124
Guainía (riv.), S. Amer.		G 3	90
Guajira (pen.), S. Amer.		F 1	90
Guam	105,979	E 4	89
Guanabacoa, Cuba	89,741	A 2	124
Guangdong (Kwangtung) (prov.), China		H 7	77
Guangzhou, China	2,300,000	H 7	77
Guantánamo, Cuba	178,129	C 2	124
Guantánamo (bay), Cuba		C 3	124
Guardafui (cape), Somalia		S 9	54
Guatemala	7,262,419	B 3	122
Guatemala (cap.), Guat.	700,538	B 3	122
Guayaquil, Ecua.	823,219	D 4	90
Guelph, Ont.	71,207	D 4	108
Guernsey (isl.), Chan. Is.	51,351	E 8	11
Guilford, Conn.	2,555	E 3	135
Guilin, China	225,000	G 6	77
Guinea	5,143,284	D 9	54
Guinea (gulf), Africa		F 11	57
Guinea-Bissau	777,214	C 9	54
Guiyang, China	1,500,000	G 6	77
Gujranwala, Pak.	360,419	C 2	70
Gulbarga, India	145,588	D 5	70
Gulf Isls. Nat'l Seashore, Fla.		B 6	136
Gulf Isls. Nat'l Seashore, Miss.		G 10	150
Gulfport, Miss.	39,696	F 10	150
Guntur, India	269,991	D 5	70
Gur'yev, U.S.S.R.	131,000	F 5	46
Guthrie, Okla.	10,312	H 3	162
Guyana	820,000	J 2	90
Gwalior, India	384,772	D 3	70
Gyor, Hung.	123,618	D 3	39

H

	Pop.	Key	Pg.
Haarlem, Neth.	164,172	F 4	25
Habik, Japan	94,160	J 8	75
Hachinohe, Japan	224,366	K 3	75
Hachioji, Japan	322,580	O 2	75
Hackensack, N.J.	36,039	D 2	156
Haddonfield, N.J.	12,337	B 3	156
Hadhramaut (reg.), P.D.R. Yemen		E-F 6	60
Haeju, N. Korea	140,000	B 4	74
Hagen, W. Ger.	229,224	B 3	20
Hagerstown, Md.	34,132	C 2	146
Hague, The (cap.), Neth.	479,369	E 4	25
Haifa, Isr.	227,800	B 2	67
Haikou, China	500,000	H 7	77
Hainan (isl.), China		H 8	77
Haiphong, Viet.	*1,279,067	E 2	81
Haiti	5,009,000	D 3	124
Hakodate, Japan	307,453	K 3	75
Haleakala Nat'l Pk., Hawaii		F 3	130
Haleb (Aleppo), Syria	639,428	G 4	64
Halifax (cap.), N.S.	*277,727	E 4	100
Hallandale, Fla.	36,517	B 4	136
Halle, E. Ger.	241,425	D 3	20
Halmahera (isl.), Indon.	122,521	H 5	83
Hama, Syria	137,421	G 5	64
Hamadan, Iran	155,846	F 3	68
Hamamatsu, Japan	468,884	H 6	75
Hamburg, W. Ger.	1,717,383	D 2	20
Hamden, Conn.	51,071	D 3	135
Hamersley (range), Austr.		B 4	86
Hamhŭng, N. Korea	484,000	C 4	74
Hamilton (cap.), Bermuda	1,617	G 3	124
Hamilton, N.Z.	91,109	L 6	87
Hamilton, Ohio	63,189	A 7	164
Hamilton, Ont.	*542,095	E 4	108
Hamm, W. Ger.	172,210	B 3	20
Hammerfest, Nor.	7,610	N 1	16
Hammond, Ind.	93,714	B 1	140
Hammond, La.	15,043	N 1	144
Hampton, Va.	122,617	M 6	170
Hamtramck, Mich.	21,300	B 6	148
Han (riv.), S. Korea		C 5	75
Handan, China	500,000	H 4	77
Hanford, Calif.	20,958	F 7	133
Hanford Atomic Energy Reservation, Wash.		F 4	171
Hangzhou (Hangchow), China	1,500,000	J 5	77
Hannibal, Mo.	18,811	K 3	151
Hannover, W. Ger.	552,955	C 2	20
Hanoi (cap.), Viet.	*2,570,905	E 2	81
Hanover, N.H.	6,861	C 4	155
Harare (cap.), Zim.	601,000	N 15	57
Harbin, China	2,750,000	L 2	77
Hardanger (fjord), Nor.		D 7	16
Hargeysa, Somalia	40,254	Q 10	54
Harlingen, Texas	43,543	G 11	168
Harpers Ferry Nat'l Hist. Site, W. Va.		L 2	172
Harper Woods, Mich.	16,361	B 6	148
Harrisburg (cap.), Pa.	53,264	H 5	164
Harrison, N.Y.	23,046	J 1	158
Harrisonburg, Va.	19,671	F 4	170
Harrodsburg, Ky.	7,265	H 5	143
Harrow, Eng.	200,200	G 8	11
Hartford (cap.), Conn.	136,392	E 1	135
Harvey, Ill.	35,810	B 6	139
Harz (mts.), Ger.		D 3	20
Hastings, Nebr.	23,045	F 4	153
Hatteras (cape), N.C.		P 4	159
Hattiesburg, Miss.	40,829	F 8	150
Havana (cap.), Cuba	1,924,886	A 2	124
Havasu (lake), U.S.		A 4	131
Haverhill, Mass.	46,865	K 1	147
Havre, Mont.	10,891	G 2	152
Hawaii (isl.), Hawaii		F 4	130
Hawaii (state), U.S.	964,691		130
Hawaiian (isls.), U.S.		J-L 3-4	89
Hawaii Volcanoes Nat'l Pk., Hawaii		F 4	130
Hawthorne, Calif.	56,447	C 11	133
Hawthorne, N.J.	18,200	B 2	156
Hay River, N.W.T.	2,863	E 3	96
Hays, Kans.	16,301	C 3	142
Hayward, Calif.	94,342	K 2	133
Hazel Park, Mich.	20,914	B 6	148
Hazleton, Pa.	27,318	L 4	164
Hebei (Hopei) (prov.), China		J 4	77
Hebrides (isls.), Scot.		C1-2	8
Hebron, West Bank	38,309	C 4	67
Hefei, China	400,000	J 5	77
Hegang, China	350,000	L 2	77
Heidelberg, W. Ger.	129,368	C 4	20
Hejaz (reg.), Saudi Arabia		C-D 4-5	60
Hekla (mt.), Iceland		B 1	19
Helena (cap.), Mont.	23,938	E 4	152
Helgoland (isl.), W. Ger.		C 1	20
Helmand (riv.), Afghan.		B 2	70
Helsingborg, Sweden	80,986	H 8	16
Helsinki (cap.), Fin.	502,961	O 6	16
Hempstead, N.Y.	40,404	B 3	158
Henan (Honan) (prov.), China		H 5	77
Henderson, Ky.	24,834	B 5	143
Henderson, Nev.	24,363	G 6	154
Henderson, N.C.	13,522	J 2	159
Hengyang, China	310,000	H 6	77
Herat, Afghan.	103,960	A 2	70
Herbert Hoover Nat'l Hist. Site, Iowa		L 5	141
Hermon (mt.), Asia		D 1	67
Hermosillo, Mex.	232,691	D 2	119
Herne, W. Ger.	190,561	B 3	20
Hershey, Pa.	13,249	J 5	164
Hesse (state), W. Ger.		C 3	20
Hialeah, Fla.	145,254	B 4	136
Hibbing, Minn.	21,193	F 3	149
Hickory, N.C.	20,757	C 3	159
Hicksville, N.Y.	43,245	B 3	158
Higashiosaka, Japan	524,750	J 8	75
Highland Park, Ill.	30,611	B 5	139
Highland Park, Mich.	27,909	B 6	148
High Point, N.C.	63,380	E 3	159
Hillsboro, Oreg.	27,664	A 2	163
Hillside, N.J.	21,440	B 2	156
Hilo, Hawaii	35,269	F 4	130
Himalaya (mts.), Asia		D-G 2-3	70
Himeji, Japan	436,086	G 6	75
Hindu Kush (mts.), Asia		B-C1	70
Hingham, Mass.	20,339	E 8	147
Hinsdale, Ill.	16,726	B 6	139
Hirakata, Japan	297,618	J 7	75
Hiroshima, Japan	852,611	E 6	75
Hispaniola (isl.), W. Indies	10,440,000	D 2	124
Hitachi, Japan	202,383	K 5	75
Hobart, Austr.	128,603	H 8	86
Hobart, Ind.	22,987	C 1	140
Hobbs, N. Mex.	29,153	F 6	157
Hoboken, N.J.	42,460	C 2	156
Ho Chi Minh City, Viet.	3,419,678	E 5	81
Hodeida, Yemen Arab Rep.	80,314	D 7	60
Hoffman Estates, Ill.	37,272	A 5	139
Hofuf, Saudi Arabia	101,271	E 4	60
Hohhot, China	700,000	H 3	77
Holguín, Cuba	190,155	C 2	124
Holland, Mich.	26,281	C 6	148
Hollywood, Calif.		C 10	133
Hollywood, Fla.	121,323	B 4	136
Holon, Isr.	121,200	B 3	67
Holyoke, Mass.	44,678	D 4	147
Homestead, Fla.	20,668	F 6	136
Homestead Nat'l Mon., Nebr.		H 4	153
Homewood, Ala.	21,412	E 4	129
Homs, Libya	66,890	J 5	54
Homs, Syria	215,423	G 5	64
Honduras	3,691,000	D 3	122
Honduras (gulf), Cent. Amer.		D 2	122
Hong Kong	5,022,000	H 7	77
Honiara (cap.), Sol. Is.	14,942	F 6	89
Honolulu (cap.), Hawaii	365,048	C 4	130
Honshu (isl.), Japan		J 5	77
Hood (mt.), Oreg.		F 2	163
Hoover (dam), U.S.		G 7	154
Hope, Ark.	10,290	C 6	132
Hopewell, Va.	23,397	K 6	170
Hopkins, Minn.	15,336	G 5	149
Hopkinsville, Ky.	27,318	B 7	143
Horn (cape), Chile		G 15	93

	Pop.	Key	Pg.
Hornell, N.Y.	10,234	E 6	158
Horseshoe Bend Nat'l Mil. Pk., Ala.		G 5	129
Hospitalet, Spain	241,978	H 2	31
Hot Springs Nat'l Park, Ark.	35,781	D 4	132
Hot Springs Nat'l Pk., Ark.		D 4	132
Houma, La.	32,602	J 7	144
Houston, Texas	1,595,138	J 2	168
Hovenweep Nat'l Mon., U.S.		E 6	169
Huainan, China	350,000	J 5	77
Huang He (Yellow) (riv.), China		J 4	77
Huánuco, Peru	52,628	E 6	90
Huascarán (mt.), Peru		E 5	90
Hubbell Trading Post Nat'l Hist. Site, Ariz.		F 3	131
Hubli-Dharwar, India	379,176	C 5	70
Huddersfield, Eng.	130,060	J 2	11
Hudson (bay), Can.		H 3	96
Hudson (str.), Can.		J 3	96
Hudson (riv.), U.S.		N 7	158
Hue, Viet.	209,043	E 3	81
Huelva, Spain	96,689	C 4	31
Hull, Eng.	276,000	G 4	11
Hull, Que.	56,225	B 4	105
Humber (riv.), Eng.		G 4	11
Humphreys (peak), Ariz.		D 3	131
Hunan (prov.), China		H 6	77
Hungary	10,709,536		39
Hŭngnam, N. Korea		D 4	74
Huntington, Ind.	16,202	G 3	140
Huntington, W. Va.	63,684	A 4	172
Huntington Beach, Calif.	170,505	C11	133
Huntington Park, Calif.	46,223	C11	133
Huntington Sta., N.Y.	28,769	B 3	158
Huntsville, Ala.	142,513	E 1	129
Huntsville, Texas	23,936	J 7	168
Huron (lake), N. Amer.		K 2	126
Huron, S. Dak.	13,000	N 5	166
Hutchinson, Kans.	40,284	D 3	142
Hyannis, Mass.	9,118	N 6	147
Hyattsville, Md.	12,709	B 4	146
Hyderabad, India	1,607,396	D 5	70
Hyderabad, Pak.	628,310	B 3	70

I

	Pop.	Key	Pg.
Iaşi, Rom.	262,493	H 2	43
Ibadan, Nigeria	847,000	G10	54
Ibagué, Col.	176,223	E 3	90
Ibiza (isl.), Spain		G 3	31
Iceland	228,785	B 1	19
Ichang (Yichang), Japan	150,000	H 5	75
Ichikawa, Japan	319,291	P 2	75
Ichinomiya, Japan	238,463	H 6	75
Idaho (state), U.S.	944,038		138
Idaho Falls, Idaho	39,590	F 6	138
Ife, Nigeria	176,000	G10	54
Iguazú (falls), S. Amer.		K 9	90
IJsselmeer (lake), Neth.		G 3	25
Iliamna (lake), Alaska		H 3	130
Illinois (state), U.S.	11,426,596		139
Iloilo, Phil.	244,827	G 3	83
Ilorin, Nigeria	282,000	G10	54
Imphal, India	100,366	G 4	70
Inch'ŏn, S. Korea	800,007	C 5	74
Independence, Kans.	10,598	G 4	142
Independence, Mo.	111,806	R 5	151
India	683,810,051		70
Indiana, Pa.	16,051	D 4	164
Indiana (state), U.S.	5,490,260		140
Indiana Dunes Nat'l Lakeshore, Ind.		C 1	140
Indianapolis (cap.), Ind.	700,807	E 5	140
Indian Ocean		H10	58
Indigirka (riv.), U.S.S.R.		P 3	46
Indio, Calif.	21,611	J 10	133
Indochina (reg.), Asia		D-E 2-4	81
Indonesia	147,490,298	G-H 7	83
Indore, India	543,381	D 4	70
Indus (riv.), Asia		B 3	70
Inglewood, Calif.	94,245	B11	133
Inkster, Mich.	35,190	B 7	148
Inn (riv.), Europe		B 2	39
Inner Mongolia (reg.), China		G-J 3	77
Innsbruck, Austria	167,200	A 3	39
Insein, Burma	143,625	C 3	81
International Peace Garden, N. Amer.		K 1	160
Inuvik, N.W.T.	3,147	D 2	96
Inverness, Scot.	35,801	D 3	13
Iona (isl.), Scot.		B 4	13
Ionian (isls.), Greece		D 6	43
Iowa (state), U.S.	2,913,808		141
Iowa City, Iowa	50,508	L 5	141
Ipoh, Malaysia	247,953	D 6	81
Ipswich, Eng.	121,500	J 5	11
Iquitos, Peru	173,629	F 4	90
Iráklion, Greece	77,506	G 8	43
Iran	37,447,000	F 3	68
Irapuato, Mex.	135,596	J 6	119
Iraq	12,767,000	D 3	68
Irbid, Jordan	136,770	D 2	67
Ireland	3,440,427		15
Ireland, Northern, U.K.	1,543,000	G-H 2	15
Irish (sea), Europe		D 4	8
Irkutsk, U.S.S.R.	550,000	L 4	46
Irondequoit, N.Y.	57,648	E 4	158
Ironton, Ohio	14,290	E 8	161
Irrawaddy (riv.), Burma		B 3	81
Irtysh (riv.), U.S.S.R.		G 4	46
Irvine, Calif.	62,134	D11	133
Irving, Texas	109,943	G 2	168
Irvington, N.J.	61,493	B 2	156
Ischia (isl.), Italy		D 4	32
Ise, Japan	104,957	H 6	75
Isère (riv.), France		F 5	26
Isfahan, Iran	671,825	F 3	68
Iskenderun, Turkey	107,437	G 4	64
Islamabad (cap.), Pak.	77,318	C 2	70
Isle of Man	64,000	C 3	11
Isle Royale Nat'l Pk., Mich.		E 1	148
Islip, N.Y.	13,438	E 2	158
Ismailia, Egypt	145,978	N 5	60
Israel	3,878,000		67
Issyk-Kul' (lake), U.S.S.R.		H 5	46
Istanbul, Turkey	2,547,364	D 6	64
Italy	57,140,000		32
Ithaca, N.Y.	28,732	G 6	158
Ivanovo, U.S.S.R.	465,000	E 3	50
Ivory Coast	7,920,000	E 10	54
Iwaki, Japan	330,213	K 5	75
Iwo (isl.), Japan		M 4	75
Izhevsk (Ustinov), U.S.S.R.	549,000	H 3	50
Izmir, Turkey	636,834	B 3	64
Izmit, Turkey	165,483	D 2	64

J

	Pop.	Key	Pg.
Jabalpur, India	426,224	D 4	70
Jackson, Mich.	39,739	E 6	148
Jackson (cap.), Miss.	202,895	D 6	150
Jackson, Tenn.	49,131	D 3	167
Jacksonville, Ark.	27,589	F 4	132
Jacksonville, Fla.	540,920	E 1	136
Jacksonville, Ill.	20,284	C 4	139
Jacksonville, N.C.	18,237	K 5	159
Jaffna, Sri Lanka	112,000	E 7	70
Jaipur, India	615,258	D 3	70
Jakarta (cap.), Indon.	6,503,449	H 1	83
Jalapa Enriquez, Mex.	161,352	P 1	119
Jamaica	2,161,000	C 3	124
Jambi, Indon.	230,373	C 6	83
James (bay), Can.		H 5	96
James (riv.), Va.		K 6	170
Jamestown, N.Y.	35,775	B 6	158
Jamestown, N. Dak.	16,280	N 6	160
Jammu, India	155,338	D 2	70
Jammu & Kashmir (state), India		D 2	70
Jamnagar, India	214,816	B 4	70
Jamshedpur, India	341,576	F 4	70
Janesville, Wis.	51,071	H10	173
Jan Mayen (isl.), Nor.		D 1	6
Japan	117,057,485		75
Japan (sea), Asia		R 6	58
Jars (plain), Laos		D 3	81
Jarvis (isl.), Pacific		K 6	89
Java (isl.), Indon.	73,712,411	D-E 7	83
Java (sea), Indon.		D-E 6	83
Jefferson City (cap.), Mo.	33,619	H 5	151
Jeffersonville, Ind.	21,220	F 8	140
Jerez de la Frontera, Spain	112,411	D 4	31
Jericho, West Bank	5,312	C 4	67
Jersey (isl.), Chan. Is.	72,629	E 6	11
Jersey City, N.J.	223,532	B 2	156
Jerusalem (cap.), Isr.	376,000	C 4	68
Jésus (isl.), Que.		H 4	105
Jewel Cave Nat'l Mon., S. Dak.		B 6	166
Jhang Sadar, Pak.	135,722	C 2	70
Jhansi, India	173,292	D 3	70
Jiamusi, China	275,000	M 2	77
Jidda, Saudi Arabia	561,104	C 5	60
Jilin, China	1,200,000	L 3	77
Jinan (Tsinan), China	1,500,000	J 4	77
Jingdezhen, China	300,000	J 6	77
Jinzhou, China	750,000	K 3	77
Jixi, China	350,000	M 2	77
João Pessoa, Braz.	290,424	O 5	90
Jodhpur, India	317,612	C 3	70
Johannesburg, S. Africa	654,232	M17	57
John Day (riv.), Oreg.		G 2	163
John Muir Nat'l Hist. Site, Calif.		K 1	133
Johnson City, N.Y.	17,126	J 6	158
Johnson City, Tenn.	39,753	R 2	167
Johnstown, Pa.	35,496	D 5	164
Johore Baharu, Malaysia	136,234	F 5	81
Joliet, Ill.	77,956	E 2	139
Jonesboro, Ark.	31,530	J 2	132
Jönköping, Sweden	131,499	H 8	16
Jonquière, Que.	60,354	F 1	105
Joplin, Mo.	39,023	C 8	151
Jordan	2,152,273		67
Jordan (riv.), Asia		D 3	67
Joshua Tree Nat'l Mon., Calif.		J 10	133
Juan de Fuca (str.), N. Amer.		E 6	117
Juan Fernández (isls.), Chile			1
Judaea (reg.), Asia		B-C 4-5	67
Juiz de Fora, Braz.	299,728	M 8	90
Julianehåb, Greenl.	3,056	D12	4
Jullundur, India	296,106	D 2	70
Jumna (riv.), India		E 3	70
Junction City, Kans.	19,305	E 2	142
Jundiaí, Braz.	210,015	L 8	93
Juneau (cap.), Alaska	19,528	N 3	130
Jungfrau (mt.), Switz.		E 3	37
Jura (mts.), Europe		F-G 4	26
Juventud (isl.), Cuba	57,879	A 2	124

K

	Pop.	Key	Pg.
K2 (mt.), Asia		D 1	70
Kabul (cap.), Afghan.	905,108	B 2	70
Kachchh (Kutch), Rann of (salt marsh), India		B-C 4	70
Kaduna, Nigeria	202,000	H 9	54
Kaesŏng, N. Korea	175,000	E 3	74
Kagoshima, Japan	456,827	E 8	75
Kahoolawe (isl.), Hawaii		E 3	130
Kaifeng, China	330,000	H 5	77
Kailua, Hawaii	35,812	C 4	130
Kaiserslautern, W. Ger.	100,886	B 4	20
Kakinada, India	164,000	E 5	70
Kalaallit Nunaat (Greenland)	49,773	B12	4
Kalahari (des.), Africa		L16	57
Kalamazoo, Mich.	79,722	D 6	148
Kalgan (Zhangjiakou), China	1,000,000	J 3	77
Kalimantan (reg.), Indon.	4,956,865	E 5	83
Kalinin, U.S.S.R.	412,000	E 3	50
Kaliningrad (Königsberg), U.S.S.R.	355,000	B 4	50
Kaliningrad, Moscow Oblast, U.S.S.R.	133,000	E 3	50
Kaluga, U.S.S.R.	265,000	E 4	50
Kamakura, Japan	165,552	O 3	75
Kamchatka (pen.), U.S.S.R.		Q 4	46
Kamloops, Br. Col.	64,048	G 5	117
Kampala (cap.), Uganda	478,895	N11	57
Kampuchea (Cambodia)	5,200,000	E 4	81
Kananga, Zaire	428,960	L13	57
Kanazawa, Japan	395,263	H 5	75
Kanchenjunga (mt.), Asia		F 3	70
Kandahar (Qandahar), Afghan.	178,409	B 2	70
Kandy, Sri Lanka	93,602	E 7	70
Kanem (reg.), Chad		K 9	54
Kaneohe, Hawaii	29,919	C 4	130
Kanin (pen.), U.S.S.R.		E 3	46
Kankakee, Ill.	30,147	F 2	139
Kannapolis, N.C.	34,564	D 4	159
Kano, Nigeria	399,000	H 9	54
Kansas (riv.), Kans.		F 2	142
Kansas (state), U.S.	2,364,236		142
Kansas City, Kans.	161,148	H 2	142
Kansas City, Mo.	448,159	P 5	151
Kaohsiung, China	1,028,334	J 7	77
Kaolack, Sen.	106,899	C 9	54
Kara (sea), U.S.S.R.		G 2	46
Kara-Bogaz-Gol (gulf), U.S.S.R.		F 5	46
Karachi, Pak.	3,498,634	B 4	70
Karaganda, U.S.S.R.	572,000	H 5	46
Karaj, Iran	138,774	G 3	68
Karakoram (mts.), Asia		D 1	70
Karakorum (ruins), Mong.		F 2	77
Kara-Kum (des.), U.S.S.R.		F 5	46
Kariba (lake), Africa		M15	57
Karl-Marx-Stadt, E. Ger.	303,811	E 3	20
Karlsruhe, W. Ger.	280,448	C 4	20
Kárpathos (isl.), Greece		H 8	43
Kashan, Iran	84,545	G 3	68
Kashi (Kashgar), China	175,000	A 4	77
Kassel, W. Ger.	205,534	C 3	20
Katahdin (mt.), Maine		F 4	145
Katherina, Jebel (mt.), Egypt		B 4	60
Kathmandu (cap.), Nepal	150,402	E 3	70
Katmai Nat'l Pk., Alaska		D 4	130
Katowice, Pol.	303,264	B 4	45
Kattegat (str.), Europe		F 8	16
Kauai (isl.), Hawaii		B 1	130
Kaunas, U.S.S.R.	370,000	C 3	51
Kawaguchi, Japan	345,538	J 6	75
Kawasaki, Japan	1,014,951	O 2	75
Kayseri, Turkey	207,037	F 3	64
Kazakh S.S.R., U.S.S.R.	14,684,000	F-J 5	46
Kazan', U.S.S.R.	993,000	G 3	50
Kearney, Nebr.	21,158	E 4	153
Kearny, N.J.	35,735	B 2	156
Kediri, Indon.	221,830	K 2	83
Keelung, China	342,604	K 6	77
Keene, N.H.	21,449	C 6	155
Kelang, Malaysia	113,611	D 7	81
Kelantan (state), Malaysia		D 6	81
Kelowna, Br. Col.	59,168	H 5	117
Kelso, Wash.	11,129	C 4	171
Kemerovo, U.S.S.R.	471,000	J 4	46
Kenai Fjords Nat'l Pk., Alaska		E 4	130
Kenitra, Mor.	139,206	E 5	54
Kenmore, N.Y.	18,474	C 5	158
Kenner, La.	66,382	N 4	144
Kennesaw Mtn. Nat'l Battlfld. Pk., Ga.		J 1	137
Kennewick, Wash.	34,397	F 4	171
Kenosha, Wis.	77,685	M 3	173
Kent, Ohio	26,164	H 3	161
Kentucky (lake), U.S.		J 3	126
Kentucky (state), U.S.	4,591,120		143
Kenya	15,327,061	O11	57
Kenya (mt.), Kenya		O12	57
Keokuk, Iowa	13,536	L 8	141
Kerala (state), India		D 6	70
Kerch, U.S.S.R.	157,000	E 5	50
Kérkira (isl.), Greece		D 6	43
Kermadec (isls.), N.Z.	5	J 9	89
Kerman, Iran	140,309	K 5	68
Kerrville, Texas	15,276	E 7	168
Ketchikan, Alaska	7,198	O 4	130
Kettering, Ohio	61,186	B 6	161
Keweenaw (pt.), Mich.		B 1	148
Key West, Fla.	24,382	E 7	136
Khabarovsk, U.S.S.R.	528,000	O 5	46
Kharagpur, India	161,783	F 4	70
Khârga (oasis), Egypt		N 6	60
Khar'kov, U.S.S.R.	1,444,000	E 5	50
Khartoum (cap.), Sudan	334,000	N 8	54
Kherson, U.S.S.R.	319,000	D 5	50
Khios (isl.), Greece		G 6	43
Khmel'nitskiy, U.S.S.R.	172,000	C 5	50
Khorramabad, Iran	104,928	F 4	68
Khorramshahr, Iran	146,709	F 5	68
Khulna, Bang.	437,304	F 4	70
Khyber (pass), Pak.		C 2	70
Kiel, W. Ger.	262,164	D 1	20
Kiel (canal), W. Ger.		C 1	20
Kielce, Pol.	125,952	E 3	45
Kiev, U.S.S.R.	2,144,000	D 4	50
Kigali (cap.), Rwanda	117,749	N12	57
Kikwit, Zaire	111,960	K13	57
Kilauea (crater), Hawaii		F 4	130
Kilgore, Texas	11,006	K 5	168
Kilimanjaro (mt.), Tanz.		O12	57
Kilkenny, Ire.	9,838	G 6	15
Killarney, Ire.	7,184	C 7	15
Killeen, Texas	46,296	G 5	168
Kimberley (plat.), Austr.		D 3	86
Kimberley, S. Africa	105,258	L17	57
King (isl.), Austr.		G 7	86
Kingman, Ariz.	9,257	A 3	131
Kings Canyon Nat'l Pk., Calif.		G 7	133
Kings Mountain, N.C.	9,080	C 4	159
Kings Mountain Nat'l Mil. Pk., S.C.		E 1	159
Kingsport, Tenn.	32,027	Q 1	167
Kingston (cap.), Jam.	106,791	C 3	124
Kingston, N.Y.	24,481	M 7	158
Kingston, Pa.	15,681	F 7	164
Kingston upon Thames, Eng.	135,600	H 8	11
Kingstown (cap.), St. Vinc. & Grens.	17,117	G 4	124
Kingsville, Texas	28,808	G10	168
Kinshasa (cap.), Zaire	1,323,039	K12	57
Kinston, N.C.	25,234	K 4	159
Kirgiz S.S.R., U.S.S.R.	3,529,000	H 5	46
Kiribati	57,500	J 6	89
Kirikkale, Turkey	137,874	E 3	64
Kiritimati (isl.), Kiribati	674	L 5	89
Kirkland, Wash.	18,779	B 2	171
Kirksville, Mo.	17,167	H 2	151
Kirkuk, Iraq	167,413	D 3	68
Kirkwood, Mo.	27,987	O 3	151
Kirov, U.S.S.R.	390,000	G 3	50

	Pop.	Key	Pg.
Kirovabad, U.S.S.R.	232,000	G 6	50
Kirovakan, U.S.S.R.	146,000	G 6	50
Kirovograd, U.S.S.R.	237,000	D 5	50
Kiryu, Japan	134,239	J 5	75
Kisangani, Zaire	229,596	M11	57
Kishinev, U.S.S.R.	503,000	C 5	50
Kishiwada, Japan	174,952	J 8	75
Kisumu, Kenya	32,431	N12	57
Kitakyushu, Japan	1,058,058	E 6	75
Kitchener, Ont.	*287,801	D 4	108
Kivu (lake), Africa		M12	57
Kjölen (mts.), Europe		K 3	16
Klaipeda, U.S.S.R.	176,000	A 3	51
Klamath Falls, Oreg.	16,661	F 5	163
Kluane Nat'l Pk., Yukon		C 3	96
Knoxville, Tenn.	175,045	O 3	167
Kobe, Japan	1,360,605	H 7	75
Koblenz, W. Ger.	118,394	B 3	20
Kobuk (riv.), Alaska		G 1	130
Kobuk Valley Nat'l Pk., Alaska		D 2	130
Kochi, Japan	280,962	F 7	75
Kodiak (isl.), Alaska		H 3	130
Kofu, Japan	193,879	J 6	75
Kokand, U.S.S.R.	153,000	H 5	46
Kokomo, Ind.	47,808	E 4	140
Kola (pen.), U.S.S.R.		E 1	50
Kolonia (cap.), Fed. States of Micronesia	5,549	F 5	89
Köln (Cologne), W. Ger.	1,013,771	B 3	20
Kolomna, U.S.S.R.	147,000	E 4	50
Kolwezi, Zaire	81,600	L 14	57
Kolyma (range), U.S.S.R.		Q 3	46
Komsomol'sk, U.S.S.R.	264,000	O 4	46
Konya, Turkey	246,727	E 4	64
Kootenay (riv.), Br. Col.		K 5	117
Kopeisk, U.S.S.R.	146,000	G 4	46
Korea, North	17,914,000		74
Korea, South	37,448,836		74
Koriyama, Japan	264,628	K 5	75
Koror (cap.), Belau	6,222	D 5	89
Koryak (range), U.S.S.R.		R 3	46
Kos (isl.), Greece		H 7	43
Kosciusko (mt.), Austr.		H 7	86
Košice, Czech.	169,100	F 2	39
Kostroma, U.S.S.R.	255,000	F 3	50
Kota, India	212,991	D 3	70
Kota Baharu, Malaysia	35,124	D 6	81
Kota Kinabalu, Malaysia	40,939	E 4	81
Kovrov, U.S.S.R.	143,000	F 3	50
Kowloon, Hong Kong	2,378,480	H 7	77
Kra (isth.), Thai.		C 5	81
Krakatau (isl.), Indon.		C 7	83
Kraków, see Cracow, Pol.			
Kramatorsk, U.S.S.R.	178,000	E 5	50
Krasnodar, U.S.S.R.	560,000	E 6	50
Krasnoyarsk, U.S.S.R.	796,000	K 4	46
Krefeld, W. Ger.	228,463	B 3	20
Kremenchug, U.S.S.R.	210,000	D 5	50
Krivoy Rog, U.S.S.R.	650,000	D 5	50
Krung Thep, see Bangkok, Thai.			
Kuala Lumpur (cap.), Malaysia	451,977	D 7	81
Kuching, Malaysia	63,535	D 5	81
Kufra (oasis), Libya		L 7	54
Kumamoto, Japan	488,166	E 7	75
Kumasi, Ghana	260,286	F 10	54
Kunlun Shan (mts.), Asia		B-D 4	77
Kunming, China	1,700,000	F 6	77
Kunsan, S. Korea	154,780	C 6	74
Kurashiki, Japan	392,755	F 6	75
Kurdistan (reg.), Asia		D 2	60
Kure, Japan	242,655	F 6	75
Kurgan, U.S.S.R.	310,000	G 4	46
Kuril (isls.), U.S.S.R.		P 5	47
Kurnool, India	136,710	D 5	70
Kursk, U.S.S.R.	375,000	E 4	50
Kurume, Japan	204,474	E 7	75
Kushiro, Japan	206,840	M 2	75
Kuskokwim (mts.), Alaska		G 2	130
Kustanay, U.S.S.R.	165,000	G 4	46
Kutaisi, U.S.S.R.	194,000	F 6	50
Kutch, Rann of (salt marsh), India		B-C 4	70
Kuwait	1,355,827	E 4	60
Kuybyshev, U.S.S.R.	1,216,000	H 4	50
Kwajalein (atoll), Marshall Is.	6,264	G 5	89
Kwangju, S. Korea	607,011	C 6	74
Kwangtung, see Guangdong, China			
Kyŏngju, S. Korea	108,431	D 6	74
Kyoto, Japan	1,461,059	J 7	75
Kyushu (isl.), Japan		E 7	74
Kyzyl, U.S.S.R.	66,000	K 4	46
Kyzyl-Kum (des.), U.S.S.R.		G 5	46
Kzyl-Orda, U.S.S.R.	156,000	G 5	46

L

	Pop.	Key	Pg.
Laayoune, W. Sahara	25,419	D 6	54
Labrador (dist.), Newf.		D1-2	99
Labuan (state), Malaysia		F 4	83
Laccadive (Cannanore) (isls.), India		C 6	70
Lackawanna, N.Y.	22,701	B 5	158
Laconia, N.H.	15,575	E 4	155
La Coruña, Spain	184,372	B 1	31
La Crosse, Wis.	48,347	D 8	173
Ladakh (reg.), India		D 2	70
Ladoga (lake), U.S.S.R.		D 2	50
Lae, Papua N.G.	61,617	E 6	89
Lafayette, Ind.	43,011	D 4	140
Lafayette, La.	81,961	F 6	144
Lagos (cap.), Nigeria	1,060,848	G10	54
La Grande, Oreg.	11,354	J 2	163
La Grange, Ga.	24,204	B 4	137
La Grange, Ill.	15,445	B 6	139
La Habra, Calif.	45,232	D11	133
Lahaina, Hawaii	6,095	E 3	130
Lahore, Pak.	2,165,372	C 2	70
Lake Charles, La.	75,226	D 6	144
Lake Chelan Nat'l Rec. Area, Wash.		E 2	171
Lake Clark Nat'l Pk., Alaska		D 3	130
Lake Forest, Ill.	15,245	B 4	139
Lake Havasu City, Ariz.	15,909	A 4	131
Lakeland, Fla.	47,406	D 3	136
Lake Louise, Alta.	355	C 4	114
Lake Mead Nat'l Rec. Area, U.S.		G 6	154
Lakewood, Calif.	74,654	C11	133
Lakewood, Colo.	113,808	J 3	134
Lakewood, N.J.	22,863	E 3	156
Lakewood, Ohio	61,963	G 9	161
Lake Worth, Fla.	27,048	G 5	136
La Manche (English) (chan.), Europe		B 3	26
Lambaréné, Gabon	17,770	H12	57
Lambeth, Eng.	290,300	H 8	11
Lamèque (isl.), N. Bruns.		F 1	102
La Mesa, Calif.	50,308	H11	133
La Mirada, Calif.	40,986	D11	133
Lanai (isl.), Hawaii		D 3	130
Lancaster, Calif.	48,027	G 9	133
Lancaster, Eng.	126,300	E 3	11
Lancaster, Ohio	34,953	E 6	161
Lancaster, Pa.	54,725	K 5	164
Land's End (prom.), Eng.		B 7	11
Lansing, Ill.	29,039	C 6	139
Lansing (cap.), Mich.	130,414	E 6	148
Lanzhou (Lanchow), China	1,500,000	F 4	77
Laos	3,721,000	D 3	81
La Paz (cap.), Bol.	635,283	G 7	90
La Pérouse (str.), Asia		R 5	58
Lapland (reg.), Europe		K-R 2	16
La Plata, Arg.	*560,341	J 11	93
La Porte, Ind.	21,796	D 1	140
Laptev (sea), U.S.S.R.		N 2	46
La Puente, Calif.	30,882	D10	133
Laramie (mts.), U.S.		F-G 3	174
Laramie, Wyo.	24,410	G 4	174
Laredo, Texas	91,449	E 10	168
Largo, Fla.	58,977	B 3	136
Lárisa, Greece	72,336	F 6	43
Las Cruces, N. Mex.	45,086	C 6	157
Las Palmas de Gran Canaria, Spain	260,368	B 4	30
Lassen Volcanic Nat'l Pk., Calif.		D 3	133
Las Vegas, Nev.	164,674	F 6	154
Las Vegas, N. Mex.	14,322	D 3	157
Latakia, Syria	125,716	F 5	64
Latium (reg.), Italy		D 3	32
Latvian S.S.R., U.S.S.R.	2,521,000	B 2	51
Lauderdale Lakes, Fla.	25,426	B 3	136
Lauderhill, Fla.	37,271	B 3	136
Laurel, Md.	12,103	G 4	146
Laurel, Miss.	21,897	F 7	150
Laurentides Prov. Pk., Que.		F 2	105
Lausanne, Switz.	136,100	C 3	37
Lava Beds Nat'l Mon., Calif.		D 2	133
La Verne, Calif.	23,508	D10	133
Lawndale, Calif.	23,460	B11	133
Lawrence, Ind.	25,591	E 5	140
Lawrence, Kans.	52,738	G 3	142
Lawrence, Mass.	63,175	K 2	147
Lawton, Okla.	80,054	F 5	162
Leavenworth, Kans.	33,656	H 2	142
Lebanon	3,161,000	F 6	64
Lebanon, Pa.	25,711	K 5	164
Leech (lake), Minn.		D 3	149
Leeds, Eng.	744,500	J 1	11
Lee's Summit, Mo.	28,741	R 6	151
Leeward (isls.), W. Indies		F 3	124
Le Havre, France	216,917	C 3	26
Lehman Caves Nat'l Mon., Nev.		G 4	154
Leicester, Eng.	289,400	F 5	11
Leiden, Neth.	99,891	E 4	25
Leipzig, E. Ger.	570,972	E 3	20
Leizhou Bandao (pen.), China		G 7	77
Le Mans, France	150,289	C 3	26
Lena (riv.), U.S.S.R.		N 3	46
Leninakan, U.S.S.R.	207,000	F 6	50
Leningrad, U.S.S.R.	3,513,000	C 3	50
Leninsk-Kuznetskiy, U.S.S.R.	132,000	J 4	46
Leominster, Mass.	34,508	G 2	147
León, Mex.	468,887	J 6	119
León, Nic.	55,625	D 4	122
León, Spain	99,702	D 1	31
Lérida, Spain	73,148	G 2	31
Lesotho	1,339,000	M17	57
Lesser Antilles (isls.), W. Indies		E-G 4	124
Lesser Slave (lake), Alta.		C 2	114
Lésvos (isl.), Greece		G 6	43
Levittown, N.Y.	57,045	B 3	158
Lewis (dist.), Scot.		B 2	13
Lewiston, Idaho	27,986	A 3	138
Lewiston, Maine	40,481	C 7	145
Lexington, Ky.	204,165	J 4	143
Lexington, Mass.	29,479	B 6	147
Lexington, N.C.	15,711	E 3	159
Leyte (isl.), Phil.		H 3	83
Lhasa, China	175,000	D 6	77
Lianyungang, China	300,000	J 5	77
Liaodong Bandao (pen.), China		K 3	77
Liaoyang, China	250,000	K 3	77
Liaoyuan, China	300,000	K 3	77
Liberal, Kans.	14,911	B 4	142
Liberia	1,873,000	E 10	54
Liberty, Mo.	16,251	R 5	151
Libreville (cap.), Gabon	105,080	H11	57
Libya	2,856,000	J 6	54
Libyan (des.), Africa		L 6	54
Liechtenstein	25,220	J 2	37
Liège, Belg.	145,573	H 7	25
Liffey (riv.), Ire.		H 5	15
Ligurian (sea), Italy		B 3	32
Lihue, Hawaii	4,000	B 2	130
Lille, France	171,010	E 2	26
Lilongwe (cap.), Malawi	102,924	N14	57
Lima, Ohio	47,381	B 4	161
Lima (cap.), Peru	375,957	E 6	90
Limassol, Cyprus	79,641	E 5	64
Limerick, Ire.	63,002	D 6	15
Limoges, France	136,059	D 5	26
Limpopo (riv.), Africa		N16	57
Lincoln, Ill.	16,327	D 3	139
Lincoln (cap.), Nebr.	171,932	H 4	153
Lincoln Boyhood Nat'l Mem., Ind.		C 8	140
Lincoln Park, Mich.	45,105	B 7	148
Linden, N.J.	37,836	A 3	156
Lindenhurst, N.Y.	26,919	E 2	158
Lindesnes (cape), Nor.		E 8	16
Line (isls.), Pacific		K-J 5-6	89
Linköping, Sweden	80,274	K 7	16
Linz, Austria	205,700	C 2	39
Lions (gulf), France		F 6	26
Lipari (isls.), Italy		E 5	32
Lipetsk, U.S.S.R.	396,000	E 4	50
Lippe (riv.), W. Ger.		B 3	20
Lisbon (cap.), Port.	769,410	B 3	31
Lithuanian S.S.R., U.S.S.R.	3,398,000	B 3	51
Little America, Antarc.		B10	5
Little Cayman (isl.), Cayman Is.	74	B 3	124
Little Colorado (riv.), U.S.		D2-3	131
Little Rock (cap.), Ark.	158,461	F 4	132
Littleton, Colo.	28,631	K 3	134
Liuzhou, China	250,000	G 7	77
Livermore, Calif.	48,349	L 2	133
Liverpool, Eng.	539,700	G 2	11
Livingston, N.J.	28,040	E 2	156
Livonia, Mich.	104,814	F 6	148
Livorno (Leghorn), Italy	170,369	E 4	32
Ljubljana, Yugo.	169,064	B 3	43
Llano Estacado (plain), U.S.		B3-5	168
Llullaillaco (vol.), Chile		F 8	93
Lockport, N.Y.	24,844	C 4	158
Lod (Lydda), Isr.	30,500	B 4	67
Lodi, Calif.	35,221	C 9	133
Łódź, Pol.	777,800	D 3	45
Lofoten (isls.), Nor.		H 2	16
Logan, Utah	26,844	C 2	169
Logan (mt.), Yukon		C 3	96
Logansport, Ind.	17,731	E 3	140
Loire (riv.), France		C 4	26
Lombard, Ill.	36,897	B 5	139
Lombardy (reg.), Italy		B 2	32
Lomé (cap.), Togo	148,443	G10	54
Lomond (lake), Scot.		D 4	13
Lompoc, Calif.	26,267	E 9	133
London, Ont.	*283,668	C 5	107
London, Eng. (cap.), U.K.	7,028,200	H 8	11
Londonderry, N. Ire.	51,200	G 2	15
Londrina, Braz.	258,054	K 8	93
Long (isl.), Bah.	3,353	C 2	124
Long (isl.), N.Y.		E 2	158
Long Beach, Calif.	361,344	C11	133
Long Beach, N.Y.	34,073	B 4	158
Long Branch, N.J.	29,819	F 3	156
Long Island (sound), U.S.		E 2	158
Longmont, Colo.	42,942	J 2	134
Longview, Texas	62,762	K 5	168
Longview, Wash.	31,052	B 4	171
Lopatka (cape), U.S.S.R.		Q 4	47
Lop Nur (Lop Nor) (dry lake), China		D 3	77
Lorain, Ohio	75,416	F 3	161
Lord Howe (isl.), Austr.		F 9	89
Los Alamos, N. Mex.	11,039	C 3	157
Los Altos, Calif.	25,769	K 3	133
Los Angeles, Calif.	2,966,763	C10	133
Los Gatos, Calif.	26,906	K 4	133
Louisbourg, N.S.	1,410	J 3	100
Louisiana (state), U.S.	4,206,312		144
Louisville, Ky.	298,840	F 4	143
Louangphrabang, Laos	7,596	D 3	81
Lourdes, France	17,685	C 6	26
Loveland, Colo.	30,244	J 2	134
Lowell, Mass.	92,418	J 2	147
Lower Tunguska (riv.), U.S.S.R.		K-L 3	46
Loyalty (isls.), New Caledonia	14,518	G 8	89
Luanda (cap.), Angola	475,328	J 13	57
Lubbock, Texas	173,979	C 4	168
Lübeck, W. Ger.	232,270	D 2	20
Lublin, Pol.	235,937	F 3	45
Lubumbashi, Zaire	318,000	M14	57
Lucerne, Switz.	70,200	F 2	37
Lucerne (lake), Switz.		F 3	37
Lucknow, India	749,239	E 3	70
Lüda (Dalian), China	4,000,000	K 4	77
Ludlow, Mass.	18,150	E 4	147
Ludhiana, India	397,850	D 2	70
Ludwigshafen, W. Ger.	170,374	C 4	20
Lufkin, Texas	28,562	K 6	168
Lumberton, N.C.	18,241	G 5	159
Luoyang, China	750,000	H 5	77
Lusaka (cap.), Zambia	538,469	M15	57
Luton, Eng.	164,500	G 6	11
Lutsk, U.S.S.R.	137,000	B 4	50
Luxembourg	364,000	J 9	25
Luxembourg (cap.), Lux.	78,272	J 9	25
Luxor, Egypt	92,748	B 4	60
Luzon (isl.), Phil.		G 2	83
L'vov, U.S.S.R.	667,000	B 5	50
Lyallpur (Faisalabad), Pak.	822,263	C 2	70
Lydda, Isr.	30,500	B 4	67
Lynbrook, N.Y.	20,424	A 3	158
Lynchburg, Va.	66,743	F 6	170
Lyndon B. Johnson Nat'l Hist. Site, Texas		F 7	168
Lynn, Mass.	78,471	D 6	147
Lynwood, Calif.	48,548	C11	133
Lyon, France	454,265	F 5	26
Lyubertsy, U.S.S.R.	160,000	E 3	50

M

	Pop.	Key	Pg.
Maas (riv.), Neth.		G 5	25
Maastricht, Neth.	111,044	H 7	25
Macapá, Braz.	89,081	K 3	42
Macau	271,000	H 7	77
Macedonia (rep.), Yugo.		E 5	43
Maceió, Braz.	376,479	N 5	90
Machida, Japan	255,305	O 2	75
Machupicchu, Peru	544	F 6	90
Mackenzie (riv.), N.W.T.		C 2	96
Mackinac (isl.), Mich.		E 3	148
Macomb, Ill.	19,863	C 3	139
Macon, Ga.	116,896	E 5	137
Ma'daba, Jordan	22,600	D 4	67
Madagascar	8,742,000	R16	57
Madeira (riv.), Braz.		H 5	90
Madeira (isl.), Port.		A 2	30
Madera, Calif.	21,732	E 7	133
Madison (cap.), Wis.	170,616	H 9	173
Madison Heights, Mich.	35,375	B 6	148
Madiun, Indon.	150,562	K 2	83
Madras, India	2,469,449	E 6	70
Madrid (cap.), Spain	3,146,071	F 4	31
Madurai, India	549,114	D 7	70

	Pop.	Key	Pg.
Maebashi, Japan	250,241	J 5	75
Magadan, U.S.S.R.	122,000	P 4	46
Magdalen (isls.), Que.		K 6	96
Magdalena (riv.), Col.		E 1	90
Magdeburg, E. Ger.	276,089	D 2	20
Magellan (str.), S. Amer.		G14	93
Maggiore (lake), Europe		G 5	37
Magnitogorsk, U.S.S.R.	406,000	G 4	46
Maiduguri, Nigeria	189,000	J 9	54
Main (riv.), W. Ger.		C 4	20
Maine (state), U.S.	1,125,027		145
Mainz, W. Ger.	183,880	C 4	20
Maipú (vol.), S. Amer.		G10	93
Majorca (isl.), Spain		H 3	31
Majuro (atoll), Marshall Is.	8,583	H 5	89
Makassar, see Ujung Pandang, Indon.			
Makassar (str.), Indon.		F 6	83
Makeyevka, U.S.S.R.	436,000	E 5	50
Makhachkala, U.S.S.R.	251,000	G 6	50
Malabar (coast), India		C 6	70
Malabo (cap.), Equat. Guin.	37,237	H11	54
Malacca (str.), Asia		C 5	83
Málaga, Spain	334,988	D 4	31
Malang, Indon.	511,780	K 2	83
Malange, Angola	31,599	K13	57
Malatya, Turkey	154,505	H 3	64
Malawi	5,968,000	N14	57
Malay (pen.), Asia		C-D 6	81
Malaya (state), Malayia	11,138,227	D 6	81
Malaysia	13,435,588	C-E 5	83
Malden, Mass.	53,386	D 6	147
Maldives	143,046	J 9	58
Male (cap.), Maldives		J 9	58
Malegaon, India	191,847	C 4	70
Mali	6,906,000	E 9	54
Malmédy, Belg.	6,464	J 8	25
Malmö, Sweden	241,191	H 9	16
Malta	343,970	E 7	32
Mamaroneck, N.Y.	17,616	J 1	158
Mammoth Cave Nat'l Pk., Ky.		F 6	143
Mamoutzou (Dzaoudzi) (cap.), Mayotte	196	R14	57
Man, Isle of (isl.)		C 3	11
Manado, Indon.	217,159	G 5	83
Managua (cap.), Nic.	398,514	D 4	122
Manama (cap.), Bahrain	358,857	E 4	60
Manassas, Va.	15,438	K 3	170
Manassas Nat'l Battlfld. Pk., Va.		J 3	170
Manaus, Braz.	613,068	H 4	90
Mancha, La (reg.), Spain		E 3	31
Manchester, Conn.	49,761	E 1	135
Manchester, Eng.	490,000	H 2	11
Manchester, N.H.	90,936	E 6	155
Mandalay, Burma	418,008	C 2	81
Mandan, N. Dak.	15,513	J 6	160
Mandeb, Bab el (str.)		D 7	60
Mangalore, India	165,174	C 6	70
Manhattan, Kans.	32,644	F 2	142
Manhattan (borough), N.Y.	1,428,285	C 2	158
Manhattan Beach, Calif.	31,542	B11	133
Manila (cap.), Phil.	1,630,485	G 3	83
Manitoba (prov.), Can.	1,026,241		110
Manitoulin (isl.), Ont.		B 2	108
Manitowoc, Wis.	32,547	L 7	173
Manizales, Col.	199,904	E 2	90
Mankato, Minn.	28,651	E 6	149
Mannheim, W. Ger.	314,086	C 4	20
Mansfield, Ohio	53,927	F 4	161
Mantua, Italy	59,529	C 2	32
Manukau, N.Z.	159,362	L 6	87
Maple Heights, Ohio	29,735	H 9	161
Maplewood, Minn.	26,990	G 5	149
Maplewood, N.J.	22,950	E 2	156
Maputo (cap.), Moz.	755,300	N17	57
Maracaibo, Ven.	651,574	F 1	90
Maracay, Ven.	255,134	G 1	90
Maraş, Turkey	135,782	G 4	64
Mar del Plata, Arg.	407,024	J11	93
Margarita (isl.), Ven.		H 1	90
Margate, Fla.	35,900	F 5	136
Marianao, Cuba	127,563	A 2	124
Maribor, Yugo.	94,976	B 2	43
Marietta, Ga.	30,829	J 1	137
Marion, Ind.	35,874	F 3	140
Marion, Ohio	37,040	D 4	161
Maritime Alps (mts.), Europe		G 5	26
Marken (isl.), Neth.		G 4	25
Markham, Ont.	77,037	K 4	108
Marlborough, Mass.	30,617	H 3	147
Marmara (sea), Turkey		C 2	64
Marne (riv.), France		E 3	26
Marquesas (isls.), Fr. Poly.	5,419	M 6	89
Marquette, Mich.	23,288	B 2	148
Marrakech, Mor.	332,741	E 5	54
Marrero, La.	36,548	O 4	144
Marseille, France	901,421	F 6	26
Marshall, Texas	24,921	K 5	168
Marshall Islands	30,873	G 4	89
Marshalltown, Iowa	26,938	G 4	141
Martha's Vineyard (isl.), Mass.		M 7	147
Martinique	328,566	G 4	124
Maryland (state), U.S.	4,216,975		146
Marystown, Newf.	6,299	C 4	99
Masan, S. Korea	371,917	D 6	74
Masbate (isl.), Phil.		G 3	83
Mascarene (isls.), Africa		S19	57
Maseru (cap.), Lesotho	71,500	M17	57
Mason City, Iowa	30,144	G 2	141
Massachusetts (state), U.S.	5,737,037		147
Massapequa, N.Y.	24,454	B 3	158
Massillon, Ohio	30,557	H 4	161
Matagorda (isl.), Texas		H 9	168
Matamoros, Mex.	165,124	L 4	119
Matane, Que.	13,612	B 1	105
Matapan (cape), Greece		F 7	43
Mata Utu (cap.), Wallis & Futuna	558	J 7	89
Mato Grosso (plat.), Braz.		K 7	90
Matsu (isl.), China		K 6	77
Matsumoto, Japan	185,595	H 5	75
Matsuyama, Japan	367,323	F 7	75
Mattoon, Ill.	19,055	E 4	139
Maturín, Ven.	98,188	H 2	90
Maui (isl.), Hawaii		E 3	130
Mauna Kea (mt.), Hawaii		F 4	130
Mauna Loa (mt.), Hawaii		F 4	130
Mauritania	1,634,000	D 8	54
Mauritius	959,000	S19	57
May (cape), N.J.		D 6	156
Mayo, Yukon	398	E 3	96
Mayotte	47,300	P14	57
Maywood, Ill.	27,998	B 5	139
Mazar-i-Sharif, Afghan.	122,567	B 1	70
Mazatlán, Mex.	147,010	F 5	119
Mbabane (cap.), Swaziland	23,109	N17	57
Mbuji-Mayi, Zaire	256,154	L13	57
McAlester, Okla.	17,255	L 5	162
McAllen, Texas	66,281	F11	168
McDonald (isls.), Austr.			1
McKeesport, Pa.	31,012	C 7	164
McKinley (mt.), Alaska		J 2	130
M'Clintock (chan.), N.W.T.		F 1	96
M'Clure (str.), N.W.T.		E 1	96
Mead (lake), U.S.		A 2	131
Mecca, Saudi Arabia	366,801	C 5	60
Mecklenburg (reg.), E. Ger.		E 2	20
Medan, Indon.	1,378,955	B 5	83
Medellín, Col.	1,070,924	E 2	90
Medford, Mass.	58,076	C 6	147
Medford, Oreg.	39,603	E 5	163
Medicine Bow (range), Wyo.		F 4	174
Medicine Hat, Alta.	40,380	E 4	114
Medina, Saudi Arabia	198,186	D 5	60
Mediterranean (sea)			34
Médoc (reg.), France		C 5	26
Meerut, India	270,993	D 3	70
Mégantic (lake), Que.		G 4	105
Megiddo, Isr.		C 2	67
Meknès, Mor.	248,369	E 5	54
Mekong (riv.), Asia		E 4	81
Melaka (Malacca), Malaya	87,160	D 7	81
Melanesia (reg.), Pacific		E-H 5-8	89
Melbourne, Austr.	2,578,759	K 2	86
Melbourne, Fla.	46,536	F 3	136
Melitopol, U.S.S.R.	161,000	D 5	50
Melrose, Mass.	30,055	D 6	147
Melville (isl.), Austr.		E 2	86
Melville (isl.), N.W.T.		E 1	96
Melville (pen.), N.W.T.		H 2	96
Memphis, Tenn.	646,174	B 4	167
Memphremagog (lake), N. Amer.		C 1	155
Mendocino (cape), Calif.		A 3	133
Mendoza, Arg.	*596,796	G10	93
Menlo Park, Calif.	26,369	J 3	133
Menominee Falls, Wis.	27,845	K 1	173
Mentor, Ohio	42,065	H 2	161
Merced, Calif.	36,499	E 6	133
Mercer Island, Wash.	21,522	B 2	171
Mergui (arch.), Burma		C 5	81
Mérida, Mex.	233,912	P 6	119
Meriden, Conn.	57,118	D 2	135
Meridian, Miss.	46,577	G 6	150
Meroe (ruins), Sudan		N 8	54
Merrick, N.Y.	24,478	B 4	157
Mersey (riv.), Eng.		G 2	11
Mersin, Turkey	152,236	F 4	64
Mesa, Ariz.	152,453	D 5	131
Mesa Verde Nat'l Pk., Colo.		C 8	134
Meshed, Iran	670,180	L 2	68
Mesopotamia (reg.), Iraq		D-E 3	60
Mesquite, Texas	67,053	H 2	168
Messina, Italy	203,937	E 5	32
Mestre, Italy	184,818	D 2	32
Metairie, La.	164,160	O 4	144
Methuen, Mass.	36,701	K 2	147
Metz, France	110,939	G 3	26
Meuse (riv.), Europe		F2-3	26
Mexicali, Mex.	317,228	B 1	119
Mexico	67,395,826		119
Mexico (gulf), N. Amer.		K 7	94
Mexico City (cap.), Mex.	9,377,300	L 1	119
Miami, Fla.	346,865	B 5	136
Miami Beach, Fla.	96,298	C 5	136
Miass, U.S.S.R.	150,000	G 4	46
Michigan (lake), U.S.		J 2	126
Michigan (state), U.S.	9,262,078		148
Michigan City, Ind.	36,850	C 1	140
Middlebury, Vt.	7,574	A 3	155
Middlesbrough, Eng.	153,900	F 3	11
Middletown, Conn.	39,040	E 2	135
Middletown, N.J.	61,615	E 3	156
Middletown, N.Y.	21,454	B 1	158
Middletown, Ohio	43,719	A 6	161
Midland, Mich.	37,250	E 5	148
Midland, Ont.	12,132	D 3	108
Midland, Texas	70,525	C 6	168
Midway Islands	453	J 3	89
Midwest City, Okla.	49,559	H 4	162
Míkonos (isl.), Greece		G 4	43
Milan, Italy	1,724,557	B 2	32
Milford, Conn.	49,101	C 4	135
Milford, Mass.	23,390	H 4	147
Millburn, N.J.	19,543	E 2	156
Mille Lacs (lake), Minn.		E 4	149
Millville, N.J.	24,815	C 5	156
Milpitas, Calif.	37,820	L 3	133
Milton, Mass.	25,860	D 7	147
Milwaukee, Wis.	636,236	M 1	173
Milwaukie, Oreg.	17,931	B 2	163
Minas (basin), N.S.		D 3	100
Mindanao (isl.), Phil.		H 4	83
Mindoro (isl.), Phil.		F 3	83
Mineola, N.Y.	20,757	B 3	158
Minneapolis, Minn.	370,951	G 5	149
Minnesota (riv.), Minn.		C 6	149
Minnesota (state), U.S.	4,075,970		149
Minnetonka, Minn.	38,683	G 5	149
Miño (riv.), Spain		C 1	31
Minot, N. Dak.	32,843	H 3	160
Minsk, U.S.S.R.	1,262,000	C 4	50
Minute Man Nat'l Hist. Pk., Mass.		B 6	147
Minya Konka (mt.), China		F 6	77
Miramar, Fla.	32,813	B 4	136
Mishawaka, Ind.	40,201	E 1	140
Miskolc, Hung.	206,727	F 2	39
Mission, Texas	22,653	F11	168
Mississippi (riv.), U.S.		H 4	126
Mississippi (state), U.S.	2,520,638		150
Missoula, Mont.	33,388	C 4	152
Missouri (riv.), U.S.		H 3	126
Missouri (state), U.S.	4,916,759		151
Misti, El (mt.), Peru		F 7	90
Misurata, Libya	102,439	K 5	54
Mitchell (mt.), N.C.		A 3	159
Mitla (ruin), Mex.		M 8	119
Mito, Japan	197,953	K 5	75
Miyazaki, Japan	234,347	E 8	75
Mobile, Ala.	200,452	B 9	129
Mobile (bay), N. Amer.		B10	129
Mobutu Sese Seko (lake), Africa		M11	57
Modena, Italy	149,029	C 2	32
Modesto, Calif.	106,602	D 6	133
Mogadishu (cap.), Somalia	371,000	R11	54
Mogilev, U.S.S.R.	290,000	D 4	46
Mohenjo Daro (ruins), Pak.		B 3	70
Mokp'o, S. Korea	192,958	C 6	74
Mojave (des.), Calif.		H 9	133
Moldau (Vltava) (riv.), Czech.		C 2	39
Moline, Ill.	46,278	C 2	139
Molokai (isl.), Hawaii		D 2	130
Moluccas (isls.), Indon.	944,240	H 6	83
Mombasa, Kenya	247,073	P12	57
Mona (passage), W. Indies		E 3	124
Monaco	25,029	G 6	26
Mönchengladbach, W. Ger.	261,367	B 3	20
Monclova, Mex.	78,134	J 3	119
Moncton, N. Br.	54,743	F 2	102
Mongolia	1,594,800	F 2	77
Monroe, La.	57,597	F 1	144
Monroe, Mich.	23,531	F 7	148
Monrovia, Calif.	30,531	D10	133
Monrovia (cap.), Liberia	166,507	D10	54
Mons, Belg.	59,362	E 8	25
Montague, P.E.I.	1,957	F 2	100
Montana (state), U.S.	786,690		152
Mont Cenis (tunnel), Europe		G 5	26
Montclair, N.J.	38,321	B 2	156
Montebello, Calif.	52,929	C10	133
Montecristo (isl.), Italy		C 3	32
Montenegro (rep.), Yugo.		D 4	43
Monterey, Calif.	27,558	D 7	133
Monterey Park, Calif.	54,338	C10	133
Monterrey, Mex.	1,006,221	J 4	119
Montevideo (cap.), Urug.	1,173,254	J11	93
Montezuma Castle Nat'l Mon., Ariz.		D 4	131
Montgomery (cap.), Ala.	177,857	F 6	129
Mont-Laurier, Que.	8,405	B 3	105
Montmagny, Que.	12,405	G 3	105
Montpelier (cap.), Vt.	8,241	B 3	155
Montpellier, France	178,136	E 6	26
Montréal, Que.	*2,828,349	H 4	105
Mont-Royal, Que.	19,247	H 4	105
Montserrat	12,073	G 3	124
Mont-Tremblant Prov. Pk., Que.		C 3	105
Monza, Italy	110,735	B 2	32
Monument (valley), Utah		D 6	169
Moore, Okla.	35,063	H 4	162
Moorea (isl.), Fr. Poly.	5,788	L 7	89
Moorhead, Minn.	29,998	B 4	149
Moosehead (lake), Maine		D 4	145
Moose Jaw, Sask.	33,941	F 5	113
Moosomin, Sask.	2,579	K 5	113
Moradabad, India	258,590	D 3	70
Morava (riv.), Czech.		D 2	39
Morava (riv.), Yugo.		E 3	43
Moravia (reg.), Czech.		L 6	39
Moray (firth), Scot.		E 3	13
Morelia, Mex.	199,099	J 7	119
Morgan City, La.	16,114	H 7	144
Morgantown, W. Va.	27,605	G 1	172
Morioka, Japan	216,223	K 4	75
Moro (gulf), Phil.		G 4	83
Morocco	20,242,000	E 5	54
Moroni (cap.), Comoros	12,000	P14	57
Morristown, N.J.	16,614	D 2	156
Morristown, Tenn.	19,683	P 2	167
Moscow, Idaho	16,513	B 3	138
Moscow (cap.), U.S.S.R.	7,831,000	E 3	50
Mosel (riv.), Europe		B 3	20
Moselle (riv.), France		G 3	26
Moses Lake, Wash.	10,629	F 3	171
Mosquito (gulf), Pan.		G 6	122
Mosquito Coast (reg.), Nic.		E 4	122
Moss Point, Miss.	18,998	G10	150
Mosul, Iraq	315,157	C 2	68
Moulmein, Burma	171,977	C 3	81
Mound City Group Nat'l Mon., Ohio		E 7	161
Mountain View, Calif.	58,655	K 3	133
Mountlake Terrace, Wash.	16,534	B 1	171
Mount Pearl, Newf.	11,543	D 4	99
Mount Prospect, Ill.	52,634	B 5	139
Mount Rainier Nat'l Pk., Wash.		D 4	171
Mount Rushmore Nat'l Mem., S. Dak.		B 6	166
Mount Vernon, Ill.	17,193	E 5	139
Mount Vernon, N.Y.	66,713	H 1	158
Mount Vernon, Ohio	14,323	E 5	161
Mount Vernon, Wash.	13,009	C 2	171
Mozambique	12,130,000	N16	57
Mozambique (chan.), Africa		O16	57
Mudanjiang, China	400,000	M 3	77
Muir Woods Nat'l Mon., Calif.		H 2	133
Mukden, see Shenyang, China			
Mulhacén (mt.), Spain		E 4	31
Mülheim, W. Ger.	189,259	B 3	20
Mulhouse, France	116,494	G 4	26
Multan, Pak.	542,195	C 2	70
Muncie, Ind.	77,216	G 4	140
Mundelein, Ill.	17,053	A 4	139
Munich (München), W. Ger.	1,314,865	D 4	20
Munster, Ind.	20,671	B 1	140
Münster, W. Ger.	264,546	B 3	20
Muonio (riv.), Europe		M 2	16
Mur (Mura) (riv.), Europe		B 2	43
Murcia, Spain	102,242	F 4	31
Mureş (riv.), Rom.		E 2	43
Murfreesboro, Tenn.	32,845	J 3	167
Murmansk, U.S.S.R.	381,000	D 1	50
Murray (riv.), Austr.		G 6	86
Murray, Utah	25,750	C 3	169
Murrumbidgee (riv.), Austr.		H 6	86
Musandam, Ras (cape), Oman		G 4	60
Muscat (cap.), Oman	7,500	G 5	60
Muscatine, Iowa	23,467	L 6	141
Musgrave (ranges), Austr.		E 5	86
Muskegon, Mich.	40,823	C 5	148
Muskogee, Okla.	40,011	M 3	162

Name	Pop.	Key	Pg.
Mwanza, Tanz.	110,611	N12	57
Mweru (lake), Africa		M13	57
Myrtle Beach, S.C.	18,446	K 4	165
Mysore, India	355,685	D 6	70

N

Name	Pop.	Key	Pg.
Nablus (Nabulus), West Bank	41,799	C 3	67
Nacogdoches, Texas	27,149	J 6	168
Nagaland (state), India		G 3	70
Nagano, Japan	306,637	J 5	75
Nagaoka, Japan	171,742	J 5	75
Nagasaki, Japan	450,194	D 7	75
Nagercoil, India	141,288	D 7	70
Nagoya, Japan	2,079,740	H 6	75
Nagpur, India	866,076	D 4	70
Naha, Japan	295,006	N 6	75
Nahuel Huapi (lake), Arg.		F12	93
Nairobi (cap.), Kenya	509,286	O12	57
Nalchik, U.S.S.R.	207,000	E 6	50
Namangan, U.S.S.R.	227,000	H 5	46
Namib (des.), Namibia		J15	57
Namibia	1,200,000	K16	57
Nampa, Idaho	25,112	B 6	138
Namp'o, N. Korea	140,000	D 3	74
Nanaimo, Br. Col.	47,069	J 3	117
Nanchang, China	900,000	J 6	77
Nanchong, China	275,000	G 5	77
Nancy, France	106,906	G 3	26
Nanda Devi (mt.), India		D 2	70
Nanga Parbat (mt.), Pak.		D 1	70
Nanjing (Nanking), China	2,000,000	J 5	77
Nanning, China	375,000	G 7	77
Nantes, France	252,537	C 4	26
Nantong, China	300,000	K 5	77
Nantucket (isl.), Mass.		O 7	147
Napa, Calif.	50,879	C 5	133
Naperville, Ill.	42,601	A 6	139
Naples, Fla.	17,581	E 5	136
Naples, Italy	1,214,775	E 4	32
Nara, Japan	257,538	J 8	75
Narmada (riv.), India		D 4	70
Narragansett (bay), R.I.		J 6	147
N.A.S.A. Space Center, Texas		K 2	168
Nashua, N.H.	67,865	D 6	155
Nashville (cap.), Tenn.	455,651	H 2	167
Nasik, India	176,091	C 5	70
Nassau (cap.), Bah.	135,437	C 1	124
Natal, Braz.	376,552	O 5	90
Natal (prov.), S. Africa		N17	57
Natchez, Miss.	22,015	B 7	150
Natchitoches, La.	16,664	D 3	144
Natick, Mass.	29,286	A 7	147
Natural Bridges Nat'l Mon., Utah		E 6	169
Naugatuck, Conn.	26,456	C 3	135
Nauru	7,254	G 6	89
Navarin (cape), U.S.S.R.		T 3	46
Navajo Nat'l Mon., Ariz.		E 2	131
Navarre (reg.), Spain		F 1	31
Náxos (isl.), Greece		G 7	43
Nazareth, Isr.	33,000	C 2	67
N'Djamena (cap.), Chad	179,000	K 9	54
Ndola, Zambia	282,439	M14	57
Neagh (lake), N. Ire.		J 2	15
Nebo (mt.), Jordan		D 4	67
Nebraska (state), U.S.	1,569,825		153
Neckar (riv.), W. Ger.		C 4	20
Needham, Mass.	27,901	B 7	147
Neenah, Wis.	22,432	J 7	173
Nefud (des.), Saudi Arabia		C-D 4	60
Negev (reg.), Isr.		D 5	67
Negro (riv.), S. Amer.		H 4	90
Negros (isl.), Phil.		G 4	83
Nei Monggol Zizhiqu (aut. reg.), China		H 3	77
Neisse (riv.), Europe		F 3	20
Neiva, Col.	105,476	F 3	90
Nejd (reg.), Saudi Arabia		C-E 4-5	60
Nelson, Br. Col.	9,143	J 5	117
Nelson (riv.), Man.		J 2	110
Nepal	14,179,301	E 3	70
Neptune, N.J.	28,366	E 3	156
Ness (lake), Scot.		D 3	13
Netherlands	14,227,000		25
Netherlands Antilles	246,000	E 4	124
		F 3	124
Netzahualcóyotl, Mex.	560,436	L 1	119
Nevada (state), U.S.	800,493		154
Nevada, Sierra (mts.), Spain		E 4	31
Nevada, Sierra (mts.), U.S.		B 3	126
Nevis (isl.), St. Chris. & Nevis		F 3	124
New Albany, Ind.	37,103	F 8	140
Newark, Calif.	32,126	K 3	133
Newark, Del.	25,247	L 2	146
Newark, N.J.	329,248	B 2	156
Newark, Ohio	41,200	F 5	161
New Bedford, Mass.	98,478	K 6	147
New Berlin, Wis.	30,529	K 2	173
New Bern, N.C.	14,557	L 4	159
New Braunfels, Texas	22,402	K10	168
New Brighton, Minn.	23,269	G 5	149
New Britain, Conn.	73,840	E 2	135
New Britain (isl.), Papua N.G.	148,773	F 6	89
New Brunswick (prov.), Can.	696,403		102
New Brunswick, N.J.	41,442	E 3	156
Newburgh, N.Y.	23,438	C 1	158
New Caledonia & Dependencies	133,233	G 8	89
New Canaan, Conn.	17,931	B 4	135
Newcastle, Austr.	135,207	J 6	86
Newcastle, Ind.	20,056	G 5	140
Newcastle, N. Br.	6,284	E 2	102
New Castle, Pa.	33,621	B 3	164
Newcastle upon Tyne, Eng.	295,800	H 3	11
New City, N.Y.	35,859	B 1	158
New Delhi (cap.), India	301,801	D 3	70
Newfoundland (prov.), Can.	567,681		99
Newfoundland (isl.), Newf.		B 2	99
New Georgia (isl.), Sol. Is.	16,472	F 6	89
New Glasgow, N.S.	10,464	F 3	100
New Guinea (isl.), Pacific		D-E 6	89
New Hampshire (state), U.S.	920,610		155
New Hanover (isl.), Papua N.G.		F 6	89
New Haven, Conn.	126,109	D 3	135
New Iberia, La.	32,766	G 6	144
Newington, Conn.	28,841	E 2	135
New Ireland (isl.), Papua N.G.	65,657	F 6	89
New Jersey (state), U.S.	7,364,823		156
New London, Conn.	28,842	G 3	135
Newmarket, Ont.	29,753	E 3	108
New Mexico (state), U.S.	1,302,981		157
New Milford, Conn.	19,420	B 2	135
New Orleans, La.	557,927	O 4	144
Newport, Ky.	21,587	L 1	143
Newport, R.I.	29,259	J 7	147
Newport Beach, Calif.	62,556	D11	133
Newport News, Va.	144,903	L 6	170
New Providence (isl.), Bah.	135,437	C 1	124
New Rochelle, N.Y.	70,794	J 1	158
New Siberian (isls.), U.S.S.R.		P 2	46
New South Wales (state), Austr.	5,126,217	H 6	86
Newton, Iowa	15,292	H 5	141
Newton, Kans.	16,332	E 3	142
Newton, Mass.	83,622	C 7	147
New Ulm, Minn.	13,755	D 6	149
New Waterford, N.S.	8,808	J 2	100
New Westminster, Br. Col.	38,550	K 3	117
New York, N.Y.	7,071,639	C 2	158
New York (state), U.S.	17,558,072		158
New Zealand	3,175,737	L 7	87
Neyagawa, Japan	254,311	J 7	75
Ngami (lake), Botswana		L16	57
Nha Trang, Viet.	216,227	F 4	81
Niagara (riv.), N. Amer.		E 4	108
Niagara Falls, N.Y.	71,384	C 4	158
Niagara Falls, Ont.	70,960	E 4	108
Niamey (cap.), Niger	225,314	G 9	54
Nias (isl.), Indon.	356,093	B 5	83
Nicaragua	2,703,000	E 4	122
Nice, France	331,002	G 6	26
Nicobar (isls.), India		G 7	70
Nicosia (cap.), Cyprus	115,718	E 5	64
Niger	5,098,427	H 8	54
Niger (riv.), Africa		G 9	54
Nigeria	82,643,000	H10	54
Niigata, Japan	423,188	J 5	75
Niihau (isl.), Hawaii		A 2	130
Nijmegen, Neth.	148,493	H 5	25
Nikolayev, U.S.S.R.	440,000	D 5	50
Nile (riv.), Africa		N 7	54
Niles, Ill.	30,363	B 5	139
Niles, Ohio	23,088	J 3	161
Nîmes, France	123,914	F 6	26
Ningbo (Ningpo), China	350,000	K 6	77
Nipawin, Sask.	4,376	H 2	113
Nipigon (lake), Ont.		H 5	108
Nipissing (lake), Ont.		E 1	108
Niš, Yugo.	128,231	F 4	43
Nishinomiya, Japan	400,622	H 8	75
Niterói, Braz.	386,185	M 8	93
Niue	3,578	K 7	89
Nizhniy Tagil, U.S.S.R.	398,000	G 4	46
Njazidja (isl.), Comoros		P14	57
Nogales, Ariz.	15,683	E 7	131
Nome, Alaska	2,301	E 1	130
Nordkapp (cape), Nor.		E 1	16
Norfolk, Nebr.	19,449	G 2	153
Norfolk, Va.	266,979	M 7	170
Norfolk I. (terr.), Austr.	2,175	L 5	86
Noril'sk, U.S.S.R.	180,000	J 3	46
Normal, Ill.	35,672	E 3	139
Norman, Okla.	68,020	H 4	162
Norman Wells, N.W.T.	420	D 2	96
Norristown, Pa.	34,684	M 5	164
Norrköping, Sweden	85,244	K 7	16
North (sea), Europe		E 3	6
North (isl.), N.Z.	2,322,989	K 6	86
North Adams, Mass.	18,063	B 2	147
North America	370,000,000		94
Northampton, Eng.	128,290	F 5	11
Northampton, Mass.	29,286	D 3	147
North Attleboro, Mass.	21,095	J 5	147
North Battleford, Sask.	14,030	C 3	113
North Bay, Ont.	51,268	E 1	108
North Bergen, N.J.	47,019	B 2	156
Northbrook, Ill.	30,778	B 5	139
North Brunswick, N.J.	22,220	D 3	156
North Carolina (state), U.S.	5,881,813		159
North Cascades Nat'l Pk., Wash.		D 2	171
North Charleston, S.C.	62,534	G 6	165
North Chicago, Ill.	38,774	B 4	139
North Dakota (state), U.S.	652,717		160
Northern Ireland, U.K.	1,543,000	H 2	15
Northern Territory, Austr.	123,324	E 3	86
Northfield, Minn.	12,562	E 6	149
North Frisian (isls.), Europe		C 1	20
Northglenn, Colo.	29,847	K 3	134
North Korea	17,914,000		74
North Haven, Conn.	22,080	D 3	135
North Highlands, Calif.	37,825	B 8	133
North Las Vegas, Nev.	42,739	F 6	154
North Little Rock, Ark.	64,288	F 4	132
North Magnetic Pole, N.W.T.		M 3	96
North Miami, Fla.	42,566	B 4	136
North Miami Beach, Fla.	36,553	C 4	136
North Olmsted, Ohio	36,486	G 9	161
North Plainfield, N.J.	19,108	E 2	156
North Platte, Nebr.	24,509	D 3	153
North Platte (riv.), U.S.		F 2	126
Northport, Ala.	14,291	C 4	129
North Providence, R.I.	29,188	J 5	147
North Saskatchewan (riv.), Can.		E-F 5	96
North Tonawanda, N.Y.	35,760	C 4	158
Northumberland (str.), Can.		D 2	96
North Vancouver, Br. Col.	*65,367	K 3	117
North West (cape), Austr.		A 4	86
Northwest Territories, Can.	45,741	E 2	96
Norton Shores, Mich.	22,025	C 5	148
Norwalk, Calif.	85,286	C11	133
Norwalk, Conn.	77,767	B 4	135
Norway	4,092,000		16
Norwegian (sea), Europe		D-E 2	6
Norwich, Conn.	38,074	G 2	135
Norwich, Eng.	119,200	J 5	11
Norwood, Mass.	29,711	B 8	147
Norwood, Ohio	26,342	C 9	161
Nottingham, Eng.	280,300	F 5	11
Nouakchott (cap.), Mauritania	134,986	C 8	54
Nouméa (cap.), New Caledonia	56,078	G 8	89
Nouveau-Québec (crater), Que.		F 1	106
Nova Scotia (prov.), Can.	847,442		100
Novato, Calif.	43,916	H 1	133
Novaya Zemlya (isls.), U.S.S.R.		F 2	46
Novgorod, U.S.S.R.	186,000	D 3	50
Novi, Mich.	22,525	F 6	148
Novi Sad, Yugo.	143,591	D 3	43
Novocherkassk, U.S.S.R.	183,000	F 5	50
Novokuznetsk, U.S.S.R.	541,000	J 4	46
Novomoskovsk, U.S.S.R.	147,000	E 4	50
Novorossiysk, U.S.S.R.	159,000	E 6	50
Novosibirsk, U.S.S.R.	1,312,000	J 4	46
Nubia (lake), Sudan		N 7	54
Nubian (des.), Sudan		N 7	54
Nueces (riv.), Texas		F 9	168
Nuevo Laredo, Mex.	184,622	J 3	119
Nuku'alofa (cap.), Tonga	18,356	J 8	89
Numazu, Japan	199,325	J 6	75
Nunivak (isl.), Alaska		E 3	130
Nuremberg (Nürnberg), W. Ger.	499,060	D 4	20
Nutley, N.J.	28,998	B 2	156
Nuuk (cap.), Greenl.	9,561	C12	4
Nyasa (lake), Africa		N14	57
Nyasaland, see Malawi			
Nyíregyháza, Hung.	108,156	F 3	39

O

Name	Pop.	Key	Pg.
Oahe (lake), U.S.		G 1	126
Oahu (isl.), Hawaii		B 3	130
Oak Creek, Wis.	16,932	M 2	173
Oak Forest, Ill.	26,096	B 6	139
Oakland, Calif.	339,337	J 2	133
Oakland Park, Fla.	23,035	B 3	136
Oak Lawn, Ill.	60,590	B 6	139
Oak Park, Ill.	54,887	B 5	139
Oak Park, Mich.	31,537	B 6	148
Oak Ridge, Tenn.	27,662	N 2	167
Oakville, Ont.	75,773	E 4	108
Oaxaca de Juárez, Mex.	114,948	L 8	119
Ob' (riv.), U.S.S.R.		G 3	46
Oberammergau, W. Ger.	4,704	D 5	20
Oberhausen, W. Ger.	237,147	B 3	20
Oberlin, Ohio	8,660	F 3	161
Ocala, Fla.	37,170	D 2	136
Ocean (Banaba) (isl.), Kiribati	2,314	G 6	89
Ocean City, N.J.	13,949	D 5	156
Oceanside, Calif.	76,698	H10	133
Oceanside, N.Y.	33,639	B 4	158
Ocmulgee Nat'l Mon., Ga.		F 5	137
Odense, Den.	168,178	D 7	19
Oder (riv.), Europe		L 5	20
Odessa, Texas	90,027	B 6	168
Odessa, U.S.S.R.	1,046,000	D 5	50
Ogaden (reg.), Eth.		P-R10	54
Ogbomosho, Nigeria	432,000	H10	54
Ogden, Utah	64,407	C 2	169
O'Higgins (lake), Chile		F13	93
Ohio (riv.), U.S.		J 3	126
Ohio (state), U.S.	10,797,624		161
Ohrid (lake), Europe		E 5	43
Oise (riv.), France		E 3	26
Oita, Japan	320,237	E 7	75
Ojos del Salado (mt.), S. Amer.		G 9	93
Okayama, Japan	513,471	F 6	75
Okazaki, Japan	234,510	H 6	75
Okeechobee (lake), Fla.		F 5	136
Okefenokee (swamp), U.S.		H 9	137
Okhotsk (sea), U.S.S.R.		P 4	46
Okinawa (isl.), Japan		N 6	75
Oklahoma (state), U.S.	3,025,290		162
Oklahoma City (cap.), Okla.	403,136	G 4	162
Okmulgee, Okla.	16,263	K 3	162
Öland (isl.), Sweden		K 8	16
Olathe, Kans.	37,258	H 3	142
Oldenburg, W. Ger.	134,706	C 2	20
Old Bridge, N.J.	51,515	E 3	156
Olds, Alta.	4,813	D 4	114
Olean, N.Y.	18,207	D 6	158
Olinda, Braz.	266,392	N 5	90
Olsztyn, Pol.	94,119	E 2	45
Olympia (cap.), Wash.	27,447	C 3	171
Olympic Nat'l Pk., Wash.		B 3	171
Olympus (mt.), Greece		F 5	43
Omaha (beach), France		C 3	26
Omaha, Nebr.	313,911	J 3	153
Oman	891,000	G 5	60
Oman (gulf), Asia		G 5	60
Omdurman, Sudan	299,000	N 8	54
Omiya, Japan	327,698	O 2	75
Omsk, U.S.S.R.	1,014,000	H 4	46
Omuta, Japan	165,969	E 7	75
Onega (lake), U.S.S.R.		E 2	50
Onitsha, Nigeria	220,000	H10	54
Ontario, Calif.	88,820	D10	133
Ontario (prov.), Can.	8,625,107		107,108
Ontario (lake), N. Amer.		D-G 3	94
Opelika, Ala.	21,896	H 5	129
Opelousas, La.	18,903	G 5	144
Opole, Pol.	86,510	C 3	45
Oporto, see Porto, Port.			
Oradea, Rom.	175,400	E 2	43
Oran, Alg.	491,000	F 4	54
Orange (riv.), Africa		K17	57
Orange, Austr.	27,626	H 6	86
Orange, Calif.	91,450	D11	133
Orange, N.J.	31,136	B 2	156
Orange, Texas	23,628	L 7	168
Orange Free State (prov.), S. Africa		M17	57
Orangeville, Ont.	13,740	D 4	108
Ordos (reg.), China		G 4	77
Ordzhonikidze, U.S.S.R.	279,000	E 6	50
Örebro, Sweden	117,877	J 7	16
Oregon (state), U.S.	2,633,149		163
Oregon Caves Nat'l Mon., Oreg.		D 5	163
Oregon City, Oreg.	14,673	B 2	163
Oregon Dunes Nat'l Rec. Area, Oreg.		C 4	163
Orel, U.S.S.R.	305,000	E 4	50
Orem, Utah	52,399	C 3	169
Orenburg, U.S.S.R.	459,000	J 4	50
Orilla, Ont.	23,955	E 3	108
Orinoco (riv.), S. Amer.		G 2	90
Orissa (state), India		E-F 4-5	70
Orlando, Fla.	128,291	E 3	136
Orléans, France	88,503	D 3	26

	Pop.	Key	Pg.
Orléans (isl.), Que.		F 3	105
Orne (riv.), France		C 3	26
Oromocto, N. Br.	9,064	D 3	102
Orono, Maine	10,578	F 6	145
Orontes (riv.), Syria		G 5	64
Orsk, U.S.S.R.	247,000	J 4	50
Oruro, Bol.	124,213	G 7	90
Osaka, Japan	2,778,987	J 8	75
Osh, U.S.S.R.	169,000	H 5	46
Oshawa, Ont.	*154,217	F 4	108
Oshkosh, Wis.	49,620	J 8	173
Oshogbo, Nigeria	282,000	H10	54
Oslo (cap.), Nor.	462,732	D 3	16
Osnabrück, W. Ger.	161,671	C 2	20
Ossining, N.Y.	20,196	D 1	158
Ostrava, Czech.	293,500	D 2	39
Oswego, N.Y.	19,793	G 4	158
Otaru, Japan	184,406	K 2	75
Otranto (str.), Europe		D 6	43
Otsu, Japan	191,481	J 7	75
Ottawa (cap.), Can.	295,163	J 7	108
Ottawa (riv.), Can.		J 6	96
Ottumwa, Iowa	27,381	J 6	141
Ouagadougou (cap.), Burkina Faso	172,661	F 9	54
Oujda, Mor.	175,532	F 5	54
Our (riv.), Europe		J 9	25
Outremont, Que.	24,338	H 4	105
Overland, Mo.	19,620	O 2	151
Overland Park, Kans.	81,784	H 3	142
Oviedo, Spain	30,021	C 1	31
Owensboro, Ky.	54,450	C 5	143
Owen Sound, Ont.	19,883	D 3	108
Oxnard, Calif.	108,195	F 9	133
Oyo, Nigeria	152,000	G10	54
Ozarks (mts.), U.S.		H 3	126
Ozarks, Lake of the, Mo.		G 6	151

P

	Pop.	Key	Pg.
Pacifica, Calif.	36,866	H 2	133
Pacific Islands, Territory of the	133,929	F 5	89
Pacific Ocean			89
Padang, Indon.	480,922	B 6	83
Paderborn, W. Ger.	103,705	C 3	20
Padre Island Nat'l Seashore, Texas		G10-11	168
Padua, Italy	210,950	C 2	32
Paducah, Ky.	29,315	D 3	143
Pago Pago (cap.), Amer. Samoa	3,075	J 7	89
Pahang (riv.), Malaysia		D 7	81
Painted (des.), Ariz.		D-E 3	131
Paisley, Scot.	94,833	B 2	13
Pakistan	83,782,000		70
Palatine, Ill.	32,166	B 5	139
Palau, see Belau			
Palembang, Indon.	787,187	D 6	83
Palermo, Italy	556,374	D 5	32
Palma de Mallorca, Spain	191,416	H 3	31
Palmas (cape), Liberia		E11	54
Palm Bay, Fla.	18,560	F 3	136
Palm Beach, Fla.	9,729	G 4	136
Palmdale, Calif.	12,277	G 9	133
Palmira, Col.	140,481	E 3	90
Palm Springs, Calif.	32,366	J 10	133
Palo Alto, Calif.	55,225	K 3	133
Pamir (plat.), Asia		J 6	58
Pampa, Texas	21,396	D 2	168
Pamplona, Spain	142,686	F 1	31
Panama	1,830,175	H 6	122
Panamá (cap.), Pan.	388,638	H 6	122
Panama (gulf), Pan.		H 7	122
Panama City, Fla.	33,346	C 6	136
Panama City (Panamá) (cap.), Pan.	388,638	H 6	122
Panay (isl.), Phil.		G 3	83
P'anmunjŏm, Korea		C 5	74
Papeete (cap.), Fr. Poly.	22,967	M 7	89
Papua New Guinea	3,010,727	E 6	89
Paradise Valley, Ariz.	11,085	D 5	131
Paradise Valley, Nev.	84,818	F 6	154
Paragould, Ark.	15,248	J 1	132
Paraguaná (pen.), Ven.		F 1	90
Paraguay	2,973,000	H 8	90
		H 7	93
Paraguay (riv.), S. Amer.		J 8	93
Paramaribo (cap.), Suriname	*67,905	K 2	90
Paramount, Calif.	36,407	C11	133
Paramus, N.J.	26,474	B 1	156
Paraná, Arg.	159,581	J 10	93
Paraná (state), Braz.		K 8	93
Paraná (riv.), S. Amer.		J 9	93
Paria (gulf)		G 5	124
Paris (cap.), France	2,291,554	B 2	26
Paris, Texas	25,498	J 4	168
Parkersburg, W. Va.	39,967	D 2	172
Park Forest, Ill.	26,222	B 6	139
Park Ridge, Ill.	33,967	B 5	139
Parkville, Md.	35,159	H 3	146
Parma, Italy	151,967	C 2	32
Parma, Ohio	92,548	H 9	161
Parnassus (mt.), Greece		F 6	43
Páros (isl.), Greece		G 7	43
Parramatta, Austr.	130,943	K 4	86
Parris Island Marine Base, S.C.		F 7	166
Parry (chan.), N.W.T.		E-H 1	96
Parry Sound, Ont.	6,124	E 2	108
Parsons, Kans.	12,898	G 4	142
Pasadena, Calif.	118,072	C10	133
Pasadena, Texas	112,560	J 2	168
Pascagoula, Miss.	29,318	G10	150
Pasco, Wash.	18,425	F 4	171
Passaic, N.J.	52,463	E 2	156
Passamaquoddy (bay), N. Amer.		J 5	94
Pasto, Col.	119,339	E 3	90
Patagonia (reg.), Arg.		F-G 12-14	93
Paterson, N.J.	137,970	B 2	156
Patiala, India	148,686	D 2	70
Pátmos (isl.), Greece		H 7	43
Patna, India	473,001	F 3	70
Pátrai, Greece	111,607	E 6	43
Pavlodar, U.S.S.R.	273,000	H 4	46
Pawtucket, R.I.	71,204	J 5	147
Peabody, Mass.	45,976	E 5	147
Peace (riv.), Can.		E 4	96
Pearl (hbr.), Hawaii		B 4	130
Pearl City, Hawaii	42,575	C 4	130
Pechora (riv.), U.S.S.R.		H 1	50
Pecos, Texas	12,855	D10	168
Pecos (riv.), Texas		F 4	168
Pecos Nat'l Mon., N. Mex.		D 3	157
Pécs, Hung.	168,788	E 3	39
Pedernales (riv.), Texas		F 7	168
Peekskill, N.Y.	18,236	D 1	158
Peipus (lake), U.S.S.R.		C 3	50
Pekin, Ill.	33,967	D 3	139
Peking (Beijing) (cap.), China	8,500,000	J 3	77
Pelée (vol.), Martinique		G 4	124
Pelée (pt.), Ont.		B 6	108
Pelly (riv.), Yukon		E 3	96
Pelotas, Braz.	197,092	K10	93
Pemba (isl.), Tanz.		P13	57
Pembroke, Ont.	14,026	G 2	108
Pembroke Pines, Fla.	35,776	B 4	136
Pendleton, Oreg.	14,521	J 2	163
Pend Oreille (lake), Idaho		B 1	138
Penetanguishene, Ont.	5,315	D 3	108
Penghu (isls.), China		J 7	77
Pennine Alps (mts.), Europe		D 5	37
Pennsauken, N.J.	33,775	B 3	156
Pennsylvania (state), U.S.	11,863,895		164
Pensacola, Fla.	57,619	B 6	136
Penticton, Br. Col.	23,181	H 5	117
Pentland (firth), Scot.		E 2	13
Penza, U.S.S.R.	483,000	G 4	50
Peoria, Ill.	124,160	D 3	139
Percé, Que.	4,839	D 1	105
Pereira, Col.	174,128	E 3	90
Périgueux, France	34,779	D 5	26
Perim (isl.), P.D.R. Yemen		D 7	60
Perm', U.S.S.R.	999,000	J 3	50
Pernambuco (Recife), Braz.	1,184,215	O 5	90
Perpignan, France	101,198	E 6	26
Persian (gulf), Asia		F 4	60
Perth, Austr.	809,035	B 2	86
Perth, Ont.	5,655	H 3	108
Perth, Scot.	43,098	E 4	13
Perth Amboy, N.J.	38,951	E 2	156
Perth-Andover, N. Br.	1,872	C 2	102
Peru	17,031,221	E 5	90
Perugia, Italy	65,975	D 3	32
Pescadores (Penghu) (isls.), China		J 7	77
Pescara, Italy	125,391	E 3	32
Peshawar, Pak.	268,366	C 2	70
Petah Tiqwa, Isr.	112,000	B 3	67
Petaluma, Calif.	33,834	H 1	133
Peterborough, Eng.	118,900	G 5	11
Peterborough, Ont.	60,620	F 3	108
Petersburg, Va.	41,055	J 6	170
Petitcodiac, N. Br.	1,401	E 3	102
Petra (ruins), Jordan		D 5	67
Petrified Forest Nat'l Pk., Ariz.		F 4	131
Petropavlovsk, U.S.S.R.	207,000	G 4	46
Petropavlovsk-Kamchatskiy, U.S.S.R.	215,000	R 4	46
Petrozavodsk, U.S.S.R.	234,000	D 2	50
Pharr, Texas	21,381	F 11	168
Phenix City, Ala.	26,928	H 6	129
Philadelphia, Pa.	1,688,210	N 6	164
Philippines	48,098,460	H 3	83
Phnom Penh (cap.), Camb.	300,000	E 5	81
Phoenix (cap.), Ariz.	789,704	C 5	131
Phoenix (isls.), Kiribati		J 6	89
Pico Rivera, Calif.	53,387	C10	133
Pictured Rocks Nat'l Lakeshore, Mich.		C 2	148
Piedmont (reg.), Italy		A-B 2	32
Pierre (cap.), S. Dak.	11,973	J 5	166
Pierrefonds, Que.	38,390	H 4	105
Pietermaritzburg, S. Africa	*174,179	N17	57
Pike's (peak), Colo.		J 5	134
Pikesville, Md.	22,555	H 3	146
Pilcomayo (riv.), S. Amer.		H 8	93
Pincher Creek, Alta.	3,757	D 5	114
Pindus (mts.), Greece		E 6	43
Pine Bluff, Ark.	56,636	F 5	132
Pinellas Park, Fla.	32,811	B 3	136
Pines (Juventud) (isl.), Cuba	57,879	A 2	124
Pingdingshan, China		H 5	77
Pingtung, China	165,000	K 7	77
Pinnacles Nat'l Mon., Calif.		D 7	133
Pinsk, U.S.S.R.	90,000	C 4	46
Pipe Springs Nat'l Mon., Ariz.		C 2	131
Pipestone Nat'l Mon., Minn.		B 6	149
Piqua, Ohio	20,480	B 5	161
Piraiévs, Greece	187,362	F 7	43
Pisa, Italy	91,156	C 3	32
Piscataway, N.J.	42,223	D 2	156
Pitcairn (isl.), Pacific	54	O 8	89
Piteşti, Rom.	125,029	G 3	43
Pittsburg, Calif.	33,034	L 1	133
Pittsburg, Kans.	18,770	H 4	142
Pittsburgh, Pa.	423,959	B 7	164
Pittsfield, Mass.	51,974	A 3	147
Piura, Peru	186,354	D 5	90
Placentia, Calif.	35,041	D11	133
Plainfield, N.J.	45,555	E 2	156
Plainview, N.Y.	28,037	B 3	158
Plainview, Texas	22,187	C 3	168
Plano, Texas	72,331	G 1	168
Plantation, Fla.	48,653	B 4	136
Plata, Río de la (est.), S. Amer.		J 11	93
Platte (riv.), Nebr.		E 4	153
Platt Nat'l Pk., Okla.		N 6	162
Plattsburgh, N.Y.	21,057	O 1	158
Pleasant Hill, Calif.	25,124	K 2	133
Pleasanton, Calif.	35,160	L 2	133
Pleiku, Viet.	23,720	E 4	81
Plessisville, Que.	7,249	F 3	105
Pleven, Bulg.	107,567	G 4	43
Ploieşti, Rom.	207,009	H 3	43
Plovdiv, Bulg.	300,242	G 4	43
Plum, Pa.	25,390	C 5	164
Plymouth, Eng.	259,100	C 7	11
Plymouth, Mass.	35,913	M 5	147
Plymouth, Minn.	31,615	G 5	149
Plymouth (cap.), Montserrat	1,623	F 3	124
Plzeň, Czech.	155,000	B 2	39
Po (riv.), Italy		C 2	32
Pocatello, Idaho	46,340	F 7	138
Podol'sk, U.S.S.R.	202,000	E 3	50
P'ohang, S. Korea	134,418	D 5	74
Pohnpei (isl.), Fed. States of Micronesia	19,935	F 5	89
Pointe-Claire, Que.	24,571	H 4	105
Pointe-Noire, Congo	141,700	J 12	57
Point Pelée Nat'l Pk., Ont.		B 5	108
Point Reyes Nat'l Seashore, Calif.		H 1	133
Poland	35,815,000		45
Poltava, U.S.S.R.	279,000	D 5	50
Polynesia (reg.), Pacific		J-M 3-8	89
Pomerania (reg.), Europe		E 2	20
Pomona, Calif.	92,742	D10	133
Pompano Beach, Fla.	52,618	F 5	136
Pompeii (ruins), Italy		F 4	32
Ponape (Pohnpei) (isl.), Fed. States of Micronesia	19,935	F 5	89
Ponca City, Okla.	26,238	H 1	162
Ponce, P. Rico	161,739	G 1	124
Pondicherry, India	90,537	E 6	70
Pontiac, Mich.	76,715	F 6	148
Pontianak, Indon.	304,778	D 5	83
Pontic (mts.), Turkey		H 2	64
Pontine (isls.), Italy		D 4	32
Poona (Pune), India	*856,105	C 5	70
Poopó (lake), Bol.		G 7	90
Poplar Bluff, Mo.	17,139	L 9	151
Popocatépetl (mt.), Mex.		M 1	119
Porcupine (riv.), N. Amer.		E 3	94
Porsangen (fjord), Nor.		O 1	16
Portage, Ind.	27,409	C 1	140
Portage, Mich.	38,157	D 6	148
Portage la Prairie, Man.	13,086	D 4	110
Port Alberni, Br. Col.	19,892	H 3	117
Port Angeles, Wash.	17,311	B 2	171
Port Arthur, Texas	61,251	K 8	168
Port-au-Prince (cap.), Haiti	306,053	D 3	124
Port Charlotte, Fla.	25,770	D 5	136
Port Chester, N.Y.	23,565	J 1	158
Port Elizabeth, S. Africa	*413,916	M18	57
Port Harcourt, Nigeria	242,000	H11	54
Port Hawkesbury, N.S.	3,850	G 3	100
Port Huron, Mich.	33,981	G 6	148
Portland, Maine	61,572	C 8	145
Portland, Oreg.	366,383	B 2	163
Port Louis (cap.), Mauritius	141,022	S19	57
Port Moody, Br. Col.	14,917	L 3	117
Port Moresby (cap.), Papua N.G.	123,624	E 6	89
Porto (Oporto), Port.	300,925	B 2	31
Porto Alegre, Braz.	1,108,883	K10	93
Port-of-Spain (cap.), Trin. & Tob.	62,680	G 5	124
Porto-Novo (cap.), Benin	104,000	G10	54
Porto Velho, Braz.	101,684	H 5	90
Port Said, Egypt	262,620	N 5	54
Portsmouth, Eng.	198,500	F 7	11
Portsmouth, N.H.	26,254	F 5	155
Portsmouth, Ohio	25,943	D 8	161
Portsmouth, Va.	104,577	M 7	170
Port Sudan, Sudan	133,000	O 8	54
Portugal	9,933,000		31
Potomac (riv.), U.S.		H 8	170
Potsdam, E. Ger.	117,236	E 2	20
Pottstown, Pa.	22,729	L 5	164
Poughkeepsie, N.Y.	29,757	N 7	170
Powell (lake), U.S.		D 6	169
Powell River, Br. Col.	*13,423	E 5	117
Poyang Hu (lake), China		J 6	77
Poznań, Pol.	469,085	C 2	45
Prague (Praha) (cap.), Czech.	1,161,200	C 1	39
Prairie Village, Kans.	24,657	H 2	142
Prescott, Ariz.	20,055	C 4	131
Presque Isle, Maine	11,172	H 2	145
Preston, Eng.	94,760	G 1	11
Prestwick, Scot.	13,218	D 5	13
Pretoria (cap.), S. Africa	*573,283	M17	57
Pribilof (isls.), Alaska		D 3	130
Prichard, Ala.	39,541	B 9	129
Prince Albert, Sask.	31,380	F 2	113
Prince Charles (isl.), N.W.T.		L 3	96
Prince Edward (isls.), S. Africa		L 8	57
Prince Edward Island prov.), Can.	122,506	E 2	100
Prince George, Br. Col.	67,559	F 3	117
Prince of Wales (isl.), N.W.T.		G 1	96
Prince Patrick (isl.), N.W.T.		M 3	96
Prince Rupert, Br. Col.	16,197	B 3	117
Princeton, Br. Col.	3,051	G 5	117
Princeton, N.J.	12,035	D 3	156
Príncipe (isl.), São Tomé & Príncipe		H11	54
Priština, Yugo.	71,264	E 4	43
Prokop'yevsk, U.S.S.R.	266,000	J 4	46
Providence (cap.), R.I.	156,804	H 5	147
Providencia (isl.), Col.		D 1	90
Provo, Utah	74,108	C 3	169
Prudhoe (bay), Alaska		K 1	130
Prut (riv.), Europe		J 2	43
Pskov, U.S.S.R.	176,000	C 3	50
Puebla de Zaragoza, Mex.	498,900	N 2	119
Pueblo, Colo.	101,686	K 6	134
Puerto La Cruz, Ven.	63,276	H 1	90
Puerto Rico	3,196,520	F 1	124
Puget (sound), Wash.		C 3	171
Pukapuka (atoll), Cook Is.	797	K 7	89
Pullman, Wash.	23,579	H 4	171
Punjab (state), India		D 2	70
Punjab (prov.), Pak.		C 2	70
Punta Arenas, Chile	2,140	F14	93
Purus (riv.), S. Amer.		H 5	90
Pusan, S. Korea	2,453,173	D 6	74
Pushkin, U.S.S.R.	90,050	C 3	50
Puyallup, Wash.	18,251	C 3	171
Puy-de-Dôme (mt.), France		E 5	26
P'yŏngyang (cap.), N. Korea	1,250,000	C 4	74
Pyrenees (mts.), Europe		C-E 6	26

Q

	Pop.	Key	Pg.
Qaanaaq, Greenl.		M 2	94
Qandahar, Afghan.	178,401	B 2	70
Qatar	220,000	F 4	60

	Pop.	Key	Pg.
Qattâra (depr.), Egypt		M 6	54
Qazvin, Iran	138,527	F 2	68
Qeqertarsuaq, Greenl.	1,012	C 12	4
Qilian Shan (range), China		E 4	77
Qingdao (Tsingtao), China	1,900,000	K 4	77
Qinghai Hu (lake), China		E 4	77
Qiqihar, China	1,500,000	K 2	77
Qiryat Shemona, Isr.	15,200	C 1	67
Qom (Qum), Iran	246,831	G 3	68
Qonduz, Afghan.	107,191	B 1	70
Qu'Appelle (riv.), Sask.		J 5	113
Québec (prov.), Can.	6,438,403		105, 106
Québec (cap.), Que.	*576,075	H 3	105
Queen Charlotte (isls.), Br. Col.		B 3	117
Queens (borough), N.Y.	1,891,325	D 2	158
Queensland (state), Austr.	2,295,123	G 4	86
Quesnel, Br. Col.	8,240	F 4	117
Quetico Prov. Pk., Ont.		G 5	108
Quetta, Pak.	156,000	B 2	70
Quincy, Ill.	42,554	B 4	139
Quincy, Mass.	84,743	D 7	147
Qui Nhon, Viet.	213,757	F 4	81
Quito (cap.), Ecua.	599,828	E 3	90

R

	Pop.	Key	Pg.
Rabat (cap.), Mor.	367,620	E 5	54
Rabaul, Papua N.G.	14,954	F 6	89
Race (cape), Newf.		D 4	99
Racine, Wis.	85,725	M 3	173
Radom, Pol.	158,640	E 3	45
Radville, Sask.	1,012	G 6	113
Rahway, N.J.	26,723	E 2	156
Rainbow Bridge Nat'l Mon., Utah		C 6	169
Rainier (mt.), Wash.		D 4	171
Rainy (lake), N. Amer.		E 2	149
Raipur, India	174,518	E 4	70
Rajahmundry, India	165,912	E 5	70
Rajkot, India	300,612	C 4	70
Raleigh (cap.), N.C.	150,225	H 3	159
Ramat Gan, Isr.	120,900	B 3	67
Rampur, India	161,417	D 3	70
Ranchi, India	175,934	F 4	70
Rancho Cucamonga, Calif.	55,250	E 10	133
Randallstown, Md.	25,927	G 3	146
Randolph, Mass.	28,218	D 8	147
Rangoon (cap.), Burma	1,586,422	C 3	81
Rantoul, Ill.	20,161	E 3	139
Rapa (isl.), Fr. Poly.	398	M 8	89
Rapa Nui (Easter) (isl.), Chile	1,598	Q 8	89
Rapid City, S. Dak.	46,492	C 5	166
Rappahannock (riv.), Va.		L 4	170
Raritan (riv.), N.J.		D 2	156
Rarotonga (isl.), Cook Is.	9,477	K 8	89
Ras Dashan (mt.), Eth.		O 9	54
Rasht, Iran	187,203	F 2	68
Ras Tanura, Saudi Arabia		F 4	60
Ravenna, Italy	75,153	D 2	32
Ravensburg, W. Ger.	42,725	C 5	20
Ravi (riv.), Asia		C 2	70
Rawalpindi, Pak.	615,392	C 2	70
Rawlins, Wyo.	11,547	E 4	174
Ray (cape), Newf.		A 4	99
Raytown, Mo.	31,759	P 6	151
Reading, Eng.	131,200	G 8	11
Reading, Pa.	78,686	L 5	164
Real (mts.), S. Amer.		G 7	90
Recife, Braz.	1,184,215	O 5	90
Red (sea)		C5-6	60
Red (riv.), Asia		E 2	81
Red (riv.), U.S.		H 4	126
Red Deer, Alta.	46,393	D 3	114
Red Deer (riv.), Alta.		D 4	114
Redding, Calif.	41,995	C 3	133
Redlands, Calif.	43,619	H 9	133
Redmond, Wash.	23,318	B 1	171
Redondo Beach, Calif.	57,102	B 11	133
Red River of the North (riv.), U.S.		A 2	96
Red Volta (riv.), Africa		F 9	54
Redwood City, Calif.	54,965	J 3	133
Redwood Nat'l Pk., Calif.		A 2	133
Ree (lake), Ire.		F 5	15
Regensburg, W. Ger.	131,886	E 4	20
Reggio di Calabria, Italy	110,291	E 5	32
Reggio nell'Emilia, Italy	102,337	C 2	32
Regina (cap.), Sask.	*164,313	G 5	113
Registan (des.), Afghan.		A-B 2	70
Reims, France	77,320	E 3	26
Reindeer (lake), Can.		N 3	96
Renfrew, Ont.	8,283	H 2	108
Rennes, France	194,094	C 3	26
Reno, Nev.	100,756	B 3	154
Renton, Wash.	30,612	B 2	171
Republican (riv.), U.S.		F 2	126
Resolution (isl.), N.W.T.		K 3	96
Réunion	491,000	R 20	57
Reutlingen, W. Ger.	95,289	C 4	20
Revelstoke, Br. Col.	5,544	J 5	117
Revere, Mass.	42,423	D 6	147
Revillagigedo (isls.), Mex.		C 7	119
Rexburg, Idaho	11,559	G 6	138
Reykjavík (cap.), Iceland	81,693	B 1	19
Reynosa, Mex.	206,500	K 3	119
Rhaetian Alps (mts.), Europe		J 3	37
Rhine (riv.), Europe		B 3	20
Rhode Island (state), U.S.	947,154		147
Rhodope (mts.), Europe		G 5	43
Rhône (riv.), Europe		F 5	26
Rialto, Calif.	37,474	E 10	133
Riau (arch.), Indon.	483,230	C 5	83
Ribeirão Preto, Braz.	300,704	L 8	90
Richardson, Texas	72,496	G 2	168
Richfield, Minn.	37,851	G 6	149
Richibucto, N. Br.	1,722	E 2	102
Richland, Wash.	33,578	F 4	171
Richmond, Calif.	74,676	J 1	133
Richmond, Ind.	41,349	H 5	140
Richmond, Ky.	21,705	J 5	143
Richmond (cap.), Va.	219,214	K 5	170
Rideau (riv.), Ont.		J 3	108
Riding Mtn. Nat'l Pk., Man.		B 4	110
Ridgefield, Conn.	20,120	B 3	135
Ridgewood, N.J.	25,208	B 1	156
Riga, U.S.S.R.	835,000	C 2	51
Rijeka, Yugo.	128,883	B 3	43
Rimini, Italy	101,579	D 2	32
Rimouski, Que.	29,120	J 1	105
Rio de Janeiro, Braz.	*9,018,637	M 8	93
Rio Grande (riv.), N. Amer.		H 7	94
Río Muni (reg.), Equat. Guin.		J 11	54
Riverside, Calif.	170,591	E 11	133
Riviera (reg.), Europe		G 6	26
Riviera Beach, Fla.	26,489	G 5	136
Rivière-du-Loup, Que.	13,459	H 2	105
Riyadh (cap.), Saudi Arabia	666,840	E 5	60
Road Town (cap.), V.I. (Br.)	2,200	H 1	124
Roanoke (isl.), N.C.		O 3	159
Roanoke, Va.	100,220	D 6	170
Roanoke Rapids, N.C.	14,702	K 2	159
Roberval, Que.	11,429	E 1	105
Rochester, Minn.	57,890	F 6	149
Rocheester, N.H.	21,560	E 5	155
Rochester, N.Y.	241,741	E 4	158
Rockall (isl.), Scot.		C 3	6
Rockford, Ill.	139,712	D 1	139
Rock Hill, S.C.	35,344	E 2	165
Rock Island, Ill.	46,928	C 2	139
Rock Springs, Wyo.	19,458	C 4	174
Rockville, Md.	43,811	F 4	146
Rockville Centre, N.Y.	25,412	B 4	158
Rocky (mts.), N. Amer.		F-G 4	94
Rocky Mount, N.C.	41,283	K 3	159
Rocky Mountain House, Alta.	4,698	C 3	114
Rocky Mountain Nat'l Pk., Colo.		H 2	134
Rogers, Ark.	17,429	B 1	132
Romania	22,048,305		43
Rome, Ga..	29,654	B 2	137
Rome (cap.), Italy	2,535,018	F 6	32
Rome, N.Y.	43,826	J 4	158
Roosevelt (isl.), Antarc.		A 10	5
Roosevelt (riv.), Braz.		H 5	90
Rosa (mt.), Europe		A 1	32
Rosario, Arg.	*954,606	H 10	93
Roseau (cap.), Dominica	9,968	G 4	124
Roseburg, Oreg.	16,644	D 4	163
Rosemead, Calif.	42,604	C 10	133
Rosetown, Sask.	2,664	D 4	113
Rosetta, Egypt	42,962	B 3	60
Roseville, Mich.	54,311	B 6	148
Roseville, Minn.	35,820	G 5	149
Ross (sea), Antarc.		B 10	5
Ross Lake Nat'l Rec. Area, Wash.		E 2	171
Rostock, E. Ger.	210,167	E 1	20
Rostov-na-Donu, U.S.S.R.	934,000	F 5	50
Roswell, Ga.	23,337	D 2	137
Roswell, N. Mex.	39,676	E 5	157
Rotterdam, Neth.	614,767	E 5	25
Rotuma (isl.), Fiji	2,805	H 7	89
Rouen, France	113,536	D 3	26
Rouyn, Que.	17,224	B 3	106
Rovno, U.S.S.R.	179,000	C 4	50
Roy, Utah	19,694	C 2	169
Royal Gorge (canyon), Colo.		J 6	134
Royal Oak, Mich.	70,893	B 6	148
Rub' al Kahli (des.), Asia		F 5	60
Ruda Śląska, Pol.	142,407	B 4	45
Rufus Woods (lake), Wash.		F 2	171
Rügen (isl.), E. Ger.		E 1	20
Ruhr (riv.), W. Ger.		B 3	20
Rukwa (lake), Tanz.		N 13	57
Rum (cay), Bah.		C 2	124
Rum (Rhum) (isl.), Scot.		B 3	13
Rupert (riv.), Que.		B 2	106
Ruse, Bulg.	160,351	H 4	43
Russell Cave Nat'l Mon., Ala.		G 1	129
Russian S.F.S.R., U.S.S.R.	137,551,000	D-S 4	46
Ruston, La.	20,585	E 1	144
Rutland, Vt.	18,436	B 4	155
Rwanda	4,819,317	N 12	57
Ryazan', U.S.S.R.	453,000	E 4	50
Rybinsk (Andropov), U.S.S.R.	239,000	E 3	50
Ryde, Austr.	88,948	K 4	86
Ryukyu (isls.), Japan		L 7	75

S

	Pop.	Key	Pg.
Saanich, Br. Col.	*78,710	K 3	117
Saar (riv.), Europe		B 4	20
Saarbrücken, W. Ger.	205,336	B 4	20
Saaremaa (isl.), U.S.S.R.		B 1	51
Saarland (state), W. Ger.		B 4	20
Sabadell, Spain	148,273	H 2	31
Sabah (state), Malaysia	1,002,608	F 4	83
Sabine (riv.), U.S.		H 4	126
Sable (cape), Fla.		E 6	136
Sable (cape), N.S.		C 5	100
Sable (isl.), N.S.		J 5	100
Sacajawea (lake), Wash.		G 4	171
Sackville, N. Br.	5,654	F 3	102
Sacramento (cap.), Calif.	275,741	B 8	133
Sacramento (riv.), Calif.		D 5	133
Sacramento (mts.), N. Mex.		D 6	157
Saga, Japan	152,258	E 7	75
Sagamihara, Japan	377,398	O 2	75
Sagamore Hill Nat'l Hist. Site, N.Y.		B 2	158
Saginaw, Mich.	77,508	K 2	148
Saguaro Nat'l Mon., Ariz.		E 6	131
Saguenay (riv.), Que.		G 1	105
Sahara (des.), Africa		E-M 7	54
Saharanpur, India	225,396	D 3	70
Saigon (Ho Chi Minh City), Viet.	*3,419,678	E 5	81
St. Albert, Alta.	31,996	D 3	114
St. Andrews, N. Br.	1,760	C 3	102
St. Augustine, Fla.	11,985	E 2	136
St. Catharines, Ont.	124,018	E 4	108
St. Charles, Mo.	37,379	N 1	151
St. Christopher (isl.), St. Chris. & Nevis		F 3	124
St. Christopher & Nevis	44,404	F 3	124
St. Clair (lake), N. Amer.		K 2	148
St. Clair Shores, Mich.	76,210	B 6	148
St. Cloud, Minn.	42,566	D 5	149
St. Croix (isl.), V.I. (U.S.)	49,725	H 2	124
St. Croix (riv.), U.S.		J 5	145
St. Croix Isl. Nat'l Mon., Maine		J 5	145
St-Denis, France	95,808	B 1	26
St-Denis (cap.), Réunion	80,075	P 19	57
Ste-Agathe-des-Monts, Que.	5,641	C 3	105
Ste-Anne-de-Beaupré, Que.	3,292	F 2	105
Ste-Foy, Que.	68,883	H 3	105
Ste-Geneviève, Que.	2,573	H 4	105
St. Elias (mt.), N. Amer.		L 2	130
Ste-Thérèse, Que.	18,750	H 4	105
St-Étienne, France	218,289	F 5	26
St-Eustache, Que.	29,716	H 4	105
St. George (cape), Newf.		A 3	99
St. George's (chan.), Europe		B 5	11
St. George's (cap.), Grenada	6,463	F 5	124
St. Gotthard (tunnel), Switz.		G 3	37
St. Helena & Dependencies	5,147		1
St. Helens (mt.), Wash.		C 4	171
St. Helier (cap.), Jersey, Chan. Is.	28,135	E 8	11
St-Hyacinthe, Que.	38,246	D 4	105
St-Jean (lake), Que.		E 1	105
St-Jerôme, Que.	25,123	H 4	105
St. John, N. Br.	80,521	E 3	102
St. John (riv.), N. Amer.		N 1	126
St. John (isl.), V.I. (U.S.)	2,472	H 1	124
St. Johns (cap.), Antigua & Barbuda	21,814	G 3	124
St. Johns (riv.), Fla.		E 2	136
St. John's (cap.), Newf.	*154,820	D 4	99
St. Joseph, Mo.	76,691	C 3	151
St-Joseph-de-Sorel, Que.	2,545	D 3	105
St. Kilda, Austr.	49,366	K 2	86
St. Kitts, see St. Christopher			
St-Lambert, Que.	20,557	J 4	105
St-Laurent, Que.	65,900	H 4	105
St. Lawrence (isl.), Alaska		D 2	130
St. Lawrence (gulf), Can.		K 6	96
St. Lawrence (riv.), N. Amer.		K 6	94
St-Léonard, Que.	79,429	H 4	105
St. Louis, Mo.	453,085	R 3	151
St. Louis Park, Minn.	42,931	G 5	149
St. Lucia	115,783	G 4	124
St-Maurice (riv.), Que.		E 2	105
St-Nazaire, France	65,228	B 4	26
St. Paul (cap.), Minn.	270,230	G 6	149
St. Peter Port (cap.), Guernsey, Chan. Is.	16,303	E 8	11
St. Petersburg, Fla.	238,647	B 3	136
St. Pierre & Miquelon	6,041	B 4	99
St. Simons (isl.), Ga.		K 8	137
St. Stephen, N. Br.	5,120	C 3	102
St. Thomas, Ont.	28,165	C 5	108
St. Thomas (isl.), V.I. (U.S.)	44,572	G 11	124
St. Vincent & the Grenadines	124,000	G 4	124
Saipan (isl.), N. Marianas	14,549	E 4	89
Sakai, Japan	750,688	J 8	75
Sakakawea (lake), N. Dak.		G 5	160
Sakhalin (isl.), U.S.S.R.		P 4	46
Salamanca, Spain	125,132	D 2	31
Sala y Gómez (isl.), Chile		Q 8	89
Salem, India	308,716	D 6	70
Salem, Mass.	38,220	E 5	147
Salem, N.H.	24,124	E 6	155
Salem (cap.), Oreg.	89,233	A 3	163
Salem, Va.	23,958	D 6	170
Salem Maritime Nat'l Hist. Site, Mass.		E 5	147
Salerno, Italy	146,534	E 4	32
Salina, Kans.	41,843	E 3	142
Salinas, Calif	80,479	D 7	133
Salinas Nat'l Mon., N. Mex.		C 4	157
Salisbury, Austr.	86,451	E 7	86
Salisbury, Md.	16,429	M 7	146
Salisbury (Harare) (cap.), Zim.	601,000	N 15	57
Salmon (riv.), Idaho		B 4	138
Salta, Arg.	260,323	G 8	93
Saltillo, Mex.	200,712	J 4	119
Salt Lake City (cap.), Utah	163,697	C 3	169
Salton Sea (lake), Calif.		K 10	133
Saluda (riv.), S.C.		D 3	165
Salvador, Braz.	1,496,276	N 6	90
Salween (riv.), Asia		L 8	58
Salzburg, Austria	213,430	B 3	39
Samar (isl.), Phil.		H 3	83
Samaria (reg.), Jordan		C 3	67
Samarinda, Indon.	264,718	F 6	83
Samarkand, U.S.S.R.	477,000	G 6	46
Sámos (isl.), Greece		H 7	43
Samothráki (isl.), Greece		G 5	43
Samsun, Turkey	168,478	F 2	64
San'a (cap.), Yemen Arab Rep.	134,588	D 6	60
San Andrés (isl.), Col.		D 1	90
San Angelo, Texas	73,240	D 6	168
San Antonio, Texas	786,023	J 11	168
San Bernardino, Calif.	118,794	E 10	133
San Bernardino (mts.), Calif.		J 10	133
San Blas (gulf), Pan.		H 6	122
San Bruno, Calif.	35,417	J 2	133
San Clemente, Calif.	27,325	H 10	133
San Clemente (isl.), Calif.		G 11	133
San Cristobal (isl.), Solomon Is.	11,212	G 7	89
San Cristóbal, Ven.	151,717	F 2	90
Sandia (peak), N. Mex.		C 3	157
San Diego, Calif.	875,538	H 11	133
Sand Springs, Okla.	13,246	K 2	162
Sandusky, Ohio	31,360	E 3	161
Sandy, Utah	52,210	C 3	169
Sandy Hook (spit), N.J.		F 3	156
San Fernando, Calif.	17,731	C 10	133
Sanford, Fla.	23,176	E 3	136
Sanford, Maine	18,020	B 9	145
Sanford, N.C.	14,773	G 4	159
San Francisco, Calif.	678,974	H 2	133
San Francisco (bay), Calif.		J 2	133
San Gabriel, Calif.	30,072	C 10	133
Sangre de Cristo (mts.), U.S.		H 6	134
San Joaquin (riv.), Calif.		E 6	133
San Jose, Calif.	629,546	L 3	133
San José (cap.), C. Rica	215,441	F 5	122
San Juan, Arg.	*290,479	G 10	93
San Juan (cap.), P. Rico	424,600	G 1	124
San Juan (riv.), U.S.		E 3	126
San Juan Island Nat'l Hist. Pk., Wash.		B 2	171
San Leandro, Calif.	63,952	J 2	133
San Lucas (cape), Mex.		E 5	119
San Luis Obispo, Calif.	34,252	E 8	133
San Luis Potosí, Mex.	271,123	J 5	119
San Marcos, Texas	23,420	F 8	168
San Marino	19,149	D 3	32
San Mateo, Calif.	77,640	J 3	133
San Miguel de Tucumán, Arg.	*496,914	H 9	93
San Nicolas (isl.), Calif.		F 10	133

	Pop.	Key	Pg.
San Pedro Sula, Hond.	150,991	C 3	122
San Rafael, Calif.	44,700	J 1	133
San Salvador (isl.), Bah.		C 1	124
San Salvador (cap.), El Sal.	337,171	C 4	122
San Sebastián, Spain	159,557	E 1	31
Santa Ana, Calif.	204,023	D11	133
Santa Ana, El Sal.	96,306	C 4	122
Santa Barbara, Calif.	74,414	F 9	133
Santa Barbara (isls.), Calif.		F10	133
Santa Catalina (isl.), Calif.		G10	133
Santa Clara, Calif.	87,700	K 3	133
Santa Cruz, Bol.	254,682	H 7	90
Santa Cruz, Calif.	41,483	K 4	133
Santa Cruz (isls.), Sol. Is.	5,421	G 6	89
Santa Cruz de Tenerife, Spain	74,910	B 4	31
Santa Fe, Arg.	287,240	H10	93
Santa Fe (cap.), N. Mex.	48,953	C 3	157
Santa Maria, Calif.	39,685	E 9	133
Santa Marta, Col.	102,484	F 1	90
Santa Monica, Calif.	88,314	B10	133
Santander, Spain	130,014	D 1	31
Santanilla (isls.), Hond.		F 2	124
Santa Rosa, Calif.	83,205	C 5	133
Santee (riv.), S.C.		H 5	165
Santiago (cap.), Chile	3,614,947	N10	93
Santiago, Dom. Rep.	278,638	D 3	124
Santiago (mts.), Texas		A 8	168
Santiago de Cuba, Cuba	362,462	C 2	124
Santo Domingo (cap.), Dom. Rep.	1,313,172	E 3	124
Santos, Braz.	411,023	L 8	93
São Bernardo do Campo, Braz.	381,261	L 8	93
São Luís, Braz.	182,466	M 4	90
Saône (riv.), France		F 4	26
São Paulo, Braz.	7,033,529	L 8	93
São Tomé (cap.), São Tomé e Príncipe	7,681	H11	54
São Tomé e Príncipe	85,000	H11	57
São Vincent (cape), Port.		B 4	31
Sapporo, Japan	1,240,613	K 2	75
Sapulpa, Okla.	15,853	K 3	162
Saragossa, Spain	449,319	F 2	31
Sarajevo, Yugo.	245,058	C 3	43
Saransk, U.S.S.R.	263,000	G 4	50
Sarasota, Fla.	48,868	D 4	136
Saratoga, Calif.	29,261	K 4	133
Saratoga Nat'l Hist. Pk., N.Y.		N 4	158
Saratoga Springs, N.Y.	23,906	N 4	158
Saratov, U.S.S.R.	856,000	G 4	50
Sarawak (state), Malaysia	1,294,753	E 5	83
Sardinia (isl.), Italy		B 4	32
Sardis (lake), Miss.		E 2	150
Sargodha, Pak.	201,407	C 2	70
Sark (isl.), Chan. Is.	590	E 8	11
Sarnia, Ont.	50,892	B 5	108
Sasebo, Japan	250,729	D 7	75
Saskatchewan (prov.), Can.	968,313		113
Saskatchewan (riv.), Can.		F 5	96
Saskatoon, Sask.	*154,210	E 3	113
Saudi Arabia	8,367,000	D 4	60
Saugus, Mass.	24,746	D 6	147
Sault Ste. Marie, Mich.	14,448	E 2	148
Sault Ste. Marie, Ont.	82,697	J 5	108
Sausalito, Calif.	7,338	H 2	133
Sava (riv.), Yugo.		D 3	43
Savannah, Ga.	141,390	L 6	137
Savannah (riv.), U.S.		K 4	126
Save (riv.), Moz.		N16	57
Sawtooth Nat'l Rec. Area, Idaho		D 5	138
Sawu (sea), Indon.		G 7	83
Saxony (reg.), E. Ger.		E 3	20
Sayreville, N.J.	29,969	E 3	156
Scapa Flow (chan.), Scot.		E 2	13
Scarborough, Ont.	443,353	K 4	109
Scarsdale, N.Y.	17,650	J 1	158
Schaumburg, Ill.	53,305	A 5	139
Scheldt (riv.), Belg.		C 7	25
Schenectady, N.Y.	67,972	M 5	158
Schleswig-Holstein (state), W. Ger.		C 1	20
Schofield Barracks, Hawaii	18,851	B 4	130
Schwarzwald (Black) (for.), W. Ger.		C 4	20
Schweinfurt, W. Ger.	56,164	D 3	20
Scilly (isls.), Eng.		A 7	11
Scioto (riv.), Ohio		D 8	161
Scotch Plains, N.J.	20,774	E 2	156
Scotia (sea), Antarc.		D16	5
Scotland, U.K.	5,117,146		13
Scottsbluff, Nebr.	14,156	A 3	153
Scottsboro, Ala.	14,758	F 1	129
Scottsdale, Ariz.	88,622	D 5	131
Scranton, Pa.	88,117	F 7	164
Scutari (lake), Europe		D 4	43
Sea (isls.), U.S.		K 9	137
Seal Beach, Calif.	25,975	C11	133
Seaside, Calif.	36,567	D 7	133
Seattle, Wash.	493,846	A 2	171
Sedalia, Mo.	20,927	F 5	151
Segovia, Spain	41,880	D 2	31
Seine (riv.), France		DC3	26
Sekondi-Takoradi, Ghana	160,868	D 8	54
Selkirk (mts.), Br. Col.		H-J 4-5	117
Selkirk, Man.	10,037	F 4	110
Selma, Ala.	26,684	E 6	129
Semarang, Indon.	1,026,671	J 2	83
Semipalatinsk, U.S.S.R.	283,000	H 4	46
Sendai, Japan	615,473	K 4	75
Seneca (lake), N.Y.		G 5	158
Senegal	5,508,000	D 9	54
Senegal (riv.), Africa		D 8	54
Seoul (cap.), S. Korea	6,889,502	C 5	74
Sept-Îles, Que.	29,262	D 2	106
Sequoia Nat'l Pk., Calif.		G 7	133
Serbia (rep.), Yugo.		E 3	43
Serpents Mouth (str.)		G 5	124
Serpukhov, U.S.S.R.	140,000	E 4	50
Sétif, Alg.	144,200	H 4	54
Sevastopol', U.S.S.R.	301,000	D 6	50
Severn (riv.), Md.		J 4	146
Severn (riv.), U.K.		E 6	11
Severnaya Zemlya (isls.), U.S.S.R.		L 1	46
Severodvinsk, U.S.S.R.	197,000	E 2	50
Sevier (lake), Utah		A 5	169
Sevier (riv.), Utah		B 4	169
Seville, Spain	511,447	C 4	31
Seward, Alaska	1,843	J 2	130
Seward (pen.), Alaska		E 2	130
Seychelles	63,000	G10	58
Sfax, Tun.	171,297	J 5	54
's Gravenhage (The Hague) (cap.), Neth.	479,369	E 4	25
Shaanxi (Shensi) (prov.), China		G 5	77
Shaba (prov.), Zaire		M13	57
Shahjahanpur, India	135,604	E 3	70
Shaker Heights, Ohio	32,487	H 9	161
Shan (plat.), Burma		C 2	81
Shandong (Shantung) (prov.), China		J 4	77
Shanghai, China	10,980,000	K 5	77
Shannon (riv.), Ire.		E 6	15
Shantou (Swatow), China	400,000	J 7	77
Shanxi (Shansi) (prov.), China		H 4	77
Shari (riv.), Africa		K 9	54
Sharon, Pa.	19,057	B 3	164
Shasta (lake), Calif.		C 3	133
Shasta (mt.), Calif.		C 2	133
Shatt-al-'Arab (riv.), Asia		E 4	68
Shawinigan, Que.	23,011	E 3	105
Shawnee, Kans.	29,653	H 2	142
Shawnee, Okla.	26,506	J 4	162
Sheboygan, Wis.	48,085	L 8	173
Sheffield, Eng.	558,000	J 2	11
Shelby, N.C.	15,310	C 4	159
Shellbrook, Sask.	1,228	E 2	113
Shelton, Conn.	31,314	C 3	135
Shenandoah (mt.), Va.		F 3	170
Shenandoah (riv.), U.S.		J 2	170
Shenandoah Nat'l Pk., Va.		G 3	170
Shenyang (Mukden), China	3,750,000	K 3	77
Sherbrooke, Que.	74,075	E 4	105
Sheridan, Wyo.	15,146	F 1	174
Sherman, Texas	30,413	H 4	168
's Hertogenbosch, Neth.	88,184	G 5	25
Sherwood Park, Alta.	29,285	D 3	114
Sheyenne (riv.), N. Dak.		O 6	160
Shijiazhuang, China	1,500,000	J 4	77
Shikoku (isl.), Japan		F 7	75
Shiloh Nat'l Mem. Pk., Tenn.		E 4	167
Shimizu, Japan	243,049	J 6	75
Shimonoseki, Japan	266,593	J 6	75
Shipki (pass), Asia		D 2	70
Shiraz, Iran	416,408	H 6	68
Shizuoka, Japan	446,952	H 6	75
Sholapur, India	398,361	D 5	70
Shoshone (riv.), Wyo.		D 1	174
Shreveport, La.	205,820	C 2	144
Shrewsbury, Mass.	22,674	H 3	147
Sialkot, Pak.	203,779	C 2	70
Siam, see Thailand			
Siberia (reg.), U.S.S.R.		H-P 3	46
Sibiu, Rom.	156,854	G 3	43
Sichuan (Szechwan) (prov.), China		F 5	77
Sicily (isl.), Italy		D-E6	32
Sidi Bel Abbès, Alg.	116,000	F 4	54
Sidra (gulf), Libya		K 5	54
Siegen, W. Ger.	116,552	C 3	20
Sierra Leone	3,470,000	D10	54
Sierra Nevada (mts.), U.S.		B 3	126
Sierra Vista, Ariz.	24,937	E 7	131
Si Kiang, see Xi Jiang, China			
Sikkim (state), India		F 3	70
Silver Spring, Md.	72,893	B 4	146
Simcoe, Ont.	14,326	D 5	108
Simcoe (lake), Ont.		E 3	108
Simferopol', U.S.S.R.	302,000	D 6	50
Simi Valley, Calif.	77,500	G 9	133
Simplon (tunnel), Europe		F 4	37
Simpson (des.), Austr.		F 4	86
Sinai (pen.), Egypt		B 4	60
Sinchu, China	208,038	K 7	77
Sind (reg.), Pak.		B 3	70
Singapore	2,413,945	F 6	81
Singapore (cap.), Sing.	2,413,945	F 6	81
Sinkiang, see Xinjiang Uygur Zizhiqu, China			
Sinŭiju, N. Korea	300,000	B 3	74
Sioux City, Iowa	82,003	A 3	141
Sioux Falls, S. Dak.	81,343	R 6	166
Siracusa (Syracuse), Italy	96,006	E 6	32
Siskiyou (mts.), Calif.		C 2	133
Sitka, Alaska	7,803	N 3	130
Sitka Nat'l Mon., Alaska		N 3	130
Sivas, Turkey	149,201	G 3	64
Siwa (oasis), Egypt		M 6	54
Skagerrak (str.), Europe		C 2	19
Skagit (riv.), Wash.		C 2	171
Skeena (riv.), Br. Col.		C 3	117
Skikda, Alg.	107,700	H 4	54
Skokie, Ill.	60,278	B 5	139
Skopje, Yugo.	308,117	E 5	43
Skye (isl), Scot.		B 3	13
Skykomish (riv.), Wash.		D 3	171
Slave (riv.), Can.		E 3	96
Sleeping Bear Dunes Nat'l Lakeshore, Mich.		C 4	148
Slidell, La.	26,718	L 6	144
Sligo, Ire.	14,080	E 3	15
Slovakia (reg.), Czech.		L 6	39
Slovenia (rep.), Yugo.		B 2	43
Smithers, Br. Col.	4,570	D 3	117
Smiths Falls, Ont.	8,831	H 3	108
Smoky Hill (riv.), Kans.		C 3	142
Smolensk, U.S.S.R.	276,000	D 4	50
Smyrna, Ga.	20,312	K 1	137
Snake (riv.), U.S.		C 1	126
Snoqualmie (riv.), Wash.		D 3	171
Snowdon (mt.), Wales		D 4	11
Sochi, U.S.S.R.	287,000	E 6	50
Society (isls.), Fr. Poly.	117,703	L 7	89
Socotra (isl.), P.D.R. Yemen		F 7	60
Sofia (cap.), Bulg.	965,728	F 4	43
Sognafjorden (fjord), Nor.		D 6	16
Solingen, W. Ger.	171,810	B 3	20
Solomon (sea), Pacific		F 6	89
Solomon Islands	221,000	G 6	89
Solway (firth), U.K.		E 6	13
Somalia	3,645,000	R10	54
Somerset (isl.), Berm.		G 3	124
Somerset (isl.), N.W.T.		G 1	96
Somerville, Mass.	77,372	C 6	147
Somme (riv.), France		D 2	26
Songhua Jiang (riv.), China		M 2	77
Sonora (state), Mex.		C1-2	119
Sorel, Que.	20,347	D 4	105
Sorocaba, Braz.	254,718	L 8	93
Sosnowiec, Pol.	144,652	B 4	45
Souris, Man.	1,731	B 5	110
Souris (riv.), N. Amer.		F 1	126
Souris, P.E.I.	1,413	F 2	100
Sousse, Tun.	69,530	J 4	54
South (isl.), N.Z.	852,748	L 7	87
South Africa	23,771,970	L18	57
South America	245,000,000		90,93
Southampton, Eng.	213,700	F 7	11
South Australia (state), Austr.	1,285,033	E 5	86
South Bend, Ind.	109,727	E 1	140
South Burlington, Vt.	10,679	A 3	155
South Carolina (state), U.S.	3,121,833		165
South China (sea), Asia		N 8	58
South Dakota (state), U.S.	690,768		166
Southend-on-Sea, Eng.	159,300	H 6	11
Southern Alps (mts.), N.Z.		L 7	87
South Euclid, Ohio	25,713	H 9	161
Southfield, Mich.	75,568	F 6	148
South Gate, Calif.	66,784	C11	133
Southgate, Mich.	32,058	F 6	148
South Georgia (isl.), Antarc.		D17	5
South Holland, Ill.	24,977	C 6	139
Southington, Conn.	36,879	D 2	135
South Korea	37,448,836		74
South Lake Tahoe, Calif.	20,681	F 5	133
South Milwaukee, Wis.	21,069	M 2	173
South Orkney (isls.), Antarc.		C16	5
South Plainfield, N.J.	20,521	E 2	156
South Platte (riv.), U.S.		H 6	126
South Pole		A 5	5
South Portland, Maine	22,712	C 8	145
South Saint Paul, Minn.	21,235	G 6	149
South Sandwich (isl.), Antarc.		C16	5
South San Francisco, Calif.	49,393	J 2	133
South Saskatchewan (riv.), Can.		C 5	113
South-West Africa (Namibia)	1,200,000	K16	57
Spain	37,430,000		31
Spandau, W. Ger.	197,687	E 3	20
Sparks, Nev.	40,780	B 3	154
Spartanburg, S.C.	43,826	C 1	165
Spirit River, Alta.	1,104	A 2	114
Spitsbergen (isl.), Nor.		C 2	16
Split, Yugo.	150,739	C 4	43
Spokane, Wash.	171,300	H 3	171
Spree (riv.), Ger.		F 3	20
Springdale, Ark.	23,458	B 1	132
Springdale, Newf.	3,501	B 3	99
Springfield (cap.), Ill.	100,054	D 4	139
Springfield, Mass.	152,319	D 4	147
Springfield, Mo.	133,116	F 8	151
Springfield, Ohio	72,563	C 6	161
Springfield, Oreg.	41,621	E 3	163
Springfield, Vt.	10,190	B 5	155
Springhill, N.S.	4,896	E 3	100
Springvale, Austr.	80,186	K 3	86
Spring Valley, N.Y.	20,537	A 2	158
Springville, Utah	12,101	C 3	169
Squamish, Br. Col.	1,590	F 5	117
Sri Lanka	14,850,000	E 7	70
Srinagar, India	403,413	D 2	70
Staked (Llano Estacado) (plain), N. Mex.		F 5	157
Stalingrad (Volgograd), U.S.S.R.	929,000	F 5	50
Stamford, Conn.	102,453	A 4	135
Stanford, Calif.	11,045	J 3	133
Stanley (cap.), Falkland Is.		J14	93
Stanley (Boyoma) (falls), Zaire		M11	57
Stanley Pool (Malebo) (lake), Africa		K12	57
Stanovoy (range), U.S.S.R.		N 4	46
Stanton, Calif.	23,723	D11	133
Stara Zagora, Bulg.	122,200	G 4	43
Starkville, Miss.	15,169	G 4	150
State College, Pa.	36,130	G 4	164
Staten (Estados) (isl.), Arg.		H14	93
Staten Island (borough), N.Y.	352,121	C 3	158
Statesboro, Ga.	14,866	J 6	137
Statesville, N.C.	18,622	D 3	159
Statue of Liberty Nat'l Mon., U.S.		B 2	156
Staunton, Va.	21,857	F 4	170
Stavropol', U.S.S.R.	258,000	F 5	50
Sterling, Colo.	11,385	N 1	134
Sterling, Ill.	16,281	D 2	139
Sterling Heights, Mich.	108,999	B 6	148
Sterlitamak, U.S.S.R.	220,000	J 4	50
Steubenville, Ohio	26,400	J 5	161
Stevens Point, Wis.	22,970	G 7	173
Stewart (isl.), N.Z.	600	K 8	87
Stillwater, Okla.	38,268	J 2	162
Stirling, Austr.	161,858	B 2	86
Stockholm (cap.), Sweden	665,550	G 1	16
Stockport, Eng.	138,350	H 2	11
Stockton, Calif.	149,779	D 6	133
Stockton (plat.), Texas		B 7	168
Stockton-on-Tees, Eng.	165,400	F 3	11
Stoke-on-Trent, Eng.	256,200	E 4	11
Stones River Nat'l Battlfld., Tenn.		H 3	167
Stoney Creek, Ont.	36,762	E 4	108
Stoughton, Mass.	26,710	K 4	147
Stow, Ohio	25,303	H 3	161
Strasbourg, France	251,520	G 3	26
Stratford, Conn.	50,541	C 4	135
Stratford, Ont.	26,262	C 4	108
Stratford-upon-Avon, Eng.	20,080	F 5	11
Strawberry (riv.), Utah		D 3	169
Stromboli (isl.), Italy		E 5	32
Strongsville, Ohio	28,577	G10	161
Stuttgart, Ark.	10,941	H 4	132
Stuttgart, W. Ger.	600,421	C 4	20
Subotica, Yugo.	89,476	D 2	43
Sucre (cap.), Bol.	63,625	G 7	90
Sudan	18,691,000	M 9	54
Sudan (reg.), Africa		F-M 9	54
Sudbury, Ont.	*149,923	K 5	108
Sudeten (mts.), Europe		C-D1	39
Suez, Egypt	194,001	N 6	54
Suez (canal), Egypt		N 5	54
Suffolk, Va.	47,621	L 7	170
Suita, Japan	300,956	J 7	75
Suitland-Silver Hill, Md.	32,164	C 5	146
Sukkur, Pak.	158,876	B 3	70
Sulawesi (Celebes) (isl.), Indon.	7,732,383	G 6	83
Sulphur, La.	19,709	D 6	144

	Pop.	Key	Pg.
Sulu (sea), Asia		G 4	83
Sulu (arch.), Phil.		G 4	83
Sumatra (isl.), Indon.	19,360,400	B 5	83
Sumba (isl.), Indon.	291,190	F 7	83
Sumbawa (isl.), Indon.	621,140	F 7	83
Sumgait, U.S.S.R.	190,000	G 6	50
Summerside, P.E.I.	7,828	E 2	100
Summit, N.J.	21,071	E 2	156
Sumter, S.C.	24,890	G 4	165
Sumy, U.S.S.R.	228,000	E 4	50
Sun (riv.), Mont.		D 3	152
Sunapee (lake), N.H.		B 5	155
Suncook (lakes), N.H.		E 5	155
Sunda (str.), Indon.		C 7	83
Sunderland, Eng.	214,820	J 3	11
Sungari (riv.), see Songhua Jiang, China			
Sunnyvale, Calif.	106,618	K 3	133
Sunrise, Fla.	39,681	B 4	136
Sunset Crater Nat'l Mon., Ariz.		D 3	131
Sunshine, Austr.	94,419	J 2	86
Sun Valley, Idaho	545	D 6	138
Suo (sea), Japan		C 4	75
Superior (lake), N. Amer.		K 5	94
Superior, Wis.	29,571	C 2	173
Superstition (mts.), Ariz.		D 5	131
Surabaya, Indon.	2,027,913	K 2	83
Surakarta, Indon.	469,888	J 2	83
Surat, India	471,656	C 4	70
Suriname	354,860	J 3	90
Surrey, Br. Col.	*147,138	K 3	117
Susquehanna (riv.), U.S.		K 6	164
Sutherland, Austr.	165,366	K 5	86
Sutton, Eng.	166,700	H 8	11
Suva (cap.), Fiji	63,628	H 7	89
Suwannee (riv.), U.S.		C 2	136
Suwŏn, S. Korea	224,145	C 5	74
Suzhou, China	1,300,000	K 5	77
Svalbard (isls.), Nor.		C 3	16
Sverdlovsk, U.S.S.R.	1,211,000	F 4	46
Sverdrup (isls.), N.W.T.		M 3	96
Swabian Jura (mts.), W. Ger.		C 4	20
Swan (Santanilla) (isls.), Hond.		F 2	124
Swansea, Wales	190,800	C 6	11
Swaziland	547,000	N17	57
Sweden	8,320,000		16
Sweetwater, Texas	12,242	D 5	168
Sweetwater (riv.), Wyo.		D 3	174
Swift Current, Sask.	14,747	D 5	113
Switzerland	6,365,960		37
Sydney, Austr.	2,876,508	L 4	86
Sydney, N.S.	29,444	H 2	100
Syracuse, Italy	93,006	E 6	32
Syracuse, N.Y.	170,105	H 4	158
Syrdar'ya (riv.), U.S.S.R.		G 5	46
Syria	8,979,000	C 2	60
Syrian (des.), Asia		A-B 4	68
Syzran', U.S.S.R.	178,000	G 4	50
Szczecin, Pol.	337,204	B 2	45
Szechwan, see Sichuan, China			
Szeged, Hung.	171,342	E 3	39
Székesfehérvár, Hung.	103,197	E 3	39

T

	Pop.	Key	Pg.
Taber, Alta.	5,988	E 5	114
Tabora, Tanz.	67,392	N12	57
Tabriz, Iran	598,576	D 2	68
Tabuaeran (isl.), Kiribati	340	L 5	89
Tacoma, Wash.	158,501	C 3	171
Taconic (mts.), U.S.		A 2	147
Tadzhik S.S.R., U.S.S.R.	3,801,000	H 6	46
Taegu, S. Korea	1,310,768	D 6	75
Taejŏn, S. Korea	506,708	C 5	75
Taganrog, U.S.S.R.	276,000	E 5	50
Tagus (riv.), Europe		D 3	31
Tahiti (isl.), Fr. Poly.	95,604	L 7	89
Tahoe (lake), U.S.		C 3	126
Tahquamenon (riv.), Mich.		D 2	148
Taichung, China	565,255	K 7	77
Tainan, China	541,390	J 7	77
Taipei (cap.), Taiwan (Rep. of China)	2,108,193	K 7	77
Taiwan (isl.), China	16,609,961	K 7	77
Taiyuan, China	2,725,000	H 4	77
Ta'izz, Yemen Arab Rep.	78,642	D 7	60
Takamatsu, Japan	298,999	F 6	75
Takasaki, Japan	211,348	J 5	75
Takaoka, Japan	169,621	H 5	75
Taklimakan Shamo (des.), China		A-C 4	77
Takoma Park, Md.	16,231	B 4	146
Takoradi-Sekondi, Ghana	58,161	F 11	54
Talbot (isl.), Fla.		E 1	136
Talca, Chile	133,160	F 11	93
Talcahuano, Chile	148,300	F 11	93
Talladega, Ala.	19,128	F 4	129
Tallahassee (cap.), Fla.	81,548	B 1	136
Tallinn, U.S.S.R.	430,000	C 1	51
Tamarac, Fla.	29,376	B 3	136
Tambov, U.S.S.R.	270,000	F 4	50
Tamiami (canal), Fla.		E 6	136
Tampa, Fla.	271,523	C 2	136
Tampa (bay), Fla.		D 4	136
Tampere, Fin.	168,118	N 6	16
Tampico, Mex.	212,188	L 5	119
Tana (lake), Eth.		O 9	54
Tanana (riv.), Alaska		K 1	130
Tandil, Arg.	78,821	J 11	93
Tanezrouft (des.), Africa		G 7	54
Tanga, Tanz.	103,409	O12	57
Tanganyika (lake), Africa		N13	57
Tangier, Mor.	187,894	E 4	54
Tangier (sound), Md.		L 8	146
Tangshan, China	1,200,000	J 4	77
Tanjungkarang, Indon.	284,275	C 7	83
Tanta, Egypt	284,636	N 5	54
Tanzania	17,527,560	N13	57
Taos, N. Mex.	3,369	D 2	157
Tapachula, Mex.	60,620	N 9	119
Tar (riv.), N.C.		K 3	159
Tarabulus, Leb.	127,611	F 5	64
Taranto, Italy	205,158	F 4	32
Tarawa (atoll), Kiribati	17,129	H 5	89
Tarim He (riv.), China		B 3	77
Tarnów, Pol.	85,514	E 4	45
Tarpon Springs, Fla.	13,251	D 3	136
Tarragona, Spain	53,548	G 2	31
Tarrasa, Spain	134,481	G 2	31
Tarsus, Turkey	102,186	F 4	64
Tartu, U.S.S.R.	105,000	D 1	51
Tashkent, U.S.S.R.	1,780,000	G 5	46
Tasman (sea), Pacific		G 9	89
Tasmania (state), Austr.	418,957	H 8	86
Tatar (str.), U.S.S.R.		P 4	46
Tatra, High (mts.), Europe		E 2	39
Taunton, Eng.	37,570	D 6	11
Taunton, Mass.	45,001	K 5	147
Taurus (mts.), Turkey		D-E 4	64
Taxila (ruins), Pak.		C 2	70
Tay (firth), Scot.		F 4	13
Taylor, Mich.	77,568	B 7	148
Taymyr (pen.), U.S.S.R.		L 2	46
Tbilisi, U.S.S.R.	1,066,000	F 6	50
Teaneck, N.J.	39,007	B 2	156
Tees (riv.), Eng.		F 3	11
Tegucigalpa (cap.), Hond.	273,894	D 3	122
Tehran (cap.), Iran	4,496,159	G 3	68
Tehuantepec, Mex.	16,179	M 8	119
Tejo (Tagus) (riv.), Port.		B 3	31
Tel Aviv-Jaffa, Isr.	343,300	B 3	67
Tempe, Ariz.	106,743	D 5	131
Temple, Texas	42,354	G 6	168
Temple City, Calif.	28,972	D10	133
Temuco, Chile	197,232	F 11	93
Tenerife (isl.), Spain		B 5	31
Tenkiller Ferry (lake), Okla.		N 3	162
Tennessee (riv.), U.S.		J 3	126
Tennessee (state), U.S.	4,591,120		167
Ten Thousand (isls.), Fla.		E 6	136
Tepic, Mexico	108,924	G 6	119
Teresina, Braz.	339,264	M 4	90
Ternate, Indon.	34,539	H 5	83
Terni, Italy	75,873	D 3	32
Terra Nova Nat'l Pk., Newf.		D 3	99
Terrebonne (bay), La.		J 8	144
Terre Haute, Ind.	61,125	C 6	140
Teton (range), Wyo.		B 2	174
Teutoburger Wald (for.), W. Ger.		C 2	20
Tewksbury, Mass.	24,635	K 2	147
Texarkana, Ark.	21,459	C 7	132
Texarkana, Texas	31,271	L 4	168
Texas (state), U.S.	14,229,288		168
Texas City, Texas	41,403	K 3	168
Texel (isl.), Neth.		F 2	25
Thailand	46,455,000	C 3	81
Thames (riv.), Conn.		G 3	135
Thames (riv.), Eng.		H 6	11
Thames (riv.), Ont.		B 5	108
Thana, India	170,675	B 6	70
Thanjavur, India	140,547	D 6	70
Thásos (isl.), Greece		G 5	43
The Dalles, Oreg.	10,820	F 2	163
Theodore Roosevelt (lake), Ariz.		D 5	131
Theodore Roosevelt Nat'l Pk., N. Dak.		D 6	166
The Pas, Man.	6,390	H 3	110
Thessaloníki, Greece	345,799	F 5	43
Thetford Mines, Que.	19,965	F 3	105
Thibodeaux, La.	15,810	J 7	144
Thiès, Sen.	117,333	C 9	54
Thimphu (cap.), Bhutan	50,000	G 3	70
Thomasville, Ga.	18,463	E 9	137
Thomasville, N.C.	14,144	E 3	159
Thon Buri, Thai.	628,015	D 4	81
Thornton, Colo.	40,343	K 3	161
Thousand (isls.), N. Amer.		H 2	158
Thousand Oaks, Calif.	77,072	G 9	133
Thule (Qaanaaq), Greenl.		M 2	94
Thun, Switz.	37,000	E 3	37
Thunder Bay, Ont.	*121,379	H 5	108
Thüringer Wald (for.), E. Ger.		D 3	20
Tianjin (Tientsin), China	7,210,000	J 4	77
Tian Shan (mts.), China		B-D 3	77
Tiber (riv.), Italy		D 3	32
Tiberias, Isr.	23,800	C 2	67
Tibesti (mts.), Chad		K 7	54
Tibet (reg.), China		C 5	77
Tientsin, see Tianjin, China			
Tierra del Fuego (isl.), S. Amer.		G14	93
Tiffin, Ohio	19,549	D 3	161
Tifton, Ga.	13,749	F 8	137
Tigard, Oreg.	14,286	A 2	163
Tigris (riv.), Asia		D 2	60
Tihama (reg.), Asia		C-D 5-7	60
Tijuana, Mex.	363,154	A 1	119
Tilburg, Neth.	151,513	G 5	25
Timaru, N.Z.	28,412	K 7	87
Timbuktu (Tombouctou), Mali	20,483	F 8	54
Timişoara, Rom.	281,320	E 3	43
Timor (reg.), Indon.	1,435,527	H 7	83
Timpanogos Cave Nat'l Mon., Utah		C 3	169
Tinian (isl.), N. Marianas	866	E 4	89
Tinley Park, Ill.	26,171	B 6	139
Tioga (riv.), Pa.		H 1	164
Tippecanoe (riv.), Ind.		E 2	140
Tipperary, Ire.	4,631	E 7	15
Tiranë (Tirana) (cap.), Albania	171,300	E 5	43
Tîrgovişte, Rom.	71,533	G 3	43
Tîrgu Mureş, Rom.	129,284	G 2	43
Tirol (reg.), Austria		A 3	39
Tiruchchirappalli, India	307,400	D 6	70
Titicaca (lake), S. Amer.		F 7	90
Titograd, Yugo.	54,639	D 4	43
Titusville, Fla.	31,910	F 3	136
Tiverton, R.I.	13,526	K 6	147
Tlemcen, Alg.	109,400	F 5	54
Toamasina (Tamatave), Madag.	77,395	S15	57
Tobago (isl.), Trin. & Tob.		G 5	124
Tobol'sk, U.S.S.R.	62,000	G 4	46
Tobruk, Libya	58,000	L 5	54
Togliatti (Tol'yatti), U.S.S.R.	502,000	G 4	50
Togo	2,472,000	G10	54
Toiyabe (range), Nev.		D 3	154
Tokelau	1,575	J 6	89
Tokushima, Japan	239,281	G 7	75
Tokyo (cap.), Japan	8,646,520	O 2	75
Toledo, Ohio	354,635	D 2	161
Toledo, Spain	43,905	D 3	31
Toluca, Mex.	136,092	K 7	119
Tomakomai, Japan	132,477	K 2	75
Tombigbee (riv.), U.S.		J 4	126
Tomsk, U.S.S.R.	421,000	J 4	46
Tonawanda, N.Y.	18,693	B 4	158
Tonga	90,128	J 8	89
Tongareva (atoll), Cook Is.	608	L 6	89
Tongue (riv.), U.S.		K 5	152
Tonkin (gulf), Asia		E 3	81
Tonle Sap (lake), Camb.		D 4	83
Tooele, Utah	14,335	B 3	169
Topeka (cap.), Kans.	115,266	G 2	142
Torbay, Eng.	109,900	D 7	11
Torino (Turin), Italy	1,181,698	A 2	32
Toronto (cap.), Ont.	*2,998,947	K 4	108
Torquay, see Torbay, Eng.			
Torrance, Calif.	129,881	C11	133
Torreón, Mex.	244,309	H 4	119
Torres (str.)		G 1	86
Torrington, Conn.	30,987	C 1	135
Tórshavn, Faeroe Is.	11,618	A 3	19
Tortola (isl.), V.I. (Br.)		H 1	124
Toruń, Pol.	129,152	D 2	45
Tottori, Japan	122,312	G 6	75
Toulon, France	180,508	F 6	26
Toulouse, France	371,143	D 6	26
Tournai, Belg.	32,794	C 7	25
Touro Synagogue Nat'l Hist. Site, R.I.		J 7	147
Tours, France	139,560	D 4	26
Towson, Md.	51,083	H 3	146
Toyama, Japan	290,143	H 5	75
Toyohashi, Japan	284,585	H 6	75
Trabzon, Turkey	97,210	H 2	64
Trafalgar (cape), Spain		C 4	31
Tralee, Ire.	13,216	B 7	15
Transkei (aut. rep.), S. Africa		M18	57
Transvaal (prov.), S. Africa		M17	57
Transylvanian Alps (mts.), Rom.		G 3	43
Traverse City, Mich.	15,516	D 4	148
Trenton, Mich.	22,762	B 7	148
Trenton (cap.), N.J.	92,124	D 3	156
Trier, W. Ger.	100,338	B 4	20
Trieste, Italy	257,259	E 2	32
Trinidad, Colo.	9,663	L 8	134
Trinidad (isl.), Trin. & Tob.		G 5	124
Trinidad and Tobago	1,067,108	G 5	124
Trinity (riv.), Calif.		B 3	133
Trinity (bay), Newf.		D 3	99
Trinity (riv.), Texas		H 5	168
Tripoli (Tarabulus), Leb.	127,611	F 5	64
Tripoli (cap.), Libya	550,438	J 5	54
Tripolitania (reg.), Libya		J-K 6	54
Tristan da Cunha (isl.), St. Helena	251		1
Trivandrum, India	409,627	D 7	70
Trois-Rivières, Que.	*111,453	E 3	105
Trondheim, Nor.	134,910	F 5	16
Troy, Mich.	67,102	B 6	148
Troy, N.Y.	56,638	N 5	158
Truckee (riv.), U.S.		B 3	154
Trujillo, Peru	354,557	C 7	90
Truk (isls.), Fed. States of Micronesia	37,488	F 5	89
Trumbull, Conn.	32,989	C 4	135
Tselinograd, U.S.S.R	234,000	H 4	46
Tuamotu (arch.), Fr. Poly.	9,052	M 7	89
Tübingen, W. Ger.	71,348	C 4	20
Tubuai (Austral) (isls.), Fr. Poly.	5,208	M 8	89
Tucson, Ariz.	330,537	D 6	131
Tula, U.S.S.R.	514,000	E 4	50
Tulare, Calif.	22,526	F 7	133
Tullahoma, Tenn.	15,800	J 4	167
Tulsa, Okla.	360,919	K 2	162
Tumacacori Nat'l Mon., Ariz.		E 7	131
Tunis (cap.), Tun.	550,404	J 4	54
Tunisia	6,367,000	H 5	54
Tupelo, Miss.	23,905	G 2	150
Tupelo Nat'l Battlfld., Miss.		G 2	150
Turin, Italy	1,181,698	A 2	32
Turkana (lake), Africa		O11	54
Turkestan, U.S.S.R.	67,000	G 5	46
Turkey	45,217,556	D 3	64
Turkey (riv.), Iowa		K 2	141
Turkmen S.S.R., U.S.S.R.	2,759,000	F 5	46
Turks & Caicos Is.	7,436	D 2	124
Turku, Fin.	164,857	N 6	16
Turlock, Calif.	26,287	E 6	133
Turtle (mts.), N. Dak.		K 2	160
Tuscaloosa, Ala.	75,211	C 4	129
Tuscany (reg.), Italy		C 3	32
Tuscarawas (riv.), Ohio		H 5	161
Tuskegee, Ala.	13,327	G 6	129
Tuticorin, India	155,310	D 7	70
Tutuila (isl.), Amer. Samoa	30,538	J 7	89
Tuvalu	7,349	H 6	89
Tuzigoot Nat'l Mon., Ariz.		D 4	131
Tweedsmuir Prov. Pk., Br. Col.		D 3	117
Twin Falls, Idaho	26,209	D 7	138
Two Rivers, Wis.	13,354	M 7	173
Tychy, Poland	71,384	B 4	45
Tyler, Texas	70,508	J 5	168
Tyre (Sur), Leb.	16,483	F 6	64
Tyrrhenian (sea), Italy		C 4	32
Tyumen, U.S.S.R.	359,000	G 4	46

U

	Pop.	Key	Pg.
Ubangi (riv.), Africa		K11	57
Ube, Japan	161,969	E 6	75
Uberaba, Braz.	180,296	L 7	90
Uberlândia, Braz.	230,400	L 7	90
Ucayali (riv.), Peru		E 5	90
Udaipur, India	161,278	C 4	70
Ufa, U.S.S.R.	969,000	J 4	50
Uganda	12,630,076	N12	57
Uinta (mts.), Utah		D 3	169
Ujjain, India	203,278	D 4	70
Ujung Pandang (Makassar), Indon.	709,038	F 7	83
Ukrainian S.S.R., U.S.S.R.	49,755,000	D 5	50
Ulaanbaatar (cap.), Mong.	345,000	G 2	77
Ulan-Ude, U.S.S.R.	300,000	L 4	46
Ulhasnagar, India	168,462	C 5	70
Ulm, W. Ger.	98,237	C 4	20
Ulsan, S. Korea	252,570	D 6	75
Ul'yanovsk, U.S.S.R.	464,000	G 4	50
Umbria (reg.), Italy		D 3	32
Umpqua (riv.), Oreg.		D 4	163
Ungava (pen.), Que.		E 1	106
Union, N.J.	50,184	A 2	156
Union City, Calif.	39,406	K 2	133

	Pop.	Key	Pg.
Union City, N.J.	55,983	C 2	156
Union City, Tenn.	10,436	C 2	167
Union of Soviet Socialist Republics	262,436,227		46
United Arab Emirates	1,040,275	F 5	60
United Kingdom	55,672,000		8
United States	226,504,825		126
University City, Mo.	42,738	P 3	151
University Park, Texas	22,254	G 2	168
Upland, Calif.	47,647	E 10	133
Upper Arlington, Ohio	35,648	D 6	161
Upper Klamath (lake), Oreg.		E 5	163
Upper Volta (Burkina Faso)	6,908,000	F 9	54
Uppsala, Sweden	101,850	K 7	16
Ur (ruins), Iraq		E 5	68
Ural (mts.), U.S.S.R.		F 4	46
Ural (riv.), U.S.S.R.		H 5	50
Uralsk, U.S.S.R.	167,000	F 4	46
Urawa, Japan	331,145	O 2	75
Urbana, Ill.	35,978	E 3	139
Urbandale, Iowa	17,869	F 5	141
Urmia, Iran	163,991	D 2	68
Urmia (lake), Iran		D 2	68
Uruapan, Mex.	108,124	H 7	119
Uruguay	2,899,000	J 10	93
Uruguay (riv.), S. Amer.		J 9	93
Ürümqi (Urumchi), China	500,000	C 3	77
Ussuri Wusuli (riv.), Asia		M 2	77
Ustinov, U.S.S.R.	549,000	H 3	50
Ust-Kamenogorsk, U.S.S.R.	274,000	J 5	46
Utah (state), U.S.	1,461,037		169
Utica, N.Y.	75,632	K 4	158
Utrecht, Neth.	250,887	G 4	25
Utsunomiya, Japan	344,420	K 5	75
Uvalde, Texas	14,178	E 8	168
Uxmal (ruins), Mex.		P 6	119
Uzbek S.S.R., U.S.S.R.	15,391,000	G 5	46

V

	Pop.	Key	Pg.
Vaal (riv.), S. Africa		M17	57
Vaasa, Fin.	54,402	M 5	16
Vacaville, Calif.	43,367	D 5	133
Vadodara, India	466,696	C 4	70
Vaduz (cap.), Liechtenstein	4,614	H 2	37
Valdez, Alaska	3,079	K 2	130
Valdivia, Chile	115,536	F 11	93
Valdosta, Ga.	37,596	F 9	137
Valencia, Spain	626,675	F 3	31
Valencia, Ven.	367,171	G 2	90
Valladolid, Spain	227,511	D 2	31
Vallejo, Calif.	80,303	J 1	133
Valletta (cap.), Malta	14,042	E 7	32
Valley Stream, N.Y.	35,769	A 3	158
Valparaíso, Chile	271,580	F 10	93
Valparaiso, Ind.	22,247	C 2	136
Van Buren, Ark.	12,020	B 3	132
Vancouver, Br. Col.	*1,169,831	K 3	117
Vancouver (isl.), Br. Col.		D 5	117
Vancouver, Wash.	42,834	C 5	171
Vandalia, Ill.	5,338	D 5	139
Vandenberg A.F.B., Calif.		E 9	133
Vänern (lake), Sweden		H 7	16
Vanuatu	112,596	G 7	89
Varanasi, India	583,856	E 3	70
Varna, Bulg.	251,654	J 4	43
Västeras, Sweden	147,508	K 7	16
Vatican City	728	B 6	32
Vellore, India	139,082	D 6	70
Venda (aut. rep.), S. Africa		N16	57
Veneto (reg.), Italy		C 2	32
Venezuela	14,313,000	F-H 2	90
Venice, Fla.	12,153	D 4	136
Venice (Venezia), Italy	108,082	D 2	32
Ventura, Calif.	74,474	F 9	133
Veracruz, Mex.	255,646	Q 1	119
Verde (cape.), Sen.		C 9	54
Verdun, France	22,889	F 3	26
Verkhoyansk (range), U.S.S.R.		N 3	46
Vermillion, S. Dak.	10,136	R 8	166
Vermont (state), U.S.	511,456		155
Vernon, Conn.	27,974	F 1	135
Vero Beach, Fla.	16,176	F 4	136
Verona, Italy	227,032	C 2	32
Versailles, France	93,359	A 2	26
Vesuvius (vol.), Italy		E 4	32
Vicenza, Italy	99,451	C 2	32
Vichy, France	32,107	E 4	26
Vicksburg, Miss.	25,434	C 6	150
Vicksburg Nat'l Mil. Pk., Miss.		C 6	150
Victoria (Mosi-Oa-Tunya) (falls), Africa		M15	57
Victoria (lake), Africa		N12	57
Victoria (state), Austr.	3,832,443	G-H 7	86
Victoria (cap.), Br. Col.	*233,481	K 4	117
Victoria (cap.), Hong Kong	1,026,870	H 7	77
Victoria (isl.), N.W.T.		E 1	96
Victoria, Tex.	50,695	H 9	168
Vienna (cap.), Austria	1,700,000	D 2	39
Vienna, Va.	15,469	M 2	170
Vientiane (cap.), Laos	132,253	D 3	81
Vietnam	52,741,766	E 3	81
Vigo, Spain	114,526	B 1	31
Vijayawada, India	317,258	D 5	70
Vila (cap.), Vanuatu	4,729	G 7	89
Villahermosa, Mex.	133,181	N 8	119
Villa Park, Ill.	23,185	B 5	139
Vilna (Vilnius), U.S.S.R.	481,000	C 3	51
Viña del Mar, Chile	281,361	N 9	93
Vincennes, Ind.	20,857	C 7	140
Vineland, N.J.	53,753	C 5	156
Vinnitsa, U.S.S.R.	314,000	C 5	50
Vinson Massif (mt.), Antarc.		B 14	5
Virgin Is. (Br.)	11,006	H 1	124
Virgin Is. (U.S.)	96,569	H 1	124
Virgin Is. Nat'l Pk., V.I. (U.S.)		G 1	124
Virginia, Minn.	11,056	F 3	149
Virginia (state), U.S.	5,346,816		170
Virginia Beach, Va.	262,199	N 7	170
Visakhapatnam, India	352,504	E 5	70
Visalia, Calif.	49,729	F 7	133
Vista, Calif.	35,834	H 10	133
Vitebsk, U.S.S.R.	297,000	C 3	50
Vitória, Braz.	144,143	N 8	90
Vitoria, Spain	124,791	E 1	31
Vladimir, U.S.S.R.	296,000	F 3	50
Vladivostok, U.S.S.R.	550,000	O 5	46
Vohimena (cape), Madag.		P 17	57
Volga (riv.), U.S.S.R.		G 5	50
Volgograd, U.S.S.R.	929,000	F 5	50
Vologda, U.S.S.R.	237,000	F 3	50
Volta (lake), Ghana		F 10	54
Volta Redonda, Braz.	177,772	M 8	93
Vorkuta, U.S.S.R.	100,000	K 1	50
Voronezh, U.S.S.R.	783,000	E 4	50
Voroshilovgrad, U.S.S.R.	463,000	E 5	50
Vosges (mts.), France		G 3	26
Voyageurs Nat'l Pk., Minn.		F 2	149

W

	Pop.	Key	Pg.
Wabash (riv.), U.S.		J 3	126
Waco, Tex.	101,261	G 6	168
Wahiawa, Hawaii	16,911	B 4	130
Wailuku, Hawaii	10,260	E 3	130
Waipahu, Hawaii	29,139	C 2	130
Wakayama, Japan	389,717	G 6	75
Wake (isl.), Pacific	302	G 4	89
Wakefield, Mass.	24,895	C 5	147
Walbrzych, Pol.	125,048	C 3	45
Wales, U.K.	2,790,462	D 5	11
Walla Walla, Wash.	25,618	G 4	171
Wallingford, Conn.	32,274	D 3	135
Wallis & Futuna	9,192	J 7	89
Walnut Canyon Nat'l Mon., Ariz.		D 3	131
Walnut Creek, Calif.	53,643	K 2	133
Walsall, Eng.	182,430	E 5	11
Waltham, Mass.	58,200	B 6	147
Walvis Bay, S. Africa	21,725	J 16	57
Waramaug (lake), Conn.		B 2	135
Warangal, India	207,520	D 5	70
Warner Robins, Ga.	39,893	E 5	137
Warren, Mich.	161,134	B 6	148
Warren, Ohio	56,629	J 3	161
Warrensburg, Mo.	13,807	E 5	151
Warrington, Eng.	65,320	G 2	11
Warsaw (cap.), Pol.	1,377,100	E 2	45
Warwick, R.I.	87,123	J 6	147
Wasatch (range), U.S.		C 3	169
Wash, The (bay), Eng.		G 4	8
Washington (mt.), N.H.		E 3	155
Washington, Pa.	18,363	B 5	164
Washington (state), U.S.	4,132,180		171
Washington, D.C. (cap.), U.S.	638,432	B 5	146
Waterbury, Conn.	103,266	C 2	135
Waterford, Conn.	17,843	G 3	135
Waterford, Ire.	31,968	G 7	15
Waterloo, Belg.	17,764	E 7	25
Waterloo, Iowa	75,985	J 4	141
Waterton-Glacier Int'l Peace Pk., N. Amer.		C1-2	152
Watertown, Conn.	19,489	C 2	135
Watertown, Mass.	34,384	C 6	147
Watertown, N.Y.	27,861	J 3	158
Watertown, S. Dak.	15,649	P 4	166
Watertown, Wis.	18,113	J 9	173
Waterville, Maine	17,779	D 6	145
Watkins Glen, N.Y.	2,440	G 6	158
Watling (San Salvador) (isl.), Bah.		C 2	124
Watsonville, Calif.	23,663	D 7	133
Waukegan, Ill.	67,653	B 4	139
Waukesha, Wis.	50,365	K 1	173
Wausau, Wis.	32,426	G 6	173
Wauwatosa, Wis.	51,308	L 1	173
Waycross, Ga.	19,371	H 8	137
Wayne, Mich.	21,159	F 6	148
Wayne, N.J.	46,474	A 1	156
Webster Groves, Mo.	23,097	P 3	151
Weirton, W. Va.	25,371	K 5	172
Welland, Ont.	454,448	E 5	108
Wellesley, Mass.	27,209	B 7	147
Wellington (cap.), N.Z.	135,688	L 7	87
Wenatchee, Wash.	17,257	E 3	171
Wenzhou, China	250,000	J 6	77
Weser (riv.), W. Ger.		C 2	20
West Allis, Wis.	63,982	L 1	173
West Bank		C 3	67
West Bend, Wis.	21,484	K 9	173
Westbrook, Maine	14,976	C 8	145
Westchester, Ill.	17,730	B 5	139
West Chester, Pa.	17,435	L 6	164
West Covina, Calif.	80,291	D 10	133
West Des Moines, Iowa	21,894	F 5	141
Westerly, R.I.	18,580	G 7	147
Western Australia (state), Austr.	1,273,624	B 4	86
Western Sahara	76,425	C 6	54
Western Samoa	158,130	J 7	89
Westerville, Ohio	23,414	D 5	161
West Fargo, N. Dak.	10,099	S 6	160
Westfield, Mass.	36,465	D 4	147
Westfield, N.J.	30,447	E 2	156
West Hartford, Conn.	61,301	D 1	135
West Haven, Conn.	53,184	D 3	135
West Indies			124
West Lafayette, Ind.	21,247	D 4	140
Westland, Mich.	84,603	F 6	148
West Linn, Oreg.	12,956	B 2	163
West Memphis, Ark.	28,138	K 3	132
West Mifflin, Pa.	26,552	C 7	164
Westminster, Calif.	71,133	D 11	133
Westminster, Colo.	50,211	J 3	134
Westminster, Eng.	216,000	H 8	11
West Monroe, La.	14,993	F 1	144
West New York, N.J.	39,194	C 2	156
West Orange, N.J.	39,510	A 2	156
West Palm Beach, Fla.	63,305	F 5	136
West Point, N.Y.	8,105	C 1	158
Westport, Conn.	25,290	B 4	135
West St. Paul, Minn.	18,527	G 5	149
West Seneca, N.Y.	51,210	C 5	158
West Springfield, Mass.	27,042	D 4	147
West Virginia (state), U.S.	1,950,279		172
West Warwick, R.I.	27,026	H 6	147
Westwego, La.	12,663	O 4	144
Wethersfield, Conn.	26,013	E 2	135
Weymouth, Mass.	55,601	D 8	147
Wheaton, Ill.	43,043	A 5	139
Wheat Ridge, Colo.	30,293	J 3	134
Wheeling, Ill.	23,266	F 1	139
Wheeling, W. Va.	43,070	K 5	172
Whiskeytown-Shasta-Trinity Nat'l Rec. Area, Calif.		C 3	133
Whitby, Ont.	36,698	F 4	108
White (riv.), Ind.		B 8	140
White (mts.), N.H.		E 3	155
White (sea), U.S.S.R.		E 1	50
White Bear Lake, Minn.	22,538	G 5	149
Whitehorse (cap.), Yukon	14,814	C 3	96
White Nile (riv.), Africa		N 10	54
White Plains, N.Y.	46,999	J 1	158
White Russian S.S.R., U.S.S.R.	9,560,000	C 4	50
White Sands Nat'l Mon., N. Mex.		C 6	157
Whitewater, Wis.	11,520	J 10	173
Whitman Mission Nat'l Hist. Site, Wash.		G 4	171
Whitney (mt.), Calif.		G 7	133
Whittier, Calif.	69,711	D 11	133
Wichita, Kans.	279,835	E 4	142
Wichita (mts.), Okla.		E 5	162
Wichita Falls, Tex.	94,201	F 4	168
Wien, see Vienna, Austria			
Wiesbaden, W. Ger.	250,592	B 3	20
Wight (isl.), Eng.		F 7	11
Wilhelmshaven, W. Ger.	103,417	B 2	20
Wilkes-Barre, Pa.	51,551	F 7	164
Wilkinsburg, Pa.	23,669	C 7	164
Willamette (riv.), Oreg.		A 3	163
Willemstad (cap.), Neth. Ant.	95,000	F 9	124
William H. Taft Nat'l Hist. Site, Ohio		C 10	161
Williamsburg, Va.	9,870	L 6	170
Williamsport, Pa.	33,401	H 3	164
Willimantic, Conn.	14,652	G 2	135
Willingboro, N.J.	39,912	D 3	156
Williston, N. Dak.	13,336	C 3	160
Willmar, Minn.	15,895	C 5	149
Wilmette, Ill.	28,229	B 5	139
Wilmington, Del.	70,195	M 2	146
Wilmington, N.C.	44,000	J 6	159
Wilson, N.C.	34,424	K 3	159
Wilson's Creek Nat'l Battlfld. Pk., Mo.		F 8	151
Wilton, Conn.	15,351	B 4	135
Winchester, Eng.	88,900	F 6	11
Winchester, Mass.	20,701	C 6	147
Winchester, Va.	20,217	H 2	170
Wind Cave Nat'l Pk., S. Dak.		B 6	166
Windhoek (cap.), Namibia	61,369	K 16	57
Windsor, Conn.	25,204	E 1	135
Windsor, Ont.	*246,110	B 5	108
Windward (isls.), W. Indies		G4-5	124
Winfield, Kans.	10,736	F 4	142
Winnebago (lake), Wis.		K 7	173
Winnetka, Ill.	12,772	B 5	139
Winnibigoshish (lake), Minn.		D 3	149
Winnipeg (cap.), Man.	*584,842	E 5	110
Winnipeg (lake), Man.		D-F 1-4	110
Winnipegosis (lake), Man.		B-C 1-3	110
Winnipesaukee (lake), N.H.		E 4	155
Winona, Minn.	25,075	G 6	149
Winslow, Ariz.	7,921	E 3	131
Winston-Salem, N.C.	131,885	E 2	159
Winter Haven, Fla.	21,119	E 3	136
Winter Park, Fla.	22,339	E 3	136
Winterthur, Switz.	93,500	G 1	37
Wisconsin (state), U.S.	4,705,521		173
Wisconsin (riv.), Wis.		E 9	173
Wisconsin Rapids, Wis.	17,995	G 7	173
Wittenberg, E. Ger.	51,364	E 3	20
Woburn, Mass.	36,626	C 6	147
Wollongong, Austr.	169,381	K 4	86
Wolverhampton, Eng.	266,400	E 5	11
Wŏnju, S. Korea	120,276	D 5	74
Wŏnsan, N. Korea	275,000	C 4	74
Woodbridge, N.J.	90,074	E 2	156
Woodbridge, Va.	24,004	K 3	170
Wood Buffalo Nat'l Pk., Can.		B 5	114
Woodland, Calif.	30,235	B 8	133
Woodridge, Ill.	22,561	B 6	139
Woods, Lake of the, N. Amer.		G 1	126
Woonsocket, R.I.	45,914	J 4	147
Wooster, Ohio	19,289	G 4	161
Worcester, Eng.	73,900	E 5	11
Worcester, Mass.	161,799	H 3	147
World	4,415,000,000		1,2
Worms, W. Ger.	75,732	C 4	20
Worthington, Minn.	10,243	C 7	149
Worthington, Ohio	15,016	E 5	161
Wounded Knee (creek), S. Dak.		E 7	166
Wrangell (mts.), Alaska		L 2	130
Wrangell-St. Elias Nat'l Pk., Alaska		E 3	130
Wright Brothers Nat'l Mem., N.C.		O 2	159
Wroclaw, Pol.	523,318	C 3	45
Wuhan, China	4,250,000	H 5	77
Wuhu, China	300,000	J 3	77
Wupatki Nat'l Mon., Ariz.		D 3	131
Wuppertal, W. Ger.	405,369	B 3	20
Würzburg, W. Ger.	112,584	C 4	20
Wusuli Jiang (Ussuri) (riv.), Asia		M 2	77
Wuxi, China	900,000	K 5	77
Wyoming, Mich.	59,616	D 6	148
Wyoming (state), U.S.	469,557		174

X

	Pop.	Key	Pg.
Xenia, Ohio	24,653	C 6	161
Xiamen (Amoy), China	400,000	J 7	77
Xi'an (Sian), China	1,900,000	G 5	77
Xiangtan, China	300,000	H 6	77
Xi Jiang (riv.), China		H 7	77
Xingu (riv.), Braz.		K 4	90
Xining, China	250,000	F 4	77
Xinjiang Uygur Zizhiqu (aut. reg.), China		B 3	77
Xinxiang, China	300,000	H 4	77
Xuzhou (Süchow), China	1,500,000	J 5	77

Y

	Pop.	Key	Pg.
Yablonovyy (range), U.S.S.R.		M 4	46
Yakima, Wash.	49,826	E 4	171
Yakut A.S.S.R., U.S.S.R.		N 3	46
Yakutsk, U.S.S.R.	152,000	N 3	46
Yalu (riv.), Asia		C 3	74
Yamagata, Japan	219,773	K 4	75
Yamoussoukro (cap.), Ivory Coast	50,000	F 10	54

	Pop.	Key	Pg.
Yangtze (Chang Jiang) (riv.), China		K 5	77
Yankton, S. Dak.	12,011	P 8	166
Yantai, China	180,000	K 4	77
Yaoundé (cap.), Cameroon	313,706	J 11	54
Yap (isl.), Fed. States of Micronesia	6,670	D 5	89
Yarmouth, Mass.	18,449	O 6	147
Yaroslavl', U.S.S.R.	597,000	E 3	50
Yazd, Iran	135,978	J 5	68
Yazoo City, Miss.	12,092	D 5	150
Yellow (sea), Asia		K 4	77
Yellow (Huang He) (riv.), China		J 4	77
Yellowknife (cap.), N.W.T.	9,483	E 3	96
Yellowstone (riv.), U.S.		E 1	126
Yellowstone Nat'l Pk., U.S.		E 2	126
Yemen Arab Republic	6,456,189	D 6	60
Yemen, People's Democratic Republic of	1,969,000	E 7	60
Yenisey (riv.), U.S.S.R.		J 3	46
Yogyakarta, Indon.	398,727	J 2	83
Yokohama, Japan	2,621,771	O 3	75
Yokosuka, Japan	389,557	O 3	75
Yonkers, N.Y.	195,351	H 1	158
Yorba Linda, Calif.	28,254	D 11	133
York (cape), Austr.		G 2	86
York, Eng.	101,900	F 4	11
York, Pa.	44,619	J 6	164
York (riv.), Va.		L 6	170
Yorktown, Va.	550	M 6	170
Yosemite Nat'l Pk., Calif.		F 6	133
Yŏsu, S. Korea	130,623	C 6	75
Youghiogheny (riv.), U.S.		D 6	164
Youngstown, Ohio	115,436	J 3	161
Ypres (Ieper), Belg.	20,825	B 7	25
Ypsilanti, Mich.	24,031	F 6	148
Yucatán (pen.), Mex.		P 7	119
Yucca Flat (basin), Nev.		E 6	154
Yucca House Nat'l Mon., Colo.		B 8	134
Yugoslavia	22,471,000	C 3	43
Yukon (terr.), Can.	23,153	C 3	96
Yukon (riv.), N. Amer.		C 3	94
Yukon, Okla.	17,112	G 3	162
Yuma, Ariz.	42,481	A 6	131
Yunnan (prov.), China		F 7	77

Z

	Pop.	Key	Pg.
Zaandam, Neth.	124,795	B 4	25
Zabrze, Pol.	197,214	A 4	45
Zagazig, Egypt	202,637	B 3	60
Zagreb, Yugo.	561,773	C 3	43
Zagros (mts.), Iran		E' 4	68
Zaire	28,291,000	L 12	57
Zambezi (riv.), Africa		M 15	57
Zambia	5,679,808	L 14	57
Zamboanga, Phil.	343,722	G 4	83
Zanesville, Ohio	28,655	G 6	161
Zanzibar, Tanz.	110,669	P 13	57
Zaporozh'ye, U.S.S.R.	781,000	E 5	50
Zaragoza, see Saragossa, Spain			
Zaria, Nigeria	224,000	H 9	54
Zermatt, Switz.	3,101	E 4	37
Zhangjiakou (Kalgan), China	1,000,000	J 3	77
Zhdanov, U.S.S.R.	503,000	E 5	50
Zhengzhou (Chengchow), China	1,500,000	H 5	77
Zhitomir, U.S.S.R.	244,000	C 4	50
Zhuzhou, China	350,000	H 6	77
Zibo, China	1,750,000	J 4	77
Zigong, China,	350,000	F 6	77
Zimbabwe	7,360,000	M 15	57
Zion, Ill.	17,861	F 1	139
Zion Nat'l Pk., Utah		B 6	169
Zug, Switz.	51,300	G 2	37
Zugspitze (mt.), Europe		A 3	38
Zululand (reg.), S. Africa		N 17	57
Zürich, Switz.	401,600	F 2	37
Zwickau, E. Ger.	123,069	E 3	20
Zwolle, Neth.	77,826	J 3	25

MAP PROJECTIONS

by Erwin Raisz

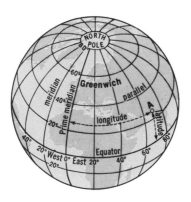

Our earth is rotating around its *axis* once a day. The two end points of its axis are the *poles*; the line circling the earth midway between the poles is the *equator*. The arc from either of the poles to the equator is divided into 90 *degrees*. The distance, expressed in degrees, from the equator to any point is its *latitude* and circles of equal latitude are the *parallels*. On maps it is customary to show parallels of evenly-spaced degrees such as every fifth or every tenth.

The equator is divided into 360 degrees. Lines circling from pole to pole through the degree points on the equator are called *meridians*. They are all equal in length but by international agreement the meridian passing through the Greenwich Observatory in London has been chosen as *prime meridian*. The distance, expressed in degrees, from the prime meridian to any point is its *longitude*. While meridians are all equal in length, parallels become shorter and shorter as they approach the poles. Whereas one degree of latitude represents everywhere approximately 69 miles, one degree of longitude varies from 69 miles at the equator to nothing at the poles.

Each degree is divided into 60 minutes and each minute into 60 seconds. One minute of latitude equals a nautical mile.

The map is flat but the earth is nearly spherical. Neither a rubber ball nor any part of a rubber ball may be flattened without stretching or tearing unless the part is very small. To present the curved surface of the earth on a flat map is not difficult as long as the areas under consideration are small, but the mapping of countries, continents, or the whole earth requires some kind of *projection*. Any regular set of parallels and meridians upon which a map can be drawn makes a map projection. Many systems are used.

In any projection only the parallels or the meridians or some other set of lines can be *true* (the same length as on the globe of corresponding scale); all other lines are too long or too short. Only on a globe is it possible to have both the parallels and the meridians true. The scale given on a flat map cannot be true everywhere. The construction of the various projections begins usually with laying out the parallels or meridians which have true lengths.

Rectangular Projection

RECTANGULAR PROJECTION — This is a set of evenly-placed meridians and horizontal parallels. The central or *standard parallel* and all meridians are true. All other parallels are either too long or too short. The projection is used for simple maps of small areas, as city plans, etc.

MERCATOR PROJECTION — In this projection the meridians are evenly-spaced vertical lines. The parallels are horizontal, spaced so that their length has the same relation to the meridians as on a globe. As the meridians converge at higher latitudes on the globe, while on the map they do not, the parallels have to be drawn also farther and farther apart to maintain the correct relationship. When every very small area has the same shape as on a globe we call the projection *conformal*. The most interesting quality of this projection is that all *compass directions* appear as straight lines. For this reason it is generally used for marine charts. It is also frequently used for world maps in spite of the fact that the high latitudes are very much exaggerated in size. Only the equator is true to scale; all other parallels and meridians are too long. The Mercator projection did *not* derive from projecting a globe upon a cylinder.

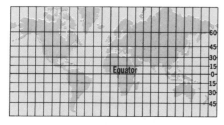

Mercator Projection

SINUSOIDAL PROJECTION — The parallels are truly-spaced horizontal lines. They are divided truly and the connecting curves make the meridians. It does not make a good world map because the outer regions are distorted, but the

Sinusoidal Projection

central portion is good and this part is often used for maps of Africa and South America. Every part of the map has the same area as the corresponding area on the globe. It is an *equal-area* projection.

MOLLWEIDE PROJECTION — The meridians are equally-spaced ellipses; the parallels are horizontal lines spaced so that every belt of latitude should have the same area as on a globe. This projection is popular for world maps, especially in European atlases.

Mollweide Projection

GOODE'S INTERRUPTED PROJECTIONS—Only the good central part of the Mollweide or sinusoidal (or both) projection is used and the oceans are cut. This makes an equal-area map with little distortion of shape. It is commonly used for world maps.

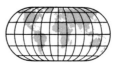

Goode's Interrupted Projection   *Eckert Projection*

ECKERT PROJECTIONS — These are similar to the sinusoidal or the Mollweide projections, but the poles are shown as lines half the length of the equator. There are several variants; the meridians are either sine curves or ellipses; the parallels are horizontal and spaced either evenly or so as to make the projection equal area. Their use for world maps is increasing. The figure shows the elliptical equal-area variant.

CONIC PROJECTION — The original idea of the conic projection is that of capping the globe by a cone upon which both the parallels and meridians are projected from the center of the globe. The cone is then cut open and laid flat. A cone can be made tangent to any chosen *standard parallel*.

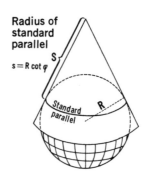

Radius of standard parallel

$s = R \cot \varphi$

Standard parallel

NORTH POLE

Standard Parallel

Conic Projection

The actually-used conic projection is a modification of this idea. The radius of the standard parallel is obtained as above. The meridians are straight radiating lines spaced truly on the standard parallel. The parallels are concentric circles spaced at true distances. All parallels except the standard are too long. The projection is used for maps of countries in middle latitudes, as it presents good shapes with small scale error.

There are several variants: The use of *two standard parallels*, one near the top, the other near the bottom of the map, reduces the scale error. In the *Albers projection* the parallels are spaced unevenly, to make the projection equal-area. This is a good projection for the United States. In the *Lambert conformal conic projection* the parallels are spaced so that any small quadrangle of the grid should have the same shape as on the globe. This is the best projection for air-navigation charts as it has relatively straight azimuths.

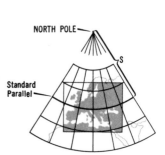

ALBERS   LAMBERT

Standard Parallels   Standard Parallels

Albers Projection   *Lambert Conformal Conic Projection*

An *azimuth* is a great-circle direction reckoned clockwise from north. A *great-circle direction* points to a place along the shortest line on the earth's surface. This is not the same as compass direction. The center of a great circle is the center of the globe.

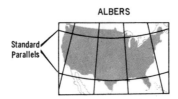

NORTH POLE

meridian   azimuth   great circle

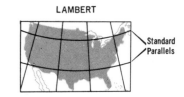

NORTH POLE   Center of parallels

Standard parallel   60°   30°   0°

BONNE PROJECTION — The parallels are laid out exactly as in the conic projection. All parallels are divided truly and the connecting curves make the meridians. It is an equal-area projection. It is used for maps of the northern continents, as Asia, Europe, and North America.

Bonne Projection

POLYCONIC PROJECTION — The central meridian is divided truly. The parallels are non-concentric circles, the radii of which are obtained by drawing tangents to the globe as though the globe were covered by several cones rather than by only one. Each parallel is divided truly and the connecting curves make the meridians. All meridians except the central one are too long. This projection is used for large-scale topographic sheets — less often for countries or continents.

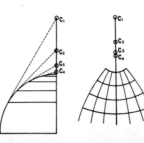

C_1 C_1
C_2 C_2
C_3 C_3
C_4 C_4

Polyconic Projection

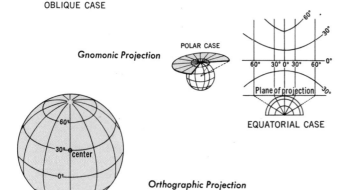

POLAR CASE

EQUATORIAL CASE

The Azimuthal Projections

OBLIQUE CASE

Gnomonic Projection

POLAR CASE

EQUATORIAL CASE

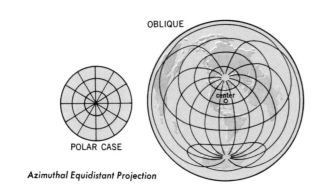

Orthographic Projection

OBLIQUE

POLAR CASE

Azimuthal Equidistant Projection

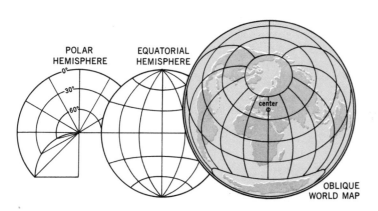

POLAR HEMISPHERE   **EQUATORIAL HEMISPHERE**

OBLIQUE WORLD MAP

Lambert Azimuthal Equal-Area Projection

THE AZIMUTHAL PROJECTIONS — In this group a part of the globe is projected from an eyepoint onto a plane. The eyepoint can be at different distances, making different projections. The plane of projection can be tangent at the equator, at a pole, or at any other point on which we want to focus attention. The most important quality of all azimuthal projections is that they show every point at its true direction (azimuth) from the center point, and all points equally distant from the center point will be equally distant on the map also.

GNOMONIC PROJECTION — This projection has the eyepoint at the center of the globe. Only the central part is good; the outer regions are badly distorted. Yet the projection has one important quality, all great circles being shown as straight lines. For this reason it is used for laying out the routes for long range flying or trans-oceanic navigation.

ORTHOGRAPHIC PROJECTION — This projection has the eyepoint at infinite distance and the projecting rays are parallel. The polar or equatorial varieties are rare but the oblique case became very popular on account of its visual quality. It looks like a picture of a globe. Although the distortion on the peripheries is extreme, we see it correctly because the eye perceives it not as a map but as a picture of a three-dimensional globe. Obviously only a hemisphere (half globe) can be shown.

Some azimuthal projections do not derive from the actual process of projecting from an eyepoint, but are arrived at by other means:

AZIMUTHAL EQUIDISTANT PROJECTION — This is the only projection in which every point is shown both at true great-circle direction and at true distance from the center point, but all other directions and distances are distorted. The principle of the projection can best be understood from the polar case. Most polar maps are in this projection. The oblique case is used for radio direction finding, for earthquake research, and in long-distance flying. A separate map has to be constructed for each central point selected.

LAMBERT AZIMUTHAL EQUAL-AREA PROJECTION — The construction of this projection can best be understood from the polar case. All three cases are widely used. It makes a good polar map and it is often extended to include the southern continents. It is the most common projection used for maps of the Eastern and Western Hemispheres, and it is a good projection for continents as it shows correct areas with relatively little distortion of shape. Most of the continent maps in this atlas are in this projection.

IN THIS ATLAS, on almost all maps, parallels and meridians have been marked because they are useful for the following:

(a) They show the north-south and east-west directions which appear on many maps at oblique angles especially near the margins.

(b) With the help of parallels and meridians every place can be exactly located; for instance, New York City is at 41° N and 74° W on any map.

(c) They help to measure distances even in the distorted parts of the map. The scale given on each map is true only along certain lines which are specified in the foregoing discussion for each projection. One degree of latitude equals nearly 69 statute miles or 60 nautical miles. The length of one degree of longitude varies (1° long. = 1° lat. × cos lat.).

AIR DISTANCES BETWEEN MAJOR WORLD CITIES
SOURCE: USAF Aeronautical Chart and Information Center (in statute miles)

	Bangkok	Berlin	Cairo	Cape Town	Caracas	Chicago	Hong Kong	Honolulu	Istanbul	Lima	London	Madrid	Melbourne
Accra	6,850	3,330	2,672	2,974	4,576	5,837	7,615	10,052	3,039	5,421	3,169	2,412	9,325
Amsterdam	5,707	360	2,015	5,997	4,883	4,118	5,772	7,254	1,372	6,538	222	921	10,286
Anchorage	6,022	4,545	6,116	10,478	5,353	2,858	5,073	2,778	5,388	6,385	4,491	5,181	7,729
Athens	4,930	1,121	671	4,957	5,815	5,447	5,316	8,353	352	7,312	1,488	1,474	9,297
Auckland	4,645	9,995	8,825	6,574	9,620	9,507	4,625	5,346	9,203	7,989	10,570	10,884	1,610
Baghdad	3,756	2,029	798	4,924	7,020	6,430	4,260	8,399	1,006	8,487	2,547	2,675	8,105
Bangkok	—	5,351	4,521	6,301	10,558	8,569	1,076	6,610	4,648	12,241	5,929	6,334	4,579
Beirut	4,272	1,689	341	4,794	6,520	6,097	4,756	8,536	614	7,972	2,151	2,190	8,579
Belgrade	5,073	623	1,147	5,419	5,587	5,000	5,327	7,882	500	7,169	1,053	1,263	9,578
Berlin	5,351	—	1,768	5,958	5,242	4,415	5,443	7,323	1,075	6,893	580	1,162	9,929
Bombay	1,870	3,915	2,717	5,103	9,034	8,066	2,679	8,036	3,000	10,389	4,478	4,689	6,101
Buenos Aires	10,490	7,395	7,360	4,285	3,155	5,582	11,478	7,554	7,608	1,945	6,907	6,236	7,219
Cairo	4,521	1,768	—	4,510	6,337	6,116	5,057	8,818	741	7,725	2,158	2,069	8,700
Cape Town	6,301	5,958	4,510	—	6,361	8,489	7,377	11,534	5,204	6,074	5,988	5,306	6,428
Caracas	10,558	5,242	6,337	6,361	—	2,500	10,171	6,024	6,050	1,699	4,662	4,351	9,703
Chicago	8,569	4,415	6,116	8,489	2,500	—	7,797	4,256	5,485	3,772	3,960	4,192	9,667
Copenhagen	5,361	222	1,964	6,179	5,215	4,263	5,392	7,101	1,252	6,886	595	1,289	9,936
Denver	8,409	5,092	6,846	9,331	3,078	920	7,476	3,346	6,164	3,986	4,701	5,028	8,755
Frankfurt	5,305	50	1,730	5,944	5,290	4,460	5,403	7,341	1,032	6,940	628	1,193	9,882
Helsinki	4,903	689	2,069	6,490	5,658	4,442	4,867	6,818	1,330	7,349	1,135	1,835	9,448
Hong Kong	1,076	5,443	5,057	7,377	10,171	7,797	—	5,557	4,989	11,415	5,986	6,556	4,605
Honolulu	6,610	7,323	8,818	11,534	6,024	4,256	5,557	—	8,118	5,944	7,241	7,874	5,501
Houston	9,261	5,337	7,005	8,608	2,262	942	8,349	3,902	6,400	3,123	4,860	5,014	8,979
Istanbul	4,648	1,075	741	5,204	6,050	5,485	4,989	8,118	—	7,593	1,551	1,701	9,100
Karachi	2,305	3,365	2,222	5,153	8,502	7,564	2,977	8,059	2,457	9,943	3,928	4,152	6,646
Keflavik	6,300	1,505	3,267	7,107	4,269	2,942	6,044	6,085	2,578	5,965	1,188	1,802	10,552
Kinshasa	5,974	3,916	2,618	2,047	5,752	7,085	6,904	11,178	3,241	6,322	3,951	3,305	8,112
Leningrad	4,718	826	2,034	6,500	5,843	4,589	4,687	6,816	1,306	7,534	1,307	1,985	9,263
Lima	12,241	6,893	7,725	6,074	1,699	3,772	11,415	5,944	7,593	—	6,316	5,907	8,052
Lisbon	6,651	1,442	2,352	5,301	4,040	4,001	6,862	7,835	2,015	5,591	989	317	11,049
London	5,929	580	2,158	5,988	4,662	3,960	5,986	7,241	1,551	6,316	—	786	10,508
Madrid	6,334	1,162	2,069	5,306	4,351	4,192	6,556	7,874	1,701	5,907	786	—	10,766
Melbourne	4,579	9,929	8,700	6,428	9,703	9,667	4,605	5,501	9,100	8,052	10,508	10,766	—
Mexico City	9,793	6,054	7,677	8,516	2,234	1,688	8,789	3,791	7,106	2,635	5,558	5,642	8,420
Montreal	8,337	3,740	5,403	7,920	2,443	746	7,736	4,919	4,798	3,967	3,256	3,449	10,390
Moscow	4,394	1,001	1,770	6,277	6,176	4,984	4,443	7,049	1,087	7,855	1,556	2,140	8,965
Nairobi	4,481	3,947	2,217	2,543	7,179	8,012	5,447	10,740	2,957	7,821	4,229	3,840	7,159
New Delhi	1,812	3,598	2,752	5,769	8,837	7,486	2,339	7,413	2,837	10,430	4,178	4,528	6,340
New York City	8,669	3,980	5,598	7,801	2,124	714	8,061	4,969	5,022	3,635	3,473	3,596	10,352
Oslo	5,395	523	2,243	6,477	5,167	4,050	5,342	6,801	1,518	6,857	718	1,485	9,934
Panama City	10,871	5,856	7,118	7,021	867	2,321	10,089	5,254	6,756	1,454	5,285	5,081	9,027
Paris	5,877	549	1,973	5,782	4,735	4,145	5,992	7,452	1,400	6,367	215	652	10,442
Peking	2,027	4,600	4,687	8,034	8,978	6,625	1,195	5,084	4,407	10,365	5,089	5,759	5,632
Rabat	6,652	1,623	2,230	4,954	4,111	4,282	6,954	8,177	2,008	5,590	1,254	474	10,856
Rio de Janeiro	9,987	6,207	6,153	3,773	2,805	5,288	11,002	8,295	6,378	2,351	5,751	5,045	8,218
Rome	5,493	735	1,305	5,231	5,198	4,823	5,773	8,040	853	6,748	892	849	9,940
Saigon (Ho Chi Minh City) ...	467	5,771	4,987	6,534	10,905	8,695	938	6,302	5,102	12,180	6,345	6,779	4,168
San Francisco	7,930	5,673	7,436	10,248	3,908	1,860	6,904	2,397	6,711	4,516	5,369	5,806	7,850
Santiago	10,967	7,772	7,967	4,947	3,033	5,295	11,615	6,861	8,135	1,528	7,241	6,639	7,017
Seattle	7,455	5,060	6,809	10,205	4,096	1,737	6,481	2,681	6,077	4,961	4,799	5,303	8,176
Shanghai	1,797	5,231	5,188	8,062	9,508	7,071	760	4,947	4,975	10,665	5,728	6,386	4,991
Shannon	6,256	940	2,534	6,188	4,320	3,583	6,246	7,006	1,938	5,992	387	884	10,826
Singapore	887	6,167	5,143	6,007	11,408	9,376	1,608	6,728	5,379	11,689	6,747	7,079	3,767
St. Louis	8,763	4,676	6,370	8,549	2,414	265	7,949	4,134	5,744	3,589	4,215	4,426	9,476
Stockholm	5,141	505	2,084	6,422	5,422	4,288	5,115	6,873	1,347	7,109	892	1,613	9,693
Teheran	3,392	2,184	1,220	5,240	7,322	6,502	3,844	8,072	1,274	8,850	2,739	2,974	7,838
Tokyo	2,865	5,557	5,937	9,155	8,813	6,313	1,792	3,860	5,574	9,628	5,956	6,704	5,070
Vienna	5,252	323	1,455	5,656	5,374	4,696	5,432	7,632	791	6,990	767	1,124	9,802
Warsaw	5,032	322	1,588	5,934	5,563	4,679	5,147	7,368	858	7,212	901	1,425	9,609
Washington D.C.	8,807	4,182	5,800	7,892	2,051	2,598	8,157	4,839	5,225	3,504	3,676	3,794	10,174

Mexico City	Montreal	Moscow	Nairobi	New Delhi	New York	Paris	Peking	Rio de Janeiro	Rome	San Francisco	Singapore	Stockholm	Teheran	Tokyo	Vienna	Warsaw
6,677	5,146	4,038	2,603	5,279	5,126	2,988	7,359	3,501	2,624	7,688	7,183	3,835	3,874	8,594	3,100	3,440
5,735	3,426	1,337	4,136	3,958	3,654	271	4,890	5,938	807	5,465	6,526	701	2,533	5,788	581	681
3,776	3,133	4,364	8,287	5,709	3,373	4,697	3,997	8,145	5,263	2,005	6,678	4,102	5,654	3,463	4,856	4,601
7,021	4,737	1,387	2,827	3,120	4,938	1,305	4,757	6,030	654	6,792	5,629	1,498	1,539	5,924	801	996
8,274	10,231	9,018	7,315	6,420	10,194	10,519	5,626	8,259	10,048	7,692	3,848	9,732	7,935	5,017	9,886	9,676
8,082	5,768	1,583	2,431	1,966	6,007	2,405	3,925	6,938	1,836	7,466	4,427	2,164	431	5,199	1,781	1,752
9,793	8,337	4,394	4,481	1,812	8,669	5,877	2,027	9,987	5,493	7,930	887	5,141	3,392	2,865	5,252	5,032
7,707	5,405	1,514	2,420	2,479	5,622	1,987	4,352	6,478	1,368	7,302	4,935	1,931	913	5,598	1,401	1,459
6,610	4,305	1,066	3,328	3,270	4,526	902	4,634	6,145	449	6,296	5,833	1,010	1,741	5,720	309	516
6,054	3,740	1,001	3,947	3,598	3,980	549	4,600	6,207	735	5,673	6,167	505	2,184	5,557	323	322
9,739	7,524	3,132	2,811	722	7,811	4,367	2,953	8,334	3,846	8,406	2,427	3,880	1,743	4,196	3,725	3,601
4,580	5,597	8,369	6,479	9,823	5,279	6,857	11,994	1,231	6,925	6,455	9,870	7,799	8,565	11,411	7,334	7,656
7,677	5,403	1,770	2,217	2,752	5,598	1,973	4,687	6,153	1,305	7,436	5,143	2,084	1,220	5,937	1,455	1,588
8,516	7,920	6,277	2,543	5,769	7,801	5,782	8,034	3,773	5,231	10,248	6,007	6,422	5,240	9,155	5,656	5,934
2,234	2,443	6,176	7,179	8,837	2,124	4,735	8,978	2,805	5,198	3,908	11,408	5,422	7,322	8,813	5,374	5,563
1,688	746	4,984	8,012	7,486	714	4,145	6,625	5,288	4,823	1,860	9,376	4,288	6,502	6,313	4,696	4,679
5,918	3,605	971	4,156	3,640	3,857	642	4,503	6,321	953	5,473	6,195	325	2,287	5,415	540	417
1,438	1,639	5,501	8,867	7,730	1,631	4,900	6,385	5,866	5,887	953	9,079	4,879	7,033	5,815	5,395	5,322
6,127	3,787	961	3,915	3,550	4,028	589	4,567	6,237	729	5,709	6,119	502	2,135	5,533	296	274
6,101	3,845	554	4,282	3,247	4,126	1,192	3,956	6,872	1,370	5,435	5,759	248	2,062	4,872	895	569
8,789	7,736	4,443	5,447	2,339	8,061	5,992	1,195	11,002	5,773	6,904	1,608	5,115	3,844	1,792	5,432	5,147
3,791	4,919	7,049	10,740	7,413	4,969	7,452	5,084	8,295	8,040	2,397	6,728	6,873	8,072	3,860	7,632	7,368
749	1,605	5,925	8,746	8,388	1,419	5,035	7,244	5,015	5,702	1,648	9,954	5,227	7,442	6,685	5,609	5,609
7,106	4,798	1,087	2,957	2,837	5,022	1,400	4,407	6,378	853	6,711	5,379	1,347	1,274	5,574	791	858
9,249	6,997	2,600	2,708	678	7,277	3,817	3,020	8,082	3,306	8,078	2,942	3,340	1,194	4,313	3,175	3,052
4,614	2,317	2,083	5,404	4,749	2,597	1,402	4,951	6,090	2,068	4,196	7,181	1,352	3,568	5,497	1,813	1,745
7,915	6,378	4,328	4,234	4,692	6,378	3,742	7,002	4,105	3,186	8,920	6,132	4,388	3,612	8,307	3,619	3,910
6,276	4,005	396	1,505	3,069	4,291	1,350	3,789	7,028	1,460	5,523	5,575	431	1,926	4,733	986	642
2,635	3,967	7,855	7,821	10,430	3,635	6,367	10,365	2,351	6,748	4,516	11,689	7,109	8,850	9,628	6,990	7,212
5,396	3,255	2,433	4,013	4,844	3,377	904	6,040	4,777	1,163	5,679	7,393	1,862	3,288	6,943	1,432	1,720
5,558	3,256	1,556	4,229	4,178	3,473	215	5,089	5,751	892	5,369	6,747	892	2,739	5,956	767	901
5,642	3,449	2,140	3,840	4,528	3,596	652	5,759	5,045	849	5,806	7,079	1,613	2,974	6,704	1,124	1,425
8,420	10,390	8,965	7,159	6,340	10,352	10,442	5,632	8,218	9,940	7,850	3,767	9,693	7,838	5,070	9,802	9,609
—	2,315	6,671	9,218	9,119	2,086	5,723	7,772	4,769	6,374	1,889	10,331	5,965	8,182	7,036	6,316	6,335
2,315	—	4,397	7,267	7,012	333	3,432	6,541	5,082	4,102	2,544	9,207	3,667	5,879	6,470	4,007	4,021
6,671	4,397	—	3,928	2,703	4,680	1,550	3,627	7,162	1,477	5,884	5,236	764	1,534	4,663	1,039	716
9,218	7,267	3,928	—	3,371	7,365	4,020	5,720	5,556	3,340	9,598	4,636	4,299	2,709	6,996	3,625	3,800
9,119	7,012	2,703	3,317	—	7,319	4,103	2,350	8,747	3,684	7,691	2,574	3,466	1,584	3,638	3,467	3,277
2,086	333	4,680	7,365	7,319	—	3,638	6,867	4,805	4,293	2,574	9,539	3,939	6,141	6,757	4,233	4,271
5,722	3,418	1,024	4,446	3,726	3,686	838	4,395	6,462	1,248	5,196	6,249	260	2,462	5,238	839	661
1,496	2,542	6,720	8,043	9,422	2,213	5,388	8,939	3,296	5,916	3,326	11,692	5,956	8,011	8,441	6,031	6,175
5,723	3,432	1,550	4,020	4,103	3,638	—	5,138	5,681	688	5,579	6,676	964	2,624	6,054	643	853
7,772	6,541	3,627	5,720	2,350	6,867	5,138	—	10,778	5,076	5,934	2,754	4,197	3,496	1,305	4,664	4,340
5,612	3,537	2,579	3,733	4,841	3,636	1,125	6,206	4,589	1,184	5,995	7,348	2,084	3,263	7,174	1,546	1,866
4,769	5,082	7,162	5,556	8,747	4,805	5,681	10,778	—	5,704	6,621	9,776	6,638	7,368	11,535	6,124	6,453
6,374	4,102	1,477	3,340	3,684	4,293	688	5,076	5,704	—	6,259	6,231	1,229	2,126	6,140	476	819
9,718	8,558	4,798	4,874	2,268	8,889	6,303	2,072	10,290	5,943	7,829	682	5,534	3,851	2,689	5,687	5,454
1,889	2,544	5,884	9,598	7,691	2,574	5,579	5,934	6,621	6,259	—	8,449	5,372	7,362	5,148	5,992	5,854
4,094	5,436	8,770	7,180	10,518	5,106	7,224	11,859	1,820	7,391	5,926	10,190	8,120	9,185	10,711	7,760	8,059
2,340	2,289	5,217	9,006	7,046	2,409	5,012	5,432	6,890	5,680	679	8,074	4,731	6,686	4,793	5,381	5,222
8,033	7,067	4,248	5,951	2,646	7,384	5,772	645	11,339	5,679	6,150	2,363	4,837	3,974	1,097	5,281	4,963
5,172	2,873	1,863	4,563	4,529	3,086	563	5,288	5,597	1,247	5,040	7,089	1,135	3,117	6,064	1,153	1,258
10,331	9,207	5,236	4,636	2,574	9,539	6,676	2,754	9,776	6,231	8,449	—	5,993	4,106	3,304	6,039	5,846
1,425	978	5,248	8,231	7,736	878	4,398	6,792	5,218	5,073	1,744	9,544	4,552	6,766	6,407	4,955	4,942
5,965	3,667	764	4,299	3,466	3,939	964	4,197	6,638	1,229	5,372	5,993	—	2,217	5,091	771	504
8,182	5,879	1,534	2,709	1,584	6,141	2,624	3,496	7,386	2,126	7,362	4,106	2,217	—	4,775	1,983	1,878
7,036	6,479	4,663	6,996	3,638	6,757	6,054	1,305	11,535	6,140	5,148	3,304	5,091	4,775	—	5,689	5,346
6,316	4,007	1,039	3,625	3,467	4,233	643	4,664	6,124	476	5,992	6,039	771	1,983	5,689	—	347
6,335	4,021	716	3,800	3,277	4,271	853	4,340	6,453	819	5,854	5,846	504	1,878	5,346	347	—
1,883	490	4,873	7,550	7,500	203	3,841	6,965	4,783	4,496	2,444	9,667	4,135	6,340	6,792	4,436	4,471

Elements of the Solar System

	Mean Distance from Sun: in Miles	in Kilometers	Period of Revolution around Sun	Period of Rotation on Axis	Equatorial Diameter: in Miles	in Kilometers	Surface Gravity (Earth = 1)	Mass (Earth = 1)	Mean Density (Water = 1)	Number of Satellites
MERCURY	35,990,000	57,900,000	87.97 days	59 days	3,032	4,880	0.38	0.055	5.5	0
VENUS	67,240,000	108,200,000	224.70 days	243 days†	7,523	12,106	0.90	0.815	5.25	0
EARTH	93,000,000	149,700,000	365.26 days	23h 56m	7,926	12,755	1.00	1.00	5.5	1
MARS	141,730,000	228,100,000	687.00 days	24h 37m	4,220	6,790	0.38	0.107	4.0	2
JUPITER	483,880,000	778,700,000	11.86 years	9h 50m	88,750	142,800	2.87	317.9	1.3	16
SATURN	887,130,000	1,427,700,000	29.46 years	10h 39m	74,580	120,020	1.32	95.2	0.7	23
URANUS	1,783,700,000	2,870,500,000	84.01 years	17h 24m†	31,600	50,900	0.93	14.6	1.3	15
NEPTUNE	2,795,500,000	4,498,800,000	164.79 years	17h 50m	30,200	48,600	1.23	17.2	1.8	2
PLUTO	3,667,900,000	5,902,800,000	247.70 years	6.39 days (?)	1,500	2,400	0.03 (?)	0.01(?)	0.7(?)	1

†Retrograde motion

Facts About the Sun

Equatorial diameter	865,000 miles	1,392,000 kilometers
Period of rotation on axis	25-35 days*	
Orbit of galaxy	every 225 million years	
Surface gravity (Earth = 1)	27.8	
Mass (Earth = 1)	333,000	
Density (Water = 1)	1.4	
Mean distance from Earth	93,000,000 miles	149,700,000 kilometers

*Rotation of 25 days at Equator, decreasing to about 35 days at the poles.

Facts About the Moon

Equatorial diameter	2,160 miles	3,476 kilometers
Period of rotation on axis	27 days, 7 hours, 43 minutes	
Period of revolution around Earth (sidereal month)	27 days, 7 hours, 43 minutes	
Phase period between new moons (synodic month)	29 days, 12 hours, 44 minutes	
Surface gravity (Earth = 1)	0.16	
Mass (Earth = 1)	0.0123	
Density (Water = 1)	3.34	
Maximum distance from Earth	252,710 miles	406,690 kilometers
Minimum distance from Earth	221,460 miles	356,400 kilometers
Mean distance from Earth	238,860 miles	384,400 kilometers

Dimensions of the Earth

	Area in Sq. Miles	Sq. Kilometers
Superficial area	197,751,000	512,175,090
Land surface	57,970,000	150,142,300
Water surface	139,781,000	362,032,790

	Miles	Kilometers
Equatorial circumference	24,902	40,075
Polar circumference	24,860	40,007
Equatorial diameter	7,926.68	12,756.4
Polar diameter	7,899.99	12,713.4
Equatorial radius	3,963.34	6,378.2
Polar radius	3,949.99	6,356.7

Volume of the Earth	2.6×10^{11} cubic miles	10.84×10^{11} cubic kilometers
Mass or weight	6.6×10^{21} short tons	6.0×10^{21} metric tons
Maximum distance from Sun	94,600,000 miles	152,000,000 kilometers
Minimum distance from Sun	91,300,000 miles	147,000,000 kilometers

The Continents

	Area in: Sq. Miles	Sq. Km.	Percent of World's Land
Asia	17,128,500	44,362,815	29.5
Africa	11,707,000	30,321,130	20.2
North America	9,363,000	24,250,170	16.2
South America	6,875,000	17,806,250	11.8
Antarctica	5,500,000	14,245,000	9.5
Europe	4,057,000	10,507,630	7.0
Australia	2,966,136	7,682,300	5.1

Oceans and Major Seas

	Area in: Sq. Miles	Sq. Km.	Greatest Depth in: Feet	Meters
Pacific Ocean	64,186,000	166,241,700	36,198	11,033
Atlantic Ocean	31,862,000	82,522,600	28,374	8,648
Indian Ocean	28,350,000	73,426,500	25,344	7,725
Arctic Ocean	5,427,000	14,056,000	17,880	5,450
Caribbean Sea	970,000	2,512,300	24,720	7,535
Mediterranean Sea	969,000	2,509,700	16,896	5,150
Bering Sea	875,000	2,266,250	15,800	4,800
Gulf of Mexico	600,000	1,554,000	12,300	3,750
Sea of Okhotsk	590,000	1,528,100	11,070	3,370
East China Sea	482,000	1,248,400	9,500	2,900
Sea of Japan	389,000	1,007,500	12,280	3,740
Hudson Bay	317,500	822,300	846	258
North Sea	222,000	575,000	2,200	670
Black Sea	185,000	479,150	7,365	2,245
Red Sea	169,000	437,700	7,200	2,195
Baltic Sea	163,000	422,170	1,506	459

Major Ship Canals

	Length in: Miles	Kms.	Minimum Feet	Depth in: Meters
Volga-Baltic, U.S.S.R.	225	362	—	—
Baltic-White Sea, U.S.S.R.	140	225	16	5
Suez, Egypt	100.76	162	42	13
Albert, Belgium	80	129	16.5	5
Moscow-Volga, U.S.S.R.	80	129	18	6
Volga-Don, U.S.S.R.	62	100	—	—
Göta, Sweden	54	87	10	3
Kiel (Nord-Ostsee), W. Ger.	53.2	86	38	12
Panama Canal, Panama	50.72	82	41.6	13
Houston Ship, U.S.A.	50	81	36	11

Largest Islands

	Area in: Sq. Mi.	Sq. Km.		Area in: Sq. Mi.	Sq. Km.		Area in: Sq. Mi.	Sq. Km.
Greenland	840,000	2,175,600	South I., New Zealand	58,393	151,238	Hokkaido, Japan	28,983	75,066
New Guinea	305,000	789,950	Java, Indonesia	48,842	126,501	Banks, Canada	27,038	70,028
Borneo	290,000	751,100	North I., New Zealand	44,187	114,444	Ceylon, Sri Lanka	25,332	65,610
Madagascar	226,400	586,376	Newfoundland, Canada	42,031	108,860	Tasmania, Australia	24,600	63,710
Baffin, Canada	195,928	507,454	Cuba	40,533	104,981	Svalbard, Norway	23,957	62,049
Sumatra, Indonesia	164,000	424,760	Luzon, Philippines	40,420	104,688	Devon, Canada	21,331	55,247
Honshu, Japan	88,000	227,920	Iceland	39,768	103,000	Novaya Zemlya (north isl.),		
Great Britain	84,400	218,896	Mindanao, Philippines	36,537	94,631	U.S.S.R.	18,600	48,200
Victoria, Canada	83,896	217,290	Ireland	31,743	82,214	Marajó, Brazil	17,991	46,597
Ellesmere, Canada	75,767	196,236	Sakhalin, U.S.S.R.	29,500	76,405	Tierra del Fuego, Chile & Argentina	17,900	46,360
Celebes, Indonesia	72,986	189,034	Hispaniola, Haiti & Dom. Rep.	29,399	76,143	Alexander, Antarctica	16,700	43,250

Principal Mountains of the World

	Feet	Meters		Feet	Meters		Feet	Meters
Everest, Nepal-China	29,028	8,848	Pissis, Argentina	22,241	6,779	Kazbek, U.S.S.R.	16,512	5,033
Godwin Austen (K2),			Mercedario, Argentina	22,211	6,770	Puncak Jaya, Indonesia	16,503	5,030
Pakistan-China	28,250	8,611	Huascarán, Peru	22,205	6,768	Tyree, Antarctica	16,289	4,965
Kanchenjunga, Nepal-India	28,208	8,598	Llullaillaco, Chile-Argentina	22,057	6,723	Blanc, France	15,771	4,807
Lhotse, Nepal-China	27,923	8,511	Nevada Ancohuma, Bolivia	21,489	6,550	Klyuchevskaya Sopka, U.S.S.R.	15,584	4,750
Makalu, Nepal-China	27,824	8,481	Illampu, Bolivia	21,276	6,485	Fairweather (Br. Col., Canada)	15,300	4,663
Dhaulagiri, Nepal	26,810	8,172	Chimborazo, Ecuador	20,561	6,267	Dufourspitze (Mte. Rosa), Italy-		
Nanga Parbat, Pakistan	26,660	8,126	McKinley, Alaska	20,320	6,194	Switzerland	15,203	4,634
Annapurna, Nepal	26,504	8,078	Logan, Canada (Yukon)	19,524	5,951	Ras Dashan, Ethiopia	15,157	4,620
Gasherbrum, Pakistan-China	26,740	8,068	Cotopaxi, Ecuador	19,347	5,897	Matterhorn, Switzerland	14,691	4,478
Nanda Devi, India	25,645	7,817	Kilimanjaro, Tanzania	19,340	5,895	Whitney, California, U.S.A.	14,494	4,418
Rakaposhi, Pakistan	25,550	7,788	El Misti, Peru	19,101	5,822	Elbert, Colorado, U.S.A.	14,433	4,399
Kamet, India	25,447	7,756	Pico Cristóbal Colón, Colombia	19,029	5,800	Rainier, Washington, U.S.A.	14,410	4,392
Gurla Mandhada, China	25,355	7,728	Huila, Colombia	18,865	5,750	Shasta, California, U.S.A.	14,162	4,350
Kongur Shan, China	25,325	7,719	Citlaltépetl (Orizaba), Mexico	18,855	5,747	Pikes Peak, Colorado, U.S.A.	14,110	4,301
Tirich Mir, Pakistan	25,230	7,690	El'brus, U.S.S.R.	18,510	5,642	Finsteraarhorn, Switzerland	14,022	4,274
Gongga Shan, China	24,790	7,556	Damavand, Iran	18,376	5,601	Mauna Kea, Hawaii, U.S.A.	13,796	4,205
Muztagata, China	24,757	7,546	St. Elias, Alaska-Canada			Mauna Loa, Hawaii, U.S.A.	13,677	4,169
Communism Peak, U.S.S.R.	24,599	7,498	(Yukon)	18,008	5,489	Jungfrau, Switzerland	13,642	4,158
Pobeda Peak, U.S.S.R.	24,406	7,439	Vilcanota, Peru	17,999	5,486	Cameroon, Cameroon	13,350	4,069
Chomo Lhari, Bhutan-China	23,997	7,314	Popocatépetl, Mexico	17,887	5,452	Grossglockner, Austria	12,457	3,797
Muztag, China	23,891	7,282	Dykhtau, U.S.S.R.	17,070	5,203	Fuji, Japan	12,389	3,776
Cerro Aconcagua, Argentina	22,831	6,959	Kenya, Kenya	17,058	5,199	Cook, New Zealand	12,349	3,764
Ojos del Salado, Chile-Argentina	22,572	6,880	Ararat, Turkey	16,946	5,165	Etna, Italy	11,053	3,369
Bonete, Chile-Argentina	22,541	6,870	Vinson Massif, Antarctica	16,864	5,140	Kosciusko, Australia	7,310	2,228
Tupungato, Chile-Argentina	22,310	6,800	Margherita (Ruwenzori), Africa	16,795	5,119	Mitchell, North Carolina, U.S.A.	6,684	2,037

Longest Rivers of the World

Length in:	Miles	Kms.	Length in:	Miles	Kms.	Length in:	Miles	Kms.
Nile, Africa	4,145	6,671	São Francisco, Brazil	1,811	2,914	Ohio-Allegheny, U.S.A.	1,306	2,102
Amazon, S. Amer.	3,915	6,300	Indus, Asia	1,800	2,897	Kama, U.S.S.R.	1,262	2,031
Chang Jiang (Yangtze), China	3,900	6,276	Danube, Europe	1,775	2,857	Red, U.S.A.	1,222	1,966
Mississippi-Missouri-Red Rock, U.S.A.	3,741	6,019	Salween, Asia	1,770	2,849	Don, U.S.S.R.	1,222	1,967
Ob'Irtysh-Black Irtysh, U.S.S.R.	3,362	5,411	Brahmaputra, Asia	1,700	2,736	Columbia, U.S.A.-Canada	1,214	1,953
Yenisey-Angara, U.S.S.R.	3,100	4,989	Euphrates, Asia	1,700	2,736	Saskatchewan, Canada	1,205	1,939
Huang He (Yellow), China	2,877	4,630	Tocantins, Brazil	1,677	2,699	Peace-Finlay, Canada	1,195	1,923
Amur-Shilka-Onon, Asia	2,744	4,416	Xi (Si), China	1,650	2,655	Tigris, Asia	1,181	1,901
Lena, U.S.S.R.	2,734	4,400	Amudar'ya, Asia	1,616	2,601	Darling, Australia	1,160	1,867
Congo (Zaire), Africa	2,718	4,374	Nelson-Saskatchewan, Canada	1,600	2,575	Angara, U.S.S.R.	1,135	1,827
Mackenzie-Peace-Finlay, Canada	2,635	4,241	Orinoco, S. Amer.	1,600	2,575	Sungari, Asia	1,130	1,819
Mekong, Asia	2,610	4,200	Zambezi, Africa	1,600	2,575	Pechora, U.S.S.R.	1,124	1,809
Missouri-Red Rock, U.S.A.	2,564	4,125	Paraguay, S. Amer.	1,584	2,549	Snake, U.S.A.	1,000	1,609
Niger, Africa	2,548	4,101	Kolyma, U.S.S.R.	1,562	2,514	Churchill, Canada	1,000	1,609
Paraná-La Plata, S. Amer.	2,450	3,943	Ganges, Asia	1,550	2,494	Pilcomayo, S. Amer.	1,000	1,609
Mississippi, U.S.A.	2,348	3,778	Ural, U.S.S.R.	1,509	2,428	Magdalena, Colombia	1,000	1,609
Murray-Darling, Australia	2,310	3,718	Japurá, S. Amer.	1,500	2,414	Uruguay, S. Amer.	994	1,600
Volga, U.S.S.R.	2,194	3,531	Arkansas, U.S.A.	1,450	2,334	Platte-N. Platte, U.S.A.	990	1,593
Madeira, S. Amer.	2,013	3,240	Colorado, U.S.A.-Mexico	1,450	2,334	Ohio, U.S.A.	981	1,578
Purus, S. Amer.	1,995	3,211	Negro, S. Amer.	1,400	2,253	Pecos, U.S.A.	926	1,490
Yukon, Alaska-Canada	1,979	3,185	Dnieper, U.S.S.R.	1,368	2,202	Oka, U.S.S.R.	918	1,477
St. Lawrence, Canada-U.S.A.	1,900	3,058	Orange, Africa	1,350	2,173	Canadian, U.S.A.	906	1,458
Rio Grande, Mexico-U.S.A.	1,885	3,034	Irrawaddy, Burma	1,325	2,132	Colorado, Texas, U.S.A.	894	1,439
Syrdar'ya-Naryn, U.S.S.R.	1,859	2,992	Brazos, U.S.A.	1,309	2,107	Dniester, U.S.S.R.	876	1,410

Principal Natural Lakes

	Area in: Sq. Miles	Sq. Km.	Max. Depth in: Feet	Meters		Area in: Sq. Miles	Sq. Km.	Max. Depth in: Feet	Meters
Caspian Sea, U.S.S.R.-Iran	143,243	370,999	3,264	995	Lake Eyre, Australia	3,500-0	9,000-0	—	—
Lake Superior, U.S.A.-Canada	31,820	82,414	1,329	405	Lake Titicaca, Peru-Bolivia	3,200	8,288	1,000	305
Lake Victoria, Africa	26,724	69,215	270	82	Lake Nicaragua, Nicaragua	3,100	8,029	230	70
Aral Sea, U.S.S.R.	25,676	66,501	256	78	Lake Athabasca, Canada	3,064	7,936	400	122
Lake Huron, U.S.A.-Canada	23,010	59,596	748	228	Reindeer Lake, Canada	2,568	6,651	—	—
Lake Michigan, U.S.A.	22,400	58,016	923	281	Lake Turkana (Rudolf), Africa	2,463	6,379	240	73
Lake Tanganyika, Africa	12,650	32,764	4,700	1,433	Issyk-Kul', U.S.S.R.	2,425	6,281	2,303	702
Lake Baykal, U.S.S.R.	12,162	31,500	5,316	1,620	Lake Torrens, Australia	2,230	5,776	—	—
Great Bear Lake, Canada	12,096	31,328	1,356	413	Vänern, Sweden	2,156	5,584	328	100
Lake Nyasa (Malawi), Africa	11,555	29,928	2,320	707	Nettilling Lake, Canada	2,140	5,543	—	—
Great Slave Lake, Canada	11,031	28,570	2,015	614	Lake Winnipegosis, Canada	2,075	5,374	38	12
Lake Erie, U.S.A.-Canada	9,940	25,745	210	64	Lake Mobutu Sese Seko (Albert),				
Lake Winnipeg, Canada	9,417	24,390	60	18	Africa	2,075	5,374	160	49
Lake Ontario, U.S.A.-Canada	7,540	19,529	775	244	Kariba Lake, Zambia-Zimbabwe	2,050	5,310	295	90
Lake Ladoga, U.S.S.R.	7,104	18,399	738	225	Lake Nipigon, Canada	1,872	4,848	540	165
Lake Balkhash, U.S.S.R.	7,027	18,200	87	27	Lake Mweru, Zaire-Zambia	1,800	4,662	60	18
Lake Maracaibo, Venezuela	5,120	13,261	100	31	Lake Manitoba, Canada	1,799	4,659	12	4
Lake Chad, Africa	4,000-10,000	10,360-25,900	25	8	Lake Taymyr, U.S.S.R.	1,737	4,499	85	26
					Lake Khanka, China-U.S.S.R.	1,700	4,403	33	10
Lake Onega, U.S.S.R.	3,710	9,609	377	115	Lake Kioga, Uganda	1,700	4,403	25	8

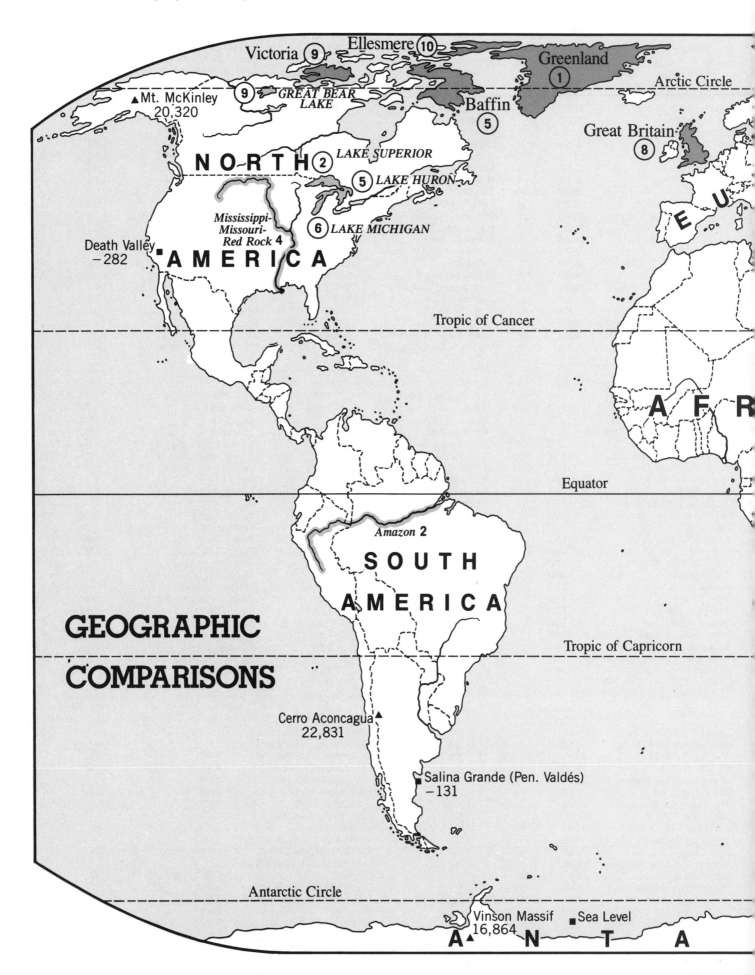

Victoria ⑨

Ellesmere ⑩

Greenland ①

Arctic Circle

▲Mt. McKinley
20,320

⑨ GREAT BEAR
LAKE

Baffin
⑤

Great Britain
⑧

N O R T H ② LAKE SUPERIOR

⑤ LAKE HURON

E U

Mississippi-
Missouri-
Red Rock 4

⑥ LAKE MICHIGAN

Death Valley
−282

A M E R I C A

A F R

Tropic of Cancer

Equator

Amazon 2

S O U T H

A M E R I C A

Tropic of Capricorn

GEOGRAPHIC

COMPARISONS

Cerro Aconcagua ▲
22,831

Salina Grande (Pen. Valdés)
−131

Antarctic Circle

Vinson Massif   ■Sea Level
16,864

A ▲   N   T   A

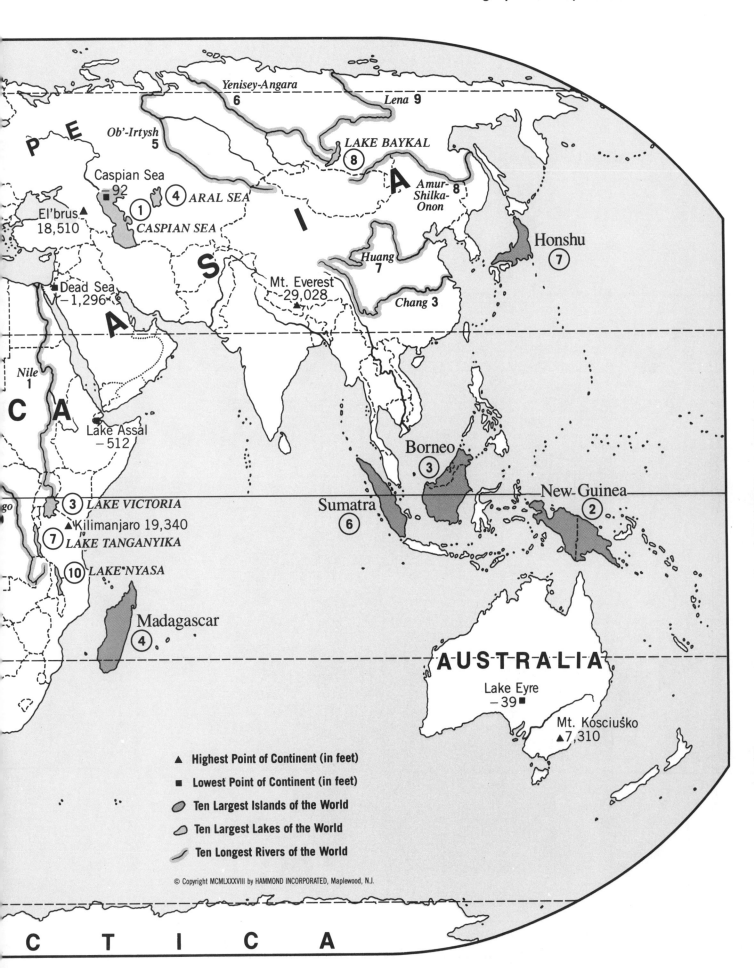

P E

Yenisey-Angara
6

Lena 9

Ob'-Irtysh
5

LAKE BAYKAL
8

A

Caspian Sea
−92

1

4   ARAL SEA

Amur-
Shilka-
Onon
8

El'brus
18,510

CASPIAN SEA

S

I

Honshu
7

Dead Sea
−1,296

Huang
7

Mt. Everest
29,028

Chang 3

C A S

Nile
1

A

C   A

Lake Assal
−512

go

3   LAKE VICTORIA

Borneo
3

New Guinea
2

▲Kilimanjaro 19,340

Sumatra
6

7   LAKE TANGANYIKA

10   LAKE NYASA

Madagascar
4

AUSTRALIA

Lake Eyre
−39

Mt. Kosciuśko
▲7,310

▲ **Highest Point of Continent (in feet)**

■ **Lowest Point of Continent (in feet)**

⬭ **Ten Largest Islands of the World**

◗ **Ten Largest Lakes of the World**

⟋ **Ten Longest Rivers of the World**

C   T   I   C   A

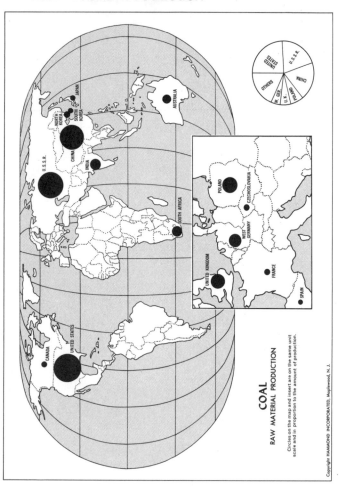

COAL
RAW MATERIAL PRODUCTION

Circles on the map and insert are on the same unit scale and in proportion to the amount of production.

Copyright HAMMOND INCORPORATED, Maplewood, N.J.

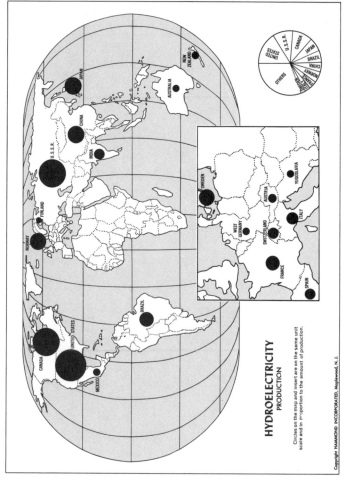

HYDROELECTRICITY
PRODUCTION

Circles on the map and insert are on the same unit scale and in proportion to the amount of production.

Copyright HAMMOND INCORPORATED, Maplewood, N.J.

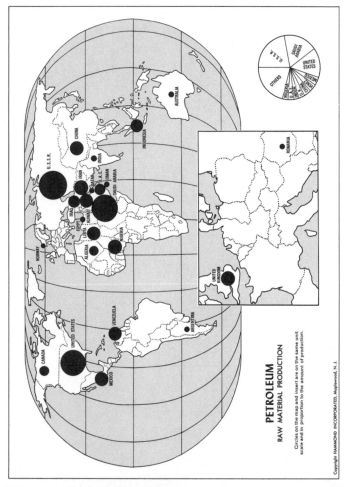

PETROLEUM
RAW MATERIAL PRODUCTION

Circles on the map and insert are on the same unit scale and in proportion to the amount of production.

Copyright HAMMOND INCORPORATED, Maplewood, N.J.

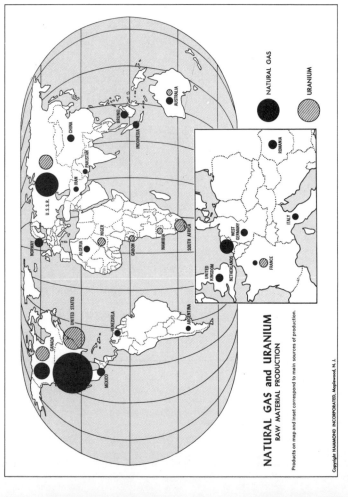

NATURAL GAS and URANIUM
RAW MATERIAL PRODUCTION

Products on map and inset correspond to main sources of production.

NATURAL GAS

URANIUM

Copyright HAMMOND INCORPORATED, Maplewood, N.J.

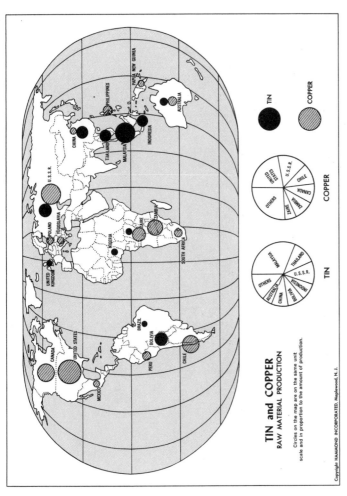

TIN and COPPER
RAW MATERIAL PRODUCTION

Circles on the map are on the same unit scale and in proportion to the amount of production.

Copyright HAMMOND INCORPORATED, Maplewood, N. J.

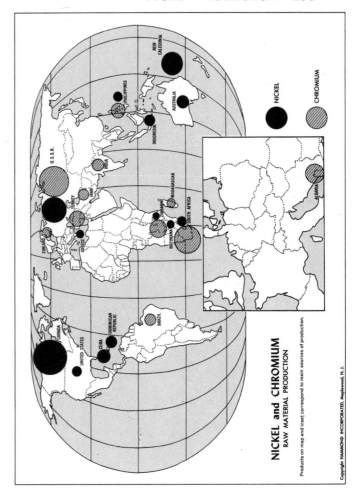

NICKEL and CHROMIUM
RAW MATERIAL PRODUCTION

Products on map and inset correspond to main sources of production.

Copyright HAMMOND INCORPORATED, Maplewood, N. J.

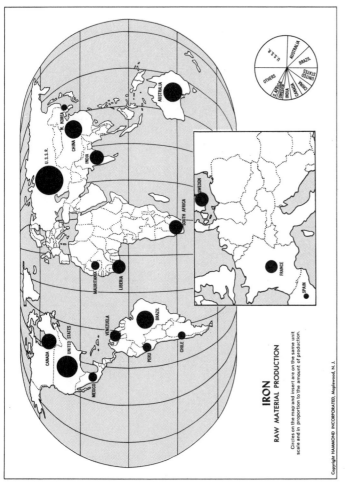

IRON
RAW MATERIAL PRODUCTION

Circles on the map and insert are on the same unit scale and in proportion to the amount of production.

Copyright HAMMOND INCORPORATED, Maplewood, N. J.

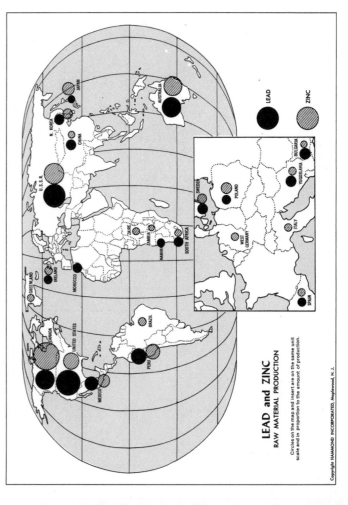

LEAD and ZINC
RAW MATERIAL PRODUCTION

Circles on the map and insert are on the same unit scale and in proportion to the amount of production.

Copyright HAMMOND INCORPORATED, Maplewood, N. J.

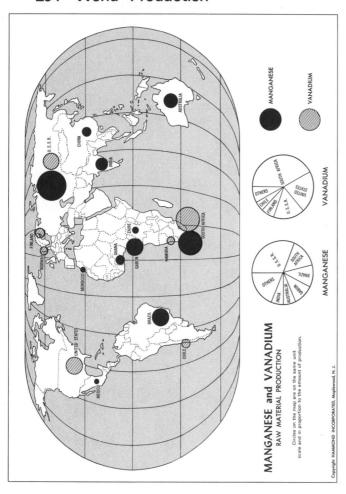

MANGANESE and VANADIUM
RAW MATERIAL PRODUCTION

Circles on the map are on the same unit
scale and in proportion to the amount of production.

Copyright HAMMOND INCORPORATED, Maplewood, N. J.

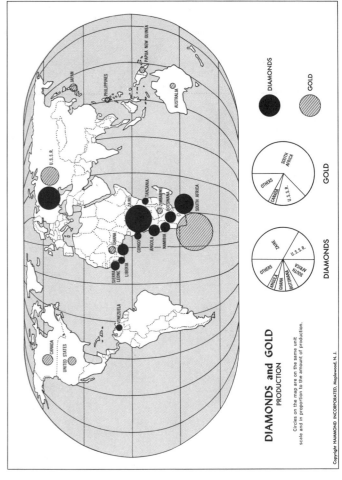

DIAMONDS and GOLD
PRODUCTION

Circles on the map are on the same unit
scale and in proportion to the amount of production.

Copyright HAMMOND INCORPORATED, Maplewood, N. J.

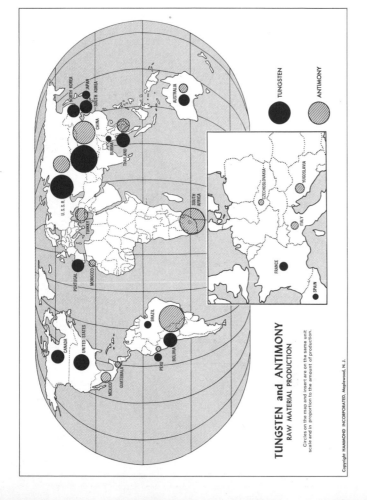

TUNGSTEN and ANTIMONY
RAW MATERIAL PRODUCTION

Circles on the map and insert are on the same unit
scale and in proportion to the amount of production.

Copyright HAMMOND INCORPORATED, Maplewood, N. J.

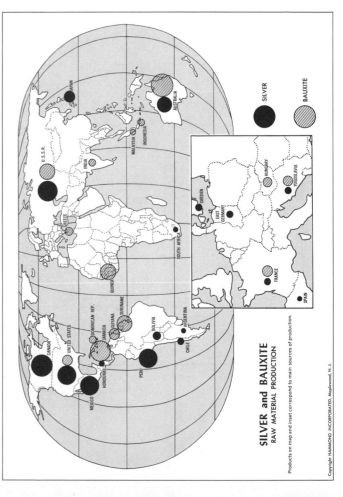

SILVER and BAUXITE
RAW MATERIAL PRODUCTION

Products on map and inset correspond to main sources of production.

Copyright HAMMOND INCORPORATED, Maplewood, N. J.

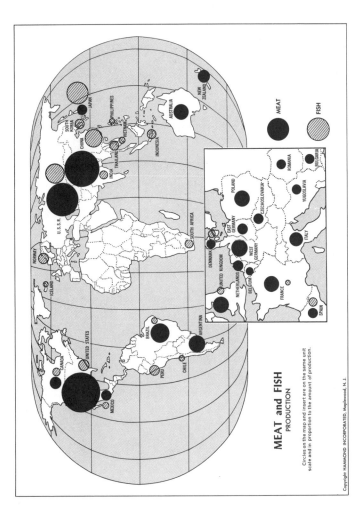

RUBBER and TIMBER
RAW MATERIAL PRODUCTION

RUBBER

S–Synthetic

TIMBER

Products on map and inset correspond to main sources of production.

Copyright HAMMOND INCORPORATED, Maplewood, N. J.

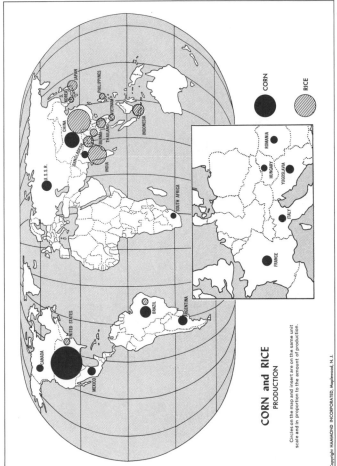

WHEAT
PRODUCTION

Circles on the map and insert are on the same unit scale and in proportion to the amount of production.

Copyright HAMMOND INCORPORATED, Maplewood, N. J.

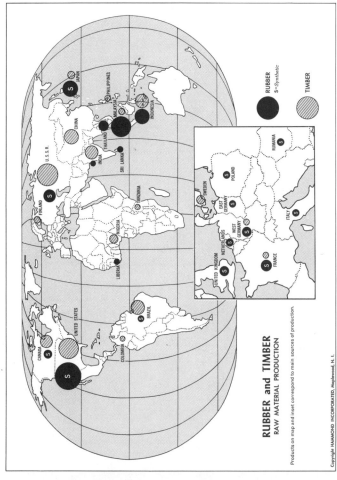

MEAT

FISH

MEAT and FISH
PRODUCTION

Circles on the map and insert are on the same unit scale and in proportion to the amount of production.

Copyright HAMMOND INCORPORATED, Maplewood, N. J.

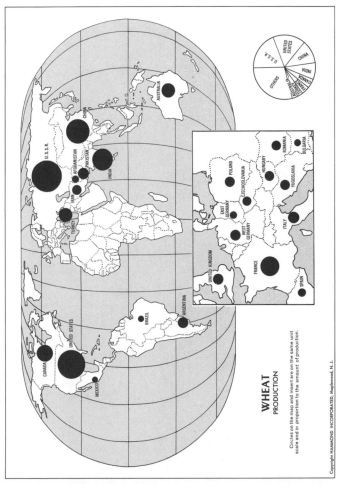

CORN

RICE

CORN and RICE
PRODUCTION

Circles on the map and insert are on the same unit scale and in proportion to the amount of production.

Copyright HAMMOND INCORPORATED, Maplewood, N. J.

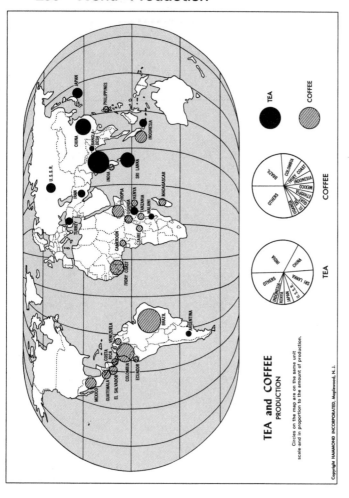

BARLEY and SUGAR
PRODUCTION

BARLEY

SUGAR (BEET AND CANE)

Circles on the map and insert are on the same unit scale and in proportion to the amount of production.

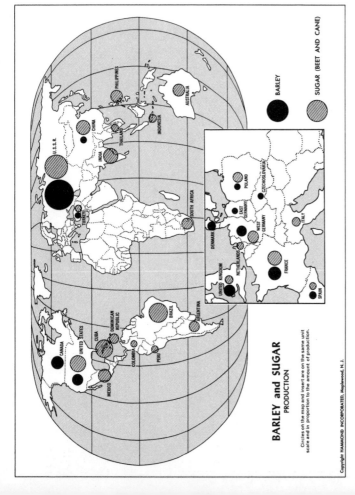

TEA and COFFEE
PRODUCTION

TEA

COFFEE

COFFEE

TEA

Circles on the map are on the same unit scale and in proportion to the amount of production.

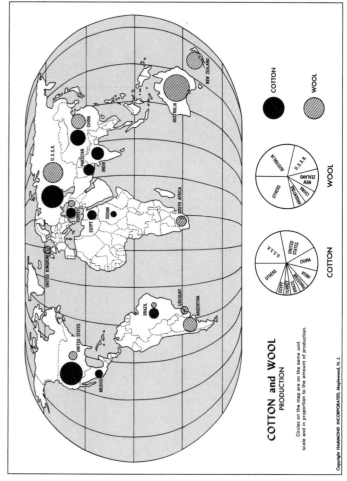

TOBACCO and COCOA
PRODUCTION

TOBACCO

COCOA

Circles on the map and insert are on the same unit scale and in proportion to the amount of production.

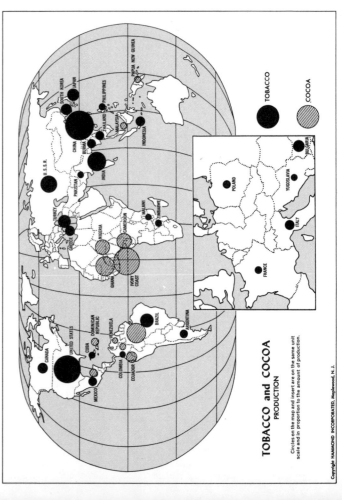

COTTON and WOOL
PRODUCTION

COTTON

WOOL

WOOL

COTTON

Circles on the map are on the same unit scale and in proportion to the amount of production.

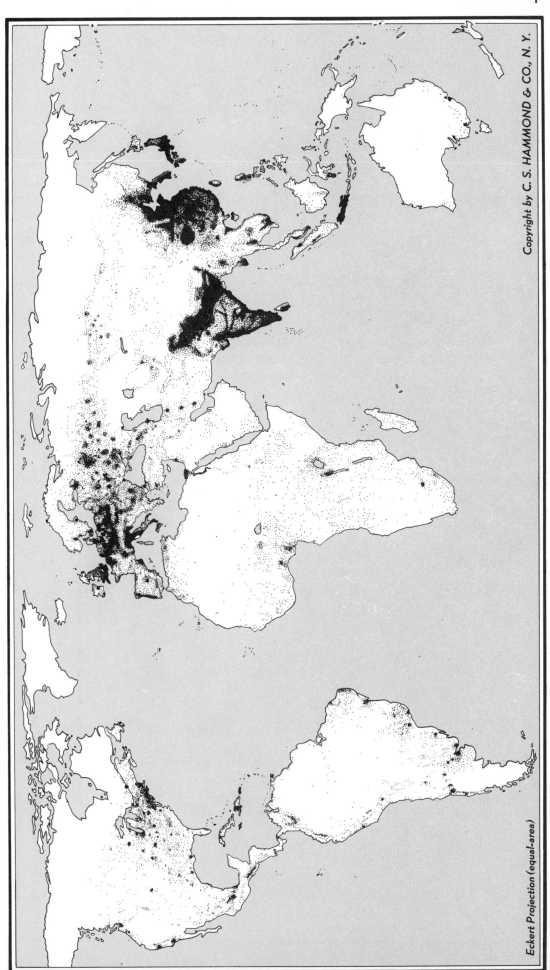

Copyright by C. S. HAMMOND & CO., N. Y.

Eckert Projection (equal-area)

DENSITY OF POPULATION. One of the most outstanding facts of human geography is the extremely uneven distribution of people over the Earth. One-half of the Earth's surface has less than 3 people per square mile, while in the lowlands of India, China, Java and Japan rural density reaches the incredible congestion of 2000-3000 per square mile. Three-fourths of the Earth's population live in four relatively small areas; Northeastern United States, North-Central Europe, India and the Far East.

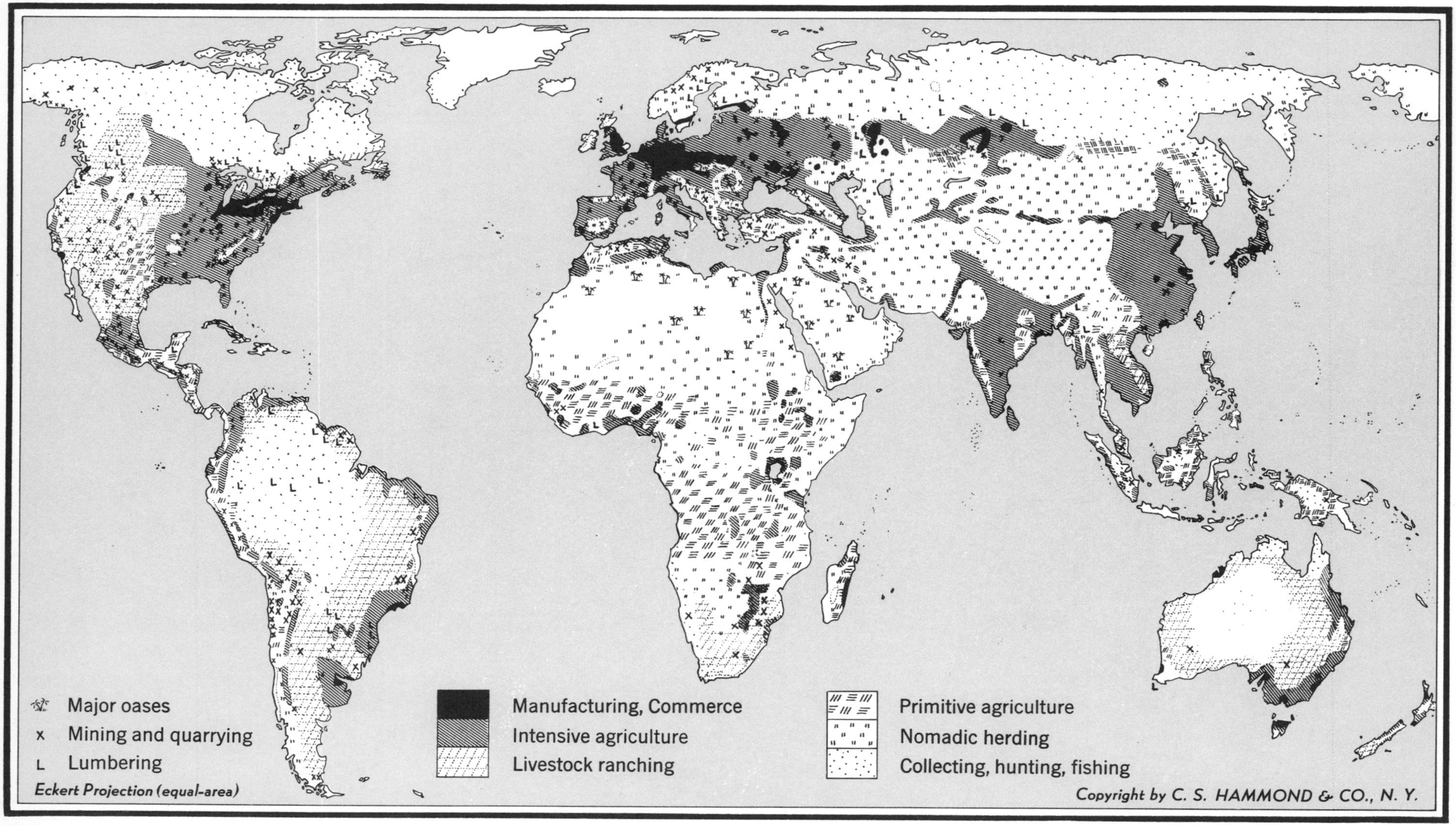

Legend:

Major oases

x   Mining and quarrying

L   Lumbering

Eckert Projection (equal-area)

■   Manufacturing, Commerce

▨   Intensive agriculture

▧   Livestock ranching

▨   Primitive agriculture

▨   Nomadic herding

⠿   Collecting, hunting, fishing

Copyright by C. S. HAMMOND & CO., N. Y.

OCCUPATIONS. Correlation with the density of population shows that the most densely populated areas fall into the regions of manufacturing and intensive farming. All other economies require considerable space. The most sparsely inhabited areas are those of collecting, hunting and fishing. Areas with practically no habitation are left blank.

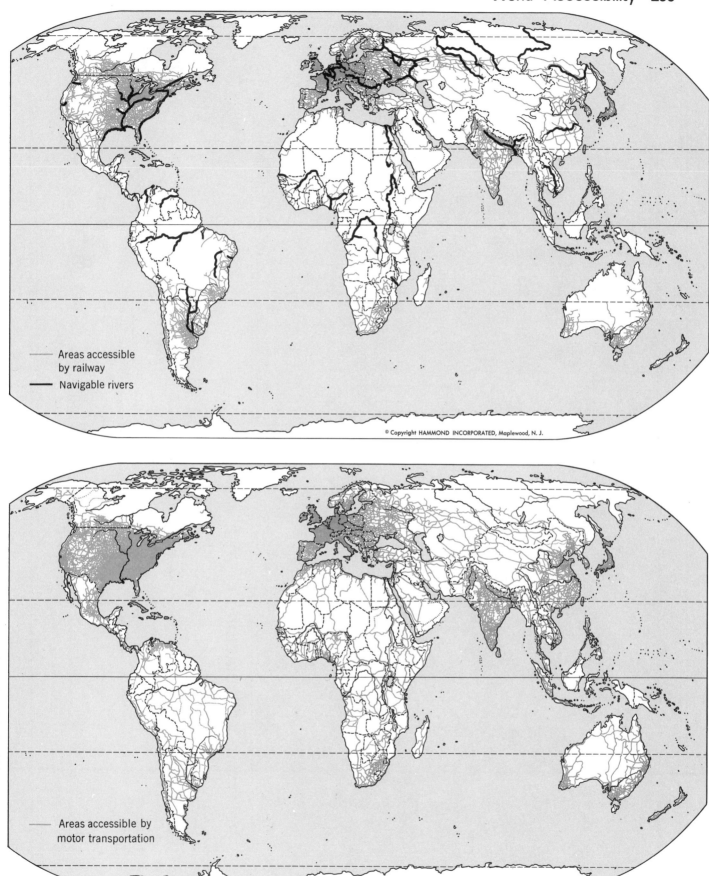

Areas accessible
by railway
Navigable rivers

© Copyright HAMMOND INCORPORATED, Maplewood, N. J.

Areas accessible by
motor transportation

© Copyright HAMMOND INCORPORATED, Maplewood, N. J.

ACCESSIBILITY. *Many regions in the world are far from railways, roads, navigable rivers or the seas. Their economic development is retarded because their products can be brought to the world's markets only at great expense. Such areas are in the tundra (alpine), the boreal forest and in the equatorial rain forest regions. Desert areas, if not too mountainous, can be crossed by tractors. The largest inaccessible area is in Tibet, on account of high mountains, the alpine climate and isolationist attitude of the people. Airplane transportation is helping to bring these inaccessible areas into the orbit of civilization.*

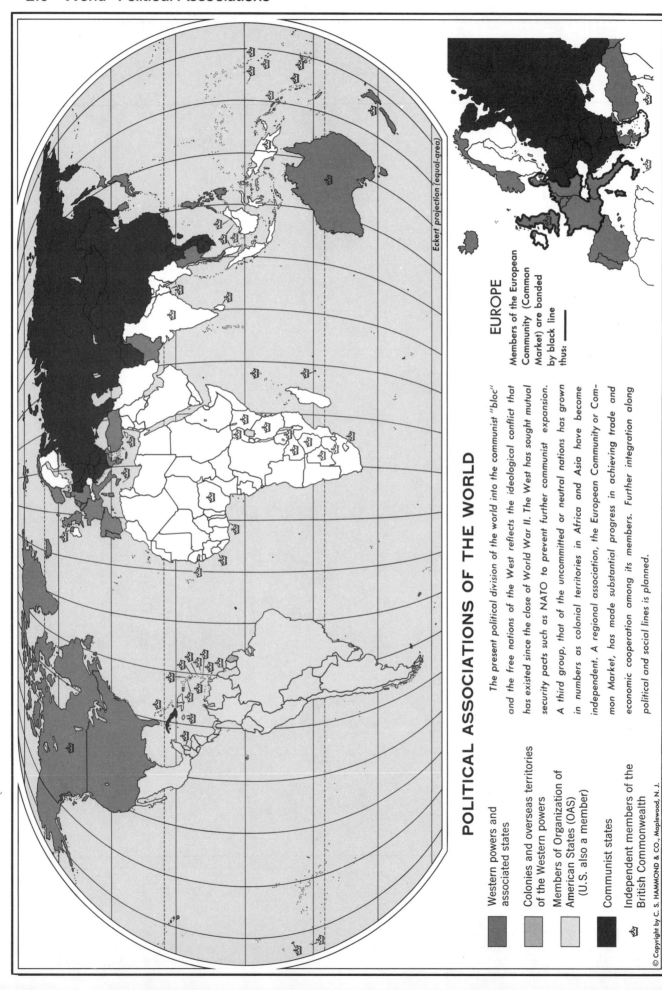

POLITICAL ASSOCIATIONS OF THE WORLD

The present political division of the world into the communist "bloc" and the free nations of the West reflects the ideological conflict that has existed since the close of World War II. The West has sought mutual security pacts such as NATO to prevent further communist expansion.

A third group, that of the uncommitted or neutral nations has grown in numbers as colonial territories in Africa and Asia have become independent. A regional association, the European Community or Common Market, has made substantial progress in achieving trade and economic cooperation among its members. Further integration along political and social lines is planned.

EUROPE

Members of the European Community (Common Market) are banded by black line thus: ▬▬▬

Western powers and associated states

Colonies and overseas territories of the Western powers

Members of Organization of American States (OAS) (U.S. also a member)

Communist states

Independent members of the British Commonwealth

Eckert projection (equal-area)

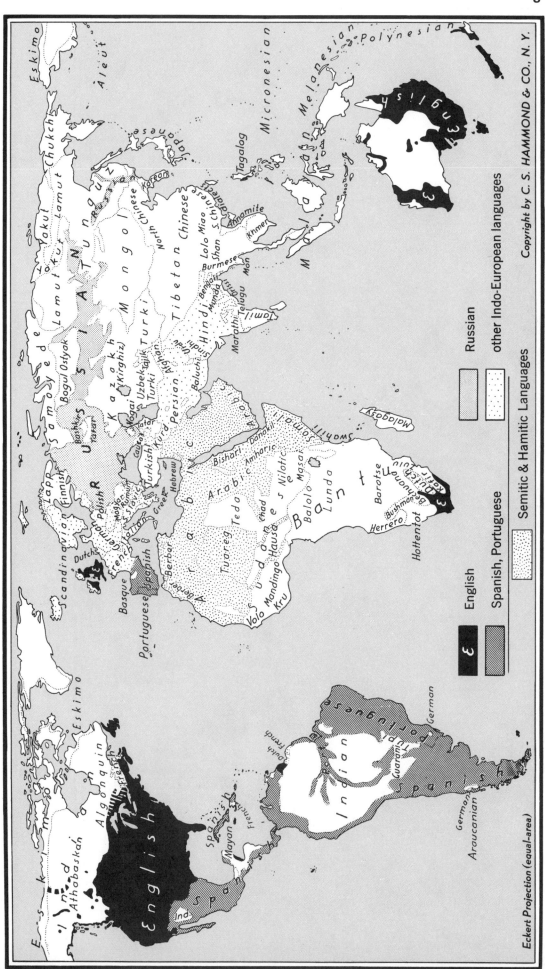

Eckert Projection (equal-area)

LANGUAGES. *Several hundred different languages are spoken in the World, and in many places two or more languages are spoken, sometimes by the same people. The map above shows the dominant languages in each locality. English, French, Spanish, Russian, Arabic and Swahili are spoken by many people as a second language for commerce or travel.*

English

Spanish, Portuguese

Russian

other Indo-European languages

Semitic & Hamitic Languages

Copyright by C. S. HAMMOND & CO., N. Y.

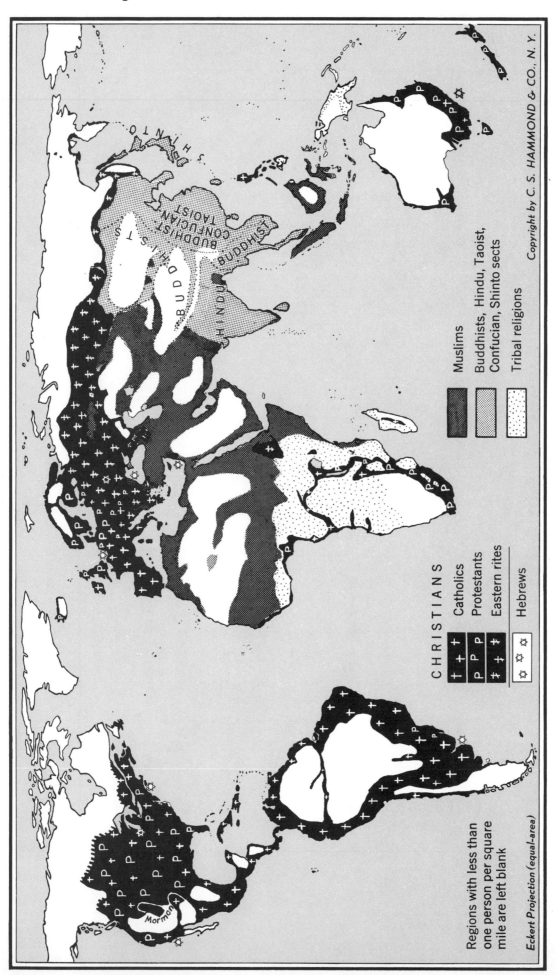

CHRISTIANS

† † †	Catholics	
P P P	Protestants	
⳥ ⳥ ⳥	Eastern rites	

Hebrews

✡ ✡ ✡

Muslims

Buddhists, Hindu, Taoist, Confucian, Shinto sects

Tribal religions

Regions with less than one person per square mile are left blank

Eckert Projection (equal-area)

Copyright by C. S. HAMMOND & CO., N. Y.

RELIGIONS. Most people of the Earth belong to four major religions: Christians, Muslims, Brahmans, Bhuddhists and derivatives. The Eastern rites of the Christians include the Greek Orthodox, Greek Catholic, Armenian, Syrian, Coptic and more minor churches. The lamaism of Tibet and Mongolia differs a great deal from Buddhism in Burma and Thailand. In the religion of China the teachings of Buddha, Confucius and Tao are mixed, while in Shinto a great deal of ancestor and emperor worship is added. About 11 million Hebrews live scattered over the globe, chiefly in cities and in the state of Israel.

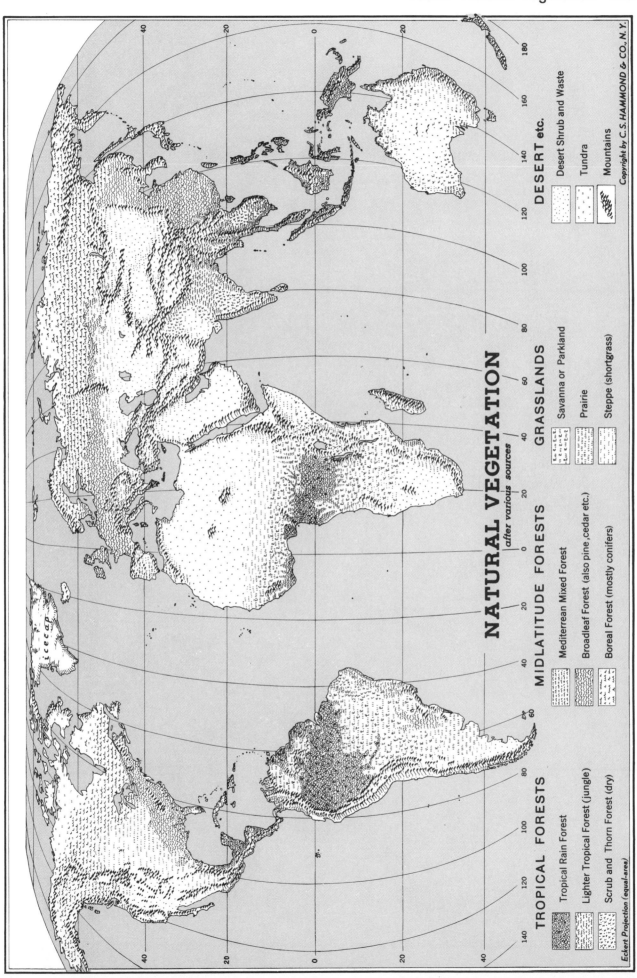

NATURAL VEGETATION
after various sources

TROPICAL FORESTS
Tropical Rain Forest
Lighter Tropical Forest (jungle)
Scrub and Thorn Forest (dry)

MIDLATITUDE FORESTS
Mediterrean Mixed Forest
Broadleaf Forest (also pine, cedar etc.)
Boreal Forest (mostly conifers)

GRASSLANDS
Savanna or Parkland
Prairie
Steppe (shortgrass)

DESERT etc.
Desert Shrub and Waste
Tundra
Mountains

Copyright by C.S. HAMMOND & CO., N.Y.

Eckert Projection (equal-area)

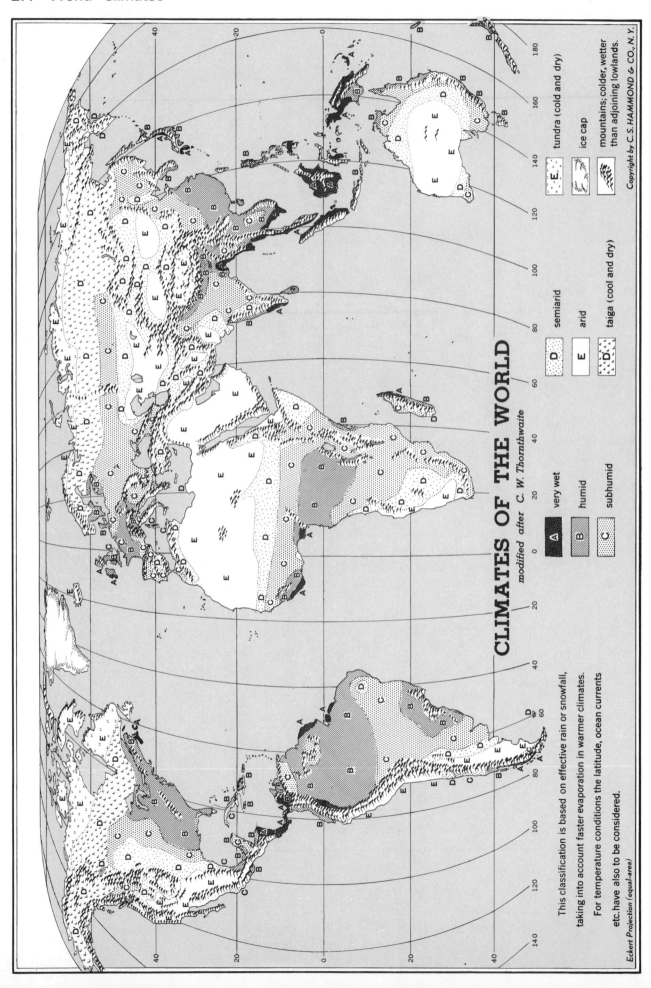

CLIMATES OF THE WORLD
modified after C. W. Thornthwaite

This classification is based on effective rain or snowfall,
taking into account faster evaporation in warmer climates.

For temperature conditions the latitude, ocean currents
etc. have also to be considered.

Eckert Projection (equal-area)

	very wet		semiarid
A		**D**	
B	humid	**E**	arid
C	subhumid	**D**	taiga (cool and dry)

E	tundra (cold and dry)
	ice cap
	mountains; colder, wetter than adjoining lowlands.

Copyright by C.S. HAMMOND & CO., N.Y.

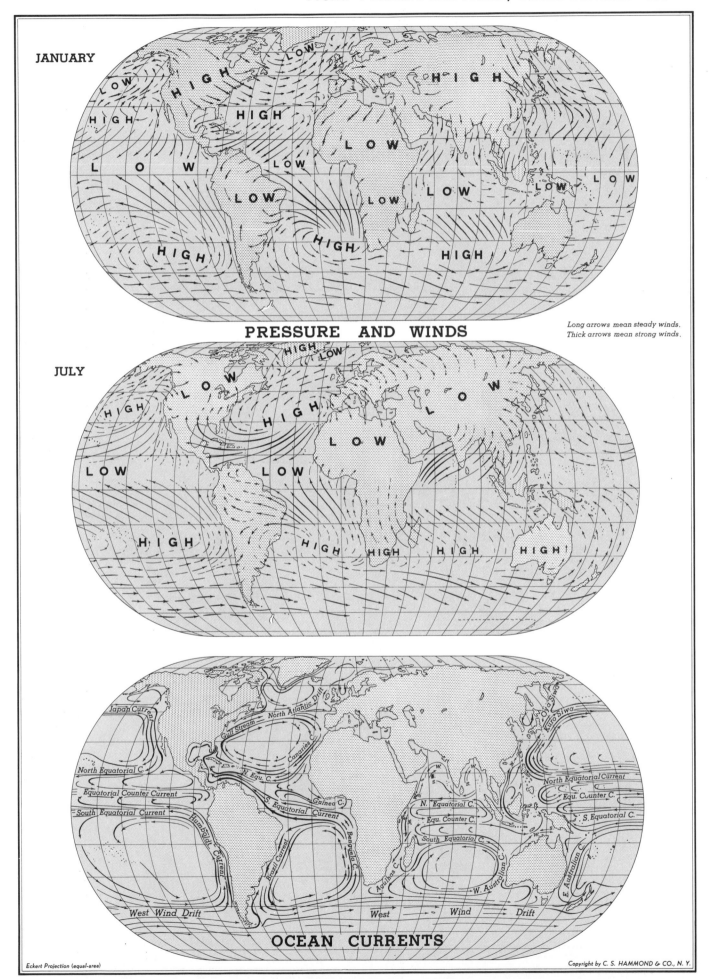

JANUARY

PRESSURE AND WINDS

Long arrows mean steady winds.
Thick arrows mean strong winds.

JULY

OCEAN CURRENTS

Eckert Projection (equal-area)

Copyright by C. S. HAMMOND & CO., N. Y.

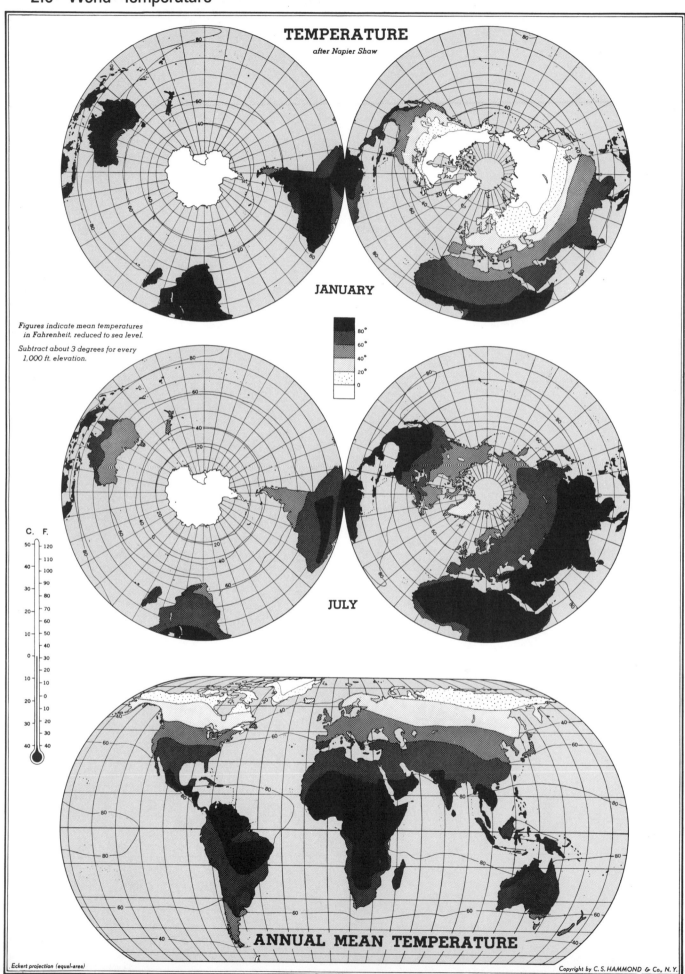

TEMPERATURE
after Napier Shaw

JANUARY

Figures indicate mean temperatures in Fahrenheit, reduced to sea level.

Subtract about 3 degrees for every 1,000 ft. elevation.

80°
60°
40°
20°
0

JULY

C. F.

ANNUAL MEAN TEMPERATURE

Eckert projection (equal-area)

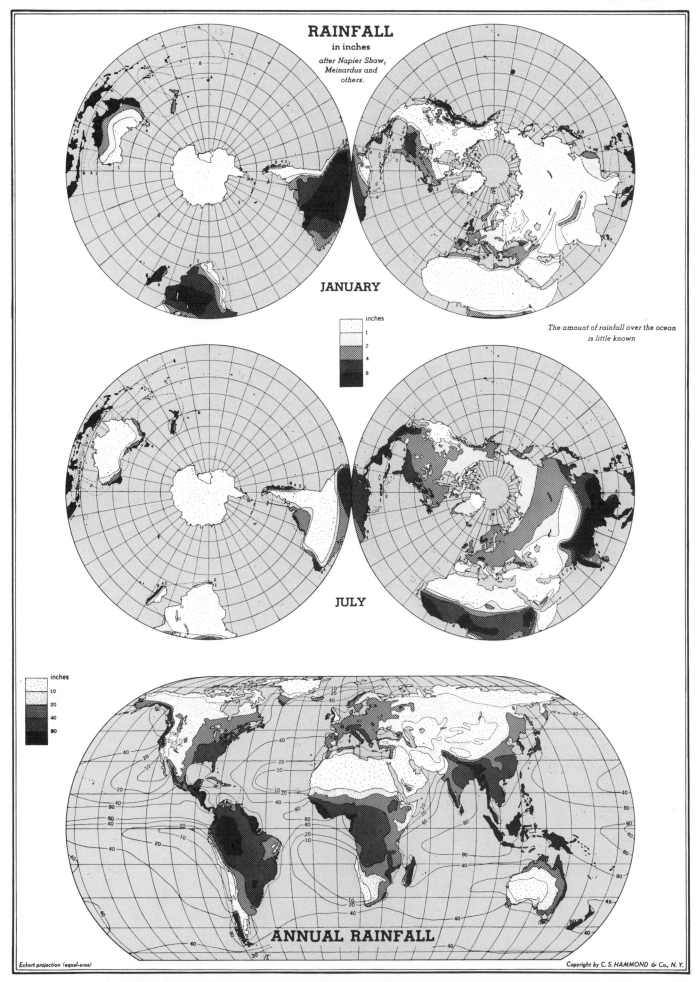

RAINFALL
in inches
*after Napier Shaw,
Meinardus and
others.*

JANUARY

inches
1
2
4
8

*The amount of rainfall over the ocean
is little known*

JULY

inches
10
20
40
80

ANNUAL RAINFALL

Eckert projection (equal-area)

Copyright by C. S. HAMMOND & Co., N. Y.

If we can envision the continents of the world as seated firmly on massive rafts of rock and moving across the surface of the earth at a rate of about 6 feet every 60 years we have a basic notion of what is meant by continental drift and the manner in which land and sea masses have been formed.

The original concept of continental drift was proposed in the 1920s, but only during the past three years or so have geologists and geophysicists accepted as fact the seemingly preposterous notion that the surface of the earth is constantly in motion.

The making of the continents began more than 200 million years ago during the Permian period with the splitting of a gigantic landmass known as Pangaea. Two continents, Laurasia to the north and Gondwana to the south, were formed by the initial division. Over a period of many millions of years these landmasses subdivided into smaller parts approximately the shapes of Africa, Eurasia, North and South America, Australia, and Antarctica as we know them today.

CONTINENTAL DRIFT

Source: R. S. Dietz and J. C. Holden

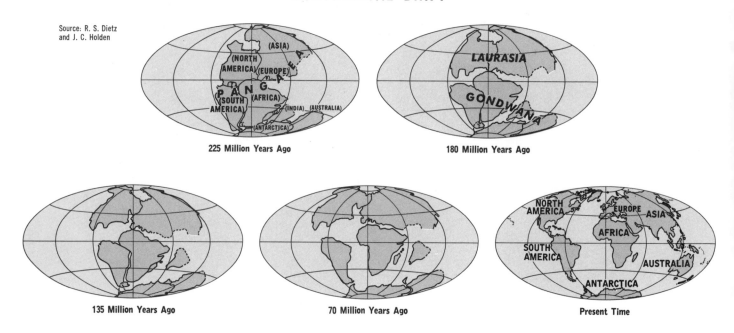

225 Million Years Ago

180 Million Years Ago

135 Million Years Ago

70 Million Years Ago

Present Time

CRUSTAL MOVEMENT

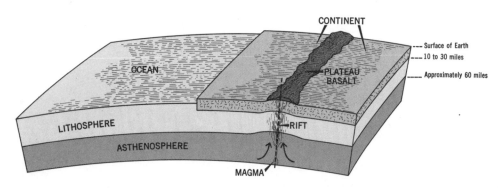

The concept of movement within the earth's crust assumes that the earth's outer layer has a firm lithosphere divided up into individual pieces called plates. These plates "float" above a weaker interior layer, the **asthenosphere**, and over vast periods of time noticeably change position, shape, size and direction depending upon forces exerted from within the earth.

Far from being an isolated instance, the movement of glaciers over the face of the earth has been a natural phenomenon for many thousands of years. Stimulated by changes in climate and resulting changes in sea level — perhaps induced by shifts in the earth's axis — glaciers have followed a rather unpredictable course of advance and retreat continuing into the 20th century.

At some point in unrecorded history during the greatest ice age, or the Pleistocene epoch, as much as 27 percent of the earth's surface was covered by glacial ice to a depth of up to 10,000 feet. The icy masses moved across the earth as far south as New York City and the Missouri River in North America, burying much of Europe and blanketing vast areas in northern Asia.

Many of the great ice sheets retreated as the climate became warmer, leaving deposits of soil and rock picked up as they traveled southward in the Northern Hemisphere. The landscape changed as the glaciers left behind their typical U-shaped valleys, amphitheater-like hollows and jagged mountain ridges, altering to a large extent the former ecological zones which changed again and again as the ice reformed and melted.

Although not enough is known about glaciers to predict accurately their future behavior, we do know that they react to climatic changes. Glaciers were advancing in Alpine regions during the 19th century until a global warm up in the beginning of this century caused their retreat. Recently the trend has been toward cooler and moister climate and, on a limited scale, glaciers are beginning to advance once more.

EXTENT OF GLACIATION IN THE NORTHERN HEMISPHERE DURING THE ICE AGES

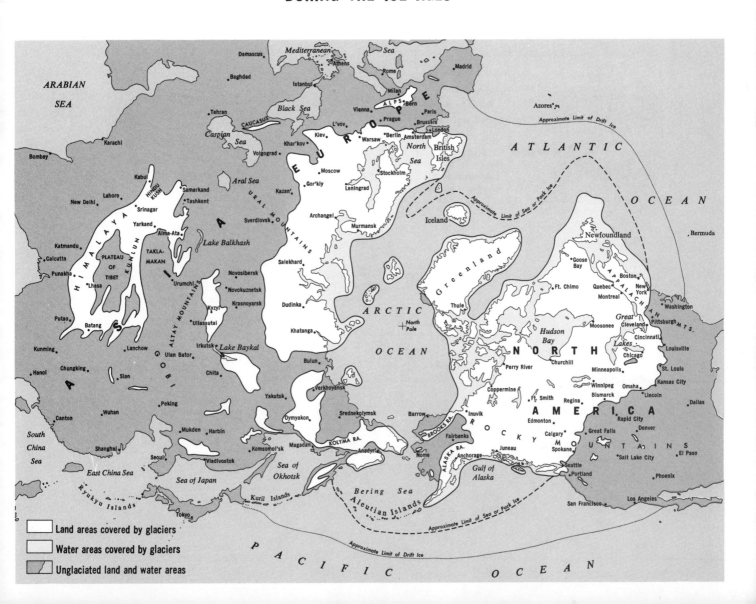

Land areas covered by glaciers

Water areas covered by glaciers

Unglaciated land and water areas

GEOLOGIC TIME

TIME DIVISION			YEARS AGO	MAJOR GEOLOGIC DEVELOPMENTS
CENOZOIC ERA	TERTIARY PERIOD	QUATERNARY PERIOD	RECENT	10,000	GREAT LAKES
		PLEISTOCENE		NORWEGIAN FJORDS
			1-2 million	ICE AGES
		PLIOCENE		BLACK SEA
			11 million	CASPIAN SEA
		MIOCENE		
			25 million	HIMALAYAS
		OLIGOCENE		
			40 million	ALPS
		EOCENE		
			60 million	
		PALEOCENE		ANDES MOUNTAINS
			70 million	ROCKY MOUNTAINS
MESOZOIC ERA		CRETACEOUS PERIOD		CHALK DEPOSITS
			135 million	COAST RANGES
		JURASSIC PERIOD		SIERRA NEVADA
				JURA MOUNTAINS
			180 million	NEW JERSEY PALISADES
		TRIASSIC PERIOD		
				CAUCASUS
			225 million	URAL MOUNTAINS
PALEOZOIC ERA		PERMIAN PERIOD		APPALACHIAN MOUNTAINS
				POTASH DEPOSITS
			270 million	
		PENNSYLVANIAN PERIOD		COAL DEPOSITS
			300 million	
		MISSISSIPPIAN PERIOD		
			350 million	ACADIAN MOUNTAINS
		DEVONIAN PERIOD		
			400 million	
		SILURIAN PERIOD		NIAGARA FALLS CAPROCK
			440 million	TACONIC MOUNTAINS
		ORDOVICIAN PERIOD		LIMESTONE DEPOSITS
			500 million	VERMONT MOUNTAINS
		CAMBRIAN PERIOD		
			600 million	ARIZONA MOUNTAINS
		PRE-CAMBRIAN		METALLIC ORE DEPOSITS
				LAURENTIAN MOUNTAINS
				ADIRONDACK MOUNTAINS

Like a giant Rosetta stone the secrets of the earth's creation lie spread in strata beneath our feet, revealing their hieroglyphic message to a few of the initiated.

For billions of years layers of rock — the sedimentary deposits of ages — have piled up on the earth's surface, entrapping the characteristics of time. Time when a lifeless nature prepared for the first microscopic living organisms; time when these organisms were destroyed or became extinct, time when, through endless subtle mutations, they evolved into new forms of life.

The Paleozoic, ancient era; Mesozoic, middle era; and

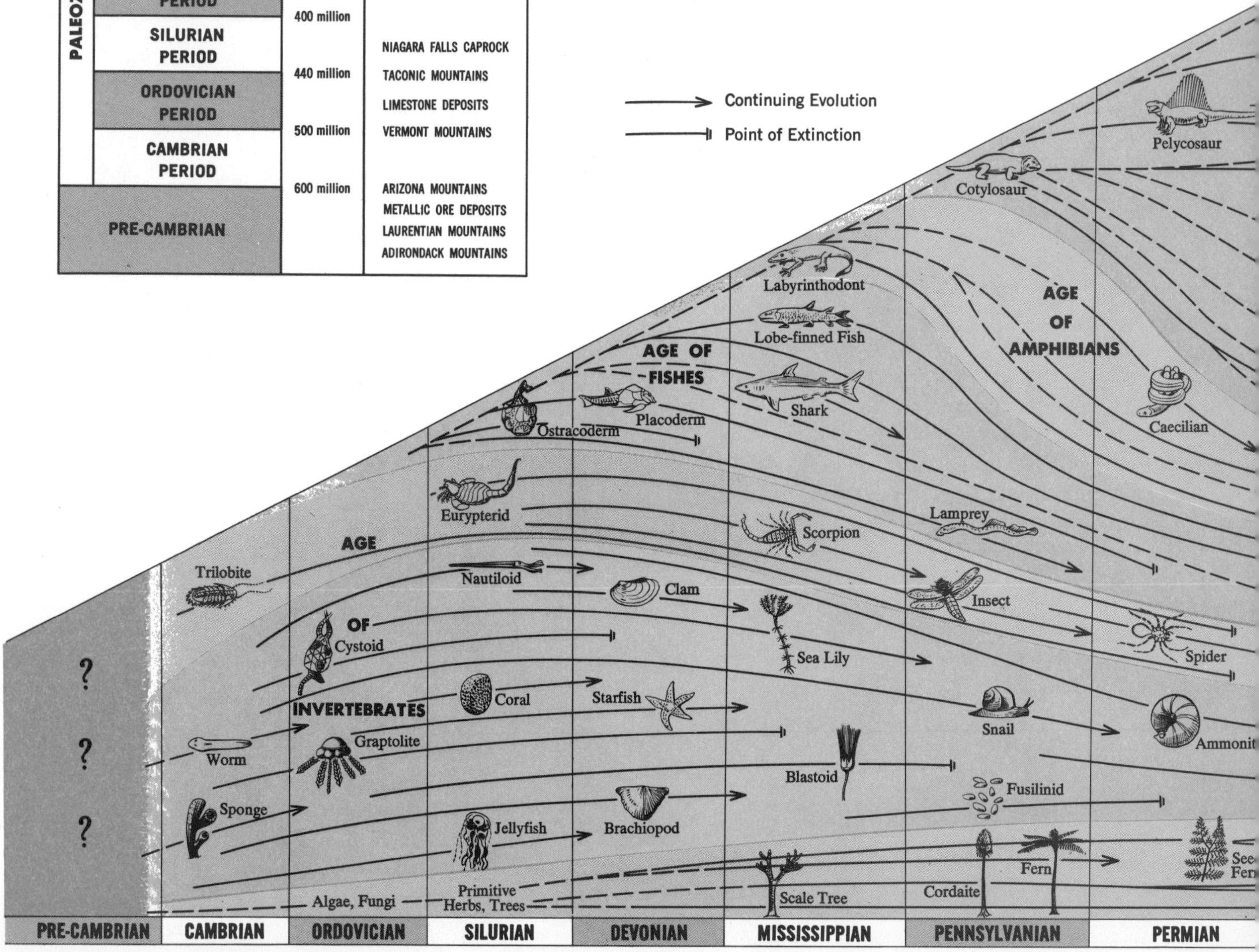

→ Continuing Evolution

⊣ Point of Extinction

PRE-CAMBRIAN | CAMBRIAN | ORDOVICIAN | SILURIAN | DEVONIAN | MISSISSIPPIAN | PENNSYLVANIAN | PERMIAN

Cenozoic, recent era, are the designations used for the broad periods of time during which life evolved. Locked within strata of rock, vestiges of life are found in the fossilized remains of creatures over a billion years old. In succeeding layers geologists and anthropologists find other clues to the mystery of time and life: the appearance of the lowest forms of animal life; the evolution of fish, amphibians, reptiles, birds and mammals. Late in the schedule of creation traces of a strange and wonderful animal appear, for it was only one million years ago that man left his first imprint on the geologic record.

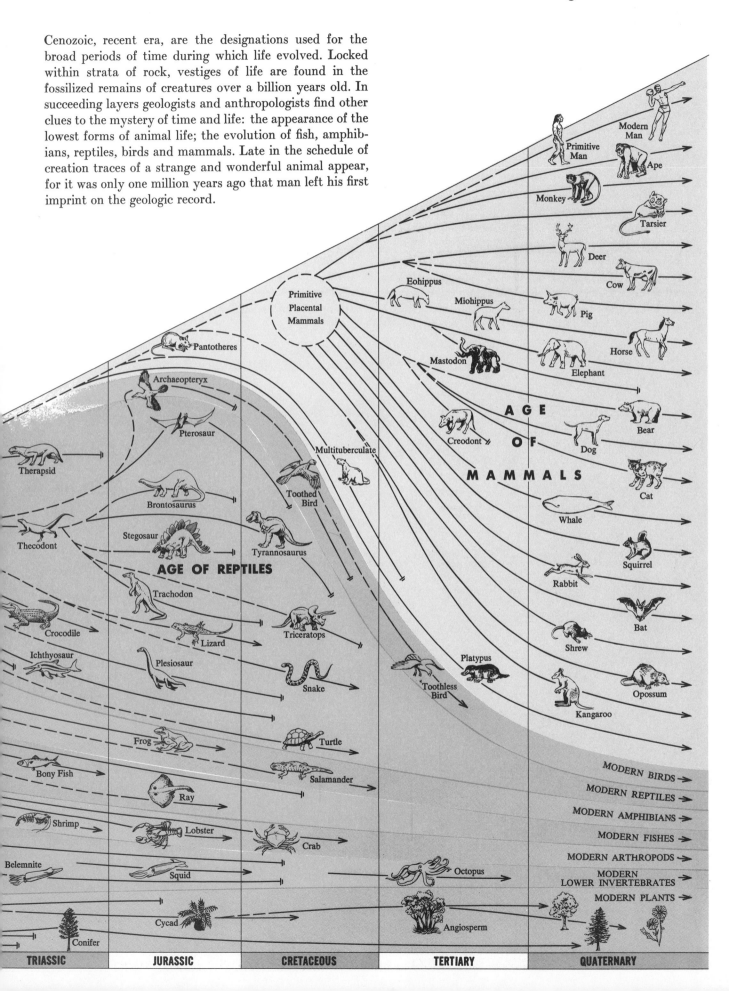

AGE OF REPTILES

AGE OF MAMMALS

Primitive Placental Mammals

Modern Man
Primitive Man
Ape
Monkey
Tarsier
Deer
Cow
Eohippus
Miohippus
Pig
Horse
Mastodon
Elephant
Creodont
Bear
Dog
Cat
Whale
Squirrel
Rabbit
Bat
Shrew
Platypus
Opossum
Toothless Bird
Kangaroo

Pantotheres
Archaeopteryx
Pterosaur
Brontosaurus
Stegosaur
Tyrannosaurus
Multituberculate
Toothed Bird
Therapsid
Thecodont
Trachodon
Triceratops
Crocodile
Lizard
Plesiosaur
Ichthyosaur
Snake
Frog
Turtle
Bony Fish
Salamander
Ray
Shrimp
Lobster
Crab
Belemnite
Squid
Octopus
Conifer
Cycad
Angiosperm

MODERN BIRDS
MODERN REPTILES
MODERN AMPHIBIANS
MODERN FISHES
MODERN ARTHROPODS
MODERN LOWER INVERTEBRATES
MODERN PLANTS

| TRIASSIC | JURASSIC | CRETACEOUS | TERTIARY | QUATERNARY |

With an intuition clearly beyond their scientific knowledge, the ancients of India developed a theory of reincarnation which, in some philosophic ways, parallels what science has learned of the workings of the biosphere. In the remarkable thrift of nature nothing is lost — in tremendous complex cycles atoms from the first life on earth still move through the biosphere.

The miracle of energy is constantly performed in the cycles of the "life-giving" elements. Carbon, hydrogen, oxygen, nitrogen, sulfur and phosphorus act together to produce all living matter. While many other elements such as calcium, iodine and iron are also found in living things, they are not absolute essentials in all cases. Carbon, hydrogen and oxygen are vital for photosynthesis and are the components of the basic food substances — carbohydrates and fats. Carbon, in its common gaseous form, carbon dioxide, is absorbed by green plants and triggers

the production of carbohydrate compounds by reacting with molecules of water.

Some "energy" is stored within the plant in the form of new tissue; other "energy," in the form of oxygen is released into the air to be used by other organisms. The seemingly inexhaustible supply of carbon dioxide available for use is replenished in the atmosphere through the respiration of all living things, and in the soil as bacteria and fungi break down plant and animal cells,

Nitrogen, sulfur and phosphorus are essential to animals and plants for the production and maintenance of protein. Nitrogen, with carbon, hydrogen and oxygen, is used for the growth and repair of tissue. Sulfur acts as a "stiffening" agent in all protein. To perform their functions proteins must be folded and shaped in a particular way, and their structure is maintained by bonds between sulfur atoms. While phosphorus is not a constituent of protein,

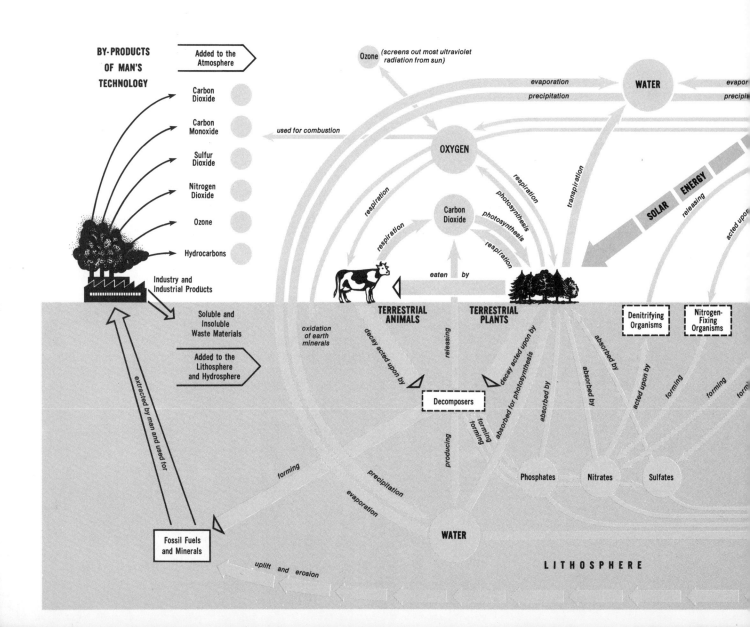

no protein can be made without it. Special phosphate compounds are the "fuel" for all biochemical work within the cell.

Although about four-fifths of the atmosphere is nitrogen, higher forms of life cannot make use of it in its "free" state and must absorb it at one or more points in its biospheric cycle. The decomposers — bacteria and fungi — act on waste matter, breaking down complex compounds into simpler usable forms including nitrogen. Some nitrogen-fixing bacteria are able to utilize atmospheric nitrogen in their own metabolism, while others convert it to those nitrogen-enriched substances necessary for all plant growth.

In nature, no part is greater than the whole and almost every element is dependent on another for some essential part of its cycle. Water, which is incorporated into every organism, is essential in the formation of free oxygen which in turn sustains the life of that organism. Water is also

the principal "carrier" in the cycling of all elements. When it evaporates, water returns certain elements to the atmosphere; when it seeps through the soil on its return to the sea, water distributes nutrients to plant roots.

Carbon monoxide, sulfur and nitrogen oxides, hydrocarbons — by-products of man's industry — are being injected into the biosphere in ever-increasing amounts. There, as the "new compounds," they must in some way co-exist with the life-support cycles established throughout millions of years of evolution. Their compatability with these cycles and the organisms they nurture will determine the future of life on our planet.

Already man has learned one thing. Although the question of reincarnation or any form of life after death remains unanswered for many, science has proved that there is no natural end to the raw materials of nature or to the "new compounds" man has made from them.

INTERLOCKING CYCLES OF THE BIOSPHERE

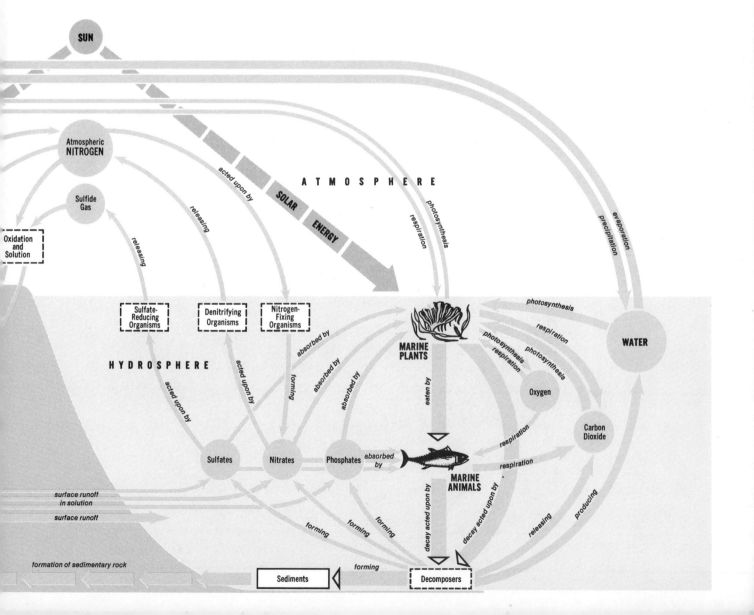

Since he could think man has been at war with death. He has fought his battles against destruction with science and technology as his weapons, virtually eliminating his own annihilation by predatory animals and from diseases such as leprosy, tuberculosis and diphtheria. He has walked into many valleys of death to fight malaria and yellow fever, and he has resolved that each year more of his own kind will live to finish out their threescore years and ten.

However, the victory over nature, which had balanced population with food supply and space, is bitter, for the population has "exploded" leaving man with the seemingly insolvable problem of providing more food and space for himself or reducing his numbers by starvation or by war.

Man outsmarted himself in many ways as he worked toward creating a more perfect world for himself without understanding that natural laws go beyond human manipulation. He has destroyed forests and meadows, polluted the water and air, eliminated organisms that tried to share his bread. However, he has yet to learn to recreate the wood and brush or the interdependent communities of bacteria, insects and animals that he learned — too late — enrich the air, the soil and the water and without which he cannot function.

Modern man knows how to manufacture "miraculous" materials to work for his pleasure or his seemingly insatiable needs, but the sophistications of technology have yet to control effectively the by-products. These new materials, still subject to the order of nature's cycles, penetrate the biosphere and eventually come to roost in his own vulnerable body.

New battles are being fought throughout the world and new standards bearing the slogans of ecology float in the "unsafe" air. It is somehow ironic to find that many people now believe that man has been fighting the wrong fight in his gigantic struggle with nature. That, after all, nature never was his enemy.

Man cannot turn back to his beginnings when he lived with, and not against, the natural world. But a compromise between technology and nature must take place for our "plundered planet" cries out for the day of reckoning.

POLLUTION CIRCLE

TYPES OF POLLUTION AND THEIR EFFECT ON THE TOTAL ENVIRONMENT

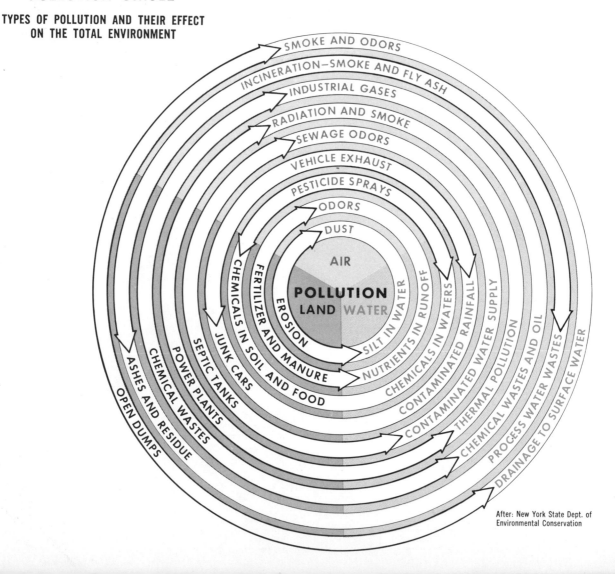

After: New York State Dept. of Environmental Conservation